D1179547

B.S.U.C. - LIBRARY

00256053

THE
Novel

Edited by Franco Moretti

Editorial Board: Ernesto Franco, Fredric Jameson, Abdelfattah Kilito,
Pier Vincenzo Mengaldo, and Mario Vargas Llosa

VOLUME 1
HISTORY, GEOGRAPHY, AND CULTURE

VOLUME 2
FORMS AND THEMES

THE

Novel

VOLUME 1

HISTORY, GEOGRAPHY,

AND CULTURE

EDITED BY

Franco Moretti

Princeton University Press

PRINCETON AND OXFORD

Copyright 2006 © by Princeton University Press

Published by Princeton University Press, 41 William Street,
Princeton, New Jersey 08540
In the United Kingdom: Princeton University Press, 3 Market Place,
Woodstock, Oxfordshire OX20 1SY

This book is a selection from the original five-volume work, published
in Italian under the title *Il romanzo*, copyright © 2001–2003 by Giulio
Einaudi editore s.p.a., Turin. Citations in these essays reflect the
substantive content of those in the Italian edition.

All Rights Reserved

Library of Congress Cataloging-in-Publication Data

Romanzo. English. Selections.
The novel / edited by Franco Moretti.
p.   cm.
A selection from the original five-volume work, published in Torino by
G. Einaudi editore, c2001–c2003.
Includes bibliographical references and indexes.
Contents: v. 1. History, geography, and culture — v. 2. Forms and themes.
ISBN-13: 978-0-691-04947-2 (cl : v. 1 : alk. paper)
ISBN-10: 0-691-04947-5 (cl : v. 1 : alk. paper)
ISBN-13: 978-0-691-04948-9 (cl : v. 2 : alk. paper)
ISBN-10: 0-691-04948-3 (cl : v. 2 : alk. paper)
1. Fiction—History and criticism.   I. Moretti, Franco, 1950–   II. Title.

PN3321.R66 2006
809.3—dc22   2005051473

British Library Cataloging-in-Publication Data is available

This book has been composed in Simoncini Garamond

Printed on acid-free paper. ∞

pup.princeton.edu

Printed in the United States of America

1 3 5 7 9 10 8 6 4 2

BATH SPA UNIVERSITY
NEWTON PARK LIBRARY

Class No.

Coutts

DISCARD

Contents

1.3. THE EUROPEAN ACCELERATION

1.4. THE CIRCLE WIDENS

1.5. TOWARD WORLD LITERATURE

On *The Novel*

Countless are the novels of the world. So, how can we speak of them? *The Novel* combines two intersecting perspectives. First, the novel is for us a great anthropological force, which has turned reading into a pleasure and redefined the sense of reality, the meaning of individual existence, the perception of time and of language. The novel as culture, then, but certainly also as form, or rather forms, plural, because in the two thousand years of its history one encounters the strangest creations, and high and low trade places at every opportunity, as the borders of literature are continuously, unpredictably expanded. At times, this endless flexibility borders on chaos. But thanks to it, the novel becomes the first truly planetary form: a phoenix always ready to take flight in a new direction, and to find the right language for the next generation of readers.

———

Two perspectives on the novel, then; and two volumes. *History, Geography, and Culture* is mostly a look from the outside; *Forms and Themes*, from the inside. But like convex and concave in a Borromini façade, inside and outside are here part of the same design, because the novel is always commodity and artwork at once: a major economic investment and an ambitious aesthetic form (for German romanticism, the most universal of all). Don't be surprised, then, if an epistemological analysis of "fiction" slides into a discussion of credit and paper money or if a statistical study of the Japanese book market becomes a reflection on narrative morphology. This is the way of the novel—and of *The Novel*.

———

A history that begins in the Hellenistic world and continues today. A geography that overlaps with the advent of world literature. A morphology that ranges euphorically from war stories, pornography, and melodrama, to syntactic labyrinths, metaphoric prose, and broken plot lines. To make the literary field longer, larger, and deeper: this is, in a nutshell, the project of *The Novel* (and of its Italian five-volume original). And then, project within the project, to take a second look at the new panorama—and estrange it. The essay on the Spanish Golden Age develops its historical argument, and then: "Wait. Why was that magical season so short?" Stating the "facts," then turning them into "problems." At the beginning of the historical arc, we wonder whether to speak of "the" Greek novel—or of a cluster of independent forms. At the opposite end, we explain why it is that the best-known African novels are not written for African readers. And so on. The more we learn about the history of the novel, the stranger it becomes.

————

To make sense of this new history, *The Novel* uses three different registers. Essays, about twenty per volume, are works of abstraction, synthesis, and comparative research: they establish the great periodizations that segment the flow of time, and the conceptual architecture that reveals its unity. "Readings" are shorter pieces, unified by a common question, and devoted to the close analysis of individual texts: *Aethiopica*, *Le Grand Cyrus*, *The War of the Worlds* (and more) as so many prototypes of novelistic subgenres; *Malte Laurids Brigge*, *Macunaíma*, *The Making of Americans* (and more) as typical modern experiments. Finally, the sections entitled "Critical Apparatus" study the novel's wider ecosystem, focusing, for instance, on how the semantic field of "narrative" took shape around keywords such as *midrash*, *monogatari*, *xiaoshuo*, *qiṣṣa*—and, why not, *romance*.

————

Countless are the novels of the world. We discuss them in two volumes. Quite a few things will be missing, of course. But this is not Noah's ark: it is a collective reflection on the pleasures of storytelling, and their interaction—at times, complicity—with social power. Now more than ever, pleasure and critique should not be divided.

F.M.

A Struggle for Space

JACK GOODY

From Oral to Written: An Anthropological Breakthrough in Storytelling

The telling of tales is often thought to be characteristic of all human discourse, and it is fashionable to speak of narrative as a universal form of expression, one that is applied both to the life experiences of individuals and to the dramas of social interaction. Storytelling in oral cultures in turn is seen as the foundation on which the novel is built in literate ones, and the activity is regarded as the focus of much creativity. Blind Homer was the model, putting all his nonliterate imagination into the epic. In discussing storytelling we are clearly leading into the topics of fiction and the novel. But not all storytelling is fictional; it can also involve personal narratives. However, although typically it is associated with oral cultures, with "the singer [or teller] of tales,"[1] in his article on the subject, Walter Benjamin sees the storyteller disappearing with the arrival of the novel, whose dissemination he associates with the advent of printing, and no longer directly linked with experience in the same way as before.[2]

The timing of the appearance of the novel is subject to discussion. Mikhail Baktin uses the term *novel* (or "novelness") in a much more extended sense. But in dealing with origins more concretely, he traces three types: the novel of "adventure time" back to the Greek romances of the second century C.E., the novel of everyday time in the story of *The Golden Ass* of Apuleius, and the "chronotope" centered on biographical time, although this does not produce any novels at this period. All three forms are harbingers of the modern novel.[3] That is basically a product of the arrival of printing in the late fifteenth century, but as we see from these early examples, the nature of storytelling had already radically changed with the coming of writing. Indeed, I want to argue that, contrary to much received opinion, *narrative* (already in 1566, according to the *Oxford English Dictionary*, used for "an account, narration, a tale, recital") is not so much a universal feature of the human situation as one that is promoted by literacy and subsequently by printing.

---

[1] Lord 1960.

[2] Benjamin 1968a: 87.

[3] Clark and Holquist 1984, chap. 13, "The theory of the novel." Doody 1997 rejects the categorical distinction, found only in English, between romance and novel, placing the origin of the latter in ancient Greece.

Today the word *narrative* has come to have an iconic, indeed a cant, significance in Western literary and social science circles. I suggest a rather different approach, using the term in a much tighter way, implying a plot with a firm sequential structure, marked by a beginning, a middle, and an end in the Aristotelian manner. Otherwise, one becomes involved in a kind of extension similar to that which Derrida has tried to give to *writing*, in which term he includes all "traces," including memory traces. That usage makes it impossible to make the at times essential distinction between written archives and memory banks. The same is true for the use of the word *literature* for oral genres, what I call standard oral forms, since this usage obscures important analytical differences. Likewise, narrative is sometimes held to include any vaguely sequential discourse. "What is the narrative?" is the often heard cry. When I employ the term, I do so in an altogether tighter sense, as a standard form that has a definite plot that proceeds by structured stages.

Let me take a recent, authoritative example of the wider usage. In his book, *The Political Unconscious* (1981), which is subtitled *Narrative as a Socially Symbolic Act*, Fredric Jameson sees his task as attempting to "restructure the problematics of ideology, of the unconscious and of desire, of representation, of history, and of cultural production, around the all-informing process of *narrative*, which I take to be . . . the central function or *instance* of the human mind."[4] There is little one can say about such a terrifyingly inclusive aim centered on such an all-embracing concept of the process of narrative. He is not alone in this usage. Some psychologists view storytelling as a prime mode of cognition; at a recent conference on competences, philosophers proposed the creation of narrative as one of the key competencies of humankind.

In attempting to query this and similar assumptions, I want also to tackle another. In an article on "the narrative structure of reality," reflecting another all-inclusive use of this term, Stuart Hall remarks, "we make an absolutely too simple and false distinction between narratives about the real and the narratives of fiction, that is, between news and adventure stories."[5] Is that really too simple and false? In my experience the distinction exists, if not universally, at least transculturally. Indeed, I would suggest it is an intrinsic feature of linguistic discourse. How do we know someone is not deceiving us, telling us a fiction, a story, if we make no distinction?

As Orwell observes about Catalonia in his "Looking Back on the Spanish

---

[4] Jameson 1981: 13.
[5] *Southern Review*, Adelaide, 17 (1984): 3–17, quoted in Sommerville 1996: 173.

Civil War," "This kind of thing is frightening to me, because it often gives me the feeling that the very concept of objective truth is fading out of the world. After all, the chances are that those lies or at any rate similar lies will pass into history."[6] Whether what we are being told is a fiction or a deliberate lie (implying intentionality), both are departures from the literal truth. It does not matter to me in this context whether there is philosophical justification for objective truth, a correspondence theory of truth. I need only an acknowledgment of the fact that the actors need to distinguish between truth and untruth.

It is true that psychology, psychoanalysis, and perhaps sociology too, have qualified our view of the lie from the standpoint of the individual, in an attempt to elicit the reasons why people do not tell the truth. But in dyadic interaction, in social communication between two or more persons, the question of the truth or untruth of a statement remains critical. Did he or did he not post the letter I gave him as he claimed? Untruth may not be a lie. It may also involve fantasy or fiction, fantasy being the latter's nonrealistic equivalent. Fantasy does not invite a literal comparison with a truthful account of events at the surface level. But fiction may do just that, may make a claim to truth value. That was the difference between romances and novels in England at the beginning of the eighteenth century. The realistic novels of Defoe and others deliberately invite an assessment of the truth or otherwise of the tale. The writers often claim truth for fiction—not the underlying experiential truth but literal, factual truth.

The distinction runs parallel to that commonly made between history and myth, marked respectively by linear and circular time; the former in effect requires the availability of documents and hence of writing, but its absence does not exclude a sense of the past in oral cultures, of which myth is only one variety of "history," in the formal meaning of a study based on the examination of documents. We might wish to qualify this distinction for our own purposes, but there can be little doubt that it emerged within the actor's frame of reference; the Homeric *mythos* was set apart from *historia* and even *logos*, both of which implied some assessment of truth.[7]

In the absence of writing, communication in oral cultures has to rely largely on speech. Yet experience in Africa suggests that such discourse rather rarely consisted in the telling of tales, if by that we mean personal and fictional stories created for adults. The LoDagaa of northern Ghana certainly make a distinction of this kind between what I translate as "proper

---

[6] Orwell 1968.
[7] Goody and Watt 1963: 321 ff.

speech" (*yil miong*) and lies (*ziiri*), between truth and falsehood. Proper speech would include what I have translated as "The Myth of the Bagre," but that recitation itself raises the question of whether what it offers is a lie or whether it is God's way, God's truth. Folktales are not referred to as lies, since they make no claim to the truth, but neither are they truth (for example, animals speak and behave like humans); as I shall claim, such tales are largely addressed to children, and they do verge upon the lie in the Platonic sense, as we see from the account of a LoDagaa writer.

For the problem with fictional narrative emerges from another angle in a rather imaginative autobiography by a member of this same LoDagaa group, Malidoma Somé, who claims his people make no distinction between the natural and supernatural or between reality and the imagined (which I doubt). Somé is described in his book, *Of Water and the Spirit*, as "a medicine man and diviner" as well as holding a Ph.D. from Brandeis and giving lectures at a spiritual center in America. He decides to test the absence of these distinctions by showing the elders of his African village a videotape of *Star Trek*. They interpret the film as portraying "the current affairs in the day-to-day lives of some other people living in the world. . . . I could not make them understand," he writes, "that all this was not real. Even though stories abound in my culture, we have no word for fiction. The only way I could get across to them the Western concept of fiction was to associate fiction with telling lies."[8] That assertion corresponds with my own experience, at least as far as adults are concerned.

Truthful narratives among the LoDagaa, in my own experience, would be those relating to one's own personal life, perhaps accounts of labor migration to the gold mines in the south of the country or those of local feuds or wars that happened before the coming of the colonial conquerors early last century. Stories of this kind are occasionally told, but their place is rather marginal; narrative and storytelling, even nonfictional, are hardly as central as is visualized by those seeking to reconstruct the forms of discourse in early literate culture and supposedly inherited from yet earlier purely oral ones.

The discussions of Derrida, Hall, and Jameson seem to me to represent the elimination or neglect of historically and analytically useful distinctions in a misguided, postmodern-influenced drive against "binarism" and toward holism. In fact the distinctions we have adopted do not threaten the overall unity of the *esprit humain*, the human mind, nor do they necessarily embody a we/they view of the world.

---

[8] Somé 1994: 8–9.

Turning more specifically to the question of narrative in oral cultures, there are five aspects I want to look at: legends, epics, myths, folktales, and finally, personal narratives. The epic is a distinctly narrative form, partly fictional, though often having a basis in heroic deeds on the field of battle. It is defined as a kind of narrative poetry that celebrates the achievements of some heroic personage of history or tradition (that is, which may have a quota of fact). The great scholar of early literature, Hector Chadwick, saw the epic as the typical product of what he called the Heroic Age, peopled by chiefs, warriors, and tribesmen (1932–40). Since this genre is usually regarded as emerging in preliterate societies, much academic research has been directed at trying to show that, for example, the Homeric poems, as epics, were composed in preliterate rather than literate cultures. During the 1930s, the Harvard classical scholars, Milman Parry (1971) and Albert Lord (1960), made a series of recordings of songs in Yugoslav cafés and aimed to show that their style, especially in the use of formulaic expressions, made them representative of epics of the oral tradition. However, Yugoslavia was by no means a purely oral culture, and its verbal forms were strongly influenced by the presence of writing, and especially of written religions. Some of the recitations actually appeared as texts in songbooks that were available to the "singers of tales," and there was reference back and forth. It is also the case more generally that the societies of the Heroic Age during which the epic flourished were ones where early literacy was present. By contrast, in the purely oral cultures of Africa, the epic is a rarity, except on the southern fringes of the Sahara, which have been much influenced by Islam and by its literary forms.

Africa south of the Sahara was until recently one of the main areas of the world where writing was totally absent; that was also the case in recent times with parts of South America (together with Australasia and the Pacific). Most of South America was transformed by the Spanish and Portuguese in the sixteenth century, though a few remote areas escaped their overwhelming, hegemonic influence. Africa offers the most straightforward case, even though influenced by the written civilizations of Europe in the West, of the Mediterranean in the North and of the Arabs in the East. It is also a continent whose oral literature has received much attention. The main work of synthesis has been carried out by Ruth Finnegan. On the epic she is very definite: "Epic is often assumed to be the typical poetic form of non-literate peoples. . . . Surprisingly, however, this does not seem to be borne out by the African evidence. At least in the more obvious sense of a 'relatively long narrative poem,' epic hardly seems to occur in sub-Saharan Africa apart from forms like the [written] Swahili *utenzi* which are directly attributable to

Arabic literary influence."[9] What has been called epic in Africa is often prose rather than poetry, though some of the lengthy praise poems of South Africa have something of an epic quality about them. Otherwise most frequently mentioned are the Mongo-Nkundo tales from the Congo; these too are mainly prose and resemble other African examples in their general features. The most famous is the Lianja epic, running to 120 pages of print for text and translation. It covers the birth and tribulations of the hero, his travels, the leadership of his people, and finally his death. Finnegan suggests that the original form might have been "a very loosely related bundle of separate episodes, told on separate occasions and not necessarily thought of as one single work of art (though recent and sophisticated narrators say that ideally it should be told at one sitting)."[10] In other words a similar type of amalgamation of short tales may have taken place under the impact of writing, as apparently occurred with the Gilgamesh epic of Mesopotamia.

We do find some poetry of a legendary kind in the *mvet* literature of the Fang peoples of Gabon and the Cameroons, as well as in the recitations of the *griot* among the Mande south of the Sahara. She concludes: "In general terms and apart from Islamic influences, epic seems to be of remarkably little significance in African oral literature, and the *a priori* assumption that epic is the natural form for many non-literate peoples turns out here to have little support."[11]

Since Finnegan's earlier book, the picture with regard to longer compositions has somewhat changed, both in respect to "mythical" and to "legendary" (including epic) material. As far as longer myths are concerned, we now have two published versions of the Bagre of the LoDagaa,[12] the first consisting of some twelve thousand short lines, and taking some eight hours to recite. This work is concerned not with the deeds of heroes (as in epics) but with the creation of the human world, with the position of humankind in relation to its God and its gods, with problems of philosophy and of life.

It contrasts sharply with the recitation of the *griots* of Bambara and Mali, whose products may well have been influenced by Islamic literature. The *griots* (the word is in general use) are a type of minstrel belonging to an endogamous castelike group. They mainly perform at the courts of chiefs but also on other secular, public occasions, for the societies in which they are found are kingdoms, unlike the acephalous, tribal LoDagaa where praise

---

[9] Finnegan 1970: 108.
[10] Finnegan 1970: 109.
[11] Finnegan 1970: 110.
[12] Goody 1972; Goody and Gandah 1981; plus a number of unpublished versions.

singing is little developed and legends are no more than migration histories of the clan or lineage.[13]

Listen to the account of his profession given by the *griot* Tinguidji, who was recorded by Seydou:

> Nous, le mâbos, nous ne quémandons, qu'auprès des nobles: là où il y a un noble, j'y suis aussi. Un mâbo ne se préoccupe pas de ce qui n'a pas de valeur: s'il voit un pauvre et qu'il quémande auprès de lui, s'il le voit dénué de tout et qu'il le loue, s'il en voit un qui en a l'air et qu'il le loue, un mâbo qui agit de la sorte, ne vaut rien. Moi, celui qui ne m'est pas superieur, je ne le loue pas. Celui qui n'est pas plus que moi, je ne le loue pas; je lui donne. Voilà comment je suis, moi, Tinguidji.[14]

It would be wrong to assume that all the activities of the *griots* were directed toward pleasing or praising the aristocracy in return for largesse. There were some who adopted an aggressive attitude toward the world in general, "griots vulgaires et sans scrupules dont le seul dessein est d'extorquer cadeaux et faveurs et qui, pour cela, manient avec autant de desinvolture et d'audace la louange et l'insulte le panégyrique dithyrambique et la diatribe vindicative, la langue noble et l'argot le plus grossier."[15] Apart from these differences of approach, *griots* differed in other ways, but all belonged to the "gens castés," the *nyeenybe*, which included smiths, woodcarvers, leather workers, weavers (who are also singers, the *mâbo*). These minstrels, "artisans du verbe et de l'art musical," included the following:

> the *intellectuel-griots* who have studied the Qur'an
> the *awlube*, or drummers, who are attached to a particular family whose
>   history, genealogy, and praises they sing
> the *jeeli* of Mandingo origin, who play many instruments, are unattached,
>   and make their living by their profession
> the *nyemakala*, wandering singers and guitarists who organize evening
>   entertainments[16]

The *intellectuel-griots* were those who studied the Qur'an, giving support to Finnegan's point about Islamic influences. The bulk of the epics in Africa

---

[13] Goody 1977.
[14] Seydou 1972: 13–14.
[15] Seydou 1972: 15.
[16] Seydou 1972: 17–20.

are found on the fringes of the Sahara where such influences are strong and of long duration. The Fulani epic of Silâmaka and Poullôri recounts the story of a chief's son and his slave together with a companion who attempt to relieve their country of its debt of tribute. It is an epic of chiefship recited within a culture that was linked to the written tradition of Islam; A.-H. Bâ has described the society of that time as village-based, with each village headed by a man who was literate in Arabic,[17] but in any case, the language and its literature were known throughout the towns of the region, influencing the nature of local life and thought, especially its artistic forms as well as its history.[18]

Under these conditions, narrative recitations of an epic kind appear. The model is provided by Islamic tradition; they are found in complex chiefdoms, the rulers of which are served by professionals of various kinds, including praise singers. Being focused on the past deeds of the chiefly ancestors (the history of the state), such songs take upon themselves a narrative format, recounting struggles of heroes of earlier times.

It should be pointed out that the content of this Fulani epic was "fixed" in certain broad features but varied enormously in its telling. Seydou describes how the legend crossed frontiers and was spread by the mouths of *griots* who, "chacun à sa guise et selon son art propre, l'ont enrichi, transformé, remanié à partir d'élements divers empruntés à d'autres récits. So the epic ended up as "une veritable geste dont il serait fort instructif de reconstituer le cycle complet, tant dans la littérature bambara que dans le peuple," that is, in Fulani.[19] As a result we find a great number and variety of versions[20] that develop one particular episode and exalt this or that hero, because it is recited for both the contending parties in the struggle, the Fulani and the Bambara. Each time the *griots* are playing to a specific but varying audience. They live by the responses of that audience; they travel, play the lute, and change their story to fit the community in which they are working. In other words, while the Fulani epic, like the epic in general, seems to occur in a society influenced by writing, the form it takes varies considerably depending on the bard, the time, the situation. Such variants should not to my mind be regarded as part of a definitive cycle, for that exists only when inventiveness has stropped and the epic has been circumscribed in text, but rather as part of an expanding universe around a narrative theme.

---

[17] Seydou 1972: 81.
[18] Hiskett 1957; Wilks 1963; Hodgkin 1966.
[19] Seydou 1972: 9–10.
[20] For example, Veillard 1931; Bâ and Kesteloot 1969.

Both Finnegan (1992) and Tedlock (1983) reject the proposition that the epic is characteristically a feature of purely oral cultures and associate it with the early literate cultures of the Old World. Finnegan works mainly on Africa, Tedlock on the Americas. The latter concludes that the only "epic texts with long metrical runs come from folk traditions within larger literate cultures."[21] However, in commenting on these conclusions, Rumsey claims that recitations found among a group of neighboring societies in the New Guinea Highlands do constitute "an oral epic tradition." The examples he gives have a strong narrative content and are marked by formulaic repetition of the kind to which Parry and Lord draw attention in their analysis of Yugoslavian songs. He discusses two kinds of story, *kange* and *temari*, which have been assimilated to the European distinction between "fiction" and "fact"[22] but which others have seen as having more to do with the distinction between the world of narrated events and the here-now world from which they are being narrated.[23] Nevertheless, some kind of "truth value" does seem to be involved. *Kange* tend to be told indoors, at night, after the evening meal. A single individual holds the floor for ten to twenty minutes, and there is a turn-taking rule with a "ratified speaker." Some stories are told by women but to children rather than to the world at large.

Rumsey compares these tales to European epics. But while they are certainly narrative and many have a central heroic character, they are short recitations, mostly running between three hundred and seven hundred lines in length. It is not part of my intent to deny the presence of fictional narrative in oral cultures, merely to say that long narratives are rare and any narrative at all less frequent than has often been thought, because I would suggest, of the inherent problems of fiction. The fact that Rumsey finds (short) epics in the New Guinea Highlands and that Finnegan denies them for black Africa and Tedlock for the Americas in itself raises a problem of presence and absence. Why should such a problem exist at all? Why are epics, defined by Tedlock as "a heroic narrative with a metrical, sung text,"[24] relatively rare in oral cultures? Why do narratives, especially fictional ones, not dominate the discourse of oral cultures, especially in artistic genres, in the way that much contemporary theory about storytelling requires? I am referring here not only to long, substantial recitations. The so-called epics from the New Guinea Highlands are quite short and involve a single speaker holding the

---

[21] Tedlock 1983: 8.
[22] Rumsey forthcoming.
[23] Merlan 1995.
[24] Tedlock 1983: 8.

floor for ten or twenty minutes. Even if we were to see these tales as epics (and they are certainly narrative), we have a problem of presence and absence that needs to be faced beyond saying that this distribution is "cultural." That is a question to which I will return later.

What about other forms of narrative, of storytelling? Legends are often linked to epics, but do not take the same metrical form. Despite their presumed association with the written word (*legenda*, what is read) and their connection with written saints tales and the like, they are also found in oral cultures—in tribal ones in the form of clan histories, and in chiefdoms in the form of dynastic ones. In the latter case they are often much more fragmentary than is often thought; in some cases the state histories take the form of drum titles for chiefs and of chronicles rather than narratives in a stronger sense.

Once again myths, which are perhaps the most studied genre, are too often assumed to be universal. Mythologies are (in the sense of universal constructions of a supernatural order) but myths in the sense of long, supernaturally oriented recitations, of the type recorded for the Zuni of North America or the Bagre of the LoDagaa, which take hours to recite, are very unevenly distributed and much less narrative in form, however, than the early Hindu Mahabratta or even the Gilgamesh "epic" of Mesopotamia (both creations of literate cultures) would lead us to suppose. Myths are standard oral forms; mythologies are bodies of beliefs in the supernatural derived from a multiplicity of sources and reconstructed by the observer, as in the case of the *Mythologiques* of Claude Lévi-Strauss.[25]

Myth does a number of different things. It has some narrative element. But the importance of that has been greatly exaggerated by the collectors of myths (and mythologies), who have asked their respondents for stories and not cared much about the philosophical, theological, and wisdom aspects of the recitation. That is an error that has led in the past, before the portable tape recorder, to considerable misconceptions. At one level I would liken the Bagre to the Bible in the number of tasks it performs. There is the etiological narrative in Genesis, the "wisdom" of Proverbs, and the ritual prescriptions of Leviticus. But there is not a sequential narrative or even continuity running throughout. Hartman (1999) writes not only of its uniqueness but of its unity. Every piece of writing is at some level unique, but that is not I think what is being said. In any case, unity is not the obvious characteristic; books have been aggregated together as a canon almost haphazardly; the unity is given by the ritual context, not by the text.

---

[25] Lévi-Strauss 1969.

What I have called "the Myth of the Bagre" found among the LoDagaa of northern Ghana will serve as an example. It concerns serious supernatural affairs, falling under the category of "proper speech," and it is associated with membership in the Bagre society, which is held to confer medical (and in a sense spiritual) benefits. This long recitation takes six to eight hours to perform in the accepted fashion, with each phrase (or "line" in my transcription) being repeated by the audience of neophytes and members (their guides), and then the whole process is repeated twice yet again by other Speakers. The time taken varies with the Speaker and the degree of elaboration he employs, as well as with the point in the ceremony at which the recitation takes place. It consists of two parts, the White and the Black. The first is an account of the different ceremonies that are held over several weeks, and it is recited up to the point in the sequence that has been reached. The Black, on the other hand, is intended only for the ears of those men (women are now excluded) who have passed through the first initiation and includes some account of how mankind was created (and how he learned to create himself) as well as how he came to acquire the basic elements of his culture, that is, farming, hunting, the raising of livestock, the making of iron, and the brewing of beer.

This is "proper speech" because it concerns man's relationship with the supernatural, especially with the beings of the wild who act as intermediaries, sometimes mischievous, between man and God. And while the outsider may look upon the recitation as "myth," as an imaginative expression of man's relationship with the world and with the divine, for the LoDagaa it is real enough, even though the possibility that it is false is often raised. Indeed, the salvation against trouble, including death itself, that the Bagre medicine offers to new initiates is subsequently shown in the Black Bagre to be an illusion; hopes are raised, only later to be crushed.

However, the point that I want to make here is that, leaving aside the question of fiction, of truth or falsehood, the narrative content of the recitation is limited. A certain framework is provided for the White Bagre, the account of the ceremonies, which explains how the Bagre was started after consultation with a diviner following a series of troubles adjudged to have divine origins. There is obviously a sequence in the account of the ceremonies and of their associated prohibitions and injunctions. But this hardly takes a narrative form. What we do find, on three or four occasions, is short narratives, resembling folktales, embedded in the recitation at certain points in the context of a particular ceremony. Denys Page has remarked upon similar modules embedded in the Homeric poems.[26] These tales do assume a

---

[26] Page 1973.

definitive narrative form, with a beginning, middle, and an end. They also seem to require a different commitment regarding 'belief' than the bulk of the recitation.

The Black Bagre begins in a more promising manner as far as narrative is concerned. The elder of two "brothers" experiences troubles that he attributes to mystical causes. He consults a diviner to find out which ones. As a result, he sets out on a long and arduous journey, which takes him to the Other World. Coming across a river, probably that separating this world from the other, he meets an old man, probably the High God, and with the aid of the spider, climbs up to Heaven (to "God's country"). There he meets "a slender young girl" and the High God shows them how a child is created in a mystical way. The recitation continues at length with the man and woman quarrelling about the ownership of the male child and his education. Meanwhile they are introduced, with the aid of the beings of the wild ("fairies"), to various aspects of LoDagaa culture, to the making of iron, the cultivation of crops, the brewing of beer, and eventually to the procreation, rather than the creation, of children. While a loose narrative frame exists, the greater part of the recitation concerns the description of central aspects of culture, especially its technological processes. And much of the rest deals with philosophical problems (like the problem of evil) and theological ones (like the relationship between the High God and the beings of the wild). Narrativity is not the dominant characteristic. And even these long recitations, myths, are very unevenly distributed. The LoDagaa have them; none of their neighbors apparently do.

What does seem to be universal, at least in the Old World, are folktales. We find these everywhere, often in a surprisingly similar form—short tales, sometimes followed by an inconsequential tail or end, involving as actors humans, animals, and often gods. We may think of the Akan Ananse stories (with the Spider as trickster) as prototypical, together with their Caribbean variants, the Nancy tales of Brer Rabbit.

Those tales have been taken by some observers as representative of primitive thought. Frequently they are envisaged as being told around the evening fire to a mixed audience. My own experience in West Africa is rather different. Such stories, like those in the works of the brothers Grimm, are mainly aimed at children and do not represent the thought of adults in oral cultures. By far the greater part are short folktales (fairy tales) of the kind told to children, not the fare of ordinary adult consumption. They represent primitive mentality only to the extent that "Jack and the Beanstalk" in Europe today can be held to represent contemporary modernity. They are set aside as children's discourse. Indeed, fiction generally is for the young;

adults demand more serious matter, not fictional stories of life or of the Other World, but truthful or near-truthful accounts. The possibility that these are the main forms of narrative fiction in many oral cultures carries another implication, that fiction itself is seen as appropriate for children but not perhaps for adults.

Finally we come to personal narratives. In psychoanalysis the "talking cure" requires both analyst and analysand to construct a case history out of fragmentary conversations, histories that appear in the form of Freud's Dora or the Wolfman. The case history is never produced autonomously but is elicited and created; and it is a creation of a literate society and of literate procedures; like the Mesopotamian Gilgamesh or the contemporary Mungo epic in all probability, it represents a piecing together of fragments to form a continuous narrative, which is never (or very rarely) given to the inquirer on a plate, except in writing.

It seems natural that we should create a narrative summary of our lives, for incorporation in a résumé, for presentation to an analyst, or for elaboration in a diary or an autobiography. But how far are such narratives called for in purely oral cultures? I can think of few if any situations where this happens. It is I, the anthropologist, the psychologist, the historian, who tries to construct life histories (like other histories) from the fragments of knowledge that have come my way, or from the arduous struggle of asking questions and getting one's respondent to respond, to articulate for me what no other situation would prompt him or her to do. Life histories do not emerge automatically; they are heavily constructed. The constructed nature of case histories is superbly bought out by Gilbert Lewis in his *A Failure of Treatment* (2000). The history does not exactly traduce the "facts," but it gives a narrative shape to the fragments of experience that present themselves in quite a different way.

The partial exceptions I have encountered are in visits to a diviner, where he provokes a response by asking what the problem is, or in accounts of past events in hearings of dispute cases in moots and courts. However, in both instances narrative recollection is not elaborated into a complete life history but focused on the situation at hand. The diviner will prompt questions from the client that his paraphernalia of divining instruments will attempt to answer; in moots and courts we have more structured narrative accounts of the dispute, but directed to that incident, even though the notion of relevance may be more inclusive than is usual in a contemporary Western court.

Narrativity, the narrative, and above all the fictional narrative, does not seem to me a prominent characteristic of most oral cultures. The rise of narrative, or of lengthy stories at any rate, is associated with written cultures. It is true that one finds, but very unevenly distributed, some recitations like that of the Bagre, but they are justified by their religious "truth." They can be regarded as fictional only in the same sense that the Old or New Testaments can be so considered.

This absence is not only a matter of the juvenile status of much fiction, of its imaginative relation with "truth." Part of the problem with long recitations is the attention they demand. The situation of an audience sitting round listening quietly to any long recitation seems to me a rare occurrence. Most discourse is dialogic; the listener reacts to what he hears, interrupting any long sequence. One may begin to listen for a short while to an individual's account of his voyage to Kumasi when he went to work down the mines or to another's account of a holiday in Mallorca. But he or she will not in real life be allowed to continue for long without some interruption, such as "I myself had an experience like that." The exception is when a monologue, because that is the nature of narrative, is validated by its supernatural character or context. One is hearing not about mundane matters but about the work of the gods. So such "mythical" accounts tend to be told in ritual contexts where attention is required for magico-religious reasons. It is ritual, ceremony, rather than narrative that is the focus of the recitation, which is often much less a purely storytelling exercise than the term narrative suggests—more like the diversity of discourse we find in the Bible. And in any case, for the listener it is not fiction.

The Novel

Walter Benjamin saw the advent of the novel as putting an end to storytelling (which he sees as basically a speech form), an end that began with the introduction of printing to Europe at the end of the fifteenth century. Lévi-Strauss considered that myth gave way to the novel at the beginning of the eighteenth century. My earlier argument has suggested that storytelling, at least to adults, and indeed narrative in general, received much less emphasis in preliterate cultures than has been assumed. The break came with the coming of the written word. Writing takes place in private. We construct an autobiography, like a diary, in private. Privacy means that we do not face the problem of direct, unmediated communication to an audience, the problem of interruption or its authoritarian suppression; we have the peace and leisure to construct. Of course later on the writing will probably become a public document. And in so doing it sets a model, an agenda, even for orally composed recollection of one's past. Literacy imposes its own pattern on the self-narrative and sets the stage for medical, sociological, psychological, analytic, inquiries where the individual is asked to provide a history, a curriculum vitae. There is feedback from what the written has encouraged and achieved. Narratives, monologues, long recitations, are encouraged by writing. The products include some brands of fiction or fictionlike forms, such as epics of a heroic character or legends like saints' lives. The problems to which fictional narratives earlier gave rise in oral cultures are still there, and that is perhaps one reason why the novel appeared so late on the scene, when printing was available to diffuse it rather than with writing alone. When it does appear, it signals the blossoming of narrative, which subsequently makes its mark in film and in the electronic media.

It is not difficult to see how narrative, the telling of true or fictional stories, was encouraged by writing. Writing automatically involves distance between the teller of tale and the audience in quite a different way from oral storytelling. Both the teller and the reader have time to reflect on what they are doing, either writing or reading, whereas the speaker is in immediate contact with the audience. A sheet of blank paper and a pen is an invitation to produce a narrative of structured recollections or of imaginative invention. One begins at the top of the page and continues to the foot, then goes on to the next. One is (relatively) uninterrupted in the writing as well as in the reading. Human discourse does not work like that; a speaker is constantly being interrupted because, except in authoritarian situations, discourse is dialogic, interactive. A story begins and is interrupted by an interlocutor: "That reminds me of a time . . ." So that the teller does not get the chance to finish a tale, or even a speech, before another breaks in. From one point of view there is no real division between speaker and audience. All are speakers, all are listeners (of a kind), and the conversation proceeeds in starts and stops, often in incomplete sentences and nearly always in unfinished narratives.

Of course there are occasions in an oral culture when a speaker commands an authoritative position and delivers a continuous speech, either directed to a specific occasion or in a standard oral form (which would be "literature" if written). These occasions are rare and special—perhaps a traveler returning from a voyage and telling of her adventures and of the knowledge she has acquired; or in politically centralized regimes, a chief or his spokesman addressing his subordinates gathered before him; or a subject offering praise songs to the ruler, recalling the deeds of ancestors, songs that perhaps verge on fiction.

Just as writing makes "history" possible, so too it promotes life histories. I do not mean to imply that oral cultures have no conception of the past on a societal or on a personal level, but organized, narrative history is rare, and without documents, fragmentary. So in terms of cultural history, what is surprising about the novel, as distinct from narrative more generally, is not simply its absence from oral cultures, but its late and sporadic appearance long after writing was introduced, followed by its great popularity despite the continuing hostility it attracted up to the nineteenth century in Europe, later elsewhere. Today we live in a culture dominated by fiction, as none other has been.

The word *novel* appears to come into English from the Romance languages in the late fifteenth century with the meaning of "news." Within ten years of the advent of the printing press to Europe, around 1486, Henry VII started to publish partisan diplomatic accounts as well as news or announcements in occasional printed broadsheets. By Elizabeth's time, various groups beside the government made use of this media, often for domestic affairs in the form of ballads. The term used for these news-ballads was *novels*, like the French *nouvelle* or the Spanish *novela*. "It only suggested something new, and did not press the issue of facts versus fiction."[27] In the sixteenth century the word is used, after the Italian, to refer to a tale or short story of the kind in Boccaccio's *Decameron*. In the seventeenth century, it comes to be employed as in contemporary English to refer to a long fictional prose narrative in contrast to the romances (the French and Italian *roman* and *romanzo* cover both), because of the close relation to real life. Nevertheless, the problem of acceptability remained. There was still a doubt, expressed by Richard Steele in the *Spectator*, no. 254 (1711) when he wrote, "I'm afraid thy Brains are a little disordered with Romances and Novels." The great diffusion of both was related to the mechanization of writing in the form of printing, reducing the need to read aloud, as many could acquire, even if temporarily from a friend or a library, their own copy for silent perusal.

It was this possibility of a disordered mind that encouraged the notion of people being led astray by fiction, to the symptom of Bovarism named after Flaubert's nineteenth-century novel, but which had arisen much earlier with regard to the romances as we see in Cervantes' *Don Quixote* of 1604, in Charlotte Lennox's *The Female Quixote* of 1751, in the many objections to the novel that were expressed in the eighteenth century, and in the preference of most male readers for nonfiction and the development of a dominantly female reading public.

The novel is clearly a product of literate cultures as well as of leisured

---

[27] Sommerville 1996: 18.

ones, yet it flourished relatively late in cultural history and certainly did not follow closely from the invention of writing itself. Early narratives appear in Greece and Rome, few in the earlier period in the Near East. But stories like Apuleius's *The Golden Ass* or Longus's *Daphne and Chloe* and the erotic romances of the Greeks were at best forerunners of the novel as we know it today.[28] Early examples of narrative fiction, often referred to as romances or novels, that were found in ancient Greek, Roman, and Egyptian literature were relatively short, very different in scope from later novels either in Europe or China. Although these works were thought to have been directed at a popular audience, the reading public was much smaller and more elitist, though it comprised women as well as men.[29] In Egypt, fictional narratives were written in Demotic (from say, the seventh century B.C.E.), but they were apparently all "of fairly modest length." Modest could mean less than six thousand words. Some were longer. "The chief structural means by which stories were made more extensive than a simple anecdote is the device of a story-within-a-story."[30] What kind of status did such fiction have? There is no evidence that narrative texts were used in education. Closer prototypes than these "novels before the novel" appeared in Europe at the end of the Middle Ages, most notably in Rabelais and *Don Quixote*, but also in the mass of French romances of the seventeenth century.

After the classical period and the long hiatus that followed in Europe, fiction seems to have revived only in the twelfth and thirteenth centuries. The historian Norman Daniel sees this revival as representing a bond with oral culture: "The sudden appearance of a fictional literature is evidence of Europe's natural links with the other cultures that derive from the ancient sources of the Near East"—in other words, the Bronze Age cultures with their invention of writing.[31] For example, the earliest example of the "boxed" story (the story-within-a-story as in the *Arabian Nights*, the frame story for which is probably Indian and the first reference from the ninth century) he sees as being Pedro de Alfonso's *Discipline Clericalis*. The author was a converted Jew who translated the tale from the Arabic and "was the first to introduce the genre of fable, a kind of subdivision of Wisdom literature."[32]

---

[28] On the novel in classical societies, see Perry 1967; Heiserman 1977; Hägg 1983; Tatum 1994; Morgan and Stoneman 1994; Holzberg 1995.

[29] Egger, "Looking at Chariton's Callirhoe," in Morgan and Stoneman 1994.

[30] Tatum 1994: 206.

[31] Daniel 1975: 310.

[32] Daniel 1975: 108.

Linked works of Indian origin such as *Kalila wa Dimna* and *The Seven Sages* [also known as the Book of Sinbad] began to appear in the thirteenth century [in Spain; in Greece in the eleventh century], and, a little later, Don Juan Manuel's *El Conde Lucaver*. European boxed stories include the *Confessio Amantis* of Gower, the *Novella* of Giovanni Sércambi [an important future name for the genre in English], Boccaccio (not only *Decameron* but *Arreto*) and, above all, Chaucer's *Canterbury Tales*, as well as the *Tale of Bergis* associated for a time with Chaucer. All these date from the later fourteenth century and represent at least what we have called "Mediterranean culture"; in some cases there are Arabic and even ultimately Indian sources.[33]

What is fascinating here is the relatively late appearance of these narrative forms at roughly the same period in different parts of the globe.

A central problem about the history of the novel is precisely its late arrival on the scene, its initially uneven distribution and its great and widespread popularity since the eighteenth century. The late arrival occurs not only in Europe but in China. Andrew Plaks remarks on "the outstanding coincidence that the rise of prose fiction occurs nearly simultaneously, step by step, in both China and Europe," namely, in the sixteenth century.[34] He tries to explain the appearance of the Ming literati novels, "the four master-works," in terms of the transformation of the Ming economy, factional politics, and the expanding educational system.[35] In other words, the form is certainly not a purely Western phenomenon. While it is not found in all earlier literate societies, the limitation of the discussion of the rise of the novel to Europe, let alone to early eighteenth-century England, has no justification.

But why the uneven distribution and why the late arrival? I suggest the problem goes back to my earlier discussion of narrative, especially fictional narrative, in oral societies. Despite the development of narrative in writing, similar doubts about its fictional forms arose. Storytelling was always an ambiguous activity, implying "telling a story" in the sense of an untruth or even a lie. It failed to represent reality, was not serious.

There were two ways around this problem. As with myth, the narrative could be legitimized in the form of an account of supernatural events, which automatically got around one objection to the reality of the representation. The earlier narratives of Christian Europe were legitimized as being accounts of heavenly miracles (the New Testament) or of the lives of saints, in

---

[33] Daniel 1975: 310.
[34] Plaks 1977: 321.
[35] Plaks 1977: 6ff.

the same way that painting and drawing became possible in the early Middle Ages if the subjects were drawn from religious sources. Even in the eighteenth century, it was this aspect of John Bunyan's *Pilgrim's Progress* that rendered it acceptable to many Nonconformist Protestants.

The modern novel, after Daniel Defoe, was essentially a secular tale, a feature that is comprised within the meaning of "realistic." The hand of God may appear, but it does so through "natural" sequences, not through miracles or mirabilia. Earlier narrative structures often displayed such intervention, which, in a world suffused by the supernatural, was present everywhere. Indeed, one can argue that in such circumstances the actors drew little distinction between natural and supernatural; it was certainly shaded, even in personal narratives. Those times had passed with the saints' tales and with the fantasy of the romance. And even earlier in the classical world, there was a separation between the two, more distinct in some fields than others.

With the coming of the Renaissance and of printing, secular romances made a definite appearance. But they were often ridiculed, seen as fare for leisured women rather than serious men, and having potentially very negative effects on their readers. In eighteenth-century England, the romances of fantasy were supplemented by the realistic novels of Defoe and his followers, more serious and less fanciful.

The early-eighteenth-century novel adopted a different strategy of legitimation, which was its claim to be true to life, to be "a history" rather than "a story." Consider Defoe's attempts to establish the details of the time and place of the tale he is telling. And in fact the tale itself, in the case of *Robinson Crusoe* or *A Journal of the Plague Year*, did oscillate between truth and fiction, incorporating details of actual events. So too with time and place in Henry Fielding or Tobias Smollett. The epistolary mode, adopted by Aphra Benn in the late seventeenth century and later by Samuel Richardson in *Clarissa*, was perhaps another example of this claim.

I have used the words *truth*, *actual*, and *reality* in their obvious, literal, commonplace, perhaps superficial, meaning. There is an equally obvious sense in which these words could be applied to fiction that purported to say something imaginatively about the human condition. But a discrimination between literal truth and poetic truth is often recognized and refers to different modes of discourse. Fictional narrative embodying the second is certainly promoted by the use of writing, but its fictional nature is sometimes concealed either by a concern with the supernatural, the nonnatural or, in the early history of the novel, by the pretence to offer literal truth. In this way the reader's bluff is called, and his or her doubts are calmed.

Despite the new realism in the eighteenth century, the novel was still heavily criticized. As fiction, the novel was widely considered to display a lack of seriousness, much as I have argued it did in many oral cultures. The resistance to the novel continued in eighteenth-century Europe. These objections to the novel and the preference for nonfiction is visible in the history of American printing. The first work in the category of fiction was that ambiguous production by Defoe, *The Dreadful Visitation in a Short Account of the Progress and Effects of the Plague . . . Extracted from the Memory of a Person Who Resided There*. This work, which as we now know was largely imaginative, was published in 1763 by Christopher Sauer of Germanstown, Pennsylvania; *Robinson Crusoe* followed only eleven years later in 1774. New novels were imported from England; they were rare in the publishing world even of the later eighteenth century in America. For early New England firmly rejected the secular trends that it saw as returning with renewed vigor to England with the restoration of the Stuarts to the throne. The Puritans objected to idleness, to the theater, to ribald literature. That included romances, which were seen as especially attractive to women. In 1693, Increase Mather wrote of this "vast mischief of false notions and images of things, particularly of love and honour." While such material was imported and diffused through circulating libraries, the moral arbiters continued to frown on all fiction.[36]

This resistance to fiction by important cultural authorities meant that its consumption and to some extent its production rested on "marginal" elements such as women. In seventeenth-century Europe, as I have pointed out, the main readers of fiction were women; French romances were often written by women, and it was women who formed the main audience of the English novel in the eighteenth century. The dominance of women among the audience was one reason it came under criticism. They were the ones more likely to be misled and deceived, especially by the lengthy romances, though such perils were not limited to women only. The great Spanish novelist Cervantes built the picareque novel, *Don Quixote*, around the deception of the hero, who was led astray as the result of reading old romances.

It was the same in the eighteenth century. As I have noted, the "realism" of the writings of Defoe and others was intended to contrast with these fanciful tales; they "deceived" in another manner, by making false claims to historical truth as a way of presenting an imaginative tale that came closer to reality. In this way they attempted to circumvent the criticism of the old romances that they misled people into not only false beliefs but into false

---

[36] Mather quoted in Daniels 1995: 46.

conduct. The statement of this position is nowhere clearer than in Charlotte Lennox's *The Female Quixote*, in which she tells the story of Arabella, who was herself misled by the reading "the great Store of Romances" left by her mother.

Such possibility of deception was not confined to the French and other romances; it was equally criticized in the Gothic novels of the later eighteenth century, above all by Jane Austen in *Northanger Abbey*. As noted by Arnold Kettle, Q. D. Leavis emphasizes "how strong a part in Jane Austen's novels is played by her conscious war on the romance. She did to the romance of her day (whether the domestic romance of Fanny Burney or the Gothic brand of Mrs. Radcliffe) what Cervantes had done in his."[37]

The heroine of the novel is Catherine Morland, who strikes up a friendship with Isabella Thorpe in the Pump-room at Bath. The relationship between the two develops rapidly. When it was wet, they read novels together. "Yes novels," declares the author, "for I will not adopt that ungenerous and impolitic custom so common with novel writers, of degrading by their contemptuous censure the very performances, to the number of which they are themselves adding. . . . Let us leave it to Reviewers to abuse such effusions of fancy at their leisure, and to talk in threadbare strains of the trash with which the press now groans. . . . Although our productions have afforded more extensive and unaffected pleasure than those of any other literary corporation in the world, no species of composition has been more decried." With this reputation, which the author herself discusses, Jane Austen contrasts that of the *Spectator* or other nonfiction ("gentlemen read better books").

All Catherine's experience comes from reading fiction. She "had read too much not to be perfectly aware of the care with which a waxen figure might be introduced [into the coffin], and a suppostitious funeral carried on." As with Don Quixote, with which the theme is often compared, reading led her away from reality into "fancy" (that is, fantasy), which turned out to be "folly."

That reading colors her entire journey to Northanger Abbey. Nothing "could shake the doubts of the well-read Catherine"; castles and abbeys were "the charm of her reveries" and with them went "the hope of some traditional legends, some awful memorials of an injured and ill-fated nun." Riding there in the curricle with her suitor, Henry Tilney, she anticipates "a fine old place, just like what one reads about." He plays on this expectation: "Are you prepared to encounter all the horrors that a building such as 'what one reads

---

[37] Kettle 1965: 112.

about' may produce?" He then goes on to elaborate all the "Gothic" possibilities of this Gothic Abbey. Her responses are fully roused by the storm that
strikes the building on her first night and by the closed chest and cupboard
that prove to contain nothing more than spare linen and a laundry list.

She suffers from "causeless terror" that results from "self-created delusion," all due to the indulgence of that sort of reading. For it was not in the
works of Mrs. Radcliffe that "human nature, at least in the midland counties
of England, was to be looked for." Her suspicions are unfounded and Henry
Tilney upbraids her. "Remember that we are English, that we are Christians.
Consult your own understanding, your own sense of the probable, your own
observations of what is passing around you." Not books but your own experience. Her disillusion is complete. "The visions of romance were over," and
Catherine is "completely awakened . . . from the extravagances of her late
fancies."

The advocacy of "critical realism" in *Northanger Abbey* is not isolated.[38]
Criticism of the novel, at least of the romantic and Gothic novel, appears in
Maria Edgeworth's *Belinda* (1801) where Lady Delacour comments, "My
dear, you will be woefully disappointed, if in my story you expect anything
like a novel." In her early writings, Jane Austen engages in burlesques that
take the form of "the direct inflation of the novel style." In *Love and Friendship* (1790), Edward's father asks, "Where Edward in the name of wonder
did you pick up this unmeaning gibberish? You have been studying Novels,
I suspect." The genre came in for heavy criticism for being either a simulacrum or a travesty of life.

The best-known literary example of this kind of deception is undoubtedly Flaubert's *Madame Bovary* (1857); indeed the predicament of the
eponymous heroine has given rise to the problem of "bovarism." Her problem is not only being misled by novels but by reading in general. Like Don
Quixote and Arabella, Emma Bovary is effectively in retirement, living in
the country, married to a boring doctor and having little to do but lead a
fantasy life of the imagination in which reading plays a dominant part. But
her imagination revolves around contemporary life, not the past; she constructs a virtual reality. She buys herself a street map of Paris, and

> with the tip of her finger, she went shopping in the capital. . . . She took out a
> subscription . . . to *Le Sylphe des Salons*. She devoured every single word of
> all the reviews of the first nights, race-meetings and dinner parties. . . . She

---

[38] A. D. McKillop, "Critical Realism in *Northanger Abbey*," in I. Watt, ed., *Jane Austen: A
Collection of Critical Essays* (Englewood Cliffs, N.J., 1963), 52–61.

knew the latest fashions . . . she read Balzac and Georges Sand, seeking to gratify in fantasy her secret cravings. Even at the table, she had her book with her, and she would be turning the pages, while Charles was eating and talking to her. The memory of the Viscount haunted her reading. Between him and the fictional characters, she would forge connections.[39]

Emma uses novels to escape from her own present into another imaginary present. Books dominate her life. She entertains the young clerk, Leon, with the fashion magazines she has brought along. He "sat beside her and they looked at the engraved plates together and waited for each other at the bottom of the page. Often she would ask him to read her some poetry. . . . And so between them arose a kind of alliance, a continual commerce in books and ballads." When a certain novel starts a fashion for cactuses, he buys some for her in Rouen. The book overshadows all and directs much of the course of events for those who immerse themselves in it. This gives rise to a dependency on fiction, to a kind of addiction, to a devaluing of the life into which one was born and a hunger for a life of luxury, of a higher stratum. These qualities were thought to be characteristic of "women in idleness," and a novelist portraying them reveals his own ambivalence toward the feminine; in criticizing them Flaubert is consciously playing with what he called his own feminine disposition.

These criticisms of the effects of fiction did not of course appear only within the pages of the novel itself. Already in 1666, Pierre Nicole, in *Les visionnaires*, describes "un faiseur de romans et un poète de théâtre" as "un empoisonneur public." One hundred years later, Dr. Pomme, in *Traité des affections vaporeuses des deux sexes* (1767), suggests that among all the causes that have harmed the health of women, "la principale a été la multiplication infinie des romans depuis cent ans." Concern about health continued. In 1900, La Baronne Staffe was still worrying about women in *Le cabinet de toilette*: "Restez assise, tard dans la nuit, à lire des romans, voilà ce qui creuse autour des yeux ces terribles petits sillons entrecroisés, qui défigurent le plus joli visage."

Moral health was even more at risk. In 1884, Gustave Claudin announced, "Ce sont surtout les dames légères qui font la plus grande consommation de romans"; while as late as 1938, Jacques Leynon protested that soon every novel would have to have a chapter taking place in a brothel.[40]

---

[39] Flaubert 1857: 45. Trans. G. Wall (Harmondsworth, 1992).

[40] These quotations are taken from G. Bechtel and J.-C. Carrière, *Dictionnaire de la bêtise et des erreurs de jugement* (Paris, 1984), for which reference I am indebted to Wolfgang Klein.

The Holy Book and Christian literature were approved. That was the fare of Roman ladies in the first centuries of Christianity, not the light novels of to-day, whose reading is so dangerous. Nor is their perusal confined to the towns: "L'on rencontre dans la lande la gardeuses de brébis qui a glissé sous son capoulet le mauvais roman passé de main et main, et qu'elle a encore la pudeur de vouloir caché."

Why were criticisms of the novel and of fiction in general especially prevalent in Europe in the eighteenth century? That of course was the time when the genre took off, so we could also expect it to be marked by pro-nounced resistance. It was also the period of the Enlightenment, of the new *Encyclopedia*, when many institutions were being queried.

Criticisms of the novel, doubts about its legitimacy, were not confined to Europe, any more than was the novel itself. Such objections lay at the root of its frequently marginal status and indeed of its failure to appear at all in many times and places. The early novel from eleventh-century Japan, *The Tale of Genji* by the Lady Murasaki, achieved a canonical status. Neverthe-less, it attracted many objections, from Confucian scholars especially, owing to "its fictional character and concentration on amorous relationships." In the Confucian tradition, the distrust of fiction is usually traced to a saying in *Analects*: "The subjects on which the Master did not talk were extraordinary things, feats of strength, disorder, and spiritual beings." Fiction was among the genres of literature scorned by Confucian literati. McMullen comments, "In part, this distrust must derive from the rational, didactic tenor of the tra-dition. Events that involved fanciful or strained credulity also lacked persua-sive, narrative power; they were falsehoods, the products of undisciplined, indulgent minds, that could undermine the truth." This view is represented in the *Genji* itself. Indeed, the novel was defended by the great commenta-tor of the early Tokugawa period, Kumazawa Banzan, as being a true record; it is not "a bookful of lies." Banzan adopts another line too, however, also found in Europe, justifying a genre where "no fact exists but where a moral truth is comprehended and a fact supplied for it"—the underlying imagina-tive or experiential truth.[41]

Similar criticisms arose wherever we find the novel—in China, for exam-ple. The concept of *wen*, imitation, is discussed in the context of narrative literature, both historical and fictional. Indeed, the preferred form of fiction is often historical; the purely fictional is doubly suspect. As Plaks remarks, the act of fiction writing is "the business of fabricating illusions of reality";

---

[41] McMullen 1999.

the opening formula of the "Heart Sutra" that appears in *Jinping mei* (*The Golden Lotus*) reads, "reality is emptiness, emptiness is reality."[42] The novels themselves offer criticisms of the way of life they describe, "the fourfold scourges of excessive indulgence in wine, women, wealth and wrath."[43] Indeed, the works themselves also contain some warnings about indulgence in fiction. As in the eighteenth-century English novel, "the simulated narrators' recurrent use of the *rhetoric* of historiography in introductory sections, asides, and concluding comments . . . to emphasize the sense of judgement going hand-in-hand with the mimetic presentation of events" may encourage the "sense that the fictional narration may convey generalized truth even where it forgoes the presumption of historical veracity."[44] Chinese literature has an important didactic component, often with Buddhist monks or Daoist recluses coming forward "to preach what seems to be the author's own message of worldly renunciation," showing "the futility of it all."[45] That moral message poses problems in the face of the manifest content, often turning on "excessive indulgence" and may lead to the introduction of warnings against fiction, at least in the hands of the young. That seems to have been more generally the view; the contents of novels were essentially frivolous, and indeed lewd and immoral. But there is a wider problem of truth and fiction that no amount of overlap (history/story) can entirely evade and that emerges in Confucian reactions, such as the criticisms of *The Tale of the Genji* in Japan. The balance that Plaks sees between the two also contains a contradiction that (under some circumstances) may lead to rejection as well as to acceptance.

Particular works might be suppressed for particular reasons. *Water Margin*, a tale of outlawry and rebellion, was thought to encourage brigands. Fiction and reality were merged; the work attacked the abuse of power and misgovernment, and is reformist in tone despite "the anarchic actions of its heroes." However, "many late Ming peasant rebel leaders were taking the names or nicknames of *Water Margin* heroes for themselves."[46] The authorities perceived this as a threat and ordered the work to be suppressed in 1642. The same happened to *The Merry Adventures of Emperor Yang*, not so much because of "its explicit descriptions of the emperor's less conventional

---

[42] Plaks 1977: 511–12.
[43] Plaks 1977: 505.
[44] Plaks 1977: 328.
[45] Plaks 1977: 352.
[46] Hegel 1981: 77.

sexual exploits" but because it raised the question of the limits of loyalty.[47] *The Prayer Mat of Flesh* was "more effectively proscribed."[48]

This constellation of opposition to the novel recalls immediately the similar set of societies I have discussed elsewhere regarding opposition to images and to the theater, as well as to relics (bones) and flowers.[49] The suspicion that we are dealing with a general phenomenon is again strengthened. It is strengthened still further when we look at recent events in China where again we find the suppression of flowers, of religious (and other) images, and of the theater. The novel shares in this history. In the Sichuan town of Yebin during the Cultural Revolution, Jung Chang's mother initially had a hard time in her party cell, being subject to continual criticism. But when she was moved to a new job and a new cell, things were better: "Instead of sniping at her like Mrs. Mi, Mrs. Tung let my mother do all sorts of things she wanted, like reading novels; before, reading a book without a Marxist cover would bring down a rain of criticism about being a bourgeois intellectual."[50]

In Islam and in Judaism objections seem to have gone deeper. The former made a firm distinction between historical truth and religious myths on the one hand, and imaginative fiction on the other. Such storytelling might be used, as in the *Thousand and One Nights*, to distract, but it consisted essentially of a distraction from more serious activities. In the Arab world there were general objections to affabulation in historical and exegetical work, and occasional and casual expression of contempt from a learned standpoint was directed at the *Thousand and One Nights*. But such tales were not only read before plebeian audiences; they seem to have been in favor at court, especially those containing mirabilia, like the voyages of Sinbad. Once again objections to fiction, ambivalences to created narrative, seem to be rooted in the fact that it "re-presents" reality and is not itself the truth. Even serious narrative may be looked down upon as a way of discovering truth more appropriate for children and for those who need guidance than for the sophisticated searcher, rather like icons for early Christians and Buddhists.

Later in nineteenth-century Europe such criticism was more muted. That was when fiction came into its own with the reading public, with the great novelists—Scott, the Brontës, Dickens, Eliot, Meredith, and Trollope

---

[47] Hegel 1981: 85.
[48] Hegel 1981: 227.
[49] Goody 1997.
[50] Jung Chang 1991: 26.

in England. This dominance of the novel has been seen as deeply transforming human emotions and behavior. While that may be partially true, it
is also accused of making such behavior more shallow, as the result of copying the actions of the characters in romances. That was a constant criticism
during the eighteenth century and remained in force during the nineteenth,
when Madame Bovary was seduced away from reality by the novel's fictions, indeed by reading itself. The defense again lay in its role in peering
below the surface at the underlying "truth" of the novel, at least of the distinguished novel. But that approach provided no defense at all against the
bulk of fiction, whether of Dame Barbara Cartland and other Mills and
Boon romances, or of most detective series, thrillers, and westerns, which
are frankly escapist, as is most film and television. That movement certainly
represents a major shift over the past hundred years or so. Until the midnineteenth century, most published books were theological in character. If
they read, most men read serious nonfictional works, whereas fiction was
left largely to women to read, and sometimes to create. The situation began
to change with the historical romances of Scott, and today the readership of
the novel is no longer gendered in the same way, although certain types may
well be.

This form has today become a completely accepted genre, largely immune
from earlier criticism. Indeed the phrase "criticism of the novel" has acquired a totally different meaning as the genre has moved from the shadows
to a dominant position on the literary scene. As with images during this the
same period, now diffused in every corner of society through printing, iconoclasm virtually disappeared, so overwhelming was the presence. Something
of the same process seems to have occurred with fiction; objections were
drowned out by the sheer quantity coming off the presses and the incorporation of the novel into daily life. However, the contradictions, which, as I have
argued elsewhere, are inherent in the process of representation, still found
occasional expression. Even in the sphere of the visual arts, where both
painting and sculpture long preceded the dominance of the novel, opposition
has continued. Walter Benjamin called attention to the recent victory of the
visual arts (perhaps especially noticeable for a Jew as for a Puritan), and he
attributed this to the tidal wave of cheap publications made available by
changes in the modes of communication. Nevertheless, resistance continued,
at least in the visual domain, taking shape in the works of French abstract
painters. For them the represented object was merely the superficial manifestation of a more profound truth, an essence, a purity, that could be expressed
only in the absence of objects, of figurative representation, of iconicity. Perhaps the same kind of resistance to pictorial representations also takes the

contemporary shape of preserving the carcass of a sheep in formaldehyde; only the real thing is truth, never the still life, *nature morte*.

Did the same process occur with fictional representations? There have been a number of attempts at the anti-novel, and radical efforts to reorganize it on less narrative lines. James Joyce, Virginia Woolf, and others too, in *le nouveau roman*, have made moves in this direction. But basically the storytelling form has endured, with volumes filling the windows of our bookshops and the newstands of our railways and airports by authors who had their roots in the late impressionists that reached their apogee in Russia with Kasimir Malevich and Wassily Kandinsky, with their philosophical justifications for the abstract as attaining purity of vision. Was the dominance of the novel, at least at the popular level, partly the result of its changing content, that is, to the elaboration of specifically sexual themes (for example, in the romantic novel) and of the murder mystery (in the detective story)? Both of these topics were often suppressed in earlier literature. Love was not suppressed but sex was, except in Chinese novels such as *Ching Ping Mei* and in the erotic novels of ancient Greece, and that too was the situation in seventeenth- and eighteenth-century Europe. This raises the question of how far storytelling is linked to seduction. In *Othello*, the Moor claims he attracted Desdemona, the daughter of a Venetian senator, by his tales of foreign lands, of

> The Anthropophagi, and men whose heads
> Did grow beneath their shoulders.
>
> . . . .
>
> She'd come again, and with a greedy ear
> Devour up my discourse.
>
> . . . .
>
> She love me for the dangers I had passed. (1.3.143–66)

Telling a story, creating one's fictional biography or personal life, is part of many a courting encounter. The story and its telling either seduces or prevents seduction, as with Shaharazad and Sinbad.

The change represents a shift of interest in reading to one in which the majority were concerned, after their time at school or at university, with "entertainment," with distraction. The sales figures for books amply illustrate the different perspective, and that has to be regarded as a change of consciousness. It is true that individuals now read more newspapers, more "serious" journalism, probably more biographies and autobiographies, and that their knowledge of the world is more profound than in earlier times. But so too is their desire for entertainment, especially home entertainment, made possible by the relative cheapness of reading matter and by the installation of the radio, television, and computer in the home, bringing there fiction and film as well as the news and commentaries, including public discussions of contemporary issues.

With the novel, one hears complaints of triviality, of escapism, rather in the same vein as the eighteenth century saw fiction as more appropriate for women in their domestic capacities than for men working in the outside world. Today, biography is perhaps more masculine, more concerned with the world. Can the novel, offering an imaginative version of experience, ever compete with the reality of everyday life, especially in the aftermath of the Holocaust? That at least is the problem raised by the novelist Wolfgang Holdesheimer, an interpreter at the Nuremburg trials. In a lecture in Dublin in 1981, he predicted the end of the novel, as fiction was incapable in his eyes of taking stock of the complexities of our age, in particular of the horrors of mass extermination. There are topics with which imaginative fiction cannot expect to deal.

Conclusions

In summary, my argument runs as follows. Narrative, and in particular fictional narrative, is not a predominant characteristic of adult intercourse in purely oral (nonliterate) cultures. Long narrative sequences, whether fictional or not, require special discourse situations. Short fictional narratives, or folktales, are aimed mostly at children—adults already know "Cinderella" and do not need it repeated, partly because the content is clearly aimed at a juvenile audience. Longer recitations, in which the narrative element is rarely the most prominent, require a ritual setting to provide an attentive audience for whom the hearing may be something of an ordeal, and require a validation beyond from the human realm. Contrary to many beliefs, the epic is characteristic not of oral cultures (though it may be presented in speech) but of early literate ones. That was also, in my view, the case with Homer and the Vedic epics.[51]

The reasons for the scarcity of long fictional narratives is different from that for long recitations in general. As with shorter folktales, the former

---

[51] Goody 1987.

may be recognized as trivial, fit for children, as compared with the weightier demands of truth. In other words, their scarcity is related to the inherent problem in representations of all kinds pointed out by Plato—but in no sense limited to the Western tradition—that fiction is not historical (self-evident) truth; it is from the literal point of view a lie, although it may aim at another kind of imaginative truth—aim at but not necessarily succeed in achieving. And for some that aim will always remain illusory; the biography, which doubtless contains its element of make-believe, may be preferred to the invented story, which may offer only a distraction, not a truth of any kind.

In real life the narrative is rarely unchallenged. The legal/jural process is perhaps the touchstone because the narrative is part of the duel: the plaintiff tells his or her story, the defendant another; one is judged to be truthful, the other a lie (or at least is not believed). Doubts about fiction, about the novel, have dogged the history of this genre, because such worries are embedded in the human situation. With the dominance of "fictionality" in Europe from the eighteenth century, with its becoming so central a feature of our lives with the advent of printing, of the rotary press, and finally of the electronic media, with the cinema and with television, resistance to fiction and the novel has become less explicit. Yet some tension remains.

For fiction is the domain of fancy and fantasy. The sharp contrast between fancy and reality is a key theme of the poems of John Keats. Fancy is highly praised in the poem of that name (1820):

> Ever let the Fancy roam,
> Pleasure never is at home;
> At a touch sweet Pleasure melteth,
> Like to bubbles when rain pelteth; . . . (1–4)

Fancy can step in when life disappoints. But it only does so in a deceptive (lying) way, as we are told in the final stanza of "Ode to a Nightingale."

> Forlorn! the very word is like a bell
> To toll me back from thee to my sole self!
> Adieu! the fancy cannot cheat so well
> As she is fam'd to do, deceiving elf. (71–74)

My interest in narrative, especially fictional narrative, arises from my interest in representations. Narrative itself I argue is not as pervasive as many recent accounts suggest, certainly not in purely oral cultures. When one thinks of it, life does not proceed like a sequential narrative. It is full of repetitions (the breakfast menu, the embrace on parting) that would make little narrative sense. The narrative, but not the sequence in a looser sense, is broken by knocks on the door, by the next e-mail message (one is bleeping its way through as I write), by scarcely relevant thoughts. Hence the stream of consciousness may be a closer representation of reality than the narrative, which I am using with a tighter meaning than pure sequence.

Fiction, as distinct from narratives of actual events, adds another dimension. At the surface level it is plainly not "true," though it may claim to be so. So in this sense it is a lie, as Plato maintained of the arts in general. To represent was not to present; it embodied an illusion. It was this doubt, lying at the core of the arts, that led not only to criticism of their achievements but at times to their virtual banishment. To this I attribute the virtual disappearance of the great artistic achievements of the classical world, of sculpture, and of three- and even two-dimensional representation in a secular context during the European Middle Ages. So too, representation in the form of the theater vanished from the scene. Physically the theater collapsed; indeed, in St. Albans and elsewhere it seems to have been deliberately destroyed early in the fourth century C.E. and did not reappear except in temporary form for some 1,500 years.

There are two aspects to these absences and doubts. The first expresses a reaction to the "luxuries" of post–Bronze Age culture, to the emergence of the stage, to the development of aesthetic activities such as reading novels and painting pictures, which were enjoyed mainly by the few who had the leisure, education, and motivation to participate. These luxury cultures were differentiated in material and cultural terms. That situation often gives rise to some kind of ideological and practical opposition, often expressed most clearly by moralists, philosophers, and theologians. But there is a second problem inherent in representation itself and therefore in fiction.

Any form of re-presentation may raise doubts and hence ambivalence about its relationship with the original. Such doubts I suggest are inherent in the human situation of language-using animals facing their environment. It is intrinsic to language, and therefore to narrative. A *horse* (the word) is never a horse (the animal). An account of events is never the events themselves. When it does not even pretend to be such an account but is fictional, the situation is aggravated. It is I think because of these general Platonic objections, reinforced in post–Bronze Age cultures by parallel "puritanical" tendencies that are generally constructed around the rejection of luxury, that fiction, including the novel, has attained the history and the distribution that has marked it worldwide. Even in oral cultures it is largely assigned to children and until recently raised widespread doubts for adults, above all for those concerned with the running of society.

Writing modifies some of those doubts; fiction and narrative expand. But doubts persist, even today where the genre has become dominant, and there remains a substantial divide between entertainment and more "serious" writing, between fiction and nonfiction.

References

Austen, Jane. [1818] 1928. *Northanger Abbey*. In *Complete Novels*, ed. J. C. Squire. London.

Bâ, A.-H., and L. Kesteloot, eds. 1969. *Kaïdara*. Paris.

Benjamin, W. 1968a [1936]. "The Work of Art in the Age of Mechanical Reproduction." In W. Benjamin, *Illuminations: Essays and Reflections*, ed. H. Arendt. New York.

———. 1968b. "The Storyteller." In above.

Chadwick, H. M. and N. K. Chadwick. 1932–40. *The Growth of Literature*. 3 vols. Cambridge.

Clark, K. and M. Holquist. 1984. *Mikhail Bakhtin*. Cambridge, Mass.

Daniel, N. 1975. *European-Arab Relations during the Middle Ages*. London.

Daniels, B. C. 1995. *Puritans at Play: Leisure and Recreation in Colonial New England*. New York.

Derrida, J. 1978. *Writing and Difference*. London.

Deshussan, P. 1998. "Monologue au désert." *Le Monde*, August 14.

Doody, M. A. 1997. *The True Story of the Novel*. New Brunswick, N.J.

Edgeworth, Maria. [1801] 1986. *Belinda*. London.

Finnegan, R. 1970. *Oral Literature in Africa*. Oxford.

Flaubert, G. 1857. *Madame Bovary*, trans. G. Wall. Harmondsworth, 1992.

Goody, J. 1972. *The Myth of the Bagre*. Oxford.

———. 1977. "Tradizione orale e ricostruzione del passata nel Ghana del Nord." *Quaderni Storici* 35:481–92.

———. 1987. *The Interface between the Written and the Oral*. Cambridge.

———. 1997. *The Culture of Flowers*. Cambridge.

Goody, J., and S. W. K. Gandah, eds. 1981. *Une récitation du Bagré*. Paris.

Goody, J., and I. P. Watt. 1963. "The Consequences of Literacy." *Comparative Studies in Society and History* 5:304–45.

Hägg, T. 1983. *The Novel in Antiquity*. Oxford.

Hartman, G. H. 1999. "The Struggle for the Text." In *A Critic's Journey, 1958–1998*. New Haven, Conn.

Hegel, R. E. 1981. *The Novel in Seventeenth-Century China*. New York.

Heiserman, A. 1977. *The Novel before the Novel*. Chicago.

Hiskett, M. 1957. "Material Relating to State of Learning among the Fulani before the *Jihad*." *Bull, S.O.A.S.* 19:550–78.

Hodgkin, T. 1966. "The Islamic Literary Tradition in Ghana." In I. M. Lewis, ed., *Islam in Tropical Africa*. London.

Holzberg, N. 1995. *The Ancient Novel: An Introduction*. Chicago.

Jameson, F. 1981. *The Political Unconscious: Narrative as a Socially Symbolic Act*. London.

Jung Chang. 1991. *Wild Swans*. London.

Keats, John. 1939. *Poetical Works*, ed. H. W. Garrad. Oxford.

Kettle, A. 1965. "Emma." In I. Watt, ed., *Jane Austen: A Collection of Critical Essays*. Englewood Cliffs, N.J.

Leroy, J. 1985. *Fabricated World: An interpretation of Kewa Tales*. Vancouver.

Lévi-Strauss, C. 1969. *Mythologiques*. Paris.

Lewis, G. 2000. *A Failure of Treatment*. Oxford.

Lord, A. B. 1960. *The Singer of Tales*. Cambridge, Mass.

McMullen, J. 1999. *Idealism, Protest and the Tale of Genji: The Confucianism of Kumazawa Banzan*. Oxford.

Merlan, F. 1995. "Indigenous Narrative Genres in the Highlands of Papua New Guinea." In P. Silberman and J. Loftlin, eds., *Proceedings of the Second Annual Symposium about Language and Society*. Austin, Tex.

Morgan, J. R., and R. Stoneman, eds. 1994. *Greek Fiction: The Greek Novel in Context*. London.

Nicole, Pierre. 1666. *Les visionnaires*. Vol. 2 of *L'hérésie imaginaire*. Liège.

Orwell, G. 1968. "Looking Back on the Spanish Civil War." In S. Orwell and I. Angus, eds., *Collected Essays*. London.

Page, D. 1973. *Folktales in Homer's Odyssey*. Cambridge, Mass.

Parry, M. 1971. *The Making of Homeric Verse*, ed. A. Parry. Oxford.

Perry, B. E. 1967. *The Ancient Romances as a Literary-Historical Account of Their Origins*. Berkeley, Calif.

Plaks, A. H., ed. 1977. *Chinese Narrative: Critical and Theoretical Essays*. Princeton, N.J.

Pomme, Pierre. 1767. *Traité des affections vaporeuses des deux sexes*. Paris.

Rumsey, A. Forthcoming. "*Tom Yaya Kange*: An Oral Epic Tradition in the New Guinea Highlands." In C. O'Neil and M. Scoggin, eds., *Politics, the Individual, and Imagination: A Tribute to Paul Friedrich*.

Seydou, C., ed. 1972. *Silâmaka et Poullôri*. Paris.

Somé, M. 1994. *Of Water and the Spirit: Magic and Initiation in the Life of an African Shaman*. New York.

Sommerville, C. J. 1996. *The News Revolution in England: Cultural Dynamics of Daily Information*. Oxford.

Staffe, La Baronne. 1891. *Le cabinet de toilette*. Paris.

Tatum, J. A., ed. 1994. *The Search for the Ancient Novel*. Baltimore.

Tedlock, D. 1983. *The Spoken Word and the Work of Interpretation*. Philadelphia.

Veillard, G. 1931. "Récits peuls du Maccina et du Kounari." *Bull, du comité d'études historiques et scientifiques de l'Afrique Occidentales Française* 14:137–56.

Wilks, I. 1963. "The Growth of Islamic Learning in Ghana." *Journal of the Historical Society of Nigeria* 2:409–17.

LUIZ COSTA LIMA

The Control of the Imagination and the Novel

An enormous difference in status separates the terms most essential to this essay: imagination, novel, and control. While *imagination*, as a psychic faculty or force whose activation would be considered decisive for the creation of the artistic product from the moment that art was conceived as autonomous, and *novel*, as the dominant literary genre since the eighteenth century, are terms of great legitimacy in literary study, *control* only recently was designated an operative analytic term.[1] Moreover, having been taken up by only a few critics in the meantime, its presence as a theoretical term has been virtually null.[2] This difference underlies the construction of this argument and constitutes its essential difficulties. Given this difference, I will restrict the preliminary presentation of the legitimized terms to the fundamental, in order to articulate more fully the term without status. Insofar as the theoretical information must be sufficiently reconciled with an empirical framework to permit me to demonstrate this latter term in action, this will require an elucidation of the particularities of Latino-American literature.

The Imagination in Antiquity and Modernity: From Aristotle to Coleridge

When and how did Western thought begin to reflect on the imagination? It was initially delineated as a secondary topos in a chapter of Aristotle's *De anima*. Victor Caston demonstrates that the philosopher needed it to show "that the content of mental states can eventually *diverge* from all that is actually in the world."[3] In other words, *fantasy* served to test a theory that

---

[1] The term was first defined in L. Costa Lima, *O controle do imaginário: Razão e imaginação nos tempos modernos* (São Paulo, 1984), trans. Ronald W. Sousa as *Control of the Imaginary: Reason and Imagination in Modern Times* (Minneapolis: University of Minnesota Press, 1988). It was subsequently developed in *Sociedade e discurso ficcional* (Rio de Janeiro, 1986) and *O fingidor e o censor* (Rio de Janeiro, 1988), works that were merged together in the English translation, *The Dark Side of Reason: Fictionality and Power*, trans. Paolo Henriques Britto (Stanford, Calif.: Stanford University Press, 1992).

[2] In this regard, see the article by Sérgio Alcides in *Portuguese Literary & Cultural Studies*, ed. J. C. de Castro, 4 (Spring 2000).

[3] Victor Caston, "Pourquoi Aristote a besoin de l'imagination," *Les Études Philosophiques* (January–March 1997): 4.

sought to demonstrate the existence of psychological error. In line with the theories of his predecessors, Aristotle's theory did not reckon with the criterion of falsifiability. Reduced to its simplest expression, his theory affirmed that *sensation* and *conceptual apprehension* constituted the base operations, respectively, of perception and of the majority of intentional states. An instrument would be necessary to prove this. Herein lay the vitality of fantasy, for "this other mental state would not be able to be identified either with sensation or with conceptual apprehension, nor would it be able to be understood according to their model: in contrast to what holds true for these two prior states, *fantasy* and all the states just mentioned (imagination,[4] association, memory, anticipation, reason, deliberation, desire, action, passions, and dreams) can diverge from reality."[5] In Aristotle's own words: "Imagination is different from either perceiving or discursive thinking, though it is not found without sensation, or judgment without it. . . . For imagining lies within our own power whenever we wish (e.g., we can call up a picture, as in the practice of mnemonics by the use of mental images), but in forming opinions we are not free: we cannot escape the alternative of falsehood or truth."[6]

Hence Aristotle's immediate task is to demonstrate the different function of fantasy relative to sensation and cognition. Aristotle's basic reasoning in *De anima* is as follows: first, feeling is a faculty or activity, while imagination occurs in the absence of both, like that which occurs in dreams (428a5–8); second, while all moving animals possess sensations, the majority do not know the imagination; third, if sensations are always true, the imagination in most cases is false (428a11–12). Insofar as cognition is concerned: imagination, capable of being false, cannot be confused with cognition or intelligence, which can never be in error (428a17–18). Nor can it be confused with opinion, since opinion supposes belief and, even when animals possess an imaginative capacity, we never find in them any evidence of belief. Hence Aristotle concludes: "It is clear then that the imagination cannot, again, be opinion *plus* sensation, or opinion mediated by sensation, or a blend of opinion and sensation" (428a24–26). For these reasons, "*fantasy* stands midway between these divers faculties. It is more fundamental than the intellectual

---

[4] For the author, *fantasy* is the general term that includes the imagination—"the meaning of interior images" ("le sens d'images intérieures")—and not, as usually translated, its synonym.

[5] Caston, "Pourquoi Aristote," 25.

[6] Aristotle, *De anima*, 3.3. 427b14–21. The English translation (cited hereafter in the text) is *On the Soul*, in *The Complete Works of Aristotle*, vol. 1, ed. J. Barnes (Princeton, N.J.: Princeton University Press, Bollingen Series, 1985).

faculties, extending to the animal kingdom, but it is also susceptible to error. From this vantage point, it functions ideally to explain errors manifest in behavior, even in those animals that are nonrational."[7]

While we can satisfy ourselves with a schematic tracing of the development of the Aristotelian concept of fantasy, we cannot do without an essential elaboration by the commentator or without commentary on a passage from *De anima* that Caston deems unnecessary. His elaboration still concerns the distinctiveness of imagination in relation to sensation: while sensation promotes a disturbance in which it is felt, the *phantasm*, that is, the product of fantasy, has the character of an echo, thus signifying a deviation from its original stimulus.[8] From this observation the commentator extracts a consequence that deserves more unfolding than I can undertake here: "*The causal chain that reconducts it* [i.e., the *phantasm*] *to its object is in no way essential*, since that which determines the content of a *phantasm* is not its causal antecedent, but its causal capability; and it can happen that this 'echo' is *modified* on the path that conducts it to the central organ in a manner that alters its causal capacities."[9] Let me add only that this property of deviating from the causal chain to which sensations are subject gives the product of fantasy a peculiarity that would be developed dramatically once it surpassed the secondary state to which it was relegated by ancient thought. The passage that Caston disdains, in fact, closes Aristotle's chapter on the history of the imagination: "Because imaginations remain in the organs of sense and resemble sensations, animals in their actions are largely guided by them, some (i.e., the brutes) because of the non-existence in them of thought, others (i.e., men) because of *the temporary eclipse in them of thought* by feeling or disease or sleep" (429a5–8, italics added). It does not matter that the philosopher considers the imaginative capacity to pertain to other animals, but rather that he affirms that its function, among men, is subordinate to the *temporary eclipse of thought*. As René Lefebvre notes, many centuries would pass before the creative capacity of fantasy would be recognized.[10] In the thinking of antiquity, the imagination is active only by default, when cognition is obscured. Thus, Aristotelian mimesis, while it might not be confounded with *imitatio*, as it would in the Renaissance

---

[7] Caston, "Pourquoi Aristote," 30.

[8] Ibid., 31, 33.

[9] Ibid., 33.

[10] R. Lefebvre, "La *phantasia* chez Aristote: Subliminalité, indistinction et pathologie de la perception," in *Les Études Philosophiques* (January–March 1997): 42.

moment of its rediscovery, would be guided by the parameters of *physis*, obliging it to be organic.[11]

As proof of the imagination's minor character, subsidiary to the theory that embraced it and subaltern in human activity, there is nothing more indicative than its presence in the poet who, more than anyone else, merged the traditions of antiquity and Christianity. In Dante, as M. W. Bundy aptly points out, the *vis imaginativa* "is a quite material faculty of representation which enables the poet and lover to keep the image of Beatrice constantly before him."[12] Bundy discusses, without distinction, a "theory of vision" or "theory of imagination," since in relation to Dante's work the imagination could only be theorized as something materially aroused. The theoretical limits of this material view of imagination are evident in the end of the *Paradiso*, when the traveler is permitted to contemplate the mystery of the Trinity:

> Ne la profonda e chiara sussistenza
> de l'alto lume parvermi tre giri
> di tre colori e d'una contenza;
> e l'un dall'altro come iri da iri
> parea reflesso, e 'l terzo parea foco
> che quinci e quindi igualmente si spiri.
> Oh quanto è corto il dire e come fioco
> al mio concetto! (33.115–22)

> Within the profound and shining subsistence of the lofty Light appeared
> to me three circles of three colors and one magnitude; and one seemed re-
> flected by the other, as rainbow by rainbow, and the third seemed fire
> breathed forth equally from the one and the other.
> O how scant is speech, and how feeble to my conception![13]

In order that the *dire* (speech) not be *corto* (scant), Dante could not restrict himself to talking of the materiality of the rings, of their three colors and identical circumference, or of their reciprocal effulgence. That is, in order that the Trinity cease to be a mystery for man, it would be necessary that imagination no longer be merged passively with vision but rather become actively creative. Dante's citation ends by strategically anticipating one of

---

[11] Cf. L. Costa Lima, *Mimesis: desafio ao pensamento* (Rio de Janeiro, 2000), 25, 206.

[12] M. W. Bundy, *The Theory of Imagination in Classical and Mediaeval Thought* (Urbana, Ill.: Norwood Editions, 1927), 226.

[13] Dante Alighieri, *The Divine Comedy: Paradiso. 1: Italian Text and Translation*, trans. Charles S. Singleton (Princeton, N.J.: Princeton University Press, Bollingen Series, 1975), 379.

the greatest difficulties confronted by the dynamic conception of imagination: the Christian vision of the world.

———

In this examination of the historical development of the imagination, consider two affirmations made by James Engell:

> From 1710 to the 1750s, the imagination had risen in stature considerably. It acquired a moral, aesthetic, and even religious value that was almost exclusively positive.[14]

> The increasing confidence in the creative imagination from about 1740 on led poets and critics to trust to and to believe in it, to sense that they had a mission not only to fabricate a new world-view, a reappraisal of man and nature, but even to swaddle this thought and energy around human feelings in the forms, colors, and sounds of a rediscovered natural world.[15]

Combined, these passages not only emphasize the relevance assumed by the imagination in the eighteenth century but also indicate the extension of its domain. And the fact that not only philosophers—aside from those considered here, Hobbes, Leibniz, Shaftesbury, and Schelling stand out—but also poets of the quality of Coleridge participate in both the redefinition and expansion of its relevance indicates that this is not a case of self-promotion on the part of artists. In fact, the latter were reacting to an orientation that developed in the domain of philosophy: the philosophy of the *cogito*, with its "haunting and almost sinister dualism" between the *res cogitans* (incarnated by man) and the *res cogitata* (reserved for nature),[16] is indirectly responsible for the importance attributed to the imagination within both Continental rationalism and English empiricism. Compounding the dualism between man and the world, Descartes added the antagonism within man himself between reason, sustaining the *cogito*, and the passions, from which the author of *Les passions de l'âme* (1649) expected nothing but the tumultuous and troubling. The lesson of Descartes would be developed by Malebranche, who would dedicate the whole of his second book of *La recherche de la verité* (1674), entitled "De l'imagination," to demonstrating "the physical causes

---

[14] J. Engell, *The Creative Imagination: Enlightenment to Romanticism* (Cambridge, Mass.: Harvard University Press, 1981), 47.

[15] Ibid., 8.

[16] Ibid., 7.

of malfunction and of errors of the imagination," as well as by the thinkers of Port-Royal, Arnauld and Nicole, in a more complex (and contemporary) work, *La logique ou l'art de penser* (1662–83), and by Arnauld and Lancelot in their *Grammaire générale et raisonée de Port-Royal* (1660). What brings them to the study of language is nothing but the uncertainty that the mobility of the passions creates for cognition. The repercussions of the praise reserved for mechanical reason in the *Discours de la méthode* (1637) helped bring about the decisive break with the unified cosmic vision that Christianity had cultivated for sixteen centuries.

Once the duality and progressive fragmentation of the world is established, especially with the development of the particular sciences, the question becomes whether it would be possible to reestablish a coherent worldview on another basis, through the primacy now conceded to the imagination. With this in mind, consider Engell's contention that "the Enlightenment's view of the imagination had one immense advantage that the later nineteenth century failed to recapture: it focused on the source of creative power, on what permits the unified operation of all faculties, and at its highest pitch, on what constitutes genius and creativity in art."[17] To speak of the failure of the nineteenth century would be improper insofar as the very proponents of the productive imagination disagreed among themselves, and the differences did not merely consist in the opposition of diverse systems but comprised also those contradictions present within each system, as maximally manifest in Kant. Insofar as *das Erhabene* (the sublime) places in check the imaginative force that it actualizes, it determines the failure of the imagination as synthesizing capacity and creates the hope in those who experience it of recourse to the supernatural, since by reinstalling within his system the figure of the divine, Kant continually reaffirms the problematic aspect of the *final cause*. The affirmation of the imagination as "source of creative power" thus upsets the justification of religion. With such a source, the new cosmic vision would have to suppose either the exclusion of religion or the Kantian divide between the certain and the problematic. It is true, nevertheless, that this dilemma would present itself in no less speculative a spirit than that of Coleridge. Coleridge would not retreat from the approximation of the "dynamic imagination" with the divine. His very divergence from Kant's conclusions lies in the demonstration that a "unified operation of all faculties" would be capable of creating "self-confidence and self-reliance" only through an unequivocal acceptance of an entity with superhuman faculties. In sum, the discrepancy between Kant and Coleridge—the

---

[17] Ibid., 79.

caution with which the former formulates what Zammito would call his utopian vision[18] weighed against the certainty with which the latter would affirm the unity of the creative in God—matters less than the insufficiency of a purely intellectual argument in its attempt to overcome the fragmentation between man and the world. It is in this sense that the creative imagination found in Christianity its great adversary.

A brief consideration of the opening of *Biographia Literaria* (1817), beginning with the initial passage of "On Poesy and Art," should suffice to advance the argument: "Art, used collectively for painting, sculpture, architecture and music, is the mediatress between and reconciler of, nature and man. It is, therefore, the power of humanizing nature, of infusing the thoughts and passions of man into every thing which is the object of his contemplation; color, form, motion, and sound are the elements which it combines, and it stamps them into unity in the mold of a moral idea."[19] The idea of the artist or poet is modified by the role conceded to the imagination, which creates a dynamic process that dissolves the separation between subject and object. As Coleridge says in *Aids to Reflection* (1825), "to *think* of a thing is different than to perceive it," as "to walk" is different than "to feel the ground under you."[20]

At first glance, the dissolution of the line differentiating subject and object touches only the human agent in both of these passages. Art has the power to "humanize nature," to extend the qualities of the producer to the object. Only attentive reading demonstrates the inverse as well: color, form, movement, and sound break beyond the bounds of the raw material. The effective fusion leads to another form of human identity: the moral idea. A "middle quality between a thought and a thing," as the poet defines art, thus maintains its human identity. This is, however, an expansive identity, significantly different from that process of absorption of the *Ichheit* with which Fichte defines man's contact with the world. While the dominion of the Fichtean *self* supposes the domination of that which the self assimilates, Coleridge argues that "in all genuine creation of art there must be a union of these separates"[21] (i.e., of similarity and difference). Such a combination of disparate elements is realized by the activity of genius, which establishes "a reconcilement of the external with the internal; the conscious is so impressed

---

[18] Cf. J. Zammito, *The Genesis of Kant's Critique of Judgment* (Chicago: Univeristy of Chicago Press, 1992).

[19] S. T. Coleridge, *Biographia Literaria, Edited with His Aesthetical Essays*, ed. J. Shawcross, 2 vols. (Oxford: Oxford University Press, 1958), 2:253.

[20] Cited in Engell, *The Creative Imagination*, 336.

[21] *Biographia Literaria*, 2:256.

on the unconscious as to appear in it."[22] Rather than defining genius in the manner of Diderot and Kant, as that which extracts from nature an *energeia* unknown to human reason, Coleridge characterizes genius by a capacity for reconciliation that, rather than mediating between subject and object, mediates between the consciousness and unconsciousness of the subject. In this way, even before merging, by means of art, with the object on which it operates, the creative subject recomposes that which was divided: "There is in genius itself an unconscious activity."

The introduction of the unconscious in Coleridge's thought, probably due to Schelling's influence, led, albeit unsystematically, to a correction of the theory of imitation. While contingent, the correction is responsible for claims of this magnitude: "A good portrait is the abstract of the personal; it is not the likeness for actual comparison, but for recollection. This explains why the likeness of a very good portrait is not always recognized."[23] Another, unfortunately unelaborated fragment indicates that the unconscious not only served Coleridge as a line of defense against an excessive emphasis on the self on the part of the romantics but also gave him the means to initiate a revision of the theory of mimesis. In an annotation in his notebooks, dated March 1810, he writes, "I wish much to investigate the connection of the Imagination with the *Bildungstrieb*—Imaginatio = imitatio vel repetitio *Imaginis*—per motum? Ergo, et motuum—The Variolae-generation—Is there not a *link* between physical Imitation—Imagination?"[24] To suppose the connection between the imagination and the image-making impulse was equal to rooting the imagination in a force—*ein Trieb*—that lay elsewhere than in the consciousness of the subject. At the same time, the intermediary phrase limits Coleridge's intuition by establishing equality between the imagination and the repetition of the image, raising the question about the possible link between the imagination and physical imitation. The interposed comparison with generation (propagation) of the *variolae* leads one to believe that Coleridge did not perceive the difference between physical and psychical movement, compromising his initial intuition. Nevertheless, to suppose a *Bildungstrieb* represented thinking along the same line that delineated the abstraction of the likeness. Thus, while the tradition of *imitatio* ultimately predominated, a divergent, albeit unconscious, force made its entrance on stage.

---

[22] Ibid., 258.

[23] Ibid., 259.

[24] Coleridge, *Notebooks*, ed. Kathleen Coburn, vol. 3: 1808–1819 (Princeton, N.J.: Princeton University Press, Bollingen Series, 1973), frag. 3744.

An earlier fragment, drawn from a passage dated October 27, 1803, helps explain the dilemma that Coleridge encountered in his new equation: "Let him have created this infinity of Infinities—Still there is space in the Imagination for the Creation of Finities—but instead of these let him again create Infinities—Yet the same Space is left—it is [in] no way filled up. I feel too, that the whole rests on a miserable Sophism of applying to an Almighty Being such words as *All*. Why were not *all*—Gods? But there is no *all*, in creation—It is composed of Infinites—& the Imagination bewildered by heaping Infinities on Infinities."[25] Coleridge raises two seemingly intertwined questions: that of divine power in relation to the power of the imagination and that of the infinite in relation to the all. To conceive of God as creator of the infinite of infinities does not impede attributing to the imagination the power to create finities. In this sense, the praise of the imagination does not collide with the conception of divinity. In contrast, the discord arises from the "miserable Sophism" inherent in the word *all*. For there is no *everything* in creation; instead, creation expresses itself through the composition of infinities. Eliminating the sophism would enable the connection between Creator and artist. The task of the imagination would then be compatible with divine conception. The reconciliation promoted by art includes that of the creative capacity—the "Creation of Finities"—with the creator of Infinities. But that harmony seems to demand a homology between the two creations. On this basis, the role of *imitatio* may be understood as the element that obstructs the way opened by the *Bildungstrieb*. *Imitatio* is preserved by Coleridge, despite his exaltation of the imagination, because it assures the preservation of a cosmology oriented by the divine.

The explication attempted above may be elucidated further by a concurring statement that Coleridge made in 1819, in which the imagination, understood as exclusively human, is seen as a power that reiterates what has already occurred in the creation of the world: "If there be aught that can be said to be purely in the human mind, it is surely those acts of its own imagination which the mathematician avails himself of. . . . The mind . . . raises that wonderful superstructure of geometry and then looking abroad into nature finds that in its own nature it has been fathoming nature, and that nature itself is but the greater mirror in which he beholds his own present and his own past being in the law, and learns to reverence while he feels the necessity of that one great Being whose eternal reason is the ground and

---

[25] Coleridge, *Notebooks*, ed. Kathleen Coburn, vol. 1: 1794–1804 (New York: Pantheon Books, Bollingen Series, 1957), frag. 1619.

absolute condition of the ideas in the mind."[26] In sum, Coleridge's "dynamic imagination" clearly represents an attempt to reconcile religious belief with an intuition that was gradually being revealed. In Coleridge's thought, Kantian reflective judgment was ceasing to function only as regulator in order to function also as determinant, and the supernatural was being affirmed, not only as problematic, but also as unquestionable.

I conclude this introduction with the renowned distinction between primary and secondary imagination, drawn by Coleridge in chapter 13 of his *Biographia Literaria*: While in "the finite mind" or primary imagination "the eternal act of creation" repeats itself, in the secondary imagination "fixed and dead" objects are revivified through combination.[27] Both, but above all the primary imagination, are associated with the act of originary creation; in contrast, fancy is vested with a lower status, precisely because it supposes an activity that unfolds exclusively within the creation: "Fancy is indeed no other than a mode of Memory emancipated from the order of time and space."[28] Coleridge's proposal—converting the imagination into a principle capable of breaking with both Cartesian and Kantian divides between reason and understanding—thus becomes untenable. If it is legitimate from the standpoint of the religious man—an attempt at an imaginatively conciliatory cosmic vision compatible with Christianity—then it is fraught with the disadvantages, first, of seeming feeble when confronted with Kant's divided system; second, of lacking any practical application insofar as it constitutes a purely intellectual engagement; and third, of requiring a retreat from its most advanced claims: the *Bildungstrieb* and the differentiation between forms of imagination that Coleridge left only sketched out.

The Novel

My concern with the novel as a genre must be limited to its capacity to elucidate the control of the imagination, both as a concept and in application. Thus, I will consider, among classical reflections on the novel, relevant contentions from Schlegel and Hegel, and among contemporary theories, even more partially, claims staked out by Mikhail Bakhtin and Paul Zumthor.

Among Schlegel's unparalleled qualities, prior to his conversion to Catholicism and to Metternich's restoration politics, is that of having

---

[26] Coleridge, *Biographia Literaria*, 2:333–34.

[27] Ibid., 1:202.

[28] Ibid.

understood the importance being assumed by the novel. One need only consider the opening of fragment 26: "Die Romane sind die sokratischen Dialoge unserer Zeit."[29] Just as Socratic dialogue revolutionized the pre-Platonic philosophical tradition, the novel would revolutionize the closed, monological forms of poetic genres. The parallel is not exact, however, insofar as the praise that Schlegel reserved for Shakespeare shows his consciousness that the dividing line did not oppose the novel to every other expressive form. In order to understand his peculiar designation of the novel, we need to subdivide his analysis into three phases:

A. The novel involves the enhancement of raw material derived not from tradition, but from individual history: "Mancher der vortrefflichsten Roman ist ein Kompendium, eine Enzyclopädie des ganzen Lebens eines genialischen Individuums" (*KA*, no. 78, p. 156).

B. While the author recognizes the umbilical cord connecting the novel with the life history of an individual, he refuses to respect the "psychological" character of its form. A psychological reading is "sehr inkonsequent, und klein" (*KA*, no. 124, p. 185). Against such a reading, Schlegel opposes the apprehension of the novelistic work as a whole, whose details, in contrast to what occurs in a "rhetorical form," matter only insofar as they contribute to its unity: "Die Lehren welche ein Roman geben will, müssen solche sein, die sich nur im Ganzen mitteilen, nicht einzeln beweisen, und durch Zergleiderung erschopfen lassen. Sonst wäre die rhetorische Form ungleich vorzüglicher" (*KA*, no. 111, p. 181). To the critic, the fragment indicates a path that Schlegel himself would take when confronted with *Wilhelm Meister.*

C. The political character attributed to "romantic poetry," in general, includes the novel: "Die Poesie ist eine republikanische Rede; eine Rede, die ihr eines Gesetz und ihr eigner Zweck ist, wo alle Teile freie Bürger sind, und mitstimmen dürfen" (*KA*, no. 65, p. 155). But if the autonomy of art participates in its politicization, it also indicates its temporality, through the absolute separation between the ancients and moderns: "In den Alten sieht man den vollendeten Buchstaben der ganzen Poesie: in den Neuern, ahnet man den werdenden Geist" (*KA*, no. 93, p. 158). Both

---

[29] Schlegel, "Kritische Fragmente" (1797), in *Kritische Ausgabe seiner Werke*, ed. H. Eichner, (São Paulo: Perspectiva, 1989), 2:147–63, cited from 149. Hereafter the quotations drawn from "Kritische Fragmente" as well as Athenäum Fragmente" (1798) (165–255 in the same volume) are cited in parentheses within the text, with the abbreviation of the title of the collected works (*KA*) and the fragment designated by number and page.

the unfinished quality of modern times and the revolutionary breath
that would shake it are recognizable in that difference. Hence the opening
of fragment 216: "Die Französische Revolution, Fichtes Wissenschaftslehre,
und Goethes Meister sind die größten Tendenzen des Zeitalters"
(*KA*, p. 198). If Fichte's elaboration or exacerbation of the self is countered by these fragments' designation of the self as merely that raw material based on which the formal totality of the work can be realized, then
the revolutionary principle is not that of a particular event: "Revolutionen
sind universelle nicht organische, sondern chemische Bewegungen" (*KA*,
no. 426, p. 248).

The relationship between the novel and history delineated in Schlegel's
"Fragments" is developed further in two finished essays, "Gespräch über
die Poesie" (1800) and "Über Goethes Meister" (1798). Taking as starting
point the affirmation "ein Roman ist ein romantisches Buch," consider the
subsequent claim: "Die alte Poesie schießt sich durchgängig an die Mythologie an, und vermeidet sogar den eigentlich historischen Stoff. Die alte
Tragödie sogar ist ein Spiel, under der Dichter, der eine wahre Begebenheit,
die das ganze Bolk ernstlich anging, darstellte, ward bestraft. Die romantische Poesie hingegen ruht ganz auf historischem Grunce, weit mehr als man
es weiß und glaubt. . . . Boccaz ist fast durchaus wahre Geschichte, ebenso
andre Quellen, aus denen alle romantische Erfindung hergeleitet ist.[30] The
hiatus that separates modern from ancient poetry, which Schlegel had already discussed in the "Fragments," now finds an added, more objective rationale: ancient poetics relies on mythology and goes so far as disdaining history; modern poetics, on the contrary, bases itself precisely on historical
material. (Taking Boccaccio as exemplar, the author demonstrates that the
term *Poesie* encompasses both prose and poetry.) Contrary to what Hegel's
homogenous vision of history would claim, the novel, as understood by
Schlegel, cannot be investigated as a variant of atemporal epic. Its homo-
geneity is unthinkable for Schlegel insofar as, even in ancient literature,
whose form is already fully realized, he finds evidence of a process of transformation to which that form is continually subject. Thus, the founders of
tragedy find their material and model in the epic and, following the example
of epic parody, in turn, develop satirical dramas.[31]

---

[30] "Gespräch über die Poesie" *Kritische Ausgabe seiner Werke*, ed. H. Eichner, (São Paulo:
Perspectiva, 1989), 2:284–339, cited from 334–35.

[31] Cf. Ibid., 292.

If we add to this discontinuous, dynamic, and transformative vision of history the unfinished character of modern times, it becomes obvious why Schlegel and the universal, progressive poetics that he proposed were antipodes to the continuous and complete conception of history that Hegel develops in *Vorlesungen über die Ästhetik*. Despite that difference, these antagonists are not so opposite might be supposed. In "Rede über die Mythologie," part of the "Gespräch," Schlegel declares that modern man lacks a center of gravity (*der Mittelpunkt*) that mythology constituted for the ancients, and that it is not enough to note this lack but also necessary to strive seriously in order to produce such a center.[32] Thus, he does not restrict himself to affirming our discontinuity, but insists that it befits humanity, fighting with all its might, "ihr Zentrum zu finden."[33] How to reconcile that demand with one enunciated just a little earlier: "Die höchste Schönheit, ja die höchste Ordnung ist denn doch nur die des Chaos"?[34] The answer may simply lie in the fact that Schlegel does not conceive of mythology as a mere horizon that encloses a meaning for life and for man. While it may contain that aspect that modern man lacks, it also has another, more relevant, trait—mythology is a "work of art of nature": "In ihrem Gewerbe ist das Höchste wirklich gebildet; alles ist Beziehung und Verwandlung, angebildet und umgebildet, und dieses Anbilden und Umbilden eben ihr eigentümliches Verfahren, ihr innres Leben, ihre Methode, wenn ich so sagen darf."[35] The ordering center, existing or yet to be constructed, rather than annulling chaos, hides it behind the harmony it makes apparent. Hence Schlegel would say that he knew no lovelier symbol of the "originary chaos of human nature" than "das bunte Gewimmel der alten Götter"[36] (the colorful bedlam of the old gods). Hence also his praise for *Tristram Shandy* and *Jacques le fataliste* as works that exceed the *Witz* and the arabesque.[37]

Schlegel's reflections on the novel as a genre presuppose that, in order for art to be understood as an actually autonomous modality of discourse, the

---

[32] Cf. Ibid., 312.

[33] Ibid., 314.

[34] Ibid., 313.

[35] Ibid., 318.

[36] Ibid., 329.

[37] In order to economize space, with respect to the role of the arabesque in the novel, I simply point the reader to one of Schlegel's posthumously published fragments: "Das Wesentliche im Roman ist die chaotische Form—Arabesken, Mährchen" (1799), *KA*, 26:276, no. 274.

critic must confront language as a constructive principle and not only as a conductive medium for content; moreover, the critic must act as an interpreter and not as a judge. Applying these principles concretely, Schlegel designates in *Wilhelm Meister* not so much this or that detail, as he might if guided by a rhetorical conception of form, but the combination of parts.[38] The novel thus forecasts the realist line, in which a quotidian, prosaic vision predominates, to the point reached by Goethe, in whose work things are as they ought to be and, at the same time, surpass that which one might demand ("und doch weit mehr als man fordern darf").[39] This does not mean that the novelist (and the critic) should turn against the world but rather toward a verbal composition that intensifies the contrasts between the world of the protagonists—Wilhelm, the dreamer of book 1, Marianne's ignoble trajectory, Philine's frivolous sensuality, Mignon's nostalgia—and the "prose of the world." The novel, as Schlegel interprets it, might be compared to the construction of a stage on which the scene played out has as its purview the process of learning how to move in life. We may add yet that Schlegel, it should be noted, preferred to the realist vision an endoscopic one, exploring the possibilities and changes suffered by each character. The autonomy of art is thus made concrete: no longer in service to some institution, it likewise does not serve to *illustrate* reality. It is a totality, "diese Harmonie von Dissonansen"[40] that, belonging to *Poesie*, cannot be confounded with one of its genres. Neither can such autonomy be exhausted in the endoscopy of the characters, since, the endoscopic demonstration of an education in the world is accomplished in both the characters and in the reader: "Mancher, dem man den Sinn nicht absprechen kann, wird sich in vieles langen nicht finden konnen: denn bei fortschreitenden Naturen erweitern, schärfen und bilden sich Begriff und Sinn gegenseitig."[41]

The principles proposed and practiced by Schlegel are antagonistic to Hegel's vision of both the novel in particular and art in general.[42] Schlegel could compete with neither the extraordinary speculative force nor the conservatism that undergirded all of Hegel's reflections on art. Limiting this discussion to the presence of these qualities in the section of his work devoted

---

[38] Cf. *KA*, no. 111.

[39] "Über Goethes Meister" *KA*, 2:126–46, cited from 127.

[40] Ibid., 130.

[41] Ibid., 135.

[42] Schlegel contended that the reflections on *Hamlet* scattered throughout the *Meister* constituted not merely criticism, but high poetry, adding a phrase that Hegel would disdain: "Das muß alle Kritik, weil jedes vortreffliche Werk, von welcher Art es auch sei, *mehr weiß als es sagt, und mehr will als es weiß*" (ibid., 140, italics added).

to romanticism, in which art could no longer be capable of satisfying the highest necessities of the spirit, this "wird sich seiner Wahrheit nur dadurch gewiß, daß er sich aus dem Äußeren in seine Innigkeit mit sich zurückführt und die äußere Realitat als ein ihm nicht adequätes Dasein setzt."[43] Thus, the "infinite value is contained by the real and individual subject, in his interior life" ("das wirkliche, einzelne Subjekt in seiner inneren Lebendigkeit ist es, das unendlichen Wert erhält," 501). But to make this affirmation is to demonstrate the unsatisfactory character that art had achieved, since, insofar as "absolute interiority" constitutes "the true content of romanticism," art begins to contain a pantheon of dethroned gods, destroyed by subjectivity, "und statt der plastischen Vielgötterei kennt die Kunst jetzt nur *einen* Gott, *einen* Geist, *eine* absolute Selbständigkeit, welche als das absolute Wissen und Wollen ihrer selbst mit sich in freier Einheit bleibt" (502). "Having achieved this level . . . , the interior is exteriorization without exteriority, invisible and, so to speak, perceptible only to itself" ("Das Innere . . . , so auf die Spitze hinausgetrieben, ist die äußerlichkeitslose Äyßerung, unsichtbar gleichsam nur sich selber vernehmend" 508). Distanced from the "free concept of the beautiful," dispossessed of the objective exteriority that contributed to the quality of Greek sculpture, art finds itself now contaminated "on every side by the accidental and particular character of the finite exterior world" (515). That fatal plunge into subjectivity accompanied by a merely accidental external world, that loss of classical equilibrium would render appreciable only those values related to individual pathos: "honor, love, loyalty, and courage, the aims and duties of romantic chivalry" (509) or, in Hegel's own world, to the struggles and aspirations proper to those so-called years of apprenticeship, of "education by that reality existing for the individual" (567).

Hegel's extraordinary speculative capacity places itself in the service of conservatism—recognizing as true only the art of the past. But this conservatism was not accidental: it was necessary for the affirmation of his system, which demanded the "demonstration" that the hour of art had passed. These brief reflections seek to establish the position of the Romanesque (*Das Romanhafte*) in the Hegelian aesthetic, but in fact, it was designated already at the beginning of the section devoted to romanticism, demonstrating the decadence of art. Art is characterized, "on one side, by the reproduction of exterior objects in the accidentalness of its form, and on the other, in contrast, by humor as the liberation of subjectivity from its internal accidentalness"

---

[43] G.W.F. Hegel, *Ästhetik* (1835), ed. F. Bassenge, 2 vols. (Berlin: Aufbau-Verlag, 1976) 1:499 (henceforth cited in the text by page numbers).

(582). Discovering ideal classical harmony lost in contemporary art, Hegel finds exceptions only in Flemish painting—with the qualification that its "objects could not satisfy anyone with a more profound sense, resulting from a content (*Gehalt*) that was in itself true" (572)—and in what he calls "objective humor." This is defined as a "penetration" (*Verinnigung*) into the object, reaching beyond the merely accidental objectivity and the subjective representation characteristic of the beginning of romanticism (cf. 582). But, he adds, "such penetration can be only partial and manifest itself only occasionally in the circuit of a *Lied* or only as a part of a greater work" (582). It is true, as Kathrin Rosenfield acutely observes, that, insofar as the *Lied* constitutes in Hegel's view an expression of "subjective comprehension, of spiritual appropriation" (*Auffassung*), one might think of it "as a hybrid form or mist," comparable to the novel, "above all when one thinks of the interminable and structurally open fragment of *Wilhelm Meister*."[44] But the fact is that Hegel did not think this. Could his failure to do so be explained simply by his conservatism or by his systematic need to take art as a surpassed form of expression? There may be a less speculative explication inherent in his conception of language as the instrumental means for conjugating the interior with the exterior: "Denn der Gehalt ist es, der, wie in allem Menschenwerk, so auch in der Kunst entscheidet" (584). Whereas Schlegel may have lacked Hegel's speculative capacity, he did understand that language is conductive and not merely a collector of content. In Hegel's thought, rather than an error in appreciation, we find a systematic incomprehension of art. It is not so strange then that Hegel's thought should have become a special source for the control of the imagination.

———

I conclude this section on the novel with a very brief analysis of two contemporary scholars, Paul Zumthor and Mikhail Bakhtin. Without delineating their full contributions to the theory of the novel, let me set in relief those among their formulations that develop the concept of the control of the imagination. Two passages from Zumthor's work suggest a point of departure:

> Formalized in ordinary language, but also shaped by high narrative or
> rhetorical demands, in fact, the novel does not renounce the supremacy of

---

[44] Kathrin Rosenfield, "Uma falha na *Estética* de Hegel: a propósito de um silêncio sobre o romance de Goethe," *A linguagem Liberada* (São Paulo: Perspectiva, 1989), 30.

Latin, the foundation and instrument of clerical power. In contrast to the folktales that sustain the common people, it demands vast dimensions: a long duration of reading and hearing, during which the developments of the plot, however entangled they may seem, are projected towards a future that is never closed and that excludes all circularity. Discourse thus discovers, at its own level, as a guarantee of the richest connotations, the trait of incompleteness and indefiniteness characterizing ordinary words.[45]

A poetry whose functioning implies the predominance of the voice manifests an indisputable truth and possesses by this means a plenitude that makes possible its perpetual renewal. A poetic discourse in which the vocal part is reduced is divided, plays against itself, engenders internal contradiction. The man who speaks it and the one who hears him begin to know that they will never know. The power of abstraction grows, nevertheless, with the role of writing in the genesis and economy of texts, but it denies every equivalence between language and truth, an equivalence that, on the contrary, exalts theatricalized performance.[46]

Born at the intersection of orality and writing, the novel in its medieval form guarantees an open discourse by opting for the vernacular. It opposes the closure—all the more closed at the moment in which Latin is known and understood only by clerics—of sacred poetic forms. By adopting the incompleteness of the spoken word of a living language, the novel prepares itself for the primordial part that it will play several centuries later, culminating in the role delineated by Zumthor in the second passage: Insofar as the novel "manifests an indisputable truth," the reduction on the part of orality stimulates contradiction and, with it, the renunciation of an equivalence between language and truth. The novel, beginning with its medieval manifestations, thematizes the role of language with respect to truth, its *constitutive incompleteness* and, consequently, its fictional status. As we will see, this will be the fundamental cog in the mechanism of control.

Drawing even more briefly on Bakhtin's work, we may denote first a difference between the novel and other genres. In his renowned essay, "Forms of Time and of the Chronotope in the Novel," Bakhtin observes that, while in other genres "the most contiguous possible position of the

---

[45] Paul Zumthor, "Et la 'littérature'? Le cas du roman—L'illusion littéraire," in *La lettre et la voix: De la littérature médiévale* (Paris: Éditions du Seuil, 1987), 300.

[46] Ibid., 302–3.

author, the point of view necessary to the shaping of the material, is dictated by the genre itself . . . , within the genre of the novel, there is no such immanent position for the author. You may publish a packet of business documents, personal letters (a novel in letters), a manuscript by 'nobody-knows-who, written for nobody-knows-who and who-found-it-and-where nobody knows.' "[47] This lack of self-characterization and consequent uncertainty of the author's position in the novel provoke, as Bakhtin immediately observed, the author's necessary adoption of a mask, which in turn places in question the conventional synonymy between fiction and acceptable falsehood. In other words, the novel upsets the traditionally recognized position of the "literary." As Bakhtin would intuit in relation to *Evgenii Onegin* in his essay "From the Prehistory of Novelistic Discourse," "literary language is not represented in the novel as a unitary, completely finished-off and indisputable language—it is represented precisely as a living mix of varied and opposing voices, developing and renewing itself."[48] "Literary" language and acceptable "fiction" (or falsehood) are questioned simultaneously, so that the novel's heteroglossia becomes a formal problem to the degree that it manifests itself as a problem related to the definition of truth. This demonstrates how the control of the imagination is umbilically linked to the history of the novel. Insofar as the question of control is a formal one concerning when fiction is acceptable and what its relation may be to factual history, it also becomes an epistemological one, concerning the nature of truth and of the real with which "serious" discourses would be obliged to correspond. It is not so strange then that the question of control should come to the fore in the highly reflexive literature of the recent decades.

---

[47] Mikhail Bakhtin, "Forms of Time and of the Chronotope in the Novel," from *Вопросы литературыи естетики*, 1975, trans. Caryl Emerson and Michael Holquist in *The Dialogic Imagination: Four Essays* (Austin: University of Texas Press, 1985), 161. Curiously, without Zumthor's having known Bakhtin's text, written decades earlier than its first publication (1937–38), this passage reinforces the former medievalist's observation concerning the novel's distinction in lacking an immanent form. This lack affects not only the position of the author, as Bakhtin insists, but has the added, more general effect of foreshadowing the a priori recognition of the genre to which the text might belong: is it the text that speaks the truth or what? (Thus, for example, Schlegel observes with incisive irony that Rousseau's *Confessions* is an excellent novel, whereas *La nouvelle Héloïse*, merely a middling one (cf. "Gespräch über die Poesie," 339).

[48] Mikhail Bakhtin, "From the Prehistory of Novelistic Discourse," in *The Dialogic Imagination: Four Essays*, trans. Caryl Emerson and Michael Holquist (Austin: University of Texas Press, 1985), 49.

Control, and the Novel as a Privileged Context for Its Comprehension

There are cultures that forbid the reproduction of both the divine and human figure. In light of that interdiction, arguments against a certain mode of artistic representation or against the thematization of a certain problem may seem to have restricted relevance. Or it may be that the question of the control of the imagination has not received greater attention precisely because Western culture has not known the prohibition against figural representation. Furthermore, if we recall that the autonomy of art is affirmed at least since the end of the eighteenth century, with the *Frühromantiker* and Kant's third critique, in which the imagination is no longer subject to the work of understanding, then it may seem that control does not deserve theoretical consideration. For these among other reasons, the hypothesis of the control of the imagination is a recent formulation,[49] which, for lack of scholarly engagement has not advanced significantly in the past sixteen years. In this context, I hope to refine the general coordinates of the hypothesis through an empirical examination in relation to the novel as a genre.

Let me begin, then, with a general delineation of the question. What is termed the control of the imagination should not be confounded with censorship either of literary works or tendencies. Censorship is rather a punctual prohibition, sanctioned by norms, and condemns the circulation of works with a given combination of characteristics. In contrast, control involves a more delicate decision: something is perceived as unacceptable, improper, or base, but its production is not simply prohibited. Since it is not, the very control applied to it can serve as a stimulus for another form of artistic expression. But at any instant, dependent on historic conjunction, control can also give way to censorship. Thus, it would make no sense to speak of the control of avant-garde art under Nazism or Stalinism or to say that Baudelaire and Flaubert were controlled. No, Baudelaire, Flaubert, and the avant-garde were censored.

A very complicated question, to which I can only allude here, concerns the principle of *imitatio*, into which Aristotelian mimesis developed, whether, indirectly, in the less speculative thinking of the Romans or with the monumental Renaissance rediscovery of Aristotle's *Poetics*. Countering any claim that Aristotelian phantasia already constituted a controlling practice, one might contend that it was rather, in Aristotle's thinking, a minor conceit, with a heuristic function, that would not even intervene in his conception of

---

[49] Cf. note 1.

mimesis. However, the reservations in the *Poetics* itself concerning Euripides, the most critical of the Greek tragedians, might make one hesitate. Could the secondary status of phantasia and its lack of articulation within the Aristotelian concept of mimesis, given the latter's evidently liberating function with respect to the Platonic conception, be sufficient in place of a theory of the control of the imagination? Or could the lack of a concept of imagination signify that its importance in the production of art was unknown? The dubiousness of this proposal grows as we abandon the Aristotelian legacy and, among the Romans, reflect on a passage in Pliny the Elder: "Non est praetereundum et nouicium inuentum, siquidem non ex auro argentoue, at certe ex aere in bibliothecis dicantur illis, quorum immortales animae in locis iisdem loquuntur, quin immo etiam quae non sunt finguntur, pariuntque desideria non traditos uultus, sicut in Homero euenit."[50] Pliny addresses the representation in public places of immortal figures whose traits— unknown—were necessarily products of the imagination. Although the author pragmatically considers the public's avid desire to see such reproductions a proof of their likeness, in fact, their favorable reception functions as an alibi for their form, which is to say that nonreproductive imagination was not in itself acceptable. Is there not a veiled form of control implied by upholding the similarity of the representation to the figure represented?

Even more reasonably, one might say that the ideal of *imitatio* propounded in Renaissance poetics, while far from confounding itself with the copy, approximated what is meant by control: perceptual data are valorized, although the work of art, whether verbal or pictorial, admittedly does not follow these to the line. An argument might even be made that control insinuates itself in classical art from the moment that Robortello, in translating passage 51a12 of the *Poetics*, substitutes *eikòs* or *anankainon* for *quod verum est et necessarium*.[51] By substituting the disjunctive function with the inclusive *et*, Robortello affirmed that discourse must satisfy, by dint of the *necessarium*, what in the Aristotelian treatise had contained also the alternative to verisimilitude. Like the sword of Damocles, control hangs over the poet's head, which, according to Robortello, ought not be restricted by the standard of verisimilitude. One may thus conjecture that *imitatio* was the root from which the classical control would develop, finding its practical justifi-

---

    [50] Pliny the Elder, *Histoire naturelle XXXV: La Peinture*, bilingual ed. (Paris: Belles Lettres, 1997), 35:9.

    [51] "Orationis mximè proprium & genuinum munus est, proferre id, quod verum est, quia aliter sese habere non potest, necessarium" (F. Robertello, *In librum Aristotelis De arte poetica explicationes* [1548], ed. B. Fabian [Munich: W. Fink, 1968], 1).

cation above all in religious reasons. Alongside Renaissance treatises on poetics, the most important work for a concrete examination of this development of control is Tasso's "Discorsi del poema eroico" (1594), but this text
still does not address the novel proper.

The novel is a particularly propitious genre for the study of control because
the author does not occupy an immanent position and is obliged to put on
masks. These leave the reader uncertain as to how to react to the "masquer-
ader" (the buffoon, the fool, the trickster), motivating authorial intervention
with an explicatory or controlling word. If this seems to suggest a control on
the verge of becoming explicit censorship, the use of masks also favors the
anarchic word,[52] and the absence of a fixed place that would permit identification and control of the author is compounded by the problem of the
genre's heteroglossia. In Bakhtin's words, "the language of the novel is a *system* of languages that mutually and ideologically interanimate each other. It
is impossible to describe and analyze it as a single unitary language."[53] While
designated as a dialogic form par excellence, the novel, nevertheless, distances itself from the ideal type of dialogic discourse conceived by Bakhtin
by dint of disciplinary control that reduces the multiplicity of languages in
the novel and, consequently, its discordant political and moral values. This
reduction was recognized also by a thinker who had no particular respect
for the novel—thus, Hegel concluded, "the truly poetic in art, then, is exactly that which we call ideal."[54] But this judgment did not work for the
genre. Rather than complying with any idealized form in the manner of classical epic and tragedy, as Hegel understood these genres, the novel, however
much it was subjected to control, concerned itself with the adventures and
misadventures of a self. Insofar as antiquity did not know the psychological
subject, classical romance recovered "an *abstract* expanse of space," in

---

[52] In an analogous manner, if modernity stimulates the development of the *Bildungsroman*—
making congruent the genre par excellence of our time and the ideal of the formation of the self—
a certain French novelist will change that entire panorama: "Flaubert killed off the novel of
'formation': and *bêtise*, with a bit of luck, gave birth to the new man" (Franco Moretti, *Oppere
mondo: Saggio sulla forma epica dal "Faust" a "Cent'anni di solitudine"* [Turin, 1994], 69, trans.
Q. Hoare as *Modern Epic: The World-System from Goethe to García Márquez* [London: Verso,
1996], 73).

[53] Bakhtin, "From the Prehistory of Novelistic Discourse," 47, italics added.

[54] Hegel, *Ästhetik*, 163.

which there was no place for a "biographical-time sequence."[55] In contrast, as recent medievalist scholarship has demonstrated, the entrance of the psychological subject onto the stage of the curtailed twelfth-century Renaissance was accompanied by the momentary recognition of the fictional as the proper subject of literature and of the romance as its proper form: "The moment when literature recognizes that its material is fiction is also . . . that in which the author enters the scene. It is the moment, par excellence, of the novel."[56] This accumulation of novelties—the psychological subject, fictive rather than mythical material, Romanesque or novelistic form—would be interrupted and gradually processed precisely because it signaled a drastic transition at the core of medieval culture, from orality to writing. Zumthor recognizes the connection between the moment of maximal crisis and the question of control:

> From an epoch that lasted, depending on location, from 1150 to around the end of the eighteenth century we find the texts of stories, songs, and liturgical pieces written in the vernacular. It may even be that some of these texts were composed with the stylus or quill in hand. By dint of this technology, what L. Costa Lima calls a "control of the imagination" was introduced discretely, though its efficacy does not become plainly apparent until after 1500, following an era of growing tensions common (in various respects) to all Western nations: tensions between traditional poetic energies and forces seeking to impose on the verb a logic of its own, to the detriment of the living word.[57]

Contemporary medieval scholarship has more to say in this respect. Eugene Vance accentuates the importance to twelfth-century narrative fiction of studies that, with Abelard, surpassed the separation of logic and grammar:

---

[55] Bakhtin, "Forms of Time and of the Chronotope in the Novel," 89. Consequently, "the world of the Greek romance is an *alien* world: everything in it is indefinite, unknown, foreign" (101). Along the same line of thought, Auden explains why Shakespeare was born at the right time: "The drama had to become secularized before any adequate treatment of human history was possible. . . . Human history cannot be written except on the presupposition that, whatever part God may play in human affairs, we cannot say of one event, 'This is an act of God,' 'This is a natural event,' and of another, 'This is a human choice'; we can only record what happens. The allegorical morality plays are concerned with history, but *only with subjective history; the social-historical setting of any particular man is excluded* (W. H. Auden, "The Globe," in *The Dyer's Hand and Other Essays*, ed. E. Mendelson [New York: Vintage Books, 1989], 180–81).

[56] L. Zink, *La subjectivité littéraire* (Paris: Presses Universitaires de France, 1985), 315.

[57] Zumthor, "Et la 'littérature'?" 315.

"Surely the prospect of systematically combining words into propositions, and of disposing propositions as valid arguments whose truth could pertain *to* reality, yet be ontologically distinct *from* reality, was invaluable to a burgeoning poetics of written vernacular fiction. For fiction, too, was a discourse whose textual utterances could presume to reflect things that truly exist, yet whose truth could be autonomous from what exists because such truth resided in the internal coherence of the story itself."[58] This passage renders more concretely Zink's idea of "literary subjectivity": a more adept manipulation of the logical resources available for configuration within the phrase permitted writers to explore subtleties of rational language as well as linguistic transgressions of language, which, as Vance adds, were transgressions through the marvelous. Vance's reflection yields yet another insight, insofar as he notes that the intercourse between logic and fictionality was not necessarily harmonious: "If twelfth-century rhetoric is strong in dealing with all of those figural resources of speech that exploit and amplify the inherent equivocity of conventional signs, the goals of twelfth-century logic are quite opposite: logic teaches us how to overcome the radical equivocity of conventional signs and to utter truths that are univocal, distinct, necessary, and permanent. One science of discourse is centrifugal, playful, relativistic, opportunistic, and subversive; the other is centripetal, serious, totalizing, constant, and recuperative. . . . The tension between them is an important constituent of twelfth-century vernacular poetics."[59]

This tension is essential to the framework on which, beginning with the Renaissance, control would be configured, as it is to our understanding of why control does not impede the appearance of intentionally fictional works. Furthermore, this tension does not appear only between discordant discursive practices, such as logical discourse and novelistic discourse. Already in *Tristan et Iseut*, in the work of writers such as Chrétien de Troyes, Robert de Boron, and the anonymous author of *Lancelot du Lac*, the effort to reconcile narrative with truth, that is, to harmonize the *récit* with an extrinsic principle of truth, is salient. This signifies that the authors of the earliest narratives in the vernacular not only benefited from the advances of logic, but also attempted to make their narrative sequences congruent with logical affirmations. Yet this is not a predictable development based on the discrepancy denoted by Vance. There is a notable effort within the centrifugal discourse

---

[58] E. Vance, "*De voir dire mot le conjure*: Dialectics and Fictive Truth," in *From Topic to Tale* (Minneapolis: University of Minnesota Press, 1987), 19.

[59] Ibid., 23.

of the nascent "literature" to reconcile narrative sequences, even when their material comprised the marvelous, with a true or immemorial referent or with a referent that declared itself factually witnessed. Whence the insistence of the narrator on declaring the fidelity of his account either to a primitive "tale" now transcribed or to what had been transmitted to him by a supposed eyewitness. Thus, in *Merlin*, the magician Merlin declares to Blaise, the narrator of the adventures of the Grail, that, in recompense for his work, his work will be recited, that is, will be viewed with respect, although "it will not be [taken as] an authority, since you are not, nor can you be [counted] among the apostles."[60] The immediately following clause makes explicit the hierarchy of texts with respect to truth: "Neither did the apostles ever put in writing anything from our Lord other than that which they had seen and heard, while you have put in nothing that you have seen or heard, other than that which I have told you." Since he did not witness that of which he writes, the narrator lacks the authority of the apostles, but his text is true because it contains what Merlin, eyewitness of the events, relates. The same control of the fiction in the name of the truth of what is being recounted reappears in *Yvain ou le Chevalier au Lyon*: "Thus, he who wishes to understand me should entrust me with his heart and his ears, for I do not wish to tell either dream, or fable, or falsehood."[61]

The preceding examples, which might be easily multiplied, demonstrate that the transition from orality to writing, that the appearance of the chivalric romance, that the exploration of the fictional vein had to take into account the reaction of purportedly hegemonic religious discourse. Hence obligatory authorial caution and play with concessions. Only a study specifically devoted to the issue could explicate the transience of the Church in permitting the circulation of such texts. The important role that popular culture would play in the work of a Rabelais, as demonstrated by Bakhtin, suggests that, despite its vast political power, in fact, the Church did not have a monopoly and so imposed control only on authors and movements that confronted it directly. As noted earlier, control supposes a sort of alibi: the circulation of something discordant in some sense with accepted truth is permissible as long as its agent domesticates its discrepancy, that is, makes it possible to integrate it.

This brief incursion into the medieval "crisis" has served as an example of the concretization of the control of the imagination. Because this notion

---

[60] R. de Boron, *Le Roman du Graal*, ed. Bernard Cerquiglinio (Paris: UGE, 1981), 105.

[61] Chrétien de Troyes, *Yvain ou le Chevalier au Lyon* (ca. 1177–81), in *Chrétien de Troyes. Oeuvres complètes*, ed. D. Poirion (Paris: Éditions de la Pléiade, 1994), 169–77.

pretends to be no more than an analytic operator, we may skip several centuries, turning to the English novel of the eighteenth century, and particularly to prefaces and critical material published between 1691 and 1778, in order to survey the situation of the novel on the eve of its affirmation as the genre par excellence of modern times.

Control in Action: The "Lamination" of the English Novel of the Eighteenth Century

We may take as entry point into the eighteenth-century English novel two brief passages from Daniel Defoe, the first of which belongs to the mini-preface to *Robinson Crusoe* (1719), and the second, to the slightly amplified preface to its continuation, published in the same year: "The editor believes the thing to be a just history of fact; neither is there any appearance of fiction in it."[62] "The just application of every incident, the religious and useful inferences drawn from every part, are so many testimonies to the good design of making it publick, and must legitimate all the part that may be call'd invention or parable in the story."[63] Three elements stand out: (a) the author assumes the mask of the editor; (b) the function of his disguise is that of negating the work's fictional status; (c) although the "invention or parable" introduced in the preface to *Farther Adventures* in some sense contradicts that negation, the account could cease being "a just history of fact" insofar as it contains "religious and useful inferences." Such inferences domesticate the fiction, conferring on it a function that would justify its use.

In 1724, in his preface to *Roxana, or the Fortunate Mistress*, Defoe notes that his tale differs "from most of the Modern Performances of this kind" in that "the Foundation of This is laid in Truth of Fact, and so the Work is not a Story but a History."[64] The insistence on negating the fictional character of the narrative and on affirming its veracity or historical reality is instigated by more than religious and biographical motives. This becomes evident in the reiteration of the topos almost thirty years later by an essayist now unknown. In the November 18, 1754, edition of *The Adventurer*, John Hawkesworth

---

[62] Defoe, Preface to *The Life and Strange Surprising Adventures of Robinson Crusoe* (London: Dent, 1964), 1.

[63] Defoe, Preface to *The Farther Adventures of Robinson Crusoe*, 1.

[64] "Preface to *Roxane, or the Fortunate Mistress*" (1724), in *Alle origini della letteratura moderna: Testi i poetica del Settecento inglese: Il romanzo e la poesia*, ed. P. Nerozzi Bellman (Milan: Mondadori, 1997), 96 (henceforth cited as *AO*).

defines both the interest in history and its limits: "History is a relation of the most natural and important events; history, therefore, gratifies curiosity, but it does not often excite terror or pity; the mind feels not that tenderness for a falling state, which it feels for an injured beauty."[65] To label a text as *history* would suffice only if readers did not feel the need to manifest their own emotions and to find in the text a cathartic liberation (exciting their "terror or pity"). The deviation of fiction from the mark is greater even than denoted by Defoe's "invention or parable," and it becomes more clear how the term *domestication* applies here: it is not simply a matter of censoring the novel, or of impeding its circulation but rather of adapting its form relative to the horizon of beliefs and values shared by critics and authors. The question they faced was how to adapt it without offending the criteria of utility and virtue. Hawkesworth continues by observing that in epic and "old romance," "truth is apparently violated" and yet "the pleasure arising from the story is not much lessened." The pleasure aroused serves as alibi, legitimizing the form. However, the critic takes a less sympathetic stance relative to the "novel," which, if it has the advantage over those genres of the past if it maintains its proximity to history, "has yet less the power of entertainment," for "it surprises us less."[66] In fact, among the authors we have considered, Hawkesworth is the least comfortable with the solution toward which the eighteenth-century English novel is headed. The role of history seems unquestionable to him, but he considers it insufficient to satisfy the imagination of the reader: "Fancy requires new gratifications, and curiosity is still unsatisfied."[67] This difficulty is compounded by another: if "the Epic Poem at once gratifies curiosity and moves the passions," but the events recovered do not represent "the fate of a nation,"[68] how, then, to shape a genre that would retain as much as possible of *real* history, release the imagination of the reader, and stimulate national sentiment? As we will see, in order for the novel to become a legitimate genre, it would be necessary that it first answer these questions.

It would be arbitrary to suppose, however, that critics and authors occupied consistently coherent positions that would facilitate an adequate response. Hawkesworth's praise of the "old romance," for example, was already, at midcentury, in some sense belated. In 1705, Mary Delarivière Manley had criticized "The Prodigious Length of the Ancient *Romances*,"

---

[65] Hawkesworth, "November 18, 1754," *The Adventurer*, in *AO*, 67.
[66] Ibid., 70.
[67] Ibid., 68.
[68] Ibid., 68.

"the Mixture of so many Extraordinary Adventures, and the great Number of Actors that appear on the Stage, and the Likeness which is so little managed, *all which has given a Distaste to Persons of Good Sense.*"[69] Here we find the respect for history, long before its manifestation in Defoe, in the connection between "so many Extraordinary Adventures" whose "Likeness is so little managed" and romances. Thus, that which was being sought out could not be in any way a continuation with the prose of the past. Rather the very term *romance* needed a replacement. That contention acquired significant strength in 1748 through the intervention of the novelist Tobias Smollett, who contended that the genre originated in "ignorance, vanity, and superstition" that had given way to "the heathen mythology, which is no other than a collection of extravagant romances."[70] Furthermore, its authors, although incapable of competing with those of epic and tragedy, "were resolved to excel them in fiction, and apply to the wonder rather than the judgment of their readers."[71] In Smollett's argument, the religious case reinforces the renunciation of fictional material, and both defer to the question of truth. In light of the gathered testimony, we can understand, even if provisionally, how the respect for history was associated with values on a philosophical-religious spectrum and, consequently, how the variables inherent in the process of controlling domestication comprised elements that were aesthetic, political (the nation), pragmatic (utility), philosophico-religious, and concerned with public interest. Yet the fact that Hawkesworth could still defend the romance demonstrates that control did not operate in accord with any official purpose, but might, on the contrary have included the entire literate community within its convergences and contradictions. This would explain the position espoused by Hugh Blair, writing "On Fictitious History" in his *Lectures on Rhetoric and Poetry* (1762). In contrast to Smollett, Blair takes the romance not as the opposite of proper customs but as having the merit "of being writing of the highly moral and heroic kind," although not of a sort that could be considered a model for contemporary society, because adapted "to the legends and superstitious notions concerning magic and necromancy."[72] It was this that motivated Blair's preference for the "familiar novel," despite the fact that its exemplars in Louis XIV's France and Charles II's England "were in general of a triffling nature, *without the*

---

[69] Mary Delarivière Manley, "The Secret History of Queen Zarah and the Zarazians," in *AO*, 59, italics added.

[70] Thomas Smollett, "Preface to *The Adventures of Roderick Random*" (1748), in *AO*, 63.

[71] Ibid., 65.

[72] Hugh Blair, "On Fictitious History," *Lectures on Rhetoric and Poetry*, in *AO*, 76.

appearance of moral tendency, or useful instruction."[73] In other words, Blair concurred, albeit not as rigorously as Smollett, with the general direction in which a prosaic genre was developing, with its useful and moral orientation and its greater proximity to the quotidian life of the common reader. This is the model that he saw incarnated both by *Robinson Crusoe*, which, captivating the imagination of the reader, stimulated it "for surmounting the difficulties of any external situation," preparing it, thus, for enterprises favorable to the nation, and, above all, by "Mr. Fielding's Novels," "highly distinguished for their humour."[74]

To the extent that Blair indicates contemporary examples of what was being sought after, we can conclude that the conditions of the novel had already supplanted the marvelous that dominated in old romance.[75] In 1785, Clara Reeve offered a synthetic taxonomy of the genre: "The Romance is an heroic fable, which treats of fabulous persons and things. The Novel is a picture of real life and manners, and of the times in which it is written. The Romance in lofty and elevated language describes what *never happened nor is likely to happen*. The Novel gives a familiar relation of such things, as pass every day before our eyes."[76] The mechanism of control emerges clearly here. It is a matter of promoting, albeit not in an intentional or conscious manner, an entertaining narrative that, while speaking in a prosaic and familiar way, would be useful, respect truth and religion, favor enterprises benefiting the nation, and maintain history, that is, fact, as its horizon. This codification is implicit already in a passage written by Holcroft in 1780: "Modern writers use the word Romance to signify a fictitious history of detached and independent adventures; . . . in a Novel, a combination of incidents, entertaining in themselves, are made to form a whole."[77] Even though Holcroft distinguishes the two terms according to "aesthetic" criteria, he concludes his argument by considering the "utility" to which "the legitimate Novel" lends itself: "The legitimate Novel is a work much more difficult than the Romance, and justly deserves to be ranked with those dramatic pieces whose utility is generally allowed."[78]

---

[73] Ibid., 76, italics added.

[74] Ibid., 78–80.

[75] This is confirmed by Michael McKeon, who observes that "it is only around the middle of the eighteenth century that 'the novel' becomes the dominant and standard term" (*The Origins of the English Novel, 1600–1740* [Baltimore: Johns Hopkins University Press, 1987], 25).

[76] Clara Reeve, *The Progress of Romance, through Times, Countries and Manners . . .* , in *AO*, 88.

[77] Thomas Holcroft, "Preface to *Alwyn; or, The Gentleman Comedian*," in *AO*, 87.

[78] Ibid., 86–88.

It is the examination of the eighteenth-century debate that demonstrates what was really at stake under the guise of an aesthetic discussion. In the meantime, even if we were to agree that the formal criterion removes the preference for certain values to a secondary plane and, with the passage of time, leads us to forget them, it must be added that there is something outlying the formal vantage point that might be elucidated simply by comparing *Tom Jones* with *Tristram Shandy*. The necessity of prefaces so imposed itself during this epoch that Fielding interposes them within his *opera magna*. Thus, in chapter 1 of book 2, he declares himself "the founder of a new province of writing," and, as such, free "to make the laws I please therein."[79] But is his freedom, in fact, so far-reaching? If we follow the chapter, we find, to the contrary, his efforts to justify his tale as a form of true narrative that is also diverting and profitable. This is why he distinguishes his work from writing by "painful and voluminous historians," who, "to preserve the regularities of [their] series" do not spare the reader the minimal, insignificant detail. In contrast, he will be a selective historian, who will treat "matters of consequence."[80] In so doing, he escapes also the "universal contempt" directed at authors "who do not draw their materials from records," in light of which he "avoid[s] the term *romance*," contending rather that "our labors have sufficient title to the name of history."[81] In order to merit the title of historian that he confers on himself, Fielding knows that he must signal his adherance to one final prerequisite: "To say the truth," the historian must avoid the incredulity caused "by falling into fiction."[82] To proclaim himself the founder of a new genre means justifying the "invention or parable" referred to by Defoe, as well as respecting the Horatian *prodesse aut delectare*. In doing so, Fielding incorporates the ideal of the control of the imagination that flourished in the eighteenth-century English novel.

In contrast, *Tristram Shandy* demonstrates the degree to which control, as such, does not impede the circulation of works that contradict it. Sterne's exception is motivated by *formal reason* that a respect for history would veil: in *Tristram Shandy*, narrative linearity is purposely violated. Without pretending to write a preface or conjugate/multiply one, the narrator comments: "In this long digression which I was accidentally led into, as in all digressions (one only excepted) there is a master-stroke of digressive

---

[79] Henry Fielding, *The History of Tom Jones, a Foundling* (1749), ed. J. Bender and S. Sterns (Oxford: Oxford University Press, 1996), 68.

[80] Ibid., 67, 68.

[81] Ibid., 423.

[82] Ibid., 349.

skill."[83] The attention devoted to digression, which will, in fact, constitute the *principio compositionis* of the book, deconstructs the entire novelistic mechanism. The reader loses the sure guide who might offer a standard for his own conduct; but the narrative gains in terms of irony what is lost in terms of utility. Wolfgang Iser, one of the work's best interpreters, points out: "Instead of demonstrating something, [the narrator] himself becomes the object of scrutiny, thus causing a shift in the narrative tradition by opening up hitherto unexplored realms: the hero, having lost his various traditional functions, is now set free to become a subject in his own right; and being thrown back upon himself, as it were, he begins to discover himself in all his difficult complexity."[84] Iser demonstrates that the linear function of history—typical of the eighteenth-century English novel and systematically disregarded by Sterne—continually subordinated the thematization of the subject to other parameters: the nation, utility, truth, and so forth. Only in rebelling against the linear treatment of history does Sterne make possible the analysis of the self in its proper internal configuration.

In sum, we can associate the function of the control of the imagination with the double instability that McKeon notes in the formation of the English novel: "the instability of generic categories" and that of "social categories." The former "registers an epistemological crisis, a major cultural transition in attitudes toward how to tell the truth in narrative." The second "registers a cultural crisis in attitudes toward how the external social order is related to the internal, moral state of its members."[85] The first case involves the necessity that the novel repudiate any sort of familiar relationship with the romance and anchor itself strongly in history. This would equal a veto of the fictional, a veto on which control would build. The second case instead involves offering the reader the novel as mirror and guide. That is, with the elevation of the self, it was a matter of domesticating the individual, making him useful and respectful of the current norms. This, in turn, would result in the importance of the novel—not only its English variant—for the formation of a national spirit. Benedict Anderson has already demonstrated that declining legitimacy of the "sacral monarchy" began in England with the execution of Charles Stuart in 1649.[86] The concept of nationalism, or of "an imagined political community—and imagined as both inherently limited

---

[83] Laurence Sterne, *The Life and Opinions of Tristram Shandy, Gentleman* (1760–67), 1, 22, 51.

[84] W. Iser, *Laurence Sterne: Tristram Shandy* (Cambridge: Cambridge University Press, 1988), 3.

[85] McKeon, *The Origins of the English Novel*, 20.

[86] Benedict Anderson, *Imagined Communities*, rev. and amplified ed. (London: Verso, 1991), 21.

and sovereign,"[87] develops as a result of the crisis of legitimacy—along with other factors that I cannot explore here, including the crisis of Latin as the language employed in the writing of books and the crisis ensuing from the development of the printing press. Anderson underlines the important part played by the novel in this process, insofar as the actions and actors in the novel are homogenized from the common vantage point of the nation: "That all these acts are performed at the same clocked, calendrical time, but by actors who may be largely unaware of one another, shows the novelty of this imagined world conjured up by the author in his readers' mind."[88]

I should accentuate one final factor: the relevance of Bacon's *The Advance of Learning* (1620) in this context of crisis and transformation. Aside from Descartes, Bacon would most inspire the configuration of seventeenth-century control. As cautious as his French contemporary, Bacon sought not to annoy religious authorities, while, at the same time, he sought to reform the processes of knowledge/cognition. For Bacon, the advancement of knowledge depended on the learner's recognizing that "words are but the images of matter: and except they have life of reason and invention, to fall in love with them is all one as to fall in love with a picture."[89] His disdain for the word reflected a greater attention owed to the world, with an emphasis on observation and the empirical, to the detriment of work on the writing itself, on those cobwebs "admirable for the fineness of thread and work, but of no substance or profit."[90] The attack launched against the fine web of words and images was augmented by the equivalence established between the sciences of the ruse and the imagination: "astrology, natural magic, and alchemy . . . have had better intelligence and confederacy with the imagination of man than with his reason."[91]

In Bacon (and in Descartes) we find the first indication of a vast crisis to which the control of the imagination would respond. While the form of control would be modified in accordance with the importance assumed by the imagination, above all after Kant's Third Critique, the suspicion awakened by the word and by the function of mere transmission associated with language would continue to act in favor of control and in hostility toward

---

[87] Ibid., 6.

[88] Ibid., 26.

[89] Sir Francis Bacon, *The Advance of Learning* (1620), ed. W. A. Wright (Oxford: Clarendon Press, 1900), 1.4.3, 30.

[90] Ibid., 1.4.6, 32.

[91] Ibid., 1.4.11, 36.

fiction. Although I have considered only the English novel of the eighteenth century, the control of the imagination that extends over the course of the century to the *Frühromantiker*, in the century's final decades, depends fundamentally on the function of language, particularly on its part in representation and communication, and on the veto of the fictional. Even a restless thinker and writer of the quality of Diderot would not escape it: "However well made it may be, the best representation, the most coherent, is no more than a fabric of falsehoods that overlie one another."[92]

Translated by Sharon Lubkemann Allen

[92] Denis Diderot, *Salon de 1793*, in *Salons*, ed. J. Seznec and J. Adhëmar (Oxford: Oxford University Press, 1975), 217.

HENRY Y. H. ZHAO

Historiography and Fiction in Chinese Culture

"All Scriptures Are Historiography"

Chinese culture has always displayed a pyramidic structure that presents it-self as a rigid generic hierarchy of discourses. The Confucianist scriptures and official dynastic histories enjoyed almost absolute authority at the top of the hierarchy and were never seriously challenged after the sanctification of Confucianism around the second century B.C. and its resanctification by the Neo-Confucianists in the twelfth century A.D. However, Confucianist scrip-tures were canons of fixed texts, leaving only a little room for textual and hermeneutic scholarship, whereas history was a continuous practice of writ-ing and interpretation. Therefore, historiography was regarded as endowed with the power of superior meaning above all the other genres.

Also, historiography used to be the supreme narrative model in China. In light of the long-standing proposition that "the *Six Scriptures*—the six generic prototypes sponsored by Confucius: *li*, ritual; *yue*, musical; *shu*, doc-umentary; *shi*, poetical; *yi*, divinatory; and *chunqiu*, chronological—are all *de facto* historiography (liu jing jie shi),"[1] historiography was then esteemed as the paramount paradigm for all cultural discourses, occupying the exalted position resembling theological writing in other cultures. Moreover, it very possibly satisfied the Chinese people's need for narratives, as China is one of the very few nations that did not have an epic, and the first Chinese novel did not appear until the twelfth century, almost two thousand years after the earliest historiography was written.

In accordance with Confucianist social philosophy, a scale of meaning-power is spread over the generic hierarchy of cultural discourses, fading off toward the end of the range and leaving the lower strata of social activities in a position very similar to what modern Western sociologists call the subal-tern or subcultural. Traditional Chinese fiction, that is, Chinese fiction be-fore its modernization in the so-called May 4 Movement—the Chinese

---

[1] The proposal that the *Six Scriptures* are all historiography was put forward very early, during the Han Dynasty (206 B.C.–A.D. 220), but it was Zhang Xuecheng (1738–1801) who spelled it out in clear terms in his *Wen Shi Tong Yi* (Shanghai: Shanghai Shudian, 1988), 5. All translations of Chinese quotations are my own unless otherwise indicated.

Enlightenment that started around 1917—had been divided into two major subgenres: works written in the archaic but culturally recognized "literary language" (*wenyan*), and those written in the vernacular (*baihua*) after about the twelfth century. The former were almost unexceptionally anecdotal short pieces, while the latter, appearing much later, were mostly novels. Though fictional texts in literary language started to be produced around the time of Christ, they had not often been considered fiction until the novel and the drama became popular genres, when frequent cross-pollination became possible.

The Chinese novel, being one of the genres at the very bottom of the generic pyramid, possesses a series of strong subcultural characteristics. Chinese literary-language stories, however, occupied a dubious position: their elegant language, the same language in which history and other privileged genres were written, attracted admiration from the elite readership, but their imagination of the nonfactual made them unsuitable as vehicles for meaning, because the very notion of fictionality conflicts with the Confucianist philosophical system. Therefore, both suffered from a similar, though to a varying degree, cultural discrimination. No problem concerning traditional Chinese fiction can be fully comprehended without considering this particular difficulty of fiction in Chinese culture.

Chinese fiction is generically subordinate to almost all the other genres—historiography, essays of all types, and poetry—so it was almost unable to function independently in cultural signification. Since historiography was the highest genre, fiction had to justify its existence by claiming to serve as its popularized illustration, or as its supplementation. Therefore, fiction hardly represented the genuine spirit of Chinese culture but rather its distorted exposition. Some critics even regard Chinese fiction as the expression of the social unconscious, which was silenced in "normal" cultural discourses but let loose in those "inferior" genres.

Chinese traditional fiction successfully conventionalized its generic particularities, turning itself into a necessary complementary element, even a safety valve, in the culture so that the interpretative codes of ideology could, to different degrees, cover the whole society. By this stabilizing ability, it won a position in that society, forcing the cultural establishment to tolerate it. The Chinese vernacular novel, for instance, routinely installed its narrator as the storyteller of an oral performance before listeners, thus making the other major narratological features also conventionalized. Its highly homogeneous manner of signification from century to century ensured effective communication based on shared codes.

The audiences of those genres were very different. Because Chinese is such a difficult language, taking many years of schooling to learn, and Chinese history is such a long and well-recorded one, generically privileged discourses, usually with abundant historical allusions, were accessible only to the professional or semiprofessional readers of the well-educated sections of society. The novel, on the contrary, employed an easy, "crude," more readily comprehensible style for the culturally and educationally underprivileged section of society. Also, their expected mode of consumption was different: most traditional fiction was unequivocally produced for leisure, while generically privileged discourses, assuming a more serious appearance, were likely to blur the distinction between work and pastimes.

This is not to deny that Chinese fiction was also a part of Chinese culture. Subcultural discourses, even in a pyramidic culture, are coded by the same hegemonic ideology. Nevertheless, two kinds of students are likely to be baffled when reading Chinese fiction—those who want to find in it a direct embodiment of the established values of Chinese culture,[2] and those who try to find a set of values subversive to the dominant cultural norms.[3] All they can find is, very possibly, a perplexing mixture of both. In most cases, an ideologically conformable framework asserts itself in the plot of the narrative, and highly entertaining but often aberrant elements dwell in localized texture. The potential subversiveness is then neutered by the ideological framework, which ensures expected interpretation on the part of the average Chinese audience. Therefore, although cultural deviations repeatedly showed up in the huge amount of traditional Chinese fiction, they were only recognizable in a limited scope and in an ambiguous manner. They rarely carried messages subversive to cultural norms until the great disruption of the May 4 Movement, when Chinese fiction became modernized and emerged as a fully qualified cultural discourse.[4]

---

[2] A typical case is the indignation shown by C. T. Hsia, author of the celebrated *The Classical Chinese Novel: A Critical Introduction* (New York: Columbia University Press, 1968), at some vernacular works such as the thirteenth-century novel about bandits, *The Water Margin* (*Shui Hu zhuan*), and the sixteenth-century erotic novel *The Golden Lotus* (*Jin Ping Mei*). He insists that they do not "represent the true spirit of Chinese culture." See also C. T. Hsia, Introduction to *Sui Shi Yiwen* (Taipei: Youshi Chubanshe), 5.

[3] Mao Zedong's criticism on *The Water Margin* is a typical case. Mao insists that the novel portrays the capitulation of the rebels to the court. His criticism, made in mid-1970s, led to another political persecution campaign during the Cultural Revolution against the "Capitulationists."

[4] The May 4 Movement, named after the political demonstration by Beijing students on May 4, 1919, is widely regarded as the Chinese Enlightenment that started around 1917 and continued until the mid-1920s.

"Fiction Is to Supplement Historiography"

Any act of signification has to be executed through a certain medium, which, however, is neither neutral nor passive, as it molds the formal features of the message into a culturally acknowledged pattern habitually called *genre*. Genre facilitates the interpretation but, on the other hand, restricts the scope of signification. Often we find in works of art and literature an inclination to break the boundaries of their own communicative patterns in an effort to achieve the effects of other genres. This extrageneric emulation may take place at an early stage of new genres—for example, early photography emulated painting, or early film emulated theatrical performance. One of the main reasons for this emulation of other discursive genres, apart from technical concerns, is that the "lower" genres have to prove that they can function in a similar fashion to more prestigious ones. They grow out of this extrageneric emulation when their own cultural position is established and recognized.

In a pyramidic culture like that of traditional China, however, extrageneric emulation by the culturally lower genres could remain an aspiration forever, as they could hardly hope to enjoy a cultural mobility to move out of the lower strata. The Chinese novel, for centuries, was situated so low in the generic hierarchy that it had to continue to emulate a prestigious genre in order to justify it own existence. In this way, the extrageneric emulation finally turned into the paradigm inherent in the genre, that is, the basic pattern that recurs in its texts and helps formulate its signification. In fact, the paradigm has little to do with the subject matter but much to do with the composition of the participants—in our case, the readers, authors, critics, editors, and publishers of the novel.

The absolute domination of historiography in traditional Chinese culture exercises great pressure on all genres, high or low. In poetry, for instance, historical allusions are so extensive that they became an overcoding essential to the genre, making its style succinct and its signification much richer, though also making it interpretable only to professional readers familiar with histories. The pressure from historiography was strongly felt in literary-language fiction. Writers of this subgenre prided themselves on producing some stories that were capable of supplementing the official histories. Most of the salient narratological characteristics of literary-language stories are ostensibly ascribable to this emulation of historiography. Always purporting to be recounting real anecdotes of real persons, the literary-language story starts with a formulaic short summary of the protagonist's family or personal history, and then the location and the date of the main event of the story are clearly provided before the story unfolds. At the end (or less often, at the beginning) of the story, a frame "situation" is installed, where the narrator, inevitably adopting the name of the author, comments on the characters and their fate, in the same manner that historians make comments on a historical character and an event.

To praise fictional works as being "historiography-like and faithful" became the greatest commendatory words among Chinese fiction writers and critics. Ge Hong of the fourth century, one of the earliest Chinese fiction writers, claimed that his collection of stories *Miscellaneous Notes from the West Capital* (*Xijing Zaji*) was compiled from the data left over by the well-known historian Liu Xin (?–23 A.D.) and that his book should be read as a supplement to Liu Xin's celebrated bibliography. Indeed, in the bibliographical supplement to the ensuing official dynastic history, *Notes from the West Capital* was always listed under the heading of "history." Almost 1,500 years later, Ji Yun (1724–1805), the preeminent eighteenth-century scholar and compiler of *Digests of the Imperial Library* (*Siku Quanshu*), praised Ge Hong's book using the reasoning that the author had wanted to hear one and a half millennia before: "Its contents, though fictional, were gathered from a wide range of material. The anthologizer Li Shan used the book to annotate *Selection of Refined Literature* (*Wen Xuan*). The educator Xu Jian alluded to it in his *Textbook for Children* (*Chu Xue Ji*). Even the great poet Du Fu, who was very careful in verifying the sources of his allusions, referred to it repeatedly. After so many hundreds of years of usefulness we can say that these notes have proved to be well-grounded historical facts, and cannot be easily ignored."[5]

Even though, as will be discussed later, some unfortunate poets who mistakenly used allusions to events seen only in vernacular historical novels had to spend the rest of their lives in pillory or in remorse, it is clear that similar allusions to at least a few of the literary-language anecdotal fictions could be less intolerable. Such cases of fiction being allowed to stand for history were very rare, however, and this flexibility was, at best, permitted only in poetry and in some lighter types of essays but not in formal essays or official documents.

If high genres felt the pressure of historiography so strongly, for a discourse in as low a position as the novel, the emulation of historiography was virtually compulsory. Being more subordinate to historiography, the best that the vernacular novel could hope for was not actually to supplement

[5] Ji Yun, *Siku Quanshu Tiyao* (Beijing: Zhonghua Shuju, 1965), 1,182.

official history by serving as its codicil (*bu shi*) but to illustrate it by being its popularized version (*yuyi xin shi*). Its restriction and its freedom both stemmed from this assigned social role, to which the well-known sixteenth-century novelist Zhu Renhuo offers an interesting explanation: "It is very true for our ancestors to think of *The Grand Chronicle* (*Tongjian*) as the great ledger of the past. But there should be both the general ledger and the small items account books. That is why novels about the past dynasties have kept coming up."[6] Here the cultural subordination of fiction is held up as something to be proud of, and indeed it became an extrinsic standard for judging the quality of novels.

Since the emulation of historiography was imperative, studying history was regarded as fundamental training for would-be novelists, even though the profession was never regarded as worth aspiring to. Luo Ye, the thirteenth-century scholar who was among the earliest compilers of Chinese novels, advised in his *Notes of a Drunken Old Man* (*Zuiweng Tanlu*): "Although a lesser scholarship, fiction requires a wider range of learning. [Fiction writers] cannot be people with scanty knowledge, but should, by necessity, be erudite. When young, they have to study the anecdotes collection *Taiping Guangji*, and when grown up, they must familiarize themselves with histories of all dynasties."[7]

This emulation of historiography continued well into the twentieth century. Liu E (1857–1909), the celebrated novelist at the turn of the century, did not care much about his great novel *The Travels of Lao Can*, which was published, as was the regular practice in traditional China, under a pseudonym. But he declared in a comment made in his own name at the end of chapter 4 of the novel: "These facts are not known to many people. Fortunately they are recorded in this book, thus providing material when an official history is to be compiled in the future. From this case we can see that there is no ground to despise the novel."[8] It is a very strange occurrence to see the last of the great masters of the traditional Chinese novel defend his art in this way, that is, expecting that a small part of it could be recognized as records of historical facts.

In the early twentieth century, using a love story to frame historical events became a popular way of writing novels, like the sugar coat for pills, in which, of course, the pills are the most important ingredients. The

---

[6] Zhu Renhuo, "Preface" to *Sui Tang Yanyi* (Shanghai: Guji Chubanshe, 1965), 4.

[7] Luo Ye, *Zuiweng Tanlu* (Shanghai: Shanghai Guji Chubanshe, 1957), 3.

[8] Liu E, *Lao Can Youji* (Taipei: Lianjing Chubanshe, 1976), 38.

best-known example is *A Flower in the Sinful Sea* (*Nie Hai Hua*) by Zeng Pu (1872–1935). The design of the novel was "to borrow a character as the thread to knit in as much as possible the history of the recent thirty years."[9] Other early-twentieth-century novelists soon followed suit: Lin Shu's *The Stench of the Sword* (*Jian Xing Lu*), Fu Ling's *The Bird That Carries Stone to the Sea* (*Qin Hai Shi*), Zhong Xinqing's *New Dame aux Camelias* (*Xin Chahua*), and others. Among them, Wu Jianren's *The Sea of Remorse* (*Hen Hai*) is a much better novel with almost all sugar and little pill—a tragic romance of two couples at the chaotic time of the Boxers Rebellion of 1900. But A Ying (1900–1977), the modern literary historian, included the novel in his anthology *Literature on the Boxer Rebellion* without any justification. In fact it is amazing to see how A Ying neatly anthologized almost all major early-twentieth-century novels into historical subject matters such as "The Opium War," "The Movement against the U.S. Exclusion of Chinese Immigrants," "The 1911 Revolution," and "The Constitutional Movement." Considering that he was a Marxist scholar active since the 1930s, we can see that the tradition of viewing the novel as "codicil to history" really died hard in China.

Indeed, the emulation of historiography grew all the stronger among early-twentieth-century novelists, to the point of becoming an infatuation. The revolutionary novel *The Lion Roars* (*Shizi Hou*) by Chen Tianhua (1875–1905) recounts the imaginary history of an island utopia, in which there are some very strange passages: "Wen Mingzhong . . . made up another song and taught his students to sing it every day, it runs. The lyric of the song is missing in the manuscripts of the novel, so we have to leave it out."[10] "Suddenly there came a lumberman who was singing while walking. The lyric of the song is not available to the author."[11] It is not easy to come up with an explanation for those clumsy statements. A novel could well leave out those lyrics without mentioning their absence at all—the first and foremost job in the narratorial mediation is to select only those details that serve to tell the story in an interesting way and to leave out the rest. Whatever the reason, the author does not have to cite the lyric in the first place. If he did not have the patience or gift to write these two lyrics (the author did compose quite a number of lyrics in the novel), his excuse only makes their absence more conspicuous. What the author is trying to achieve by this kind of awkward explanation, it seems to me, is to create an impression that

---

[9] Zeng Pu, *Nie Hai Hua* (Shanghai: Zhonghua Shuju, 1962), 4.

[10] Chen Tianhua, *Shizi Hou* (Taipei: Guanghua Shuju, 1984), 594.

[11] Ibid., 612.

everything about the history of this utopian island is faithfully recorded, so that if any document—even the song of a lumberman—is missing, its omission should still be faithfully recorded, just as proper historiography requires. This kind of "detail brimming" existed for many centuries and was one of the most salient narratological features of the Chinese novel.

The reason why the emulation of historiography culminates in such an infatuation at the beginning of the twentieth century—in the last phase of the traditional Chinese novel—is not difficult to find: the excessive social and political role imposed on the novel by the Reformists and other champions of the genre was more than the genre could bear, and this forced the novelists to draw support by posing as historians. Another interesting case is Lin Shu (1852–1924), fiction writer and the first professional translator of the Western novel at the turn of the twentieth century. He repeatedly said that his long-cherished hope was to be able to contribute to official history by writing novels: "Probably these things can serve as materials when an official history is compiled" is an aspiration of every novelist in traditional China. But when he was eventually invited by the government to be an honorary compiler of *The Official History of the Qing*, he declined, acknowledging that he was only good at producing "unofficial history" (*yeshi*).

By the late Qing, some authors apprehended the basic contradiction between historicity and fictionality. In one of the last historical novels in the traditional vein, Cheng Daoyi's *A Romance for the Leisure Time* (*Xiaoxian Yanyi*), there are a great many contradictory narratorial commentaries about these concepts. Let me select only two: "Fictionality is most misleading. In this novel of mine no groundless fictionality would be tolerated, and no libel allowed to appear. If you do not believe me, you can examine it carefully and see that every word I say is true to facts."[12] Nevertheless, a few pages after there appears a totally opposite statement: "Some people would ask how could I say that this minister was killed by the Boxers, as he was actually executed by an imperial order? My answer is: the proper way of writing the novel is that so long as it does not go far off the track, let it be as interesting as possible. We should not be too fussy over facts."[13] With such blatant self-contradictions came the end of a millennia-long persistent emulation of historiography on the part of Chinese fiction, but also the demise of the traditional Chinese novel.

---

[12] Cheng Daoyi, *Xiaoxian Yanyi*, in A. Ying, ed., *Gengzi Shibian Wenxue Juan* (Shanghai: Zhonghua Shuju, 1959), 1:337.

[13] Ibid., 405.

The Indefinability of Fiction in China

This historiographical emulation of Chinese fiction had more profound causes that may be found in Chinese thinking. Chinese historians and bibliographers all along had difficulty in categorizing fiction, which may sound ridiculous to a modern scholar. It seems that the very idea of fictionality baffled Chinese thinking. The earliest imaginative narratives were produced without any category to fit into the bibliographical appendix of history books, the only place where books were recorded as cultural products. The first categorizing attempt was made by the historian Ban Gu (A.D. 32–92), author of *The History of Han* (*Han Shu*), who actually created the Chinese word *xiaoshuo* (literally "small talk"), which gradually acquired the meaning of fiction. But he defined this subject heading as "gossip and hearsay in the streets," and *xiaoshuo* writers as the last of the ten groups of writers. Nevertheless, Ban Gu warned that "only the former nine are worth reading."[14] The fifteen books he listed under the heading, however, had all been lost by as early as the Sui Dynasty (sixth century A.D.), although we can guess from the titles that they were not fiction at all but works of various types that Ban Gu was unable to place under the other nine headings. At that time, and for centuries after that, *xiaoshuo* was actually defined by its very indefinability. The true original meaning of *xiaoshuo* should be only "miscellany."

On the contrary, there are at least two kinds of works produced in early China that would be cataloged today as fiction—fantasies like *The Book of Mountains and Seas* (*Shan Hai Jing*) and *The Book of Supernatural Things* (*Shengyi Jing*), and legends such as *The Private Life of the Hanwu Emperor* (*Hanwu Di Neizhuan*) and *The Life of Dongfang Shuo* (*Dongfang Shuo Zhuan*). Yet in the bibliographies attached to early official dynastic histories, such books were placed under "History: Geograpical Books" (*Shibu Dilei*) or under "History: Sundry Books" (*Shibu Zalei*). This absence of the category of fiction did not change until much later: in the official dynastic history *The New History of the Tang* (*Xin Tang Shu*) compiled under the general editorship of the renowned scholar Ouyang Xiu (1007–72) in the eleventh century, the books listed under *xiaoshuo* were more or less in agreement with its modern meaning of fiction. However, the inclusion of such nonfiction books as Lu Yu's *The Book of Tea* (*Cha Jing*) indicates that the term still covered a much wider area than it does today.

No matter how the categorization of *xiaoshuo* gradually edged closer to that of fiction, under the this heading one rarely finds novels written in the

---

[14] Ban Gu, *Han Shu* (Beijing: Zhonghua Shuju, 1962), 5:34.

vernacular. Hu Yinglin (1551–1602), a scholar of the sixteenth century, divided *xiaoshuo* into six types in his *Notes of Shaoshi Shanfang* (*Shaoshi Shanfang Bicong*). In his voluminous *Digests of Four-Library Collectanea* (*Siku Quanshu Tiyao*), Ji Yun, the leading bibliographer of the eighteenth century, discussed three types of fiction. Neither of them mentioned any vernacular novel at all. Actually the term *xiaoshuo* had hardly been applied to the vernacular novel in the general usage of Chinese until modern times. It used to be called *pinghua* (storytelling) or *shuobu* (storytelling books). These terms remained the formal name for the vernacular novel even in the first half of the twentieth century among the cultural conservatives, when *xiaoshuo* was already the acknowledged name for the genre of fiction.

Strictly speaking, fiction was hardly ever a well-defined genre in traditional China. Even as late as the early twentieth century, fiction was still mixed with other popular genres such as drama or balladry. Liang Qichao's essay "Scattered Notes about Fiction" ("Xiaoshuo Lingjian") includes three plays in its discussion; and Tian Liaosheng's "On the History of Chinese Fiction" ("Zhongguo Lidai Xiaoshuo Lun") covers *biji* prose of the Tang Dynasty, *zaji* prose of the Song, drama of the Yuan, and *tanci* ballads of the Qing. Similar generic confusion was common before the concept of *xiaoshuo* was redefined against its Western counterpart fiction during the May 4 Movement.

"Those Books Must Be Strictly Banned with No Exception"

As mentioned above, official historians almost never stooped to mention the vernacular novel, as if it were a disgrace to the culture. The compilers of the local histories (*fangzhi*) shared the same arrogance. They would mention all the local folk rituals and festivities, but hardly any vernacular writer or publisher. Apparently the vernacular novel was only to be tolerated in practice but not to be recognized in a record of culture such as the history of the locality, however humble the locals might feel about their area. For instance, the local histories of Anhui Province during the last years of the Qing Dynasty mention Wu Jingzi briefly in less than forty characters and say not a word about his life's work, *The Scholars* (*Rulin Waishi*), which is generally regarded as one of the greatest Chinese novels of all times. Its early-twentieth-century editions give Wu a longer entry, but *The Scholars* is still mentioned only in passing after all his other long-lost poetry and prose collections. Given that one of the best-known Chinese novelists met with this kind of treatment even as late as the early twentieth century, other fiction works and their authors had even less hope of being mentioned in the local histories of their hometown. That flagrant negligence has provided much opportunity for interesting but often futile literary detective investigations in modern scholarship since the novel unexpectedly became one the most important genres of modern Chinese culture. That is the reason why the birth and death dates of so many people—provided they did something to distinguish themselves among the literati scholars of the time—can be provided accurately in this essay, as most periods in the long history of China were indeed well documented. Nevertheless, scholars who made great contributions to the study of the novel left behind hardly anything more than their names, and many novelists simply remain anonymous.

In fact, the cultural position of the vernacular novel was not far from such activities as, for instance, prostitution. The comparison sounds strange, but it has been unequivocally documented. Many government decrees after the founding of the Ming Dynasty in the fourteenth century imposed a ban, with severe punishment, on the practice of all kinds of subcultural "discourses"—fiction, drama, balladry, popular cults, paranormal communication, and prostitution. During the Qing Dynasty, Emperor Kang Xi's decree of the fourth month of 1709 promulgated "a strict and perpetual prohibition against omen reading, magic-figure drawing, obscene balladry and novel."[15] Another decree issued by him five years later went even further: "I rule the country with an emphasis on proper mores and customs. In order to rectify social mores, it is imperative to promote the study of the Confucian Scriptures and strictly ban blasphemous books. This is an unalterable rule. Recently there have been seen in book markets numerous novels that abound in nonsense and vulgarity far from propriety and reason. Not only the foolish common people are seduced, but even gentry and scholars who browse through them are tempted. This is no small matter in regard to social mores. Those books must be strictly banned with no exceptions."[16]

Nevertheless, despite the repeated harshly phrased decrees and short periods of severe suppression, the novel, just like prostitution, was never cleared away in earnest. These works could hope to enjoy some implicit tolerance on the part of the dominant culture in traditional China because they were found "useful" for the social order. Their suppression, when enforced, was usually limited to the capital and the elite literati class. There was not much effective suppression as long as these activities stayed in not very

---

[15] Reprinted in Wang Chuanxiao, ed., *Yuan Ming Qing Sandai Jinhui Xiaoshuo Xiqu Shiliao* (Beijing: Zuojia Chubanshe, 1958), 33.

[16] Ibid., 35.

obtrusive underground. In fact, there was not too much complaint if the novel remained in subordination.

Nevertheless, Chinese culture could not stand any confusion within its strict generic hierarchy, especially the confusion between historiography and the historical novel. Hu Yingling condescended to talk about the vernacular novel, calling the novelists "vulgar hacks in the backwoods" or "petty village pedants" because their works proved that they "totally lack any knowledge of history."[17] In the eighteenth century, the great historian Zhang Xuecheng (1738–1801), in *Speculations on Literature and Historiography* (*Wen Shi Tong Yi*), criticized the novel in an attitude typical of traditional literati. *The Three Kingdoms*, according to him, was "seventy percent of historical facts mixed with thirty percent of fabrication."[18] He was lenient to the authors, because, as he commented, "these novelists are not to blame since they do not possess enough knowledge, and can hardly be free of the habit of fabricating." But he issued a stern warning on the possibility not only of confusing officially recorded historical facts with fabricated events but also of the threat of "misunderstanding history." Indeed, what was most offensive to the traditional literati-scholars was novels encroaching on the sphere of historiography through mixing fictionality with historicity, because in this way the novel confounded the generic hierarchy which was part of the definition of the Confucian social order.

Documents of the Chinese imperial government demonstrate constant efforts to preclude the possibility of this kind of crime. The Wanli Emperor of the Ming issued a decree in 1602 forbidding the use of "words of fiction" in official memorandums. In 1728, the Yongzheng Emperor of the Qing severely punished a high-ranking official by removing him from office and making him stand in the pillory in public for three months, only because the latter, in his memorandum presented to the court, made an allusion in passing to an event that could be found in the historical novel but not in the official history.

It was not only the Imperial Court that was excessively strict in applying the generic distinction. Many literati seemed to be even more finicky about it. Yuan Mei (1716–89), a scholar well known for his open-mindedness at that time, recorded in his *Talking about Poetry in the Sui Garden* (*Suiyuan Shihua*) several "true stories" about how some fine poets used historical allusions

---

[17] Hu Yingling, *Shaoshi Shanfang Bicong* (Beijing: Zhonghua Shuju, 1958), 254.

[18] Zhang Xuecheng, *Wen Shi Tong Yi*, 36.

drawn from the novel *The Three Kingdoms*, and deservedly "spent the rest of their life in remorse after being singled out as ridiculous."[19] Similar accusations can be found in Hu Yingling's book, which argued that self-respecting literati must spit on poems that unintentionally alluded to "nonsensical" fiction, and that those who committed this kind of crime "should receive the death penalty."[20]

This does not mean that the consensus of Chinese men of letters in discriminating against fiction was without exception. Some scholars launched the first serious challenge to this absolutist hierarchy of discourses in the sixteenth and seventeenth centuries (i.e., the Late Ming and the Early Qing). With such courageous critics like Li Zhi (1527–1602) and Jin Shengtan (1606–61) as their respresentatives, several generations of literati in the more liberal-minded south tried to reevaluate literature of the lower cultural strata. They carefully edited vernacular novels and invented the *bianzhu* (marginal notes), a flexible type of criticism quite effective for promoting fiction. Nevertheless, although they made a great contribution to the development of Chinese fiction, they were hardly able to cast doubt on the generic hierarchy of Chinese culture, and their witty critical remarks, though appreciated by readers of vernacular fiction, were generally regarded by mainstream literati as eccentrics' ravings.

Another challenge came at the beginning of the twentieth century before the fall of the last Qing Dynasty, when some literati-scholars started to call for a great resurgence of the novel by extolling it in high-sounding words, claiming it to be the most important tool to awaken the nation. Exaggerations of the importance of the Chinese novel did not come only from authors and publishers who wanted to boost sales, but also from political leaders of the Reformist movements, whose voice was much more influential. Liang Qichao (1873–1929), the most eloquent among the Reformists, made the following groundless claim: "Reading the history of Western civilization, we can always find that in no matter in which nation of which period, fiction writers of literature are always the greatest contributors to civilization. The people worship these masters."[21]

Liang had actually been encouraged by Kang Youwei (1858–1927), the political leader of the Reformists who urged his disciples in a poem in 1900 to adopt a new stand toward the popular novel:

---

[19] Yuan Mei, *Suiyuan Shihua* (Beijing: Renmin Wenxue Chubanshe, 1956), 67.
[20] Hu Yingling, *Shaoshi Shanfang Bicong*, 254.
[21] Liang Qichao, *Yinbingshi He Ji* (Shanghai: Shangwu Yinshuguan, 1916), 1:46.

I am eager to save the nation but short of means,
I frown in anger when the sky is overcast.

. . . .

When I visit bookstores in Shanghai
What books enjoy the best sales?
Historiography cannot compete with formulaic essays
Which in turn have to yield to novels. . . .
In our land today this new school is prevalent
Turning the Six Arts into Seven Peaks.[22]

It was more than obvious that those Reformists saw in the novel, which had more popular appeal than historiography, a new weapon most suitable for their political agenda of introducing constitutional monarchy into China.

Each promotion campaign for the novel yielded a bumper harvest: the reevaluation of the sixteenth and the seventeenth centuries heralded the great achievements of the eighteenth-century novel, with such masterpieces as *Dream of the Red Chamber, The Scholars,* and *Flowers in the Mirror,* among others; the early-twentieth-century reevaluation brought about the astonishing flood of so-called Late Qing Fiction. What remains doubtful, however, is whether those literati-scholars really appreciated the novel that much, and whether their high praise actually enabled the Chinese novel to break away from its subaltern strata. The reevaluation efforts during the sixteenth and the seventeenth centuries were isolated ones, limited to some deviant members of the literati. The failure of Late Qing reassessment was ascribable to the overly practical aim of using fiction for political education.

The Reformists at the turn of the twentieth century did not even try to cover up their true opinion about the novel, which can be seen in Liang's well-known apology: "When it is impossible to teach the barely literate common readers the Scriptures, teach them with the novel; when it is impossible to teach them historiography, teach them with the novel; when it is impossible to teach them the philosophical thesis, teach them with the novel; when it is impossible to teach them the laws, teach them with the novel."[23] Here, the traditional generic hierarchy of thousands of years is preserved absolutely intact, with the position of the novel not moved up an inch. Because their endorsement of the novel was simply to provide propaganda reading

---

[22] Kang Youwei, *Kang Youwei Shiwen Ji,* ed. Shu Wu et al. (Beijing: Renmin Wenxue Chubanshe, 1990), 232.

[23] Liang Qichao, *Yinbingshi He Ji* (Shanghai: Shangwu Yinshuguan, 1916), 1:34.

material for the "barely literate," it was only natural that as soon as their immediate political aim disappeared—when the 1911 Revolution toppled the Dynasty and replaced it with the Republic, and the contitutional monarchy was no longer a political choice—these overenthusiastic apologists of the novel completely lost interest. In 1912, a decade later after his hyperbolic praise of the novel, Liang Qichao turned around to accuse the novel of "morally debasing the Chinese people," and, when asked to recommend a list of "must-read" Chinese canons to young readers, he refused to include any novel in his list and even cautioned young students "not to read novels at all unless you want to become a novelist." He seemed to have totally forgotten his own words and, indeed, his own novel writing not long before.

Perhaps the greatest contribution of the Reformists to the development of the Chinese novel was that its promotion campaign encouraged a generic mixture in practice: starting from the beginning of the twentieth century, the same magazines could carry vernacular novels as well as literary-language fiction; the same foreign novel could be translated into either the literary language or the vernacular; the same novelist could write in both. This mixture of participants and media greatly helped the final demolition of the traditional generic hierarchy in the second decade of the twentieth century.

The May 4 Movement and the Chinese Novel

The May 4 Movement that started around 1917 demolished this hierarchy by completely scrapping the millennia-old "literary language" as the cultural language and replaced it with the modern Chinese language based on the vernacular. As history had been the top genre written in this cultural language, and the novel a genre written in vernacular for common readers, this fundamental shift of language was then not only an enormous change in the Chinese language but also in the social position of those genres. The vernacular-based language triumphantly came to function in Chinese society after it was refined by the May 4 fiction writers to such a degree and used so effectively that the archaic literary language was finally pushed into disuse, thus removing the major linguistic obstacle for the novel to rise above the subcultural level.

Hu Shi (1891–1962), one of the liberal leaders of the May 4 Movement, published his famous essay "A Modest Proposal for the Improvement of Literature" ("Wenxue Gailiang Chuyi") in the January 1917 issue of the radical magazine *New Youth* (*Xin Qingnian*). The short, seemingly casual essay ushered in the gigantic "Literature Revolution" merely by discussing the potential of the Chinese vernacular as a tool for producing decent literature. His short essay summed up the opinions in an eight-point proposal in moderate terms with no revolutionary fanfare at all. Those who try to belittle Hu Shi's contribution argue that he was by no means the first one to advocate the use of the vernacular. Indeed, it was not Hu Shi but an older scholar, Qiu Tingliang, who first suggested replacing the literary language with the vernacular in his 1898 essay "On the Vernacular as the Starting Point for Reform" ("Lun Baihua wei Weixin zhi Ben") in *Su Bao*, the well-known paper for anti-Manchu instigation. He surely raised the suggestion of "abolishing the literary language" in a more emphatic manner than Hu Shi did twenty years later. Yet his call received little response, while Hu Shi's short essay provoked a storm that completely changed Chinese culture.

It is true that May 4 Movement did not raise the proposal for the first time in history, but there is a fundamental difference between the May 4 cultural revolutionaries and the previous advocates of the vernacular. The Late Qing apologists for the novel wanted to use the vernacular only to "teach" the barely literate common people. That was why even their articles advocating the vernacular were, paradoxically, written in the literary language, because the advocacy itself was meant to convince the literati-scholars. Their proposal, then, amounted to a mere tactical maneuver within the traditional generic hierarchy. Also, before Hu Shi's proposal, the popular magazine *Fiction Pictorial* (*Xiaoshuo Huabao*) had begun in 1914 to use the vernacular exclusively. Because it was a fiction magazine, declared to be dedicated only to the entertainment novel, "suitable for everyone: housewives, students, merchants, and workers," there was no manifesto. The periodical was simply moving further along the old track of different languages for different genres.

The paradox is dramatized in Liang Qichao's utopian novel *The Future of New China* (*Xin Zhongguo Weilai Ji*), which was written and published in 1902. In it, a certain Dr. Kong—an eightieth-generation descendent of Confucius—gives a speech at the centenary celebration of the successful modernization of China, telling the history of the Reform. In his speech he quotes a debate between two leading Reformists, Huang and Li. Since Dr. Kong's speech—that is, the main text of the novel—is in the vernacular, the debate has to be reported in the vernacular too. But the novel is supposed to relate the history of the reform of China. So the inevitable generic conflict arises. The scribe of Dr. Kong's speech, that is, the narrator of the whole novel, makes such a strange intrusion. "When Mr. Huang and Mr. Li were debating this issue, Dr. Kong was of course not present. How could he know it? How could he have told the audience the whole debate without leaving out a word? Because when he was studying abroad years ago, he wrote a *biji* book with the title *Sailing with the Wind.* In Chapter Four of the book the whole text of this debate was recorded. During his speech, Dr. Kong was reading the text verbatim. All he did was to turn its literary language into vernacular. I, the scribe, saw all this with my own eyes."[24]

The leading Reformist Liang Qichao, himself enthusiastically advocating and seriously writing the vernacular novel, believed that more than one hundred years in the future, the vernacular in China would still be merely the language to address the common people and to be used in novels, and that documents of historical value—here Dr. Kong's *biji* recording the historical debate—must be written in the literary language. In his mind this was so important that he had to use a long narratorial intrusion to explain away the generic discrepancy in order to keep the hierarchy intact for the future! Against such a background, Hu Shi's "modest proposal" to adopt the vernacular, until then a tool for subaltern discourses, as the cultural language to be used in all genres, was indeed launching a extremely radical challenge to the fundamental structure of Chinese culture.

Many writers at this time started to remold the Chinese vernacular, turning it into a new language applicable for all kinds of writings. Hu Shi praised Zhou Zuoren's "literal" translation of Western fiction as "the starting-point for the Europeanization of Chinese."[25] Fu Sinian, the most active among Hu Shi's disciples, argued that "people's speech" alone was not enough for all the modern spheres and disciplines, and that only in the European languages could there be found a "more superior model."[26] Starting in 1917, some modern Chinese linguists began their controversial campaign for Europeanizing the Chinese language by adopting modified Western-type punctuation marks, as well simple but essential printing and writing conventions such as paragraphing. All kinds of linguistic experiments were tried, which, though not always successful, brought great changes to the vernacular-based modern Chinese language. It was also seriously tested how large an amount of traditional literary-language elements could still be preserved and assimilated. The Chinese writer Bing Xin was the

---

[24] Liang Qichao, *Yinbingshi He Ji* (*Collected Works*) (Shanghai: Shangwu Yinshuguan, 1916), 13:56.

[25] Hu Shi, "Wushi Nian Yilai de Zhongguo zhi Wenxue" ("Chinese Literature in the Past Fifty Years"), in *Hu Shi Wencun* (Shanghai: Yadong Tushuguan, 1924), 156.

[26] Fu Sinian, "Zenyang Zuo Baihuawen" ("How to Write Vernacular"), in *Fu Sinian Quanji* (Changsha: Hunan Jiaoyu Chubanshe, 2004), 1:343.

most refined stylist among the fiction writers of the time. She acknowledged that her language was "vernacular-turned-literary" plus "Chinese-turned-Western."[27] As a result of the massive courageous efforts of the May 4 generation of fiction writers, the vernacular was eventually raised from its subcultural vulgarity to elite refinement. It was by no means coincidental that when the novel became *the* central genre of the new culture, the Chinese vernacular—retaining many elements of Chinese classics but also fundamentally modified by Western languages—became *the* cultural language.

The Truth in History and the Truth in Fiction

Imaginative narrative texts are underprivileged in Chinese generic hierarchy because Confucius declared in *The Analects* (*Lun Yu*) that he "refrains from talking about the abnormal, the supernatural, the magic, or the weird."[28] In order to find the ground on which they can establish the essential fictionality, it is necessary for the authors of the novels to find a justification within the dominance of the historical paradigm.

Feng Menglong, the celebrated seventeenth-century Chinese scholar of fiction, made this interesting statement in his preface to *Stories of Ancient Time and of Today* (*Gujin Xiaoshuo*): "When historicity dwindles, fiction arises."[29] And he went on to point out the true lineage of fictionality in Chinese classics: "It started in the time of Zhou [ninth to fifth centuries B.C.] but flourished in the Tang period [seventh to ninth centuries A.D.]. In the Song [tenth to thirteenth centuries A.D.], it went into full blossom. Han Fei, Lie Yukou and others should be considered the ancestors of fiction."[30] Han Fei (280–233 B.C.) was one of the main rivals of the Confucian school in the pre-Qin era, and his philosophical writings, collected together as the *Han Fei Zi*, are full of imaginative fables. Lie Yukou (third century B.C. should he have been a real person) was the alleged author of the collection of stories and fables in *Lie Zi*, was probably the earliest Chinese fiction writer. Those two authors can be said to represent the non-Confucian nonhistoriographical discourses in early Chinese culture, though it has been suggested that the Taoist writings by Zhuang Zi (ca. 369–286 B.C.) provided the most treasure

---

[27] Bing Xin, "Yishu" ("The Will"), in *Bing Xin Quanji* (Fuzhou: Haixia Wenyi Chubanshe, 1994), 1:463.

[28] Kong Zi, *Lun Yu* (Shanghai: Shijie Shuju, 1934), 78.

[29] Feng Menglong, *Gujin Xiaoshuo* (Shanghai: Shanghai Guji Chubanshe, 1993), 3.

[30] Ibid., 4.

food for Chinese imaginative thought, and Buddhist discourses, which came into China in the first or second centuries A.D., greatly reinforced Chinese imaginative power. Feng Menglong shows acumen in tracing the source of the imaginative paradigm to texts regarded as heretical by the orthodox Confucianists.

Another way to justify fiction is to prove that fictionality is a mode of signification entirely different from historiography. Nevertheless, there has never been in Chinese thinking a proposition distinguishing historicity from fictionality like that put forward by Aristotle in his *Poetics*, which became the starting point of Western literary philosophy. The Aristotelian proposition, though simple in wording, led to a series of significant philosophical and aesthetic conclusions: the proposition leads to the superiority of poetry over historiography. This is not only because history is related to what has happened and literature with what could have happened, and not only because history deals with the particular and poetry with the universal, but more important, because literature is closer to truth than the narrated historical events.

The absence of an Aristotelian-like argument in Chinese philosophy reveals some important aspects of Chinese discursive structure: actuality is stored only in history, which, although managed by Heaven, is also in keeping with the basic structural rules of society (i.e., the celebrated credo *Tian Ren Heyi*—Heaven and Men Are One). The historical event (that is, the so-called actual fact) is thus imbued with the absolutism of truth and is by definition superior to fiction based on probability, whose agreement with the universal truth has yet to be proved. What has happened, as recorded in historiography, is always superior to what might have happened (as depicted by fiction), and the generic priority of historiography is unquestionable.

Wu Zimu's *Record of Dreams* (*Meng Liang Lu*), one of the first books that mentions oral fiction narratives, possibly written in the thirteenth century, vaguely suggests a comparison by saying, "The novel can tell the history of a dynasty or an era, and in a moment bring them to an end [*niehe*]."[31] Another early book that discusses oral fiction narrative, *Fascinating Things in the Capital* (*Ducheng Jisheng*, presumably written in the fourteenth century), used almost exactly the same words to describe the storytelling performance of the time, with the last word *niehe* changed to *tipo*, which can be roughly translated as "breaking suddenly onto the truth."[32] Although this is a comparison between two subgenres of oral narratives, not exactly an Aristotelian

---

[31] Wu Zimu, *Meng Liang Lu* (Hangzhou: Zhejiang Renmin Chubanshe, 1980), 3.
[32] Naide Weng, *Ducheng Jisheng* (Beijing: Beijing Guji Chubanshe, 1983), 94.

comparative speculation on the truth value in fictionality and historicity, it already touches upon the possible way to argue for the superiority of fictionality over historiography.

Jin Shengtan, in the seventeenth century, was one of the first to put forward a proposition in this direction: "The creativity of the historian is to handle events by means of narrative [*yi wen yun shi*]; whereas the creativity of the fiction writers is to fabricate events for the sake of narrative [*yin wen sheng shi*].[33] His comparison, after all, only reveals differences in the scope of the two genres, emphasising that fiction enjoys a much greater freedom. But freedom is not truth value. Zhang Zhupo (who probably lived around the end of seventeenth century), the most important critic on the novel *The Golden Lotus* in traditional China, tried another line of argument for fiction's alleged superiority: "*The Golden Lotus* is another *The Grand History* (*Shi Ji*). But in *The Grand History* there are separate biographies and treatises for each person and each important subject-matter, while in *The Golden Lotus* the one hundred chapters comprise a single biography of hundreds of characters, who share the one biography, while each one has his own story. That is why the author of *The Golden Lotus* was definitely able to write a *Grand History*. How can I be so sure? Since he was capable of the more difficult he must naturally be capable of the easier."[34]

Although boldly in favor of fiction, his enthusiasm for the genre is based on the difficulty of technique alone and is hardly a philosophical argument. One of Feng Menglong's arguments more or less in the same vein is seen in his preface to *Admonitory Stories for the World* (*Jingshi Tongyan*), which dared not declare the superiority of fiction: "Should fiction be all real? I say, 'Not necessarily.' Should it be all considered false? I say, 'Not necessarily.' Then should we delete the false and retain only the real? I say, 'Not necessarily.' . . . Real events with truth in them, are the same as unreal events with some truth in them, doing no harm to morality, giving no opposition to the sages, posing no contradiction to the canons and histories. Why should such books be abandoned?"[35] His arguments do not uphold the superiority of fiction over historiography, and in fact the conformity with historiography is listed as one condition of the raisons d'être for fiction.

Perhaps the argument put forward by Yuan Yuling, a scholar of the sixteenth century, was the only one in Chinese theoretical thinking that was

---

[33] Jin Shengtan, *Jin Shengtan Quanji* (*Collected Works of Jin Shengtan*) (Nanjing: Jiangsu Guji Chubanshe, 1985), 2:5.

[34] Zhang Zhupo, *Zhang Zhupo Piping Jin Ping Mei* (Jinan: Qilu Shushe, 1991), 5.

[35] Feng Menglong, *Jingshi Tongyan* (Beijing: Shiyue Wenyi Chubanshe, 1994), 4.

moving closer to an Aristotelian proposition: "Literature without fictionality (*huan*) is not literature. Fictionality without going to extremes is not fictionality. So we know that the most extreme fictionalized in the world is also the truest; and the most imaginative argument is the truest argument. That is why talking about reality is less worthy than talking about fictionality, just as talking about Buddha is less worthy than talking about a devil. The devil is no one else than myself."[36]

Yuan Yuling does not launch a challenge to the dominance of historiography, and his words read more like a Zen Buddhist puzzle than a theoretical argument. Small wonder that the statement appears in his introduction to a magic novel, *Journey to the West*, about a Buddhist Master's pilgrimage across the monster-infested land, the farthest Chinese novel from historiography. Yet this seems to be the highest understanding ancient Chinese fiction critics reached on the nature of the genre, although a little vague in argument, as perhaps an argument deviant to the norms had to be. It is regrettable that few modern scholar have paid attention to this interesting argument on the paradox of the truth value of fictionality in literature, and Yuan's penetrating insight in an almost heretical presentation.

Fiction criticism at the turn of the twentieth century, regretably, does not even arrive at Jin Shengtan's understanding, let alone Yuan Yuling's, even though they must have had some exposure to the Aristotelian idea. Yan Fu (1853–1921) and Xia Zengyou (1865–1924) in their well-known 1897 essay first touch on the topic: "A book recording people and events is history; a book recording people and events that might not actually have happened is fiction."[37] Five years later, Xia Zengyou published another article "Principles of Fiction" and reiterates the same proposition, but with a much more feeble explanation, which shows that he fails to come close to an Aristotelian understanding: "Fiction is the writing about the already-known truth in detail, thus it is superior. History is the writing about the already-known truth in succinct terms, and therefore is inferior to fiction."[38] Again this is a comparison of some specific technical device, not a philosophical contemplation on the truth value of the different genres.

The difficulty that Chinese critics faced in this debate is ascribable to the fact that the cultural value of historiography was considered superior beyond

---

[36] Yuan Yuling: "Preface to *Xi You Ji*," reprinted in Sun Kaidi, *Riben Dongjing Suojian Zhongguo Xiaoshuo Shumu Tiyao* (Beijing: Guoli Beiping Tushu Guan, 1931), 77.

[37] In A Ying, *Wan Qing Wenxue Congchao, Xiaoshuo Xiqu Lilun Juan* (Beijing: Zhonghua Shuju, 1960), 13.

[38] Ibid., 25.

challenge and that it was hard for the mind of traditional Chinese scholars to speculate that fictionality could hope to match it in any way. Any speculation on the comparison was simply groundless, and, so far as the cultural structure is concerned, irrelevant.

Historiographical Pressure on the Structure of the Novel

As a result of this emulation of the historiographical paradigm, the traditional Chinese novel assumes the following narratological characteristics:

Emulating the historiographer, the status of the narrator in the traditional novel must be impersonal, never a "participant" in the plot so that his narration can disguise itself as the objective record of actual facts. Since he is responsible for the factuality/truth of what he relates, the narrator, above the narrated world, intrudes at every turn. His narration is almost always thoroughly reliable, as his task is purportedly to record what has already taken place in history (or, narratologically, in *histoire*—in the prenarrated state of the story), and narratorial mediation of the time sequence is reduced to the minimum, at least in appearance.

Emulating the historiographer, he pays great attention to time in the narrative, and appears punctilious in indicating the moment of the occurrence of an event and meticulous in filling in every link in the temporal chain, giving the impression of "time brimming" and "detail brimming," that is, every link in the temporal-causal chain of events is carefully documented, though selectively reported.

He seldom feels the need to use flashbacks in his narration unless two plot lines cross. In order to maintain fundamental suspense, he frequently uses flashforwards, a habitual narrative device in historiography, as flashforwards reinforce the temporal linearity. Also, ab ovo beginnings are favored, so that the narrative can be safely anchored in historical context. Emulating historiography, the dominating type of motif tends to be more functional, making the narrative sketchy and speedy. Indeed, in the traditional novel, those events taken from historiography are narrated much faster and in a matter-of-fact tone, while those fictionalized with the help of folklore or legend are much slower.

Emulating the historiographer, he generally adopts zero-focalization (i.e., the omniscient perspective) and avoids character-focalization apart from very occasional instances, since his main purpose is supposedly to tell as objectively as possible what has really happened. The almost ubiquitous direct

quoted form of reported speech reinforces the impression of being absolutely factual.

By emulating the prestigious generic paradigms and by complying with
the hierarchy of meaning-power, narrative texts under the control of this
narrative mode aligned themselves with cultural norms, thus reinforcing the
cultural institution. Moreover, they reinforced the institution "from below,"
as they were subcultural narrative discourses and were essentially communal
to the broad masses of the lower social strata, thus ensuring a collectivized
interpretation. In this way, the narrator of the traditional Chinese novel succeeded in bringing its subculturalness into conformity with the cultural interpretive system.

It was in the May 4 period that Chinese fiction was finally relieved from
the unbearable pressure of historiography. Sneering at official historiography
became a favorite game among the movement's iconoclastic writers and critics, who relentlessly attacked Confucianism. Lu Xun (1881–1936), the first
modern Chinese writer, and until now the greatest, in his biting satire *The
True Story of Ah Q*, dealt this emulation a shattering blow, as the narrator in
this short novel, ironically posing as a historiographer, attempts to subjugate
fictionality to historicity but fails miserably. The short novel starts with a
long-winded, straightfaced discussion about what category in the rigid system of Chinese official or unofficial historiography this story of Ah Q, the
homeless farm laborer, should belong to, but finally helplessly gives up.

Lu Xun then tries to begin the story in the conventional *ab ovo*
manner—name, birthplace, lineage—and ends up in despair again that
these conventions do not fit Ah Q's life at all. Historiography is therefore
found to be not only useless but also stupid. And the narrator does not let a
chance go by without poking fun at the solemnity of historiography:
"Whenever they met, women in the village were bound to talk about how
Zhou the Seventh Aunt bought a blue silk skirt from A Q which, though
used, cost only ninety cents, and how Zhao-the-White-Eye's mother—
Another version says that it was Zhao Sichen"s mother, which remains to be
verified by future scholarship—also bought a child's crimson silk shirt which
was 70 percent new and cost only 392 coins in cash."[39]

Zhou Zuoren (1885–1968), Lu Xun's brother and also a great pioneer of
the Chinese Enlightenment, recalled in his memoirs that the "interweaving
of arguments" in *The True Story of Ah Q* was meant to be a mockery of "the

---

[39] Lu Xun, *Lu Xun Quanji* (Beijing: Renmin Wenxue Chunbanshe, 1956), 2:509.

infatuation with history" (*lishi pi*)." However, Lu Xun waged a more devastating battle against the Confucianist infatuation with historiography in his first story "The Madman's Diary." The story that was published in 1917, the very first story written in modern Chinese language, condemns the whole history of Chinese civilization as a history of cannibalism: the participant narrator's—the Madman's—surprisingly unique reading of Chinese history: "I opened the history book to have a careful reading. The history has no chronology. Scrawling on every page are written the four characters 'Benevolence and Morality.' I couldn't fall asleep anyway, so I kept on reading until the small hours before I found out from in between the lines that on every page there was written the word 'man-eating'!"[40]

So the truth is not to be found within history but without, in where the language of history could not reach, that is, the opposite side of what is recorded. In this way Lu Xun drives home a total negation of the history-cult in Chinese culture and a complete refutation of the truth value of this supreme genre in the Chinese discursive hierarchy. What is more, the edge of Lu Xun's attack was kept even sharper by the narrative form. The structure of the start of modern Chinese literature is a powerful symbol of the profound transformation that was going to take place. Viewed in terms of the narrative technique, the narrator in the modern Chinese novel is more reminiscent of a memoirist or autobiographer than a historiographer. But this madman's diary has an introductory frame story that is written in the "literary language" in a matter-of-fact style often associated with historiography, whereas the main narrative—the madman's apparent fabrication out of sheer hallucination—is written in the modern Chinese language based on vernacular. The tone of the literary-language frame story is sober, rational, and elegant, while that of the main narrative is, as acknowledged in the frame story, "chaotic and disconnected, with many mistakes." In the frame story, the madman, already recovered, has returned to the institution by taking up an official post, while in the madman's "fictional" part, he is a mentally deranged person totally isolated by society, and his hostility toward Chinese culture denied any "rational" understanding. Nevertheless, it is in the madman's narration that the verdict on traditional historiography-centred Chinese culture is proclaimed. Only those who are not contaminated by this culture—children in particular—may still be innocent enough to see through the great evil. In this way, the normality-insanity opposition is made ironical, and the fictional has been endowed with a moral power and cultural meaning infinitely superior to that of the historiographical.

---

[40] Ibid., 15.

"The Madman's Diary" is a powerful manifesto of modern Chinese fiction to denounce the institution of traditional Chinese culture. The meaning-power of fiction no longer lies in its successful emulation of historiography, but in its subversion of the latter's cultural dominance. Upon such a profound understanding, Chinese fiction finally broke away, and helped the whole Chinese culture to break away from the bondage of the oppressive generic hierarchy of traditional China.

WALTER SITI

The Novel on Trial

In Place of the Holy Book

Flamenca, the protagonist of a late-thirteenth-century Provençal romance, is kept locked up in a tower by her jealous husband.[1] The only place she can see the man who desires her is at church, during Mass. In the shelter of the Psalms, she whispers a few words to him that signify her acceptance and reciprocation of his desire. Once she is back in the tower facing the anxious questions of her ladies-in-waiting, however, she is assailed by doubts that she might have spoken too softly for her lover to hear. Her ladies-in-waiting suggest that she recreate the scene so they can see whether all went well. Laughing, Flamenca tells them to "get the book of Blancheflor," and she proceeds to act out the encounter using the romance in place of the Holy Book.[2]

This passage was written twenty years before the immortal verses of Dante's Paolo and Francesca (Canto 5 of the *Inferno*), who while reading of the loves of Lancelot and Guinevere "for pleasure," tried to duplicate the kiss of the famous lovers in an everyday realistic situation.

It might seem strange that one of the most frequently prohibited and sequestered books during the long years of the Inquisition was the Bible[3]—the Bible translated into the various national languages, of course, or the vernacular commentaries to the Bible. For the purposes of the present essay, what matters is that novels and holy books were prohibited for the same reasons and to the same category of people. As Carlo Borromeo wrote in 1582, people ignorant of Latin—immature youths, humble artisans or otherwise

---

[1] *"Flamenca": Roman occitan du XIIIe siècle*, ed. and trans. Jean-Charles Huchet (Paris: Union générale d'éditions, 1988). Available in English as *The Romance of Flamenca: A Provençal Poem of the Thirteenth Century*, trans. Merton Jerome Hubert (Princeton, N.J.: Princeton University Press, 1962).

[2] [Translator's note: "Blancheflor" refers to *Floire et Blancheflor*, a French metrical romance known in two versions from the twelfth and thirteenth centuries. The legend enjoyed pan-European fortune, the best-known version being Boccaccio's prose reworking, the *Filocolo*.]

[3] Gigliola Fragnito, *La Bibbia al rogo* (Bologna: Il Mulino, 1997). This book also carries the quotation from Cardinal Borromeo (from the edict, "May they not own vernacular Bibles, nor books of controversy with the Heretics"), 135. Unless otherwise indicated, all English translations of quoted material are by the translator of this essay.

uneducated workers, and women from every social class—had to be protected; otherwise their direct exposure to the books could "easily implicate them in various errors." In 1557, Michele Ghislieri, a "moderate" Inquisitor and the future Pope Pius V, wrote to the much more extreme Inquisitor of Genoa, saying that "to ban Orlando, Orlandino, one hundred short stories or other similar books would sooner create laughter than anything else, since such books are not read to be believed but as fiction [*fabule*]."[4] But the Inquisition took the hard line instead, to underscore its fear that the "culturally defenseless" might believe novels and allow themselves to be led astray (which is why the king of Spain prohibited the export of chivalric books to America: the *Indios*, like the lower classes and women, might believe the stories and then, once they had been disillusioned, refuse to trust any other book). Even holy books and religious books of all kinds were considered a danger to "weak minds," especially books containing multiple plots: not so much because they might conceal heretical sayings or diabolic tricks (at a 1590 trial, a man named Andrea testified that, out of a lover's despair, he had copied the text of a pact with the devil from a Life of St. Basil and signed it with his own blood[5]), as because they gave free reign to the imagination. Cardinal Bellarmino, in judging the plans for the publication of Rosweyde's *Fasti sanctorum* in 1607, found that the novelized passions of the martyrs and lives of the saints contained "many foolish, vacuous, improbable things"[6]— almost the same words that the Church would use on countless occasions between the sixteenth and eighteenth centuries to describe chivalric romances or, in general, novels and short stories. In the convents it was prohibited to read edifying books in the vernacular. Teresa of Avila confessed that she suffered greatly, "because the reading of some gave me pleasure," until the Lord appeared to her one day and said, "I shall give you a living book."[7]

At the same time, chivalric books often provided sustenance and a figurative model for "new" saints: from Francis of Assisi, who called his brothers "soldiers of the Round Table,"[8] to Teresa of Avila, who to entertain her fellow nuns invented the "interior castle," filled with "fountains, beautiful

---

[4] The Michele Ghislieri letter is quoted in Nicola Longo, "La letteratura proibita," in *Letteratura italiana*, ed. Alberto Asor Rosa, vol. 5, *Le questioni* (Turin: Einaudi, 1986), 980.

[5] Adriano Prosperi, *Tribunali della coscienza* (Turin: Einaudi, 1996), 408.

[6] Sofia Boesch Gajano, "Le metamorfosi del racconto," in *Lo spazio letterario di Roma antica*, ed. Guglielmo Cavallo, Paolo Fedeli, and Andrea Giardina (Rome: Salerno Editrice, 1990), 3:217.

[7] Teresa of Avila, *Interior Castle*, trans. and ed. E. Allison Peers (Garden City, N.Y.: Doubleday, 1961).

[8] "Compilatio assiensis," in *Fontes franciscani*, ed. Ernesto Menestò and Stefano Brufani (Assisi: Porziuncola, 1995), 1:1,643.

gardens, mazes and other charming things." It is emblematic that the bon-fire of books in front of the cathedral, through which the bishop of Santa Severina wished to celebrate the Epiphany in 1600, included three transla-tions of the Bible and one copy of *Amadís de Gaula*.[9]

The assault on the novel, as we shall see, became more indiscriminate and inflexible in times of war, when there was an enemy to shake in people's faces like a scarecrow. During the Inquisition the great enemy, of course, was the Reformation: the ideological devil was "free examination." The vast majority of books placed on the Index were thus theological books and books about the magic arts; in the case of short stories and novels, one gets the impression that the dutiful official condemnation of "obscene or lascivi-ous" pages concealed a more vague and anxious condemnation of freedom of the imagination. The textual version would be "freedom of point of view." Curiously, to illustrate France's deficit of courage to "change style," in a 1957 interview Céline cited the example of an elderly Clichy curate who in 1870 had decided to say Mass in French and was "scolded by the Commis-sion on the Liturgy."[10]

Unlike plays, novels are generally supposed to be enjoyed in private, in a one-on-one encounter with a mind inclined toward introspection and fan-tasy. Novels, according to a denigrator in Sorel's *Berger extravagant*, are "worse than Calvinist books because at least the latter speak of only one god, while novels speak of many."[11]

Perhaps it is not insignificant that in the two nations where the Inquisi-tion successfully barred individual, unsupervised reading of the sacred text, Italy and Spain, there was an irreversible decline in the romance after the sixteenth century. In the nation where the free reading of the Bible was sup-plemented by limited but substantial political freedom (the Licensing Act of 1695), namely in England, the modern novel was born.

A Self-Denying Genre

Of all the literary genres, the novel is the only one that feels the need to deny itself. The eighteenth century, when the genre was consolidated, is filled with novels that denied they were novels. "The world is so taken up of late with

---

[9] Fragnito, *La Bibbia al rogo*, 315.

[10] "Louis Ferdinand Céline vous parle," transcription of a recording made on October 22, 1957, in Céline, *Romans* (Paris: Gallimard, 1974), 2:935.

[11] Charles Sorel, *Le berger extravagant* (Paris, 1627), 26.

novels and romances, that it will be hard for a private history to be taken for genuine," according to Defoe in the preface to *Moll Flanders*. "This novel is not a novel," wrote Rousseau in the second preface to the *New Heloise*.[12] "But this is not a novel," Diderot remarks in *Jacques the Fatalist*.[13] Already at the end of the seventeenth century, Madame de La Fayette, writing to Joseph Marie de Lescheraine, said of the *Princess of Clèves*, "It is not a romance: it is more appropriately a memoir."[14] At the end of the nineteenth century, the naturalists refused to call their texts novels (at the obscenity trial for *Autour d'un clocher*, Louis Desprez defended himself in open court by stating, "the word novel is no longer appropriate to our social studies").[15]

Expressions such as "if this were a novel" or "not the way things happen in novels" became such a commonplace that some novelists flaunted a second-degree claim: Contrary to what everyone else says, my work actually is a novel. "If you are one of those for whom all it takes is someone to say that something is true for you to believe it, or for whom believing that they are fictitious ruins your pleasure in reading them, you're too serious, you're too gullible, and I wasn't writing for you." So says Giovanni Ambrogio Marini in the preface to *Calloandro fedele*, unfurling his pride in his inventiveness. With greater illuminist malice, Laclos warns, "We do not guarantee the authenticity of this story; in fact, we have good reason to think that it is only a novel," adding that the characters in *Dangerous Liaisons* behave so badly that "it is impossible to imagine that they lived in our century."

The paratext (preface, notes, postscripts, editor's note, etc.) is used to offer an apology, a justification. There are two basic reasons why the novel is ashamed of itself: (1) the novel is psychologically devastating to its readers and, in extreme cases, makes them go mad; (2) the novel has been maligned by bad, superficial novelists. Hence, when the *Berger extravagant* was introduced as an "anti-novel" and Andreas Heinrich Bucholtz presented

---

[12] Available in English as *Julie, or, The New Heloise: Letters of Two Lovers Who Live in a Small Town at the Foot of the Alps*, trans. Philip Stewart and Jean Vaché (Hanover, N.H.: University Press of New England, 1997).

[13] Denis Diderot, *Jacques le Fataliste et Son Maître*, ed. Simone Lecointre and Jean Le Galliot (Geneva: Droz, 1976), 50. The text is available in English as *Jack the Fatalist and His Master*, trans. Wesley Douglass Camp and Agnès G. Raymond (New York: Peter Lang, 1984).

[14] The letter, dated April 13, 1678, can be found in Madame de La Fayette, *The Princess of Clèves: Contemporary Reactions, Criticism*, ed. and trans. John D. Lyons (New York: W. W. Norton, 1994).

[15] Desprez's defensive memoir, entitled "Pour la liberté d'écrire," appears in the appendix to Henry Fèvre and Louis Desprez, *Autour d'un clocher* (Brussels: H. Kistemaeckers, 1885). A new edition, with a preface by Henri Mittérand, was published in Paris in 1980 by Slatikine France.

his Hercules novel [*Des christlichen königlichen Fürsten Herkuliskus und Herkuladisla*] as an "anti-Amadis novel," the first reason was invoked. *Jacques the Fatalist* and *Tristram Shandy* were labeled "anti-novels" for the second reason.

Gotthard Heidegger, a Lutheran pastor who wrote an invective against novels in 1698, was right to say, "A novel is often nothing more than a poisonous satire of another novel."[16] Could there have been a *Dangerous Liaisons* without the *New Heloise*, a *Princess of Clèves* without *Astrée*, an *Anna Karenina* without *Madame Bovary*?

Let us start with the second category: from the beginning of its history and wherever it has appeared, the novel has been a discredited genre. Although it was remarkably widespread in the Greek world, very few early novels survive today because they were considered unworthy of care and commentary, and generally inscribed on low-quality materials. In Chinese literature, while books of poetry and essays were conserved with scrupulous philological care, novels were mutilated and carelessly interpolated. Although the literary set wrote and bought them, they would have felt diminished to acknowledge their paternity of them.

Aristotle makes no mention of the novel in the *Poetics*. Nor does Horace in the *Ars poetica*. Tasso considers the genre a deviation from the epic. Boileau, with a condescension far worse than silence, says in an aside that everything can be excused in a frivolous novel because nothing can be expected, so long as it is enjoyable to read.[17] In 1774, von Blankenburg, wondering why there had not yet been a critical reflection on the novel in Germany, responded, "because people did not think that it was worth the trouble of reflecting on a genre of writing that aimed solely to entertain the masses."[18] Without rules or regulations, without requiring even the modicum of technique required for poetry, the novel ended up in anyone's hands, and anyone, indeed, could write one. "Whereas, to the composition of novels and romances, nothing is necessary but paper, pens, and ink, with the manual capacity of using them," according to Fielding in *Tom Jones* (bk. 9, chap. 1). Many of the novelists brought to trial over the centuries

---

[16] Heidegger's invective, entitled *Mythoscopia romantica; oder, Discours von den so benannten Romans*, is quoted in Ursula Bavaj, *Mythoscopia romantica: Teoria del romanzo in Germania 1629–1698* (Rome: Castelvecchi, 1996), 109. The same source carries the quotation from *Versuch über den Roman* by Christian Friedrich von Blankenburg (21).

[17] Boileau's observations are in canto 3 of *Art poétique*. To avoid excessive annotation, no specific edition is cited when there is an unequivocal reference to the canto, paragraph, or chapter number of a classic text or to its preface or afterword.

[18] Blankenburg, *Versuch über den Roman*.

were rash youths, who "write whatever comes to mind . . . they know nothing, they write off the top of their heads," as the papal nuncio Francesco Vitelli complained when he denounced Ferrante Pallavicino's *Corriero svaligiato* to the Roman curia.[19] The general accusation was that novels lowered the cultural level and promoted curiosity and gossip, to the detriment of "littérature savante." Novels wean people from the habit of thinking. "You never reread a novel," wrote Vauvenargues in 1745.[20]

On the average, novels cost less than other books, depending on large print runs and thus on popular success. Tasso told the story of how his father Bernardo had decided to rewrite *Amadís de Gaula* around a single action, according to Aristotle's precepts, except that "when he began to read, the rooms were filled with gentlemen listeners; but by the end, all of them had disappeared; from which he learned the lesson that unity of action is not very entertaining by its nature."[21] Trissino's accusation against the *Orlando furioso* was that it "pleased the common people"; in a letter to Scipione Gonzaga, Tasso admitted that in *Jerusalem Delivered* he had sought "the applause of mediocre men."[22] In Genoa in 1642, Anton Giulio Brignole Sale hastened to publish the first four books of his *Storia spagnola*, fearing that "the itch for these compositions" would stop "scratching," intending frankly to "second the torrent's current for as long as it lasts."[23] The eighteenth-century English novel would be unthinkable without the search for popular success. In *Tom Jones*, Fielding, the best educated of the novelists, reacted to attempts to discredit the novel by advising that "an author ought to consider himself, not as a gentleman who gives a private or eleemosynary treat, but rather as one who keeps a public ordinary, at which all persons are welcome for their money" (bk. 1, chap. 1). The novel (and novelists) does not want for defenders, who try to rehabilitate the genre by affiliating it with the epic or tragedy, maintaining, like Pierre-Daniel Huet in

---

[19] Vitelli's letter was published by Laura Coci in "Ferrante a Venezia: Nuovi documenti d'archivio (II)," *Studi secenteschi* 28 (1987): 306–7.

[20] Luc de Clapiers de Vauvenargues, "Réflexions sur divers sujets," in *Œvres complètes de Vauvenargues*, preface and notes by Henry Bonnier (Paris: Hachette, 1968), 256.

[21] Torquato Tasso, "Apologia in difesa della Gerusalemme liberata," *Prose*, ed. Ettore Mazzali (Milan: Ricciardi, 1959), 417.

[22] "Col Furioso suo, che piace al vulgo" ["With His Furioso, That the Common Folk Like"] is a verse from book 24 of *Italia liberata dai Goti*, quoted in Sergio Zatti, *L'ombra del Tasso* (Milan: Mondadori, 1996), 63. The same work is the source for Tasso's letter to Scipione Gonzaga of July 16, 1575 (69).

[23] The introduction to Brignole Sale's *Storia spagnola* is quoted by Q. Marini, "Romanzieri liguri e imprese editoriali nel Seicento" in *Lathè Biósas: Ricordando Ennio S. Brunori*, ed. Renato Gendre (Alessandria, Italy: Edizioni dell'Orso, 1998), 206.

1670, that a novel "is not judged by the number but by the competence of its estimators."[24] The extreme case was Rousseau, who in the second preface to *The New Heloise*, stated that "a novel should be booed, hated, torn to pieces by stylish people." In the nineteenth and twentieth centuries, the novel split into two subgenres: one for the elite, but another much vaster area for the masses. The attacks on the novel back then were not unlike the ones waged against television series today.

In condemning the novel, the civil and religious authorities were always and everywhere concerned by its broad circulation (one common legal defense of the novel was that a single novel was very expensive and written in a manner too difficult for the uneducated to grasp). They wished to protect the weak from obscenity and sedition, naturally, but also (and in this they were often allied with academic pedants and high-minded critics) to defend the culture's honor from the vulgarity of a vicious cycle that, under the pretext of adapting to market demands, ultimately perverted the tastes of the masses by supplying a shoddy product.

On second thought, however, the novel's vocation to satisfy its readers' pleasure is what steered it toward those delicate spots where pleasure rubs up against reality; its vulgarity, in short, is the condition for the antisystematic perspicacity that is its strength; to flirt with the "discourse of the ignorant" fosters the novel's "free intensities" (as Gianni Celati calls them) and promotes a particular form of knowledge that consists, rather than in a generalized "I think," in "a series of 'I feel's' that benefit from discontinuity."[25] The protean and undisciplined surrender to the folds of the present and its dishonorable status drives the novel into murky territories where other genres fear to tread. In this sense, the developments in language are exemplary. The linguistic sloppiness of the novel was criticized from the start, but it opened the gates to the "common language" in order to match character to his or her way of speaking: from the "Latin of the freedmen," in the *Cena di Trimalcione*, through the delightful coarseness of the *Facezie* of Poggio Bracciolini, the humanistic discoverer of the *Cena* ("there are things that I cannot say more elegantly because I have to report them as they were said by the characters that I have inserted in this conversation"[26]), to the attentions

---

[24] Pierre-Daniel Huet, *A Treatise of Romances and Their Original* (London: Printed by R. Battersby for S. Heyrick, 1672), 32.

[25] Gianni Celati, *Finzioni occidentali, fabulazione, comicità e scrittura*, 3rd rev. ed. (Turin: Einaudi, 2001), 46.

[26] The passage is taken from "Ne aemuli carpant Facetiarum opus propter eloquentiae tenuitatem," the preface to Poggio Bracciolini, *Facezie*, ed. Eugenio Garin and Marcello Ciccuto (Milan: Rizzoli, 1983).

shown in eighteenth-century epistolary novels to preserving the linguistic imperfections of the sender.

"Clamorous and romantic advertising is a dangerous suggestion to weak or weakened spirits. I have said the same for pairings of passionate tragedies." In this January 1926 telegram, not to novelists but to newspaper editors-in-chief, Mussolini attests to a shift in the weight of oppression.[27] The novel no longer provokes fear because it is read by a minority. At the same time, by attributing to "news stories" the same baleful influence that had always been criticized in novels, Mussolini unwittingly delivered the best possible praise of the "potential novel" that refuses to be institutionalized as a genre and stubbornly seeks to reduce (but not to annul) the distance between the uneven shapelessness of life and the absolute abstractness of beauty.

In 1735 Père Bougeant distinguished between *basse* and *haute romancie*.[28] But ever since its origins, the novel has been marked by a double destiny. Achilles Tatius and Heliodorus were already "reflected" novelists who played ironically with the trivial mechanisms of genre; the same can be said for the overbearing snobbery of Petronius. The novel denies itself because it can only seek its profundity by turning itself inside out like a glove. In his *Discorsi dell'arte poetica*, Tasso theorizes the possibility of a double level of writing that can attract both the hoi polloi and the connoisseur.

One could argue that realism itself was born with the novel because of this "obsession with doubleness": it is not Erasmian folly to say that without illusions, "You find a sow hiding behind Minerva?"[29] This was the experience of poor Don Quixote, although the refined author of *Lazzarillo de Tormes* was already purging and parodying the dreams of "other" adventures through the picaro's miseries. The popularity of *Don Quixote* in eighteenth-century England stems from the fact that the novel's modest and aggressive form is legitimized in parodistic contrast to the precious folio edition of French romance. Once it had been established that the fanciful adventures of the upper classes was little more than trivial entertainment, the problem of modern realism became how to overdetermine everyday

---

[27] Cited in Philip V. Cannistraro, *La fabbrica del consenso: Fascismo e mass media* (Bari: Laterza, 1975), 204. The book is a revision and translation of the author's 1971 Ph.D. diss. at New York University, "The Organization of Totalitarian Culture: Cultural Policy and the Mass Media in Fascist Italy, 1922–1945."

[28] G.-H. Bougeant, *Voyage merveilleux du Prince Fan-Férédin dans la Romancie* (Paris: Au Livre d'Or, 1735), 107.

[29] Desiderius Erasmus, *The Praise of Folly and Other Writings*, trans. Robert Martin Adams (New York: Norton, 1989), chap. 22.

reality in order to make it more significant and symbolic without resorting to the "tricks" of fabliaux. The opposition between the common and the interesting is only one particular instance of the opposition between the probable and the marvelous. The romance author Mademoiselle de Montpensier was forced to create a double of the exotic, fabulous place of Paflagonia in the better-known Paris ("nothing was more similar to the Place Royale than the square where her palace stood").[30] In his letters on the *Princess of Clèves*, Valincour points out that the "extravagant" refusal to marry Nemours transports the protagonist "into the kingdom of Amadis."[31] Charles Gildon reproaches Defoe by saying that *Robinson Crusoe* is basically "only a romance."[32] The author, according to Smollett in the preface to *Roderick Random*, "by representing familiar scenes in an uncommon and amusing point of view, invests them with all the graces of novelty, while nature is appealed to in every particular." But in the second preface to *The New Heloise*, Rousseau wonders, "Is it worth the trouble to register that which everyone can see every day in his own or in his neighbor's house?" The response of the Western realist novel is psychology, the "heart's surprising unfathomability."

Ambiguous by nature, when the trivial is identified with the tired repetition of pseudo-realistic stereotypes, the novel reclaims its right to fantasy. This is obviously the case with Roussel or Borges, but also with Karen Blixen or Elsa Morante (without counting the shades of "rebirth of *romance*" provoked by its intersection with non-European fiction traditions, and the "coerced *romance*" produced by Eastern Europe in response to censorial, programmatic optimism). A bastardized, parvenu, and even imperialist genre, the novel contaminates and defiles the noble genres (tragedy, the lyric) with its own needs for the ordinary, but at the same time it contaminates "positive" writing (history, the moral sermon) through its childish "wanting to be." Abbé Porée was not so far off the mark when in his 1796 lecture against the novel at the Collège Louis-le-Grand (translated into French so that women could read it, too): "Through their contagion [novels] damage all the literary genres with which they entertain relations."[33]

---

[30] The quotation from Mademoiselle de Montpensier's *Princesse de Paphalogonie* is taken from Pizzorusso, *La poetica del romanzo in Francia, 1660–1685* (Rome: Sciascia, 1962), 68.

[31] Jean-Baptiste-Henri Du Trousset de Valincour, *Lettres à Madame la Marquise *** sur le sujet de la Princesse de Clèves* (Tours: University of Tours, 1972).

[32] Charles Gildon, *The Life and Strange Surprizing Adventures of Mr D. of London* (London: J. Roberts, 1719), chap. 2.

[33] Georges May, *Le dilemme du roman au XVIIIe siècle* (New Haven, Conn.: Yale University Press, 1963), 39. May's book also contains observation on the *encanaillement* of the hero.

Head in the Clouds

In part 1, chapter 47 of *Don Quixote*, the canon, after summarizing the critiques of chivalric romance, adds that the genre still had one merit: it left the field wide open for the ink to flow unimpeded, "for the unrestricted range of these books enables the author to show his powers, epic, lyric, tragic, or comic." The chameleon-like effect of the novel, according to Huet, allows the reader not to have to concentrate on a single idea: "[Novels] do not stretch the intellect to such an extent, and they leave it in a condition to burden itself with a greater number of different ideas."[34] Because they do not demand great intellectual operations, they leave room for another faculty: "No mental strain is necessary to understand them, no great reasoning is required, no exertion of memory. All it takes is imagination."

In addition to the four traditional accusations against the novel (sedition, blasphemy, defamation, and obscenity) and the individual judicial proceedings that depend on the vagaries of tolerance, the chief accusation against the novel is that it is a waste of time. Heidegger was particularly acrimonious: "Like hornets, which respond to having their wings plucked out by devouring those of the other hornets, novelists squander ignobly the reader's precious time."[35] In other words, novels waste one's time because the novelists themselves wasted theirs in writing them. If time helps to produce wealth and moral perfection, it must be used righteously; ever since Dante's mention of "ambages pulcerrime" in the *De vulgari eloquentia*, the novel has always been the place of digression, of the labyrinth, of wandering. As Giovan Battista Pigna wrote of Ariosto in 1554, "The whole poem is about errant persons; he is likewise errant, since he is forever picking up and interrupting countless things."[36] Tasso was so tormented by the double meaning of "errore"—physical and moral—that he repudiated his own *Jerusalem Delivered*. Bossuet did not mention novels or novelists in his speech against "illicit pleasures" (quoted by the defense attorney during the *Madame Bovary* trial); instead he used the same metaphor as Tasso: "Whoever is attached to the sensible, must necessariy wander [*errare*] from object to object. . . . In this perpetual motion he will never cease to be distracted, enticed by the image of an *errant* freedom."[37] The novel, in short, offers the hypothesis of an

---

[34] Huet, *A Treatise of Romances and Their Original*, 4.

[35] Heidegger, *Mythoscopia romantica*.

[36] G. B. Pigna, *I romanzi divisi in tre libri* (Venice, 1554), 56.

[37] Jacques Bénigne Bossuet, "Contre les plaisirs illicites," in *Œvres philosophiques de Bossuet*, ed. Jules Simon (Paris: Charpentier, 1843), 65; the quotation within Sénard's harangue is Gustave Flaubert, *Oeuvres* (Paris: Gallimard, 1951), 1:664.

infinite desire (earlier in the same speech, Bossuet spoke of an "infinity irritated that it cannot be fulfilled") that is not actively directed toward a philosophical and religious truth but rather lingers in a psychic *flânerie* that is tantamount to sloth and "delectatio morose." In 1760, Claude de Marolles, examining the three roads of the perdition of the soul, wrote of the "novelistic soul . . . so reduced to fragments, fallen in the dust, that it gets lost between the pages, wandering from book to book."[38] Unhindered by the "group values" that make the epic cohere, nor torn to pieces by the radical oppositions of tragedy, the reader of novels allows himself to be seduced by the idle pleasure of variety and passivity. Novelistic identification is typically a lazy, languid identification that transports the reader to another world. In a letter of July 12, 1671, Madame de Sévigné, a rational and reasonable person, described to Madame de Grignan her reactions to a reading of La Calprenède's *Cleopatra*: "I am mad about that nonsense. . . . I find his style detestable and never stop being captivated by it like a snare. . . . Like a little girl I feel carried away by their doings and if I didn't have Monsieur de la Rochefoucauld to console me I would hang myself for discovering this personal weakness."[39]

Her remarks epitomize the first reason for the novel's self-denial: it makes you lose your head and go insane. The textbook example is obviously *Don Quixote*, the progenitor of a long series of novels ranging from Sorel's *Berger extravagant* and Marivaux's *Pharsamon* to Charlotte Lennox's *The Female Quixote*, Flaubert's *Madame Bovary*, and beyond. Twenty years before the appearance of *Don Quixote*, in his long preface to the *La conversión de la Magdalena*, Pedro Malón de Chaide wrote, "What else are the monstrous books and forests of fabulous tales and lies of Amadis, Floriseles and Don Belianis, placed in the hands of youths, but a knife in the hands of madmen?" And later, "[Girls are filled with the desire] to be served and seduced, like they were when they read their *Flos Sanctorum*, hence they turn to foul and wicked fantasies."[40] Two elements stand out: the shift of focus to female readers and the return to a sarcastic parallel between love novels and religious texts.

The novel seems to have a particular affinity with women—because they are not allowed to read more learned books; because (at least at certain

---

[38] Quoted in Pascal Quignard, *Le lecteur* (Paris: Gallimard, 1976), 31–32.

[39] Marie de Rabutin-Chantal Sévigné, *Correspondance I*, ed. Roger Duchêne (Paris: Gallimard, 1972), 294.

[40] Pedro Malón de Chaide, *La conversión de la Magdalena*, ed. Félix García, 3 vols. (Madrid: Espasa-Calpe, 1958).

times in history) they have more time to spend at home reading; because their nervous complexion seems to make them more apt to daydream; and because (and not ultimately) the weaving of the novel recalls women's work ("I am the son of an antique lace restorer," Céline tells us, "I am well acquainted with the finer things").[41] The "girl reading a novel" became a comic type as early as Richard Steele's *The Tender Husband* in 1705. Fielding believed that Lennox's novel was more credible than Cervantes', precisely because its protagonist was a woman.[42] The eighteenth century was the novel's century of women, both as readers and writers. In his review of *Cecilia* by Fanny Burney in 1784, Laclos stated that "women have a special vocation for writing this type of work."[43] Later on, in *Contemplations* Hugo saw the (literary) revolution "in the novel, while it is whispering to women."[44] George Eliot clearly distanced herself from the paradoxical but tenacious equation of a predisposition to the novel and stupidity, attacking "silly novels by lady novelists."[45] In an 1832 letter to Count Salvagnoli, Stendhal foreshadowed the theme of *Madame Bovary*: "The great occupation of provincial women in France is to read novels. . . . Since they cannot make a novel out of their lives, they take consolation by reading them."[46] But Pierre Nicole, in the twenty-second chapter of *De la comédie*, had already prophesized Emma's destiny when he spoke of women whose heads were so filled with novels that they "found the little errands of their ménage to be unbearable." When they returned home with their brains evaporated, they found "everything deplorable, especially their husbands, who since they were busy with their affairs were not always in the mood to shower them with ridiculous compliments."

Nicole's most resolute and outraged attack on novelists (whom he called "public poisoners") is the *Lettres sur l'hérésie imaginaire*, written in 1664–65 to defend the nuns of Port-Royal from the attacks of Desmarets de Saint-Sorlin.[47] On the basis of this bit of chronicle he elaborated a rigorous and

---

[41] "Entretien avec Albert Zbinden," broadcast by Radio Lausanne on July 25, 1957, in Louis-Ferdinand Céline, *Romans*, ed. Henri Godard (Paris: Gallimard, 1974), 945.

[42] "The Covent Garden Journal, 1752, no. 24," in Henry Fielding, *The Criticism of Henry Fielding*, ed. Ioan M. Williams (London: Routledge, 1970), 193.

[43] The review of *Cecilia* originally appeared in *Mercure de France* (April–May 1784); it is now in Choderlos de Laclos, *Oeuvres complètes*, ed. M. Allem (Paris: Gallimard, 1951), 525.

[44] *Réponse à un acte d'accusation*, verse 218.

[45] George Eliot, "Silly Novels by Lady Novelists," *Selected Critical Writings*, ed. Rosemary Ashton (Oxford: Oxford University Press, 1992), 296–321.

[46] Stendhal, *Correspondance II*, ed. Henri Martineau (Paris: Gallimard, 1967), 485.

[47] These quotations are taken from Pierre Nicole, Letter 11 or "First Visionary," *Les imaginaries, ou lettres sur l'hérésie imaginaire* (Liège: Beyers, 1667).

psychologically refined summation. Desmarets, a playwright and novelist, recycled himself as an exegete of the Apocalypse and Song of Songs, transferring to the sacred texts the sensual vocabulary that he had employed in his novels: "perfect love, leaping souls, divine pleasures, sweet tears, spiritual intoxication, mortal wound, amorous languor, ecstasies, raptures, liquefactions." Nicole's disdain was directed at every mystic (*alumbrados, illumines*, Quakers) who confused the infinity of the private imagination with the infinity of divine Grace: "These gentlemen, who have corrupt imaginations, calculate that things are just how they imagine them to be; not only do they subject to their own whims the will of man, whom they would have act as is pleasing to them, but they also shape the will of God to their own fantasies." This is the unforgivable sin: not only and not so much explaining the scriptures "at whim," but the arrogance (Nicole calls it the "lavish humility") of passing off as the word of God that which is instead only a literary inspiration.

One of the problems that the Church faced between the sixteenth and seventeenth centuries was "affected holiness":[48] false saints (especially women) who deceived themselves and others into believing that they were speaking with God when instead they were speaking with their own sensuality or with the devil. To remedy this, the Church came up with the doctrine of "discernment of the spirits," which taught how to distinguish between whether one was dealing with a divine, human, or diabolic spirit. In the classic treatise on the topic, *De discretione spirituum* by Jean Bona (1674), the most vulnerable categories were the young, the illiterate, and women. The "diseased imagination" induced by novels and the "inordinate fantasies" of the mystics share many points in common, such as the irresistibility of inspiration, for example. In 1585, Battistina Vernazza, in the midst of the trial of Battistina Fieschi, who had been accused of expounding "the Scriptures in her own way." wrote that, "Many times certain unforeseen impressions come to me all of a sudden."[49] What they share above all is the contagion of identification. In the autobiography he dictated to a monk, Ignatius of Loyola related that while convalescing he had asked for books of chivalry,

---

[48] Gabriella Zarri, "Vera santità: Ipotesi e riscontri," *Finzione e santità tra medioevo ed età moderna* (Turin: Rosenberg and Sellier, 1991), 9–31.

[49] The letter from Battistina Vernazza to Gasparo Scotto is quoted by Daniela Solfaroli Camillocci in "La monaca esemplare: Lettere spirituali di madre Battistina Vernazza (1497–1587)," in Gabriella Zarri, *Per lettera la scrittura epistolare femminile tra archivio e tipografia: Secoli XV–XVII*, Libri Di Viella (Rome: Viella, 1999), 252.

which he craved, but the matron of the house where he was staying only had saints lives. He began to read them saying, "Saint Domenic did this, so I shall do it, too. Saint Francis did this. So I shall do it, too."[50] His conversion began forthwith. Teresa of Avila tells the same story about herself in the *Vita*, narrating the same transition (a mimetic constant) from chivalric romances to the lives of hermits and martyrs: "We planned to run away to the land of the Moors and beg, for the love of God, in the hope that there they would decapitate us."[51] The remedy that the Church found was for the confessors to ruthlessly inspect the "spiritual memoirs" written in the convents, with an absolute exaltation of self-discipline. In 1677, Mariana Francisca de Los Angeles expressed the fear that she was "an impostor, and that everything that I had written here I had fabricated and composed as I used to compose novels and short stories.[52] In 1711, Gregoria Francisca de Santa Teresa turned herself into the Inquisition tribunal, begging to be burned in the public square for her "imaginings and folly."

Torn between the divine and the diabolic, in these cases the imagination touches its furthest point from the Earth, and the cloistered life of the convent can represent a way to seal it off. Such rarefied air leaves the novel little room to breathe. In countries where the novel flourished, instead, the relationship with the absolute was not as overwhelming. In the penultimate chapter of *The Female Quixote* (a chapter that critics suspect was penned by Samuel Johnson), novelists are accused of "dividing the world into many little pieces as it pleases them," and of "encouraging youths to place their trust in chance." The character's recovery thus takes on the characteristics of an education to continuity and responsibility, for the sake of *understanding*.

Between the seventeenth and eighteenth centuries, saints and knights came to be seen less and less as dream models. To a growing extent, the hero of the novel came to have a life and name similar to the reader's. Identification became easier but also more complex and insidious: since the hero is similar to us, he or she plunges us into introspection and invites us to regard our psyche as terra incognita. Transgression is thereby located within ordinary life; there is no need to step outside of oneself to violate taboos. As

---

[50] Ignatius of Loyola, *A Pilgrim's Journey: The Autobiography of Ignatius of Loyola*, trans. Joseph N. Tylenda (San Francisco: Ignatius Press, 2001), 23.

[51] Teresa de Avila, *Interior Castle*, 22.

[52] The quotation from Mariana Francisca de Los Angeles is taken from Isabelle Poutrin, *Le voile et la plume: Autobiographie et sainteté féminine dans l'Espagne moderne* (Madrid: Casa de Velázquez, 1995), 138.

Madame de Staël wrote in *On Germany*, "Novels are bad for us; they have taught all too well the most secret part of the sentiments. . . . The ancients would never have agreed to treat their soul as a subject for fiction."[53]

"Wanting to be something other than what you are" found ever more nuanced and flexible compromises with reality. In *Berger extravagant*, a relative of the protagonist casts the ritual curse on novels, but only because by following them the self-styled pastor neglects his business as a silk merchant on Rue Saint-Denis. The young Robinson Crusoe is slightly quixotic in his mad passion to go to sea and escape the "average condition" of his father (as Charles Gildon emphasizes in his pamphlet). His heroes are Raleigh and Drake, "heroic knights-errant of the sea."[54] But restlessness, as Locke recalls, is the driving force behind initiative and economic progress. Robinson reeducates himself to spurn "errant folly," trading it in for the adventure of hard work. Even Catherine in *Northanger Abbey* is "mad" for Gothic novels and tends to confuse novels with reality. But her malaise procures her little more than embarrassment before her future husband. Perhaps the Mediterranean countries yield more extremities, as Jane Austen ironically comments in chapter 25 of *Northanger Abbey*, than in England, where a "general though unequal mixture of good and bad" is the rule.

The reality that novelistic imagination seeks to escape is no longer the world as a whole but rather the ever more demanding and conformist bourgeois society. Rather than opposing nature, therefore, daydreams are filled with "genuine natural impulses"; "your Edward will be taken for an Don Quixote," says Rousseau's interlocutor in the second preface to the *New Heloise*, and adds, "your characters are people from the other world," but Rousseau replies, "all the worse for the world down here." Werther's *Galeotto* book is Ossian, and the adventure to which it leads him is suicide. *The Sorrows of Young Werther* is a book that teaches dissatisfaction, and Hegel was surely thinking of *Werther* when he commented on the "novelistic" in his *Aesthetics*: "These new knights are in particular young men who have to clash with the way of the world, which is realized in the place of their ideals, and that believe there is something disgraceful about the existence of family, civil society, State, laws, professions, etc."[55] Rather than offering enchanted

---

[53] Madame de Staël, "Des romans," chap. 28 of *De Allemagne*, 2 vols. (Paris: Garnier-Flammarion, 1967).

[54] Giuseppe Sertoli recalls this Conradian definition in his introduction to the Italian edition of Defoe's work, *Le avventure di Robinson Crusoe* (Turin: Einaudi, 1998), vi.

[55] Georg Wilhelm Friedrich Hegel, *Aesthetics: Lectures on Fine Art*, trans. T. M. Knox (Oxford: Clarendon Press, 1975), vol. 2, pt. 2, sec. 3, chap. 3, par. 2c.

castles and golden trees, the ideal of the novel is to offer the naked disillusioned vision of the void, of the darkness that is still preferable to a hypocritical, petty reality.

The eighteenth century was the key period for the rehabilitation of the
novel. Although Austen in the fifth chapter of *Northanger Abbey* invites
novelists to join together as an "oppressed class," the irreversible decline of
the epic undoubtedly placed the novel in the foreground. As for relations
with the theater, one has only to compare the verses from Boileau's *Art poétique* (for novels, "too much rigor would be out of place / while the stage requires a precise motivation"[56]) with this passage from a letter of Stendhal:
"Many of the sentimental nuances lent to Madame de Rênal by the author of
The Red and the Black would not have been understood by most of the spectators in the theater."[57] One-hundred-fifty years later, the hierarchy had been
reversed. The early-eighteenth-century attacks on the implausibility and di-
gressiveness of the novel (culminating in England with the full affirmation of
the modern novel and in France with a government ban on serialized novels
in 1737)[58] played an important part in the transformation of the novel and
its consolidation as a serious genre. Secret reality replaces the marvelous; in-
discretion takes the place of escapism. The end of the eighteenth century
was a major turning point, indeed, an apparent reversal in course: while up
until then the novel had been mainly accused of lying, from that moment
forth it would be accused of telling truths that were too crude.

"A Taste of Ink"

Lacking definite formal rules that guarantee and emphasize its artifice, the
novel is the literary genre that has had to struggle the hardest with the question of truth. Its elastic boundaries are, on the one side, the sheer taste for
telling wild stories and spinning yarns, on the other, the recording of history
and scientific observation. Huet specifies, like a structuralist, that stories are
narratives of things that could and did happen, fables are fictions of things
that could not happen, and novels are simulations of things that could but
did not happen. The novel's special property therefore consists in inducing
the reader to respond to the false as if it were true: the immediate and most

---

[56] Boileau, *Art poétique*, canto 3.

[57] The letter to Count Salvagnoli of November 2, 1832, is in Stendhal, *Correspondance II*, 512.

[58] The Chancellor of Aguesseau's ban is described in Françoise Weil, *L'interdiction du roman et
la libraire: 1728–1750* (Paris: Aux Amateurs de Livres, 1986).

superficial reasons why the novel denies itself is that it wishes to pass itself off as history and "deceive its readers with the appearance of truth," as Tasso says in the *Discorsi dell'arte poetica*.[59] The novel is aided in this by its unruliness and by the seeming superficiality of its writing. "The greatest defect of ordinary novels," Abbé Desfontaines explains, "is in appearing too much to be like novels. . . . Illusion is essential in a book of fiction; it is a great art to know how to avoid the appearance of art."[60]

The novel's enemies have all accused it of deceptiveness. The novel has responded either with periodic assurances of its faithfulness to the truth (sixteenth- and seventeenth-century claims of historic truthfulness, the vogue for the memoir, references to the latest news and stenographic techniques in the British eighteenth century, competition with the civil code and scientific diagnosis in the late nineteenth century, etc.) or with a reflection of the differences between fiction and lies. In 1557, Scaligero remarked precociously that the need for fiction testifies to the infinite nature of our mind, which is too great to be satisfied by the real and therefore goes "beyond the vulgar limits of truth."[61] Fiction can thus tell a deeper truth than ordinary truth: not the truth of events but of desires. "As for the sentiments and passions," Laclos writes, "history is limited to ratifying effects but it carefully hides the causes."[62] The Marquis de Sade reiterates, in his "Reflections on the Novel," that while the task of the historian is to show man as he is or how he appears to be, the task of the novelist is to show him "as he can become, as he can be modified by vice and the varied urges of the passions."[63] The twentieth century took another step, concluding that because certain truths had been repressed, they had to be introduced necessarily under the cloak of mendacity.

Too much truth can be harmful, the novel's defenders tell us. The author of *Tombeau des romans*, in 1626, used a lovely baroque metaphor: just as the sun is so bright you can only look at its reflection in the water, the truth is so cruel that you can only approach it through wine, "in vino veritas." He borrows other metaphors from the field of medicine: the novel gilds the bitter

[59] Tasso, "Primo discorso," *Prose*, 351.

[60] In vol. 29 (1742) of *Observations sur les écrits modernes*. The quotation is taken from May, *Le dilemme du roman au XVIIIe siècle*, 42.

[61] Julius Caesar Scaligeri, *Exoticarum exercitationum liber XV, De Subtilitate, Exercitatio 307, II* (Hanover: Typis Wechelianis, 1620), 835; paraphrased in F. Laglois, called Fancan, *Tombeau des romans où il est discouru 1) contre les Romans 2) pour les Romans* (Paris: Claude Morlot, 1626).

[62] Laclos, *Œvres complètes*, 524.

[63] Marquis de Sade, "Reflections on the Novel," in *The 120 Days of Sodom and Other Writings*, trans. Austryn Wainhouse and Richard Seaver (New York: Grove, 1969), 109.

pill of truth, the novelist is like the surgeon who, having to dissect the breast of a princess, hides his scalpel in a sponge.[64] (The novelist as a "surgeon of the human soul," without softening sponges, would be a prominent image in the realist and naturalist age, when the novel appropriated the traditional subject matter of its enemies to wield it against the sweet, sentimental novel.)

Hurtling between deceit and ruthlessness, illness and medicine, the novel finds an abiding compromise in reasonable constructions of the "verisimilar"; in the period of greatest splendor, between Austen and Dostoyevsky, the world of the novel is one in which the reader can believe but at the same time it is the whole universe of that in which one can believe. In other words, it restores back a reassuring image of the world, produced by a class with growing self-recognition and a growing tendency to relegate the bizarre to a higher or lower ground. However convincing the mirror that the novel holds up to the bourgeoisie may be, its vocation is not to reassure; it is rather to drape the impossible over the real or to excavate the impossible from the real, without ever being appeased. Neither Kafka's *Metamorphosis* nor Proust's *Remembrance of Things Past* is "verisimilar." At the end of *Gulliver's Travels*, Swift actually wishes for a law "that every Traveller before he were permitted to publish his Voyages, should be obliged to make Oath before the *Lord High Chancellor* that all he intended to print was absolutely true to the best of his Knowledge." This is not just paradoxical irony. Swift's misanthropy is at its most violent when the myth of the Houyhnhnms shrinks to fit the narrow, concrete reality of an English house, within the stable in whose odor the protagonist takes refuge from the repellant smell of his wife and children.

Compressing the symbol into raw fragments of reality, the story of the modern novel is a long descent toward the particular, driven by a hunger for concreteness. As long as the protagonists were princes and kings and history was the great public story, it was hard to make the fictional credible. Already in volume 1, chapter 6 of *Don Quixote*, Cervantes mocks *Tirant lo Blanc* (a judgment he would later revisit with a more "camp" sensibility), which relates the Arab conquest of England. In 1741, the Bibliothèque Française of Amsterdam attacked Prévost for the *Mémoires pour servir à l'histoire de Malte* and whoever else sought to deceive ("tromper") by passing off fictitious events as historical. One of the reasons the novel encountered problems in the eighteenth century was that by seeking to introduce the reader into the life of "characters that everyone knows," and needing to make those lives interesting, it often stumbled into the crime of slander. Only by talking about

---

[64] Fancan, *Tombeau des romans*, 512. The metaphor of the pill and the surgeon are on 63.

common people, "little people," can one tell the story of a life without being able to tell how much is true and how much is false. Obviously, as Mademoiselle de Scudéry remarked, "vraisemblance" does not always agree with "bienséance";[65] common people tend to be vulgar. In the seventh book of *Tom Jones*, Fielding warned that the tenth chapter contained "Several Matters, Natural Enough Perhaps, but *Low*." The "social singularities" that took the place of exemplarity bring out dangerous latent tendencies, from the "depths" and from "outside"; from the late eighteenth century onward, the vogue for the verisimilar and interesting would give rise to the rage for the criminal and the abject. Richardson's Pamela had already confessed, in letter 102, that she had read few novels and hadn't liked them because "either they were too amazing or unlikely or they inflamed the passions too much."

From the seventeenth to the nineteenth centuries, the more the bourgeois novel matured and became self-conscious, the more the illness spread. The complete opposition between the good and the bad guy—the lay version of the struggle between God and Satan—was replaced by a more gloomy ramification: every character contains within him- or herself unmentionable motives, and no one is truly good. Truth becomes an *unmasking*, and moral indignation at evil is succeeded by a general sense of bitterness and disgust. In 1857, one reviewer of *Madame Bovary*, to reconcile himself with life, invoked "a beautiful, fantastic and entertaining novel, full of imagination and illusions."[66] The notion of culpability for malfeasance slowly receded, to be replaced by "the nature of things," civilization or the absence of God.

The novel's strategies to defend itself from accusations that it represented evil were likewise modified. The simplest strategy, initially, was to condemn evil outright, recounting the bad ending awaiting evil-doers and making them repent. Virtue rewarded and vice punished: between the seventeenth and eighteenth centuries this formula became so standardized that it was ripe for Sade to turn it on its head. Of course the novel's enemies never let themselves be fooled, and they grasped the hypocrisy beneath this formula. Heidegger wrote, "They slowly but surely turn men into slaves of vice, thanks to the clever fiction of wanting to punish them."[67] Every condemnation of sin functions as a form of Freudian denial and entails emotional complicity with the sin itself. The cruelty of the punishment ultimately elevates the evil-doer, emphasizing the rebel's greatness.

---

[65] Mademoiselle de Scudéry's remark is cited in May, *Le dilemme du roman au XVIIIe siècle*.
[66] The review was written by A. Claveau in the *Courrier Franco-Italien* of May 7, 1857.
[67] In Bavaj, *Mythoscopia romantica*, 127.

"It is suggested there cannot be the same life, the same brightness and beauty, in relating the penitent part as is in the criminal part," Defoe candidly confesses in the preface to *Moll Flanders*. Transgression is much more enticing than order. Between the sixteenth and seventeenth centuries, even edifying novels and saints' lives preferred the great sinners, such as Mary Magdalene, as this allowed them to wallow in the details of the sinful life. The Church was concerned that this fatal ambivalence was a special case of "sollicitatio ad turpia," like the sins that entered confessionals through a penitent's detailed descriptions, or the ones that led the Inquisition to condemn, in 1611, a treatise by the Jesuit Andrea Nicosia "on caresses, on kisses, on orgasms and on pollutions."[68] Only the elderly Tolstoy, who had repudiated *Anna Karenina* and *War and Peace*, would radically reject the game of ambivalence: "An artist teaches not what he wants but what he can." What matters is not what you say but what you are; it is useless to invoke the need for evil as a bad example: evil is so omnipresent that "to counter it, one must aspire to good with all one's energy."[69] (A similar example of taking a position that went against the current and against the essence of the literature that was ironically being revindicated occurred around 1890, when Russian public opinion railed against the short stories of the Tolstoyan Nikolai Leskov, accusing him of using primitive Christian life as a pretext for staging voluptuous, sensual scenes.)

Another strategy is to play on the dynamic between characters, taking care to make a character's statements distinct from the author's positions. "This is being spoken by a wicked man," Molière writes in the margins of *Tartuffe*.[70] Barbey d'Aurevilly echoed these words at the trial for *Diabolique*, saying in his own defense, "The story was told by a wicked man."[71] "They are a hero's words, but they express Sinyavsky's thoughts," was the counterargument offered by the prosecutor in the 1966 Moscow trial.[72] This argument is usually triggered when that dynamic fails and the hero (or antihero)

[68] Prosperi, *Tribunali della coscienza*, 513.

[69] The two sentences are from Tolstoy's diary entries of July 11, 1894, and November 6, 1892, quoted in Leo Tolstoy, *Tolstoy's Diaries*, trans. Reginald Frank (New York: Scribner Press, 1985).

[70] Molière placed the famous caption, which probably also served as a cue, late in the play, next to the verses of act 4, scene 5, where Tartuffe speaks of the "accommodations" that can be reached with heaven.

[71] Barbey's interrogation of December 15, 1874, appears in the appendix to Yvan Leclerc, *Crimes écrits: La littérature en procès au XIXe siècle* (Paris: Plon, 1991), 351.

[72] *Libro bianco sul caso Daniel-Sinjavskij*, ed. Aleksander Ginzburg (Milan: Jaca Book, 1967), 201. In the same year, the Russian original of the *Belaia kniga* [*White Book*] was published (Frankfurt on Main: Possev-Verlag, 1967), as were translations into French and German.

monopolizes the field. In the whole book there is not a single character who "can make her bow her head," was the prosecutor Pinard's inadvertently admiring description of Emma Bovary. At the trial of *Lady Chatterley's Lover*, the prosecutor asked one witness, "In this novel do you see one word that implies criticism of the protagonist's deeds?"[73] An article in *Pravda* condemning Daniel-Sinyavsky underlined the emotional effectiveness of a character's statements, "if the work lacks the force to counter such sentiments."[74]

As the novel's horizon became more gloomy, its explicit condemnation of villains tapered off. It often limited itself to illustrating vice, hiding behind the excuse that the unhappiness and atrocious, livid desperation emanating from the text were sufficient warning to the reader. Early on, however, Baudelaire—who adopted a similar argument in his notes to his lawyer—questioned the wisdom of insisting on it.[75] Unhappiness itself is a sin, a form of sloth and ingratitude toward God; those who are so desperate that they would kill themselves—said Goethe in a harangue against *Werther*—show so little respect for human life that they could easily commit murder (shortly before killing himself Werther does, in fact, meet someone who had killed for love). If God is replaced by the blind myth of progress, unhappiness becomes a crime of wounded optimism; the heaviest charge brought against Solzhenitsyn for *Cancer Ward* was that it was demoralizing, but it is also present, for example, in the charges that the Second Empire brought against Eugène Sue for *Les mystères du peuple*[76] and in the ones that the Third Republic filed against Lucien Descaves for *Sous-Offs* (he was charged with "spitting on the flag," not unlike the charge of "besmirching the mother" brought against Solzhenitsyn).

To the defenders of the novel it is easy to respond that the true culprit is not the person who sounds the alarm but the one who started the fire; faced by a philistine society, it is almost a duty to give a name to evil. Faced by a society that praises utility above all else, the uselessness of the novel—an accusation made against it for centuries—becomes a badge of merit. (Gautier promptly claimed such credit in 1835, in his long preface to *Mademoiselle de Maupin*, in the years when criticism of the future became fashionable.)

---

[73] The question of the prosecutor, Griffith-Jones, to the witness, Stephen Hopkinson, is in Penguin (Firm), C. H. Rolph, and Great Britain, *The Trial of Lady Chatterley Regina v. Penguin Books Ltd.: The Transcript of the Trial* (Reading, Eng.: Privately printed, 1961), 123.

[74] *Libro bianco sul caso Daniel-Sinjavskij*, 229. Gh. Petrov's article from the February 15, 1966, issue of *Pravda* appears on 123.

[75] Charles Baudelaire, "Notes pour mon avocet," *Oeuvres complètes*, ed. Claude Pichois (Paris: Gallimard, 1975), 195.

[76] A summary of the trials of Sue and Descaves is given in Leclerc, *Crimes écrits*, 379ff. and 421ff.

Faced by a society that had lost contact with the sacred naturalness of sex, writing four-letter words became almost a therapeutic mission for D. H. Lawrence. "Staying silent," Solzhenitsyn replied to the Writers' Union, "is not a way out and it corrupts youth."[77]

"Corrupter" and "moralist" are two opposite and correlated epithets, depending on how you look at them. In 1786, Restif de la Bretonne wrote, "The novelist is a moralist."[78] Zola went one step further and said that novelists are "experimental moralists."[79] In the preface to *Jude the Obscure*, Hardy ironized, "Then someone discovered it was a moral work." During the trial of *Lady Chatterley's Lover*, a clergyman stated his conviction that the book was "a short moral treatise, in addition to being a novel."[80]

All of these vicissitudes are condensed and summarized in the fortunes of a single great metaphor, perhaps the most constant in the history of attacks on the novel: the metaphor of the vessel and the liquid it contains. Adopting a Lucretian image, Tasso in *Jerusalem Delivered* compares his métier to that of a doctor who, having to force a sick boy to drink a bitter medicine, sprinkles sugar on the lip of the glass.[81] The medicine is truth (historical and ethical); the sugar is sensuality combined with the marvelous. This metaphor is widespread in prefaces to seventeenth-century novels, inflected according to the circumstances. In the preface to *Roman bourgeois*, for example, Furetière writes that "the pleasure we feel in mocking others is what makes it so sweet to swallow the medicine that is so good for us." But to be entertained, he adds, we must be able to recognize in the characters people whom we see everyday—the sugar is therefore realism rather than the marvelous. So widespread was this metaphor that its values would soon be reversed: for the novel's detractors, the sugar is the appeal surrounding the novel, the liquid is the passionate unruliness and is no longer a medicine but a poison: "All the elements are arranged," writes Zaccaria in the *Storia polemica delle proibizioni de' libri* (1777), "to sprinkle with sweet liquor the brim of the vase in which the poison of mortality is presented to the unwary."[82] That the novel was poisonous became a commonplace redeemed only by Flaubert's formidable

---

[77] *L'affaire Soljenitsyne* (Paris: L'Herne, 1995), 244.

[78] Restif de la Bretonne, *Les Françaises* (Neuchâtel: Guillot, 1786), 2:16.

[79] Émile Zola, *Le roman expérimental* (Paris: Charpentier, 1880), 26; available in English as *The Experimental Novel* (New York: Haskell House, 1964).

[80] *The Trial of Lady Chatterley*, 103.

[81] Lucretius, *De rerum natura*, trans. W.H.D. Rouse, 3d ed., Loeb Classical Library (London/Cambridge, Mass.: Heinemann/Harvard University Press, 1966), vol. 1, vv. 936–50.

[82] Francescantonio Zaccaria, *Storia polemica delle proibizioni de' libri* (Rome: G. Salomoni, 1777), 233.

intuition that the poison imbibed by Emma Bovary "tastes like ink." As recently as 1934, in the decision permitting *Ulysses* to be published in the United States, Judge John M. Woolsey stated that Joyce's novel was "a rather strong draught to ask some sensitive, though normal, persons to take" and found that "whilst in many places the effect of *Ulysses* on the reader undoubtedly is somewhat emetic, nowhere does it tend to be an aphrodisiac."[83] Emetic: a medicine to induce vomiting, a poison turned into medicine.

According to Pinard, believing that a profound moral significance redeems the lascivious details of *Madam Bovary*, "would mean placing poison within everyone's reach, and the cure within the reach of only a few." But according to others, the cure, paradoxically, is the poison itself. Heidegger said sarcastically that if we wish to save the novel we should presume that, following the ninth epigram of Ausonious, the sum of two poisons is the antidote. Many took his observation seriously: if love is a poison and novels warn you about love, then novels are an antidote.[84] One of Laclos's female readers was convinced that she would be doing her daughter a favor by giving her *Dangerous Liaisons* on her wedding day.[85] Corrupt people need novels, said Rousseau, who contrasted the "fantastic illnesses" of his heroes to the "torrent of poisoned sayings that circulate in the cities."[86] One of the experts called upon to testify at the trial of *Lady Chatterley's Lover* stated that the work was "a true antidote to the superficial and fatuous values of sex."[87]

The End of Obscenity

Any attempt to construct a typology of the trials brought against novels at different times and places will inevitably run into a thousand exceptions. When two novels from the same period are accused of being equally harmful, sheer circumstance decides that one will be brought to trial and the

---

[83] John M. Woolsey, "The Monumental Decision of the United States District Court Rendered December 6, 1933, by Hon. John M. Woolsey Lifting the Ban on *Ulysses*," in James Joyce, *Ulysses*, new ed. (New York: Modern Library, 1961), xii.

[84] Furetière tells the story of a girl "cured of love" after having read the *Roman bourgeois* (translated into English as *Scarron's City Romance*, London: H. Herringman, 1671). At the trial of Pauvert Editions in 1956 for issuing the complete edition of Sade's works, Jean Paulhan claimed, paradoxically, that he had met a women who entered a convent as a result of reading the Marquis's works.

[85] Laclos relates this anecdote in the preface to *Dangerous Liaisons*.

[86] In the second preface to *The New Heloise*.

[87] *The Trial of Lady Chatterley*, 158.

other not, or that one will be found guilty and the other absolved. Such a map could not take into account the real social pressures on the novel because censorship is preventive where pressures are greatest and there are no trials. Typically there is often a greater "density" of trials after periods of liberalization (for example, France after the new 1881 law, England after 1959, or Russia in the early 1960s after Kruschev's thaw). It is equally impossible to briefly document the widespread phenomenon of self-censorship. Many novelists, in various periods and countries, could have easily gone through what Leonardo Sciascia describes in the afterword to *The Day of the Owl*: "I don't feel so heroic that I would challenge accusations of public offense and defamation; I am deliberate in this feeling. Therefore, when I realized that my imagination had not taken into due account the constraints imposed by the laws of the State and by the susceptibility of those who enforce them, I got busy trying to cope, to cope."[88]

At most you can identify constants and trends. The main trend in the West is clearly the transition from a society obsessed by the danger of heresy to a society confident of its power to standardize. The division of labor has relegated literature to a more and more inoffensive role, somewhere between the multiplex and the museum. In the seventeenth century you could pay with your life for having written a novel; nowadays trials against literature generally end in acquittals and embarrassment for the accusers. The suit filed against Pier Paolo Pasolini's *The Ragazzi* in 1956 was psychologically damaging to the author and changed the course of his life. This doesn't change the fact that in his sentencing the judge came close to recusing himself from the trial and emphasized that the debate had taken place "in a climate of serene elevation." In a 1968 book, Charles Rembar proclaimed "the end of obscentity," and prophesized, "nowadays if a writer has at least some talent, he and his book have nothing to fear."[89]

The banning of books has always made for good publicity. Flaubert acknowledged this with regard to *Madame Bovary*. As early as the Inquisition, people used to scan the index of prohibited books in search of interesting titles. Diderot was speaking for everyone in *Lettre sur le commerce de la librairie*: "How many times would a book-seller and author, if they had dared, have said to the judges, 'Gentlemen, please, find me guilty!' "[90] The authorities

---

[88] Leonardo Sciascia, *Il giorno della civetta* (Turin: Einaudi, 1971), 119; available in English as *The Day of the Owl*, trans. Archibald Colquhoun and Antony Oliver (London: Granta, 2001).

[89] Charles Rembar, *The End of Obscenity: The Trials of "Lady Chatterley," "Tropic of Cancer," and "Fanny Hill"* (New York: Random House, 1968).

[90] Denis Diderot, *Oeuvres complètes* (Paris: Hermann, 1976), 8:556.

played less of a role as "guardian" or "sentinel," and even the Church came to insist less on the "fragility of human nature." The problem of the "weak," for that matter, seems to have been resolved through the logic of differentiated uses. The alternative between formal beauty as a mitigating factor (in the Jesuit's *Ratio studiorum* the classics are allowed, "because of the elegance and propriety of the language"[91]) or as an aggravating factor (*Madame Bovary* is considered even more dangerous because Flaubert endowed it with "all the prestige of his style"[92]) becomes meaningless in a market that juxtaposes different and incomparable levels of formal dignity.

There has certainly been growing freedom together with a greater understanding of how a novel functions as an organism. One dividing line is the English law of 1959, which prohibits judging a book on the basis of arbitrarily excerpted sentences and requires that it be considered "as a whole." Along the same lines is the requirement to distinguish between the "results" of a text and the author's intentions. It still holds true, however, that the guarantees are never given once and for all. Accusations of obscenity, blasphemy, or defamation are often a cover for a political condemnation, and the tolerance rate is drastically lowered in emergency situations (Scholochov's lament at the twenty-third Congress of the Communist Party of the USSR is unforgettable: ". . . we were judged by the severe limits of the articles in the Penal Code, but allowed ourselves to be led by the revolutionary conscience of justice").[93]

The novel has always had a curious relationship with allegory, seeking protection through allegory at the same time as it distrusted it. Thanks to allegory, a "licentious" novel like the *Golden Ass* of Apuleius was able to survive the Middle Ages unharmed. Defoe made confusing recourse to allegory to defend *Robinson Crusoe*. An allegorical reading was proposed to defend *Lady Chatterley's Lover* (e.g., Clifford's paralysis as the paralysis of modern society). But when totalitarian regimes want to condemn a novel, they excavate allegorical readings that the author must hasten to deny. When Solzhenitsyn was facing his accusers, who interpreted *Cancer Ward* as an allegory of Soviet society (seen as an "incurable tumor"), he replied, "it has too many medical details to be a symbol" and concluded, "if one of you is hospitalized, you'll see whether or not it's an allegory."[94]

---

[91] *La "Ratio studiorum": Il metodo degli studi umanistici nei collegi dei gesuiti alla fine del secolo XVI*, trans. Giuliano Raffo, S.J. (Milan: Civiltà Cattolica–San Fedele, 1989), 192; available in English as *The Jesuit "Ratio Studiorum" of 1599*, trans. Allan P. Farrell, S.J. (Washington, D.C.: Conference of Major Superiors of Jesuits, 1970).

[92] Pinard's closing arguments can be found in Flaubert, *Oeuvres*, 621.

[93] *Libro bianco sul caso Daniel-Sinjavskij*, 81.

[94] *L'affaire Soljenitsyne*, 226.

That the religious fanaticism held up for ridicule in the *Satanic Verses* alluded to the present-day situation in Iran was one of the suspicions that led to Khomeini's *fatwa* against Salman Rushdie in 1989.[95] With a shift of a few degrees in longitude and latitude, an author is once again risking the death sentence for having written a novel. Aside from the contingent political reasons that fostered it, the sentence against Rushdie brings us back to the beginning of our discussion. The most intelligent Iranian criticism makes clear that, aside from the indignation over the insults to the Muslim religion (the city of the prophet called "Ignorance," the prostitutes who have the same names as Mohammed's wives, etc.), Rushdie's most unpardonable sin was not so much the episode of the diabolic interpolation of the verses (an episode that Rushdie did not invent but rather found in the history of the Koran's tradition) but to have treated the revealed word as if it were imaginative literature. From a philological point of view, the *Satanic Verses* is less subversive than certain studies that are accepted and discussed at Islamic universities. What is intolerable is the idea that the literary text is more powerful than the sacred text, that it can encapsulate the sacred text and turn it into narrative material, thereby inserting it into the mobile flow of the passions—and subjugating it to the novelistic law of and-and rather than to the either-or that guarantees the sacred text its fixity and authority. According to Amir Taheri, an Iranian journalist who wrote a biography of Khomeni, "for many Muslims the very idea of using the prophet Mohammed as a character in a novel is intolerable."[96]

In *La verdad de las mentiras* (1990), Mario Vargas Llosa notes that religious cultures produce poetry and plays but rarely great novels. The novel is an art that belongs to a society in which faith is crumbling. It is both modeled on the scriptures and a surrogate and parody of them. How many heroes' lives are actually imitations of Christ? The sacred text, especially our own, the Bible, is structured like a narrative. Its task is to give meaning to the world through concrete real things rather than through logical mathematical abstractions. But the sacred text has to restrain its ambivalence and perpetual germinations of reality, and guarantee its meaning once and for all.

The novel, by contrast, burns, undampered, in the friction between the contingent and absolute. Its allegory is always imperfect, always harboring an inferiority complex in its dealings with everyday life. Hardy was deliberate in naming the protagonist of *Jude the Obscure*: Jude is the "negative"

---

[95] Raphaël Aubert, *L'affaire Rushdie* (Paris: Cerf Fides, 1990).

[96] Lisa Appignanesi and Sara Maitland, eds., *The Rushdie File* (Syracuse, N.Y.: Syracuse University Press, 1990), 93.

Christ, a failed priest who casts his theology books into the fire and whose son dies atrociously because he takes things too literally.[97] The novel is a challenge to the sacred text because while it gleans the absolute from everyday reality, it also has the courage to address the thousand changing faces behind which the absolute disguises itself. In 1698, the Swiss theologian Johan Heidegger exclaimed, "Mankind is the biggest ape, thinking that it has to imitate everything." Fifteen years later, Leibniz restated the sentiment in more positive terms: "No one imitates our Lord better than the inventor of a fine novel."[98] While poetry can be a hallucinatory emanation of the divine Word, the novel is an alternative to the action of God, when God has ceased to act—an imprecise, impotent alternative: the novelist is an expelled devil, masturbating far from heaven.

The steady legitimization of the novel thus accompanied the affirmation of democracy and the transition from the need for the sacred text to the relativity of the rules of civil coexistence. In the West the freedom to narrate no longer seems to have any restrictions, except for the ones set by democracy. A difficult reception would await any story that seriously praised racism or recommended concentration camps (*Jag och min son* [*My Son and I*] by the Swedish-Kenyan writer Sara Lidman ran into problems, although its racist elements were only voiced by a single character). I do not think that anyone would get a death sentence (those who said they understood Khomeini's *fatwa* did so with a patronizing air worthy of *Uncle Tom's Cabin*), but this same fact should prompt reflections on the novel and on ourselves as Westerners.

The novel's "contagion" is almost to be hoped for in an era that cannot see the windmills behind Don Quixote's giants. In comparison with everyday unreality, the unreality of the novel preserves something noble and ascetic. In A. S. Byatt's *summa* of the novel's utility and harmfulness, *Babel Tower* (1996), the perfidious insinuation is made that even the protagonist's antiliterary choices (to marry a man who "hates words") depend on her "being a reader" (she was influenced by Forster and Lawrence), while in the

---

[97] In pt. 6, chap. 2 of *Jude the Obscure*, Sue blames herself for her stepson's suicide: "I said the world was against us, that it was better to be out of life than in it at this price; and he took it literally. . . . I wanted to be truthful. I couldn't bear deceiving him as to the facts of life. . . . Why didn't I tell him pleasant untruths, instead of half-realities?"

[98] Leibniz's sentence is in a letter of April 26, 1713, quoted in Eduard Bodemann, ed., "Leibnizens Briefwechsel mit dem Herzoge Anton Ulrich von Braunschweig-Wolfenbüttel," *Zeitschrift des historischen Vereins für Niedersachsen*, 1888, 232; Heidegger's words are in Bavaj, *Mythoscopia romantica*, 128.

end, one realizes that for the protagonist, returning to her own world of educated readers signifies rediscovering her freedom.

But the novel's unruliness is more ample and ambiguous than democratic freedom. Vargas Llosa emphasizes that in perfectly democratic societies, history and fiction should be separate and distinct; it is in totalitarian societies that they change places. The Soviet Encyclopedia was filled with as many inventions as a novel. *The City and the Dogs* was burned in a Lima square as if it were a memory to be erased. To an increasing extent Western novels (especially novelistic "stories" that are not printed on paper, like television reality shows) tend to confuse the border between reality and fiction. Is this regressive nostalgia on the novel's part, an anarchic desire to disobey, and the cowardice to say so (Dr. H. accused Céline of "lâcheté"—cowardice—when he prosecuted him for *North* in 1964[99])? Or is it a sharp sense of the passivity that is corroding our democracy?

"We grow accustomed and the shock disappears," said the prosecutor at the trial against *Lady Chatterley's Lover*, marking the point where tolerance becomes numbness.[100] Rather than an open, even harsh confrontation of opposing opinions, what is tolerable seems to be decided by the market's inertia. (Why is it considered despicable to say on the Internet how sexy an eleven-year-old girl is but acceptable to photograph a sexy eleven-year-old girl for a fashion magazine?) In its vocation to adhere to the senselessness of the world, to redeem it from close up, the novel may be undergoing a political mutation. Engaged in countering its own inoffensiveness, it seeks allies from among the products that power uses to transform information into seduction and therefore into a commodity—supinely allying itself with them but at the same time falsifying and shaming them. So is the novel a deserter or a critic of democracy? Now that would be a good subject for a novel!

Translated by Michael F. Moore

[99] Céline, *Romans*, 1,153.
[100] *The Trial of Lady Chatterley*, 283.

Polygenesis

TOMAS HÄGG

The Ancient Greek Novel: A Single Model or a Plurality of Forms?

Theme with Variations

A handbook description of what is generally called "the Greek novel" of antiquity, or more specifically, "the ideal Greek novel," might sound like this:

> These are novels of travel, adventure, and romantic love, taking place in a vaguely realistic Mediterranean or Near Eastern setting. A boy and a girl, both exceptionally attractive and of noble birth, meet and fall in love. A cruel fate separates them, and they are tossed around by land and sea, constantly longing and searching for one another. They are shipwrecked, attacked by pirates, sold as slaves, violently courted by brigands and masters, but would rather die than sacrifice their chastity. Finally, after the long series of tribulations, they are reunited and return home to a life of marital bliss.

A handbook writer who has actually read these novels, or attentively listened to those who have, will hasten to add that there are considerable variations on this theme; no two surviving novels are in fact equal in plot or attitude.

Take time, for instance. Chariton's *Callirhoe*, presumably the oldest among the five that have come down to us in its full original form (50 B.C.–A.D. 50?), is a historical novel, set in the Classical period of Greece. So is the latest one, Heliodorus's *Aithiopika* (A.D. 350–375?), though it lacks Chariton's precise references to historical characters and events.[1] In contrast, Achilles Tatius's *Leucippe and Clitophon* (A.D. 150–200?) is set in the author's own time: he pretends having met the hero and heard the story

---

[1] All the dates, and in particular those of Chariton's and Heliodorus's novels, are open to debate, since none of the authors is identified. For details and bibliography, see the handbook edited by Gareth Schmeling, *The Novel in the Ancient World*, Mnemosyne, Suppl. 159 (Leiden, 1996; rev. paperback ed., 2003). Shorter introductions to the ancient novels are provided by Tomas Hägg, *The Novel in Antiquity* (Oxford, 1983); and Niklas Holzberg, *The Ancient Novel* (London, 1995). Translations of all the texts are to be found in B. P. Reardon ed., *Collected Ancient Greek Novels* (Berkeley, Calif., 1989).

from him.[2] The remaining two, Xenophon's *Ephesiaka* (A.D. 50–150?)[3] and Longus's *Daphnis and Chloe* (A.D. 150–250?), are enacted in a diffusely contemporary world, meaning the first two centuries of the Roman Empire, though the Romans themselves are curiously absent.

Or take the geographical setting and the travel motif. Longus's pastoral, though admitting pirates into the plot, restricts the actual traveling to the groves and meadows of the island of Lesbos and the waters immediately off its coast. Xenophon's story, in contrast, chases its young travelers around the greater part of the Mediterranean, with beginning and end in Ephesus and intermediate stops (for one, or both, of the protagonists) in Samos, Rhodes, Phoenicia, Cilicia, Cappadocia, Egypt, Sicily, South Italy, Crete, and Cyprus (all in seventy pages). Achilles Tatius's novel has a north-south axis (Byzantium–Ephesus–Phoenicia–Egypt), and so has Heliodorus's (Delphi–Zacynthus–Crete–Egypt–Meroe); whereas Chariton, who notably excludes Egypt from his couple's itinerary, prefers a movement from west (Sicily) to east (Persia), with Ionia as the cherished middle.[4]

No less variable is the love motif. Although reciprocal love at first sight is usually the spectacular start of the love story, Achilles lustfully dwells on the hero's prolonged courting of his beloved. Consummated marriage precedes the separation of the lovers in Chariton and Xenophon, whereas it epitomizes the happy ending in the others. Fidelity and chastity, for male and female alike, are the professed ideals in all; but Achilles' hero is successfully seduced by Melite, the enchanting widow from Ephesus. Chariton's heroine even marries the Ionian gentleman Dionysius to be able to give birth, in legitimate marriage, to her son by Chaereas, her first (and last) husband. To escape such a fate, Xenophon's Antheia takes poison, only to become one of these novels' notorious instances of apparent death, and Heliodorus's Theagenes defiantly endures endless torture.

Xenophon creates suspense by a breathless series of outer events. Chariton, though actually admitting a similar sample of violence, torture, and

---

[2] Helen Morales, in her introduction to Tim Whitmarsh, trans., Achilles Tatius, *Leucippe and Clitophon*, (Oxford, 2001), pp. xv f., argues for a "designedly indeterminate" date of the action; but, whatever sophisticated ideas we might have about the nonidentity of the narrating "I" and author, Achilles Tatius clearly invites his readers to make such an identification and regard the story as authentic as well as contemporary.

[3] It has usually been dated in the second century A.D., but James N. O'Sullivan makes a good case for removing the supposed *terminus post quem* in Trajan's reign; see his *Xenophon of Ephesus: His Compositional Technique and the Birth of the Novel* (Berlin, 1995), 1–9.

[4] The plots are excellently mapped by Jean Alvares in Schmeling, ed., *The Novel*, 801–14.

death, embalms it all in a humane discourse, emphasizing throughout the feelings and reasoning of the characters involved. Achilles is ironic where Heliodorus is serious (though some modern critics would find him, too, more ambiguous in attitude).[5] Chariton devotes most of his attention to his heroine, while Achilles—by uniquely adopting a first-person perspective—makes his narrating hero the central character. Longus smilingly shows his readers the charming naïveté of his children of nature, in contrast to Heliodorus's missionary ethos and model characters.

The degree to which descriptive detail is allowed to slow down the tempo of the narrative is another distinctive factor—in other words, how far spatial form intrudes on the basic temporal structure.[6] Whereas Xenophon uses half a dozen lines to inform us, in his plain style, of the motifs embroidered on the canopy over the bridal couch (1.8.2–3), Achilles, with precious words, arranged according to rhythm and euphony, creates a piece of verbal art to represent, in minute detail, the erotic painting his hero is looking at (1.1.2–13). In Chariton, Tyre is captured with a fair amount of oratory but little concrete detail (7.3–4); in Heliodorus the siege of Syene is graphically depicted to fill a whole book (9). This addiction to *ecphrasis*, graphic description—be it of works of art, natural phenomena, or man-made spectacles—are among the stylistic features that have earned Achilles, Longus, and Heliodorus the epithet "sophistic" novelists, a label drawn from the dominating cultural movement of the period, the so-called Second Sophistic.[7]

In that way, the handbook writer might go on characterizing each of the novels by comparison with the others, and trying to group them by means of various distinctive criteria. But the ideal Greek novel of the general description, it turns out, is nowhere to be found.[8]

---

[5] Cf. Massimo Fusillo on the *Aithiopika* in volume 2 of this work and Gerald N. Sandy, *Heliodorus* (Boston, 1982).

[6] On spatial form in the novels, see Ingela Nilsson, *Erotic Pathos, Rhetorical Pleasure: Narrative Technique and Mimesis in Eumathios Makrembolites' Hysmine & Hysminias*, Studia Byzantina Upsaliensia, no. 7 (Uppsala, 2001), 40–43, 141–44, 242.

[7] On *ecphrasis* in the sophistic novels, see Shadi Bartsch, *Decoding the Ancient Novel: The Reader and the Role of Description in Heliodorus and Achilles Tatius* (Princeton, N.J., 1989). On the distinction between sophistic and pre- or nonsophistic novels, see J. R. Morgan, "The Greek Novel: Towards a Sociology of Production and Reception," in Anton Powell, ed., *The Greek World* (London, 1995), 130–52, at 140–43.

[8] See B. P. Reardon, *The Form of Greek Romance*, (Princeton, N.J., 1991), for an attempt at defining the genre in terms of ancient critical categories by using Chariton as the primary object of analysis.

A Single Model?

A general description of a genre, such as the ideal Greek novel, might perhaps be described as a verbal lowest common denominator. But this is a halting analogy. Even the most general description conceivable of the ideal novel appears to need some modification to be truly applicable to any of the extant exemplars. What lurks behind that description is perhaps the (mostly unspoken) belief that there "originally" existed a work that completely answered to the description, and that the surviving novels are all individual adaptations of that model itself, or of other works that ultimately go back to the model—the lost archetype.

Ben Edwin Perry has come closest to expressing in concrete terms, perhaps unwittingly, the idea of the archetype.[9] In his Sather lectures published in 1967, fed up with the evolutionary view of the origin and development of the ancient novel that had been prevalent for a hundred years, Perry envisaged the "birth" of the Greek novel in this way: "The first romance was deliberately planned and written by an individual author, its inventor. He conceived it on a Tuesday afternoon in July. . . ."[10] Earlier, Erwin Rohde had looked upon the creation of the Greek novel as a combination of two Hellenistic genres, love elegy and fabulous travel books (*Reisefabulistik*). The ground was prepared, he imagined, in the schools of rhetoric where students were trained to extemporize on fictitious topics, among them love themes in exotic settings. Eduard Schwartz, a specialist in historiography, preferred to see the novel as a result of a gradual development within that genre, from a political to an increasingly personal interest, and towards sensationalism, sentimentality, in one word: entertainment. Otmar Schissel von Fleschenberg argued for a succession of stages from short story via frame story with inserted short stories to episodic novel. Bruno Lavagnini emphasized the role of local legends as a source of material and point of departure for the first novelists. Others called attention to New Comedy, with its fictitious characters and love intrigues, as a close antecedent to the novels. Euripides' "romantic" dramas with a happy ending were also adduced. There was

---

[9] The appearance of Ben Edwin Perry, *The Ancient Romances: A Literary-Historical Account of Their Origins* (Berkeley, Calif., 1967), was an important stimulus for the development in ancient-novel studies that has gradually led to today's boom, although most scholars are now anxious to dissociate themselves from Perry's scenario. Cf. Bryan Reardon, "The Ancient Novel at the Time of Perry," *Ancient Narrative* 2 (2002).

[10] Perry, *Ancient Romances*, 175.

hardly a genre that did not lend itself to figuring, in one respect or another, as an "ancestor" of the new form.[11]

As a reaction to this kind of biological thinking among historians of Greek literature, Perry now proposed a different model of explanation. For him, the decisive driving force in the creation of any new genre is radical changes in social conditions and cultural outlook. He saw the Greek novel as the "latter-day epic for Everyman," a result of the cultural equalization and superficiality of the Hellenistic age. The closed tribal community that had fostered the epic and the classical city-state, with tragedy as its civic literary form, had given way to Hellenistic society, a vast conglomerate without common values or interests. The creation of the novel is looked upon as almost inevitable. The "spiritual and intellectual nomads" of late Hellenistic society needed this, the most formless of all so-called literary forms, the open form for the open society.

Both Perry's characterization of Hellenistic society and his view of the Greek novel as a vapid and trivial literary product would need (and have since received) much qualification. In this context, the interesting thing is that he sees fit to replace the (literary) autogenesis of the form with a (man-made) monogenesis. Yet if the social climate dominating in the vast Hellenistic world demanded this new form, might not the same idea have sprung up in more than one mind, so that there were several "inventors," a veritable polygenesis? This question of mono- or polygenesis—or something less clear-cut?—will underlie much of the discussion in this essay.[12]

Fragments and Reflections

So far, we have looked at just the five extant ideal novels—the "canon"—in isolation. Clearly, they alone are an insufficient basis for forming a theory of the emergence of the new form(s), not least because they all, or at least four of them, belong to the Imperial period, whereas there are good reasons to believe with Perry that the decisive period is late Hellenism.[13] One need not

---

[11] For the research history, see Simon Swain, "A Century and More of the Greek Novel," in Simon Swain, ed., *Oxford Readings in the Greek Novel* (Oxford, 1999), 3–35.

[12] The whole question of the novel's origins, once considered the only one worth pursuing with regard to this genre, is now bluntly dismissed as "an insoluble and vain enquiry" by E. L. Bowie and S. J. Harrison, "The Romance of the Novel," *Journal of Roman Studies* 83 (1993): 159–78, at 173.

[13] This early beginning is now doubted, on insufficient grounds, by several scholars, e.g., Swain, "A Century," referring to "current thinking on the dating of the novel" (27).

subscribe uncritically to Perry's parallels with the rise of the novel in eighteenth-century England, connected with increased literacy and leisure, to find the last century(ies) B.C. the likely formative period. It is an unduly reductionist view to believe that only what has survived has ever existed, seeing, in particular, that Hellenistic literature generally disappeared from the book market with the classicistic movement of the early empire, and has been lost ever since.

Luckily, it is not necessary only to theorize about this. There are fragments of a couple of other novels that may with some confidence be dated before the extant ones, and there are reflections of the new form in other literature. Let's begin with the latter category of *testimonia*.

Already in Neronian Rome, in the middle of the first century A.D., appear what looks like two satirical responses to the ideal Greek novel. Petronius's *Satyrica*, the fragmentarily transmitted Roman novel, seems to have had at least one of its satirical points directed against the naive idealism of the early Greek novels.[14] Like them, it features a couple of young Mediterranean travelers (from Massilia to Baiae/Puteoli and Croton in south Italy, possibly ending in Lampsacus on the Hellespont). But these are homosexual males, and chastity is replaced by promiscuity. Shipwrecks, attempted suicide, rhetorical lament, pursuing deities, and court proceedings are further common themes, though played in different keys. At about the same time, the Roman satirical poet Persius attacks popular fiction and, as a climax in his scornful denunciation of the prevalent literary taste, mentions a work entitled *Callirhoe*, which has to be Chariton's.[15] How long does it take for a new literary form to merit a parody (even in another language) or to foster a classic of its own? In the ancient literary system, we should probably reckon with (at least) several generations.

Another argument for the existence of more than has been directly transmitted may be deduced from the anonymous Latin novel *Historia Apollonii regis Tyri* (early third century A.D.?). It is more likely than not—though some would look upon such a claim as another instance of Hellenists' cultural imperialism[16]—that the *Historia Apollonii* is an adapted translation from a Greek original of unknown age. That book, to judge from the Latin version, was of a literary standard below any of the novels that have been transmitted in Greek; Xenophon's *Ephesiaka* comes closest but is still well structured in

---

[14] Cf. P. G. Walsh, *The Roman Novel*, 2nd ed. (London, 1995).

[15] Persius 1.134. See G. P. Goold in the introduction to his bilingual edition of Chariton, *Callirhoe* (Cambridge, Mass., 1995), 4–5.

[16] E.g., Gareth Schmeling in Schmeling, ed., *The Novel*, 529–31.

comparison. The *Historia Apollonii* is lacking in logic and uneven in composition and narrative style; nevertheless it had such qualities as a popular story that it experienced a successful afterlife in various languages in the Middle Ages. This would support the idea that there was a subliterary current of popular novels in Greek that never achieved even the inglorious status of those that survived. Another indication pointing in the same direction would be some of the so-called apocryphal Acts of Apostles, like *Paul and Thecla*, that may be suspected to have functioned as a Christian continuation of a popular tradition of unpretentious stories of love, travel, and adventure.[17]

These are, admittedly, speculations. But it is better to try to formulate hypotheses on the basis of all the odd traces that may be found than to be content with constructing one's building using exclusively the few blocks that have survived in their complete original shape. In the latter case, the power of selection exercised by the transmission process and its arbiters of taste is allowed to dictate unchallenged how we apprehend the ancient literary structure.

The most effective challenge, however, to the received picture does not come from internal differences within the canon or from indirect reflections in later literature, but from the fragments of lost novels. In the case of the novels, "fragments" almost always means papyrus fragments. While quotations in later literary works supply the majority of fragments in genres like historiography and biography, the novelists were not quoted by other ancient literates, at least not explicitly (the only exception is Antonius Diogenes). Some *testimonia*, it is true, have come down through Byzantine lexica and commentaries, and the Byzantines (some of whom were not afraid of admitting that they read novels) have also supplied us with epitomes of a couple of lost ancient novels and illuminating critical discussion of others;[18] but the papyrus fragments are our primary peep-hole into what lay behind the facade.[19]

---

[17] See Jan N. Bremmer, "The Novel and the Apocryphal Acts: Place, Time and Readership," in H. Hofmann and M. Zimmerman, eds., *Groningen Colloquia on the Novel* (Groningen, 1998), 9:157–80.

[18] For critical discussion, see Michael Psellus, *The Essays on Euripides and George of Pisidia and on Heliodorus and Achilles Tatius*, A. R. Dyck, ed., Byzantina Vindobonensia, no. 16 (Vienna, 1986).

[19] All the fragments discussed in this essay are to be found, with translation and commentary, in Susan A. Stephens and John J. Winkler, eds., *Ancient Greek Novels: The Fragments* (Princeton, N.J., 1995). Cf. also the indispensible critical survey by J. R. Morgan, "On the Fringes of the Canon: Work on the Fragments of Ancient Greek Fiction 1936–1994," in Wolfgang Haase and Hildegard Temporini, eds., *Aufstieg und Niedergang der Römischen Welt* (Berlin, 1998), vol. II.34.4, pp. 3,293–390.

Not-So-Ideal Greek Novels

For a long time, the fragments were duly classified according to which of the extant novels they resembled most and interpreted within that framework; a fragment that did not resemble any of them enough, risked being excluded from the category "novel (or romance) fragment" and relegated to "historiography" or simply "prose fragment." This critical *circulus vitiosus* was broken, if not earlier, with the publication in 1969 of fairly extensive papyrus fragments of a work that, though in some ways alarmingly untypical of a "Greek novel," could still hardly be denied that label. This was Lollianus's *Phoinikika*, and the papyri—one fragment from a papyrus role, long known, and one codex fragment newly identified—were written around A.D. 200, the novel itself most probably in the preceding century.[20]

Human sacrifice and cannibalism as part of rustic initiation rites, described in unemotional factual prose, are among the surprising ingredients of this story:

> Meanwhile another man, who was naked, walked by, wearing a crimson loincloth, and throwing the body of the *pais* (boy or servant?) on its back, he cut it up, and tore out its heart and placed it upon the fire. Then, he took up [the cooked heart] and sliced it up to the middle. And on the surface [of the slices] he sprinkled [barley groats] and wet it with oil; and when he had sufficiently prepared them, [he gave them to the] initiates, and those who held (a slice?) [he ordered] to swear in the blood of the heart that they would neither give up nor betray [———], not [even if they are led off to prison], nor yet it they be tortured nor yet if [their eyes] be gouged out.[21]

There is, it is true, a similar sacrificial episode in Achilles Tatius (3.15); but there, the macabre spectacle is described through the horrified eyes of the hero and is later revealed to have been a fake sacrifice. The reader must already have suspected so much, for the would-be victim is the heroine herself, and the incident occurs less than halfway through the novel. As far as can be seen from the fragments, no similar miracle saved the nameless boy (?) in Lollianus's novel.

Promiscuous sex is another topic. One Androtimus, who has just vomited

---

[20] After prepublication in 1969, the definitive edition is Albert Henrichs, ed., *Die "Phoinikika" des Lollianos: Fragmente eines neuen griechischen Romans*, Papyrologische Texte und Abhandlungen, no. 14 (Bonn, 1972).

[21] Stephens and Winkler, *Ancient Greek Novels*, 339.

out on the table the human heart he had been forced to eat, is also a witness
to the brigands' after-dinner pleasures:

> When all had passed in and there was no longer anyone outside, closing the
> [————], they sang, drank, had intercourse with the women in full view of
> Androtimus. [Some] slept exhausted, while the eleven [stationed] by the
> corpses did not drink very much—just enough to get warm (cool off?)
> [————] When it was midnight, first they stripped the bodies of the dead
> and not even leaving the band with which the girl bound her breasts; then
> hoisting them up over the windows, they let them down into [————].[22]

Tone and topics no doubt come closest to Petronius's and Apuleius's novels
among those we possess from antiquity. The neat distinction previously
made between the "ideal Greek" and "realistic Roman" novel is proven to
be (at least) unduly generalized.[23]

That this was a full-length novel is indicated both by the genre-typical title given in the codex fragment, *Phoinikika* [*Phoenician Tales*], and by the
fact that the surviving text happens to include two different book breaks,
between books 1 and 2, and between book 2 (or higher) and 3 (or higher).
The same does not apply to another fragment of similar type, usually referred to as *Iolaus*, after the name of the main character in the surviving
episode. It was first published, in 1971, under the title "A Greek *Satyricon?*"
because both content (mock initiation for erotic purposes) and form (mixture of prose and verse) are reminiscent of Petronius's novel.[24] But it is in the
nature of papyrus fragments that they only seldom provide enough clues to
judge the larger structure of the work to which they belong, unless they are
connected with a formally well-defined literary genre. Prudently, Peter Parsons in his definitive edition of the same fragment resorted to a more neutral
title, "Narrative about Iolaus."[25] If *Iolaus* was in fact a shorter composition,
the find is not so sensational; we already possessed, in much fuller form, one
such comic-realistic, erotically explicit story in Greek, *Lucius or the Ass* (second century A.D.), a condensed version of the story on which the Roman
Apuleius based his novel *Metamorphoses*.[26]

[22] Ibid., 343.
[23] Cf. Alessandro Barchiesi, "Traces of Greek Narrative and the Roman Novel: A Survey," in S.
J. Harrison, ed., *Oxford Readings in the Roman Novel* (Oxford, 1999), 124–41.
[24] Peter Parsons, "A Greek *Satyricon?*" *Bulletin of the Institute of Classical Studies* 18 (1971):
53–68.
[25] Peter Parsons, "Narrative about Iolaus," in *The Oxyrhynchus Papyri* (London, 1974), 42:34–41.
[26] Cf. Walsh, *The Roman Novel*.

This is perhaps enough to demonstrate that the ideal novel as known through the canon of five was indeed not alone on the market, and that "erotic" as a label for ancient Greek novels may sometimes correspond more to the modern understanding of the term than to what Rudolf Hercher meant when he edited the *Erotici Scriptores Graeci* in 1858–59. Susan Stephens, who lumps the *Phoinikika, Ioalus,* and a couple of other fragments together as deriving from "Criminal-Satiric Novels," interestingly suggests that Julian the Apostate, in a famous letter where he warns pagan priests against reading novels (89.301B), is in fact thinking primarily of this erotic type.[27] He says, and this is one of the very few references to the existence of novels that we find in the whole of ancient literature, "As for those fictions (*plasmata*) in the form of history (*en historias eidei*) that have been reported by earlier writers, we should renounce them—love stories (*erōtikas hypotheseis*) and all that kind of stuff."[28] Julian has first warned against the licentiousness of Archilochus, Hipponax, and Old Comedy, and when he now proceeds to the novels—lacking a generic term he has to be loosely descriptive—it is indeed natural to think that it is vulgarity and obscenity he denounces, rather than chaste love stories or "fictions" as such.[29] But it has not seemed so to anyone who has been accustomed to regard the ideal type as *the* Greek novel and taken for granted that he referred to them. Saying "in the form of history" he need not mean more than "prose narratives of book length"; that he should warn specifically against "historical novels" of Chariton's type is unlikely.

Another piece of late-antique evidence that now seems to fall into place concerns Iamblichus's *Babylōniaka*. The plot of this novel, written in the reign of Marcus Aurelius, is known chiefly through the detailed epitome that Photius, twice Patriarch of Constantinople in the ninth century, produced for his *Bibliotheke* (cod. 94). While the five extant ideal novels consist of five to ten books, or seventy to three hundred printed pages, this one ran to sixteen (Photius) or even thirty-nine books (the Byzantine lexicon *Suda*). Some of its thrilling contents, as cataloged in Photius's epitome, are vividly summarized by Susan Stephens and Jack Winkler:

---

[27] Susan Stephens, "Fragments of Lost Novels," in Schmeling, ed., *The Novel*, 669n.36.

[28] Trans. adapted from Morgan, "The Greek Novel," 132.

[29] Though he first contrasts the novels to "narratives [. . .] about deeds that have actually been done," he soon returns to what looks like a denunciation of erotic themes: "For words breed a certain sort of disposition in the soul, and little by little it arouses desires" (trans. Wilmer Cave Wright, *The Works of the Emperor Julian* [Cambridge, Mass., 1913], 2:327). The influence from Christian ethics is evident.

The hero and heroine roam throughout the Near East pursued by two eunuchs whose noses and ears have been cut off. They encounter bees with poisoned honey, a Lesbian princess of Egypt, a cannibalistic brigand, look-alike brothers named Tigris and Euphrates who happen to be exact doubles for the hero, and a rather dignified farmer's daughter whom the heroine forces to sleep with an executioner who is really a priest of Aphrodite who helps his son Euphrates break jail by dressing in the farmer's daughter's clothes. Considering the emotional tension that is constantly breaking out between the hero and heroine, culminating in her leaving him to marry another man before their final reconciliation, it is a wonder that anyone could ever refer to this work as an "ideal romance."[30]

True. We may even go one step further by trying to look behind Photius's epitome. True to his notorious interest in paradoxical phenomena and events, Photius is rather detailed about the exotic elements of the plot (the bees, for instance, 74a40). He patiently follows the countless twists and turns of the couple's adventures and conscientiously summarizes the subplots as well, where such occur. The erotic topics, on the other hand, are passed over in a rather perfunctory fashion: "the slave who is her lover and murderer," "at the beginning of their lovemaking," "how she consorted with Mesopotamia," and "she slept with Euphrates."[31] Does this reticence really reflect the true character of the novel?

It may be so. Iamblichus may well have told all this in as unerotic a manner as Xenophon of Ephesus. The extant literal fragments of the text are not particularly devoted to sexual description. Photius himself says that Iamblichus is more shameless (*aischros*) and indecent (*anaidēs*) than Heliodorus, but less so than Achilles Tatius (73b24). This would mean about the level of Xenophon. But there is a piece of evidence that points in another direction. The medical writer Theodorus Priscianus (ca. A.D. 400) recommends reading the novels of Iamblichus and similar authors as a cure for men who suffer from impotence (2.11.34).[32] This is the reverse, then, of Julian's advice to his priests. Given the recovered fragments of the *Phoinikika* and *Iolaus*, where scenes of deflowering, promiscuous sex, and

---

[30] Stephens and Winkler, *Ancient Greek Novels*, 179.

[31] Phot. *Bibl.* 76b10, 76b31, 77a20, 78b38, trans. Stephens and Winkler, *Ancient Greek Novels*, 195–98.

[32] Uti sane (sc. convenit) lectionibus animum ad delicias pertrahentibus, ut sunt Amphipolitae Philippi aut Herodiani aut certe Syrii Iamblichi, vel ceteris suaviter amatorias fabulas describentibus (p. 133.9–12 Rose).

clever seduction throng in the few surviving pages, it is easier to fill out the hints and possible omissions in Photius's epitome and let Theodorus's prescription make real sense. The *Babylōniaka*, then, while on the face of it adhering to the love-travel-adventure scheme, may have been another of those texts that negate the very concept of the ideal novel.

Parthenope: Doomed to Maidenhood?

So far we have mainly explored the diversity of novel production in the first two centuries of the Imperial period. It is time to try to reach further back in time, toward what has traditionally been called the "origins" of the Greek novel. Fragments, of various kind and age, will again be the principal guide, beginning with an inscribed potsherd, an ostracon, from Egypt. Its Greek text may be understood thus:

> "Are you [. . .], Parthenope, [he said], and forgetful of your Metiochus?
> For my part, from the day you [went away], I [. . .] and [can]not sleep, my
> eyes wide open as if glued with gum."[33]

It names the hero and heroine of a Greek novel otherwise known through some papyrus fragments and some references in later (mainly Byzantine) texts. On account of its letter forms, it has recently been given a fairly precise date, the first decades of the first century A.D.[34] Whether this ostracon is a school excercise, a private copy of a memorable passage of the novel, a free variation on a popular theme, or a quotation from a stage performance based on the novel, it necessarily presupposes that the novel in question had, by the beginning of the first century A.D., acquired a certain reputation and reached Egypt. In other words, provided the date of the ostracon is reasonably accurate, it would probably have already been written in the late Hellenistic period.[35]

---

[33] All the translations in this section are from Tomas Hägg and Bo Utas, *The Virgin and her Lover: Fragments of an Ancient Greek Novel and a Persian Epic Poem*, Brill Studies in Middle Eastern Literatures, 30 (Leiden, 2003). Most of the Greek texts, with English translation, commentary, and full bibliography, are also available in Stephens and Winkler, *Ancient Greek Novels*, 72–100, 497–99.

[34] Guglielmo Cavallo as quoted in Antonio Stramaglia, "Fra 'consumo' e 'impegno': Usi didattici della narrativa nel mondo antico," in Oronzo Pecere and Antonio Stramaglia, eds., *La letteratura di consumo nel mondo greco-latino* (Cassino, 1996), 123–24.

[35] A date in the middle of the first century B.C. had already been suggested, on linguistic and cultural-historical grounds, by Albrecht Dihle, "Zur Datierung des Metiochos-Romans," *Würzburger Jahrbücher für die Altertumswissenschaft* n.f. 4 (1978): 47–55.

This novel retained its popularity for hundreds of years. Papyrus fragments of the second and third centuries A.D. indicate that it continued to be read and copied. Pantomimic dance performances, exploiting the sentimental and tragic potentials of the plot, were staged at various places in the empire. Around A.D. 200, a wealthy man of Antioch chose to decorate a floor in his summer house at the falls of the Orontes with figures from the novel, while another man manifested the same literary inclinations in the twin towns of Zeugma on the Euphrates. And, as has recently been discovered, the novel survived long enough to serve, in the eleventh century, as the basis for a Persian epic poem by 'Unsurī the court poet of Sultan Mahmūd of Ghazna (in modern Afghanistan). Yet, in spite of its obvious popularity, it has not come down to us through the ordinary channels of medieval textual transmission. Consequently, we have to use all the sources mentioned, plus the Byzantine *testimonia*, in attempts to reconstruct its original plot and character. How this has been done in the past hundred years is revelatory for the way scholars have conceived of the genre of the ideal Greek novel, so the three principal stages in this modern recovery of the novel deserve a closer examination.[36]

When the first papyrus fragment, containing the proper names Metiochus and Parthenope, was published in 1895, the connection was immediately made with the Byzantine scholar Eusthatius's reference to an ancient love story with a hero and heroine thus named. It was also recognized that the two lovers were here engaged in a discussion of the nature of Eros. First it was supposed that the argument took place in a school of rhetoric—an idea no doubt inspired by the view prevailing since Erwin Rohde's seminal book of 1876, *Der griechische Roman und seine Vorläufer*, that the ideal Greek novel itself, as a literary genre, was a creation of the rhetorical schools of the early Roman Empire. Later it was instead suggested that the couple were discussing in front of a picture of Eros, in its turn a notion based on the important role of erotic paintings at the beginnings of Achilles Tatius's and Longus's novels, before the narrative proper starts. Both suggestions lacked support in the actual text and were to be proven wrong. They show how this novel was assimilated into the current view of the Greek novel, largely formed on the three "sophistic" specimens (and systematically disregarding the earlier ones by Chariton and Xenophon of Ephesus).

It was also taken for granted that Metiochus and Parthenope were private individuals with purely fictitious names, as seemed to be the case with all the protagonists of the five extant novels. Only Bruno Lavagnini, true to

---

[36] Details and references in Hägg and Utas, *The Virgin*, Chap. 1.

his own view of the origins of the genre, sought for connections with the Parthenopes known from Neapolitan and Samian local traditions.[37] The surprise was proportionally great when Herwig Maehler in 1976, by combining papyrus fragments then housed in East and West Berlin, respectively, succeeded in showing that this Parthenope was in fact the daughter of Polycrates, the sixth-century tyrant of Samos, and that Metiochus was the son of the Athenian general Miltiades.[38] So this was a historical novel, it was concluded, with Chariton's as its closest cognate. While Chariton had attached his love story to Thucydides, locating it in Syracuse after the defeat of the Athenian expedition in 413 and making his heroine the daughter of the Syracusan general Hermocrates, the author of *Metiochus and Parthenope* (as it was automatically called, without actual support in the ancient sources) had chosen Herodotus; for hero and heroine both appear already in his *History*, though Polycrates' daughter does so anonymously.

A date close to Chariton, that is, in the late Hellenistic or early Imperial period, was now generally accepted; and with the support of Eusthatius and Byzantine scholia, a plot similar to Chariton's was imagined. The discussion of the nature of Eros was shown to have taken place, not in a classroom or in front of a painting, but in a symposium at Polycrates' court on Samos—so, in fact, none of the extant novels but rather Plato's *Symposium*, provided the right association. The scene was located close to the beginning of the novel: the youngsters had just met and fallen in love, but they were soon to be separated and tossed around the Mediterranean in search of each other. A scholiast's reference to "Parthenope of Samos, who searching for her husband came to Anaxilaus" indicated that the tyrant of Rhegium in south Italy would be one of the stations on her way. Other parts of her itinerary were glimpsed as the scholiast added: "Parthenope is so named because she preserved her virginity (*parthenia*) in spite of falling into the hands of many men. From Phrygia, having fallen in love with Metiochos and cut off her hair, she came to Campania and settled there."[39] Another papyrus, tentatively attributed to the same novel, suggested that she passed Corfu as well. A happy ending of the usual type was taken for granted.

The normality of this reconstructed plot was, however, to be called into

---

[37] In an article written in 1921, republished in Bruno Lavagnini, *Studi sul romanzo greco* (Messina, 1950), 85n.3, 88 (suggesting a novel called *Kampanika*).

[38] Herwig Maehler, "Der Metiochus-Parthenope-Roman," *Zeitschrift für Papyrologie und Epigraphik* 23 (1976): 1–20.

[39] Scholion on Dionysius Periegetes v. 358, in K. Müller, ed., *Geographici Graeci Minores* (Paris, 1861), 2:445.

question by the discovery that the Persian epic poem *Vāmiq u 'Adhrā* ["The Ardent Lover and the Virgin"], of which a substantial manuscript fragment had been published in 1967,[40] was based on *Metiochus and Parthenope*. This now makes it possible to discern, or surmise, further parts of the plot; and they do not always turn out to have been predictable.

First, Parthenope's fate seems to have been more closely tied to the historical events and the change of rulers on her native Samos than was expected. Following Polycrates' death, she is imprisoned by his successor, the tyrant's former agent Maeandrius, and it seems that she has later also experienced her uncle Syloson as ruler of Samos. Chariton's attachment to history had appeared much looser than that. Yet it should be remembered that some of the less conventional elements of his plot have by some been explained as corresponding to (partly unknown) details of Syracusan internal history or legend.[41] Thus, when Chariton's hero and heroine are steering toward their happy homecoming, Callirhoe's infant son by Chaereas is against all expectation left behind in Miletus with her second husband Dionysius, and the boy's later return to Syracuse as a married man is foreshadowed (8.4.5–6). This constitutes a loose end in the novel and is perhaps best explained as reminiscences of a historical (or legendary) course of events. A corresponding closeness to actual history may in a more fundamental way have influenced the plot of *Metiochus and Parthenope*, making some lost parts of the novel perhaps irretrievably lost.

In particular, this may be true for its end. Parthenope, formed on *parthenos*, "virgin," is a telling name for Polycrates' daughter whom her father, according to Herodotus (3.124), condemned to a long period of maidenhood because she opposed his intention personally to meet Oroetes, the Persian satrap of Sardis. (That the scholiast thinks she is so called because she spurned unwanted suitors, is a fair guess on his side, based on Charicleia and her like.) Thus we cannot be sure that the novel really provided a happy ending in the manner of the others; perhaps she remained a virgin? We do not know, it is true, how 'Unsurī's epic ended either; but later adaptations of the story in Muslim literature exhibit a heroine who died a virgin.[42] None of the quotations in Persian lexica deriving from *Vāmiq u 'Adhrā* appears to be

---

[40] Muhammad Shafi, *Wāmiq-o-Adhrā of 'Unsurī*, Shahanshah of Iran's Grant Publications Series, 3 (Lahore, 1967).

[41] Cf. Consuelo Ruiz-Montero, "Chariton von Aphrodisias: Ein Überblick," in Haase and Temporini, eds., *Aufstieg und Niedergang der Römischen Welt* (Berlin, 1994), vol. II.34.2, pp. 1,006–54, at 1015–16.

[42] Cf. Bo Utas, "Did 'Adhrā Remain a Virgin?" *Orientalia Suecana* 33–35 (1984–86): 429–41.

culled from an impressive happy ending. Many quotations, on the other hand, are from martial contexts, so a war in which the hero—and perhaps the manly heroine as well—played an active part, may have led up to the end, much as the case is in Chariton. But that Metiochus really got his beloved after triumphing in the war, as Chaereas did, is far from certain. We may find ourselves in a period prior to the generic stereotypes that governed the extant five novels. Perhaps we are closer to the kind of romantic love story with a tragic ending that the Athenian Xenophon inserted as a subplot in his *Cyropaedia*:[43] in short installments, he tells the story of Pantheia, the faithful and loving wife, who takes her own life beside the corpse of her fallen husband Abradatas.

The beginning may also have deviated from the later uniformity. The novels that seem to offer the closest resemblance to *Metiochus and Parthenope* are all one-generation stories: the action starts when the hero and heroine have reached marriageable age and ends a few years later when they settle at home after their travels and tribulations. The atypical Longus is atypical in this respect too by commencing at the moment when the herdsmen find the exposed babies who are to grow up as Daphnis and Chloe. *Metiochus and Parthenope*, to judge from *Vāmiq u ʿAdhrā* (the reservation is necessary), was still more radical, taking as its point of departure the magnificent preparations for the wedding of Parthenope's parents, Polycrates of Samos and his bride. The wedding feast itself, the subsequent conception and birth of the heroine, and her education in various martial and liberal arts then form the first part of the novel, before the love story proper begins with the arrival of Metiochus on the island. The kind of family "prehistory" that Heliodorus incorporates in retrospect and the others lack, thus seems to have been linearly narrated in the first part of *Metiochus and Parthenope*.

The family history in question is, significantly, that of the heroine. In the Greek fragments and *testimonia* of the novel, hero and heroine seem to play equally important roles. From the Persian material—the manuscript fragment and lexical quotations as well as a summary elsewhere of part of the plot—it becomes clear that everything in fact revolves round Parthenope. Metiochus is just her preferred suitor. Before he arrives on Samos together with a trusted friend, only so much has been told about his family background as to explain why he fled from his father's home on the Chersonesus: his stepmother Hegesipyle, the Thracian woman whom Miltiades had married, machinated against him in favor of her own children. Reciprocated love at first sight, in front of the temple of Hera, is among the topoi that this novel

---

[43] On this pre-novel novel, see James Tatum, *Xenophon's Imperial Fiction: On "The Education of Cyrus,"* (Princeton, N.J., 1989).

shares with most of the others we know; but its continuation at Polycrates' court is much dependent on Parthenope's relationship with her parents and old teacher. When her parents have finally understood their lovesick daughter's predicament (another future topos) and promised to let her marry Metiochus, her mother suddenly dies and her father changes his mind (another untypical turn of events). Then, apparently, follows Polycrates' fatal journey to Oroetes at Magnesia in Asia Minor, where he is murdered as—according to Herodotus (3.125)—his daughter had foretold. Imprisonment and separation come next, and of Metiochus we hear little more. The ostracon quoted above, though, may give a glimpse of his lonely longing for his beloved.

The Evidence of the Titles

From what we have deduced about the character and emphasis of the novel, there is every reason to believe that it was originally simply called *Parthenope*. Likewise, Chariton's novel was most probably called *Callirhoe* rather than *Chaereas and Callirhoe*, the name it carries in the medieval *codex unicus*.[44] Chariton too is most interested in his heroine—in contrast to the more symmetrical *Ephesiaka* among the earlier novels—and his last words are, "So ends the story I have composed about Callirhoe."[45] The stereotyped double-name titles, with the hero's name first, were no doubt applied to these two novels later. In *Parthenope*'s case, the dual-name title is in fact just a modern guess; but the circumstance that the Persian epic poem was called *Vāmiq u 'Adhrā*, with 'Adhrā meaning "virgin," as the equivalent to Parthenope, makes it likely that its Greek model later circulated under the name *Metiochus and Parthenope*. Renaming, then, was part of the process in which the genre, when consolidated in the Imperial period, was retroactively made to include earlier compositions as well.

In fact, no titles consisting of the names of two lovers are recorded from the Classical and Hellenistic periods.[46] No epic, tragedy, or comedy carried such a double-title; there is no *Perseus and Andromeda*, no *Jason and Medea*. The common practice, if personal names were used at all for reference, was to choose the name of just one of the protagonists. In Hellenistic love elegy, this habit continued, and the female name seems to have been preferred.

---

44 Cf. B. P. Reardon, "Chariton," in Schmeling, ed., *The Novel*, 309–35, at 315–17.

45 Char. 8.8.16, trans. G. P. Goold, ed., Chariton, *Callirhoe*.

46 See the useful survey in Wilhelm Schmid's "Anhang" in Erwin Rohde, (appendix), *Der griechische Roman und seine Vorläufer*, 3rd ed. (Leipzig, 1914), 616–18; cf. also Otto Weinreich, *Der griechische Liebesroman* (Zurich, 1962), 28–29, 60.

Parthenius's prose compendium of love stories, the *Erōtika pathēmata* (first century B.C.),[47] features a number of heroines of myth and legend who lend their names to typical love plots. We are then close in time to *Parthenope* and *Callirhoe*, whatever their exact dates, and it is no wonder that writers of novels used the same formula.

Writers of novels—or *some* writers of novels. It may be that the traditional titles of the novels have further clues to offer in an exploration of diversity and plurality in the early history of the novel. Titles of the type *Daphnis and Chloe* or *Leucippe and Clitophon* do not reign supreme in the Imperial period. On the contrary, to judge from the lists in the Byzantine lexica, the *Suda* in the first place, many novels seem to have circulated under an *ethnikon* of the type already encountered in the *Phoinikika* and Iamblichus's *Babylōniaka*.[48] A combination of both kinds of title also occurs in the manuscript tradition, as when Xenophon's novel is called *Ta kata Anthian kai Abrokomēn Ephesiaka* in the *codex unicus* (while the *Suda* favors just *Ephesiaka*). Heliodorus ends with a similarly compound title: "So concludes the book of Aithiopian Tales [*Aithiopika*] about Theagenes and Chariclea." On the other hand, *Callirhoe* is never referred to as *Sikelika* (or similarly), nor is there any indication that *Parthenope* was ever called *Samiaka*. Is this titular manifold perhaps an indication of the genre's polygenesis?

Now, the geographical type of title was used for several different kinds of works, apart from these novels. There were historical epics called *Iōnika*, *Messēniaka*, and so on. In prose, regional and local histories naturally often carried such a name. More specifically, Ctesias's *Persika* (ca. 400 B.C.E.), in twenty-three books, narrated stories from Persian history in an entertaining fashion, probably using oral sources. Aristides' notorious *Milēsiaka* (ca. 100 B.C.E.) was a collection of lascivious stories;[49] Apuleius, at the beginning of his *Metamorphoses*, states that he will "weave together different tales of this Milesian mode of story-telling [*sermone isto Milesio*]";[50] and the tale of "The

---

[47] See J. L. Lightfoot, ed., Parthenius of Nicaea, *The Poetical Fragments and the "Erōtika Pathēmata,"* (Oxford, 1999).

[48] Henrichs, ed., *Die "Phoinikika" des Lollianos*, 11–12, contends that the type *Phoinikika* dominated throughout antiquity and that both single and double names are a Byzantine invention; this is to dismiss the evidence of papyri and medieval manuscripts as well as the concluding sentences of Chariton and Heliodoros. H. Morales in T. Whitmarsh, trans., Achilles Tatius, *Leucippe and Clitophon*, xvii, follows Henrichs (ibid.) in arguing that *Phoinikika* is likely to have been the original title of Achilles' novel; there is no manuscript (or other) evidence supporting that suggestion.

[49] On the implications of its title, cf. Stephen J. Harrison, "The Milesian Tales and the Roman Novel," in Hofmann and Zimmerman, eds., *Groningen Colloquia*, 9: 61–64.

[50] Trans. P. G. Walsh, ed., Apuleius, *The Golden Ass* (Oxford, 1995), 1.

Ephesian Widow" that Petronius inserted in his *Satyrica* is regarded as typically "Milesian." Incidentally, his title *Satyrica* itself is no doubt best understood as coined on the Greek novels' geographical model. Another play on the geographical type occurs when Longus's *Daphnis and Chloe* is called *Poimenika* ["Pastoral Tales"] in a couple of manuscripts, in competition with the standard coinage *Lesbiaka*. This other use, though diverse, may perhaps aid in grasping the implications of the geographical titles as applied to some of the novels. But we need first to define the nature of a complete text surviving under such a title. Leaving the fragments for the present, I will turn to Xenophon's *Ephesiaka*.

Ephesian Tales: The Formulaic and the Episodic

Anyone who reads *Callirhoe* and the *Ephesiaka* in succession, will have a curiously mixed experience. The two novels are similar enough in plot and specific motifs, or combinations of motifs, to have forced most scholars to conclude that one imitates the other. On the other hand, they are so different in style, composition, and attitude that one doubts that any one author has read the other or, at least, appreciated what he read so much as to make it his model. Did Chariton perhaps decide to "improve" upon Xenophon (if that should be the correct order), or was Xenophon poor enough a writer to misunderstand and piteously misuse the material he was so happy to take over?

The *Ephesiaka* is a short text (seventy printed pages), but packed with narrative material. For large stretches, the tempo is accordingly high; many cities and countries are seen flashing by; forty-four characters are introduced, and thirty-three of them are given a name, but most immediately disappear from sight when the short episode in which they take part is over and the hero or heroine hastens to his/her next stop. The style is mostly unadorned, and a striking repetitiousness characterizes both themes and phraseology. A typical sequence sounds like this:

> But Habrocomes remained immured in the prison (in Phoenicia), and
> Antheia was taken to Syria, along with Leucon and Rhode (their servants).
> When those in Manto's party reached Antioch, which was Moeris' country,
> she dealt maliciously with Rhode, and hated Antheia bitterly. She gave orders
> at once that Rhode and Leucon should be loaded on a ship and sold in some
> place remote from the Syrian country. Antheia she planned to join to a slave,
> and at that to the vilest sort, a rustic goatherd; this she thought a suitable

vengeance. And so she summoned the goatherd, whose name was Lampon, and delivered Antheia to his hands and bade him take her to wife, and she ordered him to use force if Antheia should be unwilling. Antheia was carried off to the country to cohabit with the goatherd. But when she arrived where Lampon kept his goats she fell at his knees and begged him to pity her and preserve her chastity. She explained who she was, and told of her high birth, her husband, her captivity. When Lampon heard these things he took pity upon the girl and swore that he would verily keep her chaste and bade her take heart. And so Anthia lived at the goatherd's in the country, lamenting Habrocomes all the while. Apsyrtus (Manto's father), rummaging through the cubicle where Habrocomes had lived before his punishment, came upon Manto's letter to Habrocomes. He recognized the writing, and realized that Habrocomes had been unjustly punished. He ordered that [. . .][51]

In another novel, this material would have sufficed to fill a book or two. In particular, the monologues and dialogues just reported here would have been developed into scenes, with their emotional and rhetorical potentials fully exploited.

The peculiarities of the text have led not only to almost universal condemnation of the author's literary talents (as always, critics have considered the three sophistic novels as the norm), but also to various efforts at explanation. The unevenness in descriptive detail and rhetorical elaboration has prompted the theory that this work may be an abbreviation of an originally fuller novel, more homogeneous and (in short) "better."[52] Others have spoken of the folktale character of the novel or suggested that it had an oral background in the practice of the *aretalogoi*, tellers of miracle stories in cultic contexts, or of other professional storytellers. Repetition and formulism have also been thought to indicate what kind of audience the first novelists addressed, people more used to listening than to reading, and thus helped in their consumption by simplicity and a certain degree of predictability.[53]

A recent study by James O'Sullivan has revealed the extent to which the *Ephesiaka* is formulaic at the thematic as well as the phraseological level:

---

[51] Xen. Eph. 2.9.1–10.1. Trans. Moses Hadas in William Hansen, ed., *Anthology of Ancient Greek Popular Literature* (Bloomington, Ind., 1998), p. 22.

[52] See the discussion in Tomas Hägg, "The 'Ephesiaka' of Xenophon Ephesius—Original or Epitome?" in my *Parthenope: Selected Studies in Ancient Greek Fiction*, L. B. Mortensen and T. Eide, eds. (Copenhagen, 2004), 159–98.

[53] For the last explanation (and references to the others), see Tomas Hägg, "Orality, Literacy, and the "Readership" of the Early Greek Novel," in Roy Eriksen, ed., *Contexts of Pre-Novel Narrative* (Berlin, 1994), 47–81.

The *Ephesiaca* is to a great extent a complex of a fairly narrow repertoire of recurrent simple happenings and concepts. These are used as building-blocks in the story, sometimes singly, sometimes in varying combinations, often in more or less standard and extensive combinations that go to make up those scenes, or themes, that recur in the romance. These building-blocks, which I shall call "theme-elements," are regularly expressed with the aid of more or less stereotyped word-combinations or at least marked by recurrent standard keywords. Thus the romance consists largely of repetitions at various levels: of verbal formulae, of theme-elements, and of themes (or scenes).[54]

Some parts, in particular book 1 and the beginning of book 2, are less formulaic in character, because, as O'Sullivan explains, they "have subject-matter that for the most part does not recur within the *Ephesiaca*" (ibid.): the couple meet, fall in love, are married, and so forth. It is the episodic structure of the rest, with a long succession of single events built up of a few recurring theme-elements (robber attack, erotic persuasion, cruel punishment, etc.), that constitutes the breeding ground for the linguistic formulae. Though seventy pages cannot house anything approaching the Homeric store of formulae, and though formulae in prose function differently from those developed within a metrically fixed form, O'Sullivan makes a convincing case for his main conclusion: the *Ephesiaka* has a background in oral composition.

This does not necessarily mean that its author was himself a practitioner of oral storytelling. We need not suppose that this novel was first told orally, then committed to writing. But, like no other extant novel, the *Ephesiaka* bears the mark of a popular, nonliterary beginning. And it is not only the formulaic structure that reveals its otherness: "Xenophon's language abounds in elements of an un-attic *Volkssprache* (the syntax in general being extremely simple and unperiodic), his work is strikingly without the texture of literary allusion typical of the other novels, and it is very strongly characterized by compositional techniques and weaknesses that link it to oral as opposed to literary practice."[55]

O'Sullivan is inclined to look for the origin of the whole genre in this same direction and to place Xenophon before Chariton and the others, at least typologically. Yet a solution that frees us from the idea of a single line

---

[54] O'Sullivan, *Xenophon of Ephesus*, 30.

[55] Ibid., 98. On Xenophon's style, see also Consuelo Ruiz-Montero, "Xenophon von Ephesos: Ein Überblick," in Haase and Temporini, eds., *Aufstieg und Niedergang der Römischen Welt* (Berlin 1994), vol. II.34.2, pp. 1,088–1,138, at 1,114–19.

of development seems preferable. If Xenophon represents oral and popular narrative, Chariton is altogether more bookish and literary, writing in what may be characterized as a historiographic style. It is true that his novel too exhibits a repertoire of repetitive material (recapitulations, in particular), but it has much less formulaic expression (there is some, for instance, in the transitions between different lines of action). Rather than viewing this as representative of a later stage in a development from popular to literary fiction, we should—with *Parthenope* in mind as well—consider the possibility that Chariton and Xenophon are exponents for two parallel novel traditions, one of bookish and one of popular origin.

Instead of a common origin with successive stages of development and gradually diverging lines, we might envisage convergent lines arriving from different directions. Chariton and Xenophon are fundamentally different (literary/popular) because they represent different lines, but superficially similar (sharing some distinct strings of motifs) because the lines have approached one another. This is not, of course, to say that Chariton's type of novel would have lacked earlier contact with popular themes. Like historiography proper (and epic, drama, elegy, etc.), and presumably to a greater extent than the other genres, it drew narrative material from popular sources; but that material was differently molded and put into a different kind of narrative framework than in Xenophon and his oral predecessors.

One external indication of their different origins, then, would be the different kinds of title they bear. The psychological, emotional, and individual-centred type of narrative that Chariton represents would choose as title a personal name, preferably (but maybe not exclusively) that of the heroine. The episodic travel-and-adventure story displaying a wider range of characters and places and with more stereotyped lovers in the lead would traditionally be called by an *ethnikon* in the collective neuter plural. The episodic structure in itself, the character of a "collection of stories" in a narrative framework, it would have had in common with other categories of works carrying the same kind of title, like Ctesias's *Persika* and Aristides' *Milēsiaka*. As we have already seen, such a description fits eminently the *Babylōniaka*, and presumably the *Phoinikika* as well. Two different lines have tentatively emerged. To find more, I turn again to the papyrus fragments.

Oriental Heroes: Ninus and Sesonchosis

The novels of Chariton and Xenophon are firmly rooted in Greek soil. Egypt is used as an exotic playground in the *Ephesiaka*, as is Persia in

Callirhoe, but the main traveling takes place between Greek cities of the Mediterranean, and the main characters as well as the other good guys participating in the action are reassuringly Hellenic (as are, to be sure, some of the villains). Two of the three sophistic novelists, it is true, were themselves non-Greek: Achilles Tatius (according to the *Suda*) was a native of Alexandria, and Heliodorus in his envoi poses as a Phoenician from Emesa (while Longus may have been a Roman). Iamblichus, according to a marginal note in one of the manuscripts of Photius's *Bibliotheke*, was a Syrian. Still, this seemed to matter little to scholars, as long as the two presumably oldest extant novels were so Greek: the genre was from the beginning Greek, and the theories of an Oriental (Egyptian, Mesopotamian, Indian) origin could be easily dismissed.

A polygenesis hypothesis, however, should more seriously take into account, perhaps not those theories of Oriental origins, because they tend to be both global in their claims and supported by the wrong arguments,[56] but at least the extant papyri that feature non-Greek heroes. Ninus, the legendary Assyrian conqueror and eponymous founder of Nineveh, is the hero—only seventeen years old—of a war-and-love story fragmentarily preserved in the most extensive (and best preserved) novel papyrus hitherto discovered.[57] The papyrus guarantees a *terminus ante quem* in A.D. 100, but it has been generally recognized that this is probably the earliest novel of which tangible traces exist, to be dated in the first century B.C., perhaps even in its first half. No title is recorded; it is usually referred to as *Ninus*, which might be correct, if the hero played the same dominating role all through the novel as in its extant parts. Ninus's thirteen-year-old cousin Semiramis, his beloved, is not only modestly silent in the fragments, but also remains unnamed (she is just referred to as "the girl," *korē*). Some identify the novel with the *Babylōniaka* by a Xenophon of Antioch referred to in the *Suda* or suggest that its supposed thematic emphasis on the ruler's childhood and education would motivate the name *Ninoupaideia* (after Xenophon's *Cyropaedia*).

There are obvious links to the canonical novels: romantic love and initially skeptical parents; separation of the lovers and obstacles sent by the

---

[56] The most recent full-scale attempt to prove an Oriental (Sumerian etc.) origin is that of Graham Anderson, *Ancient Fiction: The Novel in the Graeco-Roman World* (London, 1984), with its proud conclusion: "Rohde's great problem, the origins of the Greek novel, is now substantially solved" (217).

[57] Main papyrus first published in 1893. Other fragments have since been added; recent critical edition by Rolf Kussl, *Ninos-Roman*, in Mario Capasso, ed., *Bicentenario della morte di Antonio Piaggio*, Papyrologica Lupiensia, no. 5 (1996), 143–204. Cf. also Rolf Kussl, *Papyrusfragmente griechischer Romane*, Classica Monacensia, no. 2 (Tübingen 1991), 13–101.

goddess of chance, Tyche; a shipwreck scene; emphasis on emotional reactions; and rhetorically well-rounded speeches, as when Ninus tries to persuade his beloved's mother that it is now time to allow marriage:

"O mother," he said, "faithful to my oath I have now come into your sight and into the embraces of my cousin who is so dear to me. And first let the gods know this, as indeed they are aware, and as I shall myself confirm by this present declaration: Having traversed so much land and become master of so many peoples who submitted to my spear or because of my father's power served me and paid obeisance to me, I could have taken my full satisfaction of every pleasure. If I had done so my desire might be weaker perhaps for my cousin. But though I have returned in fact with my chastity intact, I am being defeated by the god and my maturing years. I am in my seventeenth year, as you know, and have been enrolled among the men for a year; yet to this day am I still a helpless child? Had I not become aware of Aphrodite, I might still have been rejoicing in my impregnable strength. But now, as your daughter's prisoner of war—an honorable captivity, of course, and blessed by your consent—how long must I deny that I have been captured? That men of such an age are ready to wed, no one doubts; for how many past fifteen keep their purity? But I am made to suffer by a law unwritten, one stupidly sanctioned by foolish convention, since our maidens as a rule marry when they are fifteen. But that nature itself is the best law for deciding such conjunctions, what sensible man would deny? Women at fourteen years can get pregnant, and some (God knows) actually bear children. Will your daughter not even marry? 'Let us wait for two years', you might say; let us accept this condition, mother, if Chance too will wait. I am a mortal man and have joined myself to a mortal maiden; I am subject not only to the common calamities—I mean diseases and Chance, which often strikes even those sitting quietly by their own hearth—but sea journeys too await me, and wars upon wars; and I am certainly no coward nor as an assistant to my safety will I hide behind a veil of cravenness. I am the man you know me to be, so I need not tiresomely proclaim it. Let royalty urge some haste, let strong desire urge some haste, let the uncertainty and incalculability of the times that lie ahead of me urge haste."[58]

Ninus goes on for still some time, and he speaks to willing ears, we are told. Semiramis, however, "though her feelings were similar, had no eloquence

---

[58] P. Berol. 6926 A.I.38–III.30 (+ 4.20–25). Trans. Stephens and Winkler, *Ancient Greek Novels*, 35–43.

comparable to his as she stood before Thambe (her aunt, Ninus' mother). For as a virgin [living] within the women's quarters she was unable to fashion her arguments with such finesse."[59] She cries, blushes, but cannot produce a word. This scene of silence is elaborated with similar skill and care as the preceding one of oratory. Then the two mothers meet, but the fragment (A) breaks off; presumably they decide to let their children marry.

Among all the typical elements in the speech quoted, there is also an unfamiliar ring. This hero is not, like Chariton's Chaereas, involved in war as a lover—to win back his beloved or avenge having lost her—but he is a warrior who is pursuing his personal love in the meantime, before his royal duties will again bring him out to war. His martial role is the topic of another fragment (B), describing part of Ninus's campaign against the Armenians in an informed historiographic tone, combat elephants and all. The plot thus follows, partly at least, the political course of actions traditionally connected with Ninus. It is as if Polycrates himself, rather than his daughter, had been the hero of *Parthenope* and the prime mover of its plot. Romance and history are combined in a bold synthesis. A concession to romance is the age and character of the protagonists. Semiramis, in particular, has gone through a metamorphosis from an experienced and ruthless woman, who takes Ninus as her second husband, to the archetypal maiden. Ancient Assyrian and Babylonian traditions, first presented in a Hellenized form in Ctesias's lost *Persika* (and known chiefly through Diodorus of Sicily), have obviously been further adapted to suit a Hellenistic romance concept.

Why this was done—why an ancient Assyrian king and a Babylonian queen were chosen as the hero and heroine of a Greek novel written in the first century B.C.—is perhaps the most intriguing aspect of *Ninus*. Martin Braun has suggested that the novel has a background in Syrian-Mesopotamian popular narrative literature, stories of national heroes that were first developed in the period of Persian domination and could in their later Hellenized form function as Seleucid cultural propaganda: "for the historical element appealed to the national feeling, the mythical to the need for religious background, and the novelistic to the desire for entertainment amongst the masses in the kingdom of the Seleucidae."[60] Though a Hellenized local elite rather than any "masses" would have been the primary audience (listen to Ninus's rhetoric!), the idea of a nationalistic purpose is attractive. An attempt has even been made to find a more precise historical

---

[59] Ibid., 41–43.

[60] Martin Braun, *History and Romance in Graeco-Oriental Literature* (Oxford, 1938; repr., New York, 1987), 8.

context in "the growing independence of the reformed kingdom of Babylonia after the defeat of Antiochus VII by northern invaders in 129 B.C., accompanied by an assertion of cultural identity."[61]

What makes such a nationalistic context credible is not least the fact that there seem to have been parallels in other Hellenistic countries of the East, in particular (as Braun demonstrates) in Jewish and Egyptian narrative literature. Plutarch, in his *Isis and Osiris* (360B), notes that "great deeds of Semiramis are celebrated among the Assyrians, great deeds of Sesostris in Egypt." Even if by mentioning Semiramis he does not necessarily refer to this novel (if so, its heroine must have developed into something more manly later on), this shows the strength and endurance of the nationalistic tradition; and the fact that other papyrus fragments feature precisely the Pharaoh Sesostris-Sesonchosis,[62] in situations of war and love reminiscent of those of Ninus, confirms that the Seleucid national promotion in novel form had its Ptolemaic counterpart.

A couple of the convergent novelistic lines, then, seem to have had their origin in Mesopotamian and Egyptian storytelling about national heroes. Having passed a process of Hellenization under the successor monarchies to Alexander, some of these nationalistic legends appeared as romantic love stories. Whether this happened under the influence of Greek novels of the *Parthenope* type, or vice versa, is an open question. It is anyway tempting to see the nostalgia for the Classical period of Greek history that a Chariton displays as in some way interrelated with the celebration of non-Greek national heroes in *Ninus*, *Sesonchosis*, and their likes. Was there an ideological competition, or is it rather in each case just a question of using the attractive novel form for one's own cultural purpose?

Novels without Love

Graeco-Egyptian self-assertion seems to have been an important factor behind another creation of the Hellenistic period as well, the *Alexander Romance*.[63] If Sesonchosis is a figure molded out of pharaohs of the Middle and New Kingdoms, the Nectanebo whom the *Alexander Romance*

---

[61] Pierre Grimal, review of B. E. Perry's *The Ancient Romances*, *Latomus* 26 (1967): 840–45, at 842, as reported in Morgan, "On the Fringes of the Canon," 3,336.

[62] Text and Eng. trans. of the fragments in Stephens and Winkler, *Ancient Greek Novels*.

[63] Eng. trans. by Richard Stoneman, ed., *The Greek Alexander Romance* (Harmondsworth, Eng., 1991).

constructs as Alexander's real father belongs to contemporary history: he was the last native king of Egypt, who succumbed to the Persians in 343/42 B.C., and disappeared. National myth predicted his glorious return, and the author of the *Romance* made him reappear, rejuvenated and magnified, in his son Alexander, world conqueror and founder of Alexandria.

In contrast to the nationalistic novels encountered so far, however, the *Alexander Romance* lacks an overall love intrigue. It thus serves well, as this essay draws toward its close, as a transition from novels of love to those with other basic themes. Some scholars speak of "novels proper" as opposed to "the fringe."[64] The canon of five "ideal" novels, and such fragments as may be believed to derive from similar compositions, are Greek "novels proper." As we have seen, diversity is the rule even within this group—still more so, if the "not-so-ideal" fragments and summaries are added. But Greek fiction included works of quite different character as well, "fringe novels" as Niklas Holzberg calls them, and for these the negative label "novels without love" may serve better than any more sophisticated attempt at definition. A brief survey follows, just enough not to give the impression that the texts discussed were isolated in a literary world otherwise consisting of well-defined "serious" forms such as epic, drama, and historiography. Particularly in prose, the ancient "fringes" were broad and richly cultivated.

Some of these works, like the *Alexander Romance*, had the life of a historical person as their structuring principle, they were (more or less fictionalized) biographies. Love in one form or other was of course not absent, but it was not fundamental to the plot. The Athenian Xenophon, as we have already seen, included in his *Cyropaedia* the tragic love story of the beautiful Pantheia and her soldier husband Abradatas; but this was as a subplot, with only tangential connection with the hero of the work, Cyrus the Great of Persia. The basic themes of that novel are education and leadership. The *Alexander Romance* too admits erotic topics, notably in the introductory story of how, thanks to his magical skills, the exiled Pharaoh Nectanebo in King Philip's absence succeeds in seducing Queen Olympias and fathering Alexander. But the quest that governs Alexander's life and moves the action of the novel is not for love, but for political power and wisdom.

Another novel in the form of a life story, the *Aesop Romance*, is a curious mixture of humorous satire, wisdom book, and antiquarianism; its hero, Aesop the slave and fabulist, is among other things a sexual athlete of Cynic

---

[64] See the discussion in Niklas Holzberg, "The Genre: Novels Proper and the Fringe," in Schmeling, ed., *The Novel*, 11–28.

description; but personal love has no place in his life.[65] Apollonius of Tyana, the Pythagorean sage whose largely fictitious biography by Philostratus (ca. A.D. 220) has much in common with contemporary novels, is a celibate by choice and another traveler for wisdom and political influence.[66] Among them, however, these four biographical novels have (like their heroes) little in common, except the basic biographical structure and the purely incidental role of love in their plots. Biography is a chameleonic genre, if a genre at all, and this is true of its novel-like exponents as well. Each has its specific aim and is formed by its own cultural context rather than by any inherited literary conventions, and there is little to support a view that any of them had one of the others as its model. The fringe, then, supplies further evidence of novelistic polygenesis.

The novel-in-letters is the penultimate example to illustrate that thesis. Pseudoepigraphic letters, that is, letters written in the name of a political or literary figure of the Classical period, was something of a Greek literary industry in late Hellenistic and Roman times. In the cases where collections of such fictitious letters aspire to telling a continuous story, they may be considered ancient forerunners to the modern genre of epistolary novel.[67] The best surviving example is *Chion of Heraclea*, a collection of seventeen letters from a young man who is a student of Plato in Athens. Its basic theme shows his gradually growing conviction that it is his duty to assassinate the tyrant of his hometown Heraclea (on the Black Sea). The connection with historical happenings in Classical Greece and the nostalgic attitude toward its glories makes a comparison with *Parthenope* and *Callirhoe* natural. Yet, far from being a love-and-adventure story, this is a philosophical novel, with Stoic elements mixed into the basic Platonism, and it may be that the tyrannicide topic had political actuality in the author's early Imperial milieu. Among the surviving letter collections, this is the one that comes closest to a novel, using the succession of letters for chronological development and the ego-narrative form and the different addressees for psychological characterization of the

---

[65] Eng. trans. by Lloyd W. Daly in William Hansen, ed., *Anthology*; discussion by Richard I. Pervo, "A Nihilist Fabula: Introducing 'The Life of Aesop,'" in R. F. Hock et al., eds., *Ancient Fiction and Early Christian Narrative* (Atlanta, 1998), 77–120.

[66] See Ewen Bowie, "Philostratus: Writer of Fiction," in J. R. Morgan and R. Stoneman, eds., *Greek Fiction: The Greek Novel in Context* (London, 1994), 181–99. There is a new edition and English translation of Philostratus's *The Life of Apollonius of Tyana* in the Loeb Classical Library (Cambridge, Mass., 2005).

[67] See Niklas Holzberg, ed., *Der griechische Briefroman: Gattungstypologie und Textanalyse*, Classica Monacensia, no. 8 (Tübingen, 1994); and Patricia A. Rosenmeyer, *Ancient Epistolary Fictions: The Letter in Greek Literature* (Cambridge, 2001).

letter writer. Still, it is basically a collection of letters, and thus another instance of the generic lines that, in the period around the birth of Christ, converge in the Greek novel.

Incredible Things

It is suitable to end with the greatest puzzle among Greek novels, Antonius Diogenes' *Incredible Things beyond Thule*. Probably the largest one, and certainly the most complex in structure, it has survived in some extensive quotations, a couple of papyrus fragments, and an epitome in Photius's *Bibliotheke*. It shares some of its basic elements with other novels, but again, its totality is unique. There is a separated and reunited couple, Mantinias and Dercyllis, but they are not extremely young, and they are brother and sister. The chief narrator, Deinias, falls in love with Dercyllis (as do other characters as well), but this circumstance does not seem to have influenced the continuation of the plot. All the main characters travel extensively, but not only in the familiar Mediterranean surroundings: the description of their journeys into the northern *terrae incognitae* resembles more the utopian and fantastic travel accounts of the Hellenistic age that Erwin Rohde looked upon as an ancestor of the Greek novel than anything in the surviving ideal novels themselves (the *Alexander Romance* is closer).

Some have asked if Antonius in fact meant to write a parody of the *Reisefabulistik*, as Lucian did in his *True Histories*. But some Pythagorean passages—for this is also, at least to some extent, a philosophical novel—were serious enough to be massively quoted by Porphyry in his *Life of Pythagoras*. It is a quest that sets this novel in movement too, a quest for knowledge (*kata zētēsin historias*, 109a13), and "encyclopedic" is a characterization that fits at least part of the contents. Bibliographic information about sources at the beginning of each book (111a38–40) is indeed a feature unheard of in the more typical novels. Some, wishing to give both aspects their due, talk of Antonius's "playful scholarship."[68]

The enigmas abound, and the difficulty of dating this polyphonic composition does not help in forming tenable theories. Photius thought that it was older than any novel he knew, that it was "the root and source" of both Lucian's *True Histories* and *Lucius or the Ass*, and that the "adventures and

---

[68] Stephens and Winkler, *Ancient Greek Novels*, 109. See the discussion of the various views and proposals regarding this "eccentric amalgam" in Morgan, "On the Fringes of the Canon," 3,303–18.

wanderings and loves and captures and perils" in Iamblichus, Achilles Tatius, and Heliodorus were modeled on Antonius Diogenes.[69] Since the earliest papyrus fragments make Antonius manifestly prior to A.D. 200, he anyway precedes Heliodorus, whose complex narrative structure his work resembles. But even Heliodorus looks simple in comparison: Antonius's system of chinese-box narratives comprises no less than eight different levels, if Photius's epitome is correct (and correctly understood);[70] it has been suggested that this structure was influenced by Indian narrative techniques, one of the more desperate reactions to the novel's anomalies.

Erwin Rohde made *Incredible Things beyond Thule* the cornerstone of his theory of the origins of the Greek novel: Antonius was the author who actually implanted the eroticism of Hellenistic poetry in a narrative framework of fantastic traveling, and all the other novelists built on him (much as Photius had suggested). This can easily be disproved (particularly on chronological grounds), but it is interesting as the ultimate single-model hypothesis. You take a work that is composite enough to house both serious and satirical elements, both love and paradoxography, both adventures and encyclopedic learning, both magic and philosophy, both linear narration and complex retelling, and there you have the origin of the satirical as well as the ideal novel, of simple love-and-adventure stories no less than a work as sophisticated in design and pretentious in thought as the *Aithiopika*.

It has been argued in the present essay that the reverse process is more likely. Several different lines converged in "the Greek novel": sentimental love stories in a Classical historical setting, narrated with historiographic accents, as in *Parthenope* and *Callirhoe*; popular love-and-adventure stories originating in an oral tradition and emerging in literate form in the *Ephesiaka*; erotically more explicit storytelling as in the *Phoinikika* and (perhaps) the *Babylōniaka*; nationalistic hero narratives of diverse Oriental origins as in *Ninus* and *Sesonchosis*; fabulistic travel accounts as in *Incredible Things beyond Thule*. In other words, I suggest a polygenesis that presumably took place in late Hellenistic times, with each of the forms adapting to the common cultural environment and assimilating traits from the others to create the confusing picture of similarity and diversity that face us in the surviving specimens.

From this converged "genre," in turn, each of the sophistic novelists devised his idiosyncratic variation on the theme, though keeping safely within

---

[69] Photius, *Bibl.* cod. 166, p. 111b32–42, trans. Stephens and Winkler, *Ancient Greek Novels*, 128.

[70] Its structure is displayed in ibid., 115.

the boundaries of the now consolidated genre. Too much emphasis on these second-stage novels—in which a divergent movement replaced the earlier convergence—has vitiated much modern scholarship on the emergence of the ancient Greek novel. Any attempt at reconstructing that process must start from the nonsophistic specimens and, in particular, from the fragments, however hazardous it may seem to build on such a fragile basis.

ALBERTO VARVARO

Medieval French Romance

From Storytelling as Social Practice to the Literary Novel

It is widely agreed that the history of the novel begins with twelfth-century French-language storytelling, in other words, medieval romance.[1] Before becoming a literary genre, the "novel" in the Middle Ages was an oral, recreational practice. There is no doubt that the tradition of written narrative rests—and in some ways is founded—on a long and far-reaching tradition of storytelling that began in castle halls, in farmers' stalls, and around the hearths of family groups. There is much significant evidence of such practice, but little is known regarding the conventions that governed it and the modalities in which it was carried out; nor do we know much regarding the subject matter.

We can only hypothesize (inasmuch as such a hypothesis is obvious and inasmuch as we see its impact on the subsequent written novel) that oral narrative practices offered plenty of room for folkloric and traditional themes and structures, beginning with the fairy tale. It is fascinating to think that Herodotus's master thief[2] reappeared after a thousand-year silence and without any known intermediary in the Latin work *Dolopathos* by Johannes de Alta Silva, who did not know Greek. Another fairy tale motif that reappeared in Europe during the second half of the twelfth century is the monster who is generated from an episode of necrophilia, a story that can ultimately be linked to the ancient Greek myth of the Gorgon and that seems to have reached the West via Asia Minor during the Middle Ages following the Crusades. The practice of recounting real—or reputedly real—and memorable events was surely no less common: endeavors of famous ancestors, to

---

[1] In ancient French, the term *roman* originally signified "romance language," as opposed to Latin. The expression *mettre en roman*, for example, meant simply "to translate, to vernacularize." It then began to denote "a romance-language text," and then, "romance," in the prototypical sense of "narrative" and ultimately "novel." It is worth noting that the Italian term *novella*, akin to the English *novel* (although slightly different in meaning, i.e., "short story"), is a romance-language word that first appeared in the thirteenth-century *Ritmo Cassinese*, an early Italian lyric, in the sense of "news" or "account of events that have recently occurred." This is the origin of the present meaning of the word *novel*, in the literary sense. The relationship between *romance* and *novel* is discussed below.

[2] See A. Aarne and S. Thompson, *The Types of Folktales: A Classification and Bibliography* (Helsinki, 1964), nos. 950 and 1,525.

whom noble lineage could be traced, or notable experiences of common men or great events that had recently occurred (like the Crusades).

The division between fairy tale and history is undoubtedly a stretch: it is evident that for the narrator, all of these stories referred to real events. From our point of view, "historical" tales present surprising errors in their chronology, in their identification of the characters, and in their references to well-known facts. In the "imaginary" tales, on the other hand, we are struck by the tendency to set the fairy tale in real places, by the identification of the characters with improbable exactness, and by the guarantee of veracity through presumably eyewitness accounts. In reality, these are opposite yet convergent processes that suffice to transform both types into an identically unreal reality—in other words, the sphere of the novel.

A book like *De nugis curialium* (*The Courtiers' Trifles*) by Walter Map, a Latin anthology (circa 1180) of the "courtiers' distractions" at the court of Henry II of England, gives us a rich overview of such oral narration revealed by an educated man of letters with great ability in Latin. Here these practices are clearly evident.[3] By the same measure, *De nugis* should not be confused with the performances of any old *conteur* at a manse in Picardie or Berry, whose repertoire would have been much more limited and whose abilities in constructing a text would have been infinitely lesser than Map's. The literary adornment, often of very high quality, in *De nugis* is attributable solely to him and cannot be generalized. But there are some traces elsewhere, and it is worthwhile to keep them in mind. In the first place, Map does not disdain serialization in his storytelling: he repeatedly tells the story of the fairy-wife, a theme that will later take the name of Melusina, as if to show off his ability for variation. In the second place, the blending of drafts at various stages of completion, which is certainly involuntary because the work was never finished, shows different degrees of reworking in both the fairy tale and "memorialist" material. We will see this again elsewhere. In Walter Map's laboratory, it is easy to sense the minimum requirements for reworking traditional material—albeit into Latin—as an essential condition for the narrative's qualification as a literary work, even when the original is a romance-language work.

Structure and Transmission of the Novel: As a Totality and in Episodes

The medieval vernacular texts that are usually included in the genre "romance" vary greatly in length, between five thousand lines and many tens of

---

[3] A. Varvaro, *Apparizioni fantastiche, tradizioni folcloriche e letteratura nel medioevo: Walter Map* (Bologna, 1994).

thousands of octets. Nor is there any lack of tales in prose, which occupy the space of many volumes in modern editions. When considered in their entirety, whether they are relatively short or endlessly long, there is a clearly analogous (and fundamental) dialectic between episode and tale that will later be transformed into an similar relationship between tale and anthology. I believe that these processes are analogous because there is virtually no difference in the conditions for consistency in either case, and often the difference is so inconsequential that it is incongruous with the standards of the modern reader.[4]

A situation like this is related to the ways in which the medieval tale was circulated: it was read aloud to a group of listeners over the course of a session that was limited in duration by the physical stamina of the reader and his audience. There is no lack of evidence of this, starting with the passage of *Yvain* by Chrétien de Troyes (lines 5,362ff.) in which a *pucelle* reads a tale to his parents only to finish with the tragic surprise that befell Paolo and Francesca as they were reading together (undoubtedly, with the one reading aloud to the other) "of Lancelot how him love thrall'd" (*Inferno* 5.128). A silent reading, of the type familiar to us, is incompatible not only with the limited availability of books and the ability to read them but also with the very composition of the text on the page. Originally, handwritten books were not adorned with titles, illuminated initials or rubrics. Only occasionally was the first letter of a text made larger and painted or illuminated. Little by little, by the fifteenth century, the use of rubrics for each part and the indexes had become common. These external aids facilitated the use of the text in ways that to us seem normal, but at that time, they were innovations that had appeared only with the first books intended for study (tractates, encyclopedias, etc.).

The earliest vernacular narrative works broke away from oral narrative practices for the simple reason that they were more complex and much longer, and had more complicated story lines. The fact that this was considered necessary in order to give storytelling a more literary status was probably a result of the prestige of Latin models like the *Aeneid*. In order to reach a "high" level (however "high" a vernacular work could be, despite being "low" by definition), scholastic models required that narration had to move from the short tale with a simple structure to a long one with a complex structure.

---

[4] See two of my earlier studies: A. Varvaro, "Il testo letterario," in *Lo spazio letterario del medioevo, 2: Il medioevo volgare, I/1, La produzione del testo*, edited by P. Boitani, M. Mancini, and A. Varvaro (Rome, 1999), 387–422; and A. Varvaro, "Élaboration des textes et modalités du récit dans la littérature française médiévale," *Romania* 99 (2001): 135–209.

How was the obstacle to be overcome? Oral practices offered a few solutions. The two most obvious were sequential serialization and biographical structures, both of which were linked to realist presumption of the narrative content, to which I have alluded above. A series of episodes could be ordered in chronological sequence only when you could assume that an episode narrated events that took place previous to ones narrated in other episodes, or vice versa. This was the structure employed in many of the *chansons de geste*. The most ancient and evident model is the *Couronnement de Louis* (circa 1140), which is based on five successive episodes that resulted from the highly contested imperial coronation of Louis the Pious at Aquitaine. In actually reading it, the audience perceived the text through the episodes themselves, but the author and audience both knew that each episode had its place in the group of episodes. It is therefore necessary to remember that in the *Couronnement*, the main character, Guillaume d'Orange, is still *bachelier*, unmarried, has yet to conquer Orange and Guilbourc, and does not even have the *court nes*, "short nose," that he will acquire during the duel narrated in the final episode of the *chanson* and that will become his defining feature. But in its basic elements, this sequential approach is not exclusive to epic poetry. In the *Continuations of the Old French Perceval* by Chrétien de Troyes, for example, it is applied with varying levels of sophistication: minimal in the first continuation and then substantially resolved in a succession of episodes that are practically unlinked and are not without repetition.

The reference to a biographical framework is not by its nature more sophisticated than pure sequentiality, upon which it can, at any rate, be superimposed. After all, the *Couronnement de Louis* is no less than a moment in the biographical epic of Guillaume d'Orange, just as the *Chanson d'Aspremont* is in that of Charlemagne or in that of Roland. But a much more evolved level is found in the story of Tristan and Iseut. In this case, the autonomy of the episode does not need to be merely hypothesized: it is fulfilled in the *lais*, beginning with the *Lai de Chievrefeuil* by Marie de France, whose themes are single moments in the lovers' long separation and their plotting to reach each other again. The story of Tristan and Iseut also resurfaces in the duel between Tristan and Morholt, in his battle with the dragon in Ireland, in the discovery of the notch in the sword, in the potion that they unknowingly drink, the pine from which they are spied upon, in the surprise in Morrois's hut, and so on.

Each of these episodes possesses its own narrative autonomy, but the totality of the story is implicit in all the episodes, which allude to it either tacitly or explicitly. For the listener, this totality is never an actual totality but rather virtual. The fact that it has been delivered by way of a book that few are able to read (and even fewer have the means to possess) is of little importance. By modern standards, the most surprising fact is that the awareness of this totality is not the result of *subsequent* readings of the different episodes by which it is formed. It exists *prior* to the reception of the episode. All those who listen to a passage of one of the *romans de Tristan* already know, albeit to varying degrees, the entire story; they all know that the lovers will die tragically. This also happens in epic poetry: from the outset, the audience knows that Roland will die in Roncesvalles, that Charlemagne will avenge him, and that Guillaume d'Orange will never betray an ungrateful Louis.

The constant references in the episode itself to the virtual overarching structure has an important consequence: it removes surprise from the audience's horizon. There are innumerable examples of this, like the passage where Galehaut and Lancelot have left the court of King Arthur and Galehaut pines over their separation. The narrator of the great *Lancelot* (in prose) says: "But no proof of this is needed here, for in the end, as our story will go on to show, it was clear that the grief it caused him swept away all joy and brought him death. But his death ought not be spoken of at this point, for the death of such a worthy man as Galehaut is not a thing to bring up before its time."[5] The writer makes it clear that Galehaut will die long before such an event actually comes to pass.

The relationship between the episode and the overarching structure allows for extraordinary margins of elasticity. The writer of medieval romance tolerated discrepancies and contradictions that would be unthinkable in later narrative practices. This was possible because the narrator and his audience were not so concerned by the fact that Guillaume d'Orange's nose is at times *court* even before the giant Corsolt cuts it off, or that Tristan appears to be in love with Iseut even before the two drink the potion that will be the fatal cause of their passion, or that the two continue to love each other even after the potion should have worn off. The imminence of the overarching structure thus becomes the prerequisite of the episodes' incoherence. In the overarching structure, Guillaume d'Orange is the hero with the *court nes* and Tristan and Iseut are the lovers who love each other passionately.

An extreme case of this occurs in the *Roman de Renart*, a cycle of more than twenty tales in which the main character, Renart, is generally pitted

---

[5] *Lancelot-Grail: The Old French Arthurian Vulgate and Post-Vulgate in Translation*, edited by Norris J. Lacy (New York, 1993), 2:241. Subsequent references to this work appear parenthetically in the text.

against wolf Isengrin. These texts, which are called *branches*, were composed by different authors over the course of a few decades. They are known to us in the form of two or three collections. But here the overview is not exactly biographical, even though one *branche* narrates Renart's birth and some of the others attempt to bring his endeavors to a conclusion. What holds the entire thing together is the relative regularity in the main character's personality (he is shrewd, hungry, ready for any trick or aggression, unreliable but likable) and the personalities of his rivals (the wolf is violent and stupid, his wife Hersent is lustful, and so on). Such a weak criterion for internal coherence allows for all kinds of variations and contradictions. And yet the *Roman de Renart*, however fluid it may appear, is a cohesive work. Later works, like *Renart le Nouvel* by Jacquemart Gielée (circa 1288), use different criteria of consistency even though they share the same main character.

Plot Structure

Complicated plot structure and its overarching development, whether sophisticated or not, is the first distinctive characteristic of the medieval novel that sets it apart from the short story. It is no coincidence that the first vernacular novels are adaptations of classical works. This would appear to be a paradox given that the ancient world did not know the genre of the novel, but it can be explained. The first models where Virgil's *Aeneid* and Statius's *Thebaid*, two epic poems. The first was, and remains today, a model for plot structure, as well as for its skillful application of *mise en abîme* of the entire first part of the action, from the fall of Troy to Aeneas's shipwreck, a part that is narrated by Aeneas to Dido in the first books. The *Thebaid*, instead, does not present anything so complicated. At any rate, these two ancient poems were far from the conventions of simple oral storytelling. In the *Aeneid*, the high-gear narration of what happened to the Trojans, beginning with their departure from Carthage and ending with the death of Turnus, covered not only that which took place within the walls of Troy and in Latium, but it also proclaimed and connoted the imperial destiny of Rome. Around a tale that spanned just a few years in the main character's life, an essential event in the human and divine world was lumped together *en raccourci*. Statius had set into motion a simpler mechanism. Within the walls of Thebes, the story of the world was not being decided, but there was a convergence of a host of heroes with their varying personalities and behaviors, and their destiny was being fulfilled. The third ancient model was the vernacular adaptation of the story of Alexander the Great, which allowed for a bona fide biography based in turn on supposedly medieval models (although they were actually ancient).

The importance of the highly original method used in the *Roman d'Alexandre* has perhaps been underestimated. We know nothing regarding its first author, Albéric de Besacon. He probably used multiple Latin sources instead of a single model like the *Aeneid* or the *Thebaid*. After beginning the tale in a biographical key, he found nothing strange about writing only the first part, up to the siege of Tyre: there is no indication that something or someone stopped him, despite himself, from continuing. Later, others moved the story forward, or, at least, different phases within it. A few decades later, the *Roman d'Alexandre* would become a collage of four texts by different authors, composed without any particular sequence, and with some blending by the final editor. The reference to the biographical overview is clear from the beginning, but there is no narrative link created by unforeseen circumstances. There is no reasonable proportion between the four texts. One of them, the *Fuerre de Gadres*, has no place in the biography of the Macedonian conqueror (it is linked to the siege of Tyre, but it more closely resembles one of the marginal events of the then recent Crusades). The final segment entails the alternation of two different versions, and it is followed by different continuations that prolong the biographical story beyond the death of the main character—the two *Venjances Alexandre*. The result that we read in thirteenth- and fourteenth-century manuscripts has a weak structural coherence and an unthinkable genesis by modern standards.

It is understandable that the complex narrative structure of the *Aeneid* was too sophisticated for the anonymous poet who wrote the ancient French *Roman d'Eneas*, and especially, I presume, for his audience, so much so that the transmission by means of episodes that did not correspond to the books of the Latin poem made it nearly incomprehensible. Thus, the poet reestablished the *ordo naturalis*. But as his adaptations show, he could not see any sense in respecting the source, even it were Virgil. For example, he did not have any problem in developing an independent love story between Aeneas and Lavinia entirely extraneous to the source but of great interest for listeners fascinated with the theme of love and in particular that between a mature hero and a young woman.

An equally anonymous poet, the author of the *Romance of Thebes*, did not feel the need to make such revolutionary changes. Nonetheless, he by no means respected the starting or finishing points in the plot that he was exploiting. He did offer his audience a summary of the Argonauts' story and that of Oedipus, and he continued the narrative up until the moment when Theseus arrests Creon. But it does not stop here: besides allowing room for amorous developments in a story that has darkly tragic origins, he also felt it legitimate to insert an episode entirely extraneous to Statius, namely, that of Daire le Roux, whose story examines a central point of feudal hierarchies (i.e., if love for a son can prevail over duty to one's lord) and ends in the ever popular triumph of love over justice.

Thus, in early attempts, vernacular romances relied on the Latin models simply to learn how to construct the plot. But they also treated the models with great freedom and thereby transmitted an entirely different narrative concept.

Cyclic Totality

At this point, the novel already had the necessary tools to construct plots that are not just simple sequential chains nor mere moments in a biographical parable. It could therefore freely give itself over to a tendency that it had nurtured from its beginnings. The very fact that the tale took the form of an episode in a group of episodes implicitly placed no limits on the dimensions of the totality. It is important to remember the strange outgrowth of the *Roman d'Alexandre* through successive emissions and the seemingly uncontrollable proliferation of the *branches* of *Renart*. The thirteenth century is one of the golden periods of encyclopedic ambition: it is easy to understand how the novel tended irresistibly to become a totality, to transform itself into the novel of all novels.

Cyclic patterns had already encroached on the world of epic poetry. Codices would reunite and reorder the *chansons* devoted to Guillaume d'Orange in series that, including the stories of his ancestors and descendants, reached up to twenty-four poems. The *Roman de Renart* had itself become a cycle. The *Roman d'Alexandre* could also be seen as the result of a cyclic process. Robert de Boron probably heeded analogous principles in the composition of the *Joseph d'Arimathie/Merlin/Perceval* sequence that Christianized the Graal story. But the case of the Lancelot-Grail vulgate is more complex. The rich manuscript tradition of this gargantuan cycle generally follows the sequence *Estoire du Saint Graal, Merlin, Lancelot, Quest du Saint Graal, Mort Artu*. But the sequential regularity could not contrast more greatly with the structural irregularity, which unites protracted tales like *Lancelot* with shorter texts like the *Mort* and tolerates painful ideological contradictions like that between the Cistercian spirituality of the quest and the celebration of adulterous love in *Lancelot*, not to mention the constant, if not as intense, openness to magic. If there was a gradual composition in the case of *Alexandre*, here *Lancelot* was clearly the basic nucleus. It would not be far-fetched to describe this, similarly to other cases, as a slapdash blending of ill-matched pieces, but it is also true that some insightful scholars, like Jean Frappier, have hypothesized the existence of an "architect" who was most probably the architect most foreign to Palladian symmetry imaginable.[6]

There is no question that requirements for cycle coherence were low, but they were not entirely negligible. Although each of these five romances are superficially different, they are not entirely extraneous to one another. We must suppose that although such a situation is unacceptable to us today, it was logical and tolerable at that time. In the universe of romance, this cycle lumped together the Grail and the adulterous love of Lancelot and Guenevere, which appear to be two themes in the same genre despite their incompatibility. The story ranges from the most remote origins of the Grail—the Passion of Christ—up to the *Götterdammerung*, which ultimately was caused by adultery and that marked the end of the Arthurian world. The *Roman de Tristan en prose* advances the all-encompassing cyclic tendency by including the legend of Tristan and Iseut and their other adventures in the Arthurian universe. There is also the *Guiron le Courtois*, also known as *Palamède*, a work that interested Frederick II of Swabia. Nor is there any contradiction in the existence of different or concurrent totalities.

Narrative traditions derived from the French continued in this direction. Nor was the epic tradition unaffected: the *Garin de Monglane*, for example, resumed, coordinated, and developed Carolingian tales. It is well known that in Italy, Arthurian and Carolingian material would ultimately be fused: the genealogical tree in Andrea da Barberino's *I reali di Francia* (*The French Royal House*) allowed for a different modality of totalization. In late-nineteenth-century, chivalrous literature in Sicily (the so-called theater of *pupi* and *lu cuntu*, marionettes, and storytelling), the material is bunched together in a unitary universe that is supported by its own chronology and by a dense network of kinship, hatred, and love.

We must not forget that cyclic totality in literary practice continued to be formed by episodic narrative. In actual practice, it is easy to understand how the tendency toward cyclization or totalization can be so elastic. There is no contradiction between a romance as a complete set of episodes with a specific connection to the immanence of the whole and the complete dissolution of narrative material in an open universe. The subtle difference lies in

---

[6] See J. Frappier, "The Vulgate Cycle," in *Arthurian Literature in the Middle Ages*, edited by R. S. Loomis (Oxford, 1959), 295–318 (based on much earlier studies).

the reference within the episode to the whole or in the immanence of the whole in the episode. Nothing stopped a single narrator from adding a new episode to a romance or to a cycle or from including a previously extraneous development.

Mention must be made here of the technique of *entrelacement*, or interlacing, which scholars have considered to be a typical element of romance in prose. A classic example of this is found in *Lancelot* where Gawain is taken prisoner by Caradoc; Yvain, Lancelot, and Galescalain, the duke of Clarence, set out to find him. The three knights decide to split up, and the romance recounts Galescalain's visit to his cousin and then goes backward to tell the story of Yvain with the Knight in the Coffin; then it goes even farther back to tell of Lancelot, who frees the Knight in the Coffin and then is received by Melian. Yet another step backward allows the narrator to tell the story of Gawain after his abduction and his adventures in the dungeon, and then it goes back to King Arthur's court, where Galehaut stops Lionel from leaving on the quest for the Grail, and so on.[7]

There have been many different interpretations of this technique, some of which are fascinating if not improbable, like those associating it with Panofsky's reflections on the relationship between scholasticism and Gothic architecture.[8] Bruckner was right when she noted the relationship between interlacing and the whole with the reality of the episode and the knowledge of the totality: "Interlacing . . . expresses both the impetus to segment the narrative into separate units and the equally powerful compulsion to associate and continue romance across such divisions."[9]

Besides its purely narrative function, the alternation of episodes and the connection between story lines plays an even more meaningful cognitive

---

[7] In Alexandre Micha's edition of the *Lancelot* prose cycle, this interlacing begins in book 10; see *Lancelot: Roman en prose du XIIIe siècle*, edited by Alexandre Micha (Geneva, 1978), 1:177ff.

[8] The reference is to E. Panofsky's *Gothic Architecture and Scholasticism* (Latrobe, Pa., 1951). The great scholar held that symmetrical analyzability of architectural structures corresponded to the scholastic concept of *manifestatio*. Eugène Vinaver applied this concept to the organization of the novel in overlapping chapters in *The Rise of Romance* (Oxford, 1971), 68. This hypothesis is fascinating but does not have much substance: the division into chapters and the indexing of subject matter were narrative innovations that appeared essentially sometime after 1200, but they were not taken from philosophy but rather from the mendicant orders' new approach to study (and the *mise en page* in their codices) and their needs as preachers and from the new relationship between the reader and the great texts, beginning with the Bible. See R. Rouse, "La diffusion en Occident au XIII siècle des outils de travail facilitant l'accès aux textes autoritatifs," in *Revue des études Islamiques* 44 (1976): 115–47.

[9] See M. T. Bruckner, "The Shape of Romance in Medieval France," in R. L. Krueger, ed., *The Cambridge Companion to Medieval Romance* (Cambridge, 2000), 25.

role. By means of these connections, these real processes become networks of complex relationships rather than simple linear sequences. Not by chance, the same narrative (and earlier yet, cognitive) problem was faced by historiographers who dealt with complexities of reality: but I would not say that they were able to resolve it before the narrators did. In works devoted to the Crusades, which tell the most important topical story of the age, we still have a linear narrative even up to Ambroise (the Third Crusade). Only with the Fourth Crusade, and in particular with the more worldly Ville-hardouin, does the ability to correlate simultaneous events appear. Later, the same term was used for this type of narrative insertion in the novel and historiography: incidences, like the *incidenze* in Giovanni Villani.

Alternative Space, Time, and Society

We have seen how medieval romance began with adaptations of ancient material and the legend of Tristan and Iseut. In both cases, the events narrated are situated in times, places, and societies that represent an "otherness" with respect to the French or Anglo-Norman courts of the twelfth century: prehistoric Thebes; Troy; the Mediterranean and Latium prior to the foundation of Rome; and the Cornwall, Ireland, Wales, and Brittany of an indeterminate past.

This is by no means a marginal observation: the norm for oral storytelling, whatever it was, escapes the *hic et nunc* of the poets and their audience. There is no question that Thebes, Troy, Carthage, and Tintagel ended up resembling each other and hundreds of other feudal centers and that the daily practices were the same, as were their values and problems. But this does not diminish the otherness of the world of romance, which waned only with the "comic" tale, in other words, with the *fabliau* or the *Roman de Renart*, which were based on an even more radical otherness, namely, that of the animal world. It is not far-fetched to suspect this otherness was seen as a guarantee of literary legitimacy. A fictional event that took place in the contemporary castles of Normandy or Kent around 1180 would have been considered a chronicle or a historical account.

The importance of this observation is demonstrated by the occurrence of an extraordinary phenomenon: the identification, fulfilled over the course of just a few decades, of a space, of a time, and of a society that by themselves certify the literary quality of the romance. Thus, the Arthurian world was an alternative world. This phenomenon confirms the contiguity that we can sense—more often than not—between romance and historiography. King

Arthur first appeared in written literature as a historical figure, however real he may or may not have been. In the *Historia regum Britanniae* by Geoffrey of Monmouth (1136), in which Arthur's glorious endeavors, up to his sudden demise in a fratricidal battle, are recounted with remarkable breadth, he has a definite place in the succession of British kings. The immediate widespread success of the *Historia* was aided by the French verse translation by Wace (1155), who made the first mention of the Round Table. Both Geoffrey's and Wace's works are historiographic; they both situate Arthur temporally between the fall of the Roman Empire in Britannia and the prevalence of the Anglo-Saxons, that is, between the fifth and sixth centuries. Spatially, they situate him in a predominantly western Great Britain and in some of the minor islands, which had been transformed into the Kingdom of Logres, but without any connection to the continent.[10] The origins of the legend of Tristan are even more indefinite, but the setting is nonetheless a residual of Celtic and Armoric insularity. The time line is more blurry and thus allows it to catch up quickly to the Arthurian setting (this has already happened in Beroul).[11]

The chronological and geographic framework remains the same in the romances of Chrétien de Troyes, in the subsequent romances that we call the Arthurian romances, and in the various verse and prose versions of the Grail legend. In the latter texts, however, the framework has greater breadth. The story begins in Palestine during the time of Christ, but it moves to Brittany as early as Joseph of Arimathea, and the brief succession of generations spanning from him to the Fisher King is compatible with Arthur's ancient chronology. The arc of time covered in romance is thus defined as the "time of adventure" and it extends from the birth of Merlin to Arthur's death, or rather, his disappearance. In *Lancelot* there are many references to this "time of the Adventures" as something well known: "In that land there was an evil custom that lasted as long as the Adventures lasted" (*Lancelot-Grail*, 2:259); "That evil custom started in the first year of the Adventures, when King Arthur's father went to way against King Urien" (ibid.); "By the time the Adventures began" (ibid.); and so on. The "time of the Adventures" was

---

[10] The Arthurian capitals (Carduel, Camelot, etc.) are all in Cornwall, Wales, and the western Midlands.

[11] Philippe Méneard noted rightly of *Tristan en prose*: "L'action se passe en trois lieux distincts: d'abord la Grande-Bretagne, et plu précisément le royaume de Logres, où règne Arthur et où chevauchent les chevaliers de la Table Ronde, ensuite la Cornouailles, terre du roi Marc, enfin la Bretagne armoricaine, pays du roi Hoël et de son fils Kahérdin. Des changements de perspective ou des déplacements de personnages nous transportent successivement ici ou là" (*Le roman de Tristan en prose* (Geneva, 1987), 1:46.

a finite arc of time. Indeed, there will be a hero who "completes the Adventures of Britain"; he "will be the finest knight in the world and will take the last seat at the Round Table" (ibid., 252).[12]

The "place of the Adventures" is defined with equal clarity in *Lancelot* as Great Britain ("the Adventures of Great Britain and the perilous wonders," *Lancelot-Grail*, 2:253) but it is extended to Brittany (often overlooking the fact that the English Channel lies between them). Society has maintained this ambiguous character—a theme that I will return to later.[13]

In romance, by definition, the narrator can include any event, no matter what the source. Despite the efforts of determined scholars, no one has ever proved definitively that the majority of the material comes from traditional Celtic sources. Undoubtedly, much of it comes from a generically European, traditional narrative heritage, and some individual writers show notable ability for invention. The important thing is to show how no romance subject has need for any other legitimacy than that of being set in the Arthurian world.

The consequences are important. In the first place, romance is thus able to distance itself from the binds of antiquity that defined medieval Latin literature. References to antiquity, which dominated romance in its beginnings, were easily emarginated, and they tended to lose their fertility. Second, the romance world was at once here and elsewhere (French society of that era was familiar with England, but the kingdom of Logres was foreign to English contemporaries); at once similar and different (the characters acted like us but they did not have the same habits); at once Christian and non-Christian. It was an alternative universe and place where extraordinary things could happen (*aventures* and *mervelles*, adventures and wonders) but not outside of the real.

This was not the first time that vernacular literature had invented such a solution. The same thing had happened in epic poetry. It was made up of a universe chronologically linked to the reigns of Charles and Louis (originally Charlemagne and Ludwig the Pious, but open to identification with other Charleses and Ludwigs),[14] and it was spatially defined by Paris, Laon, and

---

[12] Here Elias of Toulouse is answering Galehaut's question.

[13] I have not dealt with another point here: not everything that happens in this space and this arc of time is worthy of being retold; romance is the literary genre devoted to only those adventures worth remembering. For example, the author of *Lancelot* writes: "Lancelot rode for a long while without coming upon any adventure worth reporting" (*Lancelot-Grail*, 2:285); "they rode along until mid-morning, finding no adventure worth telling about" (*Lancelot-Grail*, 2:291).

[14] They are known as Charles Martel in *Girart de Roussillon* and Louis "from beyond the sea" in *Gormont et Isembart*.

less frequently Aachen and a border that ran from southern France toward Spain and Italy, leaving Africa and the East as faraway inexhaustible receptacles of Saracen enemies.[15]

Society and Religion

The society depicted by romance authors in this specific space and time is essentially analogous to contemporary society. Simon Gaunt was certainly not the first to make the following observation: "The characters of romance are the characters of the secular court: the king or lord, his wife, their sons and daughters, knights in his service, his seneschal, constable and retainers, his clerks, and more lowly servants.[16] But churchmen are missing in this list pertaining to contemporary reality.

There is no doubt that the world of thirteenth-century romance is a Christian world. The calendar scanning its rhythms is Christian, and is marked by the grand holidays of Christmas, Easter, the Ascension, and the Pentecost. From King Arthur and his knights on down, all the characters attend a Christian mass every day.[17] They make their vows to carry out their most important deeds on undoubtedly Christian relics—*les sains*.[18] And yet, the correspondence between the world of romance and the contemporary world of the writers ends here—at least for this fundamental aspect of the narratives.

It is also true that there is a Roman pope in Arthur's world, but he is nameless and rarely appears, except, for example, to deplore the fact that the king has sent away the real Guenevere and considers the false one to be legitimate "in disregard of the Holy Church" (*Lancelot-Grail*, 2:275). This is the least of what the pope can complain about in a weighty problem that

---

[15] The two chronotopes in the French tradition, epic and romance, are clearly distinct. But there are some rare exceptions where they overlap: Floire and Blancheflor, for example, are identified as the progenitors of Bertrada, or Bertha of the Big Foot, mother of Charlemagne (cf. *Floire et Blancheflor*, edited by M. Pelan [Paris, 1956], line 9). This is in line with anteriority of the time of romance with respect to the epic time. The inverse holds for *Partonopeus de Blois*, whose hero is a descendant of Clovis.

[16] S. Gaunt, "Romance and Other Genres," in Kreuger, ed., *The Cambridge Companion*, 47.

[17] In Chrétien, Perceval's mother admonishes him: "And above all else, I beg you, go to monasteries and churches and pray to our Lord that you live this worldly life well, and are honored, until you reach the right end to your days." Chrétien de Troyes, *Perceval, the Story of the Grail*, translated by Burton Raffel (New Haven, Conn., 1999), 19. It is worth reading the following lines, where the mother gives her son all the essential information about religion.

[18] For example, King Arthur does this in *Lancelot*. See *Lancelot-Grail*, 2:265.

touches the very sacrament of marriage. As a result, and as could be expected, "in this way King Arthur's land was placed under interdiction for twenty-one months" (ibid.). But what is unique about this is that when the moment arrives to decide which of the two Gueneveres is the real one, no one feels the need to ask the opinion of a prelate: all that is needed is the opinion of the vassals of Carmelide, who are concerned in the least-correct solution, as if the problem were purely feudal (but it is surprising that the vassals of Logres do not have a say).

The fact is that unlike in the epic world, there is no religious hierarchy analogous to the real world in the world of romance. In *Lancelot*, there is a "arcevesque de Cantorbire," most definitely supreme within Arthur's reign just as the archbishop of Canterbury in the real England of the Middle Ages and the modern age. But he has a purely ceremonial function (in the lay world!) when he goes to Sorelois to return the true Guenevere to the throne accompanied by a real "bishop of Winchester" and by a less probable bishop of Logres (*Lancelot-Grail*, 2:278). Such marginal, infrequent references to figures who played important roles in real life shows how the conventions of romance are of a different nature than those of reality.

When a man of religion is needed in a tale, a priest is not called but rather a hermit, who is invariably summoned from his cell conveniently located in the vicinity of the action or even from a unspecified *mostier* or church.[19] In the world of romance, hermits are as common as cathedrals are rare. It is normal for hermits to impart the sacraments, but this is not entirely incorrect as hermits were often ordained as priests. But it is never clear. The unknown hermit, to whom Arthur refers to as priest, turns out to be Amustan, who had been the king's chaplain for seven years (*Lancelot-Grail*, 2:276). But laymen fulfill such duties: even King Urien became a hermit at the end of his life, like so many other knights before him (ibid., 259).

As far as the ecclesiastical hierarchy is concerned, there is no doubt that the hermit is a marginal, if not external, figure. By giving him the function of mediator between the knights and the holy, romance made a choice that seems to me significantly "laical," and in any case, "other." The hermit is a figure that demarcates the border between the religious and lay world, and he often passes from one to the other. Generally, he is not bound to a church but to a building that is designated as a chapel (*Lancelot-Grail*, 2:252). Otherwise, he can be found in a forest or in a clearing—yet another form of marginalization.

---

[19] Just as happens on the page of *Lancelot* cited in the previous footnote.

Even more generally, romance often gives the impression that it is not re-spectful of the most elementary ecclesiastic prescriptions. When Galehaut explains to Lancelot why he has asked to remain alone with master Elias of Toulouse, he says (lying): "I wanted to make my confession" (*Lancelot-Grail*, 2:256–57). But Elias is only one of the *clercs* or clerks that King Arthur has sent him to interpret his dreams, "the ten wisest men of learning that could be found in his land" (ibid., 248). In other words, he has sent him as an ex-pert in the art of divination rather than as a priest.[20]

Thus, even though romance is by no means non-Christian, it is clearly nonecclesiastical. Obviously, it is a question of a convention similar to that which portrayed the Muslims of epic poetry as idolaters, and it is possible that the origins of this convention lie in the monastic rather than urban na-ture of Celtic Christendom. But what is most important to the scholar of ro-mance is not the source of these figures but their function and meaning in the texts of medieval romance. In this case, they make it possible to config-ure the world of romance as a universe with a negligible ecclesiastic compo-nent where laymen are at the center of every action, even though the central problem of romance is sin, which supposedly should be managed exclu-sively by the Church.

Sin and Perfection

The paradox is that the central focus of the great romance cycles is adultery: Lancelot with Queen Guenevere and Tristan with Iseut. It is the adulterers themselves who generate a good part of the events, and in any case, they de-termine the catastrophic outcome. However much romance authors knew and admired *fin'amor*, their subject matter had nothing to do with platonic love, the tension of desire and purification through sacrifice. The texts could not be more explicit. Guenevere says herself (and Iseut shares her con-science): "I have been hurt by the sin of going to bed with a man other than my husband" (*Lancelot-Grail*, 2:275).[21]

Modern commentators have sometimes underestimated the medieval writer's recognition of the strength of raw sexuality. A cursory reading is all it takes to appreciate it, as in the case of the following passage on the false

---

[20] I am convinced that there is no translation for the word *clerc* in this context, inasmuch as there was no word for "intellectual" in the Middle Ages.

[21] In any case, in *Lancelot*, as elsewhere, love is described as an illness: see *Lancelot-Grail*, 2:249ff.

Guenevere and King Arthur, who has been kidnapped by her: "She often came to see him, and he found her courteous and pleasant to speak with. At length, he forgot his love for the queen, and throughout the time he stayed in prison, the damsel slept with him every night" (*Lancelot-Grail*, 2:264). The narrator carefully reminds us that the king has been drugged ("the other woman had bewitched him with drugs and spells," *Lancelot-Grail*, 2:268; "The queen had so worked on the king with drugs that . . . ," ibid., 275), but the magic potions are just one of the normal tools (and perhaps symbols) of the terrible strength of feminine sexuality, which is as dangerous as it is irresistible. The Queen of Ireland's potions are a prime example of this as essential components of the uncontrollable passion between Tristan and Iseut.

In more general terms, Eve is the archetype on everyone's mind. When Galehaut says to master Elias of Toulouse that Lancelot is thinking neither of women nor damsels, the sage answers, "I know for a truth . . . that everything is bound to happen as I have said, once she puts her mind to it. In fact, I think she has already started, and she will certainly do her utmost" (*Lancelot-Grail*, 2:254).[22] No one can escape the inherent danger of feminine sexuality, from Eve onward, nor women's ability to achieve their goals.[23]

Of course, potions did not relieve one of responsibility, nor did they erase the blame, neither here nor elsewhere. Arthur witnesses an apparently mortal crisis before recognizing his wronging of the true Guenevere; the false queen becomes ill, like her evil adviser Bertoilais, with an incurable disease marked by an unbearable stench, which is the symbol of the wrongdoing. The sinners are condemned to a visible disfiguring of their bodies, a foreshadowing of their eternal damnation. The two queens, Guenevere and Iseut, receive less atrocious punishments but it is no coincidence that the latter contracts leprosy. Like their lovers, they are must endure the mortification of the continual fiction. And the lie that they live exposes them to every danger and disgrace.

Guenevere does not protest the accusation that she is not the true queen because, as we have seen, she knows that she is guilty of something else. But even more significant—and surprising—is that no one defends her openly

---

[22] His assessment of the queen is much more harsh: "She was so untrue as to dishonor the most honorable man in the world" (*Lancelot-Grail*, 2:254).

[23] Of course, the writers (and their readership) have no illusions about masculine sexuality. The greater part of evil characters—as well as many others—are rapists. The castle of Escalon the Dark, for example, is enveloped in darkness because the lord of the castle raped a damsel in the church on the first night of Holy Week (*Lancelot-Grail*, 2:295).

until the day of judgment, when Lancelot must challenge three knights of Carmelide in order to falsify the king's judgment. Privately, all the knights of Logres are favorable toward the true Guenevere, but they all have their doubts. Even after Lancelot has killed two of his three adversaries, when the barons of Carmelide remember that the two champions should have sworn that they were in the right (which was perfectly correct because "a battle of such moment, contesting a verdict, should not be undertaken without an oath," *Lancelot-Grail*, 2:272) and they propose that the duel be interrupted, Galehaut (the only one who knows that Guenevere is an adulterer) steps in so as to avoid any delay. The author tells us the reason: "and he did that because he had some lingering fear that the queen might be guilty and the condemnation [against her] just" (ibid.).

Not even Guenevere's most passionate defender, after Lancelot, is convinced that the queen is not guilty. This suspicion is insinuated throughout this society, which purports to be perfectly exemplary. They are all aware of the clamorous contradiction, which I will paraphrase in the words of Guenevere: "Our Lord pays no heed to our courtly ways, and a person whom the world sees as good is wicked to God" (*Lancelot-Grail*, 2:275). This means that there are two orders of values, courtly and religious: they are not homologous but rather antagonistic. Just think of how King Arthur is presented (for example, "King Arthur, the noblest man alive, whose house is the world's home of valor and prowess, *Lancelot-Grail*, 2:258) or how Lancelot is portrayed as he counters Arthur's judgment of the true queen: "Lancelot was extremely handsome. His dark face was radiant with gentleness and breeding; nor did he yet have a beard, as he had been made a knight only three years before, when he was no more than fifteen. His mouth was small and well shaped, and his forehead broad, his hair auburn and curly" (*Lancelot-Grail*, 2:269).

And it continues like this for a long time, with warm admiration. And yet, this young, handsome, and courageous knight is a sinner, an adulterer whose soul is in danger of eternal damnation. The character (and the writer) are aware of this. He knows that from the courtly point of view, exemplary behavior can cost eternal condemnation. This tragic conscience, therefore, envelops and embitters ever moment of courtly life, and it gives rise to a wide range of greatly varied solutions. If romances like *Tristan* or *Lancelot* seem distant from religious morality and if they appear to be shaped by courtly morality, other romances—like the quest—have a very different formation that does not conflict with the first for the reason that the awareness of the otherness is clear and the resulting tragedy—like that of King Arthur—is present in the mind of the reader.

Krueger has noted rightly that: "For an elite minority, romances were a vehicle for the construction of a social code—chivalry—and a mode of sentimental refinement—which some have called 'courtly love'—by which noble audiences defined their social identities and justified their privileges, thus reinforcing gender and class distinctions."[24] It is also true that there is an essential connection between chivalrous endeavors and love, but romance during this period is ever aware of the contradiction, or at least, of the otherness between this model and the religious model and the resulting tragedy. The world of romance is a frightful nightmare enclosed in a beautiful dream.

Centrifugal Tendencies

The preeminence of the Arthurian context as the typical setting of romance has not gone uncontested. It has its advantages, but it has clear disadvantages as well. The alternatives are marginal, but they exist nonetheless. I have already discussed the initial prevalence of ancient contextualization. To the examples already given, I must at least add one that was destined for prolonged and widespread success, the histories of Troy.[25] In *Cligès*, Chrétien de Troyes went so far as to attempt a brazen synthesis: the first part is set in Constantinople, the place where the ancient world continued to exist and where it also became Eastern (and therefore romance could be not entirely ancient and not entirely Eastern); but then the characters are transferred to Arthur's court, where the second part of the story takes place. The resulting paradox is that Constantinople become a sort of outskirts of the kingdom of Logres, a complementary but not alternative ancient world with respect to the Arthurian world. Others made choices more clearly oriented toward antiquity: Hue de Rotheland, for example, and Aimon de Varennes.

Regardless of the degree of their success, the ancient setting does not differ much from the Arthurian setting in these romances. You get the impression that the "ancient" material was either derived directly or indirectly from classic texts or it did not work as an alternative to the Arthurian world at all. Independently from Homer, the Trojan tales enjoyed great success in Latin (as in the case of Guido delle Colonne), in French (Benoît de Sainte-Maure's *Roman de Troie*), and in all the other languages, at least up to Shakespeare's *Troilus and Cressida*). But it would difficult to distinguish between this image of the world and the Arthurian. In any case, classical

---

[24] Krueger, ed., *The Cambridge Companion*, 5.

[25] See M. R. Jung's excellent book, *La légende de Troie en France au moyen âge*, (Basel, 1996).

models were too codified to allow for a flexibility in romance that was truly concurrent with the Arthurian convention.

Experiments using the East as a backdrop for romance were equally or even more limited. The resulting works were at times even more surprising. The short story, *Floire et Blancheflor*, indeed, had already enjoyed lasting success. But longer romances set in the East were never to be seen, despite the Crusades and trade with the West. The East as depicted in romance would remain that of the *Roman d'Alexandre* until Marco Polo and Jean de Mandeville (whose accounts, of course, were not fictional). We need to ask ourselves why in the modern era things have turned out differently. One hypothesis is that during the Middle Ages the degree of the East's otherness with respect to Western Christendom was excessive, perhaps because—unlike the case of *Arabian Nights*—authentically Eastern sources and models were not directly accessible, even though some scholars have speculated (and continue to do so) that they were. In any case, the Islamic world of Asia and Africa would appear in late medieval romance as setting for adventure, as will see below, but only marginally and as a variation with respect to Europe.

A more plausible hypothesis lies undoubtedly in the success of romance within noble families whose ancestors' endeavors were described in the tales, especially because such accounts represented a fundamental element of their identity. And yet literary works of this type are rare and enjoyed only limited and marginal circulation: evidently they remained within the realm of anecdotal family memory without ever crossing the threshold of literary elaboration. Only just before 1400 did the two romances of Jean d'Arras and Coudrette crystallize around the genealogy of the Lusignan line in the Melusine legend—the story of the fairy-woman and demon, half-woman and half-fish, dispenser of fortune and wealth, generator of ferocious progeny. But by then a late medieval atmosphere prevails, distant from that which has been described up until now.

The development of romance into late medieval and Renaissance "chivalric" literary forms is much different and more ancient. In the fourteenth century, on one hand, in Italy the works of a certain Andrea da Barberino and the bards set the stage for the great epic chivalric poems of the fifteenth and sixteenth centuries and the widespread popularity of this material, which continued to enjoy great success through the twentieth century; on the other hand, in Spain, an early version of *Amadis of Gaul* can be dated in the last decades of the fourteenth century, and it provides the model for subsequent works.

The geographically and formally separate traditions clearly share a dissolution of the Arthurian chronotope: their characters move through unlimited space with arbitrary conformity;[26] in these tales, time is not identifiable with a recognizable historical era; the dense kinship network is attenuated or disappears altogether; and the spreading of their adventures is transformed into a true metastasis. But the moral standards of the characters remain the same as in the Arthurian romances, and the values according to which they react are also analogous. The villains are no longer restricted to foreigners to the Arthurian world or enemies of the faith, but they do conserve the evil markings and their negation of chivalric values, elements that typified Meleagant and many more ancient characters. In these romances, love is one of the principal motors of action, even in the case of the imagined love for Dulcinea, but generally in its most abstract and cerebral form. The imminent sense of blame and ruin is erased.

Thus, the process of dehistorification of the events and characters has peaked, and it is stretched to the point that we can identify the text's diverse audience geographically, socially, and in some cases culturally. The adventure is built on data so elementary and generic that nearly any group of readers or listeners can participate thereof: this explains the vast success of this genre, but also its low literary standards, save for a few exceptions.

This itinerary moves ever distant from reality, but there is also an inverse trajectory that is much more ancient. Its first traces can be found in works like the *Roman de Guillaume de Dole* (it is also sometimes called *de la rose*, with the risk of confusing it with that masterpiece of allegorical narrative) by Jean Renart (early decdes of the thirteenth century). The innovation introduced in this romance does not lie in the plot, which once again is derived from folklore. (An envious master servant discovers the secret of a woman whom he lusts after—a mole in the shape of a rose on her inner thigh. She refuses him and he falsely accuses her of having succumbed to his desires, but then he is forced to admit that he does not even know her.) The convention is altered by the circumstance that the main characters are a plausible Conrad, emperor of Germany, and other equally real nobles, who move within their actual geographic space. By doing so, the poet dared to set the romance in the present and give the story a certainly adventurous but not unreal slant.

Romance was thus able to associate itself with another poetic but entirely different genre. The empress wrongly accused of adultery and abandoned to the beasts in the forest, but then, after many surprising twists, finally saved and protected by the Virgin Mary and by her own ability to endure and be humble—this is the story line of more than one of the "miracles," and it

---

[26] It is interesting to note that the Spaniards who first trod the unknown lands of the Americas identified them using romance place names, as in the case of California.

recurs in many different shapes in the modern era. But of greatest interest is the version by Gautier de Coincy, who used it for the longest and most complex narrative in his miracles.[27] This association demonstrates that had romance wanted not to lose its relation with contemporary reality, it could have looked to religious literature as a source, where there was no lack of vigorously realistic tales that had enjoyed widespread success. The scarcity of examples is proof of the clear preference for "other" solutions.

The first redactions of the immensely popular works *Fille du comte* and *Baudouin de Flandre* date back to the thirteenth and fourteenth centuries. The first revisits the theme of matrimonial crisis resulting from an unjust condemnation of the wife, her departure, and the suffering caused by her absence and the theme of matrimonial serenity renewed through pain and patiently tolerated adventures. The geography of the romance is the very real county of Ponthieu in Piccardy, on the banks of the Somme, and it becomes inexact and improbable only when it is extended to distant Santiago de Compostela and Almería. The second romance is a sort of genealogical chronicle. It covers a widely romanticized story of the counts of Flanders, from Philip of Alsace to Baldwin, his alleged son, to the daughters of the latter, Jeanne and Marguerite, by whom he purportedly sired a girl with clear melusine (and therefore diabolical) traits. The action then moves to the East, with Henry and Baldwin of Flanders emperors of Constantinople, concluding with the story of Jean Tristan, the purported son of Louis IX of France. This sequence of adventures, wars, and love stories is played out by real or at least plausibly real characters who live in a world recognizable to any French reader.

This type of literary production was probably only marginally successful, but during the late fourteenth to mid-fifteenth centuries, it had a starring role. Not long after 1400, the full-fledged popularity of this genre was firmly established with the success of *Paris et Vienne*, a painful love story between two very young persons of different social station (she is the daughter of the dauphin of Vienna; he is the son of a mere noble). After the dauphin refuses him, Paris goes into exile and spends the better part of his years as a victorious warrior for the sultan of Cairo; in the end, he returns to Vienna disguised as a moor and is able to corroborate the uncompromising fidelity of Vienne, who has managed to put off all of the marriages offered to her; now, the two of them can finally coronate their love. Some time later, a similar

---

[27] "De l'empeeris qui garda sa chasteé contre mout de temptations," in Gautier de Coincy, *Les miracles de Nostre Dame*, edited by V. F. Koenig (Geneva, 1966), 3:303–459 (the work is 3,980 lines long).

romance will also enjoy success: *Pierre de Provence et la belle Maguelonne*. In this case, Pierre could actually be worthy of the king of Naples's daughter, but he hides his social status because he wants to loved for his own merits; the two young people flee Naples, are separated by accident, and entirely lose touch with each other (Pierre is successful in the East) until he returns to France, where they reunite and get married.

These two examples, which have been imitated countless times with endless variations, are the fulfillment of a new formula. Here the characters are both young nobles; the innocent, virginal love is unjustly threatened; their adventures prevent them from reuniting for a long period; in the end, his military prowess and her fidelity make marriage and happiness possible. The geographic setting is realistic: in some cases, their travels could be charted on a modern map. Here the story is set in the present or in the recent past. Circulation of these romances was anything but secondary with respect to the later remakes of the Arthurian romances. Yet they were originally limited to a slightly lower social and cultural group, judging from the available information about the manuscripts' owners. It is even possible that the majority of readers of this type of story were women. But by the mid-fifteenth century, this romance model had taken hold in sophisticated spheres like that of the court of Philip the Good of Burgundy, who had many copies made,[28] and in the last decades of the century, Tirante the Knight of the White Moon also established himself, after having been depicted by Cervantes in Catalan literature—a world closely tied (at least in terms of figurative culture) to the Flemish tradition.

History and Romance

In light of the fact that medieval romance is commonly associated with fairy tales, it is important to examine its relationship, instead, to historiography. However strange it may seem to the modern reader, who views medieval romance as fiction, it is clear from the most ancient examples, like *Aeneas*, *Thebes*, *Troy*, and *Alexander*, that historical events are desirable models. If we then consider the texts that might be gathered under the label "chivalric biographies,"[29] beginning with the *Histoire de Giullaume le Maréchal*

---

[28] This is why R. Krueger's connection between late, realistic romance and its popularity in bourgeois spheres is overly simplistic (See Krueger, ed., *The Cambridge Companion*, 5).

[29] See E. Gaucher, *La biographie chevaleresque: Typologie d'un guerre (XIIIe–XVe siècle)* (Paris, 1994).

(thirteenth century) and the romanticized biographies of Bertrand du Guesclin, Marshall Bouicicaut, and even Jacques de Lalaing, it is clear that the biographical pattern is valued because it confers a license of credibility on the tale. This is true even though sometimes it is extremely difficult to distinguish between events that really happened and theatrical embellishment, which favors exemplary behavior and thus authorizes all sorts of inventions.

It is important to remember that the association of the two genres, which we tend to consider as divergent, happens in two ways. First, the standards of vernacular historiography are different and much lower than that of Latin historiography, even though the Latins were open to the fantastic and the extraordinary. In romance languages, stories that had been told only a few generations prior were then colored by the conventions of romance. The story of the conception and birth of James I of Aragon is told as a romance by the fourteenth-century historian Ramón Muntaner, but also—although with some attenuation—in the (pseudo?) autobiography of the sovereign himself, his *Llibre dels fets*. When it comes to contemporary events, interpretative models are often taken from romance. For example, historian Muntaner knew well the story of Roger de Flor because he had worked with him for a long time: an Apulian adventurer of Swedish descent, Roger de Flor had pursued a career as a pirate before becoming the head of a Catalan expedition in the East (under the aegis of the king of Sicily), and he then managed to obtain a second charge from the emperor of Constantinople only to then be dreadfully massacred with the greater part of his men. The narrative structure of Roger's parable is that of a hero of humble origins who, through his own merits, achieves glory and status and then becomes the victim of hypocrisy and betrayal. Just like the main character in any true tragedy, Roger is warned of the danger threatening him, but he is unafraid and unwilling to back down. Would the main character in a romance have acted any differently?

Some years later, Jean Froissart, a historian of the Hundred Years War, was undoubtedly well informed and attentive, but the French-English-Flemish world described by him adhered to the norms and conventions of romance to such an extent that it attenuated many realistic traits.[30] Froissart was not familiar with the classical models so well known by Boccaccio, and in his work, the great plague of 1348 plays a remarkably insignificant role, as opposed to acts of chivalry: for example, the famous scene of the bourgeoisie of Calais who is saved from decapitation only thanks to a moving

---

[30] It is important to remember that Froissart, besides being a lyric poet, was the author of a long romance, *Méliador*, the last of the Arthurian romances.

plea by the queen is constructed on a previously consolidated model (in reality, the queen was probably not pregnant). In the account by the French historian, an expedition like the one that ended tragically in Nicopolis at the hands of the Sultan's forces forgoes strategic considerations and realistic, fatalistic calculations: sublime in its coherence, it obeys only the obsolete ideology of the Crusades and thus resembles the many tales of wondrous endeavors carried out by Christian knights in the unending expanse of the East. There is no explanation for this because Bajazet's troops turned out to be much more difficult to overcome than those faced by Paris or Pierre de Provence in their respective romances (or by Tirante the Knight of the White Moon). Why ever would have Jean of Burgundy, count of Nevers, risked such a miserable and common death as a prisoner instead of basking in glory? One disastrous end for these heroes, instead of their invariable triumphs, was that which unfortunately marked the great divide between romance and reality.

This was true even in the case of a shrewd politician like poet and historian Pedro López de Ayala, who had the delicate responsibility of being ambassador and then chancellor of Castile. He narrated and probably conceived the defeat of the troops of Henry II of Trastamara and Bertrand du Guesclin at Najera at the hands of Peter I and Edward Prince of Wales, as well as the complex negotiations for the release of the Breton *condottiere* (and future constable of France), as a dialectic between courtly behavior and noncourtly behavior and as a parable in which Edward, the winner, and du Guesclin, the defeated, played their game not in accordance with their calculated convenience, but rather on the basis of chivalric models.

Therefore, as romance tended to take on the colors of the real, the accounts of events that had actually happened began to fall into the patterns and assume of the values of the conventions of romance.

Translated by Jeremy Parzen

ANDREW H. PLAKS

The Novel in Premodern China

Can There Be a "Non-Western" Novel?

To speak of the genre of full-length prose fiction that flourished in old
China—long before the advent of wholesale Western cultural influence from
the late nineteenth century onward—as the Chinese "novel" would appear
at best a misunderstanding of literary taxonomy and at worst just a sloppy
misuse of the term. It would be the logical equivalent of calling a shark a
kind of dolphin, or a small owl a bat. How can one possibly apply the name
by which we know the quintessential expression of the Western literary
imagination over the last three centuries to anything other than works of the
European and North American corpus? The novel may well be the premier
icon of recent Western culture—at least, that is, until the emergence of film
as the dominant semiotic medium of the modern age. Germinated from the
seeds of the continuous narrative tradition in the West harking back to classical epic and medieval romance, nurtured within the specific historical and
material conditions of the late Renaissance and the Enlightenment, and
reaching its mature fruition within the very particular social and intellectual
milieu that witnessed the triumph of bourgeois culture from the late eighteenth to the early twentieth centuries, the novel is inseparably linked to the
unique stages and patterns of development that define recent European cultural history. Surely one must hopelessly overextend the compass of the category "novel" beyond any degree of usefulness if one insists upon attaching
the term—already stretched to the limit to cover a vast and inconsistent
body of texts within the Western tradition alone—to forms of narrative fiction belonging to any other historical periods and cultural spheres in the annals of world literature. That is, of course, until we arrive at the age of global
canonization and the universal imitation of Western literary forms and
norms—whether out of sincere admiration or as a result of the pressure of
cultural imperialism—on the part of writers and critics throughout the rest
of the "modernizing" world.

The easiest solution to this apparent terminological impasse would be
simply to jettison the term *novel* from the baggage of comparative literary
scholarship in dealing with any non-Western or premodern texts. And yet,
the configurations of world cultural history argue otherwise. For upon examining the literary record of human civilization, we discover in times as

early as late antiquity in the Mediterranean West, and in places as far-flung as India, Persia, China, and Japan in later centuries, the existence of works of extended prose fiction that, if not perfectly consonant with all of the aesthetic conventions that comprise the common denominators of the Western novel, are at least *commensurate* with them on some of the most fundamental points of literary analysis. The remarkable flowering of the premodern Chinese "novel," in particular, forces us to reexamine and reformulate the exclusively European definitions of this literary mode. The significant areas of convergence between what we customarily call the classic novel in China and its namesake in Europe are not confined to one or two points of resemblance—as is perhaps the case when one describes parallels of a similar nature in Tokugawa Japan, for example. Rather, they cover the full range of topics of concern to literary theorists and to historians of the European novel, among these: the position of the novel within the spectrum of traditional literary genres, the structural and rhetorical analysis of its fundamental poetics, the cultural and political implications of vernacular and popular modes of narration, the roots of the new form in social and cultural history, the triumph of "mimetic" realism and then the gradual deflection of its assumed objective orientation into the dimension of internal subjectivity, the essentially ironic focus of the novel's characteristic rhetorical stance, and the relation between this inexorable shift toward interior selfhood and certain concurrent philosophical trends shaping the intellectual milieu from which the novel sprang. In the following pages, I will consider each of these dimensions in some detail, with the aim of finally justifying the application of the term *novel* to works of the Chinese fictional canon.

Full-Length Xiaoshuo: *The Generic Core of the "Classic" Chinese Novel*

Before we proceed to take a closer look at the criteria according to which the great works of prose fiction in traditional China conform to the aesthetic and intellectual substance of the European novel form, it may be helpful to present a brief overview of the scope of writings that comprise this critical and bibliographical category in the Chinese context. In this attempt to grasp the slippery outlines of the Chinese genre, we need not be deterred by the imprecision of the term *novel* or by its very broad range of cultural and geographical variation even on its own home continent. We must bear in mind that the novel in the very cradle of its birth in Europe was almost never christened with any names more apt than *novella* and its cognates, or *roman* and its cognates in the various national languages, signifying little more than that it was originally perceived in the eighteenth century to be but a new development of the earlier romance tradition—this latter genre itself being notoriously hard to define. It should therefore come as no shock to learn that what is for convenience referred to as the Chinese "novel" never had a very precise designation in the vocabulary of traditional bibliography and literary taxonomy. The most common equivalent in use in Chinese literary studies: *xiaoshuo*—and, with the necessary phonological modifications, *shôsetsu* in Japan and *sosôl* in Korea—is a very general word for fictional writing (literally "trivial discourse"). This term was used as early as the Han Dynasty (206 B.C.E.–220 C.E.) to designate various collections of anecdotal writing clustered at the edges of the serious historical and philosophical corpus. Only in a much later period—as late as the Ming (1368–1644) and Qing (1644–1911) dynasties—did it come into common use as a label for the specific genres of prose fiction it indicates today. Even here, its coverage remains very loose, with no distinction of length implied between the short story and the novel. In order to specify the longer form in contemporary academic usage, one must prefix the qualifying terms *changpian* ("full-length") or *zhanghui* ("chapter-based," literally "with storytelling-session units") to the compound locution *xiaoshuo*; or, alternatively, one may make the point by speaking of a given example using a grammatical quantifier such as *yibu* ("one entire work"), as opposed to *yipian* ("one single piece"), of prose fiction. The implications of certain other ambiguous expressions used in traditional critical writings to stand in for the indeterminate term *xiaoshuo*: *qishu* ("extraordinary books"), *baishi* ("uncultivated histories"), and the like, will be clarified as they are encountered in the following discussion.

The lack of a precise generic label for the premodern Chinese novel in either native or foreign scholarship does not mean that the genre in question remains completely amorphous and undefined—any more than the absence of a better term than *novella/roman* deprives such works of their generic integrity in Western literary theory. Quite the contrary, although we do not have a single comprehensive term or an authoritative definition of the Chinese genre, the texts that form the basis of this essay constitute a fairly distinct corpus in terms of their historical chronology, their general cultural level, and their prevailing conventions of form and content.

With regard to the time frame of the Chinese novel, we encounter very little difficulty in determining the beginning and end points of its path of development. There may remain a bit of scholarly controversy about where to set the *terminus a quo* for the new genre, depending on whether or not one views various oral storytelling traditions and antecedent narratives associated with the formation of the major texts—some of which can be dated as early as the thirteenth and fourteenth centuries—as separate literary phenomena or as integral stages in the genesis of the novels. But there is no question about the fact that the first extant editions of these works to exhibit the defining features of the classic Chinese novel genre as we know it did not appear on the scene until the late Ming period—to be more precise, from around the turn of the sixteenth century. It is a point of no small significance that this remarkable chapter in Chinese literary history opens with a grand flourish: with the appearance of two of the greatest "masterworks" of the Chinese fictional canon: *Sanguozhi yanyi* (*The Extended Meaning of the History of the Three Kingdoms*, commonly known as *Three Kingdoms*) and *Shuihuzhuan* (*Saga of the Watermargin Heroes*, commonly known as *Watermargin*) in some of their most complete, and elegant, recensions.[1] This means that, as far as we can document it by existing bibliographical and publishing information, the fullest flowering of the classic novel genre in China seems to have *preceded*, rather than followed, the spawning of a host of cruder and cheaper works of popular fiction.[2] This situation would seem to present a sharp contrast to the widely held view of the rise of the European novel as a gradual extension of chapbooks and other popular publications, although here too we note that the early history of the European genre was quickly crowned with masterpieces by the likes of Fielding and Sterne in England, Rousseau and Laclos in France, and Goethe in Germany.

It is even easier to draw a line marking off the *terminus ad quem* for the rise and fall of the traditional novel in China. One can almost pinpoint the death of old-style fiction and the birth of the "modern Chinese novel" as an event that occurred around the year 1919, when the old novel was self-consciously rejected by idealistic cultural reformers as an expression of the moribund values and effete culture of the *ancien régime,* in favor of the new Western narrative model adopted with great fervor—and no small measure of self-contradiction—as the perfect literary vehicle for promoting China's liberation from the forces of foreign domination and native reaction. From this point on, one need have no reservations about calling the major works of Chinese prose fiction novels, since they were now explicitly conceived

---

[1] Many translations of the "classic" Chinese novels exist in European languages. The best-known English renderings of *Sanguozhi yanyi* are C. H. Brewitt-Taylor's *Romance of the Three Kingdoms* (Shanghai: Kelley and Walsh, 1929) and Moss Roberts's *Three Kingdoms* (Berkeley: University of California Press; Beijing: Foreign Languages Press, 1991). Earlier translations of *Shuihuzhuan* include Pearl Buck's *All Men Are Brothers* (New York: John Day, 1933) and J. H. Jackson, *Watermargin* (Shanghai: Commercial Press, 1937). These have been superseded by Sidney Shapiro's *Outlaws of the Marsh* (Beijing: Foreign Languages Press; Bloomington: Indiana University Press, 1981).

[2] The reasoning here may get a bit circular, it must be admitted, since this excludes the earlier printings of certain fictionalized historical chronicles such as the so-called *pinghua* ("plain tales") in circulation by the fourteenth century on the grounds that they do not conform to the generic model of the mature novel form.

and unequivocally fashioned according to the European models that gave the genre its name. This watershed in Chinese literary history is set off by only a thin transitional band stretching over the last few decades of Manchu imperial rule, during which time some premature experiments with the new imported forms of prose fiction were undertaken, and certain attempts were made to introduce more "modern" story content into narratives presented in the traditional format. In the best cases, we find in late Qing fiction a bit of heady new wine in old bottles, and some mellow old wine in newfangled containers, but for the most part this period simply marks a clear break between "classic" and "modern" Chinese fiction, so that perennial attempts by scholars to trace the lingering influence of the old novel form in the age of the "New Literature" in China remain, with a few exceptions, only marginally convincing.

Over the long span of three and a half centuries—from the early sixteenth century to the late nineteenth century—that saw the brilliant initial blooming, gradual maturation, and abrupt demise of the classic Chinese novel, the historical and social changes swirling around it could not but leave their traces in the internal configurations of the genre itself. Thus one observes three distinct stages in the development of the Ming-Qing novel:

1. the first phase of spectacular creativity during the course of the sixteenth century, at the height of late-Ming "literati culture," which brought forth the superior recensions of all the so-called four masterworks out of their respective traditions of antecedent narratives and popular story-cycles;
2. a middle period from about 1600 to 1720 in which first the fin-de-siècle atmosphere that preceded the fall of the Ming (in 1644), and then bitter soul-searching over the trauma of dynastic transition, were reflected in both blithely escapist romances and darkly pessimistic satires; and
3. the age of individual and collective self-reflection that accompanied the entrenchment of Qing power in the eighteenth century, marked in the literary arena by a pronounced shift of narrative focus, in the undisputed masterpieces *Honglou meng* (*Dream of Red Mansions*, also known as *Story of the Stone*) and *Rulin waishi* (*Unofficial History of the World of the Confucian Scholars,* or by its common abbreviation, *The Scholars*) from the external dimension to the world of the inner self.[3]

---

[3] The premier English translations of *Honglou meng* include that by David Hawkes and John Minford under the title *The Story of the Stone* (Harmondsworth, Eng.: Penguin Books, 1973–86), and that by Yang Hsien-yi and Gladys Yang under the title *A Dream of Red Mansions* (Beijing: Foreign Languages Press, 1979). The sole English version of *Rulin waishi* is Yang Hsien-yi and Gladys Yang's *The Scholars* (Beijing: Foreign Languages Press, 1957).

For all the disparity in subject matter and style that sets off each of the "six classic novels" as a unique achievement, it is the continuity and consistency of their essential form that allows us to speak of a well-defined concept of genre running through each of the principal exemplars. The fact that the period that saw the consolidation of the generic form of the Chinese novel falls a good century or two earlier than the rise of its European counterpart need not inspire us to make zealous pronouncements about the precociousness and creativity of High Chinese civilization—amidst the usual litany of China's many inventions and contributions to world material culture. We shall see shortly that the parallel creation of the novel in these two cultural spheres, if slightly out of coordination in absolute historical time, was very much synchronized with respect to the configurations of cultural history out of which the new genre independently emerged.

Far more important for the purposes of this survey is the identification of the major works of the classic Chinese novel in terms of their special literary status, or what I wish to call their elevated "cultural level." When one looks over the ensemble of premodern prose fiction in China one observes, once again, a clear divide between the relatively small number of works at the high end of the scale—represented by a handful of masterworks—and on the other side of the spectrum all the rest of the corpus: a much larger quantity of works of lesser stature and more popular character that have come down to us either physically in library collections or as entries in the booklists of bibliophiles of the time. Chinese literary critics from the late Ming onward recognized that the four great novels that had come into circulation during the course of the sixteenth century—*Sanguozhi yanyi, Shuihuzhuan, Xiyouji (Journey to the West,* better known to European readers in the abridged translation *Monkey*), and *Jin Ping Mei (Golden Lotus, Lady Vase, and Spring Plum,* or simply *Golden Lotus*)—stood in a class by themselves.[4] By the first part of the Qing period, if not earlier, these works had come to be referred to collectively as the "four great extraordinary books" (*si da qishu*)—the expression I have rendered elsewhere as "the four masterworks

---

[4] There are two full English translations of *Xiyouji*: W.J.F. Jenner's *Journey to the West* (Beijing: Foreign Languages Press,1982–86), and Anthony C. Yu's *The Journey to the West* (Chicago: University of Chicago Press, 1977–83). Arthur Waley's abridged version under the title *Monkey* (New York: John Day, 1943; rpt., New York: Grove Press, 1958) has been retranslated into many European languages. An earlier full English translation of *Jin Ping Mei* by Clement Egerton under the title *The Golden Lotus* (London: G. Routledge, 1939) is being gradually superseded by David Roy's rendering of the superior Chinese recension of the novel under the title *The Plum in the Golden Vase*, first two of five projected volumes (Princeton, N.J.: Princeton University Press, 1993 and 2001).

of the Ming novel." As time went on, certain traditional critics took it upon themselves to claim the status of "extraordinary book" (*qishu*) for their own favorite fictional works outside the standard list, but the exclusive group of four remained basically unchallenged until it was subsequently expanded to include the two uncontested masterpieces of the eighteenth century: *Honglou meng* and *Rulin waishi,* yielding what have been known in more recent times as the "six classic novels." After making allowances for a small number of additional works of the seventeenth and eighteenth centuries distinguished by unusual literary quality or special thematic interest, I would put in this list *Xingshi yinyuanzhuan (A Tale of Predestined Marriage Bonds to Awaken the World), Qiludeng (The Lantern at the Crossroads), Yesou puyan (Outspoken Words of an Uncouth Old Man),* and *Jinghuayuan (The Fates of the Flowers in the Mirror).* This relegates all the rest of the traditional titles to secondary status.[5] Many of these remaining works are still reprinted and read today, and they are occasionally subjected to serious critical analysis, but they are most often registered in literary history only collectively, in generalized categories of plot and character. These include sentimental tales of the amorous adventures of "talented scholars and beautiful women" (*caizijiaren*),[6] fictionalized elaborations of notable events and exploits from history (*yanyi,* sometimes called "military romance"), martial adventures of "wandering heroes" (*wuxia*), anecdotal detective fiction presented as the "court files" (*gong'an*) of magistrates, and a considerable number of spin-offs, sequels, and imitations of the major fictional works.

As said, the literary class to which the greatest works of fiction in China belonged was conventionally referred to only by such vague terms of praise as "extraordinary books" and "classic novels." In order to set these works off from the popular tales of romance and adventure, I have elsewhere coined the expression "literati novels," on the analogy of the "literati painting" and "literati drama" that characterized the sophisticated artistic world of the late Ming and Qing periods. By this phrase I called attention not only to their specific sociocultural affinities, but also to their rich intellectual

---

[5] Only partial or abridged English translations of *Jinghuayuan* and *Xingshi yinyuanzhuan* are available, the former by Lin Tai-yi under the title *Flowers in the Mirror* (Berkeley: University of California Press, 1965), and the latter by Eve Nyren under the title *The Bonds of Matrimony* (Lewiston, N.Y.: Edwin Mellen Press, 1995).

[6] The term *caizijiaren* refers to stories, plays, and novels whose plots revolve around the amorous encounters of talented young men and the beautiful girls they meet as they struggle to make a name for themselves in the world of the Imperial examination system. Such stories had enormous appeal to Ming and Qing readers who identified—either intrinsically or vicariously—with the ideals of the "scholar-official" elite of old China.

substance, to be discussed later in this essay. The preeminence enjoyed by these particular texts among what is a very large fictional corpus may be partially attributed to the simple fact that they retell some of the most beloved tales of the Chinese tradition, hero cycles and romances known to both peasant and official alike from streetside storytelling and the popular stage. But for the purposes of this volume on the novel as a global literary phenomenon, the primary justification for focusing on this narrow set of texts alone as a test group for outlining the parameters of the classic Chinese novel as a whole—rather than extrapolating from the common denominators of more popular examples—lies in the way that these works themselves shaped the aesthetic conventions and structural paradigms that identify the *qishu,* or classic novel, in China as a distinct literary genre. Thus, paradoxically, they both set the rules and models that govern all the lesser works in the tradition, and at the same time, by their sheer literary excellence, they also push these other works effectively outside of the exclusive generic circle.

Many of the most salient structural features that define the classic Chinese novel form are conveniently—if only obliquely—summarized in the critical term *zhanghui xiaoshuo.* In this modern coinage, the word *hui* (literally, a single "session" of oral storytelling) here borrowed to refer to the typical chapter-units of old-style fiction, is often incorrectly understood to signify the origins of the art of the Chinese novel in the performance of the professional raconteur. This misapprehension may appear to be supported by the prominent use in the conventional narrator's rhetoric employed in these works of an entire set of storyteller's expressions, fixed phrases such as "now our story splits into two paths . . . ," "but let us not speak of this . . . ," and, most conspicuously, formulaic chapter-ending lines on the order of "to understand the meaning of what happened, please read [literally, 'listen to'] the next installment." The insertion of all these narrator's tag-expressions adds up to what Patrick Hanan has called the "simulated context" of oral narrative—"simulated," because far from indicating the leftover traces of popular entertainments, they are in fact contrived artistic devices deliberately applied to the aesthetic purposes of this sophisticated genre of written fiction. The most graphic example of this sort of simulation is seen in the occasional enactment of an imaginary exchange in which the hypothetical raconteur is interrupted by one of his listeners with an impatient query on the sense of the story, or the author (dropping for a moment the charade of oral performance) may simply interject: "Dear reader, you do not understand . . ." In terms of narrative structure, this sort of simulated repartee serves mainly to break up the continuous flow of the story into its constituent scenes or larger segments, but it also has serious implications for the assessment of the mimetic foundations underlying the aesthetics of the classic novel, a problem to be addressed below. Each of these paradigmatic *hui*-chapters is typically presented as a double unit, a compositional pattern highlighted by the conventional use of poetic couplets as chapter titles, further suggesting a (patently false) link between the art of the novel and the oral recitation of the streetside storyteller.

The literal sense of a "chapter-based" structure expressed in the term *zhanghui* has another, even more concrete significance for the analysis of the compositional patterns of the traditional Chinese novel. This is the fact that a large portion of the structural paradigms that define this genre are based on the assumption of a compositional scheme built up out of a string of independent narrative units. Of special importance here is the aesthetic expectation that the overall sequence of chapters will embody a certain numerical (and occasionally, numerological) logic. To be more specific: one of the abiding conventions of the full-length novel is the expectation that the total number of chapters will add up to a round and symmetrical number, typically 100 or 120. The pronounced sense of symmetry—and the aura of all-inclusive fullness—implied by these numerical parameters provide the ground for a variety of exercises in structural patterning. Most noticeable among these is the practice of contriving to divide an overall narrative sequence precisely at its arithmetic midpoint, yielding two great hemispheric structural movements. To cite just a few examples: the one hundred–chapter quest journey in *Xiyouji* arrives at its halfway mark at the crossing of the "River of Communion with Heaven" precisely at the line between chapters 49 and 50, while the strange foreign monk's bestowal of a magic aphrodisiac to the libertine hero of *Jin Ping Mei* also occurs at exactly the same midway point (chapter 49)—marking the divide between Ximen Qing's ascending and descending trajectories of gratification and self-depletion. In the same manner, the watershed Battle of the Red Cliffs in *Sanguozhi yanyi* is staged precisely at the chapter 50 mark of that work.[7] Other structural patterns that seem to flow spontaneously from these round-numbered book lengths include the unfolding of long narrative sequences based on a ten-chapter rhythm. This perception of wavelike movements punctuated at roughly ten-chapter intervals by abrupt changes of focus or direction can already be

---

[7] This last example may seem a bit anomalous, because most editions of this work stretch over 120 double-narrative units. But the observation that the most climactic scene of the book is positioned within its own sequence of chapters—at least, as they are counted in later editions—at the very same numerical point as in the former examples (chapter 50), may alert us to the fact that we are dealing with a general structural convention of the genre.

observed in a looser sense in *Sanguozhi yanyi* and *Shuihuzhuan,* but it becomes a precise grid of emplotment in *Jin Ping Mei,* where we encounter a major turning point in the fortunes of the central characters every time we reach the "nine" in a given ten-chapter sequence. Another favored pattern based on the decimal scheme of chapter sequencing is seen in the use of a one or two "decade" introductory section as a kind of extended prologue—in which the central world of the narrative with its principal actors is gradually assembled onstage—matched by a final sequence of an equal number of chapters in which the narrative framework is dismantled and the players dispersed. In the hundred-chapter compositions, this typically yields a balanced arrangement in which these opening and closing wings flank the central, slower-paced body of the text in a 20:60:20 structural scheme. Once again, the work in which this pattern is most scrupulously observed is *Jin Ping Mei*, but the same basic proportions are also quite visible in *Sanguozhi yanyi* and *Honglou meng* (and to a lesser extent in *Shuihuzhuan* and *Xiyouji*—despite their varying lengths), in that all these texts take just about twenty chapters to set up the basic configurations of their core narratives and later bring us to a point, around chapter 80, at which the main forces driving the stories have clearly played themselves out, long before the afterripples of denouement finally reach their end. Even the atypical structural outline of *Rulin waishi* (fifty-four chapters plus epilogue) observes something of these proportions, placing the "eye of the novel"—the strangely moving ritual "non-event" around which many of the episodic strands of this decentered narrative revolve—in chapter 37, just around the two-thirds point of its overall length.

These examples give only the barest outlines of the numerically based structural patterning deployed by the masters of the *zhanghui* novel form. The degree of cleverness and wit lavished on this aspect of composition takes some rather baroque forms, for instance with narrative units placed in numerically symmetrical positions counting forward and backward from the first and last chapters, special effects contrived to fall in chapters numbered with "perfect squares," and the like. It is no wonder that lesser practitioners of the Chinese novelist's art generally fail to observe these compositional patterns, producing narratives that may range from as brief as two chapters to as interminable as 140, 150, or—apparently the record—192, with a sense of structural anarchy sharply contrasting with the careful contrivance observed in the "extraordinary books."

Several other compositional conventions of the "literati novels" characterize the common narrative model reflected across the broad spectrum of traditional Chinese fiction, while, at the same time, setting in relief the unique

artistry of the greatest masterworks. To give a very noticeable example, anyone who has devoted the countless hours required to read through these
very long books soon becomes aware that their close texture of narration is
woven out of the incessant repetition of barely differentiated characters and
events. While in the hands of less gifted writers this may amount to nothing
more than the sheer redundant use of stock figures and motifs, revealing
only a poverty of creative imagination, in the greatest works of the tradition
we can observe in this same redundancy a polyphonic interweaving of
threads of narrative material designed to bring out fine nuances of meaning
through subtle cross-reflection between individual occurrences. This rich
texture of significant repetition—what I have termed "figural recurrence"—
constitutes a primary focus of analysis in traditional Chinese fiction commentaries, where critics direct considerable attention to this aspect of composition, labelling it with a variety of metaphorical expressions such as: "call
and echo," "shadow projection," and "laying an ambush," among many others. In the same vein, where the exemplars that set the models for the classic
novel genre make conspicuous use of verse passages in a variety of poetic
forms interspersed within the body of their prose narratives—a feature that
marks almost all of the genres of colloquial Chinese fiction—this is frequently taken as a further demonstration of the roots of the novelist's art in
the recitative performance of the oral storyteller. But here again the unimag-
inative use of formulaic "doggerel" verse in works of true popular fiction
serves only to highlight the remarkably inventive use of poetic expression in
the fictional masterworks—in the best tradition of the fusion of lyric and
narrative/dramatic elements in classic Chinese dramatic art—to effect the
aesthetic functions of recapitulation of plot, elevation of linguistic register,
and sheer lyric expressivity.

In the area of narrative contents as well, we can see the same great divide
between the limited corpus of texts that embodies an aesthetic model truly
comparable to that of the greatest European novels, and the host of lesser
works that fail to meet these standards and remain in the generic limbo of
popular romance. It is no surprise that we find many of the same thematic
motifs repeated across the entire range of premodern fiction, given the fact
that these are, by definition, the fixed topoi of the Chinese narrative tradition. Thus, the thematic typologies devised by Chinese bibliophiles as early
as the Ming period to categorize first oral storytelling and later written fiction were easily applied by modern literary scholars such as Lu Xun and Sun
Kaidi in their influential studies on the formation of the classic novel. But
there still remains a world of difference between the amorous adventures in
caizijiaren works such as *Haoqiuzhuan, Ping Shan Leng Yan,* and *Yu Jiao Li*

and the immeasurably more profound exploration of the mysteries of the human heart in *Honglou meng*.[8] In the same way, there is little in common between the prime model of serious historical fiction—*Sanguozhi yanyi* and the very long list of *yanyi* treatments of the historical records of other dynastic periods and other famous players on the historical stage—outside of the endless scenes of court debate on strategy and the staging of ritualized battles, replete with sensational elements of magic and the fantastic, that occupy the pages of so many lesser examples of "military romance." By the same token, the episodic adventure sagas of so many masters of the martial arts pale in comparison with the ambivalent investigation of heroic capacity in *Shuihuzhuan* and the best of the more recent martial arts sagas known as *wuxia xiaoshuo*. The same can be said of the voluminous tradition of narratives of fantastic journeys and encounters with ghosts and demons, so conspicuiously lacking in both the exuberant wit and the allegorical depth of *Xiyouji*, or the large body of erotic fiction prevalent during the late Ming, which, when compared with the unflinching exposé of the illusory core of human desire in *Jin Ping Mei*—or even the playful ribaldry in *Rouputuan* or the learned parody in *Ruyijunzhuan*—appears as little more than crude pornography.[9] In many cases the most damning mark of the lesser novels is precisely their thematic instability, as they typically begin in one category of narrative content and then slide over into another: for example, works such as *Fengshen yanyi* (*The Investiture of the Gods*) and *Xiyangji* (*Journey to the Western Sea*) start as fictional reconstructions of ancient history but quickly deteriorate into a hodgepodge of pseudo-myth and fantastic adventure.

In reviewing the above aspects of the generic scope and aesthetic underpinnings of the classic Chinese novel, we have seen that while many of the essential points that define the genre are unique to the parameters of traditional Chinese narrative, others are held in common with the (slightly later) European novel. We are now in a position to begin to assess the significance of this remarkable overlap of cultural forms. Since there would be no reason to anticipate this degree of convergence—in view of the widely divergent patterns of social, political, and cultural life in the two civilizations, with only tangential and intermittent contact between them throughout the

---

[8] These popular romances figure prominently among early translations from Chinese into European languages, partly because they happened to be in vogue in China at the height of the *Chinoiserie* craze, and partly because they matched the taste for sentimental fiction then flourishing in European salons.

[9] Two English translations of *Rouputuan* are available: Richard Martin's translation from the German of Franz Kuhn under the title *The Prayer Mat of the Flesh* (New York: Grove Press, 1963) and Patrick Hanan's *The Carnal Prayer Mat* (New York: Ballantine Books, 1990).

premodern era—it becomes even more challenging to consider what conjunctions of historical experience may account for the independent gestation of such similar narrative forms.

The Rise of the Novel and Its Roots in Social History

Among the various criteria brought to bear upon the definition of the novel as a literary form, perhaps the most tantalizing grounds for cross-cultural speculation on the conditions of its genesis are found in the extraliterary reality from which it emerged. It must be nothing if not heart-warming to critics and literary historians committed to materialist philosophy and other forms of historical determinism to see in the independent origin of the novel in China a confirmation of the organic links between the novel and various material factors in premodern social and political culture. This connection between literary and social history underlies the argument set forth in studies such as Ian Watt's 1957 monograph *The Rise of the Novel,* attributing the rapid development of British prose fiction to contemporary transformations in both the physical environment and the intellectual map of eighteenth-century England.[10] With slight adjustment for local conditions, this thesis has been extended by others to posit a social-historical basis for the consolidation of the novel genre throughout Europe in the Age of Revolution. For those whose idea of traditional Chinese society is limited to the halcyon vision of an ageless agrarian order, with benign emperors ruling placidly over contented peasants and wise, epigram-spouting "scholar-gentry," the view of the novel as an expression of the human response to poweful forces of political and economic revolution—summed up in the great polysyllables: industrialization, commercialization, and urbanization—would appear to describe a completely alien universe. And this would seem to rule out the parallel development in premodern China of a new genre of prose fiction designed to reflect all of these tempestuous upheavals, all the Sturm und Drang of a world being dragged kicking and screaming into modernity.

The picture of a timeless world of perfect order in the Middle Kingdom, envisioned so admiringly by Voltaire and with such contempt by Hegel, must be sharply corrected, however, in light of the findings of recent historical scholarship. The same centuries that saw the sudden flowering of a new genre of prose fiction in China so similar to the European novel as to justify

---

[10] Ian Watt, *The Rise of the Novel: Studies in Defoe, Richardson and Fielding* (Berkeley: University of California Press, 1957).

borrowing this Western term to name it, also witnessed a set of profound historical changes that would gradually erode the foundations of the Confucian polity and leave the empire vulnerable to as yet unforeseen forms of barbarian encroachment. Such long-range trends as population shifts to the great cities of the Yangtze Delta region and the rise of urban culture, the conversion to a silver-based money economy, commercialization, commodification, incipient industrialization—even overseas colonization, to name just the most striking factors, seem not entirely unrelated to the appearance of a new form of prose literature so well suited to questioning the values of the old order. These great changes began a century or more earlier in China than they did in Europe, and their effects were tempered—and eventually arrested—by a variety of particular aspects of the Chinese historical and cultural context, but they are still in striking accord with those historical shifts cited by Watt and others as forming the material and intellectual substrate for this new mode of literary expression. When one notes that the parallel rise of sophisticated new genres of prose fiction occurred nowhere else but in sixteenth-century China and in Europe (and to a lesser extent Tokugawa Japan) during the seventeenth and eighteenth centuries, three periods that experienced to one degree or another the significant effects of commercialization and urbanization before the modern era, while the remaining literary cultures of the world—whether trapped by native feudalism or crushed by foreign imperialism—never moved beyond the limitations of hero-cycles and courtly romance to produce a new critically oriented narrative genre until modern times, it is tempting to conclude that the causal influence of these external factors was indeed decisive.

Still, the significance of the linkage between the novel and its historical background in Europe and China rarely translates into any direct reflection of contemporary reality in the new fictional medium. Indeed, the major works of premodern Chinese fiction—with a few notable exceptions—hardly ever treat us to extended concrete reportage on current social conditions. What we get in most examples of the genre is, instead, an oblique refraction of social and political reality by means of the projection of contemporary concerns into earlier historical contexts, and by the satiric debunking or allegorical encoding of prevailing power structures and value systems. It is this function of critical cultural introspection—the rethinking of the relation between individual fulfillment and the social order catalyzed by changing empirical conditions in the external world—that marks out some of the most fertile common ground for the comparative study of the novel in China and in the West.

The Roots of the Novel in Literary History

For all that the social and political environment prevailing in early modern China and Europe may have facilitated the emergence of a new literary medium for the expression of the mentality and the sensibility of a new age, the form did not just spring up autochthonously, in either place, into a cultural vacuum. In both spheres the novel is firmly anchored in the configurations of their respective literary histories. Here, as one would naturally expect, the two paths of literary evolution, rooted as they are in two entirely independent cultural systems, diverge sharply. It is true that a measure of significant cultural influence from various Western sources can be observed in traditional China in some forms of music and dance transmitted by Central Asian performing artists arriving over the silk route to the great metropolitan centers of medieval China, in the echoes of Greek plastic aesthetics in certain kinds of Buddhist sculpture, and in other areas. But within the world of premodern classical Chinese literature, Western forms and motifs—with the exception of occasional snatches of stories passed from mouth to mouth around campfires and in caravansaries across the expanses of the Eurasian steppes—do not even show up on the screen. Most telling for the comparative cultural historian is the striking nonappearance in China of anything like an epic narrative form in prose or in verse, despite the existence of great epic songs and tales in nearly all of the cultures ringing China: Japan, Mongolia, India, even Tibet. This glaring gap in the continuity of cultural diffusion significantly weakens the theoretical presuppositions of those who would link the European novel to prior epic models. But though what we call the "novel" in each of these traditions grows out of very different literary soil, it still shares the same basic situation of being deeply rooted in its own classical heritage—making of the new genre in both cases, for all its novelty and originality, an implicitly backward-looking and intrinsically intertextual mode of expression.

The absence of an epic genre in China to serve as a fountainhead of its continuous narrative tradition is indeed inconvenient, but that is not because of any lack of *heroic* narrative in the Chinese cultural milieu. The novel taking shape in the Ming period could and did draw deeply from a very rich heritage of oral storytelling and popular hero-cycles. Far more germane to the formation of the new genre was the intersection of fictional and historical prose in the Chinese literary culture. Given the unparalleled importance of history writing in the ensemble of premodern Chinese civilization, it is not surprising that a majority of the prose works that can be classified as novels take history as their principal narrative focus. To simply state that a large portion of Chinese novels belong to the category of historical fiction may not sound very remarkable, as this is also an important subgenre of the novel in the West. But in Imperial China "history" means not just recording great deeds and events, recounting the rise and fall of kingdoms, or tracing social forces and political movements. It refers more narrowly to the so-called official histories that occupied the working lives and the literary talents of so many of the greatest minds of the empire throughout the centuries. In this spirit a great many writers and critics during the heyday of the classic novel looked back to the "Grand Historian" Sima Qian (145–86 B.C.E.) of the Han Dynasty—to whom the consolidation of the dynastic history form is usually credited—as a kind of patron saint of fictional narrative as well. Much of traditional prose narrative is framed not simply as a fictional reworking of the best-known episodes gleaned from historical sources and popular lore but more narrowly as an elaboration on the canonic texts of classical historiography themselves; this is the literal meaning of the term *yanyi* for this subgenre. Even when works of fiction are not explicitly labeled as *yanyi,* the use in their titles of generic terms for historical records (*zhuan, ji,* and the like) may also signal the fact that they are to be taken in one way or another as retellings, or critical revisions, of the great chronicles of past events. Moreover, fictional writing in general came to be designated—on a note of self-justification for the labor spent on so marginal an occupation— as "leftover history," "unofficial history," "rustic history," or "uncultivated history" (*yushi, waishi, yeshi, baishi*).

The impact of this crucial connection to the historical canon on the development of the Chinese novel works in two directions, both growing out of the fact that the vast sweep of the official histories is presented in its greater part in separate biographical chapters on important individuals rather than in continuous unified narrative. First, and most obviously, the substrate of official historiography bequeaths to the new fictional genre a primarily biographical perspective. This, in turn, provides the grounding for structural patterns oriented less to a unilinear narrative flow, and more toward the evocation of a kaleidoscope of shifting perspectives. More to the point, the tradition of classical historical writing in China sheds on the novel a decidedly *critical* stance, one in which the contemplation and ultimately the moral judgment of individual human motivation and action call forth an essentially ironic, sometimes harshly negative, view of even some of the most beloved heroes of popular lore.

A second node of interconnection between the Ming-Qing novel and earlier forms of Chinese prose concerns its genetic relation to various genres of short fiction. We have already seen that the presumption that the lengthy works of continuous narrative were generated by simply stringing together separate story units—the so-called sessions that comprise the chapter-units of *zhanghui* novels—is simply not borne out by the history of book making in late Imperial China. Rather, judging by all available evidence, it seems that the so-called *huaben* ("promptbook") form of late Ming short fiction came into full flower only *after* the appearance of the two flagship novels *Sanguozhi yanyi* and *Shuihuzhuan*. Although we do find some interesting examples of frame-tale story collections in the Ming-Qing corpus (for example, the *Decameron*-like *Doupeng xianhua*)—amidst a general tendency to combine short fiction into large anthologies with only a semblance of thematic consistency—we cannot look to chapbooks or other types of piecemeal anecdotal writings to account for the generation of the full-length novel form.

One place we can look for significant cross-generic sources of the genesis of the classic Chinese novel is in the area of traditional drama. At first glance, this connection would seem to mark yet another divergence from the story of the emergence of the novel in Europe, since a number of salient features of Chinese dramatic art—the total absence of serious drama (other than court spectacle) as a literary medium in ancient China, the nearly complete lack (with some important exceptions) of anything akin to tragedy as an aesthetic vehicle, the predominantly lyric mode of Chinese operatic drama from the thirteenth century down to the present day—all seem to pull in separate directions that weaken the case for positing a path of development parallel to that in the West. And yet in many ways the dynamic interaction between the flourishing of prose fiction and stage art in Ming and Qing China matches a comparable symbiosis in post-Renaissance European culture. In late-Imperial China, serious drama and the novel go hand in hand: they share very much the same audience, the same publishers, often the same authors and critics—not to mention by and large the same font of narrative materials and motifs. As a result, the classic Chinese novel is not only deeply imbued with the living spirit but also partakes of many of the formal structural patterns of the contemporary "literati" stage—from the smallest compositional unit of the "scene" (typically comprising one-half of a paradigmatic *hui*-chapter) to certain overarching structural schemes such as "separation and union," a staple formula of Ming-Qing drama criticism. Traditional Chinese drama, like its European counterpart, is an artistic mode that relies for its powerful effect more on rhetorical tension than on the enactment of physical conflict. This is carried over into the medium of prose mimesis, where the central clashes that motivate plot are usually played out more in dialogue than in direct narration—in this light it is entirely appropriate to borrow Bakhtin's notion of *dialogism* to describe the dialectical core of the Chinese novelist's art. The best of the classic novels in China, works like *Xiyouji* and *Honglou meng,* are profoundly immersed in the tension of unresolved dialectics of truth and falsity, reality and illusion, that they share with the great sixteenth- and seventeenth-century dramas of Tang Xianzu, Kong Shangren, and others—in a manner astonishingly reminiscent of the strikingly unconventional directions taken in vernacular prose and drama in the age of Cervantes and Calderón in Spain that were to crystallize a century or two later into the new self-referential aesthetics of the European novel.

The Novel as a Mirror of Reality

Neither their striking parallels in social and historical background, nor their ambivalent links to prior literary genres, taken alone, are sufficient to fully justify identifying the classic Chinese novel with its European counterpart. But a closer look at certain aspects of the chronological development, cultural level, and formal patterning of the Chinese genre has revealed that it is precisely on those points of aesthetic substance where the great exemplars tower above the other mediocre works of adventure and sentiment—with which they share many of the same basic formal features—that their conformance to the paradigms of the Western novel come most compellingly into view. To put this another way, what is of central importance here is not simply whether or not the Chinese and European novel emerged from analogous roots in social and cultural history, but rather the potential implications that this grounding in a concrete historical and literary context may have had on the intellectual underpinnings of the genre in the two separate spheres.

One such implication arises from the connection often inferred between the apparent coordination of the rise of the novel genre with the great historical transformations of early modern times and a certain broadening—shall we say, "democratization"—of culture. According to a commonly held picture, the meteoric rise of the novel in both China and Europe is but an outgrowth of the rapid expansion of commercial printing, the spread of popular literacy, and the creation of a vast and insatiable market for the vicarious gratification afforded by works of narrative fiction. Once one accepts this scenario (though much exaggerated and embellished by historical hindsight it is not entirely without foundation), then it is natural to attribute to the new narrative genre a shift in class affinity: that is, a drift in cultural identity away from the classical pretensions of the old elite and toward a more broadly based modern confraternity of authors and readers.

Whether or not this impression accurately describes the conditions in the literati studios of late Ming China—or, for that matter, in the literary salons of eighteenth-century England and France—this set of assumptions remains a powerful inducement to viewing the novel as an essentially popular form of expression. The very *newness* of the novel in this context seems to carry with it the implication of a reaction, even a rebellion, against the cultural and, with that, the political authority of the arbiters of the classical literary canon. That is why at the dawn of the novel we seem to hear such strident voices in both China and Europe condemning the new form as dangerous: both sexually licentious and politically subversive—something to be kept from the eyes of tenderhearted and impressionable women and children. In Ming and Qing China, these prejudices against the writing and reading of fiction were not nearly as uncomprising as is commonly believed. The occasional bans against particular works were more often observed only in the breach and were for the most part roundly ignored by leading literary figures. But the characterization of the novel as implicitly subversive remained intact, even when this was turned around by ardent political and literary reformers of the twentieth century and used to promote the novel as a positive engine of revolutionary social change.

The polemics of literature being inseparable from the politics of language, the controversy surrounding the cultural significance of the novel sooner or later comes to focus on the predominantly colloquial medium of narration upon which the new genre was based. Where the shift in literary art from the classical to the vernacular tongues of Western Europe (by the likes of Dante, Boccaccio, Rabelais, Cervantes, and Milton) had long since laid the groundwork for the emergence of the new narrative form, in China there had been very little written colloquial narrative to speak of prior to the emergence of full-blown vernacular fiction in the latter part of the Ming dynasty (with the marginal exception of the so-called *bianwen* form of popular tales in the Tang period, a handful of Song Dynasty stories and, one might add, the spoken dialogue passages in Yuan and Ming drama). Even within the corpus of Ming fiction itself, it should be noted, the dominance of the colloquial medium of expression was never total. A few notable works—the greatest being *Sanguozhi yanyi*—and a large number of mediocre ones continued to rely on classical diction for both narration and dialogue. Thus, the shaping of colloquial Chinese into an uncommonly supple and expressive literary language was only a gradual development that accompanied, rather than preconditioned, the rise of the classic novel.

At the heart of these polemics on literary language is the thesis, compellingly argued in recent Western criticism in Erich Auerbach's *Mimesis,* that level of diction (high or low style) is a principal determinant not only for rhetorical analysis, but also for probing the deeper aesthetic and intellectual substance of the "representation of reality" in narrative texts.[11] We have already seen that the conventional medium of the traditional Chinese novel is based on an imitation of the rhetoric of the professional storyteller: the so-called simulated context of oral performance. Widespread misinterpretations notwithstanding, these storyteller's tag expressions are not remnants of actual performance, but—just as the term *simulation* suggests—they comprise a set of mimetic devices self-consciously employed to achieve special rhetorical effects. Aside from the structural function of segmenting a narrative into its constituent units, what the use of these devices accomplishes is to insert into the essentially *private* domain of writing and reading an imaginary *public* ground of signification. That is, by adopting the pose of the all-knowing streetside or teashop narrator, the Chinese fiction writer can use this voice to exploit or undermine commonly held preconceptions of motivation and plausibility, and culturally shared notions of moral value and philosophical truth. This opens up to the most skilled masters of this medium great possibilities for manipulating readers' aesthetic expectations, their vicarious identification with the experiences portrayed, and their apprehension of the meaning of a given work. It is the equivalent in written prose of a playful wink or a meaningful nod to the audience from the stage or the storyteller's platform, a mode of presentation highly charged with ironic potential.

The idea that the representation of reality can be effected through rhetorical mimesis in the colloquial novel raises a number of difficult issues concerning realism as a literary criterion. Whose reality is this, and how is it conveyed? How does the novelist reconstruct the experience of reality in a way that both makes sense by commonly held standards of plausibility and moral acceptability, and at the same time unfolds before readers new insights for understanding themselves and their world?

The critical concept of realism at the aesthetic core of the novel is a double-edged tool. Before the master novelist can dissect a fictional world to reveal its inner ground of meaning (or meaninglessness), he or she must first construct it. Thus the initial and primary task of the novel, in China as in the West, is to bring forth through the conjuring arts of literary representation the convincing sense of a "real" world at the heart of its narrative fabrication.

---

[11] Erich Auerbach, *Mimesis*, trans. Willard R. Trask (Princeton, N.J.: Princeton University Press, 1953).

As we have already seen, in the history of the novel in both China and the West attempts to directly translate the immediate social and historical milieu surrounding the formation of the genre into a camera-eye depiction of the world of a given work—in the manner of Zolaesque naturalism—never defined the dominant mode. In the majority of cases the representation of reality must be understood in a manner far more abstract than glib claims of realistic portrayal might seem to indicate. At the same time, however, the attempt to capture and convey the physical enviroment of human experience in real space-time settings is as important in the classic Chinese novel as it is in the chronotopes of European fiction. Just as the distinctive urban landscapes of Balzac's Paris, Dostoyevsky's St. Petersburg, Dickens's London, and Joyce's Dublin constitute not just the mechanical backdrop but very much the essential substance of their works, so, too, the opulent gardens and back alleys of the great Chinese cities of Nanking in *Rulin waishi* and Beijing in *Honglou meng,* even the provincial backwater of Qinghexian in *Jin Ping Mei,* emerge as primary components of the reality represented in these texts—just as, in later times, the pulsating malignant metropolis of Shanghai was to embody the essential stuff-matter of a large portion of late Qing and Republican fiction. In parallel fashion, where the manor house, the hunting park, the wild heath, the great battlefield, and the pastoral bower rise to the level of living tissues of the European texture of fictional reality, in the classic Chinese novel it may be the open road between inn and wineshop, the secluded temple or monastic retreat, or the provincial yamen that takes on this function. Something bordering on the pastoral may be conveyed in vignettes of fishing villages (as in *Shuihuzhuan)* or in scenes of innocent cowherding (in *Rulin waishi*), but for some reason the vision of peasants happily toiling in their rice paddies never seems to have formed a part of the tableaux of old Chinese fiction. On a more intimate scale, where the reality of the European novel is often telescoped down to specific interiors, the drawing room or the salon, for example, in China, it is the family compound, the enclosed garden, or the scholar's study that becomes a synecdoche for the world of its principal characters.

In considering the setting of the Chinese novel, we must also take into account the human landscape: those social networks that both contain and define the narrative flow of recaptured experience. Not surprisingly, the proverbial frame of the idealized extended family ("four generations under a single roof") provides an ever-present matrix, occasionally for visions of harmony but more often for tales of tension and conflict. In its mimetic representation of the real world of Ming and Qing China, this family frame is significantly extended in works such as *Jin Ping Mei* and *Honglou meng* to take in very elastic webs of pseudo-kin: official colleagues, academic or business cronies, and assorted professional hangers-on.

This brings us to the next lower level of figures in the panorama of "reality" bodied forth in the medium of prose fiction: the individual human actors who play out the fictional representation of real experience. Here we encounter yet another striking point of convergence between the art of the classic Chinese novel and the conceptual underpinnings of the European form. I am referring to the theoretical model mapped out by Northrop Frye in his 1957 *Anatomy of Criticism* (and suggested obliquely in the theories of other critics who categorically identify the European novel with bourgeois culture), according to which the course of development of the Western narrative tradition plots a pronounced downward curve: from the divine beings and semidivine kings and warriors of epic, through the larger-than-life figures of virtue and villainy who people the romance, down to the more mundane characters in the novel, individuals whose world coincides by and large with our own—before plunging even further below this threshold into the fundamentally flawed realm of the antihero of modern and postmodern fiction.[12] Frye's discussion of these "mimetic" levels in his "theory of modes" reflects the clear assumption that the history of premodern Western narrative progresses inexorably toward its logical conclusion in the faithful representation of the outlines of human motivation and action in terms closest to common experience.

The student of full-length fictional narrative in China cannot help being struck by the analogous path of development taken by the "four masterworks" from their inception in the sixteenth century, leading us from the monumental exploits—and the monstrous crimes—of great warriors and statesmen in *Sanguozhi yanyi,* to the rough-hewn bandit-heroes in *Shuihuzhuan,* and finally to the sordid world of lust and greed at the lower rungs of the hierarchy of privilege in *Jin Ping Mei.* From that point onward, we descend yet further into the dark side of human potential savagely caricatured in *Xingshi yinyuanzhuan* and the parade of human folly and pretension exposed in *Rulin waishi.*

Frye's scheme of mimetic levels is clearly too reductive: it distinguishes only between the novel, in the most generalized sense, and its supposed progenitor genres of epic and romance, paying only passing attention to the enormous range of variation in the depiction of social levels over the breadth of the eighteenth- and nineteenth-century fictional corpus. But there still remains a rather large grain of truth in the underlying assumption

---

[12] Northrop Frye, *Anatomy of Criticism* (Princeton, N.J.: Princeton University Press, 1957).

that the novel depicts its human subjects at a remove that draws progressively closer to "normal" human experience. If we reformulate this point slightly to suggest that the novel is essentially a reconstruction of the *familiar*, a narrowing of the focus of narrative representation and the pace of narration to the parameters of common experience (whether in the recognizable settings of everyday life or the imaginable worlds of fantasy), then this may become a more useful critical tool for understanding the parallel literary phenomenon in China. The idea that the art of the novel consists in the taming or *domestication* of the exotic and the unusual through the deflation of ironic wit or the pose of matter-of-fact reportage—what one might call a *refamiliarization* of the "defamiliarized" subjects of narrative discourse—gives new meaning to the central term of traditional Chinese narrative theory: the notion of the "extraordinary" (*qi*). We may now say that with the establishment of the aesthetic canons of the novel the locus of the strange and the noteworthy is shifted from the socially or historically (or, in the case of the fantastic, ontologically) extraordinary into the realm of the ordinary, or conversely, that it finds a new way of looking at the details of daily existence in a manner that sees in the ordinary the quality of exotic eccentricity.

This inversion of the dialectics of the ordinary and the extraordinary at the heart of the fictional discourse of the novel has a special bearing on the reflection of a changing gender orientation in the new narrative genre. Obviously, this is not to say that earlier literary representation of human experience was not replete with the experience of the feminine, both as feeling and acting subjects and as objects of desire. But in the novel the new aesthetics of intimacy and familiarity take the (naive or sophisticated) unfolding of the pathways of human desire into new territory. Where the idealization of the feminine and the triumph of sentimentality dominate in both romance and mediocre novels, in the greatest exemplars of the new genre this is replaced by unstinting examination of the problematic core of human feeling and the impossibility of its perfect communication. To use another highly quotable overstatement from *Anatomy of Criticism,* when Frye asserts that the heroes of epic and romance function "near or at the conceivable limits of desire," his intention seems to be to convey the *unbounded* force of desire quickening the mythical imagination.[13] But in the novel we are brought up to those very limits, and we are made to peer over the edge into the everyday abyss of imperfect fulfillment.

In the classic Chinese novel this new gender perspective is very conspicuous. This is not because fascination with feminine sensibility was invented

---

[13] Ibid., 136.

only in the late Ming period—it had always occupied a crucial place in the aesthetics of Chinese lyricism, both in lyric poetry per se and in the lyric drama. But given the apparently exclusive male focus of so much of classic narrative,[14] the very visible way in which the feminine is thrust to the center of attention in the novel is both striking in its own right and of great significance for any comparative inquiry into the genesis of the novel in a global perspective. The traditional Chinese novelists can never quite liberate themselves from their Confucian social context—any more than their European counterparts ever shake entirely free of their own patriarchal value systems—and so the representation of female experience in China still tends to revolve around stereotypes of the abandoned lover, the devoted spouse and mother, the shrew, and the whore. But the very intimacy of the close-up perspective afforded by the new narrative mode virtually guarantees a heightened sensitivity to, and a more finely drawn representation of, the feminine half of the human condition.

In the great masterworks of the early Chinese novel this aspect of reality may be easily overlooked. The first three of the four masterworks of the Ming novel, *Sanguozhi yanyi, Shuihuzhuan,* and *Xiyouji,* are ostensibly traditional story cycles about empire builders, intrepid warriors, fierce bandits, and wandering monks presumably beyond the reach of sexual vulnerability. Yet in each of these works scenes of sexual destablization are introduced in ways that cannot be dismissed as gratuitous exercises in titillation but must be understood as attempts to delve into deeper questions of self-containment and self-mastery. Coming to *Jin Ping Mei* we plunge into one of the most profoundly negative investigations of feminine psychology in all of world literature but still one that reveals great insight into the existential truth of women trapped in the demeaning reality of concubinage, unchecked patriarchal authority, and the absolute imperative of producing male heirs—insight far more penetrating than a cursory reading of the book's notoriously explicit sexual passages alone could possibly reveal.

The supreme masterpiece of the classic Chinese novel form, *Honglou meng,* with its unique fixation on feminine sensibility, takes us even deeper into the gender complexities of traditional China. Although the young hero Baoyu apparently functions as a male center of consciousness around which all of the principal female characters revolve, he is defined, as much as his nubile cousins, by a kind of virginal self-absorption. Despite a series of

---

[14] A very important exception to this may be observed in the so-called *chuanqi* ("tales of the extraordinary") genre of short fiction that flourished during the late Tang Dynasty.

memorable lines in the author's opening remarks (and in various immature utterances voiced by Baoyu himself) that idealize the purity and innocence of young maidens, what at first sight look like naive outpourings of sentiment turn out to constitute a profoundly ambiguous search for sexual and spiritual identity. As the classic Chinese novel continues its plunge down the mimetic scale, the view of the feminine portrayed with such delicacy and sensitivity in *Honglou meng* is counterbalanced by a number of other works of roughly the same centuries in which we get a darker and darker picture of gender reality—for example, in the slightly earlier *Xingshi yinyuanzhuan,* with its grotesque pageant of female victimhood and ferocity, set into even greater relief by occasional vignettes of level-headed wives and affectionate married couples.

Continuing our descent to the ground level of the real world of human experience projected in the novel form, we arrive at the bedrock: the physical environment of material objects making up the surface texture of temporal existence. From this perspective, the realism of the novel translates into the close-up delineation of the sights, sounds, and smells of everyday life in descriptive passages evoking in all their manifold specificity—sometimes captivating, sometimes tedious—details of architecture, furnishings, clothing, food, drink, and sex. In some works of Ming and Qing fiction (especially *Jin Ping Mei* and *Xingshi yinyuanzhuan*) this minute attention to detail is of an order sufficient to make these works valuable sources for research on social history and material culture. In the finest examples of the genre, we gain the impression that this is not simply the gratuitous enumeration of details for the sake of filling in the background of the narrative canvas but that rather it serves the deeper aesthetic function of evoking the material substrate of conscious experience. Just as the exploration of material reality in the European novel is inextricably tied to the intellectual foundations of empiricism and related philosophical movements, the novel in premodern China is similarly grounded in a heightened interest in the mirror-image relation between subjectivity and objectivity in late Imperial thought—with its abiding preoccupation with the mutual implication of "self" (*wo, ji*) and "things" (*wu*). It is certainly no accident that in the heyday of Chinese colloquial fiction, beginning with its precursors as early as the late Song (960–1279) and Yuan (1279–1368) periods, the dominant literati culture witnessed a great vogue for antiquarian collecting of physical objects: rocks, seals, writing-brushes and inkblocks, and the like, as well as a new upsurge of the "poetry of things" (*yongwushi*), among other signs of fascination with the material texture of existence.

Beyond Mimesis

Just as the unstinting pursuit of objective "truth" in the macroscopic and microscopic realms of the physical universe—using ever higher powers of magnification and resolution with telescope or microscope—brings one to a point at which concrete reality reaches the limits of sensory perception and scientific measurement and gives way to sheer speculative (or mathematical) abstraction, so too, the probing of objective reality in the medium of prose fiction, when pushed to its limits, crosses over into the realms of the unreal, the irrational, the fantastic. In the language of traditional Chinese fiction theory, this may be analogous to the interface between the "ordinary" and the "extraordinary"—from the noteworthy or the exemplary to the bizarre and the grotesque. Of greatest significance for the present comparative inquiry into the conceptual underpinnings of the novel in China and the West is the literary phenomenon whereby ever closer and more minute observation of the texture of reality sweeps by the boundary separating the external from the internal and carries its pursuit of the "real" into the world of inner consciousness. This tendency of the novel as a genre to push into the territory of internal experience, as described in Erich Kahler's influential 1975 study, *The Inward Turn of Narrative*, is not just a salient feature of the later phases of development of the Western novel, but surfaces almost from the start of its parturition from epic and romance.[15] One need only think of the centrality of the bildungsroman and picaresque fiction in the formation of the genre's characteristic probing of consciousness—and the place of such early masters of the medium as Lafayette, Goethe, and Sterne in setting this basic orientation—in order to grasp this point.

In light of the preceding review of the very extensive common ground of literary aesthetics and narrative substance shared by the classic Chinese novel and its Western counterpart, it should come as no surprise that the greatest examples of the Chinese genre also take their analogous path of mimetic inquiry to its logical conclusion in the depths of consciousness. Readers of the four masterworks of the sixteenth century, bedazzled by the surface texture of their engrossing tales of heroism, ambition, greed, lust, and religious fervor, often fail to pay sufficient attention to the exploration of consciousness that takes shape between the lines of their episodic story-cycles. In the case of *Xiyouji*, those traditional and modern readers who heed the author's own allegorical signposts and apprehend in his retelling of

---

[15] Erich Kahler, *Die Verinnerung des Erzählens* (unpublished), trans. Richard and Clara Winston under the title *The Inward Turn of Narrative* (Princeton, N.J.: Princeton University Press, 1973).

the popular narrative of the quest for Buddhist scriptures in India a veiled unfolding of the progress toward enlightenment of the sentient mind can readily see that the conceptual core of this work has been turned into an internal quest for the integration of the warring elements of self. It takes a special kind of reading, however, to appreciate the degree to which even works so firmly entrenched in gripping surface narration as *Sanguozhi yanyi, Shuihuzhuan,* and *Jin Ping Mei* ultimately take us beyond the external recounting of noble and base deeds into the interior dimensions of delusion and self-awareness. When we reach the culmination of the classic novel genre in the mid eighteenth century, the two masterworks *Honglou meng* and *Rulin waishi,* as one very perceptive Chinese critic has phrased it, "put Confucian civilization on the couch."

This overlapping area of intellectual substance provides perhaps the best justification for identifying the Chinese narrative vessel dedicated to recasting the episodes and motifs of the popular narrative tradition into a new generic mold with the literary phenomenon known as the novel in the Western cultural context. When one observes the shift of focus from external acts to the inner life of the heart and mind in European fiction, one inevitably associates this development with the most important intellectual movements of the eighteenth through the twentieth centuries in Western thought: from Lockean empiricism with its Cartesian roots through the phenomenology of recent generations. To those who may be unfamiliar with the great breadth and complexity of philosophical speculation in Ming and Qing China, this intellectual backdrop to the rise of the novel in the West might appear to exclude any Chinese literary works—no matter how descriptively gripping or structurally compelling—from consideration as examples of the same literary type. But in late Imperial China, in very nearly the same way as in post-Renaissance Europe, the invention of this new literary instrument for examining the substance of reality in human experience goes hand in hand with parallel developments in the history of thought, reflecting very much the same sort of pursuit of the ground of existence down to the deepest layers of consciousness.

Within the context of premodern Chinese intellectual history, this redefinition of the object of philosophical contemplation is most meaningfully associated with developments in Confucian—or what is better known in Western sinological writings as "Neo-Confucian"—thought. This is not the narrow Confucianism of filial piety, ritual propriety, benevolent rulership, and the other social virtues by which this great cultural heritage is often reductively misrepresented. Rather, it refers to the deeper substance of Confucian learning as a system of philosophical inquiry on the nature and destiny of humankind. The Confucianism of the Imperial era was a broadly syncretic tradition so thoroughly enriched by the absorption of Buddhist metaphysics and logic, and so deeply moved by visceral attraction to Daoist aspirations to spiritual liberation, that it is best to understand it not as a narrow sectarian creed but as a rubric embracing the full range of Chinese thought of the last millennium or two. It is crucial to keep this in mind when one reads the works of Ming and Qing fiction and encounters the ubiquitous presence of Buddhist and Daoist savants exuding a sense of world-weariness and a longing for release through transcendence of, or at least withdrawal from, worldly entanglements—especially when these sentiments are neatly framed within plot structures based on schemes of karmic retribution. These elements easily give rise to the mistaken impression that such texts are designed to propagate a narrowly sectarian Buddhist or Daoist view of life. But the complex syncretic breadth of the Neo-Confucian vision provides yet another of those touchstones for distinguishing the sophisticated recasting of traditional narrative materials in the classic Chinese novels from contemporary works of less elaborate aesthetic design and more simplistic intellectual orientation.

At the heart of the Confucian system of thought—as articulated and enshrined in the so-called Four Books (*The Analects of Confucius, The Book of Mencius, The Daxue* [*Great Learning*], and *The Zhongyong* [*Doctrine of the Mean*]) that formed the scriptural core of traditional education and scholarship in Imperial China—lies the notion of the self, the object of the paradigmatic Confucian act of self-cultivation. During the phases of Chinese cultural history that led up to and then witnessed the flowering of the classic novel, the primary locus of this process of self-realization was undergoing a gradual rethinking and repositioning—from the moral integrity of the autonomous individual acting within the web of human relations (in Chinese, the physical person: *shen*) to the ideal of integral wholeness at the core of the inner self, expressed with the term *xin* ("heart" or "mind"). Many influential thinkers in the centuries of transition from the medieval world of the Tang (618–907) and Song periods through the early modern era of Ming and Qing turned their speculative attention from the external face of the self to its internal dimensions as the proper object of cultivation. Some went as far as to postulate that the eternal "principles" (*li*) underlying all reality are intrinsically lodged within—in fact, are ontologically identical to—the substrate of human consciousness, an idea summed up in the earlier dictum: "the mind is principle; principle is none other than mind" (or its sectarian equivalent: "Buddha is the mind; the mind is Buddha").

It seems to be less than historical accident that the resurgence of the so-called philosophy of mind and its powerful influence on the intellectual circles of the mid- and late Ming coincides with the consolidation of the Chinese novel as a new literary vessel for representing reality. This is not just a matter of the extreme ideological views of a handful of so-called left-wing intellectuals (as thinkers such as Wang Yangming, Wang Ji, Wang Gen, and He Xinyin are sometimes labeled today), but is an orientation that colored the thinking of virtually all members of the educated elite in China during these centuries. Given the fact that so many of the literary figures whose names are associated with the great achievements of colloquial fiction and drama in this period (including Tang Xianzu, Feng Menglong, Li Zhi, Yuan Hongdao, and others, to list just a few) are personally linked in one way or another to the most prominent contemporary exponents of this "philosophy of mind," this characteristic cannot be simply dismissed as a passing literati fashion.

In the seventeenth century many Chinese thinkers—caught up in the individual and collective soul-searching catalyzed by the traumatic fall of the Ming state to alien invaders, and then pressed by the intellectual retrenchment brought on by the insecure cultural hegemony of the Manchu rulers—tended to blame the collapse of their world on the excessively self-indulgent tendencies in both philosophical thought and artistic expression that, in their hindsight, had characterized the latest phases of Ming culture. In their eyes, both the rampant intuitionism of speculative philosophy and the licentiousness of the new sensual media of colloquial fiction and drama were tantamount to the abdication of real Confucian commitment to virtuous personal behavior and the grand vocation of ordering the world. It must be clarified, therefore, that neither the exploration of the core of selfhood in Ming Neo-Confucian thought, nor its expression in Ming and early Qing fiction and drama, represents a narrow preoccupation with the inner self in blissful isolation. Rather, both reveal the consistent Confucian understanding of the self as the intersection of the inner seat of consciousness and the outer face of its concrete interaction with the surrounding web of human relations and the broader social and cosmic order. In this light, the exploration of the reality of selfhood in the novel embodies a dual focus: the inner dimension of self-realization and the outer fulfillment of one's commitment to the integration of self and world that may be seen as two facets of the same essential reality.

This understanding is set forth paradigmatically in the canonic Confucian sources that formed the mental baggage of every educated person for more than a thousand years in traditional China. These include the brief but immensely influential text commonly known as *The Great Learning (Daxue)*, in which the "cultivation of the self" is formulated as the central link in a chain of phases of self-realization stretching in two directions of fulfillment: outward to ever broader spheres of external actualization ("regulating the family," "ordering the state," and "bringing peaceful rule to the world"), and inward to "rectifying the mind," "making whole (commonly mistranslated as "making sincere") the inner consciousness," "extending one's knowledge to the utmost," and "expanding the reach of one's apprehension of reality to all things" (literally, "reaching" things through application of the proper conceptual grid). This canonic outline of the process and substance of self-cultivation provides a convenient conceptual model for summing up the representation of the inner reality of the self in serious prose fiction, for the intellectual objective in this literary medium is precisely that of capturing the experience of the self in individual consciousness and then tracing its extension to the collective ground of being shared by us all—in other words, the complex field of intersection between the inner core of subjectivity and the changing objective circumstances of the external world.

Once again, to make such far-reaching claims for a serious intellectual purpose in what are most often read as nothing more than long episodic tales of adventure, folk-wit, sentiment, or ribaldry requires a vigorous defense. In an earlier full-length study on the four masterworks of the late Ming, I attempted to work out in considerable detail the ways in which these works engage with the problem of self. I argued that *Sanguozhi yanyi* and *Shuihuzhuan* dwell less on the external *facts* of heroic exploits and more on the problematic issues of self-image and ego-gratification that they entail; that *Xiyouji* deploys its allegorical framework to redefine the meaning of enlightenment as the reintegration of the fractious components of the self; and that *Jin Ping Mei* strips bare the core of emptiness at the heart of a world based entirely on the pursuit of material and sexual plenitude. By the middle of the eighteenth century, these thematic concerns had been reframed in light of the new intellectual preoccupations of the day, but the perennial Confucian vision of selfhood remained unchanged. Thus, in *Rulin waishi* the satiric debunking of literati pretensions in the best spirit of Dickens or Gogol turns on the more subtle and cutting issue of self-indulgence in "fame" and "profit" masked by the self-deluding pursuit of personal "authenticity." And in *Honglou meng*—as in those great works of European fiction that also study the mutual validation of self and other through the prism of romantic love—the most penetrating contemplation of the dialectics of self in the classic Chinese novel takes us beyond the naive exploration of sentiment and erotic desire characteristic of romance and popular fiction to ponder the vagaries of the realization and communication of authentic selfhood. Understanding the centrality of the conundrum of self-definition at the innermost core of the novel also helps to explain the troubling persistence of the theme of incest in works like *Honglou meng* and *Jin Ping Mei*—the same involuted pursuit of the fulfillment of self through its own replication that looms so large in certain comparable Western examples.

The ways in which the great works of Chinese fiction grapple with the central questions of the experience and communication of selfhood bring us to what is perhaps the most significant area of literary convergence between the Chinese and the European novel: the paradigmatic use of irony as its primary rhetorical mode for exploring the labyrinth of autonomous identity and defining the intrinsic limitations of self-realization. When Lukács claimed in his *Theorie des Romans* that irony in the novel functions as "the self-correction of the world's fragility," he may have been simply describing the subversive character of European fiction: its effect of cynically calling into question the collapsed ideals of the old order and their replacement by the values of bourgeois self-aggrandizement.[16] But at the same time, his insight reflects the intellectual and spiritual significance of the novel as a vessel for the contemplation of the paradox of identity defined by the uneasy interaction of Self and Other. This view of the centrality of the ironic mode among the defining aesthetic features of the novel genre lends particular weight to the characteristic rhetorical devices of novelistic discourse: such things as manipulation of point-of-view, juxtaposition of reliable and unreliable narrators, dissonant or contrapuntal layering of narrative voice (as I understand the term *heteroglossia*), deployment of multiple centers of consciousness, and the like—all of which are marshaled to grasp and convey a sense of the slippage of subjectivity and objectivity that constitutes the special preserve of the novel as a domain of literary expression.

Many of the terms employed in the preceding sentences may smack of the critical vocabulary and hobby-horses of recent Western intellectual discourse. But surprising as it may sound, some of these same expressions describe with equal validity the exploration of selfhood that lies at the heart of the classic Chinese novel. In my earlier attempt to defend an essentially ironic reading of the four classic novels of the Ming period, I dwelled at length on what I called "the limitations of valor" in *Sanguozhi yanyi*, the "deflation of heroism" in *Shuihuzhuan*, the "transcendence of emptiness" in *Xiyouji*, and the "inversion of self-cultivation" in *Jin Ping Mei*.[17] In each case I argued for an "ironic" reinterpretation of the respective texts in a double

---

[16] György Lukács, *Theorie des Romans*, trans. Anna Bostock under the title *Theory of the Novel* (Cambridge, Mass.: M.I.T. Press, 1971).

[17] Andrew Plaks, *The Four Masterworks of the Ming Novel* (Princeton, N.J.: Princeton University Press, 1987), 55, 183, 279, 361.

sense of the term: first, its relentless undermining of meaning by deflation and equivocation, and then, almost in the same breath, its capacity to effect a kind of tantalizing affirmation—if only by negative implication—of a renewed commitment to the value of human experience. It seems to go without saying that the merciless satirization of personal foibles and social ills in *Rulin waishi* carries a pronounced ironic flavor, but what is at stake in this work is not simply the destructive tearing down of false values, but a passionate projection of the ideal of authentic self-fulfillment, presented obliquely in the cameo portrait of Wang Mian in the prologue, and the vignettes of the four obscure artists in the epilogue. Traditional and modern readers of *Honglou meng* also tend to be swept along in the seductive flow of its apparent celebration of positive cultural values—this time in a seemingly blissful evocation of the glories of Chinese literary civilization and the sensual delights of a lyrical existence—and lose sight of the deeply ironic vision at its core. Here a consistent, if subtle, ironic undertone forces us to ponder very disturbing questions about the impossibility of unimpeded communication through love and the inevitable assault on innocent self-containment that in the end serve to undercut even the promise of perfect fulfillment through the extinction of consciousness and the severing of interpersonal bonds that is seemingly held out as a Buddhist "solution" to the paradox of the self.

One may well ask: what finally remains, in the debris of all this ironic undercutting, of the positive edifice of meaning so painstakingly constructed in the great Chinese novels? In grappling with this question, I have found especially illuminating the declaration in Jonathan Culler's 1975 *Structuralist Poetics* that the novel is "the primary semiotic agent of intelligibility" in the modern world.[18] Regardless of the original intention of this formulation, I would like to restate it here as a powerful assertion that, for all its ironic undermining and cynical questioning of human beliefs and values, the novel is in the final analysis inseparably tied—through its own internal structure of signs—to the projection of at least some level of *signification*. I have argued earlier in this essay that the great works of the novel genre, in China as in the West, must first construct a narrative world before they can then proceed to pull apart its very foundations. The assembling of this fictional world may be considered the primary accomplishment of the novel, but for it to work, it must be both credible in its specificity of detail and compelling in its evocation of the plenitude of reality. And at the same time it must erect a narrative framework that strikes the reader's conception of the logic of existence as

---

[18] Jonathan Culler, *Structuralist Poetics* (Ithaca, N.Y.: Cornell University Press, 1975), 189.

plausible. In a single phrase: it must *make sense*. But the very same logic of fictional narrative, in order to be intellectually engrossing and sensually engaging, not to mention entertaining, must also incorporate a strong feeling of the sheer contingency, randomness, and unpredictability of the human story. This is what confers upon the greatest novels in Europe and China their crowning achievement, their capacity to engage in the dialectical juggling of irreconcilable elements of desire and containment, causality and contingency, logic and the absurd, justice and unfathomable caprice. It is often difficult to appreciate the depth and subtlety of these dialectics in the great masterworks of the Chinese genre, since they tend to be camouflaged by the obtrusive presence of what appear to be simplisitic didactic schemes—celebration of proper Confucian values, Buddhist schemes of karmic retribution, or the simple tyranny of bland common sense and folk wisdom—until one learns to identify the essentially aesthetic function of such pronouncements as containing structures rather than expositions of doctrine. This is where the double effect of irony, simultaneously tearing down and building up a structure of meaning, weighs in with its special expressive power. In this light it may be a less astonishing coincidence that writers and readers in such remote cultural mileux as sixteenth- to eighteenth-century China and seventeenth- to nineteenth-century Europe and America exploited the same powerful rhetorical tool of irony to forge remarkably similar new literary vessels, designed in both cases to confront the unbridgeable chasms of self-contradiction—and the unfathomable gaps of contingency—that define life in a world where the eternal verities have begun to crumble.

CRITICAL APPARATUS

The Semantic Field of "Narrative"

STEFANO LEVI DELLA TORRE

Midrash

> Ezra brought the law [i.e., the Torah, literally "the Teaching"] before the assembly, both men and women and all who could hear with understanding. This was on the first day of the seventh month. He read from it facing the square before the Water Gate from early morning until midday. . . . The scribe Ezra stood on a wooden platform that had been made for the purpose . . . and when he opened it, all the people stood up. . . . Then they bowed their heads and worshipped the LORD with their faces to the ground. Also Jeshua, Bani, Sherebiah, Jamin, Akkub, Shabbethai, Hodiah, Maaseiah, Kelita, Azariah, Jozabad, Hanan, Pelaiah, the Levites, helped the people to understand the law, while the people remained in their places. So they read from the book, from the law of God, with interpretation. They gave the sense [*meforash*], so that the people understood the reading.
> —NEHEMIAH 8.2–8

This prototype of synagogal reading dates back to the mid-fifth century B.C., when, thanks to the edict of Cyrus, the Jews could return to Judea from the Babylonian exile. Their cult was renewed in that era, but since the holy language had been forgotten during their exile, the text needed to be translated aloud into the current language, Aramaic. This is an example of early exegetic reading: written Torah and oral Torah, in three forms of interpretation—the recitation (*mikrah*), in a liturgical chant; the Aramaic translation (*targum*); and the explanation of the meaning, to which we can perhaps already give the name *midrash* (pl. *midrashim*) here.[1] The term derives from the root *drsh*, which means "to investigate" or "to research."

In the passage from Nehemiah above, some characteristics of *midrash* are expressed: it is a translation into human terms of words held to be divine, and therefore, it always maintains a relation, whether direct or indirect, to the scriptures. It is a multivoiced commentary, as is indicated by the sequence of proper names of each of the Levite interpreters. It is therefore a plural interpretation, not univocal, and at times it is even divergent. At the same time, it is by no means private. On the contrary, it is intended for an

---

[1] Cf. The Babylonian Talmud, megillah 3a; *Nedarim* 37b; and *Midrash Rabbah* 36.12.

adult audience ("all who could hear with understanding"). But only half a millennium later, between the second and fifth centuries A.D., when the oral tradition was written down and gathered in the Jerusalem and Babylonian Talmuds, *midrash* became a true literary genre of rabbinical Judaism (however dishomogeneous it may be). And so too were born its set of rules and their exceptions. The *midrash* is formed by two branches, extending in two different directions: one toward the *halakah*, or the "way" of the precepts, and the other toward the *haggadah*, the narrative. The first explains that which needs to be done, including standards for behavior and ritual; the second explains that which can be understood, in other words, an interpretation of the meaning of scripture.

The following is an example of a *midrash haggadah*:

> R[abbi] Ammi and R[abbi] Assi were sitting before R[abbi] Isaac the Smith, [and] one of them said to him: Will the Master please tell us some legal points [i.e., *hakalah*]?; while the other said: Will the Master please give us some homiletical instruction [*haggadah*]? When he commenced a homiletical discourse he was prevented by the one, and when he commenced a legal discourse he was prevented by the other. He then said to them: I will tell you a parable: To what is this like? To a man who has had two wives, one young and one old. The young one used to pluck out his white hair, whereas the old one used to pluck out his black hair. He thus finally remained bald on both sides.[2]

Here we should note that the parable, including the evangelical parable, is inscribed in the category of *midrash*.

Just as generally happens in *midrash*, a question is subjected to the following procedure: one asks if and to what extent the "senile" regularity of the standards, which are intended to normalize and regulate behavior in space and time, precludes the "youthful" effervescence in the interpretation of the meaning and vice versa. The resulting bald head of the husband is also the text of the Torah, and the wives are also the persons speaking with Rabbi Isaac. The ones and the others insist on adapting both the head (of the husband) and the text to fit their private desires while excluding the others' wishes, and thus, they negate and reduce them to a single dimension. It does so at least in appearance, since visible baldness does not affect the intrinsic quality of the head, in other words, the text, which in and of itself embodies the law, the standard, and meaning.

---

[2] *Baba Kamma* 60b.

Neither *halakah* nor *haggadah* can exist without the other. The one is the structure and the support, the other is movement; the one is a grammar for Hebrew living, the other is its syntax and discourse. "I have set before you life and death, blessings and curses. Choose life" (Deuteronomy 30.19). But that life is not pure stability and mere repetition of the laws, nor is it a pure unfolding of actions and events; instead, it is both these things together. In Exodus 3, God presents himself to Moses in the burning bush by saying: "I am the God of your father, the God of Abraham, the God of Isaac, and the God of Jacob." Why does he use this formula instead of "God of Abraham, Isaac, and Jacob"? The commentators explain that the repetition shows how God reveals himself to everyone individually. Thus, the revelation is not made once and for all, nor is it ever identical to any other revelation. But it is renewed every time for every one. Thus, while the *Berit* (the "pact," the "alliance" between God and Israel) tends to be expressed in clauses (in *halakah*) in a unifying and centripetal sense, the search for truth in events and in discourse (in *haggadah*) branches out into endless dissemination.

The premise of *midrash* is that the different books of the Torah make up a unique and great organism in which every thing and every value can be found. "Deliberate over it again and again for everything is contained in it."[3] The *midrash* approaches the Torah in the same way that the natural sciences postulate that in nature there are discoverable truths. What appears to us to be *invention* or even subjective interpretation is conceived instead as a *discovery* of something that was already there but concealed. And just as the scientific mind questions nature and thus transforms the gathering of data into a question, *midrash* questions the text and tickles every little verse, word, and letter (for example, why does the Bible start with the second letter of the alphabet—the letter *bet* of *Bereshit*, "In the beginning . . ." and not with the letter *aleph*?), and thus it transforms affirmations into questions.

One interrogative filter connects but also makes a distinction between the text and its interpretation. In the Babylonian Talmud, Menahot 29b, we find, for example, the following *midrash*:

> Rab Judah said in the name of Rab, when Moses ascended on high [Mt. Sinai]
> he found the Holy One, blessed be He, engaged in affixing coronets to
> the letters. Said Moses, Lord of the Universe, Who stays Thy hand? He
> answered, There will arise a man, at the end of many generations, Akiba b
> Joseph by name, who will expound upon each tittle heaps and heaps of laws.
> Lord of the Universe, said Moses; permit me to see him. He replied, Turn

---

[3] Mishnah, Pirke Avot 5.22.

thee around. Moses went and sat down behind eight rows [and listened to
the discourses upon the law]. Not being able to follow their arguments he
was ill at ease, but when they came to a certain subject and the disciples said
to the master Whence do you know it? and the latter replied It is a law given
unto Moses at Sinai he was comforted.

There is almost a millennium and a half difference between Moses and
Rabbi Akiba (second century A.D.), but like a dream, *midrash* does not distinguish between the synchronic and the diachronic. Moses can enter
Akiba's classroom as if he were his contemporary, but at the same time, he
does not understand what is being said. It is the result of a transformation
that has taken place through the passing of the ages, a dense weaving of
threads from the Books of Moses and the actual problems that have arisen
again and again. It is the force of a *topological* deformation of the text perceived as being continuous and without interruption, a faithful mutation.
This is not Akiba's invention but rather his discovery of the same "coronets"
or corollaries that St. Benedict posited from the beginning in Moses' message, like seeds that have germinated over the course of generations.

Midrash speaks of the distance and of the link between text and commentary. There is one text, but many commentaries:

> R[abbi] Johanan said that God's voice, as it was uttered [on Mt. Sinai], split
> up into seventy voices, in seventy languages, so that all the nations should
> understand. . . . R[abbi] Tanhuma said: . . . Just see how the Voice went
> forth—coming to each Israelite with a force proportioned to his individual
> strength—to the old, according to their strength, and to the young, accord-
> ing to theirs; to the children, to the babes and to the women, according to
> their strength, and even to Moses according to his strength, as it is said:
> *Moses spoke, and God answered him by a voice* (Exodus 19.19), that is, with a
> voice which he could endure.[4]

Therefore, the Pentateuch, which was handed down by Moses, is not the
word of God but rather the meaning Moses was able to perceive in the word
of God. Then, in turn, we comprehend that which we are able to understand. "The Torah speaks in human language": it is already a *translation*, a
clue given to us by the divine voice. The investigation, in other words,
midrash, works around this clue. The message, which is unique although not
uniform, refracts differently in every culture and condition, and in every era.

---

[4] Exodus Rabbah 5.9.

It is at once universal and specific; it can be understood by all according to their ability and their inclination. Thus, the difference between emission and reception is underlined: "Once God has spoken; twice have I heard this" (Psalms 62.11). Commentary and its multiplicity are born in the space produced in this interval.

The commonly used formula, "quoting Rav X, Rav Y said," expresses the continuity in the oral transmission of the tradition. The formula *davar aher*, "another interpretation," compares different interpretations being debated. Should one interpretation be supported over another? Or would it be better to search for yet another dimension in which different interpretations can be combined into one? But, on the other hand, in the forest of discordant views, who has the authority to decide the meaning and the standards that would derive from the meaning?

For example, on page 59b of the Babylonian Talmud Bava Mezia, we find ourselves in the midst of a *midrash haggadah* that depicts a *halakah* dispute. It is a surprising *midrash* that the Maharal of Prague, one of the great Renaissance cabalists, considered particularly problematic—a discussion of "Achnai's oven," a portable oven used to bake bread, and whether or not it should be considered pure:

> On that day R. Eliezer brought forward every imaginable argument, but they did not accept them. Said he to them: "If the *halakah* agrees with me, let this carob-tree prove it!" Thereupon the carob-tree was torn a hundred cubits out of its place—others affirm, four hundred cubits. "No proof can be brought from a carob-tree," they retorted. Again he said to them: "If the *halakah* agrees with me, let the stream of water prove it!" Whereupon the stream of water flowed backwards. "No proof can be brought from a stream of water," they rejoined. Again he urged: "If the *halakah* agrees with me, let the walls of the schoolhouse prove it," whereupon the walls inclined to fall. But R. Joshua rebuked them, saying: "When scholars are engaged in a *halakic* dispute, what have ye to interfere?" Hence they did not fall, in honor of R. Joshua, nor did they resume the upright, in honor of R. Eliezer; and they are still standing thus inclined. Again he said to them "If the *halakah* agrees with me, let it be proved from Heaven!" Whereupon a Heavenly Voice cried out: "Why do ye dispute with R. Eliezer, seeing that in all matters the *halakah* agrees with him!" But R. Joshua arose and exclaimed: *"It is not in heaven."* What did he mean by this?—Said R. Jeremiah: That the Torah had already been given at Mount Sinai; we pay no attention to a Heavenly Voice, because Thou hast long since written in the Torah at Mount Sinai, *After the majority must one incline.*

R. Nathan met [the prophet] Elijah and asked him: What did the Holy
One, Blessed by He, do in that hour?—He [God] laughed [with joy], [and]
he replied saying, "My sons have defeated Me, My sons have defeated Me."[5]

Free will, secular autonomy from the voice of God in human decisions, the
democratic principle of majority rule (albeit in the context of a male oli-
garchy of wise men), criteria for relevance (in other words, if miracles and
even divine opinion are relevant to a discussion on purity standards)—these
are the problems dealt with in this passage with felicitous irony. But it will
soon turn to tragic irony when Rabbi Eliezer is chased away because he will
not accept the majority's opinion and because of the killing of some of the
main characters, including Rabbi Akiba, who will be skinned alive by the
Romans.

Does the spirit of *midrash* flourish in Kafka's fablelike short stories?
Where Sigmund Freud, in his *Interpretation of Dreams*, divides the text of a
dream into "segments" in which he searches for separate meanings, not so
much in the continuity of the onoeric discourse but in the links with other
contexts, other life and psychic events, we can find a perfect analogy with
the Hebraic exegetic modality.[6] And when he coined the expression "Oedipal complex" to denote the conflict that involves every male child because
of his attraction to his mother, Sigmund Freud was reading the Greek myth
in terms of *midrash*. He moved from Judaism toward assimilation: he openly
used terms from the socially recognized classical tradition (like the myth of
Oedipus), but then he interpreted them according to Hebraic procedures.
This allows us to clarify even further the specific elements of *midrash* by
comparison. What is the difference between myth and *midrash*? Myth is the
narration of a (symbolic) interpretation as if it were fact; *midrash* recounts a

---

[5] Deuteronomy 30.11–14: "this commandment [word] that I am commanding you . . . is not in
heaven. . . . No, the word is very near to you; it is in your mouth and in your heart."

[6] The commentary starts with the text (of the dream), which has been divided into segments.
They are almost independent from one another, like cuttings from the trunk of a tree. The
following is an example from the dream of July 23–24, 1895: "A great hall—a number of guests,
whom we are receiving—among them Irma, whom I immediately take aside, as though to answer
her letter, and to reproach her for not yet accepting the 'solution . . .' " Analysis: "*The hall—a
number of guests, whom we are receiving* . . . During the day my wife had mentioned that she
expected several friends. . . . My dream, then, anticipates this situation. . . . *I reproach Irma for not
having accepted the 'solution.' I say, 'If you still have pains, it is really your own fault.'* . . . But I note
that, in the speech which I make to Irma in the dream, I am above all anxious that I shall not be
blamed for the pains which she still suffers. If it is Irma's own fault, it cannot be mine. . . . *She looks
pale and puffy.* My patient had always a rosy complexion. I suspect that here another person is
being substituted for her."

fact as if it were interpretation. Myth is presented as an event; *midrash* as a problem, a case to be solved. Myths can have numerous versions, but they cannot compete with one another; *midrash* is a debate. Myth is a text; *midrash* is a commentary to a text. Myth does not seek, but rather finds; *midrash* is research. Myth teaches unintentionally; *midrash* wishes to teach and is often homily. The past of myth is distant and conclusive; the past of *midrash* is still active, like Freud's Oedipus ("as if it were you yourself who left Egypt today," says the Pesach Haggadah, the ritual text for Passover).

And if we are to extend this comparison to another and in many ways contiguous literary genre, that is, the fable (which is at the same level as myth and the *midrash*, inasmuch as first oral and then written), we must not let ourselves be fooled by its canonical beginning: "Once upon a time . . ." This distant past does not have the same meaning as the conclusive past in myth. The past of the fable is, rather, akin to the infantile way of saying "I was being a knight, or an astronaut, or a courageous lass . . ." It is the past imperfect with which children distance themselves from the real present. But they do so to facilitate their own self-invoked illusions, their identification with a character or role. Thus, the fable solicits identification with the main character, with his difficulties or his ultimate success. *Midrash*, on the other hand, proposes identification with the situation in which the characters find themselves rather than in the characters per se. In turn, myth is presented as a fact that is witnessed externally, and only in the theatrical form of classic tragedy is the audience involved and helped by the commentary of the chorus and universal meaning. But myth represents without judging, while *midrash* is a procedure for arriving at judgment. The fable is resolved in judgment, whereby good is rewarded and evil is punished.

The act of interpretation implies two movements. The first, and most conspicuous, shows the pertinence of understanding a text (or event) given that it can produce different versions and meanings. The second movement, which is more hidden, goes back from the interpretation to the text (or event) and reveals its objectivity and autonomy, given that no explanation is exhaustive. From the side of the subjects who interpret, there is an element of debatability; on the side of the object or the text to be interpreted, there is a reconstruction of its being within itself, which is "other" to us. For deconstruction and relativism, which consider only one side, that is, that of the subject, reality is interpretation: the object is absorbed in the interpretation, and it disappears within it. The same holds for dogmatism, which imposes a unique and orthodox interpretation on the object and ends up by forcing the object and interpretation to coincide and by replacing the object or text with the interpretation. Thus, relativism and dogmatism, which would appear to contradict one another, converge in being an *ontology of interpretation*, the deceptive triumph of a subjectivity that has lost the sense of things' autonomy from us.

Although we seem to recognize our actual thoughts in the texts of the Torah, this does not mean that its authors intended or even knew how to articulate them with divine prescience. Those who wrote them were thinking of a meaning, but instead they handed down a signifier. We are dealing with the signifier rather than the meaning. It is a signifier that no attribution of meaning can resolve or substitute for, just as no critical evaluation of a work of art can take the place of the work itself. The commentary positions itself relative to the text not in any indirect way but through the sedimentation of other commentaries and epochs that it allows to shine through as layers of the text. It reaches us consecrated by the prolonged attention of the generations. We glean its relevance to the present moment not by modernizing it but rather by retracing the intentions expressed through the linguistic and narrative material in which they are written, thus retracing the "act" to the "potency," or rather, to the possibilities offered by writing.

———————

Translated by Jeremy Parzen

MAURIZIO BETTINI

Mythos/Fabula

> If I disbelieved it, like the experts, I would not be
> extraordinary.
>
> —PLATO, *Phaedrus*, 229

From the beginnings of the Greek tradition—from Homer and Hesiod on—
the term *mythos* means "word," "discourse," and "story."[1] But whoever expected to see *mythos* defined exclusively as a fabulous or sacred story, or
simply a story in which one does not believe—all meanings to which the
subsequent history of the word has accustomed us—would be destined to
remain disappointed.[2]

In Homer and Hesiod, in fact, *mythos* does mean discourses or stories—
but not incredible ones. This is true to such an extent that, to adduce the falsity of a discourse, it is not enough to define it as a mythos, but it is necessary
to add as well that it is "deceptive" (*skolios*) (Hesiod, *Works and Days*,
190–94): the unreliability of a discourse stems from the adjective that modifies it, not in the mere fact of its being a *mythos*. On the contrary, in archaic
epic *mythoi* were even defined as discourses and stories of an indisputably
authoritative character. In fact, the discourse that the predatory falcon delivers "forcefully" to the nightingale, his prey, is a *mythos* (ibid., 206). Similarly,
in Homer the discourse exchanged vehemently by manly warriors on the
field of battle is defined as a *mythos*: when Poseidon rejects Zeus's order to
abandon the struggle, his "harsh and powerful" response is called a *mythos*
(*The Iliad*, 15.202). In the same vein, speeches given in the assembly by heroes with the requisite prestige were defined as *mythoi*, as is Agamemnon's
when he chases Criseis away while threatening him, or Achilles' when he rejects the ambassadors of Agamemnon (*The Iliad*, 1.78; 9.309). The *mythos* of
the epic is an assertive discourse that demands to be enacted. In any case, it
is an authoritative discourse.[3] One may or may not grant it authority, but not

---

[1] When Odysseus, in the palace of Alcinous, narrates to the Phaecians his own wanderings, his
story is called a mythos (*The Odyssey*, 3.94, 4.234); thus the discourses pronounced by the Homeric
heroes throughout the course of the poem are often defined as mythoi.

[2] G. Rispoli, *Lo spazio del verisimile: Il racconto, la storia e il mito* (Naples, 1988), 29ff.; G
Naddaf, "Introduction" in L. Brisson, *Plato the Myth Maker* (Chicago, 1998), pp. vii–ix; B. Lincoln,
Theorizing Myth (Chicago, 1998), 3–18.

[3] Lincoln, *Theorizing Myth*, 3–18.

because it is defined as a *mythos*. This is to say that in the archaic epic, *mythos* never indicates a discourse in which *others* believe.

Even in the philosophical texts preceding Plato, *mythos* continues to mean a reliable discourse, nor is there yet any contrast, in this sense, with the term *logos*. "The scholarly work of philosophers from Xenophanes, around 530, to Empedocles, about 450, belies the opinion of our contemporaries who attribute to 'rational thinking' the purpose of eliminating any other form of thought such as 'myth' in the sense of sacred narrative or discourse on the subject of the gods."[4] In Xenophanes, *mythoi* and *logoi* are named together, almost synonymously, as discourses containing a sentiment of devotion.[5] And other pre-Socratic philosophers refer to mythos with a rather positive connotation (like Parmenides), or at least remain neutral toward it.[6]

Pindar is a different matter—he uses the expression only three times, but always with a negative connotation. To denounce the falsity of the story of Pelops, who is dismembered and served at the table of the gods, the poet declares: "Here or there maybe the Tongues of men [*phatis*] O'erriding truth's sure word, deceive with false-spun tales [*mythoi*], the embroidery of lies" (*The Olympian Odes*, 1.45–47). Elsewhere the word *mythoi* is employed instead to denounce the seductions of Homeric poetry: "For in his lies and in his winged devices [i.e., poetry] there is an awesome power: wisdom [*sophia*] is deceptive, seducing with its *mythoi*" (*The Nemean Odes*, 7.32–34). And yet a third time *mythoi* appears in a negative context (even if this time the word is accompanied by the adjective *aimuloi*, or "deceivers," and hence deals with a different matter): "Yes, hateful slander existed long ago, partner of flattering *mythoi*, hatcher of schemes, doer of evil" (*The Nemean Odes*, 8.53–56). In Herodotus, the word *mythos* appears only twice, and he too seems to use it to mean a report in which one should not believe. To say that the Nile flows from the ocean, as Homer did, means, according to Herodotus, "carrying his *mythos* . . . back to where it vanishes," and is to affirm something that "cannot be disproved" (*ouk echei elenchon*). And when the Greeks maintain that the Egyptians wanted to sacrifice Heracles to Zeus, they are actually recounting a "foolish" mythos, and demonstrate their ignorance of nature and of the laws of the Egyptians (Herodotus, 2.23, 45).[7]

---

[4] M. Detienne, *The Creation of Mythology*, trans. Margaret Cook (Chicago, 1986), 46.

[5] Xenophanes, fr. 1, ed. H. Diels and W. Kranz, *Die Fragmente der Vorsokratiker* (Berlin, 1960). All subsequent quotations from this source will be cited parenthetically in the text as Diels-Kranz.

[6] Detienne. *The Creation of Mythology*, 46–47; Lincoln, *Theorizing Myth*, 25–32; Naddaf, "Introduction," viii.

[7] Detienne, *The Creation of Mythology*, 48–51; P. G. Bietenholz, *"Historia" and "Fabula": Myths and Legends in Historical Thought from Antiquity to the Modern Age* (Leiden, 1994), 26–27.

In order to understand these last two examples, however, it is necessary to keep in mind that, in Herodotus, as in the first Greek historians, there is no specific term to indicate discourses rejected as unreliable: still less can we affirm that the term *logos* was used to indicate discourses regarded as true and reliable. As if this were not enough, even the "father of history" made ample use of stories and reports of a fabulous nature.[8] If Herodotus, then, uses the expression *mythos* twice to define an unreliable discourse—that in which others believe—we cannot for this reason attribute to him the project of liberating his historical discourse from myths; still less can we say that, with the word *mythos*, he was identifying any discourse *whatsoever* he judged to be unreliable. As for Thucydides, he explicitly contrasts his work with those of the poets and the *logographers*, who concern themselves not with arriving at the truth but rather with pleasing their audience. They defend facts that cannot be disproved (*anexelenta*), facts whose antiquity guarantees their mythical status (*mythodes*) in spite of their credibility (Thucydides, 1.21.1).[9] The affirmation seems rather sharp: the *mythodes* characterizes the report with little authority, that which can be accepted *only by others*. Thucydides, notwithstanding his hostility towards *mythodes*, will take good care not to place in doubt the "historicity" of the stories like those of Minos or the Trojan War, which for us obviously fall into the category of the mythological. But they were not obviously mythological for Thucydides.[10]

The preceding examples are interesting, but it also necessary to warn that we can easily run the risk of overinterpreting them. In the modern perception, in fact, the distinction between what is fabulous or unbelievable and what is true and ascertainable corresponds to the distinction between what is mythical and what is not. But as I have already said regarding Herodotus, the same distinction does not hold true for the Greek writers. When they tried to tell the true from the false, the ascertainable from mere hearsay, history from fable, they not only made the distinction in a way that only partly corresponds to ours; but, in particular, they did not necessarily use the word *mythos* to indicate the rejected element. The linguistic history of the word *mythos* is one story; quite another is the *intellectual* history of the categories—true/false, historical/fabulous, hot air/documentation, written/oral—to which at a certain point the history of the word *mythos* becomes tied.

---

[8] C. Calame, *Mythe et histoire dans l'antiquite grecque* (Lausanne, 1996), 30.

[9] Detienne, *The Creation of Mythology*, 51–60; Calame, *Mythe et histoire*, 29–30; Bietenholz, "*Historia*" and "*Fabula*," 23–33.

[10] A. W. Gomme, *A Historical Commentary on Thucydides: The Ten Years' War* (Oxford, 1956–70), 149; Calame, *Mythe et histoire*, 38–39.

Having established this premise, it seems rather clear, however, that—in the transition from archaic epic to Pindar, Herodotus, and Thucydides—the term *mythos* is shifted in some way to cover the terrain of the rejected or fabulous story: a story, that is, whose credibility is placed in doubt by the one who defines it as such. Starting from the fifth century B.C., in short, we begin to see the custom of calling things said by rivals "in order to praise the superiority of one type of discourse over another" as *mythos*.[11] It is interesting that Herodotus, as much as Thucydides, attributes to *mythos* the characteristic of "being undisprovable": it is not subject to *elenchos*. Insofar as it is an "obscure" and "incredible" discourse, the *mythos* can be neither accepted nor rejected, and belongs to an order exempt from the normal procedure of investigation. Even Livy, speaking of the poetic fables transmitted concerning the foundation of Rome and the events that preceded it, will repeat that the accounts can neither be "affirmed" nor "disproved" (*refellere*) (Livy, Pref., 6). If someone wants to believe in a *mythos* or a *fabula* he is free to do so, since it is not subject to disproof: but whoever defines a story he is in the midst of narrating as a *mythos* or a *fabula* implies that he is dealing with a discourse in which *others* can believe, but in which he himself certainly cannot.

Plato's relationship with *mythos*—so extensive as to have given rise to a notoriously endless commentary—can be summarized only with difficulty. In an extremely condensed summary, we can say that, for Plato, *mythos* means above all a practical discourse used by poets, who reorganize in the form of poetry the subject matter whose memory the community wishes to preserve.[12] *Mythos* is thus an instrument of tradition. As far its characteristics, for Plato it is a discourse that speaks of distant things, located in a space remote from the audience who listens to the tale. Precisely for this reason, however, the *mythos* is subject to criticism. In the first place, the remoteness of the narrated events renders it impossible to submit the *mythoi* to the scrutiny of a critique, while the vicissitudes of their transmission are such that the *mythoi* are full of often ridiculous inconsistencies. Furthermore, *mythoi* remain prisoners of the sensible world and are inspired by all-too-human experiences, thus lacking universality. Above all, however, myths, insofar as they are narrated, do not develop a rational argument, and make an appeal rather to the emotions: their educational pretense does not go beyond a simple imitation, and hence they are similar to magic and enchantment. With *mythos* Plato therefore contrasts *logos*, rational discourse, which

---

[11] G.E.R. Lloyd, *Smascherare la Mentalita* [*Demystifying Mentalities*] (Bari, 1991), 55–58.

[12] Brisson, *Plato the Myth Maker*, 7–11; Rispoli, *Lo spazio del verisimile*, 43ff.

is grounded in the laws of deductive reasoning similar to those deduced by the geometricians of his time. This is the triumph of philosophy. Save that, confronted with the necessity of educating not only the few who are capable of appreciating rational discourse, but also all the others, even the philosopher must have recourse to *mythos* as a powerful instrument of persuasion.

With Plato, therefore, *mythos* is shifted onto the terrain of the "mythical" in the sense in which we now understand it; and yet it is important to remember that the distinctions are in reality much less sharp than they seem.[13] In our day, if we define a discourse as a *mythos*, we mean to put its credibility in doubt, to treat it as poetic and enchanting—a story of fabulous things, which still, however, remains incapable of satisfying the demands of reason. Aristotle, on the other hand, will give *mythos* a more technical meaning, one that has become valuable to literary criticism (*The Poetics*, 50a, 4ff. Cf. 47a, 9ff.; 49b, 8ff.). The term is used, in fact, to indicate the "imitation of an action" or else "the composition of deeds" in tragedy—what we would define as the "plot" of the work. It is in this very context that history—the work of the *historikos*, he who narrates the "things that have happened"—is contrasted with poetry—the work of the *poeites*, he who narrates "things that could happen" (*The Poetics*, 51a, 36ff.).[14] At other times, however, Aristotle will refer to the dimension of *mythos* in a (for us) more customary fashion, that is, in designating a discourse that does not satisfy the demands of rationality. For example, he opposes the *mythikos* procedure of Hesiod to the one used in rational argument, *apodeixis* (*The Metaphysics*, 1000a, 5ff.; 1074b, 1ff. Ecc.).[15] Yet again we see *mythos* defined as stories in which *others* believe, but not the one who defines them as such. It must be said, however, that it would be a mistake to reduce the problem of myth in Aristotle to a sharp opposition of *mythos/logos* (with the second element automatically prevailing over the first). In dealing with traditional *mythoi*, in fact, Aristotle proves in reality rather more accommodating than we might have expected.[16] This happens both because he maintains that mythical stories and science are born from the same explanatory impulse; and because, according to the rules of "endoxical" method, science can even have recourse to mythical stories in order to use them as data for its investigations.[17] But perhaps there is more here. In

---

[13] Calame, *Mythe et histoire*, 7–28.

[14] Ibid., 25–26, 44–45.

[15] Ibid., 26–27.

[16] Rispoli, *Lo spazio del verisimile*, 49ff.

[17] Th. K. Johansen, " 'Myth' and 'Logos' in Aristotle," in R.G.A. Buxton, ed., *From Myth to Reason?* (Oxford, 1999), 279–91.

accord with his cyclical vision of history, in fact, Aristotle maintained that the arts and sciences would have been discovered and rediscovered innumerable times by men, who have transmitted the acquisition of the past in the form of beliefs (*Of the Heavens*, 270b.19–20).[18] In this sense, *mythoi* might therefore present themselves as the "shards" of ancient scientific explanation, and hence could be rehabilitated by rational discourse.[19]

––––––––

And what about the Romans? The question can appear incongruous because usually the Romans are not called to the stand when we are dealing with myth. But if their autochthonous mythology was not the most productive, or the most enduring, certainly their language—which contends with Greek for primacy in the European intellectual lexicon—has made an important contribution to the definition of myth. For the Romans, in fact, the equivalent of the word *mythos* is *fabula*: the Greek myths collected by Hyginus in his work (*Fabula*) are fables, just as for Cicero's Balbus the mythological stories of the Greeks are fables, from which philosophy should keep its distance (*On the Nature of the Gods*, 2.28, 70). In the same way, Livy defines a story whose historicity one cannot trust, like that of the wolf who nurses the twins as a *fabula* (1.4, 7: *inde locum fabulae ac miraculo datum*: cf. 5.21.8; 22.6; ecc.). Theatrical compositions, those stories that are not certainly "true," however realistic they may be, are defined as *fabulae* (Varro, *The Latin Language*, 8.55); and the name *fabula* is attributed to storytelling in general, to works designed to entertain, and even to idle chit-chat and gossip. *Fabula* also therefore seems to have the same connotations as *mythos* does outside of archaic Greek epic. To define a story as a *fabula* means that whoever is speaking does not place a great deal of trust in it. Again the *fabula* is the story in which *others* believe. But was it always so?

No text provides us with a different meaning for *fabula* than the one already pointed out. One thing, however, is striking. *Fabula* is a "frivolous" substantive that derives from an extremely solemn verb: *fari*. *Fari* is related to a word of archaic use, which Cicero maintained had already died out by his own day (*The Orator*, 3.153), and which is used to define the normal act of "speaking" only in texts exhibiting an elevated rhetorical style.[20] Already this

––––––––

[18] M. Burnyeat, "Good Repute," in *London Review of Books*, November 6, 1986, 11–12.

[19] Johansen, " 'Myth' and 'Logos' in Aristotle."

[20] Of the type *fare age, quid venias?* "suvvia speaks, why have you come?" (Virgil, *The Aeneid*, 6.389).

makes us suspect that the act of *fari* presupposes a rather specific modality of speaking, distinct from those implied by *loquor*, *aio*, or *dico*. This impression is confirmed, and quite surprisingly so, by a further detailed analysis.

In the first place, the verb *fari* is used to define the speech of soothsayers, or the voice that reveals hidden secrets: as, for example, in the case of Anchises, to whom the Goddess Venus *fari donavit*, "gave the power of prophecy" (Ennius, *The Annals*, 19). In effect, ancient Roman religion recognized two deities, Fatuus and Fatua, who were known precisely as divinities of prophecy (Varro, *The Latin Language*, 6.52 and 55; Justinus, 43.1, 8), and who certainly derived their names from *fari*. The connection of this verb with prophetic declaration clearly results also in the fact that, in the present tense, it is never used in the first person (Macrobius, *Grammatical Excerpts*, 5.654.25), while in the future tense it may well be: *fabor*, never **for*. Whoever speaks in the manner of *fari* projects into the future the time of his declaration. When Jove gets ready to reveal to Venus the destiny of the Trojans in Italy, or else to recount—anticipating the event—the entire "mythical history" of Aeneas and Latium, he declares: *fabor . . . longius*, "I will speak at length." Then he adds: "and while I will explain the arcane designs of fate, I will put them in motion" (*The Aeneid*, 1.261). In the authoritative mouth of Jove, in short, prophetic *fari* corresponds directly to the *enactment* of the declaration.

Perhaps we now understand better why in Roman culture "destiny" was designated precisely in terms of "a word": a word that, surprisingly enough, belongs to the sphere of *fari*, that is to say, *fatum*. Destiny is "something said," but it is in the form of a revelation operated by a divine voice, that which belongs to the sphere of *fari*. This voice expresses a "word"—a *fatum*—which, at the same time, *enunciates and determines* the destiny of an individual. This same character of binding power can also explain the relationship of the sphere of *fari* and another quite relevant term in the institutional vocabulary of the Romans: *fas*, the substantive that means "that which is just and lawful." According to the interpretation of Emile Benveniste,[21] in fact, when the formula *fas est* is used, followed by an infinitive—in the sense of "it is lawful that . . ."—what is really meant is actually something different: "it is the divine word that . . ."[22]

---

[21] E. Benveniste, *II vocabulario delle istituzioni indoeuropee* (Turin, 1976), 2:384.

[22] For a different point of view, see A. Ernout and A. Meillet, *Dictionnaire etymologique de la langue latine* (Paris, 1967), s.v. *fari*. The ancients did not have doubts, and they reconnected to *fari* not only the noun *fas*, with its derivatives *fastus* and *ne-fastus*, but also the word *fanum* ("temple") and so on (R. Maltby, *A Lexicon of Ancient Latin Etymologies* [Leeds, 1991], 223f.).

Varro provides us with an interesting piece of information. According to him, the verb *fari* was also employed to designate the moment in which "the child emits the first voice endowed with sense. That is why, before this moment children are called *in-fantes*, and after this moment we say that 'now they speak' (*iam fari*) (*The Latin Language*, 6.52). The act of *fari* therefore distinguishes a fundamental moment in the development of the person, that which ratifies the departure of the child from *in-fantia*—a sort of prehuman stage of existence—in order to introduce her finally into the world of those who "speak." There is no doubt that, in this case, the act of *fari* defines a modality of speech that is utterly exceptional. The first word pronounced by the child—so that we exclaim "she has spoken!"—is not a word like any other. In archaic Roman culture, this moment was sufficiently important to be celebrated with a religious ceremony and was even put under the aegis of a specific divinity. The name of this divinity (truly quite "eloquent") was Fabulinus, that is, "The God of *Fabula*."[23] Elsewhere, the name of this god was transmitted to us directly in the form of Farinus.[24]

At this point, a question naturally emerges: is it not strange that, in spite of the aura of authority, religiosity, and sacredness surrounding *fari*, the noun *fabula* came to mean instead a discourse that is untrustworthy, ridiculous, or at any rate unreliable? To explain this curious contradiction, we could perhaps make an appeal to an analogy with the word *fama*—a word equally derived from the verb *fari*, just like *fabula*, and one equally oriented to define a scarcely reliable discourse (the word "belongs to the public," and as such is deprived of an individual *auctor*). But perhaps, in order to explain the negative connotation assumed by *fari* in the case of *fabula*, we can go a bit further in a simple analogy with the discredited aspects of *fama*. Let us try, in fact, to imagine that, at least in certain periods, and in certain contexts, *fabula* designated an authoritative discourse, like that which "reveals" the mysteries of fate—save that then, this authority of the *fabula* (as in the case of *mythos*?) was corroded and discredited. Perhaps we can even imagine why this happened. If *fabula* effectively covered the space of prophetic discourse, in fact, the speaker could not be anyone but the *vates*, the poet/prophet, or else the *hariolus*, the soothsayer. But as far as we can see—at least from the evidence of historical accounts—their discourse was certainly not perceived as authoritative. Ennius very colorfully defined people

---

[23] "When children begin to speak (*fari incipiebant*), one sacrificed to the God Fabulinius," Nonius, *De compendiosa doctrina*, 532 (ed. W. M. Lindsay, *Nonii Marcelli De Compendiosa Doctrina Libros 20* [Hildesheim, 1964]).

[24] Tertullian, *To the Nations*, 2.11.7: *et ab effatu Farinus.*

who "don't know where to put their feet and would like to show the way to the one following them" as "superstitious *vates* and shameless soothsayers."[25] Consistent with the discredit that the *vates* and *hariloi* suffered, the verbs derived from their names (*vaticinor* and *hariolari*) similarly mean both to "prophesize" and "to say silly things." Will there be a case when the adjective *fatuus* (silly) will be joined to Fatuus, the ancient divinity of prophecy? And where *fatuari*, aside from meaning to speak under the effect of inspiration, also means to behave foolishly? The *fabula*, in short, might have lost its authority in the same measure as the *vates* and *harioli* lost theirs, those presumptuous diviners who drag their "discourse" down the path of discredit along with them.

At this point, it is worthwhile to consider briefly what words were rivals of *fabula*, that is, what other terms identified the sphere of discourse. Let us set aside *sermo*, an expression that designates speech of a familiar, informal, and conversational character, and that therefore is less interesting. There are, on the other hand, two other terms that seem strongly to imply the sense of authority. In the first place, there is obviously *oratio*, formal and constructed discourse. Cicero had no doubts about the "true" nature of *oratio*. "Even though the speech (*locutio*) of anyone can be defined as *oratio*, still, only the *locutio* of the *orator* can be properly designated as *oratio*" (*The Orator*, 64). Speech/*oratio* refers us to the figure of the *orator*, the lawyer who defends a case in court; or, in earlier times, to the figure of the ambassador, the *legatus/orator* who came before another people in the name of the Romans. As we see here, *oratio* presupposes speakers endowed with the greatest possible authority, whose "speech" should be taken with the utmost seriousness. Next to *oratio* we find the art of *narrare*, the verb from which the noun *narratio* is derived. The verb *narro*—originally *(g)naro*—derives from a somewhat rare adjective (*gnarus*), which also appears in the form of *gnaruris*. These two adjectives lead us into the sphere of "knowledge,"[26] of "possessing experience." Speaking of Lucio Sisenna, Cicero defines him as a "learned man, devoted to the best studies, who spoke beautiful Latin and was *gnarus republicae*" (*Brutus*, 228). Evidently Sisenna was a man who had "political experience," who knew how the republic functioned in which, as an orator, he moved. Similarly, with regard to Pericles, the disciple of the philosopher Anaxagoras, Socrates maintained that in his speech he was "rich, fluent, and *gnarus*"—that which constitutes the most important element of eloquence (once again in *The Orator*, 4.15). This time *gnarus*, used

---

[25] Ennius, *Telamone*, sc. 319–23, ed. Jvahlen, *Enniae Poesis Reliquiae* (Amsterdam, 1963).
[26] Ernout and Meillet, *Dictionnaire etymologique de la langue latine*, 278.

absolutely, defines the sphere of wisdom, of prudence, of that self-awareness which is fundamental for whoever wishes to excel in the art of discourse. Hence whoever is defined as *gnarus* possesses the virtue of the experience of deeds or else that of—more abstract and absolute—"wisdom" concerning what he does or what he says. The *gnarus* gives the impression of being someone who, as we now say, is "self-assured," a person who finds himself at his ease in his own chosen field. Now perhaps we understand better what the act of "narrare" (*gnare*) implies, that is, what the specific quality of the discourse of the *gnarus* is. Whoever "narrates" or "speaks" in the manner of the *gnarus*, or else whoever makes someone *gnarus*[27] with respect to a certain thing, takes the resources of experience, of competence, and wisdom as his means. If, therefore, *oratio* presupposes the authority that comes from the orator, the "constructed" discourse of the lawyer or the ambassador, the *narrare* has on its side the virtues of the *gnarus*. In both cases, we are dealing with an extremely reliable discourse, which deserves to be heard because it comes from a source endowed with authority. Confronted with these kinds of discourses, the words of the *vates* and of the *hariolus* are destined to succumb. *Fabula* has become the discourse not to be shared and not to be trusted, associated with the speech of old women who tell stories, with marvels and gossip—enchanting and entertaining discourse, certainly, but not pertaining to us. In short, it is the discourse in which *others* can believe, but not the one who defines it as a *fabula*.

But this is the prehistory of the *fabula*—something about which we can only conjecture. When we encounter *fabula* in the sense of "mythological story," the term—together with *narratio, historia*, and *argumentum*—has already been trapped in the cages of rhetorical definitions. In the first century B.C. in fact, it is both Cicero's *On Invention* (1.19, 27) and the *Rhetorica ad Herennium* (1.8, 12ff.) that propose a scheme destined to have a great importance in the development of a rhetorical theory of narration.[28] Cicero explains it thus: "*narratio* is the exposition of what has happened, or of what could happen. . . . It is divided into three parts: *fabula, historia, argumentum*.

---

[27] Cf. Varrone, *The Latin Language*, 6.51; "*narro* when I render someone else (*g*)*narus*, by whom *narratio*."

[28] Rispoli, *Lo spazio del verisimile*, 22ff. This tripartite scheme poses in reality a problem of attribution and presents some interesting differences from one author to another: above all see ibid., 170ff., where the analogies between a similar tripartite division transmitted by Sextus Empiricus in *Against the Mathematicians*, 1.263–64, and a fragment of Asclepiade of Mirlea are illuminated; Calame, *Mythe et histoire*, 34, which inquires into Cratete of Mallo fr. 18; Bietenholz *"Historia" and "Fabula,"* 59–60ff. The tripartition appears as well in Quintilian, *Oratorical Institutions*, 2.4.

We call *fabula* a story that contains things that are neither true nor realistic, such as: 'enormous, winged serpents yoked to a wagon.' *Historia* is instead an accomplished deed, far from the memory of the age, such as: 'Appius declared war against the Carthaginians.' *Argumentum* is a fictitious narration that could still nevertheless be true, such as this passage from Terence: 'This man, his adolescence hardly past . . .' "

Fabula is in good company. Next to it appear two equally important terms: the first, *historia*, is that which—starting with Herodotus and moving all the way to Aristotle—was used to designate "history," with all of its connotations and ambiguities;[29] the other, *argumentum*, plays an important role in the rhetorical systematization of the Romans and means here the plot, the events of a theatrical text.[30] Placed under the control of history on one side, and of verisimilitude on the other, *fabula* covers the space of *mythos*, understood as an unreliable discourse. In fact, it denotes a story that deals with "things neither true nor realistic"—a story, usually, in which *others* may believe, but certainly not the one who defines it as a *fabula*. The examples chosen by Cicero are perfect. If a verse of the tragic poet Pacuvius, who with a grand display of style describes mythological animals of the most improbable kind, embodies *fabula*, for *historia* Cicero adduces one of the most prosaic and "historical" verses ever composed by Ennius: while, for *argumentum*, he gives us a citation from Terence's *Andria*, a truly respectable and lifelike comedy. The systematization of Cicero will be taken up again by Isidore of Seville (*Etymologiae*, 1.44), and thus will be transmitted to the medieval period. Isidore is concerned rather to up the ante: now *historia* deals not only with "things that have happened" but directly with "true things;" while *fabula* simply contains "things against nature." The unreliable discourse, that in which others believe, has become nothing less than a discourse against nature. Cicero had not gone quite so far: however, Isidore did not simply invent it out of thin air.

In order to criticize Varro, Augustine had taken up his tripartite division of theology (*The City of God*, 6.5):[31] "there are three kinds of theology . . . of these one is called *mythicos*, another *physicos*, and the third, *civilis*," continuing, "if Latin usage allowed, we should call the kind that [Varro] puts first *fabularis*, but let us call it *fabulosus*, for the term *mythicos* is derived from *fabulae*, since in Greek a *fabula* is called a *mythos*." Augustine thus clarifies

[29] Rispoli, *Lo spazio del verisimile*, 57ff.

[30] M. Bettini, *"argumentum,"* in *Le orecchie di Hermes* (Turin, 2000), 294–311.

[31] Cf. Varro, *Divine Antiquiies*, fr. 7–10, ed. B. Cardauns, *M. Terentius Varro Antiquitates Rerum Divinarum*, 1–2 (Wiesbaden, 1976).

once and for all that the Latin *fabula* is synonymous with *mythos*: hence *fabulosus* (and not *fabularis*, which was not to his liking) is synonymous with mythical. Varro, however, had been very honest. In the transcription of Augustine, to which we owe the survival of at least this part of *Divine Antiquities*, the great antiquarian proceeded thus: "they call the theology that is used chiefly by poets *mythicos*. . . . It has much fiction that is inconsistent with the dignity and true nature of immortal beings. In such fiction, for instance, we are told how one god sprang from the head [Athena], another from the thigh [Dionysus], another from drops of blood [Venus]; and again how gods have been thieves [Hermes], adulterers [Zeus] or slaves of a man [Apollo to Admetus]. In short, in this theology everything is ascribed to the gods that can befall a man, even the very lowest of men." Here, therefore, is where the idea of defining the stories of *fabula* as "against nature" comes to Isidore. The Bishop of Seville had read Varro in his Augustine.

The problem, however, confronted the Greeks themselves as early as the sixth century B.C. In the course of a descent to the underworld, Pythagoras would have seen the spirit of Hesiod tied, howling, to a bronze column, while the spirit of Homer, surrounded by serpents, was suspended from a tree: this torture would have fallen upon the two poets as punishment "for what they had said concerning the gods" (Diogenes Laertes, *The Lives of the Philoso phers*, 8.1.21). In more or less the same period, Xenophanes had expressly criticized Hesiod and Homer because they "had attributed to the gods all the actions which men consider shameful and blameworthy, like theft, adultery, and mutual deception" (fr. 11–12 Diels-Kranz).[32] Hence not only the Christians, but also the pagans themselves found the mythological tales concering the gods unacceptable. The Christian Augustine found in this aspect of *fabulae* only one welcome—because spontaneous—demonstration of the falsity of the pagan gods. "Can we ask for eternal life from a divinity of this kind?" he will ask ironically a little later on. But an irony of this sort could be used only by someone who considered his own theology "nonmythical," and hence had no difficulty in thinking that *mythoi* were simply stories in which others believed. But for Varro, just like for all the other "pagan" thinkers before him, this aspect of mythical theology constituted a difficult obstacle to be overcome—and compelled at the very least a deep exercise of thought. As for the modern mythologists,[33] so for the ancient ones the reflection on myth is born from a "stumbling-block." Varro had naturally tried to

---

[32] J. Pepin, *Mythe et allegorie: Les origines grecques et les contestations Judeo-Chretiennes* (Aubier, 1958), 93–94; Brisson, *Plato the Myth Maker*, 103–4.

[33] Detienne, *The Creation of Mythology*, 12ff.

downplay the extent of the scandal by separating the three different levels of his theology. If that *mythicos* is so embarrassing, however, one still had *physicos*, "the subject of many books that philosophers have bequeathed to us, in which they set forth what gods there are, where they are, what their origin is and what their nature, that is, whether they were born at a certain time or have always existed." And next, the theology *civilis*: "that which citizens in the states, and especially the priests, have an obligation to learn and carry out. It tells us what gods are to be worshipped by the state and what rites and sacrifices individuals should perform." But Augustine had made rapid work of these distinctions: "in theater," he observed, "they do mock the same gods that are venerated in the temple; nor are those to whom spectacles are offered any different from those to whom they sacrifice their victims" (*The City of God*, 6.5).

Augustine had put his finger on the wound. And Varro, as we have seen, was not the first to have to take stock of the existence of an objectionable mythical theology. A similar discourse was valid also for the mythological stories that told not of the gods, but of heroes, and of the various fantastic creatures they encountered during the course of their stories. These were full of incredible and bizarre elements. "Do you believe this *mythologema* of Boreas and Oreithyia to be true?" Phaedrus asked in a celebrated passage from the dialogue of Plato named for him. "If I disbelieved it," the philosopher had responded, "like the experts, I would not be extraordinary." After which, Socrates proposes an interpretation "out of wisdom" (*sophizomenos*) of the myth of the abduction of Oreithyia by Boreas: perhaps she simply had fallen from a rocky cliff, blown by the "wind of Boreas," and from this the story of her abduction by the god was born. Immeditaely afterwards, however, Socrates declares that he has no intention of spending his time "set[ting] the shape of the Centaurs to rights, and again that of the Chimaera," not to speak of a "mob" of Gorgons, Pegasuses, and other bizarre monsters of the kind. His motive was the following: whoever, pushed by incredulity, dedicates himself to bring back these stories "towards verisimilitude," using in this endeavor a certain "boorish kind of expertise," will end up devoting all of his time to this activity. Instead, Socrates intends to devote himself to self-reflection, and therefore in questions of mythology he preferred to "believe what is commonly thought" (*Phaedrus*, 229–30).

Hence stories about the gods appeared to be "objectionable," as much as the stories about heroes appeared to be "incredible." Myth poses itself as a problem at the moment in which traditional histories—or those composed on their model—appear to be reconsidered from the point of view of their acceptability and their credibility. In other words, when we put to ourselves the following question: can *even I* believe in these stories, as *others* do?

To describe this moment of fracture between the mythological story and its creators, we might turn, in closing, to some considerations on poetry by Samuel Coleridge in his *Biographia Literaria*. The passage that interests me occurs in the chapter in which the author recalls the experience of his collaboration with William Wordsworth on the composition of the *Lyrical Ballads*.[34] The two "neighbors," in fact, reached the conclusion that poetry can be essentially of two types: one in which the events and the forces in play are, at least in part, of a supernatural character; and the other in which characters and events are instead of a quotidian nature, those that might be found in any village. In the first type of poetry, Coleridge explains, "the particular form of perfection pursued" consists in "the interesting of the affections by the dramatic truth of such emotions, as would naturally accompany such situations, supposing them real. And real in this sense they have been to every human being who, from whatever source of delusion, has at any time believed himself under supernatural agency." It is this type of poetry—that in which the forces in play are at least in part supernatural—to which Coleridge would obviously have been devoted, leaving to William Wordsworth the task of occupying himself with the quotidian.

"My exertions," Coleridge thus continues, "would be returned to supernatural persons or characters but in such a way as to project onto them, from our familiar nature, a human interest and a pretense of truth sufficient to confer on these phantoms of the *imagination that momentary suspension of disbelief in which the poetic faith consists*." These words of Coleridge—as widely celebrated as they are suggestive—deserve to be explored further. In the first place, we should note that Coleridge, while having romantic poetry in mind—and in particular his compositions, like *The Rhyme of the Ancient Mariner* or *Christabel*—circumscribes a type of literary production that also corresponds to the *mythoi* of the Greeks: poetic texts (like those of Homer and Hesiod), in which there are supernatural personages or characters (such are precisely the fantastic creatures, the gods, or the heroes that existed in myth) who make contact with *human* beings (as also occurs in myth). According to Coleridge, in producing works of this type, the poet should have the capacity of creating in the reader what is defined as a "poetic faith," or else an attitude of belief and openness in the reader's experience of the story that widens out in a momentary "suspension of disbelief." Colderidge underlines the fact that this poetic faith can be obtained only on the condition

---

[34] S. T. Coleridge, *Biographia Literaria* (1817), ed. PI. Colaiacomo (Rome, 1991), 14.235ff.

that the writer makes the story emerge from an interior, authentic "human interest," surrounding it with a certain verisimilitude and authenticity. The literary recipe announced by Coleridge is very interesting, but, aside from this, what strikes me is that, according to him, the poetic faith is something that one produces, that is realized through the recourse to specific means. The poet should know these means if he wishes to realize his intention. In short, Coleridge is convinced that, without poetry and its arts, the telling of the supernatural is not effective.

In this sense, the perspective chosen by Coleridge is very close to that of the Greeks, for whom "the activity of mythological creation" is indissolubly linked to the poetic practice:[35] without poetry, myth would not exist. But there is another aspect of Coleridge's reflections that deserve to be highlighted: this time it concerns not the producer of the story, but the listener. According to the author of *Biographia Literaria*, in fact, the normal condition of the listener is not belief but disbelief; so much so that the space of the story—its success—is located precisely in the momentary suspension of this disbelief. The poetic faith does not correspond to a constant condition, but is achieved from time to time in making the listener take leave of her (habitual) condition of disbelief. In this respect as well, Coleridge seems rather close to the Greeks, and in particular to the role attributed to poetry by Gorgias (fr. 23 Diels-Kranz; cf. fr. 11, 9). The prince of sophists, in fact, considered poetry "a deception" (*apate*), in which "whoever deceives does better than whoever does not, and he who is deceived is wiser [*sophoteros*] than he who is not deceived." According to Gorgias, in short, in order to be able to take advantage of the possibilities offered by poetic discourse (ultimately, the achievement of *sophia*), one must surrender one's rational defenses and abandon oneself to the beneficent "deception" that is characteristic of this type of communication.

Keeping these reflections of Coleridge in mind—so Greek in nature—we can then return to the problem that interests us: that is, the fracture between the myth and its listeners, and myth's consequent demotion to the status of a discourse in which *others* believe. We can certainly say that the objections raised by Xenophanes, Pythagoras, and of Plato's Socrates to "myths" corresponds precisely to the dwindling willingness to suspend disbelief. It is as if the contract between poetry and its audience—a pact that, in Greek archaic poetry, was founded directly on the guarantee of the divinity, the Muse, with whom the singer was merely an active collaborator[36]—came in some way to

---

[35] C. Calame, *Poetique des mythes dans la Grece antique* (Paris, 2000), 38ff.

[36] C. Brillante, "Il cantore e la musa nell'epica greca arcaica," *Rudiae* 4 (1993): 7–37.

be broken. The poetic narrative and its narratee are now separated by a fracture, with the consequent waning of the poetic faith that used to generate the successful functioning of traditional myths. There is a moment in which the listener, confronted with a myth, is not able to abandon his own—natural, after all—condition of disbelief. "Do you [Socrates] believe this *mythologema* [of Boreas and Oreithyia] to be true?" It is this question that signals the decline of poetic faith and that forces myth to dwell among stories in which only *others* can believe.

———————

Translated by Simone Marchesi and Daniel Seidel

ADRIANA BOSCARO

Monogatari

A "story told" in both prose and verse: this is a *monogatari*, from *mono* (thing) and the verb stem *katari* (-*gatari* in compound tenses, to say something to someone, recount, tell).[1] Though never codified, the term was already in use in ancient Japan in the poetry anthology *Man'yōshū* (a ten thousand–page volume from the second half of the thirteenth century), emphasizing its meaning of "to chat, to converse," and demonstrating its prolonged use even though its period of greatest splendor, during which women writers made up the majority, was that spanning the tenth and eleventh centuries. These texts were originally read in circles limited to the central court, after which only a few handwritten copies were circulated. As a literary genre, given that the element linking the *monogatari* to other works is its inclusion of poetry, its nature has always remained somewhat ambiguous, and the same text might be known as *nikki* (diary), *kashū* (poetry collection), or even *zuihitsu* (free thoughts, aphorisms). But the foremost distinction of the *monogatari* is that it is fiction, nontruth, a work of fantasy, and this very lack of veracity became a point of stern critique for the era's defenders of official culture, while those who enjoyed it regarded it as an acceptable representation of quotidian life. As such, Sei Shōnagon, one of the most famous women of the court in ancient Heiankyō (today Kyoto) and author of *The Pillow Book*, still read and appreciated for both the wit of its descriptions and its fulminating intuitions,[2] joyously indulges in the opportunity to recount unknown *monogatari*, while at the same time inserting descriptions of typical pastimes such as the games *go* and snakes and ladders that helped pass the longer, emptier hours of the day.

As the origins and successes of the *monogatari* occur along the same lines as the process in which the native Japanese tongue was liberated from Chinese, a few words on this linguistic development will be useful.[3] The Japanese

---

[1] The Japanese words transcribed here accord to the Hepburn system based on the general principle of vowels being pronounced as they would be in Italian and consonants as they would be in English. Hyphens above the vowels indicate long sounds.

[2] Sei Shōnagon, *Makura no sōshi* (1020) [Eng. trans. *The Pillow Book*, New York: Columbia University Press, 1991. Trans. and ed. Ivan Morris].

[3] Details on this topic can be found in M. T. Orsi, "La standardizzazione del linguaggio: Il caso giapponese," in *Il romanzo*, 1. *La cultura del romanzo*, Turin: Einaudi, 2001, which covers the entire span of time taken into consideration here.

people acquired writing from China around the sixth century A.D. For centuries thereafter they proceeded along the same linguistic track that characterizes the development of their literary history: Chinese was the language of the literate, the cultured tongue used for documents, chronicles, essays, official poetry, and treatises, while the native language, believed to possess magical powers related to the spirit of words (*kotodama*) that made it unique and superior to any other language, was the preferred language of women writers—who found in it a rich, ductile, variegated quality—and for poetry limited to private circles. Although it would be easy to generalize the linguistic situation at the time by saying that only men could use Chinese and that Japanese was reserved for use by women, that does not necessarily correspond to the facts. Chinese was used by men for its "prestige" and as the official language of the bureaucracy, while women—given their distant remove from positions of power—had no practical need for it, even if some of the more cultured women knew and could use it. As such they opted for their native language and profited from the fact that it was beginning not only to free itself from Chinese through the acquisition of *kana* phonetic signs, but also to gain the attention of the establishment. When later the poet Ki no Tsurayuki, in a preface to the poetry anthology *Kokin wakashū*,[4] praises poetry in Japanese (*yamatouta* o *waka*) for its absolute superiority, then years later writes *Tosa niki* (*Tosa's Diary*), signaling a major shift in the development of Japanese literature (which is by now assuming, as one reads in the famous *incipit*, a feminine identity and a fictitious personality: "Diaries are written by men, I'm told, but I'm writing one to see what a woman can do"), the door is left wide open for the production of *monogatari*.

Hiragana, the phonetic system characterized by wavy, elegant writing, became the immediate prerogative for women writers and played a decisive role in the formation of *wabun*, the so-called Japanese style, that used the spoken language of the courtly aristocracy. The *wabun* excluded Chinese words entirely, and the phonetic transcription of its characters provided a wide variety of interpretational possibilities and stylistic subtleties to a largely homophonic tongue, factors of key importance to the success of the *monogatari*.

The poetic works written in Japanese (called *waka*, composed according to a syllable-per-line distribution of 5-7-5-7-7), complete with their own codified vocabulary and rhetorical expressions, quickly achieved a high degree of sociocultural importance that lasted for centuries. In a society in which relationships between men and women could only begin through

---

[4] Anonymous, *Kokinwakashū* (905) [Eng. trans. *Kokin wakashū*, Stanford, Calif.: Stanford University Press, 1985. Trans. Helen Craig McCullough].

epistolary exchange, poetry also functioned as a means of communication, and a great many writings from the Heian period (794–1185) were based on such love letters. Prose texts, for example, were interrupted by *waka*, corresponding to moments of intense emotion and high lyricism.

As has already been intimated here, not all *monogatari* were written by women. Around the year 909, an anonymous author composed what is held to be the most ancient of all *monogatari*, or rather, in the words of Murasaki Shikibu, "the forebear and first of all *monogatari*," "The Tale of the Bamboo-Cutter."[5] Murasaki even maintains the indubitable authority of this text in her *Tale of Genji*.[6] Considered the *monogatari* par excellence and perhaps the world's first psychological "novel."

Through her protagonist Prince Genji, Murasaki becomes the first writer to provide a working definition of the *monogatari* and comment on its function. This appears in chapter 25, "Hotaru" ("Fireflies"). In one of his wanderings around the palace, Genji winds up in the room of Tamakazura, who is believed to be his daughter. He finds her immersed in a reading of *The Princess of Sumiyoshi*[7] and begins to jeer at her for her interest in such stories, then admits to also be intrigued by them. And so begins the "defense" of the *monogatari*: fiction is not, as is commonly believed, made up entirely of falsehoods aimed at exploiting the naïveté of women, nor is it a collection of trifling nonsense to be used as a means for alleviating boredom on long summer days. It is not important for the writer of *monogatari* to describe characters with exacting detail; she can choose good or bad traits to highlight as might best attract and hold the reader's attention, and she isn't bound to recount events in the precise order in which they take place. Nonetheless, no matter how good or bad the context might be, no matter the order of events, the *monogatari* is always composed of things that happen in this world—enriched, of course, by the author's fantasy.

This was something highly criticized in fiction: using fantasy to decorate and make more interesting the kinds of things that happen everyday and that would normally be written up dryly and objectively in official chronicles. Moreover, the fact that women were some of the main writers of the *monogatari* cast greater doubt on their claims to truth, even if many of the details and situations they dealt with were more than credible—the same

---

[5] Anonymous, "Taketori monogatari" (ca. 909) [Eng. trans. "The Tale of the Bamboo-Cutter," *Monumenta Nipponica* 11, no. 4 (1956): 27–53. Trans. Donald Keene].

[6] Murasaki Shikibu, *Genji monogatari* (beg. eleventh century) [Eng trans. *The Tale of Genji*, New York: Vintage, 1985. Trans. Arthur Waley].

[7] Anonymous, *Sumiyoshi monogatari* (end tenth century) [No English translation available].

details and situations that furnished the stories with a base of consistency. Genji's story, for example, could have been as true and sincere as the human passions found within it.

The genre of the *monogatari* enjoyed good fortune for about four centuries (tenth through thirteenth). The production during this period totals around two hundred texts, though for many of them all that remains is the title. Clearly, not a great deal of consideration was given to the maintenance of the texts. Indicative, however, is a passage found in a treatise on the *monogatari*, "Mumyōzōshi" ("Story without a Name"), attributed to a woman writing around the year 1200, in which the genre itself is judged by a group of women who passionately discuss the qualities of various works.

Among the surviving texts are several that should be highlighted: *The Tale of Genji*; two tales dealing with relationships between mothers-in-law and daughters-in-law; the already mentioned *Princess of Sumiyoshi*, whose original copy, dating to the end of the tenth century, has been lost, but whose more than one hundred copies in following periods attest to the popularity and importance of such stories; and *The Tale of the Lady Ochikubo*, perhaps one of the most complete portraits, in which even a host of minor characters are well defined and delineated.[8] Then there is the "Utsuho monogatari" ("Story of a Hollow Tree," second half of the tenth century), which uses the music of a magic *koto* as a common thread and takes up some of the themes (such as that of the courtesans, for example) already treated in "The Tale of the Bamboo-Cutter." It is a prelude to *Genji* given its length, its description of a restricted society, and its idealization of art and aesthetics, but for the most part it underscores the contrast between old and new, between realism and idealism, between the courtly world and the "outside" world, with both of these worlds being amply treated in the following *Konjaku monogatari* (*Stories of the Time That Was*), consisting of more than a thousand tales (*setsuwa*). Then, complete with settings in both China and Japan, not to mention reincarnations and all of the intricate family drama that goes along with them, is the long, semifantastic story of "Hamamatsu chūnagon monogatari" ("The Story of One of Hamamatsu's Subadvisers"). Gathered under the title *Tsutsumi chūnagon monogatari* (*The Riverside Counselor's Stories*)[9] are ten delicate, witty, ironic tales that all share the

---

[8] Anonymous, *Ochikubo monogatari* (end tenth century) [Eng. trans. *The Tale of the Lady Ochikubo*, London: Arena, 1985. Trans. Wilfrid Whitehouse and Eizo Yonezawa].

[9] Anonymous, *Tsutsumi chūnagon monogatari* (twelfth century) [Eng. trans. *The Riverside Counselor's Stories: Vernacular Ficion of Late Heian Japan*, Stanford, Calif.: Stanford University Press, 1985. Trans. Robert L. Backus].

unifying theme of *kaimami* (literally, "view through a partition"), which is to say peeping, spying (from behind bamboo stalks, through ripped openings in tents or between branches, through little holes in paper partitions), the kind of act any gentleman would have to engage in to get a glimpse of the woman to whom he might eventually send amorous *waka* in hopes of a written response and, perhaps, a meeting with her.

One of the characteristics of Japanese culture is a predilection for detail. Rather than global, the Japanese vision of things tends toward the particular and, at the same time, the unfinished so as to avoid the realm of concrete things and explore the greatest variety of possibilities of existence (one might think of a temple in this regard, composed of various parts rather than a central body, or of the residential structures belonging to nobles of the era). Hence the *monogatari's* preference for single episodes as opposed to larger-scale, compact structures. The progression is rhapsodic with a sequential structure in which single parts intertwine into a greater whole according to certain fixed principles of the native poetry. Such a linear progression, interrupted by specific episodes, forms the *substratum* of the *monogatari*, or rather, the method of polyphonic fiction.[10] It is a process that recalls the succession of paintings on folding screens, or even the scrolled paintings (*emaki*) held between the left hand that unrolls the scroll and the right hand that rolls it back up, with the scene-by-scene movement between forming an entire narrative. The sections where the scroll's unrolling is paused for a moment, however, are the moments in which selected parts of the story are recounted, which do not always require a precise awareness of the parts immediately preceding them.

As has already been said, poetry and prose form alternating patterns in *monogatari*. Without a doubt, this was at the beginning an attempt to elevate the genre, and in cases where the sense of the story stems directly from the poetic verses, the tale's label becomes that of an *uta monogatari* (*uta* meaning "song," "poem"; it is the same character that, read in Sino-Japanese, comes across as *ka*, as in *waka*). A prime example of this is *The Tales of Ise*,[11] which, though centered on the romantic adventures of one of the era's most famous personalities, Ariwara no Narihira, is not considered fiction, rather the written expression of an authentic tradition. The same consideration is

---

[10] Noguchi Takehiko, "*The Substratum Constituting Monogatari: Prose Structure and Narrative in the* 'Genji Monogatari,'" in E. Miner, ed., *Principles of Classical Japanese Literature*, Princeton, N.J.: Princeton University Press, 1985, 130–50.

[11] Anonymous, *Ise monogatari* (mid-tenth century) [Eng. trans. *The Tales of Ise*, Tokyo: Tuttle, 1972. Trans. H. Jay Harris].

given for another form of story, the *setsuwa*, the anecdote of popular oral origins used by itinerant monks as a means of predication. Here, it is the readers' approach to the story that is different: they must believe in what the *setsuwa* says, all the while enjoying the story just as much as if they were reading a *monogatari*.

When the plot of a *monogatari* is based on historical facts, what results is the *rekishi monogatari* and the *gunki monogatari*, the style of which is a Sino-Japanese mix called *wakan konkōbun*. In both cases the narrative distinguishes itself from official chronicles (almost always written in Chinese), but given that *rekishi* means "story" and *gunki* means "army, battle," it is in the latter that the element of fiction dominates, as for example in the "Heike monogatari" ("Story of the Taira Family," thirteenth–fourteenth centuries), the tragic tale of the Taira family's succumbing to the Minamotos after years of bloody combat. The warrior heroes are glimpsed at the most crucial moment of personal defeat, and the entire work is pervaded by the Buddhist concept of *mujō*, the impermanence of things. And yet even here the internal structure of the work is composed of episodes that, once extrapolated from their context and diffused throughout the country by blind itinerant monks carrying a *biwa* (chorded instrument), were granted their own literary vitality and became important points of origin in the development of *nō* and, successively, *kabuki* theater forms.

It is significant that the term *rekishi monogatari* was coined to identify a work that escaped all labels, the "Eiga monogatari" ("The Story of Splendors"), attributed to Akazome Emon, a woman of the court who tells of courtly splendors by peppering her descriptions with anecdotes about famous people (in particular Fujiwara no Michinaga). This is apparently a historical work, but its model is undoubtedly *The Tale of Genji*. Moreover, it is the first *monogatari* to use an abstract term, *splendors*, in its title. A *rekishi monogatari* is also the most famous of the *shikkyō* (four mirrors), the "Ōkagami" ("The Great Mirror," between the eleventh and twelfth centuries), a historical work that, since it was not commissioned by the emperor himself, was written in *kana* and in the spoken tongue of the era, and by a single author who, for the first time, makes use of dialogue in which the opinions of elderly—if not over hundred-year-old—narrators are conveyed, because of their experience-based truth and validity, to inexperienced youths curious to learn about the past, such that the text was also known as the "Yotsugi monogatari," where *yotsugi*, meaning "the passing of generations," is the name given to the main protagonist.

The great tradition (which some might define as the "classic" tradition) of the *monogatari* reaches its conclusion around the turn of the fifteenth century, at which point other terms began to pop up: first *otogizōshi*, then *kanazōshi*, then *ukiyozōshi* and so forth. But *sōshi* as a descriptive term (*zōshi* in composite forms) cannot be directly compared with *monogatari*, given that it only indicates the "support" on which the text is written (such as a pamphlet or notebook), not an entire genre, and it therefore fell quickly into disuse. The proliferation of printing presses then favored the diffusion of texts whose distinguishing labels had no particular significance beyond telling the color of the texts' cover. These were readings meant for fun and entertainment, popular readings collected under the name *gesaku*. Other prose works fell under still other names, such as *sharebon*, *kokkeibon*, *kibyōshi* and *dangibon*, but those whose nature is closest to that of the *mono-gatari* are the *yomihon* (literally, "books to read," in the sense that the illustrations do not form a fundamental element to the text's meaning, as they had before) associated with two illustrious names: Ueda Akinari (1734–1809) and Takizawa Bakin (1767–1848). Akinari was among the first to make a return to the classical tradition with his *Tales of Moonlight and Rain*, the title of which already conveys the author's cultural choice and underscores the magic atmosphere in which the stories will take place. In the preface, the reference to the *monogatari* tradition is more than explicit:

> Luo Guanzhong wrote the novel *On the Water's Edge* and for this reason three generations of his descendants were born deaf and mute; Murasaki Shikibu wrote *The Story of Genji* and was therefore condemned to a certain amount of time in hell; for both of them, their works were the cause of their misfortune. But if we take a look at their prose, we find that, in creating rare forms in every detail, in approaching reality through an alternation of silence and expression with high, low and sinuous tones, it echoes in the chords hidden within the reader's soul. Here, one can see the reflection of a reality thousands of years old. Even I used to have some futile little stories that, when I put them to ink, created a fantastic world full of singing pheasants and fighting dragons. I don't personally believe that these stories have any foundation, but whoever reads them must not think that they are to be real stories; I wouldn't want them to be the reason for which descendants of mine might be born without noses or with leprous lips.[12]

The author's ironic tone is striking: it is true that prose narrative was never considered to share the same prestige as poetry and that its form was better

---

[12] Ueda Akinari, *Ugetsu monogatari* (1768) [Eng. trans. *Tales of Moonlight and Rain*, Tokyo: Tuttle, 1977. Trans. Leon M. Zolbrod].

geared toward entertainment, but that is no reason for its writers to be penalized in such crude ways. Poetry surely represents a higher level of expression of one's feelings, but prose can function similarly if one adapts to certain canons. The fact that Akinari cites Murasaki Shikibu recalls the golden years of the narrative form of the Heian court, when part of the production, as has been described here, was by women writers who were the first to voice their desire—with public and private readings, with offers of inspiration and reflection, and in particular with the language they used—for stories full of gallant plots, impossible loves, voyages, furtive courtly flirting, and poetic exchange.

When Japan opened itself up to Western culture in 1868, the term *shōsetsu* came into use to talk about the novel, but it too remained somewhat ambiguous, such that Tsubouchi Shōyō, who wrote a famous manifesto on modern fiction (*Shōsetsu shinzui*, *The Essence of the Novel*, 1885), uses rather casually the terms *monogatari*, *gesaku*, and *shōsetsu* in speaking of literary production during the classical period and thereafter. He does assert, however, that fiction is its own form of art with an autonomous nature, negating any didactic or purely entertainment-related intent.

In more recent times, in the famous debate that took place in the mid-1920s between Akutagawa Ryūnosuke and Tanizaki Jun'ichirō, their discussion dealt with the meaning of "plot" in the novel—a discussion that, given Akutagawa's premature death, did not lead to much, but did nonetheless reiterate Tanizaki's position with regard to the significance of fiction and the inherent intrigue of the *monogatari*: "That which isn't fiction does not attract" (*uso no koto de nai to omoroshiku nai*).

Translated by Paul D'Agostino

JUDITH T. ZEITLIN

Xiaoshuo

Xiaoshuo is the modern Chinese term for prose fiction of any length, particularly the novel; in its Japanese pronunciation *shōsetsu*, and its Korean pronunciation *sosŏl*, it is likewise the modern term for prose fiction or novel in Japan and Korea. As a word made up of two Chinese characters, "small," and "talk," *xiaoshuo* goes back to antiquity in China, but its significance and usage have changed repeatedly over time and space. To trace the history of the term *xiaoshuo* from its Chinese beginnings to its current pan-Asian meaning of prose fiction, then, is one way to chart the history of the novel in East Asia.

The earliest appearance of the phrase *xiaoshuo* occurs in the Daoist philosophy of *Zhuangzi* (fourth–second century B.C.E), where it means "little sayings or speeches" to contrast with "great understanding." The establishment of *xiaoshuo* as a literary category, however, occurs only several centuries later, in the bibliographical treatise of the official *History of the Han Dynasty*, compiled by Ban Gu (32–92 C.E.), where it designates the lowest class of philosophical and technical writings to be included. Ban Gu's often-cited preamble defines *xiaoshuo* as "chit-chat of the streets and alleyways, created by those holding conversations along the roadside," and he affiliates *xiaoshuo* writers with those "petty officials" (*baiguan*) who collect the "lesser understanding arising in villages" so that it will not be forgotten. He expresses his ambivalence toward it by quoting Confucius: "Even in a minor path, there is bound to be something worth considering. Taken too far, however, one fears getting mired in it; this is why the Superior Man does not engage in it." (*Analects* 19.4). *"But,"* adds Ban Gu, good historian that he is, *"neither does he destroy it."*[1]

Ban Gu's formulation became the classical definition of *xiaoshuo* in China for close to two millennia, with "petty officials" (*baiguan*) or "histories by petty officials" (*baishi*) becoming common synonyms for *xiaoshuo*. A number of basic elements in his definition continue to crop up in traditional defenses or attacks on *xiaoshuo*, even as the meaning and identity of the term change: (1) *xiaoshuo* is originally of oral provenance arising from the common people, associated with gossip and public opinion; (2) it is a minor, trivial, humble, not altogether respectable kind of literature, of dubious

---

[1] Ban Gu, *Han shu* (Beijing: Zhonghua shuju, 1962), *juan* 30, p. 1745; my emphasis.

value and veracity, but that is nonetheless worth preserving; (3) it is collected and written down by educated men of lesser rank; (4) it falls at the bottom of any classification scheme.

Ban Gu's conception of *xiaoshuo* also resembles a passage credited to another early source, *A New Treatise* (*Xinlun*, ca. 2 C.E.): "Those in the tradition of *xiaoshuo* collect fragmentary and petty utterances, and draw analogous discussions from near at hand, to make short books."[2] This description enables us to add the important qualifications of "short" and "fragmented" to the classical understanding of *xiaoshuo*. Although it is far from clear what it means "to draw analogous discussions from near at hand," it is plausible to infer that the "petty utterances" involved must have included short parables and fables, the kinds of little didactic stories that are indeed scattered in the extant writings of the early philosophers.

Nonetheless, from a modern perspective, what seems strikingly absent from these definitions of *xiaoshuo* is any overt reference to narrative or storytelling, let alone fiction. A glance at the titles Ban Gu listed in his bibliography reinforces this impression. Though none of these books are extant, their titles sound like the heterogeneous or apocryphal discourses of minor thinkers rather than collections of stories or anecdotes. By the seventh century, however, when the bibliographic treatise of the official *History of the Sui Dynasty* was compiled, the situation had changed. The *xiaoshuo* category, though still placed in the class of philosophical and technical writings, instead includes a set of titles recognizable as collections of anecdotes and joke books. One work is even entitled *Xiaoshuo*, although only portions of it survive. In these fragments and in the several extant titles on the list, we are able to see "a gradual ascendance of narrative over discursive materials,"[3] though "miscellaneous" and "minor" clearly remain salient characteristics of *xiaoshuo*, as does some connection to talk and conversation.

What is most noteworthy about *History of the Sui*, however, is the new subcategory of "miscellaneous accounts" (*zazhuan*) in the class of historical writings. The titles in this section consist mainly of *zhiguai* (records of the strange), a new genre of writing that had developed in the third through sixth centuries. These are collections of brief narratives written in the style of reportage that claim hearsay and eyewitness accounts as their sources. Their

---

[2] Translated by Robert Ford Campany in *Strange Writing: Anomaly Accounts in Early Medieval China* (Albany: SUNY Press, 1996), 131.

[3] Kenneth Dewoskin, entry on "Hsiao-shuo" (*xiaoshuo*) in *The Indiana Companion to Traditional Chinese Literature*, ed. William H. Nienhauser, Jr. (Bloomington: Indiana University Press, 1986), 424.

subject matter is primarily what we would now call the "supernatural"—an admixture of ghost stories, legends, lists of portents and their interpretations, anomalies, hagiography, miracles, and ethnographic description. The exemplary work in this vein is *Seeking the Spirits* (*Soushen ji*) by the historian Gan Bao (fl. 320), who served as official court compiler during the short-lived Jin dynasty. The operant model for both Gan Bao and the bibliographers of the *History of the Sui* is that of "leftover history" (*yushi* or *yishi*) or "marginal history" (*yeshi*), accounts that contribute to our knowledge of the world and of the past and should therefore be preserved, but whose mixture of the far-fetched and the weird preclude their inclusion in official history. Although in later dynasties some of the tales in books like *Seeking the Spirits* are rewritten as fiction or drama, at this initial stage, "records of the strange" were understood not as made-up stories but as an offshoot of historical writing.

The situation changed again in the tenth century, when Ouyang Xiu compiled the bibliographic treatise of the *New History of the Tang Dynasty*. Although he still includes a "miscellaneous accounts" section in the class of historical writings, titles in the "records of the strange" vein have been purged and removed to the *xiaoshuo* section, which is, as before, housed in the class of philosophical and technical writings. The old joke books and collections of wit are still there, but joining them are also new titles indicative of the tremendous growth in narrative literature from the eighth through tenth centuries, which produced a new genre now called *chuanqi* (tales of the marvelous), after the title of one such Tang collection. Although related to "records of the strange" in their focus on the amazing and the extraordinary, the subject matter of "tales of the marvelous" is broader, and the term can cover both longer stories that circulated independently and collections of stories. Compared with "records of the strange," "tales of the marvelous" tend to be longer, include poetry, and though they take the historical biography as their formal model and still credit hearsay and eyewitness accounts as sources, they also tend to be much more artfully crafted and sophisticated as literature.

With the tales of the marvelous we finally arrive at something close to our modern understanding of fiction—consciously made-up stories designed to entertain and edify. When in the late sixteenth century, a few Chinese scholars began for the first time to address the history of *xiaoshuo* as a genre, they pointed out that in practice it is often hard to distinguish between "records of the strange" and "tales of the marvelous," but they recognized that the Tang dynasty represented a major turning point in the creation of fictional *xiaoshuo*. As one such scholar put it: "Men of the Tang dynasty loved *xiaoshuo* and vied to devise works of the 'Mr. No-such' variety [e.g., fiction]. Yet historians lacking in scholarship still insert excerpts from them in history proper."[4]

Nevertheless, as the amalgam of titles listed under the rubric of *xiaoshuo* in the *New History of the Tang* suggests, the boundaries of *xiaoshuo* remained fluid over subsequent centuries. As a blanket term, *xiaoshuo* remained something of a catch-all and was still aligned with the qualities of miscellaneous and minor, becoming linked with the practice of individuals compiling *biji* (random jottings or notation books) as well as long romantic novellas. In his often-cited historical anatomy of the *xiaoshuo* genre, the sixteenth-century scholar Hu Yinglin defined six diverse subgroups: records of the strange, tales of the marvelous, miscellaneous anecdotes, miscellaneous notes, evidential research, and moral admonitions.

Hu Yinglin was keenly aware that the meaning of *xiaoshuo* had changed over time. He notes that the earliest titles labeled as such are not what in later periods would be called *xiaoshuo*. A careful reading of his work enables us to say that the "defining traits" of this "later *xiaoshuo*," (which would have included that of his own time, the late sixteenth century) included "narrativity, literariness, and fictionality."[5] Why this should be so has much to do with the parallel development of a separate strain of *xiaoshuo*, which Hu Yinglin pretty much ignored but which had arrived at a major turning point in the late sixteenth century. It is to this other history of *xiaoshuo* that I now turn.

All the works and genres that I have discussed so far in conjunction with the term *xiaoshuo* were composed in classical Chinese, the standard written language in China until the modern vernacular reform movement of the 1910s and '20s rendered both the literary language and the *xiaoshuo* written in it obsolete. But there also existed a substantial body of premodern narratives written in the vernacular (or in a mixture of vernacular and classical), which also came to be called *xiaoshuo*. These are the works that enable us to speak of an indigenous rise of the novel in China. (With the exception of some late-eighteenth- and nineteenth-century experiments and the brief flowering

---

[4] Mao Qiling, "*Changsheng dian* xu," in Hong Sheng, *Changsheng dian*, ed. Xu Shuofang (Beijing: Renmin wenxue chubanshe, 1986), 264.

[5] Laura Hua Wu, "From *Xiaoshuo* to Fiction: Hu Yinglin's Genre Study of *Xiaoshuo*," *Harvard Journal of Asiatic Studies* 55.2 (December 1995): 359.

of the classical romance novel in the 1910s, long fictional narratives were not written purely in classical Chinese). Unlike *xiaoshuo* composed in the classical language, which remained poised on the border between history and fiction, *xiaoshuo* written in the vernacular were understood as belonging to a clearly demarcated realm of fiction. The difference between them is not so much linguistic as ontological. The two constitute separate systems with separate histories, though there was much intermingling and mutual influence between them.

Vernacular fiction is believed to have emerged from performed oral storytelling rather than from the classical *xiaoshuo* tradition, though the precise nature of the relationship of the written to the oral medium remains highly contested, and vernacular fiction did borrow a lot of stuff-material from classical *xiaoshuo*. The most compelling arguments to date hold that vernacular fiction simulates and refers to an oral context without being a transcription of or aid for actual performance. At any rate, the adoption of a narrator loosely based on the persona of a professional oral storyteller is one of the most persistent and striking conventions of Chinese vernacular fiction, disappearing for good only in the late nineteenth century.

The bibliographies of the dynastic histories and other imperial compilations tell us virtually nothing about the vast arena of oral and written vernacular literature in China.[6] We now know that as early as the Tang dynasty (eighth through tenth centuries) stories in the vernacular were being written down, but these were not passed on in the received tradition, being only rediscovered by accident when a secret cave library in the remote desert town of Dunhuang was uncovered in 1900. These stories, known today as *bianwen*, bear clear signs of some connection with storytelling performance: they are prosimetric, alternating prose with verse passages meant to be sung or chanted, and they contain formulaic language of the sort associated with oral literature worldwide. One extraordinary example is a scroll that features pictures on the front and verses behind each one on the back, which scholars believe was used in a kind of storytelling-with-pictures, a practice that can still be found in India and other parts of Asia.

The term *xiaoshuo* appears nowhere in the *bianwen* materials at Dunhuang, although *hua* and *huaben*, two terms for "story" that are associated with later vernacular fiction, do crop up in the titles of some of the manuscripts. However, no source refers to written vernacular as *xiaoshuo* until the midsixteenth century. Prior to that we do find the term repeatedly applied to

---

[6] An exception is the gigantic early Ming encyclopedia, the *Yongle dadian*, which does include some early vernacular fiction and drama.

professional oral storytelling. There is a tantalizing isolated reference in a ninth-century miscellany to a performance of "marketplace *xiaoshuo*" (*shiren xiaoshuo*), but the first substantial evidence for *xiaoshuo* denoting storytelling performance appears on our radar only in the twelfth- and thirteenth-century memoirs of the entertainment precincts in Kaifeng and Hangzhou, respective capitals of the Northern and Southern Song.[7] The descriptions of the various kinds of storytelling (*shuoshu*) performed in these cities are still brief and somewhat confusing, but they nonetheless enable us to say with some confidence that *xiaoshuo* referred to imaginative subject matter, because the tellers of *xiaoshuo* are placed in competition with tellers of popular history and lecturers on the Buddhist sutras. These sources also indicate that *xiaoshuo* was a broad category, which included romances, fantastic stories, and tales of adventure, and suggest that the term pertained to the practice of performing short narratives in a single session rather than long narratives performed over consecutive sessions.

By the twelfth century, China already had a flourishing commercial publishing industry. From this time onward we start to find sporadic editions of what can be loosely called vernacular fiction. Because vernacular literature was, by and large, not valued in premodern China, little attempt was to made to preserve it. What imprints survive before the sixteenth century are mainly the result of accidents of history and were only rediscovered in the twentieth century when people began to look for them. Most such editions were preserved outside China, particularly in Japan and Korea; a few others have been unearthed from tombs; a fragment here and there has been found as backing paper used for other books. The point is that the imprints we do possess do not offer a good indication of the quantity or variety of what was actually published in the vernacular. Judging from the existing evidence, however, no overarching term was used to characterize early vernacular fiction, as no one at the time was interested in classifying it; instead, a range of labels are applied to individual works or groups of works in a seemingly casual manner. These works include retellings of history, prosimetric narratives, and short stories, as well as novels that emerged from oral storytelling cycles like *The Three Kingdoms* (*Sanguo zhi yanyi*) and *Outlaws of the Marsh* (*Shuihu zhuan*). A number of these labels include the word *hua* (story), especially a spoken one: *huaben* (short story), *pinghua* (plain story), *cihua* (story

---

[7] The ninth-century miscellany is Duan Chengshi's *Youyang zazu*. The relevant passages about storytelling in the memoir literature are translated and discussed in Wilt L. Idema and Stephen H. West, *Sources on Chinese Theater 1100–1450: A Sourcebook* (Wiesbaden: Steiner, 1982).

with song lyrics), *shihua* (story with poems); others use the names of historical genres: *zhuan* (biography), *zhi* (treatise), *ji* (record), *yanyi* (exposition).

The late sixteenth and early seventeenth centuries are a watershed in many respects. A major publishing boom took place at this time, which stimulated every stratum of book production, including both classical and vernacular *xiaoshuo*. The first application of the term *xiaoshuo* to vernacular fiction appears in the title of a series published in the midsixteenth century called *Sixty Stories* (*Liushi jia xiaoshuo*). Organized around the ideas of amusement and leisure, the series consists primarily but not entirely of vernacular stories (it still includes a prosimetric tale and a tale in classical Chinese). *Xiaoshuo* is used again in the title of Feng Menglong's influential collection, *Stories Old and New* (*Gujin xiaoshuo*), published about 1620. This collection, the first of three Feng published, consists exclusively of stories in the vernacular, some based on much older material dating back at least one or two centuries, and some that were newly composed by Feng or an associate.

Particularly important are the explicit statements about *xiaoshuo* that Feng Menglong provides in his preface to the collection and in the blurb on the title page. Here for the first time, the effort is made to assimilate vernacular fiction into the larger field of *xiaoshuo*, gaining for it a place on the classical literary map and a venerable history stretching back to antiquity. Thus the preface begins grandly: "*Xiaoshuo* arose when the tradition of historical writing began to weaken. It originated in the Zhou dynasty, flourished in the Tang and became widespread in the Song. The early philosophers Han Fei and Liezi are the ancestral founders of *xiaoshuo*."[8] But the preface also raises the specific question of how vernacular fiction originated. (Feng uses the term "colloquial fiction" (*tongsu yanyi*) to mark it off from the larger field of classical *xiaoshuo* here; elsewhere he uses *yanyi* and *xiaoshuo* interchangeably). A new myth of origins is supplied, which provides vernacular fiction with both an exalted pedigree by linking it to written stories collected by imperial fiat at the Southern Song court and a humble one by linking it to professional oral storytellers of that age. The preface returns to the figure of the contemporary oral storyteller at the end as part of a larger argument about the superior power of colloquial media to sway a broad audience.

Equally noteworthy is Feng Menglong's extension of the *xiaoshuo* category not only to short forms of narrative but to the long vernacular novels

---

[8] Feng Menglong, *Gujin xiaoshuo* (Beijing: Renmin wenxue chubanshe, 1981), 1. For an alternative and complete translation of the preface, see *Stories Old and New*, trans. Shuhui Yang and Yunqin Yang (Seattle: University of Washington Press, 2000).

that were starting to be acknowledged by a few critics of the day as great works of literature. Indeed, from the blurb on the title page it is clear that to Feng, the novel is *already* the dominant genre of vernacular *xiaoshuo*, since he had to defend his choice of the short story against the longer form of the novel: "Works such as *The Three Kingdoms* and *Outlaws of the Marsh* are considered the great landmarks of fiction. But the kind that concerns itself with a single character in a single action and which serves to provide entertainment should not be neglected."[9]

By no later than the 1660s, this expansive usage of *xiaoshuo* as an umbrella literary genre, covering works short and long, in both classical and vernacular idioms, had become commonplace in print. New and important collections of classical *xiaoshuo* continued to be published, but as the fashion for the vernacular story faded and as new novels and commentaries on the novel proliferated, the term *xiaoshuo* became increasingly associated with the novel. To be sure, the usage of the term remained elastic, at times still broad enough to encompass the novel-length plays known as *chuanqi*, at times so restrictive as to exclude the novel altogether. Bibliographies such as the imperial *Four Treasures* project (*Siku quanshu*) undertaken at the end of the eighteenth century could still ignore vernacular fiction entirely by insisting on an archaic, pristine definition of *xiaoshuo*. And even for liberal-minded editors of entertainment literature, *xiaoshuo* of any stripe remained at the bottom of the literary hierarchy. In a playful late-seventeenth-century piece entitled *Materia Medica Librorum* (*Shu bencao*), which classifies books as medicinal drugs in the manner of a pharmacopoeia, the Confucian classics occupy the highest category; novels and plays (*xiaoshuo chuanqi*), the lowest. The flavor of novels and plays is described as "sweet," but their effect is "highly toxic." The entry counsels extreme caution in reading such books: "This drug should be avoided because it induces insanity. It should be taken only during the summer months when suffering from a lassitude of spirits or stuffiness from overeating, when bad weather makes one feel awful, or in cases of influenza. Taking this drug can relieve ennui and dispel melancholy. It can dissipate sluggishness and open up the chest. However, it ought not be taken on a prolonged basis."[10]

Conversely, even after the late seventeenth century, alternative words for the novel, such as "unofficial history" or "histories by petty officials,"

---

[9] Translated by Patrick Hanan in *The Chinese Vernacular Story* (Cambridge, Mass.: Harvard University Press, 1981), 21.

[10] Zhang Chao, *Shu bencao* in *Xinzhai zazu*, vol. 1, pp. 1b–2a. Qing edition in the Fudan University Library.

remained in use. These terms were mainly drawn from the old discourse on classical *xiaoshuo*, and, when applied to long works of vernacular fiction in the eighteenth century, may suggest the grand literary, intellectual, and moral ambitions associated with the so-called literati novel, that flourished particularly during the eighteenth century. Epitomized by Wu Jingzi's *Unofficial History of the Literati (Rulin waishi)* and Cao Xueqin's *Dream of the Red Chamber (Honglou meng)*, these novels by literati authors for literati readers addressing literati concerns, circulated for years in manuscript among friends during their authors' lifetimes and were not conceived as commercial ventures.[11]

Dream of the Red Chamber, in particular, became a publishing sensation when it finally appeared in print in 1791, and the reading public's appetite for novels of all sorts continued to grow unabated throughout the nineteenth century. When Western missionaries arrived in China in the nineteenth century, they hit upon the idea of popularizing their own ideas through the colloquial medium of the traditional Chinese novel, in part inspired by indigenous groups who used vernacular fiction, particularly the prosimetric genre known as *baojuan* (precious scrolls), to promulgate religious cults.[12] The early Christian missionaries (which included James Legge, best known for his translations of the Confucian classics) adopted the form of the vernacular novel for their tracts because they thought their message would have a wider readership, and they appropriated the term *xiaoshuo* because it was so firmly established by this time.[13] Though largely forgotten today, their efforts may have facilitated the subsequent equation of the Chinese term *xiaoshuo* with the words for "novel" in European languages, so that later, when scores of European novels came to be translated into Chinese, they, too, were called *xiaoshuo*.

At the close of the century, late Qing social and political activists involved in journalism, attracted by the size of the audience for serialized novels in the Chinese periodical press, began to advocate the creation of a radically new type of fiction as an agent for national reform. Despite the strong influence of European and Japanese fiction in their conception of the new novel,

---

[11] Shang Wei, *Rulin waishi and Cultural Transformation in Late Imperial China* (New York: Columbia University Press, 2003), 1–4.

[12] Meir Shahar argues that vernacular novels became a major vehicle through which knowledge of the Daoist and Buddhist pantheons and local cults were propagated. See his "Vernacular Fiction and the Transmission of Gods' Cults in Late Imperial China," in *Unruly Gods: Divinity and Society in China* (Honolulu: Hawai'i University Press, 1996), 184–211.

[13] Patrick Hanan, "Missionary Novels in China," revised version in his *Chinese Fiction of the Nineteenth and Early Twentieth Centuries* (New York: Columbia University Press, 2004), 58–84.

these reformers retained the traditional term *xiaoshuo* without question and simply prefixed it with modifiers like "new" or "political," rather than coining a new word or adapting a foreign one. The earliest call for reformist novels in China came in the form of a 1895 fiction contest sponsored by the Englishman John Fryer, who placed advertisements in both the Chinese and English-language periodical press.[14]

The articles written by Yan Fu and Liang Qichao a few years later championing a new kind of fiction to reform China were much more influential and are much better known. The manifesto-like cry of Liang Qichao's editorial to the first issue of *New Fiction* (*Xin xiaoshuo*), the monthly he founded, is particularly famous: "To renovate the people of a nation, the fictional literature (*xiaoshuo*) of that nation must first be renovated. Thus to renovate morality, we must first renovate fiction; to renovate religion, we must first renovate fiction; to renovate manners, we must first renovate fiction; to renovate learning and the arts we must first renovate fiction; and even to renew the people's hearts and remold their character, we must first renovate fiction. Why? It is because fiction exercises a power of incalculable magnitude over mankind."[15]

In fact, although it was the novel that Yan Fu and Liang Qichao were most anxious to "renovate," and Liang himself produced the first published (though never completed) specimen of a "new novel," their understanding of the traditional term *xiaoshuo* was still expansive enough to include prosimetric narratives, classical tales, and even plays. It was only in the late 1910s and the 1920s, with the vernacular May 4 Movement, that the forms of the new *xiaoshuo* became fixed as the novel and modern short story, and *xiaoshuo* becames truly synonymous with prose fiction as we understand it throughout the world today.

Though *xiaoshuo* in this way became elevated as a universal category, a form of literature required of every nation, the retention of the traditional term *xiaoshuo* to denote this modern understanding of fiction placed old and new in a continuum of sorts and therefore stimulated the Chinese search for *xiaoshuo*'s past as well as its future. The writing of the new fiction went hand in hand with the writing of the first major Chinese history of

---

[14] Anonymous, "The New Novel before the Novel—John Fryer's Fiction Contest," in *Writing and Materiality in China*, ed. Judith T. Zeitlin and Lydia H. Liu (Cambridge, Mass.: Harvard Asia Center Publications, 2003), 317–40.

[15] Translated by C. T. Hsia in "Yan Fu and Liang Ch'i-ch'ao as Advocates of New Fiction," in *Approaches to Chinese Literature from Confucius to Liang Ch'i-ch'ao*, ed. Adele Austin Rickett (Princeton, N.J.: Princeton University Press, 1978), 222–23.

xiaoshuo from antiquity up to the late Qing. Lu Xun, master of the modern short story, was also the literary scholar whose pioneering work, *A Brief History of Fiction in China* (*Zhongguo xiaoshuo shilüe*), published in the 1920s, shaped this entire field of study and much of its terminology.

————

The Japanese decision to adopt the Chinese loanword *shōsetsu* as the modern term for fiction followed a different course. (*Shōsetsu* is the Japanese pronunciation of *xiaoshuo*, which is written with the identical Chinese characters in both languages). I have space only to suggest the contours of this complicated history here. Japan did not lack indigenous words for fiction. Both long narratives like the eleventh-century novel *Tale of Genji* and collections of tales were called *monogatari*, even when the tales were imitations of classical Chinese *xiaoshuo* and written much later, as in the case of the famous eighteenth-century *Ugetsu monogatari* (*Tales of the Rain and Moon*).

The term *shōsetsu* first gained currency in Japan in the late seventeenth century, when certain Japanese scholars interested in colloquial Chinese linguistics and phonology began to promote Chinese vernacular novels such as *Outlaws of the Marsh*. The term was first applied only to Chinese vernacular fiction and Japanese translations of it, but later also extended to the many vernacular Japanese imitations and creative transpositions of this fiction known as *yomihon* (books for reading). Many other words, however, were also used to designate subtypes of fiction or forms of entertainment literature at this time.

After the Meiji restoration, starting in the 1880s, political and social activists began to write "political novels" (*seiji shōsetsu*), which they saw as the most effective means to popularize their reformist ideals. Deeply influenced by the example of politically engaged European novelists like Hugo and Disraeli, they advocated a "new" kind of *shōsetsu* that would break with the old values expressed in the traditional *shōsetsu*. But the novels they actually wrote were still in the style of the *yomihon*, and though these books incorporate many European elements and locales, they are still indebted to the plots and literary conventions of Chinese vernacular fiction.

Japanese intellectuals did experiment with adopting a range of European-derived words for novel, such as *roman*, too. In the end, they kept *shōsetsu* as the standard term, in part because of the influence of Tsubouchi Shōyō's *Essence of the Novel* (*Shōsetsu shizui*) of 1885–86, a treatise that systematically "established a common ground for evaluating all existing Japanese prose fiction according to a 'universal' standard, along a nineteenth-century

Western, evolutionary axis" and that advanced a vision of how to remake the Japanese novel into "true *shōsetsu*" modeled on the nineteenth-century European novel.[16] Japanese writers went well beyond that of course, drawing inspiration from their rediscovery of older works of vernacular Japanese fiction and inventing some distinctive modern novelistic forms of their own, particularly the autobiographical "I-novel" (*shishōsetsu*).

Translations of *seiji shōsetsu*, and more important, the Japanese ideology of forging a new kind of fiction to remake culture and modernize the nation, were quickly exported to China and heavily influenced Chinese activists such as Liang Qichao in conceptualizing and promoting their vision of a "new" Chinese novel. Japanese translations of Western novels were also rapidly translated into Chinese and Korean and hence served as models for narrative in the twentieth century throughout East Asia. The Japanese usage of *shōsetsu* as the modern term for fiction must have reinforced the Chinese retention of *xiaoshuo* in a period when China was adopting quantities of loanwords coined in Japan for modern institutions and concepts. (Though, to be sure, the Chinese language has generally tended to keep the names of old literary genres for their modern counterparts).[17]

The adoption of the term *sosŏl* as the modern overarching word for fiction in Korea came both via China and Japan, though Japanese influence predominated after Japan's annexation of Korea in 1910. (*Sosŏl* is the Korean pronunciation of *shōsetsu/xiaoshuo*). A concept of *sosŏl* had previously existed in Korea, but it did not distinguish between Chinese and indigenous products, and, as in China, the term was applied to diverse kinds of writings.[18] Most types of old-style classical and vernacular Chinese *xiaoshuo* were read in Korea, and Koreans even composed their own collections of tales in classical Chinese, such as Kim Sisŭp's (1435–93) *New Stories from Golden Turtle Mountain* (*Kŭmo shinhwa*). An independent tradition of fictional narratives in Korean could only develop after the sixteenth century, however, when *hangŭl*, a proper writing system for Korean, was invented. Korean authors continued to write fictional narratives in classical Chinese after that point, but they began to develop a more distinctive tradition of their own, particularly favoring the biographical tale and first-person dream narrative.

---

[16] Tomi Suzuki, *Narrating the Self: Fictions of Japanese Modernity* (Stanford, Calif.: Stanford University Press, 1996), 20–21.

[17] Emanuel Pastreich, "The Reception of Chinese Literature in Japan," in *The Columbia History of Chinese Literature*, ed. Victor Mair (New York: Columbia University Press, 2001), 1,086–95.

[18] My account of the premodern history of *sosŏl* in Korea is indebted to unpublished research by Suyoung Son and to Pastreich, "The Reception of Chinese Literature in Korea," in ibid., 1074–78.

The high status of classical Chinese among elite men and their corresponding contempt for Korean as a written language naturally limited the forms
of literature composed in Korean. A few pioneering intellectuals, such as
Kim Manjung (1637–92), did attempt to write *sosŏl* in Korean; even so,
modern scholars are divided concerning the question of whether his novel,
A Dream of Nine Clouds (*Kuun mong*), was first written in Korean and then
translated into classical Chinese or vice versa. A tradition does exist of stories and novels written in Korean, which are known as *ŏnmun sosŏl* (*ŏnmun*
being a derogatory term for Korean). The dates of their composition are still
contested because they first circulated in manuscript, but by no later than
the eighteenth century, some of these works had probably found their way
into print. *Ŏnmun sosŏl* included heroic novels, which narrated the rise and
fall of a hero of humble origins, *p'ansori* novels, which developed out of oral
chantefable, and domestic novels written by women for upper-class female
readers, which mainly circulated in manuscript. Works in this last and most
interesting category were heavily indebted to the Chinese novelistic genres
of romance and chivalry, and still required knowledge of Chinese literary allusions, but they exhibit their own Korean emphasis on propriety in domestic life and family relations.

The late Qing movement to create a new novel to reform society had
some influence on like-minded Korean reformists, but the Japanese *shōsetsu*
was the main inspiration for them to take up the *sosŏl* in Korean as more
than entertaining or instructional reading for women. Stimulated by the
Japanese literary example and by their own experiences as part of a nation
in the throes of a painful modernization and colonization process, in the
early twentieth century, Korean writers developed their own version of the
East Asian "new novel" (*shin-sosŏl*) written in colloquial Korean, and
founded a modern fiction tradition of their own.

A few recent scholars writing in English have experimented with keeping
the terms *xiaoshuo* or *shōsetsu* untranslated to emphasize the extent to
which East Asian prose fiction differs from the dominant model of the European novel. Masao Miyoshi has made this position of ideological resistance
most explicit in his attempt to reverse the power relations ordinarily operating between Japanese *shōsetsu* and the Western novel, by making "the
'novel'" the one to be "contested against the *shōsetsu* form."[19] But the equation between *shōsetsu/ sosŏl/xiaoshuo* and "the novel" is now by far too entrenched to dislodge.

---

[19] Masao Miyoshi, *Off Center: Power and Culture Relations between Japan and the United States*
(Cambridge, Mass.: Harvard University Press, 1991), 9.

Qiṣṣa

The Arabic narrative tradition presents itself as a tangle of genres with many different names whose meaning is not always clear, such as the *khurāfa,* which denotes a fantastic tale recounted at night; the *mathal,* or fable; the *nādira,* or anecdote; and the *sīra,* or chivalric tale—to mention only those that seem easier to translate. It is of course difficult to study any one of these genres without taking the others into consideration. Consequently, this study of the *qiṣṣa,* will refer to several related genres and, in particular, to the *ḥikāya,* the *ḥadīth,* the *maqāma* and the *riwāya.* Since this last term is understood now to be the equivalent of "novel," it will lead us into a consideration of the role of narrative tradition in the formation of the modern Arabic novel.

The verb *qaṣṣa,* literally "to follow someone's tracks," means "to tell, narrate." The noun *qiṣṣa* once referred to various kinds of narratives but initially seems to have been used mostly for the edifying or religious narrative. In the Qur'ān, the term *qaṣaṣ* refers to stories of the prophets, historical narratives that carry a warning or exhortation (*'ibra*) and whose explicit goal is to strengthen the spirit of believers. Among interpreters of the Qur'ān there emerged at some point a curious figure, that of the *qāṣṣ* (pl. *quṣṣāṣ*), or popular preacher. Officiating usually in the mosques, the *qāṣṣ* would elaborate imaginatively on the stories of the prophets. In his *Kitāb al-quṣṣāṣ (Book of the Popular Preachers),* Ibn al-Jawzī (twelfth century) offers valuable details about this type of tale-teller. He describes the *qāṣṣ* as a highly colorful, unscrupulous character who paid scant attention to the authenticity of his sources and much more to flattering the taste of the crowd for the marvelous and extraordinary. He was not above donning makeup and miming gestures to have greater effect on his audience, who, listening to him, were sometimes moved to burst into tears or faint. Not surprisingly, the popular preacher was not well received by the theologians, who, outraged by his inventions and exaggerations, criticized him for not founding his stories on indisputable authorities. Despite the influence the *qāṣṣ* exerted over the crowd, his narratives did not acquire literary status. But although he was not able to establish a new narrative form, he did provide the inspiration for the figure of the eloquent vagabond (*mukaddī*), the hero of the *maqāma.*

In Arabic classical culture, it is important to note that a narrative acquires validity through an author, that is to say, a person qualified by his training to deliver a speech. An anonymous text, or one written by someone who cannot claim recommendation by acknowledged masters, has little chance of being received favorably. This explains in part the rejection of the *Thousand and One Nights*: scholars did not hide their scorn for this book, which, lacking an author, was only good for the frivolous and weak-minded. This attitude has not completely disappeared even today—far from it: Arab readers are somewhat nonplussed, even irritated, when they learn that the *Thousand and One Nights* has been adopted by Europeans and enjoys great prestige in their countries. It is, moreover, the only Arabic book Europeans know. It is an irony of history that Arabs are represented in Europe by a book in which they do not really recognize themselves, by a marginal, and, in a certain sense, illegitimate book.

Thus two kinds of narratives emerged: on the one hand, anonymous texts enjoyed by the masses, and on the other, those we could call "narratives with authors," appreciated by the literate elite. Whereas the common people were interested in stories for their own sake, the literate, at least in the classical period, sought something more, a lesson, some instruction. This explains the success of *Kalīla and Dimna*, a collection of fables of Indian origin translated from Persian in the eighth century by Ibn al-Muqaffaʿ, an author of works of great originality. In the preface, he describes the method of reading required by this book: behind the peripeteia of each story the reader is invited to discover a truth, an "aphorism" (*ḥikma*) that is not immediately apparent. This hidden wisdom provides the narrative with an alibi and grants it a certain legitimacy. A similar concern can be seen in the "philosophical novel" of Ibn Ṭufayl (twelfth century), *Ḥayy ibn Yaqẓān* (translated into Latin in 1671 as *Philosophus autodidactus*). Once again, it is the philosophical content behind the story that seems to matter. The narrative is relegated to the background and treated as a simple didactic tool, a convenient means of conveying a message. On the other hand, the *maqāma*—a genre in which both Hamadhānī (tenth century) and Ḥarīrī (eleventh century) distinguished themselves—found favor with the literate because of its learned writing and rhetorical display. In all these different cases, it was obligatory to provide a justification for the narrative, as if fictional narration were pernicious or, at the very least, suspect.

Whereas the *qiṣṣa*, originally confined to the religious domain, is a narrative whose action takes place in the past, the term *ḥikāya* refers to a narrative that relates to the present, to the author's contemporary reality. The original meaning of *ḥikāya* was "imitation, reproduction of an action or speech." (Incidentally, the mime, *ḥākiya*, specialized in reproducing the cries of animals and imitating the mispronunciations of non-Arabs in an environment where many ethnicities and languages intermingled.) In point of fact, *ḥikāya* is similar to mimesis as Plato understood it. We should mention, in this regard, two important works. The first is *The Book of Misers* (*Kitāb al-bukhalā'*) of al-Jāḥiẓ? (ninth century): the author describes the misers of his time but from their own point of view, adopting their manner of seeing and reproducing their speech even when purists would consider it grammatically incorrect. Jāḥiẓ is, moreover, careful to warn his reader: "If, in this book, you should chance upon a mistake, a vulgarism or linguistic impropriety, you should know that we have retained these because to correct the grammar would diminish the interest of the stories by distancing them from the world in which they took place. This is not, of course, the case when we record the remarks of the pretentious or learned misers."[1] The second work is that of Abū-l-Mutahhar al-Azdī (first half of the eleventh century), *Ḥikāyat Abī-l-Qāsim* (approximate translation: *The Story of Abū l-Qāsim)*. In this book, which is astonishing in many respects, the author proposes to represent the customs of Baghdad's inhabitants and reproduce their manner of speaking. The action takes place in a single location, on a single day, on the occasion of a banquet where numerous guests have gathered. Suddenly the eccentric Abū-l-Qāsim arrives, a loudmouth who dominates the conversation and behaves in such a rude and disconcerting manner that his exasperated table companions finally decide to get him drunk and thus put an end to his unbearable monologue. *The Story of Abū-l-Qāsim* is almost impossible to find in a bookstore today, probably because of the indecency of the hero's language, which is studded with phrases in dialect and riddled with pornographic and scatological expressions.

In a later semantic change, *ḥikāya* would lose the sense of "imitation" and acquire that of "story"; thus each of the tales in the *Thousand and One Nights* is introduced by its heading as a *ḥikāya*. The term *qiṣṣa* would eventually, though much later on, acquire the meaning of "novel," or, more broadly, "fictional narrative." Generally speaking, it became customary in the first half of the twentieth century to designate the novel as *qiṣṣa ṭawīla* ("long") and the novella as *qiṣṣa qaṣīra* ("short"). But another term, *riwāya*, also emerged and competed with *qiṣṣa* for the designation of "novel." Originally *riwāya* meant "the oral transmission of a poem or a narrative," but toward the end of the nineteenth century, it acquired the meaning of "dramatic work." Today it is the term used by general consent to mean "novel," while *qiṣṣa* is used only to refer to the novella.

These semantic shifts were brought about by the encounter with Western modernity. It was, indeed, in the nineteenth century that Arabs came to

---

[1] Charles Pellat, trans., *Le livre des avares de Gāḥiz*, French translation with introduction and notes by Charles Pellat (Paris: Maisonneuve, 1951), 57.

know European literature and in particular, French and English literature, for obvious historical reasons. They also discovered the theater at that time. The novel did exist in Arabic literature, it is true, in the form of the *sīra* or chivalric tale. The *Sīrat 'Antar (The Tale of 'Antar), Sīrat Sayf ibn Dhī Yazān (The Tale of Sayf ibn Dhī Yazan),* and *Sīrat Baybars (The Tale of Baybars)* are undeniably epic in inspiration and impressive in size. (The French translation of *Baybars*, an ongoing publication by Editions Sindbad in Paris, will comprise, if completed, about sixty volumes in all.) But there is scarcely a trace of these narratives to be seen in the novels of nineteenth- and twentieth-century writers.

Some researchers assert that the modern Arabic novel developed from the imitation of European novels and that its own narrative tradition played no role in its elaboration. But this statement should be corrected or, at the least, nuanced. Of the first Arab writers who tried the novel form, many turned to the *maqāma*. One of the characteristics of this genre is the constant wandering of the hero that takes him all over the Islamic world, though never beyond its borders. This trait links the *maqāma* to a genre much honored in classical literature: the *riḥla*, or travel narrative. Pilgrims, geographers, ambassadors, and adventurers would give written accounts of their wanderings, and these too, generally, were limited to the Islamic world. Europe rarely attracted these travelers; even Ibn Battūta (fourteenth century), who had traveled as far as China, had avoided European countries. But from the nineteenth century onward this would change. Arab writers stayed in Paris or London for study or other reasons, and their visits brought new perspectives and new works.

It is interesting, in this regard, to compare two Lebanese writers who, though contemporaries, had a different relationship to Europe. The first, Nāṣif al-Yāzijī (d. 1871), never left his country and learned no foreign language; consequently he remained a prisoner of the *maqāma* in his *Majma' al-baḥrayn (The Confluence of the Two Seas).* The second writer, Shidyāq (d. 1887), lived for many years in London and Paris, learned English and French, and wrote *al-Sāq 'alā al-sāq fīmā huwa al-Fāryāq*,[2] a work somewhat reminiscent of Sterne's *Tristram Shandy*. The first Arabic novels read both like travel narratives and novels of education in the sense that they described the experience of an Arab who, burdened by the weight of the past, moved

---

[2] *Al-Sāq 'alā al-sāq fīmā huwa al-Fāryāq* has been translated into French by René Khawam as *La jambe sur la jambe* (Paris: Phébus, 1991). No English translation of the novel exists, however. Roger Allen has remarked in his study, *The Arabic Novel: An Historical and Critical Introduction*, 20, that the title itself is "untranslatable": it includes a pun on the author's name "in that Fāryāq includes the first syllable of Fāris and the last of Shidyāq," and "constitutes an excellent demonstration of the revival of the proclivity of medieval Arabic prose for rhyming titles." [Translator's note.]

forward to meet Europe's present, little by little assimilating the values of modernity without completely renouncing those of the past. It is worth emphasizing that it was in Paris that Shidyāq published *al-Sāq ʿalā al-sāq*, and it was also in Paris that Haykal would later write *Zaynab* (1914).

To fully understand the transition from the *maqāma* to the novel, it might be useful here to consider a book by the Egyptian Muwayliḥī (d. 1930), *Ḥadīth ʿĪsā ibn Hishām* (*ʿĪsā ibn Hishām's Tale*), which was published first in separate installments and then in one volume (1907). This author does not define his project as either a *qiṣṣa* or a *ḥikāya* but rather as a *ḥadīth*, a term meaning "report, speech, narrative." But Muwayliḥī still relies on the *maqāma*, and particularly on the author Hamadhānī, from whom he borrows the name of his narrator, ʿĪsā ibn Hishām. Yet even while he makes reference to the *maqāma*, he distorts it and changes its design. Where the narratives of Hamadhānī are each self-enclosed and follow with no links between them, the chapters of Muwayliḥī's book are arranged chronologically. The sequencing of episodes is one of the formal traits that distinguish Muwayliḥī's project from that of authors of the *maqāma*.

A further characteristic to note in *ʿĪsā ibn Hishām's Tale* is the rejection of poetry. Whereas Shidyāq inserted poems into *al-Sāqʿalā al-sāq*, Muwayliḥī's work is completely written in prose. Later Arab novelists also banished poetry from their works, thus sacrificing one of the essential elements of the traditional Arabic narrative. Whether in the *maqāma*, the chivalric tale, *Thousand and One Nights*, or even, occasionally, simple anecdotes, the insertion or citation of poems is a constant of early narrative. The modern novel, on the other hand, does not seem to tolerate the presence of passages in verse. There are, of course, poems in *Don Quixote*, but in general the novel has tended to exclude poetry for various reasons, not the least of which is the necessity for this form to be easily translated, to pass without great loss from one language to another.

Not only was poetry set aside but so too were stylized language, archaisms, rhymed prose, and elaborate rhetoric. Classical works, such as those of Hamadhānī and Ḥarīrī were deliberately obscure and required, in addition to a lexical commentary, an explanation of cultural allusions, proverbs, and exemplary figures. Very often, authors took on the role of commentator on their own works. They wrote, moreover, with a view to receiving commentary from others or providing it themselves. With the arrival of the novel this custom would disappear, since the novelist gave up the desire to "translate" himself.

But it is the presence of the European dimension that radically transforms the ideas of the *maqāma* and invites us to consider *ʿĪsā ibn Hishām's*

Tale as a novel. The story opens with a dream: the narrator, walking one night in a cemetery, suddenly sees a tomb open, out of which emerges a pasha from the time of Muḥammad ʿAlī, Vice-Roy of Egypt. The two characters immediately embark on a series of rather droll adventures that take place first in Cairo, then in Paris. Returning from the dead, the pasha observes this world with increasing astonishment. The role of ʿĪsā ibn Hishām, his faithful companion, is to explain to him the changes that have taken place in the world and reconcile him with modern life. As we know, the resurrection of a character who views the present with a naive and dismayed gaze is an old literary topos, but in this context it has, above and beyond its mere anecdotal aspect, a deeper significance: it refers to the situation of the Arabs who, without wishing to, wake up suddenly one day in a world they have had no part in inventing or building, that they do not recognize, and that does not reflect back a reassuring self-image. Their own world lies behind them, and they must now confront that of the Europeans. A little later, Tawfīq al-Ḥakīm wrote a play entitled *The People of the Cave (Ahl al-Kahf)*, based on the Qurʾānic story of the Seven Sleepers who, after a sleep of several centuries, awoke to a new world they found utterly incomprehensible. The same writer would later publish a novel with the resonant title: *ʿAwdat al-rūḥ (The Return of the Spirit)*.

Muwayliḥī's *ʿĪsā ibn Hishām's Tale*, like *al-Sāqʾalā al-sāq* of Shidyāq, sets up a parallel between two times (the past and the present of the Arabs) and two spaces (the Orient and Europe). But the separation is not absolute, for the Orient has lost its *purity*. In Muwayliḥī's narrative, Europe lies not only on the far side of the Mediterranean but is also to be found on this side, in Cairo itself. The spectacles of Cairo astonish the resuscitated pasha no less than the spectacles of Paris. The Egyptian judicial system is grafted onto the Napoleonic Code, the streets have names and the houses have numbers, people dress in the European manner, use electric light and adopt new customs—all these surprising details and aspects suggest the passage into another time and another space. Muwayliḥī is describing, in other words, the entrance of the Arabs into modernity and the new order that prevails in the world.

Several novels published in the following years and now considered masterpieces evoke, each in its own way, an analogous situation. One thinks of *ʿUṣfūr min al-sharq (Bird from the East)* by Tawfīq al-Ḥakīm, *Qindīl Umm Hāshim (The Saint's Lamp)* by Yaḥyā Ḥaqqī, *Mawsim al-hijrah ilā al-shamāl (Season of Migration to the North)* by Ṭayyib Ṣāliḥ, and *al-Ḥayy al-Lātīnī (The Latin Quarter)* by Suhayl Idrīs. This is not all: once Europe extends south of the Mediterranean, its languages will inevitably follow, so it is not surprising when Arab novelists, particularly those of the Maghreb, write their works in French. In the past the literary elite delighted in elaborating parallels of the pen and the sword, the doctor and astronomer, the prose-writer and the poet, poetry and philosophy. Today, however, the main debate centers on the Orient and the Occident, the Arab world and Europe. For an Arab, to write a novel means to engage directly or indirectly in the debate about priority between these two spaces, two worlds.

Another debate, though a less important one, deserves mention here. The Arabs considered their poetry to be the finest aspect of their literature. Poetry was their title to fame, their *dīwān,* or register, in which were recorded their highest deeds and merits. Narrative literature, on the other hand, was accorded only a minor place. This was certainly not the opinion held by Cervantes, who imagined the Arabs to be, above all else, tale-tellers, chroniclers, and inventors of stories (which is perhaps why he attributed the composition of *Don Quixote* to a Moor, Sidi Ahmed Benengeli). This opinion was not shared by Antoine Galland either: exalting the *Thousand and One Nights* to such a point that he declared that "no one has yet seen anything as fine in this genre in any language," he still eliminated from his translation the numerous poems that were inserted into the work. Today, fictional narrative occupies an important place in the Arab literary landscape, and it is even sometimes said that the *riwāya*, the novel, is the true *dīwān* of the Arabs: *dīwān* or "divan," in all senses of the term.

Suggested Reading

Allen, Roger. *The Arabic Novel: An Historical and Critical Introduction*. (Manchester: University of Manchester Press, 1982).

Encyclopedia of Islam, new ed. Leiden: Brill, 1986. See the article by Charles Pellat on "*Ḥikāya*" (vol. 3), and that of Charles Vial, "*Ḳiṣṣa*" (vol. 5).

Translated by Mary Harper

PIERO BOITANI

Romance

"The Knight Sets Forth": this is the title of the famous chapter Erich Auerbach devoted to medieval romance more than fifty years ago in his *Mimesis*.[1] In order to demonstrate its range, as well as its continuing power of suggestiveness, I choose to begin not with one of the medieval romance's original products, of the central area from which it spread—France (for example, Chrétien de Troyes and his *Yvain*)—but with a romance of the late fourteenth-century that emerged from a peripheral region—northwestern England. Many elements of this short poem are tied to a different tradition: the rhythm and alliteration of the verses seem to descend, by ways not completely known to us, from the structure of Anglo-Saxon poetry, that is, from an archaic English world whose history, in theory, should have been left behind after 1066, the year of the Norman conquest of England.

And yet, here in this poem is a knight who sets forth on his adventure. Arthur and his companions reunite at Camelot to celebrate the joyful festivals of Christmas. All of a sudden, a green half-giant, dressed in green as well, appears in the banquet hall. He is, in appearance, a chivalrous knight who intimately knows the manners (and the pride) of the Arthurian court. In reality, he has come to put their pride to the test by presenting them with an absurd challenge. He is looking for someone who can decapitate him in three attempts with the Green Knight's axe, but who also swears for his part to receive three strokes from the same axe within one year. The only one to respond is Gawain, the "Gauvain" of so many medieval romances. Gawain lifts the weapon and without hesitating strikes off the head of the Green Knight (the romance is entitled *Sir Gawain and the Green Knight*).[2] But the stranger, as though it were completely natural, picks up his own head, tucks it under his arm, and, reminding Gawain to present himself at the Green Chapel within one year for the second part of the challenge, leaves on horseback and disappears in a flash, just as suddenly as he had arrived.

Eleven months later, Gawain, right on schedule, "sets forth." Armed to the teeth, he bears a small shield on which is emblazoned a five-pointed star, a symbol of the five virtues (multiplied by five, and again by five, until they

---

[1] E. Auerbach, *Mimesis: The Representation of Reality in Western Literature*, trans. W. R. Trask (Princeton, 1968).

[2] *Sir Gawain and the Green Knight*, J. R. R. Tolkien and E. V. Gordon, eds., 2nd rev. ed. by N. Davis (Oxford, 1967).

form an infinite knot) of the courteous knight. Gawain has a heavy heart because the thought of losing his head between Christmas and New Year's Day
does not particularly excite him, but he remains faithful to his pledge, his
loyalty (*trawthe*) pushing him onward. He goes on, like the Guidoriccio da
Fogliano against the background of the blue sky, the hills, and fortified
cities, that Simone Martini had painted in Siena not long before. On Gawain's
journey, however, there are only forests and desolate fields of snow and ice,
with dangers surrounding him on all sides. Gawain overcomes them all and
continues, but without a destination, because he does not know—nobody
knows—where to find the Green Chapel. But all of a sudden, on Christmas
Eve, he sees a marvelous castle appear, so extraordinarily similar to one of
the architectural fantasies of Ludwig of Bavaria as to seem cartoonish. In
this manor, isolated in the middle of a wasteland, so far from Camelot, a
provincial, albeit very refined court lives in great abundance, although un-
happily. There is a Lord of brilliant clothes, his wife—a beautiful, enchanting Lady of the Castle—and a wrinkled, severe old woman, whom we may
imagine as an embodied portrait of some English or American Puritan from
some centuries in the future.

Naturally, even the small court intends to celebrate the festival, so that
the Lord proposes a "game" to Gawain (whose name is obviously known to
all) that will serve to pass the time until the fateful encounter at the Green
Chapel, which can be easily reached from there, says the Lord of the Castle.
The game will consist in an exchange of gifts: the Lord will go on a hunt for
three successive days; Gawain, in order to rest himself from his toils, will remain idly at the castle. At the end of each day, the two men will exchange
what each has "won." In the three following days, the Lord of the Castle
brings home a deer, a wild boar, and a fox, while Gawain receives from
the lady one kiss the first day, two kisses on the second, and three kisses on
the third day. She courts him incessantly with her words ("You are Gawain,"
"chevalier aux demoiselles," "I want a love-story from you"), with her
clothes (at one point she comes to him while he is waking up wearing a revealing dress in front and back), and with her manners. On this last day the
Lady, who cannot obtain from Gawain what she desires (the knight thus
proves himself to be pure, and truly loyal to the Master of the House), also
gives him a green belt that will preserve his life from the mortal challenge of
the Green Knight. Gawain repays the gifts of the deer, the wild boar, and the
fox with the kisses the Lady had given him. However, he forgets to return
the belt—this he wears himself.

After having been splendidly entertained, and after having made confession, Gawain must finally depart for the fateful meeting. Following a man of

the Castle, he arrives at a kind of cairn covered by grass (the Green Chapel), and right away he is met by the mysterious and threatening Green Knight. The Green Knight does everything in his power to provoke him, in order to push him to refuse to endure the three strokes of his axe. But Gawain resists, submits himself according to the ritual, and yet he flinches when the Green Knight lowers his weapon. On the third attempt at decapitation, the axe grazes Gawain's neck, wounding him slightly. The pact has been honored, and yet Gawain is still alive. He leaps to his feet, ready for combat. Still, the Green Knight is not finished with him. After the axe strokes come the revelations and the sermon: I am the Lord of the Castle, Sir Bertilak de Hautdesert; the blows that have missed you are a reward to you for your loyalty in making restitution to me for the three kisses of my wife; that which grazed you will remind you of the green belt you failed to offer to me ("because you loved life too much"); the severe old woman is Morgan le Fay, who has devised the whole affair precisely in order to test the true substance—not merely the reputation—of the ideals and the virtues of the Round Table. Poor Gawain, humiliated, decides to continue wearing the green belt, returns to Camelot, recounts his adventure, and is consoled by the court, whose members decide to wear a green band from now on out of solidarity. The romance ends, in the only manuscript we possess, with the motto of the Order of the Garter instituted by Edward III in the second half of the fourteenth century: "Hony Soyt Qui Mal Pence."[3]

This short poem has everything we consider typical of medieval romance (even if not all romances are this perfect): the court, the knight, the ladies, the festivals, the Other, the impossible challenge, magic, the fabulous, the journey, the forest, the castle, the hunt, and the discussion of love; symbols, virtues, adventures, tests, courtly conventions, and temptation. In this romance there is, as in the romances of Chrétien de Troyes two centuries before it, a mysterious "sen" who seems to orchestrate the entire plot, an arbitrary power that seems to be sovereign and that only reveals itself at the end as causality. We could say that, if Auerbach had committed a chapter in *Mimesis* to *Sir Gawain and the Green Knight* rather than to Chrétien's *Yvain*, he would have been able to write the very same things. With one exception, perhaps: because in *Gawain* there is an additional dimension that we tend to forget when we speak of this type of romance: history, the bond with both the past and the present, and society. In fact, the anonymous author begins to narrate from the time "when the siege and assault ceased at Troy," thus

---

[3] The motto could have been added to the text of the romance, but the fact that it appears in the only surviving manuscript (of the late fourteenth century) is significant.

inserting his tale within the sphere, if not the genre, of the *roman d'antiquité*, and recalling, in the opening and in the close of the poem, the descent of Britain, through Brutus and Aeneas, from the city of the Trojan War and its exiles, exactly as many of his predecessors had done: Laymon in his English *Brut*; Wace in his Anglo-Norman *Brut*; and, the first to do so, Geoffrey of Monmouth in his *Historia Regum Britanniae*. Just as this history was composed in order to exalt the ascendance of the Angovine monarchy (Henry II and Eleanor of Aquitaine), so *Sir Gawain and the Green Knight* ends with the motto of the Garter of Edward III: perhaps it was packaged for a provincial court, but it has plenty of the refinement and the culture of the London court and of French manners—Hautdesert and Camelot.

The at least quasi-epic character of the *roman d'antiquité*, from its beginning and in all its succeeding plots, connects it to the *chanson de geste*: the subject matter of both, in fact, might be summed up as "great deeds," "great enterprises"—in a word, "arms." The first romances composed in the Middle Ages, toward the middle of the twelfth century, are "translations" of Latin epic poems (the same name of the genre derives from the expression "mettre in romans," that is to say, to translate into the vernarcular): thus the *Roman de Thèbes* (ca. 1155–65), the *Roman d'Eneas* (ca. 1160), and the *Roman de Troie* by Benoit de Sainte-Maure (ca. 1160–70). Another great theme nevertheless entered these romances as an essential element—love, which although it is overshadowed in the *chansons de geste*, is widespread in the classical models (it is enough to mention the episode of Dido in the *Aeneid*): Lavinia's love, for example, in the *Eneas*, and the love between Troilus and Brisseis in the *Troie*. In essence, the combination of heroic deeds and love is bound up with the very origins of romance, as that short period produced *Floire et Blancheflor* (ca. 1147–60), Wace's *Brut* (ca. 1150–55), Beroul's *Tristan* (ca. 1155?–87), and *Erec et Enide*, the first of the romances of Chrétien de Troyes (ca. 1170). It seems, in other words, that an intense fascination with all that is remote and strange, and yet that mirrors the present, erupts suddenly and reveals itself in a few decades: antiquity and adventures, the Arthurian world and exoticism, amorous passion and chivalry.

That such a fascination results from the flourishing of the feudal courts, from the diffusion of the so-called courtly ethic to the highest strata of the aristocracy, that it represents, even, a singular combination of "barbaric" customs (knighthood) and Christian ideals (the virtues imposed on this knighthood)—all this seems beyond dispute. Equally clear is the decisive contribution that the new figure of the "poet" brings to the growth and diffusion of the genre: a cleric, or by now a layman, who lives attached to the court, often endows his work and his themes with an innovative traditionalism, and does not hesitate to introduce himself in the middle of his work, simultaneously speaking to his audience.[4] And yet, all this is still true two centuries later, squarely in the fourteenth century, when the conditions of production and the consumption of romance had changed a great deal. Now, the central or peripheral court, feudally organized, is joined by the rich bourgeoisie and the merchants. Romantic chivalry no longer embodies a reality, however idealized, but has become, rather, a nostalgic ideal. The composer is a self-conscious and often autonomous poet.

On British soil, Geoffrey Chaucer, for example, a contemporary of the author of *Sir Gawain and the Green Knight*, is the first great classic author of English literature. He is a passionate practitioner of the genre of romance. He composed two *romans d'antiquité (The Knight's Tale* and *Troilus and Criseyde),* a fabulous-exotic romance (*The Squire's Tale*), a Breton-like lay in the manner of Marie de France (*The Franklin's Tale*), a quasi-Arthurian romance *(The Wife of Bath's Tale)*, and even a parody of romance (*Sir Thopas*). In other words, in the last decade of the fourteenth century Chaucer takes up and recapitulates the entire tradition of romance. In *The Knight's Tale*, he reconnects himself to the last epiode of the subject matter of the Theban cycle, while it is clear that *Troilus and Criseyde* confronts one of the more fascinating dramas of the subject matter of Troy. As in *Sir Gawain and the Green Knight*, here the structure and narrative technique are decisively transformed in respect to the predecessors of the twelfth and thirteenth centuries. *The Knight's Tale* does not deal with the entire history of the Theban cycle, from its very beginning to the death of Eteocles and Polynices—as the *Roman de Thèbes* had done—but concentrates only on the the vicissitudes of the last heirs of Thebes, Arcita and Palamone. They both fall in love with Emilia the Amazon when they are imprisoned by Theseus in Athens and then fight one another in fierce combat in a final tournament that also involves their respective retinues. *Troilus and Criseyde* directly and explicitly declares that it will have little to do with entire backdrop of the epic Trojan War, inviting the reader who wishes to know more about it to read Homer, Dares, and Dictys. In essence, the chivalrous "deeds" are here eliminated, and the "arms" are maintained exclusively in the background of the scene. On the other hand, the two male protagonists of these romances behave a great deal

---

[4] For the chronology adopted here and for questions addressed in this passage, see the contributions of A. T. Bruckner, C. Baswell, S. Gaunt, S. Kay, and R. Kaeuper in R. L. Kreuger, ed., *The Cambridge Companion to Medieval Romance* (Cambridge, 2000). Also important is E. Köhler, *Ideal und Wirklichkeit in der höfischen Epik* (Tübingen, 1960).

like "courtly" knights, and love assumes a cosmic and absolute value, encompassing the sublunar world, the heavens, and even the Christian God. The hero and heroine of *Troilus and Criseyde*—the knight, son of Priam, and the young widow Criseyde, the daughter of Calchas the diviner, who ends up betraying Troilus's love with Diomedes—attain an unprecedented psychological-dramatic profundity. Troilus's interior monologue foreshadows Hamlet's philosphical monologues; Criseyde's takes up and develops the model of Lavinia in *Eneas*, delineating a complexity of character of the kind we will only find in the modern novel.

In the same way, the apparently disordered, parenthetic, and obscure *Squire's Tale*, which has many loose ends, does not aspire to the structural "entrelacement" of the thirteenth-century French Arthurian vulgate.[5] The Wife of Bath's narration—preceded by an incredible (and truly revolutionary) pre-Falstaffian monologue—limits itself to inserting a folkloric tale into the Arthurian world. In short, Chaucer does not seem to be interested in following in the footsteps of the genre he nevertheless knew so well. As evidence, we can point to *Sir Thopas*, which openly makes fun of its style and structure, and, on the other hand, to *The Franklin's Tale*, in which the Breton lay is sublimated into a story of appearance and reality, of battles between conflicting loyalties in the realm of the courtly ethic, of deep nostalgia and of fundamental existential and metaphysical questions.

In *The Knight's Tale* and in *Troilus*, Chaucer even explores the relationship among author, story, protagonists, and audience—all marked features peculiar to medieval romance: he constantly addresses his heroes and heroines, commenting on their vicissitudes, and he speaks to an audience of pilgrims who represent all the social classes (in *The Knight's Tale*) and to an audience of noble lovers (in *Troilus*). Naturally, he ventures even farther than that. At times he proceeds by interrogating both audiences and discovering the vital nerves of narration, for example, advising his audience that its "epic" expectations will be disappointed, or designating a "persona" of the narrator distinct from that of the author. In essence, he creates a circle of addressees that is for the most part fictitious, that does not correspond to the historical and social reality of the time, but that is accepted by his contemporaries. Chaucer is writing for the court of Edward III, of his son the Duke John of Gaunt, of his nephew Richard II, and for the high London bourgeoisie. They love to see themselves involved in the fictions of poetry; they project onto these fictions their own idealized "self-representation," and

---

[5] On the interlace structure (*l'entrelacement* or *interlace*), see E. Vinaver, *The Rise of Romance* (Oxford, 1971).

they map "their own existence as outside of history, lacking any goal, like an absolute aesthetic creation."

As a creator of romances, Chaucer possesses an exuberant romantic personality. To find his medieval equivalent, we must go back centuries to Chrétien de Troyes to Gottfried von Strassburg, to Hartmann Von Aue, to Wolfram Von Eschenbach, or else to Boccaccio, the one who precedes the Englishman by hardly a generation. It is the French and German poets of the twelfth and thirteenth centuries who have fixed once and for all, and certainly for us moderns, the type, themes, and canon of medieval romance. We must acknowledge whoever it is who conceals himself under the name "Chrétien de Troyes" as the first to create characters and adventures endowed with an irresistible fascination, like those of Lancelot and Guinevere, of Yvain, of Eric and Enid, of Cliges, of Perceval. And if it is true that the story of Tristan and Isolde spread beyond the Celtic world, starting with Beroul's *Tristan* (ca. 1155–87) and the *Tristan* of Thomas (ca. 1170–75), there can be no doubt that Gottfried's *Tristan and Isolde* (ca. 1200–10) constitutes thematically the more complete and exalted poem, in the sense that love—as Wagner will later remember—acquires there a dimension grand enough to become an alternative to religion. In the same manner, the mysterious plot of the Grail finds a classic formulation (and in opposition to the ideology of Gottfried) in *Parsifal*, by Wolfram Von Eschenbach (ca. 1205–12), and the miraculous misadventures of Gregorius and Heinrich are narrated with an unprecedented skill by Hartmann Von Aue (1190–95) (Thomas Mann will retell those of the former).

In reality, between the end of the twelfth and the first years of the thirteenth century, the panorama of the romance seems already complete: aside from the *romans d'antiquité* already mentioned (to which should be added *The Seven Sages of Rome* compiled around 1160 and, most of all, the marvelous narrations concerning Alexander, like the *Roman d'Alexandre* by Alexandre de Paris, composed after 1180), and from the authors and works mentioned just above, it is at this moment that, together with the appearance of the romance in Spain (*The Book of Apollonius* and *The Book of Alexander*, both belonging to the period between 1220 and 1240), the so-called Arthurian prose Vulgate Cycle or Lancelot-Grail Vulgate is compiled and diffused (from *Lancelot* to *Quete* to *Mort Artu* to *Tristan*, between 1215 and 1235). The Vulgate Cycle represents a true *summa* of romance narrative: an immense cycle in its time in turn composed of intersecting cycles that, in their inner forms, articulate themselves in labyrinthine fashion, following the form of "entrelacement"—not in a causal or chronological sequence, but instead in plots that seem arabesques or like the illuminated letters of Gothic manuscripts, so that

their chivalrous and amorous adventures give the impression of extending infinitely and of coming together in fully arbitrary knots.

It is precisely these "tales of romance" (*Purgatorio*, 26.118), along with the
"verses of love," that Dante praises, using Guido Guinizzelli as his mouth-
piece. Dante—who, together with Guido del Duca in *Purgatorio* 14, recalls
with nostalgia "the ladies and the knights, the toils and sport, that love and
courtesy inspired" (14.109–10)—was a quite attentive and fascinated reader
of what he calls, in his *De Vulgari Eloquentia*, judging them peculiar to literature in the language of Languedoc, the "Arturi regis ambages pulcerrime."
He admired them to such an extent that he cited, as though it were an easily
understood and obvious reference, right in the middle of the last circle of hell
"[he] whose breast and shadow were pierced/by a single blow from Arthur's
hand," that is to say, the legendary Mordret, frozen together with the
thirteenth-century traitors Alessandro and Napoleon degli Alberti, Focaccia,
and Sassol Mascheroni; also to the extent of recording, in his *Convivio*,
Guido da Monefeltro and the "Knight Lancelot" who, in their old age, on
the verge of death (the harbor of human life), "did indeed lower the sails of
their worldly preoccupations" and "gave themselves to religious orders, for-
saking all worldly delights and affairs" (4.28.8, p.147); and to the extent, finally, of having Paolo and Francesca, in *Inferno* 5, fall in love and commit
"courtly" adultery, and hence fall into eternal death, precisely when the two
in-laws read "of Lancelot, how love enthralled him" (127–28). Francesca da
Rimini, a petty aristocrat and "provincial intellectual,"[6] is so well-versed in
Arthurian vulgate that she attributes the role of intermediary between queen
and knight to Galeotto (Galehaut), and then nimbly revises the original text,
in which Guinevere initiates the kiss, to her own version, in which the initiative is taken by "so great a [male] lover"—a revision performed in such a way
to make her mouth coincide with Paolo's trembling kiss. She is able thus to
define the "book and he who wrote it" as "Galeotto": the first example in the
world of a literary romance that draws the eyes together and drains the color
from the face to the point of overcoming its readers.

Dante, nevertheless, was a man of wide reading, and, in addition to the
romances of the Arthurian vulgate tradition, he also knew the *gestes* of that
other great branch of medieval narrative, the epic of Charlemagne and
Roland. In *Inferno* 31, to give the reader an idea of the tremendous thunder-
ing of the horn blown by the giant Nembroth, he recalls the sound that
Roland made to warn Charlemagne at Roncevaux ("After the woeful rout
when Charlemagne/had lost his holy band of knights, Roland did not sound

---

[6] G. Contini, *Un 'Idea di Dante* (Turin, 1976), 42.

so terrible a blast" [16–18]). The memory of the *Song of Roland* or of the spurious *The Chronicle of Turpin* seems precise (Ganellon will be evoked in the next canto, among the traitors). What is certain is that in the cross in the Heaven of Mars from which Cacciaguida stands out there appear, together with Joshua and Judah the Maccabee, the warriors of the Christian faith: Charlemagne, Roland, William of Orange, Renouard, Geoffrey of Bouloigne and Robert Guiscard. We do not know if Dante would have known directly of the epic cycles in which the Carolingian subject matter was amplified ("du roi," "de Guillaume," and "de Doon de Mayence"), but the list in *Paradiso* 28.43–48 almost seems to sketch out the program of chivalric, and then of the epic, narrative of the Italian Renaissance: from Pulci (Renouard is considered an antecedent of Morgante) to Boiardo and Ariosto, and finally to Tasso.

We should note, however, that in Italy—where the Arthurian stories profoundly penetrated the poetic, and even the popular, imagination until the end of the twelfth century, as the later versions of *Tristan* and *The Round Table* will attest—the reception of the Carolingian material in the Franco-Venetian territory and in Tuscany, in prose, songs, and ottava rima, has a unique development, because there are introduced into it not only indigenous motifs and themes, but also new episodes and characters—above all the themes of love and of "courtliness," the marvelous and the adventure being typical of the Breton world. Belonging to the cycle of *Gestes francor*, works like *L'entrée d'Espagne*, or *I fatti di Spagna*, or *Spagna* in rhyme, or above all Niccolò of Verona's *Prise de Pampelune* (between 1300 and 1350) constitute a fertile breeding ground of narrative-thematic cross-contamination. When, in the *Prise*, we see a Roland endowed with the amorous sensibility of a hero of the Round Table leaving for the East in search of adventures like a knight-errant, we know that we find ourselves, so to speak, between the chapter of Auerbach on Ariosto and what Cesare Segre writes on the medieval romance's capacity of adaptation and domination:

> It is indispensable to realize that the twelfth and thirteenth centuries constitute a period of extraordinary eido-genetic activity. The romance achieves its individuality, after having bordered on, with frequent interferences, analogous narratives similar to the lays (those of Marie de France and Jean Renart). It pushes itself even further in the direction of the fabliaux, elements of which are seen, for instance, in *Flamenca* and in *Joufroi*. Rather, the romance, as soon as it affirms itself as an autonomous genre, reveals clear hegemonic tendencies and aspires to engulf other genres in whatever way it can, becoming, more than a "leading" genre, a "total" genre. It is above all

the late *chansons de gestes* that tend to converge on romance by assimilating its treatment of amorous phenomenology and its openness to the comic.[7]

The interlacing of the two subject matters—of the two genres—on Italian soil continues throughout the fourteenth and intensifies in the fifteenth century. In the middle of the fourteenth century, however, an exceptional narrative personality like Boccaccio (we thus go backward in time) profoundly renovates the genre of romance. From his first literary experiments, Boccaccio demonstrates a particular predilection for romance. In *Filocolo*, for example, he takes up the tale of Florio and Biancifiore, which had been circulating in Europe for two centuries, grafting onto this "beautiful fable" rich in exoticism—"the star-crossed love but eventual happiness of two young lovers, who after many vicissitudes conquer the obstacles erected by men and Fate"[8]—a bewildering array of other stories, like those of Idalgo, Caleon, and Fileno; of "questions of love"; of embryonic novellas (those of Tarolfo and of the woman buried alive will be picked up again in *The Decameron*); of meditations and lyrical dialogues. It is, in short, a vast embroidery of the original plot according to the technique deriving on the one hand from "entrelacement" and on the other hand from the ancient novel. In his *Fiammetta*, the same tendency toward amplification leads him from the Ovidian "Heroides" and from "elegics" toward the modern psychological novel.

It is, however, to the *roman d'antiquité* that Boccaccio makes an exceptional contribution. The central insight of isolating a single event in the Trojan or Theban cycle and treating it with all its twist and turns, as in *Filostrato* and *Teseida*, belongs to him. In the first text, Troilus and Criseida's falling in love and her subsequent abandonment of him in favor of Diomedes, are taken up from Benoit (or perhaps from Binduccio dello Scelto, who had vulgarized them) and from Guido delle Colonne. But the Ovidian inspiration, however, the Dantesque and "stilnovo" lyrical borrowings, the often jongleurlike intonation (drawn from the *cantari*), the grand invocation of Venus by Troilus in part 3 (74–89), the deep exploration of the psychology of the experience of love ("autobiographical in a vague sense"), and the use of ottava rima all launch *Filostrato* toward a European renown previously unknown to Italian romance. They also brought it to the attention of Chaucer, who constructed his *Troilus and Criseyde* using it as his source (and thence transmitted to Henryson, Shakespeare, and Dryden). Even more sophisticated and meaningful is *Teseida*, as the author announces

---

[7] C. Segre, *Teatro e Romanzo* (Turin, 1984), 72.

[8] V. Branca, "Introduction," in *Tutte Le Opere di G. Boccaccio* (Milan, 1967–68), 1:49.

from the very beginning, is the attempt to bring together the inspirations of Mars and Venus in a poem intended for "noble" hearts: in short, in a clear reference to Dante in *De vulgari eloquentia*, to mix the "talk of love" with the epic "singing" of the deeds of Mars, "nel volgar lazio più mai veduti." In effect, *Teseida*, perhaps even too rich in archaic decorations, gods, and pagan customs; in lyrical elements adapted from Cino da Pistoia, and Dante; in duels and tournaments; in amorous disputations; in a long and painful agony on the model of Tristan; and in an "apotheosis" after death inspired by Lucan, constitutes a singular experiment of already classicist fusion, whose importance was grasped not only by Chaucer (who precisely in *The Knight's Tale* adapted it into English, passing it from there to Shakespeare and Dryden) but also, much later, by Tasso. Tasso often cites *Teseida* in his *Discorsi sul Poema Eroico*, mentioning it as the first true example of a "heroic poem" that had sung of "arms" and "love" together in Italian and in that "high" style enjoined by Dante for such themes, and praising the choice of ottava rima: in essence, considering it the prime model of Renaissance epic romance that he himself will practice.

Boccaccio knows the beautiful misfortunes of Tristan through and through, as some novellas from the fourth day of *The Decameron* demonstrate—the parody of the conversation under the pine tree in the story of Lodovico and Beatrice, a fragment of Lovato in the *Miscellanea Laurenzania*, and the death of Arcita in *Teseida* (all examples of themes of the romance spilling over into other genres and, as in Chaucer's *Sir Thopas*, being used ironically, well before Cervantes). He also has a thorough familiarity with the legend of Arthur, judging from when, in the *Zibaldone Magliabecchiano* and in *De casibus virorum illustrium*, he narrates the events of the Arthurian cycle, illustrating the customs and the ethos (the law [*lex*] of honor, of the defense of the weak, of the quest for monsters, of faith to one's word, of hospitality, of religion) of the Round Table and telling the story of its demise. His sources in this case are the romance *L'mort d'Arthur* (the same one used by Dante) for the death of the king and, above all, the *Historia regum Britanniae* by Geoffrey of Monmouth, the work that in the twelfth century initiated the enormous fame of the Breton subject matter in Europe.

We are now in the middle of the fourteenth century, and in a certain sense the arch of romance seems to be enclosed between two works of a "historical" nature, that of Geoffrey and that of Boccaccio. But how different the first is from the second in their attitudes toward what C. S. Lewis, following Chaucer, defined as "historial,"[9] will appear clearly when we read

---

[9] C. S. Lewis, *The Discarded Image* (Cambridge, 1964) 174–85.

the end of the chapter in *De casibus*, when Boccaccio, who has just narrated the death of Arthur following the tradition of the vulgate romance, turns back against his own source, calling the future vicissitudes of the Round Table a "legend of the common people": "The Round Table, made splendid through the heroes that had been killed, was abandoned and destroyed and reduced to a *popular legend*. The great glory and splendor of the king was, through its ruin, brought to such an ignonimy and obscurity that men—if only they were willing—could realize that nothing in the world, aside from humility, can endure."[10]

And yet, that "fable" was more alive than ever, far as it may have been from the Christian-Humanist moralism of Boccaccio. In *De casibus*, despite the caution and the doubts of the historian, the very same Certaldese tells of the Bretons' belief in the survival of Arthur "as if he were not dead, but watched over in silence, as their famous and excellent king" and reports that "they say that, when his wounds are healed, he will no doubt return."[11] Silence and return are images of a literary history that will last until our own day, the one an incubation and almost a harbinger of the other.

In reality, romance has never been silent, and the knight has continued to set forth. Shortly after the composition of *De casibus*, a splendid *Morte Arthure*, in alliterative verse, inspired by Geoffrey of Monmouth and Layamon's *Brut*, made its appearance in the north of England. And in the middle of the fifteenth century, while Pulci was drafting *Morgante* and Boiardo was conceiving of *Orlando Innamorato*, the "criminal" knight Thomas Malory, in England, reunited in his great *Mort d'Arthur* all the vulgate material, reducing its immense scope and unraveling the original "interlacement" in a "progressive" narration and miraculously ordered structure (Arthur, Lancelot, Sir Gareth, Tristan, Grail, Lancelot and Guinevere, the death of Arthur). In it, there nevertheless remain the essentials of "magic narrative"[12] and the world of "heightened significance" so typical of medieval romance, in which the knight wanders potentially without limit between the beginning and the end, which is also the reign of potential error—delusion, a loss of the senses, enchantment."[13]

Coming full circle to *Sir Gawain and the Green Knight* and to the *Yvain* of Chrétien de Troyes from which Auerbach set forth, we can now try to read

---

[10] G. Boccaccio, *De Casibus Virorum*, bk. 8, chap. 19, paragraph 16, ed. P. G. Ricci and V. Zaccaria, in Branca, ed., *Tutte le opere di G. Boccaccio*, 9:734–35; my emphasis.

[11] Ibid.

[12] F. Jameson, *The Political Unconscious* (Ithaca, N.Y., 1981), 103–50.

[13] E. Edwards, "The Place of Women in the 'Morte Darthur,'" in E. Archibald and A.S.G. Edwards, eds., *Companion to Malory* (Cambridge, 1996), 39.

an episode of Malory's *Tale of King Arthur*. After having been chased out of
the Arthurian court for the betrayals of Morgan le Fay, Iwain, and Gawain
(his cousin) meet by chance the Irish knight Sir Morhaus as they pass
through a "great forest." After Sir Morhaus defeats his adversaries, he urges
the two Arthurian knights to unite with him in his quest for marvelous adventures. Ivan and Galvano follow him into the forest:

> They rode through the forest day by day well nigh seven days before they
> found any adventure. But at last they came into a place that was named the
> country and the forest of Aroy, a country of strange adventures.
>
> "In this country," said Sir Morhaus, "came never a knight since it was
> christened who did not find strange adventures."
>
> So they rode and came into a deep valley full of stones, and nearby they
> saw a fair stream of water. Above them was the head of the stream, a fair
> fountain, and three damsels were sitting by it. The knights rode up to them
> and each greeted the others. The eldest damsel had a garland of gold about
> her head, and she was three-score winters of age or more; her hair was white
> under the garland. The second damsel was of thirty winters of age, with a cir-
> clet of gold about her head. The third damsel was but fifteen years of age,
> and a garland of flowers was about her head. After these knights had greeted
> them, they asked the cause that they sat by the fountain.
>
> "We are here," said the damsels, "for this cause: if we see any errant-
> knights we direct them unto strange adventures. Ye are three knights who
> seek adventures, and we are three damsels; therefore each one of you must
> choose one of us. And when you have done so, we will lead you unto three
> highways; there each of you shall choose a way, and his damsel will go with
> him. Then this day twelve-month, ye must meet here again, if God grants
> you your lives; thereto ye must plight your troth.[14]

Here we are, therefore, returned to knights, in the forest, traveling aim-
lessly and almost outside of time, to a mysterious spring, an enigmatic encounter with three damsels of whom we know nothing except their ages (in
geometrical proportion—sixty, thirty, fifteen). Their purpose—they declare
it themselves—is simply to be there for the three knights, to lead them to a
crossroads, to propose a further encounter: in short, to furnish them with
adventures—"great" adventures. And in fact the three knights embark on
three separate quests and confront the "tests" that their destiny places before them: Galvano meets Dame Ettard, goes to bed with her, and is then

---

[14] E. Vinaver, ed., *The Works of Sir Thomas Malory* (Oxford, 1967), 1, 61*rv*, pp. 162–63.

surprised by Pelleas, who decides that he no longer loves her; Morhaus meets a duke and his six sons, and defeats them; Ivan wins a tournament and defeats two other knights. One year later, they find themselves back at the spring, right on schedule, Galvano the only one who has lost his damsel. Twelve days later, having passed through another forest, the three go back to Camelot, where the court celebrates their return. That this is a "magic" narrative," there can be no doubt. But the space dedicated to this return, and the twists of the plot, the "laces" in which it is articulated, have been drastically reduced: from beginning to end, the entire episode takes up little more than twenty pages in a printed modern edition.

Which is to say: the "romance" is there, three hundred years after its birth, and the knight is still in his saddle. But the episode has the dimensions of a "novella," and is inserted into a consequential series of episodes that, taken together, tend toward the organization of the "novel," that is to say, of the modern romance. Furthermore, in the fifteenth century, feudal "chivalry" has now come to an end, and we can no longer speak of its "self-representation in its forms of life and its ideals." Whatever the "courtly" knight may have been, he is now on the verge of being replaced by the courtier. Finally, cannot the "entrelacement" disentangled by Malory be re-framed and rewoven into a labyrinth of tapestries, a series of spiral plots, intertwined with one another, by Boiardo and Ariosto? Once it is endowed with a historical backdrop, it will transform itself into the "heroic poem" of Tasso. Allegorized, it will become Spencer's *The Faerie Queene*. Translated with the most severe irony, it will reemerge with the title of *Don Quixote*. Whoever is inclined to substitute a duke, a prince, or a king for the knight, would produce something akin to the "romance" dramas of Shakespeare or Sydney's *Arcadia*; and conversely, hundreds of years earlier, an *Apollonius of Tyre* or, more than a thousand years earlier, the *Aethiopica* of Heliodorus. If the knight were to be replaced by a mariner or a navy captain, we would see a story close to the type of *The Odyssey*, and on the other hand to Verne, to Stevenson, to Conrad—even perhaps, a *Robinson Crusoe*. And if, finally, the knight were replaced by a picaresque hero, we would find ourselves in front of Lazarillo de Tormes or Tom Jones, perhaps also in front of Renzo from *The Betrothed*.

Translated by Simone Marchesi and Daniel Seidel

MARIA DI SALVO

Povest'

The story of Russia's *povest'*, like that of many literary genres, is comprised of myriad shifts and changes in content and function: in their wake, it seems that the only unifying element is the name itself. The only thing left for contemporary scholars to do is to search for possible common traits in this discontinuity. The generic meaning of the term (tale or narrative, from *povĕdati*, meaning to inform or to recount) has made the situation all the more ambiguous, giving rise to comparisons with modern Russian narrative, which enjoys relative autonomy with respect to other traditions, and ancient Russian narrative, which was shaped by a wide variety of functions. But an analysis of the texts reveals a much more complex overview in the earliest Russian (or Slavic-Eastern) literature, in which it is not even clear whether or not the term *povest'* denoted an actual literary genre.

In the field of ancient Russian literature, the definition of genres is one of the crucial themes of the last few decades: the question is whether or not the rhetorical-formal categories formulated in antiquity and then developed during the European Renaissance can be applied to a literature that has functioned in a prevalently nonaesthetic but rather extraliterary capacity (instructional, liturgical, political) and that has developed in an entirely peculiar fashion. There is much discussion of "types," "modes," and "protogenres," and there is even denial that genres exist in Russian literature, underscoring the polyfunctionality of the texts and their greater pertinence to the study of linguistic registers. The Slavic-Eastern Middle Ages left no descriptive or normative tractates, because the rules of the literary code were implicit in the model texts (first and foremost, the sacred scriptures). Therefore, it is necessary to refer directly to the texts themselves and their functions.

As far as the genres are concerned, the situation is made even more complex by the various transmigrations of textual materials into compilations with greater breadth and by the consequent change in function that occurs, for example, with annalistic narratives in which there is a confluence of a great number of preexistent hagiographic and narrative works, as well as chronicles.

The very titles of the works, which should provide clues as to the mode of their reception by the reader or listener, do not contribute much clarity, in part because they are often conventional definitions attributable to the copyists (if not to modern editors). Such is the case for *Povest' vremennykh let*

(*The Tale of Bygone Years*), a title derived from the incipit by which the most famous annalistic work of the Kievan period is known. It is even more difficult to evaluate the constellation of terms that seem to refer to clearly circumscribed genres but that appear alternately in the manuscript tradition without any evident reasoning behind them: the same work can be called *povest'*, *skazanie* (narration), *zhitie* (life of), or even *skazanie i povest'* (narration and tale) and *povest' ot zhitija* (tale taken from the life of), without the substitution or juxtaposition of terms indicating clear lines of demarcation or designating precise formal instrumentation. Scholars' usage of terms like "war *povesti*" and "hagiographic, historical *povesti*" is a matter of descriptive conventions limited to the classification of the multiplicity of subjects.

The difficulty of establishing a representative nucleus for *povest'* (which, at least in an intuitive sense, is the case for biographies, chronicles, and accounts of pilgrimages) is due in part to the subordinate role (of example, confirmation, and demonstration) played by narrative material that never rises to the level of genre or specific "type." This happens because, as Riccardo Picchio has observed, "the narration itself was not enough to mark semantically the higher, spiritual message."[1] Inversely and for the same reason, "narrativity" is not restricted to works labeled as *povesti* and is present in different sorts of compositions (hagiographic, homiletic, annalistic) without identifying itself exclusively with precise genres.

Even fictional and fantastical narrative strain to find an autonomous role in this context. Their presence is motivated by the truth of faith (as in the case of visions, miracles, or prophecies) or by spatial and chronological distance from the events, which are set in faraway places or in a mystical past. Fictional works from other cultures were often incorporated with seemingly harmless familiarity: translation of the Byzantine romance of Alexander the Great and epic cycle of Digenis Akritas, for example, were read as historical works and were included in manuscripts that contained chronicles and other narratives on historical subjects.

This situation remained substantially the same until the seventeenth century, the transitional era in which the gradual secularization of Russian culture created previously impossible outlets for the circulation of different subjects and new, innovative forms of writing. Once freed from rigid structural chains, *povest'* functioned as a receptacle for all sorts of narrative prose: as

---

[1] R. Picchio, "Povest' e slovo: Osservazioni sul rapporto fra narrativa e omiletica nella tradizione scrittoria dell'Antica Rus,'" in M. L. Ferrazzi, ed., "La povest' russa fra evo antico ed evo moderno," in *Atti del Convegno "La povest' antico-russa: evoluzione tipi e forme,"* Udine 6–7 dicembre 1988, *Europa Orientalis*, 9 (1990): 28.

early as the sixteenth century, these included almost always anonymous translations from Western languages (often by way of Ukrainian-Polish, but with Eastern influence as well) of chivalric romances, picaresque stories, tales, anecdotes, and witticisms that would appear in hundreds of manuscripts. Their foreign origin is reflected by their Polish-derived titles (like *istorija* or *gistorija*) and by the names of the characters who would retain their exotic colorings even in original works that appeared many years later.

The most ancient and famous of the *povesti* imported from the West is *Bova-korolevich* ("Bova, Son of the King"), based on the story of Bevis of Hampton. Still highly popular in the nineteenth century, it was often cited as an example of an "unstructured" text and consequently intended for an undemanding audience. Together with countless similar stories (from *The Three Golden Keys* and *The Fair Maguelonne* to *Paris et Vienne* and *Melusina*), *Bova-korolevich* introduced Russia to new blends of adventurous and heroic content that involved readers and favored a more direct rapport with literary texts. Satirical and humoristic *povesti* were circulated in a similar manner. They were taken from collections of tales and anecdotes or they were drawn simply from the great heritage of "wandering motifs" of European literature, but with characters familiar to the Russian readership (the merchant, the *pop*, the charlatan). Despite the condemnation of the traditionalists, these foreign tales produced imitations and even original works with indigenous heroes: the *povest'* and its considerable presence became emblems of the new Russian culture.

The *povest'*'s vitality and capacity to attract readers during this period were reflected in the frequent narrative reworkings of the lives of saints and famous episodes. The weight of tradition, however, impeded the complete emancipation of original prose, and, just as would later happen in the case of the novel, it required educational justification even for works in which the pure joy of narration prevailed. Many *povesti* were qualified in their titles with expressions like "very useful tale" or "taken from the ancient chronicles," and therefore they were believable. Instructional glosses were sometimes inserted to make the edifying content evident, and in the continuing terminological uncertainty, many anecdotal tales were entitled *pritchi* (parables).

With respect to "high" literature, which continued to develop along the lines of the medieval tradition or in the new erudite and baroque ways that arrived from the Ukraine, the *povest'* took its place in the periphery, which it shared with folklore. Together with a mutual preference for mixing imagination with a good dose of formulaity, this contiguity led to reciprocal contamination by the narrative genres of folklore (the fable or *bylina*, which was devoted to the endeavors of *bogatyri*, the mythical Russian heroes). Thus, tales imported from other countries laid their roots in Russian soil and enriched themselves with new episodes and expressive potential. Their close ties to folklore did not ensure, however, that the fruition of *povesti* was restricted to the lower or less-educated classes: this took place only in the second half of the eighteenth century, when a competing, new type of classicist literature favored other genres, especially poetical ones. At the end of the seventeenth century, chivalric tales, inasmuch as they represented a new cultural direction, were collected in the libraries of the czars and erudite aristocracy, and they were interpreted in a narrative sense, and in some cases produced imitative manners and customs.

Much has been written on the characters of the original tales of the first decades of the eighteenth century, the consonance among their main characters who seek knowledge and personal fulfillment, and the ideas that inspired the reforms of Peter the Great. It is more difficult to define their common structural traits, especially in light of the fact that many of the *povesti* of this era, influenced by folklore, were written in verse. The examination of numerous redactions and reworkings shows a coherent evolution from the initial, meager narration (similar to the *canovacci* of the *commedia dell'arte*), in which the actions are simply enunciated and the characters defined by a few stereotypical epithets. The tales were then enhanced with new narrative insertions and temporal and topographic information. Secondary characters, who had first been relegated to the role of simple extras, now took on greater autonomy. Motivation and circumstance were more developed and made more explicit. Textual cohesion in general was reinforced through repetition and anaphoric reprise that ensured greater narrative compactness. Above all, the hybrid language of the *povesti* during this period was their defining feature, a richness of lexical and syntactical elements taken from the jargon of chancellery and bureaucracy. The evolution of the Russian literary language at the height of the eighteenth century made those tales, which had introduced interlacing and invention to their readers, seem obsolete and ingenuous, and thus opened the way to the appearance of the novel.

In the 1740s, a wave of translations began to drench Russia, and in a relatively brief period of time, it brought with it a great number of varied novels with widely different origins. Before the loan translation *roman* entered into common usage, this still-new genre was labeled *basn'* (fable), *skazka* (fairy tale), and *vymyshlennaja povest'* (original tale), with the characteristic and still unresolved terminological uncertainty. The old *povest'* was an obvious term for comparison, and in the reflections of classically formed literati, the popular French novels (à la Prévost) were to be avoided and were thus likened to *Bova-korolevich*. Thanks to classicist poetics' poor view of narration, prose during this period was only indirectly touched by the evolution that profoundly changed poetic language. The traditional method for reworking the *povesti* was still alive in translations and the first original novels (beginning in 1763) by the prolific Fedor Aleksandrovich Emin, who was inspired by the great peripatetic seventeenth-century novels but lacked the linguistic tools to emulate their complex baroque ornamentation. With varying results, he tried to write a sentimental novel modeled after *La Nouvelle Héloïse*: *Pis'ma Ernesta i Doravry* (*The Letters of Ernest and Doravra*). Mikhail Dmitrievich Chulkov began his career with a collection of tales told in a unified narrative framework (1766–68) and then cultivated the model of *povesti* taken from anecdotes and witticisms. He provided the following century with an embryonic model for tales satirizing society.

The advent of the novel contributed to the partial recovery of the old *povesti* that began to be published in print and to take on sentimental traits and pathos. At the end of the eighteenth century, however, the arrival of a new linguistic taste led to the marginalization of this type of narrative, which would ultimately slip into the lowest rings of literary infamy.

A new type of *povesti* became the preferred genre for sentimentalism, which in Russia had clearly privileged the lowest forms. At the beginning of the 1790s, the leader of this movement, Nikolaj Mikhaijlovich Karamzin, provided the model for the sentimental tale, which stood in opposition to the long intricate novels by virtue of its reduced dimensions and simple plot. *Poor Liza*, the most famous of these tales, opened the way to an unending series of new *povesti*. From the outset, these tales programmatically reaffirmed their non-novelistic characteristics with titles like *spravedlivaja* or *istinnaja povest'* (true tale) or even *poluspravedlivaja* (half true). The authors themselves guaranteed this fidelity to reality and presented themselves as witnesses to the events and chroniclers who had felt the pain of the participants. They used a syntactically renewed language that was based on the colloquial usage of the elite aristocracy, which greatly contributed to the formation of modern Russian. This linguistic turning point marked the insurmountable break from the old *povest'* and was particularly evident where the interlacing of stories was similar in appearance, as in the cases of Karamzin's tale *Natalia the Boyar's Daughter*.

Even after the trend started by *Poor Liza* began to fade, Karamzin's tales (historical, satirical, societal) continued to develop their potential for innovation. The *povest'* was the predominant prose genre during the first decades of the nineteenth century, and it continued to diversify in content, often announced with a adjective in the title like "fantastic tale," "erotic," or "Eastern." It is important, however, to underscore the fluidity of these definitions, which leads back to the question posed in the beginning of this essay: can narrative during this era can be defined using distinct categories, or is it the modern reader, eager to distinguish between novel, *povest'*, tale, and fairy tale, who has superimposed these distinctions? As late as 1821, the *Slovar' drevnej i novoj poezii* (*Dictionary of Ancient and Modern Poetry*) by Nikolaj Fëdorovich Ostolopov did not include the term *povest'* (even though *povestvovanie*, or "narration," was included). Fifteen years later, critic Visarion Grigórevich Belinskij affirmed that the *povest'* was born only in the 1820s: until then it had been an imported form that had no solid roots in Russia. In saying this, he proposed that there was a continuity with the old *povesti*, but he also emphasized the importance of Western models (especially during the Romantic age). His ideas marked the first time a theoretical consciousness appeared in the pages of Russian journals.

A recurring theme in discussions of genre during this period is the question of contiguity between the novel and *povest'*: the former was still in search of an identity while the latter triumphed in all the literary journals and can be adapted to seemingly every type of exigency. Almost all of the narrative prose of the 1830s is made up of tales: from Pushkin's *Tales of Belkin*, to the fantastic tales by Vladimir Fëdorovich Odoevskij, to the ethnographic and satirical tales by Gogol. The *povesti* became a laboratory for prose narrative, and they often managed to enclose a complete novel's plot within their limited form. They began to be published in collections connected by a single narrator or by a thin thread (as in the *Tales of Belkin*) or an even stronger tie (as in Gogol's *Dikan'ka* tales). Thus, they came to embody a superior and even bold entity. From these tales that had originally appeared in journals, the first novels of the great flourishing of the nineteenth century were born, like Lermontov's *Hero of Our Time*.

The coexistence of these two genres, which had been consolidated by tradition, continued throughout the twentieth century. The shorter *rasskaz* (tale) with a more linear plot would also appear next to them. The criterion used to distinguish them is length, which positions the *povest'* between novel and tale. Attempts to define the *povest'* more rigorously from a theoretical point of view have led to conclusions often negated by literary praxis. But it is with the novel, and not with the short story, that the *povest'* entertains a competitive rapport and, in certain periods, a complementary relationship.

Translated by Jeremy Parzen

The European
Acceleration

JOAN RAMON RESINA

The Short, Happy Life of the Novel in Spain

In matters of genre, nominalism rules. You name it and it is there. Conversely, a vague designation may distort its referent and becloud its historical significance. How could one account otherwise for those "histories" of the novel that, in the wake of Ian Watt's half-century-old study on "realism," always see the novel rising in England or, in an updated, "borderless" version of the same view, in the privileged "crossing" between the chief eighteenth-century rivals: France and England. This is, at any rate, the view put forward by Margaret Cohen and Carolyn Dever in an interesting but highly restrictive "internationalization" of the "rise of the novel" (2). The reasons for the binational frame are not made less equivocal by the authors' acknowledging that "previously, isolated works from beyond the Channel zone had played a formative role in the history of the novel" (22). For one thing, to speak of isolated works is to ignore the existence of different "force fields" of cultural transactions and to forget that the novel took shape as those fields shifted *across* Europe. For another, it is hard to see what is gained by turning political borders into temporal ones and writing off "isolated works" like Cervantes' *Don Quixote* as "premodern prose" (22).

Don Quixote premodern? Critics have found, embedded in this book, practically all the features of modern narrative discourse. In his *Theory of the Novel*, Georg Lukács assigned to Cervantes' masterpiece a historico-philosophical role in the constitution of the genre as *modernity* conceived it. I use the term *modernity* as a historical category bound up with the rise of reflexivity and with the expansion of a secular viewpoint that made it possible to criticize the old theocratic institutions and the literature fostered by them. It can be reasonably maintained that *Don Quixote* is neither the first modern novel nor a premodern one, but the text that first reveals to advantage the possibilities and limits of the novel's attempt to integrate meaning and representation under the conditions of reflexivity that characterize modernity (Resina 1996).

Novel derives from the Italian *novella*, "a new story." This word is the feminine form of *novello*, from Latin *novellus*, "new." The word by which we name the most popular narrative genre is loaded with the semantics of modernity. Does that mean that a text that remained on the threshold of the new-fangled designation also fell outside the *zone* of novelistic production? If critics have no problem positing a normative language-referent correspondence, history is rarely so obliging. And are not those neat correspondences what postmodern thought taught us to relativize, soften, and suspend?

Arguments on behalf of the absolute originality of the English novel flounder on the existence of Cervantes' text, which is why efforts to establish a generic difference are aimed at framing out the *Quixote*. Lennard Davis asserts that "*Don Quixote* is not part of this new and self-conscious genre and was barely referred to as part of that genre by writers of novels until resurrected by Fielding in the mid-eighteenth century" (12). The argument *ex silentio* remains unconvincing, and Davis not only fails to establish the internal evidence by which he seeks to exclude the Spanish narrative tradition, but, as he develops his thesis, it transpires that *Don Quixote* is the more self-conscious and, consequently, the more complex of the texts he is comparing. Delayed recognition says nothing about the significance of a precursor. New forms typically bump against the current threshold of recognition and must wait until a later date before their aesthetic implications are fully grasped. Precisely because, as Davis says, "Cervantes' readers would be expected to be familiar with romances like *Amadis of Gaul*" (13),[1] they would not have exhausted *Don Quixote*'s potential as a site for the analysis of subjectivity, representation, reader-response, intertextuality, metafiction, phenomenology, and the critique of mimesis.

Margaret Anne Doody has called the bluff of the English origination of the novel:

> The English performed a wonderful trick in persuading themselves that "The Rise of the Novel" took place in England in the eighteenth century. They eliminated the predecessors once so fully acknowledged, along with the transmissions outlined by Salmasius and Huet. Such historians had made the foreignness of fiction *too* visible. That foreignness at the root must be cut off. . . . A novel must always be a somewhat inferior production because it is homely, limited, domestic, and gently emotional. Yet it cannot be allowed to exist if it is not those things, for then it supposedly becomes wild fantasy— now identified as "Romance." (Doody, 293)

---

[1] Davis wants to argue generic variance from the difference in readerly conventions. Unlike Cervantes' readers, "readers of Defoe would be more familiar with the tales of criminals that they had read in their daily or weekly newspapers" (13). By emphasizing the journalistic background, Davis neglects to mention that the English novel of marginal characters like Molly Flanders or Roxana sinks its roots into a long-standing taste for the lives of social underdogs that goes back at least as far as the translation of *Guzmán de Alfarache* by James Mabbe in 1622. Mabbe's translation was titled, significantly, *The Rogue*.

Doody is right to expose the English attempt to create an alternative history of the novel, along with a particular definition of fiction "consciously designed to obscure from view the glorious international history of the Western novel" (262), and its Spanish transmission in particular. That this alternative history arose at the same time as the British Empire is hardly a coincidence. Was not Spain, after all, the declining empire that had once threatened England with invasion and had kept its colonial ambitions at bay for a century?

Cervantes, who wrote novellas in the Italian style (cf. his *Exemplary Novels*) did not have a ready name for the new kind of text *Don Quixote* inaugurated. The book is a formidable catalogue of entertainment literature. It draws not only from chivalry books, but also from ballads, pastoral novels, Moorish romances, pilgrimage tales, proverbs, and folklore. Peppered with all the varieties of fiction known in its day and permeated by an unconventional sense of decorum, this *historia*, as Cervantes called it, was plainly not a novella, although it contained several of them. Nor was it a romance, although it parodied chivalric conventions. And it was not history, even though it sought to produce a reality effect by weaving historical characters and situations into its plot.

When it was published in 1604 (part 2 in 1615), this new specimen of prose could not be called a *novela* because the term was semantically preempted. As a result of this linguistic incident, *Don Quixote* came to seem prenovelistic in the eyes of nominalists who ignored that the founders of modern aesthetic theory, the German romantics, inferred the novel's generic traits from Cervantes' text. For Schelling, "the novel, which stirs everything in the human person, should also set passion in motion; the most tragic as well as the comic is permitted to it as long as the author himself remains detached from both" (324).[2] That Schelling had *Don Quixote* in mind can be presumed from the fact that he saw the history of the novel as an incipient aesthetic domain consisting of two works only: *Don Quixote* and *Wilhelm Meister* (327).

In calling his fictional work a *historia*, Cervantes followed established practice. In the early years of the fifteenth century, an anonymous Catalan author had written the *Història de Jacob Xalabín*, a sentimental novel full of remarkably accurate details about the Ottoman Empire. In the second half of the century, Juan de Flores' *Historia de Grisel y Mirabella*, a sentimental

---

[2] "Alles im Menschen anregend soll der Roman auch die Leidenschaft in Bewegung setzen; das höchste Tragische ist ihm erlaubt wie das Komische, nur daß der Dichter selbst von beidem unberührt bleibe." The translation of quotations is mine unless otherwise indicated.

novel, reached fifty-six editions in several languages and served as a language textbook in quatrilingual editions. The generic ambiguity inscribed in the title of these works (history or fable?) also surrounded the *Historia del abencerraje y la hermosa Jarifa* (1565), another sentimental story based on older traditions. Heliodorus's *Historia etiópica de Teágenes y Cariclea*, had been translated in 1554 and became a success among humanists. Cervantes wanted to rival it with his *Persiles*.

Cervantes made much of the equivocal meaning of *historia*. The ambiguity allowed him to play off fantasy against verisimilitude, the chief criterion of poetic merit in Alonso López Pinciano's *Philosophía antigua poética* (1596). In this matter Pinciano followed the opinion of other humanists. Earlier, Juan de Valdés had written in his *Diálogo de la lengua*: "los que scriven mentiras las deven escrivir de suerte que se lleguen, quanto fuere possible, a la verdad, de tal manera que puedan vender sus mentiras por verdades" (those who write lies must write them in such a way that they come close to the truth. Proceeding in this way they will be able to sell their lies as if they were truths) (177). Even more strictly than Valdés, Joan Lluis Vives had criticized chivalric literature as chimerical and sham. Cervantes shared these opinions. Toward the end of *Don Quixote*, when the knight watches the composition of the second part of his apocryphal story in the printer's shop in Barcelona, he wishes the book to be burned, because "las historias fingidas tanto tienen de buenas y de deleitables, cuanto se llegan a la verdad o a la semejanza della" (2:788) (works of invention are only good in so far as they adhere to the truth or verisimilitude) (878). But Cervantes, unlike the humanists, turned the censure of implausible tales into a new narrative strategy: metafiction.

In the priest's scrutiny of Don Quixote's library (bk. 1, chap. 6), verisimilitude, or what we call realism, is the touchstone for literary criticism. The books that pass the scrutiny amount to a cultural literacy list for readers of fiction. They also furnish a pretext to outline the features of the genre Cervantes is striving to shape. Singled out for its realism is Joanot Martorell's *Tirant lo Blanc* (1462),[3] a book in which "comen los caballeros y duermen y mueren en sus camas y hacen testamento antes de su muerte, con otras cosas de que todos los demás libros deste género carecen" (1:80) (the knights eat and sleep and die in their beds, and make their wills before they die, and other things as well that are left out of all other books of the kind) (60). In this book, in other words, the bourgeois viewpoint interfered with feudal idealism. To its concern with the factual and the ordinary, *Tirant* added a

---

[3] Completed by Martí Joan de Galba in 1490.

repertoire of fictionalized current events, offering, in effect, a fabled chronicle of contemporary politics.

Between *Tirant lo Blanc* and *Don Quixote* arose the aggressive realism of the picaresque novel. No longer viewed from the knight's perspective, the world now revolved around the troubles and adventures of an outcast. *El Lazarillo de Tormes* (1554), Mateo Alemán's *Guzmán de Alfarache* (1599, second part 1604), Francisco de Quevedo's *Historia de la vida del Buscón* (1626), and more than one hundred other such stories turned the world of feudal values upside down, and therewith the novel's idealizing perspective. Although *Lazarillo* still shows its seams (the juxtaposition of separate tales originating in the *fabliaux* tradition), it foregrounds the everyday in the picaro's struggle for survival in the "mean streets" of Toledo, and displays a decidedly modern reflexivity in letting the protagonist address the reader in the very discourse that frames the action and calls forth the codes in which it must be interpreted (see Resina 1991, 127–49).

In the picaresque, as in *Don Quixote*, the quotidian displaces the miraculous. A loaf of bread, a turnip, a bunch of grapes, a draught of wine become the immanent objects of desire and adventure. And unlike the Christian hero of romance, the picaro boasts that success in the quest of everyday objects is the result of his diligence and enterprise. The picaresque novel's bourgeois hubris challenged the traditional meaning of "adventure," which in the Castilian literature, from Don Juan Manuel's *El conde Lucanor* (1335) to Cervantes, always coupled chance (*fortuna*) with divine providence (see Nerlich, 323–24). Franco Moretti calls this enhancement of the everyday "revolutionary."[4] In the picaresque novel and in the *Quixote*, he says, one sees the world at the slow, road-bound pace of mules, or even at the slower pace of Sancho Panza's donkey. "The wonder of the open sea, with its extraordinary adventures, is replaced by a slow and regular progress; daily, tiresome, often banal. *But such is precisely the secret of the modern novel* (of 'realism,' if you wish): modest episodes, with a limited narrative value—and yet, never without *some* kind of value" (Moretti, 48).

Let us focus on this ordinariness. Don Quixote's world is commonplace enough, but his demeanor, his words, and his actions are hardly ordinary or banal. Although conventional in their own way, his words and actions underwrite conventions that are far from appearing normal to the world he meets on the road. The book's narrative force springs from the tension between this most extraordinary of figures and the perfectly ordinary world in

---

[4] Ian Watt considered the sustained attention to the everyday unique to the eighteenth-century English novel, asserting that this feature made *Robinson Crusoe* the first novel (74).

which he moves. Even his itinerary underscores the banality of life in the empire's hinterland, where nothing *really* happens and where, for that reason, each encounter must be endowed with transcendence by an objectless (though not aimless) will-to-action. In *Don Quixote* the disenchantment of the world, on which Lukács predicated the novel's specificity (88 passim), attains world-historical significance. In part 1, knight and squire roam through land that, one century before, had been the stage of the *Reconquista*. Don Quixote is not entirely off-track when he looks for military glory in the plains of La Mancha and the Andalusian sierra. He is, however, utterly off-date: a living anachronism. In Cervantes' day, world history had moved to a different frontier, leaving behind the epic shells of action in the ballads and romances that nourish Don Quixote's ontological desire. Wandering through the countryside, Don Quixote remains obdurately on the stage where armies once clashed and away from the stage where merchants peacefully ply their trade. It is not by chance that his travels bring him only tangentially in contact with historical figures (the encounter with the galley slaves, with the Morisco, or with the bandit Roque Guinard, who is none other than the historical Perot Rocaguinarda), or that the novel reaches its point of inflexion when the two villagers arrive in Barcelona, the only town they ever set foot in.

In Barcelona, Don Quixote makes two major discoveries: the sea and the printing press. In the harbor he boards a ship, and adventure does beckon, but then he falls into unheroic inaction as the simulacrum of chivalry is replaced by real military strife. As Moretti remarks, the wondrous seafaring adventures of a Tirant are off-bounds for the new poetics of the prosaic. Even more crucial is Don Quixote's visit to the printing shop, where he observes the technical production of his madness. Caught up in the earliest stage of the industrial revolution, adventure becomes a matter of technology. Don Quixote sees the new dream machine fabricating the popularity that confronts him in the streets. The printing revolution not only affects the volume and cost of production. It also disenchants, turning a rickety daydreamer into a sensible if duller character, and resolving the romances from which he hailed into the new genre that will shake the printing presses and, eventually, reenchant the private world.

Sobered by his visit to the powerhouse of illusion, Don Quixote wants to exit from the world of fiction: "Ya conozco sus disparates y sus embelecos, y no me pesa, sino que este desengaño ha llegado tan tarde, que no me deja tiempo para hacer alguna recompensa, leyendo otros que sean luz del alma" (2:899) (Now I know their absurdities and their deceits [of chivalry books], and the only thing that grieves me is that this discovery has come too late, and leaves me no time to make amends by reading other books, which might enlighten my soul) (935). But fiction is the essence of his world, just as dreams are the basis of Shakespeare's and Calderón's ontology. After Don Quixote's disenchantment, two roads lead again from the old narrative matrix: on the one hand, the wild cynicism of Quevedo's *Buscón*, and, on the other, Baltasar de Gracián's *El Criticón* (1651–57), the allegorical road story of another dialectical pair, Andrenio and Critilo, philosophical scions of Cervantes' wise fools. But this work, for all its ingenuity, parts with the realism that came to seem consubstantial with the novel. After Cervantes' death, long works of secular narrative appeared less and less frequently in Spain until the creative vein ran dry. By the eighteenth century, the realist novel, despite its headstart in Spain, had come to seem extraterritorial there. Had its early bloom withered overnight? Was its lifespan really that short? And what had caused it to waste?

A Change of Paradigm: The Novel and the Little Guy

If we leave aside the medieval and Renaissance narrative traditions in the peninsula, from Ramon Llull's *Llivre d'Evast e Blanquerna* to Joanot Martorell's *Tirant lo Blanc*,[5] and we turn to the Castilian picaresque novel, we are left with 1550–1646 (the years of *El Lazarillo de Tormes* and *Estebanillo González*) as the comprehensive dates for the development of a realist prose that no longer revolves around the values of the elite, or at least does not do so unproblematically. This new narrative depicts ordinary lives victimized by a society in which strategies of survival are entangled in the universal vying for prestige. Other instances of novelistic prose before and after those dates are not hard to find. However, my purpose is not to map the dissemination of novelistic features but to discern a period of creativity during which Castilian authors crafted the forms and materials out of which the seventeenth- and eighteenth-century European novel would grow. The real issue, then, is not the *duration* of the novel in early modern Spain but its *interruption*. Discontinuity is what needs explaining. Hence, the pertinent questions are: Why is there nothing rather than something? Why is the novel first there and then elsewhere, in a new *zone*?

---

[5] Llull (1233–1315) is one of the key theorists of the concept of subjectivity and freethinking that subtends the development of the novel. In his *Doctrina pueril* he observes that fate is often averted by free will (*la libertat de franch arbitre*) and by reason (186). For the implications of Llull's thought for the idea of adventure, see Nerlich, 252–55.

Let us look at that time span more closely. Do those dates, running from the middle of the sixteenth to the middle of the seventeenth century, have any broad significance? Indeed. They mark, respectively, the high point of Spanish imperial hegemony and the turning point of Spanish fortunes, the feudal bureacratization under Olivares, the war against the Catalans, and Portugal's secession. From the middle of the seventeenth to the end of the nineteenth century, Spanish history was a protracted series of military defeats and territorial losses. The correspondence between the political and the cultural downturns is remarkable, but we cannot satisfy ourselves with merely taking note of the coincidence. So, let us consider those dates again with an eye trained on the cultural sphere.

The year 1550 marks the watershed of Erasmian thought in Spain. Erasmism began to spread in Spain in 1525, and its influence lasted three-quarters of a century, disappearing with Cervantes, whom Marcel Bataillon calls the last scion of the Erasmian spirit in Spanish literature (798). Erasmism means *Devotio moderna*, criticism, the rise of individualism; in short, the forces on which the bourgeois novel thrived. Briefly, for a time roughly coincident with the reign of Charles V (1518–55), these attitudes had relative free play in a social space in which bourgeois forms of subjectivity (mental prayer, inner *light*, free examination, the *dialogism* noticed by Rodríguez) (369–70) struggled to gain ground before they were crushed by a nobility that had become an integral part of the state. However, even as the emperor was attempting to broker a reconciliation of the break-away Lutherans with the papacy, an effort to contain the spread of subjectivity was underway. In 1540, the Society of Jesus was founded in Spain to counter the advance of the Reformation.

Unquestioning obedience, hierarchical organization, mandatory eavesdropping in the private dialogue between the soul and God; the antibourgeois principles that regulated the "company" became the bulwarks of the Counter-Reformation. The Jesuits played a crucial role at the Council of Trent (1545–63), where the Spanish representatives were responsible for the conservative reform that was hammered out. Paradoxically, *liber arbitrium*, the belief in free will, became the cornerstone of the doctrinal reaffirmation at the same time that individual agency was curtailed. If the will was free, then individuals had to be protected from its vagaries. In this way, belief in subjective freedom led to a stricter surveillance of souls. To meet this need an army of confessors and directors of conscience arose. As so often in Spanish history, the philosophical affirmation of freedom was the pretext for a relentless policing of its social manifestations.

Placing the subject under scrutiny had broad and long-lasting repercussions. To account for one's actions by one's intentions gave reflexivity a new scope. A literary consequence of this reflexivity was fictional autobiography. And it was the autobiographical form, rather than its content, that became a new generic category. Now the subject, conceived as a reflecting surface, revealed the world, and only then learned something about himself. Again, *El Lazarillo de Tormes* is paradigmatic of this Copernican revolution. This fictive autobiography fulfilled (or pre-filled) Lukács's observation that "in the novel the subject, as observer and creator, is compelled by irony to apply its recognition of the world to itself and to treat itself, like its own creatures, as a free object of free irony" (75).

But the picaresque novel also reflects the world in a different sense, for, as evident as the "dialogue between souls" of bourgeois animism (Rodríguez, 369), is the confession at the behest of a director of conscience as a discursive model for this work. There is no contradiction between the two readings, since the confessor mediated (today we would say, tapped) the dialogue between the soul and the universal spirit. Lázaro is urged by some authority to engage in general confession. He must give a full account of his life. Granted, the tone of this novel is not Counter-Reformational. There is too much irony in Lázaro's compliance and in the "spirit of the letter" he addresses to "Your Eminence," taking every opportunity to criticize the feudal values. But the next work in the genre, Alemán's *Guzmán de Alfarache*, is unmistakably inspired by the Counter-Reformation. Now there is no more scoffing at the authorities. Instead, the hero's abjection leads to his spiritual redemption through secular punishment.

Before Cervantes, the picaresque novel explored the range of spiritual autonomy through physical mobility. Even so, it fell short of challenging the metaphysics that sustained the social hierarchy. The genre's orthodoxy can be appreciated in the fact that out of more than one hundred picaresque novels, only two were forbidden by the Church, and only four were expurgated (Moldenhauer, 239). First to be listed in the Inquisition's Index was *Lazarillo de Tormes,* which had been published the same year that Castilian censorship was centralized in the Consejo Real. Subsequent works were more respectful of the higher social strata and more mindful of Catholic dogma. Also forbidden was Quevedo's *El Buscón*, a demoralizing but hardly subversive work. Banned in 1640, fourteen years after its publication, it obtained the bishop of Madrid's imprimatur only four years later.

For all its relish in castigating certain social ranks, the picaresque novel advises conformity with the divine will as expressed in the iron laws of social determinism. The individual is free to acquiesce or to rebel, but he lacks the power to alter the cosmic order in which society is inserted. If adventure does not change the objective world, if it is merely the worldly sign of an eschatological destiny, if the hero remains caught in a web of appearances, how can the novel proceed? The novel depends on the illusion of agency, and its readers want to *believe* in the effect of moral choices upon the world. An allegorical field of abstract figures, of "states of the soul," falls outside the genre's purview. And yet, that field is where Castilian prose headed in the course of the seventeenth century, in Quevedo's *Sueños* and, above all, in Gracián's *El Criticón*.

To Be in the World

The answer to the question of how the novel could proceed after realism had faded into allegorical quietism is given, of course, by literary history. The genre evolved outside Spain by adapting its reflexivity to the needs of the class that took the world in its hands to mold it, lord it, and exploit it. And so, the picaresque novel ended up converging with an international narrative, and the picaro ranging all over the European map—as he does, literally, in *Estebanillo González*. In Spain, as the seventeenth century wound down, the hero's reflexivity dissociated itself from the sphere of action. The Renaissance subject-in-the-world split, precipitating, on one side, an abstract subjectivity, and on the other side, a phenomenal world deprived of ontological density. The world of cause and effect, of action and reaction, of permanence and change, the world with which the novel stands or falls, turned into a reflective surface for the subject's moral destiny. Calderón's and Gracián's world of illusion was such a screen, as was the world of the picaresque in its tapering moments. Hans Ulrich Gumbrecht observed this relinquishing of transformative action in the eighteenth-century picaro, Torres Villarroel: "Perhaps it is adequate to say that, during the course of the seventeenth century, the oscillation, characteristic of Golden Age culture, between a subject-centered and a cosmological worldview was progressively replaced by a specific figure of Subjectivity. Reading the most frequently quoted Spanish autobiography written during the eightenth century, Torres Villarroel's *Vida*, we may speculate that this was a Subjectivity that, in spite of reaching a high degree of reflexivity, never assumed a position of agency." (318).

Torres' memoirs contain the picaro's typical curriculum vitae: a succession of roles and pranks leading to the realization of life's emptiness and, by now, of Spain's decline into apathy and obscurity. The *Vida, ascendencia,*

nacimiento, crianza y aventuras del Doctor Don Diego de Torres Villarroel
(1743–58) appeared long after the emergence of the English novel. No two
lives could be farther apart than Torres' and Crusoe's. The one finds himself
caught in the ebb of a formerly dominant worldview. The other, buoyed by a
rising world power, submits to Providence and conquers fate. Crusoe is a
consummate example of agency. He does not ask if the world is real or illusory. He just observes it in order to master it. A reckless pursuer of adventure, like Don Quixote, he learns from experience and gets, like Sancho, an
island to govern. Unlike the Spanish knight, he stoops to the menial tasks
and crafts from which he draws the true measure of reality.

With the birth of the empirical hero, the novel's perspective was reversed. Instead of the marginal, the derelict, and the deranged roaming
around prosaic hamlets and cities, readers now followed the doings of a banal character who stumbled into extraordinary circumstances. Bourgeois reflexivity called for characters whose activities readers could recognize as potentially their own, but whose circumstances were complicated, alienating,
or perplexing. In the bourgeois novel, the world had to appear exotic, mysterious, or otherwise trying to an ordinary hero who must extricate himself
or herself from unexpected tribulations. Although the modern individual
was no match for the world, he could rise up to the challenge if he joined a
portentous will to a humble demeanor. Both assets were hard to come by,
but Puritanism's supply of these commodities was inexhaustible. By identifying with characters who fulfilled this condition, readers could measure
their spiritual mettle against imaginary but credible obstacles. No longer tilt-
ing at windmills, the bourgeois hero got ready for the colonies. The reader's
pleasure no longer originated in his release from illusion or in the satisfaction of his sadistic drives but in the thrill of vicariously experiencing the trials and triumphs of practical souls.

As the novel traveled north, it modified its aim and its method. Geography, as Moretti argues, was critical to the development of narrative. It hardly
needs saying that it is, above all, political geography that mattered, the juris-
dictions where different methods were tested on similar problems. "Causes
are very similar everywhere, but solutions may vary," says Braudel (488).
The novel is inseparable from the representation of social aspirations and
the limits set locally upon those aspirations. Braudel describes the century
between 1470 and 1580 as an age of accelerated social mobility throughout
Europe. In Spain, during this time, a new ethics of the autonomous subject
emerged in works like Fernando de Rojas's *La Celestina* (1499) and *El
Lazarillo de Tormes*. Such an ethics is still in evidence in Cervantes' *Exemplary Novels* (1613) and in María de Zayas's revolt against the foreclosure of

the venues for social ascent to women in her *Novelas ejemplares y amorosas* (1637). By the end of the sixteenth century, however, class barriers had been reinforced with a veto on the creation of new titles. Unsurprisingly, the halt on upward mobility coincided with the reversal of the positive economic trend. In the final years of the century the general standard of living declined significantly. A larger segment of the population now lived below the poverty line. In Arévalo, a Castilian village, 56 percent of the population were officially paupers (Kamen, 53). Even allowing for misrepresentation (a strategy to shun the burdensome taxation of peasants), the poverty rate still attests to worsening conditions at the end of the century. The fate of the novel is indissociable from this development. If Lázaro de Tormes could, at the "summit" of his career, praise those who were capable of lifting themselves by their bootstraps, half a century later Don Quixote had become the epitome of frustrated aspirations.

Critics have often observed that Don Quixote's desire for social eminence finds an outlet in his imaginary promotion (he plumes himself with the title *Don*). Yet many fail to relate the *hidalgo*'s ambition to the new barriers against social mobility. Such barriers were considerably higher for the descendants of *conversos*, to whom Cervantes, according to Américo Castro, belonged (34). Caste tensions are certainly present in the affable but irreconcilable counterpoint between Sancho Panza's bragging about his Old Christian condition and Don Quixote's retorting that each man is the son of his own works, a startling reversal of the value of genealogy for peasant and gentleman. The *Quixote* is, to a great extent, a novel about social confines and exclusion. If it is silent on the fate of the Spanish Jews, it comments explicitly on the expulsion of the Moriscos in 1609. Part 2 of the novel brings up that drama in the encounter between Ricote and Sancho Panza. The amiable embrace between the two former neighbors, one a Morisco, the other a conceited Old Christian, cloaks the hatred that had depopulated entire villages in central and eastern Spain. This passage, which is often cited as proof of Cervantes' equanimity and compassion, is ambivalent, since the embrace is purchased with the victim's justification of the victimizers. In one of the most sinister moments in Cervantes, Ricote utters the opinion that the expulsion of his own people was God-inspired, since "no era bien criar la sierpe en el seno, teniendo los enemigos dentro de casa" (2:670) (it is no good to nourish a snake in your bosom and keep enemies within your own house) (819). It is possible, of course, to speculate that Cervantes served this comment to the censors the better to introject his true feelings, sealed in the neighbors' embrace. It is possible, indeed, but if so, did the tactical critique of intolerance require Cervantes to feed the racial prejudice? Asked by

Sancho, Ricote explains that he has returned to Spain, risking the death penalty, in order to recover hidden treasure (the allusion to wealth in the Morisco's name is apparent). The contrast is telling. The descendants of the Moors thrived while Christian *hidalgos* became insolvent.

Cervantes had already given vent to ethnic prejudice in *El coloquio de los perros*, where he displays so much aversion against the hard-working and thrifty Moriscos that some critics have refused to see irony in those remarks. The same is true of the anti-Semitic raillery in the play *Los baños de argel*, which was the object of contrary interpretations until Jean Cannavaggio called a truce, proposing that "si bien no podemos llamarle antisemita, tampoco resulta lícito hablar de un claro alegato a favor de una convivencia de las dos razas" (while he cannot be considered anti-Semitic, to speak about a clear plea for the coexistence of both races is not legitimate either) (14). However the doubt is resolved, Cervantes' texts show that the Moriscos, like the *conversos* and other mobile groups, were perceived as a social threat. Prolific, frugal, and heavily taxed—often a full third of their income went to satisfy the various taxes and seigneurial duties (Domínguez Ortiz 1973, 173)—these workers and artisans of Moorish origin attracted their neighbors' hostility, especially after the Old Christian population began to decline. This group's birth rate had been sliding since 1580, and the trend would last for two generations (Kamen 51).

The demographic contraction accentuated the sense of crisis. When pressures for religious reform, for expansion at the top of society, for an end to the imperial hegemony on the continent combined with a serious slump in manufacturing and a stagnant agricultural output, Spain did what societies beset with insoluble problems frequently do: it clamped down on those elements that it identified as agents of the undesired transformations. As so often in periods of swift social change, sixteenth-century Spaniards wreaked havoc with the life of the lower strata. Someone had to pay the price of the empire. And when the time came to disburse, the dominant group knew how to play the resentful peasantry against marginal groups. In 1609, the Moriscos, blamed for the economic crisis and for imaginary dangers, were expelled from Spain.

The Wages of Fear

Purging ethnic diversity in the name of the unity of the faith preserved the spirit of the Reconquista in the modern fabric of the nation state. Some time after the expulsion of the Moriscos, rationalizations for that decision were still being offered, which suggests that the moral unity was far from accomplished. One such apology was Damián Fonseca's *Justa expulsión de los moriscos de España: con la instrucción, apostasía y traición dellos y respuesta a las dudas que se ofrecieron acerca desta materia* (published in 1612). The times, however, had changed, and neither the Church nor the monarchy could call the medieval order back into existence. A protobourgeoisie had developed new social representations (often clothed in religious garb) in its struggle against the seigneurial privileges and exemptions. The reaction must counter with new forms of indoctrination for the masses. The Church flooded the bookstores and the printing shops, the ateliers, the churches and hospitals with Catholic mythography. Pamplets, prayers, hagiographic books, ascetic texts issued from the presses in large numbers, while chisel and brush gave life to countless representations of the Inmaculate conception, Virgin with Child, moments from the life of the Virgin or the saints, crucifixions, miracles, and the like. On the secular side, the theater popularized absolutism and the values of caste so relentlessly that José Antonio Maravall was able to compare the *comedia* to an effective propaganda machine (201).

Noël Salomon surmised that the role of the Castilian peasant as hero in the *comedia* was motivated by the collapse of agriculture and the depopulation of the countryside toward the end of the sixteenth century. For Salomon the *comedia* reflected the contemporaneous physiocratic writings and their stress on the dignity of farming with the aim of encouraging agricultural production (808–9). Salomon's thesis was disputed by Castro (xix) and is still challenged by critics who are suspicious of materialist interpretations.[6] But it is indisputable that the rural exodus fostered the appearance of an audience for urban playwrights who popularized the values of the elite. In the *comedia* the king arbitrates by sanctioning the action of characters who adhere to the letter of the feudal law, codified as honor. As a result of his intervention, the social fabric is always restored.

Salomon was right to see a connection between the peasant's exaltation in the theater and his desperate plight in the real world. But no less important than the economic reasons are the values that made a rustic the object of artistic adulation. According to Castro, the Castilian peasant pitted his unblemished lineage against the nobility's racially dubious pedigree. "Lope de Vega," he claims, "hace ver, sin posible duda, que *para el vulgo* los no labriegos eran 'judíos'" (Lope de Vega shows, without the shadow of a doubt, that *for the populace* whoever was not a peasant was a "Jew") (215). "Honor" was the code word for the ideological struggle. Who had it? Under

---

[6] See McGrady lxix.

what conditions? How could it be retained? Castro's thesis is not totally persuasive, however. While there is little doubt that the Castilian peasant was religiously intolerant, it is less clear that he contested the social order, modern readings of *Fuenteovejuna* and *Peribáñez* notwithstanding. In the seventeenth century there was a reaffirmation of the aristocratic order; it is not plausible that precisely at this time the peasantry would have challenged the notion of inherited distinction that was the bedrock of that order. When Lope de Vega scoffs at the *hidalgos cansados* (tired hidalgos) in *Peribáñez* (v. 2,453), hinting at their racial impurity (in Castro's interpretation of the word *cansados*), the anti-Semitism expressed in this cryptic sentence targets a second- or third-tier of the lower gentry, which was infiltrated by recent parvenus. Infiltration had been especially frequent in the rural areas, where a rich peasant could ascend socially by purchasing a *hidalguía* (Domínguez Ortiz 1963: 267).

By impugning the honor of those who had recently escaped the condition of *pecheros* (taxpayers), the common folk helped to reassert the feudal strictures, or so they did in the theater. Lope's allusions to the "tainted blood" of the *hidalgos* were certainly not aimed at the high and mighty. Honor, states Peribáñez, is a prerogative of the *noblesse d'épée*, and let no one make any mistake about that: "Vos me ceñistes espada,/con que ya entiendo de honor;/que antes yo pienso señor,/que entendiera poco o nada" (You granted me the right to wear the sword/and now I understand honor,/whereas before, I think, Sir,/that I understood little or nothing [about it]) (vv. 2,282–85). The king bestows *hidalguía* on the peasant Peribáñez, but the message is clear: without royal sanction, which is granted only under the rarest circumstances, there is no crossing the social boundaries. The playwright's response to the growing demand of honor accords with the views of contemporary economists. Roughly at the same time that Lope wrote *Peribáñez*, Martín González de Cellorigo insisted on the need for clear class demarcations. In his *Memorial de la política necesaria y útil restauración de República de España* (1600), he warned that "al quererlo todos ygualar es lo que los tiene más desconcertados y confundida la república de menores a mediados, y de medianos a mayores, saliendo todos de su compás y orden, que conforme a la calidad de sus haziendas, de sus oficios, y estado de cada uno devieran guardar" (the craving for equality is what produces the general bewilderment and the confusion from lower to middle, and from middle to higher in the republic, with everyone leaving the compass and order that are proper to him, and which ought to be kept in harmony with the quality of the patrimony, occupation, and standing of each person) (qtd. Salomon 804).

Slurs against ennobled *conversos* are also present in Quevedo, who was not above casting racial aspersions on his literary enemies. In this rarefied environment, innovation could become a liability, and Quevedo certainly sensed the power of racial animosity when he denounced Luis de Góngora's formal experimentation and ponderous use of neologisms as "Judaic." In the previous century, the growth of the cities and the emergence of an autonomous subject had inspired the realism of the picaresque and *Don Quixote.* With the stiffening absolutism of the seventeenth century, the novel could no longer harbor the individual's quest for status or self-knowledge. Charles V's cultivation of the "autonomy of politics within absolutism" (Rodríguez, 357) had unravelled in Philip II's submission to the pope. The unified background of belief imposed with the expulsion of the Jews and the Moriscos, and with the ruthless persecution of heretics, may have bolstered the Castilian theater of the seventeenth century, but it ravaged the possibilities of the novel. Without tolerance for risk and error there is no room for adventure. After 1600, empirical knowledge and moral experimentation were no longer possible; only the formal play on stable meanings was allowed. Wit became the baroque's spiritual exhaust.

In Spain the novel withered for the same reasons that science shunned that country. An interest in "things" is essential to both enterprises, and that interest cannot blossom where free inquiry is impeded and social mobility punished. During the sixteenth century, the will to reform found a channel in the humanist critique of the scriptures (and of chivalric fables) in the name of historical and philological truth. The intellectual fluster went hand in hand with such dramatic convulsions as the revolt of the Castilian communities and of the *germanies* or brotherhoods in Mallorca and Valencia, where the rebellious artisans supressed taxes and adopted a republican constitution like those of the Italian city-states.

The seigneurial reaction was sharp and far-reaching. In the seventeenth century, the Inquisition tightened its grip on an already homogeneous society. The "triviality" of the causes brought against authors as manifestly orthodox as Quevedo and Tirso de Molina (Green 462) should not mislead us. The pettiness of the charges evinces zeal rather than restraint. The aristocracy also extended its control of the mind by confiscating the universities. In its scramble for all kinds of offices, the middle and lower nobility now took over the colleges, which had been venues for the promotion of penniless students. With the help of papal dispensations, the ruling class was able to rescind the original constitutions, which stipulated poverty as a condition for admission. From now on, candidates had to supply proof of noble origin and purity of blood in the form of an affidavit that could only be obtained through expensive procedures. The aristocratic control of the universities was consummated when student participation in the appointment of faculty was revoked in 1623. Henceforth, the Council of Castile made the appointments to the major universities, turning them into a class franchise (Domínguez Ortiz 1973, 323). Inevitably, science succumbed to dogma. In the last quarter of the seventeenth century, and in non-Castilian cities like Valencia and Barcelona, as well as in Seville, individuals working outside the universities tried to reconcile empiricism with the Catholic faith. They were called *novatores*, a pejorative term. As Angel Weruaga Prieto suggests, their conciliatory approach was probably a tactic to reform the edifice of hegemonic thought through an innocuous approach to scientific problems (47, 49). Even so, official culture retorted vehemently through its scholastic professors and theologians.

To quote Braudel once more: "Every society is shot through with currents, bristling with obstacles, with obstinate relics of the past that block the way, with long-lasting structures whose permanence is their most revealing feature for the historian" (461). This general truth is applicable to early-modern Spain. In the centuries when the West was developing its modern identity, Spain veered away from that uncharted horizon. To the risks of free examination and empirical testing of truth, the country opposed its long-standing habits and its relics. The emperor himself became a collector of relics. Philip II, the most powerful monarch on earth, sought supernatural solutions to worldly problems. In 1589, one year after the Armada's disaster, one of his ministers, Juan de Silva, count of Portalegre, criticized the government for failing to undertake realistic solutions: "todos veo que se remiten a milagros y a remedios sobrenaturales" (I see everyone turning to miracles and supernatural remedies) (qtd. in Kamen, 59).

Philip reversed the incipient differentiation of the political from the religious, which had been perceptible in his father's policies. During his reign, religion became again an affair of the state and the state a religious affair. As his life declined, his fanaticism grew, and orthodoxy filled the nation's imaginary with the lives and miracles of saints. As Sara T. Nalle puts it: "In this profoundly religious country, where one of the questions from Philip II's *Relaciones topográficas* concerned local miracles, the supernatural was the subject of endless curiosity—and curiosity sold books" (135). It sold so well that religious books accounted for well over half of the book trade. In five Castilian bookstores, between 1528 and 1581, 47 to 58 percent of the stock was on religious subjects, while in Barcelona the inventories of four printers show that between 1538 and 1595 anywhere from 46 to 73 percent of the stock was religious (Nalle, 129). A large part of this trade was in popular religion. In the course of the century, devotional materials, which accounted for nine-tenths of all religious works sold (130), became increasingly cheaper, especially those that were aimed at the poor. Religion was without any doubt the mass culture of the period.

Although interest in devotional books preceded the Counter-Reformation, it is possible to speak of a renewed culture of piety after Trent. But this culture was closely monitored by the authorities. Books of hours in the vernacular, which included large parts of translated scripture, had been immensely popular. In Barcelona, in the first half of the sixteenth century, such books accounted for two-thirds of the stock in two bookshops (Nalle, 136). In 1573, the Inquisition ordered all books of hours in the vernacular to be destroyed. The reason is obvious: the Church wanted to prevent the wayward interpretation of its canonical texts. But although certain forms of religious literature were censored or banned, other forms continued to be available at popular prices (146). The new times encouraged not only the consumption of devout works but also the appropriation of secular literature for religious purposes, a point to which I will return.

During the seventeenth century, the consumption of literature appears to have declined. After examining the records of private book collections in Salamanca from the middle of the seventeenth to the first quarter of the eighteenth century, Weruaga concludes that literature was very underrepresented, and not only among men, who normally owned professional works, mostly on law, medicine, or theology, reflecting, no doubt, the importance of the university in this town. Women's libraries, which Weruaga considers more representative of the book trade, leaned heavily toward the popular religiosity and hagiographic tradition of the baroque (160). "Literature" had little room in private libraries. Only Quevedo appears consistently among the various social groups, while Cervantes is a rare presence (Weruaga Prieto, 117). The *comedias*, on the other hand, were frequently read, but the titles were not consigned in the inventories, a detail that evinces their low cultural status and insignificant economic value (Weruaga Prieto, 119).

"Literature" increasingly had to compete with the products of popular piety. During his visit to the printing shop, Don Quixote observes the typesetting of Fray Luis de Meneses' *Luz del alma christiana*, a book of piety that had been widely read in Cervantes' youth (Bataillon, 778). The knight ostensibly approves this kind of reading: "Estos tales libros, aunque hay muchos deste género, son los que se deben imprimir, porque son muchos los pecadores que se usan, y son menester infinitas luces para tantos desalumbrados" (2:788) (Books like this, numerous though they are, are the kind that ought to be printed, for there are many sinners nowadays, and there is need of infinite light for so many in the dark) (878). But beneath the humdrum applause, one can discern Cervantes' impatience with the surfeit of such texts.

There was an objective reason for the predominance of religious books. A very high percentage of the writers belonged to the Church or to the aristocracy. Combined, these estates represented one-tenth of the population, yet they produced almost 90 percent of all literary work, with a clear predominance of the Church over the nobility. The Church's higher share was due not only to the clerics' cultural superiority but also to the fact that the religious orders often defrayed the cost of publication (Domínguez Ortiz 1973, 333). Few books turned out to be profitable in a market that was still restricted to a minority, notwithstanding the ever decreasing cost of books after the development of mechanical printing. In seventeenth-century Spain, the book trade was still far from what it would be after 1700 in countries where a flourishing bourgeoisie and increased literacy permitted the emergence of a market for secular literature.[7]

In Spain, where the novel was up against every conceivable religious genre, it also faced a more insidious competitor, the *a lo divino* adaptations. *A lo divino* writing parodied profane literature by replacing its subject matter with religious content. Imitative and adversarial at once, this form of "translation" catered to the popular taste while keeping it under control. Many writers produced religious versions of popular fiction. Bartolomé Ponce countered Jorge de Montemayor's *Diana* with his *Clara Diana a lo divino*, Jaime de Alcalá wrote a *Libro de la caballería cristiana* (1570), and Lope de Vega raided his own *Arcadia* (1598) in a religious fiction, *Pastores de Belén* (1612). Pedro Malón de Chaide wrote *La conversión de la Magdalena* (1592) explicitly to displace the "libros de amores, y las *Dianas* y Boscanes y Garcilasos, y los monstruosos libros y silvas de fabulosos cuentos y mentiras de los *Amadises, Floriseles* y *Don Belianís*, y una flota de semejantes portentos como hay escritos" (books of love, and the *Dianas* and Boscans and Garcilasos, and the monstrous books and miscellanies of

---

[7] Even in those countries, it was a long time before the novel dominated the book market. In Great Britain, the first country to develop a self-sustaining literary market, the publication of novels did not outstrip that of religious books until 1900 (Carr, 197).

fabulous tales and lies from the *Amadises*, *Florisels* and *Don Belianis*, and a fleet of such freaks as exist in writing) (qtd. in Darst, 26).

Do not Malón de Chaide's purpose and, above all, the texts that he wished to displace, ring familiar? Certainly they do. His language reminds us of Cervantes' in the prologue to *Don Quixote*, where he declares that his book aims at "deshacer la autoridad y cabida que en el mundo y en el vulgo tienen los libros de caballerías" (15) (destroying the authority and influence which books of chivalry have in the world and among the common people) (30). The connection between this intention, which critics tend to interpret in strictly literary terms, and the post-Tridentine religious intervention in the literary field transpires in the bookish auto-da-fé organized by the priest at the expense of Don Quixote's library. In this unforgettable scene, some of the titles denounced by Malón de Chaide burn in the pyre. Again, Cervantes appears to toe the line of orthodoxy, and at the same time to bring something through, like the titles he rescues from the priest's scrutiny on the merit of aesthetic value and readerly pleasure. To the "last, great and desperate mysticism" that resisted the disenchantment of the organicist world (Lukács, 104), he opposed his irony and a fiction sobered in the fires of self-awareness. But irony is an unstable talent. It could flourish in the narrow lag between the emergence of an early bourgeois autonomy and the "fanatical attempt to renew the dying religion from within" (Lukács, 104). Alternatively, it could be practiced in the narrow mental space between subjective freedom and outer conformity.

After *Don Quixote*, the life of fiction was by no means over in Spain, but the environment had become adverse to the novel. Or perhaps it was a matter of geography, as Moretti maintains. In his *Notes on the Novel* (1925), Ortega y Gasset resorted to a geographic simile to explain the enigma of the location of culture: "Imagínese a un leñador genial en el desierto del Sahara. De nada le sirve su músculo elástico y su hacha afilada. El leñador sin bosque donde tajar es una abstracción. Lo propio acontece en el arte" (Imagine a woodsman, the strongest of woodsmen, in the Sahara desert. What good are his bulging muscles and his sharp ax? A woodsman without woods is an abstraction. And the same applies to artists) (388).[8] Whether Spain could still bring forth novelists of genius was a moot question. The novel in Spain had become an abstraction. After the first quarter of the seventeenth century, Spaniards could have said, paraphrasing Kafka, there are novels, plenty of novels but not from us.

---

[8] The translation of the quotation is from the English version of "Notes on the Novel," in *The Dehumanization of Art and Other Essays on Art, Culture, and Literature*. Trans. Helene Weyl. Princeton, N.J.: Princeton University Press, 1968, 58.

Works Cited

Bataillon, Marcel. *Erasmo y España: Estudios sobre la historia espiritual del siglo XVI*. Trans. Antonio Alatorre. 2nd ed. Mexico City: Fondo de Cultura Económica, 1966.

Braudel, Fernand. *The Wheels of Commerce: Civilization and Capitalism 15th–18th Century*. 3 vols. Trans. Siân Reynolds. New York: Harper and Row, 1982.

Canavaggio, Jean. "La estilización del judío en *Los baños de Argel*." In *¿"¡Bon compaño, jura Di!"? El encuentro de moros, judíos y cristianos en la obra cervantina*. Ed. Caroline Schmauser and Monika Walter. Frankfurt on Main: Vervuert, 1998, 9–20.

Carr, Raymond. "El fin de siglo en España y Gran Bretaña." In *Visiones de fin de siglo*. Ed. Raymond Carr. Madrid: Taurus, 1999, 189–216.

Castro, Américo. *De la edad conflictiva: Crisis de la cultura española en el siglo XVII*. 4th ed. Madrid: Taurus, 1976.

Cervantes Saavedra, Miguel de. *El ingenioso hidalgo Don Quijote de la Mancha*. 2 vols. Barcelona: Luis Tasso Serra, n.d.

———. *The Adventures of Don Quixote*. Trans. J. M. Cohen. Harmondsworth, Eng.: Penguin, 1950.

Cohen, Margaret, and Carolyn Dever. "Introduction" to *The Literary Channel: The Inter-National Invention of the Novel*. Princeton, N.J.: Princeton University Press, 2002, 1–34.

Darst, David H. *Converting Fiction: Counter Reformational Closure in the Secular Literature of Golden Age Spain*. North Carolina Studies in the Romance Languages and Literatures. Chapel Hill: University of North Carolina Press, 1998.

Davis, Lennard J. *Factual Fictions: The Origins of the English Novel*. Philadelphia: University of Pennsylvania Press, 1996.

Domínguez Ortiz, Antonio. *La sociedad española del siglo XVII*, vol. 1. Madrid: Centro Superior de Investigaciones Científicas, 1963.

———. *El antiguo régimen: Los reyes católicos y los austrias*. 3rd vol. of *Historia de España Alfaguara*. Madrid: Alianza Universidad, 1973.

Doody, Margaret Anne. *The True Story of the Novel*. New Brunswick, N.J.: Rutgers University Press, 1996.

Green, Otis. *Spain and the Western Tradition: The Castilian Mind in Literature from El Cid to Calderón*, vol. 3. Madison: University of Wisconsin Press, 1968.

Gumbrecht, Hans Ulrich. "Cosmological Time and the Impossibility of Closure: A Structural Element in Spanish Golden Age Narratives." In *Cultural Authority in Golden Age Spain*. Ed. Marina S. Brownlee and Hans Ulrich Gumbrecht. Baltimore: Johns Hopkins University Press, 1995, 304–21.

Kamen, Henry. " 'El tiempo del trueno': El ocaso del siglo dorado." In *Visiones de fin de siglo*. Ed. Raymond Carr. Madrid: Taurus, 1999, 47–64.

Llull, Ramon. *Doctrina pueril*. In *Obres doctrinals del illuminat Doctor Mestre Ramon Llull*. Ciutat de Mallorca: Comissió Editora Lulliana, 1906.

Lukács, Georg. *The Theory of the Novel*. Trans. Anna Bostock. Cambridge, Mass.: MIT Press, 1973.

Maravall, José Antonio. *La cultura del barroco*. Esplugues del Llobregat: Ariel, 1975.

McGrady, Donald. "Prologue" to *Peribáñez*. In Vega, Lope de.

Moldenhauer, Gerhard. "Spanische Zensur und Schelmenroman." In *Estudios eruditos in memoriam de Adolfo Bonilla y San Martín* (Madrid: Imprenta Viuda e hijos de T. Ratés, 1927), 1:223–39.

Moretti, Franco. *Atlas of the European Novel 1800–1900*. London: Verso, 1998.

Nalle, Sara T. "Printing and Reading Popular Religious Texts in Sixteenth-Century Spain." In *Culture and the State in Spain 1550–1850*. Ed. Tom Lewis and Francisco J. Sánchez. New York: Garland, 1999, 126–56.

Nerlich, Michael. *Abenteuer oder das verlorene Selbstverständnis der Moderne*. Munich: Gerling Akademie Verlag, 1997.

Ortega y Gasset, José. "Ideas sobre la novela." In *Obras completas*, vol. 3. Madrid: Revista de Occidente, 1957, 387–419.

Resina, Joan Ramon. *Los usos del clásico*. Barcelona: Anthropos, 1991.

———. "Cervantes's Confidence Games and the Refashioning of Totality." *MLN*, 111 (1996): 218–53.

Rodríguez, Juan Carlos. *Teoría e historia de la producción ideológica: Las primeras literaturas burguesas*. Madrid: Akal, 1990.

Salomon, Noël. *Recherches sur le thème paysan dans la "Comedia" au temps de Lope de Vega*. Bordeaux: Féret et Fils, 1965.

Schelling, F.W.J. von. "Philosophie der Kunst." In *Werke*. Ed. Otto Weiß. Leipzig: Fritz Eckardt, 1907, 3:1–384.

Valdés, Juan de. *Diálogo de la lengua*. Clásicos Castellanos. Madrid: Espasa-Calpe, 1953.

Vega, Lope de. *Peribáñez y el comendador de Ocaña*. Ed. Donald McGrady. Barcelona: Crítica, 1997.

Watt, Ian. *The Rise of the Novel*. Berkeley: University of California Press, 1957.

Weruaga Prieto, Angel. *Libros y lectura en Salamanca: Del barroco a la ilustración (1650–1725)*. Salamanca: Junta de Castilla y León. Consejería de Cultura y Turismo, 1993.

DANIEL COUÉGNAS

Forms of Popular Narrative in France and England: 1700–1900

The Bibliothèque Bleue *and* Colportage *Literature*

From the sixteenth to the nineteenth centuries, printing made possible the circulation of large quantities of images and booklets (*fascicules*) throughout the urban and rural populations of Western Europe. These inexpensive publications, found particularly in Spain, Germany, Italy, and France, were distributed by *colporteurs* or itinerant peddlers—a universal feature, given the methods of travel and transportation in this period. This characteristic allows us to designate conveniently, and as we shall see, reasonably accurately, a particular type of publishing, known in France as *colportage* literature and in England as *chapbooks*.

Indisputably linked to the expansion of the artisan and merchant bourgeoisie in early capitalism, *colportage* literature offered to a public still only very partially literate a product that is interesting to examine as a commercial object. Both in France and England, this kind of literature assured the prosperity of families of printer-publishers. At the beginning of the seventeenth century in Troyes, in the Champagne region, Nicolas Oudot, who was seeking new markets for material that had proved difficult to sell because of its high price, had the idea of using secondhand printing equipment to produce small, inexpensive booklets that would be distributed by peddlers.[1] The success of this enterprise enabled a veritable Oudot "dynasty" to ensure the continuation of their business until 1769, at which time another competing family of printer-publishers, the Garniers, who had set themselves up in the venture of *colportage* literature about a century earlier, bought up the Oudot business, which they, like other smaller printers of Troyes, had shamelessly imitated. The Garnier business was in turn bought by the publisher Baudot, who would continue his business until 1863, the date that marks the end of *colportage* publishing in Troyes.[2] But the success of this literary commerce had spread throughout the northern, and even into

---

[1] Cf. Robert Mandrou, *De la culture populaire aux 17e et 18e siècles: La Bibliothèque bleue de Troyes* (Paris: Imago, 1999), ch. 1 a.

[2] Cf. Geneviève Bollème, *La Bible bleue: Anthologie d'une littérature "populaire"* (Paris: Flammarion, 1975). A table showing the great printing dynasties can be found on 397–99.

the central, region of France. Only the southwest and Brittany, for linguistic reasons, remained relatively untouched by this phenomenon. The primary explanation for these commercial and publishing successes was the high cost of traditional works that were too sumptuous, and bulky, to be easily sold. A similar phenomenon occurred in England and again had its origins in the profession of the printer-publisher. There, too, one family, the Diceys, assumed an important role and, throughout the eighteenth century, prospered from the production and distribution of chapbooks.[3]

I want to emphasize here a point I will return to: while the activities of printer and distributor were essential to this cultural phenomenon, these same publishing businesses also assumed significant editorial roles, choosing and adapting in their own workshops texts that would suit the conditions of transportation in this period, the economic capabilities of potential clients, their level of culture, and the reading practices of rural areas. I should also stress that the *colportage* booklets and other chapbooks were essentially *commercial objects*, or at least could be represented as such not only by those who produced and sold them, but more particularly by those who "consumed" them by reading them, once the works had been acquired from the peddler's basket. These booklets—which included works of imagination together with treatises, almanacs, and handbooks of a practical nature—were sold side by side with the most ordinary items. In France, for example, the *colporteur* "refurbished his supplies in Troyes itself—or in other centers where he could find haberdashery—and, as he followed his usual routes, would announce his merchandise with the sound of a horn, offering laces, needles, thread, hooks, small mirrors, and these booklets."[4] The disparate nature of the cultural products on the one hand, and their juxtaposition with material goods on the other, the desacralization of intellectual products resulting from the banal, everyday context of their sale, seems to prefigure in a striking way the role that the train-station bookshops launched by Hachette would play in the nineteenth century, and, in the twentieth century, supermarket shelves that carry, side by side, food items, handyman and cleaning products, and books.

The *colportage* booklet calls into question another representation of the cultural and literary product, that inherited from romanticism in which "the book" is distilled into "a work" generated without an intermediary by the sheer inspiration or genius of the author—the kind of author to whom,

---

[3] Cf. Gilles Duval, *Littérature de colportage et imaginaire collectif en Angleterre à l'époque des Dicey 1720–vers 1800* (Presses Universitaires de Bordeaux, 1991), ch. 2.

[4] Mandrou, *De la culture populaire*, 23.

as we shall see, the literature of *colportage* accorded little importance. Though the booklets were anonymous for the most part, they nevertheless did not appear ex nihilo. The employees of the publisher-printers, following the directives of their masters, would transcribe particular oral traditions or "adapt" works from the learned literary repertoire. But a veritable commercial and cultural circuit allowed the *colporteurs* to gauge the interest clients showed in the different types of booklets they offered, and led the printer-publishers to modulate the printing size of a particular work or genre.

How did these "adapters" operate in order to produce texts that met the norms of *colportage* literature? All the commentators note the economic logistics and conditions of reception that required short texts that could be printed in "small in-12 or in-32 booklets of a few pages each."[5] Geneviève Bollème speaks of a "staccato" (*hachée*) method of reading,[6] which required that texts be divided systematically into chapters or brief episodes. Gilles Duval makes the same observation about chapbooks in eighteenth-century England: "Even popular tales were rewritten for a public with limited faculties of concentration, divided up into chapters introduced by short summaries, whereas the original texts of Perrault and Madame d'Aulnoy were continuous."[7] These were new readers, new books—or rather, new textual versions—and new ways of reading.

At issue here is a key question—the definition of "popular" literature—that remains unresolved. Who made up the reading public of the *Bibliothèque bleue* or of chapbooks, or of *colportage* literature in general? Certainly the levels of literacy in Western Europe in this period were very low, and it is difficult to establish reliable and meaningful criteria for evaluating the degree of literacy. But as modern historians of reading have pointed out, the process of bringing literacy to the public in past centuries took place under different conditions and with different "gestures" than those familiar to us today. The appropriation of *colportage* literature depended on the reading aloud of texts to a group of listeners. This process evidently made it possible to reach a large number of people from the lower or "popular" social groups. But the low price of the *colportage* booklets and their intellectual or cultural accessibility in no way discouraged the interest of other publics. More educated, these other groups were able to practice a different mode of appropriating texts—individual silent reading—which, in the sixteenth and seventeenth centuries, developed concurrently with reading aloud, first

---

[5] Ibid., 20.

[6] Bollème, *La Bible bleue,* 25.

[7] Duval, *Littérature de colportage*, 109.

among the learned, and then among the classes of lower cultural capital.[8] The *colportage* peddlers were, then, already distributing "popular" literature, that is, "for the masses," before the term existed. These works showed certain traits that, *mutatis mutandis*, would reappear in the "easy" reading of later centuries that almost all categories of readers, not only the most modest and unsophisticated, could appropriate, each in their own way.

Let us next examine the contents of *colportage* booklets. The historian Robert Mandrou, in his careful efforts to define the contours of a "popular culture," distinguishes within the Champenois sources five main categories: "mythology and pagan marvels" (romances and fairy tales); practical works (treatises, calendars and almanacs); works of piety; "romances, farces, profane songs"; and finally, "depictions of society, trades, games, education, and historical mythology."[9] Leaving aside the very numerous works of piety (a quarter of all those studied by Mandrou) and pamphlets of a practical nature, I will examine the most strictly "literary" (in the modern sense of the term) texts of the corpus. In this group, a significant number of works were devoted to the Charlemagne cycle and drawn from highly abbreviated, fourteenth- and fifteenth-century prose adaptations of medieval *chansons de geste*. This mythical universe, whose idealized reality offered a complete contrast to the reality of the readers and listeners of the *Bibliothèque bleue*, had frequent recourse to the marvelous (magicians help heroic horsemen to fight giants and devils, etc.). Fairy tales were included in the *Bibliothèque bleue* from the seventeenth century to the end of the *colportage* period, borrowed from oral literature but also from the collections of the *Thousand and One Nights*, Charles Perrault, and Madame d'Aulnoy. The great popular myths (Gargantua, Till Eulenspiegel, Fortunatus) inscribed themselves more deeply within the daily world of these readers without, however, renouncing the world of the marvelous. The novel is rarely found in the *Bibliothèque bleue* before the end of the eighteenth century, while other genres, among them the drinking song and the love song, remain perennials.

Viewed from a pan-European perspective, *colportage* literature highlights the international success of certain works: *Till Eulenspiegel* (in Germany, England, and France); *Grisélidis* (Italy, Denmark, Sweden, Germany, France); *Robinson Crusoe, Gulliver's Travels, The Wandering Jew* (throughout

---

[8] Cf. Roger Chartier and Guglielmo Cavallo, eds., *A History of Reading in the West,* trans. Lydia Cochrane (Amherst: University of Massachusetts Press, 1999). See ch. 10, "Reading Matter and 'Popular' Reading: From the Renaissance to the Seventeenth Century." Orig. Italian edition: *Storia della Lettura nel mondo occidentale* (Rome: Giuseppe Laterza & Figli Spa, 1995).

[9] Mandrou, *De la culture populaire*, 32–33.

Europe); and *canards* ("hoaxes") or fake accounts of dramatic and bloody events.[10] Each country, however, had its own predilections, tied to its particular history, civilization, and ways of thinking. Spain, the place of passage and contact between North Africa and Europe, Muslim and Christian civilizations, gave prominence to "stories of captives and apostates (the Moor is the ancient enemy), smugglers and honorable bandits."[11] Germany seems to have introduced adaptations of novels (*Robinson Crusoe, Moll Flanders*) into *colportage* literature earlier than France—from the early eighteenth century onward. In these two countries, the popular narrative vein appears to develop alongside the higher literary register.

It is not, then, surprising that *colportage* literature and high culture, oral tradition and written text, should intersect and enrich each other in ways that are often quite complex. Thus the giant Gargantua is the hero of a narrative that appeared before 1535, the date when Rabelais granted him his literary nobility: the authors of *colportage* literature will draw successively from both sources. High literature also passes into *colportage* texts, crossing frontiers and linguistic barriers: in crossing the Channel, the English gothic novel (cf. infra), for example, is transformed into *colportage* booklets. On the other hand, oral literature leaves traces visible on several levels: in the relative brevity of oral sequences, when the text of the booklet is *read* to a group whose necessarily limited attention span must be considered; in the interpolation of tales, songs, and proverbs drawn from the tradition of vigils; and in the repetitive devices of formulas and themes that recall the presence of the oral behind the written text.[12]

In the nineteenth century, literacy, the development of the press, and the evolution of the genre of the novel simultaneously transformed the corpus of *colportage* literature and hastened its disappearance. It was the novel, and most notably the sentimental novel, that dominated all other genres of *colportage* literature. But in the last decades of the nineteenth century came changes that sounded the death-knell for *colportage* literature: technical progress in printing (rotary printing press) and transportation (railway), and a reduction in the cost of newspapers that supplied readers of modest income with information of various kinds, along with serialized novels.

Yet, at the very moment that the *Bibliothèque bleue* booklet was disappearing, some of its characteristics—which had persisted throughout the

---

[10] Duval, *Littérature de colportage*, 67.

[11] Ibid., 68.

[12] Cf. Alain-Michel Boyer, *La paralittérature* (Paris: Presses Universitaires de France, 1992), 55–61.

nineteenth century—were passed on to new forms of emerging mass literature. Among these traits, we note first and foremost the tendency of this
kind of literature to satisfy the irrepressible taste of the reader for *narrative
fiction*. As Geneviève Bollème astutely observes, the *Bibliothèque bleue* in
each of its constituent parts tries to "present everything as an anecdote,
whether it be history, novel, remedy, prayer, rule of conduct, or game . . ."
and, she notes, "this process becomes a form of narration."[13] The taste for
narration certainly contributes to the privileging of content, of the *story (la
fable)*, to the detriment of form, an aspect that explains the ease with which
colportage booklets could be adapted, transformed, reassembled, or rewritten in multiple versions. As in oral literature, to borrow the apt formulation
of Peter Burke, "the same text is different, and different texts are the
same."[14] This is literature of escapism, lacking aesthetic preoccupation and
ambivalent in its desire to give a realistic appearance to fictions of the extraordinary, spectacular, and exotic. These are also texts whose ideological
color is one of conservatism, conformism, and a certain "centrist" moderation (to borrow Robert Mandrou's term) that can be attributed both to the
threat of censorship and to the commercial desire to reach a vast public.

The "Gothic Romance"

To include the phenomenon of the gothic novel in a study of the forms of
popular narrative may seem surprising. In fact this genre of fiction, which
originated in England in the second half of the eighteenth century, did not
initially belong to the realm of "popular" literature. But its evolution, both
in form and theme, is a much more complicated issue. In the following
pages I will try to show the porosity of the genres and registers through
which the "gothic" was disseminated in the literary domain and claimed a
place in European culture. A long list of writers in the nineteenth century
and after owe their creativity and inspiration in part to the influence of the
gothic. But this influence, stimulated by the enthusiasm of readers, would
also reach the most undervalued sector of the cultural domain: narratives for
a broad readership. Indeed, it is the narrativity of the gothic, and perhaps,
most of all, a certain fantasmic, plastic aesthetic, that give the genre its exceptional quality of "transgenericity," or the potential to circulate freely
from one literary register to another, and even more, from one medium to

---

[13] Bollème, *La Bible bleue*, 34.
[14] Peter Burke, *Popular Culture in Early Modern Europe* (London: Temple Smith, 1978), 125.

another, as the cinema has revealed. Without falling into the mistaken notion—for lack of a rigorous definition of the gothic—of finding imitators of Walpole and Radcliffe everywhere, one can nevertheless follow Allan Lloyd Smith and Victor Sage and wonder whether this phenomenon, in transcending the limits of a literary genre, should not rather be described as "a broader cultural response."[15]

Paradoxically, this popular cultural tradition, a phenomenon of mass publishing (at least within the context of the norms and possibilities of the period), had its roots in "cultivated" soil. *The Castle of Otranto; A Story,* published December 24, 1764, in London without the name of its author, Horace Walpole, seems a curious literary object, a strange composite. But that is perhaps the reason why the most disparate registers and genres, even the most antithetical, recognize themselves in this work, take inspiration from it, or pay it homage. This small book has certain affinities with the fairy tale. Its characters have the same simplified, even schematic traits, although these sketchy figures lack the firm delineation of Perrault's heroes, or Grimm's. The young hero, the knight Theodore, is barely convincing, and the heroines are almost interchangeable. Only the "villain" Manfred, Prince of Otranto, who dedicates himself with dark passion to retaining an ill-gotten kingdom by all possible means, enlivens the action while occasionally revealing hesitations and doubts that lend a certain interest to his character. The narrative flows swiftly, with little description but with the occasional odd slowing of tempo when the author introduces a few fragments of comic theater that create an impression of textual heterogeneity (e.g., chapter 1, the exchange between Manfred and his servants, Diego and Jacquez). Another reminder of the fairy tale—and also, of course, of the Shakespearian world—is the manner in which Walpole dramatizes the supernatural. The medieval helmet of enormous proportions dear to Paul Eluard, the statue whose nostrils drip blood, the skeleton wrapped in a hermit's robe, the gigantic image of Alphonse rising majestically toward the Heavens: these elements among others, presented in an "objective" manner in the narrative without the least reticence, uncertainty, or respect for the rules of realist verisimilitude, appear to inscribe *The Castle of Otranto* within the realm of the marvelous. Nevertheless, elsewhere in the text the motif of the supernatural is treated differently whenever certain characters, particularly secondary ones, become hesitant and fearful in the face of mysterious events. While

---

[15] Allan Lloyd Smith and Victor Sage, eds., *Gothick Origins and Innovations* (Amsterdam: Rodopi, 1994), introduction. Cited by Cassilde Tournebize, "Le gothique et ses métamorphoses," *Caliban* 33 (1996): 4.

the doubt characteristic of the "fantastic" is not found at the center of this textual world, it is, nevertheless, not completely absent from it either, as Ann Radcliffe will remind us.

The complexity of Walpole's work derives also from its structure, which is almost superimposed on the text or is, at least, highly visible, shaping the relationships between characters—whose schematic psychology has already been noted—into parallelisms and symmetries like those of seventeenth-century Italian or French farce. But this deceptively naive textual geometry baldly dramatizes the limitless desire for power as well as the transgressive libido with its incestuous implications. It is this recurring narrative and thematic economy that contributed to the success of the gothic. In an incongruous, or quietly provocative, manner Walpole's novel reveals the inadmissible, the power of irrational forces.

But the strangest feature of Walpole's work—a novel that was to have such an extraordinary literary destiny—has yet to be described. It relates to the defining kernel of the *gothic* genre, the architectural setting—castle or abbey—that we know Walpole was dreaming of when he furnished his home, Strawberry Hill! In a remarkable essay on the gothic genre in nineteenth-century England and France, Joëlle Prungnaud notes that around 1820, "the word 'gothic' had the value of a code rather than a descriptive function."[16] We might indeed hypothesize that readers allow themselves to be easily charmed by the pleasures of rediscovery, of *repetition* and *intertextual memory*. If earlier readings had offered the reader descriptions of gothic decors that were sufficiently detailed and suggestive, these lingering mental images would reappear at the mere mention of the term *gothic,* functioning as a simple catalyst or stimulus of the imaginary. But where might we find such descriptions? If we retrace the intertextual chain, we arrive at Walpole as the point of departure for the gothic tradition. Yet *The Castle of Otranto* offers scarcely any detailed descriptions of Manfred's home, conforming in this, once again, to the aesthetic of the popular tale. Should we not conclude from this that the Gothic architectural element of the castle, or at least the deepest meanings that appear to be indissolubly attached to it, engages intimately with the psyche of the reader? Here, within the iconographic memory that predates the act of reading, these meanings are activated by the encounter with a text of great connotative force. To penetrate into the gothic castle by an act of reading is, thus, from Horace Walpole on, to undertake an interior journey that is transgressive and dangerous, a journey that, in the words of

---

[16] Joëlle Prungnaud, *Gothique et décadence: Recherches sur la continuité d'un mythe et d'un genre au XIXème siècle en Grande-Bretagne et en France* (Paris: Champion, 1997), 133.

Jean Roudaut, "however much it is presented to me as real, is for me simply the echo, in the domain of the real, of the journey which my own character undertakes within me. I become my own dream: my inner self no longer separates itself from the world where I act."[17] An eminently cultural object, that is to say a complex and crossbred one, *The Castle of Otranto* can serve both as the point of intersection for various intertextualities and as the place of origin for a genre of fiction, a sensibility, an aesthetic, that would disseminate their features through the different registers of the nineteenth-century cultural domain.

The novelist Ann Radcliffe (1764–1823) is most often credited with having given to the gothic novel the generic features that assured its success. Most notably in *The Mysteries of Udolpho, a Romance* (London, 1794) and *The Italian; or the Confessional of the Black Penitents, a Romance* (id., 1797), the novelist established a collection of *reproducible and adaptable* traits likely to please a wide public—increasingly including women—that preferred "long stories to short ones."[18] In fact, Radcliffe and her imitators adapted the formula of *The Castle of Otranto,* moving from a relatively brief and extremely pared-down narrative to novels in two, even three or four volumes. The "romance"—despite the appearance of this word at the end of the titles cited above—comes closer to the "novel," and ends up as a hybrid genre whose literary formula would enjoy a great future. From the "novel," the gothic novel borrowed the realist style—concrete, descriptive, detailed— already adopted by eighteenth-century picaresque English novelists. Unlike Walpole, Ann Radcliffe knew how to enter the psychology of her characters, notably that of her persecuted heroines, whose reactions of anxiety, anguish, terror, or hope are sympathetically described. Extended through time, the narrative could play to the maximum with the resources of a dramaturgy in which the effects of the sensational and the suspenseful captured the emotions of the reader. At the same time, in a manner that brings us gradually back again to the "romance," the curiosity of the reader is engaged in elucidating the meaning of the signs—or lures—that the novelist has strewn along the path of the mystery, leading up to the solution or denouement. And the mystery, in the Radcliffian model of the gothic novel, emanates from strange events attributable, at least in the disturbed mind of the desperate heroine, to

---

[17] Jean Roudaut, "Les demeures du roman noir," in *Ce qui nous revient: Autobiographie* (Paris: Gallimard, 1980), 159.

[18] Franco Moretti, *Atlas of the European Novel, 1800–1900* (London: Verso, 1998), 169 (see also ch. 3, sec. 5, "Theoretical Interlude: V. Center and Periphery"). Original edition: *Atlante del romanzo europeo 1800–1900* (Turin: Einaudi, 1997).

supernatural origins, before the novelist proposes to the reader, *in fine*, a rational, if improbable, explanation.

The literary—and/or paraliterary—possibilities of the works of Ann Radcliffe should now be evident. The thematics of the virtuous, persecuted heroine, which has its most notable source in Richardson, will assume other forms in the sentimental novel. The theatrical virtuosity of the narrative, its recourse to pathos and its manipulation of the reader's nerves, are all elements that resemble those of melodrama. The rhetoric of the enigma prepares the way for the detective novel. Finally, the dramatization of an imagination brought to a paroxysm of terror by events supposedly supernatural in origin looks ahead to the literature of the fantastic.

Only a few authors' names and titles of gothic novels have passed into posterity. Besides Walpole and Radcliffe, I should mention Clara Reeve (1729–1824) and *The Old English Baron* (1777), M. G. Lewis (1775–1818) and *The Monk* (1796), and Charles Robert Maturin (1782–1824) and *Melmoth the Wanderer* (1820). However, from 1790 onward, the works inspired by *The Castle of Otranto* multiplied, giving rise to a process that resembled—keeping in mind the technical limits of the period and the small number of literate[19]—a phenomenon of mass publishing and reading, accompanied by the inevitable overabundance of artifice and clichés. The repetitive suggestibility of the titles bears witness to this, and it can also be illustrated from the repertoire of several hundred gothic works indexed by Maurice Lévy.[20] The most frequent model of title falls into two parts linked by *or* in the eighteenth-century style, followed by a subtitle that indicates the genre. Thus, among many others, there is *"Correlia; or the Mystic Tomb, a romance*, by the Author of Humbert Castle, London (Lane and Newman, Minerve Press), 1802." The eponymous title (the heroine, in this case, or the "villain") is accompanied by a reference to places of action that are "gothic" in the broad sense and catalysts for recurring connotations of mystery, the supernatural, and death. The subtitle has, therefore, the function

---

[19] In his study of the "reading revolution" that occurred in Western Europe at the end of the eighteenth century, Reinhard Wittmann reviews the estimated number of readers and illiterate in this period (estimates always subject to caution). In England, the number of readers rose in 1790 to 1.5 percent of the population; in France, in 1789, at least 60 percent of the population were illiterate. In the German linguistic and cultural sphere around 1770, 15 percent of those over six years old were "potential" readers. Cf. ch. 11, "Was There a Reading Revolution at the End of the Eighteenth Century?" in Cavallo and Chartier, eds., *A History of Reading in the West*, 284–312.

[20] Maurice Lévy, "Bibliographie chronologique du roman 'gothique,' " 684–708, in M. Lévy, *Le roman "gothique" anglals (1764–1824)* (Toulouse: Publications de la Faculté des Lettres et Sciences Humaines de Toulouse, 1968).

of confirming what the reader had probably already decoded: the work's affiliation to the "gothic" genre.[21] Thus the titular strategies are already set in place that, in popular literature, are sufficiently explicit to seduce readers and confirm the sense that they are about to purchase a novel of the theme and genre they are seeking, but without destroying prematurely the readerly pleasure of discovery.

The burgeoning of the gothic novel also had a significant impact on the central feature and defining criterion of the genre: the architectural setting. We have already noted the minimal textual presence of the castle in Walpole's founding work and emphasized instead its evocative power and resonance in the reader's sensibility. Perhaps, if we are to believe readers and the conclusions of Maurice Lévy, the mere presence in the titles—and only in the titles—of terms belonging to the lexical field of Gothic architecture might have served as advertisement to incite readers to buy works that in fact did not belong to the literary category they desired. For the success of gothic novels had aroused envy among certain publishers and authors, who had sensed a windfall but had not taken care to ensure that the adjective *gothic* "always corresponded to the use of medieval architecture, the presence—more or less 'real'—of the supernatural, and an atmosphere of unease and mystery."[22] Of particular interest here is the way in which certain terms used in mass communication serve as catalysts for the oneiric and the imaginary.

The success of the gothic novel stems also from the repetition—and amplification—of the Radcliffian aesthetic formula, which combines realism and dream. The (moderately) realistic writing allows the reader easy access to the novelistic world. The referential illusion is similarly indispensable in creating the impression of familiarity against which, in contrast, the intrusion of the supernatural, real or supposed, will make the reader react. Indeed, it is certainly dream, the irrational, or escape in the broadest sense that the consumer of gothic novels seeks.

More precisely, the success of this genre is linked to its ability to offer the reader a temporary, libertarian, transgressive adventure. Once again, this type of fiction is perpetuating a long tradition of mass literature. The gothic setting constitutes a fantasmic place outside the law in which external order and morality are constantly threatened by the forces of Evil (or Desire): that is the essence of the "escape" offered to the reader by this kind of literature.

---

[21] Cf. Prungnaud, *Gothique et décadence*, 106ff.

[22] The three criteria of gothic fiction that Lévy adopts in selecting the works in his book, *Le roman "gothique,"* 388.

But whether in the middle of the narrative or at the moment of denouement, Order always ends up imposing its rule and in the most hypocritically conventional, or artificial and flamboyant manner (in *The Monk,* for example, the spectacular and edifying end of Ambrosio, who is expiating his sins when the devil, bearing him off on the wind, hurls him to his death on the jagged rocks). In the gothic novel, as in the literature of *colportage*, the commercial laws that gratify the "inadmissable" dreams of the reader must still pay the wages of morality and censorship in order to survive.

In England, as in France, the gothic and postgothic novel contributed widely to the development of the industrial publishing business. In England, the story of William Lane's Minerva Press is inseparable from the story of the gothic novel.[23] Between 1801 and 1805, this publishing house would print half of all gothic literary production, and between 1816 and 1820, three-quarters of it. William Lane promoted the diffusion of this narrative flood, in large part anonymous—Maurice Lévy speaks aptly of "collective writing"(442)—with a series of very skillful initiatives intended to revitalize the market. Not content with printing novels and selling them to booksellers, he took out newspaper advertisements to seek out new writers, then himself supplied his own network of "circulating libraries," making possible the direct loan of new books to those readers of modest social means unable to acquire the bound and costly "three-deckers" (novels in three volumes) on the regular circuit. The publishing adaptability of the gothic narrative and the success it acquired can also be measured by the fact that expensive editions and cheap popular editions existed side by side, reaching a vast public of different social levels. Some gothic texts were published as chapbooks. In France, the translators of Ann Radcliffe adapted her works in abbreviated form: long descriptions thus disappeared, foregrounding the narrative aspect of the novels and helping to accelerate their transformation into "paraliterature."[24] Later, in the last decade of the nineteenth century, the gothic novel would be published in installments at twenty centimes each, a particularly economical publishing formula.

Thus the gothic phenomenon would spread—with the possible dissolution of its original content—throughout the literary domain, from the English "penny dreadfuls" (inexpensive chapbooks, *feuilletons* in popular periodicals, or novels published in installments, between 1830 and 1860) to French *romans noirs* of the Restoration (1815–30) and Victorian novels (Wilkie Collins, Stevenson, Bram Stoker, Henry James) that adopted the

---

[23] Information drawn from Lévy, "Le marché de l'horreur," ch. 7, 468–71, in *Le roman "gothique."*
[24] Cf. Prungnaud, *Gothique et décadence*, 14.

settings and dramatic effects of the "sinister house." In the twentieth century, works as original or challenging as those of Mervyn Peake (1911–68) and his *Titus Groan* (1946) or of Julien Gracq and *Castle of Argol* (1938), also enter the realm of gothic intertextuality.

Finally, besides the fecundity of image and theme in the gothic novel, another essential characteristic is its irresistible tendency to provoke parody and pastiche. The genre's archetypal images or situations and its aesthetic of excess doubtless account for this phenomenon. The proliferation of gothic novels raises a question about the parodic character of some of them. In fact, several novels are open to a double reading: one on a first and "serious" level, the other at the meta- and ironic level. This is certainly the case with *Han d'Islande* (1823) by the young Victor Hugo.

Thus, many elements contributed to make of this genre an early sign of the industry of mass narrative that would lead to a golden age of popular reading in the second half of the nineteenth century. Among these elements were the extreme adaptability of the gothic novel, its position at the midpoint of the literary domain between literature for the educated and literature of *colportage* (at a time when the latter was progressively declining), the development of publishing into what was practically an industry, and the readerly enthusiasm this industry provoked.

The Roman-Feuilleton *from 1836 to 1900*

In the first decades of the nineteenth century, *colportage* literature remained the principal, if not the only, cultural vector to reach rural Western Europe and France in particular. In the same period, the gothic novel had exceptional publishing success thanks to the perfecting of preindustrial duplicating formulas. But with the phenomenon of the *roman-feuilleton*, mass culture would undergo an incredible evolution throughout the nineteenth century, toward the end of which the long written narrative—the novel— would arrive at a sort of golden age.

The development of mass literature and culture is directly linked to the industrial revolution, to massive displacements of rural populations to urban centers, rapid technical developments in transport and print reproduction, and to the progress of literacy. These social, economic, cultural, and technical transformations made possible the establishing of the first elements of a mass culture by means of a publishing process—the division of narrative into segments—whose history I will review. This process benefited from the support of various media and gave rise, quite rapidly, to the generic formula known as the *roman-feuilleton* or serialized novel. In the course of the nineteenth century, the serialized romantic novel centered on the character of the flamboyant hero (approx. 1836–75), would evolve into the "victim-novel" that was more realist in inspiration (approx. 1875–1900).

In France the *feuilleton* was initially a supplement to the newspaper, created by a journalist of moderate politics and a partisan of civil liberties, Louis-François Bertin, known as Bertin the Elder (1766–1841), who founded the *Journal des Débats* after the coup d'état of 18 Brumaire (November 9, 1799). The supplement made it possible to separate politics and literature at a time of strict censorship. It contained "programs of performances, advertising, booksellers' catalogues and announcements, articles of fashion, commercial offers and requests, etc., all leavened with literary trifles, charades, riddles, word puzzles, epigrams, and ephemera."[25] Two points are important to note here. On the one hand, this *feuilleton* in its original formula closely resembled an urban version of the booklets and almanacs in the *Bibliothèque bleue*, which were sold at the time in rural areas. On the other hand, we should note the entertaining character of the *feuilleton*, which aimed to distinguish itself from "serious" politics and appear "innocuous" to the censors. The *feuilleton* quickly became the "ground floor" (*rez-de-chaussée*) of the newspaper, that is, the lower part of the page, clearly separated from the rest of the paper.

From the end of the Restoration on, the publication of novels in episodes continued in literary journals, offering to a small and educated readership works by authors as varied as Balzac, Dumas, Vigny, and George Sand. But for readers who did not have the means to purchase these periodicals, or the multivolume novels costing the equivalent of a worker's monthly wage, publishers in the early 1830s proposed less expensive magazines: among these were *Le Magazin Pittoresque* (1833, publ. Hertzel) and *Le Musée des Familles* (1834, founded by Emile de Girardin).[26] Yet it was in the sector of the daily press dedicated mainly to politics, and always very expensive in the early years of the July Monarchy (1830), that a decisive change would occur. On July 1, 1836, the businessman and newspaper owner, Emile de Girardin, halved the cost of an annual subscription to a daily paper (eighty francs) by

---

[25] Cf. Gustava Vapereau, *Dictionnaire universel des littératures* (Paris: Hachette, 1876). See "feuilleton" and "Bertin (Louis-François)."

[26] On the phenomenon of the "popularization" of the press in France in the nineteenth century, there are two lucid and accessible studies in the "Que sais-je?" series of the Presses Universitaires de France: Lise Queffélec, *Le roman-feuilleton français au XIXe siècle* (no. 2466, 1989), esp. 11–12, and Alain-Michael Boyer, *La paralittérature* (no. 2673, 1992), esp. 58–59.

creating his own newspaper, *La Presse* (forty francs). His former associate, Armand Dutacq, soon after became his principal rival by creating *Le Siècle* along similar lines. Less expensive, the daily paper would also find its seductive power enhanced by the publication of serialized fictional works: its goal was, of course, to attract the mass of potential readers of modest means, whose numbers would compensate for the loss of income resulting from the lower cost of the newspaper. The goal was also to create a loyal following from this new public by condensing segments of narrative each day in the *"rez-de-chaussée."* But it should be noted that this influx of readers did not directly, or single-handedly, make the production of the newspaper profitable. From a commercial perspective this new readership simply provided an advertising base: it was the advertisements inserted into the high-circulation daily paper that made it profitable. This equation—captivating serial, *therefore* many readers, *therefore* many advertisements, *therefore* respectable profits—which was analyzed accurately by Alfred Nettement as early as 1845,[27] is worth emphasizing because it applies exactly to the mechanisms of modern media, such as television. The economic equilibrium of such media depends closely on advertising receipts, which in turn leads to a choice of programs whose "unifying" content is closely monitored by instruments measuring audience response.

Longer fiction—at the core of the new system set in place by Emile de Girardin and Dutacq, and soon imitated by all their colleagues—gradually took up increasingly more space in newspapers to the detriment of everything else, including short fiction (*nouvelles*). The first novel published in successive installments in a French daily paper, (*La Presse*) seems to have been *An Old Maid: Scenes from Provincial Life (La vieille fille; Scènes de la vie de province)* by Honoré de Balzac, which began publication on Sunday, October 23, 1836.[28] Within ten years, the public's enthusiasm for serialized novels would make it possible for the daily Parisian press to double its circulation. From 1838, *Le Siècle* began to insert advertisements to inform the public of the imminent publication of a new serial. From 1841, long works took over, and novelists had to adapt to the formal rules of this new genre, written especially to be prepublished in the dailies (cf. infra). Thus Balzac, whose narrative rhythm, thematics, and aesthetics were not easily adaptable

---

[27] Alfred Nettement, *Etudes critiques sur le feuilleton-roman* (Paris: Perrodil, 1845–46), vols. 1–3.

[28] Information drawn from a lively and well-informed article by René Guise, "Balzac et le roman-feuilleton," published 1964 in *L'Année Balzacienne* and reprinted in his book, *Balzac* (Presses Universitaires de Nancy, 1994), 57–104.

to these new conditions of publication (or to the new expectations of the public) that created among authors a frantic urge to rival and outbid each other, would find it increasingly difficult to sell his manuscripts to newspaper owners. The success of the serialized novel in the 1840s must therefore be examined carefully: while it may seem to contribute to the consecration of the genre of the novel among the wider public, it also appears to marginalize the more demanding—or less conventional—literary works. Balzac, an author in fashion in the early 1830s, despaired over his lack of success: his misfortune highlights the increasingly deeper rift in the cultural sphere around 1840 between "educated" and "popular" readers. Soulié, Dumas, and Sue reigned triumphant. "The year 1842 marks a key date in the history of the *roman-feuilleton*: one could argue that this is the moment when it wins the day."[29] The culminating event that confirms its success is certainly the exceptional enthusiasm aroused among the general public, and among writers, by the publication of Eugène Sue's *The Mysteries of Paris (Mystères de Paris)* in *Le Journal des Débats* (June 1842–October 1843). From this moment onward, the phenomenon of the serialized novel is established, determining the success, survival, or shipwreck of the dailies. The broadening of its readership, perceived both as the cultural equivalent and as the consequence of a certain political democratization, disturbed literary critics of the July Monarchy and conservatives in general, even after 1848: the *roman-feuilleton* would stimulate the imagination, dreams, irresponsibility, and individualism, and might also be the vehicle for subversive ideologies.[30] The public authorities tried to limit access to the *roman-feuilleton*: from 1850 to 1852, the Riancey Law imposed a special tax of five centimes per copy on every newspaper that published a fictional work.

The Second Empire, which censored political expression, scarcely interrupted the progress of the *roman-feuilleton* in that the genre contributed to the development of a culture that was entertaining, light, and, from an ideological point of view, innocuous. On February 2, 1863, the businessman Moïse Millaud founded a daily paper, *Le Petit Journal,* with the sale price of one sou (five centimes) a copy. Faster production, rail transport, depots in small towns, and aggressive advertising (posters, tracts) gave this new organ of the press recourse to the most modern techniques to reach the extended readership its very modest sale price required. The paper also took up again

---

[29] Guise, *Balzac,* 73.

[30] For a more detailed and nuanced study of these questions, see Lise Dumasy, ed., *La querelle du roman-feuilleton: Littérature, presse et politique, un débat precurseur (1836–1848)* (Grenoble: Presses de l'Université Stendhal, 1999). See especially the introduction, 16–19.

the old recipes from the sensationalist rags (*canards*) of the past: brief news stories, accounts of crimes and disasters, were the staple of these readers. Very quickly, *romans-feuilletons* entered the scene too. Millaud put into practice the principle of the culture industry that Edgar Morin would point to a century later in reference to modern media: the "homogenized syncretism" in which the sectors of "information" and "fiction" are brought together. Information is reduced to the *fait divers* (news item): "Everything that resembles the novelistic in real life is given priority" and symmetrically, on the fictional side, "realism dominates, or those events and fictional plots that have the semblance of reality."[31] Under the Third Republic, French daily newspapers, whether the quality press or the more popular press, were able to lower their sale price and offer serialized novels to their readers in the manner of *Le Petit Journal*, *Le Petit Parisien* (1876), *Le Matin* (1884), or *Le Journal* (1892).

The daily newspaper was, however, not the only media support for the serialized novel. During the nineteenth century, literary reviews continued to offer their readers very varied works, bringing together popular novelists and authors writing for an elite. During the Second Empire, "newspaper-novels" (*journaux-romans*)—inexpensive weekly papers, from five to ten centimes an issue—consisted essentially of two or three serialized novels. And a novel could just as readily be published in the form of illustrated installments at twenty centimes each. In these various publishing formats, which included the single- or multivolume novel more familiar to the modern reader, a particular type of longer fiction quite quickly developed and became almost fixed as a model of the genre: the *roman-feuilleton* or serialized novel, understood in the narrow, often pejorative sense of the term, whose distinctive traits—rules and constraints—I will now review. A particular *publishing procedure*—the division of the novel into sections or "installments" (*feuilletons*)—led automatically, following the logic of commerce, to the birth of a *genre of fiction*, the *roman-feuilleton*.

In 1839, when Sainte-Beuve published in *La Revue des Deux Mondes* his famous article directed against the *roman-feuilleton* and those popular authors who had "a single motto inscribed on their standard: Live by writing,"[32] he spoke of "industrial literature" but was obviously lashing out in these comments at an activity whose goals were too exclusively *commercial*. Yet it is more precisely this "industrial" character, in the literal sense of the

---

[31] Edgar Morin, "Le grand public," in *L'esprit du temps I: Névrose, 3rd ed.* (Paris: Grasset, 1975), 46–47.

[32] Cf. Dumasy, *La querelle du roman-feuilleton*, 29.

term, that defines the genre of the serialized novel. Indeed, the owners of the dailies, eager to respond to a huge demand for fiction, imposed on novelists norms of *productivity* that governed quantity, regularity, and standardization. These last two characteristics addressed in particular the insertion of the narrative into the journalistic framework. Beyond a certain number of textual characteristics that belong to the paraliterary model,[33] most notably the proliferation of events in the narrative to the detriment of description and analysis (a feature that Balzac, indulging simultaneously in a *pro domo* plea, would vigorously denounce),[34] the immutable structure of the daily "slice" of narrative should be emphasized. It aimed to provoke in the reader a sense of dissatisfaction, curiosity, frustration, and an impatience for the "to be continued . . ." episode of the next issue, the famous "suspense effect" that would make the reader of today into the buyer of tomorrow. We should also remember that the serialized novel, a finely calibrated cultural product subject to the reactions of its readers, possesses great plasticity: if unsuccessful, it can be moved quickly along to its conclusion; if successful, it can be prolonged indefinitely. The serialized novel is thus constructed on the principle René Guise has called "a relay structure"[35] whose simplest form—one that dominated in the early years (1836–1840)—juxtaposed a series of almost autonomous episodes that could be published at successive intervals. In a sort of *narrative chain*, the relay that could hold the interest of the reader (the *memory* of pleasure and the *prospect* of enjoying it again) depended generally on the reappearance of the same hero at the center of a dramatic world that remained unchanged in its settings, period, and types of narrative event. If the narrative mechanism became more complicated, the result was a *récit filé* (extended narrative) in which a new plot began *before* the resolution of the episode in progress and continued on into the next. This second kind of relay, which played more particularly on the curiosity and emotion of the reader, seems more "solid," more effective than the first mode. Finally, in an

---

[33] See the conclusion of D. Couégnas, *Introduction à la paralittérature* (Paris: Editions du Seuil, 1992).

[34] Balzac wrote: "Nothing reveals the impotence of an author more than the piling up of facts. Without forcing my observation into a theory, I would note how few facts there are in the works of skillful novelists (*Werther, Clarissa, Adolphe, Paul et Virginie*). Talent reveals itself in the depiction of the causes which give rise to facts, in the mysteries of the human heart whose emotions are neglected by historians" (from "Lettres sur la littérature" in the *Revue Parisienne*, 1840, cited by Guise, *Balzac*, 72).

[35] Cf. "Les Pléiades," roman-feuilleton?" in *Tapis-Franc, Revue du Roman Populaire* 6 (1993–94), an issue dedicated to the *Recherches en littérature populaire* by René Guise, 98ff., to which this analysis is indebted.

even more complex narrative process, plots developed simultaneously and intersected with one another from one episode to the next, even multiplying, to form a *récit tressé* (braided narrative), which enhanced the richness and suppleness of the narrative.

The great popular novelists of the July Monarchy (Sue, Soulié, Dumas), and then of the Second Empire (Ponson du Terrail, Féval), were virtuosos in exploiting all the technical possibilities of industrial literature, at times extending their narratives over more than two hundred daily "segments." Their works were, therefore, virtually *unending*: even the death of the author did not necessarily interrupt the saga if, as was the case with the Féval family, the son took up the pen in place of his father. When the publication of a serial was about to end, the editors of the dailies, anxious not to lose the interest and curiosity of the readers, would adopt the technique of the *récit filé* described above and begin to publish a new serial before the previous one had ended.[36] The desire for fiction and dream is inexhaustible, and the story of the *roman-feuilleton* bears witness to this throughout the nineteenth century: in its major incarnations (romantic-heroic, 1836–75, then realist-sentimental, 1875–1900); in the repetition of the writerly and narrative formulas that were most effective in mass communication; and in the development of subgenres that offered particular themes and fictional contexts able to attract specific categories of readers.

As the phenomenon recedes further into the past, we tend to identify the serialized novel primarily with its romantic form. This model came to the fore during the July Monarchy with Eugène Sue's (1804–57) *The Mysteries of Paris* (1842–43) and *The Wandering Jew* (*Le Juif errant* 1844–45), and continued to evolve, at the cost of an evident "deconstruction of its romantic heritage" to borrow Lise Queffélec's expression,[37] until about 1875. The last great representatives of this aesthetic, which they adapted and transformed, are Ponson du Terrail, whose hero, Rocambole, animates *Les drames de Paris* (1857–70), and Paul Féval, author of *Habits noirs* (1863–75).

With *The Mysteries of Paris*, Sue gave rise to a cultural and media phenomenon whose effects went far beyond the borders of France. What strikes readers immediately, as we follow the adventures of the fascinating and improbable Prince Rodolphe de Gerolstein, who restores some of the order of divine justice to the impoverished quarters of the Parisian capital, is the

---

[36] For more on these questions of the editorial and narrative "relays" of the serialized novel, the techniques of suspense, and the "hermeneutic" chain of the mystery novel, see D. Couégnas, *Fictions, énigmes, images: Lectures (para?) littéraires* (Presses Universitaires de Limoges, 2001).

[37] *Le roman-feuilleton français au XIXe siècle*, 60.

Ponson du Terrail, *Rocambole* (1857), vol. 1 of the series
"Les drames de Paris," cover illustration by Gino Starace
(Paris: Edition Fayard. 1905–14).

Private collection of Daniel Couégnas

extravagant, creative scope of this fictional project. The reader is taken into
a sort of literary "summa" (*oeuvre-somme*) that possesses all the characteristics, ambitions, excesses, and contrasts ascribed to the romantic sensibility
and aesthetic. It is difficult to characterize either by theme or genre this
work of fiction that traverses the most varied social milieus—worldly, popular, criminal—and prefigures all the important transformations of the serialized novel to come. While Sue's novel had recourse, day after day, to every

dramatic technique that could touch or trouble the reader, it also resonated with enormous hope for social change, hope in whose very magnitude lay the seeds of disenchantment. The tumultuous past of the characters (Rodolphe, Fleur-de-Marie), their contrasts and passionate excesses, their sins, their generosity or piety, leads the narrative toward a conclusion shaded in half-tones and bathed in a delicious melancholia. In the last chapter ("13 January, Rodolphe to Clemence"), the hero writes: "one experiences a terrible pleasure in recounting a hideous pain." And even though the novels of Dumas, equally successful, do not carry the same message of social change, they too carry traces of the sensibility of the age with their extravagant ambitions and heroic energy, tarnished, however, by the awareness of some melancholic lack, a fundamental dissatisfaction, a sense of forever-unrealized human ambition. In the last lines of Dumas's *The Vicomte de Bragelonne* (1847–48), d'Artagnan is dying, and, as he considers the limits of his actions on this earth, he murmurs: "Athos, Porthos, farewell.—Aramis, for ever, adieu!"[38] For his part, Dantès, the hero of the *The Count of Monte-Cristo* (1845), finally retreats from the theater of a world in which he has nothing more to accomplish, concluding a journey of initiation where pride has ceded the way to humility and remorse.

Such melancholic emotion does not touch readers of *Rocambole* or *Habits noirs*, works that, nevertheless, like the serialized novels of high romanticism, also display the phantasms of a Promethean omnipotence in the service of the oppressed and unfortunate. For the formal structure of these narratives had, in fact, transformed the content of the works and their scope. When throughout the Second Empire and into the beginning of the Third Republic, the *roman-feuilleton* became preoccupied with its own "interminability" above all other traits and insisted more and more heavily on its techniques to prolong the narrative and complicate the plot, the genre approached caricature and self-pastiche (sometimes deliberately, as with Ponson du Terrail) or turned to the ironic mode (Féval). In place of *feuilletons* there were "chains of *feuilletons*," series in which novelistic time became cyclical and heroes no longer aged, unlike Dumas's characters whom we would rediscover, after the long trilogy of the *Three Musketeers (Les trois mousquetaires),* in *Twenty Years After (Vingt ans après),* and then again in *Ten Years Later (Dix ans plus tard).*[39]

The elimination of this temporal dimension from the narrative, rendering

---

[38] *Les grands romans d'A. Dumas, Les mousquetaires, III,* collection "Bouquins" (Paris: Laffont, 1991), 850.

[39] Subtitle of *Vicomte de Bragelonne.*

the heroes eternal and dehumanizing them completely, certainly contributed to the undermining of the identificatory function of reading—a fundamental element of paraliterary pragmatics. That is probably one of the reasons among others, why, in the last quarter of the nineteenth century, the serialized novel, more tightly focused on the character of the victim, turned to other emotive and "lachrymose" resources and inscribed pathos within different fictional settings, imitating to some extent the realist-naturalist aesthetic. With Xavier de Montépin (1824–1902) and his *Porteuse de pain* (1884), Jules Mary (1851–1922) and *A Man's Shadow (Roger la honte*, 1886–87), Pierre Decourcelle (1856–1926) and *Le crime d'une sainte* (1889–90), Emile Richebourg (1833–98) and *L'enfant du faubourg* (1875), or Georges Ohnet (1847–1918) and *The Ironmaster* (*Le maître de forges*, 1882), it was no longer a question of defying universal Evil or Injustice by placing oneself on the margins of society to denounce it, or setting oneself arrogantly apart and above human law. The victim-novel distilled moral conformism and social conservatism. When it represented characters from the underclasses, they ended up winning the upper hand over the agents of their misfortune, individual incarnations of a timeless Evil that exonerated society from all responsibility. At the conclusion, we cannot but agree with Jeanne Fortier, the heroine of *La porteuse de pain,* who declared with emotion in the last lines of the novel: "Ah! God is good!"

It should now be evident how much the heroic-romantic novel and the realist-sentimental victim-novel differed from one another: yet such a statement is also problematic, since these two variants of the popular *roman-feuilleton* attracted, successively, similar interest from a broad readership. If the novel in the nineteenth century was "popular," it was thanks not only to the publishing vehicle of the *feuilleton*, since the works prepublished in this manner continued to inspire readers when they were published later in a volume or adapted for the theater. The division into daily installments, which shaped this fictional writing around the effects of the "to be continued" formula, does not by itself explain or describe the specific elements—if indeed there are any—that define the *unity* and *identity* of mass literature, whether heroic or sentimental. If there is any specificity—and I have spoken elsewhere of "paraliterary criteria"[40]—it was already a feature of the *Bibliothèque bleue,* of fairy tales, and of gothic fiction. For a fictional narrative to offer the best model possible for mass communication, it must possess certain paratextual features (presentation, cover, title) that instantly reveal to the potential reader the precise nature of the reading contract. Such novel-writing will

---

[40] Cf. *Introduction à la paralittérature.*

tend to exploit repetitively a repertoire of techniques (places, backgrounds, social settings, periods, dramatic situations, characters), most often without any ironic distance. The referential illusion must be established, blurring awareness of the act of reading. The text produces redundant meanings, "naturalized" into a single mode, lacking nuance or dialogism. Narrativity dominates, to the exclusive benefit of the dramatic and suspenseful. Finally, characters are reduced to allegorical Manichean figures, which encourages the most basic kinds of identification.

This description, seemingly so reductive, should not hide the fact that mass literature in general (and the nineteenth-century serialized novel in particular) is fully able, despite a strong tendency toward repetition and stereotype, to diversify and branch into subgenres that can captivate a variety of readerships. The nineteenth century thus would seem to be the century of the *roman-feuilleton*, the popular novel, and, even more, the golden age of reading, while print, with its extension into the realms of theater and song, is the main, if not the only, vehicle of mass culture. Later, at the turn of the century (the Belle Epoque), popular literature would evolve toward new fictional forms, while the narrative industry would, in a parallel development, find new direction through the medium of cinematography.

Translated by Mary Harper

CATHERINE GALLAGHER

The Rise of Fictionality

No feature of the novel seems to be more obvious and yet more easily ignored than its fictionality. Like *prose, fictional* is one of those definitive terms
("a novel is a long, fictional prose narrative") that most historians of the
form have tacitly agreed to leave unexamined; we tend to let it lie dormant
in our critical analyses as well. And yet we all know that it is active and determining in our culture, for we cannot walk into a bookstore or read the
Sunday papers without noticing that the primary categorical division in our
textual universe is between "fiction" and "nonfiction." Perhaps we imagine
that a distinction so pervasive and secure can get along without our help,
that it would be redundant to define such a self-evident trait. Or, perhaps we
find that the theories of fictionality debated by philosophers and narratologists finally tell us too little about either the history or the specific properties
of the novel to repay the difficulty of mastering them. Moreover, since none
of the theories has become dominant among the initiated, perhaps most of
us think the exercise is futile and are consequently content simply to know
fiction when we see it. Troubling this contentment, but perhaps also aug-
menting the sense of analytical futility, has been the aggressive extension of
the term by poststructural theorists to cover all forms of narration, even all
forms of meaning-production. Neglected by scholars and critics of the novel
and highjacked by philosophers and postmodernists, fictionality as a specific
feature of the genre certainly needs recovery. And yet, other reasons for its
neglect, reasons truly intrinsic to the form, also need analyzing.

This essay will try not only to retrieve novelistic fictionality for analysis
but also to explain why we have difficulty keeping it at the forefront of our
attention, why it incessantly slips behind other features or disappears into
terms like *narrative* and *signification*. As a historian of the form's British variety, I tend to approach the issue through the evidence provided by the
mideighteenth-century novel in English, in which an explicit and ongoing
discourse of fictionality developed. By entering the subject in this way, I am
following the Anglo-American practice of viewing the novel and the romance as separate genres, and I hope to show that the nature of fictionality
changed so dramatically in these mideighteenth-century British narratives
that they do constitute a new form. Moreover, the kind of fictionality they
claim for themselves became the norm throughout Europe and America in
the nineteenth century, and we still anticipate encountering it when we pick

up a new novel today. Undoubtedly the fictionality of the eighteenth-century British novel was atypical, but its atypicality established our expectations. In these works we can hear what the novel had to say about fictionality in its infancy, when it had the greatest need to differentiate itself from competing genres.

And what it had to say, both explicitly in its many metafictional digressions and implicitly in its practice, was by no means univocal. From the outset, novelistic fictionality has been unique and paradoxical. The novel is not just one kind of fictional narrative among others; it is the kind in which and through which fictionality became manifest, explicit, widely understood, and accepted. The historical connection between the terms *novel* and *fiction* is intimate; they were mutually constitutive. And yet the novel has also been widely regarded as a form that tried, for at least two centuries, to hide its fictionality behind verisimilitude or realism, insisting on certain kinds of referentiality and even making extensive truth claims. If a genre can be thought of as having an attitude, the novel has seemed ambivalent toward its fictionality—at once inventing it as an ontological ground and placing severe constraints upon it. Novelists apparently liberated fictionality, for eighteenth-century practitioners abandoned earlier writers' serious attempts to convince readers that their invented tales were literally true or were at least about actual people. Candidly and explicitly differentiating their works from the kinds of referentiality proffered by neighboring genres, these writers coaxed their readers to accept the imaginative status of their characters. And yet the same eighteenth-century novelists also seem to have imprisoned and concealed fictionality by locking it inside the confines of the credible. The novel, in short, is said both to have discovered and to have obscured fiction. Mutually contradictory as they may seem, both assertions are valid, and I hope to show that revealing and concealing fiction in the novel are one and the same process.

There is mounting historical evidence for the first, more unusual, proposition—that the novel discovered fiction. It used to be assumed that fictions form a part of every culture's life, and if evidence for the assumption were needed, one could point to the seemingly universal existence of stories that apparently do not make referential truth claims, such as fables and fairy tales. It seemed to follow that something resembling the modern acceptance of the word *fiction* must be universally comprehended and the phenomenon at least tacitly sanctioned. A general human capacity to recognize discourses that, in Sir Philip Sidney's words, "nothing affirmeth, and therefore never lieth" (Sidney 1962: 29), made the term appear unproblematically applicable to narratives from all times and places. Recent scholarship has shown, though, that this modern *concept* of narrative fiction developed slowly in early-modern Europe, a development reflected in the changing uses of the word in English. From its common use to denote, "that which is fashioned or framed; a device, a fabric, . . . whether for the purpose of deception or otherwise" (*Oxford English Dictionary*, 2nd ed., s.v. "fiction") or "something that is imaginatively invented," a new usage came into existence at the turn of the seventeenth century: "The species of literature which is concerned with the narration of imaginary events and the portraiture of imaginary characters; fictitious composition." As this sense of the word gained greater currency, mainly in the eighteenth century, an earlier frequent meaning of "deceit, dissimulation, pretense" became obsolete. Although consistently contrasted with the veridical, fictional narration ceased to be a subcategory of dissimulation as it became a literary phenomenon. If the etymology of the word tells us anything, fiction seems to have been discovered as a discursive mode in its own right as readers developed the ability to tell it apart from both fact and (this is the key) deception.

In one guise, but only one, this categorical discrimination was probably always widely practiced: earlier fictions could be distinguished from lies if they were manifestly improbable. Honest fictions, that is, were expected to distinguish *themselves* by their incredibility. If a narration did not even solicit belief, it met Sir Philip Sidney's criterion for "poesy": affirming "nothing," it could not lie. When the obvious nonexistence of its reference separated it from both truth and falsehood, even the most naive readers could recognize fiction. Sir Philip Sidney was far from naive, but even he defended "poesie" on the grounds that its "golden" creations would not be mistaken for our brazen, commonplace world.

Because of their blatant incredibility, therefore, numerous preeighteenth-century genres would meet the test set by almost all modern theorists of fictionality. Whether they conceive of fictions in terms of possible worlds, pretended illocutionary acts, gestalts, or language games, our theorists now start from Sidney's premise about "poesie": fiction somehow suspends, deflects, or otherwise disables normal referential truth claims about the world of ordinary experience. Romances, fables, allegories, fairy stories, narrative poems—all premodern genres that were not taken to be the literal truth but that obviously had no intention to deceive—may be described in modern terms as drastically modifying or altogether suspending "the 'referentialability' of assertions or claims" (Schmidt 1996: 36). They may, therefore, be retroactively and, we should notice, *anachronistically* proclaimed fictional, even though they were not so described at the time or grouped together under any single category, even that of Sidney's "poesie."

Fictionality that operates only in this one way, however, cannot be said to stand on its own as a separate concept from fantasy. Plausible stories are thus the real test for the progress of fictional sophistication in a culture, and in the early eighteenth century, a likely fiction was still considered a lie by the common reader. While the only reliable "operator" of fictionality was mere incredibility, believability was tantamount to a truth claim. As long as they did not contain talking animals, flying carpets, or human characters who are much better or much worse than the norm, narratives seemed referential in their particulars and were hence routinely accused of either fraud or slander. Most, moreover, were guilty as charged. The majority of seventeenth- and early-eighteenth-century credible prose narratives—including those we now call fictions—were meant to be read either as factual accounts or as "allegorical" reflections on contemporary people and events. When Daniel Defoe published *Robinson Crusoe* in 1719, for example, he certainly intended to deceive the public, and he succeeded. A year later, in the preface to a sequel, Defoe, under pressure to admit that he had lied, still insisted on the historical accuracy of his tale but then, inconsistently alleged that each incident in the "imaginary" story alluded to an episode in a "real Story" (Defoe 1903: xi). He accordingly clung to particularity of reference, even as he shifted the grounds of his claim from literal truth to allegorical allusion.

To take an example of the opposite form of deception, the literary field at the time was crowded with scandalmongers; one, Delarivier Manley, declared that she had published a mere work of the imagination when she was prosecuted for libeling prominent aristocrats in 1709 (Morgan 1986: 146–51). Her book had all the usual marks of libelous allegory: an imaginary kingdom populated by nobles who are monstrous but nevertheless recognizable exaggerations of well-known government ministers and ladies of the court. The "allegory" lent some legitimacy to Manley's alibi of fiction, but her work was popular mainly because readers believed that it revealed the secrets of the powerful, that it referred to contemporary individuals. A third example of the referential imperative can be found in the form that Manley parodied: romance. Personal allegory was also the mainstay of this genre, which is most often thought of as the novel's immediate fictional precursor. Despite their later associations with unbridled fantasy, the seventeenth-century French romances, on which the English modeled theirs, were originally written and read as disguised "reflections" on the great. The romances exalted particular courtly lords and ladies, turning them into exemplars of the virtues, whereas the *chroniques scandeleuse*s, as the later libelous satires à la Manley were called, mocked the romance conventions and reversed their judgments. Neither form, however, sought to dispense with referential truth claims about specific individuals. Stories that were both plausible and received as narratives about purely imaginary individuals—a category with which all nineteenth-century European publics would be thoroughly comfortable and familiar—were still exceedingly rare in the first quarter of the eighteenth century.

Two things were lacking: (1) a *conceptual category* of fiction, and (2) believable stories that did not solicit belief. Novels supplied both of these simultaneously, which explains their paradoxical relation to fiction. Fictionality only became visible when it became credible, because it only needed conceptualizing as the difference between fictions and lies became less obvious, as the operators of fictionality became multiple and incredibility lost its uniqueness. It gained a discourse of its own as it became less blatant, less likely to discover itself: the less overt it seemed, the more it had to emerge into conceptual prominence. Because the novel defined itself against the scandalous libel, it used fiction as the diacritical mark of its differentiation, requiring that the concept of fiction take on greater clarity and definition. However, since the definition included plausibility, the history of *fiction* seems simultaneously to trace a movement from greater to lesser visibility. As the novel distinguished itself through fictionality, its fictionality also differentiated itself from previous incredible forms. Hence we have another way of imagining the paradox: the novel slowly opens the conceptual space of fictionality in the process of seeming to narrow its practice.

The discursive shifts leading up to the English novel's discovery of fiction through probable narration have received considerable scholarly attention in recent decades, so we now have multiple explanations for what used to be called "the rise of the novel." Whereas an older generation of literary critics had taken fiction for granted as a transhistorical constant and viewed the novel's achievement as the addition of realism, more recent scholars have correlated the simultaneous appearance of fictionality and the novel. Lennard Davis, for example, argues that the novel developed out of what he calls the "news-novel matrix"—a tangled mass of journalism, scandal, and political and religious controversy. He points out that in order to avoid prosecution, writers like Delarivier Manley turned increasingly to the alibi of fiction, bringing the idea into sharper focus and greater respectability (Davis 1983). Despite their own bad faith in appealing to the category, they nevertheless helped install it as an innocent alternative to libelous referential stories. Even the scandalous impulses of such allegories propelled them toward increasingly more elaborate and credible settings and narratives, which could be enjoyed for their own sakes without reference to the persons satirized. No matter how insincerely invoked, therefore, the fiction alibi was connected to the vivacity and detailed complexity of the story world (Gallagher 1994). Michael McKeon, to take another example, studies a development internal to the genre of romance that eventually expanded the idea of truth to include verisimilitude. The movement from romance to novel, he demonstrates, is part of a larger epistemological shift from a narrow construction of truth as historical accuracy to a more capacious understanding that could include truth conceived as mimetic simulation. The widespread acceptance of verisimilitude as a form of truth, rather than a form of lying, founded the novel as a genre (McKeon 2002). It also created the category of fiction.

Before looking at the wider social forces surrounding these discursive processes, we should pause here to notice how limited and specific the *non-referentiality* of credible fiction was imagined to be at this stage. The global suspension of truth claims touted by Sir Philip Sidney that would make lying impossible was not yet a licensed move in the language game of the novel. Some idea of truth seems to have ruled this discourse of credible fiction, leading historians to see the eighteenth-century novel as still partially shackled by outmoded criteria. To get a clear view of the early novel's contradictory relation to fiction, we have to know exactly what form of reference it renounced and what corollary sort it embraced. Then we can see how the ban on one type of reference made another type necessary and how probability itself was rediscovered as a sign of the fictional.

The key mode of nonreferentiality in the novel was, and still is, that of proper names. Different as their tactics were, Daniel Defoe, Delarivier Manley, and even the idealizing romancers of the seventeenth century were all making moves in a previous language game that assumed a correspondence between a proper name in a believable narrative and an embodied individual in the world. Hence Defoe asserted the existence of such an individual, whether actually named "Robinson Crusoe" or allegorically referred to by that name, and Manley's style covertly made the same assertion. A cluster of midcentury novels, however, articulated a new assumption for a new form: novels are about nobody in particular. That is, the proper names do not take specific individuals as their referents, and hence none of the specific assertions made about them can be verified or falsified.

Henry Fielding's narrator in *Joseph Andrews* (1742) explicates the superiority of the new dispensation and its virtues, remonstrating that he describes "not men, but manners; not an individual, but a species." His characterizations are not intended "to expose one pitiful wretch to the small and contemptible circle of his acquaintance; but to hold the glass to thousands in

their closets that they may contemplate their deformity, and endeavor to reduce it, and thus by suffering private mortification may avoid public shame.
This places the boundary between, and distinguishes the satirist from the li-
beler: for the former privately corrects faults for the benefit of the person,
like a parent; the latter publicly exposes the person himself, as an example
to others, like an executioner" (Fielding 1967: 189). Making it clear that the
new form (Fielding called it "the comic epic in prose") must be distinguished from what had previously been called the novel (scandalous productions like Delarivier Manley's), this narrator insists that the distinction is
based on the renunciation of "malicious application" or personal reference.
At stake, as he notes, is the charge of libel, but he doesn't simply declare the
immunity of his own work from prosecution. He goes on to proclaim the
greater humanity and ambition of this new form: it can refer to a whole class
of people in general (as well as in private) because its proper names do not
refer to persons in particular.

The founding claim of the form, therefore, was a nonreferentiality that
could be seen as a greater referentiality. What distinguished the new writers
from libelers was the insistence that the human referent of the text was a
generalization about and not an extratextual, embodied instance of a
"species." Certainly the novel provided imaginary instances, but it renounced reference to individual examples in the world. The fictionality
defining the novel inhered in the *creation* of instances, rather than their mere
selection, to illustrate a class of persons. Because a general referent was indicated through a particular, but explicitly nonreferential, fictional individual,
the novel could be judged generally true even though all of its particulars are
merely imaginary. The claims to truth and fiction were not in contradiction
with each other; practitioners understood that the novel's general applicabil-
ity depended on the overt fictitiousness of its particulars, since taking examples from among real people would only confuse the issue of reference. Because they had dispensed with the individual referents, the novelists'
characterizations could only have referential value by pointing to what
Fielding calls a "species."

Fielding and his peers rarely stressed the novelty of this mode of reference. Instead, they pointed to Manley and her ilk as degenerate moderns and
harked back to Aristotle as the classical founding theorist of their own practice. Invoking the *Poetics* gave them not only a thoroughly respectable pedigree but also a ready-made equation between the probable and the fictive:

> From what has been said it is clear too that the poet's job is not to tell what
> has happened but the kind of things that *can* happen, i.e., the kind of events

that are possible according to probability or necessity. For the difference between the historian and the poet is not in their presenting accounts that are versified or not versified . . . ; rather, the difference is this: the one tells what has happened, the other the kind of things that can happen. And in fact that is why the writing of poetry is a more philosophical activity, and one to be taken more seriously, than the writing of history. For poetry tells us rather the universals, history the particulars. "Universal" means what kinds of thing a certain kind of person will say or do in accordance with probability or necessity, which is what poetic composition aims at, tacking on names afterward. (*Poetics*, ch. 9 [Else 1967: 301–2])

Aristotle also explicitly links the probability of the fable to the nonreferentiality of its proper names in one of his scattered remarks about comedy. Claiming that the nonparticularity of comic imitation is "obvious," he explains, "Now in the case of comedy this has become clear; for they construct the plot with the use of probabilities, then (and not until then) assign whatever names occur to them, rather than composing their work about a particular individual as the 'iambic' poets do" (*Poetics*, ch. 9). Reasserting Aristotle's point, midcentury novelists stressed that probability was a sign of fictionality as well as a mode of reference; it was designed to switch off the personal reference of proper names.

Of course, the elaboration of this theory ran into immediate difficulties. To begin with, novelistic personae, even when invented on purpose to exemplify classes of persons, quickly proved too specific to cover all the cases in a "species." The excessive and irrelevant detail of any individualized instance tended to obscure the view of its supposed class, and consequently mideighteenth-century authors entered into numerous disputes over how typical a character's behavior needed to be before it could be judged "probable." Samuel Richardson, replying to the Swiss writer Albrecht von Haller, for example, defended his character Lovelace against charges of improbably detestable behavior by giving details from the novel about the specific circumstances in which Lovelace operated. The exchange between von Haller and Richardson reveals what Robert Newsom calls the "antinomy of fictional probability":

> von Haller drew evidence from the real world, and Richardson responded with evidence from the novel; the evidence of the real world functions to determine the probabilities associated with the set of young men to which Lovelace belongs . . . while Richardson's evidence particularizes the individual case and so defines precisely which set Lovelace belongs to. . . .

Inevitably the set of "real" young men becomes a set with only one member
and the question ultimately posed is the circular one: How probable is it that
a young man exactly like Lovelace would behave exactly like Lovelace?
(Newsom 1994: 92–93)

Richardson, that is, preserves Lovelace's probability by reducing his referential scope to almost nothing. The problem of individuation continued to
complicate the claims of fictionality, as we will see when we take up the issue
of proper names in greater detail. Let us note for now that novelists signaled
the nonparticular referential status of their characters in a seemingly converse way: by naming them "in exactly the same way as particular individuals are named in ordinary life" (Watt 1971: 18). Given that, to quote Thomas
Hobbes, "a Proper Name bringeth to mind one thing only; Universals recall
anyone of many" (Hobbes 1964: 16), ascribing ordinary English proper
names, such as "Tom Jones" or "Pamela Andrews," is a topsy-turvy way of
referring to a type. But these paradoxes only made it all the more necessary
for novelists to explain and defend what they were up to.

In England, between the time when Defoe insisted that Robinson Crusoe
was a real individual (1720) and the time when Henry Fielding urged just as
strenuously that his characters were not representations of actual specific
people (1742), a discourse of fictionality appeared in and around the novel,
specifying new rules for its identification and new modes of nonreference.
And it is on the basis of this overt and articulated understanding that the
novel may be said to have discovered fiction. What Fielding had that Defoe
lacked was not an excuse for fictionality but a use for it as a special way of
shaping knowledge through the fabrication of particulars. Later in the century, disclaimers like Fielding's were no longer necessary, for the public had
been trained to read novels as stories about thoroughly imaginary (if representative) people, names without singular, specific referents in the world. The
transformation might have begun earlier and been completed later in France,
which had a lengthy and highly sophisticated discourse of the *vraisemblable*
to explain the manner of reference found in courtly romances but only slowly
developed a comparable conceptualization of the commonplace and quotidian fictions found in novels. Madame de Lafayette has been credited with the
presentation of characters intended and received as fully fictional in *La
princesse de Clèves* (1678), and yet Diderot's friend, the Marquis de Crois-
mare, found it difficult to conceive of the nature of *La Religieuse* (1796) not
only because he was being purposely deceived but also because the story
seemed too plausible and realistically rendered to have been invented. In his
world of discourse, probability was not yet an indicator of fiction. Fictionality

seems to have been but faintly understood in the infant United States at the end of the eighteenth century, for the work that is often identified as the first American novel, *The Power of Sympathy* (1789), is actually an instance of the earlier *chronique scandeleuse* form. In Spain, Cervantes pioneered the art of writing about nobody in the seventeenth century, but the form of the novel did not undergo a continuous development there.

As the example of *Don Quixote* demonstrates, there were novels before the eighteenth century, and as the citations of Aristotle and Sir Philip Sidney indicate, the components for an understanding of fictionality were also available. And yet, these did not gel into either a common knowledge of the concept or a sustained and durable novelistic practice until they coincided in the eighteenth-century English novel. All the elements, we might say, were present in several other times and places, but apparently no strong need prompted their assembly. What was it about England in the early eighteenth century that provided that cultural imperative? England's early secularism, scientific enlightenment, empiricism, capitalism, materialism, national consolidation, and the rise of the middle class have all been named as constituents of the general background against which the novel emerged. These have, though, usually been associated with what Ian Watt called "formal realism." England, the story goes, developed a middle-class readership earlier than other countries, and the middle class wanted to read about itself, to have the world described in elaborate circumstantial detail, as well as to imagine the simultaneous existence of others in far-flung parts of the nation (Anderson 1991: 22–36). As practical and materialistic readers, it continues, they rejected fantasy for probability and preferred the familiar to the exotic. This story thus explains, not the discovery of fiction, but its subordination to the reality principle, assuming that fiction was already an established and recognized thing that only needed to be brought down to earth by middle-class cultural hegemony.

We have just been observing, though, that early novels stressed their departure from plausible narratives with referential assumptions, not from improbable fantasies. In their competition for discursive space, they emphasized not their realism but their fictionality, so we seek some indication of what it was about early modernity in the first capitalist nation that propagated not just *realist* fiction but realist *fiction*. What is the modernity-fictionality connection? Answering this question should also help us to specify more clearly the *disposition* of novelistic fictionality, to explore what it means to read a narrative as credible while thinking it affirms nothing.

Modernity is fiction-friendly because it encourages disbelief, speculation, and credit. The early novel's thematic emphases on gullibility, innocence deceived, rash promises extracted, and impetuous emotional and financial investments of all kinds point to the habit of mind it discourages: faith. The reckless wholeheartedness of its heroes and heroines, their guileless vulnerability, solicits our affectionate concern and thereby activates our skepticism on their behalf. Hence, while sympathizing with innocent credulity, the reader is trained in an attitude of disbelief, which is flattered as superior discernment. The readers of these early novels were encouraged to anticipate problems, make suppositional predictions, and see possible outcomes and alternative interpretations. In short, the reader, unlike the character, occupies the lofty position of one who speculates on the action, entertaining various hypotheses about it. These thematically triggered reactions coincide with and magnify the more abstract formal demand that early fiction writers placed on their readers: asking them to take the reality of the story itself as a kind of suppositional speculation. They did not, to be sure, expect their readers to preface each sentence mentally with the illocutionary reservation, "the reader will suppose that. . . ," but by explaining that his characters are not to be taken for specific individuals, Fielding, for example, dispenses with the requirement that readers believe the story. In fact, he actively discourages it. Belief is replaced with what one theorist calls "ironic credulity" (Martinez-Bonati 1981: 35). Novels seek to suspend the reader's disbelief, as an element is suspended in a solution that it thoroughly permeates. Disbelief is thus the condition of fictionality, prompting judgments, not about the story's reality, but about its *believability*, its plausibility.

Novels promoted a disposition of ironic credulity enabled by optimistic incredulity; one is dissuaded from believing the literal truth of a representation so that one can instead admire its likelihood and extend enough credit to buy into the game. Such flexible mental states were the sine qua non of modern subjectivity. Everyone seemed to benefit from them. For example, they may have eased the way into the modern affective family. Since marriageable young people were given somewhat greater freedom of choice starting in the eighteenth century, and were also expected to have a genuine emotional attachment to their spouses, some form of affective speculation became necessary. Women especially would need to be able to imagine what it would be like to love a particular man without committing themselves, for loving a man before he had proposed was still considered highly improper. As in courtship, so also in commerce. One thinks immediately of merchants and insurers calculating risks, or of investors extending credit on small collateral and reasoning that the greater the risk the higher the profit, but no enterprise could prosper without some degree of imaginative play. The same suspension of literal truth claims helped even common people to accept paper money: too wise to believe that the treasury held enough specie to cover all of their paper at once, they instead understood that the credit they advanced collectively obviated the need to hoard precious metals privately. So the government, too, relied on the imaginative sophistication of its people and financed a vast military and imperial enterprise by selling national debt bonds. The spirit of "ironic" assent thus became a universal requirement. Indeed, almost all of the developments we associate with modernity—from greater religious toleration to scientific discovery—required the kind of cognitive provisionality one practices in reading fiction, a competence in investing contingent and temporary credit. One telling acknowledgment of the benefits of such mental states was the increasing use of the word *fiction* to mean, "a supposition known to be at variance with fact, but conventionally accepted for some reason of practical convenience, conformity with traditional usage, decorum, or the like," as in "legal fiction."

Expedient "fictionality" of this sort thus suffused itself throughout daily life in eighteenth-century England. But this is not to claim that the novel was just one suppositional exercise among many, for novelistic fiction had a special relation to provisionality. Whereas other forms of speculation were supposed to have practical ends—smoother economic circulation or happier marriages—novelistic fiction had no commonly agreed-upon aim, except pleasure. The other kinds of provisionality were necessary to social life; the novel seemed a voluntary luxury. There were no apparent stakes in reading a novel; one did not risk one's own heart or fortune in sympathizing with the adventures of purely imaginary beings. And when one closed the book, the emotions it generated were thought to be dispelled. In short, the novel provided its readers a seemingly free space in which to temporarily indulge imaginative play. As Coleridge would put it at the beginning of the nineteenth century, fiction solicits a *willing* suspension of disbelief, and this sensation of individual control over disbelief set novel reading apart from those mandatory suppositional acts that required the constant maintenance of active skepticism. Detaching incredulity from the guarded wariness that normally accompanies it, one could use it as an protective enclosure that would cordon off imaginary yielding from any dangerous consequences.

To be sure, the enjoyment originally willed might eventually overpower the reader and override the sense of control that the form seemed to promise. Indeed, eighteenth-century commentators and satirists routinely accused the genre of seducing its readers into imaginary experiences that were remarkably hard to exit. Coleridge, following on the heels of these critics and turning much of their censure into praise, addresses this presumed interference with volition:

> It is laxly said that during sleep we take our dreams for realities, but this is irreconcilable with the nature of sleep, which consists in a suspension of the voluntary and, therefore, of the comparative power. The fact is that we pass no judgment either way: we simply do not judge them to be real, in consequence of which the images act on our minds, as far as they act at all, by their own force as images. Our state while we are dreaming differs from that in which we are in the perusal of a deeply interesting novel in the degree rather than in the kind. (Coleridge 1960: 116)

Coleridge acknowledges that absorption in a novel is inimical to the very thing he had elsewhere aligned with fiction: willing. The will, which would allow a comparison of illusion and reality, is here said to be suspended, just as disbelief is said to be willingly suspended in the more famous formulation. We might infer that will, like disbelief, is still present under erasure, but even if we forgo this interpretation, we must note that the impairment of control has not, in Coleridge's view, led to a confusion of ontological levels. He is explicitly refuting the opinion that aesthetic receptivity encourages mistaken beliefs by arguing that the more engrossed we are in a novel, the more impossible it is to *believe* it, since we have lost the very capacity to believe anything. Belief, for Coleridge, is a judgment, and judgments cannot be made without will, so all that can be said about the cognitive status of a novel's representations when they are at their most powerful is, "we simply do not judge them to be real." Lack of belief thus always surrounds the novelistic experience, even when the suspension of disbelief can no longer be said to be willing. The element of will, meanwhile, although disabled at the psychological level, persists in the ontological status of the experience; reading a novel, like sleeping, is a controlled situation within which one needn't exercise control.

Pleasure, on this account, would partly arise from the ability to choose a state—suspended disbelief—that could then be experienced in a passive mode without risk. The volition in the initial act eliminates the traces of suspicion or calculation that would normally attach to "disbelief," causing a state of heightened receptivity to the images. This self-induced susceptibility in turn permits a more intense engagement with the fiction. Knowingly reading a novel, therefore, does not involve the continuous activity of negating its objective correspondence to reality. Quite the opposite: the knowingness conducts the reader to a greater responsiveness and more vivid perception, until one becomes, at moments of keenest involvement, too interested to care about the status of the experienced beings. Willingly entering the language game of fiction, as some theorists would now say, consequently enables a psychological state of ontological indifference, a temporary disregard for the fictional conditions of the pleasurable sensation.

Coleridge's remarks thus allow us to see how pleasure was thought to color the fictional disposition of the novel reader, who not only supposed but also supposed in a manner so intense and lively that she was no longer supposing but rather fictionally experiencing. She had the enjoyment of deep immersion in illusion *because* she was protected from delusion by the voluntary framework of disbelief. This enjoyment, moreover, disposed her to renew the fictional encounter when the next opportunity arose, even though there was no tangible profit or practical advantage in the activity.

Coleridge's observation takes us back to our opening paradox. The novel gives us explicit fiction and simultaneously seems to occlude it; the novel reader opens what she knows is a fiction because it is a fiction and soon finds that enabling knowledge to be the subtlest of the experience's elements. Just as it declares itself, it becomes that which goes without saying. Having traced the historical appearance of this paradox in order to see that it *is* a paradox and not just a flat contradiction or a pair of irreconcilable statements, I want now to probe more deeply into its workings in what I have already said is the novel's main form of nonreferentiality: the lack of individual, specific and embodied referents for the characters' proper names.

————

Fictional characters have had a bad reputation ever since Nietzsche blamed them for the decline of myth and dionysiac music in Greek drama: "Character [from Sophocles onward] must no longer be broadened so as to become a permanent type, but must be so finely individualized, by means of shading and nuances and the strict delineation of every trait, that the spectator ceases to be aware of myth at all and comes to focus on the amazing lifelikeness of the characters and the artist's power of imitation. Here, once again, we see the victory of the particular over the general." (Nietzsche 1956: 106). Walter Benjamin, following in Nietzsche's footsteps, also assailed the individuation of character, although he placed it, to be sure, in a much later period and genre, the nineteenth-century bourgeois novel. Indeed, modernists of all sorts, but especially novelists themselves, expressed a similar distaste for the carefully differentiated and minutely rendered characters of realism, devoting considerable formal ingenuity to overcoming the insufferable impression of personality that such characters are prone to make. From an altogether different perspective, Bertrand Russell, as we will see, famously claimed that all statements about them must be false and thereby touched off a long philosophical debate on the referential status of propositions about fictional entities. So when certain structuralist narratologists later began minimalizing the importance of characters and exposing their ideological import ("the 'character-person' reigns in the bourgeois novel," Roland Barthes hisses in *S/Z* (Barthes 1974: 456)), they were joining an already long tradition.

On the other side of this abuse, of course, lies the imagined cathexis: the reader's involvement in the dominant modern form of fiction has generally been thought to come about through some sort of psychic investment in, or even identification with, the characters. The fact has no doubt been taken for granted and endorsed by most critics, readers, and novelists, leading other commentators to claim that the novel encourages naive essentialism. Hence their embarrassment and the zeal in putting down the error of confusing fictional characters with persons. "The character," writes Barthes disapprovingly, "became an individual, a 'person,' in short a fully constituted 'being,' even should he do nothing and of course even before acting. Characters stopped being subordinate to the action, embodied immediately psychological essences" (Barthes 1977: 104–5). The abhorrence of essentialism was twinned with a suspicion that novel readers confuse fictional characters with real persons. Correlatively, such critics have implied that our knowledge of ontological lack would interfere with this mistaken process of identification, so structuralist demystifiers have been eager to state the obvious: "le personnage . . . n'est personne" (Grivel 1973: 113).

But far from being news, the idea that "le personnage . . . n'est *personne*" is endemic to the form of the novel. As Deidre Lynch, for example, has shown, the eighteenth-century British novel—which first established the frank fictionality that would later become normal in other literatures as well—played with the absurdity of narrating the adventures of nonexistent persons, often facetiously indicating the origins of the character-person in the "character" as a printed letter (Lynch 1998: 80–122). And, in order to distinguish themselves from romances, early novels gave us numerous Quixotic characters to laugh at for confusing textual with actual people. Early novels thus simultaneously mocked their predecessors and thumbed their noses at the many eighteenth-century critics, who, like modern ones, frequently imagined that to care for fictional personae was to mistake them for real persons. Authors sometimes did regret their readers' extraordinary readiness to sympathize with characters and warned that they might not have sufficient emotional energy to care for their actual fellow creatures if they spent it all on "the imaginary distress[es] of . . . heroine[s]," as one eighteenth-century critic put it (Taylor 1943: 53); some of them even attempted to diminish the affective response by periodically interrupting the narrative (Gallagher 1994: 273–88). But as the eighteenth century wore on and fictionality became commonly understood, writers no longer thought that sentimental readers were confused about the ontological status of characters, as earlier naive readers might have been. Instead, they tended to notice that the characters' very fictiveness had a strong emotional appeal.

That apparent paradox—that readers attach themselves to characters because of, not despite, their fictionality—was acknowledged and discussed by eighteenth-century writers. As I have already mentioned, they noticed that the fictional framework established a protected affective enclosure that encouraged risk-free emotional investment. Fictional characters, moreover, were thought to be easier to sympathize or identify with than most real people. Although readers were often called to be privileged and superior witnesses of protagonists' follies, they were also expected to imagine themselves as the characters. "All joy or sorrow for the happiness or calamities of others," Samuel Johnson explained, "is produced by an act of the imagination, that realizes the event however fictitious . . . by placing us, for a time, in the condition of him whose fortune we contemplate" (Johnson 1750). What seemed to make novelistic "others" outstanding candidates for such realizations was the fact that, especially in contradistinction to the figures who pointedly referred to actual individuals, they were enticingly unoccupied. Because they were haunted by no shadow of another person who might take priority over the reader as a "real" referent, anyone might appropriate them. No reader would have to grapple with the knowledge of some real-world double or contract an accidental feeling about any actual person by making the temporary identification. Moreover, unlike the personae of tragedy or legend, novelistic characters tended to be commoners, who would fall beneath the notice of history proper, and so they tended to carry little extratextual baggage. As we have noticed, they did carry the burden of the type, what Henry Fielding called the "species," which he thought was a turntable for aiming reference back at the reader; a fictional "he" or "she" should really be taken to mean "you." But in the case of many novel characters, even the "type" was generally minimized by the requirement that the character escape from the categorical in the process of individuation. The fact that "le personnage . . . n'est personne" was thought to be precisely what made him or her magnetic.

Some recent critics are reviving this understanding and venturing to propose that we, like our eighteenth-century predecessors, feel things for characters not *despite* our awareness of their fictionality but *because of* it. Consequently, we cannot be dissuaded from identifying with them by reminders of their nonexistence. We have plenty of those, and they configure our emotional responses in ways unique to fiction, but they do not diminish our feeling. We already know, moreover, that all of our fictional emotions are by their nature excessive because they are emotions about nobody, and yet the knowledge does not reform us. Our imagination of characters is, in this sense, absurd and (perhaps) legitimately embarrassing, but it is also constitutive of the genre, and it requires more explanation than the eighteenth-century commentators were able to provide.

Consequently, I will turn now to the twentieth-century theories that might take us beyond identification as a source of emotional response. Paradoxically, given their general hostility to the "ideology" of character, structuralist and poststructuralist writers have provided important clues to the persistence of emotional response. Although their corrective reductions of characters to actants and their discoveries of mere textuality may now seem naive in their own way, they also usefully focused attention on characters as textual effects and thereby yielded many of our most detailed accounts of the techniques of novelistic characterization. Even the more recent new historicist work (Hunter 1983; Lynch 1998) is indebted to these studies, for by repeatedly lifting the veil on the fictional apparatus, they have given us a much clearer view of the machinery.

To them we owe, for example, a long-running discussion of the structure and function of the proper name in the novel. The modern novel, it is widely acknowledged, begins with the ascription of names that conform to the "morphophonology" of those in the everyday social world (Nicole 1983: 239). As opposed to the outlandish names of characters in romances, "Tom Jones," "Clarissa Harlow," and "Pamela Andrews" sound like contemporary English names. This phonological normality is a convention alerting the reader to the fact that the name refers to nobody in particular, to a fictional entity, for individual reference at the time was normally signaled either through initials and blanks ("H———l———x" for Halifax, or "S———le" for Steele) or by pseudonyms that often referred to the moral qualities of persons. The connotations of such pseudonyms distinguished them from the usual semantics of proper names, which, as John Stuart Mill pointed out, suppress connotation in their function of denoting individuals. To be sure, names also carry quite a bit of information in social life; they are associated with region, gender, ethnic group, class status, even (in the case of given names) social ambitions, as well as family history; they generally, that is, contain the social coordinates of individual identity, but we still do not decipher

them as emblems of inner essence. This is consistent with their largely deno-
tative function, and novelistic names tend to follow the same pattern. "Tom
Jones," for example, is an assertively plebeian English name that is otherwise
remarkable for the very small amount of background information it provides.
Don Quixote begins when the protagonist resolves to escape his mundane
identity by rechristening himself, exchanging his family name, about which
the narrator is humorously uncertain, for "Don Quixote," which is a bum-
bling attempt to indicate his knighthood. Cervantes thus introduces the difference between the novel, with its fictional nobodies, and the romance, with
its exemplary individuals, as, first of all, a matter of names.

But unlike natural names, novelistic ones also seem motivated, when first
encountered, by the author's intention to produce characters; names are at
first promises of characters, and their anaphoric repetition marks the primary textual sites where we expect personages to emerge (Nicole 1983:
236). As Roland Barthes puts it, "When identical semes traverse the same
proper name several times and appear to settle upon it, a character is created" (Barthes 1974: 67). In most realist novels, these repetitions organize
the syntax of the entire work, as subjects organize the syntax of sentences,
and thus seem to be employed as if they referred to prior entities. But because we are novel readers, we understand that the givenness of the character is a convention and that the text's proper names only refer to what they
(with the active participation of the knowing reader) are simultaneously creating. We do, therefore, put more interpretive pressure on proper names in
novels than we do in life, for we take them as intentional cues to different
modes of reading. In Dickens's *Our Mutual Friend*, for example, the character named "Rogue Riderhood" generates no expectation of incipient quasi-
subjectivity; we take its bearer to be a mere functionary of the plot because
his name already reveals everything about his "character." In contrast, although there is considerable plot business surrounding the name of the initially anonymous protagonist of the same novel, the promise of subjectivity
is carried by the conspicuously bland pseudonym he adopts, "John Roke-
smith." And although the "real" name that finally carries his destiny—"John
Harmon"—resonates with multiple associations, we never read it as his
summation. Because we are conscious of their fictionality, novelistic names
not only help us to sort characters into major and minor, round and flat, serious and comic but also prompt us to begin—or not to begin—the intense
imaginative activity of reading character.

Before speculating further on the nature of that activity and its peculiar
emotional effects, I want to turn to another discourse about fictional character: British analytical philosophy. If structuralists wanted to expose the

ideology of character by specifying the literary techniques of its construction, analytical philosophers at first approached the issue as a problem for referential theories of language. Devoid of any interest in the novel for its own sake, their analyses focused on "the well known paradoxes involved in the notion of a nonreal or nonexistent object" of discourse (Martinez-Bonati 1981: 153). Early in the century, Bertrand Russell, trying to make language safe for science, declared propositions about fictional entities to be false; he therefore implicitly denied Sir Philip Sidney's defense of imaginative texts, which "nothing affirmeth, and therefore never lieth." Russell, in contradistinction, maintained that such sentences as "Mr. Pickwick is wise," could be exposed as false by translating them into their logical structure: "There exists one and only one entity such that the entity is Mr. Pickwick and whatever is Mr. Pickwick is wise." Since the first part of the conjunction, which asserts the existence of Mr. Pickwick, is false, the entire statement is, and this analysis could, of course, be repeated for every proposition about Mr. Pickwick and, cumulatively, for *The Pickwick Papers* (Pavel 1986: 14). Other analytical philosophers, who were less comfortable with the attribution of truth values to propositions about fictional entities, disagreed: P. F. Strawson maintained that such statements are spurious (illegitimate) rather than false, and Gilbert Ryle argued that the proper name "Mr. Pickwick" is a pseudo-designation, not a real one: "When Dickens says 'Mr. Pickwick wore knee-breeches,' the proper name seems to designate someone; but if no one was called 'Mr. Pickwick,' then the proposition can't be true or false of the man called Mr. Pickwick. For there was no one so called. And then the proposition is not really about someone" (Ryle 1933: 35). Although far less elegantly put, Ryle's opinion echoes Sidney's, returning us to the time-honored distinction between fictions and falsehoods without contributing anything new.

But analytical philosophers had not yet finished with fictional character. One branch of their inquiry grew out of work on modal semantics, involving counterfactuals and possible worlds, which seemed to solve some of the logical problems entailed in referring to nonexistent entities. Saul Kripke's statement that "Sherlock Holmes doesn't exist, but in other states of affairs he would have existed" (Pavel 1986: 45) helped launch a vigorous debate about the ways in which fictional characters might resemble the inhabitants of logically possible worlds. Theorists who elaborated the similarities between fictional and possible worlds sometimes also linked their ideas to Aristotle's notion of probability (Pavel 1986: 45; Wollsterstorff 1980: 134–58), but generally the concept of possibility in this tradition of thought referred only to logical possibility. Elaborating a possible-worlds approach to fiction, Thomas Pavel claimed that, like the names of beings in counterfactual statements, characters' names are rigid designators specifying only one entity who retains his or her essential qualities (parentage for Kripke) across all possible worlds in which he or she exists, although his or her accidental features may vary greatly. Although theoretically convenient for a philosophical tradition bent on reference, such creatures and their worlds proved less useful to practicing critics, and the possible-worlds account of fictionality has now been superseded. I mention it here mainly because discussions of the dissimilarities between possible and fictional worlds underscore certain features of characters that can help us understand their emotional appeal.

In the first place, analytical philosophers needed to be reminded of the very feature that was the starting point for many narratologists and poststructuralists: textuality. Characters are not ontologically different because they inhabit possible, rather than actual, worlds to which novels merely refer; they are different because they are "constructs of textual activity" (Dolozel 1988: 488). Such reminders nudged even those working inside the analytical tradition closer to the formal and stylistic concerns that had preoccupied narratologists. Moreover, the explanation of fictionality that is now dominant among analytical philosophers had a similar effect. John Searle's speech-act account marked a departure for analytical philosophy by focusing attention on "the linguistic attitude of the speaker" (Pavel 1986: 20). Instead of making what Searle calls a "serious" illocutionary act of assertion, the writer of a fiction merely pretends to perform such acts (Searle 1979: 65). Thus Dickens would only be pretending to make statements about Mr. Pickwick, who would be not an entity in a possible world or a bundle of features selected by Dickens from the set of possible features (Wollsterstorff 1980) but instead the imaginary product of these pretended assertions: "by pretending to refer to people and to recount events about them, the author creates fictional characters and events" (Searle 1979: 73). Proper names, Searle notes, are "paradigm referring expression[s]," so in using them, he maintains, novelists must be miming the speech act of referring. Various conventional markers lead communities of readers to recognize the pretended nature of these references, the serious import of which is the textual *creation* of a character. Searle thus helped move the discussion from the problem of reference ("One of the conditions of the successful performance of the speech act of reference is that there must exist an object that the speaker is referring to" [71]) to the more promising literary-critical concern of "how far the horizontal conventions of fiction break the vertical connections of serious speech" (73).

Certainly Searle's formulations have been vulnerable to a host of objections: his contentions that fictional uses of language are, in J. L. Austin's word, "parasitic" on serious uses (Derrida 1982); that the author is "pretend-ing" to do something other than write a novel (Martinez-Bonati 1980); that proper names are necessarily "referring expressions" (Rorty 1983); and that "there is no textual property, syntactic or semantic, that will identify a text as a work of fiction" (Cohn 1999; Banfield 1982) have all been met by formi-dable challenges. Searle's approach has, however, brought analytical philosophers within talking distance of narratologists (Genette 1990), and has stimulated (or provoked) further specification of the distinctive textual indexes of fictionality. Some of these bear directly on our inquiry into the af-fective appeal of the novelistic nonentity.

In third-person narratives, according to several theorists, the distinctive sign of fictionality appears when the narrator depicts the subjectivity, or con-sciousness, of a character. Narratorial omniscience, indirect discourse about the mental states of characters, and representations of interior monologues, for example, all portray the "intimate subjective experiences of . . . charac-ters, the here and now of their lives to which no real observer could ever ac-cede in real life" (Cohn 1999: 24). These modes of access to the inner life are recognizable signs that an imaginary persona is in the making (Cohn 1990, 1999; Banfield 1982; Hamburger 1973; McCormick 1988). Unlike repre-sented persons in autobiography, biography, or history, novelistic characters seem already penetrated in the very act of their construal. *Pace* Searle, sev-eral influential theorists maintain that the maximal interpenetration of the narrator's discourse with the character's subjective experience in the free in-direct style displays grammatical (not just representational) characteristics unique to fiction (Cohn 1990, 1999; Banfield 1982; Hamburger 1973). Ann Banfield's work, in particular, supports the thesis that the novel discloses rather than conceals fictionality when she demonstrates that the grammati-cal markers signifying writtenness and fictionality appear only with the rise of the European novel (225–53). In other words, competent readers under-stand that the seemingly intimate revelations of the character's depths are also revelations of its textual nature.

Characters' peculiar affective force, I propose, is generated by the mutual implication of their unreal knowability and their apparent depth, the link between their real nonexistence and the reader's experience of them as deeply and impossibly familiar. Because we know their accessibility means fictionality, we are inclined to surrender to the other side of their double im-pact: their seductive familiarity, immediacy, and intimacy. Their permeability intensifies the sense of unprecedented representational thoroughness that creates what has been called the "character-effect" (Bal 1997), the impres-sion, understood as illusion, of a preexisting creature with multiple levels of

existence, a surface and recesses, an exterior and interior. We seem to encounter something with the layers of a person but without the usual epistemological constraints on our knowledge. The character is thus what Jeremy
Bentham, in "A Fragment on Ontology," called an "imaginary nonentity,"
for its *nonexistence* sustains its effect on reality, that is to say, its effect on the
reader. If such a person did exist, the usual boundary of personhood would
be in place, and the reality created by the fiction would disintegrate. Then
there would be no inviting openness, which is always, to some extent, pathetic, and we would not be able to enter represented subjectivity while subliminally understanding that we are, as readers, its actualizers, its conditions
of being, the only minds who undergo these experiences.

In short, the attraction grows less out of a sense of identification than out
of the ontological contrast the character provides. The character's very
knowability, as D. A. Miller has remarked, produces a subtle sense of relief
when we reflect on our own comparative unfathomability (Miller 1988:
200–220). The character's appeal, we might say, thus resembles that of
Freud's fetish, because the efficacy of both resides in their imaginary status,
in the powerful combination of their contrast with and their similarity to
other entities. Both the character and the fetish reassure their knowing users
that those other things are real.

All of this pertains most fully, but not exclusively, to novels with third-
person omniscient narrators in the realist mode. Novels with first-person
narrators reveal their fictionality primarily through the techniques that indicate the difference between the narrator and an implied author, their
manifestation of what Dorrit Cohn calls "the duplicate vocal origin of fiction" (Cohn 1999: 125). Homodiegetic and intradiegetic narrators, however, must sustain the illusion of the opacity of the characters surrounding
them, and such narrators are consequently excellent vehicles for the epistemological uncertainty that modernists were anxious to produce (Bal 1997:
117). Proust's narrator can never really know Albertine; Marlowe can never
penetrate Kurtz. In these cases, sharing the narrator-character's doomed
hermeneutic struggle, often read as an allegory of reading, gives rise to an
even more intense sense of the fictionality of such intimacy as well as a
melancholy recognition of its discontents. For the technique contrasting the
insistent display of subjectivity in the narrator and its occlusion in the character who is the object of desire ensures that the reader's desire, too, is always directed beyond identification.

The differential accessibility or knowability of character is only one feature inviting cathexis with ontological difference. Another, seemingly paradoxical, pair of features is closely related and shared by all novel characters

regardless of the mode of narration: they are at once utterly finished and also necessarily incomplete. Philosopher Peter McCormick describes the first of these: "fictional characters are surprisingly exhaustible as objects of knowledge since, unlike material objects, they lack the infinity of ever receding perceptual horizons and, unlike self-conscious entities, they lack the inexorable privacy of ever changing varieties of mental states" (McCormick 1988: 240). McCormick's description of the ease and utter regularity with which characters are decoded from texts marks his description as philosophical rather than literary-critical, but the general claim remains helpful. Despite representational tactics that give the impression of layers and plenitude, characters are "peculiarly delimited" as textual beings. Persons, even dead persons, can more accurately be said to be inexhaustible. No matter how many times we reread *Anna Karenina*, there will never be more to learn about, say, the childhoods of the heroine and her brother. The proper name "Anna Karenina" is made up of a finite set of sentences no matter how much more insightful, mature, or knowledgeable our reading becomes, no matter how much more skillfully we analyze that text or how much more ruthlessly we deconstruct it. The text may be hermeneutically inexhaustible and labile; it may be indeterminate and inconstant, but this only means that a variety of "Anna"s can be produced from it, none of whom will have a more fully described childhood. We may discover that previously misattributed portions of the text should be newly laid to Anna's character code, but then she would just be finished differently.

The corollary of this delimitation is the character's incompleteness. In philosopher Ruth Ronen's formulation, "This notion of incompleteness relates to the logico-semantic status of fictional entities. The absence of a complete referent entails indeterminate areas and an impossibility to verify properties of the fictional entity not attributed to it by the fictional text itself. . . . Incompleteness is thus the reflection of the logical difference between an extraliterary real object and a fictional construct" (Ronen 1988: 497). A literary critic would probably not say that it is "impossible to verify" qualities of the character not specified by the text, since there are no such qualities, and we can, of course, object that persons, too, are incomplete if by that we mean it would be futile to try to specify and verify every detail of their existence. It is reasonable, however, to note that *in principle* we can determine, for example, the exact date on which Charles Stokes, a real-life renegade missionary to Africa, first set foot in the Congo, whereas there is no such information to be obtained about the Kurtz of *Heart of Darkness*. By definition, and not by the chance scarcity of documentation, we have no recourse to sources outside the fiction for supplementary information on characters. Various novelistic techniques can either emphasize or diminish this incompleteness. In nineteenth-century European realistic fiction, for example, we generally encounter an assumption of what Erving Goffman calls the "sufficiency" of the characterization to the needs of the narrative; for example, the text does not prompt us to wonder about what little Anna and her brother Stiva did in the nursery. Again, modernism and postmodernism tend to jettison this rule, asking us to contemplate the character's constitutional lack. The enigma of Kurtz, never to be resolved, is a case in point: our desire to know what is not stated (what Kurtz really did) can be read as a metaphor for an encounter with hollowness (the modernist emphasis) or as a reminder of textuality (the postmodernist emphasis).

Whether foregrounded or backgrounded, however, incompleteness, like uncanny accessibility and finish, invites the reader's emotional investment in the lack itself. I do not mean just that we fill in the blanks when we read novels, so that characters are partly readers' creations, as Hans Robert Jauss contends. Nor do I mean that reading requires imaginative realization, so that while we are reading we cannot tell the difference between ourselves and the protagonist, as Samuel Johnson maintained. I have in mind something closer to the position maintained by John Frow, who proceeds from psychoanalytic and semiotic considerations. "It is linguistic discontinuity [he maintains] and the field of presupposition it opens up, that constitute the condition of inscription of the reader as *unified* subject of reading" (Frow 1986: 237). Frow uses the Lacanian concept of "suture" as applied in film theory to analyze a discursive feature of characterization that we have already examined from a different angle: the movement from discourse about a character to the character as fictional producer of language. Emphasizing that the technique reveals a "discontinuity between the subject of enunciation and the subject of the enounced" Frow echoes the point made by several other critics, including Banfield: "There is . . . something essential to fiction in its representation of consciousness. The linguistic cotemporality of PAST and NOW and the coreference of SELF and the third person supplied a language for representing what can only be imagined or surmised—the thought of the other. By separating SELF from SPEAKER, this style reveals the essential fictionality of any representation of consciousness" (Banfield 1982: 260). Since the fictional character is imagined solely on the basis of these discontinuous pieces of language, readers must concentrate more intensely on their internal dynamic relations than they do when reading nonfictional genres that sometimes use similar techniques to make conjectures about the unexpressed thoughts of persons. Moreover, on those rare occasions when biographers, for example, represent consciousness, the subject position of representer and represented tend to be grammatically stabler than they are in fictional discourse (Cohn 1999: 18–37). In novels with third-person omniscient narrators, especially those using the free indirect style, the accessibility of the fictional character's mental life intensifies the uncanny separation of, to use Banfield's terms, "self " (character's mind) from "speaker" (narrator), exacerbating the instability of the subject position. The reader, to continue with Frow's theory, becomes "bound" into the text as she tries to satisfy the presupposition of unity created by the character's proper name, and yet finds herself "sliding . . . between enunciative stability and the threat of its interruption or scattering" (Frow 1986: 248). The sliding may be said to be pleasurable insofar as it stimulates and partially satisfies a reader's desire to be at once a subject of the text and independent of its various, discontinuous subjectivities. Instead of finding her own ego fragmented by such an experience, the reader of the novel is propelled by the desire to create herself as a flexible, durable subject with multiple enunciative capacities.

This account both complicates and corrects Roland Barthes's contention in *S/Z* that "what gives the illusion that the sum [of the semes connoting a character] is supplemented by a precious remainder (something like *individuality*, in that, qualitative and ineffable, it may escape the vulgar bookkeeping of compositional character) is the Proper Name. . . . The proper name enables the person to exist outside the semes, whose sum nonetheless constitutes it entirely" (Barthes 1974: 191). For Barthes, naming a character automatically imports the supplement of personhood, the ideological assumption that the character is everything attributed to it by the text, and everything else that is needed to make up a human being. Where it is not purposely prevented from doing so (as in the *nouvel roman*) the proper name draws together and unifies all the semantic material, and we have, according to Barthes, the ideologically suspect pleasure of sensing a person on the other side of the text. Incompletion, he maintains, moves ineluctably toward a desired completion through the agency of the name. However, it would be more accurate to say that the name introduces a presupposition of unity, which constitutionally cannot succeed in subduing the incompleteness and discontinuity of the changing textual perspectives. The presupposition of unity merely permits the reader's imaginative play between enunciative positions. We might add that if the embarrassing presupposition of unity, the supplement of a person-effect, were nonexistent, the reader's play would be directionless. And if, on the contrary, it actually created an impression of totality so strong that the incompleteness and disjunctions disappeared, there would be no inviting gaps for the reader to slip through, no subjective blanks to be overcome by her own idealized ego.

In addition to the gaps between shifting textual perspectives and the separation between subjectivity and speaker, we should also mention those between attempted reference and realization or typification and individuation, which hark back to Henry Fielding's Aristotelian view of fictional character as that which instances the type and therefore finds its referent in the reader. What Fielding was not quite willing to acknowledge, though, is that between type and instance, a gulf necessarily opens up, especially in the realist novel, with its double imperative to taxonomize the social body and to individualize the character. A thematic emphasis on protagonists who cannot become genuine or authentic (Stendhal's Julien Sorel, for example, or Flaubert's Emma Bovary), or who seem debarred from ordinary existence (Tolstoy's Anna Karenina or George Eliot's Dorothea Brooke) rehearses this formal difficulty, which we noted earlier, of arriving at the semblance of a unique being under the generic constraint of referential typicality. The implicit contrast between the reader, with her independent embodied selfhood that pretends to need no alibi of reference in order to achieve significance, and the character, with her notable lack of quiddity, who is therefore forever tethered to the abstraction of type, can even be played upon to produce a vicarious desire, as the imagined desire of the character, for the immanence the reader possesses. The fictional character's incompleteness can, in other words, not only create a sense of the reader's material "reality" as ontologically plentiful by helping us reenvision our embodied immanence through the condition of its possible absence, but also allows us to experience an uncanny desire to be that which we already are.

What we seek in and through characters, therefore, are not surrogate selves but the contradictory sensations of *not being a character*. On the one hand, we experience an ideal version of self-continuity, graced by enunciative mastery, mobility, and powers of almost instantaneous detachment and attachment. We experience, that is, the elation of a unitary unboundedness. On the other hand, we are also allowed to love an equally idealized immanence, an ability to be, we imagine, without textuality, meaningfulness, or any other excuse for existing.

Works Cited

Anderson, Benedict. 1991. *Imagined Communities: Reflections on the Origin and Spread of Nationalism*. New York: Verso.

Bal, Mieke. 1997. *Narratology: Introduction to the Theory of Narrative*. Translated by Christine Van Boheemen. 2nd ed. Toronto: University of Toronto Press.

Banfield, Ann. 1982. *Unspeakable Sentences: Narration and Representation in the Language of Fiction*. Boston: Routledge and Kegan Paul.

Barthes, Roland. 1974. *S/Z: An Essay*. Translated by Richard Miller. New York: Hill and Wang.

———. 1977. "Introduction to the Structural Analysis of Narratives." In *Image—Music—Text*. New York: Hill and Wang.

Cohn, Dorrit. 1990. "Signposts of Fictionality—a Narratological Perspective." *Poetics Today* 11 (4):775–804.

———. 1999. *The Distinction of Fiction*. Baltimore: Johns Hopkins University Press.

Coleridge, Samuel Taylor. 1960. *Coleridge's Shakespeare Criticism*, vol. 1. Edited by Thomas Middleton Rayson. London: Constable.

Davis, Lennard J. 1983. *Factual Fictions: The Origins of the English Novel*. New York: Columbia University Press.

Defoe, Daniel. 1903. *Serious Reflections during the Life and Surprising Adventures of Robinson Crusoe*. Vol. 3 of *The Works of Daniel Defoe*. Edited by G. H. Maynadier. 16 vols. New York: Thomas Y. Crowell.

Derrida, Jacques. 1982. "Signature Event Context." In *Margins of Philosophy*. Chicago: University of Chicago Press.

Dolozel, Lobomir. 1988. "Mimesis and Possible Worlds." *Poetics Today* 9 (3):475–96.

Else, Gerald. 1967. *Aristotle's Poetics: The Argument*. Cambridge, Mass.: Harvard University Press.

Fielding, Henry. 1967. *Joseph Andrews*. Edited by Martin C. Battestin. Middletown, Conn.: Wesleyan University Press.

Frow, John. 1986. "Spectacle Binding: On Character." *Poetics Today* 7 (2):227–50.

Gallagher, Catherine. 1994. *Nobody's Story; The Vanishing Acts of Women Writers in the Marketplace, 1760–1820*. Berkeley: University of California Press.

Genette, Gerard. 1990. "The Pragmatic Status of Narrative Fiction." *Style* 24:59–72.

Grivel, Charles. 1973. *Production de l'intérêt romanesque: Un état du texte (1870–1880), un essai de constitution de sa théorie*. Paris: Mouton.

Hamburger, Kate. 1973. *The Logic of Literature*. Translated by Marilynn Rose. Bloomington: University of Indiana Press.

Hobbes, Thomas. 1964. *Leviathan*. Abridged, edited, and with an introduction by Francis B. Randall. New York: Washington Square Press.

Hunter, Ian. 1983. "Reading Character." *Southern Review* 16 (July).

Johnson, Samuel. 1750. *The Rambler*, October 13, 318–19.

Lynch, Deidre Shauna. 1998. *The Economy of Character: Novels, Market Culture, and the Business of Inner Meaning*. Chicago: University of Chicago Press.

Martinez-Bonati, Felix. 1980. "The Act of Writing Fiction." *New Literary History* 11:425–34.

———. 1981. *Fictive Discourse and the Structures of Literature: A Phenomenological Approach*. Translated by Philip W. Silver. Ithaca, N.Y.: Cornell University Press.

McCormick, Peter J. 1988. *Fictions, Philosophies, and the Problems of Poetics*. Ithaca, N.Y.: Cornell University Press.

McKeon, Michael. 2002. *The Origins of the English Novel, 1600–1740*. Baltimore: Johns Hopkins University Press.

Miller, D. A. 1988. *The Novel and the Police*. Berkeley: University of California Press.

Morgan, Fidelis. 1986. *A Woman of No Character: An Autobiography of Mrs. Manley*. London: Faber and Faber.

Newsom, Robert. 1994. *A Likely Story: Probability and Play in Fiction*. New Brunswick, N.J.: Rutgers University Press.

Nicole, Eugene. 1983. "L'onomastique litteraire." *Poetique* 54:233–53.

Nietzsche, Friedrich. 1956. *The Birth of Tragedy*. Translated by Francis Golfing. Garden City, N.Y.: Doubleday.

Pavel, Thomas. 1986. *Fictional Worlds*. Cambridge, Mass.: Harvard University Press.

Ronen, Ruth. 1988. "Completing the Incompleteness of Fictional Entities." *Poetics Today* 9 (3):497–514.

Rorty, Richard. 1983. "Is There a Problem about Fictional Discourse?" In *Funktionen des Fiktiven*. Munich: Wilhelm Fink Verlag.

Ryle, Gilbert. 1933. "Imatinary Objects." *Aristotelian Society, Supplementary Volume* 12:18–43.

Schmidt, Siegfried J. 1996. "Beyond Reality and Fiction?" In *Fiction Updated: Theories of Fictionality, Narratology, and Poetics*, edited by C. A. Mihailescu and W. Hamarneh Toronto: University of Toronto Press.

Searle, John R. 1979. *Expression and Meaning: Studies in the Theory of Speech Acts*. Cambridge: Cambridge University Press.

Sidney, Sir Philip. 1962. "The Defense of Poesy." In *The Prose Works of Sir Philip Sidney*. Cambridge: Cambridge University Press.

Taylor, John Tinnon. 1943. *Early Opposition to the English Novel: The Popular Reaction from 1760 to 1830*. New York: King's Crown Press.

Watt, Ian. 1971. *The Rise of the Novel*. Berkeley: University of California Press.

Wollsterstorff, Nicholas. 1980. *Works and Worlds of Art*. Oxford: Clarendon Press.

FRANCO MORETTI

Serious Century

From Vermeer to Austen

In the opening pages of *The Art of Describing*, Svetlana Alpers claims that
the painters of the Dutch Golden Age had changed the course of Europan
art by "describing the world seen" rather than producing "imitations of significant human actions." Instead of the unforgettable scenes of sacred and
prophane history (like the slaughter of the innocents, often mentioned by
Alpers) these seventeenth-century paintings present still lifes, landscapes,
interiors, city views, portraits, maps on the wall . . . In brief: "an art of *describing* as distinguished from *narrative* art."[1]

It is a very elegant thesis. In at least one case, however—the work of
Johannes Vermeer—the real novelty seems to be, not really the *elimination* of
narrative, but rather the discovery of a *new dimension* of it. Take the woman
in blue, in figure 1: what a strange shape her body has; is she pregnant, perhaps? and whose letter is she reading, with such concentration? from a husband far away, as the map on the wall suggests? (but if the husband is far
away . . .) And the open casket in the foreground: was the letter in there—is
it an *old* letter, then, reread because there are no recent ones? (There are so
many letters in Vermeer, and they always suggest a little story: what is being
read here and now was written somewhere else, and earlier, about even
earlier events: three spatio-temporal layers, on a few inches of canvas.) And
the letter in figure 2, which the servant has just passed on to her mistress
(or is it the other way around?): look at their glances—worry, irony, doubt,
complicity . . . you can almost see the servant becoming her mistress's mistress. And what an odd, oblique frame: the door, the hall, the abandoned
mop—is someone waiting for an answer, out on the street? And in figure 3,
what kind of a smile is that on the girl's visage? how much wine has she had,
from the pitcher that is on the table (not a banal question, in Dutch painting; and, again, a narrative one)? what stories has the man in the foreground
been telling her? and has she *believed* him?

My gratitude to the Wissenschaftskolleg zu Berlin, where this essay was researched and written
in 1999–2000.
[1] Svetlana Alpers, *The Art of Describing: Dutch Art in the Seventeenth Century*, Chicago
University Press, 1983, xxv, xx (italics mine).

FIGURE 1. JOHANNES VERMEER, *Woman in Blue Reading a Letter,*
OIL ON CANVAS, CA. 1662–63

Rijksmuseum, Amsterdam

I stop. But a little reluctantly, because all those scenes are indeed, *pace* Alpers, "significant human actions": scenes from a story; from a *narrative.* Granted, they are not one of the memorable moments of *Weltgeschichte.* But the point is that narrative *does not consist only of memorable scenes.* This was Vermeer's stroke of genius, whose logic I will now try to unfold with the help of narrative theory.[2]

---

[2] The connection between Dutch painting and (a new form of) narrative was perfectly understood by the young George Eliot: "I turn, without shrinking, from cloud-borne angels, from prophets, sibyls, and heroic warriors, to an old woman *bending* over her flower-pot, or *eating* her solitary dinner . . . to that village wedding, kept between four brown walls, where an awkward bridegroom *opens* the dance with a high-shouldered, broad-faced bride, while elderly and middle-aged friends *look on*" (*Adam Bede,* Everyman, London 1994, 169; italics mine).

Figure 2. Johannes Vermeer, *The Love Letter*,
Oil on Canvas, ca. 1669–70

Rijksmuseum, Amsterdam

1966. Roland Barthes writes the "Introduction to the Structural Analysis of
Narratives," where he divides narrative episodes in the two broad classes
of "cardinal functions" (or "nuclei"), and "catalyzers." Terminology here
varies: Chatman's *Story and Discourse* has "kernels" and "satellites"; I will
use "turning points" and "fillers," mostly for the sake of simplicity. But terminology does not matter, only concepts do. And here is Barthes: "For a
function to be cardinal, it is enough that the action to which it refers
open . . . an alternative with consequences for the development of the
story. . . . Between two cardinal functions it is always possible to set out subsidiary notations which cluster around one or the other nucleus without

FIGURE 3. JOHANNES VERMEER, *OFFICER AND LAUGHING GIRL*,
OIL ON CANVAS, CA. 1655–60

Copyright The Frick Collection, New York

modifying its alternative nature. . . . These catalyzers are still functional . . .
but their functionality is weak, unilateral, parasitic."[3]

A cardinal function is a possible turning point in the plot; fillers no, they
are what happens *between* a turning point and the next. An example. *Pride
and Prejudice* (1813), Elizabeth and Darcy meet in chapter 3, he acts horri-
bly, she is disgusted: first action with "consequences for the development of
the story": they are set in opposition to each other. Thirty-one chapters
later, Darcy proposes to Elizabeth; second turning point: an alternative has
been opened. Another twenty-seven chapters, and Elizabeth accepts him:

---

[3] Roland Barthes, "Introduction to the Structural Analysis of Narratives," 1966, in Susan
Sontag, ed., *Barthes: Selected Writings*, Fontana, Glasgow 1983, 265–66. (Throughout the essay,
some translations have been slightly modified for reasons of fidelity to the original.)

alternative closed, end of the novel. Three turning points: beginning, middle, and ending; very geometric; very Austen-like. But of course, in between these three major scenes, Elizabeth and Darcy meet, and talk, and hear, and think about each other, and it's not easy to quantify this type of thing, but I have done my best, and have found about 110 episodes of this kind. These are the fillers. And Barthes is right, they really don't do much: they enrich and nuance the progress of the story, yes, but without ever modifying what the turning points have established, because they are indeed too "weak" to do so: just as in Vermeer, what fillers have to offer are people who talk, play cards, visit, take walks, read a letter, listen to music, drink a cup of tea . . .

Narration: but of the everyday.[4] This is the secret of fillers. Narration, because these episodes always contain a certain dose of uncertainty (how will Elizabeth react to Darcy's words? will he accept to walk with the Gardiners?); but the uncertainty remains local, circumscribed, without long-term consequences "for the development of the story," as Barthes would say. In this respect, fillers function very much like the good manners so important in Austen: they are both mechanisms designed to keep the "narrativity" of life under control—to give a regularity, a "style" to existence. And here, Vermeer's break with so-called genre painting is crucial: one looks at his scenes and realizes that no one is laughing anymore; at most a smile, but seldom, because usually his figures have the intent, composed face of the woman in blue: serious. Serious, as in the magic formula that defines realism in *Mimesis* (and already for the Goncourts, in the preface to *Germinie Lacerteux*, the novel was *la grande forme sérieuse*). Serious: what is "in opposition to amusement or pleasure-seeking" (OED); "in gegensatz von Scherz und Spasz" (Grimm); "alieno da superficialità e frivolezze" (Battaglia).

But what exactly does "serious" mean, in literature? Diderot, who introduces the *genre sérieux*, in 1757, in the *Entretiens sur le fils naturel*, places it

---

[4] In the early nineteenth century, the semantic field of everydayness—*alltäglich, everyday, quotidien, quotidiano*—drifts toward the colorless realm of the "habitual," "ordinary," "repeatable," and "frequent," in contrast to the older, more vivid opposition of the everyday and the sacred. To capture this pervasive yet elusive dimension of life was one of Auerbach's chief aims in *Mimesis*, as is made clear by the book's conceptual leitmotif of the "serious imitation of the everyday" (*die ernste Nachahmung des alltäglichen*). Although the title eventually chosen by Auerbach foregrounds the aspect of "imitation" (*Mimesis*), the book's greatest originality lies probably in the other two terms—"serious" and "everyday"—which had already been analyzed at length in the preparatory study to *Mimesis*, the essay "Über die ernste Nachahmung des alltäglichen" (where Auerbach also considered the terms "dialectic" and "existential" as possible alternatives to "everyday": see the *Travaux du séminaire de philologie romane*, Istanbul 1937, 272–73).

FIGURE 4. GUSTAVE CAILLEBOTTE, FRENCH, 1848–1894, *PARIS STREET;*
RAINY DAY, 1877, OIL ON CANVAS, 83½ × 108¾ IN. (212.2 × 276.2 CM.)

Charles H. and Mary F. S. Worcester Collection, 1964.336 *Reproduction, The Art Institute*
of Chicago

more or less halfway between comedy and tragedy.[5] It is a great intuition,
which updates the age-old connection between style and social class: to the
aristocratic heights of tragic passion, and the plebeian depths of comedy, the
class in the middle adds a form that is itself in the middle, intermediate. But
intermediate does not mean *equidistant*, and it soon becomes clear (already
in Diderot)[6] that the *genre sérieux* models itself after the "high" style of the
old ruling class. One looks at a masterpiece of bourgeois seriousness like
Caillebotte's *Paris Street; Rainy Day* (figure 4), for instance, and realizes that,
although serious may not mean tragic, it certainly means dark, cold, impassi-
ble, silent, heavy, solemn. ("All of us are attending some funeral or other,"
Baudelaire had just written in "The Heroism of Modern Life.") The class in

---

[5] "I have only one question left," we read at the end of the second *Entretien*: "it concerns the
genre of your work. It isn't a tragedy; it isn't a comedy. What is it then, and what name should we
use for it?" In the opening pages of the third *Entretien* Diderot responds by defining the "genre
sérieux" as "intermediate between the two extreme genres," "placed in their middle," and so on
(Denis Diderot, *Entretiens sur le fils naturel*, in *Oeuvres*, Bibliothèque de la Pléiade, Paris, 1951,
1,243 sgg.).

[6] "I conclude that [the serious genre] inclines rather toward tragedy than comedy" (ibid., 1,247).

the middle has closed its ranks and uses its seriousness to distance itself from the "carnevalesque" noise of the laboring classes.

But I will often return to seriousness. Now, a few more words on narrative theory.

Parting of the Ways: Unheard-of Events, Everyday Life

One hundred and ten fillers, and three turning points: 97 percent of *Pride and Prejudice* taken up by "weak and parasitic" episodes. But why? what does all this everydayness *do* in the novel? There is a conversation like so many others, in the eighth chapter of the book: people talk of Darcy's sister, how tall is she, her accomplishments, women's accomplishments in general, the importance of reading; all of this entwined with a card game, and the usual marriage strategies. And you analyze the style, the logic of conversation, the intellectual makeup of the characters—but finally have to ask yourself, What exactly has happened here? *Has* anything? And no, not really, which is absurd—a typical episode of a great storyteller (97 percent . . .), and nothing happens? It doesn't make sense; narrative theory has a very simple thesis on this, a story is worth telling if a rule is broken (a rule of conduct, or probability, or both): if it conveys an "unheard-of event," as Goethe once said. But nothing will ever be unheard-of in a polite conversation, and it is precisely this that makes Austen (and much of the nineteenth century) so puzzling: why build a story with materials that are *reluctant* to narration? Much more logical, to choose an example among hundreds, is what happens in a great best seller of late antiquity like the *Alexander Romance*: Alexander is with his friend Ephestion, the servants are brushing their horses, they have some time to fill up, and so—like the good people in Austen—the two take a walk. But unlike people in Austen, they run into a stranger, exchange a few words, and within half a page a war has been declared. The filler (the walk) is there—but only for a moment: only in order to move from one turning point to the next.[7] The everyday functions in other words as *the opposite of narrative*; a weight that cannot always be avoided (every now and then, horses must be brushed, even in novels), but has to be quickly overcome for the "real" story to be told.

And after all, this is still largely the rule in Austen's time. In Edgeworth's *Belinda* (1801), for instance, the general design of the story is clearly very

---

[7] In Heliodorus's wonderfully succinct formulation: "Now the fate that presided over the tournament of their destiny had ceased its persecutions *for a few hours* and smiled on them, but their happiness was to be short-lived" (*An Ethiopian Story*, in B. P. Reardon, ed., *Collected Ancient Greek Novels*, University of California Press, 1989, 499; italics mine).

similar to an Austen plot; but if we move from the macro-level of the marriage plot to the micro-units of its constituent episodes, we immediately realize that, in *Belinda*, the everyday hardly exists. In its place, one *coup de théâtre* after the other: the would-be husband Clarence Harvey opens a letter (Vermeer . . .), and a lock of hair falls to the ground—which Belinda misunderstands in the worst possible way. A servant walks into a room for an errand, sees some banknotes on a table—and spreads a devastating slander. A mother finds her lost daughter, a daughter her lost father, a wife rediscovers her husband, he her . . . Four pages before the end, "we might have all been making one another miserable"—explains Lady Delacour—"if it had not been for . . . captain Sunderland's humanity." "Captain Sunderland! who is captain Sunderland? we never heard of him before . . ."[8] All like this, running; a new character (and a decisive one!) invented when the novel is practically over.

And again: there is nothing strange in this. Edgeworth narrates the unheard-of, as it had long been the case—and will continue to be in the gothic, the *feuilleton-roman*, melodrama, romances . . . A diagram made in a Manhattan primary school (figure 5) is the perfect illustration of this *longue durée* of narrative conventions. Mary Foote, the teacher, and her young collaborators (*very* young) read Ann Cameron's *Julian's Glorious Summer*, visualizing the mood of the protagonist throughout the story: and the graph keeps jumping from one extreme to the other, eight times happy, fourteen sad, or

FIGURE 5. ANN CAMERON, *JULIAN'S GLORIOUS SUMMER*

Chart designed by Mary Foote, Dalissa, Janil, Michelle, Nadine, Ricky, Robert

---

[8] Maria Edgeworth, *Belinda*, Dent, London 1993, 446–47.

worried, and only four times in an intermediate state that they call "neutral," or "ok." This is how stories worked before fillers entered the scene.

But once writers began to use them, everything changed: the Elizabeth-Darcy plot in *Pride and Prejudice*, for instance, would look very much like the reverse of this chart, with some entries for "sad" and "confused," a final one for "happy," and a hundred for "neutral." It is one of Austen's great achievements, this relocation of the unheard-of toward the background of the novel, while the everyday moves into the foreground.[9] But if it's reasonably clear *what* Austen did, the *why* is not. And the same perplexity remains for that earlier novel where the new narrative hierarchy first emerged. Judging from *Robinson Crusoe*'s title page (figure 6), writes Giuseppe Sertoli, it

FIGURE 6. ORIGINAL TITLE PAGE OF *ROBINSON CRUSOE*, 1719

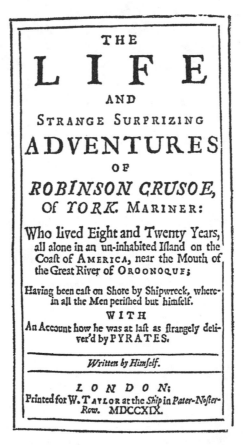

---

[9] Banned from the main plot, the unheard-of remains, however, active in the subplots of her novels (Lidia and Wickham, the Crawfords, etc.): a sedimentation of past and present that is quite frequent when a new paradigm is taking shape, but has not yet completely prevailed.

FIGURE 7. ROBINSON AND XURY ESCAPING FROM THE MOORS

seems likely that Defoe had in mind the "different narrative project" promised by the lines at the top—the life, and the strange surprising adventures—of which the part on the island was to be simply "one of the many episodes."[10] The island, in other words, was probably planned as one of several fillers *subordinated* to Robinson's unheard-of adventures (which, by the way, remained central in the countless *Robinson* chapbooks that circulated all over Europe in the eighteenth century: figures 7–10). But an "unforeseen, uncontrolled expansion" (Sertoli again) of the everyday occurred within the maritime adventure plot: the island shook off its functional subordination, and became meaningful *in itself.* Rousseau was the first to understand the magnitude of the change: his *Robinson*, "cleansed of all its hotchpotch," would begin "with the shipwreck," and be limited to the years on the island, so that Emile would not waste his time in dreams of adventure, and reflect instead on the more serious issue of Robinson's *work* ("he will want to know all that is useful, and nothing but that").[11] Which is cruel

---

[10] Giuseppe Sertoli, "I due Robinson," in *Le avventure di Robinson Crusoe*, Einaudi, Turin, 1998, xiv.

[11] Jean-Jacques Rousseau, *Emile*, 1762, in *Oeuvres complètes*, Bibliothèque de la Pléiade, Paris 1969, 4:455–56. A year before *Emile*, Rousseau's preface to the *Nouvelle Heloïse* provided another early instance of the new centrality of fillers ("Not a single bad action . . . events so natural, so simple, that can be faulted for it . . . not one *coup de théâtre*").

Figure 8. The Wreck

to children, of course, but accurate, because Robinson's work on the island is indeed the cornerstone of the entire novel.

An "unforeseen expansion" of the everyday, which takes everybody by surprise: the author (who had imagined a different novel); the readers (who, up to Rousseau, keep reading that Ur-novel); even the pirates of popular

Figure 9. Advent of Friday

FIGURE 10. LANDING OF THE MUTINOUS CREW ON THE ISLAND

literature, who literally do not *see* the new *Robinson*. Nice. And it would be even nicer if we could understand *what* made DeFoe change his plans, and enlarge the great filler of the island. But before coming to this, let's follow the transformations of the filler in nineteenth-century novels.

The Prose of the World

Goethe, *Wilhelm Meister's Years of Apprenticeship* (1796); book 2, chapter 12. The young actress Philine is flirting with Wilhelm on a bench in front of the inn; she gets up, goes toward the hotel, turns back to look at him one last time; after a moment, Wilhelm follows her—but at the door of the hotel he is stopped by Melina, the troupe's manager, to whom he has long since promised a loan. Thinking only of Philine, Wilhelm guarantees the money for that very evening, and starts to move on; but again he is stopped, by Friedrich this time, who greets him with his typical warmth . . . and precedes him upstairs to Philine's. Frustrated, Wilhelm goes to his room, where he finds Mignon; he is unhappy, careless, Mignon is upset, Wilhelm does not even notice. He goes out again, notices the landlord talking to a stranger, who is looking at him from the corner of his eye . . .

Prose of the world, will be Hegel's metaphor for a page like this: where the subject "must make himself a means to others, must subserve their

limited aims, and must likewise reduce others to mere means in order to satisfy his own interests."[12] But it's a prose where the bitterness of frustration
(Wilhelm is twice held back in his pursuit of pleasure) is curiously mixed
with a very strong sense of *possibility*. The loan to Melina, for instance, will
inaugurate the aesthetic section of the novel, with its memorable discussions
on dramatic art; the fear of losing Wilhelm sharpens Mignon's passion (and
inspires, a few pages later, the lyrical wonder of *Kennst du das Land*); the
stranger at the inn's door is preparing Wihelm's visit to the castle—where
the encounter with Jarno will lead in its turn to the novel's conclusion. And
so on.

Mind you: none of this actually *happens* in that early chapter. They are
just possibilities. But they are enough to "reawaken" the everyday, making it
feel alive, promising: and although its promises will not all be kept (the bildungsroman is also, structurally, the genre of disappointment), that sense of
openness will never be lost. It is a new, truly *secular* way of imagining the
meaning of a life: dispersed among countless minute events, precarious,
mixed to the indifference of the world: but always also tenaciously *there*. It
is a perspective that Goethe could never seamlessly reconcile with the teleological side of the bildungsroman (plenty of meaning, but all at once, at the
end). But the first step had been taken.

———

Goethe reawakens the everyday with his sense of possibility; Scott, in *Waverley* (1814), by reviving the daily rituals of the past: singing, hunting, eating,
toasting, dancing . . . Static scenes, even a little boring: but Waverley is English, he doesn't know what Scottish habits prescribe, asks the wrong questions, misunderstands, insults people—and the routine of the everyday is lit
up by small narrative ripples. Not that *Waverley* is as pervaded by fillers as
Meister; the atmosphere is still half-gothic, world history is nigh, stories of
love and death create all sorts of melodramatic echoes. But within the
melodrama—and, like Austen, in implicit rivalry with his contemporaries—
Scott manages to *slow down* the narrative, multiplying its moments of pause.
And within these pauses, let's open a window on a later section of this essay,
he finds, literally, the "time" to develop a new analytical-impersonal style—
which makes possible in its turn a new type of description, where the world is
observed with more precision and "impartiality" (*The Heart of Mid-Lothian*).

———

[12] G.W.F. Hegel, *Aesthetics*, 1823–29, Clarendon Press, Oxford 1985, 1:149.

Typical of literary evolution, this morphological cascade from fillers to the analytical style, and then to description; interacting with other aspects of the text, the new technique promotes a whole "wave of gadgets" (as has been said of the industrial revolution). Within a generation, the gadgets have redesigned the landscape.

———

Balzac, second book of *Lost Illusions* (1839): Lucien de Rubempré is (finally!) writing his first article, which will constitute an epoch-making "revolution in journalism." It is the chance he has been waiting for since his arrival in Paris. But within this euphoric turning point, a second episode is unconspicuously embedded: the newspaper is short of copy, it immediately needs a few pieces, never mind on what, as long as they fill the blank space: and a friend of Lucien's, obligingly, sits down and writes. It is almost the Platonic idea of the filler: words filling up space, period. And yet, this second article wounds a group of characters who, after many twists and turns, seal Lucien's ruin.

Balzac . . . As in the butterfly-effect of chaos theory, no matter how small the initial event is, the great city within which it takes place is so rich in variables that it magnifies its effects out of all expectation. Between the beginning and the end of every action there is always something else that comes in between, some "third person" who is pursuing his own private aims, and deviates the course of the plot in an unforeseeable direction. And so, even the most harmless moments of everyday life become chapters in a novel (but this, in Balzac, is not always good . . .)

———

The bildungsroman, and the bittersweet mix of frustration and possibility; courtship novels, and the prescribed world of good manners; the historical novel, and the daily rituals of the past; the urban novel, and the narrativization of existence in the new metropolis. It is a generalized reawakening of the everyday, that produced by nineteenth-century novels. But at midcentury, the tide turns. Reflecting on a page where Emma and Charles Bovary are having dinner—could there be a more perfect filler?—thus Auerbach: "Nothing particular happens in the scene, nothing particular has happened just before it. It is a random moment from the regularly recurring hours at which the husband and wife eat together. They are not quarrelling, there is no tangible conflict. . . . Nothing happens, but that nothing has become a heavy, oppressive, threatening something."[13]

An oppressive everyday . . . Because Emma has married a mediocre man? Yes and no. Yes, because Charles is certainly a weight in her life. And no, because even when she is most distant from him—in her two adulteries, with Rudolphe and then with Leon—Emma finds exactly "the same platitudes of married life," the same recurring hours when nothing noteworthy happens. This collapse of "adventure" into everyday banality is even more striking against the background of another novel of adultery—Ernest Feydeau's *Fanny*, of 1858—which at the time was often paired with *Madame Bovary*, but in fact constitutes its polar opposite: a constant oscillation between *extasis* and despair, infamous suspicions and celestial bliss—all conveyed in an implacably hyperbolic manner. Worlds apart from the gray neutrality of *Madame Bovary*, with its cheap clichés, its heavy awkward sentences ("they are *things*": Barthes), its *éternel imparfait* (Proust) . . . The *imparfait*: the tense that promises no surprises; the tense of repetition, ordinariness, the background—but a background that has become *more significant than the foreground itself*.[14] A few years later, in *Sentimental Education*, not even the annus mirabilis of 1848 can shake the universal inertia: what is truly unforgettable in the novel is not the "unheard-of" of the revolution, but how quickly the waters close down and the old commonplaces return, the petty egoisms, the weak aimless daydreams . . .

––––––––

The background is conquering the foreground. The next chapter, in Britain, in 1872, in a provincial town that seems ruled by the second law of thermodynamics: "imperceptible cooling of generous ardour," writes George Eliot, leading to people "shapen after the average and fit to be packed by the

---

[13] Erich Auerbach, *Mimesis*, 1946, Princeton University Press, 1974, 488. Flaubert's scene is the same that opens the 1937 essay "Über die ernste Nachahmung des alltäglichen" mentioned in footnote 4. Today, when we read *Mimesis*, the first texts we encounter are the *Odyssey* and the Bible; but in a deeper sense the book begins with the fillers of *Madame Bovary*, where Auerbach first "saw" the features of the "serious everyday."

[14] "Flaubert's novels, and more generally the narrative of realism and naturalism, are marked by a very clear prevalence of the *imparfait* in their narrative sections . . . the background becomes more significant, and the foreground less so": thus Harald Weinrich in his great study *Tempus* (1964, 2nd ed., Kohlhammer, Stuttgart 1971, 97–99). Further on, Weinrich adds that the verbal tenses that are typical of the background, and thus also of fillers ("the *imparfait de rupture* in French, and the tenses ending in *-ing* in English"), begin to spread around 1850 (ibid., 141–42).

gross."[15] Here she is musing on Lydgate, the young doctor who gave her the fantastic idea of writing the story of a life entirely ruined by—fillers: "pleasureless yielding to the small solicitations of circumstance, which is a commoner history of perdition than any single momentous bargain" (782–83). Sadness; Lydgate doesn't even *sell* his soul, as in Goethe or Balzac; he loses it in a maze of small events that he does not even see—while they are deciding his life.[16] An unusual young man was Lydgate, at his arrival in Middlemarch; a few years later, he too is "shapen after the average" like everybody else. Nothing extraordinary has happened, as Auerbach would say; and yet, everything has happened.

Finally, in the first year of the new century, the distillation of bourgeois life in Thomas Mann's *Buddenbrooks*: Tom's ironic and dismissive gestures, the wise words of the Lübeck burghers, Tony's infantile excitement, little Hanno's homework . . . by repeating themselves on every page of the book according to the technique of the leitmotif, Mann's everyday fillers lose even their "weak" narrative function to become simply—*style*. Everything declines and dies here, as in Wagner, but the words of the leitmotif remain, making that world unforgettable: just as in that other, splendid leitmotif of the Buddenbrook family book, where "respectful significance was granted even to the most modest events." Words that synthesize beautifully the almost religious attention with which the bourgeois century looked at its daily existence—and which suggest a few further reflections.

Rationalization

What a rapid transition. Around 1800, fillers are still a rarity; a hundred years later they are everywhere (the Goncourts, Zola, Maupassant, Fontane, Gissing, James, Proust . . .). You thought you were reading *Middlemarch*, but no, you were reading a great collection of fillers—which, after all, were the only narrative invention of the entire nineteenth century. And when such a modest

---

[15] *Middlemarch*, Penguin, 1994, 144–45.

[16] "Middles and mediations—what the text calls mediums ("unfriendly," "petty," "embroiled," "dim and clogging")—elude the time-killing or merely catalytic function assigned to them, and actually deflect from the ending that they were meant to reach" (D. A. Miller, *Narrative and Its Discontents*, Princeton University Press, 1981, 142).

device spreads so widely and quickly, there must be something, in the culture around it, that really "binds" to it. If fillers multiplied so successfully, I mean, European readers must have genuinely enjoyed to read them, and novelists to compose with them. But why? Strange book this *Buddenbrooks*, a reader once wrote Thomas Mann, so little happens, and yet I am not bored. True, it *is* strange. How did the everyday manage to become interesting?

To find an answer we must do a little "reverse engineering"; reverse, in the sense that the object is given, and one proceeds backward, from the solution to the problem as it were: we know *how* fillers were made, and now we must understand *why* they were made in that way. And in the process, the horizon changes. We found the how of fillers in narrative theory, in novels, in painting; but their why is outside literature, in the realm of social history, and more precisely in the history of private life. Beginning, again, with the Dutch Golden Age, when the private sphere that we still inhabit today first found its form: when houses became more comfortable and luminous, and doors multiplied, and rooms differentiated their function, and one of them specialized precisely in everyday life: the "living," or "drawing" room (which is actually the "*with*-drawing room," Peter Burke has explained, where the masters withdraw from their servants to enjoy the novelty of "free time").[17] Vermeer's room, and the novel's: Goethe, Austen, Balzac, Eliot, Mann . . . A space always ready, almost asking to generate a new story every day.

But this new story is then intersected by the growing *regularity* of private life. Vermeer's figures are clean, neatly dressed; they have washed their walls and their floors, their windows, their clothes . . . they have learned to read, to write, to understand maps, to play the lute and the virginal. They have a lot of free time, yes, but they use it so soberly that it's as if they were always *working*: "Life is dominated by what repeats itself systematically, regularly," writes the young Lukács of *Soul and Forms*, "by what must dutifully repeat itself, by what must be done without any thought of pleasure or pain. In other words: the dominion of order over mood, of what is lasting over what is ephemeral, of serene work over genius thriving on sensations."[18]

---

[17] Peter Burke, *Popular Culture in Early Modern Europe*, Harper and Row, New York 1978, 271. Free time is also one of the most significant preconditions mentioned by Jürgen Kocka "to participate fully in the values and practices of bourgeois culture": "One needs a stable income clearly above the minimum . . . the wife and mother as well as the children must be, to some degree, set free from the necessities of work . . . plenty of *space* (functionally specialized rooms in the house or apartment) and *time* for cultural activities and leisure." ("The European Pattern and the German Case," in Jürgen Kocka and Allan Mitchell, eds., *Bourgeois Society in Nineteenth-Century Europe*, 1988, Berg, Oxford 1993, 7). Kocka could be describing Vermeer's world.

[18] György Lukács, "Bürgerlichkeit und l'art pour l'art: Theodor Storm," in *Die Seele und die Formen*, Fleischer, Berlin 1911, 125.

Die Herrschaft der Ordnung über die Stimmung. Weberian shadows. After the Reformation, reads *The Protestant Ethic*, much of Western Europe moves "from a lax to a pervasive control over the everyday": "Christian asceticism . . . had already ruled the world. . . . But it had, on the whole, left the naturally spontaneous character of daily life in the world untouched. Now it strode into the market-place of life, slammed the door of the monastery behind it, and undertook to penetrate just that daily routine of life with its methodicalness."[19] A methodical routine. It's the opening chord of what Mann used to call "the bourgeois half millennium": Jürgen Kocka's "propensity toward regular work and rational lifestyles," or Eviatar Zerubavel's "hidden rhythms"—those regularly repeated activities (from work schedules to the domestic ritual of the piano lesson) that pervade "the spontaneous character of daily life" and ossify it. They are the "good" or "healthy" profits described by Barrington Moore for nineteenth-century Britain (small but regular, and arising out of a laborious attention to detail);[20] the "taming of chance" (Ian Hacking) of nineteenth-century statistics, or the irresistible diffusion of words (and deeds) such as "normalize," "standardize" . . .

Why fillers, in the nineteenth century? Because they offer *the kind of narrative pleasure compatible with the new regularity of bourgeois life.* Fillers turn the novel into a "calm passion," as in Hirschmann's splendid oxymoron for economic interest; they are part of what Weber called the "rationalization" of modern life: a process that begins in the economy and in the administration, but eventually pervades the sphere of free time, private life, entertainment, feelings (after all, the last book of *Economy and Society* analyzes the rationalization of musical language). Or in other words: fillers are an attempt at *rationalizing the novelistic universe*: turning it into a world of few surprises, fewer adventures, and no miracles at all.

One is reminded of the antithesis evoked in the *Protestant Ethic* between "adventure capitalism"[21]—impulsive, violent, confiding in fortune, and present in almost every epoch, like those narratives that in English are called "romances"—and the sober, predictable, repressed ethos of bureaucratic-rational capitalism, which is instead, like the "novel," a recent European invention. And a recent bourgeois invention are fillers, too: not however because they bring into the novel trade, or industry, or other bourgeois "realities" (which they don't), but because through fillers the logic of rationalization pervades *the very rhythm and form of the novel.* At the apex of the

---

[19] Max Weber, *The Protestant Ethic and the Spirit of Capitalism*, 1922, Scribner's, New York 1958, 154.

[20] Barrington Moore Jr., *Moral Aspects of Economic Growth*, Cornell University Press, 1998, 39.

[21] Weber, *The Protestant Ethic*, 58.

process, even mass literature falls under its spell: Holmes's "logic," "science" fiction, *Around the World in 80 Days*—"the novel of perpetual motion," as it was called, but *predictable* motion would have been more precise for this vision of a planetary punctuality, and this hero who *believes* in train schedules like a benedectine monk believed in his *horarium* . . .

But a novel is not only a story. Events and actions, important and not, are conveyed by words; they become language, style. And here, what is happening?

George Eliot Describes

Middlemarch. Dorothea is in Rome, in her room, crying; defenseless, writes Eliot, in front of this "unintelligible Rome":

> Ruins and basilicas, palaces and colossi, set in the midst of a sordid present, where all that was living and warm-blooded seemed sunk in the deep degeneracy of a superstition divorced from reverence; the dimmer but yet eager Titanic life gazing and struggling on walls and ceilings; the long vistas of white forms whose marble eyes seemed to hold the monotonous light of an alien world: all this vast wreck of ambitious ideals, sensuous and spiritual, mixed confusedly with the signs of breathing forgetfulness and degradation, at first jarred her as with an electric shock, and then urged themselves on her with that ache belonging to a glut of confused ideas which check the flow of emotion. (193)

Eighty-seven polysyllables adding up to form the single gigantic subject of the period; and that minute "her" as its only object. The disproportion between Rome and Dorothea could not be expressed better—and perhaps it couldn't be expressed at all without the *precision* so typical of Eliot's prose style. Ruins and basilicas are "set" in a present that is "sordid," and where all that is living (better: "living and warm-blooded") sinks (no: "seemed sunk") in a degeneration that is "deep," and whose "superstition" is "divorced from reverence." Each term is observed, measured, qualified, improved. "We have discovered the productivity of the spirit," writes Lukács in the *Theory of the Novel*, and he may just as well say: the productivity of *prose.*[22] Of prose as *work*, and, more precisely, as work of *analysis*. Hegel: "We may prescribe, as a general rule for prose, literal accuracy, unmistakable

---

[22] György Lukács, *Theory of the Novel*, 1916, MIT Press, Cambridge, Mass. 1990, 33–34.

definiteness, and clear intelligibility, while what is metaphorical and figurative is always relatively unclear and inaccurate."[23]

Accuracy, definiteness, intelligibility . . . it is a second semantic layer of "serious": that which "s'applique fortement à son objet" (Littré). "Seriousness has a well-defined aim," writes Schlegel in the "Athenaeum," "hence it can neither idle nor delude itself, but pursues its aim tirelessly until it achieves it . . ." (fragment 419); and one recalls Vermeer's woman in blue, with that intent face of a young Mary Ann Evans. Serious as "serious," not as "earnest," because at stake here are not the supposed good intentions of ethics *tout court*, but the sober sense of responsibility of *professional* ethics: the vocation of the specialist who—like Eliot's narrator, that great specialist of language—places herself entirely in the service of the task to be accomplished. And it's not just an external duty, the "unmistakable definiteness" of that *Middlemarch* page: half a century later, in the talk on "Wissenschaft als Beruf," Weber will explain beautifully how the vocation of the modern scientist (and artist) is so "intimately" entwined with the process of specialization "that the fate of his soul depends upon whether this, and this alone, is the right conjecture to be made."[24] The fate of his soul! And one thinks of the *mot juste*, inevitably, and of Thibaudet's cool diagnosis of Flaubert's style: "not a free, prodigious gift, but the product of a discipline which he achieved rather late."[25] (And Flaubert knew it: "This book," he wrote to Louis Bouilhet on October 5, 1856, when he saw *Madame Bovary* in print "shows much more patience than genius—work, more than talent.")

Work more than talent. This is the nineteenth-century novel. Nor the novel alone:

> Let's take for instance what you call an idea [says the devil in Mann's *Doktor Faustus*], a matter of three, four bars, no more, isn't it? All the rest is elaboration, sticking at it. Or isn't it? Good. But now we are all experts, all critics: we note that the idea is nothing new, that it reminds us all too much of something in Rimsky-Korsakov, or Brahms. So, what is to be done? You change it

---

[23] Hegel, *Aesthetics*, 2:1,005. Well before *Middlemarch*, thus Eliot in her "Ilfracombe Journal" of 1856: "I never before longed so much to know the names of things as during this visit to Ilfracombe. . . . The desire is part of the tendency that is now constantly growing in me to escape from all vagueness and inaccuracy into the daylight of distinct, vivid ideas." See George Eliot, "The Ilfracombe Journal," in *Selected Essays, Poems and other Writings*, A. S. Byatt and Nicholas Warren, eds., Penguin 1990, 228–29.

[24] Max Weber, "Science as a Vocation," 1918, in H. H. Gerth and C. Wright Mills, eds., *From Max Weber: Essays in Sociology*, Oxford University Press, 1958, 135, 137.

[25] Albert Thibaudet, *Gustave Flaubert*, 1922, Gallimard, Paris 1935, 204.

a little. But a changed idea, is that still an idea? Take Beethoven's notebooks! There is no thematic conception there as God gave it. He remolds his theme and adds: "Meilleur." Scant confidence in God's prompting, scant respect is expressed in that "Meilleur"—itself not so very enthusiastic either. (*Doktor Faustus*, 25)[26]

Meilleur. Eliot must have often whispered this word to herself. And one rereads that page from her great novel and wonders: was it really worth it? "And then urged themselves on her with that ache belonging to a glut of confused ideas which check the flow of emotion": who can really follow—who can *understand*—these sentences without getting lost in the labyrinth of precision? "Our world has become infinitely large and each of its corners is richer in gifts and dangers than the world of the Greeks," reads the *Theory of the Novel*: but "such wealth cancels out the positive meaning—the totality—upon which their life was based."[27] The gifts cancel out the meaning . . . yet Eliot keeps adding clauses, subordinates, qualifications. Why? What has made precision *more important than meaning*?

Reality Principle

A famous page from the first book of *Meister*:

> What advantages accrue to the businessman by double-entry bookkeeping! This is one of the most beautiful inventions of the human mind, and every serious housekeeper should introduce it into his business. . . . Order and clarity increase the desire to save and to acquire. A man who doesn't keep good accounts, who doesn't reckon up what he owes, easily finds himself in a foggy state, whereas [for] a good manager even a setback may be an unpleasant surprise, but does not scare him; he can balance this out with the gains he has made elsewhere.[28]

One of the most beautiful inventions of the human mind . . . For economic reasons, clearly enough, but also, and perhaps even more, for ethical ones: because double-entry bookkeeping forces people to confront facts directly:

---

[26] Vintage, New York 1971, 237.
[27] Lukács, *Theory of the Novel*, 34.
[28] Goethe, *Wilhelm Meister*, Princeton University Press, 1995, 18.

all facts, including unpleasant ones.[29] Reality principle. With their growing dependence on the market in every aspect of life, write Davidoff and Hall, the middle classes must learn to keep their income under control, and so they turn to the new "accounting books" provided by the publishing industry, which eventually leave their imprint on the rest of their existence: like that Mary Young who, between 1818 and 1844, next to her house accounts kept "a kind of profit and loss ledger of family and social life" ("children's illnesses and inoculations . . . gifts and letters received and given, evenings spent at home . . . calls paid and received").[30] Like Robinson Crusoe, in other words, who "soon begins, like a good Englishman, to keep a set of books" (Marx, *Capital*), stating "very impartially, like debtor and creditor" (and this was Defoe), the "good" and the "evil" of his state on the island.

Third face of seriousness: the *ernste Lebensführung*, the solid and responsible conduct of life that was for Mann the cornerstone of the bourgeois world. Beyond ethical gravity, beyond the concentration of the specialist, seriousness is here a sort of sublimated commercial honesty—the "almost religious respect for facts" of the Buddenbrook family book—extended to life as a whole: reliability, method, precision, "order and clarity," *realism*. In the sense, indeed, of the reality principle: where coming to terms with reality becomes, from the necessity it always is, a "principle"; a value. Containing one's immediate desires is not just repression here: it is *culture*; style. A scene from *Robinson Crusoe*, with its typical alternation of desires (bolded), difficulties (underlined), and solutions (in italics) will give an idea:

> The first time I went out I presently discovered that **there were goats in the island, which was a great satisfaction to me**; but then it was attended <u>with this misfortune to me, viz. That they were so shy, so subtile, and so swift of foot, that it was the difficultest thing in the world to come at them</u>. **But I was not discouraged at this**, not doubting but I might now and then shoot one, *as it soon happened, for after I had found their haunts a little, I laid wait in this manner for them: I observed if they saw me in the valleys, tho' they were upon the rocks,* <u>they would run away as in a terrible fright</u>; *but if they were*

---

[29] Exactly what Emma Bovary, that prototype of the consumer, will never learn: just before her final ruin, "now and again . . . she would try to make some calculations; but she would discover such exorbitant things that she could not believe it. She would start again, quickly find herself in a muddle, give it up, and stop thinking about it" (*Madame Bovary*, Penguin, 1992, 234).

[30] Leonore Davidoff and Catherine Hall, *Family Fortunes: Men and Women of the English Middle Class, 1780–1850*, Hutchinson, London 1987, 384.

feeding in the valleys, and I was upon the rocks, they took no notice of me,
from whence I concluded that by the position of their opticks, their sight was so
directed downward, that they did not readily see objects that were above
them. . . . The first shot I made among these creatures, I killed a she-goat
<u>which had a little kid by her which grieved me heartily</u>; but when the old one
fell, the kid stood stock still by her till I came and took her up, and not only
so, but when I carry'd the old one with me upon my shoulders, the kid followed me quite to my enclosure, upon which I laid down the dam, and took
the kid in my arms, **and carry's over my pale, in hopes to have it bred up**
tame, <u>but it would not eat</u>, *so I was forced to kill it and eat it.*[31]

Seven "but"s in a dozen lines. "Will; tenacious, inflexible, indomitable will
is the supreme British quality," writes in 1858 the *Revue des Deux Mondes*,
in a piece tellingly entitled "Du sérieux et du romanesque dans la vie
anglaise et américaine," and this page so full of adversative clauses—which
however don't prevent Robinson from achieving his purpose—abundantly
proves the point. Everything is here examined *sine ira et studio*, as in Taci-
tus's maxim with which Weber liked to summarize the process of rationalization: each problem is subdivided into discrete elements (the direction of
the goats' eyesight; Robinson's position in the landscape) and solved by a
methodical coordination of aims and means. The analytical style reveals here
its pragmatic origin, halfway between Bacon's nature (which can be mastered only by obeying her) and Weber's bureaucracy, with its "exclusion of
love, hatred, and all purely personal, irrational, and emotional elements
which escape calculation." And one again thinks of Flaubert: who, for his
part, would probably have welcomed the " 'objective' impersonality" of the
Weberian bureaucrat, "the more perfect, the more he is 'dehumanized.' "[32]

Parting of the Ways: Narration or Description?

"Objective" impersonality: here is a good synthesis of the analytical style.
"Objective" (in quotes: like, later, the " 'objective' seriousness" of *Mimesis*),
not because its details may ever abolish the difference between a representation and its object, of course, but because their multiplication drives the personality of the writer toward the background. Objectivity increases, because
subjectivity decreases. Hans Robert Jauss: "The flourishing historiography

---

[31] Penguin, 1985, 79.
[32] Max Weber, *Economy and Society*, 1922, Bedminster Press, New York, 1968, 3:975.

of the nineteenth century . . . followed the principle that the historian must efface himself in order for history to be able to tell its own story. The poetics of this method is no different from that of the contemporary peak of literature—the historical novel. . . . What so impressed A. Thierry, Barante, and other historians of the Twenties, in Scott's novels, was [that] the narrator of the historical novel remains completely in the background."[33]

The narrator in the background. Take *Castle Rackrent*, the 1800 (quasi-) historical novel by Maria Edgeworth, whose work was later described by Scott, in the 1829 *General Preface*, as the model for his own novels. Now, *Castle Rackrent* is entirely narrated by an old Irish *factotum*, Thady Quirk, who allows Edgeworth to create a bridge between past and present, and between the "here" of her largely English audience and the "there" of her Irish story. Half-abject, half-duplicitous, always extremely lively, Thady lends the novel much of its flavor and depth; but certainly not by allowing "history to tell its own story." Here is a description from *Castle Rackrent*, followed by one from *Kenilworth* (1821), where the presence of the same central object (a Jewish villain, with all the automatic clichés the figure evokes in a culture of widespread anti-Semitism) rules out a thematic origin for their stylistic differences:

> I got the first sight of the bride; for when the carriage door opened, just as she had her foot on the steps, I held the flame full in her face to light her, at which she shut her eyes, but I had a full view of the rest of her, and greatly shocked I was, for by that light she was little better than a blackamoor, and seemed crippled.[34]

> The astrologer was a little man, and seemed much advanced in age, for his beard was long and white, and reached over his black doublet down to his silken girdle. His hair was of the same venerable hue. But his eye-brows were as dark as the keen and piercing black eyes which they shaded, and this peculiarity gave a wild and singular cast to the physiognomy of the old man. His cheek was still fresh and ruddy, and the eyes we have mentioned resembled those of a rat, in acuteness, and even fierceness of expression. (*Kenilworth*, Penguin 1999, 185)

In *Castle Rackrent*, Thady intrudes physically in the scene ("I got the first sight . . . I held the flame . . . I had a full view"), and projects his emotions

---

[33] Hans Robert Jauss, "History of Art and Pragmatic History," in *Toward an Aesthetic of Reception*, Minnesota University Press, 1982, 55.

[34] Maria Edgeworth, *Castle Rackrent*, 1800, in *Tales and Novels*, The Longford Edition (1893), AMS Press, New York 1967, 4:13.

over the event (*"little better than a blackamoor . . .* and *greatly shocked* I was"): the point of the passage lies more in conveying his subjective reactions than in introducing a new character as such. In Scott, by contrast, the scene is largely "objectified" via its physical details: the beard is specified by emotionally neutral adjectives; its length measured against ordinary garments, of which we are told the color, the material . . . Here and there, true, an emotional spark flickers ("a wild cast . . . the eyes resembled those of a rat"); but all in all—and although Scott's character is immensely more sinister than Edgeworth's—in *Kenilworth* the decisive point is the *analytical presentation* of the character, not his emotional evaluation. Precision; not intensity.

So Jauss is right, in Scott the historian effaces himself—in comparison with his contemporaries, at least—and history (seems to) tell its own story. But "story" is the wrong word here, because the analytical-impersonal style is much more frequent in *descriptions* than in the narrative proper. And this fact opens a further line of inquiry.

———

Alongside Edgeworth, another proto-historical novelist mentioned in the *General Preface* is Joseph Strutt, whose *Queenhoo-Hall* was published posthumously (in 1808) with a "hasty conclusion" written by Scott himself at the request of the publisher. *Queenhoo-Hall* was a miserable flop, which Scott explains with Strutt's "too ancient" language (as opposed to his own, "more light and obvious to general comprehension"). But although Strutt's language can indeed be occasionally terrifying—"Away, away, ye varlets! I weened it was an idle frolic!—uncase in an instant; and off with these lozel knackeries!"[35]—these linguistic knackeries are not frequent enough to explain the book's failure. Strutt's way of (not) describing the past was probably a worse mistake. Here is how he introduces the mansion that gives the novel its title: "The Boteler family made a great figure in Hertfordshire. Lord Edward Boteler, as already noticed, was in high favour with his sovereign, and held a post of importance at court. Queenhoo-hall, the noble family-mansion, was situated about four miles from the town of Hertford; it was a spacious edifice; and large vestiges of it remain even to this day. Lord Edward was young when he married" (*Queenhoo-Hall*, 1).

A spacious edifice: end of the description. Three words. Scott would have paused for (at least) half a page, but Strutt stops as soon as possible. Nor is he the only one. In Jane West's *The Loyalists* (1812), another pre-*Waverley*

---

[35] Joseph Strutt, *Queenhoo-Hall, a Romance*, Ballantyne, Edinburgh 1808, 7.

historical novel, on Cromwell's times, we encounter the first description after 334 pages:

> The country through which they passed in their journey toward London, afforded them a full view of the miseries and crimes incident to civil war. The fields, in many places, were without any trace of culture; in others, the harvest had been prematurely seized or purposely wasted, to cut off the enemy's resources. They saw beautiful woods wantonly felled. . . . The few labourers . . . no longer exhibited the cheerful aspect of happy industry, but shewed sorrow in their faces, and wretchedness in their garb. . . . The unemployed manufacturers crowded the streets . . . shewing by the lean ferocity of their faces, and the squalid negligence of their attire, that from unpitied poverty sprang all the virulent passions of rage, envy, revenge, and disobedience.[36]

The fields, the laborers' faces, the "attire" of the "manufacturers": none of these things are really *described*. They are evoked only as a way to support those ethical abstractions (industry, ferocity, sorrow, disobedience . . .) that are West's true protagonists, and which indeed promptly reoccupy the foreground of the novel, while the next description occurs 240 pages later, and is three lines long.

Why all this resistance, on Strutt's and West's part? Probably, because descriptions interrupt the flow of events—literally: in order to describe, one must stop narrating—and a novel that gives up narration may have struck them as a contradiction in terms. It's like Edgeworth's reluctance to use fillers in *Belinda*: if one imagines novels under the sign of the unheard-of, slowing down the story with scenes of everyday life does not make sense—let alone suppressing it altogether with static detailed descriptions. And yet . . .

Yet, those description-heavy *Waverley Novels* become world best sellers, still read two hundred years later; while Strutt and West gather dust on the shelves of the British Library. Why? What did European readers find, in Scott's massive solidity?[37]

---

[36] Jane West, *The Loyalists: An Historical Novel*, Longman, Hurst, Rees, Orme, and Brown, London 1812, 334ff.

[37] On the difference between Scott's descriptions and those of contemporary gothic or historical novels (by the Porter sisters, Ann Radcliffe, Charlotte Smith) see Gary Kelly's pages on the shift from "the sublime," "costume melodrama," or "the atmospherics of subjective consciousness" to a "dense material . . . so prominent . . . that it displaces plot and absorbs character" (Gary Kelly, *English Fiction of the Romantic Period, 1789–1830*, Longman, London 1989, 98, 146–47.

"Realismus"

The answer, more than in Scott, can be found in Balzac. But there is no point in analyzing Balzac's descriptions, because no one will ever do it better than Auerbach. So: "Balzac . . . not only . . . places the human beings whose destiny he is seriously relating in their precisely defined historical and social setting, but also conceives this connection as a necessary one: to him every milieu becomes a moral and physical atmosphere which impregnates the landscape, the dwelling, furniture, implements, clothing, physique, character, surroundings, ideas, activities, and fates of men."[38]

The connection between person and things conceived as a necessity: Madame Vauquer, where "there is no separation of body and clothing, of physical characteristics and moral significance."[39] Now, the same absence of separation is also at the core of the most powerful political ideology of the early nineteenth century: conservatism. Adam Müller, writes Mannheim (sounding very much like Auerbach on *Père Goriot*), "regards things as extensions of the limbs of the human body . . . a fusion of person and thing": "a definite, vital, reciprocal relationship" between the owner and his property, as Justus Möser wrote in his essay "Of Genuine Property."[40] And the reason for this "fusion" is to be found in that other cornerstone of conservative thought that is the complete subordination of the present to the past: "the progressive always experiences the present as the beginning of the future," writes Mannheim, "while the conservative regards it simply as *the latest stage reached by the past*."[41] And Auerbach: "Balzac conceives the present as history . . . as something *resulting from history . . .*: people and atmospheres, contemporary as they may be, are always represented as phenomena *sprung from historical events and forces*."[42] In political philosophy and literary representation alike, the present is simply an external, superficial

---

[38] Auerbach, *Mimesis*, 473.

[39] Ibid., 471.

[40] Karl Mannheim, *Conservatism: A Contribution to the Sociology of Knowledge*, 1925, Routledge and Kegan Paul, New York 1986, 89–90.

[41] Ibid., 97 (italics mine).

[42] Auerbach, *Mimesis*, 480 (italics mine). As an illustration of Auerbach's point, here is a description from the beginning of *Lost Illusions*: "*For thirty years* Jérôme-Nicolas Séchard had been wearing the famous three-cornered municipal hat *still to be seen* on the heads of town-criers *in certain provinces*. His waistcoat and trousers were of greenish velvet. Finally, he wore an *old* brown frock-coat, stockings of patterned cotton and shoes with silver buckles. This costume, thanks to which *the worker was still manifest behind the bourgeois*, was . . . so expressive of his way of life, that he looked as if he had come into the world fully clad" (*Lost Illusions*, 1837–43, Penguin, 1988, 7; italics mine).

sediment of history; while the past is for its part spatialized and—instead of being gone, invisible, no-longer-existent—becomes something solid and *concrete*, to quote another key word of conservative thought (and of the rhetoric of "realism").

I have spoken of the analytical, im-personal, even "im-partial" (Scott) tone of nineteenth-century descriptions. But if individual descriptions may indeed be relatively neutral, description *as such,* as a form, embodies a project that is not neutral at all: *to bring history to a halt.* Descriptions turn the present into something so thoroughly pervaded by the past that alternatives become unimaginable. Hans Blumenberg: "'Immediate expectation' negates every type of durability [and] tears the individual free even from the historical interests of his people. . . . Assuming that this is the 'last moment,' demands can be made on every individual that are inconsistent with realism [*Realismus*] regarding the world and that would have the reverse of survival value were the world to endure."[43] Demands that are inconsistent with realism, *were the world to endure* . . . The secret source of "realistic" descriptions lies precisely in the unexpected "endurance" of the *ancien régime* into the nineteenth century. Have the "immediate expectation" of the revolutionary years challenged the "durability" of social hierarchies? It was a passing euphoria, whose verdict has been completely reversed by the Restoration. History's sudden accelerations are surface phenomena: social relationships have roots deeply anchored in the past—in a temporal stratification that only the "thick" realism of novelistic description can see and reproduce.

Realism as bourgeois reality principle, I said earlier about Defoe and Goethe; or as *Realpolitik*, one may add for the two great conservatives Scott and Balzac. A politics that "does not operate within an undefined future, but face to face with what is," wrote Ludwig August von Rochau, who coined the term a few years after the defeat of the 1848 revolutions (more or less at the same time when artistic *réalisme* begins to be discussed in France). "Realismus der Stabilität," adds, bitterly, an anonymous liberal observer: the realism of stability and of the *fait accompli*.[44] Not that Balzac is all here, of course—no, there is also the irrepressible narration that recalls Hegel's "fury of disappearance," or the paragraphs from the *Communist*

---

[43] Hans Blumenberg, *The Legitimacy of the Modern Age*, MIT Press, 1966, 42.

[44] Su von Rochau and the *Grundsätze der Realpolitik*, cf. Otto Brunner, Werner Conze, and Reinhart Koselleck, eds., *Geschichtliche Grundbegriffe*, Klett-Cotta, Stuttgart 1982, 4:359ff.; the other quotation, anonymous, can be found in Gerhard Plumpe, ed., *Theorie des bürgerlichen Realismus*, Reclam, Stuttgart 1985, 45.

Manifesto on the "everlasting uncertainty and agitation [of] the bourgeois epoch." But next to Marx's Balzac there is Auerbach's, and this strange mix of bourgeois plot and conservative description suggests something important about nineteenth-century novels (and perhaps about literature in general): its main vocation lies in forging *compromises between different ideological systems.*[45] In our case, the compromise resembles a division of labor, in which the souls of the European ruling class animate different parts of the text: capitalist rationalization reorganizes the level of the story with the pervasive regularity of fillers—while political conservatism surfaces in the novel's descriptive pauses, where the persistence of the past is the dominant reality.[46]

The bourgeoisie, and conservatism: such is the encounter at the origin of the realist novel, from Goethe to Austen, Scott, Balzac, Flaubert, Mann (Thackeray, the Goncourts, Fontane, James . . .). To this small miracle of equilibrium, free indirect style was to give the final touch.

Parting of the Ways: Politics, Style

Zeitschrift für romanische Philologie, 1887. In a long article on French grammar, A. Tobler observes, almost in passing, that the presence of the *imparfait* in interrogative sentences is often linked to a "peculiar mix of indirect and direct discourse, which draws *the verbal tenses and pronouns* from the former, and *the tone and the order of the sentence* from the latter."[47] The *"Mischung"* has no name yet (and later it will have far too many), but the decisive intuition is already there: free indirect style is a meeting ground between two forms of discourse. A passage from one of the first novels to use it in a systematic way: "The hair was curled, and the maid sent away, and Emma sat down to think and be miserable.—It was a wretched business, indeed!—Such an overthrow of everything she had been wishing for!—Such a development of everything most unwelcome!—Such a blow for Harriet!—That was the worst of all" (*Emma*, Penguin 1996, p. 112). Emma sat down to think *and be miserable.*—It was *a wretched business, indeed!* The tone and

---

[45] On literature as compromise formation, the classic study is Francesco Orlando's *Toward a Freudian Theory of Literature*, 1973, Johns Hopkins University Press, 1978.

[46] In the historical novel, this division of labor—on the one hand, a plot that decrees the pastness of the past; on the other, countless descriptions that aim at making the past visible and present—is of course particularly visible.

[47] A. Tobler, "Vermischte Beiträge zur französischen Grammatik," *Zeitschrift für romanische Philologie*, 1887, 437.

the order of the sentence, italicized, recall Emma's direct discourse. *Emma sat down* to think and be miserable.—It *was* a wretched business, indeed!—Such an overthrow of everything *she had been wishing for*!—The tenses and the pronouns, on the other hand, are those of indirect discourse. And it is strange, one feels simultaneously much closer to Emma (because the filter of the narrator's voice is gone), and much more distant (because the act of narration *objectifies* Emma, and thus somehow estranges her from her own self). It is truly "a peculiar mix," free indirect style, and with an equally peculiar history: present in the Middle Ages, but hardly in the Renaissance; widespread in La Fontaine's *Fables*, but unusual in (most of) the eighteenth century; and even in the nineteenth century, when it becomes a sort of stylistic quintessence of the European novel, the trajectory is far from linear. In Britain, for instance, around 1800 the technique is clearly in the air—and yet Austen is the only writer who truly understands and exploits its potential. Why? What is it, in that *Emma* paragraph, which is so difficult for Opie and Edgeworth, Hofland and Charlton, and so easy for Austen?

Let's look for a first answer in the relationship between the style and the narrative moment in which it occurs. Usually, in the early nineteenth century, free indirect style does not emerge randomly here and there in the text, but clusters near the plot's major turning points: moments of doubt, fear, excitement, and especially (as in *Emma*) retrospective regret.[48] And it makes sense, because in these moments the characters' emotions have that surplus intensity that is needed to "bridge" the structural gap between story and discourse. But the very same moments are also ideal for the *opposite* of free indirect style: they are a great opportunity for the narrator to draw the moral of the fable, spelling out the catastrophic effects of the character's mistakes. Moments of crisis are in other words like a narrative crossroads, where a writer can reiterate the superiority of the narrator over the character with a didactic passage—or express their tendential equality with free indirect style. One, *or* the other. Not both. And at stake, here, is not just style, but the social function of literature as such. In the first case a didactic view prevails, for which novels are fundamentally instruments of explicit (and usually stern) ethical messages. In the latter case, the vividness of emotional

---

[48] "When do [narrator and character] switch their parts? Usually [when] the hero undergoes some torments because of an uncertain and variable situation" (Giulio Herczeg, *Lo stile indiretto libero in italiano*, Sansoni, Florence 1963, 65–66). "In the novels of George Eliot," writes for his part Roy Pascal, "situations of tension and crisis almost always rely on the reproduction through free indirect style of the character's view of the problem." The same is true of Dostoevsky, where free indirect style "usually occurs at times of great inward tension, struggle, and anxiety" (Roy Pascal, *The Dual Voice*, Manchester University Press, 1977, 78, 124).

experience gains ground over the ethical message, which becomes implicit, ironic (and usually blander).

Now, most of Austen's contemporaries have a firmly didactic conception of literature: having to choose, therefore, they almost always reaffirm the narrator's ethical mission—thus barring the way to free indirect style. It's not so much that they don't *know* how to use this style: it's that they don't *want* to use it, because it contradicts their fundamental vocation. Take Mary Charlton's *The Wife and the Mistress* (1802). Lady Melville, whose husband has recently died, reflects on her situation: "a second marriage, indeed, might—yet what would a second marriage eventually do for her . . .? Renew the fetters from which she was just freed, and either make her a slave for life, or leave her, after a few years of bondage but ill-adapted to the haughtiness of her spirit, again perhaps the jointured relict of a fool, whose family regard her as a pensioned alien and an incumbrance, should she not have the good fortune to be the vehicle by which their name and honours are transmitted to posterity." So far, all is as it should be: the tone and the order of the sentence are those of direct discourse, while verbal tenses and pronouns are those of indirect discourse. It's a perfectly smooth, and in fact a rather complex instance of free indirect style. Then Charlton opens a new paragraph: "She did not reflect that this grievance extended to most women of her own rank, and even to those both in much superior and inferior gradations.—No!—her indignation arose from the consideration that the case was her individually!"[49]

Two exclamation marks in three lines, that "No!" given such odd typographic relief, a sudden animosity against Lady Melville (who a page later becomes "vain, ambitious, and unnatural"). What a mess. And one thinks that Charlton must have felt uneasy at the idea of becoming indistinguishable from her character; of representing a consciousness "unmediated by any judging point of view," as Ann Banfield has put it in her classic study of free indirect style.[50] What if some readers end up agreeing with Lady Melville's critique of marriage? God forbid. And so Charlton curtly distances herself from her character: instead of mixing her voice with hers, she raises it in condemnation—and "turns off" free indirect style. Ideological clarity trumps stylistic elegance.

And it makes sense. But then, how do we explain Austen? Why can *she* let go of didacticism, allowing free indirect style to levitate from the few

---

[49] Mary Charlton, *The Wife and the Mistress*, Minerva Press, London 1802, 3–4.
[50] Ann Banfield, *Unspeakable Sentences*, Routledge and Kegan Paul, Boston 1982, 97.

sentences of *Northanger Abbey* to the long passages of *Pride and Prejudice, Mansfield Park*, and *Emma*? Why is Austen so much more flexible than her rivals? *Pride and Prejudice*, chapter 50: the possibility of a marriage between Darcy and Elizabeth seems irrreversibly gone: "She began now to comprehend that he was exactly the man, who, in disposition and talents, would most suit her. His understanding and temper, though unlike her own, would have answered all her wishes. It was an union that must have been to the advantage of both; by her ease and liveliness, his mind might have been softened, his manners improved, and from his judgment, information, and knowledge of the world, she must have received benefit of greater importance."[51]

As a first comment, the words with which Roy Pascal elaborates Bally's thesis on free indirect style: "For Bally, simple Indirect Style tends to obliterate the characteristic personal idiom of the reported speaker; while Free Indirect Style preserves some of its elements—the sentence forms, questions, exclamations, intonations, personal vocabulary, and the subjective perspective of the character."[52] Preserving the subjective perspective instead of obliterating it. Pascal is discussing stylistic matters, here, but his words describe just as well what happens in the process of modern socialization: where individual peculiarities, instead of being erased in the name of didactic consistency, are merely toned down so as to become compatible with the super-personal syntax of social relations. In this well-known double bind of nineteenth-century capitalism—individual energies must be free to express themselves, but without threatening the stability of social relations—free indirect style functions as an excellent compromise: it leaves the individual voice a certain amount of freedom (and a *variable* amount, according to the character and the situation: just as it happens to people in flesh and blood during their socialization), while coloring individual emotions with the super-personal idiom of the narrator.[53] *His understanding and temper, though unlike her own, would have answered all her wishes* . . . who is speaking, here? Elizabeth? Austen? Perhaps neither the one nor the other, but a *third*

---

[51] Jane Austen, *Pride and Prejudice*, Penguin 1972, 325.

[52] Pascal, *The Dual Voice*, 9–10.

[53] "In free indirect style," writes D. A. Miller, "the two antithetical terms [of character and narration] stand, so to speak, as close as possible to the bar (the virgule, the disciplinary rod) that separates them. Narration comes as near to a character's psychic and linguistic reality as it can get without collapsing into it, and the character does as much of the work of narration as she may without acquiring its authority" (*Jane Austen, or The Secret of Style*, Princeton University Press, 2003, 59).

voice, intermediate and almost neutral among them:[54] the slightly abstract voice of the achieved social contract: of the *well-socialized individual*. Here, the drama and the farcical humiliations of didactic narratives have become superfluous: a little irony is enough to remind characters (and readers) of the social norms they had never really forgotten.

————

An intermediate, almost neutral third voice . . . But not quite equidistant: the premise of that *Pride and Prejudice* passage, after all, is that Elizabeth is finally seeing herself—*She began now to comprehend*—with the eyes of the narrator. She observes her own life from the outside, as if she were a third person (a third person: here, the grammar of free indirect style is really the message), and agrees with Austen. It is a tolerant technique, free indirect style, but the technique of *socialization*, not of individuality (not around 1800, at any rate);[55] Elizabeth's subjective viewpoint bows to that higher value which is the "objective" (that is, socially accepted) intelligence of the world: "une vérita-ble transposition de l'objectif dans le subjectif," as Charles Bally put it in his seminal article.[56] The Heroine Who Is Wrong, as Marilyn Butler calls her, has learned her lesson: "The anti-Jacobin plot leads to a climax in which the hero is made aware of his presumption and learns to take his place in the world as it actually is. . . . In the conservative novel . . . the most typical plot has the central character, gradually schooled to objective reality, renouncing the pri-vate delusions that once tempted him to see the world other than it is."[57]

————

[54] "With the development of modern fiction," writes Lubomír Dolezel, "the relationship between [the Discourse of the Narrator, and the Discourse of the Character] underwent a dramatic change. In structural terms, this change can be described as a process of 'neutralization' " (*Narrative Modes in Czech Literature*, Toronto University Press, 1973, 18–19). In order to define the relationship between the narrator's and the character's voice in free indirect style, adds Anne Waldron Neumann, " 'neutral' might be better than 'sympathetic,' " because "it is not meant to imply the narrator's endorsement, but simply that the two voices do not clash" ("Characterization and Comment in *Pride and Prejudice*: Free Indirect Discourse and 'Double-Voiced' Verbs of Speaking, Thinking, and Feeling," *Style*, Fall 1986, 390). On free indirect style as a "*third term* between character and narration," and on the " 'neutral' accents" of Austen's style in general, see again Miller's *Jane Austen, or The Secret of Style*, 59–60, 100. The affinity between stylistic "neutrality" and the "intermediate" position of the *genre sérieux* seems evident.

[55] Things change in the twentieth century; see my sketch in *Graphs, Maps, Trees: Abstract Models for Literary History*, Verso, London 2005.

[56] "Le style indirecte libre en français moderne," *Germanisch-Romanische Monatschrift*, 1912, second part, 603.

[57] Marilyn Butler, *Jane Austen and the War of Ideas*, 1975, Clarendon, Oxford 1987, 166, 107, 124.

Austen among the counterrevolutionaries, then? Yes and no. Yes, because the ideological arsenal of the anti-Jacobins—self-delusion, individual presumption that must end in self-criticism, the victory of the world "as it is"—is Austen's as well. And no, because if the values are the same, the historical diagnosis is however quite different. Austen is an *optimistic* conservative, at ease in the present, for whom the status quo must indeed be defended, but does not run the immediate danger that the others fear (and that leads them to the didactic intransigence so fatal to free indirect style).[58] Austen no, is not frightened. Who knows, it may just be the luck of beginning to write a decade after the others, when the revolutionary panic is over; be that as it may, her sense of reality tells her that what is on the agenda is not political anarchy, but just another adjustment within the ranks of the ruling class, such as Britain has often seen since the seventeenth century. And this compromise is well served by that "curious mix"—itself a compromise—of free indirect style, where the "truth" of the *ancien régime* subordinates the emotions of the new age, but does not quite repress them.

An optimistic conservative. Like Goethe, Scott, Balzac: all of them capable of that "strong liking for the actual" that Butler recognizes in Austen. The struggle against the revolution has been won: there is no more need of didactic drumming, nor anything to fear if a new technique allows a certain amount of ambiguity to circulate in the text. Austen's *Realpolitik* has "cleared" free indirect style; and the latter, in turn, grants her an aesthetic and anthropological depth that her rivals lack. It makes her—no question— much better. But her superiority may spring more from political cynicism than from stylistic mastery.

The Weak Style: Flaubert and Free Indirect Style

We have seen the beginnings of free indirect style. Now, a fully mature example: Emma Bovary, in front of her mirror, after her first adultery:

> But when she looked in the mirror, she was startled by her own face. Never had she had eyes so large, so black, so deep. Something subtle, transfiguring, was pervading her person.
>
> She kept saying to herself: "I have a lover! A lover!," savouring this idea just as if a second puberty had come upon her. At last, she was to know those

---

[58] "No English novels before or since have been so unremittingly ethical as the conservative novels of the generation following 1790" (ibid., 97).

joys of love, that fever of happiness which she had despaired of. She was entering something marvelous, where everything would be passion, extasy, delirium; blue immensity was all about her, the summits of sentiment were glittering in her mind's eye, ordinary appearance appeared only in the distance, far below, in the shadow, in the gaps between these heights.[59]

In February 1857, in his address to the Rouen tribunal, the prosecutor Ernest Pinard devoted to this passage—"much more immoral than the fall itself"—his harshest words.[60] And it's understandable: those sentences clash head on with "the old novelistic convention of an always unequivocal moral judgment of the represented characters."[61] Is there anybody in the novel, Pinard continues, "who may condemn this woman? No; no one. This is the conclusion. There isn't in the book a single character who may condemn her. If you can find a virtuous character, or even just an abstract principle—one—on whose basis adultery is stigmatized, then I am wrong."[62] Wrong? No, a century of criticism has vindicated him:[63] *Madame Bovary* is the logical endpoint of that slow process that has detached European literature from its didactic functions, replacing an all-wise narrator with large doses of free indirect style. But if this historical trajectory is reasonably clear, its cultural consequences are not, and critics have gravitated around two incompatible interpretations. For Jauss (and others), free indirect style places the novel in opposition to the dominant culture, because it forces readers "into an alienating uncertainty of judgment . . . turning a predecided question of public morals [that is, the evaluation of adultery] back into an open problem."[64] In this perspective, Pinard was quite right

---

[59] Gustave Flaubert, *Madame Bovary*, Penguin, 2003, 150–51.

[60] "And so, after this first crime, after this first fall, she glorifies adultery, she intones the song of adultery, its poetry, its pleasures. And this, gentlemen, is for me much more dangerous, much more immoral than the fall itself!" (Gustave Flaubert, *Oeuvres*, ed. A. Thibaudet and R. Dumesnil, Bibliothèque de la Pléiade, Paris 1951, 1:623).

[61] Hans Robert Jauss, "Literary History as Challenge to Literary Theory," 1967, in *Toward an Aesthetic of Reception*, 43.

[62] Flaubert, *Oeuvres*, 632.

[63] "In Stendhal and Balzac we frequently and indeed almost constantly hear what the writer thinks of his characters. . . . These things are almost wholly absent from Flaubert's work. His opinion of his characters and events remains unspoken. . . . We hear the writer speak; but he expresses no opinion and makes no comment" (Auerbach, *Mimesis*, 486).

[64] "Literary History as Challenge to Literary Theory," 44. Jauss's thesis is echoed by Dominick La Capra (who writes euphorically of Flaubert's "ideological crime": *Madame Bovary on Trial*, Cornell University Press, 1982, 18), and by the more measured Dorrit Cohn (*The Distinction of Fiction*, Johns Hopkins University Press, 1999, 170 sgg.).

about the stakes of the trial: Flaubert was a threat to the established order. Luckily Pinard lost, and Flaubert won.

The other position reverses the picture. Free indirect style is a sort of stylistic Panopticon, where the narrator's "master-voice . . . continually needs to confirm its authority by qualifying, canceling, endorsing, subsuming all the other voices it lets speak."[65] From this second viewpoint, Pinard and Flaubert do not stand for, respectively, repression and critique, but rather for an obsolete, stolid form of social control, and a more flexible and effective one. The trial sets them one against the other, true, but in a deeper sense they both embody a form of symbolic power; they are two versions *of the same thing*, finally.

If these were the only possible options, I would probably side with the latter; after all, my interpretation of Austen is similar. But Flaubert's case seems to me to be more extreme, more uncanny. Those sentences from *Madame Bovary* for example, that so incensed Monsieur Pinard . . . are they *Emma's* words? Of course not, they come from the sentimental novels she has read as a girl and has never forgotten (the passage continues: "Then she recalled the heroines of the books she had read"). They are commonplaces, collective myths: signs, not of her individuality, but of the *social* that is inside her. The voice we so often hear in *Pride and Prejudice* is neither Elizabeth's nor Austen's, I wrote a few pages ago, but—perhaps—the "third voice" of the achieved social contract; well, with Flaubert we can definitely drop the perhaps, because character and narrator lose their distinctiveness, and are replaced (almost) everywhere by the abstract voice of current ideology. The emotional tone, the lexicon, the shape of the sentence—all the elements on which we rely to extricate the subjective from the objective side of free indirect style—are now amalgamated in the truly " 'objective' impersonality" of the *idée reçue*.

But if this is so, then worrying about the text's "master-voice" has become superfluous: the control of Emma's soul—"qualifying, canceling, endorsing, subsuming"—is in the hands of the *doxa*, not of the narrator. In a fully homogenized society, as contemporary France is for Flaubert, free indirect style reveals, not its power, but its *impotence*: its " 'objective' seriousness" paralyzes it, making any opposition to the ruling ideology unimaginable: once the the entropic drift begins, and the narrator's voice merges with that of the characters (and, through them, of bourgeois *doxa*), there is no way back. Socialization has been *too* successful: from the many voices of the social universe, only "an average intellectual level" remains, "around which

---

[65] D. A. Miller, *The Novel and the Police*, University of California Press, Berkeley 1988, 25.

oscillate the individual intelligences of the bourgeois."[66] And it will be the anxiety of *Bouvard et Pécuchet*: no longer knowing how to distinguish a novel about stupidity from a stupid novel.

———

Thus ends the serious century of the European novel. This "Weberian" form, where temporality becomes more predictable, objects multiply, personality hides, and language is streamlined. This half-bourgeois, half-conservative form, which never really transcends its sociopolitical origin, to which it owes in fact most of its historical intelligence. This serious form, which tries with unprecedented intensity to make the European imaginary *less novelistic*.

Did it succeed? It is always difficult to draw these large balance sheets, but for what it is worth, my answer would be, No. Not in the long run, anyway. True, in the course of the nineteenth century the serious style (as a *life* style, not just a literary one) found more and more followers, even outside of the *Bildungsbürgertum* that had been its cradle. But the mass appeal of what in English is called "romance" was never really shaken by writers like Goethe or Austen or Eliot (let alone Flaubert); not in Western Europe, and even less in the southern and eastern parts of the continent, where it encountered all sorts of resistance.[67] Then, in the twentieth century, politics and the economy discarded without regrets the old bourgeois restraints; the culture industry wagered on excess, instead of measure, while the great modernist art despised realism with passionate intensity, and, later, "magical" realism re-enchanted the experience of modernity. Encircled from so many parts, and already exhausted from within, the serious style surrendered, and abandoned the scene.

In taking our leave, we should not forget how narrow it could be. Life as work, always; few smiles, few surprises. But let us also remember that bourgeois seriousness marked the discovery—half-bitter, half-proud—that nothing is ever given us for free, and that only a constant, intense attention can give form to the world. In our relaxed age of planetary superexploitation, a certain respect for this old frame of mind is perhaps in order.

———

[66] René Descharmes, *Autour de 'Bouvard et Pécuchet,'* Librairie de France, Paris 1921, 65.

[67] The general mood is well exemplified by this passage from the fifth chapter of Perez Galdos's *Fortunata y Jacinta* (1887): "Spanish society begun to flatter itself by fancying that it was "serious," that is to say, it began to dress mournfully: our happy empire of bright colors was fading away. . . . We're under the influence of northern Europe, and the blasted North imposes on us the grays that it gets from its smoky gray sky" (Penguin, 1986, 26).

WILLIAM MILLS TODD III

The Ruse of the Russian Novel

> The history of Russian literature from Pushkin's time
> not only presents many examples of departure from
> European form, it does not give a single example of the
> opposite. From Gogol's *Dead Souls* to Dostoevsky's
> *House of the Dead* . . . there is not a single work of
> literary prose that rises above mediocrity which could
> fit into the form of a novel, an epic, or a tale.[1]
> —Leo Tolstoy, "A Few Words about the Book
> *War and Peace*," 1868

"A Departure from European Taste and Method"

"The Russian novel" is truly a phrase to conjure with. Since the late nineteenth century its readers in Europe, Asia, and the western hemisphere have found it omnipresent and overwhelming, its powers little less than magical or sacred. Its first great foreign scholar, de Vogüé, writing as much against the naturalism of his native France as about a Russian realism inferred mainly from the work of four novelists (Gogol, Turgenev, Dostoevsky, Tolstoy), delivered an encomium that has shaped a century of foreign responses:

> Russian literature is creating and perfecting the instrument appropriate to its
> task, realism. While the West still hesitates to use this instrument, Russian lit-
> erature applies it with success to matters of the external world and those of
> the soul. This realism is often devoid of taste and method; it is simultane-
> ously diffuse and subtle. But it is always natural and sincere. Above all, it is
> ennobled by moral emotion, by anxiety about the divine, and by sympathy
> for human beings. None of these novelists sets himself a purely literary goal.
> All of their work is governed by a double concern: for truth and for justice.

Forests, steppes, peasants, and an elegant description of St. Isaac's Cathedral, illuminated by a stained glass representation of Christ, serve de Vogüé

---

[1] L. N. Tolstoy, "Neskol'ko slov po povodu knigi 'Voina i mir,'" in his *Sobranie sochinenii v dvadtsati tomakh* (Moscow: GIKhL, 1960–65), 7:382–83.

as stage props for this presentation of the Russian novel and the future "great word" that the Slavic race will pronounce.[2] In de Vogüé's praise and predictions readers familiar with Russian literature will, indeed, catch echoes of Gogol's sermonic digressions from *Dead Souls* (without the ironic counterpoints of the novel's more creatural passages), Dostoevsky's prophetic journalism, and the earnest demands of Russia's "radical" critics.

The crucial concepts here are realism, spirituality, sympathy, difference from the West, sincerity (manifest in an alleged absence of "taste" and "method"), and a reluctance to be merely "literary" when justice needs be served and when great truths may be pronounced. Influential Western critics have echoed this characterization in a variety of ways. Erich Auerbach in *Mimesis*, Harry Levin in *The Gates of Horn*, Georg Lukács in *The Theory of the Novel*—to cite just three instances—have looked to the great Russians for, respectively, "unqualified, unlimited, and passionate intensity of experience," "antitoxins . . . against the deadlier plagues which devastate man's spirit," and a possible departure from "the age of absolute sinfulness."[3] In each of these influential examples the crucial differences turn upon absence, be it absence from the bourgeois orientation of the Western novel, absence from the conventional density of Western society, or absence of the formal literary conventions of Western art.

At times absence becomes antithesis, and the Russian novel becomes a forum for the critique of post-Enlightenment Western society and art, as these had begun to be manifested in Russia itself. But both constructions, absence and antithesis, obscure the fact that Russian writers, coming to the attention of Europe during the age of naturalism, were drawing on trends—romantic, confessional, melodramatic, aesthetically self-conscious, gothic—that had been tried and rejected in the West by the early decades of the nineteenth century. Vladimir Nabokov was more analytic than his readers may suppose in applying such labels to Dostoevsky in his *Lectures on Russian Literature*. He could just as easily have extended them to other prominent nineteenth-century Russian novelists, who grew up on narratives by Sterne, Radcliffe, Byron, Scott, Dickens, Goethe, Schiller, Hoffmann, Poe, Rousseau, Balzac,

---

[2] Vte. E. M. de Vogüé, *Le roman russe* (Paris: Librairie Plon, 1886), 341–43.

[3] Erich Auerbach, *Mimesis: The Representation of Reality in Western Literature*, trans. Willard R. Trask (Princeton, N.J.: Princeton University Press, 1953), 522–23; Harry Levin, *The Gates of Horn: A Study of Five French Realists* (New York: Oxford University Press, 1966), 39; Georg Lukács, *The Theory of the Novel: A Historico-Philosophical Essay on the Forms of Great Epic Literature*, trans. Anna Bostock (Cambridge, Mass.: MIT Press, 1971), 153.

Sue, Sand and Hugo, whom they could read in the original languages or in abundant translations.

This paradox, that European critics failed to see that the otherness of the Russian novel was in large part their own literary past, is but one of several that emerge from a close institutional study of the Russian writers, readers, critics, publishers, and censors. In this essay I will argue that, in most cases, it is the institutional circumstances of the Russian novel that most distinguish it from, say, the English, French, or American novel of the time. By "institutional" I have in mind the roles and precedents involved in the practice of Russian fiction. I have chosen to title this essay "the ruse of the Russian novel," not its "rise," as a way of foregrounding the fragility of a literary life that, nevertheless, enabled the appearance of a handful of novels that have, both in Russia and abroad, made an indelible impression on writers and readers alike.

The period I will discuss stretches from the publication of Alexander Pushkin's *Eugene Onegin: A Novel in Verse* (by chapters, 1825–32) to Fedor Dostoevsky's *The Brothers Karamazov* (serialized 1879–80). Beginnings and ends shape the history of what comes between; why choose these? For a start, they encompass the canonical novels, the ones that survive today in the school curriculum and that were already recognized by the turn of the century as classics of Russian literature, as church, state, and intelligentsia struggled to determine the course of Russia's growing literacy: a mere 21 percent of the empire's population was able to read when literacy was first surveyed in 1897.[4] To be sure, Russians did write novels before 1825, but the names of their authors survive principally in the memory of highly learned philologists. These early novelists, such as Fedor Emin (1735?–70), Mikhail Chulkov (1743?–92), and Matvei Komarov (1730?–1812) authored assorted adventure romances, epistolary novels, and picaresques. The question marks by their dates of birth bear witness to the obscurity of their origins and to their lowly status on a literary scene dominated by imperial patronage and imported European literature. Only Komarov survived into the twentieth century, his *Tale of the Adventures of the English Milord George* (1782) having been snapped up by the chapbook trade (*Lubok*) and widely disseminated in subliterary milieux. This tale of the hero's quest to be reunited with

---

[4] Jeffrey Brooks, *When Russia Learned to Read: Literacy and Popular Literature, 1861–1917* (Princeton, N.J.: Princeton University Press, 1985), 3; Jeffrey Brooks, "Russian Nationalism and Russian Literature: The Canonization of the Classics," in Ivo Banac et al., eds., *Nation and Ideology: Essays in Honor of Wayne S. Vucinich* (Boulder, Colo.: East European Monographs, 1981), 315–34.

the Brandenburg margravine Friderika Louisa was incompatible, predictably, with the precepts of Marxism-Leninism, and it disappeared from
the book stalls with the coming of the Soviet regime.[5]

Authors, Readers, Censors, Critics

Leaving aside earlier attempts to establish a secular prose literature in Russia, who were the participants in the more successful prose fiction of the
1820s–1880s? The situation would change during these seventy years, but at
the outset most readers and writers were members of the educated Westernized gentry, later joined by civil servants who rose to noble status through
their service to the state, by members of clerical families who left their caste
to seek education in the liberal professions (law, medicine, teaching), by enlightened merchants who developed a taste for Russia's new culture, and—
far less frequently—by emancipated serfs and their children. As late as 1863,
Dostoevsky would estimate that only one Russian in five hundred had access
to this nontraditional literary culture.[6] Sales and circulation figures suggest it
was closer to one in a thousand. In assessing this cultured elite, the terms
bourgeois and *middle class* must be used with extreme caution, as Russia remained a predominantly rural society.

Who were the authors? Measured by the three principal senses of the
word *professional* (having a vocation, supporting oneself principally by
one's writing, conforming to the ethical standards of an elite occupational
group), few Russian writers would qualify. Most were landowners, civil servants, or military officers and relied on these occupations for a considerable
proportion of their income. Among the first generation of memorable Russian novelists, Alexander Pushkin (1799–1837) was the boldest and most articulate in challenging aristocratic prejudices against what he called the
"trade" of writing, but he was unable to build on the early success of his

---

[5] Viktor Shklovsky, *Matvei Komarov: Zhitel' goroda Moskvy* (Leningrad: Priboi, 1929). For a
bibliographical survey of the eighteenth-century Russian novel, see V. V. Sipovskii, *Ocherki iz istorii
russkogo romana*, vol. 1 (St. Petersburg: Trud, 1909–10); David Gasperetti provides a sophisticated
reading of Emin, Chulkov, and Komarov, *The Rise of the Russian Novel: Carnival, Stylization, and
Mockery of the West* (DeKalb: Northern Illinois University Press, 1996); and Jurij Striedter analyzes
the early picaresque tradition in *Der Schelmenroman in Russland: Ein Beitrag zur Geschichte des
russischen Romans vor Gogol'* (Berlin: Otto Harrassowitz, 1961).

[6] F. M. Dostoevsky, *Polnoe sobranie sochinenii v tridtsati tomakh* (Leningrad: Nauka,
1972–90), 5:51.

Byronic "Southern poems" to make an independent career, and he died with catastrophic debts. His "novel in verse," *Eugene Onegin*, earned significant but insufficient income; his historical novel, *The Captain's Daughter* (1835) earned little. Pushkin's younger contemporaries Mikhail Lermontov (1814–41) and Nikolai Gogol (1809–52) developed powerful literary vocations, but Lermontov was supported by family wealth and Gogol by family, friends, and imperial subsidies. Writers who came to prominence in mid-century earned higher honoraria, but—with the exception of Fedor Dosto-evsky (1821–81), who quickly resigned from imperial service and ex-changed his share of his father's estate for a thousand rubles—most could not rely solely on the income from their fiction. Leo Tolstoy (1828–1910) would inherit a significant estate (approximately eight hundred taxable male serfs); Ivan Turgenev (1818–83) divided a princely estate of four thousand serfs with his brother. Both Ivan Goncharov (1812–91) and Mikhail Saltykov-Shchedrin (1818–83) came from families that enjoyed noble status and merchant wealth, and both made significant careers in state service. Saltykov-Shchedrin, like the earlier picaresque novelist Faddei Bulgarin (1789–1859), earned more income from editing periodicals than he did from his fiction.

Toward the end of this period (1876), Serafim Shashkov, a radical journalist, would write a detailed study of literary labor in Russia. In it he asserted that writing had become a growing profession in the first and second senses of the word (vocational, financial), but that an increased number of writers resulted in lower pay, that literary honoraria had not kept pace with inflation, and that only a few writers of the upper and middle income ranges could rise above the subsistence level in remuneration (two thousand rubles a year for a writer with a family).[7] In the third—ethical—sense of the word *professional* he found Russian literature sadly lacking, as he recounted striking anecdotes of writers cheated by publishers and writers living in poverty with no support from their fellows. Shashkov could have added anecdotes of writers cheating publishers, taking advances, say, for works never delivered.

But, in fact, writers had begun to take tentative strides toward the development of professional ethics. When Goncharov accused Turgenev of plagiarizing his plans for a novel, *The Precipice*, Turgenev did not challenge him to a duel, as a gentleman might have done in an earlier decade; instead he demanded that the issue be adjudicated by a panel of fellow littérateurs,

---

[7] S. S. Shashkov, "Literaturnyi trud v Rossii: istoricheskii ocherk," *Delo* 8 (1876): 3–48.

who resolved the issue firmly in Turgenev's favor. Literature, at least in this instance, had become a professionalized occupation, one regulated by those educated in its practices.

A second step toward professionalization also involved Russia's great novelists. Knowing that Turgenev attended the annual dinners of the Royal Literary Fund in England, a fellow writer, Aleksandr Druzhinin (1824–64), asked him to describe the annual meeting for his journal. A group of Russian writers decided to draft a proposal for a Russian equivalent, The Literary Fund (Society for the Aid of Needy Writers and Scholars), which was approved by the government in 1859. The society, as its title suggests, supported writers, scholars, and their families through loans, grants, and pensions. It raised money for them from donations, from percentages of honoraria contributed by writers, and from the proceeds of public readings and performances. Dostoevsky and Turgenev became some of its most active members, taking part in fund-raising occasions until the end of their lives.

Significant as these two events are, the professional status of nineteenth-century Russian novelists was very precarious. Like publishers, they competed for a small readership, and generous honoraria paid to the very best or most popular writers often worked to the detriment of rising talents. Honoraria for writers, instituted in the 1820s, but not prevalent until the 1840s, paid writers by the signature (i.e., the large sheet that comes off a printing press), and they could range from the 500 rubles a signature that Tolstoy commanded to several rubles a signature for translators of European novels. Top honoraria tended to be public knowledge, and novelists (not unlike modern athletes) tended to equate honoraria with respect. Dostoevsky, the most professional of the great novelists, was particularly sensitive to these gradations, and his honoraria in the 1860s and 1870s fluctuated between 150 and 300 rubles a signature, behind Tolstoy and Turgenev, but on a level, more or less, with Saltykov-Shchedrin, Goncharov, Nadezhda Khvoshchinskaia (the period's best-respected woman novelist, 1824–89), and Alexei Pisemsky (1821–81). The publication of Dostoevsky's *Adolescent* in 1875 illustrates these issues. He agreed to serialize this new novel in the *Fatherland Notes* in exchange for a generous advance and a first-rate honorarium, 250 rubles a signature. His usual journal, the *Russian Herald* was already committed to *Anna Karenina* at the rate of 500 rubles. But the *Russian Herald*, wishing not to lose a valued contributor, soon proposed a compromise, although one that was hardly flattering to Dostoevsky; it offered him extra money for the new novel if he would keep silent about it, lest other writers ask for raises. Dostoevsky firmly refused and returned to the journal only with *The Brothers Karamazov*, for which he received 300 rubles a signature.[8]

This situation has a direct impact on Russian "novelistic production." No Russian novelist of the first rank matches the impressive quantitative achievements of his or her leading European contemporaries, such as Balzac, Sand, Zola, Dickens, Trollope, and Hardy. In a career that spanned roughly twenty-five years (allowing for his imprisonment and exile), Dostoevsky published only seven full-length novels; Turgenev—six in forty years; Tolstoy—only three in sixty years; Goncharov—three in twenty years. It is difficult to characterize most of Saltykov-Schedrin's books as novels, made up as they were of collections of sketches. The first generation was even less productive—two novels by Pushkin, one by Gogol, one by Lermontov.

What this suggests, in formal terms, is that Russian novelists did not have the opportunity to develop the sort of creative rhythms that sustained their European contemporaries. Only Turgenev's novels add up to the sort of comprehensive project that Balzac, Zola, and Trollope attempted with their interrelated novels—in Turgenev's case a fictionalized history of the midcentury intelligentsia, from the Hegelianism of the 1840s through the nihilism of the 1860s and the populism of the 1870s. While the novels of a Russian writer bear resemblances to each other in plotting, characterization, and description, the differences can be even more significant, as each novel rediscovers the form and exploits new possibilities.

I shall return to outline some of these struggles with the genre. Meanwhile, a snapshot of the year 1879, the first year of the serialization of *The Brothers Karamazov*, sums up the thinness of fiction writing as an institution during the "Golden Age of the Russian Novel," as Dmitri Mirsky, the most influential English-language historian of Russian literature has called it.[9] Aside from Dostoevsky's last novel, stories by Nikolai Leskov and Vsevolod Garshin, and some sketches by Saltykov-Shchedrin, the prose pickings in 1879 were slim indeed. Only thirteen other writers of fiction were reviewed in that entire year; of these only Iakov Polonsky and Nadezhda Khvoshchinskaia survive in living memory, if subcanonically—the former as a poet, the latter forgotten until recent attention to Russian women's literary efforts

---

[8] A. Reitblat, "Literaturnyi gonorar kak forma vzaimosviazi pisatelei i publiki," in his *Ot Bovy k Bal'montu* (Moscow: Izdatel'stvo MPI, 1991), ch. 5. Reitblat's information must be used with caution, as it does not account for individual contracts. The *Russian Herald*'s offer to Dostoevsky may be found in N. A. Liubimov, letter to F. M. Dostoevsky of May 4, 1874; OR GBL, fond 93, razd. II, kart 6, ed. khr. 33, sheet 14.

[9] D. S. Mirsky, A History of Russian *Literature from Its Beginnings to 1900* (New York: Knopf, 1949). The first version appeared in 1927.

(largely in the West) has restored some interest in her subtle and intelligent writing. The other eleven—at least four of them women—survive only in painstaking scholarly commentaries and in literary encyclopedias.[10]

Other institutionalized roles in the literary process remain equally elusive, especially that of the reading public. By 1835, as the growing commercialization of Russian literature began to create the "pitiless divorce" between reader and writer that Roland Barthes considered characteristic of modern literature, Gogol had asked, "what is the educational level of the Russian public, and what is the Russian public"?[11] For fiction we know that it was small, judging from print runs of separate editions (typically 1,200–2,000 throughout the period under discussion) and from the limited subscription lists of the "thick" journals that serialized fiction (rarely as many as 8,000, but—according to Dostoevsky—more than 2,500 or the journal failed). The annual reports of the Imperial Public Library give information on visitors. We can infer information about the social status and wealth of readers from the high prices of books and subscriptions to lending libraries (the most famous of which in St. Petersburg, Smirdin's, charged fifty rubles a year, or roughly 5 percent of the annual salary of a middling bureaucrat). Occasionally the archives yield a diary or correspondence that lets us follow the reading habits of our novelists' contemporaries, but such documents are few and far between. One of the most striking, Prince Vladimir Golitsyn's private diary, records this official's reaction, primarily moral and social, to the installments of the novel as it appeared in the *Russian Herald*; it shows, among other things, how deeply Anna's adultery (and Tolstoy's "realism" in depicting it) violated the literary decorum of the time.[12] Contemporary readers turned to prominent novelists for personal advice, reflecting the extra-aesthetic role of fiction in addressing social and psychological problems, but these letters, of which there are many examples in the Russian archives, give little detail on how readers processed contemporary fiction.

Two specialized types of reader, censors and critics, have, on the contrary, left ample material with which to assess nineteenth-century reading habits. Censors (charged by the censorship statutes of 1804 and 1828 with protecting religious dogma, the government, morals, and the personal honor of individuals) were far from the greatest villains of the literary process. Typically

---

[10] William Mills Todd III, "Contexts of Criticism: Reviewing *The Brothers Karamazov* in 1879," *Stanford Slavic Studies* 4:1 (1991): 296–97.

[11] N. V. Gogol, *Polnoe sobranie sochinenii* (Moscow: ANSSSR, 1937–52), 8:172.

[12] A translation of the diary appears in *Tolstoy Studies Journal* 8 (1995–96): 125–28.

writers themselves—critics, poets, professors of literature—their number included two prominent novelists: Goncharov and Sergei Aksakov (1791–1859). One of them, Aleksandr Nikitenko, has left valuable memoirs that span the period discussed in this essay. Consequently, they were not generally different in their tastes and ideologies from the educated public. As Donald Fanger has noted, they tended to read as the intelligentsia did, assuming a relationship between literature and life virtually unmediated by literary convention or the writer's imagination.[13] In fact, the official censorship left fiction relatively unscathed, directing its attention instead toward critics, journalists, and journals. At times, it may have done writers a favor. Dostoevsky complained to his brother that the censors had removed a passage on the necessity of faith from the first part of *Notes from Underground*; from Dostoevsky's description, the passage might well have weakened the novel, making it less of a challenge to the reader's powers of inference and understanding.

The government did live in fear of what the Emperor Alexander II in a pre-Foucauldian moment called "the dangers which are the result of the ungovernability and excesses of the printed word."[14] But it also lived in hope that the printed word could serve its ends, propagating the official policy of "Orthodoxy, Autocracy, and Nationality." Alternatively chaining and trying to domesticate these verbal monsters on the prowl, government policy did far more to harm the profession of letters than did its censors. During the period from 1780 to 1854, for example, private presses were permitted, banned, and reestablished; ambiguous passages in a text were held against the author, then discarded, and—de facto—held against him; the importation of foreign books was banned, permitted, then severely curtailed. And agencies with censorship powers proliferated, often contradicting one another; by the end of this period there were no fewer than twelve. But this unsettled and rapidly changing legal climate was not, in itself, the chief problem facing writers, readers, and publishers. Laws, however rapidly they changed, could enable writers, publishers, and censors to predict the consequences of their actions. Some laws could be beneficial; the copyright law of 1828, for instance, gave the Russian author rights that made writing a financially sustainable occupation. The central problem for literary people was, rather, the unpredictability, arbitrariness, and vindictiveness

[13] Donald Fanger, "Gogol and His Reader," in William Mills Todd III, ed., *Literature and Society in Imperial Russia, 1800–1914* (Stanford, Calif.: Stanford University Press, 1978), 74.

[14] Quoted in Charles A. Ruud, *Fighting Words: Imperial Censorship and the Russian Press, 1804–1906* (Toronto: Toronto University Press, 1982), 186.

of the government, from the emperor to the officials in his agencies. The censor Nikitenko—himself a critic and editor—could justly complain that "there is no legality in Russia."[15] There is no better example of this arbitrariness than a series of government actions in 1863, when the government banned Dostoevsky's moderate journal, *Time*, for a relatively innocuous article on the Polish question by one of the journal's contributors, even as it was permitting Nikolai Chernyshevsky's utopian novel, *What Is to Be Done?*—written while Chernyshevsky was imprisoned—to be serialized in a more radical journal, the *Contemporary*. Dostoevsky, a Russian nationalist who scattered unsympathetic Polish characters across the pages of his novels, was driven into crushing debt by this closing, while Chernyshevsky's novel became an etiquette manual, if not a gospel, for the radical youth, including Lenin.

The relatively—only relatively—exempt status of fiction from government suppression throughout the period under discussion helped give the novel a privileged position in nineteenth-century Russia, and a second set of specialized readers, critics, soon gave discussion of novels a central role in constituting a public sphere in Russia, a place where pressing social and cultural issues could be discussed in terms not dictated by the government. One of the first reviews of *Eugene Onegin* expressed the terms in which novels would subsequently be treated: "What is a novel? A novel is a theory of human life."[16] Aside from a few romantic essayists, who treated fiction as an art form, most reviewers—to state this bluntly—would come to treat the novelist as a sort of research assistant, gathering material that they could then reorder into critiques of Russian culture and society. Belinsky's famous treatment of *Eugene Onegin* as an "encyclopedia of Russian life" suggests the extent to which critics could come to use novels as reference works for their own research projects.[17] Research projects could, in turn, yield to polemical disquisitions, and this could lead the critics to rewrite the fictions under review. At the hands of Dmitri Pisarev, the tragic hero of Turgenev's *Fathers and Sons* acquires a longer biography, a more productive career, and greater success with women, as Pisarev uses him as a pretext for offering lessons in etiquette and life skills to the radical younger generation, thanking, however, Turgenev for being "a great artist" and an "honorable

---

[15] Aleksandr Nikitenko, *The Diary of a Russian Censor*, abridged, edited, and translated by H. S. Jacobson (Amherst: University of Massachusetts Press, 1975), 30.

[16] *Syn otechestva*, 1828.

[17] V. G. Belinsky, *Sobranie sochinenii v deviati tomakh* (Moscow: Khudozhestvennaia literatura, 1976–82), 6:425.

citizen."[18] Chernyshevsky and Dobroliubov used their literary criticism to isolate character types and typical situations for critical analysis. None of these famous and influential critics was, however, entirely blind to literary form and innovation. Pisarev makes illuminating observations about the structure of Turgenev's novel; Chernyshevsky wrote an incisive essay on Tolstoy's pioneering use of inner monologue. But, as has often been noted, literary criticism afforded them their best—often only—opportunity for social criticism. And the literary genre that offered the richest material was the novel.

The *"Thick Journal"* [tolstyi zhurnal]

From the 1840s to the 1880s, the medium that brought Russian novelists, readers, critics, and censors together was, first and foremost, the "thick journal." It had few rival modes of publication. Russians employed newspaper serialization in very short installments, as did their European counterparts, and a number of these feuilleton novels, especially those translated from French, appeared in Russian newspapers once newspapers began to appear in significant numbers in the 1860s. But the very short installments afforded by the newspapers did not appeal to the best novelists. Part publication of the sort employed by Dickens, Trollope, and others in England, that is, the publication of separate illustrated booklets that readers would buy one issue at a time without subscriptions, was out of the question in Russia, except for Pushkin's *Eugene Onegin*. Part publication required writers with large followings, economies of scale in the publishing trade, and efficient distribution networks, all of which Russia lacked. Very few novels of note were not published in the thick journals, since the proceeds of serial journal publication could be as much as ten times those from publication of separate editions. Gogol's *Dead Souls* is the most prominent exception; its author resisted serialization for fear that it would lessen the impact on Russia that he anticipated his novel would make. Within the limits imposed by Russia's small reading public and inconsistent government, the journals offered writers Russia's equivalent of the stability provided in England by the prominent

---

18 D. I. Pisarev, "Bazarov," in his *Sochineniia* (Moscow: Goslitizdat, 1955–56), 2:7–50. For enlightening analyses of the rewriting tendencies of these critics, see Edward J. Brown, "Pisarev and the Transformation of Two Russian Novels," in Todd, *Literature and Society*, 151–72; and David Michael Shapiro, "Stranger Than Fiction: Invented Narrative in Russian Literary Criticism, 1858–1871," senior thesis, Harvard University, 2001.

lending libraries, such as Mudie's, whose ability to purchase triple-decker novels guaranteed a steady income to publishers and novelists alike.[19] During Dostoevsky's four years abroad, 1867–71, the advances from the *Russian Herald* provided him something akin to a regular salary.

A handful of thick journals dominated the market for literature, periodicals such as the *Library for Reading* (1834–64), the *Contemporary* (1837–66), the *Fatherland Notes* (1839–84), the *Russian Herald* (1856–1906), the *Russian Word* (1859–66), *Time* (1861–63), the *Herald of Europe* (1866–1918), and *Russian Wealth* (1876–1918), to name the ones that published fiction that I have mentioned in this paper. Six of the eight were closed by government action—four by the empire, two by the Soviet Union. These thick journals were not, strictly speaking, literary journals like, say, Dickens's *All the Year Round*. Installments of a serialized novel—readers could expect a completed one within the subscription year—would be sandwiched between pieces on the natural sciences, technology, the social sciences, history, criticism, and essays on current events, although an increasing number of daily newspapers took over the last in the years after the Crimean War. Many of these other contributions would themselves be serialized.

For modern readers, whose sense of the differences between imaginative literature and journalism may be strong and whose only encounter with novels has been through the medium of the book, the reading of a serialized novel within its journal environment can provide a striking experience of heteroglossia, as the journals placed a variety of genres in close and familiar contact with the novel. It is perhaps not accidental that the theoretician of the novel who has best studied questions of the novel's incorporation of and interaction with other genres and discourses, Mikhail Bakhtin, should have been a Russian who came of age as the thick journals were dying out. He was able to witness a situation in which reviewers would review novels still unfinished and would review them as parts of the journal, not as separate aesthetic wholes. And fresh in memory would have been instances when a journal's review took a critical stance toward a novel undergoing serialization in that same journal—this happened to Tolstoy's *Anna Karenina* in the *Russian Herald*—or when the novel took issue with positions dear to the editors' and publishers' fundamental ideological tendencies. This, again, happened to *Anna Karenina*, the last part of which treated Russia's Balkan adventures in a highly negative fashion, incurring the wrath of the journal's jingoistic publisher, who refused to print it, compelling Tolstoy to issue it as

---

[19] J. A. Sutherland, *Victorian Novelists and Publishers* (Chicago: University of Chicago Press, 1976), 9–40.

a separate brochure. In other cases, two novels appearing in the same journal would compete in their treatment of a particular theme, as happened in the *Russian Herald* in 1866, when both *Crime and Punishment* and *War and Peace* addressed, with different negative accents, the legacy of Napoleon. Or a novel might set off a firestorm of competing narrative interpretations, as did the "Russian Monk" section of *The Brothers Karamazov*, which occasioned the publication of three competing biographies of monks in the *Russian Herald*.[20]

First Wave: Pushkin, Lermontov, Gogol

The institutional features of Russian literature that I have outlined—minimally professionalized authorship, uncertain readership, precarious publishing networks through the periodical press—evolved over the seventy years covered by this essay, so that they offered different challenges at different times. Individual novelists responded differently to them, although with attention to each other's solutions. For the sake of comparisons and to show some principal features of this evolution, I will divide the period into three moments: first attempts at the novel, the rise of the social novel, and the age of serials.

Russia's first canonical novels—Pushkin's *Eugene Onegin*, Lermontov's *A Hero of Our Time*, and Gogol's *Dead Souls*—were written for a small, elite audience that could be counted on to recognize echoes of Byron, Rousseau, Scott, Sterne, and other contemporary European writers, but that knew little Russian fiction beyond story length, and that was barely accustomed to literature not delivered orally at court or in the familiar groupings of polite society and was most probably unfamiliar with Russia's existing prose fiction. Consequently, Pushkin, Lermontov, and Gogol made the process of writing a novel part of the subject matter of their novels. They could not count on perceptive critics to explain their works to the public. Consequently, they

---

[20] For Bakhtin's treatment of heteroglossia, see "Discourse in the Novel," in M. M. Bakhtin, *The Dialogic Imagination*, ed. Michael Holquist (Austin: University of Texas Press, 1981), 272, 300. Neither here, nor in his *Problems of Dostoevsky's Poetics*, ed. and trans. Caryl Emerson (Minneapolis: University of Minnesota Press, 1984), does Bakhtin explicitly treat the problem of serialization and of novels that have not been completed when serialization begins. On the competing monastic biographies, see William Mills Todd III, "Dostoevsky's Russian Monk in Extra-Literary Dialogue: Implicit Polemics in *Russkii vestnik*, 1879–1881," in Robert P. Hughes and Irina Paperno, eds., *Christianity and the Eastern Slavs* (Berkeley: University of California Press, 1994), 2:124–33.

played the critic's role in their novels, explaining such elementary concepts as "irony" (Lermontov), "beauty" (Gogol), and "the novel" (Pushkin) to their readers. Every novelist does this to some extent, but these early Russian ones do it with unusual persistence. The heroine of Pushkin's novel, Tatiana, grows in literary understanding throughout the novel, becoming the author-narrator's "ideal" as a reader and cultural force. Lermontov's two prefaces to his novel use the technique of negative inference to create a reader who will not be "like a provincial"; and the preface to the second edition of *Dead Souls* issues a desperate plea to its readers to join the author in creative partnership, a partnership that the familiar associations could no longer provide.

Each novel presents the discovery of form as it simultaneously explores the identity of its characters and the nature of their milieu. In *Eugene Onegin*, Pushkin works with two intersecting narrative levels, a fictional level on which his characters act and a fiction-making level on which the highly self-conscious author-narrator makes them act. From its generically provocative subtitle ("A Novel in Verse") to its concluding metaphor ("life's novel") *Eugene Onegin* raises problems of the relationship between literature and life in a society aestheticized by the gentry's ideology of polite society. On each of these levels it explores the limits imposed on social action and artistic expression by the conventions, fashions, and traditions of Russia's syncretic culture. The author-narrator disconcertingly steps into his fictional world to befriend Eugene. The narrator's muse shades into Tatiana. She, Eugene, and Lensky (a poet of sorts) try to act out the patterns of the literature they read—sentimental novels, Byron and Constant, German romantic poetry. Both Eugene (a dandy) and Tatiana (the hostess of a salon) play roles that unite the social and the aesthetic. All the while the author-narrator, using a fourteen-line stanza of exceptional intricacy, charts the movement of his creative biography toward "severe prose" and the novel. Written over eight years, covering six years in the lives of its fictional characters, and published over seven years in parts, the novel uses this passage of time to present the maturation of its characters, including its author, as a process of making choices and facing the consequences of these choices. By beginning publication long before he had the ending of the novel in mind, Pushkin was able to present these processes as open, or at least, contingent, not predetermined. In this way he could incorporate reactions to unfolding events in Russian literature and history.

Lermontov's *A Hero of Our Time* was the only one of the three novels to appear in a thick journal, the *Fatherland Notes* (1839–40). But this was no ordinary serialization, as it included only three of the five short fictions and none of the prefaces that make up the complete version (1842). If any work justifies Tolstoy's view of Russian literature, quoted in the epigraph above, it is this. The five stories represent different prose genres or mixtures of them: travel notes and adventure novella ("Bela"), physiognomical description ("Maksim Maksimich"), a novella of supernatural dread (the parodic "Taman"), confession and society tale ("Princess Mary"), and philosophical tale ("The Fatalist"). They are arranged, however, in a thematically and psychologically elegant fashion, as Belinsky had already noted when they appeared: they move progressively into the hero's mind through third-person narration by a character without Pechorin's cultural resources to a third-person narration by a traveler with these resources, and, finally, to three first-person narratives by Pechorin himself, ones that allow increasing access to his innermost thoughts, as he sheds the theatricality of polite society. Lermontov reduces the world of plentiful cultural possibilities in Pushkin's novel to a minimum, constructing each of the novel's social situations as a small stage, leaving the hero but a modicum of moral conscience with which to escape the destructive competitions of society. Lukács distinguished between two types of novel, those in which the hero is broader than the world in which he moves and those in which the hero is narrower.[21] *A Hero of Our Time*, by its very title, invites commentary in these terms. A century and a half of criticism has yet to place it definitively in either category.

Gogol subtitled his great comic novel a "poema" (epic, narrative poem), in obvious contradistinction to the "novel in verse" of Pushkin, who, claimed Gogol, gave him the plot for the novel—a macabre scheme by the hero, Chichikov, to mortgage taxable serfs who had died between census revisions. At first glance—a very superficial one—*Dead Souls* may seem a throwback to the picaresques and slightly more complicated comic novels (after Fielding) of the European eighteenth century. It does, indeed, recount the passage of an orphaned, homeless outsider through a series of adventures—here visits to grotesquely individuated country estates and a provincial town—as this outsider gains knowledge of a world of dead values and hollow forms, eventually finding a place in it. If *Dead Souls* is a picaresque, however, it becomes one on multiple dimensions, a picaresque collection of interwoven picaresques, with the biographies of the dead serfs and the "poema" about the outlaw Kopeikin casting Chichikov's journey in sharper relief, cultural and ideological. Chichikov's line of the plot may be seen as a double picaresque, in which the author-narrator finally harnesses the rogue-hero in the final chapter by adjoining a conventional picaresque

---

[21] Lukács, *The Theory of the Novel*, 97.

biography to the first ten chapters of the hero's journeys, which begin and end in medias res. As a consequence, the openness of the opening estate visits, their episodic extendability, is partially "closed" by an open, extendable conclusion, which leaves hero, narrator, and reader still moving down the same road. The picaresque impetus of *Dead Souls*, however, carries even beyond its hero's imaginary serf biographies and the narrator's reverse chronological account of the hero. For in the middle chapters of the novel the narrator becomes himself a traveling, homeless outsider, first as a child, fresh of perception and imagination, then as a jaded adult. As these intertwined narratives unfold, the novel implicates not merely its characters and, at times, its narrator in its fragmented, hypocritical world, but also its fictive reader. The comic explosion of the later chapters, when the town tries to come to grips with Chichikov's fraud, blows apart signifiers and signifieds, social conventions, and the cultural aspirations of its imagined cultural elite.

In Search of a Longer Form: The Social Novel at Midcentury

This first great age of Russian fiction ended almost as suddenly as it had begun. Pushkin and Lermontov died prematurely, Gogol devoted another decade to vain attempts to continue his novel, passing from the *Inferno* of the published novel to a *Purgatorio* and *Paradiso*, hoping in his final years to redeem not only his polymorphous hero, but also himself. He burned the drafts shortly before he died in 1852; the few chapters that survived the conflagration show he was reaching for a new, more realistic style and for a more psychologically detailed treatment of his characters.

Subsequent novelists would not ignore the achievement of Pushkin, Lermontov, and Gogol. The characters and situations of their novels were frequently appropriated and made to serve different literary structures and cultural controversies. *Eugene Onegin*—set in St. Petersburg, the countryside, and Moscow—established the imaginary geography of Russian fiction, although Tolstoy, for instance, would revalue Pushkin's culturally wealthy Petersburg as a locus of hollow "form," not "content" in *War and Peace* and *Anna Karenina*. Pushkin's Tatiana, wrenched from her institutional, ideological, and fictional settings—would become an emblem of Russian womanhood in Dostoevsky's discussions of Russian culture and would serve as a model for the strong women of Turgenev's novels. Pushkin's Eugene and Lermontov's Pechorin could enter journalistic and fictional treatments of the "superfluous man," once their ready participation in the rituals and contests of society was forgotten. Gogol's Chichikov could become an incipient capitalist as new economic patterns came to the fore. Gogol's landowners—Manilov, Korobochka, Nozdrev, Sobakevich, Pliushkin—could lend their names as labels for a range of negative character traits, and they do so to this day.

But by the mid 1840s, critics would begin to find the work of Pushkin and Lermontov dated; by 1847 Belinsky came to understand that Gogol differed from the writers of the "natural school" that he thought had emerged from Gogol's work.[22] These writers, answering a demand for full-length fictions, could draw on Gogol's novel and Petersburg stories only by ignoring their grotesque humor, which confused human categories with ones from animal and inanimate realms, and by picking up instead on the more pathetic tones of Gogol's narrators or on his critical representation of a fragmented, inorganic modernity. The best writers of this school wrote their accusatory fictions against the background of German idealist philosophy and French social romanticism, including utopian socialism. They began to publish their fiction in thick journals, establishing a precedent for the greater novels of the 1860s and 1870s.

The writer who came forward with the first full-length social novel was none other than the twenty-four-year-old Dostoevsky, whose *Poor Folk* (1845) followed shortly after his translation of Balzac's *Eugénie Grandet*. Using epistolary form to develop his poor clerk and provincial girl, Dostoevsky did not so much reduce Gogol—as had other writers of his time—as he polemicized with him, for his poor clerk, unlike the scrivener protagonist of Gogol's "Overcoat," had sufficient humanity to compose letters, not just copy them, and to fall in love (however ineptly) with a woman, not an overcoat. Soon, however, Dostoevsky's work was overtaken by other young writers. Turgenev began to publish the memorable stories that would come together in his *Notes of a Hunter*; Aleksandr Herzen's *Who Is to Blame?* (1847) offered a greater range of characters than *Poor Folk*; Ivan Goncharov's first novel, *A Common Story* (1847) won critical approval for its confrontation of naive romanticism with practical life; Dmitri Grigorovich treated peasant life in unprecedented detail in two novellas, *The Village* (1846) and *Anton Goremyka* (1847); and Aleksandr Druzhinin broke new literary ground (at least in Russia) with his treatment of a liberated woman in *Polinka Saks* (1847). But much of the best prose of the late 1830s and 1840s was to be found in shorter forms—physiological sketches, fantastic tales—and in collections of shorter works.

---

[22] Belinsky, *Sobranie sochinenii v deviati tomakh*, 9:682.

For readers of the 1840s and 1850s, memoirs, autobiographies, and fictionalized autobiographies frequently offered more imaginative, better-written narratives than the novels of the day, as did Karolina Pavlova's intriguing novel in both prose and verse, *A Double Life* (1848). Sergei Aksakov produced a series of such narratives—*A Family Chronicle* (separate edition, 1856), *Childhood Years of Bagrov the Grandson* (separate edition, 1858), but he scattered parts of them in several journals, so they did not appear as continuous narratives until their publication in separate books; Leo Tolstoy's first lengthy narratives were his pseudoautobiographical *Childhood*, *Boyhood*, and *Youth*, which he did publish in the *Contemporary*, but over a five-year period (1852, 1854, 1857, respectively). These works, as Andrew Wachtel has convincingly argued, created a myth of happy childhood that would continue to be repeated well into the twentieth century.[23] More important, perhaps, in opposition to the works of the "natural school" they turned back from modernity and urban life to the life of the rural gentry. Major Russian novelists of the following decades would challenge this pastoral vision, or at least nuance it by treating aspects of rural and urban life that it neglected. Mikhail Saltykov-Shchedrin would savagely parody it in his greatest fiction, *The Golovlev Family* (serialized 1875–81 in the *Fatherland Notes*), as he turned loving patriarchy into hateful matriarchy, fertile estate into worthless productivity, happy childhood into murderous nightmare, religious faith into a pretext for theft and seduction.

A few years later Dostoevsky would take the fictionalized memoir in a very different direction with his *Notes from the House of the Dead* (serialized—in a period of lighter censorship—in *Time*, 1861–62). This turned out to be his most successful work. Taken by its contemporary readers to be a fictionalized account of Dostoevsky's own prison experience, its fictional aspects were overlooked, especially the skill with which he used a frame narrative to show the devastating effect of imprisonment on the criminal after the completion of his term. Dostoevsky, whose early fiction was shaped by utopian socialism and by its notion that crime is a product of constricting environment, took a new approach to crime in this work. While he did not neglect the crushing environmental circumstances of the prisoners, the vast majority of whom were not members of the educated gentry, he began to treat it as a phenomenon that could arise from any aspect of the human psyche— reason, will, instinct. He discovered, moreover, that the common folk treated crime as a misfortune, but one for which the criminal should take

---

[23] Andrew Baruch Wachtel, *The Battle for Childhood: Creation of a Russian Myth* (Stanford, Calif.: Stanford University Press, 1990).

responsibility. The religious terms in which Dostoevsky now viewed crime became the basis of his novelistic psychology and of the particular "realism" that he would attempt to define a few years later: "With full realism, to find the human in the human. This is primarily a Russian trait, and in this sense I am, of course, of the people, for my direction flows out of the depth of the Christian spirit of the people. . . . They call me a psychologist; it's not true. I am only a realist in a deeper sense, that is, I depict all the depths of the human soul."[24]

Dostoevsky's implicit polemic with his former views and with the more materialist version of socialism that he found on the Petersburg scene when he returned to it in 1859, meanwhile, introduces a third wave of fiction writing, one that took full advantage of the thick journals and that addressed much more closely the development of the Russian intelligentsia. Russian novelists—especially Turgenev, Tolstoy, and Dostoevsky—would learn to embody contemporary ideas in their fiction, giving fiction a central place in political and cultural discussions.

Turgenev, Tolstoy, Dostoevsky

Chronologically, Turgenev's first four novels—*Rudin* (1856), *A Nest of Gentlefolk* (1859), *On the Eve* (1860), and *Fathers and Sons* (1862)—take precedence. None is much longer than a novella, and the best of them, *Fathers and Sons*, appeared in a single issue of the *Russian Herald*. But they made the novel an instrument in contemporary debates by making ideas the subject of their drawing-room tempests over teapots. The hero of *Fathers and Sons*, Bazarov, embodied, as I have already mentioned, the ideas of Chernyshevsky, Dobroliubov, and the radical youth—to whom Turgenev gave the title "nihilists" for their unwillingness to accept any proposition that could not be empirically verified. This novel—elegantly structured around a series of visits to estates of varying size and wealth, featuring memorable characters in carefully wrought clashes—like the other novels in this series subjected its hero to the test of love. Could Bazarov's dedication to experimental medicine, to materialist views of life and art survive the experience of falling in love? No. Bazarov's failed love for Odintsova, a wealthy young widow, in turn cooled his resolve, and he dies, tragically, from an infection he receives while carelessly performing an autopsy. Turgenev gave his hero

---

[24] Quoted in Donald Fanger, *Dostoevsky and Romantic Realism: A Study of Dostoevsky in Relation to Balzac, Dickens, and Gogol* (Chicago: University of Chicago Press, 1967), 215.

the dignity of tragedy, and this set off negative reactions from all positions on the ideological spectrum of the time. The radicals, except for Pisarev, viewed the novel as a satire on their ideas; conservatives saw it as a glorification of them.

This set off a chain of textuality that would entangle Chernyshevsky and Dostoevsky and, indeed, stretch well into the twentieth century, as Nabokov's novel *The Gift*, would incorporate a devastating parody of Chernyshevsky. *What Is to Be Done?*, Chernyshevsky's utopian novel, gave the ideas of the radical youth—materialism, feminism, socialism, scientism—a different dignity, that of success. Dostoevsky followed with his first novel of ideas, *Notes from Underground* (1864), perhaps his most challenging fiction, and the fiction that was least understood or appreciated in his own time. Its first part shows its "antihero" (a term Dostoevsky coined for his Underground Man) trying to accept the ideas of the radical youth, but reducing them to absurdity as he pursues them to their ultimate conclusions; the second part depicts the Underground Man regressing fourteen years in time to perform a similarly devastating operation on the more philanthropic, utopian socialism of Dostoevsky's youth. In each case the radical ideas—like Bazarov's ideas—prove inadequate to the test of life.

All of these struggles were played out in the thick journals, focusing public attention on a set of ideas with an intensity unprecedented in Russia. Dostoevsky and Tolstoy would write their greatest fictions in the wake of this controversy of the early 1860s, but in very different ways. Tolstoy, who abandoned the editorial boards of the thick journals and urban literary life, as Boris Eikhenbaum showed in his multivolume study of Tolstoy, turned to provocatively outmoded forms of the novel—the historical novel for *War and Peace*, the drawing-room novel for *Anna Karenina*—to place contemporary ideas, Western rationality, and modernity in contexts of unprecedented breadth, in literary structures of unprecedented daring.[25] In *War and Peace*, by far his longest, he chose the Napoleonic Wars as his arena for testing the radical project of intervening in history, and he made a mockery not only of those who tried to do so (bureaucrats, military leaders, emperors) but also— in the historiographical essay that forms the second part of the novel's Epilogue—of the historians who had attempted to recount and make sense of their efforts. This novel, partly serialized in the *Russian Herald* (1865–66), then published in separate editions in 1867–78, 1873, and 1886, managed to provoke all parties, but it was also Tolstoy's greatest critical success and was

---

[25] B. M. Eikhenbaum, *Lev Tolstoi*, 3 vols. (Moscow, 1928, 1931, 1960).

generally regarded as the finest novel of its time, although Tolstoy himself objected to any generic designation to which critics tried to assign it.

Tolstoy's next serialized novel, *Anna Karenina*, was no less daring and provocative in conception and execution. The "burning issues" of the day become idle table-talk for bored and underemployed members of the gentry, as the novel centers on two principal plot lines: a plot involving Anna, her husband, and the lover with whom she runs away, and another plot centered around Dmitri Levin, an incisively critical member of the gentry who tries to modernize his estate, get married, raise a family, and make sense of his life. By choosing to commit adultery, flaunt society's rules, and abandon her family, Anna becomes the protagonist of a tragic plot that eventuates in her suicide; Levin, able to move from idea to idea, becomes the protagonist of a plot shaped more as a romance, in which the adventures are ones involving ideas, but the stakes are no less high than in Anna's plot, for he nearly commits suicide when he fails to find a belief system that will sustain him. Anna and Levin do not meet until shortly before her death, and then only briefly, but the two plots run parallel to each other, providing contrasts and "linkages," as Tolstoy called them, which provide interpretive contexts. Levin, as fortunate in his choices and accidental encounters as Anna is unfortunate in hers, pursues a quest that leaves him at the end of the novel in a new state of questioning, similar to Pierre's final position in *War and Peace*. Both of these characters join a predilection for system building with an even more powerful ability rationally to destroy systems, but they also have the saving ability to lose themselves in nature, in activity, as Levin does in the famous mowing scene in *Anna Karenina*.

By the end of his life, Tolstoy would come to question all of the institutions and discourses of secular modernity, and this is already apparent in his fiction, which places political and social reform, science, medicine, and the legal system in critical contexts, showing their inadequacy for the understanding of life and the living of it. Dostoevsky's fictions are structured very differently from Tolstoy's, but they gain much of their power from a similarly sweeping critique of the modernity that the Russian Empire was trying to assimilate from the West. They are no less daring than Tolstoy's in their formal innovation, but they take fuller advantage of the possibilities of serialization in the thick journals, and they address more directly the ideas of the radical intelligentsia. Like Tolstoy, Dostoevsky began serialization of his novels before he had completely planned them, a situation that made it possible for them both to incorporate unfolding situations into their fictions (as Tolstoy did with the Balkan Wars in *Anna Karenina*), but that made keeping to deadlines an all but impossible challenge.

Dostoevsky, far more professional than Tolstoy about meeting his obliga-tions, invented a number of narrative devices for writing toward an ending he did not yet know and mastered a new technology—dictating to a stenog-rapher (his wife)—to speed his installments to the journals. Unlike Tolstoy, who took a leisurely two and a half years to serialize *Anna Karenina*, Dosto-evsky in all but one case came close to meeting his deadlines. The exception was *The Brothers Karamazov*, written in the last years of his life, when in-creasing illness, other projects, and the need to research certain scenes in the novel (police investigation, monastic practices) delayed him.

Where Turgenev's characters can surrender ideas under the disorienting impact of love, and where Tolstoy's characters can move from idea to idea (embracing each, however, with intensity), Dostoevsky's characters *embody* their ideas, and the novels' plots are designed to bring ideas into conflict, even as they move toward their unpredictable endings. Dostoevsky's charac-ters play out their ideas in scandalous scenes, which draw them together for confrontations, then propel them apart until the next scandalous scene; they provoke each other's ideas in dialogue, but they also dream their ideas, and they encounter their ideas embodied in other characters, typically in dou-bling relationships. The term "Dostoevskian double" is something of a criti-cal cliché, and Dostoevsky used this device to structure his second novel, *The Double* (1846), but it covers a multitude of instances in his mature work—complementary and supplementary relationships, antitheses, and temporal ordering (a character represents another character's past ideas). The doubling relationship can be psychological or ideological or, most typi-cally, some combination of the two; if psychological, the doubles can repre-sent aspects of a whole human personality (heart, will, instinct). The basic requirement is uncanny recognition, such as Raskolnikov feels for Sonya and Svidrigailov (but not for the parodistic Lebeziatnikov) in *Crime and Punish-ment* (1866). All of these devices work to make ideas (nihilistic, capitalistic, nationalistic) inseparable from the characters who think (and feel and live) them, so that the hardest thing for a Dostoevskian intellectual character to do is to give up his idea, however murderous and destructive the actions it may have occasioned, against himself and his victims.

As Dostoevsky's novels unfolded, he found it expedient to employ a highly original and complicated mode of narration, one that combined se-lective omniscience (about his characters' thoughts) with ignorance (of the characters' fates). In *The Devils* (1871–72) this led him to employ a participant-chronicler, following close on the action, as does the narrator of *The Brothers Karamazov* (1879–80), at times omniscient, at times a confused witness of scandalous events. For *The Idiot*, the novel that gave him the most trouble to plot, Dostoevsky employed a narrator who gradually loses understanding of the events and characters, resorting to journalistic devices of the time (such as analyzing characters in terms of type), which are scarcely adequate for the novel's minor figures and totally inadequate to the tortuous complexity of the principal characters.

In conclusion, I would like to return to de Vogüé's pioneering assessment of the Russian novel. His sense of its ambitions holds up well to critical scrutiny. Those nineteenth-century Russian novels that have best stood the test of time are, indeed, those that, unlike the naturalist fictions of his age, developed their characters' interiority as well as their social world, that were not afraid to essay impossibly large ideas and situations, that were willing to defy "taste and method." From *Eugene Onegin* to *The Brothers Karamazov*, the Russian novels that became canonical exercised considerable freedom in narrative technique, justifying this freedom by the effects of characterization they achieved.

They turned the fragility of their institutional status to their own advantage. Where native traditions were absent, they drew creatively on foreign ones, returning them to Europe in forms that later Europeans did not immediately recognize. Where critics were absent or nearsighted, they found devices for proposing models of reading to their public. Where economics drove them to serial publication in the thick journals, they used this opportunity to invent ways of plotting and narration that kept endings and characterizations open until the very end—and at the very end.

Is there an ideology of the Russian novel? It is difficult to generalize across the many fictions that I have not had the space to discuss. But, again, the canonical texts do display a certain tendency to celebrate the open and undetermined, to hold their characters (and narrators) responsible for the consequences of their choices. This can be true even with authors such as Chernyshevsky, whose philosophy argued for environmental determinism, but whose utopian novel featured people who could rise above their surroundings. Most of the novels I have discussed do not celebrate capitalism, secular society, or the modern state (forcibly united by police surveillance and taxation, as Dostoevsky analyzed it in his *Winter Notes on Summer Impressions*, 1863)—none of which were well or long developed in the Russia of their time. Modernity's professionalized discourses (law, medicine, science) emerge as narrowly rational and inadequate to the wealth of experience. But neither do these fictions celebrate the "organic" alternatives that modernity has spewed forth in nightmare form as fascism and stalinism. They pose the questions, and their readers, domestic and foreign, continue to find them compelling.

The Circle Widens

CRITICAL APPARATUS

The Market for Novels—
Some Statistical Profiles

JAMES RAVEN

Britain, 1750–1830

By the late eighteenth century British reviewers and advertising booksellers accepted and promoted the "novel" as a distinct literary category, even though it encompassed a great many narrative forms: fables, romances, biographical and autobiographical memoirs and histories, satirical tales, and exchanges in letters. Novelists, then as now, challenged readers to engage with probability, realism, the supernatural and pseudohistory. "The word novel," wrote the Rev. Edward Mangin in 1808, "is a generical term; of which romances, histories, memoirs, letters, tales, lives, and adventures, are the species."[1] Lasting literary fame was rarely the aim. Writers, purveyors, and customers pursued amusement, diversion, and fashion. All contributed to the development of this new and sometimes shocking thing called a novel. The material contours of that formation are the subject of this essay.

In 1785, Clara Reeve, already an accomplished fiction writer, set about chronicling the history of the English novel in her *Progress of Romance.* "We had early translations of the best Novels of all other Countries," she concluded, "but for a long time produced very few of our own."[2] With exquisite confidence, Reeve argued that English novel writing had reached critical maturity and that this offered the conclusion to her "investigation of novels."[3] During the next half-century, however, the achievement of Samuel Richardson, Henry Fielding, Eliza Hayward, Tobias Smollett, and Laurence Sterne was massively extended in quantity and range. Quality was a different matter. As already evident to Reeve, these were to be years in which "the press groaned under the weight of Novels, which sprung up like Mushrooms every year."[4]

Unsurprisingly, most novelists belonged to the propertied classes, but among them also numbered humble vicars and curates, sea captains, destitute merchants' wives, high-class prostitutes, overachieving adolescents, and sanctimonious autodidacts. The diversity of writers and circumstances matched the range of success and failure. A few novels were quickly reprinted; others

---

[1] Edward Mangin, *An Essay on Light Reading, as it may be Supposed to Influence Moral Conduct on Literary Taste* (London, 1808), 5.

[2] Clara Reeve, *The Progress of Romance,* 2 vols. (Dublin, 1785), 1:108.

[3] Ibid., 1:108, 2:52.

[4] Ibid., 2:7.

were revived after a few seasons or achieved a limited success in the writer's own circle or locality. Most novels were destined for either a very dusty or a very brief shelf life following a few polite readings by friendly subscribers or meager outings from a fashionable circulatings library.

The publishing history of the English eighteenth-century novel confirms the advance of specialist booksellers and commercial circulating libraries, as well as new advertising techniques and promotional ploys. Novels, like other leisure and fashion goods, were promoted by a variety of entrepreneurs, many modestly financed but eager to exploit fresh markets.[5] For good or ill, the novel was recognized as a new cultural force, as distinctive as the theater or newspaper. Reviewers might find a tale that "affords many lessons to the youth of both sexes" but also—and far more usually—a novel deemed to be "one of those pernicious incentives to vice that are a scandal to decency."[6] Most critics regarded the novel as a separate and definable class of books.[7] In an age when Linnaeus and others categorized natural phenomena, many observers described novels according to their "order," "species," "kind," "race," or "tribe." In more military fashion, novels were assigned a "rank" or placed within a "list."[8] Commentators of the time were certainly not averse to their own exercises in novel counting and classification.

The statistical lists used in this essay—and the accompanying health warnings for their interpretation—derive from *British Fiction, 1750–1770* and *The English Novel, 1770–1829*,[9] compiled from eighteenth- and nineteenth-century review notices, booksellers' and printers' records, advertisements, and term catalogues, followed by extensive searches of *ESTC, OCLC*,[10] and hands-on stack work in many hundreds of libraries worldwide. The tallies

---

[5] See James Raven, *Judging New Wealth: Popular Publishing and Responses to Commerce in England, 1750–1800* (Oxford, 1992).

[6] *Critical Review* 33 (1772): 180, and 55 (1783): 234, on *The Cautious Lover* (London, 1772), and *Frailties of Fashion* (London, 1782).

[7] Of many examples, *Monthly Review* 44 (1771): 173; *Critical Review* 63 (1787): 308; *Monthly Review* n.s. 14 (1794): 465.

[8] Of many examples, *Critical Review* 33 (1772): 181–82; 34 (1772): 77; 44 (1777): 154; 65 (1788): 236–37; 67 (1789): 505-6, 554; n.s. 9 (1793): 118; and *Monthly Review* 45 (1771): 503; 59 (1778): 233–34; 78 (1788): 531; 79 (1788): 466.

[9] James Raven, *British Fiction 1750–1770: A Chronological Check-List of Prose Fiction Printed in Britain and Ireland*, (London, 1987); Peter Garside, James Raven, and Rainer Schöwerling, *The English Novel 1770–1829: A Bibliographical Survey of Prose Fiction Published in the British Isles*, 2 vols. (Oxford 2000), a bibliography of first editions of prose novels, listing a total of 4,185 titles. Previous volumes covering the period from 1700 to 1749 are W. H. McBurney, *A Check List of English Prose Fiction, 1700–1739* (Cambridge, Mass., 1960); and J. C. Beasley, *The Novels of the 1740s* (Athens, Ga, 1982).

[10] *English Short-Title Catalogue*, online; *Online Catalog of Library of Congress, World-Cat.*

include titles previously unknown, exclude former identifications that cannot be proved to have been published, and also list, after consultation of reviews and printing records, novels certainly published but no longer surviving in extant copy. About 7 percent of all new novel titles published between 1770 and 1800, for example, are completely lost to us.

The broadly ascendant course of publication is obvious, but the number of new novels issued each year also fluctuated markedly (see table 1). Statistical presentations must also allow for differences between the year cited in the imprints and the actual times of publication. The practice of postdating was common, designed to extend the currency of the novel. In some cases, novels printed and published in August, or even as early as April, carried the date of the following year.[11] In addition, a publishing season extended from November to May, spanning the division of the calendar year. Even so, bumper imprint years like 1771 stand out, before a steep decline in novel production in the late 1770s followed by a strong rally from the late 1780s. A slight dip in the mid-1790s precedes a late-century surge in novel output. A decline in 1801–02 was followed a few seasons later by an unprecedented peak in 1808.

The moving average of annual new novel production charted by figure 1 shows more clearly the general trends.[12] The malaise in new novel production lasted from about 1775 to 1783, coterminous, it seems, with the American war. This downturn was perhaps a reaction to a decade of poorly produced novels or to a flood of reprints in the late 1770s satisfying the market. More certainly we can chart the rise and development of novel production in Britain from the late 1780s in relation to six general considerations: a new generation of writers, the way in which certain reprints grew stale, the development of new circulating libraries, the increase in translated and cheap borrowings from foreign novels, the greater emphasis on the female and on the country market, and finally the marketing practices of a new generation of bookseller-publishers. All these features continued to sustain novel publication in the first third of the nineteenth century, although the "rise" posited in so many general surveys was by no means linear or without severe setbacks and troughs. The decline in the 1810s (a total production 15 percent lower than that of the previous decade) clearly related to the economic downturn and social disturbances of the long war years, while recovery in the 1820s was sufficiently strong to absorb the short-term shock of the 1826 crash in banking and in the book trade as a whole. Nevertheless, the high price of paper

---

[11] See, for example, *The Happy Release* (London, 1787); and *The Minor* (London, 1788).

[12] The totals include first editions of novels for juveniles and young persons but exclude publications more clearly intended to be read to very young children. The criteria by which the novel is defined is discussed in Garside et al., *English Novel*, 1: 1–5, 21–39.

TABLE 1. PUBLICATION OF NEW NOVELS IN BRITAIN AND IRELAND, 1750–1829

Year	Total	Year	Total	Year	Total	Year	Total	Year	Total
1750	23	1760	35	1770	40	1780	24	1790	74
1751	23	1761	20	1771	60	1781	22	1791	74
1752	19	1762	19	1772	41	1782	22	1792	58
1753	19	1763	18	1773	39	1783	24	1793	45
1754	30	1764	26	1774	35	1784	24	1794	56
1755	22	1765	18	1775	31	1785	47	1795	50
1756	25	1766	27	1776	17	1786	40	1796	91
1757	26	1767	33	1777	18	1787	51	1797	79
1758	16	1768	37	1778	16	1788	80	1798	75
1759	28	1769	44	1779	18	1789	71	1799	99
1750–59	231	1760–69	277	1770–79	315	1780–89	405	1790–99	701

and production continued to constrain the market. In many ways the whole eighty years considered here might be regarded as a continuing publishing 'ancien regime' in which the apparent technological breakthrough of the steam-driven printing press in the 1810s was so slowly adopted and was so circumscribed by high production costs that no real market advance was possible until the transport and distribution revolution of the 1830s.[13]

FIGURE 1. PUBLICATION OF NEW NOVELS (AND THOSE WITH ANONYMOUS TITLE PAGES), 1750–1829, MOVING FIVE-YEAR AVERAGES

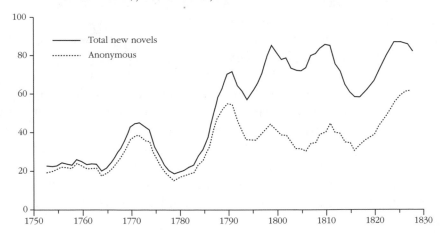

[13] For a fuller account see James Raven, "The Book as a Commodity," in Michael Suarez and Michael Turner, eds., *The History of the Book in Britain vol. V 1695–1830* (Cambridge, 2006), forthcoming; and James Raven, "The Book Trades," in Isabel Rivers, ed., *Books and Their Readers in Eighteenth-Century England: New Essays* (London, 2001), 1–34.

Year	Total	Year	Total	Year	Total		
1800	81	1810	89	1820	70		
1801	72	1811	80	1821	75		
1802	61	1812	66	1822	82		
1803	79	1813	63	1823	87		
1804	73	1814	61	1824	99		
1805	75	1815	54	1825	91		
1806	70	1816	59	1826	77		
1807	69	1817	55	1827	79		
1808	111	1818	62	1828	83		
1809	79	1819	73	1829	81		
1800–09	*770*	*1810–19*	*662*	*1820–19*	*824*		
						1750–1829	*4,185*

Almost all bookseller-publishers of the period published novels at some point in their careers. More than sixty different booksellers were the first-named publishers in the imprints of novels published between 1750 and 1770, and two hundred others were listed as partners or in other ways that implied financial involvement. In the following decades the number of different firms involved continued to increase, although many booksellers also claimed more specialist associations and about twenty booksellers became known as leading novel producers. Table 2 lists the most productive of those primarily responsible for the publication of the novels. With one nineteenth-century exception (Blackwood of Edinburgh) all were London booksellers. This is hardly surprising, given the extraordinary and long-standing dominance of London in publishing, but the neighborhoods of the booksellers are also significant. Some, like the firm of George Robinson and John Bew operated from Paternoster Row, by 1800 the main novel publishing street in London, close to the traditional stationery and book-selling center of St Paul's Churchyard.[14] Other booksellers, like Thomas Hookham (with his partner James Carpenter) and John and Francis Noble, set up shop in the newly built and fashionable squares and lanes of the

---

[14] See James Raven, "St. Paul's Precinct and the Book Trades to c. 1800," in Derek Keene, Arthur Burns, and Andrew Saint, eds., *St. Paul's: The Cathedral Church of London, 604–2004* (London, 2004), 430–38; James Raven, "Location, Size and Succession: The Bookshops of Paternoster Row before 1800," in Robin Myers, Michael Harris, and Giles Mandelbrote, eds., *The London Book Trade: Topographies of Print in the Metropolis from the Sixteenth Century* (Newcastle, Del., 2003), 89–126; and James Raven, "Memorializing a London Bookscape: The Mapping and Reading of Paternoster Row and St Paul's Churchyard, 1695–1814," in R. C. Alston, ed., *Order and Connexion: Studies in Bibliography and Book History* (Woodbridge, 1997), 177–200.

TABLE 2. LEADING BRITISH NOVEL PUBLISHERS, 1750–1829, BY PUBLICATION OF NEW NOVEL TITLES[a]

	No. new novel titles							
	1750–59	1760–69	1770–79	1780–89	1790–99	1800–10	1811–19	1820–29
Thomas Becket/Abraham de Hondt		25	17	3[b]				
John Bell			9		30	3		
John Bew			21	24	10			
William Blackwood (Edinburgh)							7	35
Thomas Cadell			16	14	4 / 14[c]	9[c]	7[c]	3[c] / 37[d]
Henry Colburn and Co.						16	43	104
Mary Cooper	18	2						
Benjamin Crosby and Co.					12	43	13	
Robert/James Dodsley	6	19	11	8	1			
Thomas Hookham			5	41	19	6[f]	9[f]	6[f]
Hughes, James Fletcher					35[e]	77	16	
William Lane (and A.K. from 1802)			3	80	217	214	163	145
Thomas Lowndes and Co.	2	19	22	8	6			
John and Francis Noble	24	38	38	21				
George Robinson and Co.			14	34	54	23	9	
Thomas Longman and Co.				1	24	53	60	84

John Roson						18
Sherwood and Co.	4	37	14			
Henry Symonds	16	23	6			
Thomas Vernor	1	9	4	5		
George Whittaker and Co.	27[g]	13[g]	1[g]	4	58	
Total primary bookseller-publishers in new novel imprints	315	405	701	773	662	830

[a] Excluding the appearance of these booksellers' names in the "sold by" advertisements to novels when not also cited in the actual imprint. Some of the novels, jointly financed, appear more than once in this table.

[b] Becket alone

[c] and Thomas Davies

[d] Thomas Cadell Jr.

[e] and James Carpenter

[f] Thomas Hookham Jr. and Co.

[g] and Thomas Hood

West End. Still others, like William Lane and his Minerva Press in Leaden-hall Street, made an address famous despite an unusual site. Some of the leading publishers of novels worked within the established network and even as prominent members of their guild, the Stationers' Company; others seemed to relish challenging the book-trade establishment and made the popular novel a weapon in their battle for commercial and public success. Self-publicists like the Nobles, Lane, and Hookham and Carpenter can be credited with pioneering efforts in the establishment of commercial circulating libraries and in the publication of fashionable, almost production-line novels. Their success was carried forward in the next century by James Fletcher Hughes (until his 1808 bankruptcy) and by Lane's successor at the Minerva, A. K. Newman, challenged by Henry Colburn from the 1810s and especially during the 1820s. In response to the development of the novel market, certain of the more established and reputable firms, most notably Thomas Longman and Sons, also made significant investments in fiction publication.[15]

The sentimental novel, the "spy" novel, and, from the 1780s, the gothic novel, counted heavily in these tallies. Gothic novels, in particular, amounted to about a third of all new novels published between 1796 and 1806 and a quarter of all those published between 1800 and 1810. Thereafter, the genre joined the spy and sentimental novels in steady decline.[16] In many ways, however, the most distinctive subset of novels before 1800 were those written in letters. The epistolary novel in English enjoyed a distinguished history, from the early models of Richardson to the translations of Françoise, Madame de Grafigny, Marie Leprince de Beaumont, and Marie-Jeanne Riccoboni.[17] As shown by table 3, between 1750 and 1760 new novels in letters averaged no more than a tenth of the annual total of new fiction, but by the mid-1760s a quarter and by 1767 more than a third of the annual crop of new novels were epistolary.[18] During the 1770s and 1780s, over 40 percent of all novels were published in letter form (and in seven of the years between 1776 and 1784 constituted at least half the annual novel output). In 1776, a year of relatively few publications, more than two-thirds of the novels were

[15] See Garside et al., *English Novel*, 2:79–90.

[16] See Raven, *British Fiction*, 11–12; Garside et al., *English Novel*, 1:28, 31–34, 2:53–59; John Mullan, "Sentimental Novels," in John Richetti, ed., *The Cambridge Companion to the Eighteenth-Century Novel* (Cambridge, 1996), 236–54; Montague Summers, *A Gothic Bibliography* (London 1948); and Maggie Kilgour, *The Rise of the Gothic Novel* (London, 1995).

[17] Robert A. Day, *Told in Letters: Epistolary Fiction before Richardson* (Ann Arbor, Mich., 1966); Frank Gees Black, *The Epistolary Novel in the Late Eighteenth Century* (Eugene, Ore., 1940); and for the early decades of the century, Ruth Perry, *Women, Letters, and the Novel* (New York, 1980).

[18] Raven, *British Fiction*, 12.

TABLE 3. PUBLICATION OF EPISTOLARY FICTION, 1750–1799

Imprint year	Total novel titles	Epistolary titles	Epistolary titles as % of total[a]
1750	23	—	—
1751	23	1	4
1752	19	1	5
1753	19	3	16
1754	30	1	3
1755	22	2	9
1756	25	1	4
1757	26	2	8
1758	16	2	13
1759	28	3	11
	231	*16*	*7*
1760	35	1	3
1761	20	3	15
1762	19	4	21
1763	18	5	26
1764	26	7	27
1765	18	4	22
1766	27	7	26
1767	33	12	36
1768	37	10	27
1769	44	16	36
	277	*69*	*25*
1770	40	14	35
1771	60	21	35
1772	41	20	49
1773	39	17	44
1774	35	17	49
1775	31	12	39
1776	17	12	71
1777	18	9	50
1778	16	7	44
1779	18	9	50
	315	*138*	*44*
1780	24	13	54
1781	22	12	55
1782	22	8	36

(*continued*)

TABLE 3. *(Continued)*

Imprint year	Total novel titles	Epistolary titles	Epistolary titles as % of total[a]
1783	24	12	50
1784	24	14	58
1785	47	20	42
1786	40	15	38
1787	51	22	43
1788	80	26	33
1789	71	27	38
	405	*169*	*42*
1790	74	27	37
1791	74	15	20
1792	58	14	24
1793	45	11	24
1794	56	12	21
1795	50	8	16
1796	91	14	15
1797	79	8	10
1798	75	8	11
1799	99	11	11
	701	*128*	*18*

[a] In this and all tables below, rounded up to the nearest percentage point

epistolary. A turning point seems to have been reached in 1791 when only fifteen (or about a fifth) of the seventy-four novels published that year were in letters, and this proportion remained about the same until a further decline to some 10 percent of the total between 1797 and 1799. By the final years of the century, the epistolary form had lost its popularity, swamped, it seems by the diversity and directness of new historical and gothic narratives that were ill-suited to relation by letters.

Such title-counting also revises histories of the relative popularity of novelists and the creation of a particular literary canon. Among the most reprinted novels of the period were both those mimicking the most feted and also well-promoted offerings from a range of prolific but now forgotten writers. Undistinguished imitations of Richardson notably proliferated in the 1750s and 1760s, but even more remarkable (and almost unnoticed by later commentators) was a later flock of would-be Frances Burneys. Of many examples, *Harcourt: A Sentimental Novel* (1780) was falsely claimed to be "by the authoress of Evelina," and the *Critical*'s reviewer identified *Oswald Castle* (1788) as "a production of the Cecilia school." Other Burneyana of the 1788 season included Anne Hughes's *Henry and Isabella* and Anna Maria Mackenzie's *Retribution*. A year later, even Elizabeth Bonhote, according to her *Critical* reviewer, "steps too nearly in the steps of Cecilia."[19] By contrast, admitted imitation of Fielding and Smollett was slender.

Of the leading novelists themselves, relative rankings will always be imprecise. Further editions varied in size, and many, where no extant copy survives, might only have been bookseller's puffs. We can at least show that the most reprinted novelists of the third quarter of eighteenth century were Sterne, Fielding, Hayward, Smollett, Defoe, Riccoboni, Kimber, and Sarah Fielding (probably in that order), while succeeding generations of novel readers favored Ann Radcliffe, Burney, Henry Mackenize, and Sir Walter Scott. The roll call of the most productive novelists, however, suggests quite another cast—one led by Anna Maria Bennett, Stéphanie Genlis, Phebe Gibbes, Barbara Hofland, Martha Hugill, Isabella Kelly Hedgeland, August Lafontaine, Francis Lathom, Mary Meeke, Henry Summersett, and George Walker.[20]

As the reviewers happily reported, the other obvious characteristic of these novels was their transience. The majority were produced in first and only editions of no more than 500 (and even some of the most successful in editions of 750 or 800). A consistent 58 to 59 percent of novels first published in the 1770s and 1780s and 66 percent of those from the 1790s did not go through a second edition, even in Ireland, where many novels were reprinted in Dublin (and occasionally elsewhere). Until 1801, Ireland was outside the Union of England and Scotland, with no copyright law in force. Dublin booksellers published cheap, undercutting reprints apparently for illegal import to England and Scotland, but many also supplied to an Irish home market.[21] Most second editions also seemed to satisfy demand with ease. Of the 40 percent of new novel titles reprinted at least once in this period, fewer than 5 percent reached further editions.

Some of the demand for further editions came from overseas. Until the early 1790s, the overwhelming strength of book exports to North America and to the Caribbean and Indian colonies, along with the handicapped state of colonial publishing ensured that both individuals and institutions were

---

[19] *Critical Review* 68 (1789): 407.

[20] Fuller discussion is given in Raven, *British Fiction*, 14–18; and Garside et al., *English Novel*, 1:39–40, 2:64.

[21] The importance of the Irish home market has been convincingly restated by Mary Pollard, *Dublin's Trade in Books 1550–1800* (Oxford, 1989).

supplied by London and other British booksellers.[22] Only from the 1790s were American editions of British novels published in significant numbers. Between 1770 and 1790, a mere three novels were reprinted on the other side of the Atlantic, but some thirty-five novels first printed in Britain during the 1790s (or 5 percent of the total) appeared in an American edition in the same season as their London publication. Thereafter, same- or next-season American reprintings increased—to nearly 10 percent of all novels first printed in Britain in the first decade of the 1800s, 18 percent in the 1810s, and 23 percent in the 1820s.[23]

In the second half of the eighteenth century, new novels were written by some 700 different authors and translators.[24] Of the 506 novelists identified with novels published between 1770 and 1799, 377 were British and 117 foreign-born (with 12 unidentified). Most were men. In eleven years only between 1750 and 1769 were fewer novels written by men than by the combined total of women *and* unknown authors. In other words, even if we count as women the large number of still unidentified authors (36 percent), male novelists are still in the majority for nine of the years 1750–69. It was also the case that in years such as 1763–64 when the popularity of women writers did increase, this was almost entirely owing to reprints of a few popular authors. In the following three decades, 1770–1800, male writers of new novels (292) greatly outnumbered female writers (189), with 25 identified authors of unknown sex. Thereafter the sociology of the novel notably altered. From about 1780, and most strikingly between 1790 and 1820, the productivity of women novelists (including those identified by later research) advanced greatly, just as the balance also changed between male and female novelists openly named on the title pages.

Variations in the public declaration of authorship are especially significant. Of the total number of novels first published in the 1770s, nearly 10 percent provided title-page or preface attribution to named men, compared with nearly 6 percent to named women, and in only one year of the decade (1775) were more novel title pages issued declaring female rather than male

---

[22] See James Raven, "The Export of Books to Colonial North America," in *Publishing History* 42 (1997): 21–49; James Raven, *London Booksellers and American Customers: Transatlantic Literary Community and the Charleston Library Society, 1748–1811* (Columbia, S.C., 2002); and Robert B. Winans, "Bibliography and the Cultural Historian: Notes on the Eighteenth-Century Novel," in William L. Joyce et al., eds., *Printing and Society in Early America* (Worcester, Mass., 1983), 174–85.

[23] Garside et al., *English Novel*, 2:98.

[24] More precise estimates can be found in Raven, *British Fiction*, 14–15; and Garside et al., *English Novel*, 1:39–65.

authorship. During the 1780s, however, this relationship was reversed, with 5 percent of all new novel titles announcing a named male author, but some 10 percent of the total naming a female author. The female title-page lead continued during the less reticent 1790s, when many more title pages or prefaces boasted names. Some 17 percent of all new novels of the 1790s were published with named male writers, but more than a fifth (21 percent) gave named female writers. In particular years a striking number of women authors were acknowledged. Between 1788 and 1790, thirty-three novel title pages (or prefaces) named women authors. Why this change came about is arguable, but the explicit promotion of female authorship seems clear, especially given that it was exactly at this time that the unprecedented number of otherwise anonymous title pages also bore the attribution to "a Lady" (however true that was).

Whatever we might now reveal about the relative numbers of men and women novelists, however, the question of what was apparent at the time is important. The overwhelming majority of the English novels of the eighteenth and early nineteenth centuries were published without attribution of authorship either on the title page or within the preface or elsewhere in the text. As also shown in figure 1, over 80 percent of all novel titles published in the 1770s and 1780s were published anonymously. Although by the 1790s more than a third (38 percent) of all novels carried some sort of specific attribution, the majority still adopted an anodyne title-page mask, with many of the anonymous novels bearing a very general and unverifiable ascription. Identities were hidden for reasons ranging from genuine modesty to fear of public ridicule and family wrath. Phebe Gibbes, one of the most prolific of novelists from this period, later declared that "being a domestic woman, and of withdrawing turn of Temper I never would be prevailed upon to put my name to any of my Productions."[25] We can only guess at the full output of such writers. Elizabeth Helme, for example, asserted that she was acknowledged as the author of ten novels and three translations but had also "translated sixteen volumes for different booksellers without my name."[26]

During the first decade of the nineteenth century, the public admission of authorship continued to increase, and the total of anonymously issued novels fell for the first time to under half of all new novels published (see figure 1). After about 1810, however, anonymity advanced again, so that by the late 1820s about 80 percent of all annual new novel titles were again

---

[25] British Library, Archives of the Royal Literary Fund, 1790–1918 (hereafter RLF), 2:74, letter of Phebe Gibbes, October 17, 1804.

[26] RLF, 3:97, letter of Elizabeth Helme, October 20, 1803.

publicly authorless. An obvious challenge, then, posed by the profiles of new novel production is to explain first, why such a very high proportion of novels were first published anonymously, and second, why anonymity was reduced and then revived in the second half of this period.

Both questions turn in part on the degree of anonymity offered in novel publication. Many novels carried references to earlier work by the same writer, declaring themselves to be "By the author of . . ." This, in fact, has been a critical aid in unraveling relationships between works, even if some of these novels remain unattributable to a specific individual. In addition, booksellers and writers adopted other devices of concealment. Among the three-quarters of all new novels of this period that were published without attribution, the vague and dubious tag of "By a Lady" or "By a Young Lady" gained special popularity. Authors and their publishers resorted to this style with particular enthusiasm in the late 1780s, when the overall publication of fiction advanced markedly. In 1785, nearly a third and in 1787 nearly a quarter of all novel titles were said to be "by a Lady." These and other general gender descriptors cannot, however, be taken at face value. Several male writers assumed "young lady" title-page identity, and a few young women pretended to be male.

A certain inclination to anonymity simply resulted from the surge in new novel writing. Given the market necessity of producing editions of only about 500 or 750 copies, the demand for new writing often seemed irresistible. Limitations of technology and the determination to avoid excessive risk encouraged booksellers to issue multiple editions of a popular work rather than an abnormally large single edition. The increase in new writing in the later years of this period inevitably brought more writers (and several popular and hack novelists also appear to have been more prolific than their predecessors). This, in turn, affected the proportion of novel titles published anonymously in as much as first-time and write-to-order authors were far more likely to withhold their names from the title page than were more proven writers.

Perhaps, however, the most obvious reason for early anonymity (and then the later defiance of it) derives from the popularity and savagery of the published critical reviews. The common charge against these novels was that they were not only "hackneyed" and "insipid," but "trifling" and "worthless."[27] Typical was the *Critical* rant against Mary Robinson's "fashionably vicious" *Widow* of 1794: "O! for a warning to prevent those, at least, in whom

---

[27] Of many examples, the negative reviews in *Critical Review* 63 (1787): 390; and *Monthly Review* 52 (1775): 187; 60 (1779): 481; and 76 (1787): 528.

age has not yet destroyed the capabilities of improvement, from dreaming away their hours in turning over publications like these."[28] Many review verdicts anticipating national moral catastrophe might be dismissed as po-faced overreaction, but some of the novels do contain episodes approaching more modern definitions of the obscene—some marvellously so. Title-page disguise or refuge in anonymity was essential given the earthy voyeurism of novels like *The Nun* (1771) and *The Adventures of a Speculist* (1788). Charges of particular lewdness were leveled against such lost novels as *Frailties of Fashion* (1782), *The Victim of Deception* (1788), and *The Adventures of Christopher Curious* (1788). The latter, according to the *English Review* "would disgrace the police of any civilised country upon earth. The mind who could rake together from brothels such a nauseous collection of filth, must be yet more depraved than even the miscreant he would describe."[29]

For the most part, however, critical scorn could be overlooked when the majority of novels were ill-written, sensationalist, or simply crude rather than obscene. In the early nineteenth century an increasing number of publishers tried to persuade authors for their own best interests either to reveal authorship of a novel or to highlight a celebrated predecessor work. Barbara Hofland whose twenty-one novels published between 1800 and 1829 made her the second-most prolific novelist of the period after Scott, opened her account with a novel published anonymously. All but one of her next seven were "by the author of" (the exception being a pseudonym), and she finally claimed public authorship in 1814. The different preferences of publishers were increasingly distinct during the 1820s, at exactly the same time as the tide of anonymity rose again. The Longmans' firm was keen on promoting female authorship, but Colburn, "himself by now far more committed to male writers, was more interested in creating a kind of mystique by not naming his authors."[30]

What was happening, therefore, was that while some publishers tapped into novel writers' fear of exposure and assisted, for their own devices, in cultivating anonymity, other publishers, adopting very different marketing strategies, were forced to take on the cult of anonymity encouraged even by successful authors like Scott. During the 1820s, many novelists of repute inclined to retreat behind anodyne camouflage or adopted complete anonymity. The final irony here was that reviewers had now begun to participate in the "outing" of novelists, contributing to the pressures, particularly for those

---

[28] *Critical Review*, n.s. 12 (1794): 102.
[29] *English Review* 14 (1789): 470.
[30] Garside et al., *English Novel*, 2:67.

writers with professional careers or society profiles, to conceal their identity from the novel-reading public. At the same time, old customs continued. Many indigent or allegedly indigent authors published anonymously as hack writers, encouraged by booksellers to hide their identity so that they could be employed again as unacknowledged writers (and translators) on-demand.

Charity and destitution were common preoccupations of the declared author. Although often disguised in part or whole by the wording of the imprint, many publications were vanity productions in which the author underwrote all or most of the edition of some 500 or 750 copies. As a career, novel writing was almost never self-supporting, despite its apparent attraction to impoverished and desperate gentry. Although most novelists in the early decades of this period lived in financially secure households, this changed markedly in the later years, with many of much humbler means attempting to live by their pen (and directly affecting the proportion of writers anxious to remain anonymous). Some of the poorest broadcast their names in order to attract subscribers or to alert readers to their plight. Charlotte Smith was perhaps the most famous of the wronged-women writers of the age, but there many others who wrote amidst or because of domestic disaster. The prolific Anna Maria Mackenzie and Eliza Parsons, for example, turned to novel writing as penurious widows with four and eight small children, respectively. When published by subscription, many novels boasted quality names in the ranks of subscribers listed at the beginning of the first (and sometimes later) volumes. The great majority, quite obviously, were published with the name of the deserving author emblazoned on the title page and preface, but sometimes a subscription was set up for an undisclosed author. Notable among these were *Emma; or, the Unfortunate Attachment* of 1773, listing 116 names, and Mary Martha Sherwood's *Traditions* of 1795, which paraded 640 subscribers' names.

Borrowing from abroad is the final important feature of novel publication in these years. We can only guess at the exact number of novels directly translated from or very largely based on foreign originals. Elizabeth Helme, for example, as already noted, claimed that she had anonymously translated sixteen works in addition to her acknowledged novels and translations. Some translations were also made indirectly (a German novel via a French translation for example) with conflicting evidence about the text used for the translation, whatever the title page or puffing advertisement decalred. We can at least show that more than a tenth of all novel titles first published in Britain in this period were translations from Continental novels. Some of the source fiction was dated and obscure, almost all from the 1750s until the mid-1790s was from the French, and foreign dependency was especially marked in the early years.

As shown in table 4, at least 95 (or 18 percent) of the 531 novels first published in Britain between 1750 and 1769 were translations. Of these, eighty-four were from the French, two from the Spanish, and only nine from other languages. In the 1770s and 1780s, a few more novels were translated from the German, but it was a popular source only at the end of the eighteenth century and at the beginning of the next. In 1794, translations from the German exceeded those from other languages for the first time, but the revolution was short-lived. Within a few seasons French translations resumed ascendancy, accounting for at least 71 of the total 770 new novels published in English between 1800 and 1809, and 21 of the 662 new titles published in the 1810s.[31] Many translations hid attempts by authors to disguise plagiarism (and lack of imagination), but their attraction to bookseller-publishers was also evident. Second-rate novels could be translated by ill-paid hacks with relative ease and cheapness. Booksellers paid most novel writers a pittance for their original manuscript, after which they had no rights to any further profit, but even this expense was avoided if the text was borrowed from abroad. Much translation was the resort of indigent writers and scholars huddled in Grub Street garrets or moonlighting from poorly paid clerical positions.[32]

The literary traffic across the English Channel was far from one way. Indeed, in reviewing one of the imports—*Innocent Rivals* (1786)—the *Critical* referred to a cross-Channel battle, each side capturing each other's voguish texts. As shown in tables 5 and 6 many English novels of the late eighteenth century were quickly translated into German, French, and other languages, although it is important to stress, first, that the tables record first and not repeated translations of the same titles. Of the 1,421 new novels known to have been published in Britain between 1770 and 1800, 500 are known to have been translated into French or German before 1850. A dozen or more titles were also translated into Spanish and Italian by the same date. In the early nineteenth century a smaller proportion of English novels seems to have been translated abroad, although the influence might also have been longer-term, with later translation and circulation than before. Of the 2,256 new novels known to have been published in Britain between 1800 and

---

[31] For full details of known translations, see Raven, *British Fiction*, 21; Garside et al., *English Novel*, 1:58; 2:41.

[32] See Josephine Grieder, *Translations of French Sentimental Prose Fiction in Late Eighteenth-Century England: The History of a Vogue* (Durham, N.C., 1975).

TABLE 4. FIRST EDITIONS OF ENGLISH TRANSLATIONS OF FOREIGN NOVELS, 1750–1829[a]

Imprint year	Total no. of novel titles	From French	From German	From other
1750	23	4	—	—
1751	23	5	—	—
1752	19	2	—	—
1753	19	7	—	—
1754	30	6	—	1
1755	22	3	—	2
1756	25	1	—	1
1757	26	2	—	—
1758	16	6	—	—
1759	28	10	—	—
	231	*46*	—	*4*
		20%		*2%*
			22%	
1760	35	5	—	—
1761	20	4	—	1
1762	19	3	—	—
1763	18	1	—	—
1764	26	4	—	2
1765	18	3	—	—
1766	27	7	—	—
1767	33	4	1	—
1768	37	3	—	2
1769	44	4	—	1
	277	*38*	*1*	*6*
		14%	—	*2%*
			16%	
1770	40	4 (5)	—	—
1771	60	1 (3)	1	2
1772	41	6 (7)	—	—
1773	39	4	2	1
1774	35	4 (5)	—	—
1775	31	4	—	—
1776	17	1	1	—
1777	18	(1)	—	—
1778	16	2	—	—

TABLE 4. (*Continued*)

Imprint year	Total no. of novel titles	From French	From German	From other
1779	18	2	1	—
	315	*28 (34)*	*5*	*3*
		9%	*2%*	
			11%	
1780	24	1	—	—
1781	22	1 (2)	—	—
1782	22	2 (3)	—	—
1783	24	3	—	—
1784	24	2	—	—
1785	47	2	—	1
1786	40	7 (8)	2	—
1787	51	4	—	1
1788	80	8	—	—
1789	71	5 (6)	2	—
	405	*35 (39)*	*4*	*2*
		9%	*1%*	
			10%	
1790	74	5 (6)	1	1 (2)
1791	74	12	1	—
1792	58	6 (7)	—	1
1793	45	3 (4)	1	1
1794	56	2 (3)	3 (4)	—
1795	50	2 (3)	4	1
1796	91	6 (8)	9	2
1797	79	7	5 (6)	—
1798	75	2 (3)	5 (6)	1 (1)
1799	99	13 (14)	10	2 (3)
	701	*58 (67)*	*39 (42)*	*9 (11)*
		8%	*6%*	*1%*
			15%	
1800	81	4	3	2
1801	72	1	1	1
1802	61	4	3	—
1803	79	20	4	3
1804	73	11	9	—

(*continued*)

TABLE 4. (*Continued*)

Imprint year	Total no. of novel titles	From French	From German	From other
1805	75	6	4	—
1806	70	4	6	1
1807	69	7	4	—
1808	111	9	1	—
1809	79	5	3	—
	770	*71*	*38*	*7*
		9%	*5%*	*1%*
		15%		
1810	89	3	—	1
1811	80	4	2	
1812	66	1	1	—
1813	63	2	2	—
1814	61	—	—	1
1815	54	2	—	—
1816	59	2	2	—
1817	55	3	—	1
1818	62	2	1	1
1819	73	2	1	—
	662	*21*	*9*	*4*
		3%	*1%*	*1%*
		5%		
1820	70	2	1	2
1821	75	3	1	—
1822	82	2	—	—
1823	87	2	2	1
1824	99	1	3	—
1825	91	4	3	—
1826	77	3	7	—
1827	79	1	2	—
1828	83	1	1	1
1829	81	2	—	—
	824	*21*	*20*	*4*
		3%	*3%*	*1%*
		6%		

[a] Includes at least one French novel that was itself a translation from the German, one doubtful translation, and one title with conflicting evidence about the source of the translation—the original German or a French intermediary. Alleged translations are in parentheses.

TABLE 5. First Translations before 1850 into German of English Novels First Published in Britain and Ireland, 1770–1799

Imprint year	Trans. same year	Trans. next year	2–5 years	6–10 years	10+ years	Total trans.	Total novels	% of trans. into German
1770	3	2	1	2	2	10	40	25
1771	2	4	2	—	1	9	60	15
1772	1	1	2	2	—	6	41	15
1773	2	3	6	3	—	14	39	36
1774	2	8	3	—	—	13	35	37
1775	4	8	3	—	1	16	31	52
1776	6	4	2	—	1	13	17	76
1777	—	10	1	1	—	12	18	66
1778	—	7	2	—	—	9	16	56
1779	2	6	4	—	—	12	18	66
1780	2	4	2	—	—	8	24	33
1781	1	7	2	—	—	10	22	45
1782	—	2	1	1	1	5	22	23
1783	—	2	2	—	—	4	24	17
1784	—	2	2	—	—	4	24	17
1785	1	2	4	1	—	8	47	17
1786	—	3	6	1	—	10	40	25
1787	1	1	5	1	3	11	51	22
1788	1	2	3	1	3	10	80	13
1789	1	5	9	—	—	15	71	21
1790	1[a]	8	4	—	—	13	74	18
1791	1	4	6	—	—	11	74	15
1792	1	5	—	1	—	7	58	12
1793	—	1	3	1	—	5	45	11
1794	1	7	2	—	—	10	56	18
1795	—	4	1	—	1	6	50	12
1796	—	6	9	2	—	17	91	19
1797	1	2	5	1	—	9	79	11
1798	—	5	3	—	1	9	75	12
1799	2	4	4	—	—	10	99	10
Total	*36*	*129*	*99*	*18*	*14*	*296*	*1,421*	*21*

[a] No date given for the foreign translation.

TABLE 6. FIRST TRANSLATIONS BEFORE 1850 INTO FRENCH OF ENGLISH
NOVELS FIRST PUBLISHED IN BRITAIN AND IRELAND, 1770–1799

Imprint year	Trans. same year	Trans. next year	2–5 years	6–10 years	10+ years	Total trans.	Total novels	% of trans. into French
1770	4	—	—	—	1	5	40	13
1771	—	2	2	1	2	7	60	12
1772	1	2	1	1	—	5	41	12
1773	—	—	3	—	—	3	39	8
1774	—	—	2	—	1	3	35	9
1775	—	—	1	—	—	1	31	3
1776	—	2	—	—	2	3	17	18
1777	—	1	1	—	—	2	18	11
1778	—	1	1	—	—	2	16	13
1779	—	—	1	—	—	1	18	6
1780	2[a]	—	1	—	—	3	24	13
1781	—		—	1	—	1	22	5
1782	—	1	—	—	1	2	22	9
1783	—	1	—	—	—	1	24	4
1784	—	—	4	—	1	5	24	21
1785	—	—	4	1	—	5	47	11
1786	1	2	7	1	1	12	40	30
1787	1	6	4	2	—	13	51	25
1788	7	5	1	1	—	14	80	18
1789	6	—	—	4	2	12	71	17
1790	—	—	—	1	—	1	74	1
1791	1	1	2	1[a]	1	6	74	8
1792	—	2	1	—	1	4	58	7
1793	1[a]	—	—	1	—	2	45	4
1794	1[a]	1	3	—	3	8	56	14
1795	—	—	2	2	—	4	50	8
1796	2[a]	8	7	—	2	19	91	21
1797	4	8	9	—	2	23	79	29
1798	7	7	4	1[a]	—	19	75	25
1799	2	6	8	—	2	18	99	18
Total	40	56	69	18	22	204	1,421	15

[a] No date given for the foreign translation.

1829, 341 are known to have been translated into French or German before 1850 (see table 7). Translations into French outnumber those into German by nearly two-to-one in the 1810s, and by more than two-to-one in the 1810s. In the 1820s, however, the battle lines were reversed, with 111 borrowings from the French compared with 134 from the German.[33]

As tables 5 and 6 also reveal, speed of translation was highly variable.[34] Notable among the slow-movers was Smollett's *Humphry Clinker* (1771), not published in French until 1826, probably as a result of his unpopularity in France in the wake of his *Travels through France and Italy* (1768). By contrast, *Humphry Clinker* was published in German the season after its appearance in English. Few notable authors were not translated into German. Another novel of 1771, Henry Mackenzie's *Man of Feeling*, delineating sensibility or, in the author's words, "the sweet emotion of pity" and "the luxury of grief," was translated into German three years later and into French the year after that. His *Man of the World* of 1773 was translated into German in the same season and into French within two years. Among titles reappearing in German in the same season were Richard Graves's *Spiritual Quixote* of 1773, Henry Brooke's *Juliet Grenville* of 1774, Charles Johnstone's *The Pilgrim*, Henry Man's *Mr Bentley* of 1775, and Elizabeth Bonhote's *Rambles of Mr Frankly* of 1776. The rage for the English novel in Germany induced translations of a range of writers from the famous to the obscure. Novels first published in Britain the 1770s also maintained greater long-term popularity in Germany than in France—well over a third of all titles from this decade were translated into German before 1850, but only 10 percent of these titles were translated into French during the same period. After some renewed interest in translating English novels in France in the late 1780s (with some retrospective translating of novels issued in London two to five years previously during the first years of the Revolution), a marked turnaround came at the very end of the century. Nearly a quarter of all novels first published in London between 1796 and 1799 were translated into French within five years of their appearance.[35] At least 274 titles were

---

[33] See Garside et al., *English Novel*, 1:65–71; 2:99–102.

[34] Because the research cutoff point was 1850, no equivalent study of the continuing translation of novels in English first published after 1800 would have been meaningful.

[35] See Lawrence Marsden Price, "English Literature in Germany," in *University of California Publications in Modern Philology* 37 (1953); James Raven, "An Antidote to the French? English Novels in German Translation and German Novels in English Translation, 1770–99," in *Eighteenth-Century Fiction* 14, 3–4 (April–July 2002): 715–34; Angus Martin, Vivienne G. Mylne, and Richard Frautschi, eds., *Bibliographie du genre romanesque français 1751–1800* (London, 1977); and Alexandre Cioranescu, ed., *Bibliographie de la littérature française du dix-huitième siècle* (Paris, 1969).

TABLE 7. FIRST TRANSLATIONS BEFORE 1850 INTO FRENCH AND GERMAN OF ENGLISH NOVELS FIRST PUBLISHED IN BRITAIN AND IRELAND 1800–1829[a]

Imprint year	Total new novels	Trans. into French & German	Trans. into French only	Trans. into German only	Total trans.
1800	81	2	7	7	16
1801	72	6	9	2	17
1802	61	—	4	1	5
1803	79	3	2	1	6
1804	73	1	3	—	4
1805	75	1	5	1	7
1806	70	3	6	3	12
1807	69	1	6	—	7
1808	111	1	4	1	6
1809	79	3	1	—	4
	770	*21*	*47*	*16*	*84*
		3%	*6%*	*2%*	*11%*
1810	89	—	4	—	4
1811	80	2	6	1	9
1812	66	—	3	1	4
1813	63	3	3	2	8
1814	61	4	6	1	11
1815	54	1	2	3	6
1816	59	3	7	—	10
1817	55	1	7	1	9
1818	62	4	8	1	13
1819	73	3	4	2	9
	662	*21*	*50*	*12*	*83*
		3%	*8%*	*2%*	*13%*
1820	70	8	5	1	14
1821	75	4	7	3	14
1822	82	8	8	5	21
1823	87	6	3	10	19
1824	99	8	5	6	19
1825	91	8	3	6	17
1826	77	6	3	9	18
1827	79	8	—	9	17
1828	83	8	4	6	18
1829	81	7	2	8	17
	824	*71*	*40*	*63*	*174*
		9%	*5%*	*8%*	*21%*
Total	*2,256*	*113*	*137*	*91*	*341*
		0. 5%	*0.6%*	*0.4%*	*15%*

[a] Based on Garside et al., *English Novel*, 2:101 (table 10).

translated into German within ten years of their appearance and a further fourteen more than ten years after first publication in English (and before 1850). By comparison, no fewer than 184 titles were translated into French within ten years of their appearance in English, with a further twenty-one titles translated more than ten years later. Translations into German were, generally, much swifter—many, within the same season or the next.

A particularly large crop of new English novels were also translated into German in a nine-year period from the mid-1770s (see the final column of table 5). In particular, novels suffering deserved obscurity in Britain were often quickly translated when styled as having been written in the manner of Richardson.[36] Of all English novels first published between 1773 and 1781, never fewer than one-quarter of all annual titles were translated into German. In the peak years of 1776 and 1777, three-quarters and two-thirds of all annual titles respectively were translated into German. By comparison, French translations of new English novels never reached even a third of the total number of English titles available in any one year of these decades. The highest total of 40, or 30 percent, of the publications with an imprint date of 1786, was also achieved slowly, over subsequent seasons. There was certainly no rush to translate English novels into French. In English terms, the most auspicious years for producing novels later to be translated into French were 1786–89 and 1796–99, but such trends are hardly explicable without a much more searching questioning of translation patterns across a broad range of literature and without more precise investigation into the actual years and circumstances of translation in Paris. Table 6 further suggests that the proportion of new English novels translated into German declined from the 35 percent of all fiction titles published in 1781 to something like an average of 10 percent in the 1790s.

It also seems clear that in years when French, and particularly German, booksellers sought foreign novels to translate to satisfy new demand, the output of particular London booksellers appealed. Most noticeable (and surprising) about the novels from table 6 that were swiftly translated into German is the number of titles first published by the Noble brothers of the newly fashionable West End of London. In Paris, Thomas Hookham advertised his "livres vendu" from his New Bond Street shop in extensive lists of French and English titles, and this contributed significantly to English-French novel exchange in the period. In addition, the later translation of

---

[36] *The New Clarissa* (London, 1771), was translated into German a few seasons later, while *The History of Sir William Harrington,* also 1771, was published in English and in German in the same year.

very obscure English titles also points to the mediating role of the periodical reviews, all exportable dictionaries of past publishing and critical assessment from London.

It is of course, important not to overrate the artistic merits of these novels. Most were lamentably written, and most were published in very modestly sized editions. Stylistic poverty and transience characterized the majority, and the majority of titles were never reprinted. All the evidence points to a very large proportion of the novels being produced to service circulating libraries—many owned and managed by the publishers of the new fiction. The short life of these "literary gad-flies" as one reviewer called them, ensured that questions of authorship were not easily pursued and very often confused, deliberately or otherwise. The history of the English popular novel in this period is one of largely impoverished writers caught between their fear of mounting critical disapproval and the varying marketing strategies of their bookseller-publishers. Male parity and, in some years, dominance, in the second half of the eighteenth century was followed by increasing female authorship of new novels during the early nineteenth century. The social background and gender of the writers clearly did make a difference to the likelihood of a name's appearing on the title page of the novel, but even this was mediated by tensions between critics and booksellers in which the financial bargaining power of the authors was usually nonexistent. Certainly, by themselves, past success and public confidence were rarely sufficient to persuade authors to countermand the advice of booksellers (even if given the choice) or to run the gamut of the periodical reviewers.

The escalating output shocked many contemporaries. Only when entertainment was combined with useful instruction might the novel escape charges of insignificance or depravity. Concern about the effects of novel-mania was a serious one and should not be dismissed with retrospective levity, however much we now enjoy the reviewers' wit and scorn. For many, the writing of a novel was an apprentice piece—and one from which they did not always recover. Much of this fiction slavishly followed model forms or lionized writers, predictably and with restrained ambition. Several novels even seem to have been put together above the print-room—a few chapters from a hack writer, other parts culled from an old romance, something more translated from a foreign potboiler. A few novels were quickly reprinted; others were revived after a few seasons or achieved a limited success in the writer's own circle or locality. The bulk of these novels were soon left to gather dust, summarily disposed of, or returned, after brief reading, to the fashionable circulating libraries for which so many of them were chiefly written.

JOHN AUSTIN

United States, 1780–1850

In 1939, Lyle Wright published a brief, ambitious, and pioneering article entitled "A Statistical Survey of American Fiction, 1774–1850." In it Wright used quantitative data drawn from his own bibliography, *American Fiction, 1774–1850*, to construct a comprehensive map of the field of American prose fiction.[1] Wright's article provides an essential point of departure for anyone interested in the use of quantitative evidence for the study of American literary history. (My first two figures are taken from data drawn from Wright's article.) But because Wright's bibliography is limited to "American fiction"—a broad category that excludes a number of important fictional forms and necessarily ignores British and European titles published in America—I have supplemented Wright's data with some additional bibliographic sources. In so doing I hope to offer a more expansive vista upon the literary field and redefine what we mean when we speak of American fiction.

Figure 1, drawing on Wright's data, breaks down 842 works of fiction according to the subtitles appearing on their title pages. According to Wright's calculations, of the 1,377 titles published between 1775 and 1850, 32 percent were offered as "tales"; 10 percent as "romances"; 6 percent as "stories"; 9 percent as a "history," "legend," "letters," "scenes," or "sketches"; and a mere 4 percent as "novels." (A whopping 39 percent carried no subtitle at all.) Significantly, the percentage of "novels" available on the market decreases over time. In the first decade of the nineteenth century, 43 percent of all titles were explicitly marketed as "novels"; in the last decade of the first half of the nineteenth century only 3 percent were. In contrast, the number of "romances" and "tales" increases dramatically over the same period, from 0 to 21 percent in the first instance and from 5 to 55 percent in the second instance. By this data, the novel can scarcely be said even to exist—in fact it steadily declines in popularity—and the "tale" is the most popular genre of American prose fiction.

But we know—or at least we think we know—that this cannot be true. American novels were published in abundance between the years 1820 and 1850—on this point every major history of American literature of the last

---

[1] Lyle H. Wright, "A Statistical Survey of American Fiction, 1774–1850," *Huntington Library Quarterly* 2 (1939): 309–18.

Figure 1. American Fiction, 1770–1850,
According to Subtitles

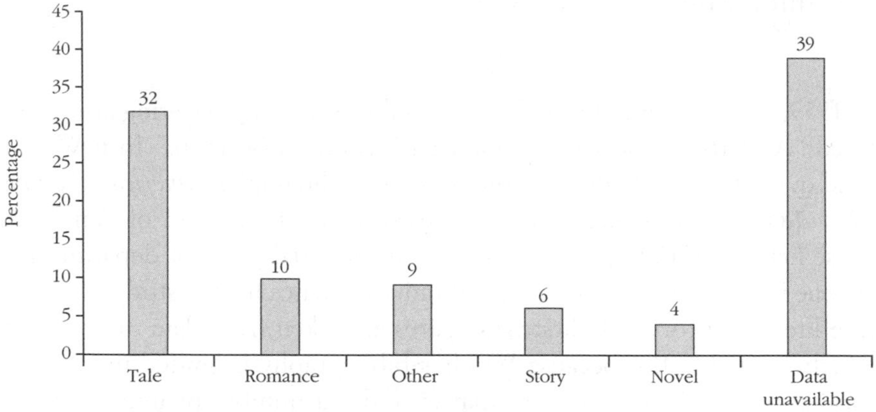

century agrees, including the most recent volume of *The Cambridge History of American Literature*. As Michael Bell argues there in his discussion of this period: "In quantitative terms at least, the period from 1820 through 1845 clearly marked the first major 'renaissance' in American fiction. More than a few of these new books were collections of tales and sketches. . . . But most were novels."[2] If Bell is correct, Wright's data probably tells us as much about the marketing strategies of American publishers—particularly their desire to package novels as either "romances" or "tales"—as its does about the actual market in fiction and the genres competing within it.

Although this data may underestimate the number novels published in this period, it does present us with an important methodological consideration: the difficulty of reading the genre of a book through its title. Titles may not be the best indicators of genre. As Wright notes: "Many short stories were called novels . . . whereas innumerable one- and two-volume novels were designated as tales."[3] The difficulty of using titles to make generic distinctions becomes even more pressing when we try to decide from a title whether a given work is a historical novel, a sentimental novel, an adventure novel, or something else entirely. But if the literary historian cannot rely on titles as indicators of genre, how does he or she proceed? How do we take the entries contained in the bibliography and organize them into taxonomies that will reveal larger patterns in the market? Here we reach an

---

[2] Michael Bell, "Conditions of Literary Vocation," *The Cambridge History of American Literature: 1820–1865*," ed. Sacvan Bercovitch (Cambridge, 1995), 37–38.
[3] Wright, "A Statistical Survey," 311.

TABLE 1. PERCENTAGE OF "SUBJECTS" IN AMERICAN FICTION, 1790–1849

	1790–99	1800–09	1810–19	1820–29	1830–39	1840–49
Life and manners	50	59	39	24	21	23
Historical fiction	23	0	26	32	18	17
Frontier	0	0	0	6	11	15
Sea tales	0	0	0	6	4	12
Temperance	0	0	0	0	12	4
Foreign	8	32	17	13	11	7
Stories of the city	0	5	4	3	3	8
Other	19	4	14	16	20	14

Source: Lyle Wright, "A Statistical Survey of American Fiction."

impasse: we can't construct a reliable, historically accurate taxonomy without reading the sample, but the sample is so large as to render it virtually unreadable. It may have been possible for Kathy Davidson to have read all the novels published by Americans between the years 1789 and 1820 (about a hundred) for her study, *Revolution and the Word: The Rise of the Novel in America*, but it would be a very difficult task indeed to read the some 1,300 titles published in the thirty years between 1820 and 1850—much less the almost 3,000 published between 1851 and 1875, or the some 6,000 titles published between 1876 and 1900. (Tellingly, Wright did not follow up his article with comparable pieces analyzing the data contained in his two subsequent volumes.)

Wright broke down his own bibliography into some thirty-two different "subject headings." In the hopes of locating some larger patterns in the market, I took Wright's thirty-two categories (some of which were too narrow to be useful) and reduced them to eight: historical fiction, life and manners, the frontier, sea tales, temperance fiction, works with a foreign setting, tales of city life, and a final miscellaneous category for the remainders. The tallies are displayed in table 1.

For the most part this data confirms what we already know: a spike in temperance fiction in the 1830s; an unsurprising rise in the number of sea tales and stories of the frontier in the 1830s and 1840s (this was, after all, a period of economic and geographic expansion); a steady decline throughout the nineteenth century in the number and percentage of titles with a foreign setting; the triumph of life and manners over historical fiction. If this data is a bit disappointing, perhaps it is because Wright's subject headings are at best impressionistic. The largest category, "life and manners," is something of a grab bag, including, as Wright himself admits, "stories of contemporary business, moral tales, scandal stories, stories of sport, and romances

TABLE 2. AMERICAN FICTION, 1785–1850

	Compilations	Two-volume novels	80 or fewer pages	81–125 pages	126 pages or longer	Totals
1785	0	0	1	0	0	1
1790	0	1	0	0	0	1
1795	1	1	0	0	1	3
1800	0	0	1	1	1	3
1805	0	0	0	0	1	1
1810	0	1	0	0	3	4
1815	1	0	0	0	0	1
1820	1	2	1	0	2	6
1825	2	1	0	1	5	9
1830	17	5	3	1	9	35
1835	17	17	7	4	12	57
1840	24	6	3	2	6	41
1845	38	7	83	18	39	185
1850	49	1	19	35	46	150

dominated by love interest."[4] Moreover, Wright's sample of 1,122 accounts for only about 80 percent of the material contained in the first volume of his bibliography of American fiction. The missing 20 percent, he tells us, represents a handful of titles he was unable to locate in the Library of Congress, a few anomalies that did not fall into any of his thirty-two subject headings, and collections of tales and sketches—a significant omission to which I return in a moment.

Table 2 offers a different sort of taxonomy—one based on other types of information easily gleaned from Wright's bibliography. This table includes the whole of the literary field in fiction, including that 20 percent originally omitted by Wright in his 1939 article. I have supplemented data from Wright with an additional bibliographic source that covers roughly the same period, Ralph Thompson's *American Literary Annuals and Gift Books: 1825–1865*. I have done so on a hint from Wright himself—his tacit admission that almost 20 percent of all titles published during this period were collections and anthologies. Wright omits annuals from his bibliography, but there are strong reasons for including them in an account of the American literary field. Although literary annuals frequently include in their contents a range of short forms—poetry, devotional essays, travel sketches, and

---

[4] Ibid., 315.

FIGURE 2. THE LITERARY FIELD, 1820–1845

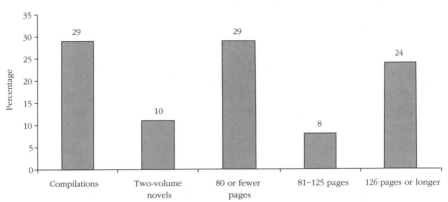

occasional dialogues—most were given over almost entirely to works of prose fiction. Moreover, they were enormously popular. Thompson counts more than 450 annuals published between 1825 and 1860 (a number that includes neither reprints nor popular titles imported from England). I have counted an additional 246 single-author collections and anthologies published between 1820 and 1850.

For the purposes of table 2, I have grouped annuals, collections, and anthologies together as "compilations." Works of prose fiction have been divided into a further four categories: novels published in two volumes or more (according to William Charvat the standard format of publication for novels during this period),[5] works of 80 or fewer pages, works between 81 and 125 pages, and works 126 pages and longer.[6]

As figure 2 reveals, the market for print commodities was much more balanced than the contemporary scholarship, which emphasizes the novel form, would lead us to believe. If we take Michael Bell's target period, 1820–45, we find a market evenly balanced between compilations (29 percent of the market), volumes of 80 or fewer pages (29 percent), and volumes 126 pages or longer (24 percent). Intermediate-length works between 81 and 125 pages constitute 8 percent of the market, while two-volume novels account for 10 percent.

---

[5] William Charvat, *Literary Publishing in America: 1790–1850* (Amherst, Mass., 1993), 80–88. Originally published 1959.

[6] Grouping books according to length is not without its dangers. One work of forty pages may be considerably longer than a different work of forty pages, especially if the former is printed in double columns (as is sometimes the case). Nonetheless, length remains a telling and important index of genre, especially in the American case, where, as we will see, an extraordinary number of single-volume fictions were between 30 and 125 pages in length.

TABLE 3. AMERICAN FICTION, 1830–1850, BY PERCENTAGE

	Compilations	Two-volume novels	80 or fewer pages	81–125 pages	126 pages or longer
1830	49	14	9	3	26
1835	30	30	12	7	21
1840	59	15	7	5	15
1845	21	4	45	10	21
1850	33	1	12	23	31

There are two surprises here: the extraordinary number of short to intermediate-length books available on the market (especially during the 1840s) and the popularity of literary compilations—annuals, collections and anthologies. Throughout this period the compilation was a major competitor in the literary market and an important rival of the novel. From 1835 to 1850 (table 2) as many or more compilations were published than two-volume novels. In 1840, twenty-four compilations appeared and only six two-volume novels; 1845 saw thirty-eight compilations and only seven two-volume novels (two of which were Cooper's). As table 3 indicates, the percentage of two-volume novels steadily declines from 1835 onward, from 30 percent in 1835 to less than 1 percent in 1850. Even when we factor in single-volume fictions 126 pages or longer, the compilation remains a major competitor in the literary market, especially between the years 1830 and 1850. In 1850, compilations still constitute one-third of the market.[7]

Print runs of individual titles, where they are available, confirm this data. For not only were extraordinary numbers of compilations published during this period, but they were also issued in unusually large editions, in some cases as large as ten thousand. Except for its first three years, *The Atlantic Souvenir*, one of the few annuals for which we possess accurate publication figures, was never issued in an edition smaller than 9,500.[8] By 1832, more than 54,000 volumes of *The Atlantic Souvenir* had appeared on the market.

---

[7] Moreover, compilations seem to have been somewhat immune to the periodical fluctuations in the economy typical of this period. While book production as a whole was declining in the final few years of the 1830s (in response to an economic recession), the number of compilations produced continues to increase.

[8] In its first three years of existence *The Atlantic Souvenir* was issued in editions of 2,000, 4,500, and 7,000. *The Token* for 1829, the only volume for which circulation figures are available, was issued in an edition of 4,000. For the first four years of its life *The Gift* was issued in editions of at least 7,000. Ralph Thompson, *American Literary Annuals and Gift Books: 1825–1865* (New York, 1936), 7 and 50.

During this same period, in contrast, most novels—the only exception seems to be those of Cooper, whose popularity guaranteed him printings as large as ten thousand—were issued in much smaller editions. Catharine Maria Sedgwick's *Clarence; or, A Tale of Our Own Times* (1830) and John Pendleton Kennedy's *Swallow Barn: or, A Sojourn in the Old Dominion* (1832), for instance, were issued in editions of two thousand.[9]

In recognizing the compilation as a literary form and a major rival to the novel during this period, we gain a more accurate view of the literary landscape and capture the true diversity of antebellum literary markets. Indeed, the popularity of the compilation—both in terms of the number of titles and size of editions published—demands that we rethink the conventional claim (again Bell in the *Cambridge History of American Literature*) that "Cooper rather than Irving provided the model most imitated" by antebellum Americans.[10] The extraordinary number of compilations published during this period suggest a second, competing line of development, one extending from Irving's *Sketch Book*, through the annuals and the collections of such authors as Child, Sedgwick, Simms, Poe, and Hawthorne, to such works as Fanny Fern's *Fern Leaves from Fanny's Portfolio* (1853), Rufus Griswold's popular *Prose Writers of America* (1847), and any number of competing anthologies.

As surprising as the popularity of the compilation is the number of short to intermediate-length works available on the market during this same period. In 1845, eighty-three titles—or 45 percent of the market—are eighty or fewer pages. The average length of these works is about fifty-two pages. The popularity of these short works, however, is short-lived—at most, a decade; by 1850 the market has swung. As table 3 indicates, the percentage of intermediate-length works increases from 10 percent in 1845 to 23 percent in 1850, while longer works increase from 21 percent to 31 percent. Short works decline to 12 percent. Moreover, longer works keep getting longer. The average length of works longer than 125 pages in 1845 is 206 pages. In 1850—the year Hawthorne published *The Scarlet Letter*—that number climbs to 265 pages. Hawthorne's relatively slim and structurally compact *Scarlet Letter* is in this context on the long side at 322 pages.

I said earlier, and in reference to figure 1 and that 32 percent of books subtitled "tales," that titles are a questionable indicator of genre. True enough, but not as true as it first appeared. Some tales are novels in disguise, but many more are not; most tales, in fact, are tales. The untold story of the

---

[9] David Kaser, *The Cost Books of Carey & Lea, 1825–1838* (Philadelphia, 1963), 83 and 115.
[10] Michael Bell, *Cambridge History of American Literature*, 38.

American market in prose fiction in these early years is the struggle between compilations and novels, tales and novels, short works and long works for generic supremacy. The publication history of Hawthorne's *Scarlet Letter* neatly captures larger tensions in the literary field between the genres of tale, compilation, and novel. Hawthorne conceived of *The Scarlet Letter* as a short story; he shopped it around as part of collection entitled *Old-Time Legends*; and finally, at the suggestion of his publisher, he expanded it into a longer work and published it as a novel. This hesitation on Hawthorne's part—story? collection? novel?—and its resolution—novel—neatly reflects the movement of the market. Short works decline in popularity, while longer works increase in number and length. Although my data stop at precisely the point where one wants to know more, the trend would suggest that the long does in fact triumph over the short.

If my data are correct, the novel emerged in a much more competitive market than hitherto believed. But what of translations and British titles? Determining the popularity of these titles is a formidably difficult task given the existing state of our bibliographies. We know that British books constituted an overwhelming majority of titles published in eighteenth-century America and that this changed dramatically over the course of the nineteenth century. According to statistics compiled in the middle of the nineteenth century by the American publisher Samuel Goodrich, works by American authors constituted 80 percent of the market in 1856, with works by British authors making up the remaining 20 percent.[11] But this estimate is based on all books, what about fiction? Did works of American fiction outsell their British and European competitors? While we know that American authors competed (in the words of Kathy Davidson) in "a market flooded with European products," we do not know the extent of this flood. Nor do we possess a systematic study telling us (again Kathy Davidson) "precisely what British books were read in America, in what numbers, by whom, and how New World writers responded individually and collectively to Old World texts."[12] Some of this information is available in the form of Charles Evans's *American Bibliography* and its supplements. Yet at dozens of volumes and thousands of pages, these data are all but irretrievable (though the ongoing computerization of it by the American Antiquarian Society might make it more accessible). Even sampling at five-year intervals proved to be prohibitively time-consuming, both because of the number of entries and because of the difficulty of sorting titles about which one knows little or, as

---

[11] Samuel Goodrich, *Recollections of a Lifetime* (New York, 1857), 429.

[12] Kathy Davidson, *Revolution and the Word* (New York, 1986), 10.

FIGURE 3. AMERICAN FICTION, BRITISH FICTION, AND TRANSLATIONS,
1770–1899 (BY PERCENTAGE)

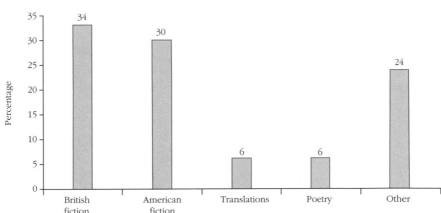

in most cases, nothing at all—even such basic information as whether a given title is a work of fiction and whether the author is American.

For these reasons I reluctantly abandoned Evans for an alternative source—an extensive list of "best" and "better sellers" that Frank Luther Mott appended to a 1947 study of the popular book.[13] Like Wright and Thompson, Mott was an early student of the literary archive who hoped, as he wrote in the first of his five-volume *History of American Magazines*, to rewrite literary history "from the standpoints of geography and the social sciences."[14] His list of best and better sellers for the years 1770–1899 contains almost six hundred titles. Although far from complete, this list offers as broad and representative cross-section of the literary field as we possess.

Figure 3 breaks Mott's list into five categories: American fiction, British fiction, European translations, poetry, and miscellaneous titles (mostly works of travel, autobiography, and history). The obvious point to emphasize here is the extent to which prose fiction—and the novel—dominates the market. Just under 70 percent of all best and better sellers were works of fiction, and of this 70 percent, 96 percent were, by my calculations, novels. But not all of these novels—not even a majority—are American novels. Of all the fiction

---

[13] Mott conceives of a best seller in terms of sales figures—which he estimated using a range of sources. He sets the minimum figure for a best seller at "one percent of the total population of the continental United States for the decade in which the book was published." His better sellers were those titles that sold well but that were believed not to have reached this 1 percent. Mott excludes from his account reference works, cookbooks, hymnals, bibles, almanacs and manuals. Frank Luther Mott, *Golden Multitudes: The Story of Best Sellers in the United States* (New York, 1947), 7.

[14] Frank Luther Mott, *A History of American Magazines, 1741–1850* (Cambridge, 1938), 1:4.

FIGURE 4. AMERICAN FICTION, BRITISH FICTION, AND TRANSLATIONS,
1770–1899 (BY NUMBER OF TITLES)

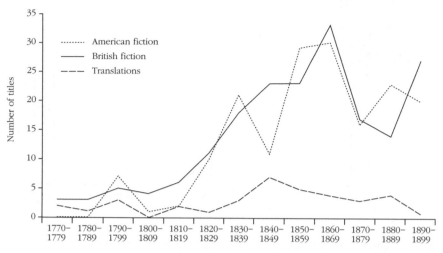

read between the years 1770 and 1899, 34 percent was British in origin. Americans, it seems, were reading as much, if not more, British fiction over the course of the nineteenth century than American fiction. Translations, in contrast, constitute (like poetry) a mcre 6 percent of the total. Nor does this change much over the course of the nineteenth century. Figure 4 breaks down the data according to decade. Although Goodrich's data would lead one to expect an increasing Americanization of the literary field, this proves not to be the case. Here a distinct pattern emerges: a rising zigzag peaking in the 1860s and then declining slightly thereafter in which British and American novels narrowly edge one another out with almost mechanical regularity. If we discount the first four decades (where data is scarce), British novels are slightly in the ascendant in the two decades between 1810 and 1830, the 1840s, the 1860s and '70s, and the 1890s; American works prevail in the 1830s, the 1850s, and the 1880s. In the 1830s, a good number of these American works are collections or books of interrelated sketches, which leaves the 1850s and the 1880s as the only two decades in which American novels best their British competitors. According to this data, the American literary market is only sporadically American.

So where does this data place the American novel in the European system described by Franco Moretti in his *Atlas of the European Novel?* Moretti argues that there was not one but three "take-offs" of the European novel, "the first around 1720–1750 (in the core: France, Britain, and a little later Germany); the second around 1820–1850 (for half dozen countries or so); and a third one, later still for all the others."[15] The emergence of the novel between the years 1820 and 1850 puts America in that second of the three "rises" hypothesized by Moretti and in the company of that half dozen or so semiperipheral European nations. Like these countries, America followed the path of the core—in this instance, Britain. Not surprisingly, America takes it cues from the British market. The two most successful American genres—the historical novel, the most popular novelistic genre in America from 1790 to 1830, and the annual, which gained popularity in the following two decades—were both British in origin. And like Britain, America was largely hostile to works in translation. From 1820 onward, the percentage of translated works never accounts for more than 10 percent of the market and hovers around 5 percent. Not only does America, like Britain, admit very few foreign works, but, as far as I have been able to determine, America and Britain read the same translations at roughly the same time. When Britain reads Sue and Dumas, so does America. As in a Henry James novel, all roads to the Continent go through London. Given the absence of both a language barrier and an international copyright law—not enacted until 1891—America's dependence on Britain should not surprise us (though its worth noting that that even in the 1890s the number of British novels in America climbs rather than falls, as the passage of the copyright agreement might lead one to predict). Still, the failure of the American novel to triumph over its British competitor and to establish cultural hegemony over the course of the nineteenth century is striking.

And, one should emphasize, markedly at odds with most accounts of "American" literature. And herein resides the usefulness of quantitative analysis; it holds forth the promise of producing some new facts, of bringing into focus new genres (like the tale and compilation) and new formations in the literary field (the competition between American and British novels). Most important, such data enriches and complicates conventional narrative accounts of national (international?) literatures.

---

[15] Franco Moretti, *Atlas of the European Novel, 1800–1900* (London, 1998), 174.

GIOVANNI RAGONE

Italy, 1815–1870

Only in the late twentieth century did Italian culture begin to recover the "full span" of the novel tradition. After the unification, once the map of narrative was traced and many times after embellished, attention shifted toward the earliest phases, giving value to the novelistic flowering of the courtly age and rediscovering the missing link of the baroque period. In the end, it has been possible to recover almost completely the corpus of narrative during the sixteenth and seventeenth centuries. At the same time, it became a critical commonplace to assert the facile prevalence of the romance over the novel, or at least the apparent absence of any "realistic" story in the Italy of the ancien régime.[1] With regard to the period that interests us here, it has of course been established that the explosion of the novel genre, in its "modern" variations, developed in the years between the Congress of Vienna and the Risorgimento. And so—even if the assertion may seem paradoxical in light of the wealth of studies on *I promessi sposi* and the fame of Grossi, Cantù, Guerrazzi, Visconti, and D'Azeglio—the overall cultural editorial picture of the narratives in the early 1800s is still largely uncertain.[2]

We are able to establish with some certainty the initial moment when the

---

[1] The corpus of seventeenth-century narrative is reconstructed in A. N. Mancini, "Saggio di bibliografia sul romanzo del'600," In *Studi Seicenteschi*, 9 (1970): 205–74, 12 (1971): 443–98, 16 (1975): 182–213; L. Spera, *Il romanzo italiano del tardo seicento*, Milan 2000; various authors, *La novella barocca*, ed. L. Spera, Naples 2001. On the subsequent period, cf. I. Crotti, "Rassegna di studi e testi sul romanzo italiano del settecento," in *Lettere Italiane*, 52 (1990): 296–331 n. 2; and L. Clerici, *Il romanzo italiano del settecento: Il caso Chiari*, Venice 1997.

[2] Among the studies of the novel 1815–1870: L. Passo', *Contributo alla storia del romanzo storico italiano: con lettere e documenti inediti*, Città di Castello 1906; G. Agnoli, *Gli albori del romanzo storico in Italia e i primi imitatori di Walter Scott*, Piacenza 1906; F. Lopez-Celly, *Il romanzo storico in Italia: Dai prescottiani alle odierne vite romanzesche*, Bologna 1929; A. Leone de Castris, *La polemica dul romanzo storico*, Rome 1978; M. Lavagetti, *Quei più modesti romanzi*, Milan 1979; L. Lattarulo, *L'intreccio: Un secolo di narrative popolare in italia*, Rome 1983; A. Arslan, *Romanzo storico, d'appendice, di consumo; Guida bibliografica 1960–1980*, Milan 1983; E. Villari (and others), *Storia su storie: Indagine sui romanzi storici*, Vicenza 1985; G. Pagliano, *Il mondo narrato*, Naples 1985; M. Cataudella, *Il romanzo storico nell'età della Restaurazione: le origini e il problema del genere*, Naples 1986; G. Rosa, *Il Romanzo melodrammatico*, Florence 1990; G. De Donato, *Gli archivi del silenzio: La tradizione del romanzo storico italiano*, Fasano 1995; G. Tellini, *Il romanzo italiano dell'ottocento e del novecento*, Milan 1999; A Cadioli, *La storia finta: Il romanzo e i suoi lettori nei dibattiti di primo ottocento*, Milan 2001.

new genre began to manifest itself, in the first years of the 1820s; it would go on to alter the entire landscape of editors and of culture in a nation still divided, functioning as a medium of an extraordinary expansion of the imagination, of the public, and of consumption. And we are able to consider events of the postunification passage toward new institutional structures, both of the market and the media, that would result in a short time (already by the 1880s) in the construction of a genuine industrial culture, in large part centered on the novel. Soon after the unification, in fact, rapid changes occurred, both in the network of the editing world and in seats of intellectual production, as well as in terms of book forms and journalistic genres. The hegemony of the Risorgimento model (above all in Piedmont and Tuscany) was falling away, and in its place appeared, following paths traveled years earlier in other metropolitan centers in Europe, a new locus of publishing in Milan. We can definitively assert that a new model of communication and culture emerged, oriented predominantly toward the bourgeois readership and the consumer in the modern sense of the word, that is, as a social group distinct within the community and separate from literary producers.[3]

During the period from 1815 to 1875, we begin to distinguish some historical-geographic coordinates, at least on the editorial side (see table 1).[4] One could say that the initial explosion of the novel should be situated in the year 1822, when in Milan nineteen titles were published, surpassing the five of the previous year. From the quantitative point of view, the growth of production is quite evident. The genre was published with regularity during this time period; an early "peak" occurs in the thirties and a second, more elevated one, in the fifties. Among the four publishing centers

---

[3] For a picture of the cultural differences between the pre- and postunification, see G. Ragone, *Un secolo di libri: Storia dell'editoria dall'Unita' al post-moderno*, Turin 1999, 3–55.

[4] One must point out the pioneering character of certain studies that attempted this reconstruction, based on three different sources: the data offered by *CLIO, Catalogo dei libri italiani dell'ottocento* (1801–1900); a survey on the "Bibliografia italiana ossia Elenco generale delle opera d'ogni specia e d'ogni lingua stampata in Italia e delle italiane pubblicate all'estero," published by Stella (Milan 1835–1971), Bari 1975; and a fairly tenable reconstruction of the corpus of Scott, across the preceding sources, with an additional bibliography compiled by F. Ruggieroi Punzo, *Walter Scott in Italia (1821–1971)*, Bari 1975. The first offers a general picture of the period 1800–1870, the second was utilized for verification purposes, the third should be consulted for significant perceptions of the most relevant novels of the first half of the century. From time to time, in addition, one is dependent on other sources to elucidate particular events and problems.

TABLE 1. PUBLICATION OF NOVELS FROM 1815 TO 1875 AND PUBLISHING
CENTERS (BASED ON CLIO DATA)

	Milan	Venice	Naples	Florence
1815	—	2	3	1
1825	13	1	6	3
1835	23	2	12	2
1845	21	4	6	6
1855	80	1	22	8
1865	45	—	10	8
1875	116	3	10	12
Total	298	13	69	40

traditionally regarded as editorial capitals of the novel in Italy, without dispute the most significant was Milan.[5] Venice was in a state of decline, and it
played a role even less important than that of Florence. The publication of
novels in Naples, on the other hand, reveals a relevant diffusion. Milan
would once again be the propulsive center of the market during the years
immediately following the unification: a phase of restructuring is registered
in the sixties, and thus a subsequent and still more intense period of publishing activity.

With table 2 we return more analytically to the "foundation" of the
genre, so to speak: the twenty years from 1820 to 1840. Another source, the
Bibliografia Italiana, worth calling the most important bibliographic journal
of the period, naturally confirms the flowering of Milanese editorial offices,
and the principal role played by the capital of Lombardy. In terms of the rest
of the country, though, it appears to offer contradictory data with respect to
the other lists available (cf. table 3).

The differences are nevertheless easily explained. With regard to Venice,
the texts listed in the Milanese journal often were not complete novels but
rather abridged versions, inserted in short collections or compendiums, designed for a different readership, in "condensed versions" as we might say
today. And with regard to the Reign of the Two Sicilies, only the "official"
data arrived in Milan, though the substantial number of editions traceable
through *CLIO* leaves few doubts: clearly Naples was the second capital of
the novel. Less clear is the role played by other Italian locations, even if

_____

[5] For a more in-depth look at the capital of Lombardy from the point of view of typography
during the restoration, see M. Berengo, *Intelletuali e librai nella Milano della Restaurazione*, Turin
1980.

TABLE 2. PUBLICATION OF NOVELS FROM 1820 TO 1840 AND PUBLISHING CENTERS (BASED ON CLIO DATA)

	Turin	Milan	Venice	Florence	Rome	Naples
1820	2	3	—	—	—	1
1821	—	5	—	—	—	3
1822	1	18	—	—	—	—
1823	—	11	—	1	—	3
1824	—	15	—	2	—	5
1825	—	13	1	2	—	7
1826	—	6	1	3	—	10
1827	2	6	1	3	2	8
1828	—	20	—	6	—	6
1829	16	39	—	3	—	12
1830	5	32	—	6	—	16
1831	2	17	—	2	—	7
1832	—	27	—	4	—	5
1833	3	18	—	4	—	6
1834	4	27	1	3	—	14
1835	2	23	—	2	—	8
1836	—	25	1	3	—	8
1837	—	21	various series	4	1	13
1838	1	25	various series	—	—	7
1839	—	16	various series	2	1	12
1840	—	33	various series	1	1	10
Total	38	400	5 (+ 4 coll.)	51	5	161

there are indications here and there of the genre's success. In Rome, for example, even within the frame of a rather limited production, there is a verifiable and significant circulation and reading of historical novels, which one can readily infer by reading reviews in specialized journals.[6] In Turin, an environment traditionally directed toward religious and erudite works, the phenomena becomes interesting toward end of the twenties and the first years of the thirties; it is a further sign of an omnipresent fashion for historical novels, even in such a peculiar milieu. Series of novels by Walter Scott, coming out in other centers, for example in Padua (Minerva Press), in

---

[6] On this point, see the observations contained in M. I. Palazzolo, "Il romanzo storico: Un best-seller di 150 anni fa," in idem, *I tri occhi dell'editore: Saggi di storia dell'editoria*, Rome 1990, 59–60. The author points to a *collana* (series) of Scott published by the editor-typographer Zampi.

TABLE 3. PUBLICATION OF NOVELS FROM 1835 TO 1844 AND PUBLISHING CENTERS

	Milan	Venice	Naples	Florence
1835	26	9	2	—
1836	18	6	—	—
1837	12	7	—	2
1838	12	2	—	—
1839	13	6	—	4
1840	4	3	4	1
1841	9	4	3	1
1842	16	3	4	—
1843	8	3	3	—
1844	13	6	—	—
Total	131	49 + 23[a] = 72	16	8

Source: *Bibliografia Italiana.*

[a] To these 49 titles one must add an additional 23, lacking specific dates of issue but occurring between 1837 and 1842.

Parma (Ducale Press), in Macerata (Cortesi Press), are further evidence of a great diffusion into more remote areas.[7]

———

Let us try now to trace a more general profile, diachronic and attentive to variations of genre and literary tastes. In the first twenty years of the nineteenth-century the titles are indeed few in number. The old best sellers of the eighteenth century are practically absent (completely missing are Chiari and Piazza, while every so often, at the turn of the century, some titles of Alessandro Verri, Defoe, and Richardson will reappear). It seems that editors and readers were taken by a taste for other typical enlightenment genres that created what could be defined as the "almost-novel" (*para-romanzesco*) more than they were by novels of the previous century.

These were mostly biographical texts that border on the scandalous (like those on Mazzarino or on Richelieu, or especially on the divorces of Henry VIII) or heroic "hagiography" (for example, regarding the controversial but still suggestive figure of Frederick the Great of Prussia). Another favorite was the report-memoir of travel and discovery in foreign lands (one could stand for them all: the genuine best seller of Prévost, *L'histoire générale des*

[7] Ibid.

voyages). Elaborate plots and fictions were destined to remain in the psychosocial world of the nineteenth-century novel, either in historical novels like Scott's, or in exotic and pre-Salgarian ones that followed, or in metropolitan and positivist-naturalistic works.

The Italian public that appreciated adventure after the restoration of European peace (1815) (in Scott and Manzoni, and then in Dumas, Balzac, even so far as in Verne) came from a long tradition that had allowed readers to collocate the events in their historical and geographical coordinates. In contrast with that of the 1700s, the public no longer was content with stylized worlds, or with rapid and stereotypical or even erotic appearances. For that public, visible information was above all fundamental, as it would be integrated into the narrative. The story of the early nineteenth century no longer is oriented toward the old concept of useful pleasure, nor does it operate in the repetitive forms of the erotic eighteenth century, so often French. Instead it articulates itself in a modern, functional syntax, where information, entertainment, and teaching converge, as it were, in the forge of the consumer: from Manzoni, Guarrazzi, D'Azeglio, up until De Amicis and Mantegazza (the ultimate break and the new subjective and visual forms will arrive in the eighties with Verga, De Roberto, and then D'Annunzio).

But of which public are we speaking? Are early-nineteenth-century readers identifiable with the "new" eighteenth-century social stratifications? The question is open to debate and still today unresolved. The idea of a "revolution of reading" that would come at the end of the eighteenth century, both in a qualitative and quantitative sense, has been considered from a variety of viewpoints. The problem is a particularly thorny one for Italy, where the geographic-cultural fragmentation and the slow growth of the bourgeois class in a modern sense render the panorama deeply uncertain. The explosion of novels after 1822, that of course is connected to a new way of reading the novel, of giving a sense to reality across *fiction*, cannot at the moment be interpreted with certainty in relation to the appearance of new social strata on the scene of reading, or a renewal and expansion of those traditional ones. For instance, are we able to accept the hypothesis of a strong (but not a monopolizing) female readership of the pathetic-sentimental kind? Nothing makes us believe in a complete and direct transfer of the female readers toward the historical novel.[8]

---

[8] See for example: L. Mascilli Migliorini, "Lettori e luoghi della lettura," in G. Turi, ed., *Storia dell'editoria nell'Italia contemporaneo*, Florence 1997, 77–112; and A. Chemello, "La Letteratura popolare e di consumo," ibid., 165–192. For a general picture of the evolution of readers during this period, see M. Lyons, "I nuovi lettori ne XIX secolo: Donne, fanciulli, operai," in G. Cavallo and R. Charter eds., *Storia della lettura,* Bari 1995, 371–410, and for the debate on the question, R. Wittmann, "Una 'rivoluzione della lettura' alla fine del XVIII secolo?," ibid., 337–69.

Some answers may be found in a "regional" observation: the prevalence of Italian historical genres in editorial centers characterized by conservative models, such as that of Florence and Turin (see table 4) seems to be evidence of a sort of "training phase" for the burgeoning editorial structures of the future united Italian states, while the richness of novel proposals from the area beyond the Alps and the north, historical and of other types, on Naples and Milan (also included in the table) reveals also a lively effervescence of the imagination in the great cities. In turn, this must be interpreted in relation to a rapid change of reading, and therefore of the strata of readers, from a more modern perspective.

Nevertheless, from at least the first years of the twenties until the forties, this public decreed above all the success of the historical novel (and, as is noted, of the historical melodrama). The general picture is rather significant with regard to the extraordinary rise of the historical novel, especially from the end of the twenties, in contrast with a paucity of traditional titles of the eighteenth century and quite circumscribed editorial experimentation in the direction of other genres. The exception, though limited, is offered once more by the "laboratory" of Milan, which in addition to the historical novel was publishing Balzac and also various titles leaning toward the pathetic-sentimental, or else the gothic novel.

––––––––

The horizon was, however, sufficiently stabilized so as to permit new editorial enterprises. Even before the restoration of peace—for instance, with the "Biblioteca scelta di opera italiane antiche e moderne" brought out by the Milanese publisher Silvestri in 1813—there were experiments along the lines of thematic *collane* (series) that presupposed a strong demand and that were guaranteed economic rewards by the formula of "association." The historical novel in *collane* was initiated according to that model and was assured of success, at least until it became more frequent, through the first half of the 1840s (from that moment the formula would be repeated in an intermittent and insignificant manner). It is worthwhile to take a more in-depth look at these *collane* that reveal the various levels of prevalence of the historical novel, sometimes giving testimony to experimentation and other editorial initiatives.

The first "battle horses" of the Milanese *collane* were the works of Scott, despite, as already noted, the wide presence of other authors, in large part foreign. The first known *collana* is that of the publishers Batelli and Bonfanti, who between 1817 and 1824 brought out the *Scelta raccolta di romanzi*, composed of ten titles in various genres. Walter Scott, for his part,

TABLE 4. TRENDS AND GENRES OF THE NOVEL BETWEEN 1820 AND 1840 IN EDITORIAL CENTERS (BASED ON CLIO DATA)

	Milan			Naples			Turin			Florence		
	Novels of the 1700s	Miscellaneous novels	Historical novels	Novels of the 1700s	Miscellaneous novels	Historical novels	Novels of the 1700s	Miscellaneous novels	Historical novels	Novels of the 1700s	Miscellaneous novels	Historical novels
1820	1	1	1	—	—	1	2	—	—	—	—	—
1821	2	1	2	2	—	1	—	—	—	—	—	—
1822	2	6	10	—	—	—	—	—	1	—	—	1
1823	3	3	5	1	—	2	—	—	—	—	1	1
1824	2	6	7	2	1	2	—	—	—	—	—	2
1825	1	5	7	2	1	5	—	—	—	1	1	2
1826	—	1	5	1	—	8	—	—	2	—	—	2
1827	—	1	5	2	1	6	—	—	—	—	—	2
1828	2	—	18	—	—	5	—	—	—	—	—	6
1829	2	5	32	—	2	12	—	—	16	2	—	3
1830	1	—	31	—	—	14	—	—	5	—	—	4
1831	2	2	13	1	1	6	—	—	2	—	—	2
1832	6	2	19	2	1	2	—	—	—	—	—	4
1833	2	2	14	2	—	3	—	—	3	—	1	3
1834	1	8	18	1	4	9	—	—	4	—	—	3
1835	1	4	18	—	2	6	—	—	2	—	—	2
1836	2	11	12	1	—	7	—	—	—	1	—	2
1837	—	4	17	—	2	11	—	—	—	1	—	3
1838	2	2	21	—	1	6	—	—	1	—	—	—
1839	—	5	11	—	2	10	—	—	—	—	—	2
1840	3	13	17	2	1	7	—	—	—	—	—	1
Total	35	82	283	19	19	123	2	—	36	5	3	43

had appeared in 1821 in a *collana* of *Opere* from the publisher Vincenzo Ferrario, followed by a similar initiative of Crespi. In 1835, Stella began a still more diverse series, that would last until 1840, entitled, "Piccola biblioteca di gabinetto," rebaptized in 1838 as "Biblioteca moderna di amena letteratura." A full twelve titles comprised authors from George Sand (for example the *Segretario intimo* of 1835) to the historical novel properly so-called in Bulwer-Lytten's *Ultimi giorni di Pompei* and the Italian "Scotians," with a text by Varese. Also in 1835, the publisher Pirotta, who had opposed Scottism from 1821–22 with his *Biblioteca amena ed istruttiva per la donna gentile*, would embark on the same route as Stella, but with attention more focused on the purely historical market: between 1835 and 1842 at least forty titles came out in the "Serie di romanzi storici e d'altro genere de' più celebri scritti moderni per la prima volta traddotti nell'idioma italiano." Compared with Stella, the initiative had a twofold strategy: the translation of foreign titles (among the most celebrated names one finds Scott, Bulwer-Lytton, Dumas, Marryat) and the selection of exclusively historical texts. The affirmation of this tendency was demonstrated by the *collana* of the publisher Truffi, already under way in 1832, and in the third series of 1834, that would be titled, not insignificantly, "Romanzi e curiosita' di tutte le nazioni" and continues until 1837, reaching twenty-seven titles. More examples could be cited: from the *collana* of Bonfanti "Scelti romanzi storici e d'altro genere de' più accreditati scrittori d'ogni nazioni e per la prima volta tradoti nell'idioma italiano," in twenty monthly volumes, commencing in 1837 and ending in 1839, to the "Ape, ossia raccolta di romanzi amenità storiche e d'altro genere" of the same editor until 1841, with an additional seven titles. In 1841, the celebrated "Florilegio romantico" was released by the editorial house of Borroni e Scotti, a strong and active firm from the 1850s, with translations of the most celebrated novelists of the age, from Balzac to Dumas, from Scott to Sue. In the wide panorama one should not overlook the *collane* dedicated to a single author, like the various Scottians and those of Fenimore Cooper from the publisher Bonfanti, as well as some others of a different sort, such as that of Silvestri, dedicated to German literature.

The same situation was occurring in Venice, where the presence of Scott was strong, with the publication by Picotti of "Raccolta di romanzi storici di Walter Scott, nuova traduzione veneta," in six volumes, from 1835 to 1836. This publisher had already brought out the *Opere di Maria di Edgeworth* in 1824. Antonelli's "Raccolta di romanzi ridotti in novella ed ornate di tavole litografiche" appeared from 1837 to 1842 with twenty-two titles, reduced in scope but ornamented with lithographs. These were followed soon after by the *collana* of Santini, with eleven titles, from Balzac to Soulié, from Masson to Marryat.[9] The publisher Tasso came out with another series of the "Florilegio romantico"-type encountered in Milan,[10] with sixteen titles, especially Balzac, Hugo, Dumas, Arlincourt, and in the end, three collections of Italian and foreign novels, but essentially almost always foreign.[11]

From what can be uncovered from the data, it didn't happen otherwise in Naples[12] or in Florence (where the prevalence of the progenitor Scott is even more evident).[13] Next to this extended phenomena we should measure the success of *I promessi sposi*, whose quantitative impact is arguable, but whose importance would be difficult to deny.[14] But what is the relationship between the translated novels and the Italian novel? (See table 5.)

In Milan, the Scottian novel represents by itself more than one-third of the titles. In Turin and Florence the ratio is 1 to 2 between foreign and Italian novels, while in Naples and Milan one encounters an inverse proportion, a sign of a distinct acceptance of models coming from over the Alps, particularly from France.

---

[9] "Serie prima di romanzi storici e d'altro genere de' più monderni scrittori francisi per la prima volta tradotti nell'idioma italiano da Giannantonio Piucco" (1837–42).

[10] "Gabinetto romantico" (1835–41).

[11] "Collezione di romanzi scelti italiani e stranieri," of Fontana (1841–44), eleven titles; "Raccolta di romanzi italiani e stranieri," of Antonelli (1839–40), four titles; "Raccolta di accreditati romanzi italiani e stranieri contemporanei," only one title in 1844.

[12] A *collana* of condensed and illustrated novels: "Raccolta di romanzi ridotti in novella ed oranti di tavole litografiche," edited by Tramater and Bianchi, from 1834–35, with two titles by Scott. Another was "Antologia storica romantica," edited by Vanspandoch, between 1840 and 1843, with eleven titles, predominantly Cooper and Hugo, but also by Italian authors, from Giacinto Battaglia to Girolomo Colleoni and D'Azeglio. Another survey seems to confirm the tendency: "Ape romanziera, o raccolta de' migliori romanzi inediti," edited by Nobile, that in 1829 presented *La sventurata di Monza*, of Giovanni Rosini; the "Raccolta di romanzi storici" of Tramater, also containing *La monaca di Monza* of Rosini (1820). Also released in 1829: Capurro Press (Pisa) and the Dettori Press (Milan); the "Collezione di nuovi racconti," of Nobile, that in 1843 presented *Brazzo di Milano*, of Frederico Borelli, and the "Collezione di nuovi racconti" also of Nobile (*Gli Eccelini e gli Estensi*, of Filippo De Boni). Worth noting is the "nuova collana di romanzi ameni e istruttivi," of Corrado, with two titles in 1830, and the "Collezione di moderni romanzi" del Trombetta, with a title in 1842.

[13] In the "Romanzi storici di Walter Scott," published by Coen between 1837 and 1840, seven titles came out; in addition, Passigli released the "Collezione di romanzi storici e poetici di Walter Scott." Finally worth pointing out is the "Raccolta di trenta romanzi stranieri dei piu' nuovi e dei piu' accreditati, tradotta per cura del bibliofilo Marco Malagoli Vacchi," with one title in 1841.

[14] See M. Parenti, *Bibliografia Manzoniana*, Florence 1936. For an interpretation of the data, see Palazzolo, "Il romanzo storico: Un best-seller di 150 anni fa," 63–64. According to the author, between 1827 and 1840 nearly seventy editions, both Italian and foreign, of *I promessi sposi* would be published, with a complete circulation of sixty thousand to seventy thousand copies. Parente estimates a figure between three hundred thousand and four hundred thousand.

TABLE 5. AUTHORS OF NOVELS IN THE PERIOD 1820–40 BY PUBLISHING CENTER (BASED ON CLIO DATA)

	Turin	Milan	Florence	Naples
Scott	5	104	7	33
Arlincourt	2	9	2	13
Cooper	3	21	2	15
Radcliffe	—	—	—	5
Dumas	—	6	—	—
Other foreign	3	48	3	23
Total foreign	12	188	14	89
Manzoni	2	3	7	5
Bazzoni	5	5	1	2
Guerrazzi	1	5	—	1
Varese	4	8	2	3
D'Azeglio	2	2	1	2
Grossi	1	6	7	2
Cantù	1	7	1	1
Rosini	2	3	—	5
Other Italian	6	56	10	13
Total Italian	24	95	29	34
Grand Total	36	283	43	123

Let's consider then the most important vector of the first explosion of the novel: Walter Scott (see figure 1).[15] Milan, as can be easily noted, inaugurated the cycle with thirteen titles between 1821 and 1823, while from 1824 to 1835 the production of Scott in Milan took off with eighty-eight titles, which represent approximately a quarter of the novels published during that period. Venice (six) and Florence (seven) remained in the margins, overtaken by Parma, a city-state in a regime of discrete tolerance with regards to the book (nineteen) and of the university city of Padua (ten). The figures for Naples (thirty-seven titles, a third of the novels published) confirm the competition with Milan and the noteworthy dimension of the publishing phenomena and the gusto for Scott. From 1836 to 1852, in short, the decline in the publication of Scott in Milan was leading the market toward a gradual decline in the publishing of novels (there and elsewhere). We are confronted

---

[15] For the reconstruction of Scott's corpus, information is taken from *CLIO*, the "Bibliografia Italiana," with those lists from Ruggiero Punzo, *Walter Scott in Italia*.

FIGURE 1. PUBLICATION OF SCOTT'S NOVELS FROM 1821 TO 1852

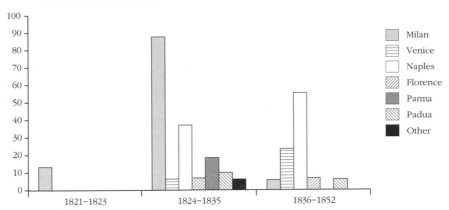

by a first restructuring and by new narrative models that will fully affirm themselves in the mid-fifties. However, Venice (twenty-four) and Naples (fifty-six) were overtaking—in retrospect—Milan in the exploitation of the line of Scott.[16]

The enormous popularity of Scott would last—in the acute phase—over ten years, beginning to decline around 1840 with the emergence of a *collana* of "letterature amena" (that is to say, of consumption) and of "letteratura romantica (that is to say, essentially Parisian). From then onward a continuous and intense growth in the genre of the novel would give Milan a near monopoly, where the number of titles would rise sixfold (from 21 to 116) between 1845 and 1865. The year 1845, for example, is still a time of transition. Although Scott is by now dead, the Italian historical novels hold their own, from Cantù's *Margherita Pusterla* to Guerrazzi's *Battaglia di Benevento*, while the most published writer is Dumas. Ten years later, in 1855, a shift has clearly occurred, and if even they reemerge—in the climate that was prelude to the war for independence—the historical novels, both Italian and Scottian (with eight titles) are destined however to feed the mythological imagination and hero-worship of the Risorgimento. Other best sellers and other tastes visibly prevail: above all (and still) Dumas (twelve titles), August

---

[16] For a geographic view of the editorial structure in nineteenth-century Italy, see G. Turi, ed., *Storia dell'editoria nell'Italia contemporaneo*, Florence 1997. In particular: M. I. Palazzolo, "Prima dell'Unita': Geografia e dinamica degli insediamenti editoriali," 11–54, and M. Infelice, "La nuova figura dell'editore," 55–76.

Ricard (thirteen), Charles Paul de Kock (eight), but also Victor Hugo (three). Isolated, in the middle of the flood of "romantic" French fiction, Charles Dickens appears as well.

It was in effect the first "period," during which a narrative model fundamentally adventurous and popular would affirm itself in the twenty years following unification, integrating itself from the seventies onward with other and new impulses, typically metropolitan. This was demonstrated above all in the extraordinary explosion of technological and science-fiction imagination (seventeen titles by Verne in 1875) and the exodus of the psychological novel and the costume novel.[17] The proto-industry of Milan pointed to the steady and gradual development of the national market for novels (and of their publication in music and in *libretti*) that would not be interrupted even by the war for independence—sensitive to the great crucible from over the Alps, and ready for innovation. The centers, on the other hand, searched for new niches of book production, orienting themselves on different communicative and cultural models for the novel. Venice would disappear from the map; Florence would remain faithful to the Risorgimento model (in 1875, of the twelve titles published in Florence, eleven are Italian historical novels, while the only foreign imprint is Voltaire's *Candide*). Naples exploited at length a very profitable Scott outside copyright, until the 1870s. Later small, local publishers that never succeeded in leaping toward the dimension of a national market were developing an authentic tradition based on short stories on the pathetic imagination and the "social" one of Mastriani.

In the events that would follow, until World War I and fascism (1875–1922), we see, not by chance, a strong polarization: on one side are the various experiments of the avant-guard, inclined toward the novel only at the moment of the apogee of the genre, in the years from the seventies through the nineties, with an oscillation of the center of gravity away from Milan toward Rome, Naples, and Florence. On the other side we see the continuity of the great industry of novel publishing in Milan and of illustrated journals, capable of absorbing and mediating new experiences directed toward a now *mass* public.

Translated by M. F. Rusnak

---

[17] For a panorama of the Italian novel during the period, see R. Bigazzi, *I colori del vero: Vent'anni di narrative, 1860–1880*, Pisa 1978.

ELISA MARTÍ-LÓPEZ
MARIO SANTANA

Spain, 1843–1900

The history of book production and consumption in nineteenth-century Spain is yet to be written. Although there are some important contributions to this subject, little is known about the publishing industry that made possible the rise of the novel in Spain or the readership that sustained it.[1] Publishers and readers are still elusive figures, and their role in the cultural process of modern Spain is yet to be determined. This lack of comprehensive studies on both the conditions of book production and the constitution and composition of the new readership for the novel determines the object and nature of the quantitative research we undertake here. It also limits considerably the scope and generality of the conclusions at which we arrive. Given the general shortage of data, it seems to us that a statistical approach to the history of the nineteenth-century novel in Spain should take up first the two most basic issues of book production still unexamined: the number of titles published and the number of reprints per title. While it is not our purpose to record the totality of titles and reprints published from 1843 to 1900—a total count of titles and reprints, even if possible, is both beyond our means and intention—we have gathered sufficient data to clearly distinguish tendencies and turning points in book production. Also, we have identified specific best-selling titles and authors, determined the hegemonic forms the novel adopted in Spain, and traced their course along those years.

Novels written and published in Spain rather than in Spanish are the main object of our study. Thus, our study shows data on novels written in Catalan and Spanish (given that very few works were published in Galician and Basque, we have excluded them for this quantitative analysis). The data on novel production in these two languages have been considered separately in order to capture the distinct moments and phenomena that characterized their particular emergence and constitution. However, we are well aware that this separation is highly artificial if considered from the perspective of readership: Catalan readers also consumed novels in Spanish. The chronological limits of our project are set to cover the period beginning in the 1840s and ending in the 1890s. Although these dates are basically arbitrary, as are

---

[1] For studies on specific issues regarding publishing activity in nineteenth-century Spain, see Bohigas, Botrel, Carrillo, Delgado and Cordón, Duran i Sampere, Escolar, Hortelano, Luxán Meléndez, Marrast, Martí-López, Milla, and Romero Tobar.

all temporal boundaries, these dates delimit a period that includes three fundamental aspects in the history of the modern novel in Spain: the takeoff of the publishing industry, the constitution of a reading public for novels in Catalan and Spanish, and the adoption and exhaustion of the modes of novel writing characteristic of the nineteenth century. The 1840s saw the rise of the first modern novelists in Spanish—Wenceslao Ayguals de Izco and Fernán Caballero (Cecilia Böhl de Faber)—the introduction of the new printing technology and methods of publication (such as serialization), and the production of the first best seller, Ayguals de Izco's *María o la hija de un jornalero* (1845–46). In the 1860s, the first novels written in Catalan were published, and by the end of the century the two modes of novel writing that had dominated the nineteenth century—melodrama and realism—were being replaced, respectively, by a new form of popular novel rooted in realism (Vicente Blasco Ibáñez) and the new modernist poetics.[2]

Our research establishes, as accurately as possible, the number of titles, editions (both in book form and in *feuilleton*), years of publication, and genre of the works written by the authors listed. Although the bibliographical sources we consulted are among the most reliable and comprehensive, there are still some areas where the information is often incomplete, confusing, and even erroneous. As is well known, the bibliographical information on nineteenth-century books is often scant or even absent. The numerous pirate editions published during these years contribute decidedly to the confusion and uncertainty that characterizes the data on novel production in Spain. Moreover, the existing catalogues present numerous deficiencies. These sources often omit the year and/or place of publication of titles and reprints (sometimes, if the work was published in different volumes, they only record the date of one of them). Frequently, also, different catalogues

---

[2] The lists of authors selected for the study of novel production in Catalan includes twenty-seven novelists (they constitute most, but not all, of the authors that published novels in Catalan during those years and represent the most prolific and best known among them). Generating a list of novelists who wrote in Spanish is a more complicated task (Ignacio Ferreras's *Catálogo de novelas y novelistas españoles del siglo XIX* provides the names of approximately two thousand authors). We have compiled a list of the thirty-seven most prolific novelists. The term *prolific*, however, needs a clarification. There is no particular number of works that defines a priori who is a prolific writer. On the contrary, we subjected this term to a historical correction. Thus, for the 1840s (when the novel in Spanish was just emerging), we consider prolific an author who published between three and six titles; for the 1850s, that number is closer to fifteen titles. After 1860, and owing to the large number of authors that published novels, we took into account not only the number of titles, but also the number of reprints by title and, in some cases, that of titles and reprints published within a particular decade. To this group of the most prolific writers we added all the authors canonized by literary history that had not already been included (see appendix).

provide different years and/or publishers for the same novel or reprint (in some cases, they give the name of the printer; in others, that of the manager of a printing house; and, yet in others, that of the bookseller involved in the publishing and distribution of a work).[3] More important, editions and reprints are hardly ever distinguished or rigorously numbered (so, for instance, there are different "second" reprints and/or editions of a novel dated in different years under the same or different publisher's name). The fact that different measuring systems are used by different library catalogues to describe the physical characteristics of the books complicates the task of identifying editions and reprints and discriminating between them. These factors have forced us to revise and consolidate the data collected, and we most probably made some mistakes in determining the exact number of prints and reprints per title to be recorded. But it is important to note that, in those cases where we were unsure about the singularity of a particular print or reprint, we always made a conservative decision: we did not count it as a different reprint, but rather we assimilated it to a record that shared with it most of its bibliographical characteristics. Thus, it is important to remember that our data is as accurate as possible and, at the same time, it represents a conservative estimate.

A couple of final comments. Faced with the very difficult dilemma of what should be considered a novel, given the loose use of the term observed in the nineteenth century and the impossibility of checking over thousand titles (most of which have not been read in practically a century), we have decided to include in our statistical study fictional narrative texts that either have been regarded as novels by critics or contemporary readers, identify themselves as novels, or are at least about one hundred pages long. With regard to the genre of the novels, we have proceeded in two ways: in the case of novels written in Catalan, and owing to the considerably smaller number of titles involved (seventy-one), we were able to identify the genre of all titles

---

[3] The common financial cooperation between printers and booksellers from different cities is hardly ever acknowledged in the bibliographical cataloging of the novels—neither are there studies on the publishing practices in nineteenth-century Spain that map this extended collaboration. The financial cooperation between the bookstore La Española y Extranjera in Barcelona and that of Fernando Fe in Madrid for the production and distribution of books is just one example of this commercial practice. Regarding the publishing role of booksellers and printers and its evolution, Hipólito Escolar says: "The increase in the number of readers and buyers allowed, at the end of the century, the consolidation of the figure of the publisher, not bound to a bookstore, although the printer/bookseller continued to play a very important role in book production well into the twentieth century" (60). It is important to remember here that, even in late-nineteenth-century Spain, authors were often their own publishers—among those most famous, Francesc Pi i Margall, Juan Valera, and Benito Pérez Galdós in his later years.

TABLE 1. NOVELS IN SPAIN, 1843–1900

	Catalan	Spanish	Total
All editions	96	2,069	2,165
Dated editions	91	1,776	1,867

but three; in the case of the novels written in Spanish, and given the difficulty of consulting secondary sources on the 966 titles selected, we decided to rely exclusively on the indications provided by the works themselves. Often the title describes the work as either a novel of manners (*novela de costumbres*) or a historical novel (*novela histórica*), those being the two major generic labels in the period.[4] In some occasions, we used paratextual indications such as the title of the collection in which the work was included. The decision we made resulted in a particular high number of novels in Spanish whose genre is not indicated (about 54 percent of editions and 59 percent of titles). Despite this, we think that clear tendencies can be perceived. The data collected for this study is summarized in table 1.

The examination of the data collected suggests some significative new insights into the history of the novel in Spain.[5] We will begin with the novel written in Spanish. Two general but important statements can be made about novels published in the Spanish language. First, 48.4 percent of total editions are first editions, or in other words, the average number of editions per title is 2.14 (see figure 1). Moreover, both numbers are pretty much constant throughout the second half of the nineteenth century. Out of the thirty seven authors, only six average 3.0 or more editions per title.[6] Unfortunately,

---

[4] *Novela histórica* is used in nineteenth-century Spain to designate three different but related subgenres: romantic imitations of Walter Scott's novels, melodramatic plots set in recognizable periods of the history of Spain, and realistic representations of past events relevant for the understanding of contemporary history. On the other hand, *novela de costumbres* also designates two varieties of writing: melodramatic plots set in contemporary contexts, and realistic works whose object of representation is the behavior of contemporary social classes.

[5] The bibliographical sources we consulted are the following: the online catalogues of the Biblioteca Nacional de Madrid, the Biblioteca de Catalunya, and WorldCat; the *Manual del librero hispano-americano* by Antonio Palau y Dulcet (the revised and expanded second edition); Juan Ignacio Ferreras's *Catálogo de novelas y novelistas españoles del siglo XIX*; and the corresponding volume of the *Cronología de la literatura española*, edited by González Herrán and Penas Valera. Finally, when they were available, we consulted also bibliographies on particular authors. Our data include all the titles written by any given author and all the reprints that were published in Spain. In some cases, we also included works printed in Paris and Leipzig, since these editions appear to have circulated in the Spanish market (as attested by their common presence in Spanish libraries) and their omission would have significantly affected the statistical outcome of some authors.

[6] For more detailed statistical information and analysis of titles and authors mentioned in this essay, see Martí-López, "Historiografía literaria y análisis cuantitativo."

FIGURE 1. TITLES AND NUMBER OF EDITIONS IN SPANISH, 1843–1900

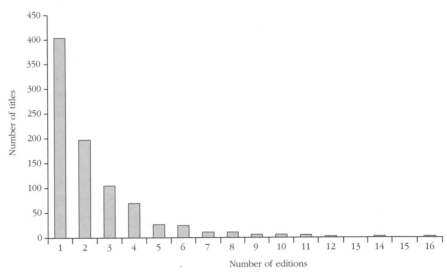

we lack information regarding the number of copies printed for each edition. There are no consistent or systematic data on copies per print run for nineteenth-century books (and novels) in Spanish, but we have some numbers. Although these numbers are either too general or too particular in their scope, they do have, however, an indicative value. In the midnineteenth century, the number of copies per print run ranged between five hundred and three thousand. The average print run of novels by popular authors might have ranged between three thousand and five thousand when first published, and between one thousand and three thousand when reprinted. Print runs of more that five thousand copies were exceptional.[7] Jean-François Botrel estimates the average print run in the last third of the century to be between twelve thousand and thirteen thousand copies.[8] Unfortunately, in our opinion, these numbers are still too general to allow us to quantify in greater detail the evolution of novel production, the movements of literary fashion and taste, or the average increase in readership, so more research needs to be done in this area.[9]

---

[7] See Carrillo, "Marketing et édition au XIXè siècle," and "Radiografía de una colección de novelas."

[8] "La literatura popular," 266.

[9] Once again, Jean-François Botrel has led the way with an excellent analysis of the production of Pérez Galdós's novels; see "Le succès d'édition des oeuvres de Benito Pérez Galdós" (published in two parts).

FIGURE 2. NOVELS IN SPANISH, 1843–1900

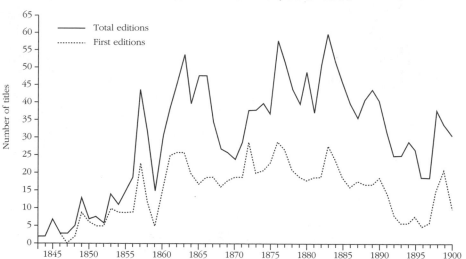

The second general statement that can be made is that there is no continuous growth in production (see figure 2). From the fluctuations shown in the figure's seesaw profile we can distinguish three distinctive periods of novel production in Spanish. It is precisely the clear configuration of these three periods that constitutes the major contribution of our statistical study to the history of the novel in Spanish. This is not to say that the publication of numerous novels after 1840 has not been widely acknowledged. What this study brings to light, however, is the quantitative (and qualitative) traits that organize novel production in these years in three distinctive periods. The identification of these three moments not only questions the traditional oblivion of works published before 1870 by most historians of the novel but makes their erasure from literary history much harder to justify.

The first period marks an *emergence of novel production* and covers the years 1843–54. The year 1854 should be specially noted because it marks a turning point: after this date, and despite the big oscillations shown in the figure, the number of editions per year will always be superior to that registered in 1854 (eleven editions). This period is characterized by a number of editions that oscillates between two and fourteen, and a number of titles that varies from two to thirteen. It is important to notice that the first best-selling novels appeared during these years, and that twelve writers (that is, the 32.4% of all the authors studied) initiate their novelistic career in these years (see figure 3). The writer Wenceslao Ayguals de Izco dominates this period with a succession of best-selling works.

FIGURE 3. AUTHORS IN SPANISH PUBLISHED BY YEAR, 1843–1900

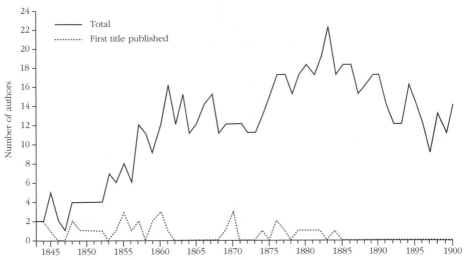

The second period marks a *radical increase in novel production* and covers the years 1855–70. The size in production in this period is significant enough to constitute an autonomous unit with a distinct aesthetics of the novel. This period is characterized by a number of editions that oscillates between fifteen and fifty-four, and a number of titles that varies from five to twenty-six. Sixteen authors (43.2 percent of all authors included) initiated their literary careers during those years. Thus, twenty-eight authors (75.7 percent of the total) published their first novel in the years 1843–70. These numbers show that a majority of novel writers had already established themselves as producers and succeeded in creating a domestic audience in the 1860s, well before it was thought (or recognized).

Three authors clearly dominate this second period: Cecilia Böhl de Faber, Manuel Fernández y González, and María del Pilar Sinués de Marco. It is interesting to note the dominant presence of women writers (two out of the three most commercially successful) in this period of novel production in Spanish. Fernández y González and Sinués de Marco will continue to enjoy an important commercial success after 1870 (but it should be noted that their numbers show a steady decline in the last third of the century, their popularity being then exceeded by that of new authors). Finally, we observe in this second period the clear hegemony of the historical novel. Of all the new titles published from 1855 to 1870, seventy-four (26.5 percent) have been identified as historical novels and thirty-four (12.2 percent) as novels of manners. Of all editions published, 173 (32.5 percent) are historical novels, and 77 (14.5 percent) are novels of manners.

The third period corresponds to *the height in novel production* and covers the longest period, 1871–96.[10] This period has traditionally constituted the main object of Spanish literary history and produced the novelists that have subsequently been canonized. While these years have been, and are, intensively studied, issues of a quantitative nature have traditionally being ignored. The period is characterized by a slightly larger number of editions per year than the previous one (between twenty-five and sixty), and a similar number of titles (from five to twenty-nine). However, our statistical study confirms that these years constitute a distinct period.

This period presents two remarkable traits with respect to novel production. First is the unquestionable commercial hegemony of Benito Pérez Galdós, the most widely published representative of the literary novel in Spanish, with 58 titles and 204 editions. Significant but lower places are occupied by Enrique Pérez Escrich and Julio Ortega y Frías (two novelists who had already published in the previous period, but that achieve their definitive commercial consecration after 1870) and once again by María Pilar Sinués de Marco. The second trait worth noting is the radical increase in the publication of novels of manners, an increase that threatens the hegemony of the historical novel: 21.5 percent of dated titles and 20.9 percent of dated editions are identified as novels of manners, while in this period 22 percent of titles and 24.5 percent of editions correspond to historical novels. Thus, the total of editions identified as novels of manners (215) is only slightly smaller than that of historical novels (252). The commercial success of the novel of manners is clearly observed from 1884 to 1895 (see figure 4). Notwithstanding the radical increase in the publication of novels of manners after 1870, it is important to notice the overall hegemony of the historical novel during this period and its commercial hegemony throughout most of the second half of the century (see table 2).

To conclude this section we must ask, what kind of history of the novel in Spanish would emerge if we focus on these (and other similar) data instead of on a few canonized works and authors? We can say, and hope to have proved, that the statistical analysis supports a new and more complex pattern of evolution for the novel in Spanish, lately suggested by some literary critics. The constitution of the Spanish novel before 1870 around three com-

---

[10] Fifty-eight percent of all dated editions were published during this third period, as compared with 4.5 percent in the first and 30.6 percent in the second. Similarly, 54.5 percent of all dated titles came out in the third period, 4.4 percent in the first, and 32.4 percent in the second.

FIGURE 4. TITLES IN SPANISH BY GENRE, 1843–1900

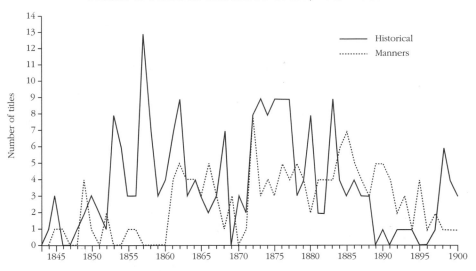

mercially successful novelists (Ayguals de Izco, Fernández y González, and Sinués de Marco) and its full development in the last decades of the century under the commercial hegemony of Pérez Galdós raise some questions regarding the total neglect of the pre-1870 novels, along with the strict distinction often made in the history of the novel in Spanish between canonical and commercial authors and, consequently, between the popular novel and the literary novel. It is clear that we cannot continue to analyze the aesthetic modes observed after 1870 as completely unrelated to market forces, as has traditionally been done. The distinction between commercial and literary authors ignores the fact that both groups share the same market-oriented publishing strategies. It also disregards the fact that the canonization of realism in Spain, as feminist critics have pointed out, depends precisely upon the marginalization of novels associated with market forces and the female reader. The exclusion of the commercial bases that sustain all novel production in the nineteenth century from the analysis of the literary novel uncritically reproduces the cultural politics of the distinction between high and low forms of art. This distinction creates a distorted view of the history of

TABLE 2. NOVELS IN SPANISH BY GENRE, 1843–1900

	Historical novel	Novel of manners	Genre not indicated
All editions	558	388	1,123
Dated editions	491	327	958

the novel in Spanish that obliterates the in-between character (both commercial and literary) of most works.

The analysis also reveals the prominence of the historical novel throughout the period. It seems therefore that this hegemony cannot be ignored without misrepresenting the history of the novel in Spanish. The traditional criticism of the genre as imitative of foreign forms and its association with the discredited *folletín* helps explain the fact that the historical novel is hardly ever studied and is generally considered no more than a by-product of romanticism. It is thus significant that the only historical novels in this period to have received some (although minimal) critical attention are the *Episodios nacionales*, novels that benefit from the prestige bestowed both upon realism and their author, Pérez Galdós. To have a better sense of the cultural phenomena and the variety of literary modes and social imaginaries that constitute the nineteenth-century novel in Spanish, we need to recover and examine the extensive production of the historical novel, leaving behind the nationalistic foundations of literary history and the prejudices of modernist poetics.

———

The statistical analysis of nineteenth-century novels in Catalan presents its own set of difficulties. The first modern novels in Catalan emerged in the 1860s as part of a cultural movement known as the *Renaixença* whose main purpose was the vindication of a national identity for Catalonia. The emergence of novels in Catalan is, then, more a political phenomenon than a commercial one. This judgment is reinforced by two particular circumstances: first, that the *Renaixença* movement made a point of using Catalan as a literary language for the first time since practically the seventeenth century; second, that all schooling was done in Spanish (there was no formal instruction in the Catalan language). Thus, the audience of the *Renaixença* and, more particularly, the readership of the novel in Catalan was highly selective, and the commercial demand for novels in Catalan quite small. We should, then, pose the question: can a quantitative method be applied to the study of the novel in Catalan? Should we apply statistical analysis to the production of a novel that by definition was not a commercial phenomenon? We believe it can and should be done. Even though more often than not the figures obtained do little more that point out what we already know—that is, the reduced circle of producers and consumers it involved—they still chart the course of the novel in Catalan and sustain some interesting remarks.

FIGURE 5. NOVELS IN CATALAN, 1862–1900

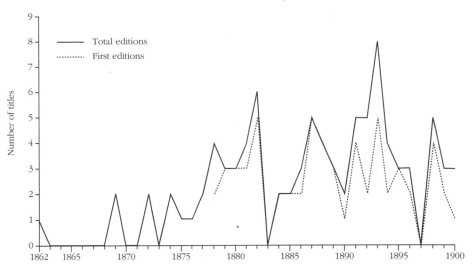

The first observation that can be made is the erratic and highly unstable growth of the Catalan novel (see figure 5). The distinct seesaw profile of the figure represents quite accurately a production that relies, as we have just mentioned, on a very small number of writers and readers. This prominent variability shows, nevertheless, a definite growth. In the first phase of novel production, during the years 1862–77, only eleven titles and editions were published (that is, an average of fewer than one per year), while for the period 1878–1900, the number of titles per year oscillates between one and five, and that of editions from two to eight (for a total of sixty titles and eighty editions).

The second observation that can be made is the absence of a few undisputably dominant figures. On the contrary, we observe that the production of novel in Catalan was mostly a collective undertaking. We can distinguish a group of eight authors who clearly were more prolific than the rest (they published between four and seven titles), but eight out of twenty-seven is hardly a sign of a production dominated by just a few. Moreover, the data indicates that they all seem to have enjoyed a similar popularity: the average number of editions per title in the whole period studied is 1.36. From the point of view of production and reception, no single author stands out—not even Narcís Oller (five titles and seven editions), who is the canonized representative of the nineteenth-century Catalan novel. Similarly, no single title seems to have captivated the readers' fancy: five titles had three editions, fifteen had two, and fifty-one had one.

TABLE 3. NOVELS IN CATALAN BY GENRE, 1862–1900

	Historical novel	Novel of manners	Genre not identified
All editions	20	73	3
Dated editions	19	69	3

The most surprising data revealed by our study is the apparent hegemony of the novel of manners over the historical novel in the production in Catalan (see table 3 and figure 6). These numbers are even more surprising when one considers the romantic character of the *Renaixença* and the essential role the historical novel has traditionally played in the constitution of a national consciousnesss. It should be noted, however, that Catalan historical topics were the subject of numerous novels written in Spanish before the 1860s (when the use of Catalan as a novelistic language was resumed). So, if we are willing to put aside the issue of language, it could be argued that Catalan writers did produce a significant number of novels on Catalan history. The hegemony of the novel of manners over the historical novel within the restricted field of works written in Catalan poses, nevertheless, important questions about the cultural strategies and aesthetic choices that guided the *Renaixença*. To these questions we can only venture here some partial answers. We could start by remembering the strong tradition of *costumisme*—narratives based on the depiction of local characters, popular events, and customs—in nineteenth-century Catalan letters. Also,

FIGURE 6. EDITIONS IN CATALAN BY GENRE, 1862–1900

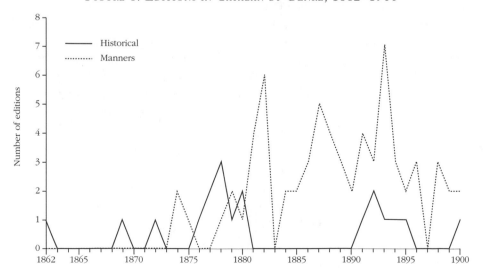

we should have in mind that, although part of the *Renaixença*, the novel in Catalan emerges at a time when the novel of manners is challenging the hegemony of the historical novel, which begins to be perceived as an outdated fictional form. Finally, the novel of manners—as the privileged form of modern fiction—suits well the discourse of Catalan nationalism, which at the end of the nineteenth century is mostly grounded on the identification of Catalonia with modernity.

It has been asked whether statistical studies on the novel will just add some numbers to the literary history we already know, or—on the contrary—if they will change it and how. We think that a quantitative analysis of literary phenomena brings to light qualitative processes not always evident. In particular, it reveals long-forgotten social imaginaires and the success their literary representations had among readers. Statistical analysis forces the reconsideration of certain acquired knowledge, raises different questions, and points to the potential interaction between commercial and literary patterns. We also think that the more complete and extensive the quantitative analysis is, and the more variables are contemplated, the more relevant statistical studies are for the history of literature. In this sense, the data and reflection provided in this study would be much more interesting and significant if it could be complemented and compared with data on the translation of foreign authors and on the establishment and development of publishing houses. We do not think that statistical analyses should substitute for qualitative ones. Neither do we think that it can or should replace the need to read each novel as a singular aesthetic object. But, at the same time, we should wonder whether the history of the novel can be appropriately written without taking into consideration the different perspectives on literary phenomena that an statistical approach brings forth.

APPENDIX: *Authors Included in This Study*

CATALAN NOVEL

Argullol, Josep d'

Bassegoda, Bonaventura

Berga i Boix, Josep

Bofarull i Brocà, Antoni de

Bosch de la Trinxeria, Carles

Boter, Francesc de

Briz, Francesc Pelai

Capella, Francesc de Paula

Careta i Vidal, Antoni

Feliu i Codina, Josep

Genís i Aguilar, Martí

Ginestà Punset, G.

CATALAN NOVEL (cont.)

Girbal Jaume, Ignasi

Girona, P. Joan

Martí i Folguera, Josep

Maspons i Labrós, Pilar

Mauricio de Xuclà, A

Monserdà de Macià, Dolors

Nadal, Lluís de B.

Olier, Narcís

Pin i Soler, Josep

Pons i Massaveu, Joan

Riera i Bertran, Joaquim

Salarich i Verdaguer, Joaquim

Soler, Gaietà

Valls i Vicens, Josep Maria

Vidal i Valenciano, Gaietà

SPANISH NOVEL (* canonized)

Alarcón, Pedro Antonio de*

Alas, Leopoldo*

Altadill y Teixidor, Antonio

Angelón y Broquetas, Manuel

Ayguals de Izco, Wenceslao

Blasco Ibáñez, Vicente

Böhl de Faber, Cecili*

Castellanos y Velasco, Julián

Castillo, Rafael de

Fernández y González, Manuel

García del Canto, Antonio

García Tejero, Alonso

López Bago, Eduardo

Macpherson de Bremón, Catalina

Martínez Barrionuevo, Manuel

Martínez Villergas, Juan

Mayo, Francisco de Sales

Mora, Juan de Dios

Moreno de la Tejera, Vicente

Muñoz Maldonado, José

Nombela y Tabares, Julio

Orellana, Francisco José

Ortega y Frías, Ramón

Palacio Valdés, Armando*

Pardo Bazán, Emilia*

Parreño, Florencio Luis

Pereda, José de*

Pérez Escrich, Enrique

Pérez Galdós, Benito*

Puerta Vizcaíno, Juan de la

Rodríguez Solís, Enrique

Saez de Melgar, Faustina

San Martín, Antonio de

Sinués de Marco, María Pilar

Tárrago y Mateos, Torcuato

Valera, Juan*

Velázquez y Sánchez, José

Works Cited

Bohigas, Pere. *El libro español: Ensayo histórico*. Barcelona: Gustavo Gili, 1962.

Botrel, Jean-François. *La diffusion du livre en Espagne (1868–1914): Les libraires*. Madrid: Casa de Velázquez, 1988.

———. "L'Espagne et les modèles éditoriaux français (1830–1850)." In *L'image de France en Espagne (1808–1850)*, ed. Jean-René Aymes and Javier Fernández Sebastián, 227–42. Bilbao: Universidad del País Vasco, 1997.

———. *Libros, prensa y lectura en la España del siglo XIX*. Madrid: Fundación Germán Sánchez Ruipérez, 1993.

———. "La literatura popular: Tradición, dependencia e innovación." In *La edición moderna: Siglos XIX y XX*. Vol. 3 of *Historia ilustrada del libro español*, 239–97. Madrid: Fundación Germán Sánchez Ruipérez/Pirámide, 1996.

———. "La novela por entregas: Unidad de creación y público." In *Creación y público en la literatura española*, ed. J.-F. Botrel and S. Salaün, 111–55. Madrid: Castalia, 1974.

———. "Le succès d'édition des oeuvres de Benito Pérez Galdós: Essai de bibliométrie (I)." *Anales de Literatura Española* 3 (1984): 119–57.

———. "Le succès d'édition des oeuvres de Benito Pérez Galdós: Essai de bibliométrie (II)." *Anales de Literatura Española* 4 (1985): 29–66.

Botrel, Jean-François, and Philippe Berger. *Histoire du livre et de l'édition dans les pays ibériques: La dépendence*. Bordeaux: Presses Universitaires de Bordeaux, 1986.

Carrillo, Victor. "Marketing et édition au XIXè siècle: La Sociedad Literaria de Madrid (Etude d'approche)." In *L'infra-littérature en Espagne au XIXè et XXè siècles: Du roman feuilleton au romancero de la guerre d'Espagne*, 7–101. Saint Martin d'Heres: Presses Universitaires de Grenoble, 1977.

———. "Radiografía de una colección de novelas a mediados del siglo XIX." In *Movimiento obrero, política y literatura en la España contemporánea*, ed. M. Tuñón de Lara and Jean-François Botrel, 159–77. Madrid: Cuadernos para el Diálogo, 1973.

Cassany, Enric. *El costumisme en la prosa catalana del segle XIX*. Barcelona: Curial, 1992.

Clemessy, Nelly. *Emilia Pardo Bazán, romancière (la critique, la théorie, la pratique)*. 2 vols. Paris: Centre de Recherches Hispaniques, 1973.

Delgado López-Cozar, Emilio, and José Antonio Cordón García. *El libro: Creación, producción y consumo en la Granada del siglo XIX*. 2 vols. Granada: Universidad de Granada/Diputación Provincial de Granada, 1990.

Dendle, Brian J. *Spain's Forgotten Novelist: Armando Palacio Valdés (1853–1938)*. Lewisburg, Penn.: Bucknell University Press, 1995.

Duran i Sampere, Agustí. *Contribució a la història de la imprenta a Barcelona*. Barcelona, 1936.

———. *Editores y libreros de Barcelona: Estivill, Piferrer, Brusi Bastinas*. Barcelona: Bosch, 1952.

Escolar, Hipólito. "La edición en el siglo XIX." In *La edición moderna: Siglos XIX y XX*. Vol. 3 of *Historia ilustrada del libro español*, 31–87. Madrid: Fundación Germán Sánchez Ruipérez/Pirámide, 1996.

Ferreras, Juan Ignacio. *Catálogo de novelas y novelistas españoles del siglo XIX*. Madrid: Cátedra, 1979.

González Herrán, José Manuel, and Ermitas Penas Valera. *Siglos XVIII y XIX*. Vol. 3 of *Cronología de la literatura española*. Coordinated by Darío Villanueva. Madrid: Cátedra, 1992.

Hortelano, Benito. *Memorias de Benito Hortelano*. Madrid: Espasa-Calpe, 1936.

Luxán Meléndez, Santiago. *La industria tipográfica en Canarias (1750–1900): Balance de la producción impresa*. Gran Canaria: Cabildo Insular de Gran Canaria, 1994.

Marrast, Robert. "Libro y lectura en la España del siglo XIX." In *Movimiento obrero, política y literatura en la España contemporánea*, ed. M. Tuñón de Lara and Jean-François Botrel, 145–59. Madrid: Cuadernos para el Diálogo, 1973.

Martí-López, Elisa. "Historiografía literaria y análisis cuantitativo: Ediciones, éxitos comerciales y novela en España, 1840–1900." *Bulletin Hispanique* 103.2 (2001): 675–94.

———. "El mercado editorial en la España de mediados del siglo XIX." *Cuadernos Hispanoamericanos* 565–566 (July–August 1997): 177–88.

———. "La orfandad de la novela española: Política editorial y creación literaria a mediados del siglo XIX." *Bulletin Hispanique* 98.2 (1996): 1–15.

Milla, Ángel. *Libreros y bibliófilos barceloneses del siglo XIX: Apuntes para una pequeña historia*. Barcelona: Gremio de Libreros, 1956.

Montesinos, José F. *Fernán Caballero: Ensayo de justificación*. Mexico City: Colegio de México, 1961.

Palau y Dulcet, Antonio. *Manual del librero hispano-americano: Bibliografía general española e hispanoamericana desde la invención de la imprenta hasta nuestros días, con el valor comercial de los impresos descritos*. 2nd ed., revised and expanded. 28 vols. Barcelona: A. Palau, 1848–1977.

Romero Tobar, Leonardo. *La novela popular española del siglo XIX*. Madrid: Fundación Juan March/Ariel, 1975.

Serrahima, Maurici, and Maria Teresa Boada. *La novella històrica en la literatura catalana*. Barcelona: Publicacions de l'Abadia de Montserrat, 1996.

Valis, Noël M. *Leopoldo Alas (Clarín)*. London: Grant and Cutler, 1986.

Xandró, Mauricio. *Vicente Blasco Ibáñez*. Madrid: Xandró, 1997.

PRIYA JOSHI

India, 1850–1900

Consumption

The novel arrived in India much as Athena did in Greek mythology, fully formed from the heads, and hands, of a paternalistic ruling power. It came in steamer trunks accompanying British officials taking possession of the territory that was soon to become the jewel in the crown. Decades later, in 1835, when the British Parliament passed an Education Act mandating the East India Company to use a £10,000 bursary for the education of Indians in the English language, it accepted the arguments of the company's chief ideologue, Thomas Babington Macaulay, to make literature the cornerstone of education policy in the subcontinent. Though English poetry and drama were Macaulay's favored tools in the infamous fabrication of "a class of persons, Indian in blood and colour, but English in tastes, opinions, morals, and intellect,"[1] it soon became clear that the novel was the favored form for leisure reading among Indian subjects, whose world of letters was dominated by epic, poetry, and drama (in that order) and where prose fiction had hitherto enjoyed an extremely negligible position. While the ancient *Panchatantra* tales and the eighteenth-century Urdu *dastan* or episodic romances were examples of prose fiction indigenous to India, the novel as such had yet to exist on the literary horizon until it was introduced in the vast textual commerce that followed the implementation of the 1835 English Education Act.

Most postcolonial critics have roundly denounced the British policy of anglicization, and Baron Macaulay along with it, for the cultural and ideological violence that, they argue, characterized the British Empire in India. Yet, few critics, if any, have actually probed what Indian readers did with or made of the British books—novels included—that flooded their shores in the decades following the Education Act of 1835. Figure 1 makes several important points clear: the original, and highly contested, education bursary of £10,000 with which English education "began" in India in 1835 was in fact a symbolic sum with dramatic consequences: by 1850, English books worth

---

[1] Thomas Babington Macaulay, *Minute on Indian Education*, in *Selected Writings: Thomas Babington Macaulay*, John Clive and Thomas Pinney, eds. (Chicago, 1972), 249.

FIGURE 1. BOOK IMPORTS INTO INDIA, 1850–1900

© Priya Joshi. Source: *Annual Statement of the Trade and Navigation of British India with Foreign Countries and of the Coasting Trade of the Several Presidencies and Provinces* (Calcutta: Government Printing Press, 1850–1901).

£148,563 were being imported into India, and these amounts would increase greatly after the 1857 Mutiny, reaching a peak in 1863–64 of £328,024. However, the sharp decline of book imports beginning in 1866 is something of a conundrum: the passage of Act 25 of 1867 (the Indian Press and Registration of Books Act that mandated the registration of all books and periodicals with a central authority) would suggest an *increase*—or stabilization—of book imports from Britain at a time when publishing activity in India was being scrutinized, yet what we see in fact is a decline in imports that has yet to be fully explained.

Imperial historians today have come to acknowledge that both commerce and culture, gunpowder and print played a role in creating and maintaining the colonial state. For these scholars, it is the forms of desire created by the circulation and consumption of European products that mark the imperial conquest—and its limits. Yet, literary scholarship, invested as it has been in its disciplinary passion for close reading, has largely ignored consumption altogether. Literary critics have mostly focused on interpreting imperial ideology as it is embedded in texts rather than on how these texts themselves may have been consumed by readers who were not the intended audience. Reading literary critics on empire sometimes reminds one of Saleem Sinai trying to understand modern India's political history in Salman Rushdie's

Midnight's Children (1980): "you've got so close to the screen," he reports, using a recurring film metaphor, "that you see nothing but the grains of the image too clearly."

Hungry for more than a few grains—or crumbs—this essay uses the methods of book history in order to probe the consumption of the novel in colonial India and to tell a fuller story of imperial influence and subaltern agency during the nineteenth century. By deferring my discipline's usual pre-occupation with close reading, I hope to show how the findings from book history make a different kind of close reading available. In it, the text does not so much disappear as reappear newly reconstituted through an encounter with forms of knowledge that are not saturated with the textual innards that conventional close reading would throw up, but with the details of a richly recovered contextual history. Consumption, I hope to show, following Michel de Certeau, might indeed be regarded as "another production" in which con-sumers manufacture new and unintended meanings from products that they themselves neither make nor fully control.

The pages that follow document the immediate and sustained enthusiasm for British fiction in the Indian subcontinent. Indian readers vigorously and unambiguously embraced the British novel for their pleasure reading, often choosing it over indigenous literary forms, discussing it in the domestic press, in literary societies, and in homes in a manner that would suggest the novel's successful conquest of the Indian literary and cultural marketplace. In examining the record more closely, however, a different pattern emerges: what we see is not an unambiguous embrace of the novel but its consump-tion through active selection. Multitudes of individual readers variously in-dicated the differences between their world and the colonial state's in two ways: first, by the specific novels they consumed (both the selections they made *for* as well as *against* certain books are revealing here); and second, by how they read, misread, translated, mistranslated the British novel. These descriptions of reading are not just writerly sleights: the historical record is full of British novels translated and adapted into Indian languages, and what got translated and how signals a form of consumption characterized not so much by opposition as by adaptation.

The Novel and Empire

Reading Edward Said, one is reminded of the considerable extent to which the novel informed, directed, and itself embodied the traffic of ideas and values between metropole, periphery, and back. As Said maintains, "imperialism and the novel fortified each other to such a degree that it is impossible, I would argue, to read one without in some way dealing with the other."[2] Said shows how the literary institution of the novel—particularly in its British manifestation—rested on a broader world of politics and economics. Through its structures, impulses, and allusions, the novel projected the world of its composition outward, giving coherence and authority to what would otherwise have been a series of discontinuous and dispersed facts of political and imperial practice.

For this, the British novel has come to be considered a particular success not just because of the cultural labor it performed in Britain but also because of the labor it performed *for* Britain, most notably for its apparently successful reception among and seduction of readers in the colonies. Some critics have suggested that British influence and prestige were so marked in the nineteenth century that Indian readers, "considered [British novels] to be far superior to anything which was available in their own languages";[3] or, in a related vein, that "Indians took to fiction as a part of their attempt to familiarise themselves with the language, style, and manners of the ruling race."[4] Yet other critics have taken a more subtly sociological approach, maintaining that the British novel opened up "a whole new world" for nineteenth-century Indian readers who discovered irresistible new possibilities in it.[5] Either way, the British novel was considered an immense success among readers in India, requested three to four times more frequently than any other printed form from Indian public libraries and liberally and visibly advertised and discussed in the local press and periodicals.[6]

---

[2] Edward W. Said, *Culture and Imperialism* (New York, 1993), 71. A few pages earlier, Said states his case about the novel and imperialism more bluntly: "Without empire, I would go so far as saying, there is no European novel as we know it, and indeed if we study the impulses giving rise to it, we shall see the far from accidental convergence between the patterns of narrative authority constitutive of the novel on the one hand, and on the other, a complex ideological configuration underlying the tendency to imperialism" (69–70).

[3] T. W. Clark, "Introduction," in *The Novel in India: Its Birth and Development*, ed. T. W. Clark (Berkeley, Calif., 1970), 11.

[4] Balgopal Varma, "Some Thoughts on English Fiction and the Reading Public," in *Fiction and the Reading Public in India*, ed. C. D. Narsimhaiah (Mysore, 1967), 6.

[5] Meenakshi Mukherjee, *Realism and Reality: The Novel and Society in India* (New Delhi, 1985), 6; also 3–18 passim.

[6] For details on Indian public libraries and their users, see chapter 2 of my *In Another Country: Colonialism, Culture, and the English Novel in India* (New York, 2002); for details on newspaper advertisements, see my preliminary findings in "Culture and Consumption: Fiction, the Reading Public, and the British Novel in Colonial India," *Book History* 1 (1998): 196–220.

TABLE 1. The Circulation of Books by Categories (Bagbazar Reading Library, 1902)

	In stock		Issued	
	English	Bengali	English	Bengali
Fiction	802	903	524	5,306
Poetry/drama	109	964	13	897
History	279	61	47	53
Biography	178	162	19	152
Science/philosophy	133	123	28	32
Travels	86	37	10	51
Literature and essays	126	134	39	63
Religion	42	241	3	119
Miscellaneous	535	488	65	445
Total	2,290	3,113	748	7,118

Source: *Report of the Bagbazar Reading Library for the 19th Year Ending on June 1902* (Calcutta: K. P. Mookerjee and Co., 1903).

Table 1 lists the circulation of books by categories for one public library patronized entirely by Indian readers in Calcutta; figures 2 and 3 illustrate visually the ratio of fiction holdings to circulation and make visible the popularity of the novel over all other categories. In the Bagbazar Reading Library's distribution, though fiction accounted for only a third of the total holdings, its circulation constituted 74 percent of the total, followed by poetry and drama at almost 12 percent of the borrowing requests, miscellaneous (6.5 percent), biography (2.1 percent), religion (1.6 percent), and history (1.3 percent). Unusually then, we see in this library that the taste for fiction

FIGURE 2. Proportion of Fiction Holdings to Circulation

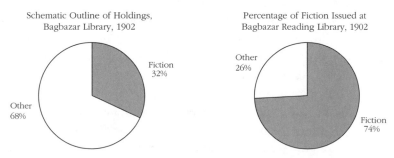

Schematic Outline of Holdings, Bagbazar Library, 1902

Fiction 32%

Other 68%

Percentage of Fiction Issued at Bagbazar Reading Library, 1902

Other 26%

Fiction 74%

© Priya Joshi. Source: *Report of the Bagbazar Reading Library for the 19th Year Ending on June 1902* (Calcutta: K. P. Mookerjee and Co., 1903).

FIGURE 3. BOOK CIRCULATION, BAGBAZAR READING LIBRARY, 1902

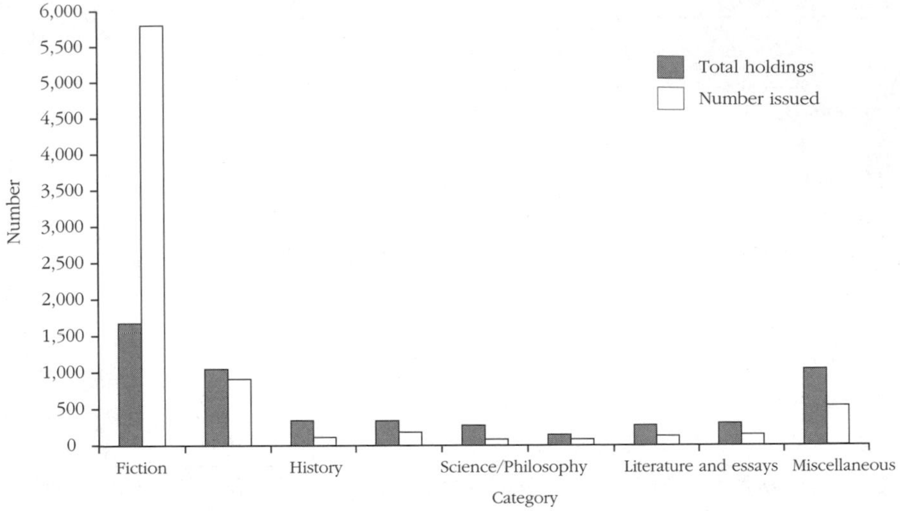

© Priya Joshi. Source: *Report of the Bagbazar Reading Library for the 19th Year Ending on June 1902* (Calcutta: K. P. Mookerjee and Co., 1903).

(over 90 percent of which circulated in Bengali) did not spill over to requesting other imaginative or narrative genres, such as travel, biography, or even history, a pattern that was often visible in British public libraries of the same period.

In order to understand the nature of what constitutes this success and to instantiate the role of culture broadly and the novel particularly in the colonial encounter, it is useful to know specifically what English novels Indians read and how they did so during the nineteenth century. The question to pose is, were literate Indians colonized by the plethora of literature arriving from Britain, or did they, through their choices and ways of reading, themselves manipulate British literary forms to their own ends, thus eluding in nimble and skillful ways the long reach of the colonizing mission? As increasing numbers of Indians started reading English books for pleasure, the novel and Indian responses to it provide ideal variables to help track the development of a population that was not just consuming the novel as a new form of literature and entertainment but was simultaneously encountering in this form a world of new values and ideas inevitably associated with Englishness, modernity, and the colonizer. Therefore, tracking how Indians consumed the novel opens a way of examining how a colonial population responded to a world of culture and priorities inherently different than and often apparently antithetical to their own. In studying the consumption of the British novel, I submit, we begin to see most clearly how ideas and ideologies were received, transmogrified, rejected, or refashioned by that small but influential part of the Indian population who had access to this world of print.

In an effort to expand the empirical base from a single region (Calcutta) to something resembling a more general pattern across India, I examined extant catalogs from fourteen public libraries catering almost exclusively to Indian users spread out in Bombay (three), Calcutta (four) and its environs (one), Madras (three), Delhi (one), Allahabad (one), and Patna (one). Using their holdings in fiction, I generated a master list of all the European novelists available to Indian readers in the second half of the nineteenth century. Working from this list, I generated a further list of notably "vendible" authors (Paul Kaufman's term) who were present in multiple copies or multiple titles at any library. A total of 207 writers, the vast majority British, fall within this short list. Finally, I isolated authors who were available in all, or virtually all, of the fourteen libraries in order to factor in (or out) any regional variances or collection eccentricities. The twenty-two novelists in this final list form the corpus of those most consistently available to Indian readers in public libraries during the period roughly between 1850 and 1900. Table 2 lists the twenty-two novelists most prevalent in extant Indian public library catalogues during the nineteenth century.

Two authors, Bulwer-Lytton and Scott, appeared in all the fourteen library catalogs; a further three, Dickens, Disraeli, and Thackeray, in thirteen out of fourteen; another eight, Corelli, Crawford, Dumas, Eliot, Kingsley, Marryat, Reynolds, and Taylor, in twelve out of fourteen collections; and a final nine, Ainsworth, Braddon, Collins, Doyle, Harte, James, Lever, Reade, and Stevenson, in eleven out of the fourteen library collections. In other words, all of these twenty-two authors appeared in at least 80 percent of the total libraries surveyed. The fourteen catalogs, as such, are a far cry from providing circulation statistics for the entire country; yet, what they do provide is a set of trends for the country that we can compare across regions, scrutinize, and evaluate alongside other data such as that on translation, which follows.

Scanning the list quickly, roughly 60 percent of the authors are recognizable today, with the remaining 40 percent (figures such as Corelli, Crawford, Marryat, Reynolds, and Taylor) known mostly to specialists and experts in Victorian literature. This fact itself merits some attention. What is immediately striking in table 2 is how *safe* and stable a list it is. Sixty percent of its authors are recognizable and still reprinted and read today. Indian readers, it seems, read fairly conventionally; either that or they were

TABLE 2. NOVELISTS MOST PRESENT IN INDIAN LIBRARY CATALOGUES

Author	Number of libraries
Edward Bulwer-Lytton	14
Sir Walter Scott	14
Charles Dickens	13
Benjamin Disraeli	13
William Thackeray	13
Marie Corelli	12
F. Marion Crawford	12
Alexandre Dumas	12
George Eliot	12
Charles Kingsley	12
Captain Frederick Marryat	12
G.W.M. Reynolds	12
Philip Meadows Taylor	12
William Ainsworth	11
Mary Elizabeth Braddon	11
Wilkie Collins	11
Sir Arthur Conan Doyle	11
Bret Harte	11
G.P.R. James	11
Charles Lever	11
Charles Reade	11
R.L. Stevenson	11

Sources: *Catalogue of Books in the Library of the Literary Society at Madras* (Madras: J. B. Pharoah, 1839); *Catalogue of the Madras Literary Society* (Madras: Government Press, 1891); *The Catalogue of Books of the Oriental and Mixed Library, Bangalore* (Madras: Addison and Co., 1899); *Catalogue of the Calcutta Public Library* (Calcutta: Sanders, Cones and Co., 1855); *Catalogue of the Calcutta Public Library. Part I. Prose Works of Fiction in the English and the French Language* (Calcutta: Bharat Mihir Press, 1894); *Catalogue of the Bengal Club Library* (Calcutta, 1889); *Catalogue of the Library of the United Service Club, Calcutta* (Calcutta, 1892); *Calcutta Chaitanya Library Catalogue of English Books* (Calcutta, 1903); *Duke Public Library, Howrah Classified Catalogue of Books* (Calcutta, 1931); *Catalogue of Books in the Uttarpara Public Library* (Calcutta: Gupta Press, 1903); *Alphabetical Catalogue of the Punjab Public Library*, rev. ed. (Lahore: Victoria Press, 1897); *Catalogue of the Printed Books of European Languages in Khuda Baksh Oriental Public Library, Patna* (Patna: Liberty Art Press, 1918); *Catalogue and Index of the Allahabad Public Library* (Allahabah: Indian Press, 1927); *The Bhuleshwar Library Catalogue of Books* (Bombay: Ripon Printing Press, 1895); *The Bombay Native General Library Catalogue of Books* (Bombay: Jehangier B. Marzban and Co., 1898); *The Jamsetjee Nesserwanjee Petit Fort Reading Room and Library, Bombay Classified Catalogue of Books* (Bombay: Captain Printing Press, 1895); *Catalogue of the Delhi Public Library* (Delhi, 1902).

very good predictors and perhaps even makers of literary canons. It is tempting at this stage to speculate that Indian readerly taste was pedestrian and imitative and that the colonial grip on culture was so marked that Indian readers stuck to the "good" books of Scott and Dickens that the colonial authorities wished them to read.

However, the fact that 40 percent of the list is composed of once-popular and noncanonical novelists such as G.W.M. Reynolds, F. Marion Crawford, and others alerts us that the colonial control of the literary market was far from absolute. Therefore, studying the list with its conservatism in mind might alert one to the possible fact that nineteenth-century Indian readers were reading with less of a free hand than they might otherwise have had, that they were reading what they ought to, not what they freely wished to. If this were the case, however, the Indian canon should be virtually identical to the British one, with colonial readers fulfilling the ideological and cultural dictates of their situation and reflecting a close-to-complete overlap with the interests of the colonial authorities. The abundance of once-popular, but often denigrated writers such as Reynolds, however, raises the question: why were imitation and docility apparent only 60 percent of the time? There is something in the Indian taste for English novels that prompts the need to scrutinize more closely not just what Indians were reading in the nineteenth century, but how, and, if possible, why. First, one final set of data on the circulation of novels before we address these larger issues.

Alongside the list of novelists available to Indian readers in English, we also have access to which writers were translated during the nineteenth century. If library catalogs index "vendible" authors, then the translation lists index the most "readable" ones, for they indicate what books were voluntarily translated into Indian languages by particularly devoted readers. In the nineteenth-century cottage industry of translation, with its paltry remuneration, a translator had to be notably enthusiastic about a book, or the book had to promise success before it was worth the expense and exercise of translation. Table 3 lists the authors, both British and foreign, most translated and "adapted" into Indian languages in the nineteenth century.

The translation lists make three points clear. First, we note the striking persistence of eighteenth-century fiction well into the nineteenth century: all of the titles, most especially Defoe and Johnson, continued to be translated throughout the next century and coexisted alongside Victorian writers, some of whom also appear in table 2. Second, the translation lists indicate that British fiction, and through it British ideas, penetrated Indian letters and interfaced with Indian readers often removed from the medium of English. When rendered into regional language adaptations and translations,

TABLE 3. WORKS TRANSLATED OR ADAPTED INTO INDIAN LANGUAGES

Pre-nineteenth-century writers	Nineteenth-century writers	Non-British works

Defoe
  *Robinson Crusoe (VLS)
	Bulwer-Lytton
	  Last Days of Pompeii
	  Rienzi
		Aesop's Fables (VLS)

Fielding
  Amelia
	Leila	Andersen, H. C.
		  Various short stories
		  (VLS)

	Collins	

Goldsmith
  *Vicar of Wakefield (VLS)
  Traveller
  Deserted Village
	Woman in White	*Arabian Nights

	Reynolds
	  *Mysteries of London
	  *Mysteries of the Court
	    of London
		Boccaccio
		  Decameron

Johnson
  *Rasselas
	*Mary Price
	  *The Seamstress
		Cervantes
		  Don Quixote

Swift
  *Gulliver's Travels
  Voyage to Brobdignag
	*Loves of the Harem
	  *Soldier's Wife
	  *Joseph Wilmot
	  *Rye House Plot
	  *The Young Duchess
	  *Mary Queen of Scots
	  *Rosa Lambert
	  *Faust
		Dumas
		  The Count of Monte
		  Cristo
		
		Lesage
		  Gil Blas
		
		Hugo
		  Les misérables

	Scott
	  Ivanhoe
	  *Lady of the Lake
	  Bride of Lamermoor
	  Kenilworth
	  *Lay of the Last Minstrel
	  *Marmion
		Saint Pierre
		  Paul et Virginie
		  (VLS)
		
		Stowe
		  Uncle Tom's Cabin
		  (VLS)

	Taylor
	  *Tara
	  Confessions of a Thug
	  One unidentified by title
		Sue
		  Les mystères de Paris

TABLE 3. (*Continued*)

Pre-nineteenth-century writers	Nineteenth-century writers	Non-British works
		Verne
		Twenty-Thousand Leagues under the Sea
		Around the World in Eighty Days

Sources: L.D. Barnett, *A Catalogue of the Telugu Books in the Library of the British Museum* (London: British Museum, 1912); Barnett, *A Supplementary Catalogue of Tamil Books in the Library of the British Museum* (London: British Museum, 1931); Barnett, and G.U. Pope, *A Catalogue of the Tamil Books in the Library of the British Museum* (London: British Museum, 1909); J.F. Blumhardt, *Catalogue of Hindustani Printed Books in the Library of the British Museum* (London: British Museum, 1889); Blumhardt, *Catalogue of Marathi and Gujarati Printed Books in the Library of the British Museum* (London: Kegan Paul, Trench, Trubner, & Co., 1892); Blumhardt, *Catalogue of the Library of the India Office. Bengali, Oriya, and Assamese Books* Vol. II (London: Eyre and Spottiswoode, 1905); Blumhardt, *Catalogue of the Library of the India Office. Marathi and Gujarati Books* Vol. II of (London: Eyre and Spottiswoode, 1908); Blumhardt, *A Supplementary Catalogue of Marathi and Gujarati Books in the British Museum* (London: British Museum, 1910.)

Note: Each of the titles was translated into at least three Indian languages.

* Denotes titles that were translated into four or more languages.

"VLS" indicates those works translated under the aegis of the Bengal Vernacular Literature Society (though it ought to be mentioned that numerous other works such as Scott's poetry and *Arabian Nights* had the clear approval, if not sponsorship, of the society).

British fiction was indigenized and stripped from the language and culture of its creation. Third, the lists further corroborate one dominant axis of readerly taste in nineteenth-century India from table 2 and renders it strikingly clear: namely, an affection for romance and melodrama, exemplified in different ways by writers as diverse as G.W.M. Reynolds (the most widely translated and adapted of all British writers), Scott (whose poetry held sway greatly over the novels), Dumas, and Sue. Indeed both the list of novelists in table 2 and translations in table 3 make clear that fiction in the melodramatic mode, with its narratology of stark social and moral contrasts, was more effective in interpellating Indian readers than a realism that depended on metropolitan conditions for its legitimacy—and indeed, for its legibility.

Melodrama in Empire

Few critics have probed why Indian readers held, and continued throughout the nineteenth and early twentieth centuries to hold, these particular novelists in such great esteem, or what special significance they carried during this period. A part of that explanation lies, I believe, in the reading tastes that Indians also had for melodrama and romance at the same time. From the array of prose that Indian readers had before them (and it was a wide array including tales, novels, fables, and short stories on one end and numerous forms of the novel such as realist, sensational, historical, romantic, didactic, social, and reformist on the other), Indian readers made certain choices that they exercised both in the marketplace and in the domestic publishing world. At the risk of reducing the diversity of Indian reading experiences into a single corpus, it seems that the manifold pattern of reading tastes that the archives document is worth scrutinizing as a set of conscious choices made both *for* certain forms and *against* certain others. What I am proposing to do then is to analyze Indian consumption as a pattern of complex but interdependent needs, with each aspect of readerly preference addressing a larger constellation that it both depended on and satisfied. By exploring colonial reading tastes *in toto*, we might be able to analyze what the affection for novelists as different as G.W.M. Reynolds, F. Marion Crawford, Wilkie Collins, and Marie Corelli satisfied in the nineteenth-century Indian reader's mind. While we can never know exactly how Indian readers read this fiction, we can at least investigate what about these novels worked in India and try to understand how it might have done so in an environment so dramatically different from the one in which the novels were produced.

What I am suggesting by invoking melodramatic form is that the fiction of Reynolds (the most popular British novelist in India) and others also invoked the content of melodrama, or what Peter Brooks has called the "moral occult" that undergirds a range of texts that sit on the uneasy divide between popular forms and a larger social conscience. Melodrama for Brooks is a "system for making sense of experience," and the moral occult, the set of intrinsic values "both indicated within and masked by the surface of reality."[7] For Brooks, as for the earlier generation of critics upon whom his work builds, melodrama is both a theatrical form and a mode for dramatizing moral issues. Melodrama's formal use of binaries such as vice and virtue

---

[7] Peter Brooks, *The Melodramatic Imagination: Balzac, Henry James, Melodrama, and the Mode of Excess* (New York, 1985), xii, 5.

serves in this context to help excavate and restore moral order on a universe that has lost it. If melodrama is a sense-making enterprise, as Brooks expresses it, then I am interested in pursuing what sense Reynolds and other popular British novelists made for their Indian readers and why and how.

In consuming melodrama of the kind that a number of British novelists provided them, Indian readers found a world that they could inhabit without contradiction or censure. In Reynolds's novels, for instance, the individual was pitted against monstrous odds, but in vanquishing them, he became prince of a newer, better, moral order, one that ought to have always been but usually was not. Reynolds's explanations of the manners of the British upper classes along with the moralizing and entertainment in his novels addressed other important needs among his Indian audience. The affection for didacticism that earlier fiction, from *Pilgrim's Progress* to *Rasselas* had provided, as well as the psychological need to find a symbolic means to resist empire found both corroboration and inspiration in novels by Reynolds, Crawford, and Corelli in the melodramatic mode. Despite elaborate plots and numerous formal variations, melodrama's cleaner-than-life modalities were evident, allowing the economy of persecution and justice to resonate even among the most unsophisticated Indian readers.

I do not mean to suggest that Reynolds, or the melodramatic mode, causes revolution. Rather, I would argue that the ways of reading these works, at least in nineteenth-century India, might do just that. What Reynolds's sustained popularity along with that of a group of other novelists such as Corelli and Crawford in nineteenth- and early twentieth-century India gestures toward is not so much revolution as the immensely powerful appeal of melodrama in a world that found great symbolic affinities with the psychological structure of the form. The melodramatic mode provided the pleasure and satisfaction of experiencing wholeness, victory, and retribution for all the wrongs that were, in reality or imagination, visited on the community of readers. Melodrama enabled its Indian readers to conceive of and give shape to the "enemy." It articulated action and projected results, however fictional. In this regard, as Robert Heilman brilliantly notes, "melodrama has affinities with politics, tragedy with religion. . . . [Melodrama] is the principal vehicle of protest and dissent."[8]

It was this clarity and singleness of vision that I would suggest was most appealing to Indian readers, who discovered in the melodramatic mode not just consolation but a way of "plotting" and seeing the world that was fully

[8] Robert B. Heilman, *Tragedy and Melodrama: Versions of Experience* (Seattle, 1968), 90, 96.

commensurate with their own fantasies and desires for wish fulfillment. That these fantasies were not just individual ones of personal grandeur and wealth, but larger cultural and political fantasies of freedom and liberation from the British in part explains the extended appeal of the melodramatic mode throughout the nineteenth and twentieth centuries in India.

"Melodrama is not an exaggeration of our dreams but a duplication of them," wrote Eric Bentley to explain the form's continued success in Britain.[9] While melodrama on the English stage (from Bentley's example) or in print quite simply embodied the dream-fantasies of its British consumers, it actually helped enact those of its Indian consumers. What I am suggesting then is that melodrama both sent and received psychological signals to Indian readers, who eventually used its tropes to fashion a liberation struggle that "really" took place, in the world and not just in dreams. The encounter with the British novel generally and the melodramatic mode in particular helped Indian readers translate themselves from a socially and politically feudal order to a modern one; from cultural and political subjection to conviction; from consumers to producers of their own national self-image. By translating and being translated by the melodramatic mode, it would seem that Indian readers used their literary landscape eventually to imagine a political one.

---

[9] Eric Bentley, *The Life of the Drama* (New York, 1964), 205.

JONATHAN ZWICKER

Japan, 1850–1900

This essay on the literary history of nineteenth-century Japan is conceived from the point of view of book history. Its most immediate inspiration came from a few lines in one of Maeda Ai's late essays, posthumously published in *Bungaku tekusuto nyûmon*. Discussing the early years of the Meiji period and the introduction of Western culture, Maeda writes: "for the ordinary Japanese, 'the West' was encountered not first of all at the level of ideology or institution but at the level of *things*."[1] Maeda goes on to mention soap and umbrellas and handkerchiefs, but for many, their first encounter with the West was with material objects of a very different sort, with books. So I began to envision a history of Meiji literature from the perspective books as *things*, as "material objects [with] symbolic forms" to use D. F. McKenzie's phrase.[2] There are, perhaps, two ways to make a history of the European novel in nineteenth-century Japan from this perspective. One would be to trace the history of a single book—a kind of test case: where it came from, how it got to Japan, who translated and who published it, how it was distributed, and ultimately who bought and read it. This approach would be anecdotal but would have the virtue of being meticulous and attentive to the various stages in the social life of a book, mapping out in real historical space one of the "communication circuits" that the cultural historian Robert Darnton has suggested as one type of model for book history.[3] The other approach would be very different: not to look at any one book in its historical singularity, but rather to survey all the extant translations and come up with some general trends. And these materials were easy enough to come by: I started with the catalog of the Meiji Collection of the National Diet Library in Tokyo, made a few simple charts and then proceeded to work on a more elaborate and exhaustive database while working through the microfilms of that collection. While both projects were appealing in their own ways, I began to be increasingly interested in what the latter, quantitative approach

---

[1] Maeda Ai, *Bungaku tekusuto nyûmon* (Tokyo: Chikuma shobô, 1996), 41.

[2] D. F. McKenzie, *Bibliography and the Sociology of Texts* (Cambridge: Cambridge University Press, 1999), 22.

[3] See "The Communication Circuit" in *The Kiss of Lamourette* (New York: Norton, 1990), 112, which also appears in *The Forbidden Best-Sellers of Pre-Revolutionary France* (New York: Norton, 1996), 183.

had to offer traditional literary history, all the while realizing that, if in the end I could not tell how a single book actually got to Japan, all of the numbers and trends would be sort of hollow. Not hollow in the sense of being worthless, but certainly not representative of the materialist strain in literary history that Maeda's work had suggested.

———

There is a well-known anecdote surrounding the first European novel published in Japanese, an edition of Defoe's *Robinson Crusoe* issued in 1857, a decade before the Meiji Restoration. *Robinsun hyôkôkiryaku*, as Yokoyama Yoshikiyo's translation was titled, was a slender volume, forty-odd pages, published by an obscure and unremarkable firm, Keika sho'oku. Little is known of the circumstances surrounding the translation: how Yokoyama, a student of the minor poet and national learning scholar Inô Hidenori, obtained the Dutch edition of Defoe's novel on which his translation was based; how that Dutch edition reached Japan and whether it had entered Japan as part of the midcentury trade in foreign books or as a personal effect. The Nagasaki customs records which may have cleared up the final point and held clues to deciphering the others are only fragmentary, and without reliable records from which to start it will probably be impossible to reconstruct the events leading up to the production of the Keika edition.

A little book, published by a little firm, translated by a minor figure, the Keika edition of Defoe's novel has remained a minor footnote in the history of the novel in Japan: yes, it anticipated the translation industry that would come twenty or thirty years down the road, but it was an isolated incident, a historical anomaly. And it is true that viewed from the perspective of traditional literary history, the Keika edition of *Robinson Crusoe* is rather uninteresting: it spawned no imitators, for instance, creating no intertextual relations, no anxieties of influence; the novel probably had a very limited readership—while there are sixteen extant copies of the 1857 edition, no copies of the book were recorded in the holdings of the Daisô library, the largest commercial lending library of the nineteenth century, when the collections were cataloged for auction in 1899; and the "novel" was not even really understood to be a novel at all but was taken to be an autobiographical account that, the preface explains, "is always used in the rearing of Western children as a basis of instruction." Yes, the novel was produced, but it was unique. It had no social life, and so what it can explain of literary history is quite limited.

Yokoyama's translation then is often mentioned, but little discussed. Viewed in a different light, however, the translation is interesting indeed.

No, it cannot yield a wealth of information and data directly, but the circumstances surrounding this "unique event" can suggest very productive ways for rethinking the material history of the European novel in Japan if one is willing to believe that these circumstances were not in fact unique. It is well known that the translation is based on a nineteenth-century Dutch edition; indeed, the title page reproduces the Dutch: *Beknopte Levensgeshiedenis van Robinson Crusoe*. So the first thing that is striking about the translation is that that book which has been unanimously hailed (by scholars from Watt to McKeon) as the origin of the English novel was translated not from the English but from the Dutch; and indeed there is extant at the University of Michigan an edition of *Crusoe* published by J. Zender of Dordrecht in the 1830s bearing the exact title that appeared in the Keika edition. Zender's edition, which is otherwise merely one of six Dutch editions published in the 1830s and '40s, is remarkable (like the Keika edition) for its brevity: only twenty-five pages. This is in contrast to William Taylor's 1719 edition that was 364 pages and to midnineteenth-century English editions that are often four or five hundred pages long, depending on page size and typography. So a second point emerges: whatever emending, redacting, and editing Defoe's novel was subjected to had already been carried out in relation to the Dutch edition before the novel arrived in Japan. Indeed Crusoe's entire diary, which was the backbone of the 1719 edition and long considered one of the most significant formal developments of the novel in terms of representing "everyday life" is already gone from the novel before it reaches Japan.[4]

What the Keika edition suggests, if it is to become part of a larger history of translation, is that during its life, a text is often subjected to various forms of mediation—linguistic, textual, contextual—that are not immediately apparent from looking only at the two bookends of that social life—the original and the final product. The extent to which the history of the life of books as things is available to later historians of course varies, but it is clear that in the end it will be much more rewarding not simply to turn back to the original edition to see what relation the translation or reproduction bears in terms of a normative fidelity, but archaeologically to trace the mediated and complex middle passage of a book as best we can. It is true, we have not achieved the harmonious circuit from author through publisher and bookseller to the reading public and back again to the author that Robert Darnton suggests is the goal of this sort of book history, but in the process we

---

[4] On Crusoe's journal, see Stuart Sherman, *Telling Time* (Chicago: University of Chicago Press, 1996), 25 and 223ff.

have discovered some valuable clues to the history of the European novel in nineteenth-century Japan and perhaps as significantly found that there are other circuits and networks that books travel that often take them far afield, and that books participate in a social life that is far more complex and mediated than literary history often admits.

But this is just one example, and it is an example, I admitted at the beginning, that is generally considered anomalous. Anomalous first because the translation was so early, because it had so little afterlife, because the history of translated literature would really start from scratch two decades after this one-shot historical dead end. This is of course true, but if we take the lessons that Yokoyama's translation teaches and use them to interrogate more closely that later history, then the anomaly begins to seem somewhat overstated.

Just two more anecdotes, then, before getting to the numbers. I would like to consider six books published between the 1880s and the first decade of the twentieth century. Only six books out of some seven hundred translated during the Meiji period: not an overwhelming number by any stretch of the imagination, but enough perhaps to extend the range of questions we might ask. Rarely do Meiji translations explain the history of their own production; but on occasion, something of that history emerges. Two translations of novels by William Le Queux, the master of the Edwardian spy novel, were published in Tokyo in 1908, and each reveals something of how the translator ended up with the novel and how he came to translate it. Ike Setsurai, the translator of Le Queux's *England's Peril*, mentions in his preface that he encountered the book first during a trip to French Indochina. He was onboard a ship named the *Hanoi* traveling from Hong Kong to Haiphong when he happened to glance through several European novels in his cabin. Le Queux's novel piqued his interest and appealed to his sense of adventure, so Setsurai translated it himself after his return and sent a copy of another of Le Queux's novels, *Confessions of a Ladies Man*, to his friend and protégé, Ikuta Kizan, who in turn translated it. Late in 1908, these two spy novels joined an ever growing group of detective fictions and sentimental and adventure novels flooding the Meiji literary market and like so many others would have seeped seamlessly into the great mass of translated literature had they not revealed in their prefaces something of how they came to be translated.

The other four books all appeared at the end of the 1880s from the publisher Hi'edô. Like the Le Queux translations, these novels are unremarkable save that each mentions in its preface that it was obtained by an F. Yano from an acquaintance in Singapore, a Mr. Joseph Clark. F. Yano turns out to be Yano Fumio, better known by his pen name Yano Ryûkei, a pioneer of political fiction in the 1870s and a prominent journalist. Joseph Clark of Singapore remains a bit of a mystery and is probably bound to remain one. Indeed, each time one tries to chart the history of a translated book one runs up against a sort of "Joseph Clark," an enigma that will not yield to historical scrutiny. But if we accept these limitations and instead focus on what we can learn about the social life of these texts, we can begin to piece together a partial but richly suggestive history. When we map, in real historical space, the geography that emerges from the prefaces and introductions to these novels, something of that history begins to emerge. Hong Kong, Singapore, French Indochina, or, in the case of *Robinson Crusoe*, the Dutch East Indies: we are no longer dealing with Japan and the West but a complex and meandering history marked by the great ports-of-call of the colonial world. Partha Chatterjee once likened European "reason" to a parasite that has "traveled the world piggyback, carried across oceans and continents by colonial powers eager to find new grounds for trade, extraction and the productive expansion of capital."[5] Well, the European novel seems to have traveled in much the same way. Edward Said's work has long suggested the importance of the "imaginary geography" of imperialism to the history of the European novel; here we come up against the real historical geography of the European novel in the nineteenth century, and not surprisingly it too bears an intimate relation to the geography of imperial expansion and power. This history is of course effaced once the novel appears in translation, and all of the mediation and complexity disappear behind the relationship that the translation bears to the original work. But if we want to situate the history of translation historically, then we must think in ways that are not bounded by dualisms such as Japan and the West, original and reproduction.

––––––––

Writing in the nineteen twenties and pondering the question of "why Italian books are not read . . . why they are considered 'boring' and foreign books 'interesting,' " Antonio Gramsci suggested that Italian literature was "subject to a foreign hegemony".[6] And, as Franco Moretti's recent work on literary markets in nineteenth-century Europe has argued, Italy was not alone—most

––––––––

[5] Partha Chatterjee, *Nationalist Thought and the Colonial World* (Minneapolis: University of Minnesota Press, 1996), 168.

[6] Antonio Gramsci, *Selections from Cultural Writings* (Cambridge: Harvard University Press, 1991), 348–49.

of southern, central and eastern Europe were under a sort of foreign literary hegemony, an almost total dominance by English and French novels: "in the crucial century between 1750 and 1850 the consequence of centralization [of the literary market] is that in most European countries the majority of novels are, quite simply, *foreign books*. Hungarian, Italian, Danish, Greek readers familiarize themselves with the new form through French and English novels: and so inevitably, French and English novels become *models to be imitated*."[7] It does not take a great leap of imagination to add to Hungary, Italy, and Denmark, India, China, and Japan, extending Moretti's argument beyond Europe.

Indeed, perhaps the most striking feature of nineteenth-century literary history and particularly of what Michael Valdez Moses has called "the global history of the novel"[8] is a sort of great "centralization" across much of the globe. This is where quantitative methods become important. By treating books as *things*, quantitative data allows access to a comparative dimension of literary history that is difficult when anecdote remains the primary mode of investigation. There is no doubt that numbers flatten out the peculiarities and individuality of their objects, but this is also part of their value, they "simplify the better to come to grips with their subject"[9] and so make accessible—through patterns and series—solutions to problems that are virtually inaccessible through the methods of traditional literary history.

Figure 1, the "rise of the novel," is based on the index to the Meiji period collection of the National Diet Library in Tokyo, and it charts the number of titles published over time for three categories: reprints of early modern (Edo) fiction, literary translations, and modern novels written in Japanese.[10] Not many surprises perhaps. After a slow start, the Japanese novel takes off, and reprints of the previous dominant form—early modern fiction—sharply drop after an initial period of dominance. But where are foreign books in all of this? This is where it gets interesting, because foreign literature never achieves—numerically at least—the sort of hegemonic position described by Gramsci. A few points: the last time there are more foreign novels published in Japan than Japanese novels is 1885; the first time there are more foreign

---

[7] Franco Moretti, *Atlas of the European Novel* (London: Verso, 1998), 187; emphasis in the original.

[8] See Michael Valdez Moses, *The Novel and the Globalization of Culture* (Oxford: Oxford University Press, 1995).

[9] Fernand Braudel, "History and the Social Sciences: The *Longue Durée*," in *On History* (Chicago: University of Chicago Press, 1980), 51.

[10] Kokuritsu Kokkai Toshokan, *Meijiki kankô tosho mokuroku* (Tokyo: Kokkai Toshokan, 1989).

FIGURE 1. THE RISE OF THE NOVEL

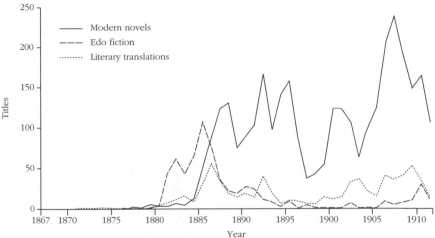

novels than reprints of early modern fiction is 1893; and the largest portion of the total number of titles that translations make is 36 percent in 1904—not insignificant, to be sure, but far from hegemonic. So the first thing that numbers tell us is that the tremendous stress laid on the importance of translated novels in literary histories of modern Japan is overstated. This is perhaps not surprising when we recall how in his pioneering work on the history of mentalities in Meiji Japan, Irokawa Daikichi argued that because most cultural and intellectual history has been written "with intellectuals at the center," "to say that modern Japan suffered to an abnormal degree from an inferiority complex or anxiety about the West does not imply that those feelings were shared by the entire nation."[11] What Irokawa's work has shown is that this stress on inferiority and "anxiety" has tended to misunderstand and misrepresent the cultural history of Meiji Japan.

Figure 2, "the novels of industrial capitalism," is based on Takuma Izuko's chronology of translations in the *Meiji hon'yaku bungakushû* and breaks down the translated novels by country of origin, contrasting those from England and France—the "core" in Moretti's formulation—with those of the rest of the world, the semiperipheral and peripheral countries.[12] What is so suggestive about this graph is not that British and French imports so totally dominate the early years of the Meiji period—this we might have

---

[11] Irokawa Daikichi, *The Culture of the Meiji Period* (Princeton, N.J.: Princeton University Press, 1985), 75.

[12] *Meiji hon'yaku bungakushû* (Tokyo: Chikuma shobô, 1972), 411–35.

FIGURE 2. THE MEIJI TRANSLATION INDUSTRY: THE NOVELS
OF INDUSTRIAL CAPITALISM

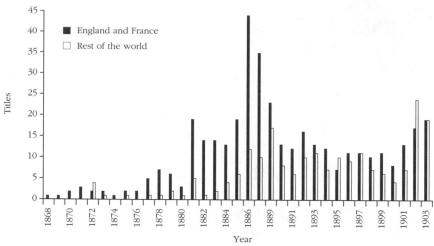

expected—but that they do not in the later years. To be sure, only once do these peripheral and semiperipheral imports attain an absolute majotity—1902—but the total dominance, the "hegemony," of the British and French ends in the late 1880s. Pierre Bourdieu writes of the emergence of a "dualist" structure in the literary market of late nineteenth-century France;[13] well, something similar seems to happen in the Meiji translation market. What I mean will become clear if we turn to figure 3—keeping the first two figures in mind. This graph plots the first 240 titles from the national diet library index. Here, the translations are broken down by genre and price rather than by country, but a very similar pattern emerges: uniformity in the first half of the Meiji period and diversity in the second. Taken together, the second and third graphs are quite striking: through the late 1880s, the market for translations is dominated almost entirely by British and French novels; after 1890 or so there are considerably more imports from Russia, Scandinavia, central and southern Europe and also proportionately more poetry, drama, and essays. And when we turn back to the first graph, we see that this great mass of translations form a sort of basso continuo beneath Japanese novels, mimicking the larger swings of these domestic products but—numerically—never challenging for hegemony. The graph seems to suggest that once the Japanese

---

[13] See Pierre Bourdieu, *The Rules of Art* (Stanford, Calif.: Stanford University Press, 1996), 47–173.

FIGURE 3. A DUALIST STRUCTURE

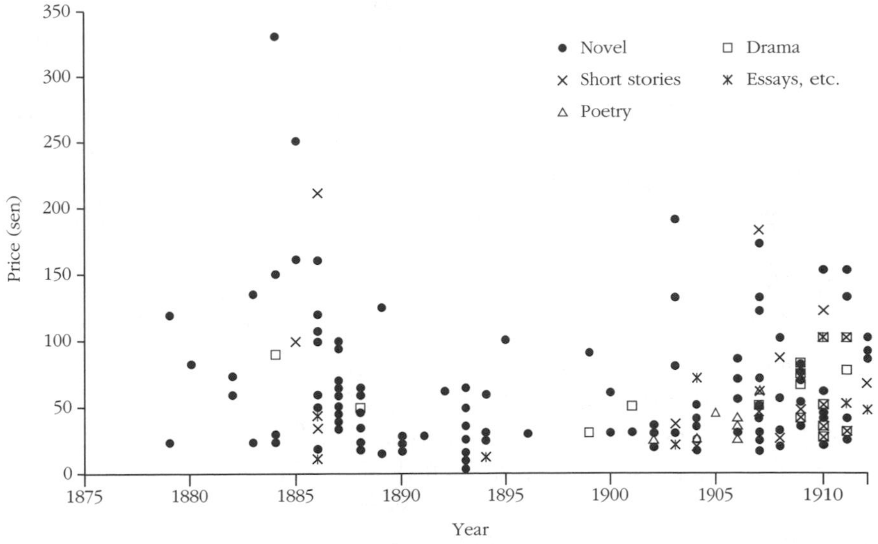

novel attains dominance circa 1890, translated literature becomes a sort of niche market catering to various curiosities and tastes but no longer wooing the hearts of the mass of the reading public. In this context we can see the rise of Shirakaba after 1910. A dualist structure indeed.

Two significant trends emerge when we consider translated works quantitatively: the first is that these translations are part of a much larger market; the second is that in the late Meiji period we seem not to be dealing with a single market but with two markets, or a fractured market. Certainly, it will be objected, hegemony is not something easily quantified: does it take 75 percent, 60 percent, or a simple absolute majority? And then again, sheer quantity does not speak to the quality of the encounter. Numbers are blind to the depth and strength of hegemony. Even Irokawa, who is suspicious of an overemphasis on elites and intellectuals, persists in describing Japan's encounter with the West as "traumatic and disruptive to a degree that is rarely found in the history of cultural intercourse."[14] Surely, these numbers do not tell the whole story, or worse yet they conceal something very important.

Rather than attempt to mitigate what the numbers suggested with any number of anecdotal accounts of the "trauma" of the encounter between

---

[14] Irokawa, *The Culture of the Meiji Period*, 51.

Japan and the West, we might gain a greater purchase on this encounter, so long misunderstood, if we are willing to take the numbers seriously and not attempt to explain them away or make excuses. Because, for all the limitations of quantitative history, its great strength, as François Furet has argued, is in the revision of "traditional general periodizations" and the "calling in question the old postulate that all elements of a society follow a homogeneous and identical evolution."[15] And this is really what the numbers suggest: "a plurality of social times."[16] And so we need not get rid of the trauma and all of the anxiety and inferiority that accompany it but simply displace it a bit and specify its parameters. The sort of cultural anxiety of which the Shirakaba writers are such a wonderful example did exist; but as Irokawa suggests the history of anxiety is a history of elites and intellectuals. The great mass of detective novels and tear-jerkers translated over the Meiji period betray no hint of unease, and it is difficult to imagine the Meiji reader as overcome by trauma and self-doubt while consuming William Le Queux, Edmond de Amicis, and Jules Verne. No, for most, the West was not first encountered at the level of ideology or institution but at the level of the pot-boiler.

———

Toward the beginning of *Capital*, in the section on "The Fetishism of the Commodity and Its Secret," Marx notes that political economists "are fond of Robinson Crusoe stories."[17] So it seems fitting to bring this Robinson Crusoe story to conclusion by thinking about what the political economist might have to teach us about literary history, that is to say by thinking about books as commodities participating in a literary market. Here, material history meets historical materialism in an effort not just to trace the social life of things but also to understand their logic and historical significance. First two brief passages from *Capital*: "The commodity is, first of all, an external object, a thing," Marx writes, "which through its qualities satisfies human needs of whatever kind. The nature of these needs, whether they arise, for example, from the stomach, or the imagination, makes no difference."[18]

---

[15] François Furet, "Quantitative History," in *In the Workshop of History* (Chicago: University of Chicago Press, 1984), 53 and 49.

[16] See Braudel, "History and the Social Sciences," 26.

[17] Karl Marx, *Capital: Volume 1* (London: Penguin, 1990), 169.

[18] Ibid., 125.

And, a little further on, he describes commodities as "social hieroglyphics," as "sensuous things which are at the same time suprasensible or social."[19] It is probably not necessary for our purposes to dwell at length on Marx's language, but the rich suggestiveness of his idiom is no doubt apparent. Because at the same time Marx stresses the physical dimensions of the commodity—its thingness—he also locates this physical thing within a web of social interaction, indeed of social meaning.

For Marx, of course, Crusoe's island is a preeminent example of a non-commodity economy, a form of production with no social dimension. But the history of Robinson Crusoe as a novel suggests that despite this stance at the narrative or discursive level, historically the book itself was participating in an ever expanding web of commodity production and distribution—both as part of "the global history of the novel" and eventually as part of a dynamic literary market domestic to Japan. In *The Modern Prince*, Gramsci writes that "in historical reality" the hegemonic relation of forces tends to be mixed "horizontally and vertically so to speak—according to economic and social activities (horizontally) and according to territory (vertically), combining and splitting up differently."[20] Gramsci's language is almost an exact model in theory of what is empirically suggested by the anecdotal and quantitative evidence of the literary market of nineteenth-century Japan—a highly complex system with both such horizontal and vertical dimensions. Literary history has to account for both of these historical dimensions although I have been suggesting from the beginning that they are in many ways very different projects. On the one hand, the literary historian would have to track down the "Joseph Clarks" of literary history and begin to map out a history of the European book trade in Asia of which Japan was a part. On the other hand, we would have to recognize that even by the time of the translation of *Robinson Crusoe* in 1857 there was already a complex literary market operative in Japan that, most scholars agree, was firmly established by the eighteenth century. What treating books as commodities allows us to do is to think at once along these two axes—the vertical and the horizontal—and so to begin to discover both the significance of the international book trade for the history of Japanese literature but also the significance of the Japanese book trade for the histories of other literatures. Because books are things but also more than things, they are commodities of the imagination.

---

[19] Ibid., 167 and 165.

[20] Antonio Gramsci, *The Modern Prince and Other Writings* (New York: International Publishers, 1992), 170.

That so often the consumption of these commodities was shared by readers in Europe and India, China and Japan should give us pause and lead us away from the binary and traumatic models of the cultural intercourse of nation-centered literary history and toward a more integrated and comparative history of the European novel in nineteenth-century Asia.

WENDY GRISWOLD

Nigeria, 1950–2000

The Nigerian novel emerged in the last half of the twentieth century, although there have been novels written in Nigeria and by Nigerians since the 1920s. Nigeria became independent from the British in 1960, so the genre is largely postcolonial. From halting beginnings in the 1950s and 1960s, Nigerian novel production exploded in the 1970s and early 1980s. Its growth faltered during the "oil bust" era following the mid-1980s, but the absolute numbers remain impressive. In the five decades following the appearance of Amos Tutuola's *The Palm-Wine Drinkard* in 1952, Nigerians have published well over five hundred novels. A Nigerian novelist, Ben Okri, has won the Booker Prize for *The Famished Road*; another novelist/playwright, Wole Soyinka, has won the Nobel Prize for Literature; and a third, Chinua Achebe, is universally recognized as Africa's premier writer. Mass-audience thrillers, romances, and pornography abound as well. No other sub-Saharan African nation has anything approaching the sheer size of Nigeria's literary production. Economic and political instability, however, have stunted the development of a popular Nigerian reading culture.

What Counts as a Nigerian Novel?

An effort to chart the emergence of the Nigerian novel must begin with definitions: what counts as a novel, and what counts as a Nigerian novel? The robust pamphlet literature of the post–World War II decades, the production of which was centered in Onitsha in the eastern region, makes the first question a difficult one. Returning soldiers, newly and sometimes barely literate, scraped together enough money to buy small printing presses and began turning out advice manuals and fiction for youth like themselves. Some of these Onitsha market pamphlets were sufficiently long as to be called novels, and a number of writers who would later be novelists of a less ambiguous sort got their start this way (Obiechina 1972).

"The novel" is usually understood to be a written work of fiction that is of some considerable length, so as a practical matter one may use number of pages to help define the Nigerian novel. A cutoff point of sixty pages—slightly more restrictive than the UNESCO definition of a book (forty-nine pages)—eliminates most, though not all, of the market pamphlets. Length is not the only criterion, however, for one must draw the line between books meant for children and those meant for adults. In Nigeria, literacy rates are higher for younger cohorts, and many people report having the leisure to read fiction only in their youth, so many novelists aim at that somewhat ill-defined category known as "young adults." In speaking of the Nigerian novel, it seems reasonable to set the age of intended readership as senior secondary school or above. Novels do not always signal their intended readers, but physical cues are common: sometimes novels indicate their intended audience on their covers or include study questions or extensive illustrations for children. These works are excluded from consideration here.

A prose fiction of significant length written for adults or young adults: this is a novel. As for what is a *Nigerian* novel, the key issue is language. With a population of about 120 million people, Nigeria is far and away the largest country in Africa. Nigerians speak an estimated 250 distinct languages (some counts go up to 400), with the three major languages—Hausa, Yoruba, and Igbo—each spoken by millions of people. Novels have been written in all three and in a number of minority languages as well. These works are accessible only to members of that ethnic group, however, and not always to them; writers often remark that they can write in English more easily than they can in their first languages. Moreover, very few novels in Nigerian languages have actually seen the light of day, not only because of their difficulty but because Nigerian authors aim at a pan-Nigerian audience. Unlike poetry and drama, novels are fundamentally commercial and have been from the start, in Nigeria as elsewhere. Authors tend to regard writing fiction in anything other than English as an indulgence.

So the Nigerian novel is fiction of sixty or more pages, intended for adults or near-adults, and written in English by someone born in or a permanent resident of Nigeria. A study of 476 of these novels constitutes the data for the following analysis (Griswold 2000).

Publishing History

Using this definition of the Nigerian novel, most people inside Nigeria and outside regard Amos Tutuola's *The Palm-Wine Drinkard*, published by Faber and Faber in 1952, to be the first Nigerian novel. Some experts regard this book as more of a strung-together collection of West African folktales than as a novel proper (Lindfors 1975). This viewpoint would give primacy to Cyprian Ekwensi's *People of the City*, which Andrew Dakers brought out in 1954 (Tutuola had a second book that year as well). Both Tutuola and Ekwensi were published in London, as were virtually all Nigerian novels

FIGURE 1. NOVELS BY YEAR AND PLACE OF PUBLICATION
(THREE-YEAR MOVING AVERAGE)

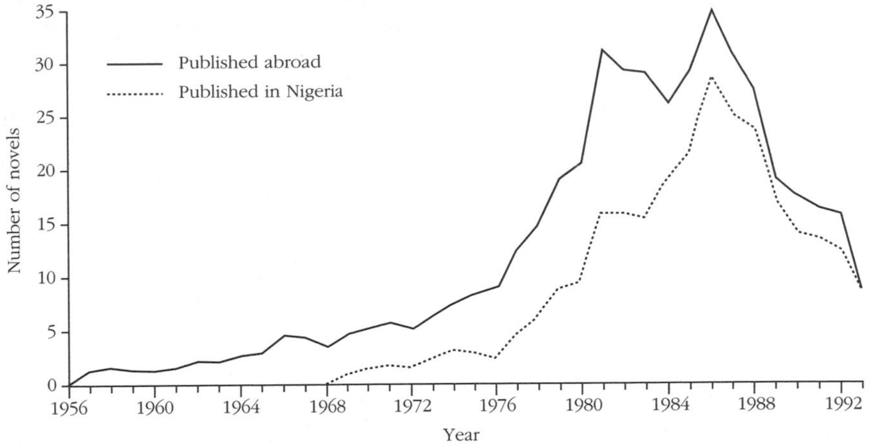

Wendy Griswold, "Bearing Witness," © *2000 Princeton University Press. Reprinted by permission of Princeton University Press.*

that came out from the 1950s through the early 1970s; a noteworthy exception was T. M. Aluko's *One Man, One Wife*, which he published himself in Lagos in 1959. Aluko is an exception that proves the rule, however, for his next six novels were all published in London by Heinemann, who brought out a new edition of *One Man, One Wife* as well. Figure 1 shows the British publishing dominance during the Nigerian novel's early years.

Only a half dozen years after independence, Nigeria was embroiled in political and ethnic conflicts. Coups, assassinations, and violence against the Igbos living in the north led to the secession of the eastern region, which proclaimed itself to be the Republic of Biafra. The civil war (1967–70) that followed, in which as many as a million people died, interrupted the rise of the Nigerian novel, especially insofar as many of the emerging Igbo writers like Chinua Achebe and Cyprian Ekwensi were caught up in the Biafran cause. Biafra lost the war and was reunited with Nigeria. The cease-fire was barely over when Nigeria entered the OPEC-generated oil boom era of the 1970s. This period was one of high hopes (and horrendous waste), and Nigerian authors and readers anticipated the long-awaited coming of a reading culture.

Educational reforms of the late 1970s seemed to promise an ever-growing number of new readers. British publishers took notice. Heinemann already dominated quality African literature with its African Writers Series, edited by Chinua Achebe since 1962. Macmillan launched a new series called

Pacesetters that was directed at the African youth market in general but focused primarily on Nigeria. At the same time Nigerian publishers sprang up
to compete with the British. New publishing operations of the late 1970s included Spectrum, Onibonoje, and Fagbamigbe; much of the new publishing
was centered in the western region, particularly in Ibadan. In addition to
general fiction these publishers created a number of local romantic and
crime series to attract the market of new readers to the likes of Spectrum's
"Panti Street Crime" series or Fagbamigbe's "Eagle Romances." Figure 1
shows that by the early 1980s Nigerian publishers had overtaken British
ones in number of titles published, as a percentage of the total.

Hopes for an ever-expanding book market and the advent of a reading
culture, along with so many other hopes in Nigeria, were dashed in the oil
bust that began in the early 1980s. The book market collapsed. British publishers backed off, as Nigerians could no longer afford books. Pacesetters,
for example, continued to publish books for the African youth, but the
number of Nigerian authors and settings plummeted. Nigerian publishers
hung on, some of them at least, but often precariously. A few wealthy authors like Flora Nwapa and Ken Saro-Wiwa were able to finance their own
publishing operations. Other people of means published a single novel at
their own expense, distributing it among their friends and leaving it to pile
up at academic stalls in markets. But for young authors trying to get established, the lack of publishing outlets has been deeply discouraging.

Some British publishers continued to publish Nigerian authors. Most
visible was Heinemann, whose African Writers Series had become (and remains) the benchmark for African literature in English. Now such publishers aimed at American and European markets, including university-level
African and world literature courses, expatriate Africans, and the handful of
Western intellectuals interested in postcolonial literature. This type of foreign publisher has been a lifesaver for established authors and for writers
with London contacts, like Ben Okri. Such high-end publishing does not
benefit formulaic writers of thrillers and romances; it has been the lowbrow
fiction—the light reading that sustains a reading culture—that has atrophied
under the oil bust era.

Authors

The question of who counts as a Nigerian author is a reasonable one to pose.
A number of writers born in Nigeria have lived much of their lives outside
the country. Buchi Emecheta and Ben Okri are well-known examples, and
both Chinua Achebe and Wole Soyinka, Nigeria's most celebrated writers,

have spent large amounts of their adult lives abroad. And a few novelists living in Nigeria were not actually born there. The late May Ellen Ezekiel, romance novelist and editor of the Nigerian women's magazine *Classique*, was born in Ghana. Rosina Umelo has lived in Nigeria for decades but was born a white Briton. And what about children of Nigerians born or raised abroad? As a rule of thumb, Nigerian birth, citizenship, or permanent residence seem to sketch out a family resemblance that can be used to define the "Nigerian author." This excludes children of Nigerians born and raised abroad; such second-generation immigrants are more properly considered, to take the most typical instances, British or American writers. The population of 476 novels that serves as the basis for this discussion were written by 261 authors. Most of these people have written but a single novel, yet a few have been extremely prolific. The top producer has been Buchi Emecheta, who published her thirteenth novel, *The New Tribe*, in November 2000.

Even when neither residence nor birth raise any questions about including someone as a Nigerian author, such authors cannot be said to "represent" Nigeria. The simplest statistical analysis confirms what every Nigerian reader suspects: a few tribes and regions dominate Nigerian fiction, while others are all but absent. Like a number of countries in the center of Africa, Nigeria divides between a largely Christian south and a largely Muslim north. It has hundreds of different ethnic groups, with three large ones dominating the three regions into which the Niger and Benue Rivers divide the country: Yoruba in the southwest, Hausa in the north, and Igbo in the southeast.

If the novelists came from a representative cross-section of their society, about half of them would be from the north and about half would be Muslim. Nigerian novelists, however, are overwhelmingly southern (80 percent, with another 10 percent from the middle belt) and Christian (81 percent). Table 1 shows how one tribal group, the Igbo, has dominated Nigerian writing, while the Hausa have been conspicuously absent. This creates a paradox, for while authors and publishers intend that the "Nigerian novel" be accessible to all Nigerians, it does not reflect the experience of all Nigerians. There was never any tradition of the Igbo novel, but as the Nigerian novel has developed, especially via British publication, it has been the development of the Igbo novel as well.

Although the novelists offer a very imperfect representation of tribe, region, and religion, the representation of gender is even more skewed. Only 15 percent of Nigerian novelists are women.[1] This statistic is more meaningful

---

[1] Based on 246 novelists whose sex is known. These women have written 17 percent of the novels.

TABLE 1. ETHNICITY OF THE NIGERIAN POPULATION AND OF NIGERIAN
NOVELISTS (PERCENTAGES)

Ethnicity	Population 1952–53	Population 1963[a]	Nigerian novelists[b]
Hausa-Fulani	28.1	29.5	5
Yoruba	16.1	20.3	34
Igbo	17.9	16.6	49
Other	37.4	33.6	12
N	30.4 million	55.7 million	200

Source: Griswold (2000).

[a] The 1963 census figures are suspect, and many regard the 1952–53 census to be the last relatively accurate count. The most recent census, 1991, did not ask about ethnicity.

[b] Of 261 Nigerian novelists, I only know the ethnicity of 200.

when compared with the situation in the West. A random sample of fiction published in the United States in 1988 found that 39 percent of the authors were women, and this probably underrepresented women authors because the data source, the *American Book Publishing Record*, did not include formulaic romances (Griswold and Hull 1998). And the picture is even more discouraging than the percentage suggests, because women's participation has remained stuck at about 20 percent since the 1970s.

Nigerians often refer to "first-generation authors," those writers who began their careers in the colonial or early postcolonial periods. Dividing the authors by generations underlines the fact that there have been three cohorts coming into their writing careers with radically different sets of expectations. The first generation was the product of missionary education. Overwhelmingly Igbo, these were the men, and a single woman (Flora Nwapa), who published fiction, usually in Britain, by the time of the civil war. They tended to be educators or civil servants; many were directly involved in the Biafran cause; and they established the African Writers Series. The best-known Nigerian authors like Achebe and Soyinka, and some of the most prolific ones like Cyprian Ekwensi and Amos Tutuola, were from this generation.

The second generation included writers who began publishing after the end of the war in 1970. This was the optimistic oil-boom generation, whose hopes were shaped by the optimism of that decade, the sense that they were "New Nigerians," modern men and women who had moved beyond the restrictions of tribe, the educational disadvantages, and the enforced poverty of the colonial era. Many of these writers published in Nigeria, with some involved in setting up publishing houses locally. Others, like Kalu Okpi, helped launch the Pacesetters series. They often had careers in the media or one of the professions.

The high hopes of this group gave way to the disillusion of the third generation, whose writing careers began in the oil bust years of the mid-1980s. Third-generation writers have no expectation of earning their living from writing. They have had to struggle, like most middle-class Nigerians, and their careers have often been patchy ones involving different enterprises. Without a Pacesetters or African Writers Series to support the most talented, few of them have been able to write more than one or two books unless they were able, like Ken Saro-Wiwa, to publish their own books independently. One way to distinguish among the three generations is to listen to what they have to say about the coming of a "reading culture" in Nigeria. The first generation expected a reading culture to arrive soon, the second generation believed they were midwives to its emergence, while the third generation no longer believes they will see a reading culture in their lives.

Readers

Nigerian readers tend to be southern, Christian, educationally and economically advantaged, urban, young, and in many cases based outside of Nigeria. This southern and Christian bias has been the case since the colonial period, and despite massive educational initiatives, it does not seem to have changed much (Schmidt 1965; Griswold 2000).

Northern Muslims are culturally conservative and suspicious about reading fiction, and many northern women lack sufficient education to read for pleasure. Southerners—Igbos, Christian Yorubas, and minority tribes—are more enthusiastic about reading novels, but the high cost of books and the poor state of libraries discourages the development of the reading habit. Nonetheless, an avid reading class exists—people who pass books around, make heavy use of libraries at the British Institutes, buy books when they travel abroad, and read whatever they can get their hands on.

The immense economic pressure felt by the middle class since the 1980s has reduced the leisure time available for fiction. It is often said that men read nonfiction for self-improvement, while women are too busy with family responsibilities to read much of anything. The people with the time and inclination to read fiction are the secondary and university students. Authors and publishers aim at this market. They especially love to see their books become "set books" required for exams, as this is the only way of actually making money on a literary work.

TABLE 2. NIGERIAN NOVELS BY GENRE

Genre	Number	Percentage of total
Crime	104	22
Romance	67	14
Village	61	13
Women and men	50	11
Politics	44	9
Intellectuals	40	8
City	34	7
Civil war	29	6
Other (cannot be categorized)	47	10
Total	476	100

Themes

Like Western fiction, much Nigerian fiction is formulaic—crime thrillers and romances. A rough thematic breakdown of Nigerian fiction is presented in table 2. To interpret these percentages it is helpful to know how they compare with Western fiction. Of the 1988 sample mentioned previously, 25 percent were crime novels, virtually identical. Only 10 percent were formulaic romances—these were undercounted—but it was nevertheless the second-largest category (Griswold and Hull 1998). Aside from the formulas, Nigerian novels were more political (only 2 percent of the American novels centered on politics) and less centered on religion (5 percent of the American novels had a religious focus). The number of political novels and novels treating social problems has been increasing, as third-generation authors have tried to consider the consequences of Nigeria's failed republics and recurrent military regimes.

The sociological characteristics of the Nigerian novel, while mediated by individual creativity, have some bearing on the thematic content of the fiction. A few examples of the relationship include the following:

1. Most Nigerian novels have urban settings, not the village settings made familiar in *Things Fall Apart*. Novels published in Britain are far more likely to use village settings than novels published in Nigeria, and this preference is holding steady. Thus Westerners, who have British novels more readily available, tend to assume that the precolonial or rural setting is typical. In fact, however, Nigerian novels are far more likely to feature traffic jams in Lagos, a boss's assaults on his secretary's virtue, or how urban youth confront temptations to easy money through crime.

2. Political novels, on the other hand, are disproportionately more likely to be published in Nigeria than in Britain, and the overall number of political novels is increasing. These two findings—village novels published and known in the West, political novels published and known in Nigeria—support Nigerian suspicions that Western readers take a highly romantic view of African life and are relatively uninterested in present-day struggles.

3. While it may be generally the rule that the history of war is told by the winners, this has not been the case in Nigeria. The Igbo have written a stunning 85 percent of the civil war novels; the fictional treatment of this war is being told by its losers. There are two reasons for this: the direct impact the war had on the Igbo (it was fought on their territory, and the entire population was mobilized) and the literary dominance the Igbo had established before the war. Aiming for a broad market, Igbo authors are circumspect, writing about microlevel war experiences and rarely discussing the structural cleavages or political causes of the war.

4. Unlike the case in the West, men have written more than half of Nigerian romance novels. Men and women write differently about love, however. Most women tell a story of a continuous relationship overcoming obstacles, following the Western formula. Only a third of the men use this pattern, however. Male-authored romances are more apt to follow the circular pattern, whereby the protagonist has another relationship before returning to the first love, or the sequential pattern, whereby the protagonist has a series of love relationships. This gender-based difference persists even though the romances are packaged as a single series (for example, Spectrum's "Sunshine Romances" or Fourth Dimension's "Heart to Heart"), suggesting that men and women have strikingly different constructions of romantic love. Both sexes write about specifically African issues, including infertility, the pain caused by polygamous marriages, and problematic in-laws demanding more grandchildren.

A Reading Class without a Reading Culture

Nigerian literature is not only an example of globally disseminated world literature but is to a considerable extent better known outside Nigeria than within it. The works of authors like Ben Okri (winner of the Booker Prize and based in London) and Buchi Emecheta (also a Londoner during her adult life, and the most prolific Nigerian novelist) are more readily available by far in New York or Toronto than in Ibadan or Kano. Foreign readers of this Nigerian literature exhibit a preference for serious literature and for novels set in villages and in the past. Meanwhile, Nigerian authors are determined to write about contemporary social and political problems at home—to "bear witness" to corruption, military arrogance, ethnic conflict, and the dislocations of urban life—but they hve difficulty getting their books published and distributed within Nigeria.

Popular fiction in Nigeria inclines toward crime and politics. These are topics of enormous concern to the Nigerian middle class, but that middle class has shrunk dramatically since the 1970s. Furthermore, its members are finding it increasingly difficult to find the money or time for novels. In Nigeria we find the persistence of a reading class in the absence of a reading culture, and there is little evidence that this reading class is growing or a reading culture emerging.

The collapse of a reading market makes this class's modernist dream— writers engaging contemporary social issues, literature as adjunct to nation building—ever more elusive. At the turn of the millennium, the restoration of democracy in 1999 and the recent rise of oil prices is giving Nigerian authors, publishers, and members of the reading class renewed reason for optimism about the future of the Nigerian novel and its role in both instructing and entertaining.

References

Griswold, Wendy. 2000. *Bearing Witness: Readers, Writers, and the Nigerian Novel.* Princeton, N.J.: Princeton University Press.

Griswold, Wendy, and Kathleen Hull. 1998. "The Burnished Steel Watch: What a Sample of a Single Year's Fiction Indicates." In *The Empirical Study of Literature and the Media*, ed. Susanne Janssen and Nel van Dijk. Rotterdam: Barjesteh van Waalwijk van Doorn.

Lindfors, Bernth, ed. 1975. *Critical Perspectives on Amos Tutuola*. Washington, D.C.: Three Continents Press.

Obiechina, E. N. 1972. *Onitsha Market Literature*. London: Heinemann.

Schmidt, Nancy. 1965. *An Anthropological Analysis of Nigerian Fiction*. Ph.D. diss., Northwestern University.

ALESSANDRO PORTELLI

The Sign of the Voice: Orality and Writing in the United States

Authority and Authenticity

Consider the following openings in two American epics, the first from Herman Melville's *Moby-Dick* in the midnineteenth century, the second from Don DeLillo's *Underworld* at the end of the millennium:

> Call me Ishmael. Some years ago—never mind how long precisely—having little or no money in my purse, and nothing particular to interest me on shore, I thought I would sail about a little and see the watery part of the world.[1]

> He speaks in your voice, American, and there's a shine in his eye that's halfway hopeful.[2]

The United States was born out of *writing*. During the colonial era, the relationship between the Puritan "city on the hill" and biblical Jerusalem, between the earthly history of the new colonies and the history of the holy people of Israel, was clearly modeled after the holy scriptures. On a political level, the royal *charter* sanctioned the colonists' autonomy and defined its terms. With the War of Independence, the birth of the nation was sanctioned by the first constitution ever written. It was drafted in such a way as to guarantee its impersonality and timelessness. This all happened in an Enlightened climate that instituted a direct relationship between reason and writing.[3] Authority, origin, order, certainty, and reason were thus entrusted to writing, paper, and the printing press.

And yet, these two texts both attempt to redefine America and the world through American eyes and both begin in the name of the voice. Melville's famous opening owes part of its effectiveness to its ingenious alliteration, and it integrates modes of orality in a dialogic appeal to the voice of the reader: it is the reader who must *call* the speaker Ishmael. But it is also

---

[1] H. Melville, *Moby-Dick* (1851) (Harmondsworth, 1988), 1.

[2] D. DeLillo, *Underworld* (1997) (London, 1999), 11.

[3] M. Warner, *The Letters of the Republic: Publication and the Public Sphere in Eighteenth-Century America* (Cambridge, Mass., 1990), 97–117.

worth noting the accurate indefiniteness—the negation of clarification and detail, the vagueness of that "watery part of the world," as if indefiniteness, fluidity, and the uncertainty of the oceans confines were already implicit in the voice's fluctuations.

And the text continues along these lines. The deixis (*"There* now is *your* insular city of the Manhattoes . . ."*) proceeds theatrically and thus implies the presence of a dialogue: a person who speaks, a person who listens, and a conversation. The deixis is intertwined with the imperative verb forms that address a dialogical and connotative appeal to an addressee ("But *look! here* come more crowds"), even to the point of inviting the reader to take it literally: "Tell me, does the magnetic virtue of the needles of the compasses of all those ships attract them thither?" The entire dialogue is sustained and scanned by the hum of anaphora and alliteration: "*Whenever* I find myself *growing grim* about the mouth; *whenever* it is a *damp, drizzly* November in my soul . . . a strong moral *principle to prevent* me from deliberately *stepping into the street.*" And again: "*C*ircumambulate the *c*ity of a dreamy *S*abbath afternoon. Go from *C*orlears Hook to *C*oenties Slip." This is a page in which sound, voice, and dialogue are evoked with a nearly maniacal obsession possible only in monologist writing that explores and pushes its limits by evoking its other: the voice.

The opening of *Underworld*, in turn, expressly evokes the beginning of *Moby-Dick*. The appeal to the reader in the second person makes an even more explicit reference to language and the act of speaking. Even here, the sentence pairs icastic efficiency with semantic indefiniteness: what does the word *American* mean? Is it an apposition (he speaks in your voice, the American language)? Or is it a vocative (hey you, American, he speaks in your voice)? Once again, only writing can use the voice in this manner: when we try to read a passage aloud, we are forced to intone and thus choose one of the two solutions. But writing has no intonation. It can contain both solutions and thus negate its destiny of discrete accuracy.

DeLillo continues to use Melvillian tones. In *Moby-Dick* the crowds converge at the sea. In DeLillo they converge at the stadium. The sea takes the place of Melville's "green fields" that have possibly been lost. In DeLillo they are now real and artificial fields of a baseball diamond. The piers wrapped around Manhattan in Melville are the iron and cement that fence in the stadium.[4] The crowd itself speaks, breathes, buzzes, and makes a deep

---

[4] If we keep reading, we find a Puerto Rican character who is called Ismael; we see the actress Jayne Mansfield defined as "a white whale"; and we suspect that the baseball, which everyone chases after and perhaps no one finds, is an equivalent of the white whale.

rumble: a primary, prelinguistic sound, anterior to articulation, alliterated, with Whitmanian echoes. "The crowd, the constant noise, the breath and hum, a basso rumble." And outside the stadium, the crowd also consists of voices, beginning with radio announcer Russ Hodges's voice: "Connected by the pulsing voice on the radio, joined to the word-of-mouth that passes the score along the street and to the fans who call the special number" (prologue, 19 and 32).

DeLillo looks for this American voice in the indefinable spaces—milk white, like the whale—of television screens and computer monitors, ancient faded pictures, ghostly presences, and the blinking oceans of the virtual universe. Melville chases a whale that runs like a *hooded phantom* through legends and oral storytelling and through wild, fabulous and strange *rumors* and *tales*. The elusive immateriality of the whale's whiteness is duplicated in the ghost and in the voice.

From the origins to the classical age of American literature, the figure of the ghost has been intertwined with that of the voice, like a "devil in the manuscript": from the "spectral evidence" of the Salem witch trials, to the headless phony ghost in the *Legend of Sleepy Hollow* by Washington Irving, reincarnated as the metaphorical ghost of Hawthorne who has been "decapitated" by the political system in *The Custom House* (preface to *The Scarlet Letter*, 1850), who "careering through the public prints, in my decapitated state, [was] like Irving's Headless Horseman; ghastly and grim, and longing to be buried."[5]

The figure of the ghost or specter has always been associated with the effects of the voice on the materiality of the real, and it has been made even more perturbing by the frequent association with decapitation, images of a revolution that has "decapitated" the state (echoes of Charles I and Louis XIV) and figures of a terrifying democracy with no head and with no visible center that has sprung from it. After all, the word *voice* also means "vote."

Therefore, the voice runs through the lines of texts and reports the crisis of political authority through the crisis of narrative authority. When Hawthorne announces that "the main facts of that story are authorized and authenticated by the document" (the manuscript discovered in the custom house), it is important not to forget that he has just said that the manuscript itself relies on "the oral testimony" of elderly persons who often tell their tales secondhand (*The Custom House*, 324, 323). Thus, every time the letter *A* (the beginning of all writings) appears in *The Scarlet Letter*, the narrative

---

[5] N. Hawthorne, *The Custom House*, introduction to *The Scarlet Letter* (1850), in *The Portable Hawthorne*, edited by M. Cowley (Harmondsworth, 1976), 335.

authority dissolves into myriad contrasting voices that put its meaning and its very existence into question. Symmetrically, after the final scene where "most of the spectators testified" that an *A* appeared on Dimmesdale's chest, "some affirmed" that he made it himself, and "certain persons" maintained that there had been no such mark, Hawthorne still ironically invokes a written source based on fluctuating orality: "The authority which we have chiefly followed—a manuscript of old date, drawn up from the verbal testimony of individuals" (541).

There is another missing "head" behind all of this: the origin. "Prior to the Revolution, there is a dearth of records," says Hawthorne, a veteran in custom house archive research (*The Custom House*, 320). At a historical moment when nation-states were searching for atavistic and ethnic origins that had been lost in the night of time in order to show that they had always existed, the United States pronounced itself to be a new reality, without a past, *constituted* by an act of writing. It is as if in this country founded on writing, writings had begun with its creation: there was nothing before—also because all that that there was before was something else (Europe's feudal past), threatening and blameful (witches and Indians). There was something comforting in the novel as a writing of the new (indeed, the *novel*).

"But the past was not dead," affirms Hawthorne in the custom house. And that which has died is destined to painfully return. It returns as a ghost, like Beloved in Toni Morrison's novel, with her head in a precarious balance on her fragile neck; and it returns as a voice. When America began to write novels, it found its narrative material amidst witches, ghosts, Indians, slaves, wars, and forests. Perhaps this is the reason that, as a long critical tradition has always maintained, America has less *novels* than *romances*, because the hum, the buzzing and the breath of a buried and repressed memory were there before the writings. The solid earth that supports us becomes fleeting and uncertain. Another Melvillian hero will see his life turned upside-down by the yell of a "voice that seems to come from under your great-grandfather's tomb."

The Shriek and the Stone

"Almost immediately following this sound, there came a sudden, long-drawn, unearthly, girlish shriek, from the further corner of the long, double room. Never had human voice so affected Pierre before. Though he saw not the person from whom it came, and though the voice was wholly strange to him, yet the sudden shriek seemed to split its way clean through his heart, and leave a yawning gap there."[6]

This is an early scene in *Pierre*, Herman Melville's complicated and controversial novel (1852). Offset by two household voices, this inhuman, feminine shriek erupts in the enchanted world of the young Pierre Glendinning and deals him an irremediable blow. Prior to this, we have read six chapters of idyllic bliss that prepare us for this moment. The shriek is inarticulate and incomprehensible. It is ghostly, and it confuses the confines and certainties of language ("but only in visible flesh, and audible breath, have I hitherto believed," 68). Ghosts and hooded phantoms again undermine the foundations of tangible reality: "He felt that what he had always before considered the solid land of veritable reality, was now being audaciously encroached upon by bannered armies of hooded phantoms, disembarking in his soul, as from flotillas of specter-boats" (73).[7]

Most read *Pierre* as philosophical allegory, but the effect of Isabel's shriek has a greater historical and metaliterary meaning that concerns the relationship between the historical foundations of the country and writing. Practically the first thing that we learn of Pierre is his family's proud patriotic heritage. The solidity of those foundations is implicit in the hero's very name: not Peter, but French—Pierre, meaning literally "stone" or "rock," the rock on which the churches and states were built. Pierre's great-grandfather, from whose tomb this voice seems to emanate, died heroically in a battle with the Indians; his grandfather was a hero of the Revolutionary War and of the war against the Indians. Although these bellicose and bloody origins could generate a sense of guilt and problems of legitimacy, such dilemmas are quickly resolved. The allusion to the marriage between Pocahontas and the ancestors of Southern farmers makes for an "underived" and "aboriginal" origin that has no origin. In particular, the writing's performative capacity has instituted a new order of law, once again without origin: "The Glendinning deeds by which their estate had so long been held, bore the ciphers of three Indian kings, the aboriginal and only conveyancers of those noble woods and plains" (12 and 5).

A *deed* is an "act," a writing that is also an action and a meeting place between language and concrete reality. The so-called rent-deeds for semifeudal properties in New York, like that owned by the Glendinnings, were granted "so long as grass grows and water runs; which hints of a surprising eternity

---

[6] H. Melville, *Pierre, or the Ambiguities* (1852), in *The Works of Herman Melville*, 16 vols. (rpt., New York: Russell and Russell, 1963), 9: 69. Hereafter cited by page number only.

[7] Melville had already described the whale as a "hooded phantom" in *Moby-Dick*.

for a deed, and seems to make lawyer's ink unobliterable as the sea" (12). Ink's eternity *seems* to connect the certainty of origin with the legitimization of the property and the certainty of the future. But up to what point can we trust it? After all, ink is a soluble liquid: we will soon see how Isabel's tears have the power to transform it into blood. And the book will end with a page of ephemeral invisible ink.[8]

In *The Scarlet Letter*, little Pearl is obsessed with the following question: "who made thee?" The Puritan authorities teach her that it was the Creator, but the question for her represents the mystery of her father and therefore, implicitly, the uncertainty of origin. In *Pierre*, Isabel's shriek reveals the sin of the father (in terms of both sexual transgression and of disloyalty and dissimulation, like Dimmesdale): Isabel is the illegitimate and unrecognized daughter of Pierre's father. The father/founder's sin brings with it a crisis of the meaning of the personal origins of Pierre and the collective origins of the country itself. It is as if Isabel's very existence revealed an entire illegitimate history that runs secretly underground and destabilizes the guarantees of an official written history. But before coming into being, the very writing itself erupts in the form of a voice in the textual order. In the end, the alliterated conclusion will be that "Pierre hath no paternity, and no past."

Writing is also a metaphor that supports the Glendinning's world as complete and stabile textuality: "So perfect to Pierre had long seemed the illuminated scroll of his life thus far, that only one hiatus was discoverable by him in that sweetly-writ manuscript. A sister had been omitted from the text" (6–7). Even long after Isabel's outburst, Pierre continues to think of himself and his life as a text: "Tear thyself open, and read there the confounding story of thy blind doltishness!" (239). He even looks for an "unraveled plot" in the mystery of Lucy (198), but he cannot find one because he has read too many novels and he is the prisoner of artificial and abstract narration.

The illegitimate sister interferes with Pierre's orderly world in the guise of inarticulation. Even when Isabel writes a letter, it is the exact opposite of the controlled order of writing: it is contaminated by her emotional state when she composed it—irregular, illegible, stained, torn, and almost bloody. The chemical reaction between the tears and the ink generates a "reddish hue— as if blood and not tears had dropped upon the sheet" (89).

No authority can be attributed to a writing of this nature. In and of itself, it is not proof, and Pierre tries to convince himself that it is a forgery. But he ends up in the uncertainty between two falsehoods: either the text he has in

---

[8] The ambiguity of the "Indian deed" as proof of legitimate ownership is also the subject of Hawthorne's *House of the Seven Gables* (1851).

his hands is false or the text of his family's and his nation's history is false. The single confirmation of the text's authenticity lies, paradoxically, in its correspondence to elusive and unverifiable oral narrations and family legends that "he had heard related by his elderly relations, some of them now dead." Hawthorne's manuscript presents the same situation: the authority of this written document can only be verified by the voices of semiforgotten dead persons.

His attempt to bring order to the situation is frustrated by writing's defeats. Printing does not guarantee the permanence of the word, nor the certainty of reason: this is proven by the "blurry ink" and the "sleazy" (that is, dirty and inconsistent) paper, and the missing final pages of the pamphlet, "Chronologicals and Horologicals." Handwriting, like that in Pierre's letter to his manservant Dates, is a disorderly and hurried "scrawl" that incorporates all the traits of orality: improvisation and composition in *performance* ("And then—let me see—then, my good Dates—why what then?" (260), parenthetical elements, anaphora, repetition, paratactical correction, and alliteration ("For that Fine Old Fellow, Dates"). It can even transform itself into voice: the last words are: "D'ye *hear*?"

Indeed, sound dominates the meeting with Isabel and the moment Pierre decides to leave his world and run away with her: "the stringed tongue of her guitar" and the "deep voice of the being of Isabel." If Pierre is a stone, then Isabel *is a bell*, sheer sound and prelinguistic vibrations.[9] Isabel's voice is not limited to upsetting the stone of origins, but it does evoke an ineffable and secret alternative origin that precedes both history and language. It erupts in the form of a pure shriek. And it reblossoms as a "low, sweet, half-sobbing voice of more than natural musicalness is heard." Ever uncertain by definition, Pierre and Pearl lose the certainty of their identities and their fathers' characters. Isabel begins the account of her life by announcing an even more essential absence: "I never knew a mortal mother." Isabel has no origin: she *is* origin.

Isabel's tale begins in a house inhabited by silences, ghosts, animal voices, and incomprehensible languages. It then moves to a house obsessed with the subterranean sounds of madness. And it culminates in every one of its narrative units with the injunction of silence. Isabel moves in a space that precedes the opposition of voice and writing. Her world is marked instead by

---

[9] She says that her name is abbreviated as Bell (177), but this never happens in the novel. At least once, her voice is described as a bell (" 'My, brother! . . .' pealed Isabel," 310). A propos names: I cannot avoid thinking that childless Pierre's last name plays on the paronomasia between Glendinning and *gelding*.

the opposition between articulated language and pure sound: in other words, the opposition of adherence to reason on one hand and emotions, passions, and instinct on the other—the whole tangle of inexpressible impulses that arise from the disproportionate distances of the infinite and the profound, from heaven and from the heart. She speaks through the "magical" music of her *mystic guitar* charged with "utter unintelligibleness, but . . . infinite significancies," "eternally incapable of being translated into words" (178 and 393). By intertwining perfect technique and total abandon, Isabel's music is a metaphor of art as performance and sound in a novel on art's failure as text and writing—of an art that is in the air and in the instrument, in a story of authorial ambition's failure.

Isabel's story relies on uncertainties, digressions, vagueness, and improvised storytelling. It is not "authorized and authenticated" by any document. The fact of "Isabel's sisterhood" to Pierre is merely "intuitively certain, however literally unproven" (195). *Literally* should be understood literally in this case (a typical Melvillian pun): there is no letter or text that proves her sisterhood. After all, the only sources are the aunt's "nebulous legend" and "Isabel's still more nebulous story" that create an "unpenetrable yet blackly significant nebulousness" around the father figure (248). The *storytelling* casts doubt on the basis of the tale itself and casts doubt on Pierre's doubt: "How did he know that Isabel was his sister?"

The shriek and Isabel's music disrupt documents and identities, but they do not offer any alternative order. This is conveyed in the final chapters, in which Pierre's story overlaps with the history of national identity. Book 17 begins with his refusal to respect the canonical order of documentation and chronology ("I write precisely as I please," he says with another pun: precisely without precision).[10] This is followed by a long parody of the literary establishment and the tools of printing, paper, ink, books, the relationship between writing and body, and the metaphorical relationship between life and biography (a nod to Franklin).

Like America, Pierre does not have enough biography to satisfy his editors, nor does he have a stable identity in his writing: "his signature did not possess that inflexible uniformity" (353). Without such a signature, no document could be deemed authentic by future readers. Writing affirms its authority in the name of invariance and immobility, but these are just illusions and conventions. In reality, literature itself is just an ephemeral pastime. Even the *sleazy* works of the celebrated (and alliterate) Plotinus Plinlimmon are poorly transcribed gossip.

---

[10] *Moby-Dick* begins: "never mind how long precisely."

The final catastrophe is announced by Isabel with another "thin, long shriek." The first had introduced disorder into the text of Pierre's life. The second shriek is like a last sign of life before order returns in the entropic guise of textualization and petrification: Pierre dies and becomes a stone (*petra*). In the arc of just a few lines from that shriek, Isabel is "petrified," and Lucy is a "marble girl." Then the prison is described as a "granite hell" with a "cumbersome stone ceiling," "stony roofs, and seven-fold stony skies." The last cynical line uttered by the turnkey also relates to stone: "Kill 'em both with one stone."[11] Symmetrically, voice and breath begin to fade with the asthmatic turnkey and Fred Tartan who rushes "wind-broken" to the prison, with Isabel's mournful groan and Pierre's last gasp. In the end, just as in the text that Pierre had ripped apart and called a mere *flatus vocis*, there is only silence: "one speechless clasp!—all's o'er!"

The order disrupted by Isabel's shriek has been finally sewn up again and recomposed in the only way possible: once her voice erupted in the book, her death was the only way to quiet it. And yet, even after the announcement of silence, the last voice that we hear is Isabel's: "All's o'er, and ye know him not!" (505).

Voices Off: Toward Huckleberry Finn

There was another memorable yell that was heard a few years prior to Isabel's, and it was accompanied by an equally memorable entrance, this time in Thomas B. Thorpe's, "The Big Bear of Arkansas" (1841):

> While I was thus busily employed in reading, and my companions were more busily still employed, in discussing such subjects as suited their humors best, we were most unexpectedly startled by a loud Indian whoop, uttered in the "social hall," that part of the cabin fitted off for a bar; then was to be heard a loud crowing, which would not have continued to interest us such sounds being quite common in that place of spirits had not the hero of these windy accomplishments stuck his head into the cabin, and hallooed out, "Hurra for the Big Bear of Arkansaw!"
>
> Then might be heard a confused hum of voices, unintelligible, save in such broken sentences as "horse," "screamer," "lightning is slow," et cetera.[12]

---

[11] Just before Isabel's last shriek, Pierre receives a rejection letter from his editors who sign with names of stones: Steel, Flint, and Asbestos.

[12] T. B. Thorpe, "The Big Bear of Arkansas" (1841), in W. J. Blair and R. I. McDavid Jr., eds., *The Mirth of a Nation* (Minneapolis, 1993), 30.

Once again, a yell has upset writing (and the order of educated conversation). There is something different in this case. The association between voice and ghost has indeed been evoked, but only to make fun of it: the *spirits* that generate the voices are those of whiskey, the ghost enters the "social hall" with his raggedy body, makes himself comfortable, and puts his feet up on the stove in the center of the room and at the center of the story. These are not nightmares from the past, but rather new flesh-and-blood subjects who invade the space of the text and the sphere of politics.

This is what always happens in frontier humor: "Quit yer kerd playin an' ritin, an' listen tu me" enjoins George W. Harris's unstoppable mountain-man Sut Lovingood. In *Georgia Scenes* by Augustus B. Longstreet (1835), the narrator's rural stroll is interrupted "by loud, profane, and boisterous voices" that unleash a "moral darkness": the frontier was indeed a house inhabited by spirits. While Hawthorne and Melville were still reflecting on the disorder generated by the democratic revolution, a second wave had already arrived from the West. The "rise of the common man" began with Jackson's presidency, and it was destined to culminate with yet another frontiersman and storyteller, Abraham Lincoln. It became impossible to avoid listening to the irreverent voice-vote vernacular of the common man. At any rate, this was the conclusion of the same process that had brought about the revolution: the eruption of carnivalesque laughter in Hawthorne's *My Kinsman, Major Molineux* (1831) alludes to his own era by remembering an episode from the late seventeenth century.

In the beginning, the voices off that come from the hall of spirits are still just an incomprehensible and fragmentary hum. But this is not because they are ineffable and inarticulate, like Isabel's shriek and her music. It is because there is a wall, an interspace, between the gentleman narrator's orderly world and that of the frontier hunter and his peers. Social distance and the refusal to listen (usually these yells did not interest us, say the narrators) hinder comprehension. In reality, these voices are anything but inarticulate: they just belong to different discursive genres and invent alternative stylistic figures. If they are unintelligible, it is because they speak different languages.

The Big Bear of Arkansas forces the gentlemen to recognize his knowledge and his experience that are incorporated into the figurative vivacity of his vocabulary, his fanciful vernacular inventions, and his tall tales. Just as he finishes upsetting one order, his voice has already begun to establish another. It is still fragmentary (these are still stories, not yet novels) and it is still formally under control (the dialect voice of the frontier is allowed into a narrative space that is framed by the educated eloquence of the gentleman narrator). But it will not be this way for long.

On the other hand, the subversive and the constitutive function of the voice are almost never separated nor are they ever inflexibly distinct. They tend rather to live side-by-side and to contend for the internal space of the texts themselves although with dramatic differences in their accentuation. This holds also for *Pierre*: the moment Isabel's voice upsets Pierre, his mother's voice tries to console him. From the very first page, Melville takes an ironic approach to the romantic relationship between voice, heart, and nature in the greeting of the two love-stricken characters—in the purity of the air and in the pastoral spontaneity of their sentiments. But then Melville himself uses sound as an expressive tool: for example, alliteration intensifies particularly in crucial moment like that in which Pierre decides to follow Isabel.[13]

The constitutive (or reconstitutive) function of literary orality depends above all on its inextricable connection to the body and therefore with time and space. The written world can distance itself from the enunciator and thus outlive its author. At least until the era of mechanical reproduction, the voice existed only in proximity to the body who emitted it, and therefore it delimited specific space and time. For that reason, in the classic novels of American literature, the power to create community is attributed to the voice. While the deep, low voice evokes the ghosts of disorder, the high voice— from the pulpit or from the commander—announces a new order, at times reassuring, and often no less unsettling: the congregation ("Father Mapple rose, and in a mild voice of unassuming authority ordered the scattered people to condense"), the marketplace (following Dimmesdale's speech, the marketplace "broke into speech" and "babbled" with enthusiasm), and the crew ("I, Ishmael, was one of that crew; my shouts had gone up with the rest; my oath had been welded with theirs").[14] This will continue, as we have seen, up to the *audience* drawn together as a community by the voice of the radio announcer who descends from the ether in *Underworld*.

The construction of a community defined by the voice brings with it the maturation of common language. Orality (especially in its dialectal and colloquial forms) stops functioning as a fragmentary and disturbing element; it is no longer the *trickster* in the manuscript or ghost in the margins or beneath

---

[13] The first section of book 10 ("The Unprecedented Final Resolution of Pierre") contains no less than forty alliterate clauses and sentences in the space of just six pages. Clearly intentional, it begins: "Glorified be his gracious memory . . ." In just one page of the Standard Edition, we read "stoically serene and symmetrical in soul," "a planned and perfect Future," "obscurely occupied," "extraordinary emergency," "from the first," and "his father's fair fame."

[14] Melville, *Moby-Dick*, 9 and 41; Hawthorne, *The Scarlet Letter*, 531; Melville, *Moby-Dick*, 181.

its foundations. It becomes, instead, a shared tool for ordinary communication. This process culminates in the moment that this orality surpasses the confines of the short story and shows itself able to support the weight of the novel. Ernest Hemingway's famous observation should be understood in this light: "All modern American literature comes from one book by Mark Twain called *Huckleberry Finn*." Of course, there had already been literary texts worthy of this name in the United States, but this novel sanctioned a paradigm change that put American literature and its languages on a new level and gave it new legitimacy. With *The Adventures of Huckleberry Finn* by Mark Twain (1884), literature began to speak "in your voice, American."

It is no coincidence that this began around the time of the Civil War. However much the formal Constitution of the country remained unaltered, the Civil War marked a deep change in the nation's true constitution and especially in its foundations of legitimacy. There was an attenuation of the constitutional principle of the states' sovereignty and there was an accentuation of popular sovereignty. The nation was no longer a contractual synthesis of multiple but partial sovereignties. It became instead a synthesis of political representation of a varied and pluralist national community.

The paradox of *Huckleberry Finn* and the literary tradition that most directly followed the same path, from Sherwood Anderson to William Faulkner, is that the new oral foundation for national literature relied not only on marginal subjects and partial languages but on the geographic margins of the country: the ever fluid frontier and especially the South, which had to be "civilized" just as Huck Finn was by the widow Douglass in order to bring it back into the fold following such a dramatic fracture. There were many reasons for this: the fact that South was closer to the frontier and farther from the cultural centers of the Atlantic coast; the influence of the great Afro-American oral culture; and a political tradition and religious emotionalism that used oratory as the privileged vehicle for public discourse even when this was no longer true in the rest of the country.

But beyond all of these causes, the effect of relocating the country's literary foundations in its most marginal sections was a reconfirmation of an essential characteristic of the voice: American literature speaks with local, marginal voices. There was a new textual order, but it was a plurilinguistic order where hierarchies were—at the least—attenuated. This is clear in *Huckleberry Finn*'s opening explanatory note:

> In this book a number of dialects are used, to wit: the Missouri negro dialect;
> the extremest form of the backwoods Southwestern dialect; the ordinary
> "Pike County" dialect; and four modified varieties of this last. The shadings

have not been done in a haphazard fashion, or by guesswork; but painstakingly, and with the trustworthy guidance and support of personal familiarity with these several forms of speech.

I make this explanation for the reason that without it many readers would suppose that all these characters were trying to talk alike and not succeeding.[15]

This is a declaration of independence sui generis (and it is reinforced by the challenge to find any form of *motive* or *moral* in the book): there is no *one* linguistic standard; dialects are not failed attempts to speak correctly but rather linguistic variants that deserve attention and that are endowed with equal dignity not only among themselves but also with respect to the variety spoken by the reader. The gentleman narrator provides the humoristic frontier setting and reaffirms the linguistic standard of the book. But in doing so, he becomes also the book's implicit reader. The use of linguistic estrangement in this text depends on the very mental adjustments that the implicit standard reader must perform in order to come into contact with Huck's words.

Once again, the beginning provides an excellent example of this: "You don't know about me without you have read a book by the name of *The Adventures of Tom Sawyer*; but that ain't no matter."[16] Here, Huck's voice works on two levels at once. On the one hand, there is the realistic reproduction of spoken language using: dialogue (the first word is *you*); prosody (the two anapests, short-short-long, in "you don't know | a-bout me"); syntax (paratactic correction); morphology (*ain't*); grammar (double negation); and semantic indefiniteness (*about*). On the other hand, the effect of estrangement imposes extra work for the standard reader: "without you have read" is perfectly smooth for the speaker of dialect, but it opens a small logical breach for the standard reader who expects a different syntactic construct after *without*.[17]

Here, the situation in "The Big Bear of Arkansas" has been partially reversed: the vernacular speaker does not burst into the space reserved for the standard reader, but it is the standard reader who, by carefully eavesdropping, must learn to understand the *hum* of the voices that come from the

---

[15] M. Twain, *The Adventures of Huckleberry Finn* (1884) (Harmondsworth, 1967), "Explanatory," 9.

[16] Ibid., 11.

[17] For a more detailed analysis of this opening, see A. Portelli, *Il testo e la voce: Oralità, letteratura e democrazia in America* (Rome, 1992), 170–72.

spirits' adjoining room. I say "partially" because this does not mean that the dialectal speaker has chosen not to invade writing's space: Huck refers to a book, and the word *book* is repeated three times in the first paragraph and then again in the first line of the second paragraph; more than anything else, Huck himself is trying to write, and he reminds us, symmetrically, in the last paragraph ("if I'd a knowed what a trouble it was to make a book I wouldn't a tackled it"). There is no doubt that Huck is slightly uncomfortable in this space, in the same way that he is uncomfortable wearing the new clothes given to him by the widow. In any case, he inhabits this space in his own unique way. The book about him does not have a title but rather a *name*: it is like a person, and this brings it even closer to the world of the voice. The relational game between dialects and normative language, combined with making a book out of a voice and a person out of a book, is an indication of how this is not an attempt to reproduce spoken language but rather an experiment in pushing the confines of writing.

The Stone and the Ghost: Beloved

As we all know, Huck has a traveling companion: Jim, a black man. Throughout the book, Jim is associated with his alienation from the world of writing and by his submission to it—from the farcical conversations on the Bible and the French kings to the final attempt to make Jim relive the hardships of the Man in the Iron Mask (Huck even asks him to write a rescue note in blood, even though he is illiterate). The black man cannot master the book, but the book can master him: "I was born in Lexington, Ky. The man who stole me as soon as I was born, recorded the births of all the infants which he claimed to be born his property, in a book which he kept for that purpose."[18]

The black presence introduces a different and more complex relationship between orality and writing in the literature of the United Sates. The opening of Frederick Douglass's *Narrative* (1845), for example, is a reversal of Hawthorne's passage on the authenticity of his manuscript drawn from oral sources. "I have no accurate knowledge of my age, never having seen any authentic record containing it."[19] On one hand, Hawthorne viewed orality as a

---

[18] W. W. Brown, *The Narrative of William W. Brown, An American Slave, Written by Himself* (1849) in *The Civitas Anthology of African American Slave Narratives*, ed. W. L. Andrews and H. L. Gates Jr. (Washington, D.C., 1999), 1:204.

[19] F. Douglass, *The Narrative of the Life of Frederick Douglass, an American Slave, Written by Himself* (1845), ibid., 117.

tool that serves to question his culture's certainties from the inside of the writing universe. On the other hand, Douglass was master of the genres and forms of orality (just think of his masterful pages on the spiritual) but was relegated to a ghettoized orality: in the very same writing that had been denied him, he was looking for certainties that could give shape to his identity. Like Pearl, Isabel, and Pierre, he had doubts regarding his father, but he knew, at least, that it was a tainted paternity. His autobiography is, therefore, the story of the arduous conquest of writing, but it ends at the moment in which he begins to speak as a preacher and an orator.

The two openings in William Wells Brown and Frederick Douglass defined a twofold internal tension between writing and orality—even before Afro-Americans began to write novels. On the one hand, writing was at once an instrument of dominance and an instrument for the building of oneself. On the other hand, orality was both the circle of communitarian identity and the fence erected to exclude others from writing. Both of these tensions traverse Toni Morrison's *Beloved* (1985). The book begins with two images that we have already encountered—the ghost and the stone—and the relationship between the body and the word (Denver's first words to Paul D. are "We have a ghost in here"; the inscribing of the baby's name on the gravestone takes "seven minutes for seven letters").

The story of *Beloved* is highly complex, but for our purposes, all that we need to know is that Sethe, a slave who has come to Tennessee after fleeing Texas, has managed to deliver her children into safety, including a still nameless baby and another to whom she gave birth while crossing the waters of the Ohio River. When the master and the slave hunters come to reclaim them, Sethe attempts to kill them all rather than let them be returned to slavery. The two boys manage to leave, while the daughter, Denver, does not have the courage to leave the house that is haunted by the ghost of the murdered baby. Eighteen years later, Paul D., an ex-slave, returns and chases away the ghost who returns in the body of an eighteen-year-old girl with the instincts of a few-months-old baby and with the same name that the mother had had engraved on the tombstone, Beloved. A reciprocally morbid and destructive fusion is generated between Beloved and Sethe until the ghost is exorcised by the voice—by the howls and the chants—of the neighborhood women.

In this story, both voice and writing are places for internal, reciprocal contradiction and conflict. The Afro-American voice is at once a communitarian and original foundation and a claustrophobic circle that is inaccessible to "others." It becomes intertwined with writing as an instrument of domination and with its achievement, as an instrument of identity and emancipation.

As we have seen, writing enters the scene in the form of a gravestone. We will find it again as the sign of the whip (the "chokecherry tree" on Sethe's back) and as the face of domination in the master's notebooks with his anthropologic observations on the slaves ("put her human characteristics on the left, her animal ones on the right. And don't forget to line them up"). Writing also represents the act of selling the slave Baby Suggs by a name other than her own (and the "good" mistress will never learn to call her by her real name rather than the one listed by the document). Writing is also found in the newspaper clipping with Sethe's portrait and the story of her action; it is also the stamp of the price paid ("Stamp Paid") by the slave who saw his wife raped and killed.

Writing, thus, is always associated with images of consolidation: the stone and the ice. "He couldn't have done it if I hadn't made the ink," says Sethe: in the end, writing is a hardened liquid; it is the life of human beings (ink made by the slave) that freezes on paper or stone, in a notebook, or in a book. The paradigmatic figure of hardened liquid alludes to the relationship between the movement of voice and the static nature of writing: the "traces" left by Stamp Paid in the snow (frozen water) around the house where Sethe and her children have holed themselves up in their delirium, the dried blood that makes the shape of a tree on Sethe's back, and even the butter (hardened milk) that her husband smears on her face after having seen her being raped by their masters who milk her breasts as if she were a beast.

Conversely, the voice is always liquid: Denver and Beloved literally suck up their mother's stories as if they were made of milk. Figures of liquidity run all around this story: the ink made by Sethe, the river where Denver is born, the flow of urine that announces Beloved's reincarnation like a new rupture, the milk that Sethe must bring for her children as she flees and the milk that the master's grandchildren steal on the plantation, and the blood of the sister that Denver sucks together with her mother's milk after Sethe kills her.

The association of liquid and voice takes place in the sign of a "semiotic" maternity: a return to the phase that precedes the daughter's separation from the body and the subject of the mother. It is invigorating, but it is also "impenetrable": the three women hole themselves up in the house in a state of madness à trois that includes vampirism and self-destruction. The interwoven painful and obsessive flows of conscience end up mixed together in a discordant polyphony that echoes the voices of black women and men who have been raped and massacred. It will take other voices yet to free them from this prison of voices. The neighborhood women, who had previously excluded Sethe from the community, decide that it is necessary to intervene, and they begin to sing and to chant around the bewitched house. "And then Ella hollered. Instantly the kneelers and the standers joined her. They stopped praying and took a step to the beginning. In the beginning there were no words. In the beginning was the sound, and they all knew what that sound sounded like."[20]

Ella's holler is one of the many yells of American literature. It is unleashed by the memory of a violent birth: "She had delivered, but would not nurse, a hairy white thing, fathered by 'the lowest yet.' It lived five days never making a sound."[21] The metaphorical relationship between voice and birth traverses American writing: the voice and the new lives are painfully emitted by the maternal body. Consider Lee Smith's *Fair and Tender Ladies* (1988): "And then right before it came out I could *hear* it. . . . I swear I could *hear* my bones parting and hear myself opening up" or Margaret Atwood's *The Handmaid's Tale* (1985): "The women's voices rise around me, a soft chant that is still too loud for me . . .'breathe, breathe,' we chant, as we have been taught. Hold, hold, hold. Expel, expel, expel." And we must not forget Emily Dickinson: "A word is dead \ When it is said \ Some say. \ I say it just \ begins to live \ That day."[22]

Giving birth is also a metaphor of an even earlier origin, that is, the birth of the world. In the beginning, there were no *words*: sound, instead of *the Word*, was the beginning of a creation that took place not in the name of the father but rather in the name—in the body—of the mother. The voice of birthing and origin is pure sound, and it precedes both the word and articulation. It is Isabel's shriek and Ella's holler; it is the indistinct hum of ghosts in the air; it is the language that human beings once shared with animals; it is the "immemorial time" when "human beings could understand what the animals said."[23] "It was all language. . . . No, it was not language; it was what was there before language. Before things were written down. Language in the time when men and animals did talk to one another."[24]

The oral origin of the world is therefore a female Afro-American (and Native American) origin; it is very different from the written male, white origin that is undermined by orality in the classical canon of Melville and

---

[20] T. Morrison, *Beloved* (1985) (London, 1978), 259.

[21] Ibid., 258.

[22] L. Smith, *Fair and Tender Ladies* (1988) (New York, 1988), 144 (italics in original); M. Atwood, *The Handmaid's Tale* (1985) (Toronto, 1985), 133; E. Dickinson, "A word is dead," poem 1,212.

[23] Leslie Marmon Silko, *Ceremony* (1977) (New York, 1988), 94–95.

[24] T. Morrison, *Song of Solomon* (New York, 1977), 281.

Hawthorne. But it is also an origin from which it is difficult to extricate one-self: assuming an individual identity distinct from the body of the mother and the collective identity is a painful and risky process, and it requires other tools.

This is why Toni Morrison is not satisfied with the certainties of the oral, maternal origin, nor is she satisfied with recognizing the oppressive func-tions of writing. Together with the maternal principles of continuity, flow, presence, fusion, and voice, she combines an equally necessary paternal principle made of discreteness, absence, distinction, and writing. As in the case of Douglass, the conquest of writing is an essential part of the process of the construction of self, partly because in the Afro-American (and Native American) tradition, there is no hierarchical difference between writing and voice. Learning how to write does not necessarily mean that you must un-learn how to speak. While a prisoner of the haunted house and the exclusive relationship between Sethe and Beloved, Denver finds the courage to es-cape, to separate herself from Sethe, and to seek a personal identity in the universe of writing and the memory of the absent father.

From the very beginning, the father, writing, and absence are linked in Denver's mind. It is an absence to which she does not even have any right because Halle's absence belongs to those who knew him and had him: Sethe, the wife, and the mother, Baby Suggs. Denver seeks both maternal stories and those that her grandmother tells her about her father. Maternal stories are at the heart of the text, but we are only given sporadic fragments of the grandmother's stories, absent stories of absence that systematically connect Halle to writing: "He loved things. Animals and tools and crops and the alphabet"; "he could count on paper." Denver knows that this was how Halle bought his mother's freedom: "If you can't count they cheat you. If you can't read they beat you." This is why, Denver concludes, "it was good for me to learn how."

Therefore, Denver's jump from the maternal semiotic to the symbolic and the construction of her distinct self takes place in the name of the *discrete* and permanent quality of writing. As she leaves Sethe and Beloved's house-prison, Denver tracks down a neighbor who had begun to teach her how to write a long time ago. It is here that Denver "inaugurated her life in the world as a woman. The trail she followed to get to that sweet thorny place was made up of paper scraps containing the handwritten names of others."[25]

---

[25] The neighbors write their names on the plates of food that they leave out of charity in front of the house for the three women. Denver looks for the persons named by the cards to return the plates to their owners and to begin to have relations with the community.

The absence that accompanies all of the male figures in this novel is a sign of their fragility and the fact that men cannot be counted on. But it is also an indication of how to begin to become a distinct and self-sufficient individual. In the works of Maxine Hong Kingston, female identity is formed in relation to a maternal presence and to the "awareness of separation" in the relationship with the father. Kingston writes of this heritage in two separate texts: in *China Men* (1980), she remembers that her father taught her how to read; and in *The Woman Warrior* (1975) she celebrates the maternal *talk-story*.[26] Morrison chooses instead to imply both in the same text. By defining paternity as alphabetized absence, *Beloved* stigmatizes men's lack of responsibility, but it also suggests that the absence is as necessary to self-building as is the presence, in the same way that orality and writing are indissolubly intertwined in the construction of an Afro-American literary tradition.

In the end, Denver meets Paul D and tells him that her abolitionist white protector is thinking of sending her to Oberlin, the "free" college in Ohio. Her access to writing seems to be complete. But, in a last ironic twist, Denver suggests that she remains within the realm of domination: "She's experimenting on me." Sending a black girl off to study is another way of testing the humanity of her race—not much different, in the end, than comparing the human and animal qualities of her mother in the anthropologist slave-owner's notebook.

The Voice's Body

So, what does this American voice sound like after all? Woody Guthrie, one of America's greatest oral poets, said: "I had rather sound like the ash cans of the early morning, like the cab drivers cursing one another, like the longshoremen yelling, like the cowhand whooping, and like the lone wolf barking."[27] A musician and a writer, Zora Neale Hurston has written that the difference between Afro-American formal speaking and singing and the art of the voice in Europe consists in the fact that while the latter tends to hide the "mechanics" of emission, the Afro-American voice features and

---

[26] S. Juhasz, "Maxine Hong Kingston: Narrative Technique and Female Identity," in *Contemporary American Women Writers: Narrative Strategies*, ed. C. Rainwater and W. J. Scheick (Lexington, Ky., 1985), 173–90.

[27] "Ear Players" (1938), in *Common Ground*, cited in the booklet included with the recording *Bound for Glory: The Songs and Stories of Woody Guthrie Sung by Woody Guthrie, told by Will Geer* (1961), ed. M. Lampell (New York: Folkways Records FA 2481).

adorns the physicality of breath.[28] It is no accident that Hurston speaks of "Europe": all of the American voice (not just Afro-American) is a tangible breath that comes from the body and then is embodied—like the living ghost of Beloved and the voice of Davy Crockett that was, wrote an English traveler, "so rough it would not be described—it was obliged to be drawn as a picture."[29]

The familiar, digressive American voice, therefore, brings with it all the signs of material living. It is rough, consumed, lacerated, full of smoke and whiskey, full of sand and gravel; it is the voice of Louis Armstrong and Little Richard (his "Long Tall Sally" is portrayed in *Underworld*); it is the voice of Tom Waits, Bob Dylan, and Lenny Bruce. It is able to coagulate in the air like that of Ichabod Crane and Isabel, or it can condense into the margins of silence like that of Hemingway's laconic heroes and Humphrey Bogart, or it can thicken like that of the dying gangster Reno Starkey in *Red Harvest* by Dashiell Hammett (1929).

This does not mean that the rough body of the voice is a prerogative of positive heroes. In hard-boiled narrative, all of the distinctions between good and evil or crime and law are questioned, and the voice confirms this as it crosses boundaries and demarcations. At the beginning of *Red Harvest*, the Continental Op goes to visit Elihu Wilsson, the "czar of Poisonville," father of his employer, who was killed the night before. The first thing that he notices is the voice, which rises up from the deep through narrow, hard lips, cutting but nevertheless indistinct: " 'What's this about my son?' His voice was harsh. His chest had too much and his mouth too little to do with his words for them to be very clear."[30]

The voice rises up from within the body, and it becomes cutting and yet indistinct as it passes through the narrow and almost motionless lips: it is the opposite of the uninterrupted column of air in the Eurocentric voice described by Hurston. Just a few lines below, the narrator makes an explicit reference to the perceptibility of breath: Elihu becomes enraged, but in the end "he still had some breath left." The harshness of the voices makes them consistently comparable to animal sounds. Elihu Wilsson "barked"; the chief of police "snarled"; the most commonly used word, shared by gangster and corrupt policemen alike, is "growl." Even Elihu's rival can be recognized

---

[28] Z. N. Hurston, *The Sanctified Church: The Folklore Writings of Zora Neale Hurston* (Berkeley, Calif., 1981), 81–82.

[29] Richard Dorson, *America in Legend: Folklore from the Colonial Period to the Present* (New York, 1976), 76–77.

[30] D. Hammett, *Red Harvest* (1929) (New York, 1992), 213.

just from the sound of his voice: a piercing, atonal "husky whisper" that earns him the name of Whisper.

The voice of radio announcer Russ Hodges in *Underworld* belongs to the same gamut of sounds:

> Russ has an overworked larynx and the makings of a major cold and he
> shouldn't be lighting a cigarette but here he goes. . . .
>
> Days of iron skies and all the mike time of the past week, the sore throat,
> the coughing, Russ is feverish and bedraggled—train trips and nerves and no
> sleep and he describes the play in his familiar homey ramble, the grits-and-
> tater voice that's a little scratchy today. (Prologue, 14–15)

These are the hard, scratchy voices of the *underworld*: the Bronx voice that "crunched, like talking through broken teeth"; the gangster voice that the hero Nick can mimic perfectly; the ironic "nasal . . . harsh and moist" voice of a girl in the Southwest desert; but they are also the electronically distorted voice of the Texas Highway Killer, the voices of loudspeakers, of crowds and motors at the airport. And at the same time, these are indefinite, blurry voices with no clear shape: the "slurred words, dropped vowels" of Italian-Americans; the "unfinished English" and the Black English of the kids in the Bronx (Sister Edgar tries to cram a hard final *g* and a few punctu-ation marks down their throats). It is the city and its story in the voice of Nick's mother: "And the voice in its factual carry, vowels extended and bent a bit, a sound out of the old streets, the old demotic song gone to the near suburbs now, and a slight Irish pitch teasing the piece from somewhere deep in childhood" (201). And all of these voices converge in the spoken jazz and mosaic rap in the voice of Lenny Bruce—abbreviated, improvised, and asso-ciative yelling and moaning:

> He did psychoanalysis, personal reminiscence, he did voices and accents,
> grandmotherly groans, scenes from prison movies, and finally closed the
> show with a monologue that had a kind of abridged syntax, a thing without
> connectives, he was cooking free-form, closer to music than speech, doing a
> spoken jazz in which a slang term generates a matching argot, like musicians
> trading fours, the road band, the sideman's inner riff, and when the crowd
> dispersed they took this rap mosaic with them into the strip joints and bars
> and late night diners. (586)

The book begins with the voice, and it finishes with the voice. On the last page, when everything seems to melt into a nuclear explosion in cyberspace, something familiar and traditional resonates in the margins of the scene. It is the beginning of a protracted, paratactical *run-on sentence* that concludes the novel: "And you can glance out the window for a moment, distracted by the sound of small kids playing a made-up game in a neighbor's yard, some kind of kickball maybe, and they speak in your voice, or piggyback races on the weedy lawn, and it's your voice you hear, essentially, under the glimmerglass sky . . ."

"He speaks in your voice," "they speak in your voice," and "it's your voice you hear." We know who "he" and "they" are. They are a black boy from Harlem in the first chapter, Bronx street urchins in the last chapter. But who is the "you" whose voice is reflected in theirs? To whom is Huck Finn, yet another emarginated boy, speaking when he says, "You don't know about me"? And whom is Ishmael addressing when he orders that person to call him "Ishmael"? As Mikhail Bakhtin has shown, in every word there is an implicit dialogue with all of those who have used it or have heard it. But in oral communication, this dialogism is no longer implicit or metaphorical but rather incarnate in the active presence of an interlocutor who hears it and who can in turn speak. And so, if we imagine, plausibly, that the "you" of the narrative beginnings is the ordinary reader of these novels ("without you have read a book"), then DeLillo and Mark Twain are saying that those who have a voice in America are the proletarian children of the Bronx, the black kids in Harlem, and the fleeing adolescents of Missouri. Through them and thanks to them, everyone speaks, because just like the underground black man in *The Invisible Man* by Ralph Ellison, "on the lower frequencies, [they] speak for [us]."[31] In times like these, maybe this is why this voice is "halfway hopeful."

Translated by Jeremy Parzen

---

[31] R. Ellison, *Invisible Man* (1952) (Harmondsworth, 1965), Epilogue, 469.

JONATHAN ZWICKER

The Long Nineteenth Century of the Japanese Novel

Tears, the Book, and the History of the Literary Function

> In the search for tears, we soon encounter the book.
> —ANNE VINCENT-BUFFAULT, *The History of Tears*[1]

Over the course of the nineteenth century, the Japanese reading public was often invited to tears. Writers frequently invoked tears in prefaces and apostrophes to the reader; in 1787, for instance, Tanishi Kin'gyo imagined that some readers of his *Keiseikai tora no maki* "would be moved, others weep, and still others be so captivated by the story that they lose the power to move their hands and their feet,"[2] while in the 1799 preface to his *Chûshin suikoden*, Santô Kyôden observed that "when the people of the marketplace see plays or read libretti, should there happen to be instances of loyalty, filial piety, virtue, or chastity they are moved and unable to hold back tears of sorrow."[3] And readers were given models of idealized weeping in the frequent tearful scenes of nineteenth-century fiction: characters might weep upon hearing or telling the unhappy fate of others or shed tears over their own misfortunes. In some texts, tears were ubiquitous while in others a well-timed scene of highly charged emotion served as a delicate counterpoint to the wide-ranging adventures of heroes and villains. At the turn of the nineteenth century, Shikitei Sanba remarked that "recently books of wit are dying out and being replaced by weeping books";[4] at the end of that century, a book reviewer might mention how he was brought to tears by a novel, and readers of serialized fiction were provided the opportunity to shed rather public tears in letters to the editor containing a range of emotions from sympathy to outrage over the fortunes of their favorite characters.

In his essay "History or Literature?" Roland Barthes suggested that "a history of tears . . . would tell us as much about those who shed them as

---

[1] Anne Vincent-Buffault, *The History of Tears*, trans. Teresa Bridgeman (New York: St. Martin's Press, 1991), 3.

[2] Tanishi Kin'gyo, *Keiseikai tora no maki*, in *Sharebon taisei* (Tokyo: Chûô kôronsha, 1980), 7:303.

[3] Santô Kyôden, *Chûshin suikoden*, in *Santô Kyôden zenshû* (Tokyo: Perikansha, 1994), 15:83.

[4] Shikitei Sanba, *Kejô suigon maku no soto*, in *Ukiyoburo; Kejô suigen maku no soto;* and *Daisen sekai gakuyasagashi*, in *Shin Nihon koten bungaku taikei* (Tokyo: Iwanami Shoten, 1989), 86:298.

about the man who made them flow."[5] Barthes's idea was that by focusing on "production, communication, and consumption," by concerning itself with "activities and institutions, not with individuals"—by "becoming sociological"—literary history would begin to reveal the "function" of literature "in the general economy of our society."[6] Barthes called this the *history of the literary function*. In the last several decades, through studies on various aspects of the culture of the book—from printing to publishing, from authorship to reading, from *colportage* to lending libraries—the sociological study of literary texts and the history of the book have produced a remarkable body of work on the social dimensions of literature. This work has, however, tended rather away from than toward the "confrontation of society and rhetoric"[7] that Barthes had in mind as the object of literary history. Instead, the study of literary forms and the history of the book have evolved as two relatively autonomous approaches to literary texts. It is in this context that Franco Moretti has recently suggested the need for a "bridge" between book history and the morphological study of forms: "there is great diplomacy between book historians and literary historians, but true engagement is still to come."[8]

In its own way, then, this essay is an attempt to contribute to such a bridge by looking historically at the situation of fiction in nineteenth-century Japan and by taking seriously the methodologies both of social history and of formal analysis. Thus the quantitative dimension of this study—my use of numbers. Numbers are often partial and partisan, "nothing more than symptoms produced by the historian himself," as Robert Darnton once put it in warning of "an overcommitment to the quantification of culture and an undervaluation of the symbolic element in social intercourse."[9] Still, they are useful for the revision of traditional periodicity, for "calling in question the old postulate that all elements of a society follow a homogeneous and identical evolution."[10] I have relied on numbers, then—primarily numbers of books published and circulated—because they tell a story that has escaped

---

[5] Roland Barthes, "History or Literature?" in *On Racine*, trans. Richard Howard (Berkeley: University of California Press, 1992), 158.

[6] Ibid., 161 and 172.

[7] Roland Barthes, "Rhetorical Analysis," in *The Rustle of Language*, trans. Richard Howard (Berkeley: University of California Press, 1989), 84.

[8] Franco Moretti, *Atlas of the European Novel 1800–1900* (London: Verso, 1998), 143.

[9] Robert Darnton, *The Great Cat Massacre and Other Episodes in French Cultural History* (New York: Vintage Books, 1984), 258.

[10] François Furet, "Quantitative History," in *In the Workshop of History*, trans. Jonathan Mandelbaum (Chicago: University of Chicago Press, 1984), 53 and 49.

traditional Japanese literary history and suggest the need to rethink quite thoroughly the way that Japanese literary history is periodized. And this is the primary value of numbers; they "simplify the better to come to grips with their subject"[11] and so make accessible through patterns and series, objects that are virtually inaccessible to traditional literary history.

This is what social history has to offer literary history. And what formal analysis has to offer the study of society is precisely that attention to the *symbolic element in social intercourse.* Tears are clues, and their traces can begin to lead us back into the symbolic world of which they were a part. If a history of tears can tell us as much about those who shed them as about those who made them flow, it is because the production of tears itself has a social dimension, it is what Frederic Jameson has called "a socially symbolic act."[12] Jameson has argued that "by construing purely formal patterns as a symbolic enactment of the social within the formal and aesthetic" it becomes possible to understand the truly social dimension of narrative, the "ideology of form."[13] Literary and cultural texts are thus historical documents in the strict sense, and by taking form seriously we can begin to have access to ideological worlds long since vanished, worlds to which quantitative history provides no access.

But to move from the traces of tears into symbolic worlds long since vanished—to move from individual texts and solitary acts of weeping to a general history of tears with a genuinely social dimension—the literary historian too has to turn to numbers. Kenneth Burke even suggests replacing "symbolic" with "statistical," arguing that, considered statistically, a group of similar texts "become but different individuations of a common paradigm. As so considered, they become 'symbolic of something'—they become 'representative' of a social trend."[14] " 'Statistical' analysis," Burke argues, "discloses the ways in which a 'symbolic' act is 'representative.' "[15] Literary historians thus properly begin with publishers' lists and guild records, with library

---

[11] Fernand Braudel, "History and the Social Sciences: The *Longue Durée*," in *On History* (Chicago: University of Chicago Press, 1980), 51.

[12] See Frederic Jameson, "On Interpretation," in *The Political Unconscious* (Ithaca, N.Y.: Cornell University Press, 1981), esp. 76–82.

[13] As Jameson writes, "Ideology is not something which informs or invests symbolic production; rather the aesthetic act is itself ideological, and the production of aesthetic or narrative form is to be seen as an ideological act in its own right, with the function of inventing imaginary or formal 'solutions' to unresolvable social contradictions" (ibid., 79).

[14] Kenneth Burke, *The Philosophy of Literary Form* (Berkeley: University of California Press, 1973), 18 and 19.

[15] Ibid., 25.

and auction catalogs, with whatever evidence they have at their disposal so that they might confront what Furet calls "the first task of serial history, the imperative of its development": the constitution of its subject matter.[16]

A literary series—Hans Robert Jauss had hit upon the idea early on in developing the idea of an "aesthetics of reception": "The theory of the aesthetics of reception not only allows one to conceive the meaning and form of a literary work in the historical unfolding of its understanding. It also demands that one insert the individual work into its 'literary series' to recognize its historical position and significance in context of the experience of literature."[17] In such a literary series, Jauss goes on, "an important work, one that indicates a new direction in the literary process, is surrounded by an unsurveyable production of works that correspond to the traditional expectations or images concerning reality, and that thus in their social index are to be no less valued than the solitary novelty of the great work."[18] We might go even further than Jauss: the "unsurveyable" bulk of literature, what Margaret Cohen has recently called "the great unread,"[19] is not only not to be less valued in its social index than the great work but much more so. If the true task of literary history is to enable the historian "to pose questions that the texts gave an answer to, and thereby to discover how the contemporary reader could have viewed and understood the work,"[20] the real emphasis of literary history has to be on those books whose now unfamiliar titles recur with such frequency in the catalogs of lending libraries and the diaries and letters of readers. "Normal literature," Franco Moretti has called it;[21] it is the perfect object for a history of nineteenth-century Japanese fiction, a literature essentially without masterpieces.

The Long Nineteenth Century of Japanese Novels

Over the course of the nineteenth century, the Japanese reading public was often invited to tears. But who were these readers and how did they read? The history of reading has gained increasing attention from scholars of literature

---

[16] Furet, "Quantitative History," 45.

[17] Hans Robert Jauss, "Literary History as a Challenge to Literary Theory," in *Toward an Aesthetic of Reception*, trans. Timothy Bahti (Minneapolis: University of Minnesota Press, 1982), 32.

[18] Jauss, "Literary History as a Challenge to Literary Theory," 12.

[19] Margaret Cohen, *The Sentimental History of the Novel* (Princeton, N.J.: Princeton University Press, 1999), 23.

[20] Jauss, "Literary History as a Challenge to Literary Theory," 28.

[21] See Franco Moretti, "The Soul and the Harpy," in *Signs Taken for Wonders: Essays in the Sociology of Literary Forms* (London: Verso, 1983), 15.

as literary history moves from an almost exclusive concern with the history of literary production and becomes more interested in the circulation and consumption of texts. But any attempt at "a history of the practices of reading" remains greatly complicated by protocols of evidence, "the scarcity of direct traces and the complexity of the interpretation of indirect evidence."[22] In its most direct form, this evidence often takes the form of the marginal notes of readers inscribed in the books they read and collected; but the existence— and legibility—of such notes varies greatly among different cultural milieux; and then again, such marginalia are themselves evidence of a practice that has ceased to be reading and has crossed over again to an act of writing.

Cultural representations of reading in both literature—in prefaces, apostrophes, asides—and in the graphic arts—in book illustrations, but also in paintings and prints—tend to offer a wealth of indirect evidence of habits and protocols of reading even if the evidence is itself ambiguous and resists simple interpretation.[23] I have reproduced two such representations of reading from the two historical bookends of this project. The first (figure 1) is a woodblock print done by Katsushika Hokusai in 1802 as an illustration for the *Itako zekkushû*, a book of verse by Fuji no Karamaro. The book was banned at the beginning of 1803, the printing blocks burned, and its author, Fuji no Karamaro, and his publisher, Tsutaya Jûzaburô, arrested.[24] The other (figure 2), is oil on canvas, painted by Kuroda Seiki during a sojourn at Gray in the east of France and displayed in the 1891 salon of the Société des Artistes Français. The painting is now housed at the Tokyo National Museum. The representations appear to illustrate not just two different practices of reading but really two different worlds. On the one hand, we have the world of the early nineteenth century, the world of woodblock printing with its attendant mode of reading: situated in the semipublic world of the demimonde, on the border between the private and public, our reader is reclining, a child peering over her shoulder, her companion in

---

[22] Roger Chartier, "Du Livre au Lire," in Chartier, ed., *Pratiques de la lecture* (Paris: Editions Rivages, 1993), 79.

[23] Again, here is Chartier: "When we are confronted with these texts and images that bring popular readers into our view, caution is indispensable. Whatever they might be, these representations never involve immediate and transparent relations with the practices they describe. All are lodged in the specific modes of their production, the interests and intentions that produced them, the genres in which they were inscribed, and the audiences at which they were aimed. To reconstruct the conventions that governed literate representations of the popular, therefore, we must decipher the strong but subtle bond that ties these representations to the social practices that are their object." Roger Chartier, "Popular Appropriations: Readers and Their Books," in *Forms and Meanings* (Philadelphia: University of Pennsylvania Press, 1995), 94.

[24] For a complete reproduction of the *Itako zekkushû*, see Nagata Seiji, ed., *Hokusai kyôka ehon* (Tokyo: Iwasaki bijutsusha, 1988).

FIGURE 1. KATSUSHIKA HOKUSAI, 1802

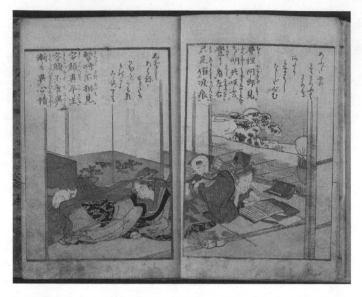

Smithsonian Institute Libraries, Freer Gallery of Art and Arthur M. Sackler
Gallery Library Special Collections

tears, distraught over her lover's absence. And on the other hand, we have the modern reader of the late nineteenth century: she sits upright and alone, shut up in a room, closed off from the outside world, the very picture of the postromantic reader.

These images appear perfectly to illustrate and to bear out in graphic detail the shift in readerly habits and sensibilities over the course of the nineteenth century that Maeda Ai has detailed in his pioneering work on the history of reading in nineteenth-century Japan. As Maeda writes, the closing decades of the nineteenth century, those following the Meiji Restoration, witnessed a radical reorganization of print culture and an attendant shift in modes of reading and apprehension, which he describes as the "emergence of the modern reader." Reading moves from an essentially uniform to a pluralistic and individual activity and from a group to a solitary activity, shifts that themselves bear an intimate relationship with what is for Maeda the hallmark of the modern reader—silent reading.[25]

Nagamine Shigetoshi has recently expanded on Maeda's argument, suggesting that two factors greatly shaped the emergence of new readerly practices at the end of the nineteenth century. The first is a shift in the spaces

---

[25] See Maeda Ai, *Kindai dokusha no seiritsu* (Tokyo: Chikuma Shobo, 1989).

FIGURE 2. "READING" BY KURODA SEIKI, 1891

"Reading" by Kuroda Seiki, Tokyo National Museum. Image: TNM Image Archives.
Source: http://TnmArchives.jp/

of reading with the development of new "public spaces"—the train, the prison, the newspaper reading room, and ultimately the public library—in which reading aloud was forbidden and in which—and through which—a generation of readers were gradually trained (we might say "disciplined") to read silently.[26] The second is an overall shift from "intensive reading" to

---

[26] Nagamine Shigetoshi, *Zasshi to dokusha no kindai* (Tokyo: Nihon editâsukûru shuppanbu, 1997), 35–76.

FIGURE 3. THE MEIJI PRINT REVOLUTION:
BOOK AND MAGAZINE TITLES, 1881–1926

"extensive reading," echoing arguments for a *Lesserevolution* in eighteenth-century Europe made by Rolf Engelsing and Erich Schön.[27] For Nagamine, this transformation in reading habits was attendant on the spread of forms of printing and publishing based on moveable type. As Nagamine writes, over the course of the 1890s, "the absolute number of publications continued to rise due to the steady development of movable type printing" leading to the birth of "a mode of reading as consumption" in which "the book—which had been an object of reverence as a 'sacred text'—was transfigured into a commodity the same as other goods."[28]

Figure 3 is based on Yayoshi Mitsunaga's statistics for the number of book and magazine titles published during the Meiji and Taishô eras and is intended to give some sense of the publishing activities in the final decades of the nineteenth century and the opening decades of the twentieth century.[29] Yayoshi's numbers, derived from statistics kept by the censoring body of the ministry of the interior, do indeed suggest a rather profound

---

[27] See ibid., 9. Nagamine's terms are *seidoku* (intensive reading) and *tadoku* (extensive reading). On the problem of a *Lesserevolution* in eighteenth-century Europe, see Rolf Engelsing, *Der Bürger als Leser: Lesergeschichte in Deutschland 1500–1800* (Stuttgart: Metzler, 1974); and Erich Schön, *Der Verlust der Sinnlichkeit, oder, Die Verwandlungen des Lesers: Mentalitätswandel um 1800* (Stuttgart: Klett-Cotta, 1987).

[28] Nagamine, *Zasshi to dokusha no kindai*, 3, 8, 5. The term for "a mode of reading as consumption" is *shôhiteki na dokushohô*.

[29] Yayoshi Mitsunaga, *Mikan shiryo ni yoru nihon shuppan bunka* (Tokyo: Yumani shobô, 1990), 5:279ff.

transformation in print culture over the final decades of the nineteenth century and the first several decades of the twentieth century; periodical titles
of one sort or another alone account for roughly 60 to 75 percent of these
titles, largely substantiating Nagamine's claim for the important place of
new media like the newspaper and magazine in the readerly world of the
early twentieth century.[30]

"The typographical industry set out to conquer the world during these
years," Henri-Jean Martin has written of the late nineteenth century, and
there is no doubt that the history of print in late-nineteenth- and early-
twentieth-century Japan was greatly impacted by this "conquest of the
world."[31] But Yayoshi's numbers fail to give any sense of the world before the
conquest, that other world suggested by Hokusai's print. What of the first
eighty years of the nineteenth century? Or the final years of the eighteenth?
What exactly was that culture of the book so completely transformed by the
modern press? Many years ago, in his history of what he called "the Chinese
World," Jacques Gernet warned of a "distortion of perspective" caused by
an excessive focus on the history of the late nineteenth century through
which "the history of the countries of East Asia fades away almost completely behind that of Western advances and conquests in this part of the
world."[32] The best solution to this "distortion" would no doubt be simply to
extend Yayoshi's numbers backward to say 1800 or 1750, but such efforts
are hamstrung by the lack of reliable data before the 1880s.[33] Not being able
to reconstruct the entire landscape of the market for books around 1800, we
must settle for the next best thing, reconstructing a part of that market and
then trying to think through the implications for the relation of a part to the
whole.

There is no reason to assume that any one segment of the book market
would necessarily be more representative than any other, but with an inquiry concerned with the emergence of reading for leisure or of reading as
consumption, fiction titles seem like a pretty good index. Nineteenth-
century reading patterns seem to suggest this. Tables 1 and 2 are based on
Nagatomo Chiyoji's pioneering work on the history of lending libraries in

---

[30] See the preface to Nagamine, *Zasshi to dokusha no kindai*, esp. iii.

[31] Henri Jean-Martin, *The History and the Power of Writing*, trans. Lydia G. Cochrane
(Chicago: University of Chicago Press, 1994), 454.

[32] Jacques Gernet, *A History of Chinese Civilization*, trans. J. R. Foster (Cambridge: Cambridge
University Press, 1982), 574.

[33] See G. Raymond Nunn, "On the Number of Books Published in Japan from 1600 to 1868,"
in *East Asian Occasional Papers* 1, Asian Studies at Hawaii 3 (Honolulu: University of Hawaii Press,
1969), 110–19.

TABLE 1. THE HOLDINGS OF THE DAISÔ LENDING LIBRARY WHEN CATALOGED FOR AUCTION IN 1898

Genre	No. of titles	% of total no. of titles	Duplicate titles	% of titles with duplicates
Medicine	352	2.0	—	—
Philosophy/ religion	2,093	12.5	—	—
Education	488	2.9	—	—
Classics	300	1.8	—	—
Fiction	3,976	23.8	2,030	51.0
Total	16,734	—	4,710	28.4

Subgenre (fiction)	Titles	Duplicates	% of duplicates
Ihara Saikaku	14	—	—
Pornography	93	—	—
Hachimonjiya	297	2	0.7
Didactic fiction	82	—	—
Sharebon	802	327	40.8
Kibyôshi/Gôkan	1,482	1,061	71.6
Kokkeibon	213	127	59.6
Ninjôbon	359	314	87.5
Yomihon	286	127	44.4

"During the century and a half that preceded the French Revolution, distribution circuits . . . devoted to a broadly based sale of low-priced books grew up throughout France. The phenomenon was universal, however: we can see it everywhere from England to Italy and from Sweden to Spain, and comparable phenomena can be found in seventeenth-century Japan." H.-J. Martin, *The History and Power of Writing.*

TABLE 2. THE HOLDINGS OF NAKAYA SHINZAEMON'S LENDING LIBRARY AT KINOSAKI

Genre	Titles	Percentage
Jôruri	181	56.0
Fiction	90	28.0
Haikai kyôka	10	3.0
Picture books	16	5.0
Popular religion	2	0.1
Sharebon	5	0.2
Essays, miscellany	20	6.0

nineteenth-century Japan and suggest the unique place that fiction titles have within the two extant catalogs of nineteenth-century lending libraries.[34] Table 1 details the holdings of the Daisô Lending Library in Nagoya, the largest lending library in nineteenth-century Japan. Daisô was founded in 1767 and remained in operation through 1898, when its holdings were cataloged for auction. Table 2 details the holdings of a library run by Nakaya Shinzaemon in the spa town of Kinosaki in present day Hyôgo Prefecture. Nakaya's library was in operation by 1802, and the collection was sold at auction in 1905. These are very different collections, composed of very different holdings, serving, no doubt, very different purposes. What they have in common is the significant position of fiction titles in their holdings; as Nagatomo himself writes, "it is clear that what we call early modern novels occupied a central position in the holdings of lending libraries."[35] In the case of Daisô, not only do these early modern novels represent an enormous section of the library's holdings in absolute terms—more than double the number of titles for philosophy and religion, almost fifteen times the number of books on medicine—but more interestingly, the number of duplicate copies of the same books suggest that fiction was subject to very different habits of circulation and ultimately of reading than were other types of books. And in the case of Nakaya Shinzaemon's library, the numbers are even more striking: if we follow the early-modern convention of including *jôruribon*, the libretti of the puppet theater, under the rubric of fiction, we find that 84 percent of the texts available to a spa patron at Kinosaki were works of fiction.[36] Nagatomo mentions a book illustrating life in Kinosaki written in the 1840s and depicting patrons of the spa leisurely reading in bed and even while in the bath, and we know statistically they were almost surely reading fiction.[37]

So what would a mapping of the nineteenth-century fiction market look like? In figure 4, I have put together Ekkehard May's statistics (based on

---

[34] See Nagatomo Chiyoji, *Kinsei kashihon'ya no kenkyû* (Tokyo: Tôkyôdô shuppan, 1982). Table 1 is based on 153–58; table 2 on 110ff.

[35] Ibid., 156.

[36] In his *Kinsei mono no hon Edo sakusha burui* (1834) (Tokyo: Yagi shoten, 1971), the most important and exhaustive taxonomy of fiction in early-modern Japan, Kyokutei Bakin had planned to devote an entire section to authors of *jôruri* and makes no distinction between such works and other genres of fiction such as *akahon*, *sharebon*, *chûhon*, and *yomihon*. Bakin had outlined four volumes for his study but completed only the first volume and part of the second. What we have then is a partial but richly suggestive record of early nineteenth-century fiction.

[37] Nagatomo, *Kinsei kashihon'ya no kenkyû*, 120–21 and 177. The book is *Ehon Ki no Saki miyage*, written in 1842.

FIGURE 4. THE LONG NINETEENTH CENTURY:
NEW FICTION TITLES, 1750–1912

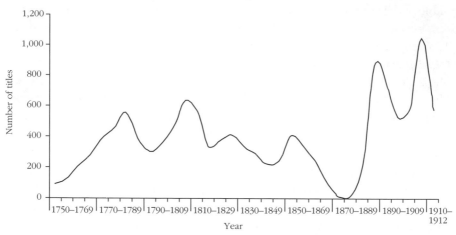

Yamazaki Fumoto's *Chronology and Checklist of Japanese Fiction)*[38] on the printing of fiction titles between the 1750s and 1868 with my own statistics (based on the National Diet Library's *Catalog of Books Published in the Meiji Period)*[39] for the period between 1868 and 1912 to show what one segment of the book market looked like across the nineteenth century, across a sort of *long nineteenth century*. This graph has several major limitations. It represents only titles with no indication of the relative size of print runs, and it represents only new titles with no sense of the reproduction or circulation of older titles. So we are not dealing even with the entire fiction market but with one segment of that market. And then too it has the limitation that—in the early-modern period—it does not represent the libretti of the puppet theater that occupied such an important place in the libraries of the time and then—in the late nineteenth and twentieth centuries—it represents only *book* titles and takes no account of fiction published in dailies (beginning in the 1880s) or periodicals (beginning in the 1890s), two elements of the emerging print culture that both Yayoshi's numbers and Nagamine's work highlight. Limitations all, and some no doubt more significant than others. But even given these limitations, the graph is immediately suggestive of a basic fact: how relatively stable the market is over the course of this long

---

[38] See Ekkehard May, *Die Kommerzialisierung der japanischen Literatur in der späten Edo-Zeit (1750–1868)* (Weisbaden: Otto Harrassowitz, 1983), 7ff.; and Yamazaki Fumoto, *Nihon shôsetsu shomoku nenpyô* (Tokyo: Yumani shobô, 1977).

[39] Kokuritsu Kokkai Toshokan, *Meijiki kankô tosho mokuroku* (Tokyo: Kokkai Toshokan, 1989).

nineteenth century, how *little* it grows even in the late nineteenth century. Indeed, there were 1,085 titles published in the first decade of the nineteenth century and 1,243 in the last decade of that century, a 14.5 percent increase. These numbers are slightly misleading because the 1890s happen to mark a sort of low ebb in the number of new fiction titles published, but even if we take instead the 1,620 published in the first decade of the twentieth century, we have only a 50 percent increase. Increases of 50 percent or even 14 or 15 percent are not insignificant, but neither are they revolutionary, certainly not when compared with the increase of fiction titles between the 1750s and the first decade of the nineteenth century, an increase of some 380 percent. There were certainly more fiction titles in 1900 than in 1800, and this number would no doubt swell if it could take account of larger print runs and a longer shelf life for books, and of the titles published in magazines and newspapers. But even given this, what these numbers suggest is that even if there was a printing revolution—if the total number of book titles published each year say doubled or trebled in the three or four decades spanning the turn of the century—this revolution had a relatively small impact on the fiction market, which continued to increase incrementally but saw no real revolutionary activity. The market is relatively stable. And more than that, the numbers seem to suggest that whatever changes the market underwent at the end of the nineteenth century—and however it was impacted by new modes of industrial print culture (from the production of paper to the advent of the steam press)—these changes have to be seen as part of the history of a fiction market that goes back to at least the seventeenth century and that took off during the middle of the eighteenth century.

The history of printing in Japan suggests the need for such a long-range approach. As Peter Kornicki has noted, the history of printing in Japan is both extraordinarily long and extraordinarily counterintuitive: "after the introduction of printing technology in the eighth century, nearly a thousand years elapsed before printing established itself as the principle [*sic*] means for the production of books."[40] Similarly, moveable type was introduced from the Korean peninsula in the late sixteenth century, and there was "a period of some 50 years in which moveable type was used extensively for the production of books" but "moveable-type printing had effectively come to an end by the 1650s. . . . As commercial publishers took over from the patronage arrangements of the early part of the [seventeenth] century, they

---

[40] Peter Kornicki, *The Book in Japan: A Cultural History from the Beginnings to the Nineteenth Century* (Leiden: Brill, 1998), 112.

reverted to block printing in order the better to respond to the demands of the market, and it is this familiar technology which governed the production of books for the remainder of the [early-modern] period."[41] It takes nearly a millennium for block printing to have a notable impact, several centuries for moveable type. This history of printing seems uncannily to bear out Fernand Braudel's conceit that "every invention that presents itself has to wait for years or even centuries before being introduced into real life."[42]

What Braudel suggests is that the history of technology—of technological change, invention, adoption—is extremely complex and extremely *slow*. That does not mean that there are no revolutionary events but that even such events are embedded within a social framework.[43] Whatever the impact new technologies had on the history of printing in late-nineteenth-century Japan, they were impacting a set of social formations that had existed in relation to one another since at least the mideighteenth century. And whatever impact these technologies had on social habits and custom was bound to be slow, complex, and uneven. Viewed from this perspective, a history of reading focused on the late nineteenth century is itself bound to "distort," and we might do well to think of the history of reading practices as more gradual, less revolutionary than is suggested either by our two readers or by Nagamine's argument.

Peter Kornicki has recently argued that reading for pleasure dates back to at least the seventeenth century and that by the mideighteenth century, "intimate reading alone, and probably in silence, was a common practice."[44] Indeed, various modes and habits of reading no doubt coexisted as is suggested by Terakado Seiken in the preface to his 1832 *Edo hanjôki*: "In the fifth month of 1831 I happened to fall sick and unable to sit properly upright and read the works of the sages, I lay idly in bed reading miscellany to chase away the gloom."[45] Intensive reading of a few sacred works on the one hand and extensive reading of miscellany on the other coexist here, serving complementary roles. But what then of our two readers who seem so distant

---

[41] Ibid., 129–30 and 134–35.

[42] Fernand Braudel, *The Structures of Everyday Life*, trans. Siân Reynolds, vol. 1 of *Civilization and Capitalism 15th–18th Century*, 3 vols. (Berkeley: University of California Press, 1992), 1:355.

[43] As Raymond Williams has put it, "A technical invention as such has comparatively little social significance. It is only when it is selected for investment towards production . . . that the general significance begins." See Raymond Williams, "Culture and Technology," in *The Politics of Modernism* (London: Verso, 1996), 120.

[44] See Kornicki, *The Book in Japan*, 262 and 266.

[45] Terakado Seiken, *Edo hanjôki*, in Hino Tatsuo, ed., *Edo hanjôki: Yanagibashi shinshi*, vol. 100 of *Shin Nihon koten bungaku taikei* (Tokyo: Iwanami shoten, 1989), 4.

one from another? How could two such representations of reading be more different? Surely something separates the experience of reading near 1900 from reading around 1800? But as distant as Kuroda's reader at Gray seems from Hokusai's reader, this distance is itself belied by certain traces of continuity—the gendering of the readers, the association of the feminine with the consumption of fiction—that suggest a degree of stability over the course of the nineteenth century to which any history beginning in the 1860s or 1880s would be blind.

The nineteenth century is itself not an object of inquiry familiar to Japanese history. Historiographically, it is conventional to think not of one "long nineteenth century" but of two "short nineteenth centuries": the one extending from the Kansei Reforms of the late 1780s through the Meiji Restoration of 1868 and the other from 1868 until the death of the Meiji emperor in 1912. But this chronology also has built into it an implicit bias for change, and it underscores the totality of the break between the early-modern and modern worlds of print. Behind this chronology is obscured a different history, a history often only visible indirectly through its traces. The idea that history is uneven and that different dimensions of historical experience require different chronologies—what Fernand Braudel once called "a plurality of social times"[46]—is now commonplace. Indeed, when the chronologies of such different histories as those of political institutions, literary form, and cultural practice coincide, as well as they do in the conventional histories of nineteenth-century Japan, it is often because something has been overlooked. Dazzled by the event, we have somehow lost track of the different calibrations of social life.

Event and Structure in Literary History

In his *History of Reading*, Alberto Manguel reflects that the chronology of reading "cannot be that of political history . . . [but] neither does the history of reading correspond to the chronologies of the histories of literature."[47] A political history broken at midcentury by the events of 1868; a history of reading—based on a different chronology—extending over the course of a long nineteenth century; and what of the chronologies of literary forms and literary history? Writing in the 1950s, Nakamura Mitsuo suggests that:

---

46 Braudel, "History and the Social Sciences," 51.
47 Alberto Manguel, *A History of Reading* (New York: Penguin Books, 1996), 22.

The interest that the history of the novel holds for us is that it has acted out, in the most representative of ways, the comedies and tragedies of Japanese culture. . . . Compared with other arts, the modern Japanese novel occupies a special position. Everyone knows that the special characteristic that runs not just through literature but also through all spheres of art in Japan is that there coexist cultural products of an indigenous tradition with modern forms developed under the influence of the West. . . . What is strange is that among all of these forms it is only in the domain of novel that we cannot see such a coexistence or contrast. There is no doubt that contemporary Japanese novels are written based on Western notions of literature and that the word "novel" itself only came to be used in its present fashion under the influence of the modern Western novel but there no longer exist any forms such as *nihonga* or *hôgaku* to oppose it.[48]

Nakamura goes on to quote the novelist Nagai Kafû that "pure Japanese literature completely died out in the late 1890s. Literature after that point was not Japanese literature. Formally, it was Western literature written in Japanese."[49] Mikhail Bakhtin has written of the novel that "it gets on poorly with other genres. . . . Wherever it triumphs, the other older genres go into decline."[50] And this is essentially what Nakamura is suggesting, that the history of the European novel in Japan (or, what amounts to the same thing, the history of the "European novel" written in Japanese) is one both of the triumph of the novel *and* of the decline of other genres of fiction. Among all of the arts, only the novel is unable to coexist with its rivals.

Turning back to figure 4, we can revisit the question of periodization from the perspective of a history of literary form. Given the rupture suggested by Nakamura, is it possible to think in terms of such a long nineteenth century? Is it possible—or useful—to chart the history of the novel along the same axis as the history of other forms of fiction, forms that emerged in the seventeenth, eighteenth, or nineteenth centuries independently of "Western notions of literature"? Perhaps terms such as *the novel* and *fiction* impose a normative relationship among genres that is ahistorical and anachronistic. This is Haruo Shirane's argument in a recent essay on the construction of the canon in Japanese literature. "We've come to use the concept of 'the novel' to refer to a wide range of texts," Shirane writes, "we've come to call such genres as

---

[48] Nakamura Mitsuo, *Nihon no kindai shôsetsu* (Tokyo: Iwanami, 1995), 4 and 5–6.

[49] Nagai Kafû, "Shin kichôsha nikki," quoted in ibid., 7.

[50] M. M. Bakhtin, "Epic and Novel" in *The Dialogic Imagination*, trans. Caryl Emerson and Michael Holquist (Austin: University of Texas Press, 1981), 4.

monogatari, setsuwa, otogizôshi, kanazôshi, ukiyo-zôshi, and *kibyôshi* medieval novels or early modern novels. But until [the introduction of various
literary concepts from Europe in the late nineteenth century] such genres
were regarded as being unrelated to one another."[51] If this is true, then the
usefulness of such concepts for a history of nineteenth-century literature is
limited or, worse yet, the possibility of writing a history of nineteenth-century
Japanese fiction is itself called into question.

The historical record suggests otherwise. In his 1834 *Classification of Recent Fiction Authors of Edo* (*Kinsei mono no hon Edo sakusha burui*),
Kyokutei Bakin, for instance, used the concept of "fiction" (*mono no hon*
物之本) to refer to an array of forms of various lengths, formats, and genres. Bakin explains that the etymology of the term goes back to the eighteenth century: "from over a hundred years ago, all narratives in book form
(*sôshi monogatari* 冊子物語) have been called *mononohon* 物之本. That
term is a contraction of *monogatari no hon* 物語之本 so as to simplify the
rhythm of the word." Bakin's *Classification* covers writers from the Kyôhô
period (1716–36) onward and includes entries (often more than one) for all
of the major writers of the late eighteenth and early nineteenth centuries—
Bakin's friend and sometime rival Santô Kyôden, Kyôden's brother Santô
Kyôzan, Ôta Nanpo, Ryûtei Tanehiko, Tamenaga Shunsui, Jippensha Ikku,
Shikitei Sanba, and, of course, Bakin himself—as well as dozens of other
writers of various degrees of fame and infamy. The *Classification* ranges
over works of various styles from short comic pieces to long historical
narratives and—significantly—was intended to include a section on the libretti of the puppet theater.[52] The most striking feature of Bakin's work is
that although it is a classification of *authors*, the primary subdivision of the
work is by *genre—akahon, sharebon, chûhon, yomihon, jôruri*—suggesting
that not only were these genres understood relationally but that they were
understood as themselves part of a larger classificatory system of *mono no
hon* or "fiction," a classificatory system designed to encompass a range of
works from the eleventh-century narrative of Murasaki Shikibu to recent
satirical writings by Shikitei Sanba.

---

[51] Haruo Shirane, *Sôzôsareta koten: Kanon keisei, kokumin kokka, Nihon bungaku* (Tokyo:
Shin'yosha, 1999), 21.

[52] "Although there are many outstanding works among the recent *jôruri* of Edo," Bakin wrote
in a note at the world of his study, "the people of the world only remember the titles of the libretti
and forget the names of the authors and writers." Not only were such libretti circulated and read
as works of fiction—as the holdings of the Daisô and Nakaya libraries suggest—but, by the midnineteenth century, they were seen to constitute a genre of fiction in their own right.

The history of discourse on fiction in nineteenth-century Japan is complicated by the fact that the late nineteenth century represents in Japan a sort of true *Sattelzeit*, to use Reinhart Koselleck's term, which the historian of English political thought John Pocock describes as a period of transition "in which old patterns of discourse persist while new arise, both interacting vigorously to produce new discursive situations and perhaps an intensified sense of their historicity."[53] Thus whatever integrity Bakin's notion of "fiction" (*mono no hon*) had within eighteenth- and early nineteenth-century discourse on literature, it had come, by the close of the nineteenth century, to be replaced by the term *novel* (*shôsetsu*) based—as Nakamura puts it—"on Western notions of literature." Tomi Suzuki, for instance, looks at the mid-1880s as representing a moment of "paradigm change": the term *shôsetsu* 小説—a lexeme with a history going back almost two thousand years—"changed radically" by having grafted onto it a new set of semantic values as a translation for the concept of the "novel."[54] Such a notion of "paradigm change" fits well with Nakamura's conception of literary history and works to substantiate claims for the totality of a break between early modern and modern worlds of fiction—between *cultural products of an indigenous tradition* on the one hand and *modern forms developed under the influence of the West* on the other. But such a conception perhaps puts the situation too simply and does not pay sufficient attention to *the intensified sense of historicity* of words and concepts in late-nineteenth-century Japanese discourse.

Before turning to what is for Suzuki the locus classicus of this "paradigm change," *Shôsetsu shinzui*, Tsubouchi Shôyô's meditation on "the essence of the novel" written between 1885 and 1886, it is worth pausing to undertake a sort of rudimentary philological exercise, a look at late-nineteenth-century dictionaries. First, two early dictionaries from the 1860s, two decades before the publication of Shôyô's essay: Hori Tatsunosuke's *A Pocket Dictionary of the English and Japanese Languages*, published in 1862, and Jack Hepburn's original 1867 *A Japanese and English Dictionary*, published by the American Presbyterian Mission Press in Shanghai. Both lexemes *novel* and "小説" are

---

[53] See J.G.A. Pocock, "Empire, Revolution, and the End of Early Modernity," in J.G.A. Pocock, ed., *The Varieties of British Political Thought 1500–1800* (Cambridge: Cambridge University Press, 1993), 311. Carol Gluck has similarly referred to the 1880s and '90s in Japan as a "time of settlement." See Carol Gluck, *Japan's Modern Myths* (Princeton, N.J.: Princeton University Press, 1985), esp. 17ff.

[54] Tomi Suzuki, *Narrating the Self* (Stanford, Calif.: Stanford University Press, 1996), 19. On the history of the lexeme in East Asia, see Cho Dong-Il's "Chungguk, Hanguk, Ilbon 'sosŏl' ui gaenyom," in his *Han'guk munhak kwa segye munhak* (Seoul: Ch'isik san'opsa, 1991), 310–49.

A Pocket Dictionary of the English and Japanese Languages compiled by Hori Tatsunosuke in 1862	A Japanese and English Dictionary compiled by J. C. Hepburn and published by American Presbyterian Mission Press, Shanghai, in 1867
Romance, s. 造り物語 Fiction, s. 小説モノ Story, s. 小説雑話 Narration, s. 物語	Novel, Kusazôshi, sakumono-gatari Fiction, Tsukurigoto, tsukuri mono gatari, shôsetsumono Narration, Monogatari Story, Hanashi, setsz [*sic*], mono-gatari Tale, Hanashi, monogatari

used but never as equivalents; "小説モノ" (*Shôsetsu-mono*) is given as a translation for "fiction" in Hori's dictionary, but the dictionary does not have an entry for *novel* as a noun;[55] Hepburn's dictionary, on the other hand, has an entry for *novel* but gives as its equivalents *kusazôshi* (草双紙) and *sakumono-gatari* (作物語) and like Hori's dictionary uses *shôsetsumono* (小説モノ) as a translation for "fiction." Before the 1880s there is indeed no equivalence between *shôsetsu* and *novel*; but afterward? Here are three dictionaries from the 1890s and the first decade of the twentieth century: the eleventh edition of Y. Shimada's *An English-Japanese Lexicon*, published by M. Ôkura, Tokyo, in 1895; Frank Brinkley's *An Unabridged Japanese-English Dictionary*, published by Sanseido, Tokyo, in 1896; and the seventh edition of Hepburn's *A Japanese-English and English-Japanese Dictionary*, published by Z. P. Maruya and Co., Tokyo, in 1903.

Shôsetsu and *novel* are indeed used as equivalents in one way or another in each of the three dictionaries; but the semantic field also becomes extremely complex and varied. Brinkley's dictionary is the best example of this complexity, although it runs through each of the dictionaries. Let us begin with *shôsetsu* 小説, which the dictionary defines as "a novel; fiction; story." So far so good, but the definition goes on to give as a synonym *tsukurib-anashi*, and in its definition for *tsukuribanashi* the dictionary gives two graphic equivalents, 作話 and 小説, suggesting the deep relationship between both concepts, but then goes on to define *tsukuribanashi* as "a made-up story, fictitious tale; fiction; fable," giving several possible equivalents of

---

[55] Hori's dictionary does have an entry for *novel* used as an adjective, for which it gives *atarashiki*.

An English-Japanese Lexicon
(eleventh edition) compiled
by Y. Shimada and published
by M. Ôkura, Tokyo, in 1895

Novel, n. 小説、人情本
Romance, n. 小説
Fiction, n.
　想像、虚構；虚説、小説、作リ話シ、虚偏

**A Japanese-English and English-
Japanese Dictionary** (seventh edition)
compiled by J. C. Hepburn and
published by Z. P. Maruya and Co.,
Tokyo, in 1903

English-Japanese
Novel, n. Kusazôshi, saku-monogatari
Romance, n. Tsukuri-mono-gatari
Fiction, n. Tsukuri-monogatari, tsukuri-
　mono, saku-mono
Narration, n. Monogatari, noberu koto
Story, n. Hanashi, setsu, mono-gatari
Tale, n. Hanashi, monogatari

Japanese-English
Shôsetsu 小説 n, A story, novel, fiction
　Syn. Kukuri-banashi
Sakumono-gatari 作物語 n, A fiction,
　novel
Tsukuri-mono-gatari 作物語 n, A novel,
　fictitious story, romance
Kusazôshi 草双紙 n, Story books, the
　name of a kind of light, fictitious
　literature; a novel, a pamphlet

Mono-gatari 物語 n, History; story;
　narration
Hai-shi 稗史 n, A novel; fictitious story
　book; romance

**An Unabridged Japanese-English
Dictionary** compiled by Frank Brinkley
and published by Sanseido, Tokyo, in
1896

Shôsetsu 小説 n, A novel; fiction; story.
　Syn. Tsukuribanashi
Tsukuri-banashi 作話、小説 n, A made-
　up story, fictitious tale; fiction; fable
Monogatari 物語 n, 1) Talking;
　conversation; collocution; dialogue;
　gossip. 2) A tale either fictitious or real;
　a narration; a romance, or novel, or
　story; a history.
Mononohon 物本 n, A book, work, or
　pamphlet
Ninjôbon 人情本 n, Novels, love-tales
　Syn. Chûhon, Sharebon
Chûhon 中本 n, Books of middle size;
　books of love stories
Saku-monogatari 作物語 n, A fiction;
　novel
Tsukuri-monogatari 作物語 n, A fictitious
　story; fable; romance; fiction; novel
Haishi 稗史 n, A novel, fiction, romance
　Syn. Kusazôshi, Shôsetsu
Kusazôshi 草双紙 n, An illustrated story-
　book (read mostly by women and
　children)

which novel is not one. Rather, *novel* reappears in several other definitions that are not given as synonyms of *shôsetsu*: the second definition of *mono-gatari* 物語; the definition of *ninjôbon* 人情本, an equivalence Brinkley's dictionary shares with Y. Shimada's dictionary; *saku-monogatai* 作物語 and *tsukuri-monogatari* 作物語, which are graphically though not semantically equivalent; and *haishi* 稗史. *Haishi*, moreover, links back to *shôsetsu* by offering it as a synonym but also branches out in another direction by offering as another possible synonym *kusazôshi* 草双紙, which the dictionary defines as "an illustrated story-book (read mostly by women and children)." Brinkley's dictionary is a veritable palimpsest of semantic change. The other two dictionaries are similar. Shimada's gives *shôsetsu* 小説 as a translation not only for *novel* but also for *romance* and even for *fiction*; Hepburn translates *shôsetsu* as "novel" but translates *novel* as "*kusazôshi*" or "*saku-monogatari*," just as in the first edition of his dictionary.

It is against the backdrop of this dense and complex semantic history that we have to situate any rereading of Shôyô's essay on "the essence of the novel" that we might better understand its historicity and its place among older and newer patterns of discourse. Because Shôyô's essay is itself—semantically—just as confused and confusing as Brinkley's dictionary. Indeed, Shôyô, at one point or another in his essay, uses virtually every lexeme that appears in the dictionaries above, in ways that are often seemingly contradictory. This has often been considered one of the great shortcomings of *Shôsetsu shinzui* as a work of literary criticism; what a look at contemporary dictionaries allows us to see is that there is a reason for this great terminological confusion: Shôyô was not working against the backdrop of a blank semantic field that had been wiped clean by some shift—paradigmatic or otherwise—but against a dense and tightly woven semantic web, labyrinthine in character, in which vocabularies and languages from various discourses overlay each other. This essay dramatizes in the most extraordinary of ways the complexity of the situation facing an author sitting down to write a history and theory of the novel in late-nineteenth-century Japan.

Suzuki suggests that *Shôsetsu shinzui*, the title of Shôyô's essay, "usually translated as "the essence of the novel," can also mean "the (Western) novel as the essence of the *shôsetsu*."[56] But is Shôyô writing here of the history of the novel in the West? Or in Japan? Or China? In his section on the "development of the novel," Shôyô draws his examples from Norman romance

[56] Suzuki, *Narrating the Self*, 20.

and Saxon ballads: the *Sumiyoshi*, *Ise*, and *Genji*; Aesop and *Zhuangzi*; the *Xiyouji* (*Journey to the West*), *Pilgrim's Progress*, and the *Faerie Queen*. For Shôyô, the "rise of the novel" does not begin with *Robinson Crusoe* in eighteenth-century England or even some centuries earlier with the Spanish picaresque; rather the novel "develops" over the course of centuries, even millennia, through a slow process of morphological evolution. Given the nature of Shôyô's project it would have been possible—perhaps even likely—for him to draw a stark contrast between the novel and all other forms of narrative—myth, romance, and so forth. Not only does Shôyô fail at every turn to do this, he takes us in the other direction. The major limitation of Shôyô's work—and the source of his terminological confusion—is also its great charm: at the same time he uses concepts ahistorically, he does so in the effort to make sense of what was for him an extremely complex empirical reality. And so he began a project to write a theory of the novel that would explain the European novel, early-modern Japanese fiction, and the great novels of the Ming and Qing, a project—whatever its merits—the possibilities of which have gone largely unexplored since the late nineteenth century.

Rather than borrowing the notion of a sort of Kuhnian paradigm change, we might more usefully approach the issue from the perspective of historical semantics. A.-J. Greimas, for instance, describes the lexeme as "a locus of an historical encounter": "in spite of its fixed character, a lexcme is of the order of an event and as such is subject to history. This means that, in the course of history, lexemes are enriched with new semes. But that same history—being, to put it most extremely, the difference which separates one action of communication from another (for diachrony can encompass a duration of five seconds as well as five centuries)—that same history may empty the lexemes of some of their semes."[57] Greimas's notion of the historicitity of the lexeme is useful because it describes the gradual and heterodox processes of semantic change for a particular lexeme—such as *shôsetsu* or *novel*—and thus makes legible the palimpsest of Brinkley's dictionary as a document of historical semantics. There is perhaps nothing revolutionary about this notion of semantic change, but in some sense that is the point: semantic change is itself rarely revolutionary and requires a methodology that is attentive to the nonrevolutionary character of semic activity.

At the same time, Greimas's notion of the lexeme as being "of the order of an event" despite its "fixed character" is useful because it allows us to situate

---

[57] A.-J. Greimas, *Structural Semantics* (Lincoln: University of Nebraska Press, 1983), 41.

the problem of the semantic history of the concept of the novel within a framework central to debates in the history of thought: *event* and *structure*. The language of paradigm change tends to highlight "events" at the expense of "structure." Thus John Pocock, one of the first historians to adapt Thomas Kuhn's work on paradigms to the history of thought and, with Quentin Skinner, one of the pioneers of a history of concepts that "places illocution at the center," has written that "text and event are for the historian nearly the same thing."[58]

> A history of the concept of, for example, "the state" will in fact be a history of the various ways in which the words *status*, *Staat*, *état*, *estate*, *stato* and so forth have been used. . . . In this history, these words will not have been used on every occasion to convey the concept of the state in any continuous or cumulative sense whatever, so that the history of the language uses and speech acts in which the various cognates of *state* have been involved is not a history of the concept of the state.[59]

The implications of Pocock's work for literary history are extremely important. One might conceive of writing a history of the *novel* or the *shôsetsu* or of *mono no hon*, but in each case these will be very different projects, and there will be—importantly—virtually no overlap. A history of the novel will be a history of the various uses of this concept in the English-speaking world and so will be different from a history of for instance *le roman*, *il romanzo*, or *der Roman*. And a history of the *shôsetsu* will again be something different, as Masao Miyoshi's work has long argued. This sort of work is the first step toward developing what Frederic Jameson once called "a new, historically reflexive, way of using categories such as those of genre, which are so clearly implicated in the literary history and the formal production they were traditionally supposed to classify and neutrally to describe."[60]

The notion of structure takes us in a very different direction, one that may seem, by contrast, to run the risk of being ahistorical. Reinhart Koselleck has

---

[58] J.G.A. Pocock, "Texts as Events: Reflections on the History of Political Thought," in K. Sharpe and S. Zwicker, eds., *Politics of Discourse* (Berkeley: University of California Press, 1987), 24 and 22.

[59] J.G.A. Pocock, "Concepts and Discourses: A Difference in Culture?" in H. Lehmann and M. Richter, eds., *The Meaning of Historical Terms and Concepts* (Washington, D.C.: German Historical Institute, 1996), 53.

[60] Jameson, *The Political Unconscious*, 107.

for instance highlighted the structural potential of concepts in historical research, arguing that

> Historical semantology shows that every concept entering into a narrative or
> representation (eg. state, democracy, army, and party, to cite only general
> concepts) renders relations discernible by a refusal to take on their unique-
> ness. Concepts not only teach us of the singularity (for us) of past meanings,
> but also contain structural potential, dealing with the contemporaneous in
> the noncontemporary, which cannot be reduced to the pure temporal succes-
> sion of history. Concepts . . . become for the historian who employs them *for-
> mal categories which are the conditions of possible histories.*[61]

Both Pocock and Koselleck are writing on the history of political thought,
but substitute the word *novel* in the above passages for *state*, and what I have
in mind will become extremely clear. What Koselleck highlights is the potential that concepts such as "novel" have for *dealing with the contemporaneous
in the noncontemporary*, that is, for seeing relations between historical objects
that at first glance appear to be of very different worlds. By grouping together
both early-nineteenth- and late-nineteenth-century narratives under the
rubric of a single concept, it becomes possible to see them relationally and so
to discover the *possibility* of a history that remains virtually inaccessible when
approached from the point of view of texts as events. Koselleck's notion of
historical semantics is important because of the potentiality he ascribes to
this sort of history: concepts are *formal categories which are the conditions of
possible histories.* A history of the concept of the novel would thus have the
potential of cutting across various borders—both spatial and temporal—and
so allow the historian to discover a potential history—or potential histories—
where none has previously existed. And it is precisely because at present the
history of nineteenth-century Japanese fiction remains only a potential history that Koselleck's notion of structure seems particularly important.

Margaret Doody has recently declared that "the Romance and Novel are
one" and that "the separation between them is part of the problem, not part
of the solution."[62] "The concept of 'Romance' as distinct from 'Novel,'"
Doody writes, "has outworn its usefulness, and . . . at its most useful it

---

[61] Reinhart Koselleck, "Representation, Event, and Structure," in *Futures Past: On the
Semantics of Historical Time*, trans. Keith Tribe (Cambridge, Mass.: MIT Press, 1985), 113,
emphasis added.

[62] Margaret Doody, *The True Story of the Novel* (New Brunswick, N.J.: Rutgers University
Press, 1996), 15.

created limitations and created blindspots."[63] What Doody is attacking is what she calls the "parochialism" of Anglophone historians of the novel, a "parochialism [that] betrays itself in the incessant assertion that the Novel should always be separated from the Romance; there is a symptomatic determination to play down the inconvenient fact that other European literary languages make no such distinction."[64] What Doody's "true" history of the novel aims at is "to help us see the range of surviving forest and not merely the individual trees or, at best, small groves": "if I emphasize continuities, it is because discontinuity, absolute division, has been harshly and hastily asserted before now."[65]

Two things are striking about Doody's "true" history. The first is the emphasis on *continuities* over a strong inclination to stress discontinuity and division, an emphasis that immediately resonates with anyone involved in the history of nineteenth-century Japan. By going beyond such generic concepts as novel and romance, it becomes *possible* to construct a different kind of literary history, one that traces the history of the novel from antiquity through modernity and one that looks at the vicissitudes of the form in the Mediterranean world of antiquity, in China and Japan, in the Islamic world, in early-modern Europe and so forth. Doody risks being ahistorical (treating "an admittedly protean form as if constantly visible from century to century") because she feels that what is to be gained—a new understanding of the novel, a *truer* history of the novel—is worth the wager.

The second striking feature of Doody's polemic is her choice of metaphors: "trees," "forests," "groves." E. R. Curtius once wrote of "a boundless realm" that he called *a garden of literary forms*; Propp borrowed his central concept of "morphology" from botany; and Barthes once suggested that "there is perhaps a certain *endogenous* development of the structure of the literary message."[66] It is as if every time literary history begins to conceive of a history beyond the narrow confines of texts and events (or *texts as events*) it turns to metaphors: metaphors from ecology, botany, biology, metaphors from the *natural* sciences. Why? Because the natural sciences provide a vocabulary

---

[63] Ibid., xvii.

[64] Ibid., 1.

[65] Ibid., xvii–xviii.

[66] See E. R. Curtius, *European Literature and the Latin Middle Ages*, trans. Willard Trask (Princeton, N.J.: Princeton University Press, 1983), 15; V. Propp, *Morphology of the Folktale*, trans. Laurence Scott (Austin: University of Texas Press, 1996), xxv; and Roland Barthes, "Rhetorical Analysis," in *The Rustle of Language*, trans. Richard Howard (Berkeley: University of California Press, 1989), 88.

and a conceptual framework—Greimas calls this a "metalanguage"[67]—which are not strictly bound by a purely historical logic or at least by the logic of history. That is to say the sciences focus on the structural potential of concepts while virtually ignoring the moments of their illocution. By taking a step outside of history and looking for purely formal patterns where traditional history has seen only discontinuity and division we can begin to conceive of a different type of history that is historical in its own right but belongs to a different register than the history of texts and events. This is what Koselleck means when he wrties that *formal categories are the conditions of possible histories*, that is, conditions for histories that do not yet exist but remain to be written.

There is really no other justification for writing a history of nineteenth-century Japanese literature than that we can discern certain formal continuities, certain patterns, certain trends that have an integrity across the century that belies the familiar history of rupture. We might begin such a history of form by choosing a relatively well-established morphological category such as Ian Watt's "formal realism," his term for what he has called "the lowest common denominator of the novel genre as a whole."[68] Thus Etô Jun, for instance, toward the beginning of his pathbreaking essay on the history of realism in Japanese literature, distinguishes between conventional histories of realism in Japan that chart the history of "theories" (*riron* 理論) of realism—and thus begin in the 1880s after the encounter with Western literature—with an approach that would look primarily at "style" (*bunshô* 文章). Etô contrasts the "style" of such works as Tsubouchi Shôyô's *Tôsei shosei katagi* (1885–86) and Futabatei Shimei's *Ukigumo*, which had adopted "realism in theory" but which "rely on a static style" with the "strangely energetic and vital" style of a passage from Katsu Shôkichi's *Musui dokugen* (1842), predating theoretical realism but practicing a sort of stylistic realism.[69] Such a generative approach to the history of realism in Japanese literature allows for the emergence of a different type of historicism, one that calls into question the notion that literary history is reducible to a history of discourse on literature.

Craig Clunas has recently put forward a similar argument in the field of early-modern Chinese visual culture, one that is instructive of the ways that an attention to form can problemetize the emphasis on discursive structures common to recent historical work in art and literature. Clunas begins like

---

[67] Greimas, *Structural Semantics*, 14–15.

[68] Ian Watt, *The Rise of the Novel* (Berkeley: University of California Press, 1957), 34.

[69] Etô Jun, "Riarizumu no genryû," *Shinchô* 68, no. 11 (October 1971): 218–20.

Etô by considering a text—in this case an anonymous sixteenth- or early seventeenth-century painting of a *Lady in a Palace Garden*—which, like Katsu Shôkichi's writing, appears to contradict the normal chronology of the history of realism in Chinese art in which "Chinese art . . . reached a point 'beyond representation' at an early date."[70] By recovering objects like *Lady in a Palace Garden* that are "within representation," Clunas is able to offer a critique of those theories of Chinese art "in which mimetic representation is relegated to a decidedly lower status":

> Such theoretical positions are strong in their ability to explicate and historicize the canon of Chinese painting over the past millennium. They are not always as successful in accounting for all the pictures we have surviving from the Ming period, and not even for all the paintings we have, leaving aside the much larger body of graphic work and of pictures in media other than painting. . . . The mainstream of Chinese art-historical theory is good at explaining why these . . . pictures have been excluded from the cannon, *but is less helpful in explaining why they were made at all.*[71]

For Clunas, the goal of such a critique is "not to argue that Chinese painting is *really* like 'this,' instead of like 'that' " but rather to begin to excavate a fuller history of representation that would account for what he calls the "huge art-historical underclass" that "are very much 'within representation,' even if this still implies a distinctive Chinese epistemology and economy of representation."[72] Both Etô's essay and Clunas's book are opening gambits of sorts, and each offers a glimpse of what an attention to form promises: the possibility of truly revolutionizing literary history, of shifting its center of gravity away from the canon and its discursive supports and toward an encounter with the huge *underclass* of literary history.

Books from Nanjing, Books from Paris

But even as "realism" seems to suggest a useful formal category from which to begin a morphological analysis of the novel, it has, in recent years, come under a series of successive critiques by literary historians like Margaret

---

[70] Craig Clunas, *Pictures and Visuality in Early Modern China* (Princeton, N.J.: Princeton University Press, 1997), 10.

[71] Ibid., 18 and 20–22 (emphasis added).

[72] Ibid., 20 and 22.

Doody and Margaret Cohen who have concerned themselves less with realism's singular triumph than with its plural failures.[73] Such an approach to literary history has the great advantage of not taking literary form for granted and so allowing the historian to develop a generative approach to literary morphology similar to that suggested by Clunas for art history. It is the perfect approach to nineteenth-century Japanese fiction, which both as a body of texts and as a set of institutions has been essentially written out of traditional literary history.[74]

When I first began working on the history of nineteenth-century Japanese literature, I came across two marginal notes that seemed to offer the beginnings of a way of approaching literary history's *huge underclass* from the perspective of literary form, suggesting a way in which formal structures had been historically encountered by reading audiences. The first example is an anecdote in Nagatomo Chiyoji's book on early-modern lending libraries. Nagatomo notes a seventeenth-century copy of Ihara Saikaku's *Kôshoku ichidai otoko*—now housed in the Waseda University Library—that had circulated in the nineteenth century as part of the collection of a commercial library run by Nakaya Shinzaemon in Kinosaki. One patron had written into the endpaper of volume 6: "long and boring."[75] The second example is from a copy of a translation of Tolstoy's *The Kreutzer Sonata*, published in 1908, which I came across in the National Diet Library in Tokyo. Punning on the translation's title—*Chôkon*, "long resentment"—the reader had quipped: "A boring book. Where is the long resentment? The resentment is having read the book. There is no value in its being translated."

---

[73] See Doody, *The True Story of the Novel* ("it is time to drop the pretence that the primary demand of a long work of prose fiction is that it should be 'realistic,'" 16); and Cohen, *The Sentimental Education of the Novel* ("if we unquestioningly equate realism with the modern novel, we give the form a retrospective teleology, perpetuating a narrative of literary history as progress," 5).

[74] Takagi Gen, one of the few literary historians who has attempted to write a history of nineteenth-century Japanese fiction, has for instance recently written: "if we do not investigate that group of works which has been neglected as not being worth looking at [in terms of literary value] then we will be ignoring the majority of nineteenth century Japanese novels." Takagi Gen, *Edo yomihon no kenkyû: Jûkyû seiki shôsetu yôshikikô* (Tokyo: Perikansha, 1995), 423. And "majority" no doubt understates the situation, as Franco Moretti has stressed in a recent article: "the majority of books disappear forever—and 'majority' actually misses the point: if we set today's canon of nineteenth century British novels at two hundred titles (which is a very high figure), they would still be only about *0.5 percent* of all published novels." Franco Moretti, "The Slaughterhouse of Literature," *Modern Language Quarterly* 61, no. 1 (March 2000): 207.

[75] See Nagatomo, *Kinsei kashihon'ya kenkyû*, 59 and 117–18.

Boredom: it is a category to which literary history has devoted little attention but one that is remarkably revealing of the ways in which readers have historically made sense of texts. Every act of reading is an encounter between a reader and a set of presuppositions, a *horizon of expectations*, which is often gratified, sometimes violated, perhaps occasionally subverted by the formal structures of the text. And this is why these two marginal notes are so suggestive: not simply because they allow a perspective on how these two individual texts were encountered by real historical readers but much more broadly because they are suggestive of the contours of a certain set of shared readerly presuppositions that governed—or at least guided—habits of reading across the long nineteenth century.

In the late seventeenth century, Saikaku was one of the most popular living authors; for most of the eighteenth century, his texts were widely circulated and read; by the nineteenth century, he has become already long and boring. Why? Or again, in Russia, *The Kreutzer Sonata* had caused a sensation: Tolstoy's eighth draft had circulated in manuscript, and "even before it had been passed for the press hundreds, even thousands of copies . . . were made, which went from hand to hand, were translated into every language and were read everywhere with incredible passion"; when the book was finally approved for publication as the thirteenth volume of Tolstoy's complete works, Pobedonostev, head of the Holy Synod, wrote to Tsar Alexander III: "On the road from Sevastopol, I saw it on sale in the station and being read in the trains. The book market is full of the thirteenth volume of Tolstoy."[76] But for the early-twentieth-century Japanese reader, it is simply a boring book, unfit for translation.

A great deal of course separates *Kôshoku ichidai otoko* and *The Kreutzer Sonata* from each other. Indeed, perhaps all that they share is that each had made its way into the hands of a reading public very different than that for which it had been originally produced and each in its own way violates the generic conventions and expectations that had come to dominate the act of reading in nineteenth-century Japan. In the case of *Kôshoku ichidai otoko* it is what Donald Keene once called Saikaku's "seriatim construction"[77] or what Ivan Morris calls the "structural weakness in Saikaku's books": "Saikaku's 'novels' lack the rigid construction that we have come to expect in the modern novel and are often close to collections of stories or

---

[76] Quoted in David McDuff, "Translator's Introduction," in Leo Tolstoy, *The Kreutzer Sonata and Other Stories* (London: Penguin, 1985), 16–17 and 19.

[77] Donald Keene, *World within Walls* (New York: Columbia University Press, 1999), 182.

sketches. . . . While most of Saikaku's works have a certain unity of theme, the individual chapters or sections are as a rule structurally independent."[78] And here is David McDuff on *The Kreutzer Sonata*: "as a work of fiction it undoubtedly suffers from numerous defects—importability, long-windedness, structural weakness and much else besides."[79] "*Structural weakness*": it is striking—indeed almost uncanny—that both Morris and McDuff should seize on exactly the same phrase to describe these two books that are in so many ways so very different; indeed, if there is one formal element that these two works share and which may have condemned them to the same fate at the hands of the reading public of nineteenth-century Japan, it is that both are rather digressive and loosely structured.

To the nineteenth-century Japanese reader, Saikaku and Tolstoy were in a sense equally foreign; and this is why nineteenth-century Japanese fiction is such a rich field for a historical morphology: it is a field bordered on one end by the works of a long tradition of Japanese prose and on the other by the introduction of European forms, and yet its aesthetic and readerly sensibilities were dominated throughout by the forms of a third tradition, the Chinese novel. It is a wonderfully rich and complex field, a true *garden of literary forms*, and at its center lies that problem raised by *Kôshoku ichidai otoko* and *The Kreutzer Sonata*, the problem of narrative structure.

The study of early-modern Japanese literature has long been governed by a paradox. On the one hand, it has been described as a "world within walls"—to use Donald Keene's great metaphor—"cut off" from literary influence originating abroad.[80] And yet despite the language with which he frames his study—"*so little foreign literature penetrated the walls with which the Japanese had surrounded their country*," "*the literature of this time developed largely without reference to foreign examples*"—Keene himself devotes a dozen or so pages in *World within Walls* to the influence of Chinese letters on the literary imagination of early-modern Japan. In his recent history of

---

[78] Ivan Morris, "Introduction," in Ihara Saikaku, *The Life of an Amorous Woman and Other Writings* (New York: New Directions, 1969), 41. And here is Donald Keene's judgment on *Kôshoku ichidai otoko*: "Judged in purely literary terms the work is a failure. The story is disjointed and the hero is a cardboard creation with scarcely a recognizable human feature" (*World within Walls*, 170). Of course, Morris rightly cautions that "we must . . . avoid judging Saikaku's books by the standards of the modern novel" ("Introduction," 41), but of course what is interesting about this piece of marginalia is that it was written before the emergence of the "modern novel" in the late nineteenth century and indeed should lead us to problematize an uncritical use of both terms *modern* and *novel* to inscribe a break at the center of nineteenth-century literary history.

[79] McDuff, "Translator's Introduction," 19–20.

[80] See Keene, "Preface to the Columbia Editions," in *World within Walls*, xii.

the book in Japan, Peter Kornicki has put this problem very clearly: "the imports [from China] were insignificant in quantity in the context of a mature
publishing industry in Japan that was producing books for a mass home
market. But the ties to China remained: they conditioned the literary imagination in the second half of the [early-modern] period."[81]

Very few books wielding an enormous influence: it is a somewhat counterintuitive situation but one that would not be without precedence in literary or cultural history. In some sense, this is the logic of the cultural field
that Pierre Bourdieu has described, the importance of books being almost
inversely proportional to their actual numbers. And it is certainly possible—
and I think productive—to think of literary forms in relation to categories
like *distinction* and *symbolic capital*. Indeed, I will return to this problem
later on. But when one runs up against the same paradoxes and contradictions in slightly different forms often enough—very few books wielding
enormous influence, a closed "world within walls" whose literary imagination is conditioned by foreign novels—it is worth investing a little time and
attempting to untangle some of the problems.

History is often complex, uneven, even contradictory. But occasionally it
is the historians themselves—despite their best efforts—who create the illusion of contradiction by posing the problem in the wrong terms. It seems to
me that the critique leveled at sociology by André Leroi-Gourham over a
quarter of a century ago in his *Gesture and Speech* is in many ways still valid:

> Our best sociologists have certainly had things to say about the ongoing rela-
> tionship between the two faces of human existence, but they have always
> said them in terms of the social sphere affecting the material one rather than
> a two-way flow springing initially from the world of matter. The result has
> been that we know more about people exchanging goods for reasons of pres-
> tige than about the kinds of exchanges that go on every day, more about rit-
> ual observances than ordinary services, more about the circulation of dowry
> money than about selling vegetables, and much more about how societies
> think than about how they are structured.[82]

In terms of literary history, it seems fair to say that we know much more
about the power of symbolic capital than that of actual capital and that we
know much more about "influence" than about how texts actually circulated,

---

[81] Kornicki, *The Book in Japan*, 299.
[82] André Leroi-Gourham, *Gesture and Speech* (Cambridge, Mass.: MIT Press, 1993), 148.

how they traveled across borders, were translated, read, even enjoyed. What I would like to do now is to turn to what we might think of as the "vegetable selling" of literary history.

In *The Forbidden Best-Sellers of Pre-Revolutionary France*, Robert Darnton has provided a wonderful example of this sort of book history—an example really and not a model, because the techniques for unraveling the literary economy of prerevolutionary France that he describes are intimately bound up with his archive, the "50,000 letters and several shelves of account books" of the Société Typographique de Neuchâtel.[83] Such an archive does not exist for nineteenth-century Japan, but we have in its place a different archive consisting of dozens of records related to the trade in Chinese books exhaustively outlined and studied by Ôba Osamu in a series of books published over the past several decades.[84] Since the mid-1960s, Ôba has collected all of the extant materials relating to the early-modern trade in Chinese books from various archives throughout Japan and put them together in a thoroughly indexed study. What we have is a very clear if highly fragmented view of the trade in Chinese books in early-modern Japan. Clear because the records supply titles, the years that the books arrived in Japan, and sometimes prices—very detailed information that makes it possible to begin to think about the traffic in Chinese novels in very concrete terms. Fragmented because we have only a scattered handful of each type of record. We know a good deal about the cargoes of particular ships in particular years but have nothing at all for other years, even decades. The outline we can assemble is very rich and detailed in some places, totally blank in others, like Conrad's map of Africa in *Heart of Darkness*. But that said, the "total" or "complete" archive is a sort of fiction or vanishing point: the historian never really begins with a complete set of data, and rather than arguing for the authenticity of our archive, it seems more useful to set its limits and recognize exactly what it can and cannot reveal.

First, some numbers. Figure 5 is based on Ôba's work on the Nagasaki customs records in *Edo jidai ni okeru Tôsen mochiwatarisho no kenkyû* and summarizes what we know of the trade in Chinese books in the century and a half between 1714 and 1855.[85] Figure 6 compares Chinese imports with

---

[83] Robert Darnton, *The Forbidden Best-Sellers of Pre-Revolutionary France* (New York: Norton, 1996), xxi.

[84] See in particular Ôba Osamu, *Edo jidai ni okeru Tôsen mochiwatarisho no kenkyû* (Osaka: The Institute of Oriental and Occidental Studies, Kansai University, 1967), which includes all of the extant records from Nagasaki as well as historical and interpretive essays and a "synopsis" in English.

[85] The figure is based on the summary Ôba gives of his findings on 227.

FIGURE 5. THE TRADE IN CHINESE BOOKS, 1714–1855

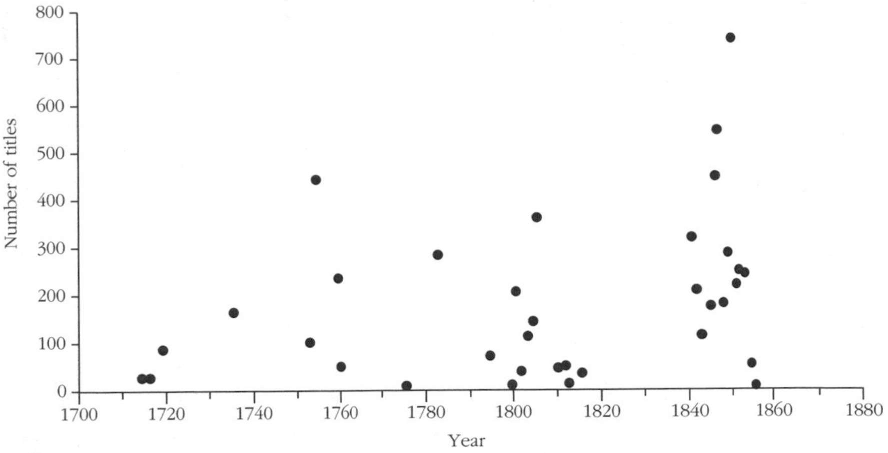

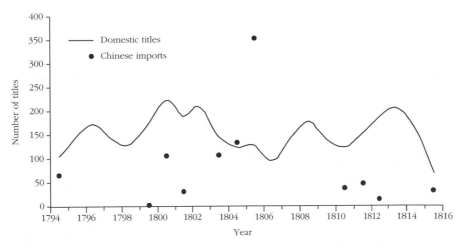

domestic book production for the two decades between 1794 and 1815, the one period for which we have relatively consistent data for both categories.[86] The data are of course very much incomplete, and it is best seen as a sort of guiding framework; still, the numbers are immediately suggestive of the relative gravity of the early-modern trade in Chinese books. A few

FIGURE 6. DOMESTIC PRODUCTION AND CHINESE IMPORTS, 1794–1815

---

[86] "Domestic titles" is based on a composite of figures for titles published in Edo (Tokyo) and Osaka given in *Kyôhô igo Edo shuppan shomoku* (Kyoto: Rinsen shoten, 1993) and *Kyôhô igo Ôsaka shuppan shomoku* (Osaka: Seibundô, 1964). It does not, therefore, include titles published in Kyoto or locally outside the two major publishing centers.

general points emerge. The first thing that this sketch suggests is that the trade in foreign books has a history long predating the Meiji period. Long before Japanese readers got their hands on *The Kreutzer Sonata*, they had been reading *The Romance of the Three Kingdoms* and *The Water Margin*. Translations and imports have to be seen as forming part of a longer history from the mideighteenth century onward, and to start from scratch at the Meiji period decontextualizes European translations. The second point is the relation between imports and domestic production: while there is no sense in which the book market is dominated by Chinese titles, as the numbers suggest, the number of Chinese titles making their way into the Japanese book market at the beginning of the nineteenth century is in no way insignificant. What the comparison with the domestic books trade suggests is that it is no longer really possible to talk about literary "isolation." There were a lot of Chinese titles making their way into Japan, and they are not in any sense overshadowed by domestic production; if anything, foreign books probably comprise a proportionately larger percentage of the book trade than during the Meiji era. It is from this perspective that we have to view the "opening" of Japan in the 1860s and the translation industry of the mid-Meiji period.

But where are the novels in all of this? Table 3 lists the extant data related to the "four masterworks" of the Ming—the *Romance of the Three Kingdoms, Journey to the West (Monkey), The Water Margin*, and the *Jin Ping Mei*—and the two masterpieces of the Qing—*The Dream of the Red Cham-*

TABLE 3. MING AND QING MASTERPIECES

Title	Years of import
Romance of the Three Kingdoms (*Sanguo zhi yanyi* 三国志演義)	1727
Journey to the West (*Xiyou ji* 西遊記)	1758, 1861
The Water Margin (*Shui hu zhuan* 水滸傳) (a)	1717, 1750, 1804, 1840, 1841, 1846, 1854
The Plum in the Golden Vase (*Jin Ping Mei* 金瓶梅) (b)	1750, 1843, 1851
The Dream of the Red Chamber (*Honglou meng* 紅楼夢) (c)	1794, 1804, 1843, 1848, 1852, 1855
The Scholars (*Rulin waishi* 儒林外史)	1850

ber and *The Scholars*.[87] The results are not really surprising: all of them are there, a steady stream of masterpieces from the beginning of the eighteenth century right up until the collapse of the *bakufu* a century and a half later. The reception of these novels in Japan has been well documented, as has their influence on nineteenth-century Japanese letters. In his catalog of illustrated fiction produced in the second decade of the nineteenth century, Tamenaga Shunsui called *The Water Margin* "the greatest of all novels."[88] But we are here only talking about half a dozen titles: important books, yes, some of the great novels of the early-modern world, but even so they would form only a tiny percentage of the hundreds of titles imported each year. This is of course essentially the paradigm adopted when approaching the early-modern trade in Chinese books—very few titles wielding a tremendous influence, a half a dozen books "conditioning" the literary imagination for several generations. But what about literary history's *huge underclass*? What about the *great unread*? Might not there be a whole other trade in "normal," "regular" novels that has essentially be written out of history, overshadowed by the great masterpieces of the Ming and Qing?

Once the question was posed in this way, it was no longer really enough to just look through the archive for titles. On the one hand, it was not always clear what I was looking for: once you stray from the well-worn path of canonical titles, it is not always easy to find one's way. On the other hand, while I was interested in what books had made it to Japan, it seemed that limiting both the starting and end points of my search entirely to the Nagasaki customs records would prove to be a somewhat circular endeavor. What I was interested in was trying to understand the contours of the early-modern trade in Chinese novels, and it is extremely difficult to see borders and overall shapes when you are approaching the problem entirely from the inside. So I decided to use the list of "best sellers" from Robert Hegel's *Reading Illustrated Fiction in Late Imperial China*[89] as a starting point for excavating the history of the early-modern trade in Chinese novels, and the results are shown in table 4. *The Water Margin*, the *Romance of the*

---

[87] (a): Includes *Shui hu zhuan* 水滸傳 (*The Water Margin*) and *Xiuxiang shui hu zhuan* 繡像水滸傳 (*Illustrated Water Margin*); (b): includes *Jin Ping Mei* 金瓶梅 and *Xiuzhen Jin Ping Mei* 袖珍金瓶梅 (*A Pocket Jin Ping Mei*); (c): includes *Honglou meng* 紅楼夢 (*Dream of the Red Chamber*) and *Xiuxiang honglou meng* 繡像紅楼夢 (*Illustrated Dream of the Red Chamber*).

[88] See the entry for Kyokutei Bakin's illustrated edition of *The Water Margin*, *Suiko gadenn*, in *Gedai kagami* (Edo: Bunkeidô, undated).

[89] See Rober Hegel, *Reading Illustrated Fiction in Late Imperial China* (Stanford, Calif.: Stanford University Press, 1998), 65.

TABLE 4. THE BEST SELLERS

Title	Years of import
Jin'gu qiguan 今古奇觀	1731, 1805, 1829, 1843, 1844, 1855
Yu Jiao Li 玉嬌梨	1697
Ping Shan Leng Yan 平山冷燕	1725
Dong Zhou lieguo zhi 東周列國志	1730, 1843, 1844, 1849
Yinglie zhuan 英烈傳	1727
Longtu gong'an 龍圖公案	1845
Shuo Tang houzhuan 説唐後傳	1754
Fengshen yanyi 封神演義	1731
Zui Puti 醉菩提	1707
Nan Bei Song zhizhuan 南北宋志傳	1779
Lü mudan 緑牡丹	(no record)
Jing hua yuan 鏡花緣	(no record)
Pai'an jingqi 拍案驚奇	1726, 1801
Haoqiu zhuan 好述傳	1731

Three Kingdoms, the *Jin Ping Mei*: that these titles were imported—and reimported—was totally unsurprising; but *Yu Jiao Li* and *Zui Puti*? But what was really surprising was not at all that this or that title had made it to Japan but that virtually all of them had. And we have records for only 36 of a 136-year period! The chance that 90 percent of these novels would be recorded in this tiny fraction of the archive is almost unfathomable. One would think just by chance the records of some might simply have been lost—and this may indeed be the case with the remaining two titles.

But even taken together, the masterpieces and the best sellers only amount to twenty titles. In an effort to expand the sample, I decided to look at three subgenres that Hegel lists: historical novels of the late Ming period, Qing military romance novels, and Qing scholar-beauty romance novels.[90] The result is figure 7. The results are of course more mixed. Scholar-beauty romances do well: we have records for just over 70 percent of the set; late Ming historical novels fare comparatively poorly: just under 40 percent; and Qing military romance novels are somewhere in between at

---

[90] See ibid., 45, 49, 50, and 65. For historical novels of the late Ming period there are eight of twenty-one titles; for Qing military romance novels, five of nine titles; for Qing scholar-beauty romance novels sixteen of twenty-two titles; for best sellers, I have followed Hegel's chart (see 65) in including the *Sanguo zhi yanyi, Shuihu zhuan, Xiyou ji, Jin Ping Mei, Rulin waishi,* and *Honglou meng,* thus giving eighteen of twenty titles.

FIGURE 7. IMPORTING THE NOVEL TO JAPAN

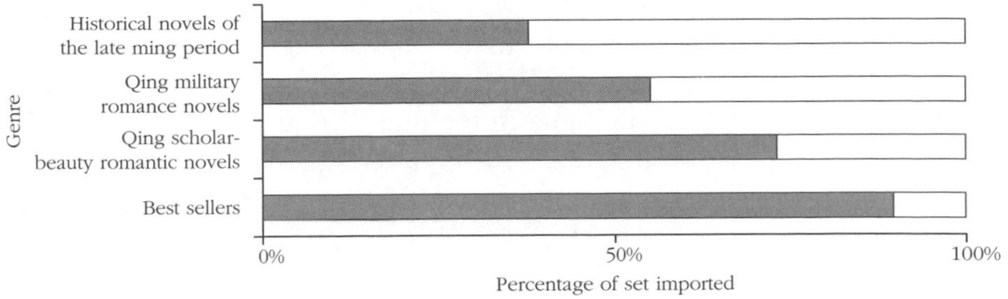

55 percent. But overall, the numbers are extremely high. In his *Edo jidai ni okeru Chûgoku bunka juyô no kenkyû*, Ôba Osamu tells an anecdote in which a Chinese merchant captain shipwrecked in 1826 estimates that some 70 to 80 percent of Chinese titles made their way to Japan;[91] and 70 percent is roughly what the numbers suggest for fiction titles: there are records for forty-seven of the seventy-two titles, or 65 percent.

Between Saikaku and Tolstoy, then, there is the Chinese novel, and it is by understanding the place of the Chinese novel within the literary ecology of nineteenth-century Japan that we can begin to understand how the tastes and the expectations of the reading public had come to be shaped in the centuries that separate the publication of *Kôshoku ichidai otoko* from that of *The Kreutzer Sonata*. What the numbers allow us to see is that it is no longer really useful to imagine the world of Japanese letters as being isolated or closed before the final decades of the nineteenth century, and perhaps even more important, these numbers should lead literary historians to undertake a more thorough rethinking of the widespread use of concepts such as "foreign" and "indigenous," endogenous and exogenous in puzzling out the subtleties of literary history. What the numbers tell us is that virtually the entire literary imagination of late imperial China—one of the richest of the early-modern world—was available to the Japanese reading public by the nineteenth century. "Comparative literature has the immense merit of combating the false isolation of national literary histories," René Wellek wrote many years ago, but it is a lesson that is only slowly being learned.[92]

And this is where the breakdown by subgenre is suggestive: the numbers are of course fragmentary, but the relative success of scholar-beauty romances

---

[91] See Ôba, *Edo jidai ni okeru Chûgoku bunka juyô no kenkyû*, 46.

[92] René Wellek, "The Crisis of Comparative Literature," in *Concepts of Criticism* (New Haven, Conn.: Yale University Press, 1963), 282–83.

is quite striking and somewhat counterintuitive. Counterintuitive because Nagatomo Chiyoji, for instance, puts military tales at the center of his study of early-modern reading habits, and there are good data to suggest that military romances were the most popular prose genre in Japan from the midseventeenth century and into the eighteenth century.[93] And of course many Chinese military and historical novels were imported, translated, and circulated in Japan from the eighteenth century onward. But the success of the scholar-beauty romances is unequivocal: we have records for sixteen of the twenty-two titles, and some, like the *Jin Yun Qiao*, were imported more than once and had a remarkable literary afterlife.

In Vietnam, the *Jin Yun Qiao* became the basis for the *Kim Van Kieu tan truyen* written by Nguyen Du in the early nineteenth century, the verse narrative that would become Vietnam's national epic. In Japan, it was imported in 1754. In just under a decade, a translation appeared, the *Tsûzoku Kingyoden*, published in Osaka in 1763 jointly by FujiyaYahei and Kichimonjiya Shihei, the two most powerful publishers of the time. In 1805, Santô Kyôden adapted the novel in his *Sakurahime akebono sôshi*, and a second and fuller adaptation was made by Kyokutei Bakin between 1829 and 1831, just after the Nagasaki custom's records show that twenty-five copies of the novel were imported in 1828. In the preface to his adaptation, *Fûzoku Kingyoden*, Bakin writes that his edition had been commissioned by the publisher Kinrindô, noting that the "*Kingyoden*, recently written by a Chinese, had become extremely popular with the reading public since appearing in a vernacular translation in 1763."[94]

The congruence of Bakin's new adaptation with the arrival of twenty-five copies of the *Jin Yun Qiao* in Nagasaki attests to the remarkable popularity that this novel and others like it had attained by the early decades of the nineteenth century and is suggestive of the place occupied by the Chinese vernacular novel within the literary landscape of early-nineteenth-century Japan. Indeed, the fate of vernacular Chinese fiction in the opening decades of the nineteenth century—translation, adaptation, often unacknowledged borrowing—is almost exactly that of the European novel in the late nineteenth century, and like the history of the European novel in Meiji Japan, the history of late imperial Chinese fiction in early-modern Japan has to be seen as something extending beyond the success of this or that particular work and beyond even the success of translations or adaptations taken as a whole.

---

[93] See Nagatomo, *Kinsei Kashihon'ya kenkyû*, 188–202 and esp. 188ff.

[94] Kyokutei Bakin, "Fûzoku Kingyoden jôhen no jo," in *Fûzoku Kingyoden* (Edo: Kinrindô, 1829). I have used the copy at the Hôsa Bunko, Nagoya.

Because like the European novel after it, it is not simply that some several dozen Chinese titles made their way into the literary market of nineteenth-century Japan after being imported, translated, and then adapted; more profoundly—and not surprisingly—the Chinese novel provided a model to be imitated. "Compared with Japanese entertainment reading," Nakamura Yukihiko writes, "Chinese vernacular fiction possessed a far superior narrative element. That excellence lay of course primarily in the fineness of the story and its structure as entertainment. For those writers who were stimulated by Chinese vernacular fiction to begin working on new forms of the novel, they began by learning and copying this."[95]

At the beginning of the nineteenth century, Japanese fiction was at a sort of formal crossroads. One need only look at *Gesaku hyôban hana no orikami* to understand this. Published in 1802, *Hana no orikami* reviews and ranks 171 fiction titles published in the last several decades of the eighteenth century. Two books receive the top rank. The first is *Keiseikai tora no maki*, a now half-forgotten book by Tanishi Kingyô, published in 1778 telling of the tragic love of Gokyô and the courtesan Segawa. The second book is *Keiseikai shijûhatte*, a collection of five short sketches of the licensed quarters by Santô Kyôden, then dean of Japanese letters and one of the most celebrated authors of the late eighteenth and early nineteenth centuries. The two books are very different in style, tone, and of course structure. On the one hand, *Tora no maki* is a "sentimemtal tragedy"—to use Nakamura Yukihiko's description—"in which true love is opposed by the power of money and the choice is for death." The overall evaluation in *Hana no orikami* sums up the book's most salient element: "a flawless plot." On the other hand, *Shijûhatte* is composed of five independent sketches centered on the relations between the men and women of the licensed quarters. The reviewer's remark: "adored throughout Edo."[96]

Both books are given equally good marks, and in a sense at the turn of the nineteenth century there existed two equally good models of writing fiction: one tightly structured and plot-driven, the other atomistic and verbally dense. Neither really had the upper hand and, as in *Hana no orikami*, the two existed side by side. But this would change. Already in 1807, Shikitei Sanba—a self-styled follower of Kyôden—sensed something of the turn:

---

[95] Nakamura Yukihiko, "Yomihon hassei ni kansuru shomondai," in *Kinsei shôsetsu yôshiki shikô*, vol. 5 of *Nakamura Yukihiko chojutsushû* (Tokyo: Chûô kôronsha, 1982), 5:363.

[96] See *Hana no orikami*, in *Sharebon taisei* (Tokyo: Chûô kôronsha, 1984), 22:135–82. For the overall evaluations of *Keiseikai tora no maki* and *Keiseikai shijûhatte*, see 138; for the full critique of the two texts, see 154–55.

"Recently, books of wit are dying out and becoming weeping books. . . . We playful writers have been put on the shelf and can only close our mouths and vainly lament that our time is over. To one side, the lending libraries say that only uncouth books are selling and are all the rage. And having stooped to the lowest common denominator, the publishers' coffers are overflowing with rice."[97] It is a marvelous description of the literary market circa 1800: wit and sentiment squared off in a sort of zero-sum game and sentiment emerging the unequivocal winner—backed not simply by the boorish reading public but by the greedy publishers and booksellers as well.

Thus even as the vernacular Chinese novel was entering the Japanese literary market in the late eighteenth century, there was already emerging a formal split within Japanese letters between the prose of wit and the prose of sentiment, between the verbally dense and ornate but structurally loose prose of the eighteenth century and the plot-driven "weeping books" of the early nineteenth century. The Chinese novel—and then the European novel after it—would simply accentuate this split. And so, not surprisingly, a writer like Saikaku spent much of the nineteenth century on the shelf, ignored by a reading public demanding plot and tears; and perhaps equally unsurprising should be the reaction of a nineteenth-century reader who had come across a copy *Ichidai otoko* at a lending library and paid a hefty six *bu* for the entire eight volumes only to discover that the book was very different from what he imagined it might be.[98] But of course, literary history is not really a zero-sum game, and, as Viktor Shklovsky writes in *Theory of Prose*, "the defeated 'line' is not annihilated, it does not cease to exist. It is only dethroned, pushed aside from its dominant position on the crest and submerged beneath it. Still it continues to move forward, always poised for a resurrection as the eternal claimant to the throne."[99] And indeed, although Saikaku would spend much of the nineteenth century on the shelf, he would reemerge at its end—in a somewhat different guise and in much different circumstances—to claim his place within literary history.[100]

And so when the European novel arrived in Japan in the final decades of the nineteenth century, it was, predictably, plot and sentiment that carried the day. In his *Culture of the Meiji Period*, Irokawa Daikichi has written that

---

[97] Shikitei Sanba, "Kejô suigon maku no soto," in *Ukiyoburo; Kejo suigen maku no soto; Daisen sekai gakuyasagashi* (Tokyo: Iwanami Shoten, 1989), in *Shin Nihon koten bungaku taikei*, 86:298.

[98] On the borrowing price of *Kôshoku Ichidai otoko*, see Nagatomo, *Kinsei kashihon'ya kenkyû*, 223.

[99] Viktor Shklovsky, *Theory of Prose* (Elmwood Park, Ill.: Dalkey Archive Press, 1991), 190.

[100] On the "revival" of Saikaku in the late 1880s and 1890s, see Suzuki, *Narrating the Self*, 26 and esp. 196 n. 50.

"the history of Meiji literature shows that during the 1880s and 1890s writers like Shakespeare, Goethe, Wordsworth, Byron, and Heine were just being introduced to Japan while works like *Crime and Punishment* were appreciated simply as detective stories."[101] But the "history of Meiji literature" also shows that hundreds of other works were known and translated in the opening decades of the Meiji period and that authors like Bulwer-Lytton, Verne, and Dumas were avidly read. And under the circumstances, it should perhaps not be surprising that *Crime and Punishment* was appreciated simply as a detective story: detective fiction constitutes one of the largest genres of European novels translated in the final decades of the nineteenth century. A fan of Eugène Sue might well have bought a novel with such a suggestive title expecting a good mystery.

In "Japan, 1850–1900" (in the Critical Apparatus section that opens part 1.4 of this volume) I give a statistical account of European translations in nineteenth-century Japan, and one of the noteworthy things to emerge from that survey is the fact that there does not seem to be a single history of European translations in nineteenth-century Japan but rather two histories, or perhaps a fractured history. In the first several decades of the Meiji period— the 1870s and 1880s and into the 1890s—the market for translations is almost entirely dominated by British and French novels. But then gradually from the 1890s onward the market begins to diversify—both geographically and generically. And viewed from the perspective of the "long nineteenth century" this makes sense: the 1870s and 1880s do not really represent a "break" but are rather an almost seamless continuation of the market that had been developing for foreign books from the eighteenth century onward—only now the foreign books were coming from London and Paris, not from Nanjing. And the public was now weeping not for Cuiqiao, the heroine of the *Jin Yun Qiao*, but for Marguerite, the heroine of Dumas's *La Dame aux Camélias*.

But then, in the 1890s, the market fractures: on the one hand there continues to be an almost unending stream of spy and detective novels, of sentiment and melodrama, adventure and science fiction; but then too there are the Romantics, there is Shakespeare, there are the great Russian novelists— Dostoyevsky, Tolstoy, Turgenev. And not surprisingly, this fracturing created its share of confusion. Thus, for our disappointed reader of Tolstoy, the title of the translation—*Chôkon*—perhaps unwittingly echoes the title of one of the great sentimental novels of the mid-Meiji period—Ozaki Kôyô's *Tajô*

---

[101] Irokawa Daikichi, *Culture of the Meiji Period* (Princeton, N.J.: Princeton University Press, 1985), 73.

takon—and it is easy to imagine how a reader familiar with Kôyô's novel and perhaps familiar too with the spate of European sentimentality translated during the Meiji period might be disappointed by the highly complex and polemical *Kreutzer Sonata*. For any reader interested in plot, *The Kreutzer Sonata* is bound to disappoint.

And yet somewhat like Saikaku—and at roughly the same time—Tolstoy too came to have his admirers in early-twentieth-century Japan. What is interesting about these two phenomena that seem so totally unrelated is that each is in a sense the result of the fracturing of the book market in the 1890s and the development of a "dualist structure" similar to that described by Pierre Bourdieu for nineteenth-century France. It is not that a taste for sentiment and melodrama dies out at the end of the nineteenth century but that a new type of reading—or perhaps something of a return to an older type of reading?—begins to emerge in the middle decades of the Meiji period. It is a moment perfectly captured by Natsume Soseki in his 1906 *Kusamakura* in a dialogue between the narrator—a painter under the spell of Shelley—and a disarming young woman, Nami, who asks him about what he is reading:

> "I see you're reading a Western book. I expect it's all about the most complicated things, isn't it?"
> "Not really."
> "Well then what is it about?"
> "That's a difficult question. To tell you the truth I'm not absolutely sure myself."
> . . .
> "I just lay the book open on the desk, and pick out passages to read at random."
> "Do you enjoy that?"
> "Yes, I enjoy it."
> "Why?"
> "Why? Well that's the most interesting way to read a novel."
> . . .
> "What's wrong with reading a novel from the beginning?"
> "Because if you start reading from the beginning, you have to read to the end."
> "That seems a peculiar reason. What's wrong with reading to the end?"
> "Nothing at all, naturally. I do it myself when I want to read the plot."
> "But if you don't read the plot, what else is left?"[102]

---

[102] Natsume Soseki, *The Three Cornered World*, trans. Alan Turney (Tokyo: Charles E. Tuttle, 1968), 122–23. I have modified the translation for the sake of consistency.

In art and plot or "art and money," as Bourdieu writes in *The Rules of Art*, "the unified literary field tends to organize itself according to two independent and hierarchized principles of differentiation: the opposition, between pure production, destined for a market restricted to producers, and a large-scale production, oriented towards the satisfaction of the demands of a wide audience."[103] And at the center of the literary field—as at the center of this dialogue—lies the novel, the "most dispersed genre" in that it alone can appeal both to a "mass audience" and an "intellectual audience"; the novel occupies the "central position of both dimensions of the literary space."[104]

And so this dialogue spells out what the numbers and graphs hint at: an emerging split in the 1890s and the first decade of the twentieth century between money and art, between commercial literature and art for art's sake, between plot and . . . and what? "If you don't read the plot, what else is left?" Nami asks, and it is a question that essentially goes unanswered. As Karatani Kojin has written, "modern Japanese literary history has been dominated by the notion that a deepened interiority and its expression are the criteria of literary merit,"[105] and so perhaps not surprisingly the literature of Nami—the literature of plot, the literature of the *nineteenth century*—has essentially disappeared from literary history and there exists a sort of long caesura between Saikaku and Tolstoy, between the works of an "indigenous tradition"—to return to Nakamura Mitsuo's terms—and those works written under the spell of Western literature, no longer works of Japanese literature in the strict sense but simply Western novels written in Japanese.

---

[103] Pierre Bourdieu, "The Emergence of a Dualist Structure," in *The Rules of Art* (Stanford, Calif.: Stanford University Press, 1996), 121.

[104] Pierre Bourdieu, *The Field of Cultural Production* (New York: Columbia University Press, 1993), 51.

[105] Karatani Kojin, *The Origins of Modern Japanese Literature*, trans. Brett De Berry (Durham, N.C.: Duke University Press, 1993), 137–38.

Epic and Novel in India

A Tangled Genealogy

The assumption that the novel in India was a borrowed genre—the indirect outcome of English education introduced in the nineteenth century by the British rulers—had remained unquestioned for a long time. From 1860 onward, the fictional texts written in different Indian languages that were identified as novels came to be evaluated largely in terms of their closeness to Western models. The canon legitimized by literary historians was constructed on the unarticulated premise that there was a universal paradigm of novel writing, and because it began in Europe, all subsequent practitioners would need to be judged by the standards set there. Thus in India, literary status was conferred and the appellation *novel* bestowed only on those long narratives that best adapted this European form to incorporate local material.

It is only very recently, in the last couple of decades to be exact, that critics have begun to address themselves to the complex question of plural heritage, the multiplicity of determinants—both indigenous and derived from other cultures—that overlapped, interacted, and fused to make the shaping of this literary form a tangled and unique process in India. Some of the narrative pulls and pressures were not as overtly visible as the stated intention of replicating the "realism" of British Victorian fiction. (Whether this realism actually amounted to fidelity of representation; whether representation can ever be true to life, or whether realism is just another narrative mode using a different set of literary conventions; whether British fiction of the period was actually reflecting life more accurately than before—these were not questions raised at that time.) The early novels in India need to be read closely, sometimes against the grain, to go beyond their stated intentions and pry open the operations of the other, often subterranean forces in their formation.

On the surface, a conscious privileging the "real" over the "fantastic" was a fairly common enterprise of these first generation of writers, as seen for example in the following passage from a novel in English written in 1875: "You are not to expect anything marvellous or wonderful in this little book. My great Indian predecessors . . . have treated of kings with ten heads and twenty arms; of a monkey carrying the sun in his arm-pit . . . of being man above and fish below, or with the body of a man and the head of an elephant; of sages, with truly profound stomachs, who drank up the waters of the oceans in one sip."[1] The vehemence of Lal Behari Day's rejection of tropes common in traditional stories almost matches Thomas Babington Macaulay's contempt for what passed for knowledge in India: "History, abounding with kings thirty feet high and reigns thirty thousand years long and Geography made up of seas of treacle and seas of butter."[2] Lord Macaulay was one of the advocates for officially adopting English as the medium for education in India and who argued against the "Orientalists" who preferred Sanskrit, Arabic, or Persian. A liberal member of the British Parliament, a historian and a critic closely associated with the *Edinburgh Review*, Macaulay was appointed a member of the Supreme Council for India from 1834 to 1838. His "Minute on Indian Education," which contained the above lines was passed in 1835 to make the study of English (and English literature) compulsory in higher education in India. Macaulay remains a frequently invoked name in educational or cultural debates in India even today, because his decision in favor of English has had far-reaching effects on subsequent intellectual and literary developments in the country. His utilitarian impatience with mythic imagination and the dismissal of traditional iconography played a role in evolving a school of thinking in Indian art and literature in the late nineteenth century that was strongly mimetic in intention.

Macaulay's echo can be heard in O. Chandu Menon's well-known manifesto on realism in the introductory pages of his *Indulekha* (1889), one of the earliest novels written in Malayalam:

> [People] asked me while I was employed on this novel, how I expected to make it a success if I described only the ordinary affairs of modern life without introducing any element of the supernatural. My answer was this: Before the European style of oil painting began to be known and appreciated in this country, we had—painted in defiance of all possible existence—pictures of Vishnu as half man and half lion . . . pictures of the god Krishna with his legs twisted and turned into postures in which no biped could stand. . . . Such productions used to be highly thought of, and those who produced them were highly remunerated, but now they are looked upon by many with aversion. A taste has set in for pictures, whether in oil or water colours, in which shall be delineated men, beasts, and things according to their true appearance, and the closer that a picture is to nature, the greater is the honour paid

---

[1] Lal Behari Day, *Govinda Samanta* (1875), quoted from a later edition reprinted as *Bengal Peasant Life* (London, 1909), 2.

[2] Thomas Babington Macaulay, "Minute on Indian Education" (1835), quoted from *Victorian Prose*, ed. S. Nagarajan et al. (Poona, 1968), 69.

to the artist. Just in the same way, if stories composed of incidents true to natural life and attractively and gracefully written, are once introduced, then by degrees the old order of books, filled with the impossible and the supernatural, will change, yielding place to the new.[3]

Despite this declaration of fidelity to nature, and insistence on delineating "things according to their true appearance," Chandu Menon's novel nevertheless veers toward the pre-novel forms of storytelling and away from the realistic mode he so admires. The idealized young lovers in *Indulekha* are paragons of beauty and virtue (it follows the Sanskrit *kavya* convention of *nakha-shikha-varnan*, that is, describing the heroine's beauty from top to toe), and their courtship is presented in a stylized manner (her heart is flint, he cannot sleep at night, they express their love in poetry). There is hardly any attempt to individualize the characters; the delay in their union is caused by purely external factors. There is no conflict within the individual or between the individual and society that often provided the plot dynamics in the novel as it emerged in Europe. The adversaries in *Indulekha* are either illusory or comic figures, and the action is propelled forward by accidents and coincidences. Once separated, the heroine languishes in illness, while the hero goes on a picaresque journey where he proves his valor and worth, following familiar fairy tale and folklore conventions. Either because of these elements, or in spite of them, *Indulekha* has remained a popular novel in Malayalam for over a century.

But the ironic gap between the author's narrative intention and textual execution is never more clear than at the end:

> Now my story is ended. . . . All the characters mentioned in the book are still alive. Madhavan has now attained a high rank in the Civil Service and he and Indulekha are blessed with two children, one a daughter and the other a son, both beautiful as harvest moon. Madhavan by his industry, uprightness and ability, and Indulekha by her devotion to her children and her husband, have reached the summit of human happiness, and May god bless us and all who read this tale. (367–68)

The last line is quite similar to the ending of the oral recitals of *puranas*, where the telling of and the listening to a story are ritual acts. For example, when Kashiram Das's Bangla version of the *Mahabharata* is read aloud, each

---

[3] O. Chandu Menon, *Indulekha* (1889), quoted from English trans. by W. Dumergue (1890) (reprint; Calicut, 1965), xiv.

recital ends with the following couplet: *Mahabharater katha amrita saman / Kashiram Das kahe, shune punyaban* (The story of the *Mahabharata* is like nectar / Kashiram Das narrates it and those who listen to it gain in virtue). Incidentally a novel in Urdu—*Umrao Jan Ada*, (1899) by Mirza Hadi Ruswa, written a decade after *Indulekha*—also ends in a similar fashion, even though the author is a Muslim. The *katha*-like[4] ending of novels links them to the tradition of Hindu sacred rituals (even though the theme or its treatment may in no way be religious), quite different from the secular realist tradition of the Western novel. In the fairy tale–like ending of *Indulekha*, the hero and heroine achieve the "summit of happiness" and live happily thereafter. What could be a greater happiness in colonial India than getting a job under the British in the Civil Service?

But to attribute such endings only to the gravitational pull of the indigenous traditions would be to deliberately overlook the fact that many Victorian novels in England also used marriage and the promise of bliss thereafter as the trope of closure. The boundary between what was absorbed from local practice by a process of osmosis and what was learned from Western models consciously is thus not such an easy line to draw.

The device of authorial intervention, for example, was as much a borrowing from the "Dear reader" convention of Victorian fiction as a continuation of the practice of the *harikatha* in Karnataka, *kathakata* in Bengal, and other oral traditions of ritual storytelling in different parts of India. In each case the narrator would occasionally keep the story on hold to establish a direct relationship with the audience in order to drive home a moral point or to share views on a character. Examples of this are common in the early Indian novel. In *Debi Chaudhurani* (Bangla, 1882), the author feigns discomfiture before readers of "modern" taste when a young man kisses his wife: "the author is a traditional man—he is not embarrassed to record this—but I assume the refined reader of the new generation will stop reading the book at this point."[5] This is evidently a dig at Victorian prudery that English education had introduced, changing the norms of propriety among the Westernized elite in Calcutta. In another novel, *Bishabriksha* (Bangla, 1873), an early chapter titled "The Reason Why the Reader Is Angry" begins thus: "Now my reader will be most annoyed. It is the custom that marriage takes place at the end of a fictional work. But we are getting Kundanandini married right away" (219). In another novel, *Krishnakanter Uil* (Bangla, 1878), the author

---

[4] *Katha* is a generic term for oral recital of stories.

[5] Bankimchandra Chatterjee, *Bankim Rachanboli*, in *Collected Works* (Calcutta, 1980), 1:747. My translation. The next two quotations are also from this volume.

makes a direct comment: "We have already told you Rohini is not a good woman. . . . Why then should we to cry at her grief? . . . But let us not be so particular. It is good to weep at the sorrow of others. God's clouds do not refrain from raining on thorny fields" (497). In such passages, the author could be emulating Victorian novels, which abound in authorial intrusions, as in Thackeray's *Vanity Fair*: "This I set down as a positive truth. A woman with fair opportunities, and without an absolute hump, may marry WHOM SHE LIKES. Only let us be thankful that the darlings are like the beasts of the field, and don't know their own power"[6]—or asides about what "our observant readers" must have already noticed (88). The Indian readers' suspension of disbelief was not affected by these interventions because s/he was quite familar with such direct communication in oral narratives.

Multiple elements drawn from divergent sources converged in the novels that became popular in India in the second half of the nineteenth century. Take the example of one writer—Bankimchandra Chatterjee (1838–94) whose fourteen novels exerted considerable influence on other writers not only in Bangla, the language in which he wrote, but also in several other Indian languages through translation. He was equally well-read in English, Sanskrit, and Bangla literatures. His novels, set in the past as well as in his own time, serve as richly productive sites for studying the complex, and often contradictory, configurations of the colonial mind, and also for understanding the process in which the emergent notion of national identity was constructed through fictional rewritings of history. Bankimchandra Chatterjee's initial and tentative attempt to write a realist novel in English about domestic life in contemporary Bengal (*Rajmohan's Wife*, 1864), based on a Victorian narrative model, was hardly noticed by anyone. Two years after this still-born English text, he switched gears—not only to write in his mother tongue Bangla but also to choose a more extravagant mode to narrate stories set in the past—and the success of *Durgeshnandini* (1866) was resounding. The reverberations continued for several decades: the novel was reprinted many times, dramatized, retold and imitated in Bangla repeatedly, and was translated and adapted in other Indian languages. Set in the late sixteenth century, *Durgeshnandini* deals with the conflict between the Mughal emperor of Delhi and his envoy in the eastern state of Bengal, evoking the color, sweep, and imaginative intensity of a romance. Its linguistic registers range from the sonorousness of Sanskrit *kavya* in the description of nature, to the earthiness of the Bangla spoken by common people of his time in the description of ordinary life, to a racy idiom peppered with Urdu and Persian

---

[6] William Makepeace Thackeray, *Vanity Fair* (1848) (Harmondsworth, 1972), 65.

words in the conversation of the Muslim soldiers. The native conventions of storytelling coexist with devices used in English historical novels. It is obvious that Bankim had read and admired Sir Walter Scott, but what he derived from the Waverly novels gets deflected by the undertow of other literary currents. Even though the processes of such coalescence, intertwining, and fusion cannot be charted accurately, it may be useful to take a look at some of the pre-novel narrative traditions present in different parts of India when the new genre called the novel made its self-conscious entry in the 1860s and 1870s.

Past Continuous: The Epics

Through the centuries, the most frequently read, recited, rewritten, adapted, interpreted, and subverted long narratives in India have been the two so-called epics: the *Ramayana* and the *Mahabharata*. To refer to these works in a discussion of the modern form called the novel might at first seem like going back too far, because the novel as a genre belongs to print culture, while epics are generally traced back to oral societies. But the oral and the written, seen as two distinct narrative traditions in the West, were not such clearly distinguished categories in the Indian past, where a written text might often have been disseminated orally or an oral tale acquired a number of written versions.

One of the recalcitrant areas in a literary discussion across cultures is that of terminology. *Epic* in the context of India means neither "primary epics" like the *Iliad* or the *Odyssey*, nor the secondary variety written by Virgil or Milton. In fact, there is no exact synonym for *epic* in Sanskrit—the language in which the *Ramayana* and the *Mahabharata* were originally composed. In English, both are referred to as *epic*, but the category for the *Ramayana* in Sanskrit is *kavya* (narrative in verse) or *mahakavya* (long narrative in verse); for the *Mahabharata*, it is *itihasa* ("thus it happened"—what is now called history) or *itihasa-purana*, which is one of the many subdivisions of the generic term *purana* (meaning stories of the gods).[7]

Thus the narrative conventions of the two texts—*Ramayana* and *Mahabharata*—are quite different, and so are their overall status in the culture. *Ramayana* in many parts of India is regarded as a sacred text, the reading

---

[7] Other such subcategories of *puranas* include *sthala-purana* (place legend), *teertha-purana* (legends connected to pilgrimages), *varna-purana* (origin myths of dominant castes). See Romila Thapar, *Situating Indian History*, ed. S. Bhattacharya and R. Rhapar (Delhi, 1986), 380.

aloud of which is a ritual act. Its hero Rama is simultaneously looked upon as god as well as a historical figure whose birthplace, many Indians believe, can be located exactly on the map of India. The space created by this ambivalence remains potent to this day, and the controversy regarding the place of Rama's birth resulted in a political impasse in the 1990s that remains unresolved even at the beginning of the twenty-first century, testifying to the continuing relevance of the *Ramayana* in contemporary India. A month-long folk performance of the story of *Ramayana* is an annual feature in many towns and villages of north India even now. Enactment of the *Ramayana* (and later also the *Mahabharata*) as a televised serial on Sunday mornings was the biggest nationwide media event of the 1980s. The *Ramayana* provides to this day certain moral paradigms, providing ideal codes of conduct in family relationships as well as in pubic life. While popular fiction and films tend to validate these values in terms of modern life, the interrogation or subversion of the role models and ethical norms contained in the *Ramayana* is also a famliar practice in serious literature and other narrative arts in our time. Both the enterprises depend equally on a widespread familiarity with the frame of reference created by the *Ramayana*.

The *Mahabharata* on the other hand is a vast storehouse of stories around the core narrative of a fratricidal battle in a royal clan, abounding in tales of deceit, aberration, transgression, deviant morality, greed, treachery, and lust, thereby problematizing the relationship between statecraft and ethics. There is hardly an ideal character in this saga. Except for the section that contains the *Bhagavat Gita*, no other part of the *Mahabharata* is considered sacred. Its appeal through many centuries lay mainly in its compelling and complex narrative. Unlike the *Ramayana*, reading *Mahabharata* aloud inside a home is forbidden in certain parts of India, because it is believed to bring about domestic strife. The length of the *Mahabharata* is some eight times that of the *Iliad* and the *Odyssey* put together. It has been subjected to substantial additions and interpolations over many centuries (according to some scholars, most of the accretions happened between 400 B.C. and 400 A.D.), and it now exists more as a tradition than as a text.[8] Several Indian languages have proverbs about the inclusiveness of the *Mahabharata*, such as "What is here may be elsewhere, but what is not here is nowhere else" or "What is not in *Mahabharata* is not in Bharata [India]." Certain concerns of the modern Indian novel—for example, conflict between an individul's social function and personal predilection, smoldering anger of strong women trapped in restrictive gender roles, questioning of caste as identity marker, transgressive

---

[8] For detailed discussion of this point, see A. K. Ramanujan, *Collected Essays* (Delhi, 1999), 162.

sexuality, corruption in politics—all seem to be prefigured in this amazing text that has existed in some form or other for at least two thousand years. There are hardly any major novelists in India in the twentieth century who have not—either directly or obliquely—deployed myths and motifs from this epic in their texts.

Over the centuries most major languages of India have rewritten (it is important to remember that these are not translations) the *Ramayana* and the *Mahabharata* to fit their regional ethos and available metrical repertoire. Even to the novelists of our time, exposed as they are to global influences, reinterpretations of episodes from these epics continue to be a creative challenge. Thus the epics in India do not belong to the past alone—they are also part of the contemporary consciousness. Some postmodern English writers from the subcontinent, who may not be ordinarily seen as part of the continuity of the narrative tradition in India, use intertextual references to the *Mahabharata* either playfully or in order to tether their novels to a larger, semimythical context.[9] Not only do novelists in many Indian languages continue to reinterpret specific incidents and derive symbols, narrative structures, and moral dilemmas from this inexhaustible reservoir; even in public life and political action the rhetoric from these epics is used to sway emotions and to aid and abet violence, and tropes from these provide material for constructing alternative ideas of the nation in currently raging ideological battles across the country.

Other Traditions

Among other popular pre-novel narrative forms circulating in different parts of India that might have enriched the protean genre called the novel, are *qissas* and *daastans*—two storytelling styles that can be traced back to Arabic and Persian but whose features underwent changes as they became incorporated in north Indian folklore and popular entertainment. *Qissa* in Arabic merely means "story," but in the Indian subcontinent it came to mean specifically a "verse-narrative telling the tragic story of two young people who love each other beyond discretion."[10] Well-known examples of this genre are *Laila-Majnu, Heer-Ranjha, Sassi-Punno, Soni-Mahiwal,* and *Yusuf-Zulekha* (written roughly between the sixteenth and the eighteenth centuries), with

---

[9] Salman Rushdie, *Midnight's Children* (London, 1981); and Shashi Tharoor, *The Great Indian Novel* (Delhi, 1989) are two examples.

[10] Sujit Mukherjee, *A Dictionary of Indian Literature* (Delhi, 1999), 302.

the names of the star-crossed lovers inscribed in each title. Most of these stories existed in different versions in north Indian languages like Panjabi, Urdu, Sindhi, and different dialects of Rajasthani and Hindi—and subsequently were also retold in Gujarati and Bangla—languages of the western and eastern edge of the Indo-Gangetic plain.

Daastan was a long prose-narrative or a chain of linked narratives. "The form was developed in Arab countries where the *daastan-go* (storyteller) had made it into a profession that was honoured by kings and nobles."[11] In India the form was patronized in the courts at Delhi and Lucknow in the pre-British days, but its popularity was not confined to elite society. The most widely circulated *daastans* were *Daastan-e-Amir Hamza*, a long interlocking prose tale featuring the character Amir Hanza written by Faizi, supposedly for the entertainment of Emperor Akbar, and *Daastan-e-Tilism-Hoshruba*, a massive prose work in seven books concerning the deeds of a brave warrior who attacks the magic (*tilism*) city of Hoshruba to defeat the forces of evil led by Afrasiayab. Another one called *Kissa Tota-Maina* used the motif of birds as the teller of tales. These popular cycles dealt with adventure, fantasy, love, and war—and were dominated by heroes of invincible courage and women of irresistible beauty. Such tales allowed freedom to the imagination in the fabled description of riches, passion, and regal splendor.

Popular reading in Hindi in the nineteenth century before the novel emerged included, apart from *qissas* and *daastans*, cycles of stories from Sanskrit also—like V*etala-pachisi* (twenty-five stories within a single narrative frame, each one ending with a conundrum), *Simhasasan-battisi* (thirty-two statues supoprting the throne of king Vikramaditya, each telling a story to prevent a less worthy king from sitting on it), and other tales featuring miraculous happenings and magical deeds. In addition to these popular cycles, there was a literary tradition in which the Sufi influence provided an added symbolic dimension to a love story, turning it into a spiritual allegory. These were written very often in medieval versions of Hindi. Examples are *Chandayan* (ca. 1370), *Madhu-Malati* (ca. 1544), and *Padmavat* (1530), some of which permeated to other languages in slightly modified versions. For example, Malik Muhammad Jayasi's *Padmavat* surfaced in the easternmost part of Bengal as *Padmaboti* (1651) as a narrative in Bangla written by Alaol, adapted to suit the local oral recital form called *panchali*.

In Bangla, popular fiction of the pre-Bankimchandra era (that is, before the 1860s) also included material like *Gul-e-Bakavali* and *Bijoy-Basanta* (the first carried over from Persian storytelling tradition and the other from

---

[11] Ibid., 86.

Sanskrit *kavya*), both mentioned by Rabindranath Tagore in his essay on Bankimchandra (1894) where the latter is credited with bringing Bangla literature out of such childish entertainment toward maturer pleasures. The same *Gul-e-Bakavali* that Rabindranath read as a child was available to the Marathi reader in the western part of India in Navalkar's translation from Gujarat, the Gujarati version itself being a translation from Persian. A similar text, *Gul-va-Sanovat*, was translated in 1867 by David Highham, an Indian Jew, from Urdu into Marathi. Tales from the *Arabian Nights* and *Hatim Tai* were available in Bangla adaptation as well as Marathi, and in quite a few other Indian languages as well. Although the major languages of India have distinctly different literary traditions, the linguistic boundaries have been in many ways porous, particularly when it comes to stories.

The popularity of the books mentioned above persisted for a long time. As a schoolboy, Premchand (1880–1936), a major Hindi novelist of the early twentieth century, read *Tilism-e-Hoshruba* and *Hatim Tai* with as much relish as the Urdu translation of the scores of volumes from the now forgotten Victorian pulp-writer G.W.M. Reynolds.[12] The best-known and most influential of Reynolds's books in India was the multivolume *The Mysteries of the Court of London*, which was read widely in English as well as in Indian language adaptations. In Hindi it was translated in fifty-four volumes as *London Rahasya* between 1905 and 1922. More than a dozen popular novels in Bangla by Harisadhan Mukhopadhyay, and a larger number in Hindi by various writers, were admittedly inspired by the success of Reynolds. The sensational and spectacular elements in these stories, particularly the description of royal splendor and the extravagance of sensual delights, could not but have left their mark on the early novels in India, making it difficult today to sift the strands of the traditional and the new, the indigenous and the foreign, the popular and the elite.

Fiction and Fantasy

The novel emerged in the second half of the nineteenth century, at first tentatively, purporting to be a vehicle of social reform or a mirror of contemporary life (it is interesting that a number of early novels were written in response to contests announced by the colonial government for depicting contemporary Indian life in the form of fiction). By the time it actually captured popular imagination, however, it had moved far from the original

---

[12] Amrit Rai, *Premchand: A Life*, trans. Harish Trivedi (New Delhi, 1982), 18.

intentions. Despite the avowed affiliation with realism, at the initial stage what attracted readers were not representations of ordinary life or novels with reformist zeal—of which there are many examples, but tales set in the real or imaginary past in which events were not restricted by the cold limits of plausibility. Elements of fantasy and intimations of history are inextricably knotted in these works. Chronicles merge with legend, events lapse into magical happenings, and kings who lived once-upon-a-time cast their spell on those who ruled at historically recognizable periods over geographically precise areas. The spectrum covered by these novels is not only wide but also varied and uneven. It ranges on one hand from Romesh Chandra Dutt's Bangla novel *Maharashtra Jiban Prabhat* (1878, roughly translated as *Dawn of Maharashtra's Glory*), a fictional rendering of Maratha power under Shivaji's leadership challenging Moghal hegemony in the seventeenth century, underpinned by the story of a romance between the daughter of a fort commander and a young subaltern in Shivaji's army, to Devakinandan Khatri's *Chandrakanta* (Hindi, 1891), a fabulous saga of the sensational and the marvelous that soon became a cult, six editions of several thousand copies selling out in a decade. Given the low literacy rate, limited reading habits, and modest buying power of the Hindi readers of the time, this sales figure is quite impressive. (Incidentally, this novel made a reappearance as a television serial after a hundred years, topping all popularity charts for many months in the 1990s.) *Chandrakanta* and its two sequels spawned a category of extremely popular novels in Hindi in the last decade of the nineteenth century, generally described as the fiction of *tilism* and *aiyari*. *Tilism* is magic, but *aiyari* is not an easy word to translate. In popular north Indian fiction influenced by Persian romances, the *aiyar* was the clever and discreet assistant of the prince who would ferret out information and negotiate between the human and the supernatural worlds to foil the enemy's plans. Francesca Orsini in her study of the commercially successful subgenre of *jasusi upanyas* (detective fiction) in Hindi has argued that the figure of the *aiyar* got conflated with that of the "detective" as found in the crime novels imported from England.[13] Through the mediation of Bangla, in which novels by Conan Doyle and other British writers of detective fiction began to get translated and adapted in the late nineteenth century, *jasusi upanyas* became the most popular category of novel in north India for many decades to come.

Critics in Hindi have generally considered the interrelated subgenres of *tilism-aiyari* or *jasusi upanyas* be too lowbrow for serious discussion, but

---

[13] This paper is about to be published. I have read it in manuscript form.

these novels obviously satisfied some deep-seated need of that time. The only insightful analysis of the *Chandrakanta* phenomenon was written by a Hindi novelist and critic of our time—Rajendra Yadav—who relates these books to the cultural and economic axes of India's colonial plight. In a forty-page essay he argues that *Chandrakanta* and its sequels are born out of a terrible feeling of national inferiority, although it had been made palatable by several layers of wrapping. Yadav thus places Devakinandan Khatri and his magnum opus in a very crucial position in north Indian culture of the time:

> When we look back at the point where history takes a turn, we usually find an event, a movement or a person who/which embodies the pressures generated by the impact of history and the forces of society. . . . Sometimes, if we look carefully, we might even find a book. . . . At the end of the nineteenth and the beginning of the twentieth century in north India, or rather, the Hindi speaking milieu, there existed such a book—*Chandrakanta, Chandrakanta-Santati* and *Bhutnath*—one book in all.[14]

Between these two poles of historical novel (Dutt) and romantic fantasy (Khatri) were scores of novels in different languages—immensely popular then, and some of them remain in print even now.[15] Past-based novels have never ceased to be written in India. Even in the late twentieth century, a few major novels have appeared that are based on historical research—written either to reinterpret accepted versions of history or to highlight the neglected aspects of a specific era, but the compulsions and concerns of our time are different from those of the British colonial period, and the massive grassroots popularity of fiction where fantasy and chronicle merge has never been replicated.

---

[14] Rajendra Yadav, *Atharah Upanyas* (Delhi, 1981), 20. My translation from Hindi.

[15] Examples are C. V. Ramana Pillai's *Marthanda Varma* (Malayalam, 1891), where the feud over the throne of Travancore is the historical backdrop but the central figure of the romantic plot turns out to be an imaginary lieutenant of the prince; Ramchandra Bhikaji Gunjikar's *Mochangarh* (1871, Marathi), where the setting is a hill-fort in Maharashtra that Shivaji succeeds in recapturing, but the plot foregrounds fictional characters and their relationships; Bankimchandra Chatterjee's *Raj Singha* (Bangla, 1882) in which some of the major characters—such as the Emperor Aurangzeb, his daughter Zebunnisa, Raj Singha, the king of Udaipur—are drawn from the pages of history, but their human dimensions are brought out through their relationship with nonhistorical figures; Umeshchandra Sarkar's *Padmavati* (Oriya, 1881), in which the accurately presented historical strand is overshadowed by the complicated love story; or Kishorilal Goswami's *Hriday Harini* (Hindi, 1890), which, despite the presence of Lord Clive, Sirajuddoula, Mir Jafar, and Amichand—actual historical personages who lived as late as the eighteenth century, is palpably a romance, weaving the supernatural and the magical in and out of its narrative strand.

Uses of History

Underlying this late-nineteenth-century fascination for creating an unspecified past in fiction—where history and imagination could mingle freely—there must be intimations of a cultural crisis that was overtaking Indian society as a result of a sudden and unprecedented impact of the West—politically through colonial rule, intellectually through the new system of education, and imaginatively through exposure to a range of literary material that became available to those who learned English. If Lord Macaulay's intention in introducing English was to ensure Britain's control over the Indian mind (to "create a class of persons, Indian in blood and colour, but English in taste, opinions, moral and intellect" and also to establish "the imperishable empire of our arts and our morals, our literature and our laws"),[16] by the end of the century, among its consequences—unforeseen by the British—were also an emerging sense of nationhood and a discontent with the subjugated present.

The novel soon came to be a dominant vehicle for articulating and consolidating the idea of the nation,[17] and in order to analyze the relation between novel and the nation, the thematic concern of the fiction written at this time needs to be looked at as closely as the narrative modes that shaped the raw material. The construction of a usable past has always been an agenda of nationalism, and the discursive process through which this is achieved enlists the services of history as well as literature. Quite noticeably in the second half of the nineteenth century there was new interest in history among fiction writers, and the desire to rewrite the British colonizers' account of India's past animated many of their novels. Bankimchandra Chatterjee, whose name has already been mentioned as the single most important architect for making the novel the major literary genre of print culture in India, was deeply interested in history and wrote no fewer than six polemical and scholarly essays on the need for an Indian perspective on historical discourse, which appeared in *Bangadarshan*, the journal he edited from 1872 to 1876. Bankimchandra's younger contemporary Romeshchandra Dutt (1848–1909), who was a novelist apart from being a civil servant and the author of the two-volume *Economic History of India* (1902, 1904), once wrote,

---

[16] The first quotation is from *"Minute,"* 1835, the second from *"Speech on the Government of India,"* 1833. Both essays are included in *Victorian Prose,* ed. S. Nagarajan et al., 70 and 65.

[17] For a contestation of this widely held view, see Dilip Menon's essay "No, Not the Nation: Lower Caste Malayalam Novels of the Nineteenth Century" in *Early Novels in India*, ed. Meenakshi Mukherjee (Delhi, 2002).

"I do not know if Sir Walter Scott gave me a taste for history or if my taste for history made me an admirer of Scott, but no subject, not even poetry had such a hold upon me as history."[18] We also know that Harinarain Apte, the author of eight past-based novels in Marathi was a serious reader of history, particularly of works by British historians, and felt dissatisfied with Grant Duff's account of Shivaji. This newly awakened interest in the past among writers coincided with a nascent nationalism among the reading public, which the novelist could address. History could, if necessary, be altered when it suited the writers' purpose better. Thus the writing of past-based fiction with varying degrees of historical accuracy was a necessary part of the writers' agenda.

Such writing was complicated by the existence of a pre-novel narrative tradition discussed in earlier sections, which also depended, as did history-based fiction, on a setting remote in time—necessary, but with quite opposite needs than that of historical fiction—for a suspension of disbelief. They worked sometimes in tandem, toward freeing the writer from the stifling conditions of the present, hedged in by the social restrictions of a hierarchical caste-based society, and lack of agency under a colonial government. Any past, historical or imaginary, was pre-British in chronology, giving the novelist a more expansive stage for heroic action, and celebration of past bravery helped to vindicate present servitude. This was the safest form a newly awakened nationalism could take.

The importance of Sir Walter Scott as a shaping force on these novels has often been taken for granted. In fact, such was the derivative mind-set of the colonial elite that the literary stature of Bankimchandra was intended to be enhanced by thrusting on him the sobriquet "The Scott of India," thereby ignoring the vastly different context and purpose of the two writers. Just because in two prominent novels of the nineteenth century—*Durgeshnandini* (Bangla, 1864) and *Marthanda Varma* (Malayalam, 1891)—sets of two contrasting heroines figure, the name of *Ivanhoe* was routinely invoked while discussing them. On a closer examination, Scott's actual influence turns out to be much less than was rumored, but perhaps Scott acted as a catalyst for the inchoate stirrings of nationalism quickening in different parts of the country.

Georg Lukács's argument about the rise of the historical fiction in Europe[19] cannot be superimposed on the very different circumstances in India,

---

[18] Quoted by Bijit Kumar Datta from *Wednesday Review*, 1905, in *Bangla Sahitye Aitihasik Upanyas* (Calcutta, 1963), 124.

[19] Georg Lukács, *The Historical Novel* (1937), English trans. by Hannah and Stanley Mitchell (Boston, 1963).

but his basic premises remain helpful for two reasons. First, Lukács connected the currents of larger political upheaval to changes in a literary form, thus liberating fiction criticism from the handcuffs of formal aestheticism. Second, he was able to theorize on the basis of texts from diverse European languages, a useful paradigm for a multilingual culture like India. He argued that behind the emergence and popularity of historical novels in Europe, there were certain larger public events rocking the tenor of normal life. He believed that in the two and a half decades between 1789 and 1814 most of the countries in Europe witnessed more political turmoil than ever before, giving rise to "a feeling that there is such a thing as history, that it is an uninterrupted process of change and finally that it had a direct effect upon the life of every individual" (23).

It may similarly be argued that a widespread consciousness about history and its effect on the lives of ordinary people happened in India during the British colonial period. Mircea Eliade has suggested a correlation in all traditional societies between the secularization of culture and the emergence of historical consciousness.[20] According to him, the mythic time of a premodern culture is cyclic and cosmological, in which the same primordial drama is continually reenacted, whereas historical time of modern peoples is linear, tracing in an irrevocable progression the events from the past, passing on to the present and future, often in a causal sequence. In literary terms mythic time is represented by the *puranas*, perhaps also in the *akhyana* works composed in Sanskrit during historical periods; but historical time, Eliade believes, had not been represented in Indian writing until colonial times. In this view, history writing and novel writing could be regarded as cognate activities, both products of a new perception of time.[21]

More than a century ago, in 1899, in an essay published in the inaugural issue of a Bangla journal on historical research called *Aitihasik Chitra* (*Images of History*), Rabindranath Tagore postulated a view somewhat similar to

---

[20] Mircea Eliade, *Myth and Reality* (1963) (reprint; New York, 1968), 134–38.

[21] It should be mentioned here that Eliade's binary conceptualization of time (cyclic and linear) as relating to traditional and modern societies and the resultant presence and absence of historical consciousness has been subjected to some questioning in recent years. The historian Romila Thapar, for example, in a monograph, *Time as a Metaphor of History* (Delhi, 1999) has examined in detail evidences of many different concepts of time in premodern eras, some of which overlapped or interlocked: "The characterising of societies as using either cyclic or linear time is inadequate explanation of the centrality or otherwise of history. Research, even into European history, has endorsed various categories of historical time, and to that extent has distanced itself from the earlier single category. Time, as conceived in cosmology and eschatology, does not exclude the use of other categories, and they can be simultaneous in the same society" (44).

Eliade's, about the inverse relationship between religious faith and historical consciousness, but without using the linear and cyclic tropes of time. According to him, when a group of people are unified mainly as a religious community, they feel the need to record their faith—which is timeless, but only when they have a secular human bond does the desire to record their daily joys and sorrows and temporal events unconnected with religion assume importance. It is the latter desire that creates the conditions for the production and consumption of novels. English education in India, as well as the new legal and administrative systems in the country in which religion was no longer central, were bringng about an altered configuration in life, at least in the urban centers. This might have engendered the urge to record these changes in people's quotidian existence quite unrelated to their faith or the preordained chain of *karma*. But Rabindranath also argued that this had begun to happen in some parts of India even before the arrival of the British. Maharashtra, for example, had a tradition of history writing (in documents called *bakhaar*) going back to the time when Shivaji successfully consolidated regional strength to confront the Mughal emperor of Delhi in military maneuvers.[22] The need to record events may thus be also linked to the rise and fall of political fortunes.

A humiliating awareness of political subjugation must have been a major factor that led to a new and unprecedented interest in history in nineteenth-century India, shared by scholars, fiction writers, and their readers alike. But several other circumstances may have also contributed. The colonial system of education exposed them to other cultures and brought in new standards of comparison. Histories of Greece and Rome, and the more recent histories of Italy, Germany, and other countries of Europe aroused an interest in understanding India's past that might suggest explanations for the present servitude. The teleology of Indian histories written by British historians commonly taught in colonial classrooms began to be seen with increasing suspicion, as the attempt to write new accounts from a nationalist perspective were set in motion. The advocates of Indian rewriting of history were quite clear that no history was completely objective, that all interpretations of events were informed by an open or concealed agenda. This is evidenced in the metaphor of the lion used by Bankimchandra in a well-known essay urging the Bengalis to write their own history: "In childhood we read a fable about a man drawing a sketch in which a human being was beating a lion with his shoes. The man showed this picture to a lion. The lion said if lions

---

[22] Rabindranath Tagore, *Aitihasik Chitra* (*Images of History*) in *Rachanaboli* (Collected Works), 5:601.

could paint, the picture would have been quite different. Bengalis have never written history. That is why the historical pictures of the Bengalis are in this condition."[23] A few decades later another major literary figure urging Indians to write their own history also emphasized the need for an Indian perspective: "In collecting facts we should have no hesitation in taking the help of accounts written by others, but in creating the context we have to use our own resources. Indians are likely to be partial if they write their own history, but hostility or lack of sympathy can distort history much more than partiality. Besides, foreign historians tend to impose the cultural ideals of one civilisation upon another, which can not be beneficial."[24]

As has been mentioned earlier, a new journal in Bangla, *Aitihasik Chitra* (edited by Akshay Kumar Maitreya), which appeared in 1899 from Calcutta attempted to initiate historical research and discussion of the past from an Indian perspective. A similar enterprise was being conducted on the western coast of the country, where scholars like Neelkantharao Kirtane, Govind Vishnu Ranade, and K. S. Chiplunkar had started a journal called *Kavyetihas Sangraha* (*Anthology of History and Literature*) in 1878 with the intention of countering the versions of British historians like Grant Duff and to posit new ways of looking at Maharashtra history. Parallel to these efforts are the works of fiction writers in Bangla and Marathi who were rewriting history through novels, going back most often to two specific periods in the past when the Rajput chieftains in the north and Shivaji in the west fought the aggression of Mughal power. These local acts of resistance were sublimated into national allegories at a time when, weighed down by the authority of another foreign culture, the self-esteem of the Indian people needed a boost. Re-creation of the episodes of native valor proved to be useful for that purpose.

Gender and Nation

Rajput bravery provided some of the most popular themes for novels in Bangla, Hindi, and Marathi in the last decades of the nineteenth century, but the trend continued well into the twentieth. *Rajput* is a generic term used to describe different warrior clans living in the arid regions of central and northern India who were engaged in warfare—with the Turk and

---

[23] Bankimchandra Chatterjee, "Bangalir Itihas Sambandhe Kayekti Katha" (A few words about the history of Bengal) in *Bankim Rachanabali*, II:337. My translation from Bangla.

[24] Rabindranath Tagore, "Aitihasik Chitra" (Historical Sketches) in *Rabindra Rachanabali*, V:601. My translation from Bangla.

Mughal invaders and also with each other—for several centuries during which the frontiers of control of each clan kept changing. The ruling families traced their myths of origin to the sun and the moon. Their genealogy, their fierce pride, chivalry, and heroic deeds were the subjects of bardic songs composed and sung by the wandering minstrels of the desert region. As in other feudal systems, the overlord demanded strict allegiance and loyalty from the chieftains, soldiers, and retainers. The most conspicuous expression of the Rajput code was in the protection of their women's honor, who in turn were expected to perform a ritual collective suicide if the men were killed or defeated in battle.

All this was heady romantic stuff for the subjugated people in colonized India constantly being reminded of their inferiority to the Europeans. The British rulers had done much to propagate the myth of effeminacy as far as Indian men were concerned. Among the earliest purveyors of this idea was James Mill, who wrote: "[Hindus] possessed a certain softness both in their persons and address that distinguished them from the manlier races of Europe."[25] The historian Richard Orme observed in 1770: "All natives in India showed an effeminacy of character, but the Bengalis were of still weaker frame and more enervated nature," and in the next century Thomas Babington Macaulay reconfirmed the sterotype by pronouncing: "The Castilians have a proverb that in Valencia the Earth is Water and Men, women; the description is equally applicable to the vast plains of lower Ganges."[26]

Another way of feminizing the colony was to emphasize the exoticism and romantic mystery by which it enticed Europe. A quotation from a novel by Maud Diver illustrates this widespread analogy that persisted well into the twentieth century: "India may truly be said . . . to be a woman country, loved of all the male lands and exercising the same irresistible magnetism, the same domination over the hearts of men. . . . India, even to her inmates seems still a veiled mystery, aloof yet alluring, like one of her purdah princesses."[27] Behind such formulations (examples could easily be multiplied) there is a desire to prove the masculinity of the ruling race in order to affirm its strength and justify the right to rule. The economic need to pillage the colonies is thus camouflaged as protective patronage, romantic attraction, or carnal longing—impulses considered legitimate in strong and virile men. In the patriarchal ideology that gave rise to imperial ventures, women

---

[25] James Mill, *The History of British India* (1817) (London, 1958), 2:149.

[26] Both Orme's and Macaulay's lines are quoted by Mrinalini Sinha in *Colonial Masculinity* (Manchester, 1995), 15.

[27] Maud Diver, *Desmon's Daughter* (London, 1916).

and land are both seen as natural properties of men, the conquest of land and the possession of women often blending into a composite metaphor.

It should also be noted that the subjugated people themselves seemed to have internalized these assumptions and smarted under a gender-based inferiority. It is in this context that the popularity of the Rajput theme in fiction needs to be examined. As a reflex reaction against the British dismissal of the Hindu male as weak and unmanly, there emerged by the end of the nineteenth century an aggressively militant nationalism that emphasized the need for physical culture, creating an ideology that linked the development of muscular strength with spiritual regeneration. By invoking *Kshatriya-hood* (*Kshatriya* = the warrior caste, only one of the four broad prescribed caste groups among Hindus) as the sole masculine model, it marginalized other ideals and tended to erase the inclusive anrdogyny of certain Hindu concepts.[28] This assertion of aggressive patriotism had as its corollary the notion of women as sacred and vulnerable—the metaphoric embodiment of the country to be protected.

One sample text may be mentioned here whose plot encapsulates this entire symbology: *Raj Singha* by Bankinchandra Chatterjee (Bangla, 1881, revised and enlarged edition 1894, subsequently translated into several other Indian languages). The story narrates how the princess of Roopnagar, a small Rajput state, writes a letter to Raj Singha, the brave ruler of Udaipur (a more powerful Rajput kingdom) for protection against the Mughal Emperor Aurangzeb, who was coming to attack Roopnagar and abduct the princess. The seed of this story was embedded in a brief paragraph of the two-volume *Annals and Antiquities of Rajasthan* (1829 and 1831) written by one Colonel James Tod, a British officer who collected folklore, bardic songs, and ballads of the Rajputs during his four-year posting (1818–1822) in that region. This seed taken from Tod's book sprouted into three full-length novels in three major languages of India, testifying to the potential of this plot to capture the imagination of a wide range of Indian readers at that point of time. The other two novels were *Roopnagarchi Rajkumari* (*The Princess of Roopnagar*) in Marathi by Hari Narain Apte (1902) and *Tara*, subtitled *Kshatrakulaka-malini* (*Tara: The Lotus of a Kshatriya Clan*) in Hindi (1901) by Kishorilal Goswami.

Thus a minor incident of Rajput valor gets expanded into a symbolic validation of Hindu resistance against Muslim invasion, employing the trope of sexual assault as a metaphor for territorial aggression. The princess of Roopnagar takes on the attributes of the motherland, and the noble Raj Singha

---

[28] For elaboaration of this idea, see Ashis Nandy, *The Intimate Enemy* (Delhi, 1983).

prevents her violation at the risk of his own life. In this semiotic logic, gender distinction has to be rigidly maintained, because men rise to their full stature of strength only if women are unambiguously defenseless. This premise underlies most heroic narratives and historical fiction depicting the so-called martial races of India.

Incidentally, Colonel Tod's two volumes played a very influential part in disseminating the romantic myths of Rajasthan to the English-educated Indians in different parts the country. Tod's work was by no means historical in the academic sense of the word. He presented an interesting blend of genealogical research on certain dynasties of Rajasthan who mythicized the past, collections of songs and legends, and documentation of social and religious practices of the region, overlaid by the romantic mind-set of a man roughly the contemporary of Byron and Scott and influenced by Henry Hallam's *View of the State of Europe during the Middle Ages* (1818), which was an attempt to understand the structures of feudalism. Tod's influence traveled in more directions than he could have imagined. His book helped the colonial administration by suggesting (see the dedication to King William IV) that the loyalty of the people of Rajasthan to their local kings could be strategically transferred to the emperor of England by supporting these feudal chiefs, and their martial skills could be used to help the empire. Quite in an opposite effect, Tod's volumes fired the imagination of the colonized people, particularly in Bengal where Tod's chronicle inspired more than a hundred novels, plays, and long narrative poems about Rajput bravery, vicariously glorifying the heroic potential of all Hindus. It has also been argued that the continuing self-perception of the Rajputs as hypermasculine warriors, the brave protectors of their land, women, and religion against foreign assault owes a lot to Tod's work celebrating their heroism.

When Rajput legends were expanded into novels, they not only fueled a burgeoning Hindu nationalism—militant in character, they also helped to define the gender codes operative in this ideology. Instead of seeing women as historicized creatures, subject to pressures of changing times, nationalist discourse invested them with a mythical dimension—making them embody the essence of a culture that became by implication eternal, unchanging, and resistant to history. Women were seen as custodians of traditional values, keeping at bay their erosion through contact with the West, which in the case of men was seen as inevitable and even desirable, because it widened their mental horizon in addition to getting them jobs in the colonial administration.[29]

---

[29] See Partha Chatterjee's essay in *Recasting Women*, ed. Kumkum Sangari and Sudesh Vaid (New Delhi, 1989).

It would, however, be an oversimplification to insist that passivity was the only available paradigm for female conduct in these heroic novels. The alternative model, that of the *veerangana* (the brave woman) is also occasionally present in the portrayal of historical and legendary women of courage from different periods and different regions—Sanjukta, Padmini, Tarabai, Sultana Razia, and a relatively recent figure, Rani Lakshmibai of Jhansi who fought against the British in the Sipahi Revolt of 1857. In the framework of Rajput lore, the women who commit *jauhar* (mass immolation after defeat in a battle) or who die fighting for their husbands' honor make the merger of history and myth possible, conflating the idea of *sati* (a woman's voluntary death at her husband's funeral pyre, misspelled *suttee* by the British) with that of the *veerangana*.

Women's courage and self-sacrifice as demonstrated in these acts of self-destruction used to be celebrated in the songs of the Rajput minstrels and ritualized in the temples that sprang up in these *sati* sites. Through Tod's narrative, some of the nineteenth-century Indian novels also came to romanticize and valorize these acts. There was something inherently contradictory in this enthusiasm for *sati* at a time when a social reform movement was propagating a transformation in Hindu society by advocating widow-marriage, women's education, and abolition of child marriage.[30] Such paradoxes were not uncommon among Indian intellectuals, caught as they were between the pulls of anticolonial nationalism and the notions of social justice inherent in modernity. In the context of the present, one fought for gender equality, but once removed in time, women's self-sacrifice became hallowed, part of the golden, heroic, and somewhat dehistoricized precolonial past.

Loyal wives, willing to die in order to uphold the honor of their husbands, and brave women with some agency (*veeranganas*) are two prevalent gender roles in the heroic fiction of the colonial era. But there was yet a third paradigm. In the nationalist agenda, the figure of the woman with the most

---

[30] This paradox may be illustrated by a quoting a passage from the last page of Romeshchandra Dutt's historical novel in Bangla *Mafarashtra Jiban Prabhat* (1878) where a woman's immolation at her husband's pyre is described lyrically and with admiration: "The fire flared upwards in a blaze of light. The tongues of the flame first gently touched Lakshmi's body and then licked it from all sides. Then it surrounded her to reach her head and proceeded heavenwards to illuminate the sky in a festival of light and sound. Not a limb of Lakshmi's body trembled, not a single hair on her body moved" (*Rachanabali* [Calcutta, 1982], 249; my translation from Bangla). At this point of ecstasy the author forgets that Lakshmi was married to a mean and revengeful man who had abducted and married her to settle a score with her father. They had never really loved each other. Surprisingly, the same author had written two reformist novels, *Samaj* and *Sansar*, set in contemporary India advocating widow-remarriage and intercaste marriage.

emotional potency was that of the mother. This resonant image brought together three different discourses: the discourse of the family with its filial aura of affection, the discourse of Hindu religion invoking *devi* or the mother goddess in a devotional fervor, and the discourse of the nation charged with motherland patrotism. The most well-known articulation of this composite sentiment was "Vande Mataram" ("Glory Be to the Mother"), an emotive song that first appeared in 1882 as part of the novel *Anandamath* and became the unofficial national anthem for the Indian freedom movement for many decades to come.

The Dialogic Mode

Evidently, the novelists who used these potent symbols and mythic motifs in their work, and the readers who responded to them either consciously or subliminally, were bound together by a belief that the Hindu upper-caste values and mores constituted the nation. Tribal and lower-caste people who had a different iconography occasionally appeared in the peripheries of these novels—for example, the Bhil aboriginals in the Rajput and Maratha stories—but their value in the narrative lay mainly in their loyalty to their feudal lords or faithfulness to the king. If people from another religion figured at all in these novels, almost invariably they did so in the role of the enemy— mostly the Mughal kings, their lieutenants, and courtiers. Occasionally one comes across Portuguese pirates, or less frequently, an errant *sahib* (white foreigner) of indeterminate origin plundering the land or abducting women.

At the time when these novels were being written, the true adversary in the domain of power were the British, but by and large, in the arena of literary representation, the Muslims continued for a long time to be the surrogate "other." Sometimes this substitution was a matter of expediency, because many of these early novelists in India were government servants by profession, and mentioning the British in any but positive terms might have been harmful to their careers. It is true that there were occasional instances of writers suffering government reprisal for their overt expression of nationalism, but such cases do not completely explain the persistent demonization of Islam in these early novels. Incidentally, the conflation of Hinduism with India continues to be a familiar ideology even at the beginning of the twenty-first century, resurfacing with a new emphasis after a mid-twentieth-century abeyance soon after the country became independent, when the idea of a secular nation and the richness of a plural heritage had gained intellectual currency.

But this notion of a nation forged by religion, although popular in the late nineteenth century, did not remain uncontested. Even in the early decades of the twentieth century, Rabindranath Tagore had offered a strong critique of this populist strain in two major novels, *Gora*[31] and *Gharey Bairey*.[32] In the latter novel, Sandeep, the flamboyant leader of a religious group spells out the cold-blooded political strategy concealed behind the cult of motherland patriotism: " 'True patriotism will never be roused among our people unless they can visualise the motherland. We must make a goddess out of her.' Sandeep's followers saw the point at once. 'Let us devise a suitable icon of the goddess to represent the country,' they said. 'It will not do if we devise a new image. We must appropriate an existing image of the goddess and convert it into the symbol of our country. The worship of the people then flow towards it along the deep-cut grooves of custom and tradition.' " This call for surrender to the mystical exaltation of the nation as mother goddess creates a collective frenzy among the people. But Nikhilesh, one of the two other central characters in the novel, stays clear of this hysteria. A liberal humanist landlord, he prefers to focus on the material conditions of the village, the concrete ground reality, rather than be carried away by symbolic abstractions. He attempts to solve the specific problems of the poor farmers and artisans (many of whom are Muslim and therefore outside the emotional ambit of Sandeep's religious patriotism) and redress the different forms of local oppression that divide and oppress the people. Refusing to be swayed by the rhetoric of "Vande Mataram" (the song from an 1882 novel mentioned earlier), Nikhilesh concentrates on economic reform at the rural level. But Nikhilesh's wife, Bimala, is drawn toward Sandeep's magnetic personality and his intoxicating brand of militant Hindu nationalism. Bimala thus becomes the crucial site for the contesting ideologies of Sandeep and Nikhilesh. Sandeep turns her into a *devi*: the spirit of the country, the motivating force behind the movement, thereby erasing her autonomy as an individual. Nikhilesh respects her as a person, and recognizes her freedom to make a choice.

Worshiping the nation as mother and essentializing women as the source of spiritual strength are parallel processes—one perpetuates the bondage of women, the other exalts the abstract notion of the country over the people

---

[31] Bangla, 1909; an erratic and partially abridged anonymous English translation appeared in 1929, which still continues to be in print. The complete English translation of *Gora* done by Sujit Mukherjee became available only recently (Delhi, 1997).

[32] Bangla, 1916; English translation as *The Home and the World* by Surendranath Tagore (London, 1919). The present passage is translated by me from the original Bangla novel in *Rabindra Rachanabali*, IV:544.

who actually constitute it. Rabindranath Tagore's two novels *Gora* and *Gharey Bairey* carry out an interrogation of the nationalistic project at three levels. These novels challenge the notion that India is exclusively a Hindu nation, they question the priority given to emotional patriotism over attempts at economic self-sufficiency and social justice, and above all they counter the model of aggressive masculinity on which the popular militant variety of *swadeshi* was predicated.[33]

Gora (1909) is the first in a new subgenre in Indian fiction: the novel of ideas, and it probably remains to this day the most important narrative reflection on the issues relating to the contesting ideologies that constructed alternative paradigms of the nation. The debate about the cultural identity of India and the place of religion, caste, class, and gender in it, which this novel had initiated in the beginning of the twentieth century, seems nowhere near a resolution even after the century is over. In India as well as in many other countries, novels have played a part in calibrating the nuances of the national idea. In polemical discourse, very often the options get congealed into structured binaries. Much of the history of Indian nationalism, for example, has been narrated through paired and oppositional categories: tradition versus modernity, religious orthodoxy versus secularism, ancient India versus the West, industrialization versus rural autonomy. Fictional texts expose the limitations of such a polarized grid. In the densely textured and webbed social contexts that novels represent, these clear-cut intellectual categories get mediated through many imperceptible forces—often emotional and irrational—some of which operate subliminally and thus remain unarticulated. This intricate and fluid process is vividly demonstrated in *Gora*.

Gora and Binoy, the two protagonists through whose spirited debates the novel moves forward, do not occupy oppositional spaces, nor are they characters who advocate Westernization or those who idealize Indian tradition presented as unitary voices. The emphasis is on the plurality of positions. Meaning in this novel lies not in individual utterances but in their dialogical negotiations. Barring one or two rigid characters whose ideas remain static, the positions of the major figures in the novel get modified gradually through mutual interaction—logic and instinct, intellect and emotional attachments often getting into each other's way to complicate both polemics and praxis. By the end of the novel this interpellation is seen to be an enrichment: the reticulation of the private arena of love, affection, and friendship

---

[33] *Swadeshi* literally means "of one's own country." But it became the name of a specific movement in the early twentieth century.

on the public domain of action and debate seems to initiate a process that might lead toward a wholeness that had been elusive so far.

Bharatvarsha (the Sanskrit name for India) is a key concept in *Gora*, denoting much more than a geographical space or an administrative unit. The emotive and abstract vision of Bharatvarsha that Gora propagates in the early part of the novel gathers around itself a louder resonance and a more febrile excitement every time he articulates it in arguments with adversaries or in exhortations to his followers. But the novel traces a gradual change in Gora. The slow drift of his idea of the nation from the abstract to the concrete, from a unitary symbol to the diversified actuality takes place in oscillatory movements. Gora eventually comes to realize the hollowness of his earlier exclusionary stand that had valorized a an aggressive Hinduism. Gora's humanization is simultaneously also a process of feminization, or at least a realization of the crucial place of the feminine principle in life. Rabindranath's attempt to inscribe the woman centrally in the narrative of the nation (in *Gora* as well as in *Gharey Bairey*) was a radical move at that historical moment, an implicit rejoinder to Bankimchandra Chatterjee's version of militant motherland patriotism and the recuperation of Hindu manhood as propagated in an influential novel like *Anandamath* (1882) in which political praxis demanded the exclusion of women and people of other religions from the sphere of action. Rabindranath's two novels with their dialogic narrative mode mark a watershed in the discourse of the nation.

Anandamath, Gora, and *Gharey Bairey*, obvious texts in any discussion of narrative and nation in India in the early phase of the freedom movement, stand in contrast to later novels written in the half-century after independence (1947–2000) with more fragmented representations of the multiplicity and contradictions in society. By the midtwentieth century, the idealized pan-Indian quest for a holistic national identity, necessitated by the priorities and strategies of the freedom struggle, was getting restructured, and at times subverted, by localized narratives, multivalent in their competing claims of voices and historically free from the need to construct a seamless and homogenized community. The charged and often inflated rhetoric gives way to a low-key account of quotidian lives that can by no means be read as national allegory. So many novels reflect this altered ethos that it is difficult to single out texts for mention. Yet at random one could refer to *Maila Anchal* (by Phnishwarnath Renu, Hindi, 1954), *Raag Darbari* (by Srilal Shukla, Hindi, 1968; translated into English by Gillian Wright, 1992), and

Bharatipura (by U. R. Anantha Murthy, Kannada, 1977; translated into English by P. Srinivasa Rao, 1996)—each text deconstructing earlier notions of nation, religion, and caste in different ways—comic, introspective, satiric, or subversive. The older markers of identity have not disappeared but have taken on newer and more complex forms. In the decentred postmodern novels of today—anticolonialism and nationalism—the twin impulses of earlier Indian fiction seem to have spent themselves, dissolving some of the binary oppositions.

One such text, *Shadow Lines* (1988) written in English by Amitav Ghosh, underlines the elusive nature of boundaries that carve up the world to confer "national" identities on people. In the Indian subcontinent, independence from colonial rule happened simultaneously with its partition into two countries, causing unprecedented physical violence at that time and long-lasting psychological repercussions on the people who migrated. Even half a century after the dismemberment of the country, writers' interest in coming to terms with this traumatic event continues unabated. Apart from being a major thematic concern in at least four Indian languages that were directly affected by partition (Urdu, Hindi, Punjabi, and Bangla) and English, which is an Indian language without regional specificity, it also changed the nature of perception and hence narrative representation. Adil Jussawala, who edited an excellent anthology of Indian writing in 1974, pointed out in his insightful introduction how metaphors of mutilation, rupture, and dislocation began to figure largely in works produced across the country.[34] People from settled agrarian communities, once displaced from their ancestral villages were jolted out of their secure collective identities to confront unfamiliar circumstances alone and in conditions of destitution. Modernist concerns about alienation and existential choice that had evolved in Europe along a very different philosophical and historical trajectory, suddenly began to seem relevant in the novels of this subcontinent, although for reasons altogether different.

In Amitav Ghosh's *Shadow Lines*, the two halves of the novel are titled "Going Away" and "Coming Home"—indicating paradoxically the difficulty displaced people face in separating the two verbs of movement. A grandmother in Ghosh's novel, about to visit her childhood home in Dhaka many years after partition has made it part of a foreign country, can only think of her journey as "Coming," causing much amusement to her grandson who thinks she does not know the difference between coming and going, between home and away. The narrative critiques the arbitrariness of all

---

[34] Adil Jussawala, ed., *New Writing in India* (Harmondsworth, 1974).

dividing lines, be it (as in a recurrent metaphor of the novel) across an ancestral home partitioned accurately right through a doorway and a lavatory, bisecting an old commode and a nameplate—or national boundaries drawn in the hope that once the borders are etched on the map, the separate bits of land would sail away from each other "like the shifting tectonic plates of the pre-historic Gondwanaland" and that eventually even memories will get neatly divided. While flying to Dhaka from Calcutta, the grandmother expected to see a visible border on the ground: "a long black line with green on one side and scarlet on the other, like it was in the school atlas" and is puzzled at finding nothing: "But if there aren't any trenches or anything how are people to know? I mean where is the difference then? And if there is no difference, both sides would be the same; it will be just like it used to be before, . . . what was it all for then—partition and all the killing and everything—if there isn't something in between?"[35] As in some other major novels in India today, a number of countries get interlocked in Ghosh's *Shadow Lines*—and people of at least three different religions and nationalities impinge on each others' lives and deaths. It is very much a text of our times, when human lives spill over from one country to another, where languages and loyalties cannot be contained within tidy national boundaries.

It has been argued that only English-language novelists can talk of shadow lines, because their language frees them from the reality of national boundaries, giving them the privilege of being a global citizen. But this interrogation of lines separating countries gets a haunting and vivid representation also in a Bangla novel, *Jochhna Kumari* (*The Girl Made of Moonlight*), written by Sunil Gangopadhyay and published in the same year as *Shadow Lines* (1988). In this novel a rural legend celebrated in folk songs about a flame-colored girl with ankle-touching black hair who is seen weeping under trees but vanishes before anyone can touch her gets telescoped into the story of a gang-raped girl found near the India-Bangladesh frontier, very likely a smuggler, but over whose identity the border security forces of the two countries get into a tangle. The narrative unfolds at various levels: the girl in question is sometimes seen as normal, sometimes as mentally deranged; she is identified alternately as Beena, a Hindu girl seeking asylum from Bangladesh, and as Fatima, a Muslim widow, running away to escape being sold to an Arab sheikh. Finally, when the border security men shoot her, the body falls—in true folktale logic—exactly halfway across the line of the national frontier, with chilling absurdity, as it had done earlier in a well-known Urdu short story by Sadat Hasan Manto called "Toba Tek Singh" (1954).

---

[35] Amitav Ghosh, *Shadow Lines* (Delhi, 1995), 151 (for all quotations).

While the soldiers of the two countries wrangle about their right over the body, arguing whether to give her the Hindu rite of cremation or an Islamic burial, the battered female body becomes radiant and whole, and like the woman of the legend vanishes into the air, reminding us that the oral and the written, the mimetic and the magical, can effortlessly merge—both in our own narrative tradition as well as in the postmodern global trend in fiction that transcends realism.

The historic event of the partition of the country has been represented in myriad ways in fiction in the subsequent five decades—documentary realism, fractured narrative, symbolic metonymy, recollection filtered through a lens of time, fabulation, allegory—each mode exploring means to impose order on an experience of incomprehensible chaos and brutality. In emphasizing the fluidity of physical and mental boundaries, these recent texts have moved a long way from the totalizing narratives of territorial nationalism. The idealism and absolute dichotomies of the early twentieth century cannot sustain a writer today, who lives in a more ambiguous, tentative, and unstable world. To accommodate a changed sense of reality, the stories have become more protean, and the mode of telling casually weaves fantasy and magic into its seemingly realist texture.

Politics and Plurality of Language

Looking at novels in a monolingual culture where a sequential axis of texts provides a definite focus of argument is a very different enterprise from tracing the foliation of narrative patterns in a subcontinent where novels in many languages, each with its distinct history and archeology, have their separate as well as interconnected existence. Whether the number of languages in India be sixteen or twenty-two,[36] the evolution of the printed form called the novel has not always followed similar trajectories. Diverse local modes of storytelling: folk as well as elite, the nature and system of education prevalent

---

[36] The Indian constitution mentions sixteen languages; Sahitya Akademi (National Academy of Letters) recognizes twenty-two. The 1981 census report enumerates over five thousand languages spoken by the Indian people, but since most of the latter do not have a tradition of printed literature, they remain outside the purview of the present essay. Among the languages that have distinct literary cultures, Hindi is spoken by over 300 million people; the next largest languages— Bangla, Telugu, Marathi, Tamil, and Malayalam—are each spoken by people whose number is very roughly comparable to those speaking French, German, or Italian in Europe. Moreover, languages like Bangla, Urdu/Punjabi, and Tamil are also used in other countries—Bangladesh, Pakistan, and Sri Lanka, respectively, complicating considerably the linguistic cartography of the subcontinent.

in the region, late or early emergence of print culture, differential nature of the public sphere, relationship with English, size of the market and effective distribution—and other intangible factors unique to each language deflected their courses in unpredictable ways.[37] The belief of the earlier decades that the sum total of the chronological accounts of different literatures (Hindi, Marathi, Bangla, Malayalam, Oriya, Telugu, etc.) will add up to a comprehensive literary history of India has begun to be challenged recently, the critics now emphasizing the need to chart overlaps, links, translations, echoes, and influences, as well as discontinuities and silences across languages with diligence and rigor.[38] There have been internal and unspoken hierarchies among the Indian languages, seen for example in the asymmetry in the patterns of translation (to take a random example: more Bangla novels have been translated over the years in Hindi or Telugu than the other way around), but these areas are still inadequately investigated.

How does a critic navigate her way through this plethora of material in so many Indian languages? As Franco Moretti argues in a context larger than India in "Conjectures of World Literature," "Reading 'more' is always a good thing, but not the solution."[39] One needs to formulate precise questions and hazard hypotheses on the basis of whatever one has read, in order to initiate the dynamics of further explorations. One of these questions relates to the changing relationship between novels in India—whatever be the language—and their putative European models. Was there a paradigm shift around the 1930s, and if so, why? Dependence exclusively on England and its literature for access to the world had begun to wane at this time—and not *only* because of the intellectual liberation made possible by the imminent decolonization at the political level. In the 1930s, the Progressive Writers Movement—the first self-conscious cross-language literary movement in India (involving four or five languages) with a left-leaning agenda had drawn attention to models from Russia and Eastern Europe. Retrospectively, earlier

---

[37] I do not fully accept Sisir Kumar Das's model for a multilingual literary history through "Prophane and Meta-phane" movements (*A History of Indian Literature* [New Delhi, 1991], 8:44–46), which assumes that literature in all the Indian languages was traveling along the same route at varying paces.

[38] See Sujit Mukherjee, *Towards a Literary History of India* (Shimla, 1976); Susie Tharu and K. Lalita, eds. *Women Writing in India* 2 vols. (New York, 1990–91); Meenakshi Mukherjee, *Realism and Reality: Novel and Society in India* (Delhi, 1985); Sudhir Chandra, *The Oppressive Present: Literature and Social Consciousness in Colonial India* (Delhi, 1992); E. V. Ramakrishnan, *Making It New* (Shimla, 1996); and Meenakshi Mukherjee, ed. *Early Novel in India* (Delhi, 2002).

[39] Franco Moretti, "Conjectures on World Literature," *New Left Review* (January–February. 2000): 55.

Russian novels (by Tolstoy, Dostoevsky, and Turgenev) with very different ideologies also began capturing the minds of Indian intellectuals and writers around this time. Neither these nor American fiction had so far been available models for the Indian novelist, whose educational curriculum had implicitly asserted the superiority of everything British. The brooding inwardness and philosophical quality of the nineteenth-century Russian novel or the intensely moral preoccupation of early American writers like Hawthorne might have demonstrated to early practitioners of Indian fiction alternative models of writing novels.

But all through the nineteenth century, the British novel—either of the eighteenth century (*Rasselas* or *The Vicar of Wakefield* were frequently translated or adapted texts)[40] or of the Victorian period with its professed emphasis on mimetic representation—had remained the official ideals of high literature. (Lowbrow literature had its own pathways of dissemination, which have been briefly mentioned earlier.) Harish Trivedi has demonstrated in his detailed and nuanced case study of Hindi how "after it lost its empire, i.e., us, England seemed to shrink for us even as the rest of the world loomed larger,"[41] and the change in perspective needs to be tested in terms of other languages too. The results may not be too different from each other, because we find quite a few novelists of the present generation from different languages, all—speaking on different occasions—reflecting on how little they have been influenced by English literature and how much more by European, American, and Latin American fiction.[42] One must also remember there has been an entire generation of powerful writers beginning their work in the 1930s and continuing for several decades who seem totally unaffected by Western paradigms, writing sagas of villages and communities, integrating local myths, and capturing the process of transformation initiated by industrialization. Shivarama Karanth in Kannada, Gopinath Mohanty in Oriya, and Tarashankar Bandopadhyay in Bangla are classic examples of such writers with indigenous sources of strength.

In the 1930s and 1940s, parallel, and sometimes in opposition, to the progressive movement in fiction was the modernist movement in which experimentation with form engaged the attention of novelists in many Indian

---

[40] In fact, the earliest and the most frequently translated English text in India was *Pilgrim's Progress*, but that was done mostly under Christian missionary initiative and may not have reflected popular taste.

[41] Harish Trivedi, "Reading English, Writing Hindi," in *Rethinking English*, ed. Svati Joshi (New Delhi, 1991), 199.

[42] For examples to illustrate this point, see Meenakshi Mukherjee, *Realism and Reality* (Delhi, 1985), 194–95 n. 23.

languages. Novels from France (albeit in English translation) came to be regarded as avant-grade reading among Indian intellectuals. Although some writers came to be identified totally with the modernist movement (for example, Agyeya in Hindi and Buddhadev Bose in Bangla), in effect these two streams—social engagement and narrative innovation—did not remain separate for too long. Among the writers who effected a unique merger of these diverse trends in highly individual narrative modes, each one bringing in an element of wonder and the inexplicable mystery in life that defies logic are Bhalchandra Nemade in Marathi, O. V. Vijayan in Malayalam, and Shirshendu Mukhopadhyay in Bangla. Each of these writers has evolved in different directions since then, but in the 1960s, when they first made their mark, it was an unparalleled defining moment for the novel in India. They were certainly exposed to foreign influence, but in their different ways they were also very much rooted in their local context. Much more recently, however, magic realism and other irreal modes of fiction writing—as practiced by Marquez, Kundera, Gunter Grass, and Calvino—have spread so widely that it has become progressively difficult to make cultural distinctions. Holding forth on what is Indian and what is absorbed from other narrative traditions is no longer a valid or legitimate critical speculation. This may well be the result of an unprecedented acceleration in global communication through electronic technology; increase in mobility across continents, making migration a common experience and *diaspora* a frequently used word; and more accommodative practices in the book trade in the last two decades of the twentieth century.

This mention of trade here is deliberate, because the process of economic globalization produces a new asymmetry—between Indian novels written in English that have gained sudden international visibility and novels in other Indian languages whose constituency, however strong and vibrant, remains confined within the country. The best-known early novelists in India did not write in English, although they were prodigious readers of English fiction. Some acknowledged their debt openly and gratefully; others carried traces of their reading in the body of their texts directly or obliquely. Translation, adaptation, and plagiarism from English flourished widely to make the novel a popular genre in India by the end of the nineteenth century. What is not remembered today is that novels at this time came to be written in English also, even though there might not have been a wide readership. While novels in Marathi, Malayalam, Tamil, Oriya, Bangla, Hindi, and other languages soon consolidated their bases and initiated literary traditions that continue to this day, the scores of English novels written in the colonial era are virtually forgotten now.[43] This is not necessarily because of numerical paucity or qualitative inferiority. There may have been a more complicated process at work here.

Not all categories of writing at a given time get equal attention and enter into literary circulation. A particular configuration of circumstances creates a momentum that gets recorded in history. Why did the Indian novel in English fail to generate that momentum in the early years of the emergence of the novel in the subcontinent? A corollary to that would be another question: why have we witnessed a reversal at the end of the twentieth century, when an ebullient proliferation of fiction in English, written both by resident and nonresident Indians has become a globally noticed and (consequently) a nationally highlighted phenomenon? Although in 1864 Bankimchandra Chatterjee felt it necessary to discard his aspiration for a literary career in English to find unprecedented pan-Indian success by writing in his mother tongue, in the 1990s Kiran Nagarkar and Mrinal Pande—trend-setting fiction writers in Marathi and Hindi respectively—switched over to English. In neither case are the reasons arbitrary or strictly literary.

Shivarama Padikkal has argued that "not all groups at all times produce artifacts which are classified as culture" and that "literary production is one of the modes by which the dominant group constructs its reality and history."[44] Because English has always been the language of power and privilege in India, the writers in English, as much in the nineteenth century as today, come from the highest social stratum. By Padikkal's logic, therefore, the early English novels should have occupied a more prominent position in Indian literary history. His statement is generally valid in the context of caste, class, and gender hierarchies, but when it comes to language, certain other determinants complicate the issues. What became popular has to be seen not only through the factors of power and control but also the emotional responses to colonial education that simultaneously generated both exhilaration and anxiety—the processes by which communities of readers were created around journals and centers of publication; the attitudes of writers toward religious, cultural, and regional identity; and similar factors generally related to the dynamics of social formation. The world represented in the

---

[43] For a detailed discussion of these early novels and a bibliography, see Meenakshi Mukherjee, *The Perishable Empire* (New Delhi, 2000).

[44] Shivarama Padikkal, "Inventing Modernity: The Emergence of the Novel in India," *Interrogating Modernity: Culture and Colonialism in India*, ed. Tejaswini Niranjana, P. Sudhir, and Vivek Dhareshwar (Calcutta, 1993), 220.

novel is not an unmediated reflection of what actually existed but an ideological reconstruction molded by an implicit political agenda in which language has, I hope to demonstrate, not a minor determining role.

Because the early English novels were hardly noticed, seldom discussed,
and never canonized, a good proportion of them (mostly published privately
by the author or by small presses with an inadequate distribution system)
are likely to have perished without a trace. Despite this, what survives in the
India Office collection in London, in the National Library in Calcutta, old
and obscure libraries around the country, and in family collections constitute no negligible archive. Two facts stand out as one glances at the title
pages of these extant books. First is the diversity and range of places from
which they appeared. Only a handful were published in the metropolitan
centers of book publication like Calcutta, Bombay, and Madras (a few were
also published in London). Most originated in smaller places not generally
connected with publishing in English (for example, Allahabad, Bangalore,
Calicut, Dinapore, Midnapore, Surat, or Vellore), indicating individual enterprise rather than the support of an organized publication/distribution
system, as well as the absence of geographical cohesion and hence a consolidated readership. The second notable feature is the propensity of the titles
to promise the unveiling of some mystery ("A Peep into," "Glimpses of,"
"Revelations," etc.) pertaining to a somewhat homogenous space called
India (or "The East," or "The Orient"), inhabited by an undifferentiated
Hindu community ("A Story of Hindu Life," or "The Hindu Wife"). Unlike
the authors in Bangla, Marathi, or Malayalam who were confident about a
sizable readership in their specific geographical region, the writer in English
suffered from an uncertainty about the audience. From the titles, as well as
the clues embedded in the text, the assumed addressee is seen to be situated
outside the culture, possibly in England, or among the colonial administra-
tors living in India. This did not of course mean that such people were the
actual consumers of this fiction, but a concern for this shadowy reader burdened these novels with an excess of ethnographic documentation and explanatory asides.[45]

The indeterminacy of the supposed readership had ambiguous effects
on the way these authors positioned themselves in the text. At a time when
one of the indirect functions of the Indian-language novel was the shaping
of an incipient nationalism, both of the national and the regional variety,
the writers in English were constricted by their anxiety not to antagonize

---

[45] I have discussed examples of both kinds in "Novel, Nation, Language" in *Perishable Empire*,
1–28.

their imagined readers by overtones of sedition. The language, English, ruled out the possibility of a regional identity, and any assertion of a broadly *Indian* identity was undertaken more to emphasize otherness or exoticism than to make a political statement. Even an explosive theme like the 1857 revolt of the Indian soldiers against the British is completely depoliticized in Soshee Chunder Dutt's novel, *Shunker* (1885), set against this historical event. It makes an implicit attempt to uphold the ordinary Indian soldier's loyalty to the Crown. Occasional insurgency is projected as a temporary reaction to the misbehavior of individual officers.

By the turn of the nineteenth century, when the novel in the "vernaculars" had become a major vehicle of political dissent, positing in fictional terms what was not yet feasible in the arena of action, novel after novel in English paid direct or veiled tribute to the imperial rule. A historical novel by K. K. Sinha, *Sanjogita or The Princess of Aryavarta* (1903), nostalgically evokes the greatness of the precolonial Hindu past and laments its eclipse during Muslim rule. But suddenly at the end of the novel there is an unceremonious switch to a different rhetoric: "India appeals to her noble foreign masters for kindness and sympathy; she is indebted to them for her rescue from a chaotic society."[46]

The early novelists in the vernacular and those who wrote in the English came from the same upper-middle-class, college-educated social segment across the country and it is very likely that they were exposed to the same English novels—both canonical and popular. Yet the language in which they wrote seems to automatically determine how this reading would be processed in their writing. Indian novelists in English displayed their acquaintance with the classics of Western literature more readily than did Indian-language novelists, parading this knowledge as validation, as it were, of their status in the eyes of the putative reader. They never mentioned the popular writers except to denounce them and took care to align themselves only with the best in ingenious ways.[47] Using epigraphs from Byron, Scott, Cowper, Moore, Shakespeare, or Coleridge at the beginning of chapters was a common practice; quotations from such writers were generously woven in whether the narrative called for them or not; veiled references were left unexplained because the readers—real and imaginary—were expected to recognize them. Apart from the British target group, the intended readers

---

[46] K. K. Sinha, *Sanjogita or The Princess of Aryavarta* (Dinapur, 1903), 267.

[47] For example, the hero of A. Madhavaiah's *Thillai Govindan* (1908) (London, 1916) describes his progress thus: "I was always fond of books and when Reynolds was discarded, Scott, Thackeray, Dickens and George Eliot took his place" (160).

probably included some Indian men as highly educated as themselves but excluded Indian women almost totally.

Gender was indeed a major factor in the different fates of these two sets of novels: in English and in the Indian languages. Knowledge of English was a gender-specific skill in nineteenth-century India, and although women's education was an important issue in the social reform movement, it was generally believed that women were best instructed through their mother tongue. One of the strengths of the novel in the Indian languages was the fact that its intended readership had a sizable percentage of women. It will not be easy to determine if as many women read these novels as was assumed, but the authors' asides and other hints in the texts seem to assume that their readers included women. It is well known that *Indulekha* (1889) an early novel in Malayalam was professedly written for a woman who had no access to the new form of entertainment called the novel that was so popular among Malayali men who knew English. The author wanted to recreate the genre in his mother tongue to enable women to share in this literary enjoyment but also to set up an idealized version of modernity for the women in his community.

There was an implicit valorization of the mother tongue as the language of naturalness and authenticity that belonged to the interior space uncorrupted by Western influence, of which women were the custodians.[48] Indian languages capitalized on the emotional resonance of this unspoken assumption by invoking regional nationalism through the merger of gender and language. The figure of *banga-janani* (*janani* = mother) embodied both the language and land of Bengal, and there were similar constructions in other parts of the country as well. One of the motivating forces behind the Kannada novel was a search for a kannada-ness: "In the novels we begin to find the god-like figure of the Kannada-matha [the Kannada mother]."[49] The figure of Kairali, which conflates the language Malayalam and the land Kerala, or the line of the popular song by Shankarambadi Sundaracharya in Andhra Pradesh, *"ma telugu thalliki malle pu danda"* (to our Telugu mother a garland of jasmine), are examples of the continuing valence of these composite images of language, mother, and regional identity in different linguistic areas of India.

Language-centered nationalism and the concept of a nation that transcends linguistic divisions reinforced each other in this period, and the novel in India emerged at the cusp of these twin impulses. One without the other

---

[48] For examples of this, see Mukherjee, *Perishable Empire*, 21–23.
[49] Padikkal, "Inventing Modernity," 220.

could not have sustained a genre that served a complex function in a colonial society, providing a vehicle for the emergence of political aspirations, imaginative adventure, and historical reconstruction, in addition to desire to comment on contemporary life. The novel as well as Indian nationalism in the early phase stood at the conjunction of English (which not only opened up a new literary horizon but introduced new knowledge) and the Indian languages that became the conduit for processing this knowledge to suit regional needs.

The Indian novel in English during the colonial era had no way of drawing sustenance from this particular configuration of the regional and the national, in which the role of gender was crucial, and this could well be one of the many reasons why this body of writing was destined to reach a dead end at that time. It took this genre in English nearly another century to come into its own in a postcolonial dispensation and globalized economy. In 1981, Salman Rushdie's novel *Midnight's Children* was a landmark text that brought vitality, velocity, and volume to Indian English novels. Thereafter, novels in English written by Indians have entered the world market—partly because of their number and quality, partly because English is a world language—the best of them getting translated into European languages and being studied as an intrinsic part of the postcolonial literary scene. Novels written in the Indian languages continue to be greater in number than those written in English, with their narrative modes as varied, or even more diverse, than their English counterparts, but their circulation remains largely confined within their linguistic region of the subcontinent. In a study of narrative modes, language need not normally be seen as a major determining factor. But for nearly two decades, Indian novels written in English and novels written in the other languages are being increasingly seen in dissimilar contexts. Whether their disparity of audience (global and local) affects their respective concerns, thematic focus, attitude toward their material, styles of representation, and fictional strategies still remains a largely unresolved area of critical debate.

GERALD MARTIN

The Novel of a Continent: Latin America

> The next day in the morning we came to the broad
> causeway that leads to Ixtapalapa. And seeing so many
> peopled cities and villages standing in the water, and
> other great towns on dry land, and that mighty road
> leading straight and flat to Mexico, we wondered
> greatly, and said that it was like the magic tales they tell
> in the novel of Amadís, on account of the towers and
> pyramids and other buildings in the water, all of brick
> and mortar, and some of our soldiers even asked
> whether they were really seeing it, or whether it was all
> a dream. . . . Now all is cast to the ground, lost, none of
> it is still standing.
> —BERNAL DÍAZ, *True Conquest of the History*
> *of New Spain*, 1568

What we call Latin American literature has been in existence for more than
five hundred years and for centuries more if we include the literatures, most
of them long since "disappeared," of the peoples who inhabited the continent before the arrival of the Spanish and Portuguese. However, for the first
three hundred years after European conquest, the colonial literatures of
what are now called Spanish America and Brazil were mainly problematical
and sometimes unruly extensions of the metropolitan literatures of Spain
and Portugal, though crucial for the understanding of everything that has
happened since. As is well known, the Spanish authorities successfully prohibited the writing of novels in the New World and did their best, with less
success, to prevent them from being imported from Europe and read in the
American colonies. From the beginning, however, and emphatically by the
eighteenth century, clear signs of an emancipatory impulse were apparent
everywhere in those "Indies," and from the early nineteenth century, following successful liberation movements and the independence of all regions but
Cuba and Puerto Rico from Spain and Portugal, there began the literary
"quest for identity" that characterized the fiction of the nations of this continent until at least the 1970s. Perhaps the single most interesting and important aspect of this history is a largely invisible one, the relation (diachronic
and synchronic) between the literatures of the twenty-one individual nations
and the construct we call "Latin American literature." This question has
been almost completely ignored by historians but will be at the heart of the

present brief account (though I have no space for details), together with an exposition of the defining family characteristics of the continent's narrative fiction that allowed the construct to be elaborated in the first place.[1]

History Made Myth

> "I shall do such things; what they are yet I know not."
> The mad king's words are the motto we have inscribed
> for a hundred years now on our flags of spiritual
> revolution. Will we overcome the discontent provoked
> by so many rebellions? Will we carry out that ambitious
> promise?
> —PEDRO HENRÍQUEZ UREÑA, *Six Essays in Search of
> Our Expression,* 1928

Latin America, viewed through the canonical works of its literature, is a continent of great dreams, vast mirages, and shattering disappointments. This pattern goes back to the earliest European chronicles. It has become a commonplace, especially since the 1992 commemorations, to say that its first European "discoverer," Christopher Columbus, was also the first of Latin America's "magical realist" writers: when he crossed the Atlantic in 1492, he did not so much discover the New World as invent it, exaggerating its marvels and giving false names to everything he saw. But though his first journal was full of wonders, the last is a bitter tale of failure and disillusionment. Three hundred years later, after leading the successful struggles for independence from Spain, the great revolutionary general Simón Bolívar saw his grandiose vision of creating a unified federation of American states come to nothing, and he died declaring that he who serves a revolution "plows the sea."

Latin America as we conceive it today had a precise date of birth with Columbus's first landfall on October 12, 1492, and most of its contemporary republics also had specific birthdays when they achieved emancipation three hundred years later. Inevitably, its subsequent official history has faithfully followed the rhythms of European periodizations, even if such classifications are just one more example of "misplaced ideas."[2] For that very reason,

---

[1] I have no space to refute, other than implicitly, the recent modish deconstructions of Latin America and its literature from the standpoint of a know-it-all, see-nothing postmodernism. I consider it, in any case, a futile task.

[2] See Roberto Schwarz, *Misplaced Ideas* (London, 1992).

beginnings and endings are commemorated there with an assiduity not found in other parts of the world. Surveyed through the continent's nineteenth- and twentieth-century narrative thematics, however, this whole erratic history is the story of a grand frustration, of newness or youthfulness repeatedly denied and repressed, of a past that has never been assimilated and a future that never seems to come or, if it does, arrives too late.[3]

The Latin American novelist who has best embodied the continent's characteristic and persistent alternation between utopia and apocalypse, euphoria and black despair—invariable though not sufficient ingredients of "magical realism"—is Colombia's Gabriel García Márquez, whose personages are direct third-world descendants of Don Quixote, invented by Miguel de Cervantes, the writer who set the pattern for the European novel as a form that would simultaneously posit both the impossibility and the necessity of self-knowledge, of distinguishing between truth and fiction. García Márquez's fabulously successful *Cien años de soledad* [*One Hundred Years of Solitude*], published in 1967, was a rare example of a work as popular with the reading public as with academics. The English critic John Berger, writing ten years later, said that, despite its "magical" reputation, it was a book that "speaks to those who are aware of the scale and turbulence of the struggles and tragedy of history."[4] Appropriately enough, García Márquez's last novel before the 1992 commemorations, *El general en su laberinto* [*The General in His Labyrinth*], published in 1989, was an imagined reconstruction of Bolívar's final despairing weeks before he departed prematurely from history into myth with his vision of continental unity unachieved. Ironically, the so-called Boom of the Latin American novel in the 1960s, of which García Márquez was the best-known representative, itself seemed to presage a vast transformation of the continent's political culture, which also failed to come about.

Before and after *Cien años de soledad*, many other famous narrative works, like Domingo Faustino Sarmiento's *Facundo: Civilización o barbarie* (Argentina, 1845) [*Facundo: Civilization and Barbarism*], Euclides da Cunha's *Os sertoes* (Brazil, 1900) [*Rebellion in the Backlands*], Miguel Angel

---

[3] Here we are speaking more specifically about Spanish America. In Brazil disenchantment has taken somewhat different forms. As José Guilherme Merquior has said, from the earliest days of settlement and colonization, "the Portuguese mind proved far less utopian than the Spanish one. . . . The masters of Brazil climbed down from the lofty dreams of high-minded Spanish *conquistadors*" ("The Brazilian and the Spanish American Literary Traditions: A Contrastive View," in Roberto González Echevarría and Enrique Pupo-Walker, eds., *The Cambridge History of Latin American Literature* [Cambridge, 1996], 3:364).

[4] *New Society*, London, April 28, 1977, 180.

Asturias's *El Señor Presidente* (Guatemala, 1946) [*Mr. President*], or Mario Vargas Llosa's *La guerra del fin del mundo* (Peru, 1981) [*The War of the End of the World*], have portrayed the historical development of Latin America as a kind of tragic-comic caricature of European history, a repetitive nightmare in which Latin Americans endlessly fail to emulate enviable European paradigms. And so the same sins and curses come to haunt the literary continent and its children through century after century—conquest, murder, violation, expropriation, dictatorship—countered by the redemptive quest for legitimacy and identity and the struggle for liberation, inevitably involving a raising of consciousness, further repression from without and within, and a new round of disillusionment and despair. Little wonder the labyrinth became a key symbol within Latin American literature.

Notice that we are already speaking, in the time-honored way, of a "Latin American literature." Notice also that, however much of a critically constructed mirage it may be, to speak in this way is very easy to do. Indeed, all the books mentioned thus far are routinely considered works that have as much—or more—to say at the level of such a "Latin American literature" as they do at the level of their national literatures: those of Colombia, Argentina, Brazil, Guatemala, or Peru. Suffice to say at this point that I see the problem posed by my title in exactly the opposite manner than do most of my fellow historians and critics. For me, after all these years of visiting the continent and reflecting on it, a unified Latin American literature does not exist because it is the unified expression of a more or less unified region (or, come to that, because it suits the purposes of literary-critical *conquistadores* concerned to control vast territories without ever working the land):[5] on the contrary, I assert that Latin America can be said to exist, in large part, beyond debatable geographical and cultural realities, because there also clearly exists a unified literature that overdetermines its twenty-one independent literatures[6] and thereby semanticizes, systematizes, and unifies, in the most material way imaginable, that historically constructed geocultural space we call Latin America. Or, to put it still more squarely, Latin American literature confirms the existence of Latin America, not the other way round. And this is a much more interesting and, for me at least, much more satisfying situation.

---

[5] It is not often acknowledged that most Latin Americanists, like most Latin Americans, have visited only a few Latin American countries; very few have experience of the entire continent.

[6] I am not concerned here with more recently formed republics like Belize, the Guyanas, Jamaica, and Trinidad, nor with the literatures written in native languages that are now merely incipient but will no doubt grow in significance in times to come.

Undoubtedly the region's semidetached and hence inherently problemat-ical and ironical relation to "Western culture" has left Latin Americans struggling over their identity (are they "Indian" or "European" Americans?) both in debate and through every form of political conflict for five hundred years, in a "subcontinent" that has never even been sure what to call itself—especially since its northern neighbors appropriated the names "America" and "Americans" for themselves.[7] In compensation, as the cosmopolitan Ar-gentinian Jorge Luis Borges put it, albeit somewhat perfidiously: "The chief advantage of belonging to a rather traditionless land (for of course we are neither Spaniards nor Indians) is that one has to fall back on the Universe or, at least, on Western culture."[8]

In fact, most Latin American republics have for almost a century repro-duced within their own borders the conflict between what for a time we called "first"- and "third"-world realities, which characterized the uneven development of twentieth-century capitalism, thereby creating a curious mise-en-abyme effect at the level of politics and economics themselves. Identity in these circumstances can seem an endless journey through looking glasses and labyrinths, prompting Borges in his fictions to show not only Latin American but all human experience as inherently irrational and inex-plicable. The search for new ways of conveying this plural and contradictory reality gave rise in the second half of the twentieth century (though there were antecedents, significantly, as early as the 1920s) to the notorious "mag-ical realist" mode, which is why so many novels these days seem to be "Latin American," even if their writers are called Calvino, Kundera, Pavic, Eco, Rushdie, or Roy.[9] In this sense, it is possible to argue that Latin American lit-erature, especially now but really since the 1920s, is the first regional narra-tive system with a truly global perspective—in contrast to European litera-ture, whose coherence until recently was achieved through the distorted unifying lens of imperialism and that simultaneous claim of uniqueness and universality that we call ethnocentrism and logocentrism, with which, for the past one hundred years, the United States has also been infected. In our new multicultural, postmodern world, with its dizzying, "magical" patterns

---

[7] The United States and Canada are rarely thought of as constituting a "subcontinent." The North wins in almost every conceptual and ideological battle (though Latin Americans themselves continue to call their subcontinent "América" and themselves "Americans"). In this essay I shall consider Latin America from the Rio Grande to Tierra del Fuego as a "continent."

[8] See *Encounter* London September 1965, 86.

[9] Franco Moretti's *Modern Epic* (London, 1996) is subtitled *The World System from Goethe to García Márquez.*

and pace of development yet disturbing, nightmarish consequences, versions of this contemporary literary mode have become frequent among writers wishing to go beyond the tired middle-class chronicles of so many European and North American novels with their petty individualism and mundane parochialism. After the 1960s, as problems of identity, influence, parody, simulacrum, and disenchantment became worldwide preoccupations, the whole planet appeared to become Latin American.

The Mestizo *Continent and Its Texts*

> We are but a small human kind, a world apart, . . .
> neither Indians nor Europeans, but a species half-way
> between the legitimate owners of the land and the
> Spanish usurpers.
> —SIMÓN BOLÍVAR, *The Jamaica Letter,* 1815

As we have seen, 1492, so recently commemorated (a date as universally portentous as A.D. 1, 1066, 1453, 1776, 1789, 1917, and, no doubt, 1989) is the historical point of departure for the vicissitudes experienced by the Latin American continent during the half-millennium since Columbus's arrival and for the ideological explanations of everything that has happened there in that time. Latin America has been in existence as an extension of "Europe" for five hundred years yet still finds itself in an essentially subaltern and even adolescent relationship to the "first world." Spanish America and Brazil were colonies of Spain and Portugal before they themselves were settled nations (Spain was for some time to be known as "the Spains" and Portugal was for some time governed by Spain). Most of its republics have been formally independent for almost two centuries, before many now-powerful European nations existed. However, their unique dialectic of biculturalism originated still earlier, at the time of discovery, when the first Indian woman was violated and the first *Mestizo* was born, a few months after Columbus's first landfall. Let us suppose the child was a male. He was also a bastard. His father was a conqueror, a murderer, and a rapist, though from an allegedly superior culture; his mother was a victim, of inferior race and gender. Her son was something less than the son of a whore. With no help from Freud, and not much from Christianity, this newly invented personage would hate, yet fear and also admire his father; he would sympathize with but despise his mother. He would resent both of them. In some guise or another he would appear in almost every Latin American cultural text—but above all, after independence, in countless Latin American novels, including most of the best-known ones—from the earliest times to the present day.[10] Shortly after his birth, African slaves would be brought to the continent, and the biological and cultural confusions would be further complicated.

If we move from the individual to the continental dimension, the development of Latin America from that time has been continuously circumscribed by external forces and colonial relationships (making Latin American literature, inescapably, a branch of "Western literature"). Inevitably, then, the oscillation between a nationalist, continentalist, or "Americanist" impulse and a European, cosmopolitan, or "universalist" impulse is the single most important phenomenon in Latin American cultural history and is reflected repeatedly in the works of the most representative novelists of the twentieth century. Once again we must emphasize: all nations, all "races" are *really* "mixed" and "impure"; all cultures, all literatures have a dynamic between an "inside" and an "outside," home and away, self and other. But only Latin Americans have been so deeply and inescapably aware of this, on a majority basis, since the very beginning of their culture, half a millennium ago. Not only is their literature structured by this reality, and by the multifold perceptions of this reality; it is also what their literature has very largely been *about*. These "imagined communities" have always been particularly difficult and painful to imagine; and, as I have mentioned, there has always been—and still remains—much confusion as to whether the community to be imagined at any given moment is a national or a continental one. This is why Benedict Anderson himself has referred to the "well-known doubleness in early Spanish-American nationalism, its alternating grand stretch and particularistic localism."[11]

Thus far, then, the image has been developed of a profoundly romantic yet disoriented and disenchanted continent, a stereotype that reached its culmination with the famous "Boom" of the Latin American novel in the 1960s. Its best-known representative, *Cien años de soledad*, was published, as it happens, in the year that a third great continental idealist (or glorious failure), the Christ-like Ernesto "Che" Guevara, died in Bolivia; and García Márquez's novel about Bolívar, *El general en su laberinto*, was published in 1989, the year that saw the symbolic end of European communism, when the island of Cuba, governed by the Bolivarian *comandante* Fidel Castro, was abandoned to its (North) American fate.

---

[10] The best-known version of this syndrome is expounded by Octavio Paz, *El laberinto de la soledad* (1950), though Paz's original version was devoted solely to Mexico; many other Latin American thinkers before and since have explored the continent's historical, geographical, and existential solitude.

[11] Benedict Anderson, *Imagined Communities*, 2nd ed. (London, 1991), 62.

Long before that, in the 1920s, Pedro Henríquez Ureña of the Dominican Republic said that Latin America—"Hispanic America," as he called it—was still in search of its own expression. He took it for granted that this quest for cultural identity was to be carried out both at the national and continental level but, significantly, gave precedence to the continental level as the only one at which Latin Americans could find a coherent focus.[12] Henríquez Ureña was only the most distinguished Latin American precursor of a form of analysis that would eventually lead to two conclusions that are of universal significance today. First, no identities are ever really fixed, as Spaniards, Frenchmen, Englishmen, and Germans were inclined to assume and colonials constrained to agree. In that sense Latin America's eternal quest for identity was potentially a good thing, not a weakness, looking forward not back. Second, and in consequence, nationalities, though an inevitable and perhaps even desirable illusion, were ideological constructs that would be more helpfully subsumed into larger continental entities on the way to the eventual formation of a universal social, economic, and cultural polity. Thus, Henríquez Ureña went on to say that Latin America, as a postcolonial region, was destined always to be searching for some future and better identity and that this was why the continent's quests always had some utopian dimension attached to them. Hence—we might add—the failures and disappointments; hence even a certain difficulty with imposed rationalities and pragmatically defined realities; but hence also that compelling romantic idealism that characterized the continent, then as now; and hence that ability to find pleasure in ordinary everyday things—a pleasure that for Latin Americans is not just a consolation for oppression and failure but a premonition of the better world that to them is always so close and that they celebrate not only through revolution but also through the festive victories of daily life.

Responding implicitly to Henríquez Ureña in the early 1930s, Peruvian critic Luis Alberto Sánchez said that Latin America had still not found its own literary expression (as France, England, and Germany had supposedly found theirs centuries before) and that it was still a vast "Novel without Novelists" (the title of his book written in 1933). The "Latin American New Novel" (from Asturias, Andrade, Bombal, Borges, and Carpentier through Arguedas, Guimarães Rosa, Lispector, Roa Bastos, and Rulfo to Cortázar, Fuentes, García Márquez, Vargas Llosa, and Allende), developing as he spoke, would resolve this problem, culminating in the Boom of the 1960s.

---

[12] Pedro Henríquez Ureña, *Seis ensayos en busca de nuestra expresión*, in *La utopía de América* (Caracas, 1978), 33.

Cuban Alejo Carpentier, in the introduction to his novel *El reino de este mundo* (1949) [*The Kingdom of This World*], presented his now-famous neo-avantgardist explanation of the "marvelous reality" of Latin America as a place where surrealism was always already redundant because the continent was a natural machine for integrating the prosaic and the poetic, the real and the marvelous. Fellow writers like Guatemalan Miguel Angel Asturias and Venezuelan Arturo Uslar Pietri were at that same time talking about a concept that was similar but destined for even greater popular success: "magical realism." And Argentina's Borges, from a country without the ethnic and mythological substrata available to Cubans, Guatemalans, or Venezuelans, had already concluded that all reality was essentially fantastic and seemed, a few decades later, to have convinced the entire world to see it his way: by now Borges has become not only an international Name but also, like Joyce and Kafka, an Adjective.

But for other Latin American thinkers, such irrational or exotic approaches to the continent's predicament were part of the problem, not the solution. The Mexican philosopher Leopoldo Zea, following Hegel, remarked that after a century of independence Latin Americans had been ashamed of their history and therefore unwilling to confront it:

> They wanted nothing to do with that series of conflicts, revolts, alternations between dictatorship and anarchy. In past history they found nothing constructive, nothing they aspired to be. And yet, in spite of everything, the Latin American was making history, not the history he would have wished for, but his own history. A very special history, with no negations or dialectical assimilations. A history full of contradictions that never came to synthesis. But history for all that. The history that we Latin Americans, half-way through the twentieth century, must negate dialectically, that is, assimilate.[13]

But another Mexican, Octavio Paz, at the end of a very pessimistic interpretation of Mexican identity, modified Zea's own pessimism by suggesting, like Henríquez Ureña before him, that Latin Americans were mistaken in thinking that their identity problems were unique:

> Zea has studied Latin American alienation, the way that we are not truly ourselves but always thought by others. This alienation, rather than our

---

[13] Leopoldo Zea, *El pensamiento latinoamericana* (Mexico City, 1965), 44. This work was an amplification of his 1949 book, *Dos etapas del pensamiento en Hispanoamérica*. (My translation. All translations from referenced Spanish and Portuguese originals are mine.)

particularities, constitutes our special way of being. But it is in reality a universal situation, shared by all men. To become aware of this is to become aware of ourselves. It is true, we have lived on the periphery of history. But today, the center, the nucleus of world society, has dissolved and we have all become peripheral beings, even the Europeans and North Americans. We are all on the margins because there is no longer a center. . . . Beyond the general collapse of Reason and Faith, God and Utopia, there are no intellectual systems old or new to be erected, capable of appeasing our anguish or relieving our dismay: there is nothing before us. We are finally alone; like all men. . . . Out there, in the open solitude, transcendence also awaits us: the hands of other solitary beings. We are, for the first time in our history, the contemporaries of all men.[14]

One might say of the characters of *Cien años de soledad* that they have not yet come to this consoling realization. Of course Paz was an archetypal Latin American intellectual, endlessly deciphering reality with the sword of reason yet leaving new myths behind him with every stroke of his blade.

For here we arrive at an essential paradox. In the period after the early Carpentier and the early Borges, after Zea and Paz, most of the great novels of the 1960s Boom—*La muerte de Artemio Cruz* (Carlos Fuentes, Mexico, 1962), *Rayuela* (Julio Cortázar, Argentina, 1963), *La casa verde* (Mario Vargas Llosa, Peru, 1966), *Cien años de soledad*, for example—carried the implicit claim that now, at long last, Latin American reality could finally be deciphered. Yet in their endlessly proliferating interviews and essays, the authors of that generation continued to feed the vast terrestrial monster of continental myth. For example, the Mexican Carlos Fuentes said of *Cien años de soledad* that it is "a true re-vision and re-creation of the utopias, the epics and the myths of America. It shows us a group of men and women deciphering a world that will devour them: a surrounding magma." Augusto Roa Bastos, of Paraguay, author of the monumental *Yo el Supremo* (1974) [*I the Supreme*], remarked that Latin America is a continent whose history offers "the features of a bitter fable whose most incredible images are, precisely, the events of its own history."[15] Still more pessimistic, Argentinian novelist Luisa Valenzuela complained: "I am afraid that my country from the moment of its discovery has been faithful to a literary tradition that has

---

[14] Octavio Paz, *El laberinto de la soledad*, 5th ed. (Mexico City, 1967), 152 and 174.

[15] Carlos Fuentes, *Myself with Others* (New York, 1988), 194; and Augusto Roa Bastos, "Entretiens," *Caravelle* 17 (1971): 208.

prompted misrepresentation and fantasy." Even Spanish America's only convincing twentieth-century narrative realist, Mario Vargas Llosa, lamented: "We are still victims in Latin America of what we could call the revenge of the novel. We still have great difficulty in our countries in differentiating between fiction and reality." And García Márquez himself spelled out the same view in his celebrated Nobel Prize speech of 1982: "Poets and beggars, musicians and prophets, soldiers and scoundrels, all we creatures of that disorderly reality have needed to ask little of the imagination, for the major challenge before us has been the want of conventional resources to make our life credible. This, my friends, is the nub of our solitude." In other words, reality and fantasy are at the best of times difficult to separate, but in the Latin American context they can seem inextricable. It hardly needs repeating that this unreality phenomenon involves a permanent and implicit comparison—and an inevitably unequal one—between Latin America and the so-called first world, between the magical and the real, a process that leaves us only a step away from the Latin American equivalent of Edward Said's "Orientalism"; except in this case the traitors are not the European enemy without but the European enemy within every Latin American.

Unity and Diversity

> The first singularity relating to Latin America is its existence as such, that is, as a body of twenty-one countries with historical, social and cultural ties which go so deep as to make them a unity in many respects. Other groups of countries are related by history or race, by language or religion or by political or economic treaties, but it is rare for them to coincide in all these aspects and still more so, as in the case of Latin America, for these common factors to be stronger than the desire for individualization or dissidence.
> —JOSÉ LUIS MARTÍNEZ, *Unidad y diversidad de la literatura latinoamericana*

Thus the globalization of identity and culture, the advent of so-called post-modernity, which most Western thinkers only began to glimpse in the 1960s, became evident earlier to Latin American observers like Henríquez Ureña, Mexico's José Vasconcelos, Brazil's Mário de Andrade (*Macunaíma*, 1928), Borges, Carpentier, Zea, and Paz, as they gazed from the periphery in that extraordinarily fertile period in Latin American thought and literature between the 1920s and the 1960s. One of the many reasons why *Cien años de soledad* was such a revelation to Latin Americans in the 1960s was that it miraculously synthesized such perspectives and suddenly showed both intellectuals and ordinary Latin American readers what they had been feeling all along about the predicament of uneven and combined development. It then went on, through translations into the principal European languages, to show other readers in the so-called centers that they themselves were not so different, after all, from these laughably underdeveloped and lovably exotic Latin Americans; and thereafter, through still further translations, the novel gave other writers in other parts of the so-called third world (Salman Rushdie was only the first and most publicized of them) a format for a new kind of writing different both from nineteenth-century realism and early-twentieth-century modernism.

Let us now deal with matters more soberly and turn to Latin America itself. We have already, in a sense, received an answer, but let us more explicitly pose the question: Does "Latin American literature" exist? Come to that, does "Latin America" exist? (In 1945, Peruvian historian Luis Alberto Sánchez published a book with this title—at a time when he was writing a general history of his Latin American "novel without novelists." Latin Americans themselves, like everyone else, call the continent in which they live "Latin America." Even the inhabitants of Brazil, always the great exception, consider themselves unreservedly to be "Latin Americans." There are departments and centers of "Latin American studies" all over the world (though fewer in Latin America than almost anywhere else!). Yet for some time theorists in many disciplines (other than geography) have been questioning the concept, and now, in an era dominated by "globalization" at one extreme and "particularism" at another, the questions are more frequently posed. What, the questioners ask, has Guatemala in common with, say, Argentina?

We could begin by remarking: more, much more, than England has in common with Poland, though both are considered part of some construction called "Europe"; more even than England has in common with France, though these are direct geographical neighbors whose history has intertwined closely for more than a thousand years. Guatemala and Argentina speak the same language. They were both "discovered" during the Renaissance when European nations began the process of colonization and settlement of other cultural spaces, and the territories they now occupy remained Spanish colonies for three hundred years. Both had preexisting native populations whom the Europeans chose to call "Indians." In both countries the overwhelmingly dominant religion has been Catholicism. Both became formally independent in the nineteenth century. Politically and culturally, they both, for long periods of their history, related more directly to Europe (especially Spain, France, and England) and later the United States than to the Latin American neighbors with whom they shared so many attributes—a curious factor to have in common but a real one nonetheless.

We may conclude, then, that whether or not we any longer think that categories can be fixed and generalizations made, if there can be said to exist any "continent" (or "subcontinent") made up of multiple countries that is, relatively speaking, unified historically and culturally, it has to be Latin America. Neither Europe nor Africa nor Asia can begin to compare in these respects. (The United States and Canada are a different case that would only complicate my argument to no good purpose.)[16] The single reason above all for this relative unity within diversity is the European Conquest that began in 1492 and changed not only the history of Latin America but of the entire planet. Moreover, the native American cultures and great civilizations of the continent themselves have many features in common because, even before the arrival of Europeans, the land mass now called Latin America was subject to less complex migratory and invasionary flows and conflicts than most other parts of the planet:

> Genetically, all native Americans living south of the intercontinental Eskimo are now recognized to have characteristic blood groups. They lack blood-group B, a highly eloquent testimony to their millennial isolation from the rest of the world after their migration from Asia. For their part, linguisticians have shown that Indian languages are closer to each other than they are to languages elsewhere; and what in the nineteenth century was thought to be a plethora of hundreds of quite distinct languages has now been reduced to five or six main groups. Further, the kind of evidence used in support of these claims also underlies the arguments of anthropologists who detect an unbroken chain of mythic thought from South to North America. In the four volumes of his *Mythologiques*, Lévi-Strauss has suggested that this ancient "syncretism" will one day shape the true history of early America, when it comes to be written.[17]

---

[16] On this topic, see Gustavo Pérez Firmat, *Do the Americas Have a Common Literature?* (Durham, N.C., 1990). My short answer is that they do not.

[17] Gordon Brotherston, *Image of the New World: The American Continent Portrayed in Native Texts* (London, 1979), 14. See also his *Book of the Fourth World: Reading the Native Americas through their Literature* (Cambridge, 1992).

Of course the many native cultures and civilizations had very diverse social structures and lifestyles at the time of the conquest. And these different
cultures and civilizations do indeed explain many of the notable differences
between the contemporary regions and republics of the continent, as do the
different degrees of African influence, depending on the extent of slavery in
each country and the provenance of the slaves themselves. But if we ask why
countries as far apart—six thousand kilometers—as Mexico and Argentina
are, despite everything, so similar in many ways to each other and so different from the United States and Canada, the explanation is, again, obvious:
because of the identities and cultures of the European countries that colonized those areas after 1492.

Latin Americans, in fact, have almost as much in common with the Spanish, the Portuguese, the Italians, and the French as United States Anglos
have with the British, the Canadians, and the Australians; but Latin Americans from different countries, united even in their own complexity, have
much more in common with each other than any of these other groups do.
In that sense Latin America is already in many material respects a shadowy
nation with twenty-one regions and therefore much more similar to the
United States than at first sight it may appear. An even more dramatic exem-
plification can be made with India: one could argue for some time whether
Latin America is more culturally united than India (even after its separation
from Pakistan), which is a single nation (as well as another subcontinent),
but no one could deny, given the number of literary languages in use in
India, that it makes much more sense to talk about "Latin American literature" than it does to talk about "Indian literature." (Indeed, the relationship
of Indians who write in English to those who write in Urdu or Bengali has a
curious asymmetrical parallelism to the relationship between Latin Americans who write with a continental vision and a continental audience in mind
and those whose horizons of reference and reception are more specifically
national.)

Latin American literary and cultural theorists have recently questioned
these alleged unities and have rejected the concept of the *Mestizo* continent—
the idea of a new human space miscegenated (and thus variably unified) not
only biologically but also politically, socially, and culturally. This identity was
most memorably theorized by Mexican thinker José Vasconcelos, with his
influential notion of the *Cosmic Race* (1925). These days the concept is considered contaminated, so other theories have been developed and explored,
like "transculturation" (Angel Rama), "heterogeneity" (Antonio Cornejo
Polar), or "hybridity" (Néstor García Canclini), not to mention the U.S.
postmodernist catch-all of now calling "multiculturalism" what used to be

called the "melting pot."[18] But it seems to me that these are all words used in a futile attempt to avoid not only (and understandably) the biological traces in a concept like miscegenation (though "hybridity," the current favorite, is hardly an improvement) but also to elide the historical implications of a— much more tractional but unfortunately Marxist—concept like uneven and combined development.

I have no space to develop these arguments. And actually there is a formula at which I have already hinted—"unity within diversity"—that has been tried and tested by Latin Americanists for almost a hundred years and that, for the purposes of this brief general essay, is probably still the best way to go.[19] Whether viewed geographically, historically, politically, socially, culturally, or linguistically, the countries of the continent make up a large, ever expanding kaleidoscope; or, as the great Mexican polymath Alfonso Reyes put it, like a constellation—some countries more prominent than others, some brighter, but all subject to the same orbital and gravitational forces and the same overall structure.[20] That is why one of the most fascinating aspects of the Latin American continent is that, geographically, historically, and culturally, most of its countries seem to replicate in miniature, albeit irregularly, the heterogeneity of Latin America as a whole: they are far more diverse than most European countries or the United States, for example. And of course within Latin America there are also regional (and cultural) groupings: for example, Mexico; Central America (Guatemala, Honduras, El Salvador, Nicaragua, Costa Rica, and Panama); the neo-Granadan republics (Colombia and Venezuela); the Andean republics (Ecuador, Bolivia, and Peru); Brazil; and the Southern Cone (Chile, Argentina, Uruguay, and, possibly, Paraguay). But this is just one pattern among many, and this exercise has been done in many different ways.[21]

---

[18] See Angel Rama, *Transculturación narrativa en América Latina* (Mexico City, 1982); Néstor García Canclini, *Culturas híbridas: Estrategias para entrar y salir de la modernidad* (Mexico City, 1990); and Antonio Cornejo Polar, *Escribir en el aire: Ensayo sobre la heterogeneidad socio-cultural en las literaturas andinas* (Lima, 1994).

[19] The concept appears in numerous titles relating to Latin America, but Mexican José Luis Martínez's use of it in his *Unidad y diversidad de la literatura latinoamericana* (Mexico City, 1972), borrowed from a 1935 lecture by Spanish critic Enrique Díez-Canedo, is the best-known application to the literary sphere.

[20] Alfonso Reyes, *La constelación americana* (Mexico City, 1950).

[21] See Brazilian Darcy Ribeiro's influential classification in *Las Américas y la civilización* (Havana, 1992): he divides Latin American countries into "testimonial peoples" (Mexico, Central America, Peru); "new peoples" (Brazil, Colombia, Venezuela, the Caribbean, Chile); and "transplanted peoples" (Argentina, Uruguay, Paraguay).

One might add that, just as it has been difficult to get a hearing in the world of readers if one is a European outside of France, England, or Germany, so a Mexican, Colombian, or Argentinian has only been able to make his voice heard if he was able to convince readers that he speaks for Latin America. Surely the most dramatic example of this happening in a historically decisive way was when, in the 1960s, the Cuban Revolution seemed to speak not only for much of Latin America but also for the whole third world (the "tricontinental" perspective).

Latin American Literature(s): The National-Continental Dialectic

> Spanish American literature is a misleading concept, largely a construction of academics writing from outside and in general institutionally tempted to think of the Third World as a homogeneous entity, of Latin America as a monolith, and of Spanish America as a unity rather than a complex whole. To be sure, since the days of Andrés Bello there has been many an effort to use culture to overcome a Balkanized polity— literary Bolivarianism has never been far away. Yet efforts are not achievements, and in the end national or regional traditions have been at least as important as supposed common elements and unifying factors. . . . Any comparison of Brazilian and Spanish American literary traditions reveals as many divergences as similarities.
>
> —José Guilherme Merquior

The above quotation, which argues directly and somewhat embarrassingly against the assumptions of the ambitious volume that contains it (not to mention my own perspective), comes, curiously, at the end of an interesting essay that seems to show quite the opposite of its own conclusion.[22] Note also that the last sentence assumes what the previous statement has already denied, namely the relative unity of Spanish American literary traditions. In fact, anyone who has attempted to write a history of Latin American (Spanish American and Brazilian) culture, including literature—and there are not many of us—may well have found the connections far easier to make than he

---

[22] Merquior, "The Brazilian and Spanish American Literary Traditions," 381. Other influential critics who have dealt with this topic, fellow Brazilian Antonio Cándido and Uruguayan Emir Rodríguez Monegal, generally disagreed with the opinion expressed by Merquior.

or she would have assumed.[23] Even in the nineteenth century there were significant mutual influences, and from the 1920s onward the two literatures, thanks especially to the work of a few heroic writers and critics (Henríquez Ureña, Reyes, Uruguayans Emir Rodríguez Monegal, and Angel Rama, Cuban Roberto Fernández Retamar, Brazilians Haroldo de Campos and Antonio Cándido, and Italian Amos Segala) trying to end the division produced by separate colonizations and consecrated by the Tordesillas division of 1494, have been growing much more closely together. At the same time it must be admitted that a novelist of world importance like the nineteenth-century Brazilian Machado de Assis is scarcely better known in Spanish America than outside Latin America, but he would certainly be better known in both places if he were French or English. Only since the 1960s has the relationship between Spanish America and Brazil become genuinely intertextual on more than an individual basis. One could say, then, that these two literatures, the Spanish American and Brazilian, have been mainly "parallel" but that they also now substantially overlap, with innumerable unnoted intertextualities. Obviously this provides a unique opportunity for a particularly fascinating exercise in comparative literature, one which has not yet been undertaken.[24] One might assert that Brazilian literature is more "complete" than any of its Spanish American equivalents but not as "self-reflexive." Its regions are part of a whole, as in the Latin America of the twenty-one republics but, surprisingly perhaps, not as dialectical: they are generally seen as complementary parts of a unified whole, which is why, despite its own vastness, Brazilian literature has a national rather than a continental dimension (no Brazilian writer has written a "Spanish American" equivalent to Peruvian Mario Vargas Llosa's "Brazilian" novel, *La guerra del fin del mundo*, 1981). At the same time, Brazilian literature is more similar to Spanish American literature than to any other literature (even to such obvious cases as the Portuguese, French or, more recently, the United States one, with which, not surprisingly, it has some quite striking features in common).

Thus in any attempt to characterize this cultural constellation for literary purposes, Brazil, which speaks Portuguese and is situated in South America,

---

[23] See my *Journeys through the Labyrinth: Latin American Fiction in the Twentieth Century* (London, 1989); and my essays on Latin American literature and culture in *The Cambridge History of Latin America*, vols. 3, 4, and 10.

[24] UNESCO attempted to launch such an initiative almost thirty years ago, with a book called *América Latina en su literatura* (Mexico City, 1972) as a kind of critical-theoretical blueprint, but all attempts to extend the project—notably by Ana Pizarro and collaborators (see below)—have been frustrated.

is a big problem—though little Haiti, which is situated in the Caribbean and speaks French, is an even bigger one. Yet there are other less decisive but still significant matters of difference to consider. For example, Spanish-speaking Mexico, one of the most prominent stars, is, in geographical theory, part of "North America." Mexican literature, however, is an obvious part not only of what we call *Spanish American literature* (adding the eighteen other Spanish-speaking countries, including the also problematical Puerto Rico, which belongs politically to the United States) but also of *Ibero-American literature* (adding Brazil) and, naturally, of *Latin American literature* (adding Haiti), as well, needless to say, of *literature in Spanish*, but not of *Spanish literature* (though possibly of *"Hispanic" literature*—here the question is, and specialists disagree, whether Portugal and Brazil should or should not be included under this rubric).

So when literary critics talk loosely about Latin American literature they are often talking about Spanish American literature, and not everything they say applies equally well or at all to Brazil or Haiti. In many respects, then, the most interesting question is the more limited one of whether there is such a thing as a "Spanish American literature" rather than the literature of nineteen Spanish-speaking countries, and this essay will concentrate heavily on that question. Pedro Henríquez Ureña noticed as early as the 1920s that "there is a fundamental unity of the Spanish American family which distinguishes it from the Spanish one (even in external signs, like pronunciation) and establishes a much closer relationship between the most dissimilar peoples of the New World than between any of them and Spain."[25] And another influential literary historian, Enrique Anderson Imbert, taking the unity of Spanish America as a given, commented that he had written a continental history of Spanish American literature quite simply because, "to group writers by countries would have broken the cultural unity of Spanish America into nineteen illusory national literatures."[26] Similar is the assertion by the editors of a prestigious recent history of Latin American literature: "National trends stress the differences and remain local. But the stronger authors and works cross frontiers or dwell in the homology. They constitute a kind of overarching literature to which all aspire. Our assumption here has been that the most significant and influential part of Latin American literature

---

[25] Pedro Henríquez Ureña, *La utopía de América* (Mexico City, 1978), 518. On the other hand, Henríquez Ureña noted in 1925 that no Spanish American had tried to write a history of Latin American literature by that time, whereas both an American and a German had.

[26] Enrique Anderson Imbert, *Historia de la literatura hispanoamericana* 2nd ed. (Mexico City, 1970), 1:10.

is the one engaged in a transcontinental intertextual exchange."[27] While this, in my opinion, is significantly overstating the case, there is no other world region about which such an assertion could be made. Nevertheless, for me the most interesting aspect of so-called Latin American literature is precisely the existence of twenty-one national literatures *and* a continental literature, and, in particular, the relationship between them.

Still, if Latin America is one continent with twenty-one relatively similar histories, cultures, and languages, it might reasonably be assumed that Latin American literature is one literature with twenty relatively similar sublitera-tures. Thus some would see so-called Latin American literature as a single world-historical cultural phenomenon with merely implicit frontiers, as if the national borders of each country were just dotted lines hardly relating to or impinging on the real topographical features underneath. Or we could see, as I tend to do, the existence of twenty-one national literatures, most of whose participants were more aware of national than international tradi-tion so that family resemblances were, so to speak, more accidental than designed—while, at the same time, within each country, though more at some times than at others, some writers would always be fully aware of the continental dimension and would therefore see themselves as contributors to a transnational Latin American literature.

Between the conquest and emancipation one sees the long, slow conver-sion of what was no more at first than the prolongation of Spanish and Por-tuguese literatures into a Spanish American and a Brazilian literature. Brazil remained an independent monarchy until 1889, but in Spanish America a particularly interesting phenomenon existed. Bolívar had argued for a united America, a "Patria Grande": "It is a grandiose idea to try to form one single nation out of the whole of the new world, with one single link to unite its parts to one another and to the whole; since they have one origin, one lan-guage, one set of customs and one religion" (*Carta de Jamaica*, 1815). And in the decades after independence many thinkers in many countries (Central American Cecilio del Valle, Venezuelan Andrés Bello, and Argentinian José María Gutiérrez, for example) thought of America first and their individual nation second. But as the century wore on, the reality of fragmentation made them turn back to national literary questions before they turned again to the idea of America with the arrival of *modernismo* in the last years of the century.

---

[27] *The Cambridge History of Latin American Literature* is a disappointingly traditional—indeed, conservative—work of literary historiography. Far more critical, imaginative, and up-to-date is Ana Pizarro, ed., *América Latina: Palavra, literatura e cultura* (Sao Paulo, 1993), also in 3 vols.

This is not to deny that there is also a constructed Latin American literature that, some would say, can sound like a myth or look like a mirage. As an
example of the uneven development of Latin America's regional or national
literatures, Mexico, a country of extraordinary historical importance and
cultural complexity, with a literary history as interesting and significant as
that of Spain itself over the past two hundred years, nevertheless has only
one work of continental importance to show in the whole of the nineteenth
century, namely José Fernández de Lizardi's *El periquillo sarniento* (1816)
[*The Itching Parrot*]. This work, which, looked at from another perspective,
has obvious "Mexican" literary and cultural characteristics, is nevertheless
considered the first "Latin American" novel, not only because of its historical precedence but also because, conveniently and symbolically, it is a picaresque novel and thus somehow compensates dialectically for that long period in which Spain, home of the picaresque novel, banned the reading and
writing of novels in its American dominions. By contrast, and paradoxically,
Argentina, a country of no historical importance in the colonial period, and
with a tiny population at the time of emancipation, boasts a nineteenth-
century literature that, in its continental importance, can sometimes seem as
significant as all the other Spanish American literatures of that period put
together. (Yet, when the crucial modernist period arrived toward the end of
the century, Argentina played a relatively minor role, and the small republics
of Central America and the Caribbean played a disproportionately large
one). Thus in this period Argentina contributed a work, the great gaucho
poem *Martín Fierro* (1872), which is considered not only Argentina's national epic but a "Latin American" epic that has become an integral (because "necessary") part of Latin American literature. By contrast, if we look
at other countries in the nineteenth century, we will find that many of them
have nothing approximating either a picaresque novel or a national epic
poem. So it is that Latin American literature, like Latin America itself, can
sometimes seem to be an illusion, sometimes a desire, and sometimes a construction; but, for me, from the earliest times it has also been much more of
a reality than, say, "European literature."

More careful scrutiny of the history reveals that many Spanish American
countries have one or two great writers plus constellations of others whom
they render almost invisible viewed from a continental perspective. This is
especially true of small countries (José Martí in Cuba, Rubén Darío in
Nicaragua, Miguel Angel Asturias in Guatemala, Augusto Roa Bastos in
Paraguay). Of course the phenomenon allows those small countries to participate culturally in something far larger than themselves. This is why, precisely in the period when Spanish American countries were coming closer

together again in the later nineteenth century and early in the twentieth, there were many thinkers and critics from small countries of continental pretensions and importance: Ecuadorean Juan Montalvo, Puerto Rican Eugenio María Hostos, Cuban José Martí, and Dominican Henríquez Ureña, to name but a few. (More recently the extraordinary phenomenon of tiny Uruguay commands attention, which in the past fifty years has produced more literary critics of continental importance than Mexico or Argentina). Sarmiento, Martí, and Darío are all "Latin American" writers. (Admittedly, there are even more "Latin American" critics!) Proust is Paris, Joyce is Dublin, but as we shall see, Asturias's *Hombres de maíz* [*Men of Maize*], Rulfo's *Pedro Páramo*, and García Márquez's *Cien años de soledad* are as much "Latin America" as they are Guatemala, Mexico, and Colombia.

Nevertheless, as I have indicated, largely unknown to those who are only concerned with the continent as a whole, twenty-one national literatures have also existed, each with its own writers, works, schools, and movements, each with its own history, each interacting also, unevenly, with the literatures of other countries within Latin America or in other continents. Many of these histories have been only imperfectly narrated, and the comparative history of their relations with each other has still, incredibly, not been related at all.[28] What has really been written is, as can be deduced, the relation of fifty or sixty canonical *writers* with one another (and even this narrative, as the next section will indicate, tends to follow the same furrows while merely changing the theoretical plowshare). There is no history of Latin American literature as a *system* or as a *process*, still less of how this process has evolved and changed over time, following the different rhythms of history, culture, and literature itself in each of the different republics and in their relations to each other.[29]

So there is no "atlas of the Latin American novel" as yet.[30] And there is no work that follows the fascinating comparative story of the narratives

---

[28] The only work that has ever brought together separate histories of each of the national literatures of the continent (including both Brazil and Haiti) is David Foster's *Handbook of Latin American Literature* (New York, 1992). No work has ever attempted to combine both this national approach and a continental approach.

[29] Chilean critic Ana Pizarro organized a series of meetings of Latin Americanist literary critics and produced a number of important publications such as *La literatura latinoamericana como proceso* (Buenos Aires, 1985), in conjunction with Brazilian Antonio Cándido and other critics; however, the eventual goal of a comparativist history of the literatures of the continent never came about.

[30] See Franco Moretti's pathbreaking snapshot, *Atlas of the European Novel 1800–1900* (London, 1998). Moretti's plans for an Atlas of World Literature have not yet found the necessary benefactor.

generated and structured by Latin America's peculiarly complex histories of the relation between provinces (with their regional capitals); nations (with their national capitals); the continent (with its four or five capitals: Mexico City, Buenos Aires, Rio de Janeiro/Sao Paulo, but above all Paris); Europe/ North America (the first world, or center); and "universality" (all the foregoing plus the third world). Notice, at any rate, that whether we make this a three-part structure (nation, continent, world) or a five-part structure (province, nation, continent, centers, world), it is the *continent*, Latin America, that is the central or pivotal term. This is of extraordinary importance for the matter under consideration here. Yet just as the national/continental history of Latin American literature has never been written, so this simple conceptual phenomenon has never been turned into a theory or a book.

Hybrid Genealogies

> Latin Americans today are the product of 2,000 years of Latinity, mixed with Mongoloid and Negroid populations, seasoned with the heritage of multiple cultural patrimonies and crystallized under the compulsion of slavery and Iberian salvationist expansion. That is to say, they are a civilization as old as the oldest in respect of their culture and as young as the newest in terms of their ethnicities. . . . Their specific contribution to the new ecumenical civilization will consist, essentially, in what they are as an ethnic configuration: more human because they incorporate more racial and cultural features of mankind; more generous because they are open to all influences and are inspired by an ideology of racial integration.
> —DARCY RIBEIRO, *Las Américas y la civilización*

Doris Sommer's New Historicist *Foundational Fictions* has studied the nineteenth-century novels that bestowed "national allegories" (Fredric Jameson) on Latin America's newly "imagined communities" (Benedict Anderson).[31] (Notice, by the way, that Sommer includes Brazil.) Each of the novels she treats was essentially a *national* romance, though many were written, no doubt, with knowledge of one another. None of the nineteenth-century works

---

[31] See Doris Sommer, *Foundational Fictions: The National Romances of Latin America* (Berkeley, Calif., 1991); Benedict Anderson, *Imagined Communities*; and Fredric Jameson, "Third-World Literature in the Era of Multinational Capitalism," *Social Text* 15 (1986): 65–88.

in her canon had a continental perspective of the kind that the 1920s "novels of the land" began to develop and that the great "new novels" of the 1940s, 1950s, and 1960s did. (By contrast Sarmiento's hybrid blueprint, *Facundo*, 1845, was at once so local and so abstract—the peculiar contradictory trait of Argentinian narrative—that the continental dimension leaps off the page, and it remains a Latin American classic down to the present).

Nevertheless, the "foundational fictions" of the nineteenth century show not only the external resemblance of the extended family, but also the intertextuality of family tradition. Moreover, one of them—the least typical, as it happens—became the first continental best seller and the first literary work to be taken to the hearts of readers everywhere in Latin America. Jorge Isaacs's *María* (1867), like a pale, weepy, backward-looking but curiously compelling Latin precursor of *Gone with the Wind*, went into forty editions all over Latin America within twenty years of publication (fifteen within Mexico alone) and by the time of its centenary in 1967 had seen more than 150 legal editions and probably as many unofficial versions. It has been filmed and turned into radio and television soap operas on numerous occasions, evidently because, as one critic has correctly observed, "no other work has so influenced the emotional life of Latin America."[32]

It was also the first example of a decisive and especially revealing phenomenon: the Latin American classic that does not travel. Here was a book that, although profoundly and recognizably Colombian, was received as if it were a defining national romance in every Latin American country by readers whose "imagined community" suddenly and almost magically became Latin America; yet it nonetheless made a minimal impact when, in view of its success "at home," it was translated into all the major European languages. Like finding one fragment of a pot that can tell an archaeologist almost everything about a given culture, the phenomenon of *María* is, in my opinion, the proof, in and of itself, that as early as 1867 "Latin America" existed; it existed because a common Latin American culture existed, with its corresponding "structures of feeling," which made this apparently unremarkable novel simultaneously beloved by middle-class readers in every country of what José Martí would call "Our America" and yet incapable at that time in history of traveling outside. No one has yet studied this phenomenon in quite these terms: why was *María* both similar to all the other national romances of the era and yet also, in its continental range, qualitatively

---

[32] Donald McGrady, "Jorge Isaacs," in Luis Iñigo Madrigal, ed., *Historia de la literatura hispanoamericana* (Madrid, 1987), 2:203.

different; and why, given its continental range, did it lack transcontinental propulsion?

By one of those curious coincidences that make Latin American literature, in its unity and diversity, such a fascinating laboratory for the cultural historian, Colombia, a country known overwhelmingly for its poets and largely arid as far as good or great novels are concerned, produced, precisely one century later, the twentieth-century novel that would not only match *María*'s achievement but surpass it. Not only did García Márquez's *Cien años de soledad* become the best-selling novel in Latin America, the literary mirror in which Latin Americans finally recognized themselves and their predicaments; it also leaped effortlessly across the cultural barriers separating Latin America from the rest of the world and became both the screen on which the first world saw Latin America and, at one remove, the mirror in which other so-called third-world countries saw themselves. In short, it is a book that readers from outside the region have been able to equate with such apparently "timeless" texts-of-the-West as *Gargantua and Pantagruel, Don Quixote, Robinsoe Crusoe, Candide, Gulliver's Travels*, or *Alice in Wonderland*.

This, then, is a curious example of parallelism within a single country's literary history. *Cien años de soledad* (1967) seems to have nothing whatever in common with *María* (1867) except that it has chalked up similar achievements. (We could speculate about implied national and continental horizons and readerships and also about implicit conservative nostalgias. In terms of financial outcome, by contrast, Isaacs received not a peso for his novel and was beset by financial misfortunes until the day he died, whereas García Márquez became a multimillionaire.) But there are thousands of Latin American intertextualities that have barely been explored and have many surprises in store for us. How about a Chilean woman who, in the 1930s, wrote two short works of fiction largely ignored by the critics that nevertheless became essential antecedents of the two best Mexican novels of the second half of the twentieth century? María Luisa Bombal, who played the girlish innocent to literary giants as different as Borges and Neruda, and who later would gain a different notoriety by shooting her ex-lover with a revolver, was the author of two lyrical novellas, *La última niebla* [*House of Mist*] (1935) and *La amortajada* [*The Shrouded Woman*] (1938), which barely figure in the standard histories of Latin American narrative; yet clear thematic, structural, and stylistic traces of these works can be found in Juan Rulfo's *Pedro Páramo* (1955) and Carlos Fuentes' *La muerte de Artemio Cruz* (1962), the two books that between them put an end to the so-called novel of the Mexican Revolution—Rulfo's a work devoted mainly to the prerevolutionary period,

Fuentes' a work devoted to the postrevolutionary period, but both of them about apparently brutal and unfeeling men who ruin the lives of the women they obsessively desire and purportedly love.

Pedro Páramo is perhaps the twentieth century's most striking example of the *María* phenomenon. Among Latin Americanist literary critics, this is perhaps, more even than *Cien años de soledad*, the most admired text in the history of Latin American fiction. However hyperbolical it may seem, this Mexican novel is repeatedly deemed a "perfect" work. No doubt Rulfo's own taciturnity and his inability ever to write another novel contributed to the book's notorious air of mystery and enchantment. Be that as it may, Latin America's two Nobel Prize–winning novelists, Miguel Angel Asturias and Gabriel García Márquez, have both told me personally that it is the novel they would most like to have written. Yet, despite the fact that it is obviously, however surprisingly, a Mexican version of a European classic (*Wuthering Heights*—and what a genealogy that book, like *Jane Eyre*, is turning out to have launched into the world: Heathcliff strides again, and in the most unlikely places), this is another example of a novel that has been hailed all over Latin America (and, interestingly enough, by Spanish critics as well) but has simply been unable to penetrate other cultural markets.

The Construction of Latin America's Grand Narrative or Continental Allegory

> What happened with Gabriel García Márquez's *Cien años de soledad* was that the vast natural space of the New World was finally conquered by a human time, an imaginative time, which was equally vast. García Márquez succeeded in combining the astonishment of the first discoverers with the irony of the last: ourselves. . . . He made us aware of the continuing hunger for history which those immense spaces evoke in us.
>
> —CARLOS FUENTES

As we have seen, Latin American history and literature show an unusually persistent alternation between utopias and dystopias. The great myth of the United States, in contrast, based on endless frontiers and unceasing exploration, is an extension of the great master narrative of Western history as a whole: the uninterrupted road to freedom, and progress and infinite development through self-realization. Latin America's myth is, inevitably, an inversion of this narrative: romantic in origin (like Latin America's nations themselves), surrealist in focus (the origins of the New Novel lay in the 1920s), and rebellious in orientation (the 1960s saw the simultaneous rise of guerrilla movements and the Boom itself). It is in essence about the subaltern relation of the New World to the Old. It tells how Mother America, aboriginal, virgin, fertile, creative, and productive—Nature's muse—was violated by the Spaniard—the European outsider; cold, rationalistic, and covetous; motivated by lust and power, not love and understanding; by theories, not experience. It tells of miscegenations despised by those who had initiated them; of discovery and conquest endlessly reproduced and repeated; and of desperate struggles, usually fruitless, to resist, rebel, and liberate. And it shows how the people's dreams, utopias, and occasional triumphs become internalized through folk memory and through art that, sometimes at least, can make itself the written record of that memory and thus unite past, present, and future at the level of representation. Naturally there are many different stories in Latin American fiction, but this is the master narrative that, combining "Joyce" and "Faulkner," reached its climax and consummation with the Boom of the 1960s.

Everyone knows that Faulkner's work is founded on and structured by the American tragedy of miscegenation. It is not sufficiently remembered that James Joyce's *Ulysses* is not only a book about Ireland but also about the relation between Ireland and Europe. Its multiple legacy involved the use of myth, both local and universal (above all the relation between roads and homes, between the local and the foreign); experimentation with language (including the parody and pastiche of all literary and social discourses); the exhaustive exploration of "consciousness"; the quest for the "Other" (the People, Woman, the Jew, etc.); an obsessive synthesis of both art and professional expertise; and an ambition for totality. Joyce himself was from a colony within Europe, and Latin America proved an especially receptive reading ground for what I have called "Ulyssean novels," with their particular form of dialogism and their typical globalizing trajectory from small town to provincial capital to national capital to international metropolis.

If we are talking of mythological journeys, however, even *Ulysses* did not take Joyce's own conception to its farthest potential limits, that is, from prehistoric times to the cosmic future (though some might argue that *Finnegans Wake* is actually such an endeavor). And although Borges' stories, taken together, may be said to amount to an atemporal version of such a project (all times are the same time), there is only one Latin American novel that seriously attempts this undertaking, namely Miguel Angel Asturias's *Hombres de maíz* [*Men of Maize*] (Guatemala, 1949), an undervalued masterwork of the twentieth century, equivalent in its achievement to Kubrick's *2001: A Space Odyssey* (the two works exemplifying, incidentally, the two different takes on the master narrative of Western history typical of Latin America and the United States). Writing in 1967, the year of *Cien años de soledad,* at the height of the "Boom," the Chilean writer Ariel Dorfman declared: "Although its origins are lost in remote regions and its socio-cultural coordinates are still debated, the contemporary Latin American novel has a quite precise date of birth. It is the year 1949, when Alejo Carpentier's *El reino de este mundo* and Miguel Angel Asturias's *Hombres de maíz* appeared. Although the latter novel is the source and backbone of all that is being written in our continent today, it has suffered a strange fate, like so many other works which open an era and close the past."[33] Needless to say, the novel's strange fate was to be rejected by many influential critics and ignored by readers. Once upon a time the same could be said of *Ulysses.*

Hombres de maíz is a book that situates its author's own experience of life within the history of his country and his continent, implying a meditation on the meaning of both Guatemala and Latin America itself within world history and, further, on the meaning of humanity's emergence from "primitive" societies on the road to our contemporary world. Asturias conceives this as a transition from tribalism and collectivism to capitalism and individualism, from matriarchy to patriarchy, from oral freedom to written tyranny, from natural myth created by the "savage mind" to rationalist history imposed by self-serving enlightenment. In other words, he captures in a single novel the essence of the anticolonial struggles that marked the entire twentieth century in their effort to invert the signs of world history—the apparently inevitable "triumph of the West"—and, while focusing on Guatemala, he also places those hopeless struggles in the context, first, of Latin America (the conquest in the fifteenth and sixteenth centuries) and, second, of the development of "Western civilization" as a whole since the Greeks and Romans and its reiterated suppression of different "barbarisms."

Inevitably, in its most elementary terms, Asturias's work (which he began in the 1920s) had to resolve, many years before the Boom, one of the most enduring problems confronted by Latin American novelists: namely, how to do justice to the essential "hybridity" or "heterogeneity" of the continent's complex cultural identity. In the case of Guatemala this meant exploring not only the great Maya civilization that dominated Central America long before

---

[33] Ariel Dorfman, "*Hombres de maíz*: El mito como tiempo y lenguaje," in *Atenea* (Santiago, 1967).

the arrival of the Spaniards in the 1520s but also its heirs, the Indians who live scattered in highland maize-based communities all over the region to the present time—as well as the European cultural traditions of the Spanish invaders and their descendants, the "Ladinos" (*Mestizos*) who have governed Guatemala since the early nineteenth century.

Asturias's solution is one of astonishing complexity but also of remarkable lucidity. Without any sort of reductionism, he shows that the struggle of the "Indians" against the *Mestizos* in the twentieth century is an endlessly reenacted continuation of the war between the Spaniards and the Maya in the sixteenth century. These two conflictive phases are then superimposed on an even vaster canvas, itself dual, in which the experience of loss undergone by every human being in the rite of passage from birth to maturity is used to chart humankind's inherently violent and tragic dialectical transition from the "state of nature" to the West's contemporary technological civilization. In practice this involves a text something like a Maya bas-relief, in which each minute glyph is multiply connected both to the glyphs surrounding it and to the aesthetic and thematic structure of the whole. At the same time, the initial tightness of this design is gradually loosened as the dense weave of tribal culture—poetic, paradigmatic, connotative, a world in which economic and kinship relations are impossible to disentangle—gradually unravels into our relentlessly linear, prosaic, and positivistic twentieth-century experience of metonymies and displacements in which individualism, alienation, transience, and death form a persistent equation.

The novel is organized symbolically in three historical phases—tribal, feudal-colonial, and capitalist-neocolonial—in each of which a dialectically modified Indian protagonist is defeated, loses his intimate relationship both to the earth and to the feminine other, and turns to alcohol and despair. Each of these phases based on modes of production is aligned mythologically with the three-part Maya structure of the universe—underworld, earth, sky (past, present, future)—which is the trajectory of Quetzalcoatl, the plumed serpent who is the Meso-American culture hero. His inherently Freudian trajectory, an endlessly repeated eruption from prehistory, is itself based on the sun's daily journey around the sky and beneath the earth.

The result of this conception is that each contemporary character lives perpetually in a cosmic eternity, whether he or she knows it or not, though Asturias is also concerned to emphasize the insistent gestural spontaneity and violence that Fanon identified as key aspects of third-world experience and revolutionary writing. The reader may conclude that, in retrospect, it is astonishing that a novel written in 1949, with such a large focus on the historical past, should also have foreseen so many central themes of Latin

America's future. The most striking of these, undoubtedly, are the doomed recourse to guerrilla warfare, the shadow of ecological catastrophe, and the rise of feminism: all are encrypted in the novel's first pages. (The mind flashes to Subcomandante Marcos and the Zapatista Indians arriving in Mexico City in April 2001.) The failure of the first, the apparent inevitability of the second, and the relative success of the third, have made it difficult in recent decades to sustain this unifying myth that crystallized in the 1920s and climaxed in the 1960s.

I brought together Asturias, Rulfo, and García Márquez in an earlier section. Let me do so again, for they are closely related. All, rightly or wrongly, have been called "magical realists," all write "national allegories" (more important, all write continental allegories), all therefore bring about the interaction of resistant third-world myth and insistent first-world history.[34] All, finally, show a Latin America trapped in the grip of nostalgias for a world definitively past. If there is a difference between Asturias and Rulfo, on the one hand, and García Márquez, on the other, it is that the former have combined a Marxist perspective (use value/exchange value, matriarchal/patriarchal, manual/mental, country/city) and a Freudian perspective (unconscious/conscious, female/male, fantasy/law) that produced surrealism (including Buñuel) in the 1920s and that eventually made the New Left both necessary and vacillating; and both situate their novels against the Lévi-Straussian context of mythological thought (nature/culture, barbarism/civilization, oral/written). *Cien años de soledad*, by contrast, is a work without such theoretical underpinnings, on the very cusp of the passage between the obvious modernism of the Boom and the postmodernism of the so-called post-Boom that was to follow.

The works of Asturias, Rulfo, and García Márquez can all be called "transcultural" or "dialogical" novels; their books are all structured by the

---

[34] See especially Fredric Jameson, "Third World Literature in the Era of Multinational Capital," *Social Text* (Fall 1986): 65–88. Jameson's theory needs some adjustment in Latin America, where the successful allegories are, as I have tried to suggest, continental rather than national in character. Part of the explanation for the *Pedro Páramo* problem mentioned in this essay may be that it is obvious to Latin Americans that this notoriously allusive novel has a continental application but not to readers outside Latin America. Aijaz Ahmad has devoted an entire book (*In Theory* [London, 1992]) to demolishing Jameson's brief article and makes many incisive points that implicitly for the kind of national/continental perspective I am advocating here. But a panoramic approach to canon-making in Latin American narrative suggests that Jameson's fundamental point stands: "All third-world texts are necessarily, I want to argue, allegorical, and in a very specific way: they are to be read as what I will call *national allegories.*" We may perhaps wish to revise it as follows, however: "All third-world texts are necessarily . . . *national* (or, in the case of Latin America, *continental*) *allegories—if they wish to be canonized at home and abroad.*"

same Latin American myth of the Unredeemed Other and the same ensuing nostalgias. (Other similarly allegorical versions, though not "magical realist" ones, are Carpentier's *Los pasos perdidos* [*The Lost Steps*], 1953; Fuentes' *La muerte de Artemio Cruz* [*The Death of Artemio Cruz*], 1962; Cortázar's *Rayuela* [*Hopscotch*], 1963; and Vargas Llosa's *La casa verde* [*The Green House*], 1966.) Asturias gives the most complete version of this "postcolonial" myth, just before the wave of decolonization in other parts of the world in the 1950s; while García Márquez writes a revised version that cursorily posits and then dismisses all mythological and biblical antecedents and presents a parodic vision of neocolonial history that speaks directly to the new versions of postcolonialism emerging from other regions (Rushdie's India, for example).

Present and Future: The Disappearance of Latin America?

> Our revels now are ended. These our actors,
> As I foretold you, were all spirits and
> Are melted into air, into thin air . . .
> —SHAKESPEARE, *The Tempest*

In the thirty years since the Boom, the Latin American novel has been extensively studied by scholars across the globe with the result that it now occupies a privileged and indeed pivotal position between "Western literature" and "third-world" (or postcolonial) literature, which no one, anywhere, would any longer seek to question. What I have called the Latin American New Novel (1920s–1970s) was a sui generis version of European modernism that, alone among world literatures, rose fully to the challenge of its times (the 1960s, the second phase of the international avant-garde), simultaneously providing the culmination of the hitherto truncated modernist avant-garde and coinciding with the rise of postmodernism, a distinctively New World phenomenon in its origins with, accordingly, both a Latin American and a United States version in those heady days of the late 1950s and the 1960s.

The authors of the Latin American New Novel—Asturias, Borges (not a novelist but crucial to the phenomenon in Latin America), Carpentier, Mário de Andrade; Rulfo, José María Arguedas, Roa Bastos, Brazil's João Guimarães Rosa and Clarice Lispector; Fuentes, Cortázar, Vargas Llosa, and García Márquez—all achieved a *grande oeuvre* in the sense that European nineteenth-century writers or international modernists pursued such a personal monument and all, accordingly, have been duly consecrated and canonized, some—like Dickens or Hemingway, for instance—in their own lifetimes.

Where the writers of the New Novel/Boom undertook a sustained critique of Latin American history and historiography from what we might call a revisionary Enlightenment standpoint, writers since the 1970s have been more inclined to deconstruct that history and the various grand narratives associated not only with the views of historians but with the role and prestige of writers and of writing itself. Not a single author has emerged with the success or influence (not to mention the *grande oeuvre*) of Borges, Asturias, Carpentier, García Márquez, Vargas Llosa, Fuentes, or Cortázar.

The fact is that Latin American utopic visions, alive as never before from the late 1950s to the mid-1970s, were brutally destroyed as never before during the late 1970s and 1980s. By the time the 1992 celebrations arrived, the grand myth collectively developed by the Ulyssean New Novel—which, unlike its original Joycean version, had not been "all in the mind" but, on the contrary, based on real political objectives with both national and continental horizons—was no longer literarily sustainable. That vision—continental revolution through a materialist inversion of many of the signs of Western history and civilization—was annulled by the ruthless counterattack of imperialism and the rise of an ideologically idealist neoliberalism preaching progress, freedom, and individual human rights. Over the decade after the Boom the literary effervescence continued, but in a less triumphal mode and against a background of military coups, foreign intervention, and economic recession throughout the region.

As soon as the momentum of the Boom began to falter in the early 1970s, and particularly after the great political and literary parting of the ways marked by the Cuban Padilla Affair in 1971, radical fictive revisions of Latin American history began to take place, initiated at first by Boom writers (and even pre-Boom writers). Utopias that had been conceived as temporarily delayed were now deemed inherently illusory. Of course *El siglo de las luces* (*Explosion in a Cathedral*, Alejo Carpentier, Cuba, 1961), *La muerte de Artemio Cruz* (Carlos Fuentes, Mexico, 1962), *La casa verde* (1966), and *Cien años de soledad* (1967) had already provided ironic interpretations of Latin American history, but the first three sustain the traditional Enlightenment view that although history is difficult to know even for the active participant, it may be understood retrospectively by the intellectual or historian—even if this is usually shown to be more difficult in Latin America than elsewhere. *Cien años de soledad*, as noted, was already more ambiguous, more "postmodern," than its fellow Boom novels.

Significantly, it is women who have reworked the great myth or master narrative of Latin America outlined above (not surprisingly, since it demanded a feminization of traditional colonialist perspectives on Latin American history), albeit fragmentarily and through new modes of writing. Chilean Diamela Eltit's *Lumpérica* (1983)[*E. Luminata*] and *Por la Patria* (1984) [*For the Fatherland*] are camouflaged, willfully degraded versions of the myth, but the myth is still alive within them, even if seen through a mirror darkly. Significantly indeed, a North American "Latino"—in this case a "Chicana" or Mexican American—lesbian writer has contributed the only recent full-fledged, nonparodic version: Gloria Anzaldúa's *Borderlands/La Frontera: The New Mestiza* (1987), while reminiscent in its hybrid form of Sarmiento's *Facundo*, and written mainly in English but with a substantial Spanish admixture, contains almost every single mytheme integral to the structure of Asturias's *Hombres de maíz*. And another Chilean woman author, Isabel Allende, has become the best-selling writer in the history of Latin America, exceeding even the sales of García Márquez, though she has not achieved academic acclaim similar to his.

Among its many other achievements, the Boom—a synthesis of the local and the modernist, like "magical realism" as a whole—effectively ended the almost mandatory division of Latin American artistic works between an "autochthonous" or "Americanist" and a "cosmopolitan" strand. Latin America was now fully in the world, and the world was now fully in Latin America. Revolutionary advances in the field of communications technology have only enhanced what was already an achieved integration. Thus no such simple divisions can be established in relation to Latin American narrative since 1970. On the one hand, admittedly, the Boom has continued to dominate the landscape through the hegemony of its principal protagonists, continentalists all. On the other hand, the new writers who have appeared on the scene since the end of the 1960s, following the demise of Cuban-inspired internationalism and Latin Americanism, have in many cases fallen back, perhaps inevitably, on their national literary, cultural, and political traditions (a phenomenon, of course, that I have no space to explore); they have thereby opened up new avenues and created a narrative literature that, although now consciously less ambitious in perspective and more minor in key, remains as innovative and diverse as any other regional equivalent in the world.

Perhaps the old dualist analysis mentioned above survives in one important respect. Instead of the distinction between a Latin Americanist and an internationalist mode it may be possible to suggest a newly accented division between those who continue to write, in a more or less traditional way, about the "Other/s" (an alleged "arrogance" for which the Boom writers have been much criticized) and those who indulge in one of the many possible forms of what we could call "self-writing" (a line that stretches back through the French *nouveau roman* and other early postmodernist excesses to the more hermetic of the 1920s avant-garde experiments and the symbolists who preceded them). But even this distinction was inaugurated in the earliest moments of the New Novel, when Asturias wrote openly about himself as writer, explorer and anthropologist (the "new Quetzalcoatl") in his *Leyendas de Guatemala* (1930) [*Legends of Guatemala*], and Borges, stimulated by the example of his compatriot Macedonio Fernández, began to talk about an eccentric character called "Borges," henceforth the implicit protagonist of all his works. But such self-reflexive forms have proliferated irresistibly since the postmodernist 1960s, and even the traditional forms of social realism have transmuted into so-called *testimonio*, in which the old "subaltern" protagonists—Indians, gauchos, blacks, proletarians, homosexuals, women—now speak with their own voices, even if the questions are still invariably put to them by academics and other intellectuals. Although writers take up widely differing positions in relation to this twin problematic, awareness of it is central to almost all writing currently appearing in the subcontinent.

The historic utopian quest for identity appears to be over, at least as traditionally conceived. In the endless dialectic between the individual subject and society, the balance in Latin American narrative appears at last to have shifted, for the time being, to the individual. The "master narratives" condemned by Lyotard, the "modern epics" exalted by Moretti, the "national allegories" vindicated by Jameson seem for the time being to have lost their purchase in Latin America. Latin Americans no longer feel the need to explain and justify themselves that was still so pressing in the 1960s. After Castro and Allende, after the Boom and the Nobel Prizes, after Borges and *Cien años de soledad*, there was no need to assert an identity, partly because Latin America's identity was finally fully globalized, and partly, paradoxically, because the utopian continental identity celebrated by the Boom novels was largely expunged from the historical agenda. These days it is language and writing, the body and sexuality, the subject and ideology, consciousness and the media that seem to be the main objects of concern in Latin American fiction.

Yet Latin America's millennial struggle between power and subalternity, between individualism and collectivism, liberalism and socialism, the Self and the Other, continues—as complex, contradictory, and fascinating as ever. There is, I think, no other region of the world where these issues, in their different historical incarnations, have been played out in narrative writing in the complex way and to the extraordinary degree in which they have appeared in Latin American literature over the last five hundred years. Today, after the West's long—and still triumphant—march to progress through logocentrism and ethnocentrism, we are almost all torn between different worlds and different identities. But Latin Americans have always consciously lived between at least two, and usually many worlds; their literature was born through and in unprecedentedly contradictory realities, and in it history and myth disputed the ground of written narrative from the very moment that Columbus landed. Latin America was destined—some would say doomed—to have a magical realism because it has never—with the sole exception of the early Vargas Llosa—had a classical (bourgeois) realism. For all kinds of reasons such "realistic" impulses have always led to other, less novelistic forms, themselves nonetheless invariably fused with the fabulatory qualities of fiction itself: chronicles (in the colonial period); hybrid works of narrative history, sociology, and philosophy by privileged witnesses, like *Facundo: Civilización y barbarie* or *Os sertões* (nineteenth century); or *testimonios* like the now world-famous *Me llamo Rigoberta Menchú y así me nació la conciencia* [*I Rigoberta Menchú*](late twentieth century). In Spanish America at least, the nineteenth century was almost entirely bereft of interesting, well-crafted novels. In the twentieth century, the "New Latin American Novel," born in the internationally avant-gardist 1920s, resolved the post-colonial ideological, structural, and technical impasses of the previous century and, while completing the mythical exploration of collective identities on behalf of their authors—writers and intellectuals—and others—oligarchs and subalterns—made a significant contribution to the universal forms of the novel and its possibilities for transformation. For the moment collective identities are taking second place to a new form of self-exploration, and for that reason the continental is again giving ground to the national, and the national in its turn is giving way to a new individuality that reaches out to the universal in a new but not entirely unpredictable way.

Near the beginning of this essay, I said that the whole planet has become infected with the formal and thematic concerns (above all, the crisis of the relation between the individual subject and her/his collective identity) of Latin America's so-called magical realism. It is somehow fitting, then, in an age of postmodern irony, that as the whole world becomes increasingly "Latin American" in an age when all identities are being deconstructed, Latin America itself has, apparently, moved on from Boom-type narratives to forms of writing that are less obviously "Latin American." And yet, unmistakably, the novels and short stories of the so-called post-Boom retain the outline of their continental identity, perhaps an equally tenacious one, at the level of writing itself. The persistent obsession with dualities and otherness, with distance and disenchantment, associated with some apparently transhistorical "baroque" style, is still visible in a continuing obsession with virtuosity embodied in a self-reflexive, multilayered and metatextual style.

So the Boom has not been superseded; it has been assimilated, dialectically negated; it is the presupposition of everything that is now written in the continent, even though much current literature ignores, writes against, or even repudiates it. Ironically enough, the Latin American narrative of the 1960s was entirely conditioned by its prescient anticipation of postmodernity and globalization; now it seems paralyzed and to some degree diminished by a phenomenon that, among many other consequences, may bring about the formal subordination of Latin America to the United States and the loss of the pivotal cultural role between the West and the third world that I mentioned above.

In one sense, then, Latin American writers no longer consider themselves special, as the Boom writers did; they no longer conceive of themselves as leaders and teachers of the people. In another sense many of them appear to think that the individual, his or her body and his or her identity, is the only currently important question in the world. It is hard to believe that this phenomenon will survive the present historical conjuncture, just as it is hard to believe that Latin America will not make a substantial and distinctive contribution to whatever is coming next. And that, we can be certain, will require a renewed awareness of the fact that Latin Americans can only achieve proper recognition when, both culturally and politically, they take full advantage of the unique dialectic between nation and continent, individual and collectivity, that is Latin America's special contribution to our planet.

EILEEN JULIEN

The Extroverted African Novel

> The colonial territories are realms of possibility, and they
> have always been associated with the realistic novel.
> —EDWARD SAID

> The moving qualities of [these] texts . . . depend not
> only on their stories of transgressive mobility but on the
> movement of the texts themselves across the border of
> the Atlantic, that watery margin which at once sealed
> and held open the ambivalent relation between the . . .
> colonies and the . . . empire. . . . Novelistic discourse
> emerges not in fixed locations or static moments but
> within a constant movement *across* borders.
> —MICHELLE BURNHAM

> Modifications of fictions . . . look for their source . . .
> in the changing world that men create, the changing
> human relations and values that accompany changes in
> economic forms, in thought, in social structure and po-
> litical relationships. The investigation of the changing
> sense of what constitutes an ending to a novel, or of [a]
> sharpened awareness of contingency, would have to
> reach into the whole world in which the novel functions.
> —ROY PASCAL

To raise the question of the novel in Africa is to invite reflection on a range
of issues that are at once literary, economic, social, and political. In particular, what is the relationship of narrative to culture and society in contexts of
radically asymmetrical power and manifestly coercive processes of exchange
and globalization?

African novels are well read, in my view, if they are perceived as a "fulfill-
ment" rather than as an "effect."[1] I borrow these concepts from Fredric
Jameson's interpretation of narrative as a "socially symbolic act" via Hayden
White. In Jameson's reading, narrative is a privileged artistic and literary

---

[1] As is sometimes pointed out, we cannot speak of an "African" novel or "the" African novel
any more (and perhaps still less) than we can speak of *Don Quixote* or *The Red and the Black*
as a "European" novel. These are useful terms, but can be misleading. There is indeed a continent that those of us outside it call Africa and that is called Africa by people who live there.
But many have argued about the justification and meaningfulness of the designation "African"
for cultural practices and products from Senegal to Madagascar and from Sudan (let alone,

form because the very ideology of narrative is to endow events with meaning, in other words, to rewrite history. White expresses it this way:

> A seizing of a past by consciousness in such a way as to make of the present a fulfillment of the former's promise rather than merely an effect of some prior (mechanistic, expressive, or structural) cause . . . is precisely what is represented in a narrativization of a sequence of historical events so as to reveal everything early in it as a prefiguration of a project to be realized in some future. . . . It is human culture that provides human beings with this opportunity to choose a past, retrospectively and as a manner of negating whatever it was from which they had actually descended, and to act as if they were a self-fashioning community rather than epiphenomena of impersonal "forces." (149)

White's remarks are helpful for an understanding of novelistic processes in Africa, as long as one keeps in mind, first, that as inherently imaginative works, novels—including historical novels—are not historical accounts in the way historians understand them; and, second, that an imaginative account of historical or social reality is not necessarily the same thing as sleight of hand, which we might infer from White's comment ("negating whatever it was from which they had actually descended"). I know of no African novels that erase the history of colonialism and the repression of contemporary regimes. On the contrary.

But the significant point here is what might be called a Borghesian effect in such imaginative accounts: the past is written through the lens of a projected future, so as to open up possibilities for it. I extrapolate from this understanding of historical accounts to the novel in broad terms. If the African novel is construed as a site of fulfillment, it is linked to human agency and self-fashioning. If it is an effect, it is part of a necessary trajectory, merely a product of historical forces beyond writers' control. The advantages of the former perspective for reading African novels are significant, but literary

---

Algeria) to South Africa. My experience is that Senegalese sometimes refer to local practices and values (be they national or ethnic) as "African," Nigerians to their local practices (again, whether national or ethnic) as "African"—where in each instance their part stands for the whole—while some South Africans seem to refer to the "rest" of Africa as "African."

There are, at the same time, broad historical experiences of colonialism and its aftermath shared by most of the fifty-odd nations on the continent, and it is on that basis in particular that Africans assert a shared identity in making common cause for economic and political justice. In a discussion such as the one that follows, then, "African" is not a settled term.

and cultural history has lent its force to the latter. Readers can accede to the first perspective, I believe, only if we ourselves rewrite the history of the novel and rethink inherited wisdom on modernity.

In order to come to terms with the practice of novel writing in Africa, then, some space clearing is called for. I want, first, to consider the story of what is commonly called "the rise of the novel," as one episode in a multi-layered narrative of European modernity's sweep of the globe; second, to note the impact of this paradigm of the novel's origins on theorizing of the relationship of African novels to African oral traditions and more generally to indigenous materials; finally, to explore a defining feature of what we have come to call "the African novel."

Ornamentalism: The Local through the Presumed Prism of the Global

In his 1982 work on European imperialism, *La conquête de l'Amérique* (*The Conquest of America*), Tzvetan Todorov, using the Spanish and the Aztecs as his case study, writes that "Western Europe worked at assimilating 'the other,' at eliminating this exterior alterity, and in large measure succeeded. [Europe's] lifestyle and values have spread around the world; as Christopher Columbus wished, the colonized have adopted our customs and have clothed themselves" (251, my translation).

I find this formulation smug, but the view Todorov articulates is nonetheless a common one among Westerners and among many Africans as well: for better or worse, modernity is a Western phenomenon. While this thinking is challenged in practice and more and more in theory (Abu-Lughod; Larkin), it still prevails, finding expression daily in newspapers, on television, and in film. In the popular imagination as in powerful and consequential agencies such as the World Bank, *democracy, science, free speech, technology*, and *development* are modern institutions and forms, synonymous with the West. African, Asian, and Latin American nations have only to copy these models, or, as Aimé Césaire writes ironically in 1939 to "get in step with the world." This paradigm is, of course, nothing other than a form of Eurocentrism, the silent, commonplace assumption of European exceptionalism, attributed ultimately, some have argued, to its Judeo-Christian heritage (Amin). In this regard, R. Radhakrishnan has written perceptively that

> Western nationalisms are deemed capable of generating their own models of
> autonomy from within, whereas Eastern nationalisms have to assimilate
> something alien to their own cultures before they can become modern

nations. Thus in the Western context, the ideals of Frenchness, Germanness, or Englishness—national essences rooted in a sense of autochthony— become the basis of a modernity that re-roots and reconfirms a native sense of identity. On the other hand, Eastern nationalisms, and in particular "Third World" nationalisms, are forced to choose between "being them- selves" and "becoming modern nations" as though the universal standards of reason and progress were natural and intrinsic to the West. . . . This divide perpetuates the ideology of a dominant common world where the West leads naturally and the East follows in an eternal game of catch-up where its iden- tity is always in dissonance with itself. (86)

The "modern" is thought to spring naturally from the various Western soils but must be imported into the non-West where culture and identity, rather than validating the modern nation, are thought to threaten and desta- bilize it. From where the third-world politician or intellectual stands, en- lightenment would always seem to come from the outside.

This formulation certainly holds in the African context. If one reads the works of any number of African and Africanist writers, philosophers, or scholars, there seems to be consensus about the exogenous origins of moder- nity and the indigenous transformations and accommodations required to become modern, despite ongoing disagreement on the causes of this imbal- ance and the nature of the accommodations to be made.[2]

Europe, so the reasoning goes, may provide the form, but Asia and Africa especially will provide culture-based modalities. This compromise seems to

---

[2] Frantz Fanon, in his address to the First International Congress of Black Men of Culture in Paris in 1956, states, for example: "On one side there is a culture which is recognised as having qualities of dynamism, expansion, depth. A culture in movement, perpetually renewed. On the other side we find characteristics, curiosities, things, but never a structure" ("Racism and Culture," 125). Fanon's remarks may be read to mean that the dual vision of European dynamism, on the one hand, and African curiosities, on the other, is an effect, first, of the Eurocentric paradigm, governing the way one *sees*, and, second, of colonialism itself, which deprived subjugated peoples of conditions in which to be creative and inventive. Fanon condemns the ideological traces and material consequences of colonialism, of course, and predicts that with the end of colonialism and racism, new possibilities will emerge. On the other hand, Richard Wright, a pan-Africanist of stature and friend of liberation movements throughout the world, could both signal Western irrationality in the form of terror and hypocrisy and nonetheless subscribe to the Eurocentric view ("Tradition and Industrialization"). And Manthia Diawara, reading Wright in the 1990s, finds Wright's embrace of European progress and rejection of African traditions unobjectionable and, in fact, salutary. Curiously, Fanon and Wright concur about the backwardness of those traditions and the necessity therefore of shedding the traditional skin. Fanon, in particular, envisions an African future in which national and class identities rout ethnic or tribal allegiances. See Julien 2000. See also Lévi-Strauss's *Race and History* for a useful rejoinder to the idea of European exceptionalism.

offer the resolution to this conflict, and we find it in various guises in a range of literary forms over several generations of African writers—Léopold Sédar Senghor, writing his collection of poems, *Chants d'ombre (Shadow Songs)* in the 1930s and 1940s; Camara Laye, writing his memoir, *L'enfant noir (The Dark Child)*, published in 1953; Cheikh Hamidou Kane, writing his masterly novel, *L'aventure ambiguë (Ambiguous Adventure)*, published in 1961; and even Wole Soyinka, for example, in his 1975 play, *Death and the King's Horseman*: young African men go off to Europe; become immersed in modern knowledge and technologies, whether scientific or political; and are tested by the extent to which they retain their cultural moorings. In fact, the protagonist's failure to negotiate a hybrid identity in several novels—*L'aventure ambiguë*, Ferdinand Oyono's *Une vie de boy (Houseboy*, 1956), and Sudanese Tayeb el Salih's *Season of Migration to the North* (1969)—results in death.

In the nearly ubiquitous tension between "the modern" and "the traditional," the latter is often represented as feminine and metonymized as woman. The following argument made with respect to India is applicable to Africa as well:

> By mobilizing the inner/outer distinction against the "outerness" of the West, nationalist rhetoric makes "woman" the pure and ahistorical signifier of "interiority" . . . the mute but necessary allegorical ground for the transactions of nationalist history. . . . Questions of change and progress posed in Western attire were conceived as an outer and epiphenomenal aspect of Indian identity, whereas the inner and inviolable sanctum of Indian identity had to do with home, spirituality, and the figure of Woman as representative of the true self. (Radhakrishnan, 84)[3]

African intellectual production has been haunted by such tensions and symbols since its inception. Senghor's early poetry—"Femme noire" is exemplary—may be read in fact as precisely the representation of the cultural treasure that must be safeguarded in order to preserve African identity

---

[3] This gendered division of symbolic labor corresponds moreover to a split in social space, between the home and the world. Chatterjee writes: "The world is the external, the domain of the material; the home represents our inner spiritual self, our true identity. The world is a treacherous terrain of the pursuit of material interests, where practical considerations reign supreme. It is also typically the domain of the male. The home in its essence must remain unaffected by the profane activities of the material world and woman is its representation." Chatterjee does not scrutinize this gendered division of labor, and Susan Andrade takes on this task in her forthcoming *The Nation Writ Small: African Fictions and Feminisms.*

amidst the alien forms and institutions of modernity. Yet, as Ousmane Sembène ironically suggests in his 1975 film *Xala*, the would-be preservation of such cultural treasure (that is, "inner identity") is no guarantee of a usable democracy or just society. In Sembène's story of a nonproductive, indeed parasitic and spendthrift Senegalese bourgeoisie, the "businessman" El Hadj takes a young third wife, with the enormous expense such a lavish event and change in lifestyle entail, only to discover on his wedding night that he has been struck impotent. Early in the story, when El Hadj invites his business colleagues to the festivities celebrating his new marriage, one of them—grasping what for Sembène is the incongruity between modernity and polygamy—justifies this soon to be unhappy marriage and declares with great pomp, "We are modern, but we are African!" To which his fellow businessmen reply with thunderous applause, "Long live Africanity!" This is precisely the status of "Africanity" within the Eurocentric paradigm: an *ornamental* detail, and as the slogan of this class, a hypocritical and exploitative strategy, as well.

Similarly, in his novel *Sardines* (1981), the Somali writer Nuruddin Farah offers an ironic reflection on such politicocultural schizophrenia through his tropes of "guest" and "host":

> *In this century, the African is a guest whether in Africa or elsewhere.* A guest. The technology; the ideology; the living cells of power which throb with confidence; the intellectual make-up from which we derive our source of power; the contradictions which breathe life into us. If not a guest, then a slave to a system of thoughts, a system of a given economic re-routing. It was too early to forecast what would happen; but a week after her arrival, [their Italian visitor] had become the host and they the guest—maybe this sufficiently indicated the precarious position of the African in his own continent. [Medina's] years in Europe were just as perilous if not worse: she was always a guest, the other person whose presence gave colour and made the dinner more interesting ("We have a *guest*, a wonderful girl from Somalia"). (218)

The narrator of *Sardines* is suggesting that the African, seen through a Eurocentric lens, is extraneous to the production of knowledge, wealth, and power that have characterized the twentieth century. The guest is invited, at best, to tag along in a gesture of altruism but has no inherent right to be there—by virtue of "having invented nothing" (Césaire). Africa is a superfluous space, marginal to the dynamic life of the century. At the same time, the figure who will bring "colour" (zest, spice, exoticism) to the European soirée is an African woman, and Radhakrishnan's citation above regarding the native "true self" makes clear this is no coincidence. Standing in for "Africa" itself, she plays ornament to Europe's preponderant role as orchestrator and inventor of substance, form and meaning. Farah's fictional scenario recurs in a number of autobiographical and fictional accounts, including Tayeb Salih's *Season of Migration to the North*; South African James Matthews's "The Party" (*Quartet: New Voices from South Africa*, ed. R. Rive, 1965); and Senegalese Ken Bugul's *Le Baobab fou* (*The Abandoned Baobab*, 1984). In the West and even in Africa, the African is ornamental, invited at the whimsy and for the pleasure of the hegemonic host.

Thus Sembène mocks his character's implicit appeal to "tradition" and claims of authenticity and, in any case, exposes authenticity's irrelevance in a context of virulent national and international capitalism. Farah, too, flatly rejects the ornamentalist vocation as an unacceptable form of marginalization. The ornamentalist scenario—alien, imported modernity, touched up with local African color—is at best a revisionist proposal that seems to justify the deep skepticism pervading the philosophical texts of Valentin Mudimbe (see also Achille Mbembe). The place of the African as ornament (or "colorful" guest) set forth in all these narratives is emblematic of the presumed tension between whatever it means to be modern and whatever it means to be African. It is this tension in fact that gives rise to and is typically the central dilemma of what we call the African novel.

I have dwelled at length on the consequences of Eurocentric paradigms and what I call an ornamentalist philosophy in the domains of culture and politics, broadly speaking, because as we turn specifically to literature and aesthetics, the effects of these modes of thinking can be better apprehended and assessed.

The Rise of the Novel Revisited

One of the serious impediments to an adequate reading of African novels is, in my view, the standard account of the origins of the novel. It is a commonplace of American literary history to describe the novel as arising autochthonously in seventeenth- and eighteenth-century Britain and Europe. The sequel to the narrative of the novel's rise is—like the movement within European novels themselves—its subsequent traveling from the "center" to the "peripheries" of the newly emerging world system, where it picks up particularities (local color, content, perhaps even formal modifications) in adapting to its new surroundings. As we have seen, tradition holds that modern institutions and cultural forms, such as the novel, come from the outside and will be adopted as societies progress to the status of modern. These forms nonetheless may or indeed should—in order to remain authentic—be ornamented with local forms, including oral traditions, national languages, and folklore. This, at least, is the dominant interpretation of the adaptations that occur with such cultural flows.

Thus while Bakhtin defines the novel as an impulse to parody and can on that basis identify novels in ancient Greece and Rome, while Harold Scheub finds in certain Egyptian texts precursors to the contemporary African novel, most scholars and readers of European and African novels embrace the account in which the novel arises in Britain and Europe and spreads to Africa along with other fruits of European modernity thanks to the otherwise unsavory episode of colonialism. Indeed, it is this particular story of the novel's rise and spread that lent such visibility and import to Amos Tutuola's *Palm-Wine Drinkard* (1952) and Chinua Achebe's *Things Fall Apart* (1957). These works seemed to demonstrate that powerful and enchanting combination of European form and local content: in the first instance, a reworking of Yoruba tales and mythology and what was called "the young English" of a low-ranking worker with only a few years of formal education; in the second, an unquestionably crafted and eloquent English, inflected nonetheless by the rhythms and metaphor of Igbo speech and oral traditions. Seen in this light and apart from whatever else these novels accomplish, their aesthetic finesse would seem to confirm both the triumph of the European model (the propagation of the novel as a literary form) and indigenization of a modern form (its very happy marriage with local modalities). Standard literary historiography thus reserves autonomy and agency (fulfillment in the Jamesonian sense) for the center, and necessary imitation with local color (the Jamesonian effect) for the peripheries.

The rise of the novel is an enshrined story—one episode, I submit, in the larger narrative discussed above that could be called the rise of Western modernity. But the account of the novel's beginnings that holds sway in the U.S. academy may be a *local* story rather than a universally recognized fact of world literary history, according to Homer Brown, who suggests the account of the novel's birth is told differently in Britain, Australia, and France than it is in the United States.

More important, what insights might be gained by shifting emphasis from the *diachronic* account of a traveling European genre to a *synchronic* account of novelistic contexts? Michelle Burnham's reading of nineteenth-century American and British captivity narratives is extremely suggestive in this regard. Is it not the crossing of borders, to which she refers in the passage cited at the beginning of this essay, that gives rise to the modern novel?

Is it not the existence of empire—of colonies as a realm of possibility, in Said's words—that enable the European novel? If the European novel arose in a context of movement across borders—a motif fundamental to the genre itself—then it is not a parochially European genre on the basis of having been scripted first in Valladolid, Paris, or London but is indeed world historical.

This is not a claim, then, for symmetry of influence on the basis of features from the far reaches of the empire or its literatures showing up on the European literary canvas. Rather, it is a claim for a condition of possibility. The movement across borders, regardless of the historical circumstances governing it—religious or political persecution, enslavement, economic promise, adventure—would seem to be the condition that enables the proliferation of the *modern* novel. In which case, it could be argued that the novel is world historical *in its inception, not in its spread.* The modern novel is *creole*, a literary "forma franca" born from the contact of peoples and cultures. It may well be the first global cultural product. I find the work of Burnham and Said intellectually stimulating and convincing, but whether one accepts their arguments or not, what is certain is that the Eurocentric account of the rise of the novel has led to stale thinking and critical dead ends where the African novel is concerned.

Carrying the Weight of the African Experience

What has this long-standing normativity of the European novel meant for an understanding of novels of the periphery, and Africa in particular?

First, this aesthetic Eurocentrism, parallel to a political Eurocentrism, has meant, as I argued above, the gendering of "local culture" as feminine and of "global form" as masculine—with all the impacts such discursive paradigms have on real women's and men's lives. South African novelist Bessie Head suggests such effects when she writes of a fictive Tswana rural community, for example: "The women were the backbone of agriculture while the men on the whole were cattle drovers. But when it came to programs for improved techniques in agriculture, soil conservation, the use of pesticides and fertilizers, and the production of cash crops, the lecture rooms were open to men only. . . . Why start talking about development and food production without taking into account who is really producing the food?" (31). Here, food production, viewed as an economic activity related to world markets and exchange, is mistakenly construed as "men's work."

Second, within the domain of literature itself, aesthetic Eurocentrism has meant a limited purview and derisory role for criticism. The novel has an especially vexed history in Africa, because it has been viewed as *the* literary form of modernity. And modernity, as many have shown, is held by definition to be that which occurred *elsewhere*. Modernity and its literary sign, the novel, must therefore be imported and reproduced (Chakrabarty). The European novel, moreover, has had a unique and dubious role as the very form through which Africa has been presented as the primitive "other" of modernity. From this point of view, the novel as a modern, urbane expressive form could be seen as especially incompatible with what might be seen in the best light as African pastoral or communal modes of living (Roscoe, 75–76), and yet, as Lynch and Warner put it, "the new nations emerging out of empires [were] required to produce novels in order to certify their distinct and modern nationhood" (5).

Thus the novel is *the* global form because it exists everywhere and is supposedly for everyone. Yet at the same time, since its proliferation on the peripheries is read typically as homage to the grandeur and potency of the novel's supposed culture(s) of origin, it paradoxically affirms European exceptionalism, thereby reinscribing the power of the center. So regardless of its extraordinary vigor in the former colonies, the novel retains its association with *European* modernity. And paradox upon paradox, there arises simultaneously an aesthetic interest in and demand for those features of local indigenous artistic traditions that would give specificity and authenticity to the "African novel." The African novel has therefore been asked to satisfy contradictory demands: to be "universal" but to display its "difference." The perceived or assumed European nature of the novel is surely responsible for one question that has dominated critical studies of the novel in Africa: "What makes the novel *African*?"

The answer set forth most often is the inclusion of traces of oral genres or African languages, felt to be distinctly or especially African. This is a problematic definition and critical practice, however, because the categories of orality and writing that have governed criticism of African literature are primarily ideological constructs. "Orality" is a nebulous, homogenizing concept that has little to do with the concrete reality of distinct oral traditions in specific contexts. Rather, it usually has been defined *essentially* and as *the opposite* of writing and the novel. Subject to the worst types of ideological pressures, orality has sometimes been viewed as a novel's weakness or its strength, as a measure of primitiveness or wholesomeness, and all the while it has come to stand for the "authentic" (Julien 1992).

Under this regime, criticism's role has often been to identify a Eurolanguage text's authenticating traces of orality or local languages. In such instances we are tempted to consider our work done when we have named and cataloged elements and made superficial comparisons without examining the transformations and uses of oral genres and forms in specific, historical contexts.

Finally, aesthetic Eurocentrism has worked toward the marginalization of oral traditions and African-language literatures. For a corollary assumption and effect of the scenario in which oral traditions supplement alien forms is that oral traditions are themselves mere precursors to modern literature, which would be written in one of the European languages. As the sign of alterity, the distinctive, ornamental "something other," oral traditions and indigenous languages exist as a reservoir of resources to be exploited by the modern writer and are superseded by the truly modern Euro-language literatures: they have no modern future of their own. Of course, the requiem for African language oral traditions and literatures is grossly premature, but this particular perspective lies at the heart of postcolonial theory, whose basic premise is that throughout the colonial world, the native writer's language is suppressed and therefore degraded by the colonial language. That conflict gags the writer—meaning, the Euro-language writer, the only writer visible to postcolonial theory—who will in time appropriate and subvert the colonial language, by infusing it with local registers so that it now speaks for the colonized. For postcolonial theory, it is this marginality, "an unprecedented source of creative energy," that is the common denominator of postcolonial writers everywhere (Ashcroft 12).

Thus while African-language literatures—in Hausa, Swahili, or Yoruba, for example—have gone ignored by most of us outside the continent, the debate on the place of African-language *resources* in Euro-language writing has raged for decades. In his well-known essay, "The African Writer and the English Language" (1964), Chinua Achebe argued that the price English would have to pay for being a "world" language, in the context of Africa, was to "carry the weight of African experience." Achebe felt that English would be up to the task, but that it would have to be "a new English, still in full communion with its ancestral home but altered to suit its new African surroundings" (103). What this has meant most often, as I have indicated, is the incorporation of proverbs, tales, colloquial speech, and a range of creole languages in Euro-language texts.

In 1986, Ngũgĩ wa Thiongo of Kenya would condemn these miscegenous linguistic exercises in his provocative book, *Decolonising the Mind*, on the grounds that, first and perhaps most important, they ignore African publics; second, that there is incompatibility between the language of oppression and the subjectivity of the oppressed; and, third, that these experiments rob

African languages themselves of the opportunity for growth. At one point, in a brilliant parodic reference to Senghor's poem "New York," Ngũgĩ ridicules the "lengths to which we were prepared to go in our mission of enriching foreign languages by injecting Senghorian 'black blood' into their [Western] rusty joints" (7). More recently, Boubacar Boris Diop expresses a similar skepticism about African language–inflected French in novels such as Ahmadou Kourouma's chronicle of a fallen Malinke prince, *Les soleils des independances* (1970). Diop states: "Aesthetically, it's very interesting, but politically it's very dangerous. You have to ask, Which language is dying, and which language is growing? That's the problem. It seems to me that African languages are dying into French, enriching it. . . . I'm suspicious of it. And I think the French love it. It saves the French language from grayness and monotony" (quoted in Sugnet, 158). Here again is a critical response to the perceived ornamentalist function of Africa via one of its signs, African languages.

Thus while Achebe points out the obvious and warns would-be keepers of the Queen's English that—in the terminology of Ashcroft et al.—"English" is a fact of postimperial life, Ngũgĩ and Diop signal their concern with the political consequences of ornamenting Euro-language texts with local languages. So we may ask, Can the sociolinguistic reality of diglossia escape the fate of commodified ornamentalism? Let me be clear that I am not writing against forms of heteroglossia in novels but against the ornamentalist interpretation of them. A text engaging the multiple, often hybrid registers of contemporary urban societies will be perceived by many readers as closer to African realities, while the standard metropolitan French or English that we infer Diop sees as the lesser of two evils—Sol Plaatje's *Mhudi* (1930) is a case in point—may be dismissed. On the other hand, as Stephanie Newell points out, South Africans writing for *Drum* magazine in the 1950s "selected English as their medium as a gesture of defiance against the language and educational policies of the Afrikaner state" (2). Certainly these are complex issues, best understood by reference to specific contexts, since meaning is context-specific, and every choice comes with costs.

Nor is it true that African languages everywhere are dying. This is certainly not the case of Igbo, Yoruba, Swahili, Hausa, or Poulaar. In current contexts, Euro-language novels may be a symptom of social stratification and unequal power relations, but it is demographics and national *language policy*, far more than hybrid linguistic registers in (or the existence of) Euro-language novels, that determine the fate of African languages and possibilities for African-language literatures.

To sum up, then, the theoretical or critical stance that sees oral traditions or African languages as "ornament" is an aesthetic equivalent of a political or cultural view that modernity and the democratic nation state are fundamentally Western and must be imported into Africa, Asia, and Latin America, where they can, at best, be "ornamented" by indigenous culture. In the political realm, Africanity will live on locally as "supplement" within alien institutions but can never be a point of reference for modern forms ("democracy," "the nation"). In the realm of culture, local products will be made modern or postmodern to the extent that they are transformed by artists (European or African) via so-called European forms—one thinks of magical realism or Afro-pop, or what has been termed the second birth of *primitive art*, its metamorphosis in the Western gallery or marketplace.[4] In African literary criticism then, drama, proverbs, written poetry, and tales are seen as more authentic because they have antecedents in African cultures historically. Novels, on the other hand, which readers associate with the crises and stresses of contemporary life, will be seen as "modern," an alien form that African writing, as it "emerges" and "matures," will and must imitate, with the proper garnish of proverbs, tales, and so forth. While many may agree about the authenticity of "traditional" forms and the "modernity" of the novel, this model tends toward a view of culture as pristine, static, and cloistered.

The relationship between "local" realities, both political and cultural, and traveling "global" forms is, of course, real and can be usefully examined. But how can this relationship be represented in a productive way? One approach to Euro-language novels that I have set forth elsewhere is to view the presence of oral genres in the novel not as the *necessary trace* of a writer's origins that is the proof of a genuine Africanness, but as an *appropriation* and *strategy* through which the writer attempts to resolve aesthetic and social questions. The revisions of the epic, for example, in Ousmane

---

[4] Howard Morphy writes of two international exhibits of Aboriginal art during the 1980s: "An integrated world economy will always produce a market that transcends the local systems and which draws products from them." But the art market, he explains, thrives on an immense contradiction between the creation of value in Western art practice and that in Aboriginal practice: With respect to European art, previous forms retain their value, while contemporary artists who work over old themes or reproduce characteristics of earlier styles are considered dated and valued negatively. In regard to Oriental, African, and folk arts, classified by ethnicity, however, their value is established "at their point of production by the West, when they were recognised [and] metamorphosed." Their value for Western art lies in their "lack of contamination by the European tradition." They remain "pristine, primeval and, as such, liberating" (213–18). Thus the value of this art requires the absence of the artist's signature, the repetition of "traditional" styles, and ultimately, stasis. Manthia Diawara illustrates and reflects on these very ironies in his story of his childhood friend, Sidimé Laye, who becomes a carver (see esp. 186–200).

Sembène's *Bouts de bois de Dieu* (*God's Bits of Wood*, 1960) and Amadou Hampâté Bâ's *L'étrange destin de Wangrin* (*The Fortunes of Wangrin*, 1973), both set in the colonial period, present in the first instance a reworking of the categories of hero and heroic action that challenges the hierarchical norms implicit in the epic and suggests the possibility, as Jameson describes it, of reinventing an order; and in the second, the mythification of an ordinary man in an emperor's tale, thus revealing a nostalgia for an old-style heroism, made impossible under colonialism.

Or, in the cases of Sony Labou Tansi's *La vie et demie* (*A Life and a Half*, 1979) and Ngugi wa Thiongo's *Devil on the Cross* (1980), both set in the postindependence period of totalitarian excess and violence, there is a deployment of popular language and the fable in which the representatives of power are portrayed through a caricature of physical appetites and bodily deformations that serves to expose them and mock the authority they represent.

In an excellent study of such transformations in Nigerian writing, Ato Quayson signals, for example, Tutuola's innovative use of traditionally *didactic* Yoruba oral storytelling motifs in his *The Palm-Wine Drinkard* to develop instead the stature of the Drinkard as hero. As the narrative progresses, then, "heroism is subsumed under compassion and community, showing that heroism centred on the individual ego is not adequate to the dictates of social existence" (54).

What is crucial in any study of Euro-language novels involving, as they do, issues of language use and literacy, social stratification, representations of the past and a context of dynamic urban cultures is to locate these texts in the vast field of cultural production and to be mindful that the African past was not exclusively "oral"; that oral traditions do not refer exclusively to "traditional" matters but are part and parcel of current social and political life; and that modern literature is not written exclusively in European languages. Artistic practices are poorly served by binary categories.

The Extroverted African Novel

Simon Gikandi has asked the provocative question, Why did Chinua Achebe's *Things Fall Apart* acquire such visibility in 1957 and herald, as it were, the birth of the African novel, when other novels by Africans—Felix Couchoro's *L'esclave* (*The Slave*, 1929), Sol Plaatje's *Mhudi* (1930), Thomas Mofolo's *Chaka* (translated from the Sesotho and published in 1931), Ousmane Socé's *Karim* (1935), and Peter Abraham's *Mine Boy* (1946)—preceded it? I have offered one answer to that question: a strong appeal of Achebe's novel is its proverbial, Igbo-inflected language that may satisfy certain readers' expectations by ornamenting what is supposedly a European form— working to suggest indigenization of the form and, paradoxically through a certain lens, to reinforce European centrality.

Gikandi offers another explanation. He has argued that Achebe was the first African writer to grasp and to exploit fully both the archeological and utopic possibilities offered by the novel as a literary form. The success of Achebe's and other such novels is surely related to the climate of the 1950s and 1960s, the historical context of decolonization that created a massive readership for these novels, because Plaatje's *Mhudi* does the same work thirty years earlier at a less auspicious moment. In any event, unearthing forgotten or willfully obscured historical truths and defining the ideals of social justice and community are dual agendas that suggest in fact the Jamesonian concept of fulfillment, to which I alluded above. Indeed, most Euro-language African writers have used the novel as a site to reconstruct the past and to project, sometimes by implication, potential or imagined futures, even in the most scandalous dystopias—Ayi Kwei Armah's *Beautyful Ones Are Not Yet Born* (1969), Buchi Emecheta's *Joys of Motherhood* (1979), Ngugi wa Thiongo's *Matigari* (1990), Sony Labou Tansi's *La vie et demie* (1979), and Bessie Head's *A Question of Power* (1973). To the extent this is true, novelists would seem to substantiate Jameson's sense of narrative as a fulfillment rather than an effect.

Here I should like to offer a working hypothesis on yet another particularity of the novel, one based neither on narrative mood, mode, nor authorial intention but on practices of production and reception governing African novels that may enable the possibilities Gikandi outlines as fundamental to the novels of Achebe and others. What African readers and readers beyond Africa think of typically as the African novel is, I submit, a particular type of narrative characterized above all by its intertextuality with hegemonic or global discourses and its appeal across borders.

Long prose narratives by African nationals abound, but only certain texts among them are recognized and admitted to the ranks of "the African novel." The bulk of these long prose narratives will be perceived as lesser novels and may be designated "thrillers," "romances," and "detective stories." That division, I submit, between the works deemed to be "novels," on the one hand, and the others deemed to be second-rank narratives, on the other, has been primarily a matter of which narratives have traveled or of what can be called their *extroversion*, "the condition of being turned outwards" (*OED*, 5:621), as correlated with a number of factors: publishing house, place of publication, and explicit engagement with—or a capacity to be read as engaging—broad critical debates. What follows is not a quantitative study but a speculation based primarily on my qualitative experience of West African literature, especially that of Senegal and the French-speaking zone more generally. This spatial paradigm (extroversion) helps focus attention on a number of conditions that may be lost when texts are seen in terms of recent history ("postcolonial"), class ("elite"), or hegemony ("Western" readerships).

I have found certain broad perspectives from political science and anthropology helpful in arriving at an understanding of the range of work literary texts may perform and the particular niches they may occupy. The first is from Immanuel Wallerstein, who describes the nation-state as being governed by two needs that force it into contradictory practices: first, the need to distinguish itself in the community of nations by projecting outward and stressing its *difference* from other nations and, second, the need to suppress internal differences of ethnicity, faith, and gender within its boundaries so as to form a reliable, *homogeneous* national citizenry.

The second perspective represents a consensus in new anthropological studies on cultural flows: specifically, consumer products and cultural practices are reconfigured creatively and take on new meanings when they are incorporated in new cultural and semiotic contexts. Writing of beauty pageants in Belize, Richard Wilk argues that "connections between localities are created by widespread and common forms of contest for the exercise of power over *what* to produce, consume, watch, read and write. These contests follow channels that put diversity in a common frame, and scale it along a limited number of dimensions, celebrating some kinds of difference and submerging others" (111). "Global" practices and institutions become the means of expressing local identities and values on a world stage; they are "structures for the expression of our common differences" (115).

The final perspective is from Arjun Appadurai, who looks at the production of culture in the current world system from the point of view of local actors rather than from the angle of the state as does Wallerstein. In his well-known study, *Modernity at Large*, Appadurai fleshes out the internal dynamics that nation-states wish to control, if not suppress. He thus focuses on the importance of *locality*, a "property of social life," in that it provides the contexts for human activities and through those activities (within evolving social, political, and environmental circumstances) is generative of new contexts. While the creation of locality is a struggle always, it is particularly so at present because of pressures brought by nation-states, massive movements of people (often refugees, or those fleeing to find greater opportunities), and the impacts of varied electronic media. "Local knowledge," Appadurai writes, "is not only local in itself but, even more important, *for* itself" (181).

What Wallerstein's, Wilk's, and Appadurai's perspectives suggest for an understanding of the novel is the simultaneous existence of multiple arenas and media of discursive self-representation—each, of course, with its different publics, although these publics clearly are not static: Many readers, both national and international, can play either part, which is to say, they are readers of "novels" and readers of "local" or "popular" novels. Therefore, although global and local worlds are interpenetrated, it would seem that the privileged and prestigious form beyond the nation's border and (possibly precisely for that reason) among a nation's intellectuals and elites may not be the leading literary form(s), in European or African languages, addressing "local" needs within the nation.

The division of literary labor I am inferring from Wallerstein's and Appadurai's arguments is confirmed by researchers on the continent. "Popular" fictions—thrillers, romances, detective stories—Stephanie Newell argues, seem to have as their explicit agenda helping ordinary people negotiate the stresses and challenges of daily living, rapid social change, and political upheaval. These forms, unlike mass-produced forms in the United States and Europe, Newell writes, are often produced locally for particular niches, and they rarely participate in the transnational exchange that characterizes what is typically called the novel. What the literary and academic establishments both within and beyond African nations dub "the African novel" is the canonical, *extroverted* novel that speaks above all in the second arena, to a nation's "others" and elites in terms (which is to say, about issues and in a language and style) they have come to expect.

For example, the connections between such novels and decolonizing nationalism in Africa are well known. Chinua Achebe, it will be recalled, writes *Things Fall Apart* precisely as a response to the kind of ideological studies represented by the ethnographic treatise, *The Pacification of the Tribes of the Lower Niger*, that the narrator cites at the end of the novel. Thus, early Euro-language novels—I'm thinking of Cheikh Hamidou Kane's *L'aventure ambiguë* (*Ambiguous Adventure*, 1961); Ferdinand Oyono's *Une vie de boy* (*Houseboy*, 1956) and *Le vieux negre et la médaille* (*The Old Man and the Medal*, 1956); Ngugi wa Thiongo's early trilogy, *Weep, Not Child* (1964), *The River Between* (1965), and *A Grain of Wheat* (1967); and José Luandino Vieira's *A vida verdeadeira de Domingos Xavier*) (*The Real Life of Domingos Xavier*, 1974)—served as the primary vehicle for African self-invention, in response to Eurocentric historical and anthropological accounts that bolstered colonial ideologies and regimes. For African readers and readers abroad, such novels legitimized newly independent nations on the rise across the continent.

Since the heady dawns of independence, novelists such as Ahmadou Kourouma of Côte d'Ivoire, Mongo Béti and Calixthe Beyala of Cameroon, Buchi Emecheta of Nigeria, Nuruddin Farah of Somalia, Henri Lopès of the Congo, Mariama Bâ of Senegal, Tsitsi Dangarembga and Dambudzo Marechera of Zimbabwe, Zoë Wicomb of South Africa, Achebe and Ngugi themselves, and countless others, have denounced the failure of communal ideals, specifically the tyranny of African patriarchies, oligarchies, and dictatorships, and the domination of foreign powers and international economic interests that have brought the hopes of independence to naught. In a context of international scholarly and policy focus on African states, of worldwide "Afro-pessimism," these fictions find ready audiences. Written by novelists who often enough are living beyond their countries' borders, they all speak outward and represent locality to nonlocal others, be they expatriate communities abroad, other African nationals on the continent, Japanese, Europeans, Brazilians, or U.S. students.

The extroverted novel is a phenomenon of what Mary Louise Pratt calls the "contact zone," a social and, I would add, discursive space "where disparate cultures meet, clash, and grapple with each other, often in highly asymmetrical relations of domination and subordination" (4). Without ignoring such relations of power, it is important to acknowledge the interactive, improvisational dimension of this space. Here novels, like colonial and colonized subjects, "are constituted in and by their relations to each other." They are characterized by "copresence, interaction, interlocking understandings and practices" (7). I wish to foreground this interactive, dialogic dimension of African novels.

The protagonists of extroverted novels are often in a liminal state. According to Victor Turner, the liminal phase of a ritual is the middle phase between separation from a settled state or cultural condition and reentry or reincorporation into the social network, with new status. Wangarĩ Wa-Nyatetũ-Waigwa uses the concept in its strict sense in her study of the autobiographical works of Camara Laye, Cheikh Hamidou Kane, and Mongo Béti. Here, I use the term more broadly, to suggest life within the contact zone. The protagonists of the extroverted novel "elude or slip through the network of classifications that normally locate states and positions in cultural space. Liminal entities are neither here nor there; they are betwixt and between the positions assigned and arrayed by law, custom, convention, and ceremonial" (Turner, 95).

In African novels the liminal space typically is fraught with psychological conflict as in Kane's *L'aventure ambiguë*, Tayeb el Salih's *Season of Migration to the North*, or Tsitsi Dangarembga's *Nervous Conditions* (1988), even as the very existence of the novels, I would argue, challenges the alienation they thematize. Less frequently, it is associated with possibility, resourcefulness, and creativity, as in Amadou Hampâté Bâ's *L'étrange destin de Wangrin* or Bessie Head's *Maru* (1971). But the space of encounter in the extroverted novel is a shifting space. The "contact zone" is not necessarily that between the imperial center and Africa—witness the novels of Bessie Head. It is increasingly a space between African ethnicities or states, between the African diaspora and the continent.

In this theorization, then, the attribute of "extroversion" is not a qualification of praise but a descriptive term. What is at work in the African novel—or more precisely, in the extroverted African novel—in my view, is not a simple matter of a novelist's intention to "write for" a hegemonic or international audience but of multiple features that traverse or inhabit a text. Following Barthes, I am arguing that what passes for the African novel is created by publishing, pedagogical, and critical practices. The novel is, like literature in general, that which is taught in African schools, but it is above all the literary narrative read, taught, and debated beyond Africa—in Europe, North America, South America, and Asia. Moreover, these practices are correlated to a text's engagement with Western or global discourses, both imaginative and scholarly.[5] It is this engagement with discourses of the Enlightenment, or on "modernity," I would argue, that has established the basis for determining what is important to read in novels—indeed, which African novels can be granted the privilege of that "curiously esteemed title" (in Homer Brown's words), rather than one of its lesser designations.

I submit, then, that "the African novel" is recognized as such precisely because it is characterized by extroversion and engagement with what is assumed to be European or global discourses: surrealism, primitivism, magical realism, cultural studies, the motifs of postcolonial theory (hybridity, exile, marginalization, dislocation), or areas of inquiry and theory integral to the social sciences, such as Marxism, feminism, democratization and governance, politics of the state, and globalization. All of this may explain the enormous appeal and prominence of African novels for social science classrooms, in the United States at least. I am not suggesting necessarily an *embrace* in such

---

[5] There are parallels between the claims I am making here and those made by Paulin Hountondji and Thandika Mkandawire with regard to African social scientific and scientific research. Franco Moretti's account and maps of the geography of colonial romances are also suggestive, since the novel typically arises in or is set in colonial port cities (59–64).

fictions of what is foreign or novel (Enlightenment ideals or what is termed "modernity"). Rather, since the 1950s and 1960s, as we have seen, the extroverted novel for the most part has foregrounded, in the terms of Ashcroft et al., "the tension with the imperial power and . . . [emphasized its] differences from the assumptions of the imperial centre" (2).

The extroverted African novel—or, as it is commonly called "the African novel"—can only be properly understood, then, as *one form among many*. It constitutes but one chapter of African narrative over the last century and, as I have argued above, is not by any objective measure the only novel produced in Africa. Nor are these other novels ("local" fictions) written *outside* global forms and discourses. Euro-language and African-language popular novels are written against the same backdrops but are different in production and tenor.

While postcolonial theory insists on the marginality of postcolonial writers and their works vis-à-vis the centers of the world system, in this theorization the extroverted African novel is also understood to be marginal—but not vis-à-vis a putative metropolitan center. Rather, it is often in the margins of (although in dialogue with) a vast local, popular cultural production. Stephanie Newell argues that three factors distinguish popular fictions and are crucial to success: cost, relevance, and marketing. Books must be affordable; a book's lesson or usefulness is often as important as its entertainment value; and the booksellers or authors must demonstrate skill and cost-effectiveness in printing, distributing, and advertising. The titles of popular works, for example, systematically put their content and lessons in plain view: *Mabel the Sweet Honey That Poured Away*, *No Condition Is Permanent*, *Dar es Salaam Usiku* (*Dar es Salaam by Night*), and *Son of Woman*.[6]

Yet the range of works and the distinctiveness of their contexts should not be underestimated. For example, Sonja Diallo, cofounder of ARED, the Pulaar-language publishing house in Dakar, Senegal, writes that the new

---

[6] It is worth noting in this regard Roger Chartier's findings in a study of "popular" works in seventeenth- and eighteenth-century France. Chartier demonstrates that elite and popular literatures were differentiated not on the basis of specific themes and values but on the basis of differing reading capacities and practices fostered by printers themselves. Printers sought to create a new market by shortening existing publications, simplifying their language, highlighting chapter themes, and making these revised texts available at lower prices. Reader-friendly length, simplicity of language, accessible themes, and cheap prices also characterize popular novels in Africa (Newell). Relying on Richard Priebe's interview of Ghanain writer Asare Konadu in the early 1970s, Leif Lorentzon also argues that Konadu produced two classes of novels, one published locally for local consumption, which the author seems to have considered "good literature books"; the other, published in the Heinemann African Writers Series for school and international readerships, dubbed by him as "books for criticism."

creative literature in Pulaar (which in many respects qualifies as "popular" by Newell's criteria) shows "an overwhelming preoccupation with 'Fulɓeness' [Fulɓe ethnic practices and ideals] and very little interest in Europe, European (or Arabic) language writing and themes, or in the impact of European language literacy on Africa." (68). The vast community of Fulɓe (also known as Peul or Fulani), who were traditionally seminomadic herders across the Sahel, still live across a swath of states from the shores of the Atlantic in Senegal through central Cameroon and are a minority community everywhere (McLaughlin). Diallo, who is a strong advocate for African-language literacy and schooling, describes the response of Haalpulaar (Pulaar-speaking) students to a translation ARED commissioned and published of the classic French-language novel by their Haalpulaar compatriot Cheikh Hamidou Kane. In Kane's philosophical, semiautobiographical novel, *L'aventure ambiguë*, the hero Samba Diallo is on the deadly cusp of two worlds, "Africa" and "the West," which Kane presents as essential opposites and to which he adds yet another layer of opposition: the spiritual transcendence of ascetic Islam versus a numbing preoccupation with material well-being. Numerous university students, according to Diallo, claimed that after reading the Pulaar translation they finally understood the book, which they had failed to understand when they read it in French, while some students were insufficiently literate in their mother tongue to read it all. More important for this discussion of the novel, readers who had "never experienced an education in French" admitted they did not understand the book and rarely bought it (70). I take this to mean that Kane's explicit engagement with European discourses of modernity ("humanism," Marxism, existentialism) and Samba Diallo's estrangement from his culture of origins and his sense of marginality vis-à-vis Europe do not resonate with the life experiences of these readers.

At the same time, new Pulaar prose narratives such as Yero Dooro Jallo's picaresque novel, *Ndikkiri Joom Moolo* (*Ndikkiri, the First-born, Owner of a Guitar*, 1993), or Mammadu Sek's *Bii Tato* (*The Child of Three Men*, 1992), focusing on the plight of a young woman in an arranged marriage and under the domination of her father, her lover, and her migrant worker husband employed abroad, are box-office hits. These popular works address modern issues of gender relations and transnational flows of labor, yet they speak to a local community, focus on individual choice or lack of it, and assert ethnic identity in the face of "local" and "global" pressures—perhaps not only thematically but in the very act of writing and reading.

Karin Barber describes a different "local" tradition of popular fiction among the Yoruba of western Nigeria. She writes that Ọladẹjọ Okediji's novel, *Atótó Arére* (*Attention, Please!*, 1981) is a powerful exploration of contemporary crisis as experienced by an urban lower class. Drawing on sources such as James Hadley Chase and exploiting what could be called modernist techniques—cinematic cuts, stream of consciousness, a feverish, dreamlike imagination—Okediji presents "the alienation, dehumanization, and dispossession of the underclass" in precise social and psychological detail (21). Barber describes the novel as revealing a starkly modern consciousness, represented in a language drawing both on long-standing repertoires and current argots. "Incorporativeness, intertextuality and generic migration are deeply characteristic of all Yoruba verbal art, oral and written, old and new. . . . The shared registers of verbal expression in modern Western Nigeria are always already hybrid" (22).

Thus while indigenous-language writers clearly take part in the global circulation of narrative, Barber is suggesting that what to Western readers might appear to be "imported" modern or postmodern narrative strategies in Okediji's Yoruba-language texts may have, rather, indigenous antecedents (and meanings). Moreover, Okediji himself points out the split between "African novels" and novels aimed at the majority of Africans, when he states that while imported English-language thrillers have had strong readerships, there has been a "well-formed and discriminating popular reading public for Yoruba-language texts which greatly exceeded that for English-language *African literature*" (17, my emphasis). It is precisely the distinction between "African literature" (such as the novel) and the literature of choice for local consumers—which apparently may be of local or foreign provenance, in an indigenous or indigenized language, deemed "serious" or "popular"—that we are striving to determine. Okediji's novel would seem to pass muster as a masterful novel in its themes and narrative acumen *and* have popular appeal—its popularity stemming in part from its reaffirmation of a cultural identity through readers' shared possession of Yoruba language, just as we have seen in the case of the Pulaar narratives.

This split between "the novel" and novels for local consumption is reproduced in the area of film and video as well. Birgit Meyer's recent research on Ghanaian videos indicates a comparable difference in focus between films that travel in international circuits and more cheaply produced and easily obtained videos that, against the same setting of urban migration and abuses of power found in films on the international circuit, address daily preoccupations of local consumers.

Karin Barber argues moreover that performance genres, such as popular theater, "sell" modernity. She writes with regard to popular theater in West African coastal cities (Accra, Lomé, Lagos) that

All the plays produced by concert parties and popular theatres in Ghana, Togo, and Nigeria are about the transformation of society wrought under colonialism (though only rarely do they represent actual European/African encounters). . . . They have produced an innovative, hybrid, opportunistic mode of expression in which the incorporation and containment of novelty is a constitutive feature. . . . The openness and novelty-seeking of modern popular genres can be understood as a specific, but perpetually repeated, conversation with the conditions of colonial and post-colonial modernity. (1997, xii)

Clearly, popular forms are situated within and acknowledge the dynamics of "local" and "global" processes as do the extroverted novel. In addition, popular and extroverted novels are in dialogue with one another: Popular novels allude to canonical texts, and canonical texts incorporate popular figures—sugar daddies and "good time girls." But the mood of many popular works is different from that of Africa's most celebrated, canonical novels. The embrace of modernity that Barber and others describe as characteristic of popular or performance genres is uncharacteristic of the extroverted novel. We will have occasion to return to this paradox.

To say, then, that local forms address local publics about local needs is not to argue about relative quality or merit. If we extrapolate from Howard Morphy's assessment of the workings of international markets with respect to Aborginal (and, as is evident, African) art, certain popular forms might well be pulled into the international circuit. With publications such as Karin Barber, John Collins and Alain Ricard's *West African Popular Theater*, an anthology of popular plays (1997), and Stephanie Newell's *Readings in Popular Fiction* (2002), containing both articles and excerpts from superbly written popular novels and novellas—*Son of Woman*, *Dar es Salaam by Night*, *The Secret in my Bosom*, and *Alhaki Kwikwiyo*—we see perhaps the beginnings of this process. It is easy to imagine that, translated into English and distributed internationally, *Atótó Arére* would take its place also in the renowned family of "the African novel" for its "postcolonial" representation of alienation.

In Africa, then—and this may be true the world over at this point—"the novel" is less a narrative genre of specific conventions or values than, in Wilk's terms, "a structure" through which we express "our common differences." While African novels are read by national elites, the novel becomes especially the vehicle through which Senegalese, Somali, or South African writers tell other Africans and the world who they and their communities are, how they think, what they do. And so the extroverted novel—which physically crosses borders and thematizes border crossings—is perhaps the most powerful literary form today in that it reaches more people beyond national boundaries. In the West and on the world stage, African novels may be read to corroborate theories or to glean information about "Africa"—information (whether in scant doses or in refracted images potentially far removed from lived experiences of most Africans)—that may seep down into popular culture and thinking or rise to corridors of power where foreign policy decisions are made. It is thus that the extroverted novel has had a disproportionate impact on thinking about Africa both *across* and *outside* the continent.

Which are these intertextual narratives or narratives arising from the contact zone? Who are the figures in the breach?

There is Sol T. Plaatje's *Mhudi*, a romance and adventure story set in the 1830s, a formative moment in the making of South Africa. Written as early as 1917 but published only in 1930, *Mhudi* was Plaatje's attempt to win over the British to the cause of black South Africans. The novel portrays the northward migration of the Barolong, a subgroup of the Tswana people now living in Botswana and modern South Africa. Plaatje places the Tswana characters, Mhudi and Ra-Thaga, in spaces of encounter with other groups, the Matabele (whose "fierceness" he relativizes) and the Boers (whose mastery is at this point far from assured). Plaatje engages, indeed rewrites—in a foreshadowing of Achebe—what Afrikaner historiography presents as a series of disorderly, violent African tribal clashes (the *mfecane*), on the one hand, and the glorious Boer "Great Trek," on the other—a binary opposition legitimizing Afrikaners' sense of imperial destiny: the takeover of African lands and their guardianship of the South African nation. At the same time, *Mhudi* functions as a South African epic, projecting a future nation composed of diverse groups. These are the archeological and utopic functions to which Gikandi refers, and yet Plaatje's progressive decolonizing agenda was premature for European quarters, and it was not well received at home. Decried for many years as an awkward mixture of fact and fiction, as conciliatory rather than radical, as assimilationist in its English prose, *Mhudi* is hailed today as precisely the type of national narrative, rehistoricizing and nonracial, that the new South Africa requires (Vaubel).

Among the best-known extroverted novels, of course, are Achebe's *Things Fall Apart* and *Arrow of God*, and Kane's *L'aventure ambiguë*, to which we have already referred, in which the hero Samba Diallo is unable to negotiate his way between the discourses and values of East and West. For Kane's Samba Diallo, this space in-between is one of great psychological anguish: "It happens that we are captured at the end of our journey, conquered by our adventure itself. Suddenly it seems to us that we have not stopped changing all along the way, and we have become someone else. Sometimes the metamorphosis is not complete, it puts us in a state of hybridity and leaves us there. So, we hide ourselves, filled with shame" (137, my translation).

In ironic counterpoint to the early Achebe, Kane, and other writers who challenge the assumptions of Eurocentrism and colonialism in a *heroic* mode, Amadou Hampâté Bâ and Yambo Ouloguem write of collaborators-cum-rivals in an *ironic* mode (Jeyifo). In Bâ's *Fortunes of Wangrin*, the eponymous hero, an interpreter under the French in colonial "Soudan," continually does his colonial masters one better, and in Ouloguem's *Le devoir de violence* (*Bound to Violence*, 1968), the villainous Saïf manipulates and murders both colonizers and local subjects in a deadly game of power.

In Ousmane Sembène's novels and films, for example, *Xala*, mentioned above, the protagonist sees himself as modern *yet* African. Or, in his *Bouts de bois de Dieu*, based on the 1947–48 railway strike that took place on the Bamako-Thiès-Dakar line, railworkers and their women, united in transethnic, transnational solidarity, inspired by Marxist principles and heroic narratives, take on their French colonizers and local collaborators. Consider also Nuruddin Farah's many novels, including *Sardines*, also cited above, in which Medina is "the guest" not only in Italy but in her native Somalia as well. Mariama Bâ's *Une si longue lettre* (*So Long a Letter*, 1979) features a heroine, Ramatoulaye, who from her home in Dakar, comes to redefine herself by writing to her friend in Washington, D.C. Then in Dangarembga's *Nervous Conditions* two cousins, Tambu and Nyasha, try to ride out the contradictions of two patriarchies—one indigenous, the other Victorian and colonial. And South African Bessie Head's heroines, Elizabeth and Margaret, and her hero Makhaya, all leave home and cross over into new countries and communities (contact zones), marked by the borrowing and piecing together of values and identities. Head writes in *When Rain Clouds Gather* (1968) that the Botswana village of Golema Mmidi, where Makhaya has come to settle, was "not a village in the usual meaning of being composed of large tribal or family groupings. Golema Mmidi consisted of individuals who had fled there to escape the tragedies of life. Its name too marked it out from the other villages, which were named after important chiefs or important events. Golema Mmidi acquired its name from the occupation the villagers followed, which was crop growing" (17). Finally, Ben Okri's Booker Award–winning, "magical realist" novel of liminality, *The Famished Road*, explores the dilemma of the spirit-child Azaro, who is torn between the corrupt Nigeria in which his parents live and the world of his spirit playmates.

New Metaphors: Le cavalier et son ombre *and* Cinéma

I want to conclude with a reference to two recent French-language novels, which offer varied perspectives on the concept of extroversion itself. The first is by Boubacar Boris Diop, a journalist, screenwriter, and author of five novels as of this writing, who lives in Dakar, Senegal. I am referring to his recent *Le cavalier et son ombre* (*The Knight and His Shadow*, 1997), a metafiction that examines the capacity of the extroverted novel for representation and self-representation and its possibilities, limits, and costs. *Le cavalier* contains a haunting image: Khadidja, an educated, penniless, and somewhat high-strung young woman in a fictional African country, is hired to go daily to a bourgeois home and speak to a figure behind a door whom she never sees and who never responds to her. She rehearses her narratives with her lover, Latsoukabé, the narrator of the novel, who plays the role of listener and responds appropriately to Khadidja's oral stories, in the vein of local storytelling conventions. In those rehearsals, Khadidja is forced to conjure up for herself an image of the figure behind the door, whom she variably sees as a man or perhaps a child or perhaps a sick child. On that basis she strives to design appropriate narratives—one of which is entitled not coincidentally, "The Knight and His Shadow"—until she suspects that there is no one behind the door. The experience is partly to blame for her going mad, or so Latsoukabé intimates, as he himself descends into madness.

The burden of extroversion in this novel derives from Khadidja's liminality and a sense of futility, the obligation to speak and to remain unheard, perhaps even uncertainty of the value of the message. Whether writers the world over in the age of globalization recognize themselves as Khadidja before the door is debatable, but it is certain that Diop sees Khadidja and Latsoukabé as emblems of modern African writers. Diop has stated that this disconnection for the African writer results from the writer's use of French (or English), which he calls "my instrument, not my destiny. . . . It's my Sunday language" (quoted in Sugnet 158). A central philosophical argument lies in that difficult choice of metaphors: Is language identity? Frantz Fanon, it will be recalled, argued that to speak a language was to carry the weight of a civilization, while Congolese writer Sony Labou Tansi, expressing a view shared by many, held that any language in which one laughs or cries is one's own. Diop insists that the French language is an instrument, but it is precisely because French comes with hegemonic baggage, leaving his native Wolof on the sidelines, that it would seem to represent a destiny and that the need for this disavowal arises.

The parable of Khadidja and the language issue are thus not unrelated to the difference between the novel and traditional storytelling or other literary forms, for Khadidja looks outward, faces an uncertain public. Is it the novelist's foreign public who is perhaps behind the door but offers no tangible response? Is it the novelist's national public who should be but is not behind the door? Because that public does not read? Or cannot afford to buy expensive books published often in Paris, London, or New York?

The second novel offering a different meditation on the nature of extroversion and liminality is Tierno Monénembo's *Cinéma* (1997), which suggests, on the contrary, the energy and resilience of ordinary youth. A Guinean national now settled in Caen, France, after many years of living and teaching abroad, Tierno Monénembo is the author of seven novels, including *Cinéma*, a beautifully written, witty, humorous work whose hero enters into a dialogue with Western texts with an eye toward appropriation and self-fashioning.

Cinéma is the coming of age story of fourteen-year-old Binguel. It is October 2, 1958, a transitional time in the history of Guinea, which, under the leadership of Sekou Touré, has broken with DeGaulle and the proposed French African community. The place is Mamou, a small port city and railway stop. As with all such ports during colonialism and after, Mamou is a crossroads, a small cosmopolitan "contact zone" that boasts, in addition to indigenous inhabitants, resident populations of French and Lebanese, and other African nationals, diverse ethnicities and faiths. It is a community aware of and responsive to world developments and events from Paris and Indochina to the USSR and the United States.

Binguel addresses his story to "the old cowboys of Arizona" and "honorable citizens." He narrates the evening's events as they occur and interrupts that narrative every so often to flash back to the history that precedes it—the portraits, foibles, episodes, and rumors that constitute the fabric of life in Mamou with all its ideologies and mythologies—religion, polygamy, ethnic and nationalist sentiment, and racial identities. By evening's end, Binguel, "the Man from the West" (as he is called by his mentor Benté) will have killed the town's villain and become, at last, a hero.

Binguel is no Camara Laye nor Samba Diallo. The son of a comfortable merchant, he finds the petty conventions of family life and the social order (represented by the French schoolmistress *and* his Muslim teacher) stifling: "I had to escape, to escape forever, to take to the road, to discover life, this puzzle of small wonders which was meant for me and not the sad tick-tock of the clock that contained my biography" (47). To the routine, well-traveled road predicated on a socially constructed and socially sanctioned identity, he prefers the call and adventure of the streets; the tales and life lessons of Ardo, the Fula shoeshine man; the excitement of the market; and the westerns at the cinema—*Shane*, *The Virginian*, *High Noon*.

Binguel thus takes the measure of his world through the metaphor of the cinema—U.S. and Indian. This neither traumatizes him nor makes him "lose" his identity. The cinema is his medium and model, but the point of reference is his very own world: "I wonder, of all the moments I've known, if I don't prefer those fleeting, extremely rare but so very rich ones, stored in the film of my memories" (29). High on the list of those personal, local souvenirs is—significantly—the compassionate, nonliterate Haalpoulaar storyteller Ardo: "Listening to him healed me of all evils, real or imaginary. . . . Words in his mouth became bunches of pink fruit that his magic alone could pluck, peel for you, so as to deliver their full flavor" (29–30).

In this liminal space that is the colonial and postcolonial port city, Binguel thus comes into contact with a multitude of ways of doing, dressing, talking, thinking; he selects among them and adapts what he selects to suit his context and needs. This openness and capacity to adopt and adapt is what we see in Seydou Keïta's photos of fashionable, urban youth in Bamako of the 1950s (Magnin). It is what we hear in the Cuban-inspired music in Senegal in the 1960s and 1970s. It is what we see in the documentary about appropriations of black American styles by black South Africans under apartheid (Davis and Riesenfeld). The cultural flows that are taken to be normal fare in the rest of the world are normal here as well, even in the face of grossly unequal power relations, be they internal or external. Binguel's story represents the quest of the human spirit for freedom.

Presenting Africa to the World

What are the implications of extroversion in the novel?

The most obvious is that to the extent its internal readership has been small (and its largest readership lies outside national boundaries, both within Africa as a whole and abroad), this extroverted novel that we think of as "the African novel" has not in most cases served the nation-building role that Benedict Anderson ascribes to "the European novel" in *Imagined Communities*.[7] In the novel's early heyday, then, novels of decolonization that addressed the Eurocentric and racist discourses that lay at the base of European imperial practices in the Americas and in Africa may thus have contributed

---

[7] An exception would seem to be Nigeria, where Achebe's early novels were an important focus of debate and helped create a national imaginary.

especially to an imagined *pan-African* community. As is well known, Frantz Fanon, writing in the 1950s, decried the *African* (as opposed to *national*) imaginary that arose in the literature of decolonization: "the native intellectual who has gone far beyond the domains of Western culture and who has got it into his head to proclaim the existence of another culture never does so in the name of Angola or of Dahomey. The culture which is affirmed is African culture" (1968, 212). Fanon continues, signaling the *racial* basis of this African identity. His disapproval notwithstanding, it is clear that if literature by African nationals took this turn and became "African" (rather than national) literature, it was because they were engaging hegemonic, racial discourses.

Compositionally, while novelistic subgenres such as the thriller or romance may have generic conventions, the canonical African novels taught in schools on the continent and abroad continue to be extroverted novels that have tended to explain Africa to the world, and especially, to a hegemonic West. In this sense, their primary feature may be their intertextuality with hegemonic or international texts of all sorts, ethnographic, historical, fictional, and travelogues, even as they may reconfigure indigenous discursive materials.

This, it seems to me, is at the root of Boubacar Boris Diop's comment, "Our literature is sad." For the novel in Africa has often been a genre of back talk or explicit engagement of discourses and cultural products come from afar, and its protagonists typically inhabit in-between spaces, contexts of liminality. As Diop explains, "I'm interested in the ways a person can be torn, the ways he can be separated from the group. And I think a writer is always separated from the group" (quoted in Sugnet, 159). It may be therefore the burden of response to hegemonic discourses and practices, the exploration of the grand motif of the (failed) nation, and a concomitant deployment of heroines and heroes who transgress various boundaries that have tended to make the novel ripe for a prevailing mood of alienation. Thus the anxieties of the contestatory, extroverted African novel; its penchant for solitary, misunderstood, and trapped heroes; and their crisis of language or that of their authors, have given it a somber cast: No exuberance here.

And since realism in African novels has tended to be taken at face value as an unmediated reflection of life in Africa, it is this novelistic theme and representation of the continent that have come to dominate perception of it on the outside. Those in the centers of the world system or elsewhere have based their understanding on these textual, most often novelistic representations that contrast sharply with the embrace of "the new" that Barber et al. describe in popular performance genres or the resilience and energy that characterize many popular fictions and the lives of ordinary people. In this one can argree with Kwame Anthony Appiah who writes, "Despite the over-whelming reality of economic decline, despite unimaginable poverty; de-spite wars, malnutrition, disease and political instability, African cultural productivity grows apace: popular literatures, oral narrative and poetry, dance, drama, music and visual art all thrive" (157).

It is easy to see how on the basis of standard extroverted novels taken to represent the whole, Fredric Jameson could claim that the third-world text is always a national allegory. Under this dispensation, the definition of "the African novel" is tautological and—because women's fictions have tended to be more complicated (Stratton, Andrade)—blind to the workings of gender: The novel is a narrative that engages discourses of modernity and nation in a mode of alienation; a narrative that engages discourses of modernity and na-tion is a novel. In his well-known response, Ahmad Aijaz signals not only the presence of such "allegories" in the so-called first world but, more impor-tant for my purposes here, the presence of other narratives, often written in local languages, invisible in standard discussions of postcolonial literatures, that have other emphases and trajectories.

Since the novel is, in the language of the anthropology of cultural flows, a form enabling an expression of differences, it permits relatively easy decod-ing and reading around the world. It arises from and reinscribes the very ex-perience of in-betweeness or liminality. As a type of "lock" operating be-tween typically unequal channels, the novel registers in its very practice, then, the formidable imbalances and inequities that characterize Africa's place in the world.

What should be clear, however, is that extroverted African novels are not to be blamed for a supposed inauthenticity, the failure to be performance, to play the part of popular culture, or for their disproportionate presence on the world stage as a megaphone for "locality"; this is their niche as a literary form. They register those inequities because they themselves are on the cusps of worlds, they negotiate semiotic systems and inscribe asymmetries of power. Roy Pascal writes in the remarks that I cite at the beginning of this essay that novels find their source in the changing world of human relations and values allied to changes in economic practices, social structures, and po-litical relationships. In order to understand the novel, he argues, one must "reach into the whole world in which the novel functions" (75). What we have come to call the African novel is this extroverted form that necessarily registers the imbalances of the world in which it arises.

This, it seems to me, is the part that "the novel" in Africa, one form among many in a complex cultural ecology, has come to play.

Works Cited

CREATIVE WORKS

Achebe, Chinua. *Things Fall Apart* (1957). New York: Fawcett, n.d.

Diop, Boubacar Boris. *Le cavalier et son ombre*. Paris: Editions Stock, 1997.

Farah, Nuruddin. *Sardines* (1981, Allison and Busby; 1982, Heinemann). St. Paul, Minn.: Graywolf Press, 1992.

Head, Bessie. *When Rain Clouds Gather*. New York: Simon and Schuster, 1968.

In Darkest Hollywood: Cinema and Apartheid. Directed by Peter Davis and Daniel Riesenfeld. Produced by Nightingale/Villon. Distributed by California Newsreel, 1993.

Kane, Cheikh Hamidou. *L'aventure ambiguë*. Paris: Juillard, 1961.

Monénembo, Tierno. *Cinéma*. Paris: Seuil, 1997.

Plaatje, Sol T. *Mhudi* (1930). Edited by Tim Couzens. Cape Town: Francolin Publishers, 1996.

Xala. Directed by Ousmane Sembène. New Yorker Films, 1975.

CRITICAL SOURCES

Abu-Lughod, Janet. "Going beyond Global Babble." In *Culture, Globalization and the World System: Contemporary Conditions for the Representation of Identity*, edited by Anthony D. King, 131–37. Minneapolis: University of Minnesota Press, 1997.

Achebe, Chinua. "The African Writer and the English Language" (1964). In *Morning Yet on Creation Day*, 91–103. Garden City, N.Y.: Anchor/Doubleday, 1975.

Aijaz, Ahmad. "Jameson's Rhetoric of Otherness and the 'National Allegory.'" *Social Text* 17 (1987): 3–27.

Amin, Samir. *Eurocentrism*. Translated by Russell Moore. New York: Monthly Review Press, 1989.

Anderson, Benedict. *Imagined Communities: Reflections on the Origin and Spread of Nationalism*. London: Verso, 1991.

Andrade, Susan. *The Nation Writ Small: African Fictions and Feminisms*. Durham, N.C.: Duke University Press, forthcoming.

Appadurai, Arjun. "The Production of Locality." In *Modernity at Large: Cultural Dimensions of Globalization*, 178–217. Minneapolis: University of Minnesota Press, 1996.

Appiah, Kwame Anthony. *In My Father's House*. New York: Oxford University Press, 1992.

Ashcroft, Bill, Gareth Griffiths, and Helen Tiffin. *The Empire Writes Back: Theory and Practice in Post-colonial Literatures*. London: Routledge, 1989.

Bakhtin, Mikhail. *The Dialogic Imagination*. Translated by Caryl Emerson and Michael Holquist. Edited by Michael Holquist. Austin: University of Texas Press, 1981.

Barber, Karin. "African Language Literatures and Postcolonial Criticism." *Research in African Literatures* 26 (1995): 3–30.

———. "Introduction." In Karin Barber, John Collins, and Alain Ricard. *West African Popular Theater*. Bloomington: Indiana University Press, 1997.

Brown, Homer. "Why the Story of the Origin of the (English) Novel Is an American Romance (if Not the Great American Novel)." In *Cultural Institutions of the Novel*, edited by Deidre Lynch and William B. Warner, 11–43. Durham, N.C.: Duke University Press, 1996.

Burnham, Michelle. "Between England and America: Captivity, Sympathy, and the Sentimental Novel." In *Cultural Institutions of the Novel*, edited by Deidre Lynch and William B. Warner, 47–72. Durham, N.C.: Duke University Press, 1996.

Césaire, Aimé. *Cahier d'un retour au pays natal* (1939). Paris: Présence Africaine, 1956.

———. "Culture and Colonisation." *Présence africaine* 8–10 (1956): 193–207.

Chakrabarty, Dipesh. "Postcoloniality and the Artifice of History: Who Speaks for 'Indian' Pasts?" *Representations* 37 (1992): 1–26.

Chartier, Roger. "Texts, Printings, Readings." In *The New Cultural History*, 154–75. Berkeley: University of California Press, 1989.

Chatterjee, Partha. "The Nationalist Resolution of the Women's Question." In *Recasting Women: Essays in Indian Colonial History*, edited by Kumkum Sangari and Sudesh Vaid. New Brunswick, N.J.: Rutgers University Press, 1990.

Diallo, Sonja Fagerberg. "Milk and Honey: Developing Written Literature in Pulaar." *Yearbook of Comparative and General Literature* 43 (1995): 67–83.

Diawara, Manthia. *In Search of Africa*. Cambridge, Mass.: Harvard University Press, 1998.

Fanon, Frantz. "On National Culture." In *Wretched of the Earth*, translated by Constance Farrington, 206–48. New York: Grove Press, 1968.

———. "Racism and Culture." *Présence africaine* 8–10 (1956): 122–31.

Gikandi, Simon. *Reading Chinua Achebe: Language and Ideology in Fiction*. London: Currey; Portsmouth, N.H.: Heinemann, 1991.

Hountondji, Paulin. "Producing Knowledge in Africa Today." *African Studies Review* 38 (1995): 1–10.

Jameson, Fredric. "Third World Literature in the Era of Multinational Capitalism." *Social Text* 15 (1986): 65–88.

Jeyifo, Biodun. "Determinations of Remembering: Postcolonial Fictional Genealogies of Colonialism in Africa." *Stanford Literary Review* 10 (1993): 99–116.

Julien, Eileen. *African Novels and the Question of Orality*. Bloomington: Indiana University Press, 1992.

———. "*Terrains de rencontre*: Césaire, Fanon, and Wright on Culture and Decolonization." *Yale French Studies* 98 (2000): 149–66.

Larkin, Brian. "Indian Films and Nigerian Lovers: Media and the Creation of Parallel Modernities." In *Readings in Popular Fiction*, edited by Stephanie Newell, 18–32. Bloomington: Indiana University Press, 2002.

Lévi-Strauss, Claude. *Race and History*. Paris: UNESCO, 1952.

Lorentzon, Leif. "Asare Konadu and His Two Levels of (Popular) Literature." Paper delivered at "Popular Fictions: Versions and Subversions." International Conference on African Literature, Humboldt University. Berlin, May 4, 2002.

Lynch, Deidre, and William B. Warner, eds. *Cultural Institutions of the Novel*. Durham, N.C.: Duke University Press, 1996.

Magnin, André. *Seydou Keïta*. Zurich: Scalo Editions, 1997.

Mbembe, Achille. "African Modes of Self-Writing." *Public Culture* 14.1 (2002): 239–73.

McLaughlin, Fiona. "Haalpulaar Identity as a Response to Wolofization." *African Languages and Cultures* 8.2 (1995).

Meyer, Birgit. *Translating the Devil: Religion and Modernity among the Ewe in Ghana*. Edinburgh: Edinburgh University Press, 1999.

Mkandawire, Thandika. "Problems and Prospects of Social Sciences in Africa," 129–40. *International Social Science Journal*. Oxford: Blackwell Publishers, 1993.

Moretti, Franco. *Atlas of the European Novel 1800–1900*. London: Verso, 1998.

Morphy, Howard. "Aboriginal Art in a Global Context." In *Worlds Apart: Modernity through the Prism of the Local*, edited by Daniel Miller, 211–39. London: Routledge, 1995.

Mudimbe, V. Y. *L'écart*. Paris: Présence Africaine, 1979.

———. *The Invention of Africa*. Bloomington: Indiana University Press, 1988.

Newell, Stephanie. *Readings in Popular Fiction*. Bloomington: Indiana University Press, 2002.

Ngũgĩ wa Thiongo. *Decolonising the Mind*. London: Currey/Heinemann, 1986.

The Oxford English Dictionary. Prepared by J. A. Simpson and E.S.C. Weiner. 2nd ed., vol. 5. Oxford: Clarendon Press, 1989.

Pascal, Roy. "Narrative Fictions and Reality: A Comment on Frank Kermode's *The Sense of an Ending*." In *Why the Novel Matters: A Postmodern Perplex*, edited by Mark Spilka and Caroline McCracken-Flesher, 65–75. Bloomington: Indiana University Press, 1990.

Pratt, Mary Louise. *Imperial Eyes: Travel Writing and Transculturation*. London: Routledge, 1992.

Quayson, Ato. *Strategic Transformations in Nigerian Writing: Orality and History in the Work of Rev. Samuel Johnson, Amos Tutuola, Wole Soyinka and Ben Okri*. Oxford: James Currey; Bloomington: Indiana University Press, 1997.

Radhakrishnan, R. "Nationalism, Gender and the Narrative of Identity." In *Nationalisms and Sexualities*, edited by Andrew Parker, Mary Russo, Doris Sommer, and Patricia Yaeger. New York: Routledge, 1992.

Roscoe, Adrian. *Mother Is Gold*. Cambridge: Cambridge University Press, 1971.

Said, Edward. *Culture and Imperialism*. New York: Knopf, 1993.

Scheub, Harold. "A Review of African Oral Traditions and Literature." *African Studies Review* 28.2–3 (1985): 559–75.

Stratton, Florence. *Contemporary African Literature and the Politics of Gender*. London: Routledge, 1994.

Sugnet, Charles J. "Dances with Wolofs." *Transition* 87 (2001): 138–59.

Todorov, Tzvetan. *La conquête de l'Amérique*. Paris: Seuil, 1982.

Turner, Victor. *The Ritual Process: Structure and Anti-Structure* (1969, Aldine). Ithaca, N.Y.: Cornell University Press, 1991.

Tutuola, Amos. *The Palm-Wine Drinkard*. London: Faber, 1952.

Vaubel, Natasha. "Truth, Reconciliation and History: Looking Back from the 'New' South Africa to Sol T. Plaatje's *Mhudi*." Thesis, Indiana University, 2001.

Wallerstein, Immanuel. "The National and the Universal: Can There Be Such a Thing as World Culture?" In *Culture, Globalization and the World System: Contemporary Conditions for the Representation of Identity* (1991), edited by Anthony D. King, 91–105. Minneapolis: University of Minnesota Press, 1997.

Wa-Nyatetũ-Waigwa, Wangarĩ. *The Liminal Novel: Studies in the Francophone African Novels as Bildungsroman*. New York: Peter Lang, 1996.

White, Hayden. *The Content of the Form: Narrative Discourse and Historical Representation*. Baltimore: Johns Hopkins University Press, 1987.

Wilk, Richard. "Learning to Be Local in Belize: Global Systems of Common Difference." In *Worlds Apart: Modernity through the Prism of the Local*, edited by Daniel Miller, 110–33. London: Routledge, 1995.

Wright, Richard. "Tradition and Industrialization: The Plight of the Tragic Elite in Africa." *Présence Africaine* 8–10 (1956): 347–60.

Toward World Literature

MICHAEL DENNING

The Novelists' International

As the age of three worlds (1945–89) reached its midpoint, the novel looked dead, exhausted. In the capitalist first world, it was reduced to increasingly arid formalisms alongside an industry of formulaic genre fictions. In the communist second world, the official conventions of socialist realism were ritualized into a form of didactic popular literature. Into the freeze of this literary cold war erupted Gabriel García Márquez's *Cien años de soledad* [*One Hundred Years of Solitude*] (1967), the first international best seller from Latin America and perhaps the most influential novel of the last third of the twentieth century. In its wake, a new sense of a world novel emerged, with *Cien años de soledad* as its avatar, the "third world" as its home, and a vaguely defined "magical realism" as its aesthetic rubric.[1]

Like "world music," the "world novel" is a category to be distrusted; if it genuinely points to the transformed geography of the novel, it is also a marketing device that flattens distinct regional and linguistic traditions into a single cosmopolitan "world beat," with magical realism serving as the aesthetic of globalization, often as empty and contrived a signifier as the modernism and socialist realism it supplanted. There is, however, a historical truth to the sense that there are links between writers as unlike as García Márquez, Naguib Mahfouz, Nadine Gordimer, José Saramago, Paule Marshall, and Pramoedya Ananta Toer, for the work of each has roots in the remarkable international literary movement that emerged in the middle decades of the twentieth century under the slogans of "proletarian literature," "neorealism," and "progressive," "engaged," or "committed" writing. The African-American novelist Richard Wright (1908–60) captured the sense of political and literary enfranchisement that marked this novelists' international in his autobiography:

> It was not the economics of Communism, nor the great power of trade
> unions, nor the excitement of underground politics that claimed me; my at-
> tention was caught by the similarity of the experiences of workers in other

---

[1] Gregory Rabassa's English translation (1970) had immense influence in breaking up the formalisms that dominated the official modernism of the U.S. literary world; in the USSR, the 1970 *Foreign Literature* translation made it a model for writers trying to break with bureaucratic socialist realism. Katerina Clark, *The Soviet Novel: History as Ritual* (Chicago: University of Chicago Press, 1985), 267.

lands, by the possibility of uniting scattered but kindred peoples into a whole. . . . Out of the magazines I read came a passionate call for the experiences of the disinherited, and there were none of the lame lispings of the missionary in it. It did not say: "Be like us and we will like you, maybe." It said: "If you possess enough courage to speak out what you are, you will find that you are not alone." . . . Out of step with our times, it was but natural for us [writers] to respond to the Communist party, which said: "Your rebellion is right. Come with us and we will support your vision with militant action."

(Indeed, we felt that we were lucky. Why cower in towers of ivory and squeeze out private words when we had only to speak and millions listened? Our writing was translated into French, German, Russian, Chinese, Spanish, Japanese. . . . Who had ever, in all human history, offered to young writers an audience so vast? True, our royalties were small or less than small, but that did not matter.[2]

This international of writers was allied to, and often organized by, the international communist movement, and its failures and successes—"the horror and the glory" in Wright's phrase—echoed the checkered history of that movement: both the local communist parties, legal and underground, and the revolutionary regimes ruled by communist parties in the wake of 1917. Nevertheless, its history is by no means congruent with that of the official "socialist realisms" of the communist regimes. And though the novelists of this movement were deeply influenced by the experimental modernisms of the early decades of the century, they rarely fit into the canonical genealogies of Western modernism and postmodernism. Though the royalties were small, the writers were not all proletarians, and the audience was often more a promise than a reality, the movement did, by imagining an international of novelists, transform the history of the novel. It enfranchised a generation of writers, often of plebian backgrounds, around the world, and it was the first self-concious attempt to create a world literature. In looking at how the geography of the novel was transformed in the twentieth century, the history of this first "world literature" is central. From Maxim Gorky to Gabriel García Márquez, from Lu Xun to Praemoedya Ananta Toer, from Richard Wright to Ngugi wa Thiong'o, from Patrícia Galvão to Isabel Allende: the novelists' international spans the globe and the century.

To sketch the history of this novelists' international is a daunting task. First, literary histories usually focus on its dramatic and still controversial literary politics: the formation and splitting of writers' organizations and

---

[2] Richard Wright, *Later Works: Black Boy (American Hunger), The Outsider* (New York: Library of America, 1991), 302, 303, 328.

unions; the brief ascendency of the idea of a "proletarian literature" and the shift to "socialist realism" at the 1934 Soviet Writers' Congress; the famous writers' congresses in Kharkov (1930), Moscow (1934), Paris (1935), New York (1936), Lucknow (1936), Madrid (1937), Tashkent (1958), Cairo (1962), and Havana (1968); the struggles over the writers' place in revolutionary regimes from Stalin's Soviet Union to Mao's China and Castro's Cuba. One can easily collect the manifestos in which writers, critics, militants, and bureaucrats tried to define the proletarian novel and the forms of a radical or revolutionary realism—critical, social, socialist—and announced their intention to produce a committed, engaged, partisan writing; but the novels actually written under these literary charters rarely matched the manifestos and often provoked further controversy.

Second, though the aesthetic ideologies of "proletarian literature," "socialist realism," or "engaged" writing are found around the globe in the twentieth century, most literary histories focus on a single national tradition, and there is little comparative work that would indicate whether the novels share common modes, forms, and styles. Mainstream literary criticism has generally taken one of two stances: either arguing that proletarian or social realist novels share a transnational formula that marks them as less-than-literary outsiders to the national literature, or claiming that the finest left-wing writers transcend the generic formula and are thus best understood within the particular linguistic and cultural tradition that makes up the national literature. Moreover, the two leading transnational aesthetic terms—realism and modernism—were so embedded in the cultural cold war that they became mere honorifics, with little actual meaning. In the communist world, favored writers were proclaimed realists; in the capitalist world, they were deemed modernists. The discoveries that apparent modernists were actually realists— think of the cases of Picasso or Brecht—and the reverse claim that classic social realists were actually modernists (as in contemporary reinterpretations of Lu Xun) have regularly been part of the ideological battle conducted through these terms.

Third, the novel itself has an uncertain relation to politics and social movements. Radical writers have usually chosen shorter and more public forms, writing plays, poems, journalism, and short stories. Novels take time; as Gerald Martin notes in his history of Latin American fiction, "a great historical novel usually requires at least thirty years' distance from its subject matter. Great realist works will always exist . . . [but] they will not appear during the era to which they refer."[3] The great novels of the revolutionary

---

[3] Gerald Martin, *Journeys through the Labyrinth: Latin American Fiction in the Twentieth Century* (London: Verso, 1989), 94.

movements that erupted around 1917 often did not appear until the 1950s and 1960s, when the political energies of the movements had receded. A history of this literary movement must thus move between two moments: the moment of the breakthrough books, the landmark "proletarian novels," short, often crude, but electrifying works often written by figures who did not go on to careers as novelists; and the moment of fruition when writers shaped by the radical literary movement produced major works, long after the manifestos and polemics had been forgotten.

Thus, if "proletarian literature" came to world attention in the brief moment in the late 1920s and early 1930s when young writers like Wright founded communist literary circles and magazines, and the fledgling Soviet regime attracted writers to literary congresses and published *Literature of the World Revolution* in several languages, its roots lay in the first alliances between writers and the socialist movement at the beginning of the twentieth century, and its legacies reach to the magical realisms and postmodernisms of the age of three worlds.

The First Socialist Realism

The massive historical presence of the communist regimes and movements often screens out world socialism *before* the Bolshevik revolution. Though the phrase "socialist realism" is rightly linked to the 1934 Soviet Writers' Congress that formally adopted it as the new aesthetic and thus as a central part of the consolidation of the Stalinist regime, the idea of a socialist realism was, as Régine Robin has argued, the culmination of decades of socialist debate over a new aesthetic.[4] Gorky's presence as the chair of the 1934 Writers' Congress was emblematic because he represented a generation of socialist realists who preceded the Bolshevik revolution of 1917, a generation who came of age at the turn of the century just as the powerful labor movements and socialist parties of the Second International were forming. They also preceded the experimental modernisms that exploded around the world in the 1910s; their slogans were "realism" and "naturalism." Some affiliated themselves with the emerging socialist and labor parties, and others were adopted by them. If Gorky (1868–1936) and the Chinese writer Lu Xun (1881–1936) were to become international communist icons (Gorky's *Mother* [1907] would be a central book in this tradition), this generation would also

---

[4] Régine Robin, *Socialist Realism: An Impossible Aesthetic* (Stanford, Calif.: Stanford University Press, 1992).

include Europeans like H. G. Wells (1866–1946), George Bernard Shaw (1856–1950), Anatole France (1844–1924), Romain Rolland (1866–1944), Martin Anderson Nexo (1869–1954), Pio Baroja and the authors of classic antiwar novels of World War I, Henri Barbusse (1873–1935), and Jaroslav Hasek (1883–1923); North Americans like Theodore Dreiser (1871–1945), W.E.B. Du Bois (1868–1963), Upton Sinclair (1878–1968), and Jack London (1876–1916); and South Asians like Rabindranath Tagore (1861–1941) and Prem Chand (1880–1936). By the 1920s and 1930s, they were "the grand old men of socialist literature," the classic "fellow travelers."[5] Though several (including France, Dreiser, and Du Bois) were to join the communist party just before their deaths, it is worth emphasizing that the generation of Gorky marked the beginnings of an international socialist literary culture before 1917.

It was this generation that brought the novel to forefront of socialist literary culture. In the latter half of the nineteenth century, the novel was not central to socialist cultural thought. Poetry and drama were the heart of socialist notions of *Bildung*, which stressed the appropriation and mastery of the classics by working people rather than the development of an independent radical or working-class art. Following the lead of Marx and Engels, socialist critics championed the classics of the epoch of an ascendent and revolutionary bourgeoisie—Lessing, Schiller, and Goethe—against the bourgeois culture of the time. The novel was generally seen as merely a form of entertainment, and socialists both criticized and tried to supplant the commercial dime novels and *Schundliteratur* that proliferated in working-class culture. The main exception to this disregard of fiction was provoked by the social novels of Zola and his naturalist followers. The Marxist debate over naturalism—now largely associated with the writings of Lukács in the 1930s—began among German socialists (including Franz Mehring) in the 1890s.[6]

By the turn of the century, the immense popularity of Zola's novels among working-class socialist militants and the emergence of the generation of Gorky brought the novel to the fore in socialist culture. The realists of the turn of the century were hailed as the heirs of Balzac and Tolstoy, and the first two decades of the twentieth century saw the hegemony of realism among socialists: this was the source of the notion of "critical realism" that Lukács would defend. Novels of turn-of-the-century industrial cities like

---

[5] Jürgen Rühle, *Literature and Revolution: A Critical History of the Writer and Communism in the Twentieth Century* (New York: Frederick A. Praeger, 1969).

[6] See H.-J. Schulz, *German Socialist Literature 1860–1914: Predicaments of Criticism* (Columbia, S.C.: Camden House, 1993).

Gorky's *Mat* (*Mother*, 1907) (set in the shipworks of Nizhni-Novgorod), Sinclair's *The Jungle* (1906) (set in Chicago's meat-packing plants), Nexo's *Pelle Erobreren* (*Pele the Conquerer*, four volumes, 1906–10, narrating the migration to working-class Copenhagen), and Baroja's *La lucha por la vida* (*The Struggle for Life*, three volumes, 1903–05, set in Madrid) became internationally famous.

In the early 1910s, the first calls for a "proletarian literature"—writing by workers—appeared among Russian social democrats in exile and Yiddish-speaking socialists in New York, and soon resonated with the younger "lefts"—syndicalists, maximalists, and bolsheviks—who emerged in the strike waves of the 1910s. This marked a radical break with the classicism of Second International socialist *Bildung*, which had maintained a suspicion of both proletarian cultural iconoclasm and agitational or "tendentious" literature. In their rejection of received aesthetic canons, the young advocates of proletarian writing shared much with their dadaist, cubist, and expressionist contemporaries.

Nevertheless, there were few attempts to organize left-wing writers before the First World War; the socialist subcultures of newspapers, clubs, and party schools rarely brought together young worker-writers, and the Second International did not organize international writers' congresses. If an incipient socialist realism had taken shape, a novelists' international lay in the future.

1917: Toward a Proletarian Novel

The turning point was the world upheaval of 1917–21. In the wake of the European slaughter, regimes and empires were challenged: there were revolutions in czarist Russia and Mexico; brief-lived socialist republics in Germany, Hungary, and Persia; uprisings against colonialism in Ireland, India, and China; and massive strike waves and factory occupations in Japan, Italy, Spain, Chile, Brazil, and the United States. The "imaginative proximity of social revolution" electrified a generation of young writers who came together in variety of revolutionary and proletarian writers groups.[7] Three initiatives were particularly influential. The first was the formation of the first international writers' association, *Clarté*, in 1919 by Henri Barbusse, which symbolically enrolled many of the established writers of the prewar years

---

[7] The phrase comes from Perry Anderson's account of the coordinates of the modernist conjuncture in his "Modernity and Revolution," *New Left Review* 144 (March–April 1984): 104.

including Gorky, Sinclair, and Tagore, and which led to a series of international writers' congresses. The second was the emergence of a proletarian culture movement in revolutionary Russia, a loose federation of clubs, educational societies, and workers' theaters that held its first national conference in Petrograd just a week before the storming of the Winter Palace, and that soon became known by the epithet Proletkult. The Proletkult movement reached its peak in the Soviet Union in the early 1920s, spawning workshops, journals, and rival groups, and its example resonated around the world. By the time of the 1930 Kharkov conference of revolutionary writers, there were active unions of proletarian writers not only in the Soviet Union, but in Japan, Germany, Hungary, Poland, Austria, Korea, China, and the United States.

The third initiative was the Baku conference of 1920, which marked the turn by the communist inheritors of European socialism to the anticolonial movements in Asia and Africa, generating the powerful alliance of communism and anticolonialism that was to shape the global decolonization struggles of the twentieth century. The importance of the anticolonial movements for European radical artists did not register immediately; at the Kharkov conference, the delegates from Egypt and Brazil argued that "European revolutionary and proletarian writers do not pay sufficient attention to the colonial question" and to "one of the most important branches of world proletarian literature—the development of revolutionary literature in colonial countries."[8] In many ways, the proletarian literature movement was to have a deeper impact on the national literatures of the colonized countries than it would in Western Europe.

In the wake of the upheavals of 1917–21, the slogans of revolutionary and proletarian literature were adopted by young avant-gardes around the world. The early Proletkult groups were usually organized around theaters or small magazines publishing poems, short stories, reportage, and workers' correspondence. However, by the late 1920s and early 1930s—just as the world plunged into economic depression—a group of landmark proletarian novels appeared, announcing a new form: among them were Feodor Gladkov's *Tsement* (*Cement*, 1925) in the Soviet Union; Mike Gold's *Jews without Money* (1929), Agnes Smedley's *Daughter of Earth* (1929), and John Dos Passos's *The 42nd Parallel* (1930) in the United States; Kobayashi Takiji's *Kani Kosen* (*The Factory Ship*, 1929) and Tokunaga Sunao's *Taiyo no Nai Machi* (*The Street without Sun*, 1929) in Japan; Alfred Döblin's *Alexanderplatz*

---

[8] "Second International Conference of Revolutionary Writers," *Literature of the World Revolution* (special number, 1931): 180, 176.

(1929) and Willi Bredel's *Maschinenfabrik N&K* (*Machine Factory N&K*, 1930) in Germany; the controversial story collections *Los que se van* (*Those That Leave*, 1930) by Ecuador's Quayaquil group of social realists; *Angarey* (*Embers*, 1932) edited by the radical Urdu writer Sajjad Zaheer; César Vallejo's *El tungsteno* (*Tungsten*, 1931) in Peru; Patrícia Galvão's *Parque industrial* (*Industrial Park*, 1933) and Jorge Amado's *Cacau* (*Cacao*, 1933) in Brazil; Lamine Senghor's *La violation d'un pays* (*The Violation of a Country*, 1927) in French West Africa; Paul Nizan's *Antoine Bloyé* (1933) in France; Ding Ling's *Yijiu sanling nian chun Shanghai* (*Shanghai, Spring 1930*, 1930) and Mao Dun's *Ziye* (*Midnight*, 1933) in China; Yi Kiyong's *Kohyang* (*Hometown*, 1934) in Korea; Mulk Raj Anand's *Untouchable* (1935) in India; Jacques Roumain's *La montagne ensorcelée* (*The Bewitched Mountain*, 1931) in Haiti; and C.L.R. James's *Minty Alley* (1936) in Trinidad.

The polemics that tried to define the revolutionary or proletarian novel—did one define it by subject matter, by the writer's class origins, or by its implicit or explicit proletarian or revolutionary stance?—hardly illuminate this flowering of books that were widely translated and read and that served as an inspiration to other radical writers. Some of the novelists, like Gold, Bredel, and Tokunaga, grew up in working-class families and found their literary vocation in the radical labor movement; others, like James and Anand, were the "talented tenth" of colonized peoples; still others, like Dos Passos, Galvão, and Döblin, were children of bourgeois families and elite schools who had come to the left from the ranks of the the modernist avant-gardes: dadaism, German expressionism, French and Latin American surrealism, Brazilian *antropofagia*. Many had traveled widely: the plebian writers as soldiers, migrant workers, or seamen; the young colonials as students in the imperial capitals; the modernists as artist expatriates, tourists, and journalists.

Their books were experiments in form, attempts to reshape the novel. Several challenges immediately presented themselves: the attempt to represent working-class life in a genre that had developed as the quintessential narrator of bourgeois or middle-class manners, kin structures, and social circles; the attempt to represent a collective subject in a form built around the interior life of the individual; the attempt to create a public, agitational work in a form that, unlike drama, depended on private, often domestic consumption; and the attempt to create a vision of revolutionary social change in a form almost inherently committed to the solidity of society and history. The early novels are often awkward and un-novelistic. They had their roots in the reportage of worker correspondents, first-person testimonies of working life, and they adopted its plotless, loosely linked sketches of shop floors and tenement neighborhoods. As Gorky had put it at the beginning of

Mother: "it was clear that the life of working people was the same every-where. And if this was true, what was there to talk about?"[9]

Thus, this emerging novelists' international and its proletarian novel is neither a sociological entity—all novels written by proletarians—nor a fully formed genre, but is a continuing dialectic between a self-conscious literary movement and the literary forms it developed. In the three decades between the victory of the Russian bolsheviks in 1917 and the victory of the Chinese communists in 1949, this proletarian literature spread around the world, as both a movement and a mode, a formation and a form. In the midst of the Cold War, literary historians tended to read this as a single story, whether in the Soviet literary historian Ivan Anisimov's triumphant sense (in 1966) that the "literary movement set in motion by the Russian Revolution" marked "a new epoch in world literature," or in the German literary historian Jürgen Rühle's tragic judgment (also of the 1960s) that the "alliance between left-wing art and left-wing politics" was a complete failure.[10] More recent schol-arship has focused on the place of these movements in national literary traditions, and we now have many fine revaluations of specific national pro-letarian literatures. However, a survey of these literary histories suggests that there were several common trajectories, and allows us to sketch a prelimi-nary set of hypotheses about the movements and the forms.

Movements

Not surprisingly, the presence of a proletarian literary movement in a country usually correlates with the presence of a communist movement, even though communist parties were often skeptical, even suspicious, of their literary al-lies. But proletarian literary movements seem to have had their greatest im-pact in countries that experienced major cultural upheavals in these decades, conflicts that challenged the legitimacy of dominant cultural forms. More-over, there seems to be an inverse relation between the impact of the prole-tarian novel on a culture and the earlier importance of the novel in a culture. In countries with a long-established tradition of the novel—and that did not see overwhelming cultural crises (England, for example)—the proletarian novel left little mark. Thus, the most significant proletarian literary move-ments emerged in four types of situations: those in countries where commu-nist regimes came to power; those in countries where fascist or authoritarian

---

[9] Maxim Gorky, *Mother*, trans. Margaret Wettlin (New York: Collier Books, 1962), 13.

[10] Anisimov quoted in Rühle, *Literature and Revolution*, 464; Rühle, *Literature and Revolution*, 3.

regimes came to power; those in the creole countries of the Americas; and those in colonized regions of Asia and Africa.

The trigger for the proletarian literary movement was the bolshevik revolution of 1917, and the history of the Russian movement casts a long shadow around the globe.[11] However, in a number of ways, the Russian proletarian literary movement was not typical but exceptional. The Russian writers of the proletarian moment had perhaps the most daunting literary forebears, the prerevolutionary reinvention of the novel by Tolstoy and Dostoyevsky, not to mention the pioneering working-class novels of Gorky. It is not clear that any of the writers of the proletarian generation succeeded in creating a space of their own. Second, in Russia, the literary movement developed largely after the revolution, in alliance (in varying degrees) with the new regime, rather than as an oppositional avant-garde. As a result, proletarian novels were more about reconstructing the nation and building socialism than about struggling against capitalism or colonialism: the production novel—the tale of "how the plan was fulfilled or the project was constructed"—not the strike novel dominated.[12] Third, the early and often experimental proletarian novels of the Soviet cultural renaissance of the 1920s—like Gladkov's *Cement*—became canonized by the Stalinist state as models for a didactic and formulaic "socialist realism." "Many forties classics," Katerina Clark notes, "read like reruns of either *Cement* or *How the Steel Was Tempered*."[13] In the communist states established after World War Two, works of the local proletarian literary movements were similarly canonized, and some of

---

[11] Four distinct moments emerge from the historiography: the original Proletkult, formed in the midst of the revolution by left-wing bolsheviks who had developed circles of worker writers in exile, and which became a state-funded haven for socialist intellectuals during the civil war, before evaporating in the wake of the Kronstadt uprising; the post–civil war Soviet cultural renaissance of 1921–28, which saw the emergence of several rival proletarian literary groups in Moscow and Leningrad, publishing journals (*Na Postu* [*On Guard*], *October*, *Kuznitza* [*Smithy*]) and the first celebrated proletarian novels, particularly Gladkov's *Cement*; the Stalinist "cultural revolution" of 1928–32, as Fitzpatrick calls it, a turbulent moment when the promotion of young workers into higher education and the arts created a new Soviet intelligentsia, and when one wing of the proletarian literature avant-garde, RAPP, was unleashed to conduct a literary class war against the older, established intelligentsia; and the end of the "cultural revolution" after 1932, when the advocates of proletarian literature were purged, traditional Russian culture was reasserted, and a middlebrow sense of "socialism realism" was officially sanctioned. See Lynn Mally, *Culture of the Future: The Proletkult Movement in Revolutionary Russia* (Berkeley: University of California Press, 1990); and Sheila Fitzpatrick, *The Cultural Front: Power and Culture in Revolutionary Russia* (Ithaca, N.Y.: Cornell University Press, 1992).

[12] Clark, *The Soviet Novel*, 256.

[13] Ibid., 192.

the writers became bureaucrats of an official socialist realism in state-run Writers' Unions: one can see this in the careers of Mao Dun in China, of Johannes Brecher in East Germany, and of Han Sorya in North Korea.[14]

The experience of fascism marked a second trajectory. The earliest proletarian literary movements to appear outside the Soviet Union—those in Japan and Germany—came to world attention in the middle 1920s before being crushed by fascist and authoritarian regimes in the early 1930s.[15] The vibrant left-wing cultural worlds of Weimar Germany and Taisho Japan had developed out of dramatic alliances between modernist intellectuals and young working-class writers, spurring passionate debates over the shape of a revolutionary or proletarian novel (like the debates in *Die Linkskurve* sparked by Lukács over the novels of Bredel and Ottwalt), and producing

---

[14] In China, the radical literary movement emerged out of two moments: the cultural renaissance associated with the student May 4 movement of 1919 and the turn to the Marxist left following the suppression of the Shanghai strikes of 1927. A number of left literary circles and journals appeared in the late 1920s, most notably the League of Left Writers, founded in Shanghai in 1930, and led by Lu Xun, a key figure of the New Culture movement of 1919. Its major figures, including Mao Tun (1896–1981) and Ding Ling (1904–86), became central literary figures in the early People's Republic after the victory of the communists in 1949. See Tang Tao, ed., *History of Modern Chinese Literature* (Beijing: Foreign Languages Press, 1993); Liu Kang, *Aesthetics and Marxism: Chinese Aesthetic Marxists and Their Western Contemporaries* (Durham, N.C.: Duke University Press, 2000). The Korean proletarian literary movement began among Korean students studying in Japan in the early 1920s; the Korean Proletarian Art Federation (KAPF) was founded in 1925. See Brian Myers, *Han Sorya and North Korean Literature: The Failure of Socialist Realism in DPRK* (Ithaca, N.Y.: Cornell University East Asia Series, 1994); Kim Yoon-Shik, "Phases of Development of Proletarian Literature in Korea," *Korea Journal* 27.1 (January 1987): 31–36.

[15] In Japan, the strike wave of 1917–19 had led to the formation of the Japanese Socialist League in 1920, and an explosion of Marxist discussion and debate. The left-wing literary journal *Tanemaku hito* [*The Sower*] appeared in 1921, directly inspired by Barbusse's *Clarté*. Though it ceased publication during the crackdown on the left that followed the Tokyo earthquake in 1923, a successor journal, *Bungen sensen* [*Literary Arts Front*] appeared a year later, helping to organize the Japanese Proletarian Literary Arts League in 1925. The movement was crushed in the early 1930s, as writers were arrested and forced to issue a *tenko*, a disavowal of their politics. After the war, however, members of the proletarian writers' movement, like Nakano Shigeharu (1902–79), organized left-wing writers' groups that became a major force in Japanese literature. See Cecil H. Uyehara, "Proletarian Cultural Movement," in his *Left-Wing Social Movements in Japan: An Annotated Bibliography* (Tokyo: Charles Tuttle, 1959); G. T. Shea, *Leftwing Literature in Japan: A Brief History of the Proletarian Literary Movement* (Tokyo: Hosei University Press, 1964); Miriam Silverberg, *Changing Song: The Marxist Manifestos of Nakano Shigeharu* (Princeton, N.J.: Princeton University Press, 1990). In Germany, the League of Proletarian-Revolutionary Writers (BPRS) with its journal *Die Linkskurve* emerged in Weimar Germany as an alliance between former expressionist poets and playwrights and working-class writers in the orbit of the communist party; forced into exile by the Nazi regime, many of these writers became the core of an international antifascist cultural front. See Rühle, *Literature and Revolution*.

classic proletarian novels, like Tokunaga Sunao's (1899–1958) *The Street without Sun*, which was translated into German in 1930 and into Spanish in 1931. Fascism extinguished this culture—Kobayashi Takiji (1903–33) became a martyr of the international proletarian literature movement when he was arrested and tortured to death in 1933—forcing it underground and into exile. For these movements, the resistance to fascism became a central literary topoi, displacing the factory and tenement novels of earlier years: one sees this in Anna Seghers's enormously popular novel of the antifascist underground, *Das Siebte Kreuz* (*The Seventh Cross*, 1942), written and published in exile.

After the defeat of fascism, the experience of the resistance, as well as the story of collaboration, haunted the work of left-wing writers who revived the energies of the proletarian literary movement under the new slogans of "neorealism," and "committed" or "engaged" literature. In Italy, where the early rise of fascism had prevented a proletarian literary movement from emerging out of the factory occupations of 1919, a "neorealism" in fiction and film—closely connected to the cultural prestige of the postwar communist party—created new modes of representing working-class life, in such works as Vasco Pratolini's *Cronache de poveri amanti* (*A Tale of Poor Lovers*, 1947) and Cesare Pavese's *La luna e i falao* (*The Moon and the Bonfire*, 1950). Neorealism had a powerful impact throughout the Mediterranean, on the Iberian penisula, and in Latin America. Even though, when Iberian fascism gave way in the the early 1970s, the great left-wing writers of Spain and Portugal, Juan Goytisolo and José Saramago, seemed more in the tradition of Latin American magical realism, echoes of Mediterranean neorealism persisted: indeed Goytisolo's early novels of the 1950s were written in that tradition.[16]

The third trajectory of the proletarian literary movement was that of the creole nations of the Americas, where neither communism nor fascism came to power, but where communist movements of varying strengths found themselves facing nationalist, populist regimes ruling societies whose proletariats were colored by the ethnic and racial legacies of slavery, Indian conquest, and the recruitment of immigrant labor. American proletarian literary movements developed in the early 1930s, in the face of the Great Depression and political leaders like Roosevelt (United States), Cárdenas (Mexico), Vargas

---

[16] Margarida Lieblich Losa, "From Realist Novel to Working-Class Romance: An Introduction to the Study of the Brazilian, Italian, and Portuguese New Social Realist Novel, 1930–1955, in Light of New Critical Theory on Realism, Fiction and Reader-Response" (Ph.D. diss., New York University, 1989).

(Brazil), and Perón (Argentina), who attempted to incorporate insurgent labor movements into populist parties.[17] If left-wing writers of the Americas were at turns bitterly hostile and deeply sympathetic to these New Deals and Estavo Novos, they also inherited the messianic exceptionalism and cultural inferiority complex that characterized settler societies. Thus, they, like the celebrated Mexican muralists, helped to constitute a national imaginary of the "people" by importing European modernisms, reviving American folk traditions, and adopting the proletarian musics of the New World metropolises: jazz, samba, son, and tango.

The "proletarian" novels of the young American radicals often proved indistinguishable from the emergence of "regional" or "ethnic" fiction: "Negro writers," Richard Wright wrote in his classic "Blueprint for Negro Writers," "must accept the nationalist implications of their lives, not in order to encourage them but in order to change and transcend them."[18] The renaissance of African-American writing in the United States—from Claude McKay and Langston Hughes through Richard Wright and Ralph Ellison to Gwendolyn Brooks and Paule Marshall—grew out of a host of left-wing black writers' organizations and created links with radical black writers in

---

[17] In the United States, the John Reed Clubs and magazines like the *New Masses* brought together young modernists like Dos Passos, Josephine Herbst, and John Steinbeck (whose epic tale of southwestern migrant farmworkers, *The Grapes of Wrath*, 1939, became internationally known) with a generation of plebian writers, children of a largely immigrant working class, including Pietro di Donato, Tillie Olsen, and Henry Roth. In the Andean republics, Ecuador's Guayaquil Group, including Enrique Gil Gilbert, Joaquin Gallegos Lara, and Demetrio Aguilera Malta, launched radical writing with the celebrated collection, *Los que se van*, and the historic 1922 general strike and massacre became the subject of Gallegos Lara's *Cruces sobre el agua* [*Crosses on the Water*] (1946). In Brazil, proletarian writing became associated with the "novel of the Northeast," including the works of Rachel de Queiroz (1910–), Graciliano Ramos (1892–1953), and Jorge Amado (1912–). All three were imprisoned at various points in the 1930s. De Queiroz had been a member of the communist party in 1931 but was expelled for Trotskyist sympathies; both Amado and Graciliano Ramos joined the communist party during the war years. If Amado was to become Brazil's most widely read novelist, Graciliano Ramos's brief and stark novel of refugees, *Vidas secas* [*Barren Lives*] (1938), stands as a landmark of Brazilian modernism. Like Brazil, Chile had a strong communist and Marxist tradition, based in the militant nitrate miners of the north and figured by the great poet Pablo Neruda; the election of Latin America's only Popular Front government in 1938 marked the emergence of a slightly younger "generation of 1938," which included the proletarian novelists Nicomedes Guzmán (1914–64) and Volodia Teitelboim (1916–), both of whom wrote novels of the nitrate mines. See Michael Denning, *The Cultural Front: The Laboring of American Culture in the Twentieth Century* (London: Verso, 1997); Martin, *Journeys through the Labyrinth*; Lon Pearson, *Nicomedes Guzmán: Proletarian Author in Chile's Literary Generation of 1938* (Columbia: University of Missouri Press, 1976).

[18] Richard Wright, "Blueprint for Negro Writing," *New Challenge* 2.2 (Fall 1937): 58.

the Caribbean: Hughes translated and rallied support for the imprisoned Haitian Jacques Roumain. In the Andean republics, proletarian writing fused with the tradition of *indigenista* novels in César Vallejo's widely read novel of Indian miners, *El tungsteno*, and Jorge Icaza's *Huasipungo* (*The Villagers*, 1934). In Brazil, Jorge Amado's cycle of six "novels of Bahia" ranged from cocoa plantations to the waterfront of Salvador and put black culture at the heart of Brazil. It included *Jubiabá* (1935), a popular tale of a black boxer who becomes the leader of a stevedores' strike.

The fourth kind of proletarian literary movement emerged in the Asian and African colonies of the European empires. Small left-wing, anticolonial writers' groups emerged among students in both imperial and colonial cities in the 1930s, as strikes and popular uprisings not only registered anticolonial ferment but became the subject of early novels like Mulk Raj Anand's *Coolie* (based on a 1935 Bombay textile strike) and Thein Pe Myint's *Thabeik-hmauk kyaung-tha* (*The Student Boycotter*, 1938), based on the 1936 Rangoon student strike. The imperial crisis created by the Second World War and the subsequent era of national liberation struggles—the age of three worlds—turned these small groups into major cultural movements. The All India Progressive Writers Association, conceived in London in the mid-1930s by the émigré writers Sajjad Zaheer and Mulk Raj Anand and founded at the 1936 Lucknow conference (addressed by Prem Chand [1880–1936], South Asia's equivalent of Gorky or Lu Xun, just before his death), became a powerful force in postindependence Indian culture; though Anand's novels in English received the most attention outside India, the left-wing literary movement influenced writers in many South Asian languages throughout the age of three worlds and was a major force for literatures in Bengali, Malayalam (particularly the figure of Thakazhi Sivasankara Pillai), and Urdu (including figures like Zaheer, Ismat Chugtai, Sa'adat Hasan Manto, and the poet Faiz Ahmad Faiz). Similarly, Indonesia's LEKRA (*Lembaga Kebudayaan Rakyat*, Institute for People's Culture), formed in 1950 and suppressed in 1965, was a key institution in developing a radical postindependence culture, figured in the work of Pramoedya Ananta Toer (who also translated Gorky's *Mother* into Indonesian in 1956).[19]

---

[19] On India, see Priyamvada Gopal, "Midnight's Labors: Gender, Nation and Narratives of Social Transformation in Transitional India, 1932–1954" (Ph.D. diss., Cornell University, 2000); Sudhi Pradhan, ed., *Marxist Cultural Movement in India* (volume 1, Calcutta: National Book Agency, 1979; volume 2, Calcutta: Navana, 1982; volume 3, Calcutta: Pustak Bipani, 1985); and Carlo Coppola, ed., *Marxist Influences and South Asian Literature*, 2 vols. (East Lansing: Michigan State University Asian Studies Center, 1974). For Indonesia, see Keith Foulcher, *Social Commitment in Literature and the Arts: The Indonesian Insititute of People's Culture 1950–1965*

After the Bandung conference of 1955, these literary movements of decolonization began to create a new novelists' international—"the links that
bind us," in the words of Ngugi wa Thiong'o—through a series of Afro-Asian
writers' congresses and journals (particularly *Lotus*, published in Cairo beginning in 1967).[20] The novels by this generation of writers enfranchised by
the proletarian literary movements often became the founding fictions of the
new national literatures: for example, Pramoedya's *Perburuan* (*The Fugitive*,
1950), the tale of an underground fighter appearing as a beggar in his home

---

(Monash University Center for Southeast Asian Studies, 1986); Keith Foulcher, "Literature,
Cultural Politics, and the Indonesian Revolution," in D. M. Roskies, ed., *Text/Politics in Island
Southeast Asia* (Athens: Ohio University Center for International Studies, Southeast Asia Series
Number 91, 1993). Proletarian literary movements emerged throughout Southeast Asia, including
the Marxist Thakin movement in Burma, the Angkatan Sasterawan 50 founded in Singapore, and
the Philippine Writers League, organized in 1939: see Anna J. Allott, "Continuity and Change
in the Burmese Literary Canon," in David Smyth, ed., *The Canon in Southeast Asian Literatures*
(Richmond, Surrey: Curzon, 2000); Robert H. Taylor, *Marxism and Resistance in Burma 1942–1945*
(Columbus: Ohio State University, 1984); Tham Seong Chee, ed., *Essays on Literature and Society
in Southeast Asia* (Singapore University Press, 1981); Manuel E. Arguilla et al., eds., *Literature
under the Commonwealth* (Manila: Philippine Writers' League, 1940); Milagros Guerrero,
"Proletarian Consciousness in Philippine Literature, 1930–1970," in Wang Gungwu, M. Guerrero,
and D. Marr, eds., *Society and the Writer: Essays on Literature in Modern Asia* (Canberra:
Australian National University Press, 1981); E. San Juan, *Towards a People's Literature: Essays in
the Dialectics of Praxis and Contradiction in Philippine Writing* (Quezon City: University of the
Philippines Press, 1984). In the British Caribbean, the impulse dates from the circle around C.L.R.
James and *The Beacon* in the early 1930s but reaches a flowering in the figures of the early 1950s:
George Lamming, Roger Mais, and V. S. Reid, among others. In the French Caribbean, the major
figures include the poet Aimé Césaire and the novelist Edouard Glissant. See Hazel V. Carby,
"Proletarian or Revolutionary Literature? C.L.R. James and the Politics of the Trinidadian Renais-
sance," in her *Cultures in Babylon* (London: Verso, 1999); and Selwyn R. Cudjoe, *Resistance and
Caribbean Literature* (Athens: Ohio University Press, 1980). In Africa, Peter Abrahams was the
pioneering figure among writers in English, and Ousmane Sembène among writers in French.
See Chidi Amuta, *The Theory of African Literature* (London: Zed Books, 1989); George M.
Gugelberger, ed., *Marxism and African Literature* (Trenton, N.J.: Africa World Press, 1985); and
Neil Lazarus, *Resistance in Postcolonial African Fiction* (New Haven, Conn.: Yale University Press,
1990). In West Asia and North Africa, there were major left-wing literary movements in Turkish
literature, whose key figures include the poet Nazim Hikmet and the novelist Yashar Kemal, and in
Arabic, where the socialist ideas of Salamah Musa had a powerful impact on a generation of young
social realists in the 1940s, including Naguib Mahfouz. See Yashar Kemal, *On His Life and Art*
(Syracuse, N.Y.: Syracuse University Press, 1999); M. M. Badawi, ed., *Modern Arabic Literature*
(Cambridge: Cambridge University Press, 1992); and Edward Said, "After Mahfouz," in *Reflections
on Exile and Other Essays* (Cambridge, Mass.: Harvard University Press, 2000).

[20] Ngugi wa Thiong'o, "The Links That Bind Us," was an address to the 1973 Afro-Asian
Writers' conference, reprinted in his *Writers in Politics* (London: Heinemann, 1981). See also
Akram Aminov, "Afro-Asian Writers' Movement in its 15th Year," *Freedomways* 12.3 (1972).

village in the final hours of the struggle against Japanese occupation, adopts the outline of the traditional Javanese shadow-puppet play to narrate an allegory of resistance and collaboration.

The culmination of the proletarian literary movements in the decolonizing world might thus be seen in the grand trilogies and tetralogies of the age of three worlds: Miguel Angel Asturias's Banana trilogy, which encompasses the entire world of United Fruit, culminating in a banana workers' strike (Asturias won both of the competing prizes of the Cold War, the Nobel and the Lenin); Naguib Mahfouz's Cairo trilogy, a generational saga that narrates Egyptian society and politics from 1917 to 1944 through a single family, eventually divided between rival brothers, the communist Ahmad and the Muslim Brother Abd al-Munim; and Pramoedya Ananta Toer's Buru Quartet, composed in prison, an epic of Indonesian nationalism in the early twentieth century, told through the life of Minke, a fictional portrait of the nationalist journalist, Tirto Adi Suryo.[21]

Forms

Given this diversity of proletarian literary movements, are there any common modes, forms, or genres? At first, it seems unlikely, given the multitude of linguistic, literary, religious, political, ethnic, and national traditions from which the "proletarian" or "progressive" writers came. On the other hand, unlike many novelists around the world, these writers held an explicitly internationalist aesthetic ideology; they sought links across continents and actively translated each other. The novelists' international certainly imagined the possibility of common forms and modes, and attempted to develop them. Nevertheless, here my conclusions are tentative, based on a mere sampling of the novels, mostly in translation, and on a survey of the critical studies of proletarian literature traditions.

---

[21] Miguel Angel Asturias's *Viento fuerte* (1949), *El papa verde* (1954), *Los ojos de los enterrados* (1960); Naguib Mahfouz's *Bayn al-Qasrayn* (1956), *Qasr al-Shawq* (1957), *al-Sukkariyya* (1957); Pramoedya Ananta Toer's *Anak semua bangsa* (1980), *Bumi manusia* (1981), *Jejak langkah* (1985), *Rumah kaca* (1988). Similar multivolume novels that are written in this period by inheritors of the left-wing writers' movements include the Anatolian village trilogy of Turkish novelist Yashar Kemal—*Ortadirek* (1960), *Yer Demir Gök Bakir* (1963), *Ölmez otu* (1968)—and the Rosario saga of Filipino writer F. Sionel José—*The Pretenders* (1962), *Tree* (1978), *My Brother, My Executioner* (1979), *Mass* (1982), *Po-on* (1984).

It is fair to say that if the masterplot of Soviet socialist realism—the production novel with its heroic militants—informed the officially sanctioned literatures of the communist states, it had little presence in the genealogies of proletarian or engaged fiction elsewhere. Indeed, novels of militants and organizers were relatively rare, and those written were not particularly successful. Could one synthesize the realism of the novel with an engaged, agitational stance? The classical Marxist tradition, represented in these years by Lukács, was skeptical, and argued for realism at the expense of agitation. Gorky had pulled it off in *Mother*, making revolutionary organizers central characters; but perhaps it only worked if working-class or anticolonial struggles reshaped a society's history, if the organizers and militants became, in Lukács's sense, typical. It was more common for militants and organizers to be secondary characters, providing guidance like the donor in folktales.

Rather, two kinds of works quickly emerged: novels of, to use the capitalized personifications of Pietro di Donato's *Christ in Concrete*, Job and Tenement.[22] Representing the factory and its collective laborer was not only a central formal and political challenge, but it offered a microcosm, a knowable community that might found a new realism. "There are no heroes in this work—no leading characters or persons such as you would find in works dealing with the lives of individuals," Kobayashi Takiji wrote about his *Kani Kosen*, a landmark of Japanese proletarian literature, banned in Japan and translated around the world. "The collective hero is a group of laborers. . . . I have rejected all attempts at depicting character or delving into psychology."[23] The narrative is a sequence of incidents in the daily life of the factory ship, culminating in a strike.

The strike narrative becomes, not surprisingly, a core element in these works, representing the interruption in daily life—a festival of the oppressed—that creates a story. Certain actual historical strikes—the 1927 Shanghai strikes and the 1929 Gastonia (U.S.) textile strike, for example—became the subject for a cluster of novels. If the strike is often defeated, it is because it stands as a figure for a promised revolution. In the early, simpler novels, the strike serves as the climax, often meriting only a few pages; by Ousmane Sembène's *Les bouts de bois de Dieu* [*God's Bits of Wood*] (1960),

---

[22] It is striking that the two novels by Willi Bredel that were the subject of Lukács's famous critique were a factory novel and a tenement novel. See Georg Lukács, "The Novels of Willi Bredel," in Lukács, *Essays on Realism* (Cambridge, Mass.: MIT Press, 1981).

[23] Kobayashi Takiji, *The Factory Ship, and The Absentee Landlord*, trans. Frank Motofuji (Seattle: University of Washington Press, 1973), xvii–xviii.

the strike (a fictional account of the 1947–48 railway strike in French West Africa) becomes the subject of the entire novel, its own form of daily life and struggle, a totality that encompasses not a single workplace but an entire land connected by the railway.

The other formal option was to represent the tenement, the crowded and chaotic collective households of urban workers that spilled out into the streets of proletarian quarter. "When I think," Michael Gold wrote, "it is the tenement thinking."[24] A few of the radical writers—following the celebrated examples of Dos Passos and Döblin—attempted to write what might be called the novel of the metropolis by juxtaposing the workers' districts to the city of the bourgeoisie. In Mao Dun's sprawling portrait of Shanghai, *Midnight*, an omniscient narrator tries to weave together the family sagas of silk factory owners and workers; in Patrícia Galvão's brief and staccato montage of São Paulo street life, an omniscient editor splices together maps, statistics, conversations, and speeches under chapter headings like "In a Sector of the Class Struggle," "Where Surplus Value Is Spent," and "Where They Talk about Rosa Luxemburg."

But the novel of the metropolis was far outnumbered by the novel of the ghetto, the tale of working-class districts isolated from the "city," that is to say, the commercial districts whose department stores, skyscrapers, and theaters served as emblems of modernity. Early twentieth-century socialist and communist subcultures were usually found in class-isolated mining and textile towns, and the class-segregated urban waterfronts and metal-working districts, and this became the characteristic landscape of the proletarian novel: Johannesburg's Malay Camp in Peter Abrahams's narrative of a South African miner, *Mine Boy*; the immigrant patchwork of New York's Lower East Side in the novels of Michael Gold and Henry Roth; or a single street like Florence's Via del Corno—"fifty yards long and five wide"—in Vasco Pratolini's *A Tale of Poor Lovers*. Often, the protagonist of these novels was not an adult worker, but a child growing up in the streets and tenements. Equally common were accounts of the intellectual outsider watching and learning from the life of the "barrack-yards," as in C.L.R. James's *Minty Alley*.

Both of these modes were forms of subaltern modernism, as writers abandoned established family plots and the individual bildungsroman to create an experimental collective novel based on documentary and reportage (both

---

[24] Michael Folsom, ed., *Mike Gold: A Literary Anthology* (New York: International Publishers, 1972), 64–65.

terms were coined in this period). This impulse continued throughout the age of three worlds, manifesting itself in the aesthetic of neorealism—in fiction and film—at midcentury, and then in the testimonial literature of the 1960s and 1970s.[25] However, these often powerful documentary portraits of factory and tenement were, like many modernist fictions, curiously ahistorical, and rarely produced the temporal and spatial sweep of grand historical fiction or generational epics. A larger historical sensibility first emerged among the proletarian writers with the resistance narratives of antifascist and anticolonial wars, but it fully developed in the novels that grew out of the recognition that the new proletarians of the century were not simply factory workers and tenement dwellers, but were migrants from the countryside.

The worldwide migration from country to city was one of the central historical events of the age of three worlds: as Eric Hobsbawm writes, "the most dramatic and far-reaching social change of the second half of this century . . . is the death of the peasantry. . . . With the exception of Britain, peasants and farmers remained a massive part of the occupied population even in industrialized countries until well into the twentieth century." In 1940, Hobsbawm notes, there were only two countries—England and Belgium—where farmers were less than 20 percent of the population; in Latin America, peasants were a majority at the end of World War Two. But by the 1980s, farmers constituted less than 10 percent of the population in almost all the countries of Western Europe, and peasants were a minority throughout most of Latin America. "In Japan . . . , farmers were reduced from 52.4 percent of the people in 1947 to 9 percent in 1985."[26] Like the Leninist communisms of the twentieth century that inspired them, the proletarian literary movements were hybrid concoctions, at once peasant and proletarian, completely entangled in this worldwide migration. Many of the novelists were themselves products of the migration, peasant children who moved to cities for work or education, or the city-bred children of peasant migrants.

---

[25] It is beyond the scope of this essay, but it is worth noting the profound impact this literary movement had on world film, from postwar Italian neorealism and the noir films of the Hollywood left to the various new cinema movements of the third world. The new Indian cinema of Satyajit Ray, Ritwik Ghatak, and Mrinal Sen was closely connected to the Marxist cultural movement; the Brazilian *cinema novo* followed the radical novelists in filming the Northeast, with Nelson Pereira dos Santos filming Graciliano Ramos's novel, *Vidas secas*; and Ousmane Sembène moved from the novel to become one of Africa's leading directors.

[26] Eric Hobsbawm, *The Age of Extremes: A History of the World, 1914–1991* (New York: Vintage Books, 1996), 289–91.

Thus, in the decades after the initial factory novels of the proletarian avant-garde, the social and cultural uprooting that accompanied the migration from rural villages to the vast proletarian metropoles became the key historical experience behind the works of the novelists' international. At times it took the form of a quasi-autobiographical tale of a young man, as in the trans-Pacific migration of the Filipino proletarian novelist Carlos Bulosan, recounted in his *America Is in the Heart* (1944), or the migration of the student nationalist Minke from a Javanese village to the port city of Surabaya and the capital city of Batavia that structures Toer's *Buru Quartet*. At other times, it becomes the quasi-epic saga of a migrant family: John Steinbeck's *The Grapes of Wrath* (1939) narrates the exodus of a southwestern Dust Bowl family to California's "factories in the fields," and Harriette Arnow's *The Dollmaker* (1954) follows an Appalachian hill family to the war plants of Detroit. The migration was present even if it was not directly represented: it was the subtext to the contemporary murder mysteries that structure Richard Wright's *Native Son* and Ngugi wa Thiong'o's *Petals of Blood*.

The contemporary experience of migration is one reason why many of the earliest proletarian novels were actually novels of the peasantry, like Jacques Roumain's *Gouverneurs de la rosée* (*Masters of the Dew*, 1944) or the Brazilian novels of the "Northeast." "The urban masses are, on the whole, only rarely the central focus of Latin American narrative," one literary historian notes, and even the radical self-consciously "proletarian" writers often represented those who, metaphorically, stood between the peasantry and the urban working classes: rural proletarians like miners, plantation workers, sharecroppers, and tenant farmers. Mining novels, sugar novels, banana novels (including Asturias's classic Banana trilogy) became entire genres in the middle decades of the twentieth century.[27]

When the radical writers turned to historical fiction, they also returned to the countryside, writing narratives of the epoch Marx had called "primitive accumulation." In his classic *Terras do sem fim* (*The Violent Land*, 1942), Jorge Amado turned away from the proletarian naturalism of his early novels to fashion a historical romance of the founding of the cacao plantations, a "land fertilized with human blood": "It was the last great struggle in connection with conquest of the land, and the most ferocious of them all. For this reason it has remained a living reality down the years, the stories concerning it passing from mouth to mouth. . . . At the fairs in the towns and

[27] Martin, *Journeys through the Labyrinth*, 376n.11. See also Joe Lockard, " 'Sugar Realism' in Caribbean Fiction," *Journal of Commonwealth and Postcolonial Studies* 2.1 (Fall 1994): 80–103.

the cities blind musicians sing of these gun-frays which once upon a time drenched with blood the black land of cacao."[28]

Out of the clash of peasant and proletarian worlds came the most powerful new form to emerge from the proletarian literary movements, magical or marvelous realism. Though magical realism is often considered as a successor and antagonist to social realism, its roots lay in the left-wing writers' movements. The idea and practice of magical realism was developed by two left-wing novelists from the Carribean and Central America, the Cuban Alejo Carpentier (1904–80) and the Guatamalan Miguel Angel Asturias (1899–1974), both of whom had been briefly imprisoned as young radicals in their native countries and both of whom were influenced by the communist surrealists during periods of exile in Paris. Carpentier's notion of *"lo real maravilloso"* was an explicit attempt to capture the temporal dislocations, the juxtapostion of different modes of life, mythic and the modern, that had resulted from a history of conquest, enslavement, and colonization. "What is the entire history of America if not a chronicle of the marvelous real?" he asked in the 1949 preface to *El reino de este mundo* (*The Kingdom of This World*) where he coined the phrase; the novel that followed was a tale of the Haitian revolution, a central turning point in that history, and a narrative that the proletarian writers often retold.[29]

The magical realism of Carpentier and Asturias is perhaps best seen as a second stage of the proletarian avant-garde: if the first moment in the wake of the upheavals of 1917–19 was dominated by a paradoxically ahistorical modernism that tried to document the lived experience of radically new factory and tenement (Chaplin's *Modern Times*), the magical realism of 1949 is the return of the repressed history—lived and witnessed by the exiles and migrants—and the consequent insistence on the specific reality of the colonized world at the moment of liberation in India, Indonesia, and China, a moment that finds its historical precursor not in the French Revolution (as the bolshevicks did) but in the Haitian revolution.

If this is true, then one can see why the notion of magical realism resonates far beyond the Caribbean islands and coasts where it began. The term comes to represent a larger shift in the aesthetic of the novelists' international from the powerful censoring of desire in the early novels—for the

---

[28] Jorge Amado, *The Violent Land*, trans. Samuel Putnam (New York: Alfred A. Knopf, 1945), 333, 249–50.

[29] Alejo Carpentier, "On the Marvelous Real in America," in Lois Parkinson Zamora and Wendy B. Faris, eds., *Magical Realism: Theory, History, Community* (Durham, N.C.: Duke University Press, 1995), 88.

works of the epoch of worldwide depression are novels of lack, of hunger (the utopian novel is rare, and Louis Aragon's earlier move from surrealist desire to the socialist realism of his aptly named cycle *Le monde réel* is emblematic)—to an unleashing of desire and utopia, foreshadowing the liberation ideologies of the New Left (this is why it is common to see magical realism as the antithesis of an earlier social realism). One can see the shift in individual writers: in Brazil, Amado remains loyal to the communist left while creating a fictional equivalent of carnival, beginning with *Gabriela, carvo e canela* (*Gabriela, Clove, and Cinnamon*, 1958); in Egypt, Naguib Mahfouz turned from the urban realism and generational saga of his Cairo trilogy to a series of allegorical tales on the betrayal of the 1952 revolution, beginning with *Awlad haratina* (*The Children of Our Quarter*, 1959). It is also evident in the work of the left-wing writers of the postfascist Iberian penisula, Juan Goytisolo and José Saramago, in the turn to surrealism and magical realism in the post-1965 Indonesian novel of figures like Iwan Simatupang, and in the work of the contemporary English-language inheritor of the Marxist traditions of India's Kerala, Arundhati Roy.

Magical realism finds its most celebrated avatar in Gabriel García Márquez's *Cien años de soledad*. The 1967 novel, part of the celebrated Boom in Latin American fiction, came to stand for the moment of third-world hopefulness in the wake of decolonization, the 1955 Bandung conference, and the 1959 Cuban revolution, peaking at the Havana cultural congress of 1968, a moment that died with the coups in Brazil (1964), Indonesia (1965), and Chile (1973). The literary analogue of the 1960s "dependency theory" of Latin American Marxists, *Cien años de soledad* is a tale of primitive accumulation and desire, of the origins of the capitalist world system with its wonders and its monsters; the house of the Buendías is neither factory nor tenement. Nevertheless, it could be said to contain the classic proletarian novel, for at its heart lies a strike story. The climax of the novel—"the events that would deal Macondo its fatal blow"—is directly based on the 1928 strike by Colombian banana workers against United Fruit, and the subsequent massacre of the workers by government troops. The curious nature of García Márquez's strike sequence suggests that *Cien años de soledad* is both the culmination and overturning of the half-century of the proletarian literary movements.[30]

---

[30] Gabriel García Márquez, *One Hundred Years of Solitude*, trans. Gregory Rabassa (New York: HarperPerennial, 1992), 315. I am indebted to the discussions in Gene H. Bell-Villada, "Banana Strike and Military Massacre: *One Hundred Years of Solitude* and What Happened in 1928," in his *Gabriel García Márquez's* One Hundred Years of Solitude: *A Casebook* (New York: Oxford University Press, 2002); and Franco Moretti, "Epilogue: *One Hundred Years of Solitude*," in his *Modern Epic: The World-System from Goethe to García Márquez* (London: Verso, 1996).

In 1928, the strike might have inspired one of the original proletarian novels; for García Márquez, a generation later (he was born the year of the strike), it is a history suppressed by the "official version . . . : there were no dead, the satisfied workers had gone back to their families." The strike stands not as a figure for future revolution, but for social amnesia, as it is swept away in the torrential five-year rains that bring ruin to Macondo: "Nothing has happened in Macondo, nothing had ever happened, and nothing ever will happen." Indeed, the strike has a contradictory place in the novel, at once central and marginal, memorialized in a single brief chapter, a climax that is forgotten by nearly every character. There is no preparation for the strike, and the massacre seems to take its place among the myriad magical events that constitute Macondo's reality. Unlike Asturias in his Banana trilogy, García Márquez makes no effort to represent either United Fruit or the banana workers; the only link between the strike and the novel's larger narrative is that one of the more "colorless" and anonymous Buendías—José Arcadio Segundo—becomes a leader of the strikers and the sole survivor of the massacre, keeping its memory alive.[31]

Thus, *Cien años de soledad* stands as both a sign of the crisis in the literary desire to represent workers that had animated a generation of plebian writers, and an attempt to bear witness to that desire. On the one hand, not only does García Márquez not represent the banana workers; he testifies to the "hermeneutical delirium" in which "by a decision of the court it was established and set down in solemn decrees that the workers did not exist." On the other hand, García Márquez, like the child witness to the massacre, continues to recount the tale "to the disbelief of all."[32] Nearly a century after the first calls for an international "proletarian literature" and "socialist realism," that desire seems not only defeated, but nonexistent, unimaginable. Yet like the strike story in *Cien años de soledad,* the aspirations and aesthetics of the novelists' international remain the forgotten, repressed history behind the contemporary globalization of the novel.

---

[31] García Márquez, *One Hundred Years of Solitude*, 333, 320.
[32] Ibid., 324, 327.

ATO QUAYSON

Fecundities of the Unexpected: Magical Realism, Narrative, and History

> The manner of seeing is also a detail, the detail of a
> perspective.

Magical Realism, Unheimlich, and Violence

Even though there are several potential genealogies to be traced for the term
magical realism,[1] it is now generally agreed that its contemporary usage can
be attributed to the German art critic Franz Roh, in his 1925 introduction
to postexpressionist painting.[2] Roh's own term, the *Magischer Realismus*
(magic real), which he coined to describe the intense focus of the postexpressionists on a detailed evocation of reality, was itself gradually assimilated
in Germany to the term *Neue Sachlichkeit* (New Objectivity). By 1958, when
he published his *Geschichte der Deutschen Kunst von 1900 bis zur Gegen-
wart* (published in English as *German Art in the Twentieth Century*) he had
opted for the second term. But it is in his description of what he describes as
the magical real in painting that he laid the foundation for later usages of the
term. The central point in Roh's account is the idea that in paying close
attention to the minutiae of their painted objects, postexpressionists revealed a deeper layer behind the real. At various points Roh seems inspired
by images from the new scientific discussions of atomic structure, suggesting

---

[1] Though the genre of magical realism is mainly associated with Latin American writers and
Salman Rushdie, there is no doubt that it is a rapidly growing area and extends far beyond the
handful of texts normally used to exemplify it. Because of the limitations of this essay, however, I
shall be referring only to a clutch of authors and their works. This is necessary for purposes of organization. I hope that generalizations can fruitfully be made from the many examples I will try to
give. I would like to seize this opportunity to thank the many students of my "Magical Realism:
Postcolonialism and Postmodernism" lectures at Cambridge University over the past five years.

[2] One could for instance trace the concept to the romantic philosophy of Novalis, seeing in
romanticism generally the germ of a peculiarly "magically idealist" attitude to phenomenal reality.
Another possible route might be to look at the genre of medieval romance, taking as a starting
point the chivalric romance of Cervantes' *Don Quixote*, and then to see how the apparatus of
narrative magic gets gradually residualized in the process of the secularization of narrative form.
For a contextualization of Roh's term and its subsequent impact on definitions of magical realism,
see Irene Guenther's superb essay in Zamora and Faris (1995).

for instance that postexpressionism "offers us the miracle of existence in its imperturbable duration: the unending miracle of eternally mobile and vibrating molecules" and that this art admires and highlights the "enigma of total quietude in the midst of general becoming, of universal dissolution" (22). This reliance on scientific imagery is itself telling, for far from preaching a new form of mysticism in art, Roh is claiming that the invisible world is a part of the rational universe, only cursoriness preventing us from perceiving it in its fullness.

But it is to another idea underpinning Roh's account that I want to draw attention in setting out my own sense of the implications of magical realism for literature, narrative, and history. This is the often barely acknowledged assumption that the magical operates in a relation of hierarchical differentiation to the real, either behind, after, beneath, anterior to, or generally in a relation of secondariness to reality. In many ways this notion of the spatialized relations between reality and the magical is an effect of the language that we are obliged to use to describe something that is not easily discernible in reality. This is so primarily because we are often condemned to narrativize experience in terms of a sequence. But it is also due to certain forms of rational thinking, perhaps the main legacy of Enlightenment rationality, one of whose central impulses was to privilege rationality above all else and to dismiss anything that was not clearly submissible to the discourse of reason to the domain either of the evolutionarily backward or to the domain of that which had not been fully grasped in its rationality. As Johannes Fabian (1983) points out, it is this legacy that formally shaped the evolutionist tendencies in anthropology when it aspired to the status of a "science" in the early stages of its disciplinary formation. Enlightenment thinking helps to establish what Dipesh Chakrabarty in his essay "The Time of History and the Times of the Gods" (1997) has termed the disenchanted time of history, one that is opposed to a view of time as saturated with ghostly or spiritual significance. It is evident that magical realism disrupts any such easy hierarchies and oppositions, thereby generating problems for the language by which to describe it.

After the translation into Spanish of Roh's essay in Ortega y Gasset's *Revista de Occidente* in 1927, his notions were appropriated by Alejo Carpentier as a means to describe what he saw as the marvelous reality (*lo real maravilloso*) of the Americas. For Carpentier, America is the site of an ontological marvelous reality because of the mixing of cultures and imaginations that produces a particularly fertile kind of *criollo, mestisaje*, and hybrid existence. But hybridity for him is no mere issue of the mixing of races; it is the very fabric of existence itself, making it more extraordinary than anything to be found in literature. It is a marvelous reality encountered at every step. In his own *The Kingdom of the World* (1949), in which the prologue is dedicated to an elaboration of this reality, and subsequently in novels like Cortázar's *Hopscotch* (1963), Asturias's *Men of Maize* (1949) and Fuentes' *The Death of Artemio Cruz* (1964) and others, this key idea of a special reality is reaffirmed and provides the foundations for the development of the genre of magical realism.

The assertion of Latin America as being the privileged site of magical realism is one that is frequently echoed by critics who operate on the assumption that the Boom of Latin American writings in the 1960s marked the expression of a special form of literary sensibility that was postcolonial, counter to the protocols of Western realism, and thoroughly immersed in indigenous forms of storytelling (see, for a wide-ranging discussion, Martin 1989). Though this is hard to contest, it does not easily address the problem as to how to account for the mixture of fantastical with real elements in literatures from across the world and from different epochs, ranging from Cervantes' *Don Quixote* (1604) and the tradition of medieval romance, Shakespeare's *Hamlet* (1601) and *Macbeth* (1605–6), Bram Stoker's *Dracula* (1897), Tolkien's *Lord of the Rings* (1966), Amos Tutuola's ghostly stories from the 1950s, and the science fiction of Isaac Asimov from the 1960s and 1970s to name just a few eclectic examples.

All these can arguably be said to a combination of the fantastic and the real that contests any settled consensual realism, but the central distinction to be drawn between all these and magical realism proper is what I want to define as the principle of equivalence. For it is not that magical realism does not share elements of the fantastic with other genres, but that in confounding any simple or clear sense of spatial, ethical, or motivational hierarchies between the real and the fantastic, magical realism generates a scrupulous equivalence between the two domains. In an insightful essay first published in the late 1980s, Stephen Slemon (1995) notes that the term is essentially an oxymoron and marks a "battle" between two contrasting and mutually exclusive codes of representation. He identifies some of the implications of this:

> The term "magic realism" is an oxymoron, one that suggests a binary opposition between the representational code of realism and that, roughly, of fantasy. In the language of narration in a magic realist text, a battle between two oppositional systems takes place, each working toward the creation of a different kind of fictional world from the other. Since the ground rules of these two worlds are incompatible, neither one can fully come into being, and each

remains suspended, locked in a continuous dialectic with the "other," a situation which creates disjunction within each of the separate discursive systems, rending them with gaps, absences, and silences. (409)[3]

An important qualification has to be made to Slemon's definition here. This is to the idea that there is a "battle" between two oppositional discursive modalities. As we will see in our discussion, conceptualizing the two domains in terms of a battle raises serious problems about the equivalence that often governs the narrative relationship between them. It is better to speak of an interplay between the two representational regimes, with an equal emphasis on both parts of the word *inter/play*. The idea that they are in a battle undermines the notion of equivalence, since it implies that the reader is invited to switch sides in a shifting hierarchical relationship, either of an ethical, motivational, or indeed, spatial kind, between the real and the fantastic.

Another distinction to be made with regards to magical realism has to do not so much with the overlaps between magical realist devices and those of cognate areas as to the status of the uncanny within the genre. In Freud's 1919 essay on the subject he notes the curious observable overlap between *heimlich* (homeliness) and *unheimlich* (unhomeliness/uncanny). The uncanny is the unsettling recognition of the strange within something that is normally perceived as *heimlich* or ordinary. In his account the uncanny is assimilated primarily to a repressed memory, often a castration anxiety. This is one of the main observations he draws from his discussion of E.T.A. Hoffman's "The Sandman." Among other things he also notes the negative affect that attends our perception of objects that seem to combine human and nonhuman qualities (such as machines that seem to have human qualities or viceversa) and suggests that in this we see the potential for our own negation. Pushing these two elements a bit further, we might say in extending Freud that it is not only (a) the perception of blurring between man and machine or (b) the strength of a castration anxiety as it is assimilated to some aspect of reality that generates the sense of the uncanny, but, more generally, *the conversion of the perception of a systemic disorder into a negative affect.* In the face of persistent physical or social violence brought on either by acute

---

[3] By far the best collection on magical realism to date has been *Magical Realism: Theory, History, Community*, edited by Lois Parkinson Zamora and Wendy B. Faris (1995) in which they put together a broad range of essays on the genre spanning the earliest contemporary usage in Roh, Carpentier, Flores, and Leal to various explications of the term from different scholars and critics. As the collection shows, there have been many attempted definitions of the term, a detailed survey of which is beyond the scope of this essay but that could prove useful in itself.

political chaos or the general collapse of the social order there is an internal-
ization of these perceived disorders in terms either of guilt, an inexplicable
terror, or a general sense of disquiet which does not seem to have a clear
source. This idea finds some support in the work of psychoanalysts such
Gampel and others who have concentrated on social violence and the prevalence of the uncanny. For, as he notes from his wide-ranging clinical work
with survivors of the Holocaust and their children and from consultations
with children and adults undergoing traumatic situations in Israel, South
America, and the former Yugoslavia, people feel safe when they exist in a
constant social context, the feeling of uncanniness overwhelming them
when they are thrust into "a fragmented, violent social context, one without
any continuity and which transmits extremely paradoxical messages" (2000,
55). The effect of such acute social fragmentation varies, but predominantly
it involves various psychic mechanisms that define a breaking down of the integrated ego, with a new ego structure of an ambiguous nature formed in its
place (Bleger 1967; cited in Gampel). Under conditions of social dissolution, this ambiguous ego restructuring often takes place in a space between
anxiety and terror. This space is the space of the uncanny.

Two key features of magical realism need to be accounted for in relation
to the location of the uncanny. These are the general instability of the
perceived world, and the nature and range of the blurring of boundaries
between the animal and human worlds. In both cases we find that magical
realism normalizes what in other contexts would be patently abnormal and
deeply unsettling. Thus even though in the represented worlds of the texts,
anything can happen and instability and fragmentation are the norm, there
is no sense that this instability is a converted perception of systemic disorder. On the contrary, the instability and fragmentation produce what in
One Hundred Years of Solitude is referred to several times as a "penetrating
lucidity beyond the bounds of formalism" (40, 164, 202–4, 283). In other
words, the regular fragmentations are an invitation for us to look beyond
any settled norms of epistemological ontological forms, rather than as a
means of instituting a desire for normality, however this may be defined.
The same applies to the examples of metamorphosis that we find in magical
realist texts. In cases such as Muriol Rubiao's *The Ex-Magician and Other
Stories* (1965) or Miguel Angel Asturias's *Men of Maize* (1949; of which
more later), metamorphoses and the blurring of boundaries between the
human and animal worlds are meant to suggest the harmony of heterogeneous life forms. They are rarely if ever the conversion of a perception of
systemic disorder.

A clear contrast, then, can be seen in the effects such blurrings between say Kafka's "Metamorphosis" and Robert Kroetsch's *What the Crow Said* (1978). Even though Márquez cites Kafka's story as an inspiration behind his work (1983, 48–49; see also Leal 1995), Kafka situates the uncanny in a completely different way than any of the magical realists I am aware of. When Gregor Samsa wakes up one morning to find himself transformed into a bug, he is progressively assimilated by the narrative to the category of the uncanny. This is particularly so in the eyes of his family members. In his own eyes, Gregor still has the central humane impulses that have presumably always defined him prior to his metamorphosis. Not so for his family. After the incident with the apples, in which one of them is lodged painfully in his back, his father has to force himself to suppress his disgust: "The serious injury done to Gregor, which disabled him for more than a month—the apple went on sticking in his body as a visible reminder since no one ventured to remove it—seemed to have made even his father recollect that Gregor was a member of the family, despite his present unfortunate shape, and ought not to be treated as an enemy, that, on the contrary, family duty required the suppression of disgust and the exercise of patience, nothing but patience" (Kafka, 45). The "ought" in his father's mind is precisely the signal of the near impossibility of suppressing his sense of the uncanny in the face of this metamorphosis. In a magical realist text the metamorphosis would have quickly been normalized by the family.

Significantly, however, Kafka also establishes a more complex discursive source for the uncanny in the story that goes beyond Gregor's unexpected metamorphosis. The family's confrontation with the metamorphosis is paralleled by our own recognition of the disabling conditions within which they have to exist. They are shown to be mired in the problems of survival and under the impress of unfavorable working conditions. We are encouraged to see Gregor's condition as the symbolization of a systemic disorder. The negative affectivity of this systemic disorder is captured in the malaise and emotional aridity brought on by the oppressive and mechanical forms of economic labor that members of the family have to struggle under. Their attitudes toward Gregor get progressively worse as they are inserted more deeply into the oppressive economic conditions. In fact, it is notable how his sister completely shirks her earlier responsibilities toward him once she gets engrossed in weaving the items for the shop in which she has found work. His metamorphosis, which at one level is a metaphor for an unexpected physical disability that his family members have to cope with, is simultaneously paralleled by the disabling conditions that figure their existence more generally.[4] The *unheimlich* of boundary blurring between the human and animal/insect worlds is then a dimension of a larger social disorder against which the family members futilely struggle. They are themselves like insects trapped in the webwork of economic oppression, Gregor's condition being the materialization in their midst of something that transcends their powers of comprehension. When at Gregor's death they grant themselves a tram journey in the open country and begin to imagine the brighter things that are available to them, the immediate relief is in the apparent recession of the uncanny. But because we are aware of its wider source, we can only conclude that this is an ironic ending that serves to merely temporarily conceal the sense of systemic disorder. For the struggles of survival under a dehumanizing capitalism will still remain to be contended with.

A contrastive handling of the blurring of boundaries between the human and the animal/insect worlds is provided in Kroetsch's *What the Crow Said*, where the description of the potentially uncanny and disconcerting rape of the young Vera by a swarm of bees is rendered in such an aestheticized way as to take it out of the domain of the uncanny. The narrator first speculates about "what her terror must have been at the soft caress of those touching bees; what ultimate desperation caught in her throat at the ferocious and innocent need of those homeless bees" something that it seems "she never told," thus leaving the matter of her response to the unusual event purely speculative (8). Later on, she is described as actively participating in an act that is simultaneously oppressive and pleasurable:

> Her eyelids were each a bee. Her armpits opened to the nuzzling bees. They found the spaces between her fingers, between her toes. Her body was not hers now, it moved with the surge of grass in the wind, a field of green oats, a flowering of clover. Her moving crushed the blue-purple petals of the crocus bed, broke the hairy stalks, the blossoms, into dizzying sweetness of her own

---

[4] It is useful with regards to the relationship between physical disability and magical realism to recall here Patrick Suskind's *Perfume* (1985). Suskind uses Grenouille's incredible powers of smell to define a sense of anomalousness rather than normality. This is so particularly as he also turns out to be a serial killer. Thus his fantastic power of smell is assimilated to a moral order of good and evil. This is further complicated by the fact that Grenouille is physically deformed and quite abominable in his appearance. With this Suskind falls into a tradition of reading physical disability as a sign of metaphysical disorder, something that has a long history in many cultures (see Linton 1997). Thus, contrary to the opinions expressed about the work in Wendy B. Faris's "Scheherezade's Children: Magical Realism and Postmodern Fiction" (1995), I would not regard *Perfume* as a magical realist text. The moral hierarchy that discursively defines Grenouille enjoins disgust and judgment rather than normalization.

desire. The hum of wings melded earth and sky into the thickness of her skin. She had no mind left for thinking, no fear, no dream, no memory. The bees had closed her mouth, her ears. The bees found the swollen lips between her thighs; she felt their intrusive weight and spread farther her legs.
Then she gave her cry. (11)

The passage defines a highly sensuous expressive field, full of color (the field of green oats, purple petals), with words suggestive of tactility (nuzzling, crushed, broke, melded) as well as of sounds (hum), all of which combine with the sense of her pleasure (dizzying sweetness, no mind left for thinking, no fear, no dreaming, etc.) such that the cry she gives at the end is orgasmically suspended between pleasure and pain. The main achievement of the passage is to aestheticize what should really be a highly disturbing experience, thus successfully assimilating a fantastic incident—her transformation into a queen bee—into a normal register of lovemaking. This aesthetic effect is not dissimilar from what Yeats achieves in "Leda and the Swan," mainly because what is an essentially uncanny occurrence (the rape of a young woman by a swan) is written so as to invite us to contemplate it as an aesthetic tableau amenable to multiple interpretations and irreducible to a code of the uncanny. In *What the Crow Said* this (rape? lovemaking?) is further normalized by virtue of the fact that Vera always refers lovingly to bees. The son she gives birth to from this encounter seems to be merely a lonely idiot with a speech defect that produces a buzzlike confusion of sounds. But this seeming idiocy is redeemed by his having the unusual ability to predict the turns of the weather, which for the largely agricultural community of Big Indian, makes him an indispensable member of the community.

Having noted these distinctions, however, we are also obliged to attend to the varying ways in which violence is registered in magical realist texts. Violence often relates to a wider political domain, which in itself is either rendered parodically, as is the case in *One Hundred Years of Solitude*, or as an apparently transcendental signified that is only partially assimilated to the magical domain of the genre. In such cases its nonassimilation puts it in relief in order to problematize and destabilize its assumed transcendental status. As we shall see, there are at least two ways in which the represented political discourse resists assimilation. First is when the systemic disorder engendered by political violence is not routed through the consciousness of any character but retains the essential features of the motor of history itself. Such is the case with Allende's *The House of Spirits*. The represented political domain institutes a historical causality but does not establish a direct relation to the magical real. In such cases the magical realist discourse transcends the ability of the political to become a motivational explanation for it. There is thus no direct conversion of a sense of systemic disorder into the affect of the uncanny. In Rushdie's *Midnight's Children*, on the other hand, a nonviolent but confusing political domain is the direct motivation of the magical real, but such that the political domain itself is continuously supplemented by a magical interpretation of history to the extent of being evacuated of any certifiable meaning. Thus when Saleem Sinai pauses from his narration to note that he has reported Gandhi's assassination on the wrong date, he refuses to correct it, suggesting that Gandhi's death was "untimely" anyway, and being untimely cannot be assigned to the correct date. Toni Morrison's *Beloved* (1987) stands between these two modes of assimilation of violence into the discourse of magical realism. In the novel the character of the spirit of Sethe's daughter is figured both as Sethe's repressed desire to escape her traumatic history and as a product of the systemic violence of slavery. Beloved is thus a supplement to the dangerous traumatic history of slavery. To a certain extent Toni Morrison's novel institutes a curious boundary confusion between the real and the esoteric, mainly because it for the most part naturalizes Beloved within the sphere of everyday domestic relations in the household of 124, even though she is the spirit of a two-year-old child killed by her mother who has returned now as an eighteen-year-old girl, but then moves to expose her as an ghostly and dangerous figure. She becomes almost imperceptibly but progressively uncanny until the people in the community come together to collectively exorcise her and free Sethe from her grip. In that sense *Beloved* starts off by producing equivalence between the real and the esoteric and then proceeds to privilege the real. This rehearses the movement of waking up from the nightmare of traumatic history, at the same time as suggesting that its essential contours will not easily go away. As the final, highly lyrical two pages of the novel tell us, the community decided on a strategic collective forgetting that was bound to fail: "So they forgot her. Like an unpleasant dream during a troubling sleep. Occasionally, however, the rustle of a skirt hushes when they wake, and the knuckles brushing a cheek in sleep seem to belong to the sleeper. Sometimes the photograph of a close friend or relative—looked at too long—shifts, and something more familiar than the dear face itself moves there. They can touch it if they like, but don't, because they know things will never be the same if they do" (275). The everyday become uncanny because of the return of the repressed of traumatic slave history.

In the rest of this essay I want to illustrate four narrative problems. I shall label them issue clusters for ease of reference. They will involve the following: (1) the implications of various boundary-blurring devices in magical realism; (2) the motivations behind the metaphorical/literality chain; (3) the representation of space and time in magical realism; and (4) magical realism and the implications for a philosophy of history. For each issue cluster I shall be drawing on specific texts, my main ones being Márquez's *One Hundred Years of Solitude*, Rushdie's *Midnight's Children*, Isabel Allende's *The House of Spirits*, and Ben Okri's *The Famished Road*, with many references to other texts. Finally, I shall spend a brief section discussing what might be thought to be the different sources of magical realism and whether, in considering these varying sources along with the various experiments in narrative form, we could describe a poetics of the genre. At all times I shall use the analysis of textual features to establish the hermeneutical and theoretical framework within which questions of the relationship between magical realism, narrative, and history will be discussed.

Issue Cluster 1: Generic Blurrings and the Status of the Real

Borges' preeminent standing in Latin American literature is acknowledged by both writers and critics. He was not a magical realist in the terms in which we describe it here, since in much of his work what was central was the production of secular parables. These were significant not for the secret or kernel they might be thought to conceal, but for their processual structures that enjoined a regular renegotiation of meanings. It is in fact this careful blurring of boundaries between form and content, between fiction and reality and between reader and character that provides the fertile ground for later explorations in both magical realism and postmodernism more generally. Borges' boundary blurrings were meant to indicate how tenuous our grasp is on what we call reality. Even the will-to-knowledge and the taxonomic impulse by which the world is organized are gently mocked by him. In his much-cited essay, "The Analytical Language of John Wilkins" (1964), he refers to the taxonomic organization to be found in "a certain Chinese encyclopedia" entitled *Celestial Emporium of Benevolent Knowledge*: "On these remote pages it is written that animals are divided into (a) those that belong to the Emperor, (b) embalmed ones, (c) those that are trained, (d) suckling pigs, (e) mermaids, (f) fabulous ones, (g) stray dogs, (h) those that are included in this classification, (i) those that tremble as if they were mad, (j) innumerable ones, (k) those drawn with a very fine hari brush, (l) others, (m) those that have just broken a flower vase, (n) those that resemble flies from a distance." What this points to is that all representations are dictated by certain conventions, simply because, as he puts it, "there is no classification of the universe that is not arbitrary and conjectural. The reason is very simple: we do not know what the universe is" (133–34).

This incredible taxonomic grid, which has itself been the object of a fascinating exploration in the preface to Foucault's *The Order of Things* (1970), finds an echo in Márquez's Nobel Prize acceptance speech in 1982. Márquez opens his speech with a reference to Antonio Pigafetta, a Florentine navigator who accompanied Magellan on the first circumnavigation of the world, and in whose log-book is recorded his observations about things seen in Southern America. These include "pigs with their umbilicus on their backs and birds without feet," "a monstrosity of an animal with the head and ears of a mule, the body of a camel, the hooves of a deer and the neigh of a horse" and the first native they met in Patagonia and "how that overexcited giant lost the use of his reason out of fear of his own image" (207). After a list of further fantastical observations, this time drawn from different chroniclers, Márquez goes on to point out that the reality of Latin America, "that great homeland of deluded men and historic women whose infinite stubbornness is confused with legend," makes fantastical things quite commonplace, such as the dizzying number of coups d'état, the number of children that die before the age of two (twenty million in the twelve years prior to his speech, he says) and the many tens of thousands that disappear without trace. He suggests that perhaps it is this unusual state of affairs that has attracted the attention of the Swedish Literary Academy. In other words, Márquez draws a direct parallel between his magical realist universe and the reality of Latin America, suggesting that not only does this have a long geneaology in chronicles of the region, but that it is being recognized as such by the august bodies in the rest of the world. We are reminded of the blurrings of Borges as well of the claim first made by Carpentier that Latin America is the supreme ontological cite of the *lo real maravilloso*.

In Borges, structural and generic blurrings are mirrored by blurrings at other levels of the text. "The Garden of Forking Paths" (1964) for example, is at various levels a spy thriller (of the fugitive spy Yu Tsun's attempt to escape Richard Madden to send a coded message to his masters in Germany during World War I), a quasi-gothic quest, a parable about labyrinths, and an oedipal story about the discovery and murder of a father-figure in the person of the sinologist Stephen Albert. It is told mainly by Yu Tsun and is supposed to be his signed statement. But it is in Borges' careful cultivation of "objectivity" that paradoxically the boundaries between fact and fiction are blurred. From the opening of the story there is reference to "page 22 of Liddell Hart's *History of World War I*" to which the story we read is supposed to be providing a corrective detail. This factual framing is further buttressed by a footnote on the bottom of the first page attributed to "the editor" hypothesizing on the murder motive of another spy not directly represented in the story. The footnote, however, immediately undermines the distance of the framing narrator, because it is essentially a partisan explanation of an event that we do not see for ourselves. But there is something more than this taking place. Essentially, the footnote and the device of objective framing have the effect of assimilating the paratextual apparatus enframing the story into the narrative text that unfolds slowly before our eyes.

This is reproduced at the level of the story itself, where the narrator, Yu Tsun, frequently pauses to make metanarrative philosophical observations about the events in which he is entangled. But given this discursive mirroring of the narrative impulses of "editor" and "narrator," how do we know who is really responsible for the story that unfolds before us? More important, what value do we assign to the words *For Victoria Ocampo* and *Translated by D.A.Y.* that appear at the bottom of the last page of the story? Because of the assimilation of the paratextual apparatus to the textual, these proper names themselves suddenly seem fictional. This then draws us in as readers into the domain of the various blurrings that have taken place in the course of the story, for if we cannot decide whether the proper names at the end of the story are part of reality or part of the fictional world, how do we know whether we as readers are ontologically real or merely fictional?

These generic and structural blurrings, which can be found in many of Borges' stories, are repeated in Márquez's *One Hundred Years of Solitude*. At one level the blurrings are dictated by the range of dizzying repetition of similar names across different generations. We encounter, time again, the following: José Arcadio Buendía, Aurieliano (and seventeen of his children, all male and all called Aureliano), José Arcadio, Arcadio, Aureliano José, José Arcadio Segundo, Aureliano Segundo, Remedios, Remedios the Beauty, Renata Remedios, Amaranta, Amaranta Úrsula and Úrsula. So many names get repeated so often, and with such curious implications for their repeated predispositions that Úrsula, indomitable matriarch of the Buendía household, is led to exclaim at one point: "I know all this off by heart. It's as if time had turned around and we were back at the beginning" (162).

It is however through the figure of Melquíades that the problem of the blurring of boundaries is most acutely articulated. Melquíades first comes into the story as the leader of the first band of gypsies to arrive in Macondo. Unlike the subsequent bands of gypsies that come to the town as purveyors of pleasure, Melquíades and his group are heralds of science and progress. After instigating in José Arcadio Buendía a zest for social development through scientific discovery (admittedly of an alchemical kind), he goes through various deaths and returns (all casually reported) until a final death on a visit to Macondo, upon which he is buried in a room in the Buendía house. But this turns out not to be the end of Melquíades. His ghost guides first the third-generation José Arcadio Segundo to his secret manuscripts while he is in hiding from the authorities for claiming to have witnessed the banana plantation massacre, something that they were keen to airbrush out of history. Then, much later, Melquíades also guides the fifth-generation Aureliano, condemned to be hidden from view by Fernanda, his frigidly religious grandmother. In his seclusion Aureliano happens upon the Melquíades manuscripts and begins to laboriously decipher them. He is temporarily diverted from his task by the passionate but incestuous affair he has with Amaranta Úrsula, his aunt. Many years previously, his great-grandparents had been warned that incest in the family might lead to the birth of a child with the tail of a pig. This is exactly what happens. The child is a sign of a coming apocalypse, something that is itself foretold in the manuscript that Aureliano is translating. The apocalyptic ending read in Melquíades' manuscript is important, for it bears directly on the blurring of boundaries we have noted. What Aureliano is reading is the history of the house of the Buendías written by Melquíades not "in the order of man's conventional time, but . . . concentrated [in] a century of daily episodes, in such a way that they coexisted in one instant." As he unravels the key to deciphering the manuscript, apocalypse is upon him:

> Macondo was already a fearful whirlwind of dust and rubble being spun about by the wrath of the biblical hurricane when Aureliano skipped eleven pages so as not to lose time with facts he knew only too well, and he began to decipher the instant he was living, deciphering it as he lived it, prophesying himself in the act of deciphering the last page of the parchments, as if he were looking into a speaking mirror. Then he skipped again to anticipate the predictions and ascertain the date and circumstances of his death. Before reaching the final line, however, he had already understood that he would never leave the room, for it was foreseen that the city of mirrors (or mirages) would be wiped out by the wind and exiled from the memory of men at the precise moment when Aureliano Bablionia would finish deciphering the parchments, and that everything written on them was unrepeatable since time immemorial and forever more, because races condemned to one hundred years of solitude did not have a second chance on earth. (335)

One particular element in the apocalyptic description that speaks to the blurring of boundaries is the idea of a "speaking mirror." A speaking mirror is curiously misplaced in this context, because what "speaks" is a written text. The image of a speaking mirror places us in the face of clairvoyance, a clairvoyance perhaps best figured in a crystal ball. For what is a crystal ball but a speaking mirror, one that mirrors past, present, and future and collapses the boundaries between the three temporalities? But if what Aureliano deciphers is the novel we have just read, this makes him our surrogate in the text. In that case our entire reading process has been the figuration of an encounter with a crystal ball, a reading process in which we are both the objective facts of our own existence and the figment of hoped for and imagined futures *as they unfold within the text.* Aureliano is the surrogate for the reader limited by the contingencies of narrative unfoldment. You cannot know what lies in the future of the narrative before you arrive at it, and yet that future is already coexistent with the present that unfolds slowly before your reading. With the reader-function mirrored in Aureliano, there is the suggestion of a conceptual scaling-down of the real reader into a liminal existence partially inside and partially outside the text.

Going back to the repetition of names, we might suggest that part of the reason for this is that the narrative is affected by Melquíades' old age and senility, for time, like Melquíades, "also stumbled and had accidents and could therefore splinter and leave an eternalized fragment in a room" (283). The eternalized fragment in a room also recalls Melquíades' room, since it is here that the manuscript, like a crystal ball, tells past, present, and future simultaneously. Melquíades is like Shakespeare conjuring Prospero who in turn conjures into being the imaginary universe that surrounds him. And beyond him stands Márquez himself. And beyond Márquez? We stop posing the question only so that we can impose closure on what is essentially an open-ended processual question that forces a blurring of epistemological boundaries.

Issue Cluster 2: Metaphorical-Literality Chains

Etymologically, metaphor involves the transfer and transposition of meanings. It derives for the Greek *meta* (trans) + *pherein* (to carry) and from Aristotle onward has been taken to be a means of comparing two terms. It is an indispensable part of language use, as Lakoff and Johnson (1980) and others have adroitly shown. Linguists have also elaborately defined the notion of code-switching, which, basically, involves the switching between two or more languages within a single communicative environment. Code-switching occurs when people commanding more than one common language move quickly between one language and another, either at the level of single phrases, sentences, or within larger demarcated levels of exchange. Code-switching is also evident in literatures where writers attempt to move between two very different languages, sometimes creating what Chantal Zabus (1991) has termed literary palimpsests. From the examples from African literature she draws upon (Chinua Achebe, Amos Tutuola, and others) it might also be argued that these literary palimpsests involve not just the translation of terms, but the translation of entire cultures of cognition between languages. One such culture of cognition derives from the nature of metaphoricity, for it could be argued that different languages have different ways of generating metaphors. In that sense the translation of cultures of cognition between different languages also involves the interplay of different codes of metaphoricity. Metaphor-as-discourse, then, becomes the subject of code-switching as much as does language itself. In this regard, the various shifts between foreground and background, and tenor and vehicle (to invoke I. A. Richards) is the mechanism that defines the tensions in this code-switching or transfer. Disney's *Aladdin* (1992) and Rushdie's *Midnight's Children* help us to explore these aspects of metaphor and metaphoricity a bit further.

A particularly fertile point of transfers and transpositions occurs in Disney's *Aladdin*, when the hapless Aladdin, now seemingly trapped in the cave of treasures into which he has been tricked by the wizard Jafaar, rubs the lamp that was the object of his quest. There is a terrifying whoosh, a sudden shaking of the lamp, and lo and behold! a blue genie emerges out of the lamp. Aladdin suspects he must have bumped his head, but the genie moves to assure him that he is for real and, beyond that, also a friend. Now, as the older variants of the Aladdin story have long established, the genie of the lamp is supposed to signify the possibility of wish fulfilment; but is combined with the limitation to such fulfilment, since there are only so many wishes that can be delivered. Thus the story is also about the exercise of wisdom. This element remains the same in the Disney version, except for one very significant difference: Disney's genie sets out to display the full range of possible wishes that he can fulfill, thus defining a kaleidoscope of tantalizing possibilities. In this wish/ful kaleidoscope a particular play with language is central. Its main feature is that any idiomatic expression that the genie uses is immediately literalized. Thus when he tells Aladdin to "hang on a minute" he picks him up and hangs him on a peg, and when he describes himself as "self-contained" (among other things) he transforms himself into an ice cube. These rapid literalizations of metaphor are not idle, for they lend themselves to the definition of the genie as a showman, a performer who likes to put his wares on display, as it were. But what is of interest here is the degree and scale to which the rapid literalizations of the metaphorical also stand-in for the frenetic collapse of foreground and background, the literal and the metaphorical.

A similarly persistent literalization of the metaphorical helps define the peculiar quality of Rushdie's *Midnight's Children*. The analogy with the story from the *Thousand and One Nights* is itself justified by the fact that Saleem Sinai frequently likens himself to Scheherazade. (We also recall that the Midnight's Children are a thousand and one). There are at least three such modes of literalization. The first literalization relates to the midnight children themselves, precisely because they are physical manifestations of certain repressed potentials in Indian history. As Saleem says at one point, "Midnight's children can be made to represent many things, according to your point of view" (200). The second type occurs when a particular idea is repeated at different points but in such a way as to accrue more and more meanings. Such is the case with the hole in the middle of the protective white sheet that is held before Naseem, Aadam Aizziz's future wife, on his medical trips to her protective father's home to examine her; subsequently she becomes something of a jigsaw puzzle to him, a hole in his attempts to achieve marital and sexual fulfilment. As he grows older, he is reported to have a shadowy hole in his stomach, especially when the light falls on him from a particular angle. But all these holes are essentially transformations of the hole he sustains in his faith as a Muslim physician educated in Germany. The many "holes" that proliferate around him are only materializations of this metaphysical hole. This kind of literalization of metaphor could be described in terms of incremental repetition, in the sense that the image or idea once repeated, is both a reiteration of what has come before and a supplement to it. The third mode of literalization is connected to the first but this time relates mainly to the fact that Saleem Sinai's life is a direct parallel of Indian history. He is, as he tells us from the beginning, "handcuffed" to it.

These three modes of literalization of metaphor come together in different configurations in the course of the narrative, so that it is no straightforward matter to set up a typology of their occurrences. However, there is at least one instance when the several threads are woven together so adroitly as to produce a careful balance between the tragic and the comic, and to establish the contours of the metaphorical-literal chains that saturate the narrative. I refer here to the moment when Ahmed Sinai, Saleem's father, comes upstairs to the breakfast table from his basement office with a letter announcing the freezing of his assets. It is a fascinating scene that deserves lengthy quotation:

> Red eyes at breakfast were followed by the shaven chin of the working day; footsteps down the stairs; alarmed giggles of Coca-Cola girl. The squeak of a chair drawn up to a desk topped with green leathercloth. Metallic noise of a metal paper-cutter being lifted, colliding momentarily with telephone. The brief rasp of metal slicing envelope; and one minute later, Ahmed was running back up the stairs, yelling for my mother, shouting:
>
> "Amina! Come here, wife! The bastards have shoved my balls in an ice-bucket!"
>
> In the days after Ahmed received the formal letter informing him of the freezing of his assets, the whole world was talking at once. . . . "For pity's sake, janum, such language!" Amina is saying—and is it my imagination, or does a baby blush in a sky-blue crib?
>
> . . .
>
> "Come on now," Amina interrupts him; her dedication rising to new heights, she leads him towards her bedroom. . . . "Janum, you need to lie for some time." And Ahmed: "What's this, wife? A time like this—cleaned out; finished; crushed like ice—and you think about . . ." But she closed the door; slippers have been kicked off; arms are reaching towards him; and some moments later her hands are stretching down down down; and then, "Oh my goodness, janum, I thought you were just talking dirty but it's true! So cold, Allah, so coooold, like little round cubes of ice!" (135–36)

We notice first of all the telegraphic nature of the opening paragraph. This connects to certain cinematic techniques of narration. Rushdie frequently uses a plethora of details to rapidly set a scene or establish atmosphere. As Saleem Sinai points out, "nobody from Bombay should be without a basic film vocabulary" (33). But it is Ahmed Sinai's strange assertion that his balls have been "shoved in an ice bucket" that is of interest here. Several tightly related moves from the literal to the metaphorical and back again are taking place. I want to set them out in the form of numbered points for ease of reference:

1. First is that Ahmed Sinai has had his economic assets frozen. However, far from announcing this in a straightforward fashion he transposes the idea of "assets" onto a sexual register of physical "endowment" as is the case in a phrase like "he is physically well endowed." This could be taken either as a description of athleticism or as a euphemism for the size of the sexual organs.

2. However, behind this particular metaphorical transposition is another move, which is that of suggesting that by freezing his economic assets, the government has done damage to his libido. This seems perfectly rational, except that there has been a leap from the immediate "foreground" of economic mishap to the "background" of sexual and libidinal implications.

3. The third move centers on Amina Sinai's skepticism about the state of her husband's sexual organs. In this she represents a skeptical interlocutor, much like the reader who might be reluctant to make the brisk leap from economic foreground to sexual background. When she takes him into the room, her husband protests that she is trying to be sexual at a time of mishap. He is in his turn taking her interest in the state of his genitals at sexual face value, and thus fails to recognize her skepticism. When she touches his balls and announces that they are "so coooold," the literal-metaphorical chain is complete because what was the metaphorical background (that is, the sexual register) has now become the literal foreground, achieving a complete inversion of the economic and sexual codes with which the extract opened. This move also mocks us if we had harbored the thought that Ahmed Sinai was somehow deluded in thinking it was his balls that had been shoved in an ice bucket.

4. This metaphorical-literal-metaphorical chain could be explained in terms of the narrative motivations of the story itself, that is, in terms of the general structure of metaphoricity that governs the novel in general. However, this curious scene is also explicable with reference to a moment in India's political history. In 1975, Indira Gandhi announced a state of emergency that lasted for several months. Among the many things she did was to freeze people's assets as a means of clamping down on corruption. At about the same time, Rajiv Gandhi, her first son, took it upon himself to spearhead a highly controversial birth control scheme whose centerpiece was compulsory male vasectomy. These two highly unpopular moves in Indian history resonate behind the scene we have just looked at. In other words, the motivation behind the scene is the fusion of two particularly controversial political moments in Indian history. In this sense, the scene has yet another "background," which is the background of History itself.

Issue Cluster 3: Magical Realism and the Representation of Space, Time, and Space-Time

As we noted earlier, the interplay between the real and the fantastic in the genre of magical realism produces constitutive *aporia* as part of it. These *aporia* can be felt most strongly in the conduct of time and temporality, since it is these that most capture our sense of consensual realism. Elizabeth Deeds Ermath notes that in postmodern narrative, temporality is experienced as "an imaginary ambience containing tensions, fields, tectonics, values" (1983, 22).[5] Time is a function of positionality in which temporality itself becomes part of a system of value and emphasis. Okri's *The Famished Road* exemplifies at different levels the ways in which time and temporality become part of a system of variegated emphases.

Okri's novel is narrated entirely in the first person through the eyes of Azaro, an *abiku* child.[6] The *abiku* is a child believed to be a "born-to-die," one that has an umbilical connection to the otherworld, and, trapped in a restless cycle of rebirth, is born only to die again and be reborn to the same mother. Belief in the phenomenon is common in southern Nigeria and has figured prominently in Nigerian literature. The key difference between Okri's use of the concept and its treatment by others is that, in his novel, there is a free interaction between the real world and that of spirits that disobeys all notions of boundaries or of a clear narrative teleology.

The novel opens with a time reference evocative of myth that is thoroughly atemporal in its invocation of quasi-biblical beginnings: "In the beginning there was a river." Using a formulaic opening pushes the events of this opening section far beyond the realm of the events that will later follow and also beyond any recognizable time scheme. The mythical opening gives way to a more time-bound ordering of temporality in chapter 2, where Azaro recounts his early childhood. Even here his childhood is plotted in the iterative, showing isolated examples of repeated events. Thus the events are an embodiment of repeated time located within moments in the temporal flow of the narrative proper. They are a tissue of the repeated and the habitual:

> When I was very young I had a clear memory of my life stretching to other lives. . . . Sometimes I seemed to be living several lives at once. (7)

---

[5] For the purposes of the following sections, I am going to follow the example of several scholars of postmodernist fiction (Brian McHale, Linda Hutcheon, Elizabeth Ermath, and Elizabeth Dipple, among others) in assuming that magical realism is an expression of post-modernism. In the work of many such scholars, the texts of magical realism are often adduced to exemplify key features of postmodernism. I will thus not be going into an elaborate definition and justification of my usage of the term in this context.

[6] For a fuller discussion of Okri's work, see chapters 5 and 6 of my *Strategic Transformations in Nigerian Writing* (1997).

As a child I could read people's minds. I could foretell their futures. Accidents happened in places I had just left. One night I was standing in the
street with Mum when a voice said: "Cross over." (9)

These references to iterative incidents within a generalized time frame resolve themselves into a specific framework when the text focuses on one of
the various incidents and expands it to become the trigger for the rest of the
events in the narrative. A nocturnal conflagration and the ensuing riots offer
this framework. Time indices are employed to locate the incidents that en-
sue after the riots in relationship to that inaugural event. The conflagration
and the riots occur on the same night:

On another night I was asleep when the great king stared down at me. I
woke up, ran out of the room, and up the road. My parents came after me.
They were dragging me back when we discovered that the compound was
burning. On that night our lives changed. . . .
   It was a night of fires. . . . Three policemen . . . fell on us and flogged us
with whips and cracked our skulls with batons. (9–10)

The narrative undertakes a massive digression shortly after this section to relate Azaro's adventures at the hands of the "cult of women" who capture
him when he is separated from his mother by the milling and riotous crowd
that gathers because of the fires. (The word *digression* in this context is
somewhat clumsy since it insinuates a normative scale with the events of the
real-world of the novel being the point from which the esoteric digresses.
This is inescapable because it is only the texture of real-world events that remains recognizable and to which we are always returned after forays into the
esoteric. However, the novel renders all such notions of priority provisional;
I only stick to the word as a means of imposing an organizational perspective on the discussion.) Azaro manages to escape the women, is later taken
into custody by a policeman and his wife, and is finally rescued by his
mother. He has stayed in the policeman's house for "several days" when his
mother comes for him. As a means of bridging the gap between the time of
their separation during the riots and their coming together again, his mother
later relates the incidents that occur after his being lost on the night of the
riots, thus updating us on all the events that have transpired and also locating the mass of events in relation to the main frame of the fires and riots.
   Throughout all these myriad events, no specific time indices are given.
All the time indices are vague references to "that night," "the next morning,"

"during that time," and so on. Subsequently, the narrative makes concessions to temporality by referring to a sequence of days such as "Saturday"
and "Sunday" as a frame for the occurrence of certain events.[7] It is clear that
the narrative imposes a framework of temporality on the narrated events
rather reluctantly, for, as it progresses, temporal indices become less and less
prominent. The central operation of the narrative in this respect is to recall
significant events that come to mind without necessarily noting time's passage. This mode of organization has a telling effect on overall plot structure,
rendering it loosely episodic not only because of the massive esoteric digressions, but also because of the marked absence of temporal indices.

There is an even more complex implication of the relative paucity of temporal indices in the text. Because we are not given an indication of what period of time each event spans, it is difficult if not impossible to define the
relative duration of each event. Narratologists have mapped out how duration is grasped by the reader, linking it to the relationship between the clock
time consumed in reading a passage and the temporal frame given by the
passage itself.[8] If the duration of three hundred years is plotted in three
paragraphs, it signals a short duration and the telescoping of a long time
span. The lavish description of an hour's incident in thirty pages shows a
long duration, slowing down the pace of the narrative. In *The Famished
Road*, however, the lack of definite temporal indices in relation to events ensures that a mode of equivalence is insinuated as definitive of the relationships between various events. In other words, no event is subordinated to
another in terms of temporal duration. Thus, a homogenous sense of atem-
porality, only relieved by the vaguest time indices, is spread throughout the
narrative.

Yet another formal textual feature that helps enforce a sense of homo-
geneity is the relative absence of character recall of earlier events. At no
time, for instance, do any of the characters ever refer back to the conflagration of the earlier stages of the narrative in constructing a sense of life in the

---

[7] The events that occur from Azaro's homecoming party on page 41 to the end of book 1, page
71 take about four days, but it is difficult to be sure. Again, chapters 5 and 6 contain references
to the Rich People's Party's milk distribution on a Saturday evening; on Sunday the entire
neighborhood react to food poisoning. After that there is an abandonment of this temporal
framework, with chapter 7 opening on page 133 with a vague "the next time I went to Madame
Koto's bar . . ."

[8] Gerard Genette gives the most exhaustive analysis of the relationship between narrative time
and clock time, and it is his model I draw upon here. See his *Narrative Discourse* (1980), 86–112;
also Meir Sternberg, *Expositional Modes and Temporal Ordering in Fiction* (1978), 236–305.

ghetto. After the food poisoning brought on by the powdered milk of the Party of the Rich (130–32), no reference is made later in the narrative to this traumatic event as a means of defining the character of the party. That the party is populated by hooligans is never forgotten, but this is continually demonstrated by the text rather than being recalled. As a third instance of this structural feature, we must note that even at the second house party thrown by Azaro's father there is no reference whatsoever to Azaro's welcoming party, which occurs much earlier in the narrative and seems to be a discursive precursor of the later one. There are also no flashbacks or what Genette calls "anachronies" in the novel in the sense of an event appearing later in the sequence of the narrative but indicated to have occurred earlier in the story (1980, 35–36). It is as if there is an effort not only to disperse a series of discrete events across time but also to enforce a sense of a continual forward narrative movement. And yet, simultaneously, this teleological narrative impulse is disturbed by the constant recurrence of extended esoteric moments that do not follow any teleological trajectory. Rather, there is a pervasive sense of the interpenetration of the essence of the two realms of the real and the esoteric.

It is this interpenetration that provides the ground for the anamorphic conception of time in the novel. Okri's many digressions are not that different from the ones that can be plotted for Márquez, Rushdie, and other magical realist writers. What distinguishes his conception of time from that of the others is that in *The Famished Road*, every moment has an esoteric latency. Every moment is potentially enchanted such that moments are experienced differently. This is not the case in other magical realists, where, despite the confusing randomization of temporal sequence, each moment is experienced as durationally homogenous. The use of time in these others is not different from that in operation in consensual realism. The experiences *in* time may be different, but time itself is the same. Not so with Okri, where time itself is different. Closely connected to this enchantment of time is the fact that space is also rendered anamorphic and enchanted. Whereas space in the other magical realist texts is shown to be merely background spectacle, in Okri's novel, space itself is enchanted. Thus, in one instance, when Azaro is in Madame Koto's room drying himself from the rain, he notices that "on a wall the form of an enormous sunflower changed into the shape of a bull" (290). These sudden esoteric modulations of space occur repeatedly. They are completely unpredictable and call for a constant openness as to the ontology of space, time, and space-time.

But the anamorphization of space-time carries with it the mark of a particular mythopoiesis. It is the mythopoiesis of an indigenous cultural system that assigns spiritual value to every living thing. Okri extends this essentially animist conception of the universe to cover every imaginable object both living and nonliving, thus rendering everything potentially enchanted. What's more, it is not only living and nonliving things that show this enchanted potential; even abstract states are sometimes shown to posses some form of enchanted excess. Thus it is that at one point, in weeping for his mother's despondency, he becomes his mother's grief:

> Her words came too late. I could not separate myself from unhappiness. I became my grief. I wept in advance for all the things that would happen, the unimaginable things beyond the horizon of all the narratives of our lives. Misery filled me like water fills a deep well after a heavy downpour. I started to choke. My spirit companions drank of my grief and filled me with sweet songs to make my wretchedness more sublime. My heart stopped beating. I froze, became rigid, didn't breathe, my mouth open, eyes wide. Darkness rushed over me, a powerful wind from the forest. Darkness extinguished my consciousness. (229)

He is dissolved into this brief moment, and entering by way of his mother's grief goes on a sublime journey in which he moves through darkness and back into light. But the starting point was an abstract feeling, which in itself becomes codified as harboring its own potential for esoteric transport. In Okri, then, everything is potentially enchanted, whether space, time, feelings, or abstract states. The magical and the real are equivalent because both of them are articulations of what cannot be reduced to a predictable sequence of laws. Anything can happen, and we ought to be prepared for this at all times.

Brian McHale has noted that there is an oscillation between epistemological and ontological perspectives that defines the difference between modernism and postmodernism. The two genres are marked by different aesthetic dominants, namely, the impulse toward articulating epistemological problems and that toward the expression of ontological ones, respectively. Thus, as he demonstrates through detailed textual analyses, the aesthetic devices that the two genres use are regulated by specific epistemological or ontological predispositions. However, at the same time, McHale is conscious of the fact that it is not possible to demarcate radically between the two orders of questions. As he notes, "Intractable epistemological uncertainty becomes at a certain point ontological plurality or instability: push epistemological questions far enough and they 'tip over' into ontological questions. By the same token, push ontological questions far enough and they tip over into epistemological questions—the sequence is not linear and unidirectional, but bidirectional, and reversible" (McHale, 11, 9–10). With Okri in particular we find ontological questions pushed to the extreme, because in rendering the real equivalent to the nonreal or fantastic, it is suggested that the ontological status of the real is itself thrown into question.

Issue Cluster 4: Magical Realism and the Philosophy of History

With the term *historiographic metafiction*, Linda Hutcheon attempts to define the various ways in which postmodern fiction incorporates and assimilates historical data in order to simultaneously affirm and subvert the historical. Unlike the traditional historical novel, it is the unsuccessful assimilation of historical data that is foregrounded in historiographic metafiction. Historical details are not referred to in order to produce a patina of verifiability; rather they are there to show how difficult it is to verify history in the first place (see Hutcheon 1988). In magical realism, historiographic metafiction often also embraces various processes and contradictions by which the historical is established, producing what, to echo Raymond Williams, is a structure of (absurdist) feeling with respect to history. All the magical realists we are concerned with here do this to varying degrees, but it is perhaps only in Allende's *The House of Spirits* that a consistent and abstractable philosophy of history is made constitutive of the historiographic metafiction of the text.

   The House of Spirits is the most explicitly political of all the novels we have looked at. There are three reasons for this: (1) it maps out the evolution of a series of political orders; (2) it sets out a series of explicit debates on political ideology; and (3) it illustrates the movement of what seems on first encounter to be a Marxist dialectic of history. However, there is one significant problem that does not allow it to become a mere Marxist propaganda document, and that is the fact that the movement of the dialectic she sets out does not deliver the proletariat and the subaltern working classes into the glory of power, but rather takes power from them effectively and puts it in the hands of the military class. This military class is shown to harbor the synthesis of the negative aspects of both liberal and conservative ideologies as figured in the novel. It is thus not the dialectical synthesis of positive elements but that of negative ones. In collusion with external forces, here imagined as the United States, the military class becomes almost invincible. In this Allende is imaginatively rendering the essential movement of the political history of South American totalitarian regimes. In many respects, however, her model can be extrapolated to apply to other totalitarian military regimes in Africa, Asia, and in the third world more generally. One only thinks of the rationale given by coup leaders in many parts of Africa to see how close Allende's model is to the violent spasmodic processes of postcolonial nation-state formation.

This essentially dialectical process of unfoldment is, however, situated via particular characterological dispositions. When the novel opens, we are ushered into the household of the del Valles and encounter a clutch of very curious characters. There is Rosa, who is born with green hair and exudes all the qualities of a mermaid. She commits herself to embroidering a giant tablecloth with all the animals of paradise. There is her sister Clara who possesses powers of telekinesis and clairvoyance; their mother Nívea, constantly fussing about her children but unable to do anything to prevent them from developing in their own uncontrollable ways; Nana, endearing but absent-minded; and their dog Barrabás, frolicsome as a kitten but with the claws of a crocodile, very sharp teeth, and to whom the popular imagination lends mythological characteristics: "Some people believed him to be a cross between a dog and a mare, and expected him to sprout wings and horns and acquire the sulfuric breath of a dragon, like the beasts Rosa was embroidering on her endless tablecloth" (33). This household firmly establishes the world of the magical. At the same time, it also establishes a certain contradiction between the interests of a subaristocratic household, which the del Valles clearly are, and those of the laboring classes whom we persistently encounter in the course of the novel. Since this is clearly a subaristocratic household, there are very few references to work, unless they pertain to the work done by the various housekeepers. This magical and subaristocratic universe is contrasted sharply with that of Esteban Trueba, whose mother is literally rotting from arthritis. He has to go out to the mines far from home to make money to look after her and also to attempt to win the hand of Rosa, with whom he has fallen in love at first sight. His world is that of sickness, decay, putridness, and ultimately death, and is marked by the rigors of labor necessary for survival. Esteban Trueba appears as a strongly opinionated self-made man but also turns out to be a die-hard conservative right-winger, a chauvinist, and a bully. His attitude to the world is diametrically opposed to everything that the del Valle household represents.

The third generation of the Trueba household produces Alba, who is the product of a disapproved alliance between Blanca, Clara's daughter, and Pedro Tercero, former tenant on Esteban's farm turned revolutionary. She has green hair, thus recalling her great-aunt Rosa. At the same time that Alba is discursively situated as the privileged legatee of the magical real, the processes of political unfoldment ensure that mythology is also put to different political uses. For there is also myth and magic among the ordinary people. Some of it produces a sense of conservatism and powerlessness; for a long time the peasants are unable to take their destiny into their own hands but rely on their overlords such as Esteban Trueba to shape it for them. However, it is the channeling of the popular imagination, partly through a discrete liberation theology and partly through the revolutionary folk songs of the guitar-wielding Pedro Tercero, that a new revolutionary consciousness is shaped. When the radicals win a surprise election, they are led by a man simply called The Poet (with whom the mild-mannered Jaíme has long political disquisitions along with interminable chess games). Sadly, this order of the working class and the peasantry is overthrown by the military, who are shown to be the only class who have both the coherence and the means to force their narrow strategic interests on the populace. They also deploy a form of myth-making, but this is in the interests of cynicism and oppression (434).

By the end of the novel things look dire. The student movement is in disarray with key leaders on the run, the political opposition on both the Right and Left are decimated, and the poor are crushed by the immensity of their disillusionment. Alba is arrested by García Trueba, bastard son of Esteban Trueba fathered with one of the peasants he raped on the farm. García has grown up with an implacable hatred of the other Trueba children whom he feels have usurped his birthright. But, more worryingly, he has become a senior police officer in charge of the general repression of the dissidents. García's brutal intrusion into the lives of Alba and the other Truebas partly represents the return of a repressed past of misdemeanor, and, on a more discursively symbolic level, the maturation of the cynicism that is the product of the exploitation of the peasantry by the exploiting master class represented by Esteban. García is the negative synthesis of certain historical processes of exploitation, Alba the synthesis of the more positive values of the alliance between the magical and the political. Alba is raped repeatedly in detention, by him and others and finally finds herself pregnant. She doesn't know whether this is her left-wing student boyfriend Miguel's child or that of one of her detested violators. All seems dark and lost to her, and thus, we would conclude, for the positive synthesis that she represents— except for one seemingly tenuous line of hope, whose ramifications transcend her dire circumstances. This line emerges in a crucial reinterpretation of her past that occurs at two epiphanic moments toward the end of the novel. The first is when she recognizes in the poor woman sent by her grandfather to arrange her release an indomitable spirit that is shared by all the nameless women who, though abandoned by men are still able to take in "other people's abandoned children, her own poor relatives and anybody else who needs a mother, a sister, or an aunt; the kind of woman who's the pillar of many lives, who raises her children to grow up and leave her and lets her men leave too, without a word of reproach, because she has more pressing things to worry about" (487). In this woman she sees an image of motherhood that transcends the violations of the political. She concludes that "the days of Colonel García and all those like him are numbered, because they have not been able to destroy the spirit of these women." The second epiphanic moment is perhaps more complicated and involves situating herself in relation to the fantastic women in her own lineage, starting from Clara:

> When I was in the doghouse, I felt as if I were assembling a jigsaw puzzle in which each piece had a specific place. Before I put the puzzle together, it all seemed incomprehensible to me, but I was sure that if I ever managed to complete it, the separate parts would each have a meaning and the whole be harmonious. Each piece has a reason for being the way it is, even Colonel García. *At times I feel as if I had lived all this before and that I have already written these very words*, but I know it was not I: it was another woman, who kept her notebooks so that one day I could use them. I write, she wrote, that memory is fragile and *the space of a single life is brief, passing so quickly that we never get a chance to see the relationship between events*; we cannot gauge the consequences of our acts, and we believe in the fiction of past, present, and future, but it may also be true that everything happens simultaneously— as the three Moira sisters said, who could see the spirits of all eras mingled in space. That's why my Grandmother Clara wrote in her notebooks, in order to see things in their true dimension and to defy her poor memory. . . . It would be very difficult for me to avenge all those who should be avenged, because my revenge would be just another part of the same inexorable rite. *I have to break that terrible chain*. (490; emphases added)

Like *One Hundred Years of Solitude*, this novel is pieced together from the notebooks of another, this time of her grandmother Clara. Like Melquíades Clara does not impose any clear order on her notebooks. They have to be rearranged, and even then there is no full continuity between events, because she had always been in a liminal existence. But the lesson for Alba is that the space of a single life is all too brief to understand the full meaning of life and the intricate interconnections that shape it. With this she comes to the conclusion that even revenge would be only part of a meaning that is never capable of full disclosure. With this she escapes the hubris traditionally associated with the classic revenge hero from the Greeks to the present day, thus transcending both the inexorable rites of history as they have been disclosed in the novel, and also the image of a particular kind of heroine. A cynical way of reading this of course would be to suggest that Allende declines a full critical engagement with the traumatic historical unfolding she has so poignantly detailed. However, following her careful subversion of Marxist historiography, it is better to suggest that she returns the individual consciousness to the center of history. But it a consciousness refusing to acquiesce in history's imposed linearities, thus transcending its limitations to be able to imagine a future not dictated by it. With this Allende asserts the preeminence of choice for the human spirit, a choice that might ultimately help to dialectically shape history itself, even as it affects the individual's consciousness.

Conclusions

As can be seen from the discussion so far, magical realism is no single and simple discourse. It is full of surprising twists and turns and also constantly evolving. What is more, it draws its inspiration from a variety of sources. Thus, in the earliest magical realist texts of Latin American writers such as Miguel Angel Asturias and Alejo Carpentier, a thoroughly indigenous worldview was used to saturate the writing at all levels. In Asturias's *Men of Maize*, for instance, we find that the voice of the narrator melds completely with that of a subtle and evocative mythical cosnciousnes of the native peoples of Guatemala such that it is almost impossible to distinguish between what the narrator says, the thoughts and sensibilities of the characters he is describing, and, more significant, the native discourse in which all this is dissolved in the production of a mythical worldview. We are invited to piece the lines of the story together by paying close attention to the mythical worldview, even though this is highly elusive and calls for a detailed labor of attention. And, to complicate matters, even as we are focusing intently on this discourse, we are also meant to note the ravages of capitalism and the new modes of exploitation whose effects are to transmogrify human relations and the structures of feeling that they encode into through the brutal work of capitalist reason. By interpreting, then, we are both entering that universe of local mythmaking *and* witnessing its regrettable passing away.

One Hundred Years of Solitude, on the other hand, fuses motifs and metaphors from Greek mythology, the *Arabian Nights*, biblical tales, and Catholic iconography (we remember Remedios the Beauty's ascent into heaven as a parallel to the Ascension of the Madonna) to produce a shifting and labile resource for his text. Rushdie also draws from the *Arabian Nights* but combines these with references from the sacred Hindu texts, Bollywood, and popular advertising to generate a partially recognizable but largely elusive resource base. And with Okri, the transposition of an animist realism into the genre serves to indicate his debt to a long tradition of Nigerian orality. And there are many others, all differently cast and of different inspirations: D. M. Thomas's *The White Hotel* (1981), Laura Esquivel's *Like Water for Chocolate* (1989), Günter Grass's *The Tin Drum* (1959), and Mikhail Bulgakov's *The Master and Margarita* (1967) among many others. All these point to the inexhaustible nature of the matrices that can be drawn upon for magical realism. But beyond that, they also hint at the means by which humanity may renew itself: not by subsuming the fruits of the nonrational under the impress of rationality, but to celebrate and open itself to the fecundities of the unexpected. For, as the Brazilian journalist Paulo Coelho (1997) puts it: "The skeptic says that the world is mad. But the wise man knows that the real difficulty is in choosing well your own madness."⁹

References

PRIMARY TEXTS

Allende, Isabel (1986). *The House of Spirits*. Translated by Magda Bogin. London: Black Swan.

Asturias, Miguel Angel (1949). *Men of Maize*. Translated by Gerald Martin. Pittsburg: University of Pittsburg Press, 1993.

Borges, Jorge Luis (1964). "The Analytical Language of John Wilkins." In *Other Inquisitions, 1937–1952*, translated by Ruth L. C. Simms. Austin: University of Texas Press.

——— (1964). "The Garden of Forking Paths." In *Labyrinths: Selected Stories and Other Writings*. Harmondsworth: Penguin, 1980.

Disney, *Aladdin* (1992).

Kafka, Franz (1916). *Metamorphosis and Other Stories*. Translated by Willa and Edwin Muir. London: Penguin, 1988.

Kroetsch, Robert (1978). *What the Crow Said*. Don Mills, Ontario: General.

Márquez, Gabriel García (1967). *One Hundred Years of Solitude*. Translated by Gregory Rabassa. New York: Harper Collins, 1998.

---

⁹ I have paraphrased here from *Manuale del guerriero della luce*, the Italian edition of *Manual do guerreiro da luz* with the aid of Valentina Napolitano, to whom many thanks.

———— (1982). Nobel Prize acceptance speech. In *Gabriel García Márquez: New Readings*. Edited by Bernard McGuirk and Richard Andrew Cardwell. Cambridge: Cambridge University Press, 1987.

Márquez, Gabriel García, and Plinio Apuleyo Mendoza (1983). *Fragrance of the Guava: Conversations*. London: Faber.

Morrison, Toni (1987). *Beloved*. London: Chatto and Windus.

Okri, Ben (1991). *The Famished Road*. London: Vintgage.

Rushdie, Salman (1981). *Midnight's Children*. London: Cape.

Suskind, Patrick (1985). *Perfume: The Story of a Murderer*. Translated by John E. Woods. London: Hamilton.

SECONDARY TEXTS

Chakrabarty, Dipesh (1997). "The Time of History and the Times of the Gods." In *The Politics of Culture in the Shadow of Capital*, edited by Lisa Lowe and David Lloyd. Durham, N.C.: Duke University Press.

Dipple, Elizabeth (1988). *The Unresolvable Plot: Reading Contemporary Fiction*. New York: Routledge.

Ermath, Elizabeth (1983). *Realism and Consensus in the English Novel*. Princeton, N.J.: Princeton University Press.

Fabian, Johannes (1983). *Time and the Other: How Anthropology Makes Its Object*. New York: Columbia University Press.

Faris, Wendy B. (1995). "Scheherazade's Children: Magical Realism and Postmodern Fiction." In Zamora and Faris.

Freud, Sigmund (1919). "The Uncanny." Standard ed., vol. 17. London: Hogarth.

Gampel, Yolanda (2000). "Reflections on the Prevalence of the Uncanny in Social Violence." In *Cultures under Siege: Collective Violence and Trauma*, edited by Antonius C.G.M. Robben and Marcelo M. Suarez-Orozco. Cambridge: Cambridge University Press.

Genette, Gerard (1980). *Narrative Discourse*. Translated by Jane E. Lewin. Oxford: Basil Blackwell.

Guenther, Irene (1995). "Magic Realism, New Objectivity, and the Arts during the Weimar Republic." In Zamora and Faris.

Hutcheon, Linda (1988). *A Poetics of Postmodernism: History, Theory, Fiction*. New York: Routledge.

Lakoff, George, and Mark Johnson (1980). *Metaphors We Live By*. Chicago: University of Chicago Press.

Leal, Luis (1995). "Magical Realism in Spanish American Literature." In Zamora and Faris.

Linton, Simi (1997). *Claiming Disability: Knowledge and Identity*. New York: New York University Press.

Martin, Gerald (1989). *Journeys through the Labyrinth: Latin American Fiction in the Twentieth Century*. London: Verso.

McHale, Brian (1987). *Postmodernist Fiction*. London: Methuen.

Quayson, Ato (1997). *Strategic Transformations in Nigerian Writing*. Oxford and Bloomington: James Currey and Indiana University Press.

Roh, Franz (1995). "Magic Realism: Post-Expressionism." In Zamora and Faris.

Slemon, Stephen (1995). "Magical Realism as Postcolonial Discourse." In Zamora and Faris.

Sternberg, Meir (1978). *Expositional Modes and Temporal Ordering in Fiction*. Baltimore: Johns Hopkins University Press.

Zabus, Chantal (1991). *The African Palimpsest: Indigenization of Language in the West African Europhone Novel*. Amsterdam: Rodopi.

Zamora, Lois Parkinson, and Wendy B. Faris, eds. (1995). *Magical Realism: Theory, History, Community*. Durham, N.C.: Duke University Press.

Traditions in Contact

ABDELFATTAH KILITO

Al-Sāq ʿalā al-sāq fīm ā huwa al-Fāryāq
(Aḥmad Fāris Shidyāq, Paris, 1855)

In 1855, Aḥmad Fāris Shidyāq (1804–87), a writer of Lebanese origin, published *al-Sāq ʿalā al-sāq fīm ā huwa al-Fāryāq*, a work that is generally considered to be the "first" modern Arabic novel.[1] Shidyāq is also the author of
a travel narrative to Europe in which he recounted the following misadven-
ture: during a visit to London, he composed a panegyric in honor of Queen
Victoria and succeeded, not without some difficulty, in having it sent to her,
together with an English translation. But, alas, he received neither a reward
from the queen nor even a reply. A little later, in Paris, he wrote another
panegyric, this one to Louis-Napoléon, who had just executed the coup d'é-
tat of December 2, 1851. As a dutiful prince, Louis-Napoléon acknowledged
receipt of the poem but nothing more. Obviously, Shidyāq was hoping for
some remuneration, which never came. However, not losing heart, Shidyāq
composed a second panegyric to the glory of Louis-Napoléon when the latter reestablished the empire and had himself proclaimed Napoléon III on
December 2, 1852. But a member of the emperor's entourage, deeming the
poem untranslatable, dissuaded Shidyā q from sending it.

This was indeed an episode worthy of Don Quixote! For the first time
in history, an Arab poet had composed panegyrics in honor of European
princes. In the midnineteenth century, in two of the great European capitals,
Shidyāq was conducting himself in the manner of poets of the first Islamic
centuries, who would praise the caliphs and receive a reward in return. In
his praise of Napoléon III, Shidyāq turned to the same images, the same poetic formulas as those used by his early predecessors to laud the merits of a
Hārūn al-Rashīd. He was, in fact, seeking to perpetuate the image of the
court poet when that figure had already disappeared in Europe and the contract with the prince had been replaced by a contract with the reader. This

---

[1] Translator's note: *Al-Sāq ʿalā al-sāq fīmā huwa al-Fāryāq* has been translated into French by
René Khawam as *La jambe sur la jambe* (Paris: Phébus 1991). There exists, however, no English
translation of the novel. Roger Allen has remarked in his study of *The Arabic Novel: An Historical
and Critical Introduction* (Manchester: University of Manchester Press, 1982), 20, that the title itself
is "untranslatable": it includes a pun on the author's name "in that Fāryāq includes the first syllable
of Fāris and the last of Shidyāq," and "constitutes an excellent demonstration of the revival of the
proclivity of medieval Arabic prose for rhyming titles."

was doubtless a painful experience for Shidyāq: in rejecting him, Europe was rejecting all Arabic poetry. Indeed, Shidyāq's poetic production was a synecdoche for the entire corpus of Arabic poetry. If Europeans could not accord recognition to Shidyāq, they would not be able to welcome other Arab poets either, whether contemporary or earlier. Beyond the limits of its own sphere, Arabic poetry would not be accepted. This complete rupture between the Arabs and the Europeans was for Shidyāq a narcissistic wound, both personal and cultural.

Immediately after abandoning his attempts to send his panegyric to Napoléon III, Shidyāq began to write *al-Sāq ʿalā al-sāq*. Why did he move from poetry to prose? What revenge was he seeking in turning from pane- gyrics to a work where he talks of . . . of what, exactly? Leaving aside the question of whether *al-Sāq ʿalā al-sāq* is an autobiography in the third per- son, a novel of education, or a travel narrative, suffice it to say, for the mo- ment, that this work offers a new relationship to space, or at least one that is different from the space of the traditional Arab narrative. This feature can be illuminated by a brief reference to the *maqāma*, as it was developed by Hamadhānī in the tenth century and Harīrī in the eleventh.

In the works of both these authors, characters travel constantly, moving across countries and stopping off in towns. The space of the *maqāma* is open, available, welcoming. Yet at the same time, it is the closed space of "the empire of Islam" (*mamlakat al-Islām*), where everyone speaks the same language, Arabic, and the main subject of discussion is *adab*, literary culture. No one travels beyond the boundaries of this empire, nor does anyone feel the need or desire to. At the borders (*thaghr*) war is waged half-heartedly against the Rūm: that is, the "Byzantines" in Hamadhānī's work, and the Crusaders in Harīrī's. Vaguely menacing in Harīrī's works, the Rūm are in- visible; they are referred to on a few occasions but remain faceless. Indeed, the only source of surprise in the world of the *maqāma* is the spectacle of the beggars, eloquent and rascally tramps who are called the "Children of Sāsān." Otherwise the journey offers nothing truly surprising. The world evoked by the *maqāma* is, essentially, a static one: self-sufficient, redundant, enclosed within its own fullness.

The genre of the *maqāma* was said to have reached perfection with Harīrī, and to imitate this author was an act as desperate as it was futile. Everyone knew this, but continued to write *maqāmāt* nevertheless. In the nineteenth century, Nāṣif al-Yāzijī collected together sixty *maqāmāt*, or ten more than Harīrī, in *Majmaʿ al-bahrayn* (*The Confluence of the Two Seas*). His work, published in 1856, is certainly worthy of note, but disappointing reading when compared with Shidyāq's *al-Sāq ʿalā al-sāq* published one year earlier in Paris. With this book, Shidyāq introduced the novel into Arabic literature, though he probably never imagined the success the genre would find with those who came after him.

The break between the *maqāma* and the novel is, I should emphasize, not an absolute one. In *al-Sāq ʿalā al-sāq* the characters continue to travel. The hero, Fāryāq (a contraction of "Fāris" and "Shidyāq") leaves Lebanon for Egypt where he settles for a while before visiting Damascus and Tunis; the novel ends as he is about to embark for Turkey. Though it is true that in Shidyāq's works the traditionally vast dimensions of space displayed by Hamadhānī and Harīrī are reduced, this shrinking world is offset by the emergence of another world unsuspected by the authors of the *maqāma*, that of Europe, the world of the Franks or the *Ifranj*, to use Shidyāq's term. A new dimension appears, a space hardly glimpsed by the literate elite of the past. The world is no longer what it was; the notion of *thaghr*, of a dangerous and impassable frontier, has lost its usual meaning. Fāryāq remains a considerable time in Malta, as well as in England and France.

Most of Fāryāq's travels take place by "light-ship" (*safīnat al-nār*), while in the *maqāma* a maritime journey is the exception. But the most profound difference lies in the significance of the journey, in the relationship to space. Though the protagonists of Hamadhānī and Harīrī are continually in motion, they do not give the impression of moving forward but rather of circling around. Whether the action takes place in Samarqand, Bukhārā, Basra, or Balkh has no particular significance: towns and other places are interchangeable and therefore not described. In Shidyāq's works, on the contrary, the hero moves from one surprising discovery to another, and each country, each town, has a special, distinctive status. Since everything forcefully engages his gaze and provokes his astonishment, space itself becomes the object of description: not only the foreign space of the Franks, but also Arab space, which, when observed carefully, reveals its great variety. The journey becomes the occasion for a whole series of discoveries about languages, religious beliefs, customs, conjugal relations, costumes, table manners, and so on.

Each space is different from all other spaces: that is the revelation of Shidyāq's book and perhaps the feature that most distinguishes it from the *maqāma* and makes of it a novel. The quest for the *other* replaces the quest for the *same*. The Arabic novel is said to be of European inspiration. This is correct, but one should add that the form was borrowed from Europe precisely in order to speak about Europe. The discovery of Europe, and of the novel, are two simultaneous and correlative operations: one could not happen without the other. It is perhaps no exaggeration to say that the theme of the Arab novel, its main subject, is the relationship of Arabs to Europe.

Hamadhānī and Harīrī, as we know, speak of the familiar world, the world of the "Islamic Empire," and only of this world. The Arab novelist from Shidyāq onward considers it absolutely essential to establish a comparison between Europe and his own world, the latter a world that he had thought was familiar but that has suddenly become strange because he now observes it with eyes that are informed, blurred, or sharpened by Europe.

This new perspective on the world leads to a new vision of women and a new relationship between the sexes. In the *maqāma*, women do not appear, or very little; on their travels, the protaganonists of Hamadhānī (Abū-l-Fath of Alexandria) and Harīrī (Abū Zayd of Sarūj) do not burden themselves with the company of their wives, if they even have one.

Abū-l-Fath mentions a wife once or twice in passing. Abū Zayd has a son. He claims also to have a daughter who was abducted by the Crusaders, but their mother (if she is indeed their mother) only appears once during an argument before a judge (*qādī*). Women have no place in the *maqāma*: they appear only fleetingly; their presence is ephemeral and contingent. The *maqāma* is a male genre; neither gynaeceum nor harem has any place in it.

Everything changes with Shidyāq, whose declared intent is to consecrate his book to women, who are in fact present in it from beginning to end. Mapped onto the comparison of the Arab world and Europe, the author superimposes a comparison between men and women. *Al-Sāq ʿalā al-sāq* is a novel that promotes and valorizes women; even the hero regrets, at times, that he is not a woman. The author gives the heroine the name Fāryāqiyya, the feminine form of Fāryāq. She accompanies Fāryāq on almost all his travels; they are a pair and travel as a pair. In the *maqāma* we also find this theme of the double: the hero and the narrator are inseparable, or they separate only to find each other again. But this is a male duo, whereas in Shidyāq's work the couple is androgynous, achieving the blissful reconciliation of masculinity and femininity. The title of the book is significant in this regard: it means, approximately, "the pairing of two legs." At the beginning, Fāryāq plays the role of attentive and amused teacher with his wife, but he quickly realizes she is making tremendous progress: she is learning English, she participates in men's discussions and expresses her opinion on various aspects of European civilization. *Al-Sāq ʿalā al-sāq* is thus a novel of education about a young woman as much as it is about a young man.

Shidyāq constantly repeats that women are the equals of men, just as he constantly argues that they should receive the same education. One of his greatest regrets is that, despite the fact that his book is dedicated to women, it will not have women readers: "They will not be able to understand a word—not that it is written in a difficult language, but simply because they do not know how to read." However, in raising the question of women's education, in trying to change their status and their lot, it is society as a whole one is seeking to change. This is indeed a goal of *al-Sāq ʿalā al-sāq* and, in general, a characteristic of the first Arab novels. The novelist is, in this sense, a reformer who casts a stern gaze over his society and offers a remedy for the ills with which it is afflicted.

Here again we can see a difference between the early Arab novel and the *maqāma*. The novelist is optimistic; he believes society can be corrected, amended, and improved. The author of the *maqāma* is pessimistic; he cannot imagine any process of improvement because he considers society completely degraded. It is true that the *maqāma* presents a satire on manners, which finds expression mainly in the sermon. But while the sermonizer generally addresses a crowd, his edifying speech is aimed at the individual, the worshiper as a distinct person. Moral reform is the responsibility of the individual, and what is at stake is not only his earthly destiny but also his fate in the world beyond. In Shidyāq's novel, on the other hand, the reform that is sought is essentially social in nature; it is the collectivity, above all, that must be reformed. The novel genre is, moreover, mostly preoccupied with the surrounding reality, with the present of this world, and only secondarily with the next. The beyond, the afterlife, does not fall within the competence or scope of the novelist. The sermon is thus no longer a viable form in the novel; devalued, it gives way to a discourse on society and its problems.

In *al-Sāq ʿalā al-sāq* the devaluation of the sermon is expressed humorously in the attribution of a moralizing discourse to a non-Arab priest who is incapable of pronouncing certain letters and sounds: the words he uses turn into other sounds that have obscene meanings. The result is a comic speech, and laughter instead of the tears the sermon was supposed to provoke. At another moment, the narrator seems to deliver a sermon on well-known themes: evils of all kinds that afflict men, the fragility of life, and so forth. In the traditional sermon, the melancholic meditation on the vanity of the world is also an exhortation to reflect on *maʿād*, or the afterlife. But in Shidyāq's work, this meditation ends with an appeal for tolerance among the various faiths and for understanding among people. The emphasis is placed on the community, and its fate here and now. Resistant to the sermon, the novel can only integrate this genre by parodying it or perverting its aims. One could perhaps even risk the hypothesis that the novel is a secular genre.

Shidyāq is aware of the novelty of his own project. For him this is a subject of pride; he is convinced that his work is completely distinct from that of his contemporaries. His claim to originality, however, mingles with the fear, which he expresses repeatedly, that his work might be received badly or even burned because of passages that might be judged licentious or heretical. The readers he fears are all those whose horizon is limited by a fossilized tradition, most particularly the clergy, whom he never misses an occasion to attack.

Al-Sāq ʿalā al-sāq is divided into four parts, each composed of twenty chapters. In the thirteenth chapter of each part, Shidyāq has placed a *maqāma*. But these four *maqāmāt* seem to have been composed unwillingly, as if he did not really believe in them and included them more as a concession to literary tradition and to the prevailing taste. Moreover Shidyāq expresses openly his dissatisfaction with the devices of rhetoric and warns the reader he will them use them only if necessary, since the description of women's beauty will excuse him, he says, from having recourse to these vain ornaments. For the reader who finds himself dissatisfied, he advises him to turn to Ḥarīrī and Zamakhsharī. Another concession to tradition is the philological digression: when the reader least expects it, the narrative is interrupted by a long list of synonyms or homonyms. This lexicographic piling up of words induces a sense of vertigo and takes on an air of parody: the author is not unaware that the reader will be tempted to "skip over" these didactic passages. Finally, Shidyāq scatters through his work poems he has composed for various occasions. However, several signs suggest that he also anticipates (or invents) another reader, one who is open to European culture. Hence he includes English and French citations, excerpts from Lamartine, Chateaubriand, and Byron. Yet one senses he is closer to three authors he also cites in his book: Rabelais, Swift, and Sterne. Several readers, moreover, have underscored the affinity between *Tristram Shandy* and *al-Sāq ʿalā al-sāq*, and it is clear that Shidyāq has numerous points in common with Sterne: erudition, digression, eclecticism, humor, parody, bawdy stories, and jokes. *Al-Sāq ʿalā al-sāq* could have been titled, like Sterne's novel, *Life and Opinions of Fāryāq*.

It is not easy to determine the genre of *al-Sāq ʿalā al-sāq*, which incorporates several: travel narrative (*riḥla*), anecdote, autobiography in the third person, *maqāma*, dissertations on several subjects, portrait, poem, lexicology lesson. Certainly the *maqāma* is itself a complex genre, but *al-Sāq ʿalā al-sāq* leaves far behind the model set in place by Hamadhānī and Ḥarīrī. Shidyāq himself underscores this fact since, as we have just seen, only four chapters out of eighty are presented as *maqāmāt*. His book is also distinguished by another element: in Hamadhānī and Ḥarīrī's works, each *maqāma* is autonomous and, from the narrative perspective, has little to link it to the others. In Shidyāq's the narrative follows a chronological order: events succeed each other from the birth of the hero up to the eve of his departure for

Turkey. The description of childhood, rarely represented in classical Arabic literature, is another trait of his modernity.

Shidyāq's narrative goal is to move lightly, with ease, so it is no accident that he refers to a "leg" in the title of his work, nor is it surprising that he compares rhymed prose (*sajʿ*) to a wooden leg that makes movement awkward, difficult. The novel is as resistant to rhymed prose as it is to the sermon. Yet Shidyāq's freedom of tone is not without anxiety: might he not be reproached with futility, frivolity? We know the small value Valéry accorded to the novel: "The Marquise went out at five o'clock . . ." For completely different reasons, classical Arabic literature also looked askance at narrative fiction. Shidyāq does not use the word *novel* to characterize his own work, but he does explore various literary possibilities unfamiliar to his predecessors and practiced by Europeans. For example, he remarks humorously that European writers do not fail to register the smallest detail of daily life, nor would they see any reason to criticize the writer who relates that an old woman left her house in the morning, returned at ten o'clock, accompanied by her dog, in the midst of wind and rain. One could daydream forever before such a portrait of a mysterious old woman, scurrying along one morning, as fast as her legs would carry her.

Translated by Mary Harper

NORMA FIELD

Drifting Clouds
(Futabatei Shimei, Japan, 1887–1889)

Can you pick a fight in the national language? commit robbery? seduce a woman? These are some of the questions posed in Inoue Hisashi's 1986 comedy, *Kokugo gannen*, or *National Language Year One*. Set in 1874, the seventh year in the reign of Emperor Meiji, the play invokes the Babelian scene of samurai-turned bureaucrats converging on Tokyo, the capital of the recently unified nation-state. The protagonist, an education ministry official, is charged with the task of establishing a national spoken language. The newly constituted Japanese subjects already exhibited a literacy rate remarkable in world history, but there was no Japanese language as such to be spoken throughout the archipelago. It was urgent, therefore, for the young state to develop a language supple enough to implant conformity and flexibility—to meet the demands of an authoritarian capitalism driven to "catch up and overtake [the West]," as the slogan of the day put it.

But of course, language development is never the exclusive province of the state. The capaciousness of the novel has made it a useful form around the world for the project of language production and its twin, subject formation. This essay will consider a pioneering work by Futabatei Shimei (1864–1909) titled *Ukigumo* [*Drifting Clouds*] and commonly labeled "Japan's first modern novel." Before exploring the prominence accorded this apparently unfinished work about a downsized young man's entrapment in speechless inaction, it is worth noting some of the signposts of the Meiji period (1868–1912). By the seventh year of the Meiji Restoration, the new state had managed to suppress several rebellions and agrarian uprisings, open the first railway and silk mill, and send off a mission to the United States and Europe to seek the abrogation of unequal treaties and to study the institutions enabling the imposition of unequal relations. By 1887 (the twentieth year), when the first volume of the then twenty-four-year-old Futabatei's *Drifting Clouds* was published, Japan had imposed its own unequal treaty on Korea, Tokyo Imperial University was established, and a national songbook had been compiled for primary schoolers. Foreign (European) literature in translation and political novels flooded the market, while older forms of popular fiction and theater, including Chinese fiction and poetry, continued to be eagerly consumed.

Predictably, the appetite for novelty—call it knowledge—factual and not, local or foreign, entertaining and didactic, went hand in hand with the explosion of print culture. Intellectuals, writers, and bureaucrats became obsessed with the relationship between writing and speech, which came to be captured by the term *genbun itchi*, literally, the "unification of speech and writing." *Drifting Clouds* was hailed for its implementation of *genbun itchi*. Twenty years later, its author admitted he had adopted this form because even though he had been wanting to write something, he had "always been a poor writer and didn't know where to begin." So he had followed the advice of his mentor and adopted the style of a popular raconteur.[1]

Even though the term *genbun itchi* had been coined just a few years before *Drifting Clouds*, its informing impulse can be traced back to pre-Restoration scholars whose contact with the West led them to conclude that the rationality of alphabetic writing promoted civilizational advance. The modernization frenzy following the Restoration produced polemic that, on the one hand, argued for simplifying the writing system (even to the extent of adopting the Roman alphabet) and, on the other, the vernacularization of writing. The latter begged the question of which vernacular, since Japanese speech to this day is inflected for class, gender, and age, not to mention region. The development of Japanese-style shorthand in the 1880s to "completely" record speeches, legislative deliberations, and lectures enabled the performed storytelling of a celebrated raconteur—the model recommended to Futabatei—to be produced as wildly successful books. Political novels, newspaper serializations, all experimented with vernacularization.

There is a fundamental ambiguity, for the most part usefully unnoticed, in the formulation "unification of speech and writing": it can mean standardization or vernacularization, and usually it refers to some combination of the two. If for bureaucrats a language spoken and written uniformly throughout the national territory was the dream of modern, rational, and evenly penetrating governance, for writers, it held different possibilities. Women writers could masquerade as men in the unified, ostensibly neutral voice or emphasize their gender by writing first-person women's speech (Hirata, 196). The most influential argument yoking *genbun itchi* to fiction came from Futabatei's mentor Tsubouchi Shôyô (1859–1935), essayist, novelist, dramatist, literary theorist, and translator of Shakespeare. At the age of twenty-three, he embarked on a polemical work, *Shôsetsu shinzui*, or *The Essence of the Novel* (1885–86), with the aim of enhancing the prestige of fiction. Fiction, which had flourished as falsehood, had a role to play in the

---

[1] "Yo ga genbun itchi," 412. All translations are my own.

nation-building project. The object of fiction was first and foremost human emotion, and second, social conditions and mores. To be adequate to the age, fiction needed to deal with reality, including and especially psychological reality, and it needed to present this reality realistically, deploying the colloquial language of the day despite its taint of vulgarity (Tsubouchi Shôyô, 54–55, 115). That Tsubouchi and those who followed in his wake were producing a self (mistakenly) thought to be hidden and awaiting exteriorization in language is the foucauldian thesis of Karatani Kojin's justly influential *Origins of Modern Japanese Literature*. Like most productive arguments, this one misses by overstating its case. In suggesting that interiority or subjectivity per se, rather than a particular kind of subjectivity, namely bourgeois, was initiated in Japan by Western modernity, it paradoxically undermines its own case for historicity.

Drifting Clouds opens after catastrophe has befallen the hero. Bunzô ("letters"),[2] the son of a samurai displaced by the Restoration, is an earnest young man who has just been dismissed from his position in the government machinery. No justification is given other than the need to reduce personnel, but both his shrewd aunt Omasa ("rule") and his colleague and rival in love, Noboru ("climbing"), are confident that his failure to curry favor with his superior is the cause. Not surprisingly, Bunzô's tenuously promising courtship of his cousin Osei ("energy") crumbles, and the enterprising Noboru picks up the pieces. The action revolves around Bunzô's struggle to speak: to confess to his aunt about his dismissal, to declare his love to Osei, and to ascertain what are to him, her maddeningly elusive feelings.

Most of the novel takes place in the aunt and uncle's two-story house, with the women downstairs and Bunzô upstairs in a shabbily furnished room (Maeda, 267–70). His spatial isolation is accentuated by the absence of supporters: his mother, a long-suffering widow lives in the provinces, and his uncle, who runs a teahouse in Yokohama, never visits the household that he heads. In his stead, Omasa, the former servant-mistress turned second wife, manages the household with effortless efficiency, collecting both rent and interest. Calculating that she has another source of income in her daughter's good looks now that she is on the marriage market, Omasa wastes no time redirecting Osei toward Noboru once it is evident that the provincial nephew's symbolic capital (education) has already exhausted its potential. In the end, Omasa and Noboru are the only happy couple, intimately chatting about their favorite topic, money.

---

[2] Walker calls attention to the allegorical quality of character names in *Clouds* (161).

So, on the ground level, women and worldly exchange; above, a brooding, castrated male who has translated his socioeconomic crisis into a psychoerotic one. Connecting and separating the two levels is the stairway. Osei, a proto-New Woman, boldly ascends to Bunzô's room to discuss equal rights for men and women and the hopelessness of the uneducated (her mother, their maid). Bunzô, whenever the urge to speak his mind grows strong enough, descends. More often, though, he listens: listens from upstairs, listens downstairs, but still outside the sliding paper doors.

This, in other words, is a claustrophobic novel—all the more so because it is noisy, mostly from the unspoken words circling inside Bunzô's head. This brings us back to the matter of language. Three broad categories of text make up the novel: narrator's commentary, dialogue, and quoted or narrated thought. First, the conspicuous narrator: the reader who opens the book having heard ad nauseam about its modern language will be astonished by its forbidding rhetorical density. Fixed epithets and exuberant lists in rhythmic prose reflect Futabatei's immersion in the language of an earlier theater and popular fiction. (Such recalcitrant expressions do not make it into Marleigh Grayer Ryan's courageous translation of 1965.) The extravagant language, at odds with the object of description, namely, office workers making their way home, vivifies the irreverent narrator's keen sociological sense. The initial distance we feel from the characters becomes psychological as well as spatial, for the narrator's jocular cynicism keeps us from identifying with any of them. This is a narrator who feels free to address us directly and yet soon disappears from sight or, rather, is absorbed into the text to become a disembodied conduit drawing us steadily closer to Bunzô.

Flipping through the pages of *Clouds* reveals chunks of extended dialogue. As in earlier comical and satirical prose fiction that often read like plays, dialogue carries a heavy narrative load, interspersed with the equivalent of stage directions. There are two differences, however. In the old fiction, the townspeople traded slapstick with each other and directed cynical humor at the pretentious. In *Clouds*, the cynical humor comes from the narrator, and the dialogue itself tends to be serious. The other, related, difference has to do with the distribution of kinds of language. Quoted speech in earlier popular fiction was in the vernacular. Indeed, those texts demonstrated the very possibility of representing a rich variety of actually spoken language well before the intellectual frenzy over *genbun itchi*. The pseudo–stage directions, however, were given in literary language well into the Meiji era. Futabatei boldly resorted to colloquial language—Tokyo dialect, as he himself described it—in narration as well as dialogue. What was the resistance to using ordinary spoken language in narration? In *Clouds*, the narration is conducted in casual verb forms, of the sort used by males on equal footing. The polite, or wanting-to-be-respectable reader might have recoiled before the vulgarity of unadorned statement, an unsettling harbinger of the mixed-up social world in which the novel would flourish. On the other hand, with sentences ending more and more frequently in -*ta*, which comes to be experienced as the (past-tense) marker of modern fiction, Futabatei seems to be galloping his readers to the modern illusion of immediate access to the fictional world.[3] And while that might have been thrilling, it might also have evoked an unacknowledged ambivalence about the truth-status of an account seemingly unmoored from a narrator—then, as today, often experienced as the author.

At any rate, the abundance of dialogue and the use of unobtrusive narration prepare the way for the increasingly insistent representation of thought as speech. Dialogue cedes easily to monologue, which in turn blurs into narrated thought and back again. The movement from one to the other is subtle because quotation marks are sometimes used for quoted monologue as well as dialogue but at other times for neither. The presentation and representation of thought are among the most memorable of the novel's features. Mostly, it must be admitted, it is Bunzô's thought, endlessly and exasperatingly circular. He is, moreover, given to repeating Osei's or Noboru's words in order to confirm his own hopes and fears. Nearly trapped in Bunzô's mind, we are nonetheless kept short of sharing in his self-deception. In an important development, part 3 delivers glimpses of Osei's mind, which almost delivers her from the role of Bunzô's callous manipulator: her agonizing hints at the substance as well as the style of the New Woman. Indeed, the emerging focus on psychic process is moving, which comes as a surprise, because for the most part the characters in *Drifting Clouds* are not only uninteresting but unappealing and even repellent. This is in part, but not entirely, the consequence of our early conditioning by the cynical narrator. Bunzô is evidently going mad at the end, but this cannot evoke our sympathy, either. Then what makes the later chapters of parts 2 and 3 so compelling?

It is the evident passion to represent mental process. It is as if the pains taken to represent character intonation and rhythm with the phonetic syllabary and marks of ellipsis find worthy purpose in representing thought as speech. The proliferating use of ellipses (also missing in translation)

---

[3] A concise discussion can be found in Karatani, 72–73. But see Kamei, especially chapter 1, for the sociohistorical implications of narrative decisions in *Clouds*.

suggests not only faltering voice but faltering thought. Futabatei tries to make visible gaps in speech and, increasingly, gaps in thought—the silence of the mind. What pushed him in this direction? And what is the meaning of such passion?

In "Confessions at Midlife," published more than twenty years after *Clouds*, Futabatei says that the writing in part 1 was drawn from ("imitated" is also a word Futabatei uses, in keeping with his self-announced penchant for honesty) a mixture of eighteenth- and nineteenth-century Japanese writers of popular fiction such as Shikitei Samba and Hiraga Gennai; part 2 from Goncharov and especially Dostoyevsky; and part 3 from Goncharov ("Yo ga hansei," 428). Such passages have long been used to subsume *Clouds* under the paradigm of the Russian superfluous hero; Futabatei himself, a gifted student of Russian, calls this a work "founded in argument," written while immersed in Belinsky and driven to expose the "underside of Japanese civilization" (ibid.). From a first foundation in Confucian ethics and early identification with Japanese imperialist goals, he had been drawn to Russian literature's concern for social issues, thence to socialism, which simultaneously prompted him to philosophical reflection on human fate as well as to psychological study. We need to keep in mind the uncannily familiar glimpse of bureaucratic life and capitalism's relentless sorting of human beings with which *Clouds* opens before it turns inward.

In an essay on translation from the same period, Futabatei talks about how, in training himself as a translator, he had studied punctuation—periods and commas—in order to understand what made sentences in European languages so attractive when read out loud, in contrast to sentences in Japanese, which he found "monotonous" ("Yo ga hon'yaku," 405–6). In his language academy days, texts were unavailable for the students of Russian, so their teacher read out loud from the classics of Russian literature, after which the students were asked to write character analyses. Futabatei's sensitivity to the aural dimension of language would also have been honed by listening to the performances of raconteurs and later, reading their texts from shorthand transcripts. His translations from Russian have been so highly regarded that they are often credited with inaugurating modern Japanese literature. He was evidently a translator not only of sense but the senses, traveling between sight and sound, and between these and human character.

But for the most part, character is not quite what we get in *Drifting Clouds*, that is, the sense of a being with a life beyond what we are literally shown. The passion to make thought visible gives mounting force to the novel, but it also keeps our attention at the surface, at the mode of representation. What readers experience as wearying is in part the result of Futabatei's meticulous rendering of obsessional thought, but we can see that myopia is method from much earlier in the novel. In a moonlit scene, Bunzô stares at Osei's profile. So absorbed is he by her beauty that he fails to notice that her face is twisting toward his, until his own eye is startled by hers—an eyeball-to-eyeball moment that is, needless to say, anything but romantic. Next, we learn that her mouth, already compared to the opening of a turbo shell, is concealed by a fan held in a "hand resembling five white fish arranged on a slender *daikon*" (these similes, not surprisingly, have been omitted in translation; *Ukigumo*, 30; Ryan, 218). The distancing humor of the narrator is here applied at such close range that it skips registers and becomes unnerving. Even when that narrator has been absorbed into the text so that we seem to stare directly at the characters' verbalized minds, it is precisely a staring at rather than a seeing into. Myopia blocks depth.

I would not want to suggest that Futabatei had a prescient understanding that language, or representation, was all there is, and that he was accordingly pursuing an aesthetic of surfaces. By most accounts *Drifting Clouds* is unfinished. Futabatei abandoned the idea of making a living by writing, continuing to translate from the Russian and not producing another novel for twenty years. In response to a reporter's questions during that fictional hiatus, he repeated what he had earlier said, that *Clouds* was boring. He still wanted to write, but this time without imitating others. The theories of aestheticians and philosophers had to be suspended, and the writer needed to focus his concentration on life itself. Ordinarily, a curtain hung between onself and life, but in moments of life-and-death crisis, that curtain would tear asunder; it was then that one could feel oneself staring life in the face. And the task of the novelist or the poet was to "seize by saying" the feel of that moment ("Sakka," 50). But a 1908 essay, "I Am a Skeptic," declares the impossibility of writing the truth, because things necessarily come out wrong in the instance of transmission to speech or writing ("Watashi wa," 417). A believer in thought, science, and art for life's sake (ibid., 422), Futabatei, like all writers, knew the impossibility of life's accurate capture, and as well, the impossibility of evading the challenge.

Futabatei was an obsessive observer, and like other moderns, anxious about the tools for seeing and for showing what had been seen. *Clouds* lets us watch him grasp the psychic effects of socioeconomic trauma misrecognized. Futabatei did this in part by vernacularizing the mind, letting it speak (in Tokyo dialect) and falter (with ellipsis points). But he could not find his way out of the mind he had made visible, an entrapment that proves to have been historic insofar as it paved the way for the deluge of male intellectual introspection, otherwise known as the I-novel, the perduring core of modern

Japanese literature. The know-it-all narrator in the early parts of *Clouds* sustained a sense of inside-outside, but after he disappeared, probably for good reason, Futabatei was stuck. What would have allowed him to reconnect inside and outside—to keep the curtain torn beyond moments of crisis? The question must have haunted this pioneering translator, who never lost his hunger for "great action" in the world ("Yo ga hansei," 437).

Works Cited

Futabatei Shimei. "Sakka kushindan" ["Tales of a Writer's Struggles"]. 1897. In *Sakka no jiden 1: Futabatei Shimei* [*Autobiography of a Writer*], edited by Hata Yûzô, 48–54. Tokyo: Nihon Tosho Centâ, 1994.

———. *Ukigumo* [*Drifting Clouds*]. 1887–89. In Tsubouchi Yûzô, 4–220.

———. "Watashi wa kaigiha da" ["I Am a Skeptic"]. 1908. In Tsubouchi Yûzô, 416–23.

———. "Yo ga genbun itchi no yurai" ["How I Came to Write *genbun itchi*"]. 1906. In Tsubouchi Yûzô, 412–15.

———. "Yo ga hansei no zange" ["Confessions at Midlife"]. 1908. In Tsubouchi Yûzô, 424–37. Also, "Midlife Confessions," translated by Mamiko Suzuki in *From Japan's Modernity: A Reader*, 81–89. Center for East Asian Studies, University of Chicago Select Papers 11, 2002.

———. "Yo ga hon'yaku no hyôjun" ["My Standards of Translation"]. 1905. In Tsubouchi Yûzô, 405–11.

Hirata Yumi. *Josei hyôgen no Meijishi: Higuchi Ichiyô izen* [*A Meiji History of Women's Expression: Before Higuchi Ichiyô*]. Tokyo: Iwanami Shoten, 1999.

Inoue Hisashi. *Kokugo gannen* [*National Language Year One*]. Tokyo: Shinchôsha, 1986.

Kamei Hideo. *Transformations of Sensibility: The Phenomenology of Meiji Literature* [*Kansei no henkaku*, 1983]. Translated and edited by Michael Bourdaghs. Ann Arbor: Center for Japanese Studies, University of Michigan, 2002.

Karatani Kojin. *Origins of Modern Japanese Literature* [*Nihon kindai bungaku no kigen*, 1980]. Translated and edited by Brett de Bary. Durham, N.C.: Duke University Press, 1993.

Maeda Ai. *Toshi kûkan no naka no bungaku* [*The Literature of Urban Space*]. Tokyo: Chikuma Shobô, 1982.

Ryan, Marleigh Grayer, trans. *Japan's First Modern Novel: Ukigumo of Futabatei Shimei*. UNESCO Collection of Representative Works, Japan Series. New York: Columbia University Press, 1965.

Tsubouchi Shôyô. *Shôsetsu shinzui* [*The Essence of the Novel*, 1885–86]. Edited by Yanagida Izumi. Tokyo: Iwanami Shoten, 1936.

Tsubouchi Yûzô, ed. *Futabatei Shimei*. Tokyo: Chikuma Shobô, 2000.

Walker, Janet. "Futabatei Shimei's *Ukigumo* as a Vehicle of Cognitive and Emotional Reorientation in a Period of Cultural Change." In *Literary Intercrossings: East Asia and the West*, edited by Mabel Lee and A. D. Syrokomla-Stefanowska. University of Sydney World Literature Series 2. Sydney: Wild Peony, 1998.

JALE PARLA

A Carriage Affair
(Recaizade Mahmut Ekrem, Turkey, 1896)

The novel entered the Ottoman culture during the last three decades of the nineteenth century with the works of its major Turkish forerunners, namely Ahmet Mithat Efendi, Namık Kemal, and Recaizade Mahmut Ekrem. The period is also marked by the official Westernization of the empire when literature, along with other institutions, became the object of the modernizing efforts of a new, Westernized intelligentsia that replaced the previous bureaucratic Ottoman elite. Although the first novelists turned to European models (especially French) as they introduced the new genre, the fact that they were reproducing the literary practice of a foreign culture did not bother them much, at least, on the surface. As far as they were concerned, the Western literary models could be used with moderation in order to borrow a few practical writing techniques and a couple of interesting plots. The genre, these early modernizers insisted, no matter how new it was as a narrative mode, must certainly be informed by their own superior cultural heritage.

At a deeper level of the encounter, however, lay hidden a sense of insecurity and threat that was engendered by the incompatibility between Ottoman communitarian norms and Western individualism, between Islamic a priori scholarship and Western scientific positivism; in short, between Ottoman idealism and Western realism. This sense of insecurity and threat found expression in plots of truancy, in which wayward sons of respectable Ottoman families spent the family fortune in pursuit of sensual pleasures offered by a Westernized way of life, thereby bringing tragedy upon themselves at the same time that they brought about the fall of the house. When this favorite and much-repeated plot of the early Turkish novels is read allegorically, the house stands for the Ottoman culture from which the figure of the traditional father (the Sultan with his obvious weakening of authority) is absent and is not yet replaced by another. The steady decline of the empire has made its culture all the more vulnerable and the need for a father all the more urgent in the face of the assault from the West that is threatening to change manners, morals, art, and politics, by imposing a new way of life based on extravagance. The writer, in this picture, volunteers to substitute the missing father and admonishes the son (who stands for the future of the empire) by warning him of the dangers of the confrontation with the West.

The plot of Recaizade Mahmut Ekrem's *A Carriage Affair* (1896) is no different from the standard truancy structure. Ekrem's goal, in reworking the familiar plot, was to give an example of the "realistic" novel; what he achieved, however, went far beyond that modest objective. Among the other novels of the Tanzimat period, *A Carriage Affair* occupies a unique place: its writer was totally aware of the cultural chaos of his age and perceived the dark space at the meeting point of not only two opposing cultures, but more significant, of two different epistemologies. Moreover, Ekrem felt that it was impossible to represent any kind of reality from that space. He was convinced that the distance between illusion and reality could not be bridged by the writing strategies of his contemporaries, and he expressed this conviction in this novel, which he composed in the form of a parody of writing and reading activities. What made Ekrem unique among his contemporaries was his transformation of all practices into futility, all aspirations into failure, all emotion into meaningless emotionalism, and imagination into nothingness. As such, *A Carriage Affair* must also be called the first modern Turkish novel. Here I am using the term *modern* to mean the display of a consciousness that views the consciousness of the age from outside, that directs its analytic edge to itself as well as to the other practices of its time, that employs questioning at the same time as self-questioning. This modern approach led Ekrem to reject the current practices related to form and plot in the novel, to parody the older narrative forms, and to ironize his own narrative. He extends his irony by weaving into his text a rich fabric of intertextuality that consists of allusions to the classical Ottoman Divan poetry; the French romantics, such as Lamartine and Hugo; as well as his contemporary Tanzimat literature. In order to convey the slippery epistemological ground on which the first Turkish novels are constructed, he creates a sense of precipice over which any narrative strategy will fall and perish: the themes, characters, relationships, even the very plot itself. In *A Carriage Affair*, all things are fated to dissolve; carriages disappear, loves are lost, the beloveds vanish, love letters are not read but crushed and discarded. All personal relationships follow a futile circularity, mimicking the routes followed by the carriages in which the *nouveaux riches* and the Westernized fops go round and round to flaunt their latest Parisian acquisitions.

The protagonist of *A Carriage Affair* is another one of the frequently satirized *beaus* who disparage everything Turkish and extol everything French. He has a quixotic dimension to his character with a difference: he is petty. But like Don Quixote, he is a character who models his life on textuality—in his case, French romantic poetry. However, as opposed to Don Quixote, who is well versed in chivalric literature, Bihruz Bey of *A Carriage Affair* is pathetically ignorant of French language and literature. To make matters worse, he is totally cut off from his own language and literature as well.

During one of his carriage excursions in Çamlıca, Bihruz Bey becomes enamored of a beautiful woman he glimpses in another carriage. He decides the woman is a modern, French-educated young girl of a noble family and, therefore, fit for his amorous attentions. As Bihruz Bey builds castles in the air about the "refined" affair that has come his way, the reader finds out that, far from being a well-educated girl of a good family, the woman in the carriage (which is, by the way, a rented one) is one of the best-known courtesans of İstanbul. Her name is Periveş (fairy), as befits women of her profession. Although warned by a friend about Periveş's true identity, the misguided Bihruz does not heed the advice and loses himself in elaborate dreams of a fantastic affair to be culminated in marriage.

Obsessed by the image of Periveş Bihruz Bey comes back to the place he first saw her, but she does not appear. The frustration of not seeing her again leads the young man to distraction as his dreams about Periveş invade his days and nights. These dreams are crucial in revealing the tragicomic confusion he is in, for they come in a melange of Turkish and French words that make no sense:

> The carriage of Periveş speeds so fast down the slope that leads to Beylerbeyi that the wheels do not touch the ground. The fantastic animals that pull the carriage do not look like horses. . . . Bihruz Bey, riding a steed, follows the carriage but cannot catch up. He spurs his horse, drives it on, but just as he is about to catch up, his horse begins to run backwards. Bihruz Bey turns around to find out that an old woman (perhaps Madame Pierre) is hanging onto the tail of his horse and pulling the horse back! In the meantime, M. Pierre, wearing a long robe de chambre and a woman's hat adorned with colored feathers, with a Bordeau bottle of wine under each arm, appears. Mme. and M. Pierre jump and dance as they sing: "Que est-ce que l'amour? C'est un tambour! C'est un tambour! . . . Mais mon cher chavalier! J'ai vu enfin que le beau sex vaut mieux qu'un lapin!" And as they jump, they turn the carriage over. From within the carriage rush out a couple of turtles and a little dog. And then Bihruz Bey's steed frees itself and flies into the air, the turtles begin to dance, and the little fino barks to the tunes of the opera *La belle Hélène*.[1]

---

[1] Recaizade Mahmut Ekrem, *Araba Sevdasi* (*A Carriage Affair*), edited by Seyit Kemal (Istanbul, 1985), 54. All translations from this text are mine.

Following this dream that signifies the confusion of Bihruz Bey's consciousness and his frustration in reaching the unattainable object of his desire, Ekrem employs a series of parodies that mock the high-flown language of the "academic" Tanzimat novels, with their rhetoric of love and of noble aspirations. The subject of all this grandeloquence is Bihruz Bey, who finally decides to put theory into practice and sits down to compose a love letter to his beloved Periveş.

The composition of this love letter by the ignorant Bihruz parodies the confusion that Ekrem believes his contemporary literary practice is in. The frustrations of writing the letter surpass the frustrations of the pursuit of the carriage. Bihruz Bey first asks his French tutor, M. Pierre, to help him compose it. Finding him unwilling to cooperate, Bihruz resorts to his own resources. He picks up two books from his library, Rousseau's *La nouvelle Héloise* and *Secretaire des amants*, whose author is not known. Bihruz finds *La nouvelle Héloise* too dificult to read and sets it aside. Nevertheless, he tries to improvise on a couple of sentences he copies from Rousseau's text and produces an absurd, meaningless letter. Somewhat aware of the shortcomings of this epistle, he turns to the *Secretaire des amants*, which he finds more appropriate for his purpose. He struggles through this text by often resorting to a dictionary and produces a second text that surpasses the first in its incoherence and senselessness. Nevertheless, he likes this one better. Its only fault, he believes, is that it lacks some love poems. He loots the *Secretaire* for one that will serve his purpose and picks up a poem to translate. The translation he achieves after an enormous effort he finds totally incomprehensible. The translation reads thus:

> I name a rose
> That woman who confuses my mind
> If the word owes to represent the thing
> That woman deserves that name of beauty
> Like a rose.

In this poem, there is one line that makes absolutely no sense to Bihruz Bey: "If the word owes to represent the thing." He puts the *Secretaire* aside as he mumbles to himself: "Tous les poètes sont fous." He now turns to classical Ottoman poetry, which he finds impossible to decipher and has to make do with popular songs. He finds one that he thinks will beautifully serve his purpose. It is a song composed for a certain *siyehçerde* which means dark, handsome young man. Ignorant of the meaning of the word, he addresses his beloved as *siyehçerde*, and finally content with his epistle, he waits for the opportunity to deliver it. He frequents the site for many days until he spots Periveş's carriage approaching his own. He runs and delivers the letter. Agonizing days follow as Bihruz waits for a response from his beloved. He imagines all kinds of reactions except for the actual one: upon receiving the letter, Periveş has not even looked at it but has thrown it into the old cemetery nearby, after tearing it to pieces.

Bihruz Bey waits for Periveş at the appointed place in his letter, but she never appears. He decides he must have unwittingly insulted her. When he is finally enlightened about the true meaning of *siyehçerde*, he wishes to kill himself for his blunder. Now he knows what went wrong. The thing to do, he decides, is to write another letter and apologize. In this letter he puts the lines that he had decided not to put in the first letter, including the line that reads, "if the word owes to represent the thing." He still does not understand what these words mean, but hopes that they will remedy the blunder of the *siyehçerde*. And poor Bihruz begins his search anew, with another senseless letter in his hand, in a determined effort to find its reader, a reader who is not in the least interested in what Bihruz is trying to say in words that are far from representing the thing.

Yet Periveş does not appear. To amuse himself with Bihruz's obsession, a friend tells him she has died. Bihruz is thrown into despair. He now plunders anthologies of French poetry to find verses about women who died young. He recites Lamartine's *Graziella* near a grave where he thinks Periveş must be buried. The subtitle "Le premier regret" he misinterprets and searches to find the second and the third regrets. Failing, he moves on to Hugo's *La chute d'un ange*. Totally ignorant of the subject matter of Hugo's epic, he believes it to be a poem about the death of a beautiful woman. He roams the streets of İstanbul reciting the only line he can remember from *Graziella*: C'est bientôt pour mourir.

One day, as he roams the streets in sadness, the bereaved Bihruz runs across Periveş. Stunned, he stands facing her only to be met with her derisive laughter. A red carriage turns the corner at full speed, and Bihruz Bey, who is forced to step aside, pronounces the last word of the novel: "Pardon!"

The unread letter of *A Carriage Affair* is a subtext, in a way another missing text, the composition of which parallels the familiar plot of wayward sons doomed to ridicule or disaster because of their zeal for overmodernization. The letter undermines that zeal by taking the critical intent of the novelist a step further than simply satirizing or condemning unchecked enthusiasm for the adaptation of Western culture. Bihruz's poorly composed, incomplete, and unread epistle signifies the mimetic crisis that Ekrem perceived was engendered by cultural and linguistic chaos, by an epistemological dead end where *the word fails to represent the thing.* The voice of *A Carriage Affair* is neither the communal, conciliatory voice of the typical Westernizing elite, nor the iconoclastic, blasphemous one of the more dedicated Westernizer. It is the voice of an alienated narrator that reduces "everything" to "nothing" and has no solution to offer except for the apology of the last word: "Pardon!"

The Heartless
(Yi Kwangsu, Korea, 1917)

In Korea the development of the novel resembles that of Christianity. Both the novel and Christianity were transmitted from modern Europe, began to find their supporters among those on society's periphery, and then played a substantial role in the formation of Korea's cultural modernity. Just as Christians in Korea found in Protestantism a new religious and ethical ideology necessary for the project of "civilizing" their homeland, so writers in Korea discovered in the European novel and its Japanese variation a new literary language that would define, represent, and rouse their nation according to the terms of modernity. At the center of the "new literature" that these writers took upon themselves to create, lay the idea of the European novel that had begun to be translated and to circulate in Japan from the second half of the nineteenth century. With his *Shōsetsu Shinzui* (*The Essence of the Novel*), published between 1885 and 1886, Tsubouchi Shōyō, a critic sometimes acclaimed as the founder of modern Japanese literature, had established the idea of the novel as an art that existed for its own sake and had set forth a program for the reform of Japanese fiction based on this idea. In the most important section of the book he declared that the main work of fiction was not to follow the principle of "encouraging virtue and chastising vice," but to depict in depth "human emotions" by which he meant the interiority of individuals. In some of his essays, which signal the birth of a modern view of literature, Yi Kwangsu (1892–1950) also adopted the position of separating fiction from morality and viewing it as an art, and declared that the objective of literature lay in the realistic representation of people's actual thoughts and emotions. There is no doubt that in Korea the appearance of the novel comprises an attempt to free human life from the chains of Confucian ideology and to organize that life anew. Similar to Christianity, in Korea the novel was a project that worked toward the transformation of people by seeking in an interior life, which had been concealed and oppressed by Confucianism, some new human possibility in accord with the demands of modernity.

In Korea's first full-length novel *Mujŏng* (*The Heartless*), serialized in a daily newspaper in 1917, this search for the modern man constitutes the major impulse for Yi Kwangsu's story of the self-formation of a youth named Yi Hyŏngshik. Hyŏngshik is orphaned as a child and wanders the world helplessly until he meets Pak Ŭngjin, an enlightened activist and scholar in a small village in Pyŏng'an province. With Pak's help, Hyŏngshik's fortunes change; he receives an education and even studies in Japan before returning to Korea where, as the novel begins, he is working as an English teacher at Kyŏngsŏng High School in Seoul. As suggested by his orphan status and study abroad, Hyŏngshik is excluded from all the privileges and culture of traditional Korean society and stands a good chance of success in the contemporary society, which is undergoing full-scale reorganization with the imposition of Japanese colonial rule.

The story begins with an event that seems to hint that an opportunity for advancement is coming his way. Kim Kwanghyŏn, a Presbyterian church elder and one of the richest men in Seoul, has asked Hyŏngshik to tutor his daughter, Sŏnhyŏng, in English before she leaves to study in the United States. When Hyŏngshik first meets the beautiful Sŏnhyŏng at her father's house, he is unwittingly overcome with the expectation of erotic fulfillment, but his excitement is interrupted by another woman, named Yongch'ae, who suddenly appears at his boarding house after an interval of over seven years and tearfully tells him about the deaths of her father and brothers and her wretched life ever since. Hyŏngshik is thrown into mental turmoil by the appearance of the daughter of the man who had saved him from starvation and ignorance and who had also once promised his daughter in marriage to him. In his unconscious, he is attracted by the happiness and success that marriage to Sŏnhyŏng seems to promise him, but consciously he persuades himself that he must rescue Yŏngch'ae from her unhappy fate by marrying her. The desire to realize his self is pitted against his sense of duty, individualism against Confucian morality. In other words, Hyŏngshik represents the modern ego, which may be fragile but is still growing in the womb of colonized Korea at the beginning of the twentieth century, where the fall of one culture and the birth of another was simultaneously experienced.

As befits his job as a schoolteacher, Hyŏngshik appears to be a well-disciplined person, but his heart harbors desires that conflict with his morals. Hyŏngshik's self-observation, self-censorship, and the hiding of his desires from other people makes him the first interiorized character to appear in Korean fiction. But the conflict between those desires and morals is not developed dramatically throughout the plot. Despite her occupation as a *kisaeng* entertainer, a female entertainer trained in traditional Korean arts of poetry, music, and dance, Yŏngch'ae has protected her chastity in preparation for marriage to Hyŏngshik, but when she is raped, she leaves for Pyongyang, leaving behind a letter, in which she explains her shame and intention to commit suicide. Hyŏngshik follows her to Pyongyang, but returns to Seoul believing that she is dead, having made little effort to search for her. The day after his return, he receives word from Elder Kim that the old man wishes him to marry Sŏnhyŏng and go with her to the United States. In the presence of a pastor at Kim's house, Hyŏngshik pledges to marry her. He then berates himself as a "heartless" person, ultimately responsible for the death of the tragic Yŏngch'ae, who gave her heart to him but whose love was never reciprocated.

However, this does not mean that he condemns his desires that caused him to betray Yŏngch'ae. The description of Hyŏngshik's consciousness following the meetings with Sŏnhyŏng and Yŏngch'ae tends to focus on moments when he affirms his own desires. In a scene where he visits Pak's grave while in Pyongyang, he strengthens his resolve to pursue pleasure and advancement by deciding "not to be sad at the sight of the poor Pak's remaining bones, but to enjoy the flowers which have bloomed on the grave and fed on his rotted flesh."[1] And in the train returning to Seoul from Pyongyang, when his thoughts reach the conclusion that he must not yield to social custom but instead follow his own discretion and judgment, he is stirred: "Now he had finally become aware of his life. He had become aware of his self." This self-awakening, which results from the separation of desire and morality, proves decisively that Hyŏngshik has parted with the Confucian idea of self-cultivation that aims at harmony with the moral order of nature.

The Heartless simultaneously documents the appearance of the modern ego and critiques narratives grounded on Confucian doctrines. The character with the most richly developed history in the novel is Yŏngch'ae, who belongs to the type of the ill-fated woman from premodern prose fiction. Like her literary foremothers, she embodies femininity as constructed within Confucian culture. She has grown up with a Confucian education, beginning with the study of *The Biographies of Virtuous Women* from an early age; become a *kisaeng* in order to save her father and brothers, who were imprisoned on false charges; and protected her chastity while awaiting the marriage to Hyŏngshik in line with her father's wishes. Although she undergoes great hardship and temptation after the death of her protectors, she still clings to her belief that good and bad are clearly distinguishable in the human world. Her act of protecting her chastity for Hyŏngshik reveals her determination to confirm a reality in her own life that complies with that belief.

The Confucian belief in an unchanging moral order in the human world makes her into a symbol of the old Korea, along with the old-fashioned world of sensual pleasure expressed through her status as a *kisaeng*. In this way *The*

---

[1] Yi Kwangsu, *Mujŏng* (*The Heartless*) (Seoul: Munhakdongne, 2003). All quotations are from this edition, and the translations are my own.

Heartless, which professes enlightenment along the lines of Western and Japanese models, feminizes Confucian Korea much in the same way that Orientalist discourse feminizes the Orient. The vulnerability of a pure and moral Korea is clearly exposed in the incident where Yŏngch'ae is raped by the Kyŏngsŏng High School governor and headmaster, the benefactors of colonial authority. Although the world of ordered morality is portrayed with affection, it is already no longer a reality. Therefore, although Hyŏngshik feels attraction and pity toward Yŏngch'ae after she sacrifices herself in pursuit of the ideals of the virtuous women, he does not carry through with the promise to marry her. His "heartlessness" not only perceives the perishing of Confucian Korea to be inevitable, but as a merciless pose of enlightenment pursued in the name of civilization. In the latter half of *The Heartless*, with the help of Pyŏng'uk, Hyŏngshik's female equivalent, Yŏngch'ae realizes that her life has amounted to no more than enslavement to conventionality and begins to undergo a metamorphosis for the sake of an autonomous life.

The new person pictured in *The Heartless* is a free man or woman who tries to define him or herself according to his/her own cognitive and moral capacities. This person is conscious of his/her own self, which tries to throw off the constraints of custom and the system in order to assert and expand itself; s/he tries to organize her/his own individual and social life in order to satisfy these desires. At the time he was writing *The Heartless*, Yi Kwangsu understood the desire to assert and expand the self to be the way of the world. In common with many other enlightened thinkers in Korea and Japan, he was heavily influenced by social Darwinism and believed that the liberation of desire was necessary for both individuals and nations to survive in the modern world. However, the program to liberate desire can all too easily push individuals' and nations' lives into a Leviathan state, as suggested by the actions of the school governor and headmaster, who rape Yŏngch'ae, and the students who mock Hyŏngshik.

And so *The Heartless* moves toward regulating individual desire and advances a political and ethical principle for limiting freedom. That principle is nationalism. Hyŏngshik, Sŏnhyŏng, Yŏngch'ae and Pyŏng'uk meet again by chance when they all take the same train at the beginning of their journeys to study abroad. As they reach the Samnang ferry, they witness the devastation wrought on one village by a flood. The tragic sight of the villagers helpless in the face of the violence of nature brings to a head the images of Korea as a backward and uncivilized society, images that are stressed repeatedly throughout the novel. While their train is held up by the flood, the four young people go about trying to raise money to help the villagers, and in the process the seeds of conflict that have been growing for a while in the hearts of

Hyŏngshik, Yŏngch'ae and Sŏnhyŏng are eased. This latent conflict in their relationships is dissolved in their shared realization of their duty to master Western scholarship and art with the goal of saving their poor and ignorant compatriots. The new person who *The Heartless* tries to reveal to the world seems to appear in a relatively whole form for the first time when these young people regard themselves as free individuals yet build a form of cooperation by committing themselves to the task of bringing civilization to their nation.

The author of *The Heartless* belongs to the first young generation in Korea who lost faith in their ancestors' culture (whose decrepitude seemed to have been proved by their country's submission to Japanese colonialism) and saw the opportunities for a new life opened up by the study of Western culture. Raised on the Western-style educational institutions both within Korea and abroad, this new generation not only asserted their prerogatives for self-expression and social advancement, but considered it to be their duty to be political and intellectual leaders. In a society where history was felt all the more keenly as traditional authority collapsed under colonial rule and every sphere of life was drawn into the maelstrom of change, they discovered possibilities for self-development along with the duty of self-reliance. By depicting characters who liberated their desires from the constraints of morality and went on to unite those desires with the will of the nation, Yi Kwangsu provided a heroic type of youth that would legitimate his generation's demands. He did not hesitate to describe Hyŏngshik's experiences of restlessness and capriciousness, of suspicion and consideration, and of hypocrisy and passion as a process of growth.

The Heartless is a Korean version of *bildungsroman* in that its narrative revolves around a young man whose self-formation ultimately merges into the nation's self-strengthening. However, Hyŏngshik's maturity is both politically and morally dubious, because the fact is that his youth, or his upwardly mobile life depends on Japanese colonial administration for its realization. The criticism of Korea as miserably backward, which is the enabling condition of his heroic youth, is rather similar to the thinking of Japanese colonialists, who in propaganda presented their oppression and exploitation of the Korean people as the blessings of civilization. Consequently, Hyŏngshik's maturity remains no more than another term for adaptation to the colonial regime. *The Heartless* thematized the self-formation of youth against the background of a society in turmoil, and by doing so it propelled the dynamics of modernity into Korean fiction, but at the same time it failed to endow a narrative language to Koreans' efforts to make their own history and decide their own fate. Much more time was needed before the novel form became adequate for Koreans' self-expression.

M. KEITH BOOKER

Chaka
(Thomas Mofolo, South Africa, 1925)

Thomas Mofolo's *Chaka* is a historical novel based on the career of the great Zulu leader, Chaka (a.k.a. Shaka), who was the principal chief of the Zulu nation from about 1816 until his death in 1828, leading the Zulus during that time in a number of campaigns of conquest that led to the establishment of an extensive empire in southern Africa. However, Mofolo's narrative is highly fictionalized, and many aspects of Chaka's career as related in the book have been modified, omitted, or invented, presumably for dramatic effect.[1] Written in the Sesotho (Southern Sotho) language, *Chaka* also draws in important ways on folk traditions and on the conventions of African oral epics. In many cases, however, it subverts those conventions, repudiating traditional African culture in favor of the Christian culture Mofolo learned at the Morija mission, in Lesotho, South Africa, where he wrote the book. It is, therefore, reasonable to consider the book a novel, despite its complex mixture of generic elements. Indeed, based on the work of Mikhail Bakhtin, one could argue that *Chaka* is an exemplary novel that perfectly illustrates Bakhtin's vision of the novel as an inherently multigeneric form that derives much of its force from its ability to incorporate different social points of view (including different genres) and to set them into dialogue with one another.[2]

In its incorporation of elements from African oral narratives, *Chaka* anticipates such later phenomena as the Nigerian novelist Chinua Achebe's use of Igbo proverbs and folktales in *Things Fall Apart* (1958) or the Kenyan novelist Ngugi wa Thiong'o's use of Gikuyi oral narrative structures and styles in *Devil on the Cross* (1980) and *Matigari* (1986). Albert Gérard notes the historical importance of *Chaka*, arguing that "the foundation of the novel in Southern Sotho must be ascribed" to the work of Mofolo.[3] In addition,

---

[1] For a succinct survey of some of Mofolo's deviations from the historical record, see Daniel P. Kunene's introduction to his translation of *Chaka* (Oxford, 1981). For a further discussion, including speculation on the historical sources Mofolo might have used, see C. F. Swanepoel, "Historicity and Mofolo's *Chaka:* A Comparison of Text and Possible Sources," *South African Journal of African Languages* 8, no. 1 (1988): 23–27.

[2] See Mikhail Bakhtin, *The Dialogic Imagination*, trans. Caryl Emerson and Michael Holquist (Austin, Tex., 1981).

[3] Albert S. Gérard, *Four African Literatures: Xhosa, Sotho, Zulu, Amharic* (Berkeley, Calif., 1971), 108.

having been completed in manuscript form by Mofolo some time before 1910, *Chaka* has some claim to being the first novel written by a black African to receive any sort of widespread attention.[4] However, *Chaka* was not published until 1925, after a somewhat complex history that apparently saw much of the original manuscript excised before publication.[5] A full English translation of *Chaka*, by F. H. Dutton, was published in 1931, though the most widely read version now is the later English translation by Daniel P. Kunene.[6] Abridged versions of the novel have since been published in English, German, French, Italian, and Swahili. It has become generally acknowledged as a classic, described by Gérard as a "major landmark in the literary history of black Africa and as "the first novel written in an African language which was to have an international circulation."[7]

In this sense, *Chaka* is a landmark text in the history of African literature and in the efforts of African writers to contribute to the development of positive African cultural identities that escape the domination of the colonialist culture of Europe. Among other things, *Chaka* addresses early on many of the issues that would be faced by postcolonial African writers. For example, as a novel, the book raises questions about the suitability of that quintessential European bourgeois genre for African writers, who are seeking to overcome the cultural domination of the European bourgeoisie. Bakhtin's work is again relevant here, because his vision of the novel depicts it as a form rooted in folk cultural energies that go back thousands of years, thus suggesting that the genre transcends bourgeois ideology, even if it does experience a special "flowering" during the rise of the European bourgeoisie to power in the eighteenth century. Bakhtin's vision of the novel as an ever-evolving, infinitely flexible form also suggests that the genre can move beyond bourgeois ideology in the future, whether that movement be toward the development of socialist novels in Bakhtin's own Soviet Union or toward the development of postcolonial novels in Africa. Events would bear out his supposition: the novel would be central to the impressive literary achievements of Soviet socialist realism from the 1920s to the 1950s, just as it has

---

[4] However, Mofolo himself had already written and published two other (now obscure) novels in Sesotho by this time. See Thomas Mofolo, *Moeti oa Bochabela* (Morija, South Africa, 1907); and Thomas Mofolo, *Pitseng* (Morija, South Africa, 1910). For a brief survey of Mofolo's writings, see Daniel P. Kunene, *The Works of Thomas Mofolo: Summaries and Critiques* (Los Angeles, 1967).

[5] For a detailed account of the history of the manuscript, see Daniel P. Kunene, *Thomas Mofolo and the Emergence of Written Sesotho Prose* (Braamfontein, South Africa, 1989).

[6] Thomas Mofolo, *Chaka*, trans. Daniel P. Kunene (Oxford 1981). Quotations from this work are cited parenthetically in the text.

[7] Albert Gérard, "Rereading *Chaka*," *English in Africa* 13, no. 1 (1986): 1.

been the most important genre of postcolonial literature from the 1950s onward.[8]

Chaka, by incorporating so many elements of traditional African oral narrative into its novelistic framework, well illustrates the flexibility of the novel as a genre. As outlined by Kwame Ayivor, these conventions include "the noble ancestry of the hero, the mysteriousness of his birth and early youth, his supernatural and magical endowments, his pre-eminence as hero, his ability to invoke supernatural agents to aid him in his destiny, and his heroic martial ferocity." In addition, Ayivor notes that Mofolo supplements this characterization of his hero through the use of crucial epic narrative techniques, including images of epic horror and the representation of praise singing.[9] On the other hand, Mofolo's use of techniques and motifs from traditional African oral narratives is complicated by his largely negative characterization of the protagonist Chaka, especially after his rise to power. It is thus not entirely clear whether *Chaka* enacts a dialogic encounter between African and European culture, in the dialogic mode praised by Bakhtin, or whether it introduces African culture in order to demonstrate, in monologic fashion, the ultimate inferiority of that culture to the culture of Europe.

At first glance, the historical subject matter of *Chaka* might seem to make it a forerunner of the numerous late African novels that would attempt to contribute to the reconstruction of the African past from positive perspectives, overcoming the legacy of European colonialist historiography. For example, each of Ngugi's novels focuses on a particular moment in the history of Kenya, and together his novels, ranging from *The River Between* (1965) to *Matigari*, constitute a sweeping historical narrative that tells the story of Kenya from the early days of British colonization to the contemporary postcolonial period, highlighting the strong Kenyan tradition of resistance to oppression. Similarly, Achebe, in works such as *Things Fall Apart*, seeks to provide his African readers with a realistic depiction of their precolonial past, free of the distortions and stereotypes imposed on that past in European accounts. Meanwhile, Senegal's Ousmane Sembène, in *Les bouts de bois de Dieu* (1960), dramatizes a 1947–48 railway strike in French colonial Africa, thus providing his contemporary readership with an example of effective

---

[8] For a discussion of the ways in which Bakhtin's theories of the novel suggest the relevance of that genre to the project of developing postcolonial cultural identities in emerging third-world nations, see Timothy Brennan, "The National Longing for Form," in *Nation and Narration*, ed. Homi K. Bhabha (London, 1990), 44–70.

[9] Kwame Ayivor, "Thomas Mopoku Mofolo's 'Inverted Epic Hero': A Reading of Mofolo's *Chaka* as an African Epic Folktale," *Research in African Literatures* 28 (1997): 49.

resistance to European domination. And Ayi Kwei Armah's *Two Thousand Seasons* (1979) attempts to construct, through fiction, the past glories of the Ashanti Empire in what is now Ghana.

Indeed, Mofolo's book is in many ways an important forerunner of such later African novels. If nothing else, *Chaka* is an impressive literary achievement marked by a strong imaginative vision and dramatic power. It thereby demonstrates that the African past can serve as effective material for literary representation. Moreover, as discussed by Mbongeni Malaba, Mofolo's presentation of the story of Chaka served as a direct inspiration for a number of later works on the same subject, including an entire family of "Chakan" poems and plays by Francophone African writers.[10] However, these later Francophone writers largely treat Chaka as a heroic figure, whose representation contributes to the attempt to construct a positive vision of the African past. Their works thus foreshadow the attempts of writers such as Ngugi and Sembène to use the African past as a source for viable African cultural identities in the present, surmounting the legacy of negative European colonialist representations of African history. Yet Mofolo presents Chaka as a seriously flawed character, whose violent reign exemplifies a savage African past that, in fact, seems to confirm typical colonialist stereotypes.

In fact, Ayivor concludes that Mofolo's book functions as a "literary subversion" of recent attempts to develop positive models of African history that can serve as counternarratives to European colonialist histories.[11] In this sense, Mofolo's *Chaka* is less a precursor of the works of writers such as Ngugi and Achebe than of a work such as Yambo Ouologuem's somewhat notorious depiction of African history as a never-ending cycle of abject violence in *Le devoir de violence* (1968).[12] Indeed, Mofolo's Chaka is more villain than hero, even though his villainy is motivated in Mofolo's narrative by a justified resentment over the rejection and abuse he suffers in childhood, then exacerbated by the manipulation of the conniving Isanusi, an African "doctor" and sorcerer, from whose charms Chaka derives a considerable portion of his power. No doubt part of Mofolo's negative view of Chaka comes from the fact that he sees his own Sesotho people as the historical victims of the Chaka-led campaigns of Zulu expansion. Another source of this view may be the fact that Mofolo probably gained much of his historical information from

---

[10] Mbongeni Malaba, "The Legacy of Thomas Mofolo's *Chaka*," *English in Africa* 13, no. 1 (1986): 61–71.

[11] Ayivor, "Mofolo's 'Inverted Epic Hero,'" 49.

[12] Yambo Ouologuem, *Le devoir de violence* (Paris, 1968).

biased European accounts that sought to diminish Chaka's achievements by depicting them as typical examples of African savagery and barbarism.[13]

Mofolo depicts pagan magic as a crucial element of both traditional African culture and Chaka's rise to power. Such magic is also crucial to the moral decline suffered by Chaka after he achieves power. Early on, though he is an amiable, regal child, Chaka has a difficult childhood and is much abused by the other boys—and even the adults—in his village. However, fortified by magical charms and medicines, he eventually becomes fierce and strong enough to rout his tormentors and to perform several heroic deeds, gaining fame, but also increasing the resentment that is directed toward him, especially by his half-brothers. Ultimately, he is forced to flee into the forest, after an altercation in which he nearly kills his half-brother, Mfokazana. There he meets the mysterious and powerful Isanusi, who fortifies him with additional charms and informs him that he will become a great king if only he will pursue that kingship with ruthless intensity. For his own part, Isanusi pledges to aid Chaka in any way that he can, for the promise of some future, unspecified, payment.

Isanusi then helps Chaka make his way to the capital city of the greatest king in the region, Dingiswayo, who is depicted as a paragon of virtue and an enlightened leader. He will ultimately serve in the text as a counterpart to Chaka, whose overarching ambition eventually makes him an extreme figure of cruelty and ruthlessness. Soon after his arrival, Chaka uses an enchanted spear given him by Isanusi to slay a dangerous madman who has been tormenting the locals. Chaka then joins Dingiswayo's army, and, aided by Isanusi's magic, soon distinguishes himself in battle against Zwide, Dingiswayo's chief enemy. Meanwhile, Isanusi sends his minions, Malunga and Ndlebe, to aid Chaka in his efforts to pursue his ambition to be a great king. They are, in fact, of great help to Chaka, even though Dingiswayo is suspicious of them and regards them as evil.

As he gains more and more power, Chaka, partly owing to his immersion in the magic of Isanusi, becomes less and less human. So, as he begins his rise to power, he puts aside all other values except his quest for a great kingship: "He had already resolved that, however ugly a deed might be, he would do it if only it led him towards that kingship" (55). Chaka thus gains his first throne by finally killing Mfokazana, who has succeeded their father,

---

[13] For a discussion of some of these possible sources, see Swanepoel, "Historiocity and Mofolo's *Chaka*."

Senzangakhona, a local king. Chaka then launches an increasingly savage and ruthless series of campaigns of conquest, extending his rule in all directions and wreaking havoc as he goes. Chaka's legend as a ruler grows, and his people begin to suspect that he has been sent by the gods to carry out their will. However, his ruthless treatment, not only of his enemies, but of supporters whom he views as a possible threat to his power, eventually turns the people against him. On the advice of Isanusi, Chaka sacrifices his own wife, Noliwa (the sister of the now-deceased Dingiswayo), in order to use her blood as a charm to fortify his armies. After her death, we are told, "the last spark of humanity remaining in him was utterly and finally extinguished" (127). Chaka then goes on to kill his own mother when she attempts to identify and protect the unacknowledged offspring that he produces via his numerous liaisons with young courtesans.

Chaka rules with an iron hand, and anyone whom he even vaguely suspects of less than enthusiastic support for his regime is likely to be put to death. Meanwhile, Chaka's reign of terror leads to great suffering and hardship. For example, the ravages of Chaka's wars destroy crops and lead to widespread starvation. Desperate, the people of the region begin to resort to cannibalism in order to survive: "On account of hunger, people began to eat each other as one eats the flesh of a slaughtered animal; they hunted each other like animals and ate each other; they started because of hunger, but afterwards continued with their cannibalism out of habit" (137). Mofolo thus attributes to Chaka the beginnings of a practice that would serve as one of the central themes of European colonialist visions of Africans as primitive savages. Finally, Chaka is assassinated by his remaining half-brothers, Dingana and Mhlangana. As he dies, he warns his killers that they will not succeed him as powerful kings, but that they will, in fact, be supplanted by the coming of new white rulers to the land. After his death, Chaka's body is ordered left in the open plains, so that it might be devoured by the wild beasts. However, when it is discovered that the beasts refuse to touch the corpse, Dingana orders it buried. The text then ends with an announcement of the coming end of Chaka's great Zulu kingdom. Indeed, the text appears to make clear the historical inevitability of both the fall of Chaka's kingdom and the eventual rise of European colonial rule in Africa.

Given Mofolo's treatment of traditional African oral narrative forms and the vivid extent to which he evokes pagan magic and superstition as contributing factors to Chaka's moral decline, one might see his novel as a thorough rejection of traditional African culture in favor of the Christian culture he had learned from the missionaries at Morija. As Malaba notes, the entire text can be seen as an illustration of the Christian text, "what shall it profit a man if he gain the whole world but lose his soul?"[14] In addition, many aspects of the text recall European culture in ways that tend to suggest that Mofolo was striving to mimic European literature in writing the book. For example, numerous critics have noted the obvious Faustian resonances in Mofolo's portrayal of Chaka, while Gérard suggests that Chaka's trajectory follows a "tragic pattern on the classical Aristotelian model," while also resembling Shakespearean tragedies, such as *Macbeth* and *Othello*.[15]

Of course, Mofolo was working within severe constraints. His only available publishing outlet was the missionary press at Morija, and that press was obviously not interested in publishing anything that did not further its Christian message. Indeed, Mofolo apparently had considerable difficulty in getting *Chaka* cleared for publication, which contributed to the long delay between the original writing and the actual publication of the book. For one thing, despite the negative characterization of Chaka, the text still provides reminders that the achievements of the African past went well beyond what is typically granted in European historical accounts. In addition, Mofolo's evocation of witchcraft and other aspects of traditional African culture is so dramatic that the missionaries apparently felt that it might entice some readers, despite Mofolo's clear rejection of African magic. In addition, the Christian message of *Chaka* is not nearly so clear as the message of Mofolo's two earlier books, both of which contained much more overt and unequivocal Christian moral messages—and both of which were published by the missionary press without hesitation.

Meanwhile, *Chaka* contains numerous complexities that threaten to undermine its apparently pro-European message. In particular, Chaka is presented as a unique, almost superhuman figure, so that his savagery cannot be taken as representative of African culture. Moreover, the sheer literary merit of *Chaka* poses a strong challenge to the legacy of colonialist visions that Africans and African languages were too primitive to produce genuine literature. In addition, the book's reminder of Chaka's achievement in building a vast African empire radically undermines the colonialist notion that traditional African cultures were incapable of large-scale political organization. In this sense, Mofolo's novel made an important contribution to the preservation of the memory of Chaka and to later positive representations of the great Zulu king, ranging from the Francophone plays of the 1950s and

---

[14] Malaba, "The Legacy of Thomas Mofolo's *Chaka*," 66.
[15] Gérard, "Rereading *Chaka*," 10.

1960s to the positive (if problematic) dramatization of Chaka's career in the 1983 British television miniseries (later released as a theatrical film), *Shaka Zulu* (directed by South African William C. Faure). As such, Mofolo's *Chaka* can be considered an important forerunner of the African postcolonial novel, despite its ostensible endorsement of European culture and European rule in Africa.

M. R. GHANOONPARVAR

The Blind Owl
(Sadeq Hedayat, Iran, 1941)

When the French translation of *The Blind Owl* was published in 1953, it was heralded by many French critics as a masterpiece that, according to one reviewer, was sufficient to place its author, Sadeq Hedayat (1903–51), "among the most eloquent and expressive writers of the present century." The same reviewer further observes: "I think this novel has left a special impression on the literary history of our century."[1] In contrast, the initial reaction of British critics to the English translation, which was published in 1958, was generally negative.[2] One reviewer wrote: "This narrative is a rambling, inchoate mass, a sort of verbal bouillabaisse. A western nightmare is a small marvel of lucidity beside this eastern fable. Mescaline before reading might help, but don't try." Another reviewer describes this novel as a mixture of opium dream and fatalism in which the phrases "repeat like the coils of a serpent" and further observes that "reading the hallucinations and fears is like sipping from a bottle of poisoned wine." Since its first publication in Iran in 1941, this novel has evoked either extreme praise or utter contempt in that country as well, mirroring the conflicting reactions abroad. Some have regarded it as the most brilliant expression of the Iranian collective psyche, while others have scorned its author, who committed suicide in Paris, as a psychologically deranged man and the symbol and even the cause

---

[1] The original version of Sadeq Hedayat's *Buf-e Kur* [*The Blind Owl*] first appeared in photocopied form in 1937 in India, because the author thought that the censors in Iran would not have allowed its publication, and was sent by the author to his close friends in Iran. After the abdication of Reza Shah Pahlavi and the Allied occupation in Iran, it was published for the first time in printed format in 1941 in Iran. The French version, translated during World War II by Roger Lescot as *La chouette aveugle*, was not published until 1953. All the information regarding the French and English reviews is found in Hassan Kamshad, *Modern Persian Prose Literature* (Cambridge: Cambridge University Press, 1966), 177–81.

[2] The first English version was translated by D. P. Costello (London: Calder, 1957; New York: Grove Press, 1957), a new edition of which has been reprinted frequently (New York: Evergreen, 1969). Another translation is found in *"The Blind Owl" and Other Hedayat Stories*, compiled by Carol L. Sayers (Minneapolis: Sorayya Publishers, 1984). However, Costello's translation remains the most widely circulated version in English and is the one to which I refer in all parenthetical page citations to the novel.

of the social alienation and nihilism of the younger generations. Such diverse reactions may be owing to the fact that *The Blind Owl* is perhaps the first truly modern Persian novel and by its very nature challenges the traditions and conventions of a millennium of literary expression in the neo-Persian language.[3]

The Blind Owl is a first-person narrative with a simple plot. The un-named narrator and protagonist is a lonely young man who lives in an iso-lated area outside the city of Tehran. He begins his story with the descrip-tion of what he terms an incurable disease, which the reader soon learns is his obsessive love for an imaginary, beautiful woman whom he has seen only once by a strange accident through an imagined window in the dark closet of his room. This "ethereal girl," as he refers to her, appears before his eyes motionless, in a picture reminiscent of scenes frequently depicted in clichéd Persian miniature paintings: a stooped old man sits under a cypress tree and a young woman stands before him, leaning forward and offering the old man a blue morning glory flower across a stream. The old man is biting the nail of the index finger of his right hand. The girl is slender and graceful; she has radiant slanting Turkoman eyes, prominent cheekbones, a high forehead, and full half-open lips. Her face is as pale as the moon, and one strand of her black disheveled hair is clinging to her temple. She is gazing straight ahead with a vague smile.

The narrator then goes outside his house looking for this girl, whom he feels he has known all of his life, but to no avail. There is no sign of the ethereal girl, the old man, the cypress tree, or the stream. Obsessed with finding the object of his love, he searches for her for many days until finally, upon returning home from one of his nocturnal walks in quest of his beloved, he finds her waiting by the door of his house. Without uttering a word, she walks into the narrator's room and lies down on his bed. In a state of stupor and disbelief in his good fortune he tries to be hospitable, but instead, he inadvertently kills her with poisoned wine. The narrator is a painter of pen boxes on which he draws repeatedly the same scene, similar to the one in which he saw the ethereal girl. Ever since that encounter, he has been trying unsuccessfully to capture in his paintings the supernatural quality of her eyes. Now that she is dead, he is finally able to do so. Soon

---

[3] Numerous articles exist in English on *The Blind Owl*. A relatively recent in-depth, book-length study of this work is Michael Beard, *Hedayat's "Blind Owl" as a Western Novel* (Princeton, N.J.: Princeton University Press, 1990). See also Iraj Bashiri, *The Fiction of Sadeq Hedayat* (Lexington, Ky.: Mazda Publishers, 1984).

after, fearing the consequences of the murder, he cuts the body into pieces, places it in a suitcase, and buries her in an isolated spot on the outskirts of the city.

At this point in the story, a change occurs in the setting and characters. We find the narrator in a different world, or as he calls it, "a new world," with a variety of different characters. In this section, the narrator is married and lives in a house with his old nanny. The rather surrealistic and mysterious surroundings and environment of the first part of the novel are now replaced with a more realistic setting and characters. But the narrator's wife, whom he refers to as "the slut," has the same physical appearance as the ethereal girl in the earlier part of the novel. In contrast to the ethereal girl, however, there is nothing supernatural, mysterious, or transcendental about his wife, and while he did not wish to have any physical contact with the ethereal girl, he is sexually obsessed with a wife who feels nothing but contempt for him and has always refused any relationship with him. The narrator thinks that "the slut" has all sorts of lovers, and he is full of disdain for all other people, whom he refers to as the riffraff, including his wife's lovers. He describes the riffraff as nothing more than a stomach and intestines ending in genitals, capable only of eating, sleeping, and copulating. Eventually, his sexual desires for the slut are satisfied when one night he disguises himself as one of his wife's lovers. However, the sexual act functions to transform him physically and emotionally, and as he looks at himself in the mirror, he is appalled to find that he too in fact has ironically become one of the riffraff, the rest of the human race that he despises. The second part of the story also ends as does the first part: the narrator, upon attaining the object of his desire, inadvertently murders his wife.

Numerous critics have observed that the two parts of *The Blind Owl* are in fact two versions of the same story, the first part being a hallucinatory and even idealistic description of the narrator's thoughts and emotions and his relationship with others, and the second part a more realistic albeit psychotic version of the same events. For this reason, in order to better comprehend and decode this enigmatic tale, some critics suggest that the second part should be read first in order to facilitate an understanding of the illusive first part. Perhaps the book itself provides the key for an interpretation of the story. There are two central metaphors, namely, "disease" and "writing," that are crucial to any reading of this work. The novel opens with the subject of disease: "There are sores which slowly erode the mind in solitude like a kind of canker." This is an agonizing disease from which the narrator tells us he suffers. This nameless disease is described merely as a "sore" of some kind.[4] But, it is not a physical ailment; rather it is a disease of the mind. Further, the narrator explains that this disease is usually considered imaginary and is relegated "to the category of the incredible" (1). To the narrator, however, this illness is not imaginary but very real. And although he is unable to name the disease, he attempts to describe it by setting down the case that concerns him personally that may, he thinks, clarify the nature of his disorder. The first part of the story he tells can be described as a fantastic tale, in the tradition of romanticism. His excessive yearning for the unattainable ethereal girl, characteristic of both traditional Persian as well as Western poetry, is not unlike the pains that the European romantics suffered from the so-called *Weltschmerz*, or romantic malady.[5] Like the romantics, the narrator in the first part of the novel feels that he is not understood by others. His "self" is most important to him, again like the romantics, for whom the self is the center of the universe, and he writes his story for his shadow, the projection of his "self" on the wall.

Although the pain and suffering brought on by the narrator's disease, along with the beloved ethereal girl and other constituent elements of the first part of the novel, seem very real to the narrator, they appear irrational and unreal to those who adhere to everyday notions of reality, as the narrator himself recognizes. But in the second part of the novel, the constituent elements of the story, the setting and characters in general, and the disease of the narrator in particular, materialize, become concrete in a sense. Driven by his wife's adverse behavior toward him, he confines himself to his room, abandons all activities, and begins to waste away, as he puts it, from day to day. Here, the narrator provides a description of his physical symptoms: "My body was glowing with heat and the expression of my eyes was languid

---

[4] Although the narrator never names his disease in medical terms, Leonardo P. Alishan in his "The *Ménage à Trois* of *The Blind Owl*" in *Hedayat's "The Blind Owl" Forty Years After*, ed. Michael C. Hillmann (Austin: University of Texas Press, 1978), 179, identifies the disease as tuberculosis. Whether the disease is actually a split identity, as Michael Beard suggests in "Character and Psychology in Hedayat's *Buf-e Kur*," *Edebiyat* 1 (1976): 207–18; the result of his homosexuality, as Carter Bryant posits in "Hedayat's Psychoanalysis of a Nation," in *Hedayat's "The Blind Owl" Forty Years After*, 151–67; or hysteria, as Hassan Kamshad intimates in his chapter, "Hysterical Self-Analysis," in *Modern Persian Prose Literature*, 165–81, the identification of the narrator's disorder in medical or technical terms does not conflict with the argument at hand, the point being that the narrator himself has identified it as a disease of the mind.

[5] See Hushang Golshiri, "Si Sal Romannevisi" ["Thirty Years of Novel Writing"], *Jong-e Esfahan* 5 (Summer 1967): 196, and Bahram Meghdadi and Leo Hamalian, "Oedipus and the Owl," in *Hedayat's "The Blind Owl" Forty Years After*, 142–43.

and depressed" (65). As his condition worsens, the family physician is sent for, who prescribes certain medicines and measures to be taken. The illness, however, grows progressively worse. The narrator's cheeks become crimson, and he explains: "My body was burning hot and I coughed—how deep and horrible my cough was" (67). He suffers from hallucinations of a feverishly sick man. In his semiconsciousness, he even imagines a visit by Azrael, the Muslim angel of death.

The relationship between the mental state and the physical condition of the narrator is noteworthy. Whereas his mental agonies because of his wife were the original cause of his physical ailment, his illness now becomes the cause of his mental disorder, nightmares, and hallucinations. Although in this part of the story the narrator mostly describes his reflections and emotions, he is intently aware of his physical illness, even to the extent that he worries about Nanny, the woman who nurses him, smoking in his room (81). In effect, the disease in the first section, the dreamlike enigmatic part of the novel, is basically one of the mind or the psyche, whereas in the second, it is essentially a physical illness that brings about psychological effects on the narrator.

Suffering from and conscious of his disorder and disease, the narrator is also concerned about a remedy. From the very beginning of the novel, immediately after his opening statement about his disease, he reveals his preoccupation with its cure and treatment. Temporary relief, he explains, "is to be found only in the oblivion brought about by wine and in the artificial sleep induced by opium and similar narcotics" (1). Of permanent cure, the narrator knows none, and his only hope seems to be to "diagnose" his disease by "disentangling the various threads" of his story, by writing the events or the history of his case as truthfully as he can remember for his shadow, hoping to attain better knowledge of himself. He is, in effect, playing the amateur psychologist, prescribing therapeutic writing as a possible cure. Through writing a sort of distorted, idealistic love story, he arrives at the root of his disease. The world of dreams disappears, and he awakens in "a new world" where everything he finds is "perfectly familiar and near" to him (44). "My previous surroundings and manners of life," he notes, "have been only the reflection of my real life" (44). But more powerful than any other concern—the blood on his clothing, the fear of the police discovering the crime that he has committed—is his need to write. "I hoped by this means," he says, "to expel the demon which had long been lacerating my vitals, to vent onto paper the horrors of my mind" (45). Through therapeutic writing his eyes open to his "real life" wherein the woman in his life is no longer viewed under a glorifying, supernatural light as the ethereal girl. She is, in actuality, his wife the slut. What he had imagined her to be, the ethereal girl, can be viewed in Freudian terms as a "substitute gratification" for his slut-of-a-wife. His disease is also demystified in this real, new world. He now recognizes exactly what led up to the onset of his malady. Tortured and distraught by his wife's attitude toward and rejection of him, he confines himself to his room. In this semidark, damp room, his mental anguish brings about his pitiable physical condition, hallucinations, and mental depression.

The physician who is brought in is only concerned with the physical aspects of the narrator's illness. His "lengthy prescriptions of herbal extracts and weird and wonderful oils" (65), along with Nanny's homemade remedies acquired from neighbors, magicians, and fortune-tellers, might have some effect on the physical condition of the patient, but not on his mental disorder. In fact, the narrator feels nothing but contempt for anything—the medicine, even the religion—of "the riffraff." The only prescription of the physician that the narrator applauds is opium, since it gives him temporary relief from the mental anguish from which he suffers. But why does the narrator, who is aware of the temporary effect of narcotics such as opium and who knows that "after a certain point, instead of alleviating the pain, they only intensify it" (1), welcome this prescription toward the end of the novel? Has he now abandoned all hope of finding a cure? The answer can be found in the opening paragraphs of the novel. The disease is not merely of the mind, but of the *ruh*, a word rich with connotations in Persian, encompassing the psyche, the mind, the soul, and the spirit. Thus, the disease is not simply mental or psychological, but spiritual, even metaphysical. And it is from the first word he puts down on paper that the narrator begins his therapy.

To recount what was stated: in the first part of the novel, the narrator writes about the most profound incident in his life. The effect of therapeutic writing in this section results in the "rebirth" at the start of part two, where he attributes his excitement to his need to write (45). But this time he is not going to write about one incident in his life; he intends to write it all for his shadow, to be able to tell him, "This is my life" (47). It is for his shadow, for himself, that he writes, and he explains that it is "the best means I have of bringing order and regularity into my thoughts" (47). Hence, we are led to assume that in the end writing has in some way brought a degree of order and regularity to his mind and that he is faced with the unexpected realization that his shadow encompasses more than the mere reflection of his "self"—it is also a reflection of all those he has despised, "the riffraff." As he puts it, all of them, including his wife the slut, "were shadows of me, shadows in the midst of which I was imprisoned" (123). Indeed, the story he writes, whether it deals with the "sores which slowly erode the mind" or with his life, is more than the story of his own life and his own malady; it is also the story of all those who, he believes, are shadows of himself. If writing about his disease or about his life has been therapeutic in any way, it involves more than the narrator exclusively. He explains: "I wish now to squeeze out every drop of juice from my life as if from a cluster of grapes and to pour the juice—the wine, rather—drop by drop . . . down the parched throat of my shadow" (46). In this light, the story that he writes is intended as a treatment not only for himself but his shadow, which can be said to represent the characters in the story as well as the reader and even his nation as a whole.[6]

"The god of writing is the god of *pharmakon*," observes Jacques Derrida, and he sees *pharmakon* as a double-edged word, comprising both good and evil, medicine and poison.[7] In *The Blind Owl*, as well, the function of writing is double-edged, both remedy and poison. Writing brings knowledge to the narrator that both treats and posits the disease at the same time. With *The Blind Owl*, Hedayat provides his compatriots with a diagnosis of what is ailing them as a nation and the challenges of historical and cultural, individual and collective identity that they were encountering and continue to encounter in the modern world. In this light, the object of love and desire, which appears in *The Blind Owl* first as an idealized beloved and then as a whore, may indeed represent for the modern artist and other offspring of an ancient civilization their beloved homeland, Iran.

Since the Arab invasion of the Persian Empire in the seventh century, which resulted in the almost total conversion of the Iranian people from Zoroastrianism to Islam, and up to the recent centuries, Iranians had viewed themselves and defined their identity vis-à-vis their Arab neighbors. After all, similar to people in many other parts of the world, they had lived in relative isolation. For intellectuals and thinkers in particular, this identity was schizophrenic, partly defined in terms of the new religion they had helped to spread to other parts of the world and partly in terms of a sense of nostalgia for the glories of the lost empire coupled with resentment toward those who had brought about its downfall. Through increasing contact with the world outside the Islamic region, in particular the West, which began in the eigh-

---

[6] Concerning the owl-like shadow of the narrator as representative of the characters in the story as well as the reader, see M. R. Ghanoonparvar, "*Buf-e Kur* as a Title," in *Hedayat's "The Blind Owl" Forty Years After*, 68–75.

[7] Quoted in Gian-Paolo Biasin, *Literary Diseases* (Austin: University of Texas Press, 1975), 31. Also see Gayatri Chakravorty Spivak's "Translator's Preface" to Jacques Derrida's *Of Grammatology*, 2nd ed. (Baltimore: Johns Hopkins University Press, 1977), especially xlix and lxxiii–lxxiv.

teenth century and continued in the nineteenth and the twentieth centuries, Iranians became more aware of their isolation, and more important, of their backwardness in contrast to the advances of the Western world, not merely in science and technology but in all aspects of social life. This awareness of the outside world and such new concepts as the nation-state, patriotism, nationalism, and modernism also brought about the need for self-assessment, for understanding their ambivalent and schizophrenic attitude toward their pre-Islamic and Islamic heritage, a diagnosis of the causes of their backwardness, and a redefinition of their individual and collective identity. Hedayat's novel is the record of a sensitive artist's systematic effort at such a self-assessment, albeit symbolically through the mind of a schizophrenic, perhaps psychotic, narrator.

ALESSANDRO PORTELLI

Uncle Tom's Cabin
(Harriet Beecher Stowe, United States, 1852)

Tom and Uncle Tom

> He was a large, broad-chested, powerfully-made man,
> of a full glossy black, and a face whose truly African
> features were characterized by an expression of grave
> and steady good sense, united with much kindliness
> and benevolence. There was something about his whole
> air self-respecting and dignified, yet united with a
> confiding and humble simplicity.[1]

So this is the famous Uncle Tom, the docile old slave who was used, as Malcolm X put it, "to keep the field Negroes in check" and the eponymous ancestor of all the "black Uncle Toms telling us to lay down our guns when the police are out there killing us"?[2] In a famous essay, James Baldwin called him "jet-black, wooly-haired, illiterate."[3] Nowhere in the book is he described as having white hair. From the beginning we find him intent on learning to read and, later, on writing letters to his former masters. He is a strong, muscular, majestic, "broad-chested, strong-armed fellow" able to jump in the Mississippi River and rescue little Eva (128), to bear a flogging soundlessly, and to exceed his daily cotton quota enough to help another person (306). He has two little children and a baby girl on his knee. He's not old. The children are the only ones to address him using the honorific, "Uncle," reserved for older slaves. Tom's mythic stature derives in part from his seeming ability, from one moment to the next, to be any age. He ranges from

---

[1] Harriet Beecher Stowe, *Uncle Tom's Cabin: Authoritative Text, Backgrounds and Contexts, Criticism*, ed. Elizabeth Ammons (New York: Norton, 1994), 18. All subsequent in-text citations are from this edition.

[2] Malcolm X, "Message to the Grass Roots," in *Malcolm X Speaks* (New York: Grove Press, 1965), 3–17; Keith Peddler, spokesman for the Piru Nation Gang, speech to the leadership of the African American gangs, Kansas City, April 30–May 2, 1993, quoted in R. C. De Prospo, "Afterword / Afterward: Auntie Harriet and Uncle Ike—Prophesying a Final Stowe Debate," in *The Stowe Debate: Rhetorical Strategies in "Uncle Tom's Cabin,"* ed. Mason I. Lowance, Ellen E. Westbrook, and R. C. De Prospo (Amherst: University of Massachusetts Press, 1994), 271.

[3] James Baldwin, "Everybody's Protest Novel," originally published in *Partisan Review* 16 (June 1949): 578–85, quoted from *Uncle Tom's Cabin*, ed. Ammons, 497.

being a "sort of patriarch in religious matters" (26) to "simple and childlike" (127) to "uncle" and biological and spiritual father: Cassy calls him "Father Tom" (343). It is only on his deathbed that he talks about, "this poor old body" (357).

The characterization of the stereotypical Uncle Tom as servile and elderly derives not so much from the novel as from theatrical adaptations, minstrel shows, regional writing, and large-circulation political journalism that turned him into an awkward figure of the collective imagination. Duke Ellington once said, "An American audience is trained to expect a Negro on stage to play the clown or 'Uncle Tom'; the task of the Black artist is thus to 'take Uncle Tom out of the theater.' "[4] A later film version produced by African Americans reverses the stereotype through the simple act of choosing actors who match the novel's description of the characters and their actions.[5] Without attributing to Tom either an action or a word that is not in the text, the film makes him a hero of the "interior resistance" that for slaves was often the only possible rebellion, and of the nonviolent revolution that his contemporary Thoreau postulated.[6] His clash with Simon Legree begins with an act of solidarity toward a slave woman; he helps Cassy and Emmeline to escape and in the end dies protecting the location of their hiding place; he agrees to being sold only to prevent the same destiny from striking his fellow slaves. This is hardly servility: this is a man who dies so as not to betray his peers or his self-respect: "Mas'r, if you mean to kill me, kill me; but, as to my raising my hand agin any one here, I never shall,—I'll die first!" (309).

While the vilification of Uncle Tom represents a biased reading, filtered through the ideology of the civil rights movement, it is not entirely arbitrary. When Cassy urges him to kill Legree, Tom replies that, "The dear, blessed Lord never shed no blood but his own" (344). Martin Luther King once said, "If blood must flow, better that it be our blood," and was branded an "Uncle Tom." "Tom had a remarkably smooth, soft voice, and a habitually respectful manner, that had given Legree an idea that he would be cowardly,

---

[4] Eric Lott, "Uncle Tom Fooleries: Racial Melodrama and Modes of Production," in *Love and Theft: Black Face Minstrelsy and the American Working Class* (New York: Oxford University Press, 1993); Harry Birdoff, *The World's Greatest Hit: "Uncle Tom's Cabin"* (New York: S. F. Vanni, 1947); Duke Ellington is referring to his 1941 musical review, *Jump for Joy*, in this quotation taken from Michael Denning, *The Cultural Front: The Laboring of American Culture in the Twentieth Century* (London: Verso, 1996), 312–13.

[5] *Uncle Tom's Cabin*, 1987, directed by Stan Lathan, screenplay by John Gay.

[6] Ann Douglas, "Introduction: The Art of Controversy," in *Uncle Tom's Cabin: Or, Life among the Lowly* (New York: Penguin, 1981).

and easily subdued" (308–9): too many readers and critics make the same mistake, confusing his character with his tone of voice and the voice that describes it.

A defiant, dignified Tom does indeed exist; but the groveling language and the material that envelop him and turn him into "Uncle Tom" are anything but transparent or insignificant. Stowe pulled no punches when she wrote; any sense of moderation is an occasional guest of her prose style. The book contains an abundance of tears and bloodshed, religious and political proselytizing, visions, prayers, and maternal, filial, and universal love, as well as the pathetic topos of absolute injustice and otherworldly hope constituted by the death of innocents and children.[7] Baldwin exaggerates when he says that Tom's "sentimentalism" is the "ostentatious parading of excessive and spurious emotions," a "mark of dishonesty" and "cruelty."[8] But he does make us understand that "Tom" and "Uncle Tom" are distinct yet inseparable.

Text, Hors-Texte, Metatext

"So you are the little woman who wrote the book that started this great war," was Abraham Lincoln's famous greeting to Harriet Beecher Stowe when he received her at the White House in the midst of the Civil War. Mark Twain notoriously blamed the war on Walter Scott instead. Both men were obviously speaking in jest, yet they still suggested the now obsolete idea that novels have a direct, concrete impact on the surrounding world: Had they really instilled indignation for slavery in the North and the heroic-chivalric ideology in the South, Stowe and Scott would have contributed not so much to fomenting the conflict as to shaping it.[9]

Uncle Tom's Cabin refuses to function as a self-sufficient icon constructed from words, a possible world of pure textuality. Stowe believed in a *hors-texte*, and very much so! The world of the book and its readers knew the same pain of separation (by sale or death) and were disturbed by the same laws (the "Fugitive Slave Law" that required the return of runaway slaves to their legal owners): these same two factors propel the plot. To condemn slavery without acting to abolish it, whether through the idle skepticism of

---

[7] For a definition of the pathetic in literature, see Alessandro Portelli, "Dai diamanti nella polvere all'angelo dei sotterranei: per una tipologia del patetico," in *Calibano* 6 (1981): 101–33.

[8] Baldwin, "Everybody's Protest Novel," 496.

[9] Ellen Moers, *Literary Women* (New York: Oxford University Press, 1985), 14; Beniamino Placido, *Le due schiavitù: Per un'analisi dell'immaginazione americana* (Turin: Einaudi, 1975), 41–50.

Augustin St. Clare or the passiveness of public opinion, was tantamount to helping to perpetuate it. The text draws us in through embarrassingly direct apostrophes: "Just such tears, sir, as you dropped into the coffin where lay your first-born son; such tears, woman, as you shed when you heard the cries of your dying babe" (34). It populates the text with the conversions, illuminations, repentances, and redemptions that generate the change of heart in the readers that will make them "feel right" and act consequently. Such a work could only become illegible to critics and readers, like Baldwin, accustomed to seeking in the text "the disquieting complexity of ourselves . . . this web of ambiguity, paradox," rather that its projections toward us.[10]

These projections are more ambiguous, however, than they appear at first sight. The introduction and conclusion of the book explain that its purpose is to rouse "sympathy" and to invite the readers to cultivate their own sympathies. In beween we are also treated to the hypochondriacal and egotistical Mrs. St. Claire's lament that no one has sympathy for her grief (43–44, 154). The key words of sentimental and democratic rhetoric are placed in the mouths of odious characters: the slave trader Haley is the first to use the words *religion* ("I consider religion a valeyable thing in a nigger, when it's the genuine article, and no mistake") (2) and *humanity* ("humanity, sir, I may say, is the great pillar of *my* management") (5); the narrator ironizes on the "humanity" of legislators who prohibit the foreign slave trade but protect it within the States (115); the slogan of American freedom sounds paradoxical in the mouth of the cruel slaveholder Mr. Harris: "It's a free country, sir; the man's *mine*, and I do what I please with him,—that's it!" (12).

It is as if we were being invited to suspect the text's and thus our own rhetoric by a form of metatextual irony. If we congratulate ourselves on our compassion, the irony suggests that our sentiments may be as spurious as those of Haley, Harris, and Mrs. St. Clare. The poetics of the pathetic invites the spectators to contemplate the suffering of others and to identify with it by imagining themselves in their place ("If it were *your* Harry, mother, or your Willie, that were going to be torn from you by a brutal trader . . . how fast could *you* walk?" 43–44). But if we seek consolation in the thought that they and not us are in their place—that the child on the auction block is Eliza's and not ours—the irony sets off new alarm bells, telling us to look at the place that we are in: "The trader had arrived at that stage of Christian and political perfection which has been recommended by some preachers

[10] Baldwin, "Everybody's Protest Novel," 496.

and politicians of the north, lately, in which he had completely overcome every humane weakness and prejudice. His heart was exactly where yours, sir, and mine could be brought, with proper effort and cultivation"(112).

While the book presents itself as an empathetic intervention on material reality, the only behavior it proposes belongs to the order of immaterial reality: faith and sentiment ("But, what can any individual do? . . . They can see to it that *they feel right*," 385). To a reader who does not share this faith or this emotional grammar, the proposed behavior and states of mind can appear painfully inadequate, and the characters can seem to be little more than hagiographic or demonological allegories: "No one, except in dreams, has ever been as good as Tom, as demonic as Topsy, as unremittingly evil as Simon Legree."[11] This is the substance of a project that should not be measured by the canons of the realistic novel but by those of religious typological narrative.[12] If we suspend our disbelief and accept that the immaterial realities of religious spirituality and sentiment are as true and operative as those of the body and social relations, that salvation and damnation are not less tangible and true than floggings and chains, we can read this novel provisionally, the way it demands to be read, and if not make it our own at least take it seriously.

Faith

"This is all real to you!" Augustin St. Clare says in amazement to Tom. What makes Tom and Eve so implausible is that they truly believe in their world's professed beliefs. Tom's absurd claim is that he takes seriously Christianity's highest and most difficult commandment: to love thy enemy. Because of this conviction he tells Simon Legree that he would shed the last drop of his blood to save his soul, and he kneels before St. Claire, beseeching him to redeem himself, in a scene that would otherwise be abject and embarrassing.

The novel, according to Jane Tompkins, "rewrites the Bible in the form of the history of the black slave." Tom becomes a figure of the imitation of Christ: his humanity, tempered by suffering, is a humanity that approaches the divine. Stowe thought that the book itself was an act of communication between heaven and earth ("God wrote it," she once said); Tom and little

---

[11] Leslie A. Fiedler, *The Inadvertent Epic: From "Uncle Tom's Cabin" to "Roots"* (Toronto: Canadian Broadcasting Company, 1979), 34.

[12] Jane Tompkins, "Sentimental Power: *Uncle Tom's Cabin* and the Politics of Literary History," in *Uncle Tom's Cabin*, ed. Ammons, 501–22.

Eva are, in turn, vehicles of communication between earth and heaven. Eva is so spiritual that she can only die and go to heaven; from her eyes shines "the light of immortality," and through her eyes, in the crucial passage to death, we can see immortality: "When that thar blessed child goes into the kingdom, they'll open the door so wide, we'll all get a look in at the glory," says Tom (255).

Tom represents the figure of Christ dying on the cross, not Christ driving the merchants from the temple: "Our suffering is redemptive," said Martin Luther King, and it is on this point that he, and Tom, are taken to task by the critics.[13] His virtues of meekness, simplicity, and humility are those of the Sermon on the Mount, and for this, Baldwin writes, "his triumph is [only] metaphysical, unearthly."[14] What's more, Stowe fully participates in the "romantic racialism" of her times, according to which Tom's virtues are attributed not only to his personal disposition but to the intrinsic characteristics of the "Africans": "Tom . . . had the soft, impressible nature of his kindly race, ever yearning toward the simple and childlike" (127). Eva and Topsy are "the representatives of the two extremes of society. The fair, high-bred child, with her golden head, her deep eyes, her spiritual, noble brow, and prince-like movements; and her black, keen, subtle, cringing, yet acute neighbor. They stood the representatives of their races. The Saxon, born of ages of cultivation, command, education, physical and moral eminence; the Afric, born of ages of oppression, submission, ignorance, toil and vice!" (213).

The text is embroidered with generalizations that attribute metahistorical and hereditary qualities to both the "Anglo-Saxons" and the "Africans": the former, especially in the South, possess innate tendencies to action and domination, "a high and indomitable spirit"; the latter are instead "filled with passion and imagination," "not naturally audacious and enterprising but homey and affectionate," "shy, patient," "sensitive and impressionable," "compassionate and imitative," endowed with "instinctive affects," and, since they are "exotics of the most splendid and superb countries in the world," they possess an instinctive, though rough, sense of beauty. Stowe says all of this in order to praise, going so far as to imagine a millennium in which Africa, "called to the crown of thorns, the scourge, the bloody sweat, the cross of agony . . . by this shalt thou reign with Christ when his kingdom shall come on earth" (345). Moreover, "the negro race . . . will, in their gentleness, their

---

[13] Quoted in Josephine Donovan, *Uncle Tom's Cabin: Evil, Affliction, and Redemptive Love* (Boston: Twayne, 1991).

[14] Baldwin, "Everybody's Protest Novel," 497.

lowly docility of heart, their aptitude to repose on a superior mind and rest on a higher power, their childlike simplicity of affection, and facility of forgiveness . . . exhibit the highest form of the peculiarly *Christian life*, and, perhaps, as God chasteneth whom he loveth, he hath chosen poor Africa in the furnace of affliction, to make her the highest and noblest in that kingdom which he will set up" (155–56).

This is the classic American form of the jeremiad: God puts his chosen ones to the test, and the fall is thus the renewed sign of this mission.[15] What a pity that the whip, sweat, and torment are not only metaphors but actual tangible experiences, while the millennium of the completed mission and of spiritual reward is deferred to a time yet to come.

Influences

The epitome of the virtues attributed to the "Africans" is the curious lexical invention *impressible*. Like the wax that carries the imprint of the seal, the Africans are bearers of affective and passive virtues—virtues, in other words, that are branded as feminine. Leslie Fiedler writes that Tom represents "all in the author which yearns toward 'womanly' forgiveness and love as endless accommodation." Tom is "the true 'Good White Mother' of the book," in a "shamanistic shifting of sex roles."[16] Baldwin concludes somewhat more hastily that Tom "has been robbed of his humanity and divested of his sex."[17] We have remarked how Tom is manly enough to have a wife and little children: while it may be true that their main purpose is to dramatize the family separation, once they have been admitted into the text, for whatever reason, we cannot pretend that they do not exist. Moreover, to demonstrate that Tom has been feminized, Fiedler notes how Stowe confers on him, "the gentle, domestic heart, which—woe for them!—has been a peculiar characteristic of his unhappy race" (35). What could be more feminizing than domesticity? But Fiedler does not notice that a few lines later, when Tom meets Chloe and her children, Stowe comments, "Ah, brave, manly heart,—smothering thine own sorrow, to comfort thy beloved ones!" (81).

In other words, a man can be domestic and affectionate without ceasing

---

[15] Sacvan Bercovitch, *The American Jeremiad* (Madison: University of Wisconsin Press, 1978); for a proposed reading of *Uncle Tom's Cabin* as a jeremiad, see Tompkins, "Sentimental Power."

[16] Fiedler, *The Inadvertent Epic*, 33 and 35. Fiedler interprets the scene of Tom's torture as a rape in which the feminized protagonist plays the victim's role (36).

[17] Baldwin, "Everybody's Protest Novel," 498.

to be masculine. If we were to interpret Tom not through Baldwin and Fiedler but through bell hooks, he might be seen as prefiguring a possible alternative black masculinity. She writes that for black men, the impossibility of exercising the patriarchal role has led to a tendency to prove their manhood in the form of domination over women, leaving room, nevertheless, for alternative projects: "Throughout the history of black males in the United States, there have been men who were not at all interested in the patriarchal ideal. In the black community in which they were raised, there was no monolithic standard of black masculinity."[18]

The feminization of Tom is based on the explicit analogy between the conditions of women and blacks (and children): having no rights in patriarchal society, they assert a moral superiority based on alternative metahistoric values. Tom's distance from the patriarchal ideal could thus strengthen the recent reassessment of *Uncle Tom's Cabin* on behalf of a female "sentimental power" and a "maternal" economy in opposition to the masculine economy of the market. Hence Jane Tompkins sees the domestic scene of the Quaker kitchen as a utopia of feminine power administered through "delicate morality," "loving maternal kindness," perfect efficiency, and harmony: the only masculine figure is "in the corner," intent on the "anti-patriarchal operation of shaving" (120–22).[19]

Nevertheless, as a male reader, I don't feel especially threatened by the fact that while I am shaving the women of the house are busy making my breakfast.[20] I am also aware that the time of vindication is near, and that it coincides with the persistent male monopoly over the active sphere. Mrs. Bird persuades her husband to help the fugitives, but he is the one who prepares the wagon and leads them through the swamps and woods till they reach the Quaker settlement. The Quaker kitchen may be a female utopian space, but it is the men who will later transport George and Eliza to the border, and it will be thanks to George's good aim with a pistol that they will be saved from the slave hunters in pursuit.

The relationship between action and sentiment governs all the thematic couplings in the novel: Anglo-Saxon and African, male and female, adult and child. The most important term of mediation concerns gender relations, going under the rubric of influence—the ability of women, through

---

[18] bell hooks, "Reconstructing Black Masculinity," in *Black Looks: Race and Representation* (Boston: South End Press, 1992), 88.

[19] Tompkins, "Sentimental Power."

[20] On the limits of matriarchal, domestic utopia, see S. L. Roberson, "Matriarchy and the Rhetoric of Domesticity," in *The Stowe Debate*, 116–57.

sentiment, to persuade men to take action. In this sense, influence also defines the function of the book. Through sentiment, a woman's words persuade men to take the masculine action of war. Here, too, there is no lack of evidence to the contrary. Even Cassy has influence over Legree, but it can hardly be considered beneficent, and Mrs. Shelby's influence and sympathy are not enough to stop her husband from selling Tom and little George. Nor does it appear that Senator Bird, after saving Eliza, has any intention of acting to repeal the Fugitive Slave Law for which he voted: influence can generate exceptions but almost never can change the rules.[21]

Endings

Like many American classics, *Uncle Tom's Cabin* has a multiple ending, in homage to the open form of the country and the impossibility of finding single replies to its contradictions. Tom dies; George, Eliza, and Topsy go to Africa as missionaries; the other slaves are emancipated *motu proprio* by George Shelby Jr. This combination of death, expatriation, and emancipation betokens Stowe's failure to accept the image of free African Americans present in America. The return to Africa was opposed by the black abolitionists precisely because it seemed driven by Americans' desire to rid themselves first of slavery and then of the slaves. Apart from the fact that Stowe knew and interacted with many free African Americans (listing their names at the end of the book), it should be observed that George explains his decision in terms of black nationalism: "The desire and yearning of my soul is for an African *nationality*. I want a people that shall have a tangible, separate existence of its own" (374–75). Three-quarters of a century later, Marcus Garvey would speak in these very terms.[22]

---

[21] Douglas, "Introduction"; Elizabeth Barnes, *States of Sympathy: Seduction and Democracy in the American Novel* (New York: Columbia University Press, 1997); E. O'Connell, "The Magic of Real Distress: Sentimentality and Competing Rhetorics of Authority," in *The Stowe Debate*, 13–36.

[22] Michelle Burnham, *Captivity and Sentiment: Cultural Exchange in American Literature, 1682–1861* (Hanover, N.H.: University Press of New England, 1997); Robert S. Levine, "A Nation within a Nation: Debating *Uncle Tom's Cabin* and Black Emigration," in *Martin Delany, Frederick Douglass, and the Politics of Representative Identity* (Chapel Hill: University of North Carolina Press, 1997), 58–98; Placido, *Le due schiavitù*. The George Harris character has been read, and not arbitrarily, as a confirmation of the superiority attributed to white "blood," which only makes people able to rebel. I believe that it is closer to the intention of the text, and to a postmodern sensibility, to see also an attempt (heavily compromised by "racialist" ideology) at synthesis and overcoming: the representation of an identity that is neither all black nor all white but a little of both.

Despite these misgivings, would we be satisfied by another solution? Alive and free in America, Tom and George would be an optimistic simplification; alive and enslaved (or dead), they would confer tragic irreparability on a text that wants to invest hope in salvation. If Tom and George can only die and emigrate, it is because America, rather than Stowe, has no place for them. It would have taken a catastrophic shake-up in the American system for a different ending to be possible. Later, Stowe would support John Brown's attempted insurrection. But *Uncle Tom's Cabin* came out at the darkest moment for abolitionist hopes: the Fugitive Slave Law, the new compromise between North and South, and the election of a president with Southern sympathies (Pierce) were some of the motivations that drove her to write.

Which brings me back to the contradiction between intervention into reality and the sense that any action, in the given conditions, would be a palliative. The result might be rage and despair (George's atheistic temptations), or a denunciation accompanied by moral, sentimental sympathy. A much less sentimental writer, Nathaniel Hawthorne, believed that slavery would die out through the will of Providence, independent of any human action: "One of those evils which divine Providence does not leave to be remedied by human contrivances but which, in its own good time, by some means impossible to be anticipated, but of the simplest and easiest operation, when all its uses shall have been fulfilled, it causes to vanish like a dream."[23] Stowe was also convinced that the disappearance of slavery depended on divine Providence, but she did not conclude that she should then wash her hands of all involvement.

Stowe's moral contradictions are highlighted by both her forcefulness—no compromises are possible—and her limits. Influence can only be exerted if the moral base is shared by the addressees; the morals to which Stowe appeals are the same domestic, Christian morals in which America allegedly believes and that it delegates to powerless subjects such as women, blacks, and children. By accusing America of violating its own values, she reiterates the fundamental values of the American ideology. This is the grammar of the jeremiad, but also the grammar of sentimentalism, which, as Ann Douglas writes, affirms that the values denied by the functioning of a given society are precisely the same ones that the society claims to treasure. The poetics of the pathetic consists in dramatizing the suffering of weak subjects that are

---

[23] From Hawthorne's *Life of Franklin Pierce* (417), quoted in Eric Cheyfitz, "The Irresistibleness of Great Literature: Reconstructing Hawthorne's Politics," *American Literary History* 6, no. 3 (1994): 545.

bearers of values. Their sufferings are unjust to bring out the virtue of the sufferers; inevitable because the victims are weak and their weakness is what makes them bearers of values; necessary because it is the suffering—the martyrdom and the crown of thorns—that leads straight to the triumph to come.[24]

A sense of injustice still remains. While the instruments that Stowe proposes to fight injustice may seem inadequate or even counterproductive, this is still no reason not to take her seriously. What remains ultimately is the imposing figure, soft in his ways and unshakeable in his principles, of an "Uncle" Tom who is ready to die rather than betray his fellows or betray himself. He may not be a role model for revolutionaries and liberators, but he nevertheless deserves our full respect.

Translated by Michael F. Moore

[24] Ann Douglas, *The Feminization of American Culture* (New York: Knopf, 1977), 10; Portelli, "Dai diamanti nella polvere."

ROBERTO SCHWARZ

Posthumous Memoirs of Brás Cubas
(J. M. Machado de Assis, Brazil, 1880)

Between 1880 and 1908, Joaquim Maria Machado de Assis wrote four or five novels and several dozen stories of world-class caliber, masterpieces much above what Brazilian literature—inclusive of Machado's own earlier production—had offered up to that time. These are works that distance themselves from the romantic mixture of local color, the romanesque, and patriotism, or rather, from the facile and infallible formula in which the reading public of this young nation reveled. The difference, which is not merely one of degree, has a great reach and deserves reflection.

In this case, the change did not exclude necessary continuities, but transfigured them. As one critic astutely observed, Machado de Assis "meticulously steeped himself in the work of his predecessors," acutely conscious of their adroit description of social customs and accurate analytic effort.[1] The limitations and inconsistencies of those same models, similarly, did not escape Machado. With a spirit notably aimed at overcoming those limitations, he sought to correct and—discreetly—ironize, by reprising in a less innocent key, the thematic and formal framework developed by his predecessors, and for that matter, in his own previous works. The justness of his rectifications stems from his malicious sensitivity to social functions and to the specificity of the country, suited to satirical study.

Thus, a localized and recent tradition, permeated with European models and bearing the signs of recent decolonialization, culminated in an unanticipated series of masterpieces. Machado's rearrangement of material and form elevated a modest, secondhand fictional universe to the level of complexity of the most advanced contemporary art. In order to underscore the particular interest of that transformation, one could say that Machado's action on the literary plane incorporates an overcoming of the sorts of alienation proper to colonial heritage.

Machado's daring was timid at first, limited to the sphere of family life, within which he analyzed the perspectives and inequities of paternalism Brazilian-style, supported by slavery and vexed by liberal ideas. Without being disrespectful, he subjected to examination the unacceptable deprecation

---

[1] Antonio Candido, *Formação da literatura brasileira* (1959) (São Paulo: Martins, 1969), 117.

of dependents and, at the opposite pole, the arbitrariness of proprietors, equally unacceptable, though under the guise of civilization. As far as genre, his fiction represented a decorous realism, whose reading public was the Brazilian family. As far as content, Machado set his sights on and incisively investigated a characteristic complex of relationships resulting from the renewal of colonial inequalities in the newly independent nation, commited to the new concepts of freedom and progress.

Subsequently, from 1880 onward, Machado's daring becomes more encompassing and spectacular, *affronting the presuppositions of realist fiction*, that is, the nineteenth-century scaffolding of the bourgeois status quo. The novelty of his work lies in the narrator, humorous and aggressively arbitrary, functioning like a *formal principle*, subjecting characters, literary convention, and even the reader, not to mention the authority of the narrative form, to periodic feints. The narrator's intrusions range from light impertinence to unbridled aggression. Very deliberate, his infractions neither ignore nor cancel the norms they affront; but, at the same time, these are derided and rendered inactive, relegated to a status of half-valence that aptly encapsulates the ambivalent position of modern culture in peripheral countries. Necessary to that *rule of composition*, transgressions of every kind repeat themselves with the regularity of a universal law. The devastating sense of a Nothingness that forms in the wake of this composition deserves a capital letter, insofar as it is the final sum of an experience, in anticipation of other rules remaining to be trampled. As for the artistic climate of the epoch, this ending in a Nothingness is a replica, under a different sky, of what was being done by the French postromantics, described by Sartre as "knights of nonbeing."[2]

At first glance, Machado was trading an awkward and provincial sphere for another that was emphatically universal and philosophical, which lent itself to interpolations, digressions, and doubts of the kind that haunted Hamlet. This was a sphere that, incidentally, did not lack the note of cheap metaphysics, rediscovering a provincial tone on a more literate level (a splendid and *modern* finding). We might note that in this second mode, that of his great works, the first universe remains present, as anecdotal material—but not only that.

In their most conspicuous aspects, Machado's provocations recycled an erudite and refined range of prerealist conventions, in open defiance of the nineteenth-century sense of reality and of its objectivity. According to the

---

[2] Jean-Paul Sartre, *L'idiot de la famille* (Paris: Gallimard, 1972), 3:147.

Author's own warnings, he now adopted "the free form of a Sterne, or of a Xavier de Maistre," referring, above all, to the *digressive arbitrariness* of the eighteenth-century European novel.[3] Nevertheless, and contrary to what a breaking of rules might make one suppose, the spirit of Machado's work was incisively realist, propelled as much by an implacable social logic as by the task of capturing its peculiarly Brazilian character. And it was also postrealist, interested in reflecting in a poor light the verisimilitude of the bourgeois order, opening up to visitation its unconfessed aspects, unmasking it in the modern manner that would prevail at the end of the century. The degree of historical paradox in this mode of composition is high, but functional in its own way, as we will see. Be that as it may, it presupposed a new kind of literary and intellectual culture in the country.

Ironic dealings with the Bible, the classics, philosophy, and science; continual formal experimentation, fed by advanced ideas on the dynamics of the unconscious, by a disabused perspicacity with regard to material interests and by personal social reflection cognizant of national particularities and of the dubious sides of nationalism; independence also in the adoption of foreign inspiration, sought outside the contemporary French and Portuguese *mainstream* and, moreover, adapted to Brazilian circumstance with memorable ingenuity; competition with naturalism, whose simple determinisms (so convincing and wrong in the context of the tropical ex-colony) Machado countered with complex causations no less powerful (but clear of racism): confidence in the potency of "free form," whose effects his narrator does not comment on in their most essential aspects or who does so only with the intent of confounding, compelling the reader to establish and reexamine them for himself—all of these were more or less unscripted innovations. If we add to this the cosmopolitan mien of his prose and the superior intelligence of his formulations in a country in which even today intelligence does not seem to be counted among artistic faculties, we have a basis to imagine that there is no common denominator between this universe and that of the fiction that preceded it.

Until the *Posthumous Memoirs of Brás Cubas* (1880)—the work that marked Machado's turnabout—the Brazilian novel was narrated by a compatriot worthy of applause, whose speech was set loose by the beauty of the country's beaches and forests, the grace of its young maidens and its popular customs, not to mention the stupendous achievements of Rio de Janeiro. Beyond being an artist, the person who directly or indirectly extolled the country was an ally in the civic campaign for a national identity and culture. The

---

[3] J. M. Machado de Assis, *Memórias pósthumas de Brás Cubas* (1880), in *Obras completas* (Rio de Janeiro: Aguilar, 1959), 1:413.

narrator of *Posthumous Memoirs* is of another type: deprived of credibility (insofar as he presents himself in the impossible position of being defunct), Brás Cubas is spiteful, partial, intrusive, absurdly inconsistent, given to mystification and indignant insinuation, capable of baseness in relation to other characters and the reader, and, at the same time, notably cultivated—setting a sort of standard of elegance—and capable of composing the best prose on the market. The internal disparity is disconcerting and highly problematic, resulting in a figure unequal to the previous national standard.

In principle, the obligation to respect the reader, verisimilitude, temporal and spatial continuities, coherence, and so forth, transcends geographical and linguistic borders. The same thing goes for the transgressions against common sense, in which the Machadian narrator revels: these are also situated in the abstract and transnational sphere of social standars, in which *universal* (as opposed to Brazilian) questions concerning civilized humankind are at play. Whether deeming Machado's narrator correct or incorrect, arguing against him or in favor, this was the common view among the critics of the day. The literary pirouettes performed by Brás Cubas, who does not lend himself to being respected, are plotted by these critics in terms of coordinates related to metaphysical and cosmopolitan lines, unattached to *local* material, on which they lean, nevertheless. According to one adversary, Machado took refuge in philosophical and formalist affectations, and peculiarly English ones, in order to avert the battles of the Brazilian writer. Others, fed up with the picturesque and provincial, and desirous of civilization proper (that is, European and unashamed of the backwardness around them), greeted Machado as the country's first writer in the full sense of the term.

In sum, the arguments were more or less the following. In changing the rules of the game in the very face of the reader, only to change them again immediately, the narrator engages in a kind of dissolute jesting, in poor taste, unworthy of a serious Brazilian, and poorly disguising both an intellectual incapacity and a lack of narrative stamina. In the other camp, the same affronts indicated a formally adept artist, a skeptical and civilized spirit, for whom the world lent itself to doubt and was not reduced to narrow national limits. Thus, sympathizers and opponents were both of the opinion that Machado retreated from Brazilian particularity, whether to interrogate the human condition or to devote himself to "the comedy of the almanac, the pessimism of ephemeral hack writing, which manages to delude those few simpletons who find it marvelous."[4] The idea that Brazilian reality did not pose universal problems, and vice versa, was common to both sides, *reflecting*

---

[4] Sílvio Romero, *Machado de Assis* (1897) (Campinas: Unicamp, 1992), 160.

the persistence of colonial segregation. "The instability to which I refer stems from the fact that in America the landscape, life, the horizon, architecture, everything that surrounds us lacks a historical basis, a human perspective; and from the fact that in Europe we lack our homeland, that is, the form in which each of us was cast at birth. On one side of the sea we feel the absence of the world; on the other, the absence of the country."[5]

The dissonance between the local note and ostensible universalism was discomfiting, but not uncharacteristic. For whomever had ears to hear, the mutual estrangement comprised a necessary and representative accord that formalized, in microcosmic terms, an alienation of world-historical proportions as much as a dissonance. Machado comprehended the comic impasse inherent in this tonal disparity and, instead of avoiding it, made of it a central element in his literary art. Thus, the erudite, highly experienced narrator, the humanist disdainful of the idiocies and inconsequentialities in which our humanity is wrapped up, and intimately familiar with the Bible, Homer, Lucian, Erasmus, Shakespeare, the French moralists, Pascal—is just half of the picture, and a less absolute part than it might seem. The other half emerges when we consider him as one character among others, defined by characteristics typical in their manifestation of local malformation, the very characteristics that the narrative playfulness and the corresponding climate of metaphysical farce make us overlook as irrelevant details. One need only put together these two halves for the picture to change. We then observe

---

[5] Joaquim Nabuco, *Minha formação* (1900) (Rio de Janeiro: José Olympio, 1976), 26. To have an idea of the extent of the problem, it suffices to note how José Veríssimo, a critic who insisted on the great superiority of Machado, nevertheless stated that his works had little to do with Brazil: "Machado's literary work cannot be measured against criteria which, if you allow me the expression, one might call nationalistic. These criteria, which constitute the main tenet of the *História da Literatura Brasileira*, as well as of the whole of Sílvio Romero's critical work, consist of, when reduced to their simplest expression, looking into the ways in which a writer contributes to the shaping of the national character, or, in other words, to what extent his works aid the development of a literature which, due to its particular nature, one might call Brazilian. These criteria, when applied by our critic, as well as by others, to the works of Machado de Assis, would certainly place them in an inferior position in our literature." Later, Veríssimo would change his mind: "Albeit not explicitly, it was Machado who provided us with the deepest and most perceptive explanation of the Brazilian soul . . . representing Brazilian society with a talent for synthesis and generalization which raised his works to the category of great universal masterpieces." The romantic and dialectical scheme, according to which, the more universal, the more local a writer is, integrated Brazil with civilization. By offering a different evaluation on a superior level, Veríssimo somewhat agreed with Sílvio Romero's criteria. For the quotations, see, respectively, *Estudos brasileiros, segunda série (1889–1893)* (Rio de Janeiro: Laemmert, 1894), 198; and *Estudos de literatura brasileira*, 6th ed. (Belo Horizonte: Italiaia, 1977), 106.

that in *real life* (within the fiction) the virtuoso of literary-philosophical feints is a proprietor Brazilian-style, master of slaves, versed in relations of clientelism, adherent to European conceptions of progress, and partner in the postcolonial joint venture of domination.

The montage is slightly unforeseen, but transforms the terms that integrate it, bringing into focus a remarkable social type, with similarly remarkable social repercussions and a profound historical reach. The infractions against narrative equity take on different dimensions: through the narrator, they are assimilated to a sui generis group of proprietary prerogatives, proper to the *national* picture of class distinctions, differing significantly from the universalist terrain of rhetorical art and at odds with civilized social standards. From the liberal and European standpoint, from whose authority there was no means of escape, these prerogatives were insulting—which did not keep them from taking part in the *douceur de vivre* passed on by the colony and, on the other hand, from echoing the new moral carelessness cultivated by imperialism. In its own way, creating a rhythm with its own rules, the affront to literary *fair play* metaphorically stood for the admixture of regal privilege and illegitimacy that the nineteenth century linked to direct personal domination. Inserted in the field of international inequities, the capacity for coinage began to be exercised at a pole that until then had not exercised its power, a *peripheral pole*, that inverts perspectives and forces the recalibration of standards of measurements: the Western literary tradition is solicited and deformed in such a way as to manifest the delights and moral contortions, or simply the differences, linked with that historically reproved form of class domination, and it imprints on that tradition, together with its vitality, its contravening stamp. One substantial critical consequence of the flexibility with which high culture lends itself to this role is that high culture itself is then seen in a less estimable, or more sarcastic, light. At the same time, this social type, which might be considered exotic and remote, and more of an operetta-like cliché than a problem, is developed in terms of the magnitude of its effects in contemporary world culture, within which it comes to be a discrete pivot.[6]

---

[6] For the historical reach and expansive impulse of that order of digressions, cf. an observation by Marx on the U.S. Civil War: "Already in the years between 1856 and 1860, that which the political spokesmen, jurists, moralists and theologians for the side of slavery sought to prove was not so much the justice of black slavery, but rather that the color in play is irrelevant, and that it is the working class, everywhere, that is made for slavery" (Karl Marx, "Der Bürgerkrieg inden Vereinigten Staaten" (1861), in Marx Engels Werke [Berlin: Dietz, 1985], 15:344). I am grateful to Luis Felipe de Alencastro for the reference.

In other terms, the liberties taken with formal convention represent, beyond rhetorical caper, what had been a dimly lit sector of the contemporary scene. They extend to the plane of culture and to the presuppositions of nineteenth-century civility—the uncivilized power enjoyed by Brazilian proprietors in relation to poor or enslaved dependents. The literary accent falls back on aspects of irresponsibility and arbitrariness, as well as on the ins and outs of intra-elite connivance, which is its complement. In this case, there is an affinity between imaginative license and irresponsible power, or, along a parallel line, between disregarded literary forms and abused dependents, setting up an extraordinary play of mirrors. It is as if Brás Cubas were saying that the culture and civility that he esteems and of which he considers himself a part could continue to function in its own way without impeding him from taking advantage of his privileges—or even as if he were demonstrating, through the operation of scandal and everyday practice on the consecrated body of universal culture, the consequences of those same privileges. Thus, far from exchanging a small, irrelevant world (nevertheless, ours) for the prestigious (but falsified) universality of the being-or-not-being of forms, Machado linked the two planes, in order to open up, *in the spirit of critical exposure*, the sequestered universe that had been his point of departure. This is a heterodox example of the universalization of the particular and of the particularization of the universal, or of dialectic.

The narrator's intellectual range and ease, incommensurate with the backward world of his characters, compensates for their historical isolation. Situations that might appear picturesque or peculiarly colonial are interwoven with anecdotes in the classical tradition, philosophical arguments, religious dogma, paradoxical or cynical maxims of a bourgeois order, recent European fashions, scientific innovations, and news of imperialist conflicts, *composing a peculiarly mixed narrative structure and speech* that then came to be the trademark of the Author. Always a little forced (but the humor lies in this), these approximations achieve a release from the confinements of the local reality. It is a matter of deprovincialization and universalization in the literal sense of these terms. The resulting hit, precisely on target, includes a factitious and laughable note, insofar as the detachment from the surroundings exposes the incompatibility of the two spheres. Be that as it may, we witness the insertion of the country within the modern human perimeter, an insertion achieved through insolent narrative devices, now strident, now subtle. As far as models go, beyond digressive eighteenth-century prose, another closer one exists in the flittering style of the weekly French *feuilleton*, whose Parisian frivolity Machado wanted to infuse with "American color," or rather, with the poison of local class relations.[7]

The abrupt step taken—let us suppose—from Catumbi [the elegant outskirts of Rio de Janeiro, where Brás Cubas lives comfortably] to metaphysics, from the latter to the punishment of a slave, moving on to the cosmos or to parliamentary Europe, to the crooked dealings of war or to the beginning of time, is indebted to Brás Cubas's intellectual outbursts and resources. While great, the latter are at the same time ambivalent in every respect, tending toward baseness, exhibitionism, and class impertinence. Thus, the country's incorporation by the contemporary world is operated by a dubious character, who makes a mockery of the credibility that the reader invests in him. Gone is the somewhat careless and hypocritical supposition that narrators are men of worth, not to mention worthy of posts of national leadership, or, by extension, the supposition that national leaders and the readers themselves are worthy. In this sardonic constellation, progress and victory over colonial isolation acquire an unanticipated perverse coloration: the former do not cease to exist, but their usefulness to a modernized reproduction of colonial inequalities, with which they show themselves compatible, does not provide any sense of having overcome the latter. This has nothing to do with denying advances, but with acknowledging that these constitute inglorious achievements—depending on one's point of view—in the scope of the most precious national aspirations. The critical and counterideological daring of this anticlimax, or of this second-rate regionalism that incorporated the degradation of cosmopolitanism, is disconcerting even today. In my opinion, it is this that determines the eminence of Machado's great works.

But let us return to the contrast with the awkwardness of Machado's first novels.[8] These earlier works also were engaged in a search for modernity, albeit from a different perspective. The aspirations for progress and freedom had to do with the discomforting state of the *dependents*, in particular of the most talented among them, whom only "an error of nature" had caused to be born into inferior circumstances.[9] The narrative represents these dependents

---

[7] In one of his first critical essays, Machado discussed the "acclimatization" of the *feuilleton* in the country "To write a *folhetim* and remain Brazilian in truth is difficult. Meanwhile, as all difficulties level off, it could well take on more local color, more of an American character. Thus, it would do less wrong to the independence of the national spirit, so captive to those imitations, to that mimicry, to that suicide on the part of originality and initiative" (Machado de Assis, "O folhetonista" (1859), in *Obras completas*, 3:968–69).

[8] *Ressureição* (1872), *A mão e a luva* (1874), *Helena* (1876) and *Iaiá Garcia* (1878).

[9] *A mão e a luva*, in *Obras completas*, 1:142.

in their fight for personal dignity, enmeshed in the sphere of proprietary families, to whose number, in this case, civilization seemed reduced. At the center of intrigue, poor heroines, intelligent and lovely—not to mention susceptible—confronted the injustices to which they fell victim; or rather, they maneuvered in order to be adopted by a well-situated clan. They neither lacked sincerity, nor allowed themselves to be disrespected, within the bounds of a prickly situation. Rebelliousness and criticism, inspired from abroad by romanticism and the Rights of Man, found their practical limits in the destitution of these young girls. On the other hand, the loyalty that they owed their patrons and protectors, tinged with filial piety and Catholic obligation, marked a moral boundary that it would be indecent to cross. Woven into everything was the lordly suspicion, derisive and debasing, that the heroines might be motivated by pecuniary interests—which obligated the poor things to endless demonstrations of disinterested abnegation. The ambiguities of this rearguard combat raised unsavory questions, exasperating in their conformity, and always fell short of the modern emancipation of the individual. How to confront without humiliation the inevitable despotism of patriarchs (or matriarchs) and their close relatives? Why would the girl without means, who insinuates herself and instigates an adoption by well-situated neighbors, without whom she would have no access to the world, not be respectable; or better, why would she be calculating, in the bad sense of the word? Does a poor man's taste for Sevres vases and cashmere curtains constitute an index of insolence or, worse, place his honor in doubt? Could a preference for luxury, by chance, not be spontaneous and natural, in the good sense, clear of the baser aspects of money? What is the dose of insolence that gratitude requires one to accept without scandal? In sum, how to disarm the preconceptions of the well-off against those who have nothing? Although these were glaring questions, the social scheme made any direct confrontation taboo for the protagonists and narrators of Machado's early fiction.

By and large, the main adventures belong to the repertoire of the more trivial romantic novel, in which love is put to the test by chance social happenings and distances, with marriage always in view. Nevertheless, if we attend to the motivations woven into the fabric of the text, we will note that it is not really this that is at stake, but rather the relation between *dependent* and the *family of means*, the former's status burdened by the oppressive sign of protection that at any moment can be revoked. In this case, love matters less than dignity, always at risk of not being recognized (but why?). In order to understand the latent issues here, we need to distance ourselves. Let us say that Machado was rearranging the paraphernalia of romantic fiction in order to render it consonant with a real historical question, embedded in the characteristic lines of Brazilian society, which gave them their peculiar tone. Bourgeois and slaveholding at the same time, Brazil gave mercantile form to material wealth but did not develop salaried labor, resulting in the special problem *of class* alluded to in these novels. Supported by an agricultural economy dependent on a slaveholding system, whose structures extended into urban life, the country required that men who were free but poor— neither proprietary, nor proletarian—live in a peculiar state of privation or semiexclusion. They had no means to renounce the shelter of patronage, under whose protection they continually returned, despite the fact that the liberal-romantic fashion of the century, the depository of contemporary sentiment, designated that kind of dependence as a degrading sign of backwardness. To carry this point further, let us say that, in the absence of proprietorship, only patronage could save somebody from being nobody, but without making him an equal. Thus, *relationships based on favors*, incompatible with the impersonality of law, or, seen from the other side, inseparable from an exaggeration of the personal sphere, mediated the material reproduction of one of the largest social classes as well as its access to the sphere of modern civilization. A different standard of modernity was being developed, *falling short of general legal guarantees*, with outlets and impasses that were likewise sui generis. The sense of discrepancy that resulted from this would outlive the abolition of slavery and last into the present era, expressed sometimes as inferiority, sometimes as originality, depending on the circumstances. In this case, the loss of dignity would be less of an indignity than the falling back into the condition of a marginalized people.

In other words, the conventions of the romantic novel served Machado as tools with which to study and recast, within a restricted terrain, a problem of national life. In fact, in spite of the conventional genre and its moralizing attitude, seemingly impermeable to actual social complexity, Machado's analytical acuity makes these books serious and representative, engaged on their own terms. They suggest replacing traditional authoritarian paternalism, according to which the proprietor disposes of his dependents without consulting them in a way that naturally mutilates and humiliates, with enlightened paternalism, in which mutual respect civilizes the relationship, although without questioning the systemic inequality and especially the slave labor that sustain it. It is a matter of the modernization of paternalism, echoing at a distance, that is, from within the country's anomalous position, the formal equalities that have emerged in the course of development in model European countries. More specifically, Machado rehearsed case by case the pros and cons of an alliance between proprietors and the educated, talented poor, achieved through co-optation based on the well-understood interests of the involved parties. He suggested to those involved a more intelligent and somewhat less barbarous society.

The conservatism of that idea of progress speaks for itself. Intrigue and analysis must be congruent with the structural circumstances of the dependents, whose aspirations to co-optation impose the narrow perspective of personal affiliation as well as a low tolerance for signs of disagreement. The aesthetic price is fixed by the corresponding rule of decorum, sugary and anachronistic, according to which the familial structure in which slave ownership is vested is essentially pure, with no room for dispute. To be sure, there is egoism and materialism (modern defects), as well as traditionalism and authoritarianism (defects resulting from backwardness), but these are no more than individual deviations. They represent blemishes on the social canvas that well-intentioned observation ought to correct, without, in the meantime, engaging in dangerous generalizations, or rather, without pointing out the discretionary and antiquated nucleus of power of the patriarch. Artistically, despite the evident talent of the writer, the policed expression of dissatisfaction is a disaster that paralyzes spirited thrusts and weakens the whole of Machado's first attempts at the novel. On the other hand, the restrictions on criticism are themselves instructive, imbued with mimetic accuracy, since they give literary form to the pressure exerted on the intellect by the real social scheme, which left no room for the exercise of modern freedoms.

The respectful prose, with its elevated and antimaterialist tone, always silencing the essential, expresses in various guises the historical dead end in which the dependents find themselves. A mediating term between Catholic discretion and aesthetic norm, accentuated decorum seeks to pare down the cruelties connected with proprietorship in its colonial aspect. Without attenuating the disequilibria between the diverse aspects of proprietorship, decorum functions as living reproof to the disregard of personhood and to the crude primacy of money, fatal to those who live in a weak position in the shadow of favor. As for the dependents, decorum helps them to maintain their stature and not slide back into the "Gogolian" indignities of resentment, compensatory fantasy, and abject personal subjection, more or less implicated in the condition of incomplete equality. Beyond this, decorous composure postulates a dubious common cause, casting the dependents' adherence to the demands of the protector-oppressor as a contribution to the smooth working of things, which ennobles everyone and, at its limit, manages to benefit the fatherland. On those terms, progress would consist of self-reform on the part of proprietors who had been converted to an enlightened attitude under the civilizing pressure of a relationship with dependents full of merit, albeit lacking anything they might call their own. There would be, in sum, a possible path for overcoming social infelicities, or for *Aufklärung* by half. Modernization would be of a spiritual nature, linked to the distinguished effort of the poor and the receptive disposition of the well-situated, or in other words, to a moment of comprehension between classes, far from the fight for any rights, as well as from any frank formulation. The deliberate grading of the conflicts, in its turn, sugars the pill in terms of dramatic composition. The coarseness and material calculations of the proprietors are restricted to the margins, where they resound like heavy threats but represent the exception. In contrast, at the center of intrigue, as a rule, the encounter of souls who elected each other under the sign of reciprocal obligation constitutes an idealized version of cooption. Romanesque and poignant, bordering on the domain of melodrama, this mutual understanding remains superior to clearly condemnable considerations of self-interest. Naturally, the victory of exemplary manners is not convincing and confers on the narratives the aura of lost causes, giving them some pungency.

In order to strengthen this line of argument, let us say that the lovely little Rio estate, "semiurban and semiforested," represents the general scene.[10] In the background, we see slaves and poor dependents, together with a few flickers of life among the godforsaken poor; in the parlor and the garden, conversing politely, are the proprietors and their satellites: baronesses, counselors, well-furnished widows, factotums, numerous supporters and hangers-on, self-seeking neighbors, and functionaries of various sorts, plus the marriageable youth and the heroine with a "soul above her destiny," that is, without a birthright.[11] The conventional weaving of the plot and the buttoned-up writing muffle the contentious texture of the material, or better, leave unexplored the internal connection between the civility of the parlor and the ancien régime outside, which would give the intrigue denser Brazilian dimensions. Even so, more or less by its very absence, the connection makes itself felt and constitutes the objective complexity of a novelistic universe, making the books almost good. From another perspective, this substantial unity constitutes the very blind spot of the composition, since the emphatic dignity of both the central figures and the narrator could not possibly surrive, had the necessary connections been made explicit. Imprisoned in the idealizing vision of co-option necessary to those who seek to be co-opted, the narrative point of view cannot latitudinally

---

[10] *Ressureição*, in *Obras completas*, 1:33.
[11] *Iaiá Garcia*, in *Obras completas*, 1:315.

expound the antisocial interests of proprietorship—or the rather unromantic calculations of the candidate for adoption—whose diffuse presence nevertheless is the center of the prose. Such calculations would offend the edifying idea that both people of means and candidates hoping to become people of means have of themselves and of their alliance. We might note, moreover, that the veto extends to irreverence in general, and, with it, to the crucial operations of freedom of spirit and of humor in an ex-colony: the meritorious and civilized character of the elite should not be subjected to open scrutiny, or rather, should not be compared to the semicolonial relations that sustain it, nor be confronted in detail with the metropolitan models that give it a passport of modern stamp. *However, the intellect neither reaches the height of its era, nor escapes a position of colonial subservience without that order of sensitive and relativizing comparisons, always double-faced, that were and are the genius of the critical spirit in peripheral societies.*

Halfway between idealization and criticism, the touchstone of progress would lie in respect on the part of proprietors for dependents, differing from the mere importation of the innovations of bourgeois civilization. Improvement of morals would help paternalism to play the sanitizing roles expected from free labor and a law equal for all—a pious hope, attuned to the lack of a material base of the poor, while at the same time inconsonant with those liberal evaluations aligned with the commodities and ideas from abroad. That said, Machado's insistence on dignity in these early fictions manifested not only the social vacuum in which those who had no means of earning a salary lived in destitution, but also the suspicions about a copied modernity, or rather, a fear that, despite progress, or even with the help of progress, everything would remain as before. This apprehension had a real basis, insofar as the Europeanization of society peacefully coexisted with the colonial disqualification of a part of the country's inhabitants. Let us say that the moralist wrinkle of these first novels countered the local course of the world with a thesis that was simultaneously on the cutting edge and conformist. It maintained that there would only be progress in the event that a rigid *internal* dialectic reformed the relation between proprietors and dependents (but without getting to the base of everything, slavery), or, alternatively, that any changes occurring without this kind of reform, even if imported from advanced countries, would not be sufficient to overcome the nation's backwardness.

In the preface to his first novel, Machado announced that he wanted to *contrast characters* rather than narrate customs.[12] Perhaps in keeping with the

---

[12] *Ressureição*, 32.

self-love of dependents who found themselves in less precarious situations, he took the artistic-moral position of giving greater value to personal disposition than to external conditioning. In order to imbue that perspective with realism, he would dissect all possible options in every corresponding circumstance, thus establishing a set of offensive complementarities. Armed with intelligence and valor, the heroine could not remain in the no-man's land of poverty. She must make herself accepted "in society" but also defend herself against the fantasies of her benefactors, which ranged from offers of good counsel to offers of marriage and attempts to deflower her, whereas the proprietor chose, depending on the occasion, to treat her civilly, as an equal, or barbarously, as an inferior to whom nothing is owed ("Who was she to affront him that way?").[13] It was up to him to decide whether he was standing before a subaltern without greater rights, equivalent to the rest of the colonial rabble, or before a modern young woman, whom he might even marry. The absurd distance between the alternative terms indicates the degree of social insecurity of the poor, as well as the degree of social irresponsibility permitted to their protectors, maddening in its own manner. The burlesque and indecorous substance of the country would find its way back into the fiction through the back door, diverging from the well-behaved narrative form, conceived according to the *contrast of characters*, with which it would produce an involuntary irony.

The sentimental plot ought to humanize this uncivil society. The heroines' confrontations with their patrons' abuses of authority, whether those patrons, often godparents, are male or female, offers itself under a different sign in each of the four novels, which also illustrates the experimental and systematic spirit of Machadian literature. The attempt to moralize patriarchal power through the worth of young women of low birth depended, successively, on trusting frankness, on calculating but civilizing ambition, on Christian purity, and on severity without illusions. Despite the disparity between the plots, in all four cases the presumption of equality, sustained above all by love, coexists with humiliating, panic-inducing deviance from that ideal, leaving the social destiny of the dependent to the discretion of the proprietor. The proprietor's decision may be made indifferently, "between two cups of tea," or in a state of agitation, in the midst of a moral confusion, in which the imperatives of patronage mix with the appetites of the lover or with aspirations to greatness.[14] There are odd passages, undeniable high

---

[13] *Iaiá Garcia*, 316.
[14] Ibid., 402.

points, altogether surprising in books so chained to decency. Separated from the conventional mold, the dissociations between self-consciousness and social rationality might well figure in a Russian novel or amid the daring of modern literature, on its way to discovering the unconscious. Under the pretext of chronicling the ins and outs of sentiments of distinguished people, the writer tried his hand at the psychological drifts and ideological rationalizations that would later lie at the center of his great novels, where they would oil the day-to-day workings of a fractured society. Be that as it may, the romantic adventure in the European tradition occupied the preeminent position in the plot without, for that matter, avoiding the clichés of second-class conformist fiction. Meanwhile, the complementary side, restricted to dimly lit margins by the very law of the genre, gained ground for disabused observation and analysis, in which the unjustifiable and antiheroic realities of local privilege were faced head on, in an adult spirit, with an evident heightening of literary quality.

At the end of *Iaiá Garcia*, the final novel of the first block, the heroine breaks with the advantages and humiliations of dependency: "for her cup of gratitude was full."[15] She seeks an outlet in a teaching post that permits her to move to another part of the country, far from the influence of her benefactors. She asks that her father accompany her and leaves "the life . . . of servility that he had lived until then."[16] The decision reflects the reconfiguring of the horizon afforded by salaried labor, which represented an alternative to clientelism, casting light on the connection, always overlooked, between the humiliations of dependency and the slave system. This is the future, arriving with exasperating delay. From another perspective, regarding the coherence of the plot, the decision also has retrospective reach. It seems as though in the end the heroine considers deluded and pointless her fight (comprising hundreds of pages) in which she has fought to redeem the contentiousness characterizing the relationship between protected and protector, which turned out to have no remedy after all. There is a reflux of the lesson with respect to the earlier novels, where the just objectives and mental clarity of the female protagonists also tried to correct the disorientation of proprietors, excellent folk by definition, but drowning in a viscous world of familial prejudices, retrograde suspicions, satisfied indolence, and unconfessed appetites.

In the abstract, the confrontation between reason and obscurantism, with the connotations of class peculiar to each case, promised to end well.

---

[15] Ibid., 315.
[16] Ibid., 406.

The young women's longing for dignity suited everyone, resulting in any case from the education that they had been able to acquire thanks to their proximity to the wealthy, whereas the half-tyrannical aspect of the latter seemed part of the general backwardness of Brazilian society rather than a manifestation of conservatism incarnated—in other words, nothing that tolerance and good counsel could not overcome. In *Iaiá Garcia* the conflict becomes both deeper and more complex. The whims of the authorities, as well as the equally arbitrary favors are still there. Both are portrayed realistically, for routine insult is part of the situation of clientelism, inevitable until the arrival of free labor. The novelty, which halts the course of paternalist relations and points in a more radical direction, although it appears a retreat, is that now the heroine thinks it inadmissible to marry above her situation. This is not because she considers herself inferior—very much the contrary: the problem is that her pride will not permit her to accept this "kind of favor," since she cannot recognize the professed qualities of her erstwhile benefactors, who, as notorious representatives of dignity and reason, do not know what these may be.[17]

On the one side, with its antiromantic aspect, there is nothing more romantic than that objection to unequal marriage. It is a matter of not consenting to the degradation of love, which must be preserved against the system of favoritism and brute force that determines Brazilian backwardness. In this respect, the heroine presents that which elsewhere the modern individual owes herself. As for everything else, she makes concessions fitting to the local lifestyle, as long as these do not compromise her at the core. In the form of the divided self, which opposed the just but impossible to the backward but possible, some of the great international lines of difference and hierarchy were being internalized, transforming what seems a picturesque condition into a contemporary moral impasse, proper to the peripheral world.

On the other side, the objection is the result of a class experience. There is a ravine between the situation of the dependent, one step from the excluded populace, and the situation of the established lady, enjoying the guarantees and benefits of modern civilization. Although not impossible, the passage from one side to the other depended on the good graces of a superior. But how to owe such a change of state—no less than an insertion in the present world—to the hazards of personal sympathy? By dint of the excessiveness of the debt, the corresponding hope must harm the self-esteem

---

[17] Ibid., 402.

of the dependent. Pricked by illusion, the dependent forgets what she owes herself and is capable of submitting herself, bound hand and foot, to the whim of her patron, *who in his turn may, but need not, keep the promise that he made in a moment of caprice.* Even in the favorable case, in which—let us suppose—the eldest son of the family does not go back on his word and marries the obscure young maiden, the ghost of class humiliation remains. The most legitimate of impulses, that is, the dependent's aspiration to dignity, always runs the risk of being disdainfully treated, increasing the feeling of indignity, which needs to be avoided at all cost. In other words, the object of intellectual-ideological aversion in these novels is the moment in which the mirage of individual emancipation, or of liberal and romantic values, raised by the daydreams of personal favor, functions to the contrary, as the instrument of paternalist domination, leading the dependent to lower her guard and become usufructuary. Out of self-respect, the latter ought not to respect the liberal promise on the lips of her patrons.

The historical conclusion reached in *Iaiá Garcia* sums up an apprenticeship of class, while depersonalizing the issue. We may note that the source of humiliation has changed place, no longer following from this or that exorbitance in which the protector falls short of fulfilling his duty. Now it is linked to an irreconcilable duality of functions, with a structural basis: the patriarch, to whom the protected owes loyalty, is also a proprietor in the modern meaning of the term, for whom that order of obligations is relative. The dynamic of paternalist involvement shows itself to be only one side of the situation, whose other aspect, dictated by the ownership of property, belongs to a discrete orbit to which the reasons of the dependent do not correspond and to which the dependent, furthermore, has no independent access, *which consubstantiates the social fragmentation.* The systematization of the point of view of those underneath, taken to its extreme by the novelist, qualifies negatively the promise in the relationship, whose seductions, made up of degrading class mechanisms, it is better to flee. The moral debt does not have the same value on both sides of the equation. The breast of Brazilian proprietors lodges two souls.

In *Posthumous Memoirs of Brás Cubas* this fund of frustration and backwardness is transformed into great literature through the recombination of its elements. The strike of genius consists—if I am not mistaken—in delegating the narrative function to the old class adversary, the very one who does not know, according to his enlightened dependents, what dignity and reason may be. After having been one *subject* among others, or a collection of anecdotes concerning local anachronisms, always with some reflection on the existence of those without rights, the oscillations of the Janus-faced man of property, civilized in European fashion and uncivilized in Brazilian, or senti-mental in a Brazilian manner and objective in a European—enlightened and arbitrary, distant and intrusive, Victorian and given to cronyism—define the very *form* of the prose, conditioning the world to their regular tic-tock. The elegant or ignoble alternation of the models no longer determines only the relation with dependents in circumscribed moments of crisis, well lo-cated in the unfolding of the plot. Now it is ubiquitous and comes to be the general ambience of life in all of its moments, on an incredible scale, whose rhetorical achievement is a technical feat. Vertiginously, encyclopedically, it is applied to the foundations of literary representation, to the gullibility of the trusting reader, to contemporary norms of decency, to minisyntheses of Western tradition, as well as to the trivial day-to-day existence of the ex-colony. At its extreme, nothing is left untouched. It is true that the incon-stant narrator, lacking credibility, constantly engaged in skirmishes with the reader, is part of an illustrious comic tradition, independent of Brazil. Yet Machado polarized that tradition's repertoire of maneuvers by making it a function of the class ambivalence of the Brazilian elite, giving those maneu-vers a realist imprint and, above all, limning a process of social formation, locked into a lagging destiny, but modern nevertheless.

From an evolutionary perspective, or that of the fight against backward-ness with its stages following in foreseen sequence, the solution was unex-pected. Free labor, which at the conclusion of *Iaiá Garcia* reconfigured the canvas, promised dependents the independence that they needed for a revi-sion, without subterfuge, of a passé society. After slavery and disenfran-chised poverty, the grievances were ending and true freedom was coming, married with progress. However, Machado did not write the conclusive book that seemed the order of the day—but neither did the country take the higher path. Contrary to the expectations of abolitionist optimism, the end of captivity did not deliver the blacks and the poor to citizenship, a national duty that would be delayed indefinitely. What prevailed, with the aid of im-migration, were forms of semiforced and precarious salaried labor, which gave new life to the preceding patterns of authority. With some rearrange-ment, the dissonant combinations of liberalism and exclusion, of bourgeois property and fondness for clientelism ("I didn't think very highly of that al-liance of manager of a bank and father to a dog"), of elegance and raw power ("because I want it and can have it that way") entered into the new times unchecked, reacquiring trust for the future.[18] Let us say that in the

---

[18] Machado de Assis, *Memorial de Aires* (1908), in *Obras completas*, 1:1,068 and 1,047.

brief period between *Iaiá Garcia* (1878) and *Posthumous Memoirs* (1880), almost ten years before the abolition of slavery (1888), the writer took notice of the disappointing course of things, which was not going to be shaped by the secular providentiality of doctrines of progress, nor by the good counsel that dependents might have given to their patrons. In that sense, the delegation of the narrative role to the satisfied classes signaled a turnabout as well as a desire not to insist on exhausted perspectives.

Of course, there would be no extraordinary artistic invention if everything could be summed up by the exchange of (moderated) criticism for apologetics or of the perspective of the oppressed for that of the oppressors. The passage to an opposing class viewpoint, which in its way represented an adhesion to the stronger side, a turncoat operation, or a slap at justice, in fact played a role—scandalous or discreet—in the new formal apparatus, within which it also combined a disconcerting dose of socioliterary perfidy. Handled with absolute virtuosity, the latter reequilibrated the mix by means of the indirect truths that it allowed to escape, to the detriment of the well-situated and their society, through an organized and impressive, not to mention humorous, leakage. In negative fashion, the narrator, now positioned at the top of the local system of inequalities, functions (with respect to his condition and the consequences of these inequities as well as through his adherence to both new and old theories that might be brought to bear) as an all-embracing conscience, who incites a reading against the grain and the formation of a contrary superconscience, if it is possible to say that. Under the guise of conformity, the part played by provocation is great.

Let us say that the Machadian narrator realizes to a superlative degree the aspirations to elegance and culture characteristic of the Brazilian elite, but only in order to compromise that society and let it make a poor show of itself. In the exercise of his refinements, he mingles with a representative gallery of national types, or rather, a scarcely presentable set of class relations, outside the norm (if the criteria applied to it are *exigent* and *imported*, or Anglo-French), yet at the same time familiar and normal—if the standard is quotidian Brazilian life. The catalog of ambiguities that distance the country's own well-off from the modern model—but not from that modernity devoid of evens model—is exemplified in action. Bordering on didacticism and also sarcasm, the character-narrator's thoughts and deeds are illustrations designed to authenticate the worst suppositions held about him by diverse categories of dependents, including slaves as well as his consorts in paracolonial domination—relatives or not, liberals or supporters of slavery who were not fooled by civility, and also by the sincere or hypocritical foreigner, to whom all this seemed barbarous—this ensemble constituting the network of viewpoints relevant in this circumstance. Thus, the new artistic equation did not forget the humiliations suffered by dependents, for which it functioned as an oblique spokesman. Contrary to appearances, these dictated the hidden staff of the narrator's histrionic performance, who had as his function the role of representing them in their full gravity, with the accompaniment of the egoistic, niggardly, or abject reflections that the victims, hopeful of cooption, could not bring themselves to articulate or even to imagine.

The maliciousness of this procedure, which unites subtle irony and gross farce, class travesty and treason, intimacy and hostility, is more salient in those novels written in the first-person singular (*Posthumous Memoirs* and *Dom Casmurro* [1899]). Albeit less ostentatious, the method equally serves impersonal, third-person narrative, often called objective, but as capable of partiality and baseness as the other.[19] However that may be, the accelerated verve of the prose ought to satisfy objectives of an opposing order, whose stitching is a miracle of dexterity. From a *spontaneous* point of view, the narrator revels at whim, on many planes and remorselessly, in the advantages and facilities apportioned to him by local injustice and by his power to speak with impunity, without letting go of anything—from peccadillo to atrocity—and, moreover, without being incognizant of the fact that in the eyes of the European superego, he is playing a parodied part, which only accentuates the piquancy of his position. The extreme cultivation of his speech does not diminish the injustices but confers on them an urbanity and a special type of poetry, which, according to the preference of the critic, betters or worsens the picture. From the point of view of composition, highly manipulated by an Author who maintains an epic distance, the anecdotal and reflexive frame of these erratic feints ought to sketch out a social totality. It also ought to inspire the ill will of the disaffected, among them the reader, drawing toward the narrator and his form of elegance a lukewarm version of universal dislike. This is owing to complacency in the historical slough, a peripheral variant of the Baudelarian conscience in evil. That said, the narrator's elegance does not disintegrate into sheer caprice, since beyond semicolonial affectation it is the valid demonstration that civilized qualities are compatible with the transgressions to which they give cover. The implacable visibility that

---

[19] *Quincas Borba* (1891), the second of Machado's great novels, is written in the third person. *Esaú e Jacó* (1904) constitutes a complex halfway construct: the narrative is in the third person, but was found among the diaries of Conselheiro Aires, its main character. *Memorial de Aires* has the form of a diary but is better understood if read against the grain of its pseudo-author's elegant opinions.

this elegance confers on these transgressions—a considerable demonstration and also a contribution to truth—has no parallel in Brazilian literature and may be rare even in other literatures.

In abandoning the well-behaved, moralizing narrator of his first novels, connected to the cause of dependents, Machado anticipated the scarcely edifying lessons of abolition, which would not have as its objective the social integration of the country. The accuracy of his prognosis, which in and of itself constitutes no guarantee of literary quality, in this circumstance would lead to intellectual verification of forms then in effect and to the invention of new ones, equal to the times. Delineated by the Author at a critical distance, the highly refined narrator, who represents the flower of civilization but who is indulgent not only with himself but also with the screaming injustices within his society, is one of these actualizing inventions. There one can see, with a superior verisimilitude, a different version of the enlightened and generous guardianship that the country's landed gentlemen believed they exercised.

The deepening of the likeness and of historical judgment is notable, albeit little understood. In relation to the Brazilian referent, there is a clear *progress of mimesis*, sustained by a daring ensemble of formal operations, which in turn presupposes a high conjugation of artistic and social criticism. This chain, if it is exact, has the merit of indicating the reflexive and constructive component of the mimetic effort, unknown to literary theory of the last decades, which has confronted imitation from the banalizing angle of photographic fidelity. That said, it is clear that the artistic value and the truth of the work do not reside in the similarity of the portrait but in its new perspectives and in the reconfigurations occasioned by the search for verisimilitude. In this case, these perspectives and reconfigurations belong to several orders.

As far as focus and proportions, the inversion is general: the new procedure brings to the forefront the elusive oppression that in the earlier novels had remained in the background and that constituted their best part, while it mocked the illusions—"dry your glasses, sensitive soul!"—of the romantic impulse that occupied the first plane.[20] Along the same line, the emphasis on the costs of injustice suffered by dependents is replaced by the testimony to its *utility*, made in the first-person singular by its *enlightened* beneficiary, whose objectives lie in another sphere, but also in this. The novelistic fantasies of personal amends give way to the somewhat cynical experience of a

---

[20] *Memórias póstumas de Brás Cubas*, 456.

dissociated social mechanism. The insult did not cease to exist but gained a solid foundation. As far as the desegregation of the country itself, the limited universe of the semiexcluded, deprived of a public existence, was not propitious ground for civilization's new developments. Recent philosophies, railway projects, historical studies, financial operations, mathematical sciences, and parliamentary politics figured only in the margin, as conventional indices of modernity and social class, in the same way as did fashion magazines, the tail-coat, and the cigar. With the new narrator, these and other innovations of the epoch acquire a reality and invade the scene in a spectacular way, always framed by his own caprice, or better, to function according to the regime of a heterodox class, creating a special atmosphere of ostensible and lowered actualization, which is an extraordinary mimetic and artistic accomplishment. The proprietors participate intensely in contemporary progress, but this is *thanks* to the antiquated relationships on which they lean, and not *despite* them, and even less *in opposition to them*, as common sense might dictate. With this last rectification, we arrive at the modern perplexity and truth of the new Machadian configuration. The narrator who is integrally sophisticated and free, in possession of his means and of tradition (one could almost call him emancipated), reiterates in thought and conduct the *backwardness* of the social formation, rather than overcoming it—in part out of spite, in order that these delays be present as lamentable facts, accentuating the sensation of foolishness; in part out of nostalgia (another form of spite?), in order not to distance himself from them, even though they have been surpassed; and in part because heightened consciousness is essential to this ensemble, which has a direction, but no purpose. Rather than deceiving ourselves about the progress of a backward society, we witness the reproduction of backwardness in a sphere of the greatest clairvoyance available.

A schematic recapitulation would say the following. In a foundational moment, romantic fiction discerned the peculiarities of Brazilian family life under the sign of the picturesque and of national identity, over which it superimposed more or less *folhetinesque* confabulations. The success of the combination, well adapted to the necessities of the young country, was great. Even with an irreverent cast, the reflection and its somewhat regressive complicities conferred a positive sign on the traces that differentiated the society. One generation later, Machado recovered that thematic, ideological, and aesthetic complex in new terms, without the protective fog of local color and patriotic self-congratulation. The extended Brazilian family began to be confronted according to the prism of the instructed dependent, who was part of it and transformed it into a *problem*. In this there was a special system of relations, with its own structure, outlets, and impasses, demanding analysis. Its difference indicated backwardness, insofar as the tacit values of the dependent were determined by the Rights of Man, which, at least in principle, had currency elsewhere. The narrator's sympathy was devoted to the wronged heroine's struggles, which were partly formed according to the mold of the *folhetim*. Meanwhile, in the opposing field, it was inevitable that the configuration of the conflict, according to its progress from book to book, should look into the negative aspects of the figure of the proprietor. These negative aspects internalized and reflected with precision, in the form of *defect*, the absurd disequilibrium between the classes. By analyzing the consequences of this very disequilibrium, which showed no signs of internal regeneration, Machado invented the formula that would characterize his mature work and make a great writer out of him. Just as he had not accommodated himself to the facile enchantment of the romantic picturesque, he now renounced the unanimous deference due the moderate narrator who was the friend of good causes.

The new artistic apparatus gave an indirect account of the frustration of dependents and a direct account of their abandonment by the proprietors, with resonating allusion to a peripheral society incapable of integrating itself. The reach of the formal arrangement, which affronted the superstitions of the secular spirit, particularly the trust in progress and its benevolence, is disconcerting even today. The cunning personification of an elite narrator, enviably civilized and very involved in the relations of oppression that he himself configures and judges, is a move that upsets the narrative board, making the game more real. The artifice challenges readers along every line: it teaches them to think for themselves; to debate not only the subject matter but also its mode of representation; to consider at a critical distance both narrators and authorities, who are always interested parties, even when well-spoken; to doubt the civilizing national engagement of the privileged, in particular in new countries, where this pretension plays a great part; and to develop an aversion for the imaginary consolations of the novel, manipulated by narrative authority out of self-interest. The artifice teaches, above all, that the combination of the cosmopolitan sphere and that of the excluded can be stable. It also shows that there is no prospect of overcoming this combination in view. The demonstration is particularly succulent because it illustrates and investigates the national mechanisms—"delicious" ones, to use Machado's term—of nonbourgeois reproduction of the bourgeois order; and these are not only national but also universal mechanisms, since on a world scale, contrary to what seems self-evident, this reproduction is the rule, not the exception.

The heroines of the first novels are not very interesting, insofar as their precarious social position is disfigured by romantic cliché. Their vicissitudes, nevertheless, make evident the class characteristics of the antagonist, whose figure has literary originality. In the novels of the second phase, in which the perspective is inverted, it is the turn of the poor to figure in the subjective mirror of the proprietors, in which the prisms of bourgeois individualism and paternalist domination take turns according to the shamelessness of egoistic convenience. In that light the figure of the dependent acquires extraordinary relief. These are portraits of a kind of destitution that does not count on the recognition of the value of work, on the protection of rights, or on the compensations of divine providence. It is a matter of the social vacuum set up by modern slavery for a freedom without means, another theme that, *mutatis mutandis*, has not been exhausted. Along the same line of strangely advanced resonances of backwardness, we might note how the extrabourgeois aspect of local affairs and of the narrative relation itself functions: now it may seem merely a deviation from the rule, but then it has a movement with its own slant, which escapes dominant definitions and discovers unknown ground. To get an idea of this, see the role played by authority in the definition and dissolution of the person, one's own or that of another; the relation between the experience of time and personal disintegration, often of the authority issuing the mandate; the extrascientific dimensions of science, with its authoritarian and sadistic functions; and the radical difference constituted by the point of view. In this respect, Machado's fiction converges with the advanced literature of his time, which also applied itself to laying bare other realities underlying bourgeois reality. We might simply notice, a little haphazardly, affinities in the field of innovations with Dostoevsky, Baudelaire, Henry James, Chekhov, Proust, Kafka, and Borges. Machado's classical borrowings are endless and have led critics to seek his merit in that domain, to our loss in comprehending the contemporary and advanced character of his experimentation.

The manifestation of intelligence, technical refinement, and general culture of the Machadian narrator is discomfiting at first contact, though it later imposes itself as a great finding. On a somewhat laughable plane, it was a demonstration of literary proficiency that served his country's patriotic effort toward accelerated cultural formation. Here was an educated narrator among the educated, who shamed no one and who contributed to the elevation of national culture to a new level, above the sympathetic modesty that had come to be the rule. Above all in his first, most spectacular moment, in *Posthumous Memoirs*, this finally provincial aspect, which captures the aspiration of a young country, plays a significant part in inciting and sustaining our interest. Meanwhile, the most substantial aspect of the work was another.

The universalizing program, which in its way represented an ideal standard, presupposed the encyclopedic assimilation of all that had to do with the *generally human*. The Bible, philosophy, humanist rhetoric, the eighteenth-century analysis of egoism, scientific materialism, ancient and recent historiography, and the philosophy of the unconscious—all these, coupled with disabused commentary on actuality and with local notation, entered into the package. The result could not be more socially flattering. But then, in a daring thrust of his art, Machado would not confer a positive sign on this great accumulation. Despite all that it might have cost, he made it an integral part of the prestige and arbitrary action of his narrator. Linked to local class domination, the very process of enlightenment changed its sign, beginning to resound in accord with an underlying stave, which is left to the reader to decipher and that even today leaves us without response.

Translated by Sharon Lubkemann Allen

JONATHAN ARAC

Adventures of Huckleberry Finn
(Mark Twain, United States, 1884)

Everyone thinks they remember the story, but the voice is what really lingers. Huckleberry Finn, the preteen boy who narrates the novel, and his companion Jim, a runaway slave, are floating on a raft down the Mississippi in the American South of the 1840s. Jim is in danger of being captured and re-enslaved, so they need to lie low, and they travel at night. Despite the danger, Huck finds beauty. "It's lovely to live on a raft," Huck says,[1] and the sentence might be the alliterative, eight-syllabled opening line of a ballad. The book's language is poetic, but not often so close to verse. The next sentence broaches quite a different rhythm, extending itself with unexpected turns that give a sense of unforced, widely ranging speech and thought alike: "We had the sky up there, all speckled with stars, and we used to lay on our backs and look up at them, and discuss about whether they was made or only just happened—Jim he allowed they was made, but I allowed they happened; I judged it would have took too long to *make* so many" (chapter 19; here and in all subsequent quotations, emphases are Twain's).

Huck's narrative is not only oral in rhythm, it is local in vocabulary. "Allow" in the sense of *think* or *conclude* is a regional usage of the U.S. South and Midwest. Huck's grammar breaks the rules of the schoolroom, a discipline to which he has been subjected back at home, but that he prefers to evade. Standard English dictates *lie* where Huck has "lay"; abjures the pleonasms of *about* after "discuss," of *he* after "Jim"; requires the plural *were* instead of "was"; demands the participial form *taken* instead of "took." Against all this bossiness, Huck's speech feels free, and yet he and Jim are also engaged in reflection, and their conversation is about judging. Alone on the river, left to their own devices, they discuss the nature of things in bold cosmological debate between equals: "Jim said the moon could a *laid* [all the stars]; well, that looked kind of reasonable, so I didn't say nothing against it, because I've seen a frog lay most as many, so of course it could be done." Social hierarchies of free and slave, black and white, are suspended in a democratic utopia. These memorable passages feel timeless, a scene of

---

[1] Mark Twain, *The Adventures of Huckleberry Finn* (New York: Penguin Books, 2003). All subsequent quotations are from this edition and are cited parenthetically in the text.

mythmaking itself mythical, but they are part of a sequence measured as "two or three days and nights," in a few pages set between the force of murderous feuds and the fraud of con men claiming to be royalty.

When the impending dawn forces Huck and Jim to pull over and hide, they

> slid into the river and had a swim, so as to freshen up and cool off; then we set down on the sandy bottom where the water was about knee deep, and watched the daylight come. Not a sound, anywheres—perfectly still—just like the whole world was asleep, only sometimes the bull-frogs a-cluttering, maybe. The first thing to see, looking away over the water, was a kind of dull line—that was the woods on t'other side—you couldn't make nothing else out; then a pale place in the sky; then more paleness spreading around; then the river softened up, away off, and warn't black any more, but gray; you could see little dark spots drifting along, ever so far away—trading scows, and such things; and long black streaks—rafts; sometimes you could hear a sweep screaking; or jumbled up voices, it was so still, and sounds come so far; and by and by you could see a streak on the water which you know by the look of the streak that there's a snag there in a swift current which breaks on it and makes that streak look that way; and you see the mist curl up off of the water, and the east reddens up, and the river, and you make out a log cabin in the edge of the woods, away on the bank on t'other side of the river, being a wood-yard, likely, and piled by them cheats so you can throw a dog through it anywheres; then the nice breeze springs up, and comes fanning you from over there, so cool and fresh, and sweet to smell, on account of the woods and the flowers; but sometimes not that way, because they've left dead fish laying around, gars, and such, and they do get pretty rank; and next you've got the full day, and everything smiling in the sun, and the song-birds just going it!
>
> A little smoke couldn't be noticed now, so we could take some fish off of the lines, and cook up a hot breakfast. And afterwards we would watch the lonesomeness of the river, and kind of lazy along, and by and by lazy off to sleep. Wake up, by and by, and look to see what done it, and maybe see a steamboat, coughing along up stream, so far off towards the other side you couldn't tell nothing about her only whether she was stern-wheel or side-wheel; then for about an hour there wouldn't be anything to hear nor nothing to see—just solid lonesomeness. Next you'd see a raft sliding by, away off yonder, and maybe a galoot on it chopping, because they're most always doing it on a raft; you'd see the axe flash, and come down—you don't hear

nothing; you see that axe go up again, and by the time it's above the man's head, then you hear the *k'chunk!*—it had took all that time to come over the water. So we would put in the day, lazying around, listening to the stillness. (chapter 19)

Huck responds with all his senses: you can taste the fish for breakfast; smell the flowers or the rotting gars; feel the cool water or the sand underfoot; hear the quiet, broken by frogs a-cluttering, sweeps screaking, steamboats coughing, or galoots k'chunking; and above all, see the many things he and Jim see. What might be summarized as a single noun—*dawn*—opens into an extended process, punctuated by emergences. First a "dull line," then a "pale place," next "little dark spots" and "long black streaks," before the "east reddens up" and images can at last be categorized more precisely as "mist" and a "log cabin." The process is registered through a second-person narration: "you couldn't make nothing else out" but then "by and by you could see." Together with the "we" of Huck and Jim, the reader is invited also to share the experience of wonder and pleasure.

Mark Twain here naturalizes, as part of the American frontier landscape taken in and uttered by an uneducated youth, the techniques of impressionist prose so important in Western art writing from Flaubert to Conrad and beyond. The privilege of sensitive spectatorship is extended from the leisure class down the social scale, bringing to fulfillment an experiment that in the early nineteenth-century British poetry of William Wordsworth had met a far more mixed response. The risk, overcome by Twain, is that the putatively natural perceiving consciousness will seem to be ventriloquized by the highly cultivated author. Marks of the authorial vocabulary and sensibility may be felt in the abstract nouns so important in composing the passage: *paleness*, *lonesomeness*, and *stillness*. Samuel Clemens, as a young man before he had become Mark Twain, learned to read the river, as he recounts in *Life on the Mississippi*, and his active working skill becomes Huck's power to explain "a streak on the water which you know by the look of the streak that there's a snag there in a swift current which breaks on it and makes that streak look that way." The sequence is full of work, but always by others.

The flow of language is the sign of Huck's voice, felt in his words and intonation, while the author has constructed the sentences, in all their intricacy. The second paragraph of the quotation above, beginning with "a little smoke," starts with a rather short sentence and moves through three sentences of increasing length, until concluding with the shortest in the sequence, "So we would put in the day, lazying around and listening to the stillness."

The first paragraph features a Faulkner-length sentence 269 words long (starting with "the first thing to see" and running to the end), splattered with commas to set its microrhythms and built sequentially onto eleven semicolons, the punctuation mark most associated with high literacy.

Twain uses the story situation to motivate Huck's hyperattentiveness. He and Jim are on the lam, and danger lurks anywhere, so they need to notice everything. Hiding during the day enforces an idleness usually enjoyed only by rich people. Lowly men at leisure, singing the praises of their simple life—this is backwoods pastoral, guarded against the dangers of evident idealization by its awareness of stinky smells in nature and wood-yard cheats in society. The unusual verb form *to lazy* marks the enforced idleness, and names it with an ordinarily pejorative word, but Huck's blithely reiterating the term sets at ease any Protestant ethic anxieties. The euphoric narration transfigures a state of deprivation ("nothing to hear nor nothing to see") into satisfying plenitude ("just solid lonesomeness"), and the catachresis is imperceptible except to critical analysis. Huck and Jim, "lazying around, listening to the stillness," bring into informal, everyday prose something like what Wordsworth in "Tintern Abbey" had achieved only through elevated verse: for *lazying*, read: "the breath of this corporeal frame / And even the motion of our human blood / Almost suspended, we are laid asleep / In body"; and for *listening to the stillness*, read: "with an eye made quiet by the power / Of harmony, and the deep power of joy, / We see into the life of things."[2]

Adventures of Huckleberry Finn is not a visionary lyric, though it memorably incorporates such moments. Its title suggests a picaresque novel, which signals not only roguery but also comedy. The book is very funny, as well as comic, in many ways. The large comic frame depends on the history separating the time of Huck's adventures, in the 1840s, from the time of Twain's writing, which began in 1876, and the book's publication, first in England, for copyright purposes, in 1884, and then in the United States in 1885. The Civil War (1861–65) had abolished slavery in the United States, and therefore every reader has had a different perspective on the laws and customs of slave society than was possible for anyone in the time of the book's action. When a rich, famous, worldly author entrusts his narrative to a provincial outcast of limited literacy, it already produces the structural potential for irony, but when everyone in the author's world knows more and sees differently

---

[2] *The Poetical Works of Wordsworth*, ed. Thomas Hutchinson (New York: Oxford University Press, 1933), 206.

from everyone in the novel's world, it multiplies ironic possibilities. Huck's distance from the norms and mores of his time may, in this instance, bring him closer to us. His alienation from his society seems a strength rather than a ground for pathos. There is also a trick here to flatter the readership: if Huck is relatively uncultured, he is therefore, by a common logic, necessarily more natural, and if he is also more like us, then we allow ourselves credit for his good nature.

Huck is not wholly formed by his culture, yet he is shown to believe in the social customs governing slavery, even though he breaks them in allying himself with Jim, and at several points quite specifically acting to protect Jim. Readers applaud his actions and laugh indulgently at his self-doubts and self-castigations. The worse he thinks he is, the better we know he is.

Late in the book, this pattern of opposites stretches its farthest. Jim has been separated from Huck and betrayed; he is locked up on a farm way down river from his home in Missouri. Huck imagines that it might work better for Jim if Huck sends a letter back to the owner Jim has run away from. That way, if he must be re-enslaved, at least he can be reunited with his family and the community he knows. But then Huck realizes that if he returns home with Jim, he will be known as someone who helped a slave to escape. This fantasy of social "shame" awakens thoughts of moral guilt: "That's just the way: a person does a low-down thing, and then he don't want to take no consequences of it. Thinks as long as he can hide it, it ain't no disgrace" (chapter 31). The rhetorical stakes are raised. Huck's "conscience" kicks in, and his mind becomes a theater in which several versions of small-town Missouri and all-American, religious talk play themselves out, while he listens and tries to duck.

The language of religious admonition morphs into Huck's language, and the interference between different registers of speech raises a laugh. Huck preserves the formal model of the periodic sentence. The main verb ("dropped") is suspended for nearly one hundred words from the sentence's start, but the rhythms are bent into breathlessness, and the words, too, are twisted:

> At last, when it hit me all of a sudden that here was the plain hand of Providence slapping me in the face and letting me know my wickedness was being watched all the time from up there in heaven, whilst I was stealing a poor old woman's nigger that hadn't ever done me no harm, and now was showing me there's One that's always on the lookout, and ain't agoing to allow no such miserable doings to go on only just so fur and no further, I most dropped in my tracks I was so scared. (chapter 31)

The conventionally dead metaphor of the "hand of Providence" comes to life to slap Huck one, while the alien syntax suspends his identity and transports him into a space of moral agonizing.

Next Huck hears in his mind the voice of the schoolmarm, given a twist by his own dialect and by a wavering in personal pronouns: "There was the Sunday School, you could a gone to it; and if you'd a done it they'd a learnt you, there, that people that acts as I'd been acting about that nigger goes to everlasting fire" (chapter 31). Huck's imperfect impersonation causes the voice of authority to condemn itself out of its own mouth ("as I'd been acting"), rather than condemning him. Moreover, it is both comic and true to social hegemony that even though he hasn't gone to Sunday school, he knows what he would have learned if he had.

Then the rapid repetitive rhythms of preacherly exhortation take over: "It was because my heart warn't right; it was because I warn't square; it was because I was playing double." And one of his most famous lines still seems part of the preaching voice, "You can't pray a lie." By this point, he feels compelled to write the letter, and afterward he purrs in the voice of revival testimony, "I felt good and all washed clean of sin for the first time" (chapter 31).

But Huck can't stay saved. Once he has written the letter, he remembers all that Jim has meant to him on their travels together. The form parodies visions of the devil, as images of the black man arise to keep the young soul from heaven's path, and the rhetorical modeling is seductive—not breathless, nor haranguing, nor pushy, like the churchy voices, but an artful balance of overlapping doublets and triplets: "I see Jim before me, all the time, in the day, and in the night-time, sometimes moonlight, sometimes storms, and we a floating along, talking, and singing, and laughing." All the commas make it sound like Huck again, ventilating the sentence and easing its movement. As this string of memories unrolls, Huck decides to help Jim escape again. The language of this decision gains force from its sudden snap back to the discarded religious idiom. Huck concludes, "All right, then, I'll *go* to hell" (chapter 31). The syntax has the direct simplicity of the memories of Jim, but the key word, deferred to the end, returns to the language that is alien to Huck's own human sympathy.

Huck melodramatically, in a gestural extravagance equal and opposite to what he rejects, chooses hell over heaven, Jim over the society that enslaves him, and yet he does it in language that seems to modern readers racist. He calls Jim a "nigger." This term was not nearly so essential to Samuel Clemens's speech, in his adult life, as it is to Huck's. Over the course of the book, the term appears hundreds of times. The word is part of the historical and social distancing between author and character, and yet the word is not now a dead relic of slavery, nor was it when the book was written. Rather, the word did and still does active damage in the long working through a legacy of brutal inhumanity.[3]

Twain's use of the word is both willful and constrained. In part, it seems a rhetorical strategy of deidealization, keeping a dirty face on Huck so he does not seem too angelic. This may be given a polemically higher name as realism, as if one merely recorded what was there, but in the management of Huck's decision to "go to hell," there is evidently much calculation. To make the comic miracle of Huck's decision seem the pure act of natural goodness that socially misknows itself as damned, Huck has been allowed to hear only some of the voices possible in the 1840s, or even in the novel. Back home in Missouri, Widow Douglas speaks for the established hellfire religion, but Aunt Polly offers a gospel of love that might have inspired Huck, as it did many abolitionists. The American national credo, "all men are created equal," was celebrated every July Fourth. Huck knows this holiday, and it comes during his river trip (which begins with the river's June rising). The word *nigger* may have permeated Huck's environment as deeply as *muthafucka* does some now (and may have in Huck's time, too, had we the sources to tell us), but writers, even realists, find the means they need to achieve the effects they wish. Contrast two scandalous eighteenth-century novels, *Les liaisons dangereuses* and *Fanny Hill*: does Laclos's purer language make his novel less truthful about sexuality? Twain made great art out of dreadful history, and his work survives its time of writing, but it bears the scars of a racist society. Its language implies a literary world in which it was unthinkable that African Americans would ever form a consequential part of Twain's readership.

The character of Jim presents some of the same problems. Jim is shown as a brave man and a good man, and at moments he and Huck are treated as equals. Yet the representation of Jim also draws on comic traditions that were highly disrespectful to the African Americans that made up their subject matter. In particular, American minstrel shows, an immensely popular form of entertainment from the 1840s through the rest of century, offered musical numbers and comic sketches in which white performers, in blackface makeup, masqueraded as African Americans.

Blackface minstrelsy underlies some of the way Jim appears, but worse trouble comes in the long sequence that ends the book. Tom Sawyer has

---

[3] See Jonathan Arac, *"Huckleberry Finn" as Idol and Target: The Functions of Criticism in Our Time* (Madison: University of Wisconsin Press, 1997).

come down from Missouri to where Jim is being held. Tom knows that Jim is no longer a runaway but "free as any cretur that walks this earth" (chapter 42), because the woman who had owned him has died and freed him in her will. But Tom insists on staging elaborate schemes "to set a nigger free that was already free" (chapter the last), casting Jim as a noble prisoner, and Huck and Tom as his rescuers. *The Count of Monte Cristo* is one of many literary models for Tom's ideas of "style." This scheming is not the book's best comedy, and it leads to "a raft of trouble" (chapter 42): Tom gets shot and Jim risks his freedom to save him.

In this most fantasticated portion of the book, as in earlier sequences, Twain deploys a fundamental gesture of realism. *Huckleberry Finn* criticizes other books, so that we think it is realer than they are. The fraudulent scoundrels who join Huck and Jim claim to be a king and a duke, cheated of their lands and identities and outcast to the wilderness. Their phoniness comes from little bits of European history and culture, including butchered versions of Shakespeare. If this nonsense is high culture, than Huck's ignorance and unimaginativeness, which mean he responds only to what is before him, seems far preferable. Yet Huck defers to Tom Sawyer, who always plays out his life on themes from his reading. If Tom is Quixotic, then Huck is a juvenile Sancho Panza. He heeds the good sense of life against the folly of books. Such juvenilization means that sexuality has far less role in American realism than in its European counterparts. Realism as polemic propels Twain's formidable rejection of the historical romances of Walter Scott and Fenimore Cooper. *Life on the Mississippi* asserts that Scott had undone Cervantes's critique of romance, and caused the Civil War, by filling the heads of Southern readers with false ideas of chivalric valor. Twain's elaborate demolition of "Fenimore Cooper's Literary Offenses" (1895) makes one of the funniest critical essays ever written.

In its time, *Huckleberry Finn* was understood as realistic for its evident refusal to idealize. It shows life in the lower reaches of society, and it shows that life as grim. It also shows the moral value of Huck and Jim, despite their lowly status and lack of education. This may also seem, from another perspective, idealization. It may be impossible to adjudicate this book's realism, but it is worth testing how it fits the various frames that have defined realism, the crucial term in the history of Western thinking about the novel. The most influential theories of literary realism were codified by several European critics, born in the late-nineteenth-century years when realism became a slogan, who then in the 1930s and 1940s gave it scholarly basis. *Huckleberry Finn* makes trouble for these ideas. It does not behave, and its acting up casts doubt on old books.

For Erich Auerbach, realism violates classical rhetorical norms that treated socially low characters in low style and that associated low life with the comic. Through its new effects of style, realism could represent the existential seriousness of everyday life. But Twain's style serves other uses. The sunrise passage, discussed above, is idyllic, and more sober-toned passages are melancholic. When Huck approaches a farm, he is oppressed by the feeling of a ghost town, which is only exacerbated by a sign of life: "I heard the dim hum of a spinning-wheel wailing along up and sinking along down again; and then I knowed for certain I wished I was dead—for that *is* the lonesomest sound in the world" (chapter 32). Huck's decision to go to hell, as discussed above, is made comic, and it is relieved of any decisive role in the plot.

For Mikhail Bakhtin's language-based analysis of realism, *Huckleberry Finn* would also fail the test of seriousness. Bakhtin found in Dostoevsky's set-pieces of scandal the footprints of "reduced laughter," but Twain makes you laugh out loud. Twain loves to clash together different ways of talking. On the page before the novel begins, he explains that the characters speak seven different dialects that are "pains-takingly" differentiated. He pretends to fear that otherwise "many readers would suppose that all these characters were trying to talk alike and not succeeding." But this is not what Bakhtin means by the speech of the other. Dostoevsky, for Bakhtin, exemplified heteroglossic realism because he made the voices of his villains as compelling, or more so, than those of his heroes. What might be an ideological weakness becomes a literary strength—many good readers have not recognized that Dostoevsky was on the side of Christianity, not nihilism. No one has ever thought Twain favored slavery, or that any character in the book presents a serious alternative to Huck. Colonel Sherburne denounces the cowards who people his town, echoing views that were often Twain's own, but then he shoots a harmless fool. Jim is a good man, and he acts more bravely than Huck ever does, but African-American readers, just like white readers, have chosen Huck rather than Jim as their place of identification. Huck's voice prevails.

Georg Lukács would have valued Twain's critical satire against many features of bourgeois life, and yet Twain does not show human beings making their history, which for Lukács is the fundamental reality to which literature is responsible. The means by which Jim is freed—not by Huck's efforts but by the will of a far-off woman who died months earlier—if read as historical allegory, would suggest that the Civil War, the means by which all American slaves were freed, had been an extrinsic accident, not a collective action. The failure of action in *Huckleberry Finn* puts it in Lukács's negative category of "naturalism" together with Flaubert and Zola, rather than in his positive category of realism with Balzac and Tolstoy and Thomas Mann. Maybe Lukács also had a problem with funny books. But maybe Twain pulled his works' punches so that they would be bought and read; his literary clowning did not just sugarcoat a message but made sure it was not there. Twain laid down the law to critics in the "Notice" immediately following the title page: "Persons attempting to find a motive in this narrative will be prosecuted; persons attempting to find a moral in it will be banished; persons attempting to find a plot in it will be shot."

Huckleberry Finn contains tensions that arise from its compromises. This does not make it unique among novels of the United States or of the world. Novels are acts of communication and also items of commerce. They must answer to authorities different from those of the author. This problem extends even to the question of what exactly a proper edition of the novel should include. Mark Twain's *Life on the Mississippi* (1883) contains a passage of some five thousand words recounting songs and repartee on a raft in the old days on the river. He explained that this came from a book he was writing about Huckleberry Finn (already known to readers as Tom Sawyer's companion in Twain's 1876 novel), but then this "Raftmen Episode" did not appear in *Huckleberry Finn*. Should it be put in later editions? The reason it was omitted is adequately, if tersely, documented: the novel's publisher thought it might be left out, and Twain agreed. By one theory of editing, this means that the omission was an external imposition on the author's intention; but it could equally be argued that the author changed his mind. Twain had plenty of chances in the remaining thirty-five years of his life to restore the passage if he had wished to. The publisher was a young nephew of Twain's whom Twain himself had set up in charge of the publishing house, which primarily published Twain's works. So the idea of an alien commercial intrusion does not make sense; Twain treated his work commercially through and through. Samuel Clemens's pen name was registered as a trademark. No less than Charles Dickens in England, his fellow great philistine comic humanist, Mark Twain aimed to sell.

Since 1942, some editions of *Huckleberry Finn* have included the Raftmen Episode, and the established scholarly edition does, but many editions still do not, and the inclusion or exclusion of the passage has not made any difference to how people read the book. The passage contains wonderful American dialect humor writing and a rich summary of folklore traditions, so it fits in, but it is simply an episode. Aristotle long ago argued that episodes are not essential, although they may contribute to a work's excellence.

If so substantial an episode may be present or absent, it raises questions about the book overall. Is it primarily episodic, or does some strong principle of unity organize it? From the book's opening in Missouri, through the trip downriver, to the ending, some change of fortune occurs—Jim is freed, and Huck is liberated from anxiety about his alcoholic, abusive father. Yet the book's narrative economy muffles the process by which these changes occur. As in Shakespeare's comedies, both Jim's manumission and the death of Huck's father are revealed only in the very last pages of the book. They happened some time earlier and were concealed, Jim's freedom by Tom Sawyer so as to allow for the charade of Jim's "evasion" (chapter 39) from imprisonment, and Huck's father's death by Jim, for reasons left to the reader's speculation. So all that Huck did on Jim's behalf has not been essential to this plot. Whether or not Huck decided to go to hell, Jim was already free, and Tom Sawyer would in any case have arrived with the news at the farm where Jim was held.

Rather than seeking organic unity, it seems better to recognize that *Huckleberry Finn* operates discontinuously, by repetition and difference more than by beginning, middle, and end. The strongest moments of the book, including the passages I have discussed above, are sublime, as defined by the classical critic Longinus. By sublime, Longinus does not mean highfalutin. The sublime may arise from the representation of silence and from terse, simple language: his treatise praises the opening of the Hebrew Bible (" 'Let there be light,' and there was light.") The sublime means simply the greatest literary experience. It does not depend on unity. Like a "whirlwind" or thunderbolt it tears up any smooth pattern or texture, so it stands out from the work in which it occurs. For Longinus, the sublime depends on a series of identifications: the words of a great moment seem "the echo of a great soul" that is the author's, and in reading such passages, we are "uplifted" by feeling as if we had ourselves produced those words. Longinus's key term in Greek is *ekstasis*, literally getting out of one's place, a "transport" into a new state or position.[4] Longinus's analysis helps explain how Mark Twain became identified with Uncle Sam and known in the United States as "Our Mark Twain," while *Huckleberry Finn* has become not only the best-known and most-loved work of American literature, but also the most vehemently defended. To have to answer questions about the impact of Twain's racial language has seemed to some readers to foul their own moral decency.

---

[4] "Longinus," *On the Sublime*, ed. D. A. Russell (Oxford: Clarendon Press, 1964). My translations are from this Greek text.

It is a wonderful, and yet rather puzzling, feature of liberal culture that America's most-beloved novel, the most American of novels, so savagely mocks life in the United States. This without even considering slavery, which the book treats with no nostalgia or apologetics. Slavery has been abolished in the United States, so there is some ground for feeling better about things, but the book offers little comfort. Through Huck's narration, the small-town decencies in Missouri seem confining if not wholly pointless, compared to the pleasures of hanging out with friends or fishing. And on the river, Huck encounters no society, except Jim's, preferable to what he left behind. The Southern gentry life of the Grangerfords is appealing until he realizes that they are caught up in a senseless and deadly feud with the Shepherdsons, and in Arkansas, which was in Twain's America a byword for rural idiocy, the riverfront life is not only murderous but also mean-spirited. The King and Duke provide many laughs, but they also sell Jim back into slavery.

The American institution that *Huckleberry Finn* most unremittingly attacks is the Christian church. Twice the novel stages false scenes of conversion, the pretense of a sinner redeemed, but Huck's pap and the King are just fooling the holy to make a buck off them. When Huck decides to go to hell, it is against the voices of religion. Even if some American readers now criticize Twain's treatment of racial matters, many have taken inspiration from Huck's relation to Jim and have found in it the possibility of interracial friendship and social commitment alike. The years of the American civil rights movement, from after the Second World War to the 1960s, were also the time in which academic critics brought *Huckleberry Finn* to the forefront of established American literature, as many readers had already placed it in their own hearts long before it became required reading. Yet perhaps American secular intellectuals on the left were flying the race flag as camouflage. Far more than it fosters progressive interraciality, *Huckleberry Finn* attacks the social cowardice of the religion that was in Huck's 1840s and Twain's 1880s and that remains, in the new millennium of George W. Bush even more emphatically, the core religion of the United States, a Bible-based Christianity committed to the drama of the individual soul choosing heaven or hell. Twain represents this religion as ignorant and, above all, selfish.

This attack matters only if literature does, but the understanding of literature that had begun to prevail in Twain's time, and that dominated the twentieth century, suggests it may not. This notion of literature, nowadays second nature to cultivated readers, is a fairly recent cultural product. In the English language of the eighteenth century, the term *literature* referred to all of value that was written, including nonfictional, even scientific and religious writing. Beginning in the era of romanticism, poetry, fiction, and drama came to define the more restrictive sense of literature as imaginative belles lettres. This new sense of literature asserted autonomy: literature was valued for being original, not for effectively following the rules; for being the work of a unique imagination rather than part of a social transaction. Writers were supposed to answer to their own will rather than to any other set of expectations. This autonomy, however, diminished writing's social role. Literature offered the splendors of a world that was its own, but it therefore no longer exercised any direct claim on the world in which its readers pursued their political and economic lives. Before Samuel Clemens was born, in the United States of the 1820s, the historical fiction of Fenimore Cooper was understood as participating directly in debates about how the nation had come into existence and what that might mean for life in the present, but by the time he died in 1851, Cooper already seemed a relic, ripe for Twain's later debunking of his "literary offenses."

As Twain came of age in the midnineteenth century, national narrative, as practiced by Cooper, was challenged by an emergent mode of narrative that was literary in the new sense. The decisive new fiction of 1850, *The Scarlet Letter*, by Nathaniel Hawthorne, like Cooper looked back to American history, but the work deliberately guarded itself from direct involvement in the politics of its day, with which Hawthorne himself, in his nonauthorial role, was much involved. Dedicated to Hawthorne, Melville's *Moby-Dick* (1851) is the encyclopedic literary narrative of this moment, and it has come to dominate American literary study. In contrast, the comprehensive national narrative *Uncle Tom's Cabin* (1852) made far more impact at the time, but has only recently begun to receive the academic study that it merits. The figure of the sensitive spectator is crucial in literary narrative, whether Miles Coverdale in Hawthorne's *The Blithedale Romance*; Ishmael, the narrator of *Moby-Dick*; or, as noted above, Huck himself. This figure invites identification by a sensitive reader. In Stowe's novel the scope of this figure is limited to Augustine St. Clare, who occupies only the middle third of the novel, and is killed off as a dangerous failure.

Works by Hawthorne, Melville, and above all Twain, became models for American literature, even though they were written at a tense distance from the actually existing United States. American writing of the nineteenth century is full of distinctive voices, whether in the essays and journals of Emerson and Thoreau, the poetry of Whitman and Dickinson, or the fiction of Melville and Twain. In the 1960s and 1970s, the civil rights movement and the women's movement struggled to enlarge what it means to be American, who may count as American. This transformation has allowed readers now to recognize that the works of Harriet Beecher Stowe and Frederick

Douglass, produced to combat slavery, are not just propaganda about a dead issue but are also great and valuable, despite lacking such distinctive voices. *Huckleberry Finn*, by contrast, satirizes slavery after its abolition. It offers an unforgettable voice that has echoed through later American writing. But what has it meant that literature traded power for voice?

ERNESTO FRANCO

Pedro Páramo
(Juan Rulfo, Mexico, 1955)

Pedro Páramo is a work made of less.[1] It is a study in continuous subtraction, a narration without the shrewdness of a novel. It is a page of history without any date or hero. An immovable time. A metaphysics without a world. Not just a book with few pages but a book with fewer pages. But this is one of the reasons that this book, like a mountain pass, represents a dividing line in twentieth-century Latin American narrative.

The story begins much earlier. Together with a collection of stories entitled *The Burning Plain* published in 1953 (the only other book completed by Juan Rulfo), *Pedro Páramo* appeared between two periods of prolonged and laborious silence. During the first such period, he was occupied with his novel *El hijo del desconsuelo (Desolation's Son)*, which he began to write in 1938 and then destroyed; the second period, spanning thirty years until his death in 1986, was fruitful but also full of indiscretions, interviews, and rumors regarding a work in progress entitled *La cordillera*, of which only the title remains. And there is more: every time Rulfo spoke of the one hundred-odd pages of *Pedro Páramo*, he would say that he had eliminated at least one hundred pages, including much of the dialogue and many of the shadowy characters. The result was a book made of fragments—seventy fragments to be exact—and blank spaces. The first elements to be dissolved were the voices of the author and the narrator, the verisimilitude of the events, and the logic of the plot—in other words, the work's narrative grammar.

In a conversation with Jorge Ruffinelli, Rulfo commented: "This is why there are loose ends; if I hadn't removed all those pages, everything in the book would be explained perfectly."[2] But Rulfo was not interested in explanations or performances. He was not a *costumbrista* or regionalist writer, nor was he a "Revolutionary novelist," even though his subjects were those very same poor farmers; the physical and metaphysical desolation of a territory— Jalisco and, by synecdoche, all of Mexico—abandoned by history and by mankind; the postrevolution era with its countless disappointments; the

---

[1] *Pedro Páramo* (1955), edited by J. C. Gonzales Boixo (Madrid: Catedra, 1994).

[2] J. Ruffinelli, "La leyenda de Rulfo: Cómo se construye el escritor desde el momento en que deja de serlo," in J. Rulfo, *Toda la obra* (Madrid, 1992), 469.

cristeros war; the brutal direct power exerted over small and large *cachiques* alike; and the impotence of a man who has repeatedly lost everything he had. His was a social fabric in total disintegration over a backdrop of a landscape that knew no mediation: it was a desert, it was absolute light, stone, and aridity, in a word, it was that very same landscape that Rulfo had attentively and uniformly photographed during his long pilgrimages through Mexico in the guise of an Immigration Office agent.

With *Pedro Páramo*, Juan Rulfo revealed the way in which the culture of an entire continent first found its own voice. It is possible that this began with the contraction of new debts, first and foremost to William Faulkner, and with the simultaneous creation of future credits, like that of the much-cited fragment 41: "Many years later, Father Rentería would remember the night in which the hardness of his bed would keep him up and oblige him to go out."[3] This would become the model for the famous opening of *One Hundred Years of Solitude*: "Many years later, as he faced the firing squad, Colonel Aureliano Buendía was to remember that distant afternoon when his father took him to discover ice."[4] Once this voice had been found, Latin America could finally converse with the rest of the world, regenerate that world, and introduce new roads, tales, and voices. Let us not begin at degree zero but rather from zero—in other words, from history.

"I came to Comala because I had been told that my father, a man named Pedro Páramo, lived there. It was my mother who told me."[5] Juan Preciado promises his dying mother that he will return to his roots to find his father, whom he has never met and whose memory is tinged by violence and by his chilling absence. As soon as he arrives in the town's outskirts, Juan Preciado meets a stranger who provides him with some information on Comala and Pedro Páramo, "living bile."[6] Before he disappears, the stranger tells him that there is no one living in the town and that "Pedro Páramo died years ago."[7] Despite this, as if there were a strange misunderstanding—an impalpable, protracted disconnect between words and experience—Juan Preciado goes into the town, meets the townsfolk, and listens to their stories.

---

[3] J. Rulfo, *Pedro Páramo*, translated by Margaret Sayers Peden (New York: Grove Press, 1994), 68.

[4] Gabriel García Márquez, *One Hundred Years of Solitude*, translated by Gregory Rabassa (New York: Harper and Row, 1970), 1.

[5] Rulfo, *Pedro Páramo*, 3.

[6] Ibid., 6.

[7] Ibid., 7.

There is the story of Miguel Páramo, who died falling from a horse; he was Pedro's only legitimate son and the innocent inheritor of his only hubris, that of sexual violence: "I'm beginning to pay. The sooner I begin, the sooner I'll be through."[8] There is the story of Father Rentería, the impotent man of God, who can neither receive nor grant absolution because he has been overwhelmed by the madness that he was supposed to fight; there is the story of Susana San Juan's murky, endless delirium; she is the woman for whom Pedro Páramo feels his only obsessive but muted passion.

They are all stories of landlocked shipwreck. Susana San Juan's unreachable, murky world is Pedro Páramo's shipwreck and his limitation. Yet he is the omnipotent dictator of the whole affair and at times he is a tiger: he kills, he pays, he commands, and in the end it is he who allows Comala to extinguish itself: "I will cross my arms and Comala will die of hunger."[9] But everything, every little detail of the Comala cosmos, is written in the name of less.

The stories, the characters, and even objects present themselves to Juan Preciado through an uninterrupted vanishing act—a disappearing of the senses primarily. Touch: "I lifted my hand to knock, but there was nothing there. My hand met only empty space, as if the wind had blown open the door."[10] Hearing: "Because until then, I realized, the words I had heard had been silent. There had been no sound, I had sensed them. But silently, the way you hear words in your dreams."[11] The entire body: " 'This is the end of the road,' I told it. 'I don't have the strength to go on.' And I opened my mouth to let it escape. And it went. I knew when I felt the little thread of blood that bound it to my heart drip into my hands."[12] The name, Comala, means literally the town that "sits on the coals of the earth, at the very mouth of hell."[13] There is really no one left there. They have all died. At a certain point, the only living thing seems to be the tale told by Juan Preciado, who perhaps alone can hear the chorus of silent voices. But it is Juan Preciado himself who announces his own end and who, at that moment, becomes just another murmur among the many others.

Los murmullos, the murmurs, was the original title of the book, said Juan Rulfo. It was changed to *Pedro Páramo* for editorial reasons. But

---

[8] Ibid., 68.
[9] Ibid., 117.
[10] Ibid., 9.
[11] Ibid., 47.
[12] Ibid., 66.
[13] Ibid., 6.

"murmurs"—that is, something less than a voice—is the most fitting formal definition for Rulfo's work. With the demise of Juan Preciado's character and his narrative voice, the last principle guiding the time and space of the story vanishes. The various voices that appear in the narration from the very beginning overlap the different times and places of the stories, and they juxtapose partial moments of the same event, which is never narrated from the beginning to the end. By the same token, as long as there is a main voice in the story, a guiding cause-and-effect temporal principle persists, or at least a notion of such a principle is still present. But when Juan Preciado announces that what he has just retold "was the last thing I saw,"[14] even this apparent subject vanishes and with it does too any concept of monologue or dialogue, which, by definition, requires two speakers and a sequence in speaking. Even the most complex monologue or the most absurd dialogue must begin with clearly defined subjects. By forcing things a little, one could say that monologues and dialogues tend not to exist in *Pedro Páramo*: there are only murmurs, like a continuous fabric without beginning or end and in which forgotten passages of stories are recomposed over and over again. "We are in a world of effects without causes," observed Luis Harss, "a world of shadows without substance."[15]

The dispersion of any idea of a beginning or any guiding principle is reflected in Comala's weather, which is insistent but undefined and is the only true landscape in the novel

> During the night it began to rain again. For a long time, he [Pedro Páramo] lay listening to the gurgling of the water; then he must have slept, because when he awoke, he heard only a quiet drizzle. The windowpanes were misted over and raindrops were threading down like tears. . . .
>
> The rain turned to wind. He heard ". . . the forgiveness of sins and the resurrection of flesh. Amen."[16]

Rain continuously loses its substance, and even though it can be seen, it is listened to and heard as if it were made of the same stuff as murmurs, and it actually needs a brief alchemic process in order to "convert itself" into wind. "The winds continued to blow, day after day. The winds that had brought the rain. The rain was over but the wind remained. . . . By day the

---

[14] Ibid., 58.
[15] L. Harss, *Los nuestros* (Buenos Aires, 1977), 30.
[16] Rulfo, *Pedro Páramo*, 14–15.

wind was bearable; it worried the ivy and rattled the roof tiles; but by night it moaned, it moaned without ceasing."[17] In a manner more natural than the rain's, even the wind converts itself into an impalpable acoustic element. In every other tale, landscape and history, persons and things, and life and death move the events forward through contrast, or, at least, they are a counterpoint to one another. In *Pedro Páramo* they are made of a homogeneous substance, and they follow one another in a sort of continuity without progress. They are like the fragments of the text. The symbolic force and imagery of the book reside in this formal compactness of every aspect of the narration. There is one important element that looms over all things in the book or rather pervades the basis of everything in the book: death.

There is not one living subject in *Pedro Páramo*, nor is there any cause; as we have observed, there are only effects. Except for the anecdotes of Miguel Páramo and Susana San Juan, even death is deprived of its tragic dimension, in other words, the only thing that binds it to life if not for anything else than as life's cessation. Even death is traversed by murmurs and can feel the wetness of the rain and the blowing of the wind. The murmurs speak of bodies and souls as something different from them. They are neither the ones nor the others and thus even death is deathless. Carlos Monsiváis said it perfectly when he wrote that Comala "is not the after-life but rather the here-forever."[18] In his wonderful, however "brief reminiscences of Juan Rulfo," Gabriel García Márquez also pointed out the necessary narrative consequences when he wrote that "no one can actually know how long the years of death will last."[19]

Following *Pedro Páramo*, Latin America was freed from its colors and folklore, from the cage of its chronology and the blood of its horrors. Its story could then be recounted as universal myth that touches the imagination of all men and not just that of "connoisseurs." This is another reason that it is not so farfetched to think of Juan Rulfo as an ancient Greek lost along the equator.

Even if this is only partly the case, it is worthwhile to ask oneself what story is told by the tales and murmurs of Comala. It is a story of dissimulation. Octavio Paz wrote of this in an essay published in another book that is central to understanding twentieth-century Mexican culture, *The Labyrinth*

---

[17] Ibid., 91–92.

[18] C. Monsiváis, "Sí, tampoco los muertos retoñan, desgraciadamente," in Rulfo, *Toda la obra*, 837.

[19] G. García Márquez, "Breves nostalgias sobre Juan Rulfo," in Rulfo, *Toda la obra*, 801.

of Solitude, originally published in 1950—a book that in my opinion is closely related to *Pedro Páramo*. In Paz's view, simulation—just like its more pragmatic twin sister, lying—is a powerfully creative undertaking. It is the invention of a universe that requires its own coherence, however virtual it may be. Contrarily, dissimulation is the subtraction of being: "the person who dissimulates is not counterfeiting but attempting to become invisible, to pass unnoticed without renouncing his individuality. The Mexican excels at the dissimulations of his passions and himself. He is afraid of others' looks and therefore he withdraws, contracts, become a shadow, a phantasm, an echo."[20] The origin of such negative passion lies in the Indian who is faced with the horrors of the Conquistadores and colonialism and who wishes to blend in with the earth upon which he walks: he "turns into a stone, a tree, a wall, silence, and space."[21] "The act of spreading oneself out, of blending with space, of becoming space, is a way of rejecting appearances, but it is also a way of being nothing except Appearance."[22] So strong is the feeling of dissimulation in Mexican culture that there exists even a paradoxical, transitive version of it, which addresses the other but never itself. There is even a word, *ninguenear*, which could be translated as "to change into nobody, into nothingness": "Nobody is the blankness in our looks, the pauses in our conversations, the reserve in our silences. He is the name we always and inevitably forget, the eternal absentee, the guest we never invite, the emptiness we can never fill. He is an omission, and yet he is forever present. He is our secret, our crime, and our remorse."[23]

One seemingly enters the world of *Pedro Páramo* by accident. As many have noted, Comala, a ghost town, slowly becomes the main character of the book. This is because it is a place that exists only in murmurs, where, after all those years of death, there is vanishing, subtraction, and where even death wishes it could disappear.

The feeling of dissimulation has deep historical roots for Mexico and Latin America. This sentiment is translatable in both collective and private terms, and for this reason, it can travel beyond historical contexts and latitudes. This is the road that has been opened but never closed by *Pedro Páramo*.

Among the many photographs taken by Juan Rulfo, there is one dated 1955 that belongs to a sequence entitled *The Musicians*. In the foreground is

---

[20] Octavio Paz, *The Labyrinth of Solitude*, translated by Lysander Kemp (New York: Grove Press, 1985), 42–43.

[21] Ibid., 43.

[22] Ibid., 44.

[23] Ibid., 45.

a large drum aslant as well as plates slanted at the same angle, a trumpet, and to the right, almost disappearing from the frame, two trombones. Also at an angle, rays of twilight can be seen. Hills are in the background, but lower. We are on a high plain. Scattered here and there, standing on tripods, are simple music stands without musical scores. They are like skeletons standing upright. Men appear in the distance, their backs to the viewers. They are leaving. This is Juan Rulfo's gaze onto the world. Not quite a real place.

Translated by Jeremy Parzen

STEPHANIE MERRIM

Grande Sertão: Veredas
(João Guimarães Rosa, Brazil, 1956)

For the phenomenal literary productivity that resulted in his creating a Spanish national theater, seventeenth-century writer Félix Lope de Vega y Carpio has come down through history as the "Monster of Nature." No less, and for similar reasons, does contemporary Brazilian author João Guimarães Rosa (1908–67) warrant the epithet. In the midst of a frenetic career as a medical doctor, diplomat, and civil servant, over the course of only twenty writing years, the formidably erudite Guimarães Rosa managed to craft the stories,[1] novellas, and the blockbuster novel that transformed the Brazilian literary landscape. The year 1956, in which Guimarães Rosa accomplished the improbable feat of launching both the two-volume collection of novellas, *Corpo de Baile* (*Dance Corps*), and the monstrously long and dense novel of some 450 pages, *Grande Sertão: Veredas* (literally translated, *The Great Backlands and Their Paths*; to be abbreviated *GS:V*)[2] is often considered the "miraculous year" of Brazilian literary culture. *GS:V*, something of a miracle unto itself for the magnificent innovations that it embodies, brings to bear a sinuous Faulknerian plotting and Joycean linguistic experimentation on the Brazilian heartland. Inaugurating the "Nuclear Age of Brazilian Fiction" (Gledson, 190), *GS:V* now stands as *the* Brazilian novel both inside and outside the country.

In a meandering confession told to an ever-silent interlocutor, *GS:V*'s protagonist, Riobaldo, recounts his experiences as member and then chief of one of the nomadic bands of men known as *jagunços* who roamed the *sertão*, the backlands or vast interior area of Brazil, during the formative period of modern Brazil (the 1880s to the 1920s). Riobaldo details at length the battles

---

[1] Guimarães Rosa's collections of stories include *Sagarana*, 1946; *Primeiras Estórias*, 1962; and *Tutaméia*, 1967. Guimarães Rosa's editions published by José Olympio contain essential bibliographical references for works by and about the author.

[2] The linguistically impoverished, expurgated English translation of *GS:V* bears the unsatisfactory title *The Devil to Pay in the Backlands*. I encourage the reader to read the novel in Portuguese or in its superior French, Spanish, German, or Italian versions. Edoardo Bizarri's Italian translation is particularly notable, and yielded the illuminating *Correspondência com o tradutor italiano* (Sao Paulo: Instituto Cultural Ítalo-Brasileiro, 1972). All translations from Portuguese in this article are mine.

between his *jagunços* and the bands captained by Hermógenes and Ricardão, whom the text vilifies as "monsters." At the same time, Riobaldo presents the stories of his forbidden love for Diadorim, a fearless *jagunço* who only after her death is revealed to be a woman, and of a purported pact with the devil to gain the courage necessary to defeat the "monsters" and bring peace to the *sertão*. Implicated in the work's epic, sentimental, and metaphysical aspects, the *sertão* at once provides the setting of the novel and assumes a leading role in it. Guimarães Rosa's masterpiece thus inscribes itself in the tradition of the Latin American regionalist *novela de la tierra*, the novel of and about the earth, such as the Colombian *La vorágine* (*The Vortex*, 1921) or the Venezuelan *Doña Bárbara* (1929). As is apparent, *GS:V* *anachronistically* enacts the *novela de la tierra*, an undertaking fraught with shadings and consequences. In what follows I will therefore explore the dynamics, both natural and "monstrous," of this revisiting of the *novela de la tierra*.

As a *novela de la tierra*, *GS:V* draws upon an entrenched line of thought that imputes to *nature* the legitimation of Latin American *civilization*. The ostensible contradiction accrues from the fact that the modern Latin American state and its concomitant discourses of self-definition came into being in the aura of a romantic ideology that valorized nature. Although, as we will see, romantic and regionalist texts called for the defeat of autochthonous barbarism by civilization, they also invoked their region's nature as its signal claim to distinction, source of its positive difference, and "myth of its legitimacy" (González Echevarría, 41). In the words of Brazilian critic and novelist Antonio Cândido, "the idea of *patria*, of "fatherland," was clearly linked to that of nature and in part took its justification from this. Both led to a literature which compensated for material backwardness and the weakness of institutions by the supervaluing of 'regional' aspects. . . . One of the ostensible or latent assumptions of Latin American literature was this connection, greatly exalted, between the land and the *patria*—taking for granted that the greatness of the second would be a kind of natural unfolding of the might attributed to the first" ("Literature and Underdevelopment," translated in González Echevarría, 42). Similarly, in his paradigmatic essay, "Nuestra América" ("Our America," 1891), Cuban José Martí catapults the legitimating myth of nature into a model for the major components of Latin America's incipient postcolonial existence. Martí exalts the "natural man," who will predicate Latin American institutions on natural law and embody a natural intelligence. Adherence to foreign models, he says, creates monsters ("monsters, not nations, derive from them; we must live off ourselves," 136).

Guimarães Rosa himself was a dedicated naturalist, utterly imbued with the flora and fauna of his native backlands, Minas Gerais. The author's personal love of nature, which conceivably led him to frame the text as a *novela de la tierra*, also profoundly affects the formal dimensions of *GS:V*. To achieve the semblance of a natural, unconstructed narrative while still aspiring to novelistic coherence, *GS:V* incurs extreme structural complexity. The first eighty pages of the novel manifest an associative, stream-of-consciousness organization in which Riobaldo lays out the major themes of the novel, the events closest to his heart and most pertinent to his being (*GS:V*, 79). A chronological account of his life takes over after Riobaldo recounts his first meeting with Diadorim, in their youth. The chronological narration then acquires its own complexity as events related in its first half repeat themselves but are reversed in the second half, when Riobaldo becomes the chief and accomplishes what his predecessor could not. Throughout, as mentioned above, the plotting is Faulknerian. It presents last things first and expounds all things in slowly unfurling wrinkles.

The structural scaffolding of *GS:V*, sufficiently imbricated in its own right, can barely be discerned amid the effluent chaos that dominates the novel. With its goal of presenting the *sertão*, or life itself, as irreducibly multiple, *GS:V* insistently vitiates any will to order. The narrative thread routinely gives way to exquisite, minute descriptions of the natural phenomena of the *sertão*, to the lyrical "song and plumage" (*Sagarana*, 238) of botanical nomenclature. Identifying nature with Riobaldo's beloved Diadorim (who taught him to appreciate the beauty of the *sertão*), and as God's handiwork, *GS:V* offers its audience a seemingly unmediated "prose of the world." Among natural elements, rivers hold special import for Riobaldo as the loci of milestone events in his life. Appropriately, the novel charts an alluvial course that curves and branches into byways. The intensely nonlinear novel spirals back time and again to Riobaldo's reflections on his loves and the devil. Anecdotes, exemplary "cases" of individuals extraneous to the novel's action, rosters of warriors' names reminiscent of the medieval epic—in sum, digressions—all overwhelm the action of the novel, even at its culminating moments.

With these various centrifugal maneuvers, *GS:V* deviates from traditional epic action to enact the digressive and encyclopedic functions of the *modern* epic, as construed by Franco Moretti ("the digressions have themselves become the main purpose of the epic Action," 49). In *GS:V*, however, the thrust toward the modern epic is not entirely salutary. For the novel, so intent on appearing natural, often feels monstrously capacious, egregiously amorphous.

GS:V undertakes to counter its own confounding amorphousness by means of a rhythm of expansion and contraction, the latter affording the reader the illuminating paths through the labyrinthine *sertão* to which the novel's title alludes. Recurring verbal leitmotifs, such as "to live is very dangerous," purvey the novel's axial philosophical concerns. Significantly, *GS:V* employs popular poetry to the same end. In a corrective gesture to both the distension and the erudite character of the novel, Guimarães Rosa repeatedly showcases shards of folkloric poetry (*cantigas*) and songs. Though the author romantically views popular poetry as arising directly from nature, he employs the *cantigas* not as transparent bearers of the text's concerns but as tantalizing, enigmatic parables for the reader to decipher (see Merrim 1988). As such, *GS:V*'s folkloric poetry joins energies with the other "natural" or popular genre that underwrites the text: the *cordel* folktale, which revolves around a character's responses to or "readings" of the life-defining challenges that constitute the stuff of the tale (see Slater).

Being a *novela de la tierra* so laden with gestures to nature, *GS:V* does not fail to engage with the polemic of civilization versus barbarism that weighed heavily on both Spanish-American and Brazilian texts of the early twentieth century by virtue of their involvement with Domingo Faustino Sarmiento's influential *Facundo* (1845). *Facundo*'s largely Manichean oppositions pit the city, progress, inventions, and law of imported "civilization" against the alleged backwardness, violence, and lawlessness of the native provinces.[3] *GS:V* resuscitates and replays the debate through the character of Zé Bebelo. A large portion of the novel revolves around Riobaldo's contests with Zé, an outsider who champions the positivists' agenda of bringing "order and progress" to the uncivilized *sertão*. At the very center of the novel, the unmistakably God-like *jagunço* chief, Joca Ramiro, banishes Zé from the Edenic backlands, thereby forestalling the crisis of modernity. After Ramiro's assassination by the "Judases" (Hermógenes and Ricardão), however, Zé returns as a *jagunço* chief, his agenda still intact. For his part, Riobaldo, who oscillates between fear and lucid courage, strives to arrive at an understanding of the slippery Zé. When in fear's thrall, Riobaldo admires Zé and longs for the city; he becomes an unreliable narrator and the text a map of his misreadings. Ultimately, however, a strong Riobaldo defeats Zé, whose thinking and chatter "nauseate" him, displaces him as chief, and avenges Joca Ramiro's death.

---

[3] However, one cannot fail to note, as have most commentators of *Facundo* (and even *Os Sertões* and *Doña Bárbara*), that their romantic valorization of nature at times leads the works' authors to undo their own clear-cut oppositions by expressing admiration for rural lands and their inhabitants.

From within its modernist-inflected unreliable narration and from the heart of the twentieth century, we realize, *GS:V* takes a stand against the supposed barbarism of the Latin American backlands. As distinct from *Facundo*, *Doña Bárbara*, and the Brazilian masterpiece, Euclides Da Cunha's *Os Sertões* (1902), and in alignment with "Nuestra América," his compatriot Oswald de Andrade's "Anthropophagy" of the late 1920s, and Argentine Ezequiel Martínez Estrada's *Radiografía de la pampa* (1933), Guimarães Rosa imputes to "barbarism" its own civilization, a better civilization because natural. Even Zé Bebelo by turns concedes the *jagunços*'s intrinsically civilized nature and the rightness of their justice.

Yet Guimarães Rosa knows that the Zé Bebelos of the world will never abandon their "civilizing" mission. They will always return to the *sertão*—as Zé in the end does once again, as a cotton planter possessing "all the modern qualities" (460). The crisis of modernity cannot be forever forestalled. Indeed, by the 1950s, it had overtaken the *sertão*, obliterating the *jagunços* and displacing the cattle farming that previously united the region. Faced with this, Guimarães Rosa takes the two interrelated ecological measures to which we now turn. In view of the inevitable demise of the *sertão* as a way of life, he reterritorializes and immortalizes it as a metaphysical entity associated with the devil;[4] the author not only comes out on the side of nature in the dispute between civilization and barbarism, but as a prescient postmodernist also dispels the dualistic logic that sustains the dispute, placing categories themselves in crisis. The latter tactic allies *GS:V* with the antipositivism and antirationalism that so drive Latin American fiction, including the omnipresent magical realism.

GS:V opens with the shooting of a "monster." A defective calf has been born with the "face of a person, the face of a dog: they decided—it was the devil. . . . They killed it" (9). Reminiscent of the early modern construction of monsters as hybrids that defy categorization, *GS:V*'s emblematic "monster" bespeaks the novel's central philosophical conundrums. Just as the calf is malignantly multiple, so Riobaldo experiences the world as fearsomely complex, mercurial, arbitrary, and inscrutable. The *sertão*, nature, people, even his own life story that Riobaldo labors to tell, all partake of what José Carlos Garbuglio, in one of the best exegeses of the novel, has called the "moving world." Impelled by the moving world's apparent disorder,

---

[4] On p. 68 of his correspondence with Bizarri, cited in note 2, Guimarães Rosa outlined and prioritized the aims of *G:SV* as follows: Scenario, the reality of the *sertão* = 1 point; Plot = 2 points; Poetry = 3 points; metaphysical-religious value = 4 points.

Riobaldo strives to apportion life into neat categories, to separate good from evil, the beautiful from the ugly, happiness from sadness (169). Salient among these categories is the devil, the motor of the entire novel. Whatever Riobaldo perceives as incomprehensible and thus terrifying, he denominates as the devil. Crucially, he persists in viewing the polymorphous *sertão* as the devil's territory. For example, "*Satan!* . . . and I only said—S . . . —*Sertão* . . . *Sertão* . . ." (449). And like those who shot the monstrous calf, Riobaldo attempts to destroy what unnerves him.

To gain strength and become chief of the *jagunços*, Riobaldo allegedly makes a pact with the devil. That very act, however, will expose the nonexistence of the devil and explain that entity's enigmatic presence in the text. Rendering his novel a metaphysical thriller, Guimarães Rosa laces *GS:V* with conceptual riddles such as "the devil needn't exist to be" (49) or "The devil. Does he exist and not exist?" (11). The riddles find resolution in an existential formulation: the devil only exists inside us, as fear itself and particularly as fear of the unknown. In other words, the devil emerges as both a heuristic category and a spurious construct. When Riobaldo executes his latter-day Faustian pact with the devil, then, he summons the courage in himself to confront the unknown, embraces the *sertão*'s shifting grounds, and defeats the devil of his own making. At the same time, he renounces the dualistic thinking that has imprisoned him. "God or the devil? God and the Devil!" (318). "Nonada" (nonothing), an archaic locution that appears in the first and last paragraphs of the novel, echoes and nullifies the category crisis that inheres in *GS:V*'s devil.

That Riobaldo, fortified by the pact, triumphs over the Judases yet fails to act on his love for Diadorim tenders a cautionary tale that warns against false constructs. *GS:V* abounds in category-crossings around gender issues (praising matriarchs, love-giving prostitutes, and the courageous Diadorim, who dies killing Hermógenes). Yet Riobaldo has erected his love for Diadorim into a taboo, believing that a man does not carnally love another of his sex. Had Riobaldo found the strength to risk his strictures and logical structures by fully loving Diadorim, another devil—signifying the nonexistence of any devil—would have been proven fraudulent with the discovery of Diadorim's true sex. Guimarães Rosa would thus appear to concur with Michel Foucault's understanding that order "has no existence except in the grid created by a glance, an examination, a language" (xx). Accordingly, *GS:V* explicitly invokes *and* conflates the heterogeneous grids that over the ages have performed an order-endowing function for humanity, including Christianity, existentialism, Hinduism, and Platonism. The fluvial *GS:V* weaves them together, becoming multiply allegorical and denying any single thought-system ultimate explanatory power. The novel only privileges non-order, that is, anti-Cartesian thought, intuition, and the knowledge imparted by the body (26).

GS:V's "monstrously" category-defying natural project nevertheless attains its fullest life in the novel's extreme linguistic innovations. From a post-Saussurean world, Guimarães Rosa resolutely attempts to remotivate language, to restore language to its natural, Adamic state. "What is a name? A name doesn't give: a name receives" (121), he writes. In the author's praxis, to remotivate or return language to nature entails remaking it, and, paradoxically enough, remaking it by transgressing linguistic norms almost to the point of unintelligibility. On every page and at every turn, the novel's notoriously hermetic, seemingly "diabolical" language ruptures normative syntax, punctuation, and semantics. *GS:V*'s fragmented, planar, sound-ruled diction invests modern prose with the attributes of baroque poetry, with its linguistic crises. Guimarães Rosa imports to the *sertão* Joyce's equally baroque "verbivocovisual" neologisms, crafting magnificent coinages such as the name "Diadorim," which encapsulates the character's whole plight (*dia* = light of day and *diabo*, devil; *adorar*, adore; *dor*, pain).[5] At the same time, the author naturalizes the verbal texture of the novel by amalgamating it with a rural, oral Portuguese, bursting with onomatopoeias that reproduce the sounds of nature and its creatures. Reading *GS:V*, if one can, in sum perforce and constantly involves crossing between the written/the oral, elite/popular culture, Eden/Babel, hermeticism/transparency, nature/culture, the law and its transgression. Crossing (*travessia*) is in fact the last word of the text, followed by an infinity sign.

To conclude, we might recall that Hermógenes, the preeminent "monster" of *GS:V*, also figures in Plato's *Cratylus* as a proponent of the arbitrary, nonnatural constitution of language. During the reign of Roman Emperor Diocletian, a later Hermogenes performed another task that is anathema to *GS:V* in drawing up codes for the imposition of boundaries on lands. These classical antecedents, no doubt familiar to the omniverously learned Guimarães Rosa, signal the Brazilian author's mission to serve as an intermediary between different realms—not a Hermogenes but a Hermes. He guides the reader through the *sertão*, which he resites onto metaphysical grounds to preserve it. A weaver of geographical, literary, and philosophical topoi, he mobilizes the resources of modernism and beyond to reinvent the

---

[5] I follow Augusto de Campo's superb "Um lance de 'Dês' do Grande Sertão" in *Guimarães Rosa*, ed. Eduardo F. Coutinho, 321–49 (Rio de Janeiro: Civilização Brasileira, 1983).

novel of the land, bodying forth rather than effacing the divide between the original and his restaging of it. Clearly, Guimarães Rosa has inaugurated the "Nuclear Age of Brazilian Fiction" with a consummately sophisticated apologetics of primitivism, an oxymoronic achievement that renders the novel a worthy, and appropriately hermetic, secular scripture for Brazilian *lettres*.

Works Cited

Foucault, Michel. *The Order of Things: An Archaeology of the Human Sciences.* New York: Random House, 1970.

Garbuglio, José Carlos. *O mundo movente de Guimarães Rosa.* Sao Paulo: Ática, 1971.

Gledson, John. "Brazilian Prose from 1940 to 1980." In *The Cambridge History of Latin American Literature*, edited by Roberto González Echevarría and Enrique Pupo-Walker, 3:189–206. Cambridge: Cambridge University Press, 1996.

González Echevarría, Roberto. *The Voice of the Masters: Writing and Authority in Modern Latin American Literature.* Austin: University of Texas Press, 1985.

Martí, José. *Ensayos y crónicas.* Edited by José Olivio Jiménez. Madrid: Anaya, 1995.

Merrim, Stephanie. "Desire and the Art of Dehumanization: Macedonio Fernández, Julio Cortázar and João Guimarães Rosa." *Latin American Literary Review* 31 (1988): 45–64.

Moretti, Franco. *Modern Epic: The World-System from Goethe to García Márquez.* Translated by Quintin Hoare. London: Verso, 1996.

Rosa, João Guimarães. *Grande Sertão: Veredas* (1956). 10th ed. Rio de Janeiro: José Olympio, 1976.

———. *Sagarana.* 17th ed. Rio de Janeiro: José Olympio, 1974.

Slater, Candace. *Stories on a String.* Berkeley: University of California Press, 1982.

JOSÉ MIGUEL OVIEDO

The Death of Artemio Cruz
(Carlos Fuentes, Mexico, 1962)

In 1962, the year in which *The Death of Artemio Cruz* appeared, Mexican writer Carlos Fuentes (b. Panama, 1928) was thirty-four years old and had published a few books, among which *Where the Air Is Clear* (*La región más transparente*) and the phantasmagoric story "Aura" stand out. The interest that these initial works had awakened turned into widespread admiration with *The Death of Artemio Cruz*, and it enthroned him as one of the undisputed members of the so-called Latin American literary Boom. More than forty years later, during which time Fuentes has produced a large and varied body of literary work, this novel remains one of his fundamental works.

The Death of Artemio Cruz typifies the novelistic craft of the author, distinguished by verbal lavishness, the vastness and depth of his fictional world, the intense reworking of symbols and myths, and an agonizing vision of Mexican history. The book is a biography of the title character, whose multiple roles inside the Mexican Revolution reflect its contradictory phases: leader, elected official, peddler of political influence, international businessman, and so forth. But the novel intends something very different from a conventional biography. It synthesizes the life of a character and of the society in which he happened to live through a selection of privileged moments that shaped both him and Mexican society.

Three aspects of this biographical scheme should be emphasized. The first is that the recounting of Artemio Cruz's public and private deeds is made from his deathbed. He lies in a hospital bed, after undergoing an emergency operation. His mind wanders, and he remembers his life in a confused manner. The book, then, is about biography made from the perspective of death, which colors the entire story with a mournful and tragic tone: we first arrive at the end and from there we begin to make our way backward until we reach the beginning. In the hands of Fuentes, the motif of death—that predominant presence in all forms of the Mexican imagination—is a burning question full of ancestral and symbolic echoes. The beginning is the end, the end is the beginning, time is cyclical.

Second, the biographical reconstruction is enigmatic, fragmentary, and chaotic. Chronological leaps are the constant rule, which creates a vertiginous oscillation between times and spaces lived and relived by just one persona but through various and contradictory perspectives. Readers have to solve the puzzle in their own minds and come to their own conclusions because—as we will see—the final piece is missing, denying us access to any definitive truth about the character. Who was Artemio Cruz? A hero of the revolution, or a traitor to it? A pragmatic leader, or a corrupt manipulator? We don't know with any certainty, and perhaps what the novel tells us is that the protagonist was all of those things and, being all of them, negated himself. Essentially, his case coincides with that other paradigm—of lost opportunities, of the exhaustion of possibilities, until arriving at the point where death finds us.

Third, beyond the biography of Cruz is also the political biography of a country caught up in a violent revolutionary process that goes through many phases and transformations and that ultimately also negates itself. In other words, the novel is a reflection on political power and on the individual, and on the painful condition of being part of history, from which we cannot escape.

In his final hours, Artemio Cruz relives his life, but the narrative gives us only a synthesis of the totality by centering itself on a set of decisive moments when Cruz makes a choice or suffers a defining crisis of either his private persona or his historical role. The novel presents a series of snapshots of Cruz at crossroads—and here the name Cruz, meaning *cross* in Spanish, may have symbolic resonance—that form (or deform) a public figure and that only in part reflect the private man. That personal contradiction is analogous to another more dramatic contradiction that pervades the revolution itself. It began as a legitimate reaction of the people against the dictatorship of Porfirio Díaz and then gave way to a terrible bloodbath that is presumed to have been the necessary price to pay so that a more humane society, reconciled with its indigenous past, could be born—only to end, after a series of compromises and tactical abdications, with the absolute control of a party in cahoots with the new national bourgeoisie and the growing economic influence of the United States.

Fuentes reviews the life of Artemio Cruz and of postrevolutionary Mexico from the critical perspective of the great political, social, and economic changes brought about by the regime of President Miguel Alemán, which began in 1946, the same year in which the official party adopted the paradoxical name Institutional Revolutionary Party (Partido Revolucionario Institucional, or PRI). Thus began an era during which the few remaining reforms and ideals true to the original revolutionary spirit were cast aside in favor of the powerful new political clientele of the system and its North American allies. Mexico's definition of itself as a "modern" society dependent on foreign capital began then as well. In his final phase, Artemio Cruz is the very incarnation of the "Alemanist" politician. The dedication of the book reveals the ideological position of Fuentes at this historical juncture. It reads, "To C. Wright Mills, true voice of the United States of America, friend and companion in Latin America's struggle."[1]

The portrait of Artemio Cruz shows us that he is the product of a series of chance events and personal choices, of historical circumstances and acts of his own volition, of successes and errors whose consequences he can no longer control. This complex reality is summoned up by the flickering conscience of the dying protagonist, at the moment when no exits remain nor any possible modifications to the tragic situation that he himself, as actor, witness, and subject of history has created. The most characteristic feature of the novel is the "I" of Artemio Cruz. It fragments and disperses into three different points of view or narrative discourses that require the reader to participate in a search to discover, organize, and evaluate the clues that each scene contains. This central "I" disintegrates into three persons or voices. Each one of these voices forms a distinct series of sequences—instead of interlinked episodes or chapters proper—that communicate among themselves, both complementing and contradicting the other voices.

The sequences of the "I," "You," and "He" series are immediately recognizable because each always begins with one of those words: *I, You*, or *He.* They alternate throughout with absolute regularity and in that same order. Each series has a corresponding time (*I* is the present, *You* is the future, and *He* is the past) as well as different levels of perception (the subconscious, collective unconscious, and the conscious, respectively). The changing stylistic features assure a precise identification for each sequence, which orients the reader in the midst of an otherwise labyrinthine construction.

The I in the present is the dying Artemio Cruz, reduced to basic physical sensations and confusing perceptions of what happens beyond his weakened body, which is close to death. The stylistic form that this series uses is stream of consciousness, hesitant and each time more halting and obscure. The You is the most complex series because it adopts a form of poetic meditation that, by moving in an increasingly mythical or virtual dimension, escapes all the trappings of historical time and reaches the time of the possible, then able to ignore the objective fact of death. Through it a cyclical horizon unfolds, where what has happened will happen again, without end. (It is also

---

[1] The American sociologist C. Wright Mills was among the most prominent critics of U.S. policy toward Latin America during the Cold War. He suffered a heart attack in December 1960 while preparing for a television debate on Latin American policy. He died fifteen months later, in 1962, just before Fuentes' novel was published.

possible to interpret the You as a splitting of the I, in dialogue with itself or with the reader, whom it seems to invoke or conjure.) The He is, from the narrative point of view, the series that carries the greatest weight of factual or historical events because it contains the fundamental episodes of Cruz's public and private life. The facts that it narrates happen in the historic past (they are dated with great precision), use the third person of traditional narration, and are configured as flashbacks out of chronological order. The first three sequences of this series, for example, correspond to the years 1941, 1919, and 1913.

The best way to appreciate the changes in form, tone, and perspective among the three series is to quote their opening passages. The I series begins: "I wake up. . . . The touch of that cold object against my penis wakes me up. I didn't know I could urinate without being aware of it. I keep my eyes shut. I can't even make out the nearest voices. If I opened my eyes, would I be able to hear them?" (3).

The You series begins: "Yesterday you did what you do every day.[2] You don't know if it's worthwhile remembering it. You only want to remember, lying back there in the twilight of your bedroom, what's going to happen: you don't want to foresee what has already happened" (7).

The He series begins: "He was on his way to the office. The chauffeur drove, and he read the newspaper. Traffic stopped; he raised his eyes. He saw the two ladies enter the shop. Squinting, he watched them, and then the car moved forward, and he went on reading the news about Sidi Barrani and El Alamein" (12).

The novel is strictly symmetrical. Each of the three series is composed of twelve sequences, for a total of thirty-six sequences. But in fact there are two additional sequences, very brief, that function like a closing—however incomplete—to the novel: sequence 37 of the I series, which has only four lines; and the last of the You series (sequence 38), which blends the three voices in a final attempt to find irrevocable meaning. The novel closes with these disjointed lines: "all three . . . We shall die . . . You . . . are dying . . . have died . . . I shall die." In other words, sequence 39, which would correspond to the He, is missing, and thus the puzzle remains forever open. The enigma of Artemio Cruz has not been fully resolved. As a whole, the

---

[2] Translator's note: The Spanish original begins "*Tú, ayer, hiciste . . .*" The English translation requires a change in word order so that *tú* is no longer in its original place at the beginning of the sentence. Thus, the point of the pronoun beginning each series is lost in the English translation. Page numbers refer to Carlos Fuentes, *The Death of Artemio Cruz*, trans. Alfred MacAdam (New York: Farrar Straus, 1991).

structural design can be compared to that of a mosaic in which each piece—save the last—has its exact place, its own meaning, and its value within the whole picture, as can be seen in the following diagram:

Present	1 4 7 10 13 16 19 22 25 28 31 34 37	subconscious / I
Future	2 5 8 11 14 17 20 23 26 29 32 35 (38)	collective unconscious / You
Past	3 6 9 12 15 18 21 24 27 30 33 36 X	conscious / He

It is easy to observe, following this diagram, that the reading of the sequences implies constantly changing points of view and shifts of time, space, and narrative styles. Rhetorical patterns mark these shifts: the triadic formulas of the I, the leitmotifs and the recurrences of the He, the lyrical texture of the You, and the convergences and disparities between the three voices, which are in reality only one. In a traditional story, the dominant relationship between chapters is a linear progression; in this novel the values of contrast, opposition, displacement, and contiguity are assembled together. Each sequence functions as a crossroads between a "horizontal" reading (that connects the narration within the same series) and another "vertical" reading (that jumps from one series to another). Thus, it is possible to say that the novel has a polyhedral structure: each piece of the mosaic generates multidimensional contacts with the others and earns a relative or positional value in addition to its own.

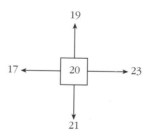

It is obvious that this type of relationship is in the realm of the cinematographic montage, where the disjunctions, confluences, and fragmentations are an essential part of the visual story. Fuentes' interest in film is well known. He has written scripts, and some of his novels have been written with film versions of them in mind, such as *Sacred Zone* (*Zona sagrada*, 1967) and *The Old Gringo* (*Gringo viejo*, 1985), without forgetting either the constant references to film classics in *A Change of Skin* (*Cambio de piel*, 1967), which even contains stills from movies. In the case of *The Death of Artemio*

Cruz, there is something more profound: the novel follows a structural pattern inspired by a recognizable cinematic model. That model is of course Orson Welles's masterpiece *Citizen Kane* (1949). Like *Artemio Cruz* it begins with the death of a powerful public figure based on a real person, the magnate William Randolph Hearst. Soon after his death, a group of journalists try to find the appropriate "angle" to reconstruct his life and to discover who the man really was. They begin from the final word that Kane utters on his death bed, *Rosebud*, a clue that alludes to his humble origins (comparable to those of Artemio Cruz, an illegitimate child).[3] The film gives the same impression of disconnected episodes and everything being uncertain as does the reading of the novel. There are visible analogies between the scene of Kane seeing himself repeated in the mirrors of his opulent palace at Xanadu, and the notable one in Artemio Cruz's Coyoacán mansion, where the aged protagonist celebrates the New Year and senses the emptiness of his own power.

The narrative works of Fuentes tend to draw on particular models, literary or cinematic, over which he tries to build an original story. This tendency is based in his conviction that all creative work is, at its base, a rereading, a new version of something already existing—a great example of which is his novel *Terra nostra* (1975). In his stories there is a system of citations, echoes, and multiple cultural references, which is why he tends toward the palimpsest, to symphonic composition, and textual variegation. *Artemio Cruz* is no exception and typifies what Fuentes' output is: a baroque labyrinth that seems to absorb everything. But it is a Latin American baroque that itself has a model: the ancient art of Mexico congested with hieroglyphics, intricate symbols, and serpentine forms. At the same time, his work has close and deep ties with other Mexican traditions: the cult of death, the rites of courage and defiance echoing the *corridos*, the poetry of José Gorostiza and Octavio Paz, and so forth. And, finally, one has to see this work as a splendid variant of an eternal and universal story: the rise and fall of the hero who drags with him, tragically, his entire nation. Or is it the other way around?

Translated by Mary Murrell

---

[3] The word *Rosebud* had, apparently, a sexual meaning for Hearst, which Welles knew when he was shooting the film.

CLARISSE ZIMRA

Lone Sun
(Daniel Maximin, Guadeloupe, 1981)

Published in 1981 by the prestigious Editions du Seuil, *L'isolé soleil* was the first work of Guadeloupean-born Daniel Maximin, a young high school teacher who had undertaken a Ph.D. in anthropology at the Sorbonne. Edouard Glissant, a major French Caribbean writer in his own right who was part of the editorial team, had given it high marks. The well-known red and white cover carried the subtitle *roman* (a novel). But such a subtitle was somewhat misleading, and most French readers would have known that, in the unpredictable world of Parisian publishing, marketing editors with more regard for prospective sales than formalist accuracy often make the decisions about titles. In these post-post-*nouveau roman* times, as long as the work was not pure rhyming verse, the term *novel* would suffice.

Indeed this first work did proffer some verse, along with a splendid variety of literary and extraliterary modes that, at times, barely remained this side of pastiche. It displayed multiple writing styles, jumped linguistic registers, and switched narrative personae, while moving along criss-crossing plots and exuberantly looping subplots. It borrowed openly from the oral tradition, glossed over folk songs and tales wittily retold; quoted, misquoted and parodied Creole proverbs; used or even invented excerpts from works by the Negritude fathers, Aimé Césaire and Léon-Gontran Damas, whom it sometimes identified as such, sometimes not. In a further show of authorial hubris, it pilfered their famous lines to encode them as messages of black resistance against the Vichy occupation of the islands. Finally, it threaded some of their well-known characters through its own pages—for example, one Charley Hannah, this "nègre COMIQUE ET LAID, pour sûr" ("negro, COMICAL AND UGLY for sure") of Césaire's *Cahier d'un retour au pays natal*.[1] This move unfolded a highly self-referential intertext, since the original Hannah, whom Césaire had encoded in his famous 1937 poem, really did exist. An ebullient medley that would have done *The Saragossa Manuscript* proud "riffed" through multiple flashback maneuvers against a thick sociopolitical

---

[1] See the bilingual edition, *Notebook of a Return to the Native Land* in *Aimé Césaire: The Collected Poetry*, trans. Clayton Eshleman and Annette Smith (Berkeley: University of California Press, 1984), 62–63.

subtext. Animated by what seems like a revolving cast of thousands, it was enough to make the head spin.

In this exuberant scope, ambitious grasp, and sheer lyricism, a young writer was discovering the principles of his craft; one attentive to the fact that the Greek *poiesis* likewise stressed the crafted, constructed nature of all imaginary writing. At the center of *L'isolé soleil* stand two childhood friends, young Adrien, now departing to study in Paris as the novel begins and, to remain on the island, Marie-Gabriel, who has just turned seventeen. They will exchange letters, confidences, journals, and, eventually, scriptive projects: she will undertake the biography of Louis-Gabriel, the natural father she has seen but once; he'll draft a biography of Guadeloupe's historical father, Louis Delgrès, who died resisting slavery. They discuss home life, local politics, and the cultural scene in Paris, such as the premiere of Césaire's *La tragédie du roi Christophe*, or Soyinka's early plays in which Adrien (like Maximin himself) works as a stagehand. Children of the 1960s who weep for the entangled destinies of Vietnam and Algeria, they are impatient with the glacial waning of an empire that has lost none of its lethal power. For all of their legally protected status as full French citizens by birth, the pair nevertheless feels vulnerable, part of an ever-expanding diasporic world under attack. They fear for young James Meredith standing up to racism in an Alabama school, admire Stokely Carmichael's African exile, and mourn Frantz Fanon who has just died, alone, in a Washington, D.C., hospital. They even manage to assist in spiriting Angela Davis away from the clutches of the island political police. Returning from Cuba, her ship had been forced to transit by way of Guadeloupe.

Marie-Gabriel begins the biography of her long-gone father, a dissident exile whose plane has just exploded over the island volcano, as Adrien meditates on "a dream deferred," Delgrès's failed uprising. An officer in the Army of the Republic, who hailed from the sister island of Martinique, this "free man of color" briefly embodied pan-Caribbean freedom. Biological father of a fictional character and real historical father of a nation yet to come, they share a first name, a dream, and a death of mythical proportions. Maximin's grand narrative accordingly spans continents and centuries in this poetic quest for origins, and in so doing discovers that in the Caribbean this poetic return is always already overdetermined by the official version of the past. Witness the fact that, until a generation ago, Afro-Caribbean history was not part of the curricula in the French islands and, on Guadeloupe, there was no monument honoring Delgrès's last stand. Blurring the mimetic distinction between history and fiction, the writer's imagination will therefore embroider on what faint traces are left in oral history to recover the long-silenced collective memory. Art must become the anamnestic ritual wherein the past reveals itself.

L'isolé soleil opens accordingly with a "true" missing piece of modern history upon whose symbolism Maximin embroiders fully with a series of implied resonances. The biological father's plane explodes over Delgrès' Matouba fortress. On this hallowed ground, 160 years earlier, the ancestral father, along with the last five hundred of his men, their women, and children, had lured the enemy. They blew themselves up, taking along with them three hundred of Napoleon's finest in a ritual repetition of the more successful conflagration on the sister island of Haiti. Volcanic symbology is never far from the awareness of a pan-Caribbean identity.[2] Toussaint Louverture had predicted the failure of the French expeditionary forces, "dancing on the volcano." Before his demise, Delgrès pens an apocalyptic call directed at Haiti, a real archival document that Maximin incorporates in his fictional universe: "A l'univers tout entier le dernier cri de l'innocence et du désespoir" ("To the entire universe, the last cry of innocence and despair").

In the Caribbean, history does repeat itself, but never exactly. There was no apocalyptic rebirth into real freedom in 1802; there will be none now. Among the real victims of the conflagration of 1962, we find the leaders of a nascent independence party, Niger and Cataye. These real historical figures are presented as childhood friends of Louis-Gabriel, a fictional character, all three plotting to trigger another pan-Caribbean uprising that would repair the mistake of history, the defeat of Matouba. History and fiction fuse again as the real Angela Davis, briefly setting foot in Guadeloupe, bequeaths her name and her fiery temper to a reappearing set of fictional characters. The first fictional Angela is birthed by the African-born priestess who presides over the final *obeah* ritual for the fateful night on Matouba. Entrusted with Delgrès's last words, little Angela becomes the embodied memory of the tribe, a mythical foremother whose blood flows, fictionally, through both Adrien and Marie-Gabriel, and, by symbolic implication as well, through the real Angela Davis a century and a half later. Likewise interweaving the interdiegetic and the intradiegetic, Davis's Soledad Brothers, George and Jonathan Jackson, are "reborn" a century and a half earlier as the prophetic twins who are part of Delgrès's last night. Twins are obsessive figures in this corpus. The pattern metonymically subtends pairing figures of doubling and

---

[2] A constellation of images very much on the mind of Césaire, Maximin's literary father, who has called himself "péléen" in several interviews. Exactly one century after Delgrès's suicidal conflagration, the Pelée explosion on Martinique buried an entire town in 1902, leaving only one survivor. With less lethal results, Guadeloupe's Soufrière blew open its crater in 1976.

repetition. *Primus inter pares*, we find Martinique-born Delgrès, self-mirrored in Guadeloupe as freedom's putative father. The island itself, shaped like an open-winged butterfly, reinforces this quest of the dislocated Caribbean subject for an other that is also himself.

This nonlinear structure places *L'isolé soleil* on the cusp of the postmodern, a mode that it nevertheless resists in its insistence on clear political references. It unfolds patterns of doubling and repetition carried further by paired characters—that is, real siblings, like the Matouba officers; or putative ones, like Marie-Gabriel and Adrien, who are related but do not know that they are both descended from little Angela; and, all the successive Angelas, who are symbolically reengendering one another in loop after loop. A fragmented narrative consciousness gleefully floats up and down the moebius strip of collective memory wherein, says Maximin, "the present always invents itself a past out of its own desire."[3] In this universe, time moves neither chronologically nor predictably. The end is contained in the beginning, but because each loop changes both present and past simultaneously, the resulting figure is helicoidal rather than simply circular. There is more than a passing resemblance between *L'isolé soleil* and another famous Caribbean meditation on history, García-Márquez's *Cien años de soledad*, in their common urge to destabilize well-constructed narratives by pushing the limits of their representational envelopes, their determination to refuse the materiality of time. Maximin, who reads Spanish, is an avid admirer of Latin American fiction.

Following the French islands' faltering steps toward an independence that did not materialize with Césaire's election to power in 1946, the fated year of "departmentalization," the work coils back several times to the original failure. The text operates what Edouard Glissant, another writer-historian born in Martinique, calls "the prophetic reading of the past" ("lecture prophétique du passé").[4] Offering lengthy dramatic re-creations, a brutally successful slave rebellion on an imaginary plantation but with real historical participants, for example, alongside fictional excerpts presented as newly retrieved authentic archival documents, Maximin's counterpoetics eviscerates the heroic gesture that would validate the violent Fanonian polarization of the colonizer-colonized paradigm. The dyadic exchange between Marie-Gabriel and Adrien follows the same trajectory. At his prompting, she jettisons the singular heroics of the male-centered plot in favor of an alternative narrative,

---

[3] The title of his interview by C. Zimra for the American version of the novel, *Lone Sun* (Charlottesville: University of Virginia Press, 1989), xvi–xxxii.

[4] See the first preface, dated 1961, to his play *Monsieur Toussaint* (Paris: Seuil 1986), 7.

female-centered and plural. In the resulting collaborative project, the narrator might be said to be both Adrien and Marie-Gabriel, *animus-anima* of a regendered Caribbean corpus-to-be. And we realize that the multigenerational narrative they intend to write is the very one we are reading.

Not only does *L'isolé soleil* contain a large number of literary features that neoclassicist formalists would maintain do not belong together, it also takes extravagant liberties with mimetic referentiality, boasting an ever-larger number of characters enmeshed in dialogical relationships among themselves and with common ancestors, biological or symbolic, real or imagined, known or unknown. And, across an equally huge time frame, from the pre-Columbian to Guadeloupe's current postcolonization status, this "novel" seeks to recover "une histoire d'archipel, attentive à nos quatre races, nos sept langues et nos douzaines de sangs" ("a story in the shape of an archipelago traced by our four races, seven languages and dozens of bloods").[5] This is a text that, in the original French ("histoire"), glides smoothly between story and history. Maximin's method, to use Russian formalist terms, collapses the classical distinction between *fabula* (the old Aristotelian plot in its cause-and-effect sequence) and *sjuzhet* (the plot resequenced by the writer's imagination and acted out by any number of narrative personae). Characters multiply versions of the past that do not necessarily contradict but that, nevertheless, never exactly coincide. Rather, these versions operate as a series of infinitely refracting mirrors. It comes as no surprise, then, to discover that the Guadeloupean writer admires Borges and has often declared himself in thrall to a South American novel whose challenge to singular heroics he finds hard to resist.[6]

In homage to his masters, Maximin issues his readers a formal challenge that spills over into his three novels to date, *L'isolé soleil* (Seuil, 1981); *Soufrières* (Seuil, 1987); and *L'île et une nuit* (Seuil, 1991). He has admitted that his third novel was conceptualized before the first, so that to read the trilogy in its published sequence is truly a return to origins. In *L'isolé soleil*, this discovery of a novel yet to be written takes us to its very last chapter, titled, simply, "One." It is signed with the writer's first name, "Daniel," and a self-identifying oscillation between continents and cultural identities, "Paris. Guadeloupe." The thirteen preceding chapters that make up the final part of the book are numbered backward; that is to say, the first one is titled "Fourteen," the next one "Thirteen," and so forth. They invite reading either in ascending or descending order; a regime that demands the simultaneity of an

---

[5] *Isolé*, 7; *Sun*, 3.

[6] *Isolé*, 92–93; *Sun*, 82–83. In the accompanying interview, he also singles out Fuentes and Asturias (xxiii).

either *and* or, mimicking both the coiling quest and its open-ended finale. For, in that very last chapter, on that very last page, "Daniel" concludes with a last sentence that stands conspicuously alone and begins with a lowercase letter: "et la feuille prend son vol au risque de sa verdure" ("and the leaf flies off at the risk of losing its green").[7] The French *feuille* further facilitates the symbolism, as it can mean simultaneously "leaf" and "page." The lowercase letter indicates a fragment that continues a prior exchange whose beginning we find, not surprisingly, on the first leaf/page of the novel's own beginning, that of its unpaginated prologue: "Les mots sont des feuilles envolées au risque de leurs racines" ("Words are leaves blown off at the roots' risk"). The circular motion spirals out and the concluding sentence turns into the first sentence of the next book, *Soufrières*.

This time, the uncapitalized phrase is preceded by an ellipsis mark that underlines its implied reference to a prior text (". . . et la feuille" / ". . . and the leaf"). Punning on the fused meaning, leaves flown off a real tree as well as imaginary leaves of this yet-to-be-written book we've just perused, these reiterative sequences punctuate the contrapuntal structure of the first novel. In turn, the last novel will reveal a familiar organizing principle early on, which its ending will eventually engage: "Chaque livre en appelle un autre pour offrir un lendemain à sa faim" ("Each book calls forth another to present it with a tomorrow against hunger").[8] Animated by a similar call-response movement and similar epistolary premises (the exchanges between Marie-Gabriel and Adrien), the three novels acquire full synergistic power when read together and in any order, since one always calls forth the other two. This plural narrative elaborates its own mise-en-abyme, that is, a how-to-read as well as a how-to-write. Metafictive in its juxtaposition of other "send and receive" features, such as letters, diaries, journals, and excerpts of work in progress that must be shared and responded to before becoming final, the procedure stresses the desired fusion between the "letter" as object sent, a metonymic leaf unafraid to fly away at the risk of foundering, and the semiotic sign, this page-leaf that is the very site of fluid self-representation. Mirror and echo, the sentence is quoted again in the concluding pages of *L'île et une nuit*, this time in a fuller version lifted verbatim from the first pages of *L'isolé soleil*, a version that now insists on the concrete presence of words: "Les mots ne sont pas du vent. Les mots sont des feuilles envolées au risque de leur verdure" ("Words are not wind. Words are leaves blown off at the risk of losing their greenness").[9]

---

[7] *Isolé*, 311; *Sun*, 283.

[8] *L'île et une nuit*, 48.

[9] Ibid., 163.

In public as well as in private, the writer has explained that he wanted to slough off both the straitjacket of a Rousseauesque autobiography, latent in the epistolary model, and the phony omniscience of a Flaubertian narrator, the god-in-his-creation emplotment model. Answering questions from the floor in 1998, he expostulated:

> Je n'ai pas voulu me mettre au centre, en auteur qui présente ses personnages comme un montreur de marionnettes. . . . En parlant pour les autres, on leur impose silence. Je me suis donc dit, "je ne puis être porte-parole, parce que je ne veux pas me retrouver en position de pouvoir." Le cyclique est venu remplacer le linéaire. Mon livre a échappé à la loi du livre et mon roman à la loi du roman. La fin imposait de revenir au début.

> (I did not want to install myself at the center, as the author who shows off his characters like the puppet master. . . . When one speaks for others, one silences them. Therefore, I told myself: "I cannot be a spokesman, because I do not want to find myself occupying a power position." The cyclical came to replace the linear. My book escaped its prescribed law and my novel *its* prescribed law. The ending demanded a coming back to the beginning.)[10]

Eschewing the single stance in a not-so-veiled borrowing from the Barthesian persona that, in effect, collapses narrator and author (what the French critic called, writing, degree zero), Maximin creates, he says, "a polybiography," a form punctuated by a profusion of narrative voices that modulate without warning among *all* of the singular and plural subject pronouns available to the French language, further redoubled by the fact that the original can differentiate between singular and plural vocatives. In further homage to Camus's famous challenge, the in-your-face thrust of Meursault's very first line ("Mother died today, or was it yesterday"), Maximin refuses a tired form that does not ask enough of us (and of him):

> Le roman classique, style Balzac, nous installe d'abord dans une histoire bien campée; et donc, c'est toujours par la troisième personne qu'il démarre. Avec en plus quarante pages pour décrire un paysage, ou camper un intérieur, il ne demande rien, ou pas grand chose à notre imagination. Moi, je crois au

---

[10] Maximin was one of the keynote speakers for the 1998 Würzburg Symposium on autobiographies. These quotations are culled from my own notes, taken as chair of one of the roundtables devoted to his work. All translations are mine. A slightly different French version, "Sous le signe du colibri," can be found in the first of the two-volume proceedings, *Postcolonialism and Autobiographie*, ed. Alfred Hornung and Ernstpetr Ruhe (Amsterdam: Rodopi, 1998), 203–19.

contraire que le roman moderne, en comparaison, doit tout de suite postuler la connivence, comme Camus dès les premiers mots de *L'étranger*. Il peut commencer par le "je," le "nous," aussi bien le "tu," parce qu'il accueille l'altérité au lieu de nous y repousser. Si bien que moi, en choisissant le "tu," en entrant dans mon texte, j'ai choisi tout de suite de commencer par le dialogue et de n'en plus sortir.

(The classical novel, à la Balzac, situates us, first, within a well-crafted story; therefore, it always has to start in the third person. Using up to forty pages, on top of it all, to describe a landscape or cover the inside of a house, it never asks anything, or hardly a thing, of our imagination. As for myself, I happen to believe that the modern novel, by comparison, must postulate a complicitous state; as Camus does with the very first words of *The Stranger*. It can start with an "I," or a "we," as well as a singular "you," because it welcomes the other instead of repelling otherness. So that by choosing to start with a "you," I've entered my text and chose to begin immediately with a dialogue I never intended to leave.)[11]

To establish this "complicitous state" in the first novel, he had selected for its opening, a second-person singular: "Tu cherches la clé de tes fruits dans la forêt des rêves" ("In the forests of your dreams, you seek the key to your fruits").[12] He will then openly draw again on Camus's famous beginning in the third novel, *L'île et une nuit*, by way of a conclusion that seems to kill off the dyadic pair: "Aujourd'hui Marie-Gabriel est morte. Ou peut-être hier, je ne sais pas . . . Et lui aussi, plus qu'elle peut-être, puisque né sur une terre sans aieux et sans mémoire, une pure passion de vivre affrontée à une mort totale" ("Marie-Gabriel died today. Or was it yesterday, I don't know . . . As did *he*, also and perhaps more than she, since he had been born on a land without ancestors and without memory, a pure passion for life confronting an absolute death").[13] However, with this clear intertextual echo, the helix continues its boundless trajectory because it is, in essence and in structure, infinitely dialogical. The *punctum* (to use another of Barthes's concepts) may well be the mantralike sentence that resurfaces, once more, in the preface to his 2000 collection of poems, *L'invention des désirades:* "et la feuille prend son vol au risque de sa verdure" ("and the leaf flies off at the risk of losing its green").

---

[11] Ibid.

[12] *Isolé*, 11; *Sun*, 5.

[13] *Ile*, 165; punctuation, his; translation, mine.

L'isolé soleil starts with this elusive second-person singular vocative: "In the forest of *your* dreams . . ." Who speaks here? And to whom? Who reads here? To whom? And for whom? This first sentence implies a prior exchange for which it is already a response. The first sentence of the next chapter finds Adrien responding, in turn, on the ship that takes him away: "Pour ma part, je rêve souvent d'un livre à écrire dont les pages de droite accueilleraient mes pensées, et celles de gauche, les tiennes en regards" ("As for me, I often dream of writing a book with your thoughts on the right-hand pages and mine on the left, looking at each other").[14] Shuttling from right to left and back, the exchange structures a mirrored recursive chain that Adrien signs, "je serai toujours à tu et à toi," an untranslatable pun on their degree of intimacy as well as on the fact that they are each other's alter-ego (I am you as you are I; as well as, I am yours as you are mine). The translation wisely keeps it in the original French. Simultaneously sender and receiver, each reflected back to the other, they embody all the looping back and forth subplots to come and adumbrate the spiral of the whole. Theirs should be the pronominal shifts by which Benveniste, following Saussure, identifies the post-Enlightenment subject as divided in language; and Glissant, a Caribbean self dislocated from its missing authentic core. However, these mutually reflexive enunciations become, on the contrary, signifiers of a utopian potentiality that heals.

To overcome the epistemological violence that the autobiographical mode of the singular voice would perpetuate, Maximin chooses a narrative that welcomes, instead, what he had called earlier, "an alterity that is a complicitous postulate." This is not the Rimbaldian conviction that "I" is another but, rather, the glorious possibility that "I" might be able to enfold all others in an almost Levinassian ethics of generosity. To quote another of his Würzburg comments on *L'étranger*, "Je est un autre. À prendre littéralement et dans tous les sens" ("I is another. To be understood literally and in all senses")—that is, the senses of the polyvalent word as well as of the corporeal imagination; a live work-in-progress.

We have now come full circle, back to the days when Schlegel applauded in the newly born *roman* the dawning of a plural form whose extraordinary plasticity could include all others; when, mindful of the fact that Plato had praised the mimetic versatility of the theater, Nietzsche marveled in turn that the ancient philosopher ingeniously foresaw its portmanteau character.[15] To

---

[14] *Isolé*, 19; *Sun*, 12.

[15] See *The Birth of Tragedy and the Genealogy of Morals*, trans. Francis Golffing (Garden City, N.Y.: Doubleday, 1956), in particular, chapter 14.

define itself in the teeth of neo-classicist epistemological suspicion, the romantic praxis called forth a dual strategy: one, to transcend boundary markers; and, two, to hypostasize the plurality of genre/s into a singular, protean *dichtung*. This is, to use Lacoue-Labarthe and Nancy's phrase, "literature's absolute" ("l'absolu littéraire"), a form organically "equal to the task of containing its own reflection and including the theory of its own 'genre.'"[16] Maximin's first novel certainly fits this definition of the boundless text, a form often suspected of aesthetic antihistoricism. But far from adopting the apolitical stance of the postmodern subject, it demands that we attend to the historical conditions that dictated its writing. In the interview that accompanies the American translation, the writer muses on his own stunned discovery, while a graduate student in Paris, that he was caught in the master narrative of empire: "I had started to work on my doctoral dissertation . . . an inquiry into the nature of the social sciences, or rather, an inquiry into its object. I wanted to examine the way in which a center defines its periphery, what we call the Third World, the wild man, the colonized man; in a word, the 'Other.' . . . I found myself writing, not on this 'exotic object,' this object of European scientific discourse, but on what I soon called the exotic 'subject.'"[17] Discovering that he was that "object," he abandoned the anthropological project.

Trapped within an empire that carefully guards its margins, Maximin developed instead "novels," fluid forms whose shuttling back and forth among time, space, personae, narrators, and narratees simultaneously makes and unmakes all authorial centers; forms wherein axes are provisional and none (and no one) may hierarchize the open-ended structure of the whole. We are no longer in the old postcolonial margin/center paradigm that so annoyed Salman Rushdie. We have entered a fractal universe of infinite reverberation and multiplicity: "Literally and in all senses," indeed. And we suddenly remember that the butterfly effect is one of the major dissemination figures of chaos theory as well as, in its open-winged beauty, the very shape of Guadeloupe, Maximin's imaginary universe.

---

[16] See Philippe Lacoue-Labarthe and Jean-Luc Nancy's joint introduction to the proceedings from the Strasbourg Colloquium, on "l'absolu littéraire," *Genre: Glyph Textual Studies* 7 (Baltimore: Johns Hopkins University Press, 1980), 4–5.

[17] Interview (see note 3), xix.

ALESSANDRO PORTELLI

Beloved
(Toni Morrison, United States, 1987)

> She didn't mind a little communication between the
> two worlds, but this was an invasion.
> —TONI MORRISON, *Beloved*

"124 was spiteful. Full of a baby's venom. The women in the house knew it
and so did the children. For years each one put up with the spite in his own
way, but by 1873 Sethe and her daughter Denver were its only victims."[1]
The unusual incipit of *Beloved* is a number. Three lines later there is another.
One designates a house that is haunted by a spirit; the other, a historical period. In *Beloved*, the spirits erupt into the story with transformative violence,
and Beloved—a little girl who becomes a ghost, a ghost that is reincarnated
in a woman's body, a body that dissolves into air and water—is the vehicle
for contact between the immaterial world of ghosts and the concrete world
of the story.

Number 124 Bluestone Road in Cincinnati, just beyond the border between slavery and freedom, is the home of Sethe, an escaped slave from Kentucky, and her daughter Denver. In 1855, Sethe killed her unnamed baby girl
and tried to kill her other children to keep them away from the slave hunter.
The murdered girl fills the house with a lustful ghost's rage until Paul D,
Sethe's partner from her slave days, reappears and expels her. But she returns
in the body of a young woman who says that her name is Beloved, the only
word that Sethe was able to write on the gravestone (which she paid for by allowing the stonecarver seven minutes of sex). The year is 1873. Beloved is as
old as the years gone by since her death, eighteen. But she has the impulses
and desires of a living baby who still does not know how to walk.

Quiet as it is kept, *Beloved* is also a historical novel that is accurate in
its references and setting. This ghost story is also true: the former slave
Margaret Garner really did kill her children to keep them from being
forced back into slavery.[2] Still, in what reality does a mother kill her children

---

[1] Toni Morrison, *Beloved* (New York: Alfred A. Knopf, 1987), 3. Subsequent references to page
numbers from this edition are made parenthetically in the text.

[2] Toni Morrison includes Margaret Garner's story in the historical anthology that she edited,
The Black Book, compiled by Middleton Harris (New York: Random House, 1974). The 1850
Fugitive Slave Law authorized the restitution of escaped slaves to their owners, even if the slaves
had taken refuge in states where slavery was illegal, requiring the state authorities to comply.

to prevent them from living within it? In what reality can a mother continue to live who has made such a decision? What kind of love is this? How do you talk about it?

"Unspeakable thoughts unspoken": this is *Beloved*. The unspeakable thought of a historical institution like slavery; the unspeakable thoughts of an archetypal relationship like motherhood. To speak them, one has to evade tangible reality and view things through the eyes of one who has crossed that border. In what reality does a baby girl live who, before she knew her own body apart from her mother's, had her throat slit by her mother without knowing why? How could she not go back to fill the house with her anger, her desires, and her pain?

In the end, after Beloved has been exorcized, Paul D asks Denver whether the girl really had been her sister. Denver answers, "At times I think she was—more." More: the "sixty million and more" Africans who were deported, evoked in the epigraph. Outside of the house where Sethe had been locked up with her two daughters, the survivor Denver and the rediscovered Beloved, her neighbor Stamp Paid hears the cries of the unavenged black souls stirring. The ghostly grief of Beloved is the historic, concrete grief of all: "Not a house in the country ain't packed to its rafters with some dead Negro's grief," says Baby Suggs, the mother of Sethe's lost husband. "We lucky this ghost is a baby. My husband's spirit was to come back in here? Or yours? Don't talk to me. You lucky" (5).

Through the interweaving of the streams of consciousness of Sethe, Denver, and Beloved, we realize that Beloved's passage through death is also the Middle Passage, the Atlantic crossing. The hold of the slave ship is an overcrowded tomb. All the Africans and their descendents brought to America passed through death and came out on the other side—from where they remember and speak.

The text is organized around the relationship between history and the ghost, starting with the many time frames into which it is divided: the linear time of the story, a chronological plot punctured by the metahistoric time of memory and archetype. The linear plot begins in 1873 with the reappearance of Paul D, continues with the start of his relationship with Sethe, their tragic revelations to each other, crisis, separation, and the exorcism of the returned ghost by the women of the community. It concludes with the reunion of Paul D and Sethe and a new attempt to collate their stories.

This sequence of events is constantly interrupted, however, by the nonlinear time of memory, to such an extent that the text takes on the form of memory, in which all past time coexists and enters into consciousness through uncontrollable associations, short circuits, and insistent yet unanswerable questions. The daily labor of Sethe's wounded conscience is an attempt to control these memories, "put the past behind," as if she were struggling to drive away an undercurrent that keeps washing ashore. But the past comes back through the return of Paul D and his tales, the involuntary epiphanies, Denver's and Beloved's insistence that Sethe tell them stories, the presence of a ghost in the house, and finally through its reincarnation. Sethe carries her memories on her body: floggings cut the shape of a tree into her back. It is hidden from view and invisible to the touch but there nevertheless, just beyond the threshold of conscience. Her relationship to this memory is the opposite of repression: it is irrepressible, always there, even when she thinks she is not thinking about it.

But the ghost is "more": if memory makes the past ever more present, the novel makes this story present in narrative time and the reader's time. Here the ghost becomes the return of something repressed—the slave trade, human bondage, racism—in an America that is afflicted by deliberate amnesia. While some might want these horrors to be buried and expelled from our present, the ghost made flesh gets in the way. Literally, as in Faulkner (a crucial reference for Toni Morrison), not only is the past not dead, it is not even past.[3]

For Sethe, keeping the past at bay and elaborating her grief are truly a question of life and death. The reappearance of Beloved is not only the fulfillment of her desire to have her lost daughter back. Above all it is an opportunity for her to explain herself, to find peace and be able to have "a life" with Paul D and herself. What Beloved wants from her mother is not an explanation but rather a return to the preoedipal bonding of the flesh, exclusive physical possession, transforming her loving relationship with her mother into a destructive vampirism. Beloved's return is thus only the first step toward the elaboration of mourning. The next step, which does not complete the process but may initiate it (for Sethe and, perhaps, for Beloved, too), is her exorcism and redisappearance.

Hence the ambivalence of the closing admonishment, "it was not a story to pass *on*," not a story to keep telling, or "it was not a story to *pass* on," it was not a story that could be ignored (274–75). This emblematic story of slavery should be forgotten and remembered at the same time: without forgetting slavery, its victims still need to be emancipated from this memory so as not to be paralyzed by it; but for American and Western memory and

---

[3] American literature is filled with flesh-and-blood ghosts, from Brom Bones, the fake ghost in Washington Irving's *The Legend of Sleepy Hollow* (1819) to Ralph Ellison's *Invisible Man* (1952), who seems like a ghost until we run into his heavy fists. I would also include Bruce Springsteen's Tom Joad, a memory of the Depression made flesh.

identity, this story remains like a boulder in the road that cannot be walked around.

"She's mine, Beloved. She's mine"; "I am Beloved and she is mine." So begin the interior monologues of Sethe and Beloved (210–14). The relationship between historical and metahistorical time in *Beloved* is also the result of two relations built on the idea of possession: slavery and maternity. Slavery and maternity contend for the possession of Sethe's children: "Maybe I couldn't love em proper in Kentucky because they wasn't mine to love" (162). Slavery radicalizes and distorts the possessiveness of maternal love: raised to think of property as the paradigm for relationships between persons, Sethe does not hesitate to decide the life and death of a child who is finally *hers*.

The slave is "an extension of the master's will."[4] The mother and her newborn child are parts of each other, and Sethe's possessiveness corresponds to Beloved's vampirelike, devouring desire. White people do not know where to stop, says Baby Suggs. Paul D thinks that Sethe does not know where she ends and the world begins. Both of them, like ghosts, have neither form nor limits. Beloved remembers the whites on the slave ship as "men without skin" (211). The killing of Beloved, supreme act of possession, is manifested, however, through an act of separation: to keep her from being taken away, Sethe has to cut her away from herself. The paradigm of maternal (and slave) possession is intertwined with the pain and violence of separation. The ultimate subject of *Beloved* is the difficulty of being a person, of distinguishing oneself from others, the living from the dead, individuals from the group, the present from the past, human beings from ghosts and animals. The most difficult word, which Sethe cannot pronounce until the end, is "Me? Me?" (273).

Denver and Beloved suck on Sethe's tales like mother's milk: orality (associative, nonlinear, evocative expanse of memory) and the ever-present figures of liquids (ink, blood, milk, water, urine, amniotic fluid) are the vehicles and symbols of blending. The blending flow of liquids stands in contrast to the violent figures of separation (decapitation, strangling). The flow of voices is controlled by the stable materiality of the writing: the footprints that Stamp Paid sees on the snow, the traces of whippings on Sethe's body, the mark on the mother's body, the name Beloved paid for in flesh and engraved on stone. The congealing and consolidation of voices in writing (of

---

[4] At the Sweet Home plantation from which Sethe escaped, the slaves had alphabetical names—Paul D, E, F—to suggest their owner's difficulties in distinguishing between them (another slave, Sixo, is given a number for a name).

memory in a book) completes the dizzying exchange between the concrete and the immaterial, between spirits and history, which pivots on the oxymoron of the ghost incarnate.

The association of voice, maternal presence, and fusion is also related to the association of writing, paternal absence, and identification. As Jean Wyatt points out, Denver is the one who "takes the normal road to separation, substituting signifiers [literacy] for a physical connection with the mother's body."[5] She is the one who is able to extricate herself from the vortex of desire unleashed by Beloved, to leave the house, to give herself a form distinct from her mother's in order to save her. And she does so in the sign of writing and the absent father.

The first words that Denver says to Paul D are, "You know my father?" (12). The relationship with the father is immediately designated in terms of a double absence: not only is he missing, but she who has never known him does not even have the right to miss him. Soon the paternal absence is connoted in terms of another form of absence, writing: "He loved things. Animals and tools and crops and the alphabet" (208). Denver ultimately finds the road back to relations with others and the reconstruction of herself, returning to the teacher who had taught her to read and to communicate with neighbors who, sight unseen, had donated solid food and written names: "[She] inaugurated her life in the world as a woman" following a pathway "made up of paper scraps containing handwritten names of others" (248). The last time that we see her, Paul D remarks that she looks more like her father than ever (266).

The tension between the immateriality of the ghost and the voice, and the materiality of the body and writing is thus articulated in the tension between the physicality of the mother-daughter bond and the cultural construction of paternity. This women's novel thus also has to redefine masculine identity. On the one hand, the mother-daughter relationship of Sethe, Beloved, and Denver stands in contrast to a series of father-son couples united in the name of rape, as if the absence of a physical connection to the father's body could only be filled through the violent possession of the woman's body.[6] On the other hand, in the sign of absence—of self-control, restraint—*Beloved* outlines a possible alternative masculinity: the men of Sweet Home are men

---

[5] Jean Wyatt, *Reconstructing Desire: The Role of the Unconscious in Women's Reading and Writing* (Chapel Hill: University of North Carolina Press, 1990), 200.

[6] The stonecarver and his son in the cemetery, Ella's masters, the "schoolteacher" and his nephews who steal Sethe's milk. I have written a detailed analysis of this theme in "Figlie e padri: Scrittura e assenza in *Beloved* di Toni Morrison," *Acoma* 5 (1995): 72–84.

because they abstain from imposing themselves sexually on Sethe. One cannot depend on men because they break down, disappear, go mad; but it is Paul D's awareness of his own inadequacy that ultimately makes of him a "gentle" man with whom it is possible to hope.

Beloved is the arrival point of two African-American narrative traditions. It reconnects to the legacy of denunciation that goes back to the nineteenth-century slave narratives and is passed down to Richard Wright and the black aesthetic of the 1960s: a tradition in which the artist assumes the role of spokesperson for the community, especially in addressing the outside world.[7] But it rejects the idea that oppression has annihilated the humanity, culture, and community of its victims, leaving the artists oppression itself as their only theme.[8] In the wake of Zora Neale Hurston and Ralph Ellison, *Beloved* is instead a deeply felt reconstruction of the richness of a culture and a world of relations that exist beyond oppression and help one to survive. Toni Morrison does not believe, however, that to affirm black culture with love and pride it is necessary to put the context of oppression between brackets. Relationships between blacks, and not with whites, is at the heart of *Beloved*. Yet these relationships are invaded, distorted, and violated by slavery, and amid this violence they regain shape in the ways that are possible and that are necessary to resist it.

Morrison holds everything together thanks to language, relating moral horrors in a Black English charged with life and love for beauty, fantastic metaphors and rigorous syntax, and without orthographic distortions or phonetic approximations. It is a book meant to be read aloud, in which the syntax and vocabulary dictate the rhythm in which we find the book's linguistic and cultural specificity. Hear the voice of Baby Suggs: "Not a house in the country ain't packed to its rafters with some dead Negro's grief. We lucky this ghost is a baby. My husband's spirit was to come back in here? Or yours? Don't talk to me. You lucky" (5).

A voice made flesh like the ghost, writing does not separate itself from the place of the greatest violence and extreme resistance, the body. The tautology, repetition, complement of the internal object, and literalization of the

---

[7] Bernard W. Bell, *The African American Novel and Its Tradition* (Amherst: University of Massachusetts Press, 1987); Addison Gayle, *The Black Aesthetic* (Garden City, N.Y.: Doubleday, 1971). On the responsibilities of the African-American artist, see "La nostra amatissima: Intervista con Toni Morrison," ed. Bruno Cartosio and Alessandro Portelli, *Acoma* 5 (1995): 67–71.

[8] Langston Hughes, "The Negro Artist and the Racial Mountain," first published in 1926 in *The Nation*, and now available on many Web sites; James Baldwin, "Everybody's Protest Novel," *Partisan Review* 16 (1949): 578–85.

metaphor (Sethe literally circles around Paul D the way she metaphorically circles around the story of her act) are all forms of a "semiotic" language that resists the separation between signified and signifier, between body and word. With her body she pays for the name of Beloved, on her body the mark and the whip do their writing; with her body, bearing milk, Sethe communicates with her children. In the plenitude of African-American sacred eloquence, Baby Suggs invokes the love for one's own body and the memory of the violence that it suffers: "Here,—she said,—in this here place, we flesh; flesh that weeps, laughs; flesh that dances on bare feet in grass. Love it. Love it hard. Yonder they do not lover your flesh. They despise it. . . . And O my people they do not love your hands. These they only use, tie, bind, chop off and leave empty. Love your hands! Love them. Raise them up and kiss them. Touch others with them, pat them together, stroke them on your face 'cause they don't love that either. *You* got to love it, *you*!" (89).

Translated by Michael F. Moore

Contributors

JONATHAN ARAC, Harriman Professor of English and Comparative Literature, Columbia University

JOHN AUSTIN, Academic Dean, St. Andrew's School (Middletown, Delaware)

MAURIZIO BETTINI, Professor of Greek and Latin Philology, University of Siena

PIERO BOITANI, Professor of Comparative Literature, University of Rome "La Sapienza"

M. KEITH BOOKER, Professor of English, University of Arkansas

ADRIANA BOSCARO, Professor of Japanese Literature, Ca' Foscari University (Venice)

LUIZ COSTA LIMA, Professor of Comparative Literature, Universidade do Estado do Rio de Janeiro (U.E.R.J.) and Pontifíficia Universidade Católica (P.U.C., Rio de Janeiro)

DANIEL COUÉGNAS, Professor of General and Comparative Literature, University of Nantes

MICHAEL DENNING, William R. Kenan Jr. Professor of American Studies, Yale University

MARIA DI SALVO, Professor of Slavic Philology, University of Milan (Italy)

NORMA FIELD, Robert S. Ingersoll Professor of Japanese Studies, University of Chicago

ERNESTO FRANCO, Editorial Director, Einaudi (Turin)

CATHERINE GALLAGHER, Eggers Professor of English Literature, University of California, Berkeley

M. R. GHANOONPARVAR, Professor of Persian and Comparative Literature, University of Texas at Austin

JACK GOODY, Professor of Social Anthropology, Emeritus, St. John's College, University of Cambridge

WENDY GRISWOLD, Professor of Sociology, Comparative Literary Studies, and English, Northwestern University

TOMAS HÄGG, Professor of Classical Philology, University of Bergen (Norway)

JONGYON HWANG, Professor of Korean Literature, Dongguk University (Seoul)

PRIYA JOSHI, Associate Professor of English, Temple University (Philadelphia)

EILEEN JULIEN, Professor of French, Comparative Literature, and African Studies, Indiana University

ABDELFATTAH KILITO, Professor of Literature, Mohammed V University, Rabat-Agdal (Morocco)

STEFANO LEVI DELLA TORRE, Lecturer in Architecture and History of Art, Polytechnic of Milan

ELISA MARTÍ-LÓPEZ, Associate Professor of Spanish, Northwestern University

GERALD MARTIN, Andrew Mellon Professor of Modern Languages, University of Pittsburgh

STEPHANIE MERRIM, Professor of Comparative Literature and Hispanic Studies, Brown University

FRANCO MORETTI, Professor of English and Comparative Literature, Stanford University

MEENAKSHI MUKHERJEE, formerly Professor of English, Jawaharlal Nehru University, New Delhi (now based in Hyderabad, working as an independent scholar)

JOSÉ MIGUEL OVIEDO, Professor of Spanish American Literature, Emeritus, University of Pennsylvania

JALE PARLA, Professor of English and Comparative Literature, Istanbul Bilgi University

ANDREW H. PLAKS, Professor of East Asian Studies and Comparative Literature, Princeton University

ALESSANDRO PORTELLI, Professor of American Literature, University of Rome "La Sapienza"

ATO QUAYSON, Professor of English and Director, Diaspora and Transnational Studies Centre, University of Toronto

GIOVANNI RAGONE, Professor of Media and Literature, University of Urbino "Carlo Bo"

JAMES RAVEN, Professor of Modern History, University of Essex

JOAN RAMON RESINA, Professor of Romance Studies and Comparative Literature, Cornell University

MARIO SANTANA, Associate Professor of Spanish, University of Chicago

ROBERTO SCHWARZ, writer, São Paulo (Brazil)

WALTER SITI, Professor of Contemporary Italian Literature, University of L'Aquila (Italy)

WILLIAM MILLS TODD III, Harry Tuchman Levin Professor of Literature and Harvard College Professor, Harvard University

ALBERTO VARVARO, Professor of Romance Philology, University of Naples Federico II

JUDITH T. ZEITLIN, Professor of East Asian Languages and Civilizations, University of Chicago

Henry Y. H. Zhao, Professor, Sichuan University, China

Clarisse Zimra, Associate Professor of English, Southern Illinois University at Carbondale

Jonathan Zwicker, Assistant Professor of Japanese Literature, University of Michigan

Author Index

Works Cited Index